Property of
Four Seasons Library

Anthony John Monaco

The Testimony of the Major Prophets

By

Anthony John Monaco

authorHOUSE

1663 LIBERTY DRIVE, SUITE 200
BLOOMINGTON, INDIANA 47403
(800) 839-8640
www.authorhouse.com

© 2004 Anthony John Monaco
All Rights Reserved.

No part of this book may be reproduced, stored in a retrieval system, or transmitted by any means without the written permission of the author.

First published by AuthorHouse 06/30/04

ISBN: 1-4184-6326-4 (e)
ISBN: 1-4184-6324-8 (sc)

Printed in the United States of America
Bloomington, Indiana

This book is printed on acid-free paper.

The Testimony Of The Major Prophets

The Symbolic Version Of
Isaiah

The Symbolic Version Of
Ezekiel

The Symbolic Version Of
Jeremiah & Lamentations

The Symbolic Version Of
Daniel

Anthony John Monaco

A Stars of the Scriptures Series

Published Books of the Author

The Challenge of Moses
The Symbolic Version Of Genesis

The Symbolic Version Of Exodus

The Symbolic Version Of Job

The Mission of Jesus and John
The Symbolic Version Of The Parables Of The Master

The Symbolic Version Of John

The Symbolic Version Of Revelation

The Songs and Wisdom of David and Solomon
The Symbolic Version of Psalms

The Symbolic Version of Proverbs

The Symbolic Version Of Ecclesiastes &

The Symbolic Version Of The Song of Solomon

The Testimony of the Major Prophets
The Symbolic Version Of Isaiah

The Symbolic Version of Ezekiel

The Symbolic Version of Jeremiah &

The Symbolic Version of Lamentations

The Symbolic Version of Daniel

The Recitations of Mohammed
The Symbolic Version of the Koran

The Scriptures from the Orient
The Symbolic Version of the Dhammapada

The Symbolic Version of the Tao Te Ching of Lao Tzu

The Symbolic Version of the Kitab-i-Aqdas

The Symbolic Version of the Bhagavad Gita

The Leadership of Joseph Smith
The Symbolic Version of the Book of Mormon

The Truth of Nanak and the Sikhs
The Symbolic Version of the Guru Granth Sahib Part I

The Symbolic Version of the Guru Granth Sahib Part II

The Symbolic Version of the Guru Granth Sahib Part III

The Interpretations of Anthony John Monaco

THE SPIRIT IS in the Form
Stop Dying and Start Living

Hey There! Here I Am!!

The Symbolic Version of the Wizard of Oz

(The Motion Picture)

COPYRIGHTED BOOKS OF THE AUTHOR

Stop Dying and Start Living

Hey There! Here I Am!!

The Symbolic Version Of Genesis

The Symbolic Version Of Exodus

The Symbolic Version Of Job

The Symbolic Version Of Isaiah

The Symbolic Version Of John

The Symbolic Version Of Revelation

The Symbolic Version Of The Parables Of The Master

The Symbolic Version Of Ecclesiastes &

The Symbolic Version Of The Song of Solomon

The Symbolic Version of Psalms

The Symbolic Version of Proverbs

The Symbolic Version of Ezekiel

The Symbolic Version of Jeremiah &

The Symbolic Version of Lamentations

The Symbolic Version of Daniel

The Symbolic Version of the Bhagavad Gita

The Symbolic Version of the Koran

The Symbolic Version of the Dhammapada

The Symbolic Version of the Tao Te Ching of Lao Tzu

The Symbolic Version of the Kitab-i-Aqdas

The Symbolic Version of the Wizard of Oz

(The Motion Picture)

The Symbolic Version of the Book of Mormon

The Symbolic Version of the Guru Granth Sahib Part I

The Symbolic Version of the Guru Granth Sahib Part II

The Symbolic Version of the Guru Granth Sahib Part III

The Testimony of The Major Prophets

PREFACE

Isaiah, Ezekiel, Jeremiah and Daniel were major prophets whose books are listed in the Holy Bible (which means, "a collection of many books") filled with words that should lead the reader to experience the true spiritual nature of man while he or she is on earth. These four prophets, as Four Stars of the Scriptures, are aptly named: the name, Isaiah, means "the salvation of the LORD"; the name, Ezekiel means, "God is my strength"; the name, Jeremiah, means, "one who gives glory and exaltation to the LORD"; and the name, Daniel, means, "God is my judge".

The word, prophet, contains two definitions. One definition is a person who is born on earth and who can foretell the future. This ability to foretell future events is described as "prophecy" and this advance knowledge would certainly satisfy the self-active human minds which desire to know what the future holds in advance of everyone else. Many people in all religions would like to know beforehand the future events that will come to pass. Another definition of prophet is a person, inspired and appointed by God, with the ability to prophesy; the ability let the spirit of the LORD--which is everywhere and moving through the human consciousness of everyone--produce instruction and guidance for those who are willing to receive the ongoing blessing that flows constantly and continuously from above, from the divine source, from the LORD.

Isaiah is known as the Evangelical Prophet. He invited everyone to be an angel of the LORD. As he personally allowed the spirit of the LORD to move unhindered through his earthly equipment to reveal the divine nature of the LORD in his own experience, he is also aware that the same creative process is available to everyone. In his ministry, Isaiah offers the Salvation from the LORD to everyone. His teaching to others is described as "Arise, shine, for thy Light is come and the glory of the LORD is risen upon thee". Isaiah invites everyone who listens to him to join him in spirit to experience the covenant of the LORD and, consequently, be moved on earth by the higher power from the LORD.

The writings of <u>Ezekiel</u> reveal in his personal living that, indeed, "God is his strength".

Ezekiel was far away from the material temple in Jerusalem when he experienced his personal covenant with the LORD. The spirit of the LORD was with him and in him as he used many earthly symbols to explain the connection of spirit to human forms.

<u>Jeremiah</u>, "one who gives glory and exaltation to the LORD", was aware that he could not add any glory to the LORD of heaven: he could only magnify the glory of the LORD on earth as he Let the Spirit of the LORD shine through himself and thus inspire others. Jeremiah and Ezekiel are known as "the prophets of individual responsibility".

Finally, <u>Daniel</u>, whose name means "God is my Judge", was willing to live his life trusting the LORD so that the operation of Divine Law was his salvation in his times of trouble.

Let us consider the lives of these "major" prophets who understood that the spirit of the LORD that came directly <u>to</u> them must indeed come <u>through</u> them if they are to have the ability to prophesy and give testimony to the LORD.

The Symbolic Version of
Isaiah

Anthony John Monaco
A Stars of the Scriptures Series

FOREWORD

Isaiah, the prophet, had a vision. He saw something from a high point of spiritual awareness within himself, something that was not generally seen by his contemporaries, even though, the information was available to be seen. This spiritual vision prompted him to preach, to write and to record the Book of Isaiah twenty-seven centuries ago at approximately 740 BC. Whatever he saw, whatever came to focus in his consciousness long ago, and whatever he presented to his contemporaries can and does have meaning to us today if we look beyond the physical interpretation of his words to the spirit behind the words. It is the spirit behind the words which can give an understanding in the here and now of the present moment when we read the words of Isaiah. This spiritual interpretation would be true to all of mankind even if the physical words were written in Hebrew, Greek, Latin, English, or translated from one language to another. The meaning is in the spirit of the words and not in the physical words themselves. The physical words in any language are the bridge to the spirit that is a Reality within every person. The purpose of the Book of Isaiah is to lead the reader toward the Reality, to experience the Reality of Spirit.

If there is such a thing as the spirit behind the words from many different languages, then the spirit is the treasure which contains the real meaning. The truth of Isaiah's words would be in the spirit of the words and not the words per se. The spiritual treasure of the words of Isaiah can be proven and understood in this generation just as surely as when the words were first spoken or written. It is possible for us to re-prove the spirit carried in the words of Isaiah using the spirit which is in ourselves. There is spirit within ourselves: the Spirit of Life. We are alive. If Isaiah had a message to convey "way back then", and the message carried the spirit of Truth, then, it would be possible for us to see and understand his message if we could consider his words in the very same spirit which he used when he first thought, spoke or wrote the words. The spirit of Truth brought understanding to Isaiah and an understanding of Isaiah's words can lead us to the Truth. Although Isaiah discusses people, events and locations widely known in his day, he does so to enable his contemporaries to rise up and participate in his vision that comes from the flow of the spirit.

If the vision of Isaiah were based upon an experience which he had with the LORD while he was alive and which enabled him to speak with authority, then the authority is in the spirit behind the words and not in the words themselves. His words which have come down to us, as recorded in the King James Version of the Holy Bible, are only the carriers of the spirit which he represented on earth. His words are the evidence, the clothing of the spirit, which convey his understanding of divine principles. His words conveyed and impressed some of his audience that he understood something about the Way of the LORD. If we examine the clothing of his words, we might discern the spirit which was used to formulate the words. It is said that spiritual things are spiritually discerned. It is necessary that we discern from a standpoint of the invisible world of spirit rather than from a standpoint of the visible world of form.

The very same words used to describe the world of form can also be used as carriers for the world of Spirit. Let us consider the written words of the Book of Isaiah that exist in the world of form, and see whether we can discern the spirit from which the words were delivered, and, the spirit which brought the words into form. There were people who walked on earth who knew something of the world of spirit. They had names such as Abraham, Isaac, Jacob, Moses, Jesus, John and Isaiah. They walked on earth as human beings. Each of them spoke of the spirit, of the LORD, of God which was "above" the world of form. Isaiah knew that the Being within each human form originated from a Divine Source. The human form carries a spiritual Being. Some people are aware of the presence of the spirit; the majority of the people are not consciously aware of their own spiritual nature. Isaiah tried to tell us that the spirit and the form are not separated; they are connected. The conscious awareness and experience of the dynamic oneness between spirit and form is the covenant-agreement with the LORD. Let us consider the many ways in which Isaiah tried to tell us this many centuries ago. Let us consider *The Symbolic Version of Isaiah.*

CHAPTER 1

1 The vision of Isaiah the son of Amoz, which he saw concerning Judah and Jerusalem in the days of Uzziah, Jotham, Ahaz, and Hezekiah, kings of Judah.

Isaiah the prophet had a vision. He saw the world of his environment from a high point of spiritual awareness within himself which prompted him to speak with authority, to preach, to record for all those with ears to hear at that time over twenty-seven centuries ago. Whatever he saw, whatever came to focus in his particular consciousness long ago, and, whatever he presented to his contemporaries can have meaning to us today if we look beyond the physical interpretation of the words to the spirit which conveys understanding from a higher point of view. Isaiah looked out into his environment and he saw very clearly the conditions in the land of Judah and the city of Jerusalem. For the historical record, the scriptures reveal that a human being named Isaiah saw these things in the days when Uzziah, Jotham, Ahaz and Hezekiah were kings of Judah. The point is that earthly kings ruled in Judah, and they were doing the best that they knew how to do, but peace and harmony did not prevail. Isaiah observes very accurately the conditions and circumstances of the world immediately around him and he offers some sage advice.

2 Hear, O heavens, and give ear, O earth: for the LORD hath spoken, I have nourished and brought up children, and they have rebelled against me.
3 The ox knoweth his owner, and the ass his master's crib: but Israel doth not know, my people doth not consider.
4 Ah sinful nation, a people laden with iniquity, a seed of evildoers, children that are corrupters: they have forsaken the LORD, they have provoked the Holy One of Israel unto anger, they are gone away backward.

Isaiah has something very important to say and he makes a pronouncement in the fashion of a town crier: "Hear, O heavens, and give ear, O earth." Isaiah is speaking to those people who have the ears to hear him and listen to him. The spirit of Isaiah is speaking to the spirits within the people, the spirits that reside in the heavens within each person; and he is also speaking to the earth of the spiritual people which we know as the human portion consisting of a physical body, with its mind and emotions. Isaiah declares the Source for his authority to speak when he tells his listeners that it is the LORD who has spoken. Isaiah is indicating that the LORD has spoken to him; the LORD has made Isaiah aware of some information which Isaiah chooses to announce to his fellow citizens. What is the message of the LORD?

The message is that the LORD has nourished and brought up His children to the present condition in which they find themselves. But, the children, who are the property of the LORD, have rebelled against the LORD. The LORD is the Cause, the Father, of all the children on the face of the planet; the individual beings within the children originate and derive from the GREATER BEING of God, the Father; but, the children of the Father have rebelled against the nature of the Father, the Way of the LORD. Isaiah is aware that he, personally, as a child of God, belongs to the Father, but, the children to whom he is speaking, do not know their Owner. It seems inconceivable that so-called dumb animals such as the ox knows his owner and the ass knows its master's crib, but the crowning creation of man, male and female, the people in general, and Israel in particular, do not consider to Whom they belong. The people do not emulate or reveal their Father's nature, a nature of love, and they, therefore, have become a sinful nation; a people laden with iniquity, a seed of evildoers, children that are corrupters: they have forsaken the LORD. It is perfectly observable to Isaiah that Israel, the inhabitants whom he sees in Jerusalem and Judah, have forsaken the Way of the LORD.

As the people forsake their Owner, they have provoked the Holy One of Israel, God, when, in their rebellious state, they have gone away backward from Him. The people have turned their backs on their purpose to represent the LORD on earth. Instead, they want to represent themselves, the rebellious children which they have become, false selves. If they do not represent the LORD of love and harmony, it is only natural that the people who have fallen away from the LORD should produce an environment filled with chaos.

The people at the time of Isaiah, like the people of today, are not truly aware of the fact that they are the children of God; they may have some beliefs about it; but a belief is not the state of knowing the Truth. This lack of awareness manifests in a condition on earth in which man does not know who he is, why he is on earth, and where he is going. The evidence of deteriorating conditions in the world is proof of man's fallen state of consciousness. The fallen consciousness produced the turmoil, the trials and the tribulations which are observable everywhere. The inhabitants of the earth are so very ill that they claim not to know that the conditions which they have made collectively have indeed been created solely by them.

The inhabitants of the earth are and have been a sinful nation, laden with the iniquity inherited from previous generations with the result that the whole world is deceived. The whole world has become contaminated with concepts formulated by the rebellious, self-active collective human mind referred to in the Bible as a great red dragon, the accuser, the Devil, and Satan. The children of the LORD have indeed forsaken Him and have fallen down to worship the self-concocted vain imaginings which proclaim that there is nothing higher than man in the evolutionary scheme of things. Man, in this sick condition, has produced all of the present circumstances, all the miseries, and all the distortions; he blames these horrible effects on a supernatural Devil, that is separate from himself, whom he mentally created to contend with God. Man has indeed gone away backward; he is on the road to destruction.

The present conditions, miseries and distortions observable on every hand are the evidence of the absence of the true condition from which the distortion has derived. Man's true purpose on earth is to create the true manifest conditions which represent the Father. There is only one right way, a way of the LORD, in which man creates material forms on earth acting in the spirit of love rather than the evil spirits, which are the absence of love. The message of Isaiah is that man is out of position, out of alignment, out of attunement with the spirit being supplied to him or her by the Creator. The power of the LORD is being used for destructive expressions through man instead of creative expressions. The results of a sinful nation need not continue indefinitely to pollute the whole world. Isaiah calls upon the people to change, to repent, to sow a new cause that will reap a new harvest. If man does this, then there is no need for him to be stricken any more by a self-induced illness. Mankind is stricken with an illness caused by rebellion from God and he has been harming himself. Mankind is sick and Isaiah has the prescription for the cure.

5 Why should ye be stricken any more? ye will revolt more and more: the whole head is sick, and the whole heart faint.
6 From the sole of the foot even unto the head there is no soundness in it; but wounds, and bruises, and putrifying sores: they have not been closed, neither bound up, neither mollified with ointment.
7 Your country is desolate, your cities are burned with fire: your land, strangers devour it in your presence, and it is desolate, as overthrown by strangers.
8 And the daughter of Zion is left as a cottage in a vineyard, as a lodge in a garden of cucumbers, as a besieged city.

Isaiah has been speaking to all the hosts of mankind, who are embodied into a worldwide creature, called Man. Isaiah asks why should Man be stricken any more now that he knows the nature and the cause of his illness? It is predictable that Man in his state of illness will continue to revolt more and more, because the whole head of Man is sick, and the whole heart, the whole emotional realm, is faint for lack of the love from the LORD. This is not a disease of only a few people who have observable, physical diseases. If we can envision all men and women on earth as personified as a large single Man, then, Man is sick from the sole of his foot to his head, from bottom to top, there is no soundness of the divine design in the body of mankind. The body of mankind, while it appears outwardly healthy, is filled with wounds, and bruises, and putrefying sores: these ill conditions have not been closed, bound up, nor mollified with soft ointment. Most people do not consider themselves, individually, as being ill. The condition of man in his fallen state has gone untreated.

Here, in symbolic language, it is beautifully and graphically portrayed that **spiritual** man is not providing the proper care for the body of which he is a member. This is the reason that your country is desolate, your cities are burned with fire: strangers devour your land in your presence, and your world is desolate, as overthrown by strangers. This is the reason that the daughter of Zion, the potential beautiful bride for the LORD which Jerusalem and the whole earth should be, has been left as an unattended cottage in the vineyard, overgrown as a lodge in a garden of cucumbers, as a besieged city that has been overgrown with the growth that destroys the city. Zion and Jerusalem,

The Testimony of the Major Prophets

likes ships, are referred to as females, or daughters, available for men. How is it that Isaiah knows of the true value and potential that lies within man?

9 Except the LORD of hosts had left unto us a very small remnant, we should have been as Sodom, and we should have been like unto Gomorrah.
10 Hear the word of the LORD, ye rulers of Sodom; give ear unto the law of our God, ye people of Gomorrah.

Isaiah announces that the LORD of hosts has left a small remnant, a very small portion of the body of mankind, who represent the true nature of man so that it has been possible to avoid total destruction as was the result for Sodom and Gomorrah when Abraham was unable to find one righteous person in either city. The people who listen to Isaiah are advised to hear the word of the LORD; Isaiah has the courage and the audacity to refer to the sinners and hypocrites of his day as "rulers of Sodom"; and he advises others to listen as he refers to them as the "people of Gomorrah". Isaiah does not want any of the people to misunderstand the basic fact that he is referring to all of them as rulers of Sodom and people of Gomorrah. The inhabitants of Jerusalem and Judah are sick and they are not aware of it. In the LORD's view, they are just as wicked as the people in the two cities which were destroyed. Of course, the people to whom Isaiah is speaking believe themselves to be "good" people, who are "normal", and "only human" as they continue to remain self-satisfied. There is no doubt that Isaiah is speaking to all those with ears to hear, those with the integrity to admit that they are in a fallen state of consciousness; that they know not the LORD; and that they are sinners. Isaiah understands that these people are making ritualistic sacrifices unto the LORD as they have been taught by their religious leaders. These people believe that they are "good in the eyes of the LORD" because of their ritualistic practices which they have been doing for generations. What does the LORD, speaking through Isaiah, think of these offerings from the people?

11 To what purpose is the multitude of your sacrifices unto me? saith the LORD: I am full of the burnt offerings of rams, and the fat of fed beasts; and I delight not in the blood of bullocks, or of lambs, or of he goats.
12 When ye come to appear before me, who hath required this at your hand, to tread my courts?

The Lord wants to give us the kingdom which He has prepared for us in heaven to be made manifest on earth, through His earthly creation, men and women, because He is a God of love, order and beauty. He very pointedly asks man in his fallen state the purpose of his many sacrifices of animals? Who has required this pattern of sacrifice to a God of Love? It is the nature of the Father to give the kingdom to His children on earth. Surely, this practice of making sacrifices to God has been a distorted concept of man in the fallen state: men who have behaved in a destructive manner; who has reaped the destructive results of his own behavior; who has implied that God is responsible for the terrible conditions on earth; and, then, who has offered sacrifices to God so that God will take away these chaotic conditions. Man has sown destructive seed and he wants to blame God or propitiate God with burnt offerings of His property for the purpose that God will be "bribed" to take away the bitter harvest.

This pattern of accusation and blame is a characteristic of the accuser, the one who blames, the Devil; and it is not a characteristic of the LORD and His offspring. It is not the LORD's will that man should offer sacrifices of material treasures through a process of destruction, the burning of incense and other nefarious practices designed by fallen man to appease God. This is a distorted concept of man. One wonders why so many churches continue to burn incense and for what purpose other than to call God's attention to the terrible conditions on earth so that God will take away the harvest which was sown by the behavior of men and women. Isaiah speaks the word of the LORD very clearly when he very accurately conveys the wrath of the LORD at man's behavior who continues to offer the stench from the burnt offerings of rams, the fat of beasts and the blood of animals, all of which have a better purpose on earth other than to be killed, burned and destroyed by converting the animal bodies to smoke and ashes to appease the LORD. Does the LORD want this practice of sacrifice to continue? What is the LORD's command to the people in regard to these practices?

13 Bring no more vain oblations; incense is an abomination unto me; the new moons and sabbaths, the calling of assemblies, I cannot away with; it is iniquity, even the solemn meeting.
14 Your new moons and your appointed feasts my soul hateth: they are a trouble unto me; I am weary to bear them.
15 And when ye spread forth your hands, I will hide mine eyes from you: yea, when ye make many prayers, I will not hear: your hands are full of blood.

These material offerings of the destruction of physical animal forms are vain oblations, offerings proffered by men and women based in their own vanity. The LORD doesn't want an offering of man's possessions. He wants an acknowledgment by man that man is the LORD's possession and that man was created for the LORD's purpose. Men and women are included in the instruction that "the earth is the LORD's and the fullness thereof". Oblations and incense are an abomination to the LORD. All the meetings and all the ceremonies that destroy the forms of animals to give honor to the LORD are an iniquity that the LORD cannot do away with. The LORD's soul hates the new moons and appointed feasts; they are a trouble unto the LORD and He is weary to bear them. The rebellious people started these meetings and the people must end them.

When the people hold their hands in allegiance to the LORD and they continue to remain sinners, the LORD will hide his eyes from the people and will not hear their prayers of vanity because their hands are full of the blood of destructiveness. The people are sinners comparable to the inhabitants of Sodom and Gomorrah. The people are sinners because they do not allow the spirit of God to flow through His creation, man, into the earth. God's kingdom cannot come on earth as long as men and women withhold themselves from participation in this creative process that will bring the true design. There is only one course of action available for sinners in any generation, but, the action must begin with the admission that the person is a sinner.

16 Wash you, make you clean; put away the evil of your doings from before mine eyes; cease to do evil;

Each child of the Father, each son or daughter of God, must begin with himself and herself and wash the iniquities, the sins, the destructive feelings and thoughts that are not of the spirit of God from one's own mind and heart. There can be no other starting point! The individual heart is not pure; it harbors the attitudes and feelings of fear, greed, resentment, hatred and other feelings which are not characterized by the spirit of God, which is love. The individual must put away the evils of his doings, his distorted expressions, before the ever-watchful eyes of the LORD and cease to do evil. Man has the ability to choose; he can choose to cease to do evil. Isaiah knew the requirement of the need for purity of heart so that the word of the LORD can manifest on earth. A person needs to learn to do well by being doers of the Word of God, as the spirit of God flows through each person. Actions and deeds are the fruit of the tree called man by which he is known on earth. Words of prayer that call upon God to change conditions on earth, except as they can be changed through each person, mean nothing unless they are substantiated by deed—the end result of the thought, word and deed sequence. When Isaiah instructs us to cease to do evil, he points us in the direction of personal cleanliness in our own consciousness, the content of our own minds and hearts. What begins in consciousness has immediate effect in our behaviors and our actions.

17 Learn to do well; seek judgment, relieve the oppressed, judge the fatherless, plead for the widow

Learn to do well by being doers of the word. Isaiah calls attention to the need to learn to do well from the divine standpoint, not from the human standpoint. The divine standpoint is that a person must monitor his or her actions by learning what the spirit of God would do if it had unrestricted access through the person into the earth. The spirit of Love expressed into the earth would have an immediate observable impact and it would have a direct effect on the fatherless child, the widow, the oppressed and those who were judged by the unholy standards of human nature. The fatherless child symbolizes the irresponsible actions set in motion by males and females who did not provide a clear channel for the Father. The widow symbolizes the beginning of a divinely inspired action which is subsequently terminated and left alone to perish.

It is obvious why the LORD has no use for the rituals of meetings and the burning of incense and animal bodies: this time-consuming busy-work prevents the blessings from God to flow into the earth through man because mankind is so preoccupied with the sacrifices which are an abomination unto the LORD. The cessation of the sacrifices allows for the LORD to come into the earth through the person who "sacrifices" his human capacities in dedicated service for the LORD to come through him into the earth. A person who allows the spirit of the LORD, the spirit of love, to come into the earth in his momentary living will let the nature of heaven come into the earth. Heaven is heavenly! How shall the heaven of the true design come into the earth?

18 Come now, and let us reason together, saith the LORD: though your sins be as scarlet, they shall be as white as snow; though they be red like crimson, they shall be as wool.
19 If ye be willing and obedient, ye shall eat the good of the land:
20 But if ye refuse and rebel, ye shall be devoured with the sword: for the mouth of the LORD hath spoken it.

The teaching and preaching of Isaiah, who is a spokesman for the LORD, invites people to, "Come now, and let us reason together". There must be sufficient interest on the part of the listeners to hear the invitation to come to Isaiah. The time to come to Isaiah when Isaiah spoke the word of the

LORD was "now". As we read and hear the spirit of Isaiah, it is "now" for us. It is always now! The LORD through Isaiah offers man, who is in a fallen state of consciousness, and who does not know his true place of position in relationship to the LORD, an opportunity to return to his true position. The true position of man, made in the image and likeness of God, is to stand with God in man's rightful place as the connecting link between the heaven and the earth. The LORD invites man to, "Come now, and let us reason together", let us reason from the same vantage point where man will become aware of his true responsibility in relationship with the LORD, in which man will allow the spirit of the LORD to come into the earth. Of course, the present conditions on earth are proof that man has not been fulfilling this responsibility. Man has been doing something else; man has been doing his own thing.

The invitation of the LORD through Isaiah is very simple to understand: a person who has not been living the correct way on earth needs to change his ways; he needs to repent. Even though the person's sins of the past be as scarlet or crimson, they shall be as white as snow and as wool as the spirit of the LORD is allowed to flow through the heart and the mind. A person can choose to change behavior, but the person must be willing and obedient to the instruction of the LORD through the words of Isaiah. If a person does change, if a person does repent and adopt a new behavior, that person shall eat of the good of the land. As the spirit of the LORD passes through any individual, the spirit will bring health and prosperity through the open channel that delivers the spirit into the earth. But if a person refuses and rebels against the delivery of the spirit of the LORD into the earth, which is the responsibility of everyone, then the person will be devoured by the spirit which is experienced as a destructive fire as it flows through a person who is out of alignment with the spirit of the LORD. The choice for man is to be blessed by the spirit or devoured by the sword of Truth which will cut away distortions. The choice is with each person to choose the road of expression which he will follow. This is such a simple and straight-forward invitation by Isaiah for his listeners to let the spirit of the LORD to come into the earth to produce beauty; or, to let horrible distortions to enter the world to produce ugliness.

21 How is the faithful city become an harlot! it was full of judgment; righteousness lodged in it; but now murderers.
22 Thy silver is become dross, thy wine mixed with water:
23 Thy princes are rebellious, and companions of thieves: every one loveth gifts, and followeth after rewards: they judge not the fatherless, neither doth the cause of the widow come unto them.

At one time on earth, every person on earth allowed the spirit of the LORD to come freely into the earth to produce the kingdom of heaven, the Garden of Eden, the faithful city which is built when the citizens of the earth allow the spirit of the Father to enter the earth. How could the faithful city become an harlot?! At one time, the faithful city was full of righteous judgment; righteousness lodged in the city because the people let the LORD's rightness into the city; but, now the world is filled with murderers, people who murder the spirit of the LORD as it passes through each person into the earth, and the environment reflects the contents of the minds and hearts of the people very accurately. The Truth of people, which is symbolized by beautiful shiny silver, has become dross, tarnished with blackness; the true wine of life has been mixed with water to produce an inferior diluted product. Isaiah gives further examples of the fallen state of man.

The Testimony of the Major Prophets

The princes who should represent the king are rebellious from their father, the King; they do not behave as royal children. A King knows and loves the fact that his people are well and that they prosper. The princes have become the companions of thieves in their desires to want treasures from the environment. Everyone loves earthly gifts and they always want a material reward. They are so busy in their wants of material things that they have lost their concern and compassion for people; they do not care for the fatherless children or the widows. Does the LORD have anything to say about these distorted conditions on earth that have been transpiring for so long a time that everyone considers these circumstances to be normal?

24 Therefore saith the Lord, the LORD of hosts, the mighty One of Israel, Ah, I will ease me of mine adversaries, and avenge me of mine enemies:
25 And I will turn my hand upon thee, and purely purge away thy dross, and take away all thy tin:
26 And I will restore thy judges as at the first, and thy counsellors as at the beginning: afterward thou shalt be called, The city of righteousness, the faithful city.

Isaiah gives us some insight into the divine organization for planet Earth. The spirit, the Being, who lives within the physical form of Isaiah is a Lord (notice the small letters). Each of us, like Isaiah, is a Being, a Lord, within a human form. The GREATER BEING to whom the Lord Isaiah is responsible is the LORD of hosts. The hosts have reference to all the Beings on planet Earth who are either in human form or not presently in human forms. The LORD of hosts is responsible to the mighty One of Israel, God Almighty, or the Father. All spiritual Beings in heaven are always in agreement! Isaiah teaches us that there is a divine "chain-of-command" in the world of spirit and the spirits are all of the same substance or composition but at different levels of power and intensity. It is expected that these "three spirits who are one" should speak as with one voice. The Lord, the LORD of hosts and the Almighty are all connected and they are one spirit. Let us hear the message of the "three" spirits.

Therefore, the Lord, the LORD of hosts and the mighty One of Israel, declare that He will ease himself of the people in the fallen state who are functioning as adversaries and enemies of the LORD. This will be done by the LORD turning the hand of right control against the rebellious people, who are under the wrong control, which will take away the tarnish, the blackness, the dross which stains the silver. Silver is the symbol of Truth. Shiny silver symbolized the Truth; the blackness on the silver symbolizes the impurities that tarnish man, made in the image and likeness of God. Silver symbolizes the truth of man. The shiny tin is not silver. As silver symbolizes the Truth of man, shiny tin symbolizes the counterfeit man in the fallen state who tries to be good by his many rituals. The LORD shall take away all the shiny tin, all the vanity of man who will continue to function as a counterfeit self that is symbolized by shiny tin.

The people who prepare the way of the LORD on earth shall ascend to the positions of true righteousness and their consciousness shall be restored. This new state of consciousness is compared to the judges being restored to their true positions and the counselors would function as they did in the beginning before the fall of man into this distorted condition. Afterward, after the behavior has changed to reveal the way of the LORD through people, then the city of righteousness, the city of the right-use-ness of the capacities of man, shall create the faithful city because man has become faithful once again to his true purpose on earth. As long as man remains in the fallen state unfaithful to the Spirit of the LORD on earth, he can never build the faithful city

27 Zion shall be redeemed with judgment, and her converts with righteousness.
28 And the destruction of the transgressors and of the sinners shall be together, and they that forsake the LORD shall be consumed.
29 For they shall be ashamed of the oaks which ye have desired, and ye shall be confounded for the gardens that ye have chosen.
30 For ye shall be as an oak whose leaf fadeth, and as a garden that hath no water.
31 And the strong shall be as tow, and the maker of it as a spark, and they shall both burn together, and none shall quench them.

Zion is considered to be another name for the city of Jerusalem, but **Zion** relates to the **spiritual** level of the city and **Jerusalem** refers to the **material** level. The city, whether it is referred to as Zion or Jerusalem, is personified, or symbolized, as a woman which is called the daughter of **Zion**, or the daughter of **Jerusalem**. Isaiah tells us that she, the city, shall be redeemed with the correct judgment of the people and she shall be converted to the faithful city with righteousness, the righteousness of the people. The converts of Zion indicate that a conversion is necessary from the present distorted state, known as the normal human nature state, to be replaced by a true state that is available in spirit as a potential even though it is not yet known by fallen human minds. At the same time that the conversion of the sinners is taking place among the people who return to righteousness, the destruction of the transgressors and the sinners shall also take place simultaneously. There shall be an integrative and a destructive cycle taking place simultaneously depending exactly on the choices of the people. The people who forsake the LORD shall be consumed.

The presence of those who provide the right example will cause the sinners to be ashamed of the oaks, the symbol of strength, the things of the environment which loom large and desirable in the fallen consciousness of those who make the wrong choices. The sinner will be confounded by the gardens of wrong expression which they have produced by reason of their wrong choices. Their gardens shall wither and die as an oak or a garden that has no water. The sinner is symbolized by the deterioration and decay of a garden without water; it shall lead to death. On the other hand, the strong, the persons who allow the way of the LORD to be expressed through them are symbolized by the tow, the dry grass-like hemp, which is strong as rope and burns easily. When the spark is added to the tow, fire results. How impressed the ancients must have been with the magic of fire, with its heat, warmth and light. Isaiah states that this combination of tow and spark, the form and the spirit of the LORD, symbolized by the physical form and the fire, that burn together in controlled expression and that none shall quench them. Is this not an example of living in a controlled manner, rather than the chaotic out-of-control state, which man calls living, but which is a dying state? What a beautiful beginning point! It is only logical that, with this true beginning, Isaiah can prophesy future glories for those who will choose to love and serve the LORD; and, tribulations for those who choose to serve themselves.

CHAPTER 2

1 The word that Isaiah the son of Amoz saw concerning Judah and Jerusalem.
2 And it shall come to pass in the last days, that the mountain of the LORD's house shall be established in the top of the mountains, and shall be exalted above the hills; and all nations shall flow unto it.

The word that Isaiah saw because he was in position on earth in the covenant-agreement with the LORD allowed him to speak truly and accurately concerning the conditions in the city of Jerusalem and in the nation of Judah. Isaiah could see conditions as they were and with an understanding of how the conditions in the environment were created. Isaiah could see with divine vision, spiritual vision, which begins with the premise that everything on earth comes through the power of the LORD. This source of power from on high is symbolized as coming from the mountain top of the LORD's house established in the top of the mountains. All nations of the earth shall receive the flow from this mountain top, the Holy Mountain which symbolizes the Divine Source of Power. There is no other source of power than the LORD God Who is everywhere

Isaiah, in his position of covenant-agreement with the LORD, could readily see that the fallen state of consciousness of all the people was responsible for the conditions which appeared in manifest form in Jerusalem and Judah. All conditions are created by the power of God moving through the consciousness of the people. The conditions of the city of Jerusalem were produced by the present inhabitants, or their fathers before them. How else could the sins of the fathers be visited upon the children generation after generation except through the consciousness of the inhabitants? Isaiah has discovered that it is not necessary to continue the destructive patterns of behavior simply because these patterns had become customs and traditions. Isaiah has experienced the victory over the inherited traditions, by not being bound and controlled by them, and he could see the habitual patterns moving through the many generations that formed the culture of the people. The ability to rise above customs and traditions is to see with the LORD's vision which is available in the covenant-agreement.

A change in customs, behavior patterns and traditions, which have been imposed upon the present generation by the process of the "sins of the fathers", is the new order of the present day. If this change is to occur, then the old ways, the old habit patterns, the traditions of the fallen state of consciousness (such as the burnt offerings!), would be in their "last days" because new ways, new patterns and new conditions would herald the beginning of the "new days". But the new effects and the new ways will only result from a new state of consciousness. Things must change in consciousness **before** the changes occur in physical form. There is a need for the last days of the traditions in the old state of consciousness to be relinquished before the new ways can put in an appearance. It is traditional to think of the "last days" as the end of the world that comes by reason of some great destructive holocaust. A spiritual discernment of the last days is the change in the consciousness of the people from the fallen state to a new state: the "last days" of self-active people who are certain that they have been right all along must be replaced with the day of the LORD, which is an understanding that what comes forth is absolutely due to the state of consciousness which is expressed into the world..

Isaiah is teaching people that since the population of Jerusalem is comprised of individuals, it is obvious that the change in the mass consciousness must be accomplished on an individual basis. In this manner, an individual is responsible to God for preparing the way of the LORD and making His path straight through that individual's heart, mind and body. The overwhelming majority of people, then and now, do not want to be spiritual pioneers who begin the process. If they never begin, they can never ascend the mountain of the Lord which leads to the covenant. The LORD speaking through the prophet Isaiah is extending the invitation to all people, with the desire that many people will use their ability to choose to let the spirit of the LORD flow through each of them as an individual. The spirit of the LORD will produce new forms as it flows through the consciousness of each person.

3 And many people shall go and say, Come ye, and let us go up to the mountain of the LORD, to the house of the God of Jacob; and he will teach us of his ways, and we will walk in his paths: for out of Zion shall go forth the law, and the word of the LORD from Jerusalem.
4 And he shall judge among the nations, and shall rebuke many people: and they shall beat their swords into plowshares, and their spears into pruninghooks: nation shall not lift up sword against nation, neither shall they learn war any more.
5 O house of Jacob, come ye, and let us walk in the light of the LORD.

Isaiah is preaching that the desire of the LORD is that many people shall come together to talk, and to agree to ascend into a new state of consciousness with the LORD, by letting the LORD's consciousness lift them up into the house of the God of Jacob. Isaiah uses the name of Jacob to symbolize the fallen state of man, who thinks that he is only human, but who has the potential to rise up to the state of the spirit which is symbolized by the name change to Israel where he will know the LORD. It should be stimulating to learn that the God of Jacob, who lived many generations ago, is being offered at the time of Isaiah indicating an eternal God. The God of Jacob will teach us His ways and we will walk in His paths with the result that when the LORD teaches us His ways, then, out of Zion, the place of spiritual expression within a person and among people, there shall go forth both the law and the word from the city of Jerusalem. The LORD's spirit must go forth through a body of people who carry the spirit of the LORD. The LORD needs a body of

The Testimony of the Major Prophets

people to speak the word of the LORD and to exemplify the way of the LORD on earth. A body of people develops from a single cell. An individual is a cell in the body of mankind.

The people who carry the LORD's spirit will be the means through which the LORD will be able to judge among the nations, rebuke many people with the old state of consciousness, influence the people to beat their swords of war into plowshares and their spears into pruning hooks: instruments of war need to be converted into implements of peace. After this change has been done in the consciousness of the many, then, nation will not lift up their swords against nation any more. It would be foolish to expect the implementation of peace among nations before the consciousness of the people has changed. So, Isaiah, calls to the house of Jacob to come to him as he extends the invitation from the LORD to walk in the light, the understanding, of the LORD. The path to be walked is the way of the LORD. The house of Jacob was designed to be the body of God on earth. The people are not fulfilling their purpose on earth by walking in the light of the LORD; they are walking in darkness. A cursory observation of the environment of Jerusalem reveals to Isaiah and to those who hear his message, that the inhabitants of the land are on the wrong path; they are in the fallen state of man, they are in the house of Jacob.

6 Therefore thou hast forsaken thy people the house of Jacob, because they be replenished from the east, and are soothsayers like the Philistines, and they please themselves in the children of strangers.
7 Their land also is full of silver and gold, neither is there any end of their treasures; their land is also full of horses, neither is there any end of their chariots:
8 Their land also is full of idols; they worship the work of their own hands, that which their own fingers have made:
9 And the mean man boweth down, and the great man humbleth himself: therefore forgive them not.

The LORD has forsaken His people, the house of Jacob, because they are not revealing the spirit of the LORD in their living of life on earth. If the people of Judah, who are descendants of the house of Jacob, (who became Israel after his experience with the angel of the LORD), are not revealing the way of the LORD in their living, then they must have replenished, replaced, their spiritual purpose with what Isaiah describes as the soothsayers of the Philistines, a warlike people who once had a champion called Goliath. The Philistines please themselves in the children of strangers after they have defeated the strangers. Isaiah further describes the Philistines as a people who desire material treasures described as silver and gold, horses and chariots, idols that they have made with their own fingers and they worship these man-made creations. The people who should be the house of Jacob, a spiritual house that loves the LORD, has become as the Philistines. The people have become mean in their ways and the mean men bow themselves down to earthly treasures and earthly images; and people, who should be great men on earth in representation of the LORD, humble themselves before those with material treasures. Isaiah states that people who are trapped in these ways cannot be forgiven. What shall the people who desire to listen to Isaiah do in order to avoid the sins of the majority of people who have forgotten the purpose of the house of Jacob—who became the children of Israel—and the teachings of the LORD through Moses? What is the teaching of the LORD through the prophet, Isaiah?

10 Enter into the rock, and hide thee in the dust, for fear of the LORD, and for the glory of his majesty.
11 The lofty looks of man shall be humbled, and the haughtiness of men shall be bowed down, and the LORD alone shall be exalted in that day.
12 For the day of the LORD of hosts shall be upon every one that is proud and lofty, and upon every one that is lifted up; and he shall be brought low:
13 And upon all the cedars of Lebanon, that are high and lifted up, and upon all the oaks of Bashan,
14 And upon all the high mountains, and upon all the hills that are lifted up,
15 And upon every high tower, and upon every fenced wall,
16 And upon all the ships of Tarshish, and upon all pleasant pictures.
17 And the loftiness of man shall be bowed down, and the haughtiness of men shall be made low: and the LORD alone shall be exalted in that day.

Isaiah advises those with ears to hear, the people who are willing to follow his teaching, to enter into the rock, the rock of the covenant which is the solid place within one's self. The people are also to hide in the dust of the material self for fear and awe of the power of the LORD and for the glory of His majesty which has created the material person which each one is in the present state. This is a direction to enter into the "closet within" to do two things: to shut out the opinions and beliefs of the fallen material world in which one finds one's self; and, to contemplate on the relationship between yourself and the LORD, your God. There is no one else within the solid-rock relationship of the covenant-agreement that is available between man and Creator, between the material human self and the spiritual Self of the true identity that man is made in the image and likeness of God. The opinions and beliefs of the others should be left "outside".

In the outside world of human nature with all of its distortions, the lofty looks, the lofty views, of man shall be humbled when the Truth of the covenant-agreement is known in one's own experience. The people in their mistaken beliefs that they are material creatures in a world without the LORD which gives them their attitudes of haughtiness shall be bowed down and brought low when the Truth is known. When the Truth is known, the LORD alone shall be exalted because it will be known that the earth is the LORD's. There is a material self that shall be brought low; and there is a spiritual Self that shall be lifted up. The material self cannot be brought low unless it presently occupies a high position in which it does not belong.

This error in the position of the false human-ego material self shall be brought low in the day of the LORD of hosts. When it is discovered that there is a LORD of hosts, who is a LORD of all the hosts of people everywhere, then, in that day, everyone who is falsely lifted up to where he is proud and lofty, shall be brought low. The cedars of Lebanon and the oaks of Bashan are tall trees which are used as symbols of men and women who have exalted themselves into high positions in the human nature world in the man-made scheme of things. Other symbols of wealth and affluence in the material world are symbolized by high mountains, hills, towers and fenced walls, the great ships of Tarshish, and pleasant pictures. These are all symbols of fallen man in his effort to raise himself back to the position from whence he has fallen. Man in the false high and elevated position in the fallen world shall surely be made low and the LORD shall be exalted in that day. When a man knows the LORD, he shall do certain things to demonstrate his new values.

The Testimony of the Major Prophets

20 In that day a man shall cast his idols of silver, and his idols of gold, which they made each one for himself to worship, to the moles and to the bats;
21 To go into the clefts of the rocks, and into the tops of the ragged rocks, for fear of the LORD, and for the glory of his majesty, when he ariseth to shake terribly the earth.
22 Cease ye from man, whose breath is in his nostrils: for wherein is he to be accounted of?

When a man knows his relationship in covenant-agreement with the LORD, then man shall cast his gold and silver idols—which were creations made by him so that he could worship them—to the moles, to the bats and to clefts in the rocks. The idols shall be utterly abolished without fear of reprisal from the false gods. The knowing of the presence of the LORD shall shake terribly the earth of one's body because man is no longer controlled by the false gods of the earth. The shaking results from the increased surge of spirit which is allowed to flow through the heart, mind and body as the allegiance to traditional customs are relinquished. Man is now controlled by the heaven of the spirit of the LORD. The spirit is symbolized by the breath that is in man's nostrils. The spirit and the breath of life come from the LORD. Man is accountable only to the LORD. The idols are unnecessary.

CHAPTER 3

1 For, behold, the Lord, the LORD of hosts, doth take away from Jerusalem and from Judah the stay and the staff, the whole stay of bread, and the whole stay of water,
2 The mighty man, and the man of war, the judge, and the prophet, and the prudent, and the ancient,
3 The captain of fifty, and the honourable man, and the counsellor, and the cunning artificer, and the eloquent orator.
4 And I will give children to be their princes, and babes shall rule over them.

Isaiah tells his listeners to behold, to observe for themselves, that the LORD of hosts, the LORD of everyone, Who is the Source of Life for everyone, has taken away the spiritual substance from the people of Jerusalem and Judah, their spiritual substance which has made them, in the past, a holy people and a holy nation. There is such a thing as spiritual substance which accumulates and builds in the human form. Isaiah refers to this spiritual substance, which is the result of the covenant with the LORD, as the stay and the staff, the mainstay of the populace who should be expressing this bread of life which comes from the Lord into the earth. Just as bread is the symbol of the spirit of Life which comes from the LORD, "water" is the symbol of the spirit of Truth which comes from the LORD. If the people stray from their allegiance to the LORD, and they leave the position where they receive the blessings of Life and Truth, the bread and the water, then, the LORD takes these two vital spirits away from the people. Actually, the LORD does not take the blessings away as much as the people remove themselves from the place of the covenant where the blessings would be received. This foolish action on the part of the people who depart from the covenant has removed the strength of the spirits of Life and Truth from the leaders who, previously, had strength and wisdom; the mighty man, the man of war, the judge, the prophet, the prudent, and the ancient, the captain of fifty, and the honorable man, and the counselor, the cunning artificer, and the eloquent orator. If the people move away, abandon their position of being the LORD's people, then they become weaker and less talented. In this instance, the LORD will give immature children to be their princes, their leaders, and spiritual babes shall rule over the weakened populace.

The Testimony of the Major Prophets

5 And the people shall be oppressed, every one by another, and every one by his neighbour: the child shall behave himself proudly against the ancient, and the base against the honourable.
6 When a man shall take hold of his brother of the house of his father, saying, Thou hast clothing, be thou our ruler, and let this ruin be under thy hand:
7 In that day shall he swear, saying, I will not be an healer; for in my house is neither bread nor clothing: make me not a ruler of the people.
8 For Jerusalem is ruined, and Judah is fallen: because their tongue and their doings are against the LORD, to provoke the eyes of his glory.

A people who do not carry the spiritual substance of Life and Truth, which come from the LORD, shall be an oppressed people because of their weakness due to the reduction of the spirit of Life, and the reduction of the spirit of Truth. This reduction of the "bread" of Life and "water" of Truth from the covenant with the LORD shall result in distortions which manifest among the people. The divine order inherent in the covenant shall be replaced by chaos: people and neighbors oppress each other; children behave with false pride against the ancient and ignore their wisdom; base and coarse people contend with the honorable. These are the conditions of the day and they are the signs of the times, the events which Isaiah asks the people to behold, and see the deterioration which is everywhere

At a time of deterioration and decay, such as this, a man will take hold of his brother of the house of his earthly father, a person that he knows who has material wealth, and on that basis alone, appoint that person to be the ruler. The person with material wealth is placed in charge of the ruin which has occurred because the people have moved away from the LORD. The people want the wealth and prosperity, which is exemplified by a wealthy man, and they elect him to be their ruler. In the day that the person is elected to be the ruler, he shall declare by oath to the people that he will not be a healer of the ruined conditions. In the house of his being and in the house where he lives, that person does not have the quality of leadership, neither the bread of life within or the clothing of ideas, to do the job that they want done. He will ask his brothers not to make him a ruler of the people because he does not have enough material wealth or the talent and ability to make them all wealthy. It should be obvious that Jerusalem is ruined and Judah is fallen because their tongue and their doings, the words and the actions of the people, are against the purpose of the LORD and the eyes of His glory, the vision of the LORD. It is impossible for people to succeed if they ignore the LORD. Isaiah asks his listeners to look at the faces of the people!

9 The shew of their countenance doth witness against them; and they declare their sin as Sodom, they hide it not. Woe unto their soul! for they have rewarded evil unto themselves.
10 Say ye to the righteous, that it shall be well with him: for they shall eat the fruit of their doings.
11 Woe unto the wicked! it shall be ill with him: for the reward of his hands shall be given him.

The countenances of the people are a witness against them; their facial expressions declare their sin openly, as was the case with the people who lived in Sodom, and they do not hide their sins anymore. They believe that their way is preferable to the Way of the LORD. Of course, woe must come unto their soul! for they have rewarded evil unto themselves. They have sown evil and they reap evil. This is the law of the LORD: as you sow, so shall you reap. Isaiah tells his students, his disciples, those who will be instructed by his advice, to tell the righteous that it shall be well with them because they shall "eat" the fruit of their doings; the people shall reap what they express and they shall know what they express. But woe unto the wicked! The same law applies to the wicked and it shall be ill with him because the reward of his hands, the behaviors that he makes that are under his own control, shall be given in kind to him. This is the working of the Law of the LORD and it is very, very just. The problem is the mindset of the people; they want to sow evil and reap a different and pleasing harvest.

12 As for my people, children are their oppressors, and women rule over them. O my people, they which lead thee cause thee to err, and destroy the way of thy paths.
13 The LORD standeth up to plead, and standeth to judge the people.
14 The LORD will enter into judgment with the ancients of his people, and the princes thereof: for ye have eaten up the vineyard; the spoil of the poor is in your houses.
15 What mean ye that ye beat my people to pieces, and grind the faces of the poor? saith the Lord GOD of hosts.

Isaiah, who speaks the word of the LORD, observes that His people, spiritual beings in human forms, the men of the LORD, are immature, undisciplined children of the fallen human nature state. The children of men oppress the spiritual beings who are in the human forms, usurp their power, divert their true purpose and rebel against the LORD by doing whatever they feel like doing. These human egos are symbolized by the term, women, the women rule over the spirits, beings or the adult men. Lack of true leadership and the material desires of the human state are the faults that cause the people to err in their ways and to destroy the true path of strength in their own experience. The LORD speaking through Isaiah stands up to plead with the people and to judge the behaviors of the people objectively, as the LORD would assess their behaviors, in an attempt to help them to return to their spiritual roots as a people, which would return their strength.

The Law of the LORD is always at work in the affairs of the people and the true judgment from the LORD has been ignored by the ancients and princes of the past who should have provided spiritual leadership. Consequently, a greedy people have eaten up the vineyard, symbolizing the fruits of their environments, without providing proper care for the vine, and this inconsiderate action has brought the spoil of the poor, emptiness and nothingness, into their houses. Isaiah sounds the word of the Lord GOD of all the hosts of people when he asks why the people are behaving in such a manner that beats the LORD's children to pieces and grinds the faces of the poor as their actions of taking from the environment, without planting new seed, makes matters worse. The LORD speaking through Isaiah has more to say!

16 Moreover the LORD saith, Because the daughters of Zion are haughty, and walk with stretched forth necks and wanton eyes, walking and mincing as they go, and making a tinkling with their feet:
17 Therefore the LORD will smite with a scab the crown of the head of the daughters of Zion, and the LORD will discover their secret parts.
18 In that day the Lord will take away the bravery of their tinkling ornaments about their feet, and their cauls, and their round tires like the moon,

The Testimony of the Major Prophets

19 The chains, and the bracelets, and the mufflers,
20 The bonnets, and the ornaments of the legs, and the headbands, and the tablets, and the earrings,
21 The rings, and nose jewels,
22 The changeable suits of apparel, and the mantles, and the wimples, and the crisping pins,
23 The glasses, and the fine linen, and the hoods, and the vails.

The "daughters of Zion" symbolize the people of Jerusalem, male and female, who have fallen away from the spiritual covenant-agreement with the LORD and they have descended into the actions of human nature. Their proud, materialistic and selfish ways are described by Isaiah as women who are haughty, walking with stretched-forth necks to observe what they can get, walking in a manner that makes their feet, adorned with ornamental bells, tinkle to attract attention to themselves. They are filled with the desires that they want some of the material treasures of the world which have been placed there by the efforts of someone else. This selfish action cannot go unpunished by the LORD and the operation of His law.

In symbolic language, Isaiah describes the retribution that comes from breaking the law—you can't really break the law since you always reap what you sow— as the scab on the crown of the head of the daughters of Zion. The people of Jerusalem have been wounded by their collective behavior and the scab of their wound is observable in the character of the people. The scab, the evidence of the wound, is not the same physical wound on all the people; but it is a wound on their heads to symbolize that the minds and the hearts of the people are not being used for the purpose of the LORD which would make the people a mighty nation. The LORD can see what the people believe to be are the secret parts of their selfish desires. It is only a matter of time, until the people lose the material treasures with which they adorn and decorate their bodies, such as various jewels, ornaments, chains, stylish clothing, etc. These items are used to conceal the inner worthlessness of the people when they feel the emptiness which results from their separation from the covenant with the LORD. These displays of material affluence are a cover-up; signs of the moral disintegration of true character and an attempt to hide or ignore the facts from one's self.

24 And it shall come to pass, that instead of sweet smell there shall be stink; and instead of a girdle a rent; and instead of well set hair baldness; and instead of a stomacher a girding of sackcloth; and burning instead of beauty.
25 Thy men shall fall by the sword, and thy mighty in the war.
26 And her gates shall lament and mourn; and she being desolate shall sit upon the ground.

Isaiah predicts that the deterioration of the society of Jerusalem and Judah shall progress from the sweet smell of apparent success to a stink of decay; that instead of a beautiful girdle, there will appear a rent, a torn cloth; baldness shall replace well-set hair; a girding of sackcloth shall replace a decorative stomacher, the apparel that is worn to add bulk to the breast and waist as a sign of wealth; and burning of the bare skin when there is no protective clothing shall replace the beautiful coverings of fine raiment. The deterioration shall go much further than the loss of personal clothing and ornaments. The people are weak. The men of the weakened fallen state shall fall by the sword and by those who are mighty in war. The gates of the beautiful city that Jerusalem could have been shall lament and mourn at the fate of a city in weakness, disintegration and decay.

The people being desolate shall do nothing to help itself. A demoralized people shall simply sit upon the ground and do nothing.

CHAPTER 4

1 And in that day seven women shall take hold of one man, saying, We will eat our own bread, and wear our own apparel: only let us be called by thy name, to take away our reproach.
2 In that day shall the branch of the LORD be beautiful and glorious, and the fruit of the earth shall be excellent and comely for them that are escaped of Israel.

In that day of disintegration, demoralization and decay in Jerusalem, when a dejected people know not what to do, there is a need for a leader to rise up among the down-hearted people. This very special leader is described as a branch of the LORD who would reveal a beautiful and glorious spirit. The spirit that this person carries will originate in the LORD; the person will not have to create the spirit of the LORD which already exists; he will simply have to be a branch of the spirit and allow the spirit of the LORD to flow into the earth through him, through his heart, mind and body. This action will produce a result, an observable effect, the fruit of the earth from his living branch of the LORD, that will be excellent and comely among the fallen, demoralized people who are demoralized because they have fallen from, or escaped from, the spirit of Israel, the divine spirit that Jacob became years ago when he became a branch of the LORD. The person who would allow the spirit of the LORD to flow through him would be a real man, a real leader among the people of Jerusalem and Judah who have lost the spirit of their forefathers, Abraham, Isaac and Jacob, who became Israel.

If the real man, the person who carries the spirit of the LORD from the vine into his particular branch that allows the spirit to flow through his heart, mind and physical body, then, the demoralized people in male physical bodies are not "real men" who carry the spirit of victory; the demoralized people are symbolized by women, the weaker sex. In that day, Isaiah said that seven women shall take hold of one man. In the symbolism of numbers, the number, "seven", has reference to the completion of a cycle. The seven "women", symbolize the demoralized people who are looking for a leader to whom they can connect with, give their allegiance to, and follow the man out of the depressed state in which they find themselves. The fallen people, who are sitting on the ground doing nothing for themselves, need a visible point of orientation to follow and to emulate. The completed cycle by the seven women will produce a man of the LORD who has the seven spirits before the throne of God. (See "The Symbolic Version of Revelation")

Some of the fallen people are willing to eat their own "bread" of life that comes from the LORD, the spirit that will strengthen them; they are willing to wear their own "apparel", the symbols of their own hearts, minds and bodies; but the one thing that they really need is to take "Thy" name, the name of the man, of the branch of the LORD, of the point of orientation so that they will develop the strength that he is displaying, and this strength in their own experience will take away the reproach that they feel in their demoralized condition. If the people of Jerusalem and Judah, symbolized by the seven women, will listen to Isaiah, a branch of the LORD, then, conditions will change as the people change from their fallen, demoralized, decadent state to a holy state.

3 And it shall come to pass, that he that is left in Zion, and he that remaineth in Jerusalem, shall be called holy, even every one that is written among the living in Jerusalem:
4 When the Lord shall have washed away the filth of the daughters of Zion, and shall have purged the blood of Jerusalem from the midst thereof by the spirit of judgment, and by the spirit of burning.

And it shall come to pass, that he, the real spiritual leader, and his followers, who remain in Jerusalem shall be called holy. They will be holy if they allow the spirit of the branch of the LORD, which is a holy spirit, to flow through them in their living. The spirit of the LORD shall bring forth new life in His people who let this phenomenon occur. The holy people will be those who allow the holy spirit to produce what is called, "every one that is written among the living in Jerusalem". They will certainly be alive because the spirit of the LORD is moving through them.

The people who were in the fallen state have undergone a re-creative process as the spirit of the LORD washes away all the filth of the sinful state which built up in each person's experience when the spirit of the LORD did not flow through the people of Jerusalem. These "women", who are the men and women that did not allow the spirit of the LORD flow through them, but who are now willing to let the spirit of the LORD flow through them, are now known as the daughters of Zion. Zion is a place of high spiritual consciousness which is a place where the people enter when the filth of the fallen human nature state is washed away from them. Isaiah states that the blood of Jerusalem in its fallen and filthy condition must be purged. This is not real blood; it is the culture and the behavior of the fallen state of desolation and decay which have accumulated in the people. The wrong function of the people, the accumulated sins, must be eliminated from the people by the spirit of judgment and the spirit of burning.

The spirit of judgment has reference to its source as an aspect of the spirit of the LORD which is the spirit of Truth, that can be symbolized as the scales of a balance; and the spirit of burning has reference to an aspect of the spirit of the LORD, which is the spirit of Love, symbolized by fire. These two spirits, Love and Truth, blended with the third aspect of spirit, the spirit of Life, comprise the triune spirit of the LORD. The LORD's spirit is a triune spirit of Love, Truth and Life which are intertwined together. The purification of the daughters of Zion, the washing away of the filth that contaminates the daughters of Zion, is accomplished by the spirits of Truth and Love. The Truth will replace the deceit and the lies contained in the filthiness of the fallen nature; and the spirit of Love will burn away the negative emotions, such as anger, despair, hopelessness,

The Testimony of the Major Prophets

hatred, etc., which are the absence of Love. The spirit of the LORD moving through the people can accomplish this purification which is the fourth spirit before the throne of God. (See "The Symbolic Version of Revelation" for a detailed discussion of the seven spirits before the throne of God.)

5 And the LORD will create upon every dwelling place of mount Zion, and upon her assemblies, a cloud and smoke by day, and the shining of a flaming fire by night: for upon all the glory shall be a defence.
6 And there shall be a tabernacle for a shadow in the daytime from the heat, and for a place of refuge, and for a covert from storm and from rain.

As the spirit of the LORD is allowed to flow through the human capacities of the people in Jerusalem and Judah, then, the power of the LORD will create a dwelling place for the LORD on mount Zion, the symbol of a high and pure state of consciousness, on a person and upon her assemblies, the people who are in agreement with that particular person. This new state of consciousness is symbolized by a cloud of smoke that can be seen by day, and the light shining from the fire at night; the evidence of the burning fire can be seen day and night. This fire that burns, the light that glows and the cloud of glory which can be seen on a mountain far away can be called the Shekinah, which is the evidence of the Presence of the One who dwells, the LORD. When this evidence of spirit in manifestation is available to be seen, then the presence of the radiance will create a holy place, a tabernacle, that is a result of the shining of the light

This tabernacle, this spiritual tabernacle, can be used as a calm cool place which is available for a shadow in the daytime from the heat, the heat of emotionally heated circumstances; it can also be available as a hidden place of refuge, a covert shelter from the storm and the rain, the storms and difficulties that rain down on people that each person must weather. Isaiah is telling his listeners, students or disciples that every one, every dwelling place of mount Zion, within the consciousness of every person builds their own tabernacle of the LORD by means of spiritual expression, the way in which each person allows the spirit of the LORD to flow and find expression through each of them. Each person must do this through his or her own individual experience. Isaiah will teach his listeners how to do this by telling the parable of the vineyard.

CHAPTER 5

1 Now will I sing to my wellbeloved a song of my beloved touching his vineyard. My wellbeloved hath a vineyard in a very fruitful hill:
2 And he fenced it, and gathered out the stones thereof, and planted it with the choicest vine, and built a tower in the midst of it, and also made a winepress therein: and he looked that it should bring forth grapes, and it brought forth wild grapes.

In order to understand this parable of Isaiah, it is necessary to know the names and the places, as follows: "I" has reference to Isaiah who is teaching us by means of a parable. Isaiah is a Being or Spirit in a human form on earth, just the same as each of us. The well-beloved is the heart, mind and body of the spirit which is known on earth as the physical form of Isaiah, which is made of the dust of the ground that we know today as atoms and molecules. The spirit, Isaiah, will sing a song to his three capacities, his well-beloved. The spirit of Isaiah has a BELOVED. The BELOVED is the name of the LORD, the LORD of hosts, the LORD of everyone. The BELOVED has a large VINEYARD called planet Earth and all the constellations in the sky, that are observable to Isaiah. The spirit of Isaiah is contained within the VINEYARD of the LORD. The well-beloved physical form of Isaiah is under the direct control of Isaiah. Isaiah, who is made in the image and likeness of the LORD, has a Vineyard which is his immediate environment on the earth that is built in a very fruitful hill, which means that the land is able to reproduce.

The BELOVED, the LORD of the VINEYARD, has fenced His vineyard, gathered the stones out of it, planted the choicest vine which is the vine of life, built a tower in the midst of the garden so that a person could see that which is coming to pass, and made a winepress in the garden so that a person could make wine to drink and to enjoy the garden. The vine symbolizes the people who live in the garden and the purpose of the people is to bring forth grapes, the symbols of the behaviors of people. The winepress symbolizes the collective expression of the people which comes forth through the hearts, minds and bodies by means of the LORD's power. However, the LORD, the BELOVED, has observed that the grapes are wild grapes. The behaviors of the people are not tender grapes; the behaviors are wild grapes. The quality of the grapes are sub-standard. The LORD has observed that the quality of the grapes are "wild"; like the people of Jerusalem in their

The Testimony of the Major Prophets

wild conditions. The stage has been set by Isaiah and he prepares to tell the people of Jerusalem the remainder of the parable from his BELOVED, the LORD.

3 And now, O inhabitants of Jerusalem, and men of Judah, judge, I pray you, betwixt me and my vineyard.
4 What could have been done more to my vineyard, that I have not done in it? wherefore, when I looked that it should bring forth grapes, brought it forth wild grapes?

The LORD asks the inhabitants of Jerusalem and the men of Judah to judge between the LORD who has built such a perfect vineyard and the wild grapes, the wild behaviors, the behaviors which do not represent the LORD, which are coming forth from the vineyard. What more could the LORD have done to His vineyard that He has not done? Why did the LORD's vine bring forth "wild fruit", the erratic behavior of people who are weak rather than strong? The Owner of the VINEYARD, the Husbandman can not tolerate this poor crop of wild grapes in his garden. The LORD will speak to inform the people of his plans, by means of this parable, about how he intends to address the unacceptable conditions, unacceptable to the LORD, within the present vineyard.

5 And now go to; I will tell you what I will do to my vineyard: I will take away the hedge thereof, and it shall be eaten up; and break down the wall thereof, and it shall be trodden down:
6 And I will lay it waste: it shall not be pruned, nor digger; but there shall come up briers and thorns: I will also command the clouds that they rain no rain upon it.
7 For the vineyard of the LORD of hosts is the house of Israel, and the men of Judah his pleasant plant: and he looked for judgment, but behold oppression; for righteousness, but behold a cry.

Up until now, the LORD has maintained a hedge of protection around the VINEYARD, but it is the LORD's intention to remove the hedge so that the inhabitants of the city can learn that they must reap what they sow. When the hedge of protection is removed, then the garden, which symbolizes Jerusalem and Judah, shall be eaten up from external forces; the walls shall break down from the internal forces which manifest as a lack of maintenance from within; and it shall be trodden down from without, from people who want to control this particular garden for their own desires. Through internal forces stemming from a lack of prevention, and from external forces, stemming from outsiders who desire the land, the operation of the Law of the LORD shall lay the garden waste; the reason is given that the garden has not been pruned or dug to remove the weeds; it is only natural that the briers and thorns shall come to fill the garden with weeds, the evidence of the lack of care. The LORD will command the clouds not to rain the divine inspiration to the people and the resulting drought will destroy the garden even further. Rain, water from above, is a symbol of the truth that flows from God to water the earth. The absence of "water" through people illustrates a further lack of care and concern by the people.

The message of the parable is given when it is revealed that the vineyard of the LORD of hosts is the house of Israel, and the men of the territory of Judah is the LORD's pleasant plant. The LORD has looked for the true judgment of the Owner to come forth from the plant in the vineyard but His observation sees only oppression; instead of righteousness and right behavior, the Lord observed a cry of the unhappy and the unfulfilled children of Israel, particularly those of the house of Judah

The Symbolic Version of Isaiah

in the city of Jerusalem. Due to the unrighteous behavior of the people of Jerusalem and Judah, it should be expected that woes will come upon them because of the operation of the Law.

8 Woe unto them that join house to house, that lay field to field, till there be no place, that they may be placed alone in the midst of the earth!
9 In mine ears said the LORD of hosts, Of a truth many houses shall be desolate, even great and fair, without inhabitant.
10 Yea, ten acres of vineyard shall yield one bath, and the seed of an homer shall yield an ephah.
11 Woe unto them that rise up early in the morning, that they may follow strong drink; that continue until night, till wine inflame them!
12 And the harp, and the viol, the tabret, and pipe, and wine, are in their feasts: but they regard not the work of the LORD, neither consider the operation of his hands.

There will be woe unto those people that join house to house and field to field. The houses and the land are all connected and the parcels of land are permanently held by families. Land in Israel was almost never sold; it was always leased so that the control would stay in the possession of the family. If the leader of the family has lost his way, his leadership skills, then it is logical that the occupants on the family land will deteriorate simultaneously. If there is no room for expansion, then other people will always be on the alert to seek new lands for the expansion of each family group by marriage or by force. The LORD of hosts says that if the conditions of the individual gardens continue to deteriorate, then, many houses will become desolate due to ill repair and improper maintenance from within and foreign invaders from without.

The productivity of the land will shrink in its annual production. This is quantified by statements such as 10 acres of vineyard shall yield one bath of wine, a bath is an ancient Hebrew liquid measure that is equal to one-tenth of a homer, approximately 8 ½ gallons; and an omer of seed, approximately a gallon, will yield only an ephah, an ancient Jewish measure of capacity which refers to a little over a bushel. An omer is a tenth of an ephah. The people shall rise up early in the morning not to go to work and be productive, but to follow strong drink that continues until night, and the wine inflames them with its ability to produce drunkenness. The people enjoy their ability to party among their friends and to listen to the sound of musical instruments that proclaim the feasts, but they do not regard the work of the LORD, nor do they consider the work of His hands. These actions describe a people who are living similarly to the people of
Sodom and Gomorrah and they surely are on the way to decadence, weakness and decay which shall make them vulnerable. The people are getting weaker and unable to defend themselves.

13 Therefore my people are gone into captivity, because they have no knowledge: and their honourable men are famished, and their multitude dried up with thirst.
14 Therefore hell hath enlarged herself, and opened her mouth without measure: and their glory, and their multitude, and their pomp, and he that rejoiceth, shall descend into it.
15 And the mean man shall be brought down, and the mighty man shall be humbled, and the eyes of the lofty shall be humbled:
16 But the LORD of hosts shall be exalted in judgment, and God that is holy shall be sanctified in righteousness.

The Testimony of the Major Prophets

17 Then shall the lambs feed after their manner, and the waste places of the fat ones shall strangers eat.

The people in this weakened condition are taken into captivity by other forces because the people have no knowledge, no awareness of their weakness; their leaders have become weak for lack of food because they are not growing enough food to feed themselves and their leaders are famished for lack of vision to protect the people, and the multitude of people for whom they are responsible have dried up for lack of "water"; the symbol of spiritual truth that flows from the LORD.

These progressively worsening conditions are described as the enlargement of hell, which is indication that the conditions of hell are in the environment on this side of the grave, and the mouth of hell is getting larger due to lack of effort and lack of care on the part of the people. In their good times, celebrations and their glories, the people, who are engaged in the riotous living, shall descend into the mouth of hell which they have made. This is the path of the mean man, the "normal man" of the fallen state, who shall be brought down, and the once mighty man shall be humbled. This is the description of a destructive cycle that is in operation and it is directly related to the behavior of the people who do not love and serve the LORD. But the LORD of hosts shall be exalted in his judgment of the law of sowing and reaping. God that is holy shall be sanctified in his righteousness and his righteousness is the working of the One Law, the law of reaping whatever it is that man has sown. The lambs shall continue to feed after their manner, and the herds of the fat ones shall be available to those strangers that may come upon them and take them because nobody is providing for their care. The care, concern and responsibility of the people continue to diminish and decline; and the woes shall continue to come in a more rapid manner. The destructive process continues.

18 Woe unto them that draw iniquity with cords of vanity, and sin as it were with a cart rope:
19 That say, Let him make speed, and hasten his work, that we may see it: and let the counsel of the Holy One of Israel draw nigh and come, that we may know it!
20 Woe unto them that call evil good, and good evil; that put darkness for light, and light for darkness; that put bitter for sweet, and sweet for bitter!
21 Woe unto them that are wise in their own eyes, and prudent in their own sight!
22 Woe unto them that are mighty to drink wine, and men of strength to mingle strong drink:
23 Which justify the wicked for reward, and take away the righteousness of the righteous from him!

The people in the fallen state are drawing woe, wrong function toward them as iniquity and wrong behavior is drawn by a person who has cords of vanity in their living; and the people pull sin along with them and toward themselves as people pull a cart of sins as though it were a cart rope. Vain people are really attached to their sins. The people in the fallen state call upon the LORD to make speed and hasten His work as though the LORD should be working for the people instead of the other way around. The people want the LORD, the Holy One of Israel, to draw near to them as a people so that they may see and know the LORD as the LORD does things for the fallen people. Fallen people want the LORD to serve them as though He were a magic genie out of a bottle. People pray for the LORD to serve them!

The Symbolic Version of Isaiah

The conditions of the environment are disordered and chaotic. The people are calling evil, good; and, they are calling good, evil, which is the eating of the forbidden fruit that the LORD has forbidden man to eat; behaviors of darkness are called light; and conditions of light are called darkness; the bitter things are called sweet and the sweet things are called bitter. Everything is all mixed up and topsy-turvy. The people in the fallen state are all wise in their own eyes, and they are prudent in their own sight. Woe to the mighty who drink wine from their wild grapes, and the men of strength who mingle strong drink because drunkenness and strength produce damage: these people justify their wicked behavior for a reward; and the behaviors of righteousness are taken away from the righteous. This wrong behavior cannot continue indefinitely before the fire of God's love and truth moving through His people constantly will destroy the false design.

24 Therefore as the fire devoureth the stubble, and the flame consumeth the chaff, so their root shall be as rottenness, and their blossom shall go up as dust: because they have cast away the law of the LORD of hosts, and despised the word of the Holy One of Israel.
25 Therefore is the anger of the LORD kindled against his people, and he hath stretched forth his hand against them, and hath smitten them: and the hills did tremble, and their carcases were torn in the midst of the streets. For all this his anger is not turned away, but his hand is stretched out still.

The fire of the true design which is inherent in the spirit will destroy the evil patterns of the false or the counterfeit design as a fire devours stubble and the flame consumes the chaff so that the roots of the wrong plants, the weeds, shall be consumed because of their rottenness and the blossom of the wrong behavior shall go up as dust. All of this destruction shall occur because the people have cast away from their behaviors the law of the LORD, and they have not listened to the Holy One of Israel. Therefore, the anger of the Lord is kindled against the people and the LORD seems to have stretched His hand of control against the people and strike the people who have rebelled against the way of the LORD in their living to cause the destruction which even the people in the fallen state can easily observe. The hills, the high points of the fallen consciousness of man, do tremble at the destruction which has been caused by his own behavior, the seeds of which have been planted by him and his immediate ancestors. The LORD is able to see all of this destruction which is directly linked to man's behavior and the Lord continues to stretch out His hand still to offer a helping hand to man to cease to create these horrible conditions in his living. If fallen man will not change his ways directly, then the LORD will use force from outside the city of Jerusalem and the country of Judah.

26 And he will lift up an ensign to the nations from far, and will hiss unto them from the end of the earth: and, behold, they shall come with speed swiftly:
27 None shall be weary nor stumble among them; none shall slumber nor sleep; neither shall the girdle of their loins be loosed, nor the latchet of their shoes be broken:
28 Whose arrows are sharp, and all their bows bent, their horses' hoofs shall be counted like flint, and their wheels like a whirlwind:
29 Their roaring shall be like a lion, they shall roar like young lions: yea, they shall roar, and lay hold of the prey, and shall carry it away safe, and none shall deliver it.
30 And in that day they shall roar against them like the roaring of the sea: and if one look unto the land, behold darkness and sorrow, and the light is darkened in the heavens thereof.

The Testimony of the Major Prophets

The LORD will lift up an ensign, a banner, in the consciousness of the people from afar off, and will call unto them through the hiss of the serpent, the sound of their own self-active minds so that they will come with great speed to take control of a weakened people who do not have the power to protect the land which the LORD has given to the children of Israel. The people who come to invade shall be a strong people who will not be weak and weary; they shall not slumber or sleep, nor will they be unprepared with loose girdles and broken shoe latchets as they come to take control of land people and herds. They shall be prepared for war: their arrows are sharp, their bows bent, their horses hoofs shall be hard as flint and the wheels of their chariots shall move like the whirlwind.

They shall be ready for war as they have the ferocity of the lion and the roars of the young lions who are ready to lay hold of their prey and carry it away because they know that none but themselves can deliver to them what they want. In that day of war, they shall be the prepared aggressor who shall come like the roaring of the sea: and if one looks to the land, they shall see darkness and sorrow, and the light from the LORD in the heavens shall be darkened because there is very little of His light shining through the people.

CHAPTER 6

1 In the year that king Uzziah died I saw also the Lord sitting upon a throne, high and lifted up, and his train filled the temple.
2 Above it stood the seraphims: each one had six wings; with twain he covered his face, and with twain he covered his feet, and with twain he did fly.

Isaiah tells us that in the year that king Uzziah died, 740 B.C., he saw a vision of the LORD sitting on a throne, high and lifted up into a high place, so that Isaiah had to look up to see the LORD in the form of a material person, who is in a higher position than where Isaiah is located. The LORD's train filled the temple, the holy place. Of course, where the LORD is present, with his train, that place would be a holy place, a temple. In his vision, Isaiah perceives that the train of the LORD is composed of other people in physical bodies, who are arranged in an orderly manner around the LORD and who compose the LORD's train of people. Above the train of individual people are angels, seraphims, angelic beings made of the same spiritual substance as the LORD, and there is a spirit associated with each person in the train of the LORD. Each one of the seraphim, the angelic beings, has six wings: two wings cover the face (the face is the symbol of a person's identity) of each Being to symbolize that the angels have no separate identities of their own—they are spirits of the LORD above the physical bodies in the material train of people. Two wings cover the feet; feet are the symbol of understanding to illustrate that the angels have divine angelic understanding. Two wings are used by the angel to fly, not literally, over the bodies of the physical form and remain above that person in the train to give that individual, divine guidance and understanding from the LORD. The angels are aware of each other and they have the ability to communicate with each other in angelic joy.

3 And one cried unto another, and said, Holy, holy, holy, is the LORD of hosts: the whole earth is full of his glory.
4 And the posts of the door moved at the voice of him that cried, and the house was filled with smoke.
5 Then said I, Woe is me! for I am undone; because I am a man of unclean lips, and I dwell in the midst of a people of unclean lips: for mine eyes have seen the King, the LORD of hosts.

Isaiah sees the angels in his vision cry joyfully to one another and their uniform cry, their uniform message, is Holy, holy, holy is the LORD of hosts who is the LORD of all the hosts of angels who are flying above the train of people on earth: and the whole earth is filled with the glory of the LORD since each angel is composed of the same spiritual substance of the LORD. The angels are the spiritual body of the LORD. Isaiah realizes in that moment that his vision is the vision of the angel who is above his particular human form and that he is in the presence of other angels and he has seen the spiritual divine design of the LORD. It is the angel that is above Isaiah that has cried to the other angels. When the angelic being, the seraphim, of Isaiah cried out, the posts of the door that separated the earth from the heaven moved and the house of Isaiah's physical form was filled with the smoke, the spiritual incense, the spiritual substance, of the holy place.

Isaiah realizes that he is in a holy place of the angels of the LORD and he expresses his woe because he, as a material person, is undone; he realizes that he is a part of the angelic train of the LORD and he is no longer a separate human form who can do whatsoever he pleases on earth. Isaiah is very upset because he has been a man of unclean lips who has been dwelling in the midst of a people of unclean lips, and his lips are the symbols of an expression that has not been true to the angel or the LORD. The eyes of Isaiah, which symbolize his vision and understanding, have seen the King, the LORD of hosts, and Isaiah understands that he is not only the earth of his physical form, but he is the seraphim within his physical form. Isaiah has discovered that the earth and the heaven of him are connected and that he is now aware that he is a part of the body of the King. Isaiah is ashamed of his uncleanness, his sins and his iniquities; he feels great remorse and sorrow.

6 Then flew one of the seraphims unto me, having a live coal in his hand, which he had taken with the tongs from off the altar:
7 And he laid it upon my mouth, and said, Lo, this hath touched thy lips; and thine iniquity is taken away, and thy sin purged.

Isaiah is functioning at a divine level, an angelic level of consciousness, and he sees one of the seraphim come to him with a live spiritual coal of fire and light, symbolizing love and truth, which the seraphim had taken from the altar, laid it upon the mouth of Isaiah and said that the vision of the live coal from the altar of the LORD (a spiritual coal, not a literal coal) has touched his lips, his expression, which has taken away all the iniquity of the past; and all the sins of the past have been purged away from Isaiah. Isaiah has been forgiven for everything that he has done while he was in the state of spiritual darkness, the state of not knowing the LORD. Isaiah realizes that there are many, many people on earth who do not know what Isaiah has discovered: that the earth is truly the LORD's, that there is a LORD and that Isaiah is aware of this fact. Isaiah hears the voice of the LORD directly for the first time.

8 Also I heard the voice of the Lord, saying, Whom shall I send, and who will go for us? Then said I, Here am I; send me.

Isaiah has heard the voice of the LORD, who understands and knows that His fallen people on earth do not really know the LORD and that there is a divine plan for the earth. The problem has been that there is no one to tell the people who believe that the LORD's kingdom can be accessed only by dying to get there. The people need to know that heaven and earth are one and the LORD wants them to know that the connection exists. The LORD's question to his angels is, "Whom shall I send, and who will go for us?" Isaiah heard himself accept the divine commission to go to his people and tell them that the LORD is real. Isaiah says, "Here am I; send me". The LORD commissions Isaiah, who has experienced the covenant with the LORD, with divine authority. He has been ordained by the LORD.

9 And he said, Go, and tell this people, Hear ye indeed, but understand not; and see ye indeed, but perceive not.
10 Make the heart of this people fat, and make their ears heavy, and shut their eyes; lest they see with their eyes, and hear with their ears, and understand with their heart, and convert, and be healed.

Isaiah has been commissioned to go, and tell the people who need to be told that they have heard the word of the LORD before through other messengers that the LORD has sent and they do not yet understand; the people have seen those who proclaimed the message of the LORD and they do not perceive what they had seen before their own eyes. The people who do not want to see, hear or feel the message of the LORD because they have hardened their hearts, do not hear with their ears or see with their eyes because if they do receive what is offered to them they will convert their behaviors from unholy nature to a holy nature and be healed of their iniquity and sin.

It is the LORD's desire that the hearts of the people, who hear His word through His messengers, that their hearts will become fat with the word of the LORD and that their ears will be made heavy from many people who proclaim the words; and that the people shut their eyes to the material treasures of the earth which blinds them to the treasures of the spirit. Isaiah wants to know how long he should preach the word of the LORD to the people who do not know?

11 Then said I, Lord, how long? And he answered, Until the cities be wasted without inhabitant, and the houses without man, and the land be utterly desolate,
12 And the LORD have removed men far away, and there be a great forsaking in the midst of the land.
13 But yet in it shall be a tenth, and it shall return, and shall be eaten: as a teil tree, and as an oak, whose substance is in them, when they cast their leaves: so the holy seed shall be the substance thereof.

The LORD wants his message to be offered to the people in the fallen state until the cities are totally wasted without a single inhabitant, people are no longer in the houses, the land is desolate because the LORD has taken men far away, and the LORD has forsaken the land. In symbolic language, this means that it is Isaiah's function to express the spirit of the LORD even if he were the last person on earth. The tenth part, the completion of the divine plan shall always be present as a potential and the divine design of the LORD shall return. The LORD says that the true design shall be "eaten", accepted by man as the teil tree (the linden tree) and the oak, whose seed is within themselves and the seed is distributed when they cast their leaves. In like manner, the substance of the LORD is within man and the holy seed shall be spread as the substance of divine action is planted on earth.

The Testimony of the Major Prophets

Isaiah has experienced the covenant of the LORD and he shall go to his people and speak for the LORD on earth. Isaiah will soon have an opportunity to speak for the LORD to Ahaz, the king of Judah.

CHAPTER 7

1 And it came to pass in the days of Ahaz the son of Jotham, the son of Uzziah, king of Judah, that Rezin the king of Syria, and Pekah the son of Remaliah, king of Israel, went up toward Jerusalem to war against it, but could not prevail against it.
2 And it was told the house of David, saying, Syria is confederate with Ephraim. And his heart was moved, and the heart of his people, as the trees of the wood are moved with the wind.

Ahaz—whose name means, "one that takes and possesses for himself", or greedy and self-centered—is the king of Judah during times of the moral and physical deterioration of the people in the area. Ahaz's father was King Jotham, whose name means, "perfection of the LORD", and his grandfather was King Uzziah, whose name means, "strength of the LORD".

The names of the kings indicate that the two rulers before Ahaz had some relatedness with the LORD if only in name. King Ahaz is faced with the fact that two other kings have attempted, unsuccessfully, to war against Jerusalem and Judah but they did not prevail. The two other kings were Rezin, the king of Syria, and Remaliah, king of Israel, who is working through his son, Pekah. The name Remaliah means, "rejected by the LORD" and his son's name, Pekah, means, "opens the eye" or "at liberty" to do the bidding of his father the king, which, as we have seen, is to war against Jerusalem for the purpose of capturing it.

It was told to the house of David, of which Ahaz is a descendent, that a foreign country, Syria, is confederate with Ephraim, a brother of Judah, in the assault against Jerusalem. The heart of Ahaz is moved with fear as was the heart of his people and the fear is compared to the movement of the trees as they are moved by the wind. Their hearts are shaken at the prospect of the people of Ephraim in alliance with a foreign country, Syria. The name Syria means, "deceives" and the name Ephraim means "fruitful". These two territories believe that their collaboration to 'deceive fruitfully' to attack Jerusalem will be successful. Ahaz is in need of some wise counsel that will be provided by the LORD through Isaiah.

The Testimony of the Major Prophets

3 Then said the LORD unto Isaiah, Go forth now to meet Ahaz, thou, and Shearjashub thy son, at the end of the conduit of the upper pool in the highway of the fuller's field;
4 And say unto him, Take heed, and be quiet; fear not, neither be fainthearted for the two tails of these smoking firebrands, for the fierce anger of Rezin with Syria, and of the son of Remaliah.
5 Because Syria, Ephraim, and the son of Remaliah, have taken evil counsel against thee, saying,
6 Let us go up against Judah, and vex it, and let us make a breach therein for us, and set a king in the midst of it, even the son of Tabeal:

The LORD working through Isaiah has been directed to go forth, with his elder son, Shearjashub, whose name means, "the remnant shall return", and meet Ahaz. The three men are directed to meet at the end of the conduit of the upper pool in the highway of the fuller's field. The fuller's field is very close to the wall of Jerusalem and this field is used to wash and cleanse the garments that people wore and whiten them in the sunshine. The word of the LORD to Ahaz through Isaiah is to take heed and be quiet, be still, be calm: particularly in the emotional realm of Ahaz; he is instructed to fear not, and not to be fainthearted especially with regard to the smoking firebrands, Rezin of Syria and Pekah, the son of Ramaliah of Israel, who are now very angry because they have taken evil counsel and waged a war against Jerusalem and Judah and lost the war against Judah. The plan of Rezin and Pekah is to go to Jerusalem, provoke or vex the people, create a breach among the people and set a king in Judah who would be loyal to the new alliance. The person that Syria and Israel wanted to put in charge as the new king was the son of Tabeal. An alliance of enemies is building and in action against Ahaz. The Lord GOD has some information and advice for Ahaz.

7 Thus saith the Lord GOD, It shall not stand, neither shall it come to pass.
8 For the head of Syria is Damascus, and the head of Damascus is Rezin; and within threescore and five years shall Ephraim be broken, that it be not a people.
9 And the head of Ephraim is Samaria, and the head of Samaria is Remaliah's son. If ye will not believe, surely ye shall not be established.

The word of the Lord GOD speaking through Isaiah is that the alliance shall not stand, it will fail, and the son of Tabeal shall not become king for the following reason: the head of Syria is Damascus and the head of Damascus is Rezin; and within 65 years, the land of Ephraim shall be broken and it shall no longer be a people. The demise of Ephraim will come to pass because of the deportation of the Israelites and the intermarriage of the Israelites who remained with foreign colonists, who settled there on order of the king of Assyria, to produce the Samaritans. Ephraim was in the process of being taken over from within. The head of Ephraim is the city of Samaria, and the head of Samaria is Remaliah's son, Pekah. If Ahaz does not believe the Lord GOD speaking through Isaiah, then Ahaz shall not be established as a successor in Ephraim and he will not be established in new lands. The LORD speaking through Isaiah speaks to Ahaz once again.

10 Moreover the LORD spake again unto Ahaz, saying,
11 Ask thee a sign of the LORD thy God; ask it either in the depth, or in the height above.
12 But Ahaz said, I will not ask, neither will I tempt the LORD.
13 And he said, Hear ye now, O house of David; it a small thing for you to weary men, but will ye weary my God also?

The Symbolic Version of Isaiah

When The LORD speaking through Isaiah requests Ahaz to ask for a sign from the LORD his God, Ahaz refuses to ask for a sign from the LORD either from the depth of the earth or the height of the heaven, Ahaz refuses to ask because he will not tempt the LORD. Isaiah replies that Ahaz, the grandson of the king of Judah, should listen and heed the word of Isaiah when he is speaking for the LORD. Ahaz can weary his people of the house of David when he speaks to them because it is a small thing, but will Ahaz weary the God of Isaiah also by speaking to God in the same manner that he speaks to the house of David?

14 Therefore the Lord himself shall give you a sign; Behold, a virgin shall conceive, and bear a son, and shall call his name Immanuel.
15 Butter and honey shall he eat, that he may know to refuse the evil, and choose the good.
16 For before the child shall know to refuse the evil, and choose the good, the land that thou abhorrest shall be forsaken of both her kings.

Isaiah tells Ahaz that the LORD himself shall give Ahaz a sign; the sign is that a virgin shall conceive and bear a son and his name shall be called Immanuel, which means, "God with us". Isaiah, who has experienced the covenant with the LORD, knows by his own realized experience that the covenant is available to be experienced by a person who is willing to let the spirit of the LORD flow through that person. The willingness of a person who has never before experienced the flow of the LORD's spirit through his particular human form is a "virgin", a virgin to the experience of the spirit of the LORD as that spirit flows through him for the first time to establish the covenant. Immanuel, or God with us, is the experience of God in the covenant agreement that is available to Ahaz to be experienced.

A person who experiences the spirit of God in the covenant, Immanuel, so that he knows, really knows, by a realized experience knows the joy of the experience that is symbolized by the butter and honey, the pleasant sensation of the experience. After the spiritual experience, Ahaz will be able to refuse the evil of the material world with all its treasures, and he will be able to choose the good of the spiritual world because he will be a part of the divine design that is to return to the earth. But before the boy knows enough to reject the wrong choice of the material approach and choose the right direction of the spirit of the LORD in action, the land that Ahaz abhorred, Syria and Ephraim, shall be forsaken of both their kings.

17 The LORD shall bring upon thee, and upon thy people, and upon thy father's house, days that have not come, from the day that Ephraim departed from Judah; even the king of Assyria.
18 And it shall come to pass in that day, that the LORD shall hiss for the fly that is in the uttermost part of the rivers of Egypt, and for the bee that is in the land of Assyria.
19 And they shall come, and shall rest all of them in the desolate valleys, and in the holes of the rocks, and upon all thorns, and upon all bushes.

The action of the LORD shall bring upon Ahaz and his people, and upon his father's house, days of prosperity that have not come since Ephraim departed from Judah; or, the days of the King of Assyria. In that day, it shall come to pass, that the working of the law of the LORD shall bring in the flies from the uttermost parts of the rivers in Egypt and the bees that are in the land of

The Testimony of the Major Prophets

Assyria. They shall come and inhabit the desolate valleys, the holes in the rocks, the thorns, and the bushes.

20 In the same day shall the Lord shave with a rasor that is hired, namely, by them beyond the river, by the king of Assyria, the head, and the hair of the feet: and it shall also consume the beard.
21 And it shall come to pass in that day, that a man shall nourish a young cow, and two sheep;
22 And it shall come to pass, for the abundance of milk that they shall give he shall eat butter: for butter and honey shall every one eat that is left in the land.

In times of mourning, a person would shave his own head and beard to signify his sorrow. But the forcible shaving of the hair from the top of his head to the hair of the feet was considered a great insult, especially, if the shaving was done by the razor of a person who was hired to do the job by them beyond the river, by the king of Assyria. In that day, a man shall nourish a young cow for milk and two sheep; everyone left in the land shall subsist on butter and honey. The desolation of the land and the shame shall continue.

23 And it shall come to pass in that day, that every place shall be, where there were a thousand vines at a thousand silverlings, it shall even be for briers and thorns.
24 With arrows and with bows shall men come thither; because all the land shall become briers and thorns.
25 And on all hills that shall be digged with the mattock, there shall not come thither the fear of briers and thorns: but it shall be for the sending forth of oxen, and for the treading of lesser cattle.

It shall come to pass that in places where once there were a thousand vines worth a thousand silver shekels, there will be only briers and thorns. The land will become so rugged that men will come with bow and arrows to hunt in the wilderness filled with briers and thorns that the land has become. On all the hills that were once cultivated with the mattock, the hoe, people will no longer go there to cultivate the land due to the briers and the thorns: the land will be used as grazing land for oxen and the smaller animals.

CHAPTER 8

1 Moreover the LORD said unto me, Take thee a great roll, and write in it with a man's pen concerning Maher-shalal-hashbaz.
2 And I took unto me faithful witnesses to record, Uriah the priest, and Zechariah the son of Jeberechiah.
3 And I went unto the prophetess; and she conceived, and bare a son. Then said the LORD to me, Call his name Maher-shalal-hashbaz.
4 For before the child shall have knowledge to cry, My father, and my mother, the riches of Damascus and the spoil of Samaria shall be taken away before the king of Assyria.

Isaiah is in a covenant-agreement with the LORD and he has dedicated his life to letting the spirit of the LORD find expression on earth through him. The impulse of the spirit of the LORD instructs Isaiah, through divine inspiration, to take a great roll, a large scroll, and write on it with a man's pen concerning the new and true expression of the spirit of the LORD, which will hastily make changes in the conditions of the fallen world, the sinful world that is the result of the distortion of the spirit of the LORD as it flows through the consciousness of His people. This true flow of the spirit of the LORD through people will eliminate the prey of wrong conditions and circumstances, the distortion which is known as human nature, and the flow of undistorted spirit will result in a new world, the divine world on earth. This birth of a new "child" on earth which is fathered by the LORD and "mothered" by Isaiah, who would be in the position of a spiritual "virgin" or a bride of the Bridegroom, is called, Maher-shalal-hashbaz. Maher-shalal-hashbaz means, "making speed to the spoil or the prey". The spoil or the prey from the viewpoint of the LORD is the distortion which man, in the fallen state, has made as the LORD's spirit passes through the polluted consciousness of men and women.

As Isaiah writes of his experience with the LORD into a scroll, he takes into his confidence two witnesses which are required to corroborate that the written words are true and written by him in the same manner as a Last Will and Testament requires two witnesses to the event. Isaiah is in the process of making a written record of the spirit of the LORD as he allows the spirit of the LORD to find expression through his heart, mind and body. Isaiah chooses Uriah, the priest, whose name

The Testimony of the Major Prophets

means, "light of the Lord", and Zechariah, whose name means, "memory of the Lord", as his two witnesses. It is the intention of the LORD to build a body of people who will live in covenant-agreement with the LORD. This body of people would carry the spirit of the LORD in the human flesh of the people who would offer themselves to this divine purpose. The purpose would be **to live** so the spirit of the LORD would be made manifest on earth. The purpose is not **to die** for the LORD; the purpose is to live for the LORD. As people express human nature, they are **dying**; as people express divine nature, they are **living. A choice is available!**

It would take time for this spiritual body to form on earth. It would begin as a seed with Isaiah and grow into an infant, and then into a child as the spiritual body grew on earth. Each person in the body would have experienced the covenant-agreement with the LORD, which is a personal relationship with the LORD. It would not be enough to say that a person is "born again" of the spirit in one's imagination; the person would have a realized experience of the LORD moving through his or her body, mind and heart in momentary living. It is easy to see that before, prior to, this body of people, this spiritual "child" on earth, shall have the knowledge to cry, to proclaim its spiritual message, the expressions and actions of previous generations, symbolized by Isaiah's mother and father, the riches of Damascus, and the spoil of Samaria shall be taken away before the king of Assyria. The distortion of the much greater power, symbolized by the power of the king of Assyria, shall prevail over the power of the body of people who compose the "child of God" on earth whose name is Immanuel, or "God with Us".

5 The LORD spake also unto me again, saying,
6 Forasmuch as this people refuseth the waters of Shiloah that go softly, and rejoice in Rezin and Remaliah's son;
7 Now therefore, behold, the Lord bringeth up upon them the waters of the river, strong and many, even the king of Assyria, and all his glory: and he shall come up over all his channels, and go over all his banks:
8 And he shall pass through Judah; he shall overflow and go over, he shall reach even to the neck; and the stretching out of his wings shall fill the breadth of thy land, O Immanuel.

The spirit of the LORD spoke to Isaiah again saying, that since the people have refused to express the spirit of the LORD as it moves through each of their hearts, mind and bodies, which is symbolized as the flowing waters of Shiloah that go softly, which would bring peace on earth (Shiloah means, "peace"), then, the people have accepted and rejoiced in human nature symbolized by the leadership of Rezin and Pekah, Remaliah's son, whose names mean that they have been at liberty to reject the way of the LORD to carry out their own plans of war, which is not peace. The "waters" of the truth of the spirit of the LORD shall continue to flow constantly. The distorted, angry waters of the polluted river of consciousness symbolized by the many strong people of the king of Assyria shall come and overflow its banks and pass through Judah; he shall spread his wings and fill the breadth of the land. All of this is done by the power of God on earth which is used to create a distortion of the true design of God. God's power can be used on earth to create the distortions of the fallen state. It is all God's power; there is no other power. However, fallen man has the ability to divert and distort the power to produce evil creations. "O Immanuel" is an exclamation that the power of God on earth has been used to produce horrible conditions. People who do not associate with the spiritual body of the LORD on earth can associate themselves into other bodies with "good purposes".

9 Associate yourselves, O ye people, and ye shall be broken in pieces; and give ear, all ye of far countries: gird yourselves, and ye shall be broken in pieces; gird yourselves, and ye shall be broken in pieces.
10 Take counsel together, and it shall come to nought; speak the word, and it shall not stand: for God is with us.

People are called to join into many different types of associations which have a higher priority, in their view, than the release of the spirit of the LORD into the earth. People have the ability to form and to choose earthly, human associations which are not centered in the LORD. The people who do this, who do not put the LORD first, shall be broken into pieces. The people can gird themselves to fight to keep their earthly associations and they will be broken into pieces. They can take counsel together, mentally, into associations of the mind, and it shall come to nothing. People can speak words of association and it shall not stand. The reason that all these organizations shall come to nothing and fall to pieces is that they are organizations of the material body, the material mind of the material body or the emotions associated with the physical body and they, being material, shall always fall apart. The spiritual body is eternal and it shall stand because God is with us, the body of Immanuel.

11 For the LORD spake thus to me with a strong hand, and instructed me that I should not walk in the way of this people, saying,
12 Say ye not, A confederacy, to all them to whom this people shall say, A confederacy; neither fear ye their fear, nor be afraid.
13 Sanctify the LORD of hosts himself; and let him be your fear, and let him be your dread.

The LORD has spoken to Isaiah with a strong spiritual hand of control and instructed him not to walk in the way of this people who band themselves together into earthly associations which they may call a confederacy. A confederacy is a group of people who stand equally within a loosely-held organization for some "good" earthly purpose to advance a particular point of view. The purpose of the confederacy is to develop group pressure and power. Isaiah is instructed to fear not, to not be afraid of their collective power which is designed and used to coerce you to their opinions and their ways. Isaiah is instructed to sanctify the LORD of hosts himself, the LORD of all the people on earth who is supplying the power to everyone on earth because He is the LORD of everyone on earth. Isaiah is instructed to fear the LORD and to let the LORD be your fear and your dread. Isaiah is instructed to keep the LORD's spirit first.

14 And he shall be for a sanctuary; but for a stone of stumbling and for a rock of offence to both the houses of Israel, for a gin and for a snare to the inhabitants of Jerusalem.
15 And many among them shall stumble, and fall, and be broken, and be snared, and be taken.

Isaiah is to **let** the moving spirit of the LORD be his sanctuary, his retreat, his rock, in his individual relationship with the LORD which is the covenant; there is safety in the spiritual agreement which is eternal. The spirit of the LORD can be a sanctuary that can hold a person upright or a stone to cause a person to stumble and fall; it can be a rock of offense, of transgression and sin, to both houses of Israel, the northern and the southern houses of Israel and Judah who are fighting with each other to gain control. This conflict is the evidence of a gin that separates the people or a snare that traps the people who are the inhabitants of Jerusalem.

Many among the people of Jerusalem who take sides with Israel or Judah shall indeed stumble, fall, be broken, snared and be taken prisoner because this "war" between two sides is the way of the fallen state; it is not the design of the LORD. What should be done if the people do not take one side or the other, and both sides believe that they are right? There are no conflicting sides in the harmonious design of the LORD. Man in the fallen state is unable or unwilling to see this heavenly potential.

16 Bind up the testimony, seal the law among my disciples.
17 And I will wait upon the LORD, that hideth his face from the house of Jacob, and I will look for him.
18 Behold, I and the children whom the LORD hath given me are for signs and for wonders in Israel from the LORD of hosts, which dwelleth in mount Zion.

Isaiah is offering an alternative of the LORD in action through the people which will bind the testimony of the people, what they are saying and doing, if they will seal the law of the LORD among the disciples of the LORD. Isaiah will wait upon, he will serve, the spirit of the LORD into His environment. Presently, the LORD is hiding his face from the house of Jacob, the material form of the body of Jacob, which is not truly Israel because it lacks the spirit of the LORD Who transformed Jacob into Israel.

Isaiah will look for the people who will serve the LORD. The people are instructed to observe and see that Isaiah and the children of the LORD, the people that the LORD has given to Isaiah in the emerging spiritual body, who will be for signs and for wonders in Israel from the LORD of hosts because the spirit from the LORD of hosts is flowing through the people who let it be so. These people are the ones who dwell in mount Zion, the monument of the LORD on earth, the place of high spiritual consciousness where the covenant is known. Their right example will generate opposition from the majority of the people who will try to attract them to their "good" positions in the fallen state.

19 And when they shall say unto you, Seek unto them that have familiar spirits, and unto wizards that peep, and that mutter: should not a people seek unto their God? for the living to the dead?
20 To the law and to the testimony: if they speak not according to this word, it is because there is no light in them.
21 And they shall pass through it, hardly bestead and hungry: and it shall come to pass, that when they shall be hungry, they shall fret themselves, and curse their king and their God, and look upward.
22 And they shall look unto the earth; and behold trouble and darkness, dimness of anguish; and they shall be driven to darkness.

When the people who are in the majority position due to the sheer numbers of their associations or their confederacy advise you to seek those who have the familiar spirits, the familiar ways which everyone else is doing; when you are advised to listen to wizards who chirp their earthly magic tricks to influence you, or those who mutter that they are receiving advice from the dead; then, the people who are wise will seek unto their God who is supplying them with life from within themselves; they will seek a LORD of the living and not look to people who have died.

They should look to the law of God and to the testimony of those who keep the law in their living. If they do not speak according to this word, then it is because there is no light from the LORD in them. And it shall come to pass, that the people who have taken their particular sides of a dispute shall espouse their positions when everything is going well and they are not tired and hungry, but when they are hungry and upset, they shall curse their God and their king and look upward for help. They shall look into the earth and see the trouble and the darkness of the fallen materialistic state that surrounds them and they shall be driven into the darkness of it.

CHAPTER 9

1 Nevertheless the dimness shall not be such as was in her vexation, when at the first he lightly afflicted the land of Zebulun and the land of Naphtali, and afterward did more grievously afflict her by the way of the sea, beyond Jordan, in Galilee of the nations.
2 The people that walked in darkness have seen a great light: they that dwell in the land of the shadow of death, upon them hath the light shined.

The Assyrian invasion of the land of Zebulun and the land of Naphtali is described as a lightly affliction, at first, but afterward, the Assyrians did more grievously afflict her boundaries by the "way of the sea", which was the major highway between Egypt and Damascus, beyond the river Jordan that would bring deep distress on all Israel.

The people of Israel who walked in the darkness of this invasion by Assyria saw a great light: they who dwell in the land of the shadow of death were able to see the light from the LORD through Isaiah and his followers shine upon them in contrast to the darkness that was expressed by themselves. Isaiah and his followers expressed the light from **within** them: the people who looked at the conditions of the environment and were saddened by what they saw experienced the darkness. Both groups were in the same environment observing the same conditions.

3 Thou hast multiplied the nation, and not increased the joy: they joy before thee according to the joy in harvest, and as men rejoice when they divide the spoil.
4 For thou hast broken the yoke of his burden, and the staff of his shoulder, the rod of his oppressor, as in the day of Midian.
5 For every battle of the warrior is with confused noise, and garments rolled in blood; but this shall be with burning and fuel of fire.

The Assyrian invasion and victory has multiplied the size of their nation but it has not increased the joy among the people: the Assyrians are joyful according to the joy of the harvest of their victory as men divide the spoils of war. It is a one-sided joy for the aggressor who is the winner. But the followers of Isaiah who express the spirit of the LORD have broken the yoke of the burden of defeat, and the rod and the staff of the oppressor because the oppressors were not able to break the spirit of the LORD as it shines in the darkness. This is a victory over the circumstances in which they find themselves. It is a victory as decisive as the victory of Gideon over the hordes of Midian when he broke their domination over Israel. Every battle of a warrior is with confused noise, not harmony. The garments of the warriors are rolled in blood from the battle; but this victory of the LORD through the people shall be with the burning spirit of the LORD and the fuel of the fire of the LORD's love being expressed into the darkness of these conditions of defeat to light the world. What a strange new doctrine! Isaiah goes on to explain that he is in the process of building a totally new body of people which at present is like a new child.

6 For unto us a child is born, unto us a son is given: and the government shall be on his shoulder: and his name shall be called Wonderful, Counsellor, The mighty God, The everlasting Father, The Prince of Peace.
7 Of the increase of his government and peace there shall be no end, upon the throne of David, and upon his kingdom, to order it, and to establish it with judgment and with justice from henceforth even for ever. The zeal of the LORD of hosts will perform this.

Isaiah describes for his followers that unto them, the developing, emerging body of people is a child that has been born on earth, unto them a son, a body of the son of God which contains the LORD's spirit, is given to them to care for: and the government of the divine body shall be on the shoulder of the LORD: and his name shall be called Wonderful, Counselor, The mighty God, The everlasting Father, and The Prince of Peace because the LORD's spirit which is coming forth through the body is all of these attributes. Each person in the body is to let the spirit of the LORD come forth through himself or herself. As this is allowed to occur, regardless of the conditions in which the body finds itself, then the size of the body will increase the LORD's government on earth and there shall be no end to the peace that will find expression through a peaceful people. The son or the child is described as the throne of David and upon his kingdom, to order it and to establish it on earth with judgment and with justice from henceforth as the people in the body bring forth the way of the LORD in their living always, forever. The building of the body of the son of the LORD will require zeal and Isaiah says that the zeal of the LORD of hosts will perform this great work through individuals who compose the body. The spirit of the LORD working through an individual has been done before this particular time of Isaiah.

8 The Lord sent a word into Jacob, and it hath lighted upon Israel.
9 And all the people shall know, even Ephraim and the inhabitant of Samaria, that say in the pride and stoutness of heart,
10 The bricks are fallen down, but we will build with hewn stones: the sycomores are cut down, but we will change them into cedars.

The LORD has sent his word into and through the physical body of Jacob and it lighted, it converted and transformed Jacob into Israel, who was the father of the children of Israel, that should have become a great nation if the LORD's spirit would have been allowed to work through His people. All the people who let the LORD find expression through them shall know the LORD, even Ephraim, who was at war with Jerusalem, or, the inhabitant of Samaria. Isaiah wants the people to know that the LORD of hosts is the LORD of **all** people. The divided people can say, in their false pride and their hardness of heart, that the "bricks", the people, are fallen down and that they will build a new body of people with hewn stones; and they will replace the sycamore trees that are cut down with cedars. The symbolism of the two trees as it applies to two types of people is that the sycamore tree has a thorny ball for a seed and readily sheds its bark while the cedar tree does not readily shed its bark, its wood resists decay and has a fragrant odor. But will the LORD be allowed to build his body of people on earth using the LORD's spirit? or will it be built according to the ways of men who fight between and among each other?

11 Therefore the LORD shall set up the adversaries of Rezin against him, and join his enemies together;
12 The Syrians before, and the Philistines behind; and they shall devour Israel with open mouth. For all this his anger is not turned away, but his hand is stretched out still.
13 For the people turneth not unto him that smiteth them, neither do they seek the LORD of hosts.

If the people do not use the spirit of the LORD to build the body of the child on earth, then the LORD shall set up adversaries of Rezin against him and join his enemies together to defeat him. The Syrians on the north and the Philistines on the south shall form an open mouth to devour Israel in a battle. Even if this occurred, the anger of the aggressors would not be turned away, they would stretch out their hand for "more" land and people. The people will not turn to the leaders who defeat them, nor do the defeated people seek the LORD of hosts to lead them because they want revenge for their defeat. The way of the aggressors is the way of war. The way of the LORD, the way of letting the LORD build the house on earth, is the way of victory without war.

14 Therefore the LORD will cut off from Israel head and tail, branch and rush, in one day.
15 The ancient and honourable, he is the head; and the prophet that teacheth lies, he is the tail.
16 For the leaders of this people cause them to err; and they that are led of them are destroyed.
17 Therefore the Lord shall have no joy in their young men, neither shall have mercy on their fatherless and widows: for every one is an hypocrite and an evildoer, and every mouth speaketh folly. For all this his anger is not turned away, but his hand is stretched out still.

The advice of the ancient and the honorable leaders of the past is identified as the head; the prophets that teach lies of what they believe will happen are identified as the tail of the beast that leads the people in the wrong direction. These false leaders of the people who base their conclusions on the ways of the past or the great expectations of the future through fighting and war cause them to make mistakes in judgment and to err; the people who are led of them will be destroyed. Therefore, the LORD shall have no joy in their young men, neither shall the LORD have mercy on their casualties of battle such as the fatherless and the widows because every one of the leaders is a hypocrite and an evildoer and every mouth speaks folly. Even when all this destruction comes to pass, the anger of the enemy is not turned away, the enemy wants "more" and his hand is still stretched out to get "more" of everything. The leaders of the fallen state are wicked and they do not love the people.

18 For wickedness burneth as the fire: it shall devour the briers and thorns, and shall kindle in the thickets of the forest, and they shall mount up like the lifting up of smoke.

19 Through the wrath of the LORD of hosts is the land darkened, and the people shall be as the fuel of the fire: no man shall spare his brother.
20 And he shall snatch on the right hand, and be hungry; and he shall eat on the left hand, and they shall not be satisfied: they shall eat every man the flesh of his own arm:
21 Manasseh, Ephraim; and Ephraim, Manasseh: and they together shall be against Judah. For all this his anger is not turned away, but his hand is stretched out still.

Wickedness within fallen man burns as a raging fire in the affairs of men to eliminate the wickedness in the people as fire devours the thorns and the briers, the thickets in the forest. The effect of the destruction of the people shall be seen as clearly as the smoke that rises up from the fire that clears the land. This destructive action is the wrath of the power of the LORD when the true nature of the spirit of love is not expressed. The people who do not let the spirit of the LORD come into the earth shall be as fuel for the fire: the conflagration in which no man shall spare his brother because man in the fallen state is greedy and unclean.

He shall snatch with his right hand and still be hungry for more, because greed is never satisfied. He shall eat with his left hand, which is unclean, and he shall not be satisfied after his unclean acts. These fallen men shall eat of the flesh of his own arm because each person is an arm in the body of the LORD of hosts. Brothers are fighting each other. Whether the brothers are Ephraim fighting Manasseh, or, Manasseh fighting Ephraim, they are still brothers. If they join together to fight against Judah, they are fighting their uncle. It is all one family of the LORD. Their anger will not be turned away no matter who wins the battle. The greedy person, who thinks that the earth is his personal possession instead of the LORD's, will continue to stretch out his hand for more because material things will not satisfy the thirst for the spirit of the LORD.

CHAPTER 10

1 Woe unto them that decree unrighteous decrees, and that write grievousness which they have prescribed;
2 To turn aside the needy from judgment, and to take away the right from the poor of my people, that widows may be their prey, and that they may rob the fatherless!

Isaiah is aware that when a country is invaded by an enemy who has superior forces, the people must learn to live with the tyrants who have devastated the land and who will rule with harsh decrees. Isaiah prophesies woe to the invaders who issue unrighteous decrees and who write the records of the grievousness which they themselves have prescribed for the people that they have conquered. The conqueror has done away with any mercy for the needy, any rights for the poor, the widows are taken advantage of and the fatherless children are robbed of their possessions. The invaders have brought woe upon the people and Isaiah is prophesying that they will reap woe according to the law of the LORD.

3 And what will ye do in the day of visitation, and in the desolation which shall come from far? to whom will ye flee for help? and where will ye leave your glory?
4 Without me they shall bow down under the prisoners, and they shall fall under the slain. For all this his anger is not turned away, but his hand is stretched out still.

Isaiah is concerned about the behavior of his friends, neighbors and countrymen in Jerusalem, Judah and the house of Israel. What will they do in the day of visitation by the conquerors and in the desolation which shall come from rulers from far away? To whom shall the people turn for help? Where will the people leave their glory when they are a defeated people? Without the help of Isaiah who knows the covenant of the LORD, the people shall bow down under the burden of being prisoners and they shall fall just as the slain have fallen in battle. Isaiah knows that in these desolate times, the LORD's anger, which is the wrath of the LORD that is directed against the people through the invaders from Assyria, is not turned away and eliminated but the LORD's hand is still stretched-out in the invitation to a covenant-agreement to those who will accept His hand.

The Symbolic Version of Isaiah

5 O Assyrian, the rod of mine anger, and the staff in their hand is mine indignation.
6 I will send him against an hypocritical nation, and against the people of my wrath will I give him a charge, to take the spoil, and to take the prey, and to tread them down like the mire of the streets.

Isaiah speaks the word of the LORD when he tells the Assyrian invader that the rod of the LORD's anger is being made manifest through the staff in the hand of the Assyrians. The wrath is the indignation of the LORD's power, which, if it is not used to produce the harmony of love and truth, will surely be used to demonstrate the LORD's ire and displeasure. The working of the law of the LORD shall send the Assyrians against the hypocritical nation that the children of Israel have become. The power of the LORD
is utilized to bring pressure to bear upon the children of Israel who did not build the holy nation of the LORD when they had the opportunity. The children of Israel fought among themselves and they lost their strength. The balance of power is in the hands of the Assyrians who have taken charge, who take the spoils of war, who take their prey and who tread on the people as mud in the streets. The power of the LORD must manifest on earth: it can either be in a true design which will result in a kingdom of peace and harmony among the people; or, it can be in the chaos produced by the individual leaders in the fallen state, fallen away from the covenant of the LORD, who formulate their own plans to divide, conquer and subjugate the people. The law of the LORD works fairly among all the people on earth, because all the people on earth are the LORD's people. The people can either reveal the true design of the LORD; or, a distortion of the true design. The choice is left with the people. Thus far, except for Isaiah and a small band of followers, or disciples, the people have not chosen the true design and they must reap what they sow.

7 Howbeit he meaneth not so, neither doth his heart think so; but it is in his heart to destroy and cut off nations not a few.
8 For he saith, Are not my princes altogether kings?
9 Is not Calno as Carchemish? is not Hamath as Arpad? is not Samaria as Damascus?
10 As my hand hath found the kingdoms of the idols, and whose graven images did excel them of Jerusalem and of Samaria;
11 Shall I not, as I have done unto Samaria and her idols, so do to Jerusalem and her idols?

The path of destruction is not in the heart of the LORD; it is a heart filled with love and the true design is a lovely design. However, the power of the LORD must work through the hearts and minds of the people and they choose to use the LORD's power to destroy and to fight among nations and not restrict the fighting and disagreement to the few in a restricted area. Is this not true in all cities where people abide? From the LORD's point of view, which is the King's viewpoint, all of his princes are kings of their particular areas if they are in covenant-agreement with the King. The true King treats his subjects fairly by the working of the Law. Is not the law at work in Calno and Carchemish? Is not the law at work in Hamath as Arpad? Is not the law at work in Samaria as Damascus? Is not the law at work everywhere?

As the LORD has found the kingdoms of idols and graven images that the people worship in Jerusalem and Samaria, shall the LORD not do to Jerusalem and her idols as He has done to Samaria and her idols? During the present invasion by the Assyrians, the idols and the graven images of the fallen state that are not of the covenant are in the process of being destroyed. Does that mean that Assyria will go unharmed?

12 Wherefore it shall come to pass, that when the Lord hath performed his whole work upon mount Zion and on Jerusalem, I will punish the fruit of the stout heart of the king of Assyria, and the glory of his high looks.
13 For he saith, By the strength of my hand I have done it, and by my wisdom; for I am prudent: and I have removed the bounds of the people, and have robbed their treasures, and I have put down the inhabitants like a valiant man:
14 And my hand hath found as a nest the riches of the people: and as one gathereth eggs that are left, have I gathered all the earth; and there was none that moved the wing, or opened the mouth, or peeped.

Isaiah tells his people that when the LORD has performed his whole work upon mount Zion and Jerusalem, then He will punish both the hard heart of the king of Assyria and the glory of his high looks, his grand vision to build a large empire which ignores the spirit of the LORD. The king of Assyria says that all that has been done has been done by the power of his own hand and his own wisdom. The king of Assyria, like Pharaoh, knows not the LORD. The king of Assyria has been prudent in his plans to remove the boundaries of the people, robbed their treasures and conquered the inhabitants like the valiant person that he believes himself to be. The king of Assyria—all on his own—has found the nest of the riches of the people, and, as one gathers eggs, he has gathered all the riches of the earth. There was not one of the eggs and the little birds that he picked among the house of Israel who gave him any opposition by moving a wing, opening a mouth or giving a peep. There was no objection by anyone. Isaiah points out the error in the thinking of the king of Assyria.

15 Shall the axe boast itself against him that heweth therewith? or shall the saw magnify itself against him that shaketh it? as if the rod should shake itself against them that lift it up, or as if the staff should lift up itself, as if it were no wood.

Isaiah compares the king of Assyria as an ax without a person to swing it; as a saw who believes that it is shaking itself; as a rod which should shake itself against the person that lifts it up; as a staff that could lift itself up as if it were not wood. Isaiah is emphasizing the point that the king of Assyria is like a material tool in the hand of the LORD, but, the king does not know it and he obscures the obvious fact by thinking that he has done these things all aone without the power of the LORD.

16 Therefore shall the Lord, the Lord of hosts, send among his fat ones leanness; and under his glory he shall kindle a burning like the burning of a fire.
17 And the light of Israel shall be for a fire, and his Holy One for a flame: and it shall burn and devour his thorns and his briers in one day;
18 And shall consume the glory of his forest, and of his fruitful field, both soul and body: and they shall be as when a standardbearer fainteth.
19 And the rest of the trees of his forest shall be few, that a child may write them.

The Symbolic Version of Isaiah

Therefore, in due time, the LORD of hosts shall send among his (King of Assyria) fat ones, the ones who believe that there is no LORD, leanness. The fat spoils of their self-activity shall be replaced with leanness; and under his (King of Assyria) self-proclaimed glory, the LORD shall kindle the burning like the burning of a fire because the LORD is within the person and causing the desire that burns within the king of Assyria and all self-active fallen people who have fallen away from the way of the LORD. The true design that is contained within the fire of the LORD is the Light of the LORD and the Holy One, who is the individualized aspect of the LORD within, is the flame, the spirit within the form. The emergence of this flame shall burn and devour the thorns and the briers of the fallen person in one day; the day that the experience occurs. When a person comes to know the glory of the covenant within himself, this knowledge shall consume the glory of the forest that the person has built for himself, and the fruitful field that the person has done all by himself with his own body and soul without any help. The knowledge of the presence of the LORD in the covenant-agreement within a person shall produce an effect as when a standard bearer faints; they fall on their face and are unable to stand before the LORD. The rest of the trees, the symbols of what he thought he had grown all by himself, will be so few in number that a child may count them and write them because they will be so few in number.

20 And it shall come to pass in that day, that the remnant of Israel, and such as are escaped of the house of Jacob, shall no more again stay upon him that smote them; but shall stay upon the LORD, the Holy One of Israel, in truth.
21 The remnant shall return, even the remnant of Jacob, unto the mighty God.
22 For though thy people Israel be as the sand of the sea, yet a remnant of them shall return: the consumption decreed shall overflow with righteousness.
23 For the Lord GOD of hosts shall make a consumption, even determined, in the midst of all the land.

And it shall come to pass in that day, the day when the people are being ruled by those leaders who have no regard for the dominion of the LORD in their lives, that the remnant of Israel, the people who know of their spiritual heritage of the covenant with the LORD, along with those of the house of Jacob, who are not consciously aware of the covenant but they move closely with the people who are, shall no longer be focused on the invaders who have defeated them or threatened to defeat them, but rather they stay focused on letting the way of the covenant with the LORD, the Holy One of Israel, be the truth of experience in their daily lives.

In this way, the remnant of Israel shall return to the people, even including the remnant of Jacob who are not consciously aware of the covenant but they will learn to experience the covenant with the LORD, the mighty God, as the spirit of God is allowed to flow through them in their living. For as the people of Israel be as scattered and divided as the sand of the sea, yet a remnant of them shall return to build the body of God on earth. This body of people shall overflow with righteousness because it carries the righteousness of the LORD in their midst and they will be consumed with the righteousness from the LORD. It is the LORD of hosts which makes the consumption, the divine attributes, that will be in the land of the people and their surroundings who carry the spirit of the LORD through the covenant agreement. In this way, the LORD shall be with his people in times of trouble and tribulation by the invaders.

The Testimony of the Major Prophets

24 Therefore thus saith the Lord GOD of hosts, O my people that dwellest in Zion, be not afraid of the Assyrian: he shall smite thee with a rod, and shall lift up his staff against thee, after the manner of Egypt.
25 For yet a very little while, and the indignation shall cease, and mine anger in their destruction.
26 And the LORD of hosts shall stir up a scourge for him according to the slaughter of Midian at the rock of Oreb: and as his rod was upon the sea, so shall he lift it up after the manner of Egypt.

Therefore, the Lord GOD of hosts shall indeed be with his people in the living covenant-agreement and the people shall know of His living presence in their own individual consciousness, and they will know that the LORD says to them, "O my people that dwell in Zion," (Zion is the place of spiritual awareness and oneness with the LORD), "be not afraid of the Assyrian" and his domination and occupation of the land. The Assyrian shall afflict you with his rod of power and control, but the presence of the LORD in your hearts, minds and bodies shall lift up his staff of oppression against thee after the manner of the children of Israel in Egypt under the leadership of Moses. Isaiah is providing a leadership similar to that which was provided by the LORD through Moses approximately 800 years earlier. The spirit of the LORD is eternal; the material forms of the leaders and the people are different.

The people are advised to be patient and to let the spirit of the LORD work through their forms for a little while in the eternal scheme of things and eventually, the indignation will cease as well as the LORD's anger in the destruction of the forms that are oppressing His body of people that carry a conscious awareness of His spirit. The Lord of all the hosts of people shall stir up a scourge for the Assyrians, who are a distortion of the true design that should be on earth, and they will be eliminated in a similar manner to the slaughter of Midian at the rock of Oreb; and as the LORD's rod of control through Moses that was upon the sea, so shall the LORD lift away the burden of the oppressor after the manner in Egypt. *(See The Symbolic Version of Exodus.)*

27 And it shall come to pass in that day, that his burden shall be taken away from off thy shoulder, and his yoke from off thy neck, and the yoke shall be destroyed because of the anointing.
28 He is come to Aiath, he is passed to Migron; at Michmash he hath laid up his carriages:
29 They are gone over the passage: they have taken up their lodging at Geba; Ramah is afraid; Gibeah of Saul is fled.
30 Lift up thy voice, O daughter of Gallim: cause it to be heard unto Laish, O poor Anathoth.
31 Madmenah is removed; the inhabitants of Gebim gather themselves to flee.
32 As yet shall he remain at Nob that day: he shall shake his hand against the mount of the daughter of Zion, the hill of Jerusalem.

And the LORD promises that it shall come to pass that the burden of the Assyrian invaders shall be taken off the shoulder of the body of people who carry His spirit and his name on earth; and the yoke of the Assyrians shall come off thy neck and they will be destroyed because of the anointing of LORD's spirit that comes to the body of people through the covenant. Isaiah is telling his people that the Assyrians invaders are on the march and they are moving to and through Aiath, Migron and Michmash, which is only seven miles from Jerusalem: they are moving through the passage of lands quickly with the result that they have taken up lodging at Geba; Ramah, the home of Samuel that is only five miles from Jerusalem, is afraid; Gibeah of Saul, which had been the first capital of Israel's first king, only three miles from Jerusalem, has fled.

The people of Jerusalem and Judah will lift up their voices in sadness at the coming of the invaders who are moving quickly over the lands that were under the control of historical leaders of Israel. Anathoth, the hometown of Jeremiah; Madmenah is removed and the people of Gebim gather themselves together to flee. And yet Isaiah shall remain at Nob, the high place of spiritual consciousness of the LORD in Jerusalem that day of invasion and represent the LORD. Isaiah shall be able to observe what is happening to Jerusalem as a part of the unfolding outworking of the law of the LORD without fear. He has also advised his followers not to panic or flee but to observe the invasion with his vision, which is the vision of the LORD.

33 Behold, the Lord, the LORD of hosts, shall lop the bough with terror: and the high ones of stature shall be hewn down, and the haughty shall be humbled.
34 And he shall cut down the thickets of the forest with iron, and Lebanon shall fall by a mighty one.

The action of the LORD of hosts shall change the face of the environment which is symbolized by the removal of, the lop, of the bough of the material tree which is observed with terror among the people who are not of the LORD; the high and mighty leaders of stature shall be hewn down and the haughty shall be humbled by the defeat of the invasion of Jerusalem. Isaiah and his followers observe this change in the leadership and environment of Jerusalem and Judah as the working of the law as the LORD. It is the LORD's power at work as He trims the thickets of His forest with iron, the unbending will of the invaders, and removes the tall tree of Lebanon, who symbolizes the leadership of Jerusalem and Jerusalem itself as the highest tree in Judah, by a mighty force. Isaiah sees all of this as the outworking of the LORD according to the law of the LORD when seen with a true perspective of bringing the divine design into form on earth. Isaiah and his followers will hold steady in the spiritual covenant with the LORD so that the LORD will have some physical substance of His people to make a new beginning.

CHAPTER 11

1 And there shall come forth a rod out of the stem of Jesse, and a Branch shall grow out of his roots:
2 And the spirit of the LORD shall rest upon him, the spirit of wisdom and understanding, the spirit of counsel and might, the spirit of knowledge and of the fear of the LORD;
3 And shall make him of quick understanding in the fear of the LORD: and he shall not judge after the sight of his eyes, neither reprove after the hearing of his ears:
4 But with righteousness shall he judge the poor, and reprove with equity for the meek of the earth: and he shall smite the earth with the rod of his mouth, and with the breath of his lips shall he slay the wicked.
5 And righteousness shall be the girdle of his loins, and faithfulness the girdle of his reins.

The covenant of the LORD in the heaven of the spirit with the spirit of a person on earth is a covenant-agreement that exists in spirit; The LORD is always in agreement with the spirit that is in man. The evidence of the agreement in spirit must manifest in and through the physical form on earth. The physical manifestation of the spirit on earth is known as a rod out of the stem of Jesse. Jesse means, "that which is" or "exists". The spirit of Man is, and the spirit of Man exists. He is a branch of the Tree of Life and he shall grow out of the roots of the LORD on earth. The spirit of the LORD in the spiritual realm shall rest upon him, man, who is in form on earth. It is the spirit of the LORD which will bring the spirit of understanding and wisdom, the spirit of counsel and might, the spirit of knowledge and the fear, the awesomeness, of the eternal LORD into the earth to a person who fulfills the earthly requirement of the covenant-agreement. The spirit of knowledge has a direct application to the mind of a person; the fear and awe have application to the emotions, the heart. Man has a mind and a heart that can be turned to the LORD.

The divine intelligence and attributes of the LORD which come to focus in a person on earth, such as Isaiah, shall give that person a quick, lively understanding that is obtained when one is in agreement with the fear, the awesome power, of the LORD: the person has spiritual vision which is higher than an earthly, material vision. The person will not judge what he sees on earth with his material vision called the sight of his eyes or to reprove anyone with the hearing of his ears. The person with spiritual vision has it because of his experience of the covenant which allows him to see from a higher level that puts everything into a new perspective based upon the operation of the Law of the LORD. The mind and the heart are turned to the LORD.

The spiritual vision which the person in covenant-agreement has with the LORD produces an action which is based upon the new vision: he has a righteousness which will be used to judge the poor and to reprove with equity, with fairness, the poor of the earth who function at the material level since they can not see as clearly as a person with spiritual vision. The reproof which is offered to a person who needs reproof is accomplished through a spirit of understanding that is offered to help the poor person, who is poor in spirit. The correction of a person who has been smitten by the spirit is done through the rod of his mouth or the control of his lips, his expression; it is never accomplished through an intention to physically harm a person. If physical correction or damage comes, it is always done physically through the expression of someone else through the working of the Law unless the person with spiritual vision acts to protect himself. Only with the breath of the lips, a word of correction done out of love, shall a person in the covenant harm or slay the wicked. The slaying of the wicked is accomplished when the wicked person is transformed from material orientation into spiritual identity. Righteousness shall be the tool of the person on earth who is in the covenant-agreement and faithfulness to the spirit of the LORD shall be the girdle of his loins and the girdle of the reins that control how and what he expresses in life.

6 The wolf also shall dwell with the lamb, and the leopard shall lie down with the kid; and the calf and the young lion and the fatling together; and a little child shall lead them.
7 And the cow and the bear shall feed; their young ones shall lie down together: and the lion shall eat straw like the ox.
8 And the sucking child shall play on the hole of the asp, and the weaned child shall put his hand on the cockatrice' den.
9 They shall not hurt nor destroy in all my holy mountain: for the earth shall be full of the knowledge of the LORD, as the waters cover the sea.

It is possible for human beings on earth who are in the fallen state to live in a harmonious balance with each other but not if they remain the way they are. A great change needs to take place from their fallen material behavior to an ascended spiritual behavior. In their present state, which is described in symbolic terms, the people are identified with the characteristics of animals: they can live together **after** they come to the LORD's holy mountain. Then, the people with previous faults can be as the wolf, a ravenous person, dwelling with the lamb, who was his prey; the leopard can lie down with the young goat; the calf and the young lion can abide together; and a little child, the symbol of the spiritual body of the covenant, Immanuel, God with us on earth, shall lead the way to bring the divine design, the harmony from heaven into physical manifestation on earth. These "animals" who need to learn to live together apply to people who can change, rather than to the literal animals who function at a balanced level for their survival. The covenant of the LORD is not designed for just one earthly person but, for everyone on earth. Let us consider the expansion of the covenant to other people that Isaiah personifies as animals.

The cow, the person who gives, and the bear, who kills and takes with the power of his paw, shall feed together and their offspring, their young ones shall lie down together: and the person who was as a destructive lion shall eat straw like the ox who used to be his prey. The sucking child shall safely play on the hole of the asp, the poisonous snake of a person who would do him harm, and the weaned child, the child who no longer needs the divine example from Isaiah, shall put his hand of control that he has internalized on the den of the cockatrice, the poisonous serpent of the devil of his self-active mind that led him to do the horrible things of which fallen human nature is capable. The destructive characteristics of human nature must rise up, ascend, to the nature of the spirit for the divine design to return to the earth in manifest form. Then, and only then, shall the fallen creatures on earth neither hurt nor destroy in all the LORD's holy mountain of spirit which has been brought to earth: for the earth shall be full of the knowledge of the LORD, that everyone and everything is a part of the LORD's earthly form as the waters cover the sea. Only the LORD's spirit moving through His creation, Man, produces His divine design for the planet.

10 And in that day there shall be a root of Jesse, which shall stand for an ensign of the people; to it shall the Gentiles seek: and his rest shall be glorious.
11 And it shall come to pass in that day, that the Lord shall set his hand again the second time to recover the remnant of his people, which shall be left, from Assyria, and from Egypt, and from Pathros, and from Cush, and from Elam, and from Shinar, and from Hamath, and from the islands of the sea.
12 And he shall set up an ensign for the nations, and shall assemble the outcasts of Israel, and gather together the dispersed of Judah from the four corners of the earth.
13 The envy also of Ephraim shall depart, and the adversaries of Judah shall be cut off: Ephraim shall not envy Judah, and Judah shall not vex Ephraim.

In that day, there shall be a root of Jesse, a person who shall stand as an ensign, a human banner of the spirit of the LORD, a flag or a symbol to be observed by others and that person (or people) shall serve as a point of orientation, for the purpose that the Gentiles shall be attracted and seek the treasure that will be glorious in their experience on earth. This person, this banner, JEHOVAH-nissi, which means, "the LORD our banner" is the leader, Isaiah, who, at this time, would be the instrument of the LORD, the sword of the LORD, on earth as an example for others to follow to return the earth to the LORD once again.

It shall come to pass that the LORD shall set his hand upon his people on earth once again, the second time, to recover the remnant of his people, the people who are willing to return to the LORD. The people who are willing to return are not limited to Jerusalem and Judah; there is a remnant of people, others, outside the covenant who want to return to the LORD from places described as Assyria, Egypt, Pathros, Cush, Elam, Shinar, Hamoth, and the islands of the sea.

Each of these seemingly separate nations shall have an ensign, a leader, a point of orientation, to reassemble people, who are considered the outcasts of Israel, so that the dispersed of Judah from the four corners of the earth shall be gathered together in oneness of spirit. The envy of Ephraim shall depart from the people, and the adversaries of Judah shall be cut off and be no more. The fighting between Ephraim and Judah shall cease because the envy and the vexation of one for the other shall cease only in the covenant.

14 But they shall fly upon the shoulders of the Philistines toward the west; they shall spoil them of the east together: they shall lay their hand upon Edom and Moab; and the children of Ammon shall obey them.
15 And the LORD shall utterly destroy the tongue of the Egyptian sea; and with his mighty wind shall he shake his hand over the river, and shall smite it in the seven streams, and make men go over dryshod.
16 And there shall be an highway for the remnant of his people, which shall be left, from Assyria; like as it was to Israel in the day that he came up out of the land of Egypt.

In togetherness and oneness of spirit, the united people, united in the LORD's spirit, shall fly upon the shoulders of the Philistines, the symbol of a tall and powerful people, toward the west; they shall spoil the people of the east together as they move into the country of Edom and Moab; and the children of Ammon shall obey the orders of the people in the covenant-agreement.

The expansion of the spirit of the LORD into the affairs of greedy men shall destroy the tongue of the Egyptian sea, the sea of people who were guided and governed by the words of a materialistic people of Egypt. The wind of the spirit of the LORD shall move and shake His hand of control over the river of wrong function that is the river of fallen consciousness, and He shall break it into seven streams, seven different directions and differentiations from the LORD's spirit to reduce its power, and make men go over the land in a new way of behavior based in the spirit of the LORD. There shall be a highway, a spiritual path for the remnant of the LORD's people from Assyria and other places to walk on earth and the way shall not be narrow, but wide, only as more people will be walking in the Way of the LORD. Leadership is needed so that the people can see and follow as it was to Israel when the children came forth from captivity out of the land of Egypt. It is the way of the people from an unholy to a holy nation.

CHAPTER 12

1 And in that day thou shalt say, O LORD, I will praise thee: though thou wast angry with me, thine anger is turned away, and thou comfortedst me.
2 Behold, God is my salvation; I will trust, and not be afraid: for the LORD JEHOVAH is my strength and my song; he also is become my salvation.
3 Therefore with joy shall ye draw water out of the wells of salvation.

In the day (which could be today!) when the people will know that there is a path for the remnant of the LORD's people to walk on earth, then the people shall say, O LORD, I will praise thee in my moment to moment living of life: though I thought that the LORD was angry with me when I was on the wrong path, out-of-position to see and understand the way of the LORD; now that I have changed behavior, I see my experience of anger is turned away and the power of the LORD is comforting me. Behold, God is my salvation: I will trust the LORD and not be afraid: for the LORD JEHOVAH is my strength and my song because I am one with the LORD's strength of spirit and I am singing the song of the LORD on earth.

The word JEHOVAH means, "God in action on earth through man" in general and to the individual man or woman in particular. There is no difference between the covenant-agreement of the LORD and JEHOVAH. Both words describe the condition in which the person is letting, or allowing, the spirit of the LORD in the heaven of the spirit to find expression in earth of the person's heart, mind and body to flow into the environment. This is the way of salvation and the way that the LORD becomes "my" individual salvation; the salvation of the person who allows it to happen. The water of the truth of the LORD is buried deep within everyone. Now that a person has heard of the location of the water that symbolizes the truth of the LORD that satisfies the thirst for the LORD, then the people can draw out of the wells of salvation from the abundance of water which is within.

4 And in that day shall ye say, Praise the LORD, call upon his name, declare his doings among the people, make mention that his name is exalted.
5 Sing unto the LORD; for he hath done excellent things: this is known in all the earth.

6 Cry out and shout, thou inhabitant of Zion: for great is the Holy One of Israel in the midst of thee.

And, in the day that a person understands that the location of the LORD is within everyone, then the wise person shall praise the LORD, call upon His name, and declare the LORD's doings among the people by letting the LORD's spirit flow from within one's self to other people. A person who chooses to do this is a "Chosen one", who has chosen to let the spirit of the LORD flow out from him to the people and in so doing, the name of the LORD is exalted.

The person is to sing unto the LORD, using the LORD's spirit of love in action on earth, and that expression will do excellent things: once the expression of the LORD's spirit is released into the earth, then it is known on earth because the LORD's spirit has been wrapped in material forms of thoughts, words and deeds on earth where the spirit becomes observable.

The instruction of Isaiah is to cry out and shout, to the inhabitant of Zion, the high holy place of spiritual consciousness, because a person has chosen to let the spirit of the LORD take form on earth. The person who does this in an inhabitant of Zion, which is not a physical place, it is a spiritual place within one's self where the Holy One of Israel, Who is great, dwells in the midst of you. A person who chooses to allow the LORD's spirit to flow through him or her does not magically transform the environment immediately. The same burden of the conditions in the environment are still with the person who made the choice to serve the LORD. However, if a person chooses to serve the LORD's spirit into the environment, it is the flow of the spirit that transforms the conditions of the earth. When the spirit is not being expressed, there is no creative spiritual change. Everything that is being done by fallen human beings is simply rearranging the "furniture", the things of the environment, of the fallen state.

CHAPTER 13

1 The burden of Babylon, which Isaiah the son of Amoz did see.
2 Lift ye up a banner upon the high mountain, exalt the voice unto them, shake the hand, that they may go into the gates of the nobles.

Isaiah, the point of focus of a visible person on earth who is letting the spirit of the LORD flow through him continues to see very clearly the distorted conditions in the environment. This is described symbolically for the conditions of the whole world as "the burden of Babylon". Babylon is used as a symbol for a confused state of affairs made by the people who live in the city. The conditions of the environment are exactly the way that they are at that moment in time. (The conditions of the environment in this moment of observation are exactly the way they are!) Isaiah's words to his followers are to lift up a banner upon a high mountain of spiritual consciousness within one's self, to make contact, or to bring the focus of their attention to the spirit of the LORD within them, so that they can exalt the voice of the LORD. This can be done easily as the person can shake the hand of the LORD, or shake the physical hand of a person such as Isaiah who is in agreement with the LORD, so that they can be in oneness with the spirit of the LORD and have the courage to go into the gates, the hearts and minds, of the nobles.

3 I have commanded my sanctified ones, I have also called my mighty ones for mine anger, even them that rejoice in my highness.
4 The noise of a multitude in the mountains, like as of a great people; a tumultuous noise of the kingdoms of nations gathered together: the LORD of hosts mustereth the host of the battle.
5 They come from a far country, from the end of heaven, even the LORD, and the weapons of his indignation, to destroy the whole land.

Isaiah, speaking the word of the LORD, has said that the LORD has commanded His sanctified ones, the people who are in agreement with the LORD, and, Isaiah has called the mighty spiritual ones within those who choose to serve the LORD to become an army of people that can, in combined expression, radiate the spirit of the LORD, a spirit of love in action, which will be perceived as

The Symbolic Version of Isaiah

anger by those who are against the way of the LORD. The LORD, Isaiah and his followers are calling all those who rejoice in the highness and the supremacy of the LORD on earth.

The LORD through Isaiah is mustering an army of his followers who will band together to create a noise of a great multitude in the mountains of spiritual consciousness, as a great people. Many people are needed to make a tumultuous noise of the kingdoms of nations gathered together. The LORD of hosts must muster a host of people who will represent the divine nature of the LORD on earth to do battle with, to counter the effect of, the greed and self-centeredness of human nature. The people who choose to come to the LORD may come from a far country, from the end of the heaven, which is the beginning of the earth, since heaven and earth are one. In any event, there needs to be a body of people on earth to carry the spirit of the LORD on earth with the weapons of the LORD's "indignation" in order to do "battle" with the majority of the fallen people who are presently in control. Isaiah cannot do what needs to be done on earth all by himself, which is to destroy the evidence of human nature on the earth. Additional people are needed in the LORD's army to allow the spirit of the LORD to flow into the earth.

6 Howl ye; for the day of the LORD is at hand; it shall come as a destruction from the Almighty.
7 Therefore shall all hands be faint, and every man's heart shall melt:
8 And they shall be afraid: pangs and sorrows shall take hold of them; they shall be in pain as a woman that travaileth: they shall be amazed one at another; their faces shall be as flames.

Isaiah is looking for people to "howl", to rejoice and release the spirit of the LORD through themselves because the day of the LORD is at hand, available, from the LORD who is constantly and continuously sending His spirit into the earth of His people. The flow of the LORD's spirit comes as a destruction from the Almighty to eliminate the human nature conditions which have been created by men and women in the fallen state. While people may envision the battle as a battle between the participants who are either the "good" or the "evil" people, the great battle is between the spirit of the LORD and the human nature habits within one's self. It is the hand of control of human nature, that must become weaker and faint; it is every man's evil heart which shall melt. The people who come to the way of the LORD shall be afraid to let go of their old familiar ways; they will suffer pangs and sorrows as they experience the withdrawal symptoms of the human nature state that will be replaced by the true nature of man. Their experience will be like the pain of a woman that travails in the pain of childbirth. The people who go through the process shall be amazed at one another; their faces shall be as flames, the people will know the flames of the internal fire that consumes human habits, due to the process and the action of giving birth to the spirit of the LORD.

9 Behold, the day of the LORD cometh, cruel both with wrath and fierce anger, to lay the land desolate: and he shall destroy the sinners thereof out of it.
10 For the stars of heaven and the constellations thereof shall not give their light: the sun shall be darkened in his going forth, and the moon shall not cause her light to shine.
11 And I will punish the world for their evil, and the wicked for their iniquity; and I will cause the arrogancy of the proud to cease, and will lay low the haughtiness of the terrible.
12 I will make a man more precious than fine gold; even a man than the golden wedge of Ophir.

The Testimony of the Major Prophets

Isaiah tells his followers that the day of the LORD comes into the experience of each person and it may seem cruel, both with wrath and fierce anger by the LORD, as the changes take place **within the person to lay the human nature land desolate: he shall destroy the sinners out of it, the fallen human nature state that one offers to the LORD.** The land that the spirit of the LORD flows through must be a new land, a holy land, and not a sinful land. The "land" of the human form must be cleared.

Isaiah warns his new followers that if the LORD is envisioned as the stars of the heaven and the constellations thereof, or as the sun and the moon, these heavenly bodies cannot give forth their light to shine through the land where clouds dwell and dim the light. As the spirit off the LORD moves through the consciousness of the fallen human nature state of man, then the spirit will punish the world for the evil that is contained within the heart of man for the wickedness, the iniquity, the arrogance of the proud and the haughtiness of the terrible that will be pushed aside by the moving spirit of the LORD as it is expressed in daily living. This process may seem difficult to the carnal, human nature mind and heart but the process will make a man more precious than fine gold; even a man worth more than the large golden wedge of Ophir where Solomon obtained his gold. There is earthly gold, which does not tarnish, considered a valuable ornamental metal by human nature and it is used as a symbol of love; and there is the spiritual gold of the true state, which is God's love and power that is pure, eternal, and invaluable. It does not need to be symbolized. One is of the material earth; and one is of the heaven.

13 Therefore I will shake the heavens, and the earth shall remove out of her place, in the wrath of the LORD of hosts, and in the day of his fierce anger.
14 And it shall be as the chased roe, and as a sheep that no man taketh up: they shall every man turn to his own people, and flee every one into his own land.
15 Every one that is found shall be thrust through; and every one that is joined unto them shall fall by the sword.
16 Their children also shall be dashed to pieces before their eyes; their houses shall be spoiled, and their wives ravished.

Therefore, in order to gather people on earth who will represent the spirit on earth, the LORD will shake the heavens of the consciousness and the earth shall remove out of her place the distortions that resided there. The distortions will perceive their ejection from the heavens of the consciousness as the wrath of the LORD and the day of his fierce anger. But the truth of God is love. Love does the cleansing that seems like animals scurrying back to their wilderness homes. This symbolic language illustrates that the sins or distortions of human nature are driven out of the LORD's house, which is man in the process of being restored.

The thoughts of fallen man, which do not belong in the LORD's house, turn and flee to their own fallen land. The distorted thoughts which do not run away, when they are found, they are thrust through or fall by the sword of truth: they are destroyed. The children, who symbolize the immature thoughts that will eventually mature and grow, shall be dashed to pieces before their eyes; their houses of human nature spoiled and their wives, the symbols that connect their consciousness with the fallen state, shall be ravished and discarded. The distortions of fallen man have been ejected by the LORD from the consciousness of His heaven into the consciousness of fallen man symbolized

The Symbolic Version of Isaiah

by Babylon. The destructive consciousness of Babylon is more concentrated with distortions and it will wreak additional havoc there. The law of the LORD has increased the destructive consciousness in the fallen human nature state.

17 Behold, I will stir up the Medes against them, which shall not regard silver; and as for gold, they shall not delight in it.
18 Their bows also shall dash the young men to pieces; and they shall have no pity on the fruit of the womb; their eye shall not spare children.
19 And Babylon, the glory of kingdoms, the beauty of the Chaldees' excellency, shall be as when God overthrew Sodom and Gomorrah.

The law of the LORD in action will stir up the Medes against the distortions. The distortions hold no regard for silver, the symbol of truth, and gold, the symbol of love. Truth and love are the enemies of all distortions because if truth and love were taken up by the distortions they would not be distortions any longer. The distortions among people are the cause of the fighting against each other. Distortions are self-destructive. This is symbolized by the use of bows as the young men dash each other to pieces with the use of them. The distortions have no pity on the fruit of the womb, the new divinely inspired solutions which come forth in creative process: and, their eye shall not spare the children, who symbolize the young ideas that may have promise when they mature. In this manner, the distortions in the consciousness of fallen man are self-destructive. Babylon, the symbol of the environmental fallen state, is perceived by fallen man as the glory of the earthly kingdoms and the beauty of the Chaldees' excellency which can be traced back to Abraham. Isaiah's view, which he is teaching his followers, is that this so-called beauty of Babylon is comparable to the conditions that existed when God overthrew Sodom and Gomorrah.

20 It shall never be inhabited, neither shall it be dwelt in from generation to generation: neither shall the Arabian pitch tent there; neither shall the shepherds make their fold there.
21 But wild beasts of the desert shall lie there; and their houses shall be full of doleful creatures; and owls shall dwell there, and satyrs shall dance there.
22 And the wild beasts of the islands shall cry in their desolate houses, and dragons in their pleasant palaces: and her time is near to come, and her days shall not be prolonged.

The distorted environmental state of human nature shall never be inhabited peacefully nor shall it be dwelt in from generation to generation: neither shall the Arabian pitch their tent there, nor the shepherds make their fold there because the true design from the LORD keeps flowing into the environment through the consciousness of his people where the fallen state of consciousness distorts the true design into a self-destructive counterfeit state. Until the true design puts in an appearance through man who has been restored to his true position in covenant-agreement with the LORD, the environment shall remain a wilderness. The environment of a wilderness will be fit for wild beasts of the desert who shall lie there; the houses of the inhabitants of the human nature state shall be full of doleful creatures filled with sadness woe and melancholy. Owls, the symbols of the creatures of the night who sleep in the light of day, and the satyrs, the symbols of monstrosities and fiends, shall dance there. The people of the fallen state shall be as wild beasts who cry in their houses of desolation, and as dragons as they dwell in their environmentally pleasant palaces but they will not be happy. The woman who symbolizes human nature, is Babylon the great. Her time is come and her days on earth shall not be prolonged when the people who carry the spirit of the LORD put in an appearance.

CHAPTER 14

1 For the LORD will have mercy on Jacob, and will yet choose Israel, and set them in their own land: and the strangers shall be joined with them, and they shall cleave to the house of Jacob.
2 And the people shall take them, and bring them to their place: and the house of Israel shall possess them in the land of the LORD for servants and handmaids: and they shall take them captives, whose captives they were; and they shall rule over their oppressors.

Isaiah is not speaking about Jacob who lived many years ago and died in Egypt. Isaiah is using Jacob as the personification of the people in the fallen state of mankind who are interested in the service of the LORD. The LORD will have mercy on the people who are like Jacob because, even though they do not know the LORD, they want to continue in the holy ways of Abraham and Isaac. Jacob, as he relinquished his self-centeredness, became a new person, Israel, as a result of his experience with the covenant of the LORD. Israel symbolizes the people who have a spiritual experience with the LORD and they know the LORD through an internal revelation similar to the covenant relationship which existed many years ago when Jacob became Israel. The original Jacob and Israel changed physically, but the LORD is the same LORD always.

The LORD will choose Israel, the LORD will choose the people who desire and are in focus to experience a relationship in spirit with the LORD which puts them into their own land, the land of the spiritual experience of Israel. Either a person is in the land or he isn't; either a person has the covenant-experience or he has not. The people who have experienced the transition from the body of Jacob to the body of Israel know that they are spiritual beings in material forms. Strangers are those people who have never experienced the land of the spirit. Strangers shall be associated with the physical people who represent Israel but they do not know the spiritual Israel: they will be associated with, they will cleave to, the personification of the physical form of Jacob, but there is no conscious awareness that the spirit of the LORD is in the spiritual body of Israel that exists within the physical body of people who compose "Jacob".

The strangers to the LORD, the people who represent Jacob, shall be taken by those who know the way to their place: the place where the house of Israel shall possess them in the land of the LORD,

The Testimony of the Major Prophets

the land of knowing the LORD, as servants and handmaids of the LORD. Once the servants and handmaids discover that they are a representative of the LORD's body, then the strangers shall take "captives", as they were taken "captives" in the service of the LORD. When the person becomes a "captive" of the LORD, they receive power from the LORD in the covenant and they shall rule over their oppressors. The LORD uses the body of Israel to capture the people in the body of Jacob, who are associated with the people in the body of Israel and bring them to the experience of the covenant with the LORD where they become members of the body of Israel, the spiritual body in a material form. The previous members of the body of Jacob have been slain by the spirit. Jacob (human nature) is no more; Israel (divine nature) lives in his place.

3 And it shall come to pass in the day that the LORD shall give thee rest from thy sorrow, and from thy fear, and from the hard bondage wherein thou wast made to serve,
4 That thou shalt take up this proverb against the king of Babylon, and say, How hath the oppressor ceased! the golden city ceased!

It shall come to pass, in the day of the covenant, that the LORD shall give a person rest from the sorrow, the fear and the hard bondage which is associated with an earthly identity in which the person was made to wander in the wilderness of not knowing the LORD to serve other people instead of serving the LORD. After the people have undergone the change in identity from what is described as the Jacob to Israel transition, then, they are able to take up the proverb against the king of Babylon, who symbolizes any person with a big self-centered ego that is omnipresent in human nature, which asks, How has the oppressor ceased his function of being an oppressor? and how has the golden city, the state of fallen consciousness that is searching for earthly treasures, ceased?

5 The LORD hath broken the staff of the wicked, and the sceptre of the rulers.
6 He who smote the people in wrath with a continual stroke, he that ruled the nations in anger, is persecuted, and none hindereth.
7 The whole earth is at rest, and is quiet: they break forth into singing.
8 Yea, the fir trees rejoice at thee, and the cedars of Lebanon, saying, Since thou art laid down, no feller is come up against us.
9 Hell from beneath is moved for thee to meet thee at thy coming: it stirreth up the dead for thee, even all the chief ones of the earth; it hath raised up from their thrones all the kings of the nations.

The realization of the LORD in covenant-agreement with an individual is the action that has broken the staff of the wicked and the scepter of the individual kings of their environments, the rulers of the human nature state. The person in the human nature, or Jacob state, who in false identity did smite the people in anger with a continual stroke of the sword when he rules the people in anger, is persecuted by his own anger; and no one has the power to hinder him from doing so. Not even the LORD can stop a person from using divine power to create anger in lieu of beauty except through the death of the person.

But after the transition from the body of Jacob to the body of Israel, from human nature to divine nature, then, the whole earth is at rest, and it is quiet and still; the people burst forth into singing. Yes, the fir trees and the cedars of Lebanon rejoice in that no one comes to fell, to cut down, the

The Symbolic Version of Isaiah

trees that were once considered to be in one's way. Hell from beneath, which represented the location of hell that a person believes he goes to after he is dead, is seen as the chaos that the person will meet as he comes into his heavenly position in the spiritual state. The divine design of heaven can be seen as a person becomes a part of it. The location of hell is moved from a place beneath the earth at some future time when death occurs to a location on the earth's surface in the present moment for the person to handle, the person who is coming in the name of the LORD. Heaven is available as light to illuminate the hellish worldly conditions. Others may join the body of Israel thereby increasing the shining of the light which decreases the darkness of hell because of the increased shining of the light.

The person who has experienced the new state of spiritual consciousness in which he is in covenant-agreement with the LORD and therefore a member of the body of Israel can begin to see the "dead" in a new light. It can be seen that the spirits within the "dead" are not really dead; they are alive because you know that you are alive in the LORD forever. All the chief ones of the earth are seen as playing a role in the transition from the fallen state back to the divine state and the actions of people either help or hinder the process. This realization of an everlasting spiritual identity raises the kings of nations, every spirit, within a human form, their earthly throne, to membership in the one spiritual body of Israel which belongs to the LORD.

10 All they shall speak and say unto thee, Art thou also become weak as we? art thou become like unto us?
11 Thy pomp is brought down to the grave, and the noise of thy viols: the worm is spread under thee, and the worms cover thee.

The kings of the nations are the people in the fallen human nature state. Each person is a king over his individual nation, his or her individual environment, but they are not aware that they are a spiritual being with everlasting life, a piece of the LORD, a member of the spiritual body of Israel on earth. They can only envision themselves in the fallen state that they know. It seems logical for those in the fallen human nature state to ask if you have become as weak as we? Have you become like us? The pomp of the kingly egocentric state has been brought down to the grave and the noise of the viols which are played at the funeral. The human nature view is that everybody dies and the worm is spread under you in death and the worms shall cover you and devour your material body because you are dust of the ground; you are not a spirit from heaven. How could this change in identity have occurred where spiritual beings believe that they are only material forms?

12 How art thou fallen from heaven, O Lucifer, son of the morning! how art thou cut down to the ground, which didst weaken the nations!
13 For thou hast said in thine heart, I will ascend into heaven, I will exalt my throne above the stars of God: I will sit also upon the mount of the congregation, in the sides of the north:

The question is directed to the person who is in the fallen state of consciousness, which is outside the covenant-agreement where one would know the LORD, as to how did the person fall from heaven? The person who is asked that question is symbolized by the name, Lucifer, and that he was the son of the morning. The name, Lucifer, means, "the light bearer", or "the bearer of the Light". The son of the morning bears the light of the reflection of the morning "star", symbolized by the planet Venus that reflects the morning sun to reveal its brightness. In this analogy, the sun represents the LORD, and the morning star, the planet Venus, should reflect the sun to produce an earthly object that reflects the light of the sun. People are designed to reflect the light of the LORD, just as Venus reflects the light of the sun.

The question is asked as to how the morning star, Lucifer, the personification of all the spiritual beings, fell from the heavens, where he rightfully belongs, to the ground, to the earth, which did weaken the nations on earth who are now in a fallen state of consciousness. The star, which fell to the ground, has said in his heart that he would love to ascend into heaven and "I will exalt my throne above all the stars of God". The fallen star will sit itself above the mount of the congregation of people in the sides of the north (which is the direction of the north side of the tabernacle that leads to the unified promise land). The fallen angel, the son of the morning, Lucifer, wants to be higher than the stars of God: not of the LORD but, as the LORD.

14 I will ascend above the heights of the clouds; I will be like the most High.
15 Yet thou shalt be brought down to hell, to the sides of the pit.
16 They that see thee shall narrowly look upon thee, and consider thee, saying, this the man that made the earth to tremble, that did shake kingdoms;
17 That made the world as a wilderness, and destroyed the cities thereof; that opened not the house of his prisoners?

The fallen angel, Lucifer, who once occupied a very high place in the heavens wants to ascend above the height of the clouds to a point where he will be like the most High. The fallen angel is not content to be **of** God; the fallen angel wants to be **as** God. This desire to be higher than God is the action that brought Lucifer the bearer of the light down into the darkness, down to hell which is the sides of the pit, the cave, where there is no light from the LORD, and, his consciousness is covered with darkness instead of light. The people who do observe Lucifer in this fallen and degraded condition say that this is the man who made the earth tremble, and that did shake kingdoms which were ruled over by the personification of the one who, out of his true position, to reflect the light of the LORD, made the world as a wilderness. His refusal to serve the LORD destroyed the cities; and opened not the house of his prisoners? The world of Lucifer, the angel who has fallen, is a prison and the inhabitants of his world are prisoners. In other books of the Bible, Lucifer, the Light-bearer who has fallen from grace, becomes known as Satan, the prince of darkness as he ceases to bear the light of the LORD and predictably descends into the world of darkness.

18 All the kings of the nations, even all of them, lie in glory, every one in his own house.
19 But thou art cast out of thy grave like an abominable branch, and as the raiment of those that are slain, thrust through with a sword, that go down to the stones of the pit; as a carcase trodden under feet.
20 Thou shalt not be joined with them in burial, because thou hast destroyed thy land, and slain thy people: the seed of evildoers shall never be renowned.
21 Prepare slaughter for his children for the iniquity of their fathers; that they do not rise, nor possess the land, nor fill the face of the world with cities.

All the kings of nations, even all of them, lie in glory in his own house. But Lucifer, the fallen angel, is cast out of his grave like an abominable branch, and dressed with the raiment of those who are slain, thrust through with a sword, that go down to the stones of the pit as a carcass thrown underfoot. You shall not be joined with them in burial because you have destroyed the land and slain the people. The seed of evildoers shall never be renowned. The children of his house, his behaviors and actions, shall be slaughtered for the iniquity of his fathers; they shall not rise, they shall not possess the land and they shall not fill the face of the world with cities. The fallen Lucifer is the personification of the fallen state of man. It is impossible for Lucifer, the fallen angel, to win or succeed in a contest with the LORD. Lucifer is the ruler of his restricted state which is called Babylon.

22 For I will rise up against them, saith the LORD of hosts, and cut off from Babylon the name, and remnant, and son, and nephew, saith the LORD.
23 I will also make it a possession for the bittern, and pools of water: and I will sweep it with the besom of destruction, saith the LORD of hosts.
24 The LORD of hosts hath sworn, saying, Surely as I have thought, so shall it come to pass; and as I have purposed, so shall it stand:

The LORD of hosts will rise up against them, who compose the body of fallen Lucifer on earth, and cut off Babylon, his clothes, and son and nephew. I will also make it a possession of the bittern, a bird of the heron family on pools of water with a melancholy, night-booming voice that symbolizes the sadness of sound: and I will sweep it with the besom, the broom of destruction, says the LORD of hosts. The LORD of hosts has said, Surely, as I have thought, so it shall come to pass; and as I purposed, so shall it stand. The LORD's thought and purpose is to keep Lucifer and his followers as prisoners on earth until each of them repent and return to the LORD through the body of Jacob on earth to the body of Israel on earth to the covenant with the LORD on earth. There is much for people on earth to do while they are on earth.

25 That I will break the Assyrian in my land, and upon my mountains tread him under foot: then shall his yoke depart from off them, and his burden depart from off their shoulders.
26 This is the purpose that is purposed upon the whole earth: and this is the hand that is stretched out upon all the nations.
27 For the LORD of hosts hath purposed, and who shall disannul it? and his hand is stretched out, and who shall turn it back?
28 In the year that king Ahaz died was this burden.

The ultimate victory of the LORD of the universe is inevitable over the kingdoms of men on earth, specifically, the Assyrians. The LORD will break the Assyrian in the LORD's land and he shall be tread under foot. The Assyrian yoke shall depart from off them, and his burden shall depart from off their shoulders. This victory for Isaiah and his followers is the purpose that is the purpose for all the inhabitants of the whole earth: and this is the hand of control that is stretched out upon all the nations. If the LORD of hosts has purposed it, then, who shall turn it back? In the year that King Ahaz died, this burden of leadership was placed upon the shoulders of Isaiah. Isaiah has accepted the role to aid in the restoration of the people to the LORD.

The Testimony of the Major Prophets

29 Rejoice not thou, whole Palestina, because the rod of him that smote thee is broken: for out of the serpent's root shall come forth a cockatrice, and his fruit shall be a fiery flying serpent.
30 And the firstborn of the poor shall feed, and the needy shall lie down in safety: and I will kill thy root with famine, and he shall slay thy remnant.
31 Howl, O gate; cry, O city; thou, whole Palestina, art dissolved: for there shall come from the north a smoke, and none shall be alone in his appointed times.
32 What shall one then answer the messengers of the nation? That the LORD hath founded Zion, and the poor of his people shall trust in it.

Israel is not to rejoice because the rod of him that smote thee is broken: out of the serpent's root in the garden of Eden shall come forth a cockatrice, an unidentified species of a deadly serpent, which we have seen is the eating of the forbidden fruit and his fruit shall be like a flying serpent that flies through the air to spread its evil fruit among the people. This is the spread of evil in the fallen state. The firstborn of the poor shall feed and the needy shall lie down in safety. The root of the tree of the knowledge of good and evil will be struck by famine and he, Lucifer, the fallen state, shall slay the remnant of the way of the LORD on earth. In symbolic language, we are being told that the elimination of one serpent is replaced by a bigger and more deadly one. In the battle for the earth between the LORD and Lucifer, the LORD will strike the root of the tree of people with famine and difficult times on earth, and Lucifer will try to eliminate the remnant of people who carry the spirit of the LORD.

Howl, O gate, the gate to the consciousness of true divine identity with the LORD on earth; cry, O city, the city is the symbol of the consciousness in the whole of Palestine until the evil within is dissolved. There shall come forth from the north a smoke, the evidence of the burning that symbolizes the evidence of the action of the burning of the LORD, and no one shall be alone in these appointed times. What shall one answer the messengers of the nation that the LORD will build? The LORD has founded Zion, the high point of spiritual agreement on earth between the LORD and his people who are willing to build Zion in manifest form, and the poor of His people, the "poor" of the desires of the material things of the fallen state on earth, trust in the establishment and the building of the LORD's kingdom on earth.

CHAPTER 15

1 The burden of Moab. Because in the night Ar of Moab is laid waste, and brought to silence; because in the night Kir of Moab is laid waste, and brought to silence;

Isaiah informs his readers that, within his consciousness, he is carrying the burden of Moab. Burdens are carried in the consciousness, in the heart and the mind of the person who is burdened. On occasion, there is something that needs to be done physically, but most "burdens" are carried in the mind as soon as a person becomes aware of the information, and then, that information is pondered in the heart of one's emotional realm where the burden can become a heavy one at the moment that the information enters into the heart and it can be pondered there for many years or a lifetime.

The country of Moab and the people who live there have been an enemy of Israel for many years. Isaiah, as a point of focus for the LORD on earth, would not have the prevailing attitude of the majority of people who consider the Moabites as "enemies". The teaching of the LORD is to love your enemies. This would free an individual of the bitter, hateful and angry feelings associated with having an enemy. Incidentally, the maintenance of enemies will keep a person out of the focus which is necessary to achieve a covenant-agreement with the LORD. Isaiah is aware of the burdens which are carried by the people in his sphere of influence who are caught in this trap of hating other people and, subsequently, being controlled by them. But, Isaiah will not hate the people who would be hating him because Isaiah understands that the generation of hatred perpetuates the fallen state, the ungodly state, on earth.

Isaiah is aware of the circumstances that have befallen the Moabites, when, in the night, Ar of Moab and Kir of Moab are laid waste and they are brought to silence. There is not a single sound of life in these two cities which are on the south-to-north route on the eastern side of the Dead Sea. This burden which Isaiah carries is not solely or totally his burden. The Moabites also feel this burden very heavily because of the devastation caused to their lands and to their people and property. Isaiah feels the pain in their troubled hearts because from Isaiah's perspective, everyone is in the same spiritual family of the LORD regardless of the different beliefs and cultures which they hold deeply in their minds and hearts.

2 He is gone up to Bajith, and to Dibon, the high places, to weep: Moab shall howl over Nebo, and over Medeba: on all their heads shall be baldness, and every beard cut off.
3 In their streets they shall gird themselves with sackcloth: on the tops of their houses, and in their streets, every one shall howl, weeping abundantly.
4 And Heshbon shall cry, and Elealeh: their voice shall be heard even unto Jahaz: therefore the armed soldiers of Moab shall cry out; his life shall be grievous unto him.

The leadership and the people of Moab have gone up to the high country of Dibon and Bajith to weep. The country of Moab shall howl, cry loudly for all to hear, their sadness with regard to the loss of Nebo and over Medeba. This shame, sadness and grief shall be demonstrated as the people shave the hair off their heads and their beards off their faces. The loss has afflicted everyone. The sadness of the defeat and destruction of their cities prompt the people to gird, or wrap themselves in sackcloth to demonstrate their melancholy. The people want everyone to know of their misery. They moan, weep and howl abundantly from the tops of their houses and in their streets because of the loss of their material treasures and possessions.

The enormity of the defeat is extended by the loss of the cities of Heshbon and Elealeh who will cry at their loss; and their voices of sadness and wailing shall be heard unto Jahaz. The armed soldiers of Moab shall cry out because they are faced with superior numbers from a large united force and the soldiers understand and comprehend that each soldier's life will be filled with grief.

5 My heart shall cry out for Moab; his fugitives shall flee unto Zoar, an heifer of three years old: for by the mounting up of Luhith with weeping shall they go it up; for in the way of Horonaim they shall raise up a cry of destruction.
6 For the waters of Nimrim shall be desolate: for the hay is withered away, the grass faileth, there is no green thing.
7 Therefore the abundance they have gotten, and that which they have laid up, shall they carry away to the brook of the willows.
8 For the cry is gone round about the borders of Moab; the howling thereof unto Eglaim, and the howling thereof unto Beerelim.
9 For the waters of Dimon shall be full of blood: for I will bring more upon Dimon, lions upon him that escapeth of Moab, and upon the remnant of the land.

Isaiah states that his heart shall cry out for Moab and the people who live there, along with their circumstances. Isaiah is particularly sad because he has the vision of the potential beauty available to be born into the earth when people allow the way of the LORD to come into the earth. Isaiah knows that this is not the case; the Moabites flee as fugitives unto Zoar with a heifer for a burnt offering to the LORD. The requirement needed was for the people to offer themselves as a the true offering, not to die, but to live and to bring the kingdom of the LORD on earth many years ago, which would have produced a totally different outcome than the present disaster of the Moabites. There has been too much talk of sacrifice and dying in the Bible which is a Book to teach people how to live and how to bring the LORD's kingdom on earth.

The weeping shall be extended to include Luhith and Horonaim as they are destroyed. The waters of Nimrim shall be desolate which in turn will cause the hay to wither away, the grass will fail and there will be no green thing because water is absent, not available. The prosperity which the Moabites had, temporarily, while they were a nation unto itself, was insufficient against a superior force. What food and supplies that they have laid up, they must take to the brook of the willows where there is some water
to keep them alive.

The cry and the weeping about the disaster has gone round about all the borders of the country of Moab; the howling of the people shall reach to Eglaim, and to Beerelim. The waters of Dimon shall be full of blood, the blood of the wounded, who would be bathing their wounds and make the waters red. Isaiah predicts that the law of the LORD shall bring more desolation upon Dimon, and destructive lions, the beasts which symbolize the king of the warring tribes, upon the people of Moab who escaped destruction. This would also include the spiritual remnant of the people of the LORD who are also in the land.

CHAPTER 16

1 Send ye the lamb to the ruler of the land from Sela to the wilderness, unto the mount of the daughter of Zion.
2 For it shall be, that, as a wandering bird cast out of the nest, so the daughters of Moab shall be at the fords of Arnon.
3 Take counsel, execute judgment; make thy shadow as the night in the midst of the noonday; hide the outcasts; bewray not him that wandereth.

Isaiah continues to advise Moab to pay a tribute of lambs to the Assyrians, who were the victors over Moab and the ruler of the land from the city of Sela, near Petra, to the wilderness unto the mount of the daughter of Zion. Zion symbolizes the high point of spiritual consciousness where Isaiah dwells. Isaiah, the servant of the LORD, has the primary responsibility to offer the daughter of Zion, an offering of peace that is available in the covenant with the LORD to everyone. A daughter of Zion is anyone who will accept the spiritual consciousness that Isaiah exemplifies. It shall be, that, as a wandering bird cast out of a nest with no place to go, so the daughters of Moab shall be on the banks of the river of Arnon available to become one spiritual family by making a new beginning.

Moab should take the counsel of Isaiah and execute, carry out, the advice given to him and execute the judgment of Isaiah: the Moabites are instructed to stand up tall with their backs to the sun so that they can see their shadows, as clearly as the night, in the midst of the noonday which can only occur when the sun, as a symbol of God, is allowed to cast its shadow through the body of Moab. Moab is instructed by Isaiah to hide the outcasts and do not bewray, do not disclose or betray, the people who wander into the camp of the Moabites. Do not remain warlike; protect the lives of the people of Judah that come into your camp who are trying to escape the Assyrians who are in Judah and the outskirts of Jerusalem.

4 Let mine outcasts dwell with thee, Moab; be thou a covert to them from the face of the spoiler: for the extortioner is at an end, the spoiler ceaseth, the oppressors are consumed out of the land.

5 And in mercy shall the throne be established: and he shall sit upon it in truth in the tabernacle of David, judging, and seeking judgment, and hasting righteousness.

Isaiah tells Moab to allow his outcasts dwell with the Moabites; let the Moabites be a covert, a refuge from the face of the spoiler, the Assyrians who have invaded and pillaged the land. Isaiah tells Moab that the time of the extortionist, the Assyrian invader who holds hostages for tribute, is at an end. The spoiler of the land who uses his superior physical force shall cease his activity, and the oppressors are consumed out of the land because they have already taken everything which is of value.

A new throne will be established after the conquering Assyrians leave the area and the new throne will be established in mercy: and the new ruler who sits on the new throne shall sit upon it in the truth that was demonstrated when the holy person, the tabernacle, of David sat on the throne judging, seeking judgment and hasting righteousness because he wants to do the right thing that is fair to all the LORD's people, everyone.

6 We have heard of the pride of Moab; he is very proud: even of his haughtiness, and his pride, and his wrath: but his lies shall not be so.
7 Therefore shall Moab howl for Moab, every one shall howl: for the foundations of Kirhareseth shall ye mourn; surely they are stricken.
8 For the fields of Heshbon languish, and the vine of Sibmah: the lords of the heathen have broken down the principal plants thereof, they are come even unto Jazer, they wandered through the wilderness: her branches are stretched out, they are gone over the sea.

Isaiah states that he has heard of the pride of the people of Moab; in fact, Moab, as a people, are very proud: He is proud of his haughtiness, his pride and his wrath. As a people, the Moabites are proud of these attributes of their culture: but lies shall not be so; the Moabites do not embrace lies as a character traits. Therefore, the Moabites shall moan and howl for the subservient position in which they find themselves. Their howling is evidence of how badly they feel about their loss to the Assyrians. The Moabites shall moan for the devastation of their city Kirhareseth, the city of Hareseth, because the people of that city have been stricken in battle and defeat. In addition, other cities have been defeated: the fields of Heshbon languish; the lords of the heathen people, the Assyrians, have defeated the vine of Sibmah; and the city of Jazer. The Assyrian invaders have penetrated and sacked these Moabite cities and then they wandered through the wilderness: her branches are stretched out as they have grown from the wealth and plunder of the cities and they continue on to the Dead Sea.

9 Therefore I will bewail with the weeping of Jazer the vine of Sibmah: I will water thee with my tears, O Heshbon, and Elealeh: for the shouting for thy summer fruits and for thy harvest is fallen.
10 And gladness is taken away, and joy out of the plentiful field; and in the vineyards there shall be no singing, neither shall there be shouting: the treaders shall tread out no wine in their presses; I have made their vintage shouting to cease.

Isaiah says that he will bewail the weeping of the people of Jazer and the vine of Sibmah: Isaiah will water with his tears the cities of Heshbon and Elealeh: for the expressions of the loss for their summer fruits and the harvest of the people is fallen to the invader as they plundered the Moabite cities. The gladness of the people has been taken away and the joy that prevailed, because of the plentiful fields, has ceased. There shall be no singing and shouting: the treaders shall make no wine in their winepresses; the working of the law of the LORD has made their vintage shouting, the happy singing noises that they make while making wine, to cease.

11 Wherefore my bowels shall sound like an harp for Moab, and mine inward parts for Kirharesh.
12 And it shall come to pass, when it is seen that Moab is weary on the high place, that he shall come to his sanctuary to pray; but he shall not prevail.
13 This is the word that the LORD hath spoken concerning Moab since that time.
14 But now the LORD hath spoken, saying, Within three years, as the years of an hireling, and the glory of Moab shall be contemned, with all that great multitude; and the remnant shall be very small and feeble.

Isaiah empathizes for the fate of Moab. He describes his emotional discomfort as his bowels which are in an uproar concerning the fate of Moab because his bowels sound like a harp for what has occurred to the land and the people: Isaiah's inward parts grieve for Kirharesh. When it is come to pass, that the people of Moab are weary on the high place in their consciousness where they moan and wail because of the fate and the defeat that they have experienced, the LORD shall come to his sanctuary to pray with the Moabites, but the LORD shall not prevail. The Moabites will refuse to accept the covenant of the LORD under these horrible conditions. The LORD is willing under any external conditions; but Moab is not willing.

This is the word that the LORD has spoken concerning Moab since that time and Isaiah carries the Moabites in his heart. But now the LORD has spoken, saying, Within three years, as the years of an hireling, the glory of Moab shall be condemned, despised and scorned, with all the great multitude of the people because they will not forget their defeat and humiliation due to their pride. The remnant of the way of the LORD on earth shall remain very small and feeble because the people, such as the Moabites, are not willing to forgive the wrongs that have been inflicted on them in the past and to make a new beginning, a new creation of the LORD's people in action on earth. The LORD has been willing to offer the covenant but the people have not been willing to accept the covenant with the LORD that is always available to be received by those who are willing to accept the spirit of the LORD into their hearts. The people are not willing to accept the LORD's terms, the LORD's spirit, for a symbolic three years, the years of a hireling to work for his master. If people would adopt the LORD's spirit and terms for three years, how great could be the glory of the LORD on earth!?

CHAPTER 17

1 The burden of Damascus. Behold, Damascus is taken away from being a city, and it shall be a ruinous heap.
2 The cities of Aroer are forsaken: they shall be for flocks, which shall lie down, and none shall make them afraid.
3 The fortress also shall cease from Ephraim, and the kingdom from Damascus, and the remnant of Syria: they shall be as the glory of the children of Israel, saith the LORD of hosts.

In the spirit of the LORD, Isaiah is carrying in his consciousness the burden of his view of the city of Damascus, the capital of Aram (Syria). The Aramaeans of Damascus were frequent enemies of Israel since the time of King David. At this time, Damascus is a city in transition; it is in a process of disintegration; it is taken away from being a city to what is described as a ruinous heap. The disintegration is not limited to Damascus. The cities of Aroer, about 15 miles East of the Dead Sea, are the southern-most boundary of Aram's sphere of influence are also forsaken: the people who live in these cities shall be treated like flocks, which shall lie down, and be as a flock of people to whomsoever is in control. Their lives are lived in a simple fashion; none shall be make them afraid because of their circumstances.

The fortress of Ephraim shall also cease to be a force and a power as is the case with the kingdom of Damascus and the remnant of Syria because Ephraim was allied with Damascus against Assyria. In 732 B.C., Damascus was captured by Tigleth-Pileser III and made a province of Assyria along with a remnant of Syria. The expansion of the empire shall be like the glory of the children of Israel says the LORD of hosts.

4 And in that day it shall come to pass, that the glory of Jacob shall be made thin, and the fatness of his flesh shall wax lean.
5 And it shall be as when the harvestman gathereth the corn, and reapeth the ears with his arm; and it shall be as he that gathereth ears in the valley of Rephaim.

The Testimony of the Major Prophets

6 Yet gleaning grapes shall be left in it, as the shaking of an olive tree, two or three berries in the top of the uppermost bough, four or five in the outmost fruitful branches thereof, saith the LORD God of Israel.

And in that day the glory of Jacob, son of Isaac, shall be made thin, his influence and prosperity begins to decline, and the fatness of his flesh, not the flesh of his physical body but rather the people who comprise his body of followers, shall grow lean. The transition that is taking place is compared to a time when the harvestmen of the Assyrian invader shall gather corn and they reap the ears with his arms full. Furthermore, it is like he that gathers ears in the fruitful valley of Rephaim, which is a valley in Jerusalem. The invaders pick the crops rapidly to reap the majority of the harvest of the land. But the gleaning-grapes shall be left on the vine. Gleaning-grapes are those which are gathered from a field after the main crop that is easily picked has been reaped; what remains is lean pickings. The grapes on the outer-most branch or the on the highest branches which are difficult to reach and would slow the person down as they gather the fruit. It is similar to the shaking of the olive tree where two or three berries are in the top of the uppermost branch or four or five olives in the outmost fruitful branches says the LORD God of Israel. This illustrates that the work required to get the fruit is not worth the effort for one who is in a hurry.

7 At that day shall a man look to his Maker, and his eyes shall have respect to the Holy One of Israel.
8 And he shall not look to the altars, the work of his hands, neither shall respect that which his fingers have made, either the groves, or the images.
9 In that day shall his strong cities be as a forsaken bough, and an uppermost branch, which they left because of the children of Israel: and there shall be desolation.
10 Because thou hast forgotten the God of thy salvation, and hast not been mindful of the rock of thy strength, therefore shalt thou plant pleasant plants, and shalt set it with strange slips:

In that day of adversity, a man shall look to his Maker, and his eyes shall have respect for the Holy One of Israel who is the LORD of hosts. In that day of tribulation, man shall not look to the altars of images of strange Gods, nor worship the work of his own hands, nor that which his own fingers have made, either the groves of trees or the images. In that day shall his strong cities be as a forsaken bough which has little wealth, a small amount of fruit, on it, and the uppermost branch, which they left because of the children of Israel. The result is that there shall be desolation after the invaders have taken most of the crops. The desolation of the people has occurred because the people have forgotten the God of their salvation from times past, and that they have not been mindful of the Rock of the LORD's strength. The people who are not aligned, not attuned with the spirit of the LORD, shall plant pleasant plants, plants that are pleasant in the sight of their own eyes and they shall set up the planting with slips, cuttings or grafts, that shall produce strange plants.

11 In the day shalt thou make thy plant to grow, and in the morning shalt thou make thy seed to flourish: but the harvest shall be a heap in the day of grief and of desperate sorrow.
12 Woe to the multitude of many people, which make a noise like the noise of the seas; and to the rushing of nations, that make a rushing like the rushing of mighty waters!

13 The nations shall rush like the rushing of many waters: but God shall rebuke them, and they shall flee far off, and shall be chased as the chaff of the mountains before the wind, and like a rolling thing before the whirlwind.
14 And behold at eveningtide trouble; and before the morning he is not. This is the portion of them that spoil us, and the lot of them that rob us.

In that day, the plants shall grow as life from the LORD moves through the plants and eventually, the seed shall flourish; but the harvest shall be a heap of desperate sorrow. Isaiah says that there shall be woe in the land among the multitude of many people who will make noise like the noise of the seas. The seas are a symbol for the many people, a sea of people, whose complaints and moans are like the waves of the seas; and the rushing of the waters symbolizes the rushing of the nations.

The nations shall rush as the rushing of many waters; but God shall rebuke them, and they shall flee and be chased as the chaff of the mountains flee before the wind, and like a rolling thing before a whirlwind. The material things symbolized by the chaff are being moved by the power of the spirit of the LORD symbolized by the wind. And behold, see, at the end of the day, at eveningtide; and before morning, he is no longer present. Isaiah says that the harvest that is taken by the invaders is the spoil of war and the portion of material goods taken by the invaders, who spoil the people, but they are gone in the morning. Isaiah tells the people that this is the portion of them that rob and pillage. It is to be expected that invaders will ravage and pillage. Isaiah calls the people to rise above this circumstance which could cause them to feel like helpless victims. Isaiah will continue to share his vision of the LORD with his people.

CHAPTER 18

1 Woe to the land shadowing with wings, which is beyond the rivers of Ethiopia:
2 That sendeth ambassadors by the sea, even in vessels of bulrushes upon the waters, saying, Go, ye swift messengers, to a nation scattered and peeled, to a people terrible from their beginning hitherto; a nation meted out and trodden down, whose land the rivers have spoiled!
3 All ye inhabitants of the world, and dwellers on the earth, see ye, when he lifteth up an ensign on the mountains; and when he bloweth a trumpet, hear ye.

Isaiah calls the attention of his followers to the land covered with the shadowing with wings of the vultures over the death associated with the dry land beyond the rivers of Ethiopia: These lands send ambassadors by the sea in ships made of bulrushes, boats of papyrus, upon the waters. The ambassadors are to go as swift messengers to a nation that is scattered and peeled, stripped of its treasures, due to recent wars which devastate and humiliate a land and its people. The people recovering from an invasion begin with a terrible beginning with a new ambassador from a land far away; the defeated land and its people are like a land that has been meted out and trodden down as the people and the land have been spoiled by an army flowing through the land as a moving river causes destruction and despair!

Isaiah warns the people, all the inhabitants of the world and the dwellers of the earth, to see and observe when the ambassador from a foreign land comes and lifts his ensign, his flag, on the mountains to observe the conditions of weakness in your land; and when the ambassador from another country blows his trumpet to announce his presence so that the people will listen to what the ambassador has to say.

4 For so the LORD said unto me, I will take my rest, and I will consider in my dwelling- place like a clear heat upon herbs, and like a cloud of dew in the heat of harvest.
5 For afore the harvest, when the bud is perfect, and the sour grape is ripening in the flower, he shall both cut off the sprigs with pruning-hooks, and take away and cut down the branches.
6 They shall be left together unto the fowls of the mountains, and to the beasts of the earth shall winter upon them.

7 In that time shall the present be brought unto the LORD of hosts of a people scattered and peeled, and from a people terrible from their beginning hitherto; a nation meted out and trodden under foot, whose land the rivers have spoiled, to the place of the name of the LORD of hosts, the mount Zion.

The LORD said to Isaiah that the He will take His rest, He will be patient, and He will consider in His dwelling-place like a clear radiant heat from the sun upon herbs, and like a cloud of dew in the heat of harvest; the power and the water will be present but almost unnoticeable. And before the harvest, and the sour grape is ripening in the flower, He shall trim the sprigs with pruning hooks, and take away and cut down the branches that interfere with a good harvest. The LORD is using an analogy to illustrate the way that He trims the people on the Tree of Life to produce a good harvest. Just as the vine of grapes is trimmed of the branches, so the people that are removed from the vine shall be left for the fowls of the mountains and the beasts of the earth, the predators, who will winter on them as food.

In that time, the present shall be brought upon the LORD of hosts and the present is a body of people who are scattered and peeled, and from a people who have a terrible beginning. It will be a nation that has been meted out and trodden down under foot, a body of people who the armies of the rivers have spoiled. It is this body of people that will be led to the place of the name of the LORD of hosts, the mount Zion. The LORD wants to preserve this body of people.

Isaiah will share with his people his views on Egypt.

CHAPTER 19

1 The burden of Egypt. Behold, the LORD rideth upon a swift cloud, and shall come into Egypt: and the idols of Egypt shall be moved at his presence, and the heart of Egypt shall melt in the midst of it.
2 And I will set the Egyptians against the Egyptians: and they shall fight every one against his brother, and every one against his neighbour; city against city, and kingdom against kingdom.
3 And the spirit of Egypt shall fail in the midst thereof; and I will destroy the counsel thereof: and they shall seek to the idols, and to the charmers, and to them that have familiar spirits, and to the wizards.
4 And the Egyptians will I give over into the hand of a cruel lord; and a fierce king shall rule over them, saith the Lord, the LORD of hosts.

The LORD of hosts speaking through Isaiah shares with the people the burden in his consciousness of Egypt. It is the design of the LORD that the spirit of the LORD shall ride on a swift cloud and spread, come into, Egypt: and the idols of Egypt shall be moved at the presence of the LORD. If the reality of the presence of the LORD, the true God, becomes known in Egypt, then the idols of Egypt cannot stand in the presence of the LORD. They shall be seen as material idols with no power over anything. The heart of Egypt shall melt in the midst of the power of the LORD in Egypt. When the sword of Truth puts in an appearance, the beliefs about the Truth cannot stand when the Truth of the LORD is present through a servant of the LORD. This will result in a clash among people of different beliefs: it is described as the fighting of Egyptian against Egyptian, brother against brother; neighbor against neighbor; city against city, and kingdom against kingdom. The fighting will range from an individual basis to increasingly larger groups of people who are fighting against their different beliefs about the Truth.

And the spirit of Egypt that was prevalent, before the spirit of the LORD came into Egypt, shall fail in the midst of the people who know the spirit of the LORD in themselves. The presence of the Truth of the LORD shall destroy the counsel of those who are not of the LORD. The people with the false beliefs and concepts will seek to the idols, and the charmers, and them that have familiar spirits and beliefs, and the wizards. The people who share similar beliefs and concepts will band together into groups. The result of the process, when the Truth is present, is that the followers of the customs, opinions and beliefs shall follow a leader who is not representing the Truth and these followers, the Egyptians, will be led by a cruel lord and a fierce king who will rule over them says the LORD of hosts. If the people do not accept the true LORD, they will surely be led by a false lord. The conditions that will naturally follow when the Truth is rejected can be compared to the earth when there is no water for the land: everything dries up.

5 And the waters shall fail from the sea, and the river shall be wasted and dried up.
6 And they shall turn the rivers far away; and the brooks of defence shall be emptied and dried up: the reeds and flags shall wither.
7 The paper reeds by the brooks, by the mouth of the brooks, and every thing sown by the brooks, shall wither, be driven away, and be no more.
8 The fishers also shall mourn, and all they that cast angle into the brooks shall lament, and they that spread nets upon the waters shall languish.
9 Moreover they that work in fine flax, and they that weave networks, shall be confounded.
10 And they shall be broken in the purposes thereof, all that make sluices and ponds for fish.

The absence of the Truth of the LORD in expression is like the absence of water in a desert land. As water is needed for the activities of life, so is the Truth needed in the affairs of men to sustain life. The waters that come from the sea shall fail to produce rain, and the water in the river shall waste away and dry up. The rivers shall be turned away from their normal flow; and the brooks of defense that fill the moats shall be emptied and dry up also: the reeds and the flags that grow by the rivers and brooks shall wither. The paper reeds by the brooks and everything sown by the brooks, the seeds that are sown by the brooks shall wither and be driven away by the winds as fertile land turns to dust without any water. Just as water is needed for growth on earth, so is the Truth needed for the LORD's people to survive.

The people who fish shall mourn and all the people who cast their lines into the brooks for food shall lament, and they who cast their nets on the water shall languish for food. Moreover, those people who work in the making of fine flax, which requires large quantities of water, shall be confounded as to how they can survive without water. All the people that make sluices and ponds to grow fish shall be broken in their purposes. We can readily understand that water is the symbol for the Truth that originates in the LORD. The picture that is being painted by Isaiah is the failure that is sure to come when the Truth of the spirit of the LORD, symbolized by water, is not flowing into the affairs of men.

11 Surely the princes of Zoan are fools, the counsel of the wise counsellors of Pharaoh is become brutish: how say ye unto Pharaoh, I am the son of the wise, the son of ancient kings?
12 Where are they? where are thy wise men? and let them tell thee now, and let them know what the LORD of hosts hath purposed upon Egypt.
13 The princes of Zoan are become fools, the princes of Noph are deceived; they have also seduced Egypt, even they that are the stay of the tribes thereof.

The princes of Zoan are not following the advice and the direction that comes from the LORD which makes them fools. As the city of Zoan which is on the eastern border of lower Egypt as part of the Nile delta that thrives on water, the princes of Zoan do not see the analogy between the source of their material wealth from water and the importance of the source of life from the LORD. The princes of Zoan are the effects of the counsel, which they receive from the wise counselors of Pharaoh, whose advice carries the power of brute force: how can a person say to Pharaoh and his wise counselors that with the wisdom of the spirit of Truth from the LORD, "I am the son of the wise, the son of ancient kings" who has the spiritual wisdom to see clearly?

Where are these so-called wise men that offer counsel to Pharaoh, the symbol of the fallen self-active mind? where are your wise men who offer counsel from the LORD within you? Let them tell you now so that you can let the counselors of Pharaoh know what the purpose of the LORD of hosts has in store for Egypt. The princes of Zoan are fools and the princes of Noph are deceived when they choose to go the way of the counselors of men and ignore the way of the LORD. As they follow the wrong counsel, Egypt is seduced by their counsel and the leaders, the mainstay of the tribes are seduced also which will surely lead to destruction. Why will the paths other than the path of the LORD lead to destruction?

14 The LORD hath mingled a perverse spirit in the midst thereof: and they have caused Egypt to err in every work thereof, as a drunken man staggereth in his vomit.
15 Neither shall there be any work for Egypt, which the head or tail, branch or rush, may do.
16 In that day shall Egypt be like unto women: and it shall be afraid and fear because of the shaking of the hand of the LORD of hosts, which he shaketh over it.

The LORD has mingled a perverse spirit in the midst of His perfect plan! If the LORD's plan is not followed, then, a perverse spirit of destruction mingled with the LORD's plan will cause Egypt to err in every work so that the result will be as a drunken man who staggers in the vomit caused by the intoxication of his wrong choice to drink something that he likes to a great excess. If this wrong path is followed, there shall be no work for Egypt, from the head to the tail of it, from the branch of the tree to the rush that grows out of the water, that will do satisfactorily. In that day of retribution, when the results of the wrong choices have been made manifest, then, the men of Egypt shall be like unto women: the people shall be afraid and fearful because the shaking of the hand of the LORD is the cause of the changes that the LORD of hosts is causing to take place over the entire land off Egypt.

17 And the land of Judah shall be a terror unto Egypt, every one that maketh mention thereof shall be afraid in himself, because of the counsel of the LORD of hosts, which he hath determined against it.
18 In that day shall five cities in the land of Egypt speak the language of Canaan, and swear to the LORD of hosts; one shall be called, The city of destruction.
19 In that day shall there be an altar to the LORD in the midst of the land of Egypt, and a pillar at the border thereof to the LORD.
20 And it shall be for a sign and for a witness unto the LORD of hosts in the land of Egypt: for they shall cry unto the LORD because of the oppressors, and he shall send them a saviour, and a great one, and he shall deliver them.
21 And the LORD shall be known to Egypt, and the Egyptians shall know the LORD in that day, and shall do sacrifice and oblation; yea, they shall vow a vow unto the LORD, and perform it.

The land of Judah which does follow the way of the LORD shall be a terror unto Egypt because of the people who hear the word of Isaiah, which is the word of the LORD. Everyone of the Egyptians shall be afraid within himself because he has heard the counsel of the LORD of hosts and has chosen, has determined against it. In the day that this occurs, five cities in the land of Egypt shall speak the language of Canaan, which is the word of the LORD and swear to the LORD of hosts; the city, the consciousness of the people in the city, shall be called the city of destruction because the consciousness of the city of Egypt has been destroyed and replaced with a consciousness of the way of the LORD of hosts.

In that day, there shall be an altar to the LORD in the midst of the land of Egypt, the symbol of the fallen state, and a pillar at the border to the LORD. The change, the altar and the pillar is in the consciousness of each person and these changes within the consciousness will be the witness for the LORD in the land of Egypt. The people who know the LORD in their own consciousness shall cry unto the LORD because of the oppressors around them and the LORD shall send them a savior, a great one, and he shall deliver them from the oppressors. In this manner, the LORD shall be known in Egypt and the Egyptians shall know the LORD and do sacrifice, make the things that they handle sacred for the LORD. Yes, they shall vow a vow that everything that they do will done in the spirit of the LORD and it will be performed for the LORD of hosts.

22 And the LORD shall smite Egypt: he shall smite and heal it: and they shall return even to the LORD, and he shall be intreated of them, and shall heal them.
23 In that day shall there be a highway out of Egypt to Assyria, and the Assyrian shall come into Egypt, and the Egyptian into Assyria, and the Egyptians shall serve with the Assyrians.
24 In that day shall Israel be the third with Egypt and with Assyria, even a blessing in the midst of the land:
25 Whom the LORD of hosts shall bless, saying, Blessed be Egypt my people, and Assyria the work of my hands, and Israel mine inheritance.

In this manner, the LORD's spirit moving through His people **to** the Egyptians shall smite Egypt: He shall smite it and heal it in the minds and heart of the people who accept the spirit of the LORD: and they shall return to the LORD and they will be healed as the spirit of the LORD flows **through** them. In that day, in the day when the consciousness of the LORD and the consciousness of Egypt shall become one in the covenant-agreement of the LORD, then, the agreement shall expand even further. There shall be a highway out of Egypt to Assyria and the Assyrian shall come into agreement with the consciousness of the Egyptian, and the Egyptian into Assyria, and the Egyptians shall serve with the Assyrians. They will serve the spirit of the LORD of hosts. In that day, Israel shall be the third with Egypt and Assyria, even a blessing in the midst of the land: The agreement is a spiritual agreement with the LORD among all people, especially those who have been at war with each other for generations. The LORD of hosts will bless all people whether they are from Egypt or Assyria or Israel. From the view of the LORD, Egypt are His people, Assyria is the work of His hands and Israel has received the inheritance of the spirit of the LORD of hosts. The Truth of the LORD, like water in the material world, flows through all His people. No one is excluded. If people choose to exclude themselves, then, they will surely wither and die. The LORD of hosts includes everyone.

CHAPTER 20

1 In the year that Tartan came unto Ashdod, (when Sargon the king of Assyria sent him,) and fought against Ashdod, and took it;

In the year, probably 711 B.C., Tartan, the supreme commander sent by Sargon the king of Assyria, came to Ashdod, a Philistine city about 18 miles northeast of Gaza near the Mediterranean Sea which housed the temple of Dagon, the fishGod; Tartan fought against Ashdod and took control of it. At this time, the LORD has a mission for Isaiah:

2 At the same time spake the LORD by Isaiah the son of Amoz, saying, Go and loose the sackcloth from off thy loins, and put off thy shoe from thy foot. And he did so, walking naked and barefoot.

The LORD speaking on earth by means of Isaiah instructed him to Go, remove the sackcloth, that symbolizes sadness and shame, from off his loins and to remove the shoe from his foot. Shoes are symbols of concepts that bind the feet and the foot is the symbol of understanding. Isaiah is being told to drop all of his concepts and human understanding and to symbolically walk barefoot, so that the movement of the spirit of the LORD will provide Isaiah with the understanding in the moment that he needs it. Isaiah is walking naked and unashamed in the spiritual clothing of the LORD so that the LORD will be with him. Here is a clear differentiation between the difference between a literal translation and a symbolic, spiritual translation of the same words to produce two completely different meanings. The letter of the word kills (the meaning), the spirit gives life. Isaiah is an example of a prophet of the LORD who walks naked and unashamed to represent, to re-present, the LORD's spirit wherever he goes. Isaiah is walking barefoot and naked of all his human concepts and beliefs to make a point.

3 And the LORD said, Like as my servant Isaiah hath walked naked and barefoot three years for a sign and wonder upon Egypt and upon Ethiopia;
4 So shall the king of Assyria lead away the Egyptians prisoners, and the Ethiopians captives, young and old, naked and barefoot, even with their buttocks uncovered, to the shame of Egypt.

The king of Assyria has lead away Egyptian prisoners and Ethiopian captives, young and old, naked and barefoot even with their buttocks uncovered to the shame of Egypt. The only way that Egypt could be shamed is if the prisoners and captives of the King of Assyria would be ashamed. The prisoners and the captives of the King of Assyria are naked and ashamed while at the same time, Isaiah has been walking about naked and barefoot for the LORD for three years for a sign and a wonder upon the people of Egypt and Ethiopia. Isaiah is in the same physical condition that they are in but he is in a state of glory to represent the LORD. Isaiah is a "prisoner" of the LORD and he is in his glory; the Egyptians and Ethiopians are prisoners of the king of Assyria and they are filled with shame. They have other thoughts also.

5 And they shall be afraid and ashamed of Ethiopia their expectation, and of Egypt their glory.
6 And the inhabitant of this isle shall say in that day, Behold, such is our expectation, whither we flee for help to be delivered from the king of Assyria: and how shall we escape?

The prisoners of the King of Assyria are afraid and ashamed because they do not meet the expectations of the people of Ethiopia and the glory of the people of Egypt. And Isaiah, the inhabitant of this small isle of earth, the barefoot and naked body of earth which he occupies, shall offer some very divine advice in that day. The advice is: Behold, see me as I am. Such is my expectation. This is my present condition and Isaiah is at peace in that circumstance. This is the circumstance that Isaiah has to reveal the spirit of the LORD. There is no other circumstance to reveal the LORD's spirit flowing through him into the earth to be seen of other men. This is their circumstance: whether the people hope to be delivered from the king of Assyria; or, whether they ponder how they shall escape. If Isaiah can get the prisoners to let the spirit of the LORD flow through themselves simultaneously, he has magnified the action of the LORD on earth.

CHAPTER 21

1 The burden of the desert of the sea. As whirlwinds in the south pass through; so it cometh from the desert, from a terrible land.
2 A grievous vision is declared unto me; the treacherous dealer dealeth treacherously, and the spoiler spoileth. Go up, O Elam: besiege, O Media; all the sighing thereof have I made to cease.

Isaiah shares his vision of the LORD through him which he observes as the burden of the desert of the sea. As whirlwinds from the south pass through their lands; so this burden comes from the desert, from a terrible land. Isaiah describes the vision declared to him from the LORD as a grievous vision that will bring much grief with it. The previous vision that Isaiah shared was a vision that concluded in harmony as Egypt, Assyria and Israel all let the spirit of the LORD work through themselves to produce a condition of harmony for everyone because the people were expressing the spirit of the LORD which produced harmony. The grievous vision has reference to what will occur if the people do not express the spirit of the LORD but rather, they choose a different path.

Just as the treacherous dealer deals in treachery and the spoiler will spoil whatever he touches, it can be expected that the people who do not express the LORD's spirit will produce chaos and war. As certainly as it is possible for Egypt, Assyria and Israel to live in harmony, it is just as certain that people can choose to express ways that lead to chaos. This way to chaos is symbolized by Elam and Media: Elam is in the desert area south of Assyria and east of Persia; Media is the vast region between Persia and the Caspian Sea. The Elamites, who were descendants of Shem, were perpetual enemies of Assyria and Babylon; while the Medianites, were descendants of Japheth. In *The Symbolic Version of Genesis*, Shem and Japheth, two of the sons of Noah, symbolized the physical body and the emotions. When the negative emotions unite with the physical force, chaos and war will develop. Sufficient time has elapsed from the time of Noah, that the LORD has allowed any sighing, any expression of sadness, with regard to the past to cease.

3 Therefore are my loins filled with pain: pangs have taken hold upon me, as the pangs of a woman that travaileth: I was bowed down at the hearing of it; I was dismayed at the seeing of it.

4 My heart panted, fearfulness affrighted me: the night of my pleasure hath he turned into fear unto me.
5 Prepare the table, watch in the watchtower, eat, drink: arise, ye princes, and anoint the shield.

As Isaiah sees the possibility of the devastation from the east which will occur if the people do not use the spirit of the LORD in their creations, his loins are filled with pain; pangs of pain and suffering have taken hold of Isaiah as a woman in labor; and his body was bowed down at the hearing of it and he was dismayed at the seeing of it. Isaiah is experiencing an anxiety attack as fear overtakes him, his heart panted quickly, fear has overtaken him and the night of his pleasure has turned into fear. Isaiah calls for his friends and followers to prepare the table for nourishment before the battle, set a watch in the watchtower, eat, drink to prepare yourselves for battle and anoint your shields with oil so that the arrows and spears will glance off their shields.

6 For thus hath the Lord said unto me, Go, set a watchman, let him declare what he seeth.
7 And he saw a chariot with a couple of horsemen, a chariot of asses, and a chariot of camels; and he hearkened diligently with much heed:
8 And he cried, A lion: My lord, I stand continually upon the watchtower in the daytime, and I am set in my ward whole nights:
9 And, behold, here cometh a chariot of men, with a couple of horsemen. And he answered and said, Babylon is fallen, is fallen; and all the graven images of her gods he hath broken unto the ground.
10 O my threshing, and the corn of my floor: that which I have heard of the LORD of hosts, the God of Israel, have I declared unto you.

Isaiah has said that the LORD has told him to set up a watchman and the watchman is to declare honestly what he sees. The watchman saw a chariot with a couple of horsemen, a chariot of asses and a chariot of camels which he interpreted as an advance group who were searching the area prior to an invasion. The watchmen listened diligently with much caution and he cried, A lion: a lion is the symbol for a destructive advance force from the east. The watchman reports to Isaiah that he stands continually all day to observe the enemy and he is set in his ward, his instruction, whole nights. The chariot of men with a couple of horsemen deliver the message that the city of Babylon is fallen; and all of her graven images of her gods have been broken to the ground. Isaiah has delivered the news that he has heard from the LORD of hosts, the God of Israel, has been declared to the listeners. Threshing of grain was a common metaphor for the judgment and the destruction which resulted on the people following a war.

11 The burden of Dumah. He calleth to me out of Seir, Watchman, what of the night? Watchman, what of the night?
12 The watchman said, The morning cometh, and also the night: if ye will inquire, inquire ye: return, come.

Isaiah is concerned about the burden of Dumah. Dumah means silence or stillness, which is a burden of insufficient information. He calls to me out of Seir, Watchman, what of the night? Watchman, what of the night? What is transpiring in the darkness that we do not know what is happening and what are the plans of the enemy? Are they marching upon us?

13 The burden upon Arabia. In the forest in Arabia shall ye lodge, O ye travelling companies of Dedanim.
14 The inhabitants of the land of Tema brought water to him that was thirsty, they prevented with their bread him that fled.
15 For they fled from the swords, from the drawn sword, and from the bent bow, and from the grievousness of war.

Isaiah shares the burden in his consciousness which he calls the burden of Arabia. When Isaiah has insufficient information, he must lodge in the trees, which symbolizes that he cannot see clearly because the trees obstruct his vision. In this lack of information as to whether or not he will be attacked is like unto the people of Dedanim, Arabia, a merchant tribe who had never before been attacked by the Assyrians until the first time that they were attacked in 732 B.C

The inhabitants of the land of Tema, an oasis in northern Arabia about 400 miles southwest of Babylon, brought water to him that was thirsty and the bread that they offered to the people that were fleeing prevented the exodus of the people who wanted to leave. The people who were fleeing fled because of the swords which were drawn to do battle, from the bows of the Assyrians which were superior to the simple bows of the Arabs; they were also leaving because of the grief that comes from war.

16 For thus hath the Lord said unto me, Within a year, according to the years of an hireling, and all the glory of Kedar shall fail:
17 And the residue of the number of archers, the mighty men of the children of Kedar, shall be diminished: for the LORD God of Israel hath spoken it.

The LORD has said to Isaiah that, Within a year, according to the years of a hireling, all the glory of Kedar shall fall. Kedar was the second son of Ishmael, the son of Abraham and Hagar the handmaid, whose land was known for its flocks. Kedar was the home of Bedouin tribes of Arabia. The remaining number of archers, the mighty men of Kedar, who used to protect Kedar with their bows, shall be diminished through the war with the Assyrians who had superior bows, for the LORD God of Israel has spoken it. The message is that while the word of the LORD is spreading on the west to produce **harmony** among Egypt, Assyria and Israel; while on the east, the Assyrians are **fighting** with the Arabs.

CHAPTER 22

1 The burden of the valley of vision. What aileth thee now, that thou art wholly gone up to the housetops?
2 Thou that art full of stirs, a tumultuous city, a joyous city: thy slain men are not slain with the sword, nor dead in battle.
3 All thy rulers are fled together, they are bound by the archers: all that are found in thee are bound together, which have fled from far.

Isaiah shares with his followers the burden of the valley of vision. This is vision which is not of the mountain but of the valley and consequently, a person cannot perceive as clearly as a person with "high" vision; not physically high but spiritually high. Isaiah asks those with the vision of the valley what ails them now that the person has gone up to the housetops, he has gone as high as he can with physical perspective while they are in the valley. The people in high places are full of stirs, emotional stirs, about everything that they see and observe. This produces a tumultuous city when people are emotionally down and a joyous city when the people are emotionally up. The slain men in this city are not physically dead; they are not slain with the sword, nor dead because they have been in battle. All the rulers of the city have fled together and they are stopped dead in their tracks by the archers; they are afraid to move for fear of death. All the people that are found in you, are captured, are bound together which have fled from far and they are trapped together.

4 Therefore said I, Look away from me; I will weep bitterly, labour not to comfort me, because of the spoiling of the daughter of my people.
5 For it is a day of trouble, and of treading down, and of perplexity by the Lord GOD of hosts in the valley of vision, breaking down the walls, and of crying to the mountains.
6 And Elam bare the quiver with chariots of men and horsemen, and Kir uncovered the shield.
7 And it shall come to pass, that thy choicest valleys shall be full of chariots, and the horsemen shall set themselves in array at the gate.

Isaiah asks all of the people to look away from him while he weeps bitterly over the fate of Jerusalem and the condition that it is in. The people are not to try to comfort him because of the

The Testimony of the Major Prophets

spoiling of the daughter of his people, the "daughter of his people" is the symbol of the city of Jerusalem. It is a day of trouble that has been reaped based upon the previous behaviors of the people; the treading down by the feet of the invaders who have taken control of the city; and the perplexity by the Lord GOD of hosts in the valley of vision, the low point of vision, which must be accepted because the actions of the inhabitants brought Jerusalem to this state which could have been avoided if the people would have served the God who could have given them strength. The breaking down of the walls has already occurred and the crying to the mountains at the sadness of the situation, after the fact, is a total waste of time and effort. Invasion and occupation has happened to other cities.

The city of Elam bare the quiver, endured the experience of the shaking, caused by chariots of men and horsemen and the city of Kir uncovered the shield to protect themselves from the invader, but they were unsuccessful. It shall come to pass that the choicest valleys shall be full of the chariots of the invaders and the horsemen shall set themselves in array at the gate to prove that they are the rulers of the city and to control the entrance to and the exit from the city which they have conquered. The enemy has been preparing for a successful invasion of Jerusalem, the seat of power of Judah.

8 And he discovered the covering of Judah, and thou didst look in that day to the armour of the house of the forest.
9 Ye have seen also the breaches of the city of David, that they are many: and ye gathered together the waters of the lower pool.
10 And ye have numbered the houses of Jerusalem, and the houses have ye broken down to fortify the wall.
11 Ye made also a ditch between the two walls for the water of the old pool: but ye have not looked unto the maker thereof, neither had respect unto him that fashioned it long ago.
12 And in that day did the Lord GOD of hosts call to weeping, and to mourning, and to baldness, and to girding with sackcloth:

The potential invader discovered the covering of Judah, the total defenses and the amount of resistance available that covered the land of Judah, and the people of Jerusalem did look in that day of invasion to the armor and armaments available in the house of the forest, the Palace of the Forest built by King Solomon from the trees of the cedars of Lebanon.

The people of Jerusalem have seen that the breaches, the breaks, in the defenses of the city of David were many: and you gathered together the water of the lower pool which was used as a moat or barrier against invasion. You have numbered, counted, the houses in Jerusalem for the purpose of breaking down the houses to fortify the wall to keep out the invaders. You also made a ditch between the two walls for the water of the old pool: but you have not looked to the Maker of the water and the land, you have not looked to the LORD nor did you have respect for the One that fashioned it long ago. In that day, the day when the people turned away from the LORD, was the beginning of the events that led to the weeping, mourning, the tearing out of hair to produce baldness as a sign of shame, and the wearing of sackcloth to demonstrate your misery.

13 And behold joy and gladness, slaying oxen, and killing sheep, eating flesh, and drinking wine: let us eat and drink; for to morrow we shall die.
14 And it was revealed in mine ears by the LORD of hosts, Surely this iniquity shall not be purged from you till ye die, saith the Lord GOD of hosts.

The people were content with the defenses of the city before the invasion. They celebrated with joy and revelry, slaying oxen, and killing sheep, eating flesh, and drinking wine: their attitude was one of eat, drink and make revelry because tomorrow, you may be dead. This is the outlook and vision of a people who expected to lose and expected to be defeated. It is not the attitude of the LORD's people who draw strength from the LORD. It was revealed into the ears of Isaiah by the LORD of hosts that, Surely this iniquity in the people shall not be purged from them until they die. It is sad that death must come to remove the attitude of defeat from the consciousness of the people of Jerusalem and Judah. Is there any way out, any salvation, for a people who carry this attitude and culture of defeat in their consciousness?

15 Thus saith the Lord GOD of hosts, Go, get thee unto this treasurer, even unto Shebna, which is over the house, and say,
16 What hast thou here? and whom hast thou here, that thou hast hewed thee out a sepulchre here, as he that heweth him out a sepulchre on high, and that graveth an habitation for himself in a rock?

The Lord GOD of hosts says that the way out of defeat is to adopt an attitude of victory. The change of attitude is described as a change in consciousness where the people of Jerusalem must have the attitude to Go, get themselves to the treasury, the source of the wealth that has given the invader the victory, even to Shebna, the head of the house of the invaders and say to him: What do you have here in Jerusalem? Who do you have here in Jerusalem that you want this land so badly that you are willing to stay here until you die and your body is buried in a sepulcher and you will end up in a rock? Dead and buried!

17 Behold, the LORD will carry thee away with a mighty captivity, and will surely cover thee.
18 He will surely violently turn and toss thee like a ball into a large country: there shalt thou die, and there the chariots of thy glory shall be the shame of thy lord's house.
19 And I will drive thee from thy station, and from thy state shall he pull thee down.

The people of Jerusalem who turn to the LORD for strength will have the strength of the LORD. They will be able to say to their captors that the LORD will carry the invaders away with a mighty captivity by a mighty and victorious people who will surely cover the invaders. The LORD's people will surely use the power of the LORD to violently turn from their captivity and weakness, and toss the invader like a ball into a large country far away from Jerusalem and Judah. There you shall die, and there the chariots which were the symbols of your strength and glory shall be the shame of the house of your lord and god. And I, the LORD working through many people, will drive you from your present station, and, from your present high state, shall the LORD and his body of people pull you down. The process of victory utilizing the power and the wisdom of the LORD must begin in the consciousness of the LORD's people.

The Testimony of the Major Prophets

20 And it shall come to pass in that day, that I will call my servant Eliakim the son of Hilkiah:
21 And I will clothe him with thy robe, and strengthen him with thy girdle, and I will commit thy government into his hand: and he shall be a father to the inhabitants of Jerusalem, and to the house of Judah.
22 And the key of the house of David will I lay upon his shoulder; so he shall open, and none shall shut; and he shall shut, and none shall open.

And it shall come to pass, if the people of Jerusalem meet the requirements of the LORD, that the LORD will provide a leader, Eliakim the son of Hilkiah, whose name means, "power of the LORD", will be clothed with the robe and strengthened with the girdle presently worn by Shebna. The government of the people of Jerusalem will be placed into his hand: and he shall be a father to the inhabitants of Jerusalem and to the house of Judah. The LORD will give the key to the city of David to rest upon his shoulder; and he shall open the gates to the city and none shall shut them; and he shall shut the gates to invaders from outside, and none shall open them again. He will be a point of stability in his representation of the LORD among his people. The key of the house, the key to the city of David symbolizes the spirit and the power of love.

23 And I will fasten him as a nail in a sure place; and he shall be for a glorious throne to his father's house.
24 And they shall hang upon him all the glory of his father's house, the offspring and the issue, all vessels of small quantity, from the vessels of cups, even to all the vessels of flagons.
25 In that day, saith the LORD of hosts, shall the nail that is fastened in the sure place be removed, and be cut down, and fall; and the burden that was upon it shall be cut off: for the LORD hath spoken it.

The LORD will fasten Eliakim as a nail in a sure place, the place where he will represent the LORD on earth. In this position of representation, he shall be a glorious throne to his father's house, the house of the LORD. The people of Jerusalem shall hang upon him all the glory of his father's house, the offspring and the issue, the descendants, the vessels of small quantity that range in size from the vessels of small cups to the vessels of larger flagons. These things shall occur if the nail is fastened in a sure place, not physically, but spiritually, in true representation of the spirit of the LORD. But, if that stable nail that is fastened in the sure place be removed, cut down and fall, or if the spirit of the LORD be ignored, removed or discarded; then the burden of success and power that was upon it shall be cut off. The people have two choices: to be faithful to the LORD and prosper; or, to go their own way and be taken into captivity. The LORD has spoken the only two possible outcomes.

CHAPTER 23

1 The burden of Tyre. Howl, ye ships of Tarshish; for it is laid waste, so that there is no house, no entering in: from the land of Chittim it is revealed to them.
2 Be still, ye inhabitants of the isle; thou whom the merchants of Zidon, that pass over the sea, have replenished.
3 And by great waters the seed of Sihor, the harvest of the river, is her revenue; and she is a mart of nations.

The spirit of the LORD speaking through Isaiah shares the burden of the distorted conditions and circumstances of Tyre which he carries in his consciousness as he views the world of his environment. Tyre is an ancient city on the Mediterranean Sea which was founded by the Sidonians about 240 years before Solomon's temple. Tyre possessed astonishing enterprise and material wealth since it was the main seaport on the Phoenician coast located 35 miles north of Mount Carmel and 25 miles south of Sidon. Part of the city of Tyre was built on two islands about ½ a mile from shore which provided a protected island fortress that was not taken by force until Alexander the Great destroyed it 400 years later in 332 B.C. Ships from foreign lands arrived in Tyre with their goods and their cultures. Since the world is not revealing the design of the LORD, many distortions and aberrations came to focus in Tyre which is a burden to the consciousness of Isaiah. The part of the city of Tyre, which was not part of the island, has been destroyed as Isaiah speaks of it to his followers. After a long sea voyage, the ships of Tarshish were looking forward to the pleasures which were available in Tyre.

Isaiah calls to the occupants of the ships from far-away Tarshish, a maritime city in southern Spain, to howl, to give a loud cry of grief, because Tyre is destroyed and left without house, or a place of entering in, a harbor. This information has been revealed to the ships of Tarshish from the land of Chittim, from the island of Cyprus, which had close trading ties with Tyre. Isaiah's advice to the inhabitants of the isle of Tyre is to be still, be patient of mind and quiet of heart during these times of trouble. The merchants of Sidon, the Phoenician city to the north of Tyre, have replenished the city. From the south, from the region of the easternmost branch of the Nile River in Egypt, the seed of Sihor, the grain from this Egyptian area which is the harvest of the river, is the revenue of

The Testimony of the Major Prophets

Tyre that came over the great waters of the sea. Tyre has become a trading market place of nations. Isaiah is calling attention to the fact that the people of Tyre are so involved with their trading and commerce and the material wealth which it has brought to the people of Tyre, that there is no thought of the LORD of hosts in their lives. This is shameful behavior.

4 Be thou ashamed, O Zidon: for the sea hath spoken, even the strength of the sea, saying, I travail not, nor bring forth children, neither do I nourish up young men, nor bring up virgins.
5 As at the report concerning Egypt, so shall they be sorely pained at the report of Tyre.
6 Pass ye over to Tarshish; howl, ye inhabitants of the isle.
7 Is this your joyous city, whose antiquity is of ancient days? her own feet shall carry her afar off to sojourn.

The people of Zidon, (Isaiah uses the Greek spelling of Sidon to indicate that the people have entered into the ways of the world instead of the way of the LORD,) are called to be ashamed at their movement away from the LORD. The ways of the sea, the culture of the people who come from the sea, have spoken, and the strength of the peer pressure has prevailed upon the people of Tyre. The people who are not of the LORD say that they do not travail in the path of the LORD, they do not bring forth children in the way of the LORD, they do not nourish their young men in the way of love, nor do they bring up their young women to be virgins. They are a materialistic people who have never seen the LORD and they are not interested in the possibility that there might be a LORD over them, a LORD who has sent them here for a purpose. They are the kings of the sea. Tyre has become a place where the LORD has been forgotten. As the report, the news, from Egypt being a symbol of the fallen state of mankind which is far removed from the way of the LORD, so shall the people who are interested in the LORD be pained that the people of Tyre have gone the way of Egypt.

Isaiah tells the people of Tyre to pass over to the ways of the people of Tarshish who are far removed from the LORD; howl in your love of the material world of trading and commerce without any thought of the LORD, you inhabitants of the isle of Tyre. You have chosen to do this. Is this your joyous city? Is this city going the way of antiquity, the way of the people of ancient days, before they heard of the LORD? The feet of the people, and the understanding of the people in the city, are walking in a direction that they have chosen to sojourn, to go as they move through life. Isaiah is speaking an unpopular doctrine to the people of a wealthy and prosperous seaport which has become wise in the ways and the pleasures of the world.

8 Who hath taken this counsel against Tyre, the crowning city, whose merchants are princes, whose traffickers are the honourable of the earth?
9 The LORD of hosts hath purposed it, to stain the pride of all glory, and to bring into contempt all the honourable of the earth.

Who has taken this counsel and advice against Tyre, the crowning city of the Mediterranean Sea, whose merchants are so successful in material goods that they are princes of the world and whose workers, that traffic in this great endeavor, are perceived as the honorable people of the earth? Isaiah announces his authority for speaking as he has against Tyre, against the people of Tyre, as the LORD of hosts. The LORD has purposed it, allowed it to transpire, to stain the pride of all the

The Symbolic Version of Isaiah

glory of the world and to bring into contempt all the so-called honorable people of the earth who have been "successful" in their endeavors. The growth of the materialistic world from external sources, from people with cultures that are not of the LORD, shall magnify and grow.

10 Pass through thy land as a river, O daughter of Tarshish: there is no more strength.
11 He stretched out his hand over the sea, he shook the kingdoms: the LORD hath given a commandment against the merchant city, to destroy the strong holds thereof.
12 And he said, Thou shalt no more rejoice, O thou oppressed virgin, daughter of Zidon: arise, pass over to Chittim; there also shalt thou have no rest.
13 Behold the land of the Chaldeans; this people was not, till the Assyrian founded it for them that dwell in the wilderness: they set up the towers thereof, they raised up the palaces thereof; and he brought it to ruin.

The land is available for this fallen culture to pass through as a river and the city of Tyre will become as a daughter of Tarshish: there is no more strength of people who will reveal the LORD and the true design which is contained in the spirit of the LORD. If the true design of spirit is absent, the predictable will happen when the power of the LORD moves through a distorted design. The LORD stretched out his hand of control over the sea of all the people in the fallen state and He shook their kingdoms which are not the Kingdom of the LORD. The LORD has given a commandment against the merchant city to destroy the strongholds of the city. What the people are building contains the seed of self-destruction.

The working of the law of the LORD in the affairs of fallen men will end the rejoicing in the conditions which are called the oppressed virgin, the daughter of Sidon. The oppression is brought about and expressed by the people who live there. The end of the rejoicing is the beginning of misery. The misery will arise and pass over to Chittim (Cyprus); and they shall have no rest because the conditions created by the people who have fallen away from the LORD, are not restful. This process of the spread of a culture is not very much different from what happened in the land of the Chaldeans; these people were not very learned or wise until the Assyrians founded a new culture for the people who dwelled in the wilderness: the Assyrians set up the towers and raised up the palaces thereof; and, eventually, the Chaldeans returned to their wild ways and brought the enlightened state to ruin.

14 Howl, ye ships of Tarshish: for your strength is laid waste.
15 And it shall come to pass in that day, that Tyre shall be forgotten seventy years, according to the days of one king: after the end of seventy years shall Tyre sing as an harlot.
16 Take an harp, go about the city, thou harlot that hast been forgotten; make sweet melody, sing many songs, that thou mayest be remembered.

So Isaiah tells the people of Tarshish, the people who are going the wrong way on the sea that belongs to the LORD, to howl. The howl may appear to be revelry for a while but the howl will turn to grief when the circumstances disintegrate and their strength is laid to waste; the strength of the LORD will destroy what is not the true design. It will come to pass that Tyre shall be forgotten for 70 years, the life span of the average man, the king of the environment, the king of this material

The Testimony of the Major Prophets

world, whose actions and behaviors created the conditions. After the 70 years have passed, people will forget that they have created the conditions of the environment in which they find themselves and they sing the song of a harlot. A harlot is the symbol of a person who has done something wrong for such a long time that she believes that what she is doing is right, and "normal", for her.

She shall take her harp, an instrument that plays music, which is also a symbol for her body, and the person who has become a harlot by his or her own choice and his or her own behavior, has been forgotten. It has been forgotten that the person who has fallen away from the Way of the LORD because the fallen way of life is now acceptable behavior; the harlot will make sweet melody, make pleasurable tunes, sing many songs, that the fallen state shall be remembered and become an accepted part of the new culture.

17 And it shall come to pass after the end of seventy years, that the LORD will visit Tyre, and she shall turn to her hire, and shall commit fornication with all the kingdoms of the world upon the face of the earth.
18 And her merchandise and her hire shall be holiness to the LORD: it shall not be treasured nor laid up; for her merchandise shall be for them that dwell before the LORD, to eat sufficiently, and for durable clothing.

And it shall come to pass after 70 years, after an old generation has passed and a new generation has put in an appearance, that the LORD will visit Tyre through the people who will let it be so. The representation of the LORD revealed by a few of the people will allow the harlot to turn to her hire, the people who will hire her for her services, and she shall commit fornication with them. The fornication of mixing and blending is not limited to sexual behavior. The fornication can also be a symbol of the intimate contact by the harlot, the symbol of the fallen human nature state with all the people who represent the evils of the world described as all the kingdoms of the world upon the face of the earth. What is the LORD's viewpoint in regard to mankind behaving this way and doing these things?

It may be shocking to some people to see that the harlot of human nature and her hire, the people who are intimately involved with her, shall be considered a holiness to the LORD. The LORD knows that all things work together to perfection including the wrong behavior which enables certain creations to self-destruct. It is possible to see these things transpiring with a vision of observation of a fact: this does not mean that the behavior that one is observing is to be treasured by a representative of the LORD nor laid up as a desire in one's heart. The merchandise of the harlot is for those that dwell before the LORD in the fallen state and they eat sufficiently of the "good" fruit of the tree of the knowledge of good and evil. These people in the fallen state have taken this type of behavior into themselves with the result that it has become second nature to them to be a part of the durable behavior which they call their way of living. Isaiah is telling his followers that the LORD can tolerate the sins of human nature, that there is no need to fight against the wrong behaviors of human nature because it carries the seed of self-destruction with its expression into the earth. Isaiah wants his followers to understand that the power of the LORD is behind everything; He is the author of everything.

CHAPTER 24

1 Behold, the LORD maketh the earth empty, and maketh it waste, and turneth it upside down, and scattereth abroad the inhabitants thereof.
2 And it shall be, as with the people, so with the priest; as with the servant, so with his master; as with the maid, so with her mistress; as with the buyer, so with the seller; as with the lender, so with the borrower; as with the taker of usury, so with the giver of usury to him.
3 The land shall be utterly emptied, and utterly spoiled: for the LORD hath spoken this word.
4 The earth mourneth and fadeth away, the world languisheth and fadeth away, the haughty people of the earth do languish.

Isaiah wants his followers to behold, to observe, that it is the power of the LORD that is distorted by fallen human beings who makes the earth empty, makes it the waste that it is, turns it upside down, and scatters the people to the ends of the earth. The power of the LORD is the power that produces all these conditions. The power of the LORD moving through the consciousness of man produces conditions: whatever is in the consciousness is eventually revealed in form on earth. This is the working of the law of the LORD: it is the law of sowing and reaping. The LORD does not interfere or intervene with the working of the law. This is the way it shall be on earth with everyone: as with the people, so with the priest; as with the servant, so with his master; as with the maid, so with her mistress; as with the buyer, so with the seller; as with the lender, so with the borrower; as with the taker of usury, so with the giver of usury to him. The law works always with everyone.

What is in the consciousness of the people is expressed into their emotional, mental or physical forms on earth. The law of the LORD will continue to work even if the earth mourns and fades away; even if the world languishes and fades away. This law will continue to work even though the land shall be utterly emptied, utterly spoiled and totally devastated: because the LORD has spoken this word. As man sows, so shall he reap and not one jot or one tittle shall escape the working of the law. By observation, it can be seen that the people of the earth, the haughty people of the earth, do languish in the fallen nature which they have chosen for their expression.

The Testimony of the Major Prophets

5 The earth also is defiled under the inhabitants thereof; because they have transgressed the laws, changed the ordinance, broken the everlasting covenant.
6 Therefore hath the curse devoured the earth, and they that dwell therein are desolate: therefore the inhabitants of the earth are burned, and few men left.

The earth is defiled under the control of the inhabitants who live on earth. The LORD has given total power to man in this regard. If men and women transgress the law of sowing, they shall reap what they have sown. It is man who has changed the ordinance and broken the everlasting covenant that man is to represent the LORD on earth. If the earth is defiled, man has done it and he should not blame or accuse anyone else for what he has done as a collective body. Therefore the curse of man's behavior has devoured the earth and the people who dwell on earth are a desolate people, a devastated and a ravaged people who have done this terrible thing to themselves. This is the reason that the inhabitants of the earth are burned by the fire of the LORD's love in action through an untrue design. The burning experience is blamed on an "imaginary, supernatural devil" created by man who will not accept responsibility for his own actions. Man has even given the devil that he has created the name of the Accuser. Almost everybody wants to blame or accuse someone else for the conditions on earth, but mankind has done it all. There are only a relatively few men left on earth who will admit that the law is at work and that the LORD will not change the constant working of the law. Man, male and female, are the only people, the grapes, on the vine of life. The expression of the grapes produces the wine of life; the wine comes from the grapes; people make the wine that they drink; people create the conditions in which they must live.

7 The new wine mourneth, the vine languisheth, all the merryhearted do sigh.
8 The mirth of tabrets ceaseth, the noise of them that rejoice endeth, the joy of the harp ceaseth.
9 They shall not drink wine with a song; strong drink shall be bitter to them that drink it.
10 The city of confusion is broken down: every house is shut up, that no man may come in.
11 There is a crying for wine in the streets; all joy is darkened, the mirth of the land is gone.

The new wine, the newest expression that comes from the people who are symbolized by grapes, mourn because of the poor quality of the wine. The vine languishes for lack of proper care and all the merry-hearted people do sigh because they sense that conditions could be much better than they are in the present moment. Sadness and bitterness prevail: the mirth of the people who play music ceases; the noise of them that rejoice ends; and the joy of the harp ceases. Each person has a harp consisting of a heart, a mind and a body and people should be playing this harp to produce beauty.

These fallen people shall not drink wine with a song in their hearts; they drink strong drink to try to obtain happiness but the drink is a drug that is bitter to them that drink it for this purpose. Addiction results. The city is in a state of confusion because the people are confused and this confusion is the cause for the breakdown of society. The person in every house is shut up tight so that everyone is right in their own eyes and no man, man made in the image and likeness of God, may come in because the occupant of the house, the spiritual person who resides inside, will not allow the divine man to come in. There is a crying for the good wine of life in the streets; everyone wants the good wine, but no one will make it. This is the reason that all joy is darkened because joy is a product of light and light comes from the LORD. It is easy to see why the mirth of the land is gone; the people are not expressing mirth into their environments. They are singing sad songs about the conditions of their environments which have been made by men.

12 In the city is left desolation, and the gate is mitten with destruction.
13 When thus it shall be in the midst of the land among the people, there shall be as the shaking of an olive tree, and as the gleaning grapes when the vintage is done.
14 They shall lift up their voice, they shall sing for the majesty of the LORD, they shall cry aloud from the sea.
15 Wherefore glorify ye the LORD in the fires, even the name of the LORD God of Israel in the isles of the sea.

It is clear to see why the city is left in desolation because the people are expressing their desolation into the environment of the city. The gate that lets the inhabitants into the city is mitten, is allowing the expression to be destructive. When these conditions have been produced by the people of the land, there shall be very little fruit as what occurs when the olive tree is shaken or the grapes that are gleaned when the harvest is done. There is little harvest and the people will want more than is available to them.

The people who want more shall lift up their voices, they shall sing for the majesty of the LORD to intervene, they shall cry aloud from the sea of people who will gather to present a unified voice, but to no avail. If you understand the working of the law of the LORD, you can see that it is useless to glorify the name of the LORD in the fires of sacrifice that are burned to entreat the LORD, even the LORD God of Israel, to intercede for the isles of individual physical forms in the sea of people who call on the LORD for help in an attempt to get what they want.

16 From the uttermost part of the earth have we heard songs, even glory to the righteous. But I said, My leanness, my leanness, woe unto me! the treacherous dealers have dealt treacherously; yea, the treacherous dealers have dealt very treacherously.
17 Fear, and the pit, and the snare, are upon thee, O inhabitant of the earth.

From the uttermost parts of the earth, we have heard songs of praise and glory to the righteous actions that have appeared through others. But Isaiah has looked to his own leanness, the lean expression of righteousness that has come from him and he has said, woe to himself! Isaiah has a sense that he has been the source of his lean expression of the spirit of the LORD that would produce abundance. Isaiah was a dealer of what he expressed into the earth. Treacherous dealers deal treachery; treacherous dealers have dealt very treacherously into the earth. This is why things are the way they are. This is the reason that fear is on earth, and that fear is in the pit that surrounds each person, which they can fall into, and have difficulty extricating themselves from it. This is the reason that following the wrong example and behavior of others is a snare upon one's self, O inhabitant of the earth.

18 And it shall come to pass, that he who fleeth from the noise of the fear shall fall into the pit; and he that cometh up out of the midst of the pit shall be taken in the snare: for the windows from on high are open, and the foundations of the earth do shake.
19 The earth is utterly broken down, the earth is clean dissolved, the earth is moved exceedingly.

The Testimony of the Major Prophets

20 The earth shall reel to and fro like a drunkard, and shall be removed like a cottage; and the transgression thereof shall be heavy upon it; and it shall fall, and not rise again.

And it shall come to pass because of the working of the law that he who flees from the noise of fear shall fall into the pit of fear because the person is expressing fear into his world. And he who comes up out of the midst of the pit shall be taken in the snare, the trap, of the fear that was created when it was expressed into the earth. The reason should be obvious to those who know the working of the law of the LORD: the windows of the power of creation are open and the foundations of the earth do shake when the power of the LORD moving through the fear in a person creates fear in an earthly form.

The earth is utterly broken down by what is expressed upon it by the power from the LORD moving through the consciousness of man. The earth can be either clean and dissolved of fear or the earth can be moved exceedingly. The power is not in the earth, the power is in the person's expression which has control over the earth if the person will take the control that is available. The earth can reel to and fro like a drunkard who is out of control. The earth can be removed like a cottage can be removed because man has dominion over physical form. The transgression of the physical form of things shall be heavy and decisive upon it because once it falls, it cannot rise again by itself. It cannot be rearranged into exactly the same pattern.

21 And it shall come to pass in that day, that the LORD shall punish the host of the high ones that are on high, and the kings of the earth upon the earth.
22 And they shall be gathered together, as prisoners are gathered in the pit, and shall be shut up in the prison, and after many days shall they be visited.
23 Then the moon shall be confounded, and the sun ashamed, when the LORD of hosts shall reign in mount Zion, and in Jerusalem, and before his ancients gloriously.

Isaiah tells his followers that if they understand the working of the law of the LORD's spirit into the world of form then they can see how the LORD will punish the host of the high ones that are on high and they create conditions that affect many people, and the kings of the earth who have great control upon the earth. The high ones and the kings are responsible for their creations just as surely as each individual is responsible for his expression. Everyone should understand that they shall be gathered together on earth, as prisoners are gathered in a pit, and they shall be shut up as in prison. The whole earth is as a prison of the LORD and, after many days, when the behavior of the prisoners produce conditions in which all the people must live, then they will be visited by a higher authority who will review the results of their behavior.

When the people really see, really observe, the results of their combined behavior, they will be confounded. The moon which symbolizes the reflected light of the behavior copied from other people, peer pressure, and the sun, which symbolizes the radiant light of one's own behavior, shall be a cause for shame as the expressions are reviewed. Who will conduct the review? The LORD of hosts who shall reign in Mount Zion, the eternal, spiritual holy place, and in Jerusalem, which should be a holy city containing the expressions to the LORD in physical manifestation. The ancients who set a glorious example for the people of this generation shall be seen for what they have done. Isaiah is teaching his followers that the power of the LORD of hosts is with them to review their behavior and their creations, and that the power from the LORD can be used to shape the earth of their immediate environments.

CHAPTER 25

1 O LORD, thou art my God; I will exalt thee, I will praise thy name; for thou hast done wonderful things; thy counsels of old are faithfulness and truth.
2 For thou hast made of a city an heap; of a defenced city a ruin: a palace of strangers to be no city; it shall never be built.
3 Therefore shall the strong people glorify thee, the city of the terrible nations shall fear thee.

Isaiah reveals to his followers the way in which he prays to the LORD by making obeisance to Him and placing himself in service to the purposes of the LORD. Isaiah commits himself totally to the LORD whom he acknowledges as his God. The heart, mind and physical body of Isaiah are totally available to let the spirit of the LORD find expression through Isaiah who will exalt the name of the LORD in the living of his life. Isaiah will praise the name of the LORD who has done wonderful things: because Isaiah is in position to let the spirit of the LORD flow through his capacities of heart, mind and body, the counsels of the prophets of old, such as Moses, have been proven to be faithful and the truth. Isaiah has learned in his service to the LORD that all power that comes to living things on earth comes from the LORD.

It is the power of the LORD, used incorrectly, that has made the city a heap of distortions and disintegration that is a manifestation of a partial release of the spirit that cannot produce wholeness in form; wholeness would bring strength in the power of the LORD while the partial release of the spirit through people brings weakness. It is the weakness of spiritual expression that brings an inadequately defended city to ruin; the leadership in a palace of strangers, strangers to the Way of the LORD, that results in no more city under the control and the blessing of the LORD because the blessing will not come if the people are not under the LORD's control; the holy city of the LORD will never be built unless the people, the inhabitants of the city, let the LORD's spirit with its divine design and control, build the city.

4 For thou hast been a strength to the poor, a strength to the needy in his distress, a refuge from the storm, a shadow from the heat, when the blast of the terrible ones is as a storm against the wall.

5 Thou shalt bring down the noise of strangers, as the heat in a dry place; even the heat with the shadow of a cloud: the branch of the terrible ones shall be brought low.

Isaiah acknowledges that it is the LORD who has been the source of strength to the poor, to the needy in his distress, a refuge from the storm in a person's life, a shadow of bearable comfort from the emotional, mental and physical heat that is experienced by people when the blast of the terrible ones in the environment is like a storm against the wall of the place where each individual lives.

It is the LORD whose spirit is constantly flowing through Isaiah that will bring down the noise, the absence of harmonious behavior, of strangers, the distorted behavior of people who do not know the LORD's spirit as the heat in a dry place is more bearable than in a damp place with high humidity; this difference in heat can also be experienced as the increase in comfort when the shadow from a cloud blocks the heat of the sun. Isaiah offers the teaching to his followers that the brand of the terrible ones, the branch of people who produce terrible behaviors will brought low, brought down, by the working of the spirit of the LORD in the affairs of men on earth.

6 And in this mountain shall the LORD of hosts make unto all people a feast of fat things, a feast of wines on the lees, of fat things full of marrow, of wines on the lees well refined.
7 And he will destroy in this mountain the face of the covering cast over all people, and the vail that is spread over all nations.

Isaiah teaches his followers that in this holy mountain, the mountain of spiritual consciousness where the spirit of Isaiah and the spirit of the LORD are in oneness, in agreement, in the covenant, the LORD of hosts makes, for all people who are in spiritual agreement, a feast. The feast is described in earthly terms as a feast of the choice fat animals full of marrow, the wines that are grown from grapes on the lee side of the mountain where the choicest grapes are grown and made into the finest wines.

The LORD's spirit working through Isaiah and other servants of the LORD shall destroy in this holy mountain of spiritual agreement the face of the covering cast over the people of the earth who believe that oneness with the LORD is not possible. The person who experiences the presence of the LORD in his own heart, mind and body can understand that a veil of blindness is spread over all the nations and covers all the people who do not know the LORD. The face of the covering, that prevents a realized experience with the LORD's presence with His people, shall be destroyed. It is the LORD's desire that everyone should know of the LORD's constant presence with His people, but the presence of the power and the truth of the LORD with each individual is not known because of the veil of self-centeredness.

8 He will swallow up death in victory; and the Lord GOD will wipe away tears from off all faces; and the rebuke of his people shall he take away from off all the earth: for the LORD hath spoken it.

The true nature of man is spirit, not physical form. Isaiah is calling his followers to oneness with the LORD by expressing the LORD's spirit through themselves so that they, too, will know what they express. In this way they will discover that they are spirit that inhabits the body. The body

The Testimony of the Major Prophets

"dies" in what is known on earth as death, but if a person has experienced the spirit that is in the body as one's own spirit, then the victory of identification with the spirit eliminates the fear of death because the person knows that he is the spirit in the body and he is not the body. His individual spirit is a part of God's spirit. When a person experiences this victory over physical form, in the covenant-agreement with the LORD, then, the Lord GOD will wipe away tears from off all the faces of the people who have experienced spiritual identity, a person's true identity, the truth of one's self; and the rebuke of his people, the nightmare experience on earth when man was "separated" from the LORD shall be taken away from off all the earth of a person who has experienced his relationship with the LORD: a person has never, ever been separated from the LORD except in that person's consciousness. In this state of separation, which exists only in the mind of a person, a person expressed distortions that have been painful and unpleasant, which is the rebuke of the LORD. Isaiah has said that the LORD has spoken these things to call His people home to the holy mountain where the LORD and His server, Isaiah, are one.

9 And it shall be said in that day, Lo, this is our God; we have waited for him, and he will save us: this is the LORD; we have waited for him, we will be glad and rejoice in his salvation.
10 For in this mountain shall the hand of the LORD rest, and Moab shall be trodden down under him, even as straw is trodden down for the dunghill.

And it shall be said in that day, the day of the experience of the covenant, Lo, this is our God because the person has experienced God within himself that cannot be denied. This is accomplished because the people have waited for Him, served Him and His spirit on earth, in momentary living as the LORD's spirit is released on earth. This is how a person is saved and how the LORD saves us. A person knows what he expresses; if he expresses the LORD's spirit, he knows the LORD to the extent that the spirit is expressed. The completion of this process is a knowing of the LORD so the person can say, "this is the LORD". We have waited (served His spirit) for Him, we will rejoice in the service of the LORD's spirit and be glad in the salvation of the LORD that is offered through one's heart, mind and body.

This service is done in the mountain of spiritual consciousness where the consciousness of the LORD, the hand of the control of the LORD, meets the consciousness of the person, who offers his consciousness to the LORD, so that they become one, in agreement, to do the LORD's will. It is Thy will that is to be done, not "my" will be done. When the consciousness of the LORD and man are one, then the distortions, symbolized by Moab, are eliminated from the experience in the consciousness and the distortions shall be trodden down under him, even as straw is trodden down for the dunghill. The distortions that are under your feet are trampled into the fertilizer that is used for a new creative process. The LORD will have true priests, helpers, waiters, servers, representatives, emissaries, etc., on earth to release His spirit on earth.

11 And he shall spread forth his hands in the midst of them, as he that swimmeth spreadeth forth his hands to swim: and he shall bring down their pride together with the spoils of their hands.
12 And the fortress of the high fort of thy walls shall he bring down, lay low, and bring to the ground, even to the dust.

The Symbolic Version of Isaiah

Isaiah tells his followers that the LORD can now spread forth His hands of spiritual control in the midst of the people on earth, and the people who are swimming in unison of spirit with the LORD's spirit can spread forth his or her hands to swim in unison as fish in a school of fish without bumping into each other. This concerted spiritual activity on earth is the spiritual action that shall bring down the people who are controlled by their pride and the spoils of the distortions of their hands that have defiled the earth. The evidence of the distortions produced by man in the fallen state, who has such great pride in his accomplishments, must be replaced with a new creation.

The new creation must come down from the Holy Mountain of spiritual consciousness from the LORD which has a strength of design that cannot fall. It is described as a fortress to indicate its strength in physical terms and as a fort with high walls that shall be brought down from the high place of the covenant, where it will lay low, bring to the ground, even to the dust, the physical forms which were the distortions built by mankind in the fallen state. The power and the design of the LORD are now in the earth.

CHAPTER 26

1 In that day shall this song be sung in the land of Judah; We have a strong city; salvation will God appoint for walls and bulwarks.
2 Open ye the gates, that the righteous nation which keepeth the truth may enter in.
3 Thou wilt keep him in perfect peace, whose mind is stayed on thee: because he trusteth in thee.

Isaiah tells his followers that in that day, the day when the people begin to let the spirit of the LORD find expression through the hearts, minds and bodies of His people, then a new song will be sung in the land of Judah; the song that will be sung is a song of the spirit of the LORD which is both strong and wise. A single individual who is releasing the spirit of the LORD will not have the strength and the wisdom of ten people, or 100 or 144,000. The strength of the LORD is in the size and the wisdom of the body moving in unison with the spirit. The power is the power of love that comes from the LORD which is coordinated and does not fight among its various parts. In time, it is possible to sing from a physical standpoint, "We have a strong city". However, from the spiritual standpoint of only one person, it is possible to sing the same song internally without attempting to do anything prematurely. Salvation will be appointed by God for walls and bulwarks for the spiritual city that is putting in an appearance through the physical forms of his children and the people of the LORD are appointed for walls and for bulwarks. This city is built primarily by walls of people, not physical walls. It is a living city with people as its walls, and the walls are moveable!

The responsibility of the people is to open the gates, the gates through which the LORD can enter, consciously, into the earth, so that the righteous nation, the nation that carries the LORD's spirit which keeps the truth of the LORD's spirit may enter into the earth and be observed through the people who carry the spirit. Isaiah instructs each of his followers to keep the spirit of the LORD in perfect peace. The LORD has His mind stayed on each individual and He trusts each individual to release the spirit and the wisdom which He sends to each of His children. The LORD trusts all His children. The question is do we trust the LORD enough to let His spirit flow into the earth? Isaiah entreats his followers to trust the LORD.

The Symbolic Version of Isaiah

4 Trust ye in the LORD for ever: for in the LORD JEHOVAH is everlasting strength:

Isaiah brings his instruction to a sharp point of focus for each individual when he asks each of them to trust in the LORD for ever. Forever does not mean for an hour of a religious service, a 24 hour day which is called the Sabbath Day limited to a Friday, Saturday or Sunday or any single day of the week. Forever means **all the time**. As long as a person is alive on earth, the LORD is with that person moment by moment: Isaiah asks his followers to do the same for the LORD moment by moment so that the covenant with the LORD can be revealed constantly and consistently on earth. The moment by moment living, forever, with the spirit of the LORD would provide everlasting strength from the LORD. The moment to moment expression is given a name, LORD JEHOVAH. Jehovah means that God is in action on earth through man. Man is composed of males and females. The LORD is present with every single person in physical form on earth simultaneously; men and women do not release, let, the spirit of the LORD come out of them into the earth simultaneously, but the people are not aware of the LORD's omnipresence. Isaiah is calling his followers to trust in the LORD and release the LORD's spirit on earth so that JEHOVAH can be known on earth. What will be the effect on earth of a people who bring the LORD's spirit through the earth of their hearts, minds and bodies?

5 For he bringeth down them that dwell on high; the lofty city, he layeth it low; he layeth it low, even to the ground; he bringeth it even to the dust.
6 The foot shall tread it down, even the feet of the poor, and the steps of the needy.

Isaiah says that the LORD functioning consciously through a group of people shall bring down those people who dwell on high within themselves where they are self-centered in their earthly egos. The lofty city that has been built by self-centeredness will be laid low, brought down to the ground and return to the dust from which it was built. The foot, the people who walk in the way of the LORD allowing the spirit to manifest, shall tread it down; even the feet of the poor and the steps taken by the needy. The cumulative result of spiritual expression will produce changes in the physical form of things because the true material design is in the design which originates in spirit. The spirit of the LORD contains the pattern for right behavior.

7 The way of the just is uprightness: thou, most upright, dost weigh the path of the just.
8 Yea, in the way of thy judgments, O LORD, have we waited for thee; the desire of our soul is to thy name, and to the remembrance of thee.
9 With my soul have I desired thee in the night; yea, with my spirit within me will I seek thee early: for when thy judgments are in the earth, the inhabitants of the world will learn righteousness.
10 Let favour be shewed to the wicked, yet will he not learn righteousness: in the land of uprightness will he deal unjustly, and will not behold the majesty of the LORD.

The way, in which the people who are just, walk on earth is called, uprightness. The LORD is the most upright and He does weigh the path that the just people on earth will walk. Isaiah states for himself and his followers that the way of the judgments of the LORD is what they have been waiting for; the desire of the soul, the hearts, minds and bodies, of this small group is to carry the spirit of the LORD and the remembrance of His name in their living.

The Testimony of the Major Prophets

Isaiah says that with his individual soul he has desired the LORD in the night and early in the morning; Isaiah seeks to do the will of the LORD even while he is asleep. Isaiah knows that when the LORD's judgments are released into the earth through himself and his followers, then, the inhabitants of the earth will learn righteousness from the example that has been established. If favoritism is shown to the wicked, then that person will not learn righteousness. Righteousness— the right-use-ness of the heart, mind and body— is a very exact translation of the LORD's spirit by people who express righteous behavior. If any favor is shown to the unrighteous, than righteousness will never be learned. In the land where everyone is expressing the righteousness of the LORD, the LORD will not deal unjustly with the person who is unjust. The people will not be able to observe the majesty of the LORD that could have been revealed through the person who has been unjust. The majesty of the LORD has been withheld from the earth by the person who has been unrighteous.

11 LORD, when thy hand is lifted up, they will not see: but they shall see, and be ashamed for their envy at the people; yea, the fire of thine enemies shall devour them.

Isaiah announces his understanding that when the hand, the control, is lifted up out of the earth, the people on earth will not be able to see the way of the LORD as long as it remains in spirit which is invisible: but the people shall see the way of the LORD because Isaiah and his followers shall release the spirit of the LORD on earth where the action is observable. Once the people do observe the spirit of the LORD in action on earth, which is JEHOVAH, then the people who do not allow the spirit of the LORD to come on earth through themselves shall be ashamed because they envy the people who let the spirit of the LORD come on earth. The right example expressed on earth shall be like an internal fire within the enemies of the LORD who do not express the LORD's spirit. The power of love, the power of the LORD, when it is not expressed on earth by the enemies of the LORD shall devour the people who do not express love.

12 LORD, thou wilt ordain peace for us: for thou also hast wrought all our works in us.
13 O LORD our God, other lords beside thee have had dominion over us: but by thee only will we make mention of thy name.
14 They are dead, they shall not live; they are deceased, they shall not rise: therefore hast thou visited and destroyed them, and made all their memory to perish.
15 Thou hast increased the nation, O LORD, thou hast increased the nation: thou art glorified: thou hadst removed it far unto all the ends of the earth.

Isaiah knows from his own experience of letting the LORD's spirit move through his heart, mind and body that this flow will produce peace in the person who lets the process occur. Isaiah knows that it is the LORD's spirit that has brought about all the works that come forth from man. Isaiah acknowledges that other "lords", idols, the pressure from the environment have had dominion in the past over him and his group: but in the present moment, the LORD only shall be mentioned, by name, as the LORD. The influences of the other "lords", idols from the environment are dead; they are deceased, they shall not rise because they are out of the past and they have no life in them. As the spirit of the LORD is allowed to be expressed, the spirit of the LORD has visited and destroyed any allegiance to any false lords. The memory of the controls from the past have been destroyed by the movement of the spirit of the LORD moving through the memory facilities. In this way, the

The Symbolic Version of Isaiah

LORD has increased his nation; the LORD is glorified as His spirit is expressed where it is moved and travels to the ends of the earth.

16 LORD, in trouble have they visited thee, they poured out a prayer when thy chastening was upon them.
17 Like as a woman with child, that draweth near the time of her delivery, is in pain, and crieth out in her pangs; so have we been in thy sight, O LORD.
18 We have been with child, we have been in pain, we have as it were brought forth wind; we have not wrought any deliverance in the earth; neither have the inhabitants of the world fallen.

Isaiah tells his followers that there are people who cry to the LORD when they are in trouble, they pour out a prayer when the chastening of the LORD, the discomfort of the LORD, was upon them. Isaiah acknowledges that we have been as a pregnant woman near the time of her delivery who cries out due to the pains of her labor. We have been that way also, LORD. We have been with child, we have been in pain from the worship of other lords of the earth, and we have brought forth the wind of nothingness insofar as the spirit of the LORD is concerned. When we are not bringing forth the spirit of the LORD, the delivery of the LORD, His spirit on earth, then, we failed in our individual mission. It is totally on us. The other inhabitants of the earth have not fallen because they are being sustained by the LORD and they must answer to the LORD for their behavior.

19 Thy dead men shall live, together with my dead body shall they arise. Awake and sing, ye that dwell in dust: for thy dew is as the dew of herbs, and the earth shall cast out the dead.

The dead men, the people who are spiritually dead because they do not know that the spirit of the LORD is with them, shall live. The LORD shall continue to send life to them to keep them alive on the vine of life. They are alive to the things and the treasures of the earthly environment but they are not aware of the presence of the LORD. But with the "dead" body of Isaiah, which is dead to the influences of the material world that have once controlled him, these people shall live because Isaiah has become alive to the world of the spirit which is the source of life. The people around Isaiah shall live because Isaiah is alive in the spirit of the LORD while he is "dead" to the controls of the lords of the things in the environment. Isaiah was once "dead" to the LORD's spirit, but now he can say, Arise and sing, you people who dwell in the dust of the material world. The spirit of the LORD lives in the body that you know as Isaiah. Isaiah will give them the water of truth from the LORD while, previously, they have been content with the water they have received from the environment, which is as sparse as the dew from the herbs; and the earth of the material world shall cast out the people who are dead to the controls of the material world and they will be attracted to the world of the spirit. Isaiah issues an invitation.

20 Come, my people, enter thou into thy chambers, and shut thy doors about thee: hide thyself as it were for a little moment, until the indignation be overpast.
21 For, behold, the LORD cometh out of his place to punish the inhabitants of the earth for their iniquity: the earth also shall disclose her blood, and shall no more cover her slain.

Isaiah invites his friends, the people around him to "Come" and enter in to your chambers, the secret place within one's self, and shut the doors around yourself: hide yourself from the controls, the external influences, of the material world for a little moment until the indignation, the anger of the false self which will complain when you turn off its pleasures from the environment, has passed over you.

Behold, the LORD comes out of His place within his children to punish the inhabitants of the earth, the people who were so wrapped up in the material things of the earth, which is the iniquity committed by the LORD's people. The material earth of the environment shall disclose her blood, the lifeblood of the LORD's people who have been held captive by the earth. The earth has been exposed for what it is, as powerless dust. She shall no more cover her slain, the people who are dead, to the fact that they are spirits of the LORD.

CHAPTER 27

1 In that day the LORD with his sore and great and strong sword shall punish leviathan the piercing serpent, even leviathan that crooked serpent; and he shall slay the dragon that is in the sea.

Isaiah tells his followers that the day of the LORD is the day when the LORD has a fierce, great and strong sword, an instrument of action on earth composed of a person or people, which the LORD can use on earth. A spiritual LORD needs an earthly instrument of action that is symbolized by a sword. The LORD shall punish leviathan with the sword. (Leviathan is a term used in *The Symbolic Version of Job* as the distorted state of mankind.) The sword is the symbol of the earthly portion of JEHOVAH while the LORD can be visualized as the spiritual portion of the JEHOVAH. The sword on earth, JEHOVAH, has three functions to perform: he must punish leviathan the piercing serpent; he must punish leviathan the crooked serpent; and he must slay the dragon that is in the sea. In order to punish the two serpents which are leviathan and slay the dragon, we must know what they are and where they can be found.

Leviathan is the symbol for the fallen state of consciousness which is contained within the physical body of mankind. There are two aspects to leviathan which we know as the conscious mind and the subconscious mind. Each of us has a conscious mind which is a part of the mass conscious mind that is contained within all of mankind; each of us has a subconscious mind which is a part of the mass subconscious mind. In *"The Symbolic Version of Genesis"*, we have identified the mind as symbolized by a serpent. The conscious aspect of the mind, which can bring the mind into a sharp focus on any particular situation or circumstance, can be called the **piercing serpent**. The subconscious mind with all of its twists and turns in the labyrinth of the subconscious is symbolized by a **crooked serpent**. The mind needs to punished because it has led man into the fallen state. Man needs a "serpent", a mind to function intelligently on earth but the mind must be used for the purpose of the LORD and not the self-centered purpose devised by man in the fallen state. This is why the two serpents, the two aspects of the conscious and the subconscious mind need to be punished and not slain because there is a divine purpose for the mind. There is a need to slay the dragon that is in the sea.

The Testimony of the Major Prophets

The dragon that lives in the sea, under the surface of the water of consciousness where it cannot be seen, represents the sub-conscious. The dragon is the symbol of the conglomeration of all the negative feelings which are contained within the false self. The negative emotions are the horrible fire-breathing type of emotions which always feel terrible: such as hatred, anger, resentment; jealousy, bitterness, greed, fear, etc., which are stored in the heart of the false self. In fact, the negative emotions are the primary reason why there is a false self. It is the dragon in the sea, the reservoir of the negative emotions of the false self that needs to be slain so that it no longer exists. As long as the dragon of the false self is alive, it will use these emotions to create thoughts and physical forms that are based upon or filled with the negative emotions. It is the responsibility of JEHOVAH, the person who represents the sword of the LORD, to slay the dragon that lives within each person. The sword identity, JEHOVAH, the true self, the truth of love, which is the true state of man made in the image and likeness of God, can slay the dragon and thereby eliminate the control by the negative emotions which are the power of the dragon. The person who does this can experience man in his true state on earth. The material form of a person in the true state on earth can be symbolized as a woman, while the spiritual state is the male that is contained within the female material state. The material form, the woman, is to be responsive to the spirit, the man. The man and the woman in this connection, as Adam and his help-meet, compose Man on earth, who is made in the image and likeness of God. The material form is referred to as a female and the entire physical body of mankind on earth is referred to as a woman.

2 In that day sing ye unto her, A vineyard of red wine.

In the day that this is seen and experienced by an individual, then, JEHOVAH, the spiritual self is able to sing harmonious songs to her, the individual person or the entire physical body of mankind, who is like a vineyard of red wine. The vineyard contains the vine of life composed of all the physical people whose grapes produce the wine of life on earth. The physical manifestation of the vine is kept alive by the spirit of the LORD.

3 I the LORD do keep it; I will water it every moment: lest any hurt it, I will keep it night and day.
4 Fury is not in me: who would set the briers and thorns against me in battle? I would go through them, I would burn them together.

Isaiah taught his followers that the LORD keeps the vine; and the LORD will water the vine every moment. No one is able to hurt the spiritual vine that comes from the LORD. It is the spiritual vine that has eternal life from the LORD; the physical form is the material clothing of the spirit of the LORD and it experiences what appears to be death. This is true regardless of the distortions that may have been produced on earth. The LORD does not get furious over the behavior of the people on earth. Fury is not in the nature of the LORD. The LORD God is love. The material forms, who do not perform the purpose of God on earth, are like briars and thorns against the LORD in battle. These fallen people cannot stand against the power of the LORD whose power can go through them and burn them together in the burning process, the disintegrative process, called death which is the process of the rearrangement of matter to create a new form for the spirit of the LORD. The people in the fallen state do not have to be destroyed by the power of the LORD. They have the freedom of choice if they choose to use it.

5 Or let him take hold of my strength, that he may make peace with me; and he shall make peace with me.
6 He shall cause them that come of Jacob to take root: Israel shall blossom and bud, and fill the face of the world with fruit.

The people in the fallen state may take hold of the LORD's strength which is flowing through them as long as they are alive and they can make peace with the LORD. The only way to make peace with the LORD is to harmonize with the LORD's purpose; and the people who hear the word and advice of the LORD shall make peace with the LORD. The people must be willing to harmonize with the path of the LORD and follow His example in living. The willingness begins in the heart, in the emotional realm.

The LORD shall cause them that come of Jacob, those whose hearts are willing, to receive the words of the LORD as seeds that will take root in one's heart. A transformation will occur as was the fact when Jacob turned into Israel. Israel, the one who was lifted up to the LORD, shall blossom and bud, and eventually will fill the face of the world with fruit, the fruit of Israel. The face of the world does not apply initially to the whole world, but, only to those people whose faces of response are turned to the LORD to hear and do what is instructed of them. The potential of the whole world returning to the LORD does exist.

7 Hath he smitten him, as he smote those that smote him? or is he slain according to the slaughter of them that are slain by him?
8 In measure, when it shooteth forth, thou wilt debate with it: he stayeth his rough wind in the day of the east wind.

Isaiah asks his followers to consider whether the LORD has smitten the people on earth to destroy them? Has the LORD smote those who smote Him in thought, word or deed? or is a man slain according to the slaughter and ill treatment of those others who are slain and injured by the perpetrator himself? A person who hates or fears his neighbor is destroyed by his own hatred and fear. The people are destroyed by their own misuse of the power of the LORD that flows through them. The LORD has not harmed them directly; the misuse of the LORD's power does the damage.

If a person desires to measure the effect that the LORD's power has in his own experience, when the power shoots forth through the human equipment, the person can debate with the misuse of the power that harms him as it comes forth through him in moment by moment living, but the damage is done by the misuse of the LORD's spirit that is not used for the LORD's purpose. The LORD stays His true course even through the rough wind created by a rebellious person, who wants to go his own way instead of the Way of the LORD which is symbolized by the east wind, the wind that comes out of the future which carries the true design. The east is the direction of the sunrise and the direction of the new day of the LORD. The wind is the symbol of the power of the LORD moving through the people. It has its own direction. A person can move with the LORD's power or try to go against it in a totally different direction, which is foolish and futile. The difficulties of people who want to go their own way are the evidence of going at cross purposes with the LORD's

The Testimony of the Major Prophets

way. The difficulties, so-called, can be seen as warnings for a person to straighten their course, the course of man in the fallen state symbolized by Jacob.

9 By this therefore shall the iniquity of Jacob be purged; and this is all the fruit to take away his sin; when he maketh all the stones of the altar as chalkstones that are beaten in sunder, the groves and images shall not stand up.
10 Yet the defenced city shall be desolate, and the habitation forsaken, and left like a wilderness: there shall the calf feed, and there shall he lie down, and consume the branches thereof.
11 When the boughs thereof are withered, they shall be broken off: the women come, and set them on fire: for it is a people of no understanding: therefore he that made them will not have mercy on them, and he that formed them will shew them no favour.

By this built-in warning system that is sensed by the emotional realm, the heart, the iniquity of Jacob, symbolizing fallen man, can be purged from one's own expression; and this warning system is all the fruit that is needed to take away one's sin, the behavior that is off-the-mark. A person who truly desires to serve the LORD will make an altar to the LORD by means of behaviors, that are pleasing to the LORD; the behaviors of his own self-centered plans shall be broken asunder into pieces with the result that the images and the trees on the groves of his self-determined daydreams shall not stand up as the LORD's plan take precedence. Some examples of these self-centered plans that have come to nothing, are the defended cities which have become desolate, the people forsaken and left like a wilderness: in this area where self-centered planning was demonstrated, the calf shall feed, he shall lie down and consume the branches of the destructive process that was planned by the beast of the self-active human minds. When the bough of the branches of the wrong design are withered, they shall be broken off the tree of life, and the women will come and set them on fire because they are useless. It is of a people with no understanding. The LORD that made the plans will not have mercy on them and the LORD that formed them will show them no special treatment for the plans not made by the LORD.

12 And it shall come to pass in that day, that the LORD shall beat off from the channel of the river unto the stream of Egypt, and ye shall be gathered one by one, O ye children of Israel.
13 And it shall come to pass in that day, that the great trumpet shall be blown, and they shall come which were ready to perish in the land of Assyria, and the outcasts in the land of Egypt, and shall worship the LORD in the holy mount at Jerusalem.

And it shall come to pass that on that day, the day when the person shall see that his self-centered way is not the way of the LORD, then there shall be a change of direction in the flow of the spirit of the LORD as it flows through that person. The channel of the flow in the wrong direction is symbolized as the stream of Egypt that leads to the fallen state. The LORD will beat off, change the wrong channel, into the correct channel. The result of the new direction is the children of Israel, the children who are interested in the risen state shall be gathered one by one. It shall come to pass that the great trumpet shall be blown and the people shall come to the sound of the trumpet. The people who come are those who were ready to perish in the land of Assyria and who are the outcast of the land of Egypt. These are the people who are not self-satisfied with their present conditions. They are the ones who are ready to accept the invitation of the trumpet of JEHOVAH and they shall worship the LORD in the holy mount of Jerusalem because the trumpet has sounded on earth.

The trumpet is the sound made by JEHOVAH, the people who reveal the spirit and the word of the LORD in their living. The people who respond to the call of the trumpet will be blessed. There are those who will hear the sound of the LORD's trumpet on earth and will ignore the call to continue in their proud and wicked ways.

CHAPTER 28

1 Woe to the crown of pride, to the drunkards of Ephraim, whose glorious beauty is a fading flower, which are on the head of the fat valleys of them that are overcome with wine!
2 Behold, the Lord hath a mighty and strong one, which as a tempest of hail and a destroying storm, as a flood of mighty waters overflowing, shall cast down to the earth with the hand.
3 The crown of pride, the drunkards of Ephraim, shall be trodden under feet:
4 And the glorious beauty, which is on the head of the fat valley, shall be a fading flower, and as the hasty fruit before the summer; which when he that looketh upon it seeth, while it is yet in his hand he eateth it up.

Isaiah tells his followers that the people who have the crown of pride, who have such pride in their own self-centered ways, that they are compared to the drunkards of Ephraim, whose glorious beauty from times past is a fading flower. Their vision is compared to the low, restricted ,valley view of people who are overcome with wine and in their drunken state, they imagine that things are better than they actually are.

The LORD has a strong and mighty channel in the ever-flowing spiritual river of correction for the drunkards of Ephraim who will be trodden underfoot because of their pride: the channel of correction in the river of life shall be like a tempest of hail and a destroying storm that brings a flood of mighty waters overflowing the banks of the river which shall cast down the earth with the hand of control of the LORD in action. The vision of a person with the crown of pride distorts the vision as one who is drunk: the glorious beauty that they think they see, is in the head of the fat ego which sees with restricted vision. They do not see the fading flower, the deterioration of the circumstances around them. His view is like the hasty fruit of summer that a person holds in his hand and imagines that it is sweet and delicious before he actually tastes it to determine whether it is sour and not yet ripe.

5 In that day shall the LORD of hosts be for a crown of glory, and for a diadem of beauty, unto the residue of his people,

6 And for a spirit of judgment to him that sitteth in judgment, and for strength to them that turn the battle to the gate.
7 But they also have erred through wine, and through strong drink are out of the way; the priest and the prophet have erred through strong drink, they are swallowed up of wine, they are out of the way through strong drink; they err in vision, they stumble in judgment.
8 For all tables are full of vomit and filthiness, so that there is no place clean.

In that day, the day when there are two different visions when observing the same thing, the view of the LORD of hosts shall be for a crown of glory and a diadem, a sign of royalty for the beauty, that shall be shown to the residue, the remnant of the LORD's people who are not afflicted with the faulty vision of pride. The LORD shall also have the true spirit of judgment when he sees those who sit in judgment through the faulty vision of pride; and the LORD shall have strength to give to those who desire to turn the battle of pride in their fading material environment to the battle of the gate to the LORD's spirit which brings clear vision. In addition to having their vision impaired by pride, they also have erred in their vision through the use of strong drink which takes them out of the way of the LORD. The priest and the prophet have erred in the drunken view produced by strong drink; they stumble in their drunken judgment and the tables around them are full of vomit and filthiness so that there is no clean place around them. Both pride and wine are distorting the vision of the people that Isaiah wants to teach.

9 Whom shall he teach knowledge? and whom shall he make to understand doctrine? them that are weaned from the milk, and drawn from the breasts.
10 For precept must be upon precept, precept upon precept; line upon line, line upon line; here a little, and there a little:
11 For with stammering lips and another tongue will he speak to this people.
12 To whom he said, This is the rest wherewith ye may cause the weary to rest; and this is the refreshing: yet they would not hear.

Isaiah has knowledge of the LORD to teach to the people in the fallen state. Whom shall he teach this knowledge? and whom shall he make to understand the doctrine of the LORD? them that are so young that they are weaned from milk and drawn away from the breasts of their mothers. Isaiah is looking for some innocent people who are like children, childlike, without the sins of pride and drunkenness that cloud the vision.

Isaiah knows that he needs people with clear minds to understand the word and the teaching of the LORD: precept must be built upon precept, line upon line, a little here and a little there so that people can understand the way of the LORD on earth. The way of the LORD is a spiritual way and not a material way; it is like speaking with stammering lips that are searching for words to convey the spirit and it is like speaking in another tongue, a new language with which the people are unfamiliar. Isaiah is trying to offer people a condition of rest wherewith the weary can come to a place of rest; this would be refreshing to them, if they would listen, but they would not hear; they had ears to hear but they would not listen.

The Testimony of the Major Prophets

13 But the word of the LORD was unto them precept upon precept, precept upon precept; line upon line, line upon line; here a little, and there a little; that they might go, and fall backward, and be broken, and snared, and taken.
14 Wherefore hear the word of the LORD, ye scornful men, that rule this people which is in Jerusalem.
15 Because ye have said, We have made a covenant with death, and with hell are we at agreement; when the overflowing scourge shall pass through, it shall not come unto us: for we have made lies our refuge, and under falsehood have we hid ourselves:

Isaiah has spoken the way of the LORD to them over and over again; precept upon precept; rule upon rule; line by line; here a little, there a little; teaching as clearly as he could that they might go forth in the way of the LORD, and fall backward from where they had progressed, and be broken in their lack of immediate progress, and snared back into the trap of their human nature and taken away from the way of the LORD to the ways of fallen man.

Isaiah wants the people to hear the way of the LORD that he is bringing to them and the leaders of the people of Jerusalem have received him with scorn and contempt. The leaders have said that they have made a covenant with death and they are in agreement with hell, the hellish conditions of their present environment and the inevitable conditions that are to come. They say that when the overflowing scourge, the working of the law of the LORD that will bring the results of their previous actions, when the corrective spirit of the LORD passes through, it shall not come to them because they have taken refuge in their lies that it will not happen to them and they have hidden themselves from the working of the law of the LORD in their falsehoods which state that it will not affect them.

16 Therefore thus saith the Lord GOD, Behold, I lay in Zion for a foundation a stone, a tried stone, a precious corner stone, a sure foundation: he that believeth shall not make haste.
17 Judgment also will I lay to the line, and righteousness to the plummet: and the hail shall sweep away the refuge of lies, and the waters shall overflow the hiding place.
18 And your covenant with death shall be disannulled, and your agreement with hell shall not stand; when the overflowing scourge shall pass through, then ye shall be trodden down by it.
19 From the time that it goeth forth it shall take you: for morning by morning shall it pass over, by day and by night: and it shall be a vexation only to understand the report.

The reply of the LORD God through Isaiah is, Behold, see, the LORD lays a foundation stone in Zion, a tried stone, a precious corner stone, a sure foundation who is Isaiah. He that believes the word of the LORD shall not make haste to go in some other direction. The judgment of the LORD through the working of the law shall follow the line that states the what is sown must be reaped; and righteousness will plummet if wrong behavior is expressed. The impending storms in which the hail, the symbol of cold hard truth in action, shall sweep away the refuge of lies that the people have built for themselves and the waters of truth will surely find you in your hiding place.

Your covenant with death shall be dis-annulled and your agreement with hell shall not stand; when the overflowing scourge of the working of the law that states that destructive expression shall bring destructive results, you shall not escape the working of the law and you will be trodden down by it. The law will work from the time that an expression, a behavior goes forth, it shall take you with it because you are the originator of the expression. Morning by morning the working of the law of the LORD shall pass over: it continues working day and night: it shall be a vexation to people who hear the consistent working of the law of the LORD and they understand the report of the working of the law is inevitable; and it works exactly, it fits the expression exactly.

20 For the bed is shorter than that a man can stretch himself on it: and the covering narrower than that he can wrap himself in it.
21 For the LORD shall rise up as in mount Perazim, he shall be wroth as in the valley of Gibeon, that he may do his work, his strange work; and bring to pass his act, his strange act.
22 Now therefore be ye not mockers, lest your bands be made strong: for I have heard from the Lord GOD of hosts a consumption, even determined upon the whole earth.

Isaiah wants the people to understand that the working of the law of the LORD is exact and fitting. The expression by a man produces a predictable effect based upon the nature of the expression. The result must fit the expression. A man of a certain stature in height cannot stretch himself, recline, on a bed that is shorter than he is; and the covering cannot be narrower than the man can wrap himself in; the bed and the covering that the person uses must fit the person.

The LORD shall rise up as in mount Perazim, where He broke out against the Philistines, and He shall be wroth as in the valley of Gibeon where he sent hail to demolish the Amorites to provide for the working of His law. This may appear to be strange work and a strange act to the understanding of fallen man but this is the law of the LORD. Isaiah cautions the people not to be mockers so that the bands of your beliefs do not become too strong because Isaiah has heard from the LORD God of hosts that a consumption, a destructive force, has been determined for the whole earth.

23 Give ye ear, and hear my voice; hearken, and hear my speech.
24 Doth the plowman plow all day to sow? doth he open and break the clods of his ground?
25 When he hath made plain the face thereof, doth he not cast abroad the fitches, and scatter the cummin, and cast in the principal wheat and the appointed barley and the rie in their place?
26 For his God doth instruct him to discretion, and doth teach him.
27 For the fitches are not threshed with a threshing instrument, neither is a cart wheel turned about upon the cummin; but the fitches are beaten out with a staff, and the cummin with a rod.
28 Bread corn is bruised; because he will not ever be threshing it, nor break it with the wheel of his cart, nor bruise it with his horsemen.
29 This also cometh forth from the LORD of hosts, which is wonderful in counsel, and excellent in working.

Isaiah asks the people to listen with their ears to his voice and to hear his speech. Does a plowman plow all day to sow? does he open and break the clods of his ground for no purpose? When he has leveled the surface and the land is ready for seed, does he not plant the fitches and the cummin, the vines and the seeds for condiments that he uses on his table to season his food? does he not put wheat, barley and rye in their appointed places? God has instructed man to do this and teaches him. There is a sense of fitness and rightness. The fitches of caraway seed are not threshed with a sledge, nor a grinding cart rolled over the cummin; the correct instrument is used for the harvest, such as a staff for the fitches and a rod for the cummin. Bread corn is bruised to make bread with the proper implement; not with threshing, or breaking it with a cart wheel or with his horsemen. This wisdom comes from the LORD of hosts, a wonderful counsel, who will teach man if man will let him.

CHAPTER 29

1 Woe to Ariel, to Ariel, the city where David dwelt! add ye year to year; let them kill sacrifices.
2 Yet I will distress Ariel, and there shall be heaviness and sorrow: and it shall be unto me as Ariel.
3 And I will camp against thee round about, and will lay siege against thee with a mount, and I will raise forts against thee.

Isaiah instructs his followers on the present woes that are the conditions of Ariel, which means, "lion of God", and is another name for Jerusalem. Ariel is the city where King David dwelt in times of greater glory! The expressions and the people have been added year to year to produce the woes that are the present experience. The people continue to kill sacrifices of animals as an offering to God which Isaiah stated are a stench and an abomination to the LORD. These sacrifices do nothing to change the working of the Law. The LORD, working through His Law, will continue to distress Ariel, the conditions of Jerusalem, and there shall be heaviness and sorrow because the people are filled with heaviness and sorrow. The conditions before the LORD shall be according to Ariel, the people of Jerusalem, and also the people who are the invaders of Jerusalem. The conditions are determined by the expressions that come through the people in the area including the invaders. The spirit of the LORD works through all people. The LORD will lay siege against Jerusalem through the invaders who have a mount, who have towers that they push up against the city wall so that they can fight at the same level; their strategy will also include the raising of forts against the people of Jerusalem.

4 And thou shalt be brought down, and shalt speak out of the ground, and thy speech shall be low out of the dust, and thy voice shall be, as of one that hath a familiar spirit, out of the ground, and thy speech shall whisper out of the dust.
5 Moreover the multitude of thy strangers shall be like small dust, and the multitude of the terrible ones shall be as chaff that passeth away: yea, it shall be at an instant suddenly.

The invaders shall bring down the people of Jerusalem and the defeated people shall speak out of the ground of their defeat, their speech will be low out of the dust, and their voice shall be as of one with a familiar spirit of defeat as they whisper their woes to each other. The invaders, the enemy, shall come like fine dust and settle over the people, and the multitude of the horrible ones, the horde of the invaders, shall be as chaff, as undesirable and unwanted substance, that blows in large quantities around them. This action by the invaders shall occur suddenly, in an instant.

6 Thou shalt be visited of the LORD of hosts with thunder, and with earthquake, and great noise, with storm and tempest, and the flame of devouring fire.
7 And the multitude of all the nations that fight against Ariel, even all that fight against her and her munition, and that distress her, shall be as a dream of a night vision.
8 It shall even be as when an hungry man dreameth, and, behold, he eateth; but he awaketh, and his soul is empty: or as when a thirsty man dreameth, and, behold, he drinketh; but he awaketh, and, behold, he is faint, and his soul hath appetite: so shall the multitude of all the nations be, that fight against mount Zion.

Isaiah describes the invasion of Jerusalem as being visited by the LORD of hosts with destructive results symbolized by thunder, earthquakes, great noise with storm and tempest, and the flame of devouring fire. These terrible conditions are brought to the people by the multitudes of nations that fight against Ariel, even all the invaders that fight against her, and her armaments, to produce the conditions that disturb the people shall be as a dream of a night vision. a nightmare experience. The invaders shall capture Jerusalem but they will not be satisfied.

The invaders will have an experience similar to the dream of a hungry man who eats in his dream but when he awakens, his soul, his body, mind and heart are empty and unfulfilled. Or, when a thirsty man dreams that he drinks, but upon awakening, he is still thirsty, faint for want of drink and his appetite is still in his soul. Isaiah teaches his followers that the invaders, the multitude of nations, shall not be satisfied after their fight against mount Zion. They will still hunger and thirst for more territory after the fight because the fulfillment that assuages the longing is not material; it is spiritual. Mount Zion symbolizes the treasure of the spirit that is to be experienced on earth by man.

9 Stay yourselves, and wonder; cry ye out, and cry: they are drunken, but not with wine; they stagger, but not with strong drink.
10 For the LORD hath poured out upon you the spirit of deep sleep, and hath closed your eyes: the prophets and your rulers, the seers hath he covered.

Isaiah tells his followers to stay yourselves, hold steady, and remain in the flow of the spirit of the LORD which cannot be touched, captured or defeated by material means. Isaiah's followers are to cry out that the invaders are drunken, but not with wine; they stagger, but not with strong drink. They stagger in a material darkness that is due to the absence of the light that comes from the spirit of the LORD. If a people do not have the light from the spirit, it is as though the LORD has poured upon them the spirit of a deep sleep, which closes the eyes of the invaders so that they cannot see clearly. They stagger as they go through life because they have a perceptual blindness and they cannot perceive and observe the works of the spirit. This perceptual blindness is not limited to the enemy invaders; the prophets, the seers and the rulers of Jerusalem are also covered with the same spirit of the deep sleep from the LORD which makes people function in a dream state, a state in which they cannot see the reality of the spirit of God at work on earth.

11 And the vision of all is become unto you as the words of a book that is sealed, which men deliver to one that is learned, saying, Read this, I pray thee: and he saith, I cannot; for it is sealed:
12 And the book is delivered to him that is not learned, saying, Read this, I pray thee: and he saith, I am not learned.
13 Wherefore the Lord said, Forasmuch as this people draw near me with their mouth, and with their lips do honour me, but have removed their heart far from me, and their fear toward me is taught by the precept of men:

Isaiah further states that the materialistic vision of all the people has become to them as the words of a book that is sealed, which men deliver to one that is learned saying, Read this: and he replies, I am not learned. The LORD replies that this parable is similar to the people who draw near to the LORD with their mouths and their lips pay honor to the LORD, but their hearts are far removed from the spirit of the LORD. The people will not let the spirit of the LORD pass through their hearts which would give them spiritual vision and wake them from the deep sleep. The spirit of the deep sleep from the LORD came upon the people because the spirit of the LORD could not flow through the hearts of the people who been moved away from the reception of the spirit of the LORD. The LORD is love; the fear of the LORD has been taught to the people by the precepts of men, particularly, the prophets, the rulers and the seers.

14 Therefore, behold, I will proceed to do a marvellous work among this people, even a marvellous work and a wonder: for the wisdom of their wise men shall perish, and the understanding of their prudent men shall be hid.

Isaiah's followers are instructed to observe this wonder, this marvelous work that the LORD performs among his people. Behold, look and see, the LORD whose spirit is moving through all of His people to give them life and wisdom and love, the LORD has produced the deep sleep on them so that they are not aware of His presence. The wisdom of their wise men shall perish and the understanding of their prudent men shall be hidden from them. The people have the wisdom and understanding but the internal wisdom and prudence is not available to them while they are in the dream state. The dream state is caused by a materialistic viewpoint; the awakened state is the result of spiritual vision. Isaiah and his followers are to cry loudly to wake the people who are in a dream state.

15 Woe unto them that seek deep to hide their counsel from the LORD, and their works are in the dark, and they say, Who seeth us? and who knoweth us?
16 Surely your turning of things upside down shall be esteemed as the potter's clay: for shall the work say of him that made it, He made me not? or shall the thing framed say of him that framed it, He had no understanding?

Woe is the natural result of those who seek, with deep selfish desire, to hide their counsel, the things that they know, from the purpose of the LORD. This leaves their works in the dark because they have not brought them to the light. The people who do this say, Who sees us? and Who knows us as we really are? People cannot be known if they keep their counsel from the LORD by not expressing the counsel which they have to give. They try to hide their light under a bushel and they do not let their light shine on earth where it needs to shine to eliminate the darkness of the fallen state. Surely, people can begin to see that the turning of the events of the environment upside down can be compared to the potter's clay. The clay is the material that the potter works with to produce the creation that the potter has in his consciousness. Can the object made by the potter say, He made me not? or shall the thing that was framed or formed, say of him that formed it, He had no understanding? Can the material effect be separated from the spiritual cause?

17 Is it not yet a very little while, and Lebanon shall be turned into a fruitful field, and the fruitful field shall be esteemed as a forest?
18 And in that day shall the deaf hear the words of the book, and the eyes of the blind shall see out of obscurity, and out of darkness.
19 The meek also shall increase their joy in the LORD, and the poor among men shall rejoice in the Holy One of Israel.
20 For the terrible one is brought to nought, and the scorner is consumed, and all that watch for iniquity are cut off:
21 That make a man an offender for a word, and lay a snare for him that reproveth in the gate, and turn aside the just for a thing of nought.

Is it not a very little while, and Lebanon shall be turned into a fruitful field and the fruitful field be esteemed as a forest? There is a creative process at work which is the spirit of the LORD bringing about the material forms of the earth. When people begin to see and understand that the spirit of the LORD is at work constantly on earth, then, in that day, the deaf shall hear the words of the book, and the eyes of the blind shall see out of obscurity, that which was obscured by the materialistic viewpoint, the material darkness, that shut out the spirit of the LORD from one's own conscious awareness. The spirit of the LORD was present all the time. The meek also shall increase their joy in the LORD because His presence will give them strength; and the poor among men shall rejoice in the Holy One of Israel because they will understand that the LORD has been with them all the time even though they have few possessions.

22 Therefore thus saith the LORD, who redeemed Abraham, concerning the house of Jacob, Jacob shall not now be ashamed, neither shall his face now wax pale.
23 But when he seeth his children, the work of mine hands, in the midst of him, they shall sanctify my name, and sanctify the Holy One of Jacob, and shall fear the God of Israel.
24 They also that erred in spirit shall come to understanding, and they that murmured shall learn doctrine.

Isaiah cautions his followers that the LORD who redeemed Abraham has this to say concerning the house of Jacob who also did not know that the LORD was present all along: the people who are symbolized by Jacob are not to be ashamed now that they have been made aware that the LORD has been with them always. Their faces are not to grow pale with guilt and remorse. When the people see the work of the LORD's hands in their midst, they shall sanctify the name of the LORD, and sanctify the Holy One of Jacob who became consciously known when Jacob became Israel. Jacob is the material form, Israel is spirit. The people who erred in spirit shall come to understanding and they that murmured that they did not understand shall learn the true doctrine of the LORD on earth.

CHAPTER 30

1 Woe to the rebellious children, saith the LORD, that take counsel, but not of me; and that cover with a covering, but not of my spirit, that they may add sin to sin:
2 That walk to go down into Egypt, and have not asked at my mouth; to strengthen themselves in the strength of Pharaoh, and to trust in the shadow of Egypt!
3 Therefore shall the strength of Pharaoh be your shame, and the trust in the shadow of Egypt your confusion.

The LORD speaking through Isaiah tells his followers that woe is the experience of the rebellious children that take the counsel of men in the fallen state but not the counsel of the LORD as revealed through his prophet, Isaiah; people in the fallen state cover themselves with the trappings of the material world while ignoring the spirit of the LORD. This approach adds sin to sin. A sin is accurately described as the word is used in archery: to be off-the-mark. The mark is the spiritual mark and not a material mark. The people who go down into Egypt and have not asked if the journey is fitting for the mouth, the expression of the LORD, or is the trip to strengthen themselves in the ways of Pharaoh, the symbol of the materialistic state? Is the purpose of the trip to trust in the shadow, the material possessions and orientation to the materialistic state? If this is the case, then the strength of Pharaoh, the amount of material goods which you own, can be your shame because the amount of material goods can reveal where the heart is. The trust in the material possessions, the shadow of Egypt, can be your confusion.

4 For his princes were at Zoan, and his ambassadors came to Hanes.
5 They were all ashamed of a people that could not profit them, nor be an help nor profit, but a shame, and also a reproach.

The princes of Pharaoh, the leaders of the materialistic philosophy amd control, who were at Zoan and his ambassadors came to Hanes. These cities are places where the Israelites served as slaves, where they were the material possessions of the Egyptians. The Egyptians were ashamed of a people that could not profit them, nor be a help nor a profit, to the materialistic purposes of the Egyptians. The Israelites were perceived as a shame and a reproach by the Egyptians. In contrast, the spirit of the LORD loves and flows through all people equally; everyone has a direct connection with the LORD who is the LORD of hosts of all people in the entire earth which has the potential of making all men on earth brothers because they are fathered by the omnipresent spirit of the same LORD. The materialistic approach degrades man, male and female, and treats selected groups of men and women as beasts.

6 The burden of the beasts of the south: into the land of trouble and anguish, from whence come the young and old lion, the viper and fiery flying serpent, they will carry their riches upon the shoulders of young asses, and their treasures upon the bunches of camels, to a people that shall not profit them.
7 For the Egyptians shall help in vain, and to no purpose: therefore have I cried concerning this, Their strength is to sit still.

The burden of the beasts of the south is the burden of materialism that excludes the spirit of the LORD. Egypt has been used as the symbol of the materialistic, fallen state of man but it applies to materialistic values and fallen people everywhere and in every time period. It is a land of trouble and anguish from whence comes the destructive young and old lions who symbolize the power of the fallen state of man, the viper, the symbol of the self-active mind that inflicts the poison of the fallen state, and the fiery, flying serpent that symbolizes the negative emotions which are the controls used by Egypt. These controls are used to accumulate material treasures that are carried on the asses and camels to a people that shall not profit from having them because the material treasures prevent the people from seeking the treasures of the spirit which are eternal. The Egyptians shall help the people in vain, out of their own vanity, and to no purpose other than their own self-interest. Isaiah has cried, spoken out, concerning this by saying that the strength of the Egyptian position is to sit still, do nothing, maintain the status quo because it benefits their materialistic position.

8 Now go, write it before them in a table, and note it in a book, that it may be for the time to come for ever and ever:
9 That this is a rebellious people, lying children, children that will not hear the law of the LORD:
10 Which say to the seers, See not; and to the prophets, Prophesy not unto us right things, speak unto us smooth things, prophesy deceits:
11 Get you out of the way, turn aside out of the path, cause the Holy One of Israel to cease from before us.

After Isaiah has instructed his followers about the evil of the materialistic approach as symbolized by Egypt, he tells them to go, and write it before them in a table, and note it in a book, that the message of choosing the spirit of the LORD over the treasures of the material earth shall not be lost for ever and ever. This action is an action of a rebellious people and they are in rebellion against the LORD. They are lying children who do not reveal the truth that is within them; they are children who do not hear the law of the LORD. They say to seers, See not the truth; and they tell the prophets not to prophesy right things but rather speak to us of smooth easy things that are pleasing to the ears of fallen people; continue to preach and prophesy deceits and lies. The deceitful teaching is to get out of the way of the LORD, turn aside the path of the LORD, cause the Holy One of Israel to

The Testimony of the Major Prophets

cease from being before the children of Israel. The purpose of the true teaching for people in the fallen state is so that they can repent and return to the LORD.

12 Wherefore thus saith the Holy One of Israel, Because ye despise this word, and trust in oppression and perverseness, and stay thereon:
13 Therefore this iniquity shall be to you as a breach ready to fall, swelling out in a high wall, whose breaking cometh suddenly at an instant.
14 And he shall break it as the breaking of the potters' vessel that is broken in pieces; he shall not spare: so that there shall not be found in the bursting of it a sherd to take fire from the hearth, or to take water withal out of the pit.

Wherefore, the Holy One of Israel says that because the people have despised this word from the LORD and they trust in oppression and perverseness and they stay fixed upon these methods; therefore, this iniquity shall be upon you as a break that is ready to fall, the swelling can be seen in a high wall and the break will come suddenly. The power of the working of the Law shall break the materialistic civilization as a potters vessel is broken into many pieces; the LORD shall not spare the power of the bursting of it so that not even a shard of a piece can be large enough to use to take fire from a hearth or to take water out of a pit, a well.

15 For thus saith the Lord GOD, the Holy One of Israel; In returning and rest shall ye be saved; in quietness and in confidence shall be your strength: and ye would not.
16 But ye said, No; for we will flee upon horses; therefore shall ye flee: and, We will ride upon the swift; therefore shall they that pursue you be swift.
17 One thousand shall flee at the rebuke of one; at the rebuke of five shall ye flee: till ye be left as a beacon upon the top of a mountain, and as an ensign on an hill.

Isaiah teaches that the LORD God, the Holy One of Israel shall save those who return, who rest in the flowing spirit of the LORD and who will let the spirit find expression into the earth. The person who dwells in the flowing spirit will experience a quietness and a confidence that shall be one's strength: and there were many people of Jerusalem who would not take the advice of Isaiah. They were terrified at the thought of the invasion of Jerusalem by the Assyrians. They said, No; they would flee upon horses, and they would ride the most swift; and the pursuers who follow you would be swift. In the fallen state, everything must be done quickly because materialistic people sense that they have a limited time on earth. As the invader rebukes only one of Jerusalem, a thousand inhabitants will flee. If five inhabitants of Jerusalem are rebuked, then more people will leave the city until only a remnant of those that remain will be like a beacon atop a mountain and as an ensign, a banner on a hill. The people who are willing to let the spirit of the LORD flow through them in any circumstance will be alone and isolated from the people who left the city, but the LORD will be with them.

18 And therefore will the LORD wait, that he may be gracious unto you, and therefore will he be exalted, that he may have mercy upon you: for the LORD is a God of judgment: blessed are all they that wait for him.
19 For the people shall dwell in Zion at Jerusalem: thou shalt weep no more: he will be very gracious unto thee at the voice of thy cry; when he shall hear it, he will answer thee.

20 And though the Lord give you the bread of adversity, and the water of affliction, yet shall not thy teachers be removed into a corner any more, but thine eyes shall see thy teachers:
21 And thine ears shall hear a word behind thee, saying, This is the way, walk ye in it, when ye turn to the right hand, and when ye turn to the left.

Therefore the LORD will wait, will serve, His spirit to you whose hearts are open to receive His spirit so that He will be gracious to you. The LORD will be exalted on earth through you because you have let the spirit of the LORD find expression. This is the way that the LORD has mercy upon the person who lets the spirit of the LORD flow into the earth. The LORD is a God of judgment: blessed are all they that wait for Him, that serve His spirit into the earth. The people who do this are the people who dwell in Zion at Jerusalem: these people shall weep no more. The LORD will be very generous to you at the voice of your cry because, since you are connected to the LORD in the covenant-agreement—JEHOVAH—then, when He hears your voice He will answer you because your heart is open to the LORD to receive His answer.

The external circumstances will be what they will be according to the working of the law. If the LORD gives you the bread of adversity or the water of affliction, you shall not seek out your teachers: instead, your eyes shall see your teachers: and your ears shall hear the word behind you, saying, This is the Way, the Way of the LORD, the Way that the LORD would walk in this situation or circumstance whether you walk physically to the right or physically to the left makes little difference if you walk in agreement with the spirit of the LORD. The LORD is behind you, supporting you, in every circumstance. The teachers mentioned here are symbolic for the external circumstances presented for right handling by the spirit of the LORD which is behind you. Even though one receives spiritual experience by rightly handling difficult situations, one is not to chase after the circumstance to become its apprentice.

22 Ye shall defile also the covering of thy graven images of silver, and the ornament of thy molten images of gold: thou shalt cast them away as a menstruous cloth; thou shalt say unto it, Get thee hence.
23 Then shall he give the rain of thy seed, that thou shalt sow the ground withal; and bread of the increase of the earth, and it shall be fat and plenteous: in that day shall thy cattle feed in large pastures.
24 The oxen likewise and the young asses that ear the ground shall eat clean provender, which hath been winnowed with the shovel and with the fan.
25 And there shall be upon every high mountain, and upon every high hill, rivers and streams of waters in the day of the great slaughter, when the towers fall.

A person who is in covenant-agreement with the LORD, who knows that he or she is a part of the sword of the LORD, shall defile the covering of the graven images of silver and of gold. The person who knows that he is a member of the covenant shall cast the idols and images away as he would a menstrual cloth; you shall say to these images, Get thee hence. The symbols of silver and gold are not needed when the reality of the spirit of Truth and the spirit of Love from the LORD are known to be present in the spirit that is behind you. Then shall the LORD give to you the rain of the seed of thoughts and ideas, that you shall sow into the ground around you. In that day, all of your cattle shall feed in large pastures, your actions will have large spheres of influence. The oxen

The Testimony of the Major Prophets

and the asses that are a part of the material property shall be well cared for with clean provender that has been winnowed with the shovel and the pan.

There shall be on every high mountain and every high hill, every high viewpoint, rivers and streams of water which represent the streams of consciousness and inspired ideas in the days of the great slaughter when the towers of the invader of Jerusalem fall.

26 Moreover the light of the moon shall be as the light of the sun, and the light of the sun shall be sevenfold, as the light of seven days, in the day that the LORD bindeth up the breach of his people, and healeth the stroke of their wound.
27 Behold, the name of the LORD cometh from far, burning with his anger, and the burden thereof is heavy: his lips are full of indignation, and his tongue as a devouring fire:
28 And his breath, as an overflowing stream, shall reach to the midst of the neck, to sift the nations with the sieve of vanity: and there shall be a bridle in the jaws of the people, causing them to err.

Moreover, the light of the moon, the reflected light on the people of the LORD who are turned toward Him, which is the effect of the consciousness of the LORD, shall be as the light of the sun, the symbol for the radiance of the LORD. The combination of the spirit of the LORD coming from both radiant light and reflected light shall be sevenfold, as the light of the seven days of creation when the LORD brought more Light into the earth. This is the day and the Way that the LORD binds up the breaches, the breaks, of his people, and how His spirit shall heal the stroke of the wound that the person has sustained in the service of the LORD.

Once the breach has been closed on the body of mankind through a person or people who have closed the breach, then the name of the LORD comes from afar, and the burning of the spirit of the LORD who has an open window into the earth is like a person burning with anger and the new burden in heavy. The new burden is to remove the generations of the false design which have accumulated around the window of heaven which has been closed. The LORD's lips are full of indignation and his tongue as a devouring fire to illustrate the desire to eliminate the false design. The breath of the LORD, the spirit flowing through the world of spirit into the world of form, shall reach into the midst of the neck of the body of mankind to sift the nations with the sieve of vanity to eliminate the vain and the profane from the body of the LORD. The presence of JEHOVAH shall be a bridle, a means of controlling the direction, in the jaws of the fallen people that will cause fallen man to err as he goes his materialistic way through life.

29 Ye shall have a song, as in the night when a holy solemnity is kept; and gladness of heart, as when one goeth with a pipe to come into the mountain of the LORD, to the mighty One of Israel.
30 And the LORD shall cause his glorious voice to be heard, and shall shew the lighting down of his arm, with the indignation of his anger, and with the flame of a devouring fire, with scattering, and tempest, and hailstones.
31 For through the voice of the LORD shall the Assyrian be beaten down, which smote with a rod.
32 And in every place where the grounded staff shall pass, which the LORD shall lay upon him, it shall be with tabrets and harps: and in battles of shaking will he fight with it.

The Symbolic Version of Isaiah

33 For Tophet is ordained of old; yea, for the king it is prepared; he hath made it deep and large: the pile thereof is fire and much wood; the breath of the LORD, like a stream of brimstone, doth kindle it.

The person who is a member of the sword of the LORD, of the covenant, of JEHOVAH, shall have a song, a holy song which only that person can sing on earth, in the night when a holy solemnity is kept between the LORD and His creation. The person will experience gladness of heart, as one goes with a pipe to make music by blowing on it to come into the mountain of the LORD, to the mighty one of Israel. The person has become a part of the mountain of God on earth. In the covenant agreement, the LORD shall cause His glorious voice to be heard and the power of the LORD, moving through the form of the people, can be perceived as lightning, indignation, a flame devouring the material of the false design, with scattering, tempest and hailstones.

The voice of the LORD is heard on earth as there are people who let the spirit of the LORD use their forms to create the sound as of a trumpet that can be heard on earth by others. In this manner, the Assyrian shall be smote with a rod. In every place that the grounded staff shall pass, the staff who are grounded in the spirit of the LORD, which the LORD shall lay upon a person who serves the LORD, it shall be a celebration of a victory with harps and tabrets: but in battles of shaking and rearranging the physical forms of things, the way of the LORD will fight with the designs that resist His spirit. Any material thing which resists the movement of the LORD's spirit will, in time, perish.

Tophet, a region outside of Jerusalem where children were sacrificed to Molech, a god of the Ammonites, is ordained of old and it was prepared for the king. The place of the sacrifice of the children was deep and large: the pile is made of fire and much wood; the breath of the LORD was the power that kindles the fire that made human sacrifice to kill the children. Isaiah is making the contrast between the sacrifice of a person to the spirit of the LORD which leads to everlasting life, so that the person can know and serve the LORD in and through his own physical form: and the sacrifice of the physical form as a burnt offering to Molech which leads to the death of the physical form. The true Lord wants you to have life through your human form and to have it more abundantly.

CHAPTER 31

1 Woe to them that go down to Egypt for help; and stay on horses, and trust in chariots, because they are many; and in horsemen, because they are very strong; but they look not unto the Holy One of Israel, neither seek the LORD!
2 Yet he also is wise, and will bring evil, and will not call back his words: but will arise against the house of the evildoers, and against the help of them that work iniquity.
3 Now the Egyptians are men, and not God; and their horses flesh, and not spirit. When the LORD shall stretch out his hand, both he that helpeth shall fall, and he that is holpen shall fall down, and they all shall fail together.

Isaiah tells his followers that woe is on them that go down to Egypt, to the symbol of the material state, for help. Their minds are stayed, fixed, on horses, and their trust in chariots, because they are many; their trust in horsemen, because they are strong in physical strength; but they do not look to the spirit, to the Holy One of Israel and they do not seek the LORD.

The LORD also is wise, He will bring evil, and He will not call back His words of the working of the law: but He will arise against the house of the evildoers who distort the divine design on earth: He will be against the work of those that work iniquity. The LORD cannot use people who will try to do the purpose of the LORD but utilize methods and acts of iniquity. Now, the Egyptians are men and they use the ways of men in what they build; they are not God; the horses of the Egyptians are flesh and not spirit. The LORD must use the ways of God, the spirits of love and truth, in His creation. When the LORD shall stretch out His hand, both He that has helped shall fall, and He that is holpen (past participle of helpeth) shall fall down and they all shall fall together. The LORD's design in spirit shall not hold the wrong design of form in physical manifestation. The result will be disintegrative and not integrative. The true design exists in spirit and the incorrect physical design is a distortion, a counterfeit of the true design which is destined to fall apart.

4 For thus hath the LORD spoken unto me, Like as the lion and the young lion roaring on his prey, when a multitude of shepherds is called forth against him, he will not be afraid of their voice, nor

abase himself for the noise of them: so shall the LORD of hosts come down to fight for mount Zion, and for the hill thereof.
5 As birds flying, so will the LORD of hosts defend Jerusalem; defending also he will deliver it; and passing over he will preserve it.
6 Turn ye unto him from whom the children of Israel have deeply revolted.
7 For in that day every man shall cast away his idols of silver, and his idols of gold, which your own hands have made unto you for a sin.

Isaiah says that the LORD has spoken to him with this parable. When a lion and a young lion are roaring on the prey for something that they want to eat, and a multitude of shepherds are called forth to prevent them from harming the sheep, the lions on the prey will not be turned aside by the fear of many voices of the shepherds, nor do the lions change their plans because of the noise that the shepherds make to frighten them away from the sheep. In like determination, shall the LORD of hosts come down and fight for mount Zion and for the hill of spiritual expression on earth that is being built. The LORD wants His people for creative purposes as much or more than the lions want the sheep for food to satisfy their hunger. As birds flying on high, shall the LORD of hosts hover above the people who defend Jerusalem; and while the LORD is defending Jerusalem through His people, He will also deliver it; and passing over it, He will preserve it. The LORD needs shepherds with physical bodies on earth to reveal the spirit of the LORD.

The people, who are not of the LORD by revealing His spirit in living, are called by Isaiah to turn to the LORD. The people being called are the children of Israel who have revolted and rebelled. In the day when the revolt has ended is the day that every man shall cast away his material idols of silver, and his idols of gold, which you have made with your own hands and then, worshipped your own creation, which is a sin of worshipping false gods.

8 Then shall the Assyrian fall with the sword, not of a mighty man; and the sword, not of a mean man, shall devour him: but he shall flee from the sword, and his young men shall be discomfited.
9 And he shall pass over to his strong hold for fear, and his princes shall be afraid of the ensign, saith the LORD, whose fire is in Zion, and his furnace in Jerusalem.

Isaiah tells his followers that the Assyrians who are outside the walls of Jerusalem shall fall with the sword. The sword, the spiritual sword, is not the sword of a mighty man, it is the sword of the LORD on earth, JEHOVAH. The sword is not the sword of a mean man; it is the sword of the LORD. It is by this sword that the Assyrian will fall and be devoured: The Assyrian will flee from the sword, and his young men, shall be discomfited, baffled, perplexed and bewildered by the way of the LORD. In the parable of Isaiah, the old lion is the king of Assyria and the young lions are the fighting soldiers who invaded Jerusalem. The sword of the LORD, the manifestation of JEHOVAH, is the ensign, the banner, Jehovah-nissi, whose fire is in Zion, the place of spiritual expression within the people, and his furnace is in Jerusalem, the place of material manifestation where the people dwell. This spiritual design in form is a cause of fear to the king of Assyria who will pass over, return to, his stronghold because he is fearful.

CHAPTER 32

1 Behold, a king shall reign in righteousness, and princes shall rule in judgment.

Isaiah asks his followers to behold, to visualize, that in the true state of man on earth, which is JEHOVAH or God in action on earth through man, that the focus of the LORD shall be in a king on earth who would represent the LORD. This person would re-present the spirit of the LORD in physical form where the action of spirit would be made manifest on earth so that people could observe the emotional representation, the mental representation and the physical representation in a king. This king would reign in righteousness—in right-use-ness—where the right use of the heart, mind and body of the king would re-present the LORD's spirit on earth. This king would not be an earthly king who would want the treasures of the earth for his own pleasure at the expense of others who would serve his wants or his whims. A true king would serve as a pattern, a role model, so that other people would observe and learn how to let the spirit of the LORD move through their bodies accurately.

The people who would truly learn how to do this and then actually do it would be in position to experience the covenant with the LORD. The people who experience the covenant would have the victory over the selfish desires of the human condition and they would dedicate themselves to serving the LORD's spirit on earth in the same manner that the king does in his moment-by-moment living. The people with the victory, the people who are in covenant-agreement with the LORD are the princes who shall rule over their immediate environments in true judgment. Their judgments would be true because it is the judgment of the spirit of the LORD through them. They would be a true representation of man made in the image and likeness of God because the LORD God is finding expression through them. A true man, a divine man, would be on earth.

2 And a man shall be as an hiding place from the wind, and a covert from the tempest; as rivers of water in a dry place, as the shadow of a great rock in a weary land.
3 And the eyes of them that see shall not be dim, and the ears of them that hear shall hearken.

This true man, the divine man which everyone is in spiritual identity, shall be as a hiding place from the wind of change in the physical conditions of the earth which includes the mental and the emotional distortions which are called "problems". These problems of the earth are the tempest and the true man shall be a covert, a secret hiding place of the spirit; the spiritual man is not here on earth to be a secret and do nothing. He is here to serve the LORD to his fellow man and the environment which he centers. He is to be a comfort to others which is described by Isaiah as rivers of water in a dry place to satisfy the thirst of many; and as the shadow of a great rock which will provide shade for many people in distress from the heat of the day in the weary human nature land in which they dwell. The eyes of them that see and understand the theory of the covenant shall not be dim because they will move in the direction of the covenant, and the ears of them that hear Isaiah's message shall hearken to begin to express the spirit of the LORD as made manifest through Isaiah. There is more to spiritual expression than seeing and hearing about it with the eyes and the ears. A person must take the teaching to heart.

4 The heart also of the rash shall understand knowledge, and the tongue of the stammerers shall be ready to speak plainly.

The heart of a person must get involved. This is the level of deep feeling and commitment to the expression of the spirit of the LORD which Isaiah is representing for them. A person must begin where he is and man in the fallen state is not in the true state. This means that the person's heart is filled with emotions that should not be there and the feelings that are not of the LORD's spirit must be relinquished. If these feelings are not relinquished, then the spirit of the LORD that flows through the heart, the emotional realm, will be distorted by the condition of the human heart. Isaiah calls this a rash heart. The heart of the rash, the "normal" human nature heart, that is present in the fallen state in which man finds himself, shall understand the knowledge that Isaiah is conveying to his followers.

The challenge is whether or not the person will do anything with the knowledge that Isaiah has brought to the people from the LORD. People have freedom of choice. The question for each one individually who hears the word of the LORD through the mouth and words of Isaiah is whether or not they will do what they understand. There was no fault in the people before Isaiah brought the truth of the LORD to their attention, but, once Isaiah has made them aware and given each person a choice, then the responsibility is with the person who understands how the spirit of the LORD comes into the earth through man who was created for this purpose. The true nature of man on earth is now known and offered as a choice which was not previously available. The normal, human nature person is now identified by Isaiah as a vile person.

5 The vile person shall be no more called liberal, nor the churl said to be bountiful.
6 For the vile person will speak villany, and his heart will work iniquity, to practise hypocrisy, and to utter error against the LORD, to make empty the soul of the hungry, and he will cause the drink of the thirsty to fail.
7 The instruments also of the churl are evil: he deviseth wicked devices to destroy the poor with lying words, even when the needy speaketh right.
8 But the liberal deviseth liberal things; and by liberal things shall he stand.

The Testimony of the Major Prophets

Isaiah uses the examples of a liberal and a churl to make his point with people who are trapped in the materialistic earthly state of their consciousness who have now been given a choice to serve the LORD's spirit. The vile person with a rash heart shall no more be called and labeled "liberal", and a "churl"; a churl is a low-bred surly and miserly person said to be bountiful because he has a lot of material wealth. A vile person with a rash heart will speak villainy and his impure heart will work iniquity. He will also work hypocrisy, to accuse the LORD of error in regard to the terrible conditions of the world are the fault of the LORD whom he does not know. This vile person will take away food from the hungry and be the cause that the thirsty will not get water because he withholds the spirit of the LORD that could be on earth through himself.

The instruments of the churl, the miser, the greedy low-life, are evil: he devises wicked devices, schemes, and legal documents to destroy the poor with lying words, even when the needy people speak what is right. The churl is interested and motivated by getting more material goods for himself at the expense of others. But the liberal is not guided by getting material goods for himself; he devises liberal things to give material things to people who do not have material things; the liberal will stand by the liberal things which he devises as being the right thing to do. Many times the liberal is giving away the property that belongs to someone other than himself, while he contributes only the idea and the words and refuses to give his own money and goods, which is hypocrisy. This giving and receiving of material goods locks a person into the material state and the busy activity of involvement in the matters of the earth is not expressing the spirit of the LORD into the affairs of the earth which is the LORD's. People are stuck at the earthly level of activity and Isaiah will call upon them to rise up to the level of the spirit of the LORD.
Isaiah is telling them that they are not men, made in the image and likeness of God; they are acting as people whose interest is in things. He refers to them as weaker than they should be; he refers to them as women.

9 Rise up, ye women that are at ease; hear my voice, ye careless daughters; give ear unto my speech.
10 Many days and years shall ye be troubled, ye careless women: for the vintage shall fail, the gathering shall not come.
11 Tremble, ye women that are at ease; be troubled, ye careless ones: strip you, and make you bare, and gird sackcloth upon your loins

The people who are stuck in their materialistic positions, whether miserly or liberal, are referred to as "women". This is not done to accuse them of wrong function but rather to invite them to rise up like a man and serve the LORD. The careless daughters are asked to hear the voice of Isaiah and to give ear to message that his speech is attempting to teach to them. If the people continue in the way that they are going, the way of fallen human nature, then the working of the law will bring troubled times for many days and years because the daughters of the earth have been careless with the use of the spirit of their spiritual father, the LORD. It can be expected that the vintage from the vine of life shall fail and the gathering of the harvest shall not come. It is ordained that the material way without the spirit of the LORD shall fail. It is right for the women who are presently at ease, with the material possessions they have, to tremble; it is proper that the people be troubled because they are careless with the LORD's creative spirit. The working of the law of the LORD will strip you of the earthly treasures that you have, make you bare, and you should prepare to put sackcloth on your loins to demonstrate your loss and your shame. They will lose their riches and the "good life" with which they are at ease, with which they are complacent, smug and self-satisfied. The loss of their material possessions will lead to their sadness.

12 They shall lament for the teats, for the pleasant fields, for the fruitful vine.
13 Upon the land of my people shall come up thorns and briers; yea, upon all the houses of joy in the joyous city:
14 Because the palaces shall be forsaken; the multitude of the city shall be left; the forts and towers shall be for dens for ever, a joy of wild asses, a pasture of flocks;
15 Until the spirit be poured upon us from on high, and the wilderness be a fruitful field, and the fruitful field be counted for a forest.

The people who have lost ownership of their possessions shall lament for the loss of the good life from the teats that bring forth milk, the pleasant fields that bring forth the crops and the fat cattle and the fruitful vine that brings the fruit of plenty of material things. The land of the LORD's people shall come up thorns and briers very quickly when an enemy invades the land and strips the people of their earthly treasures. Then the houses that were filled with joy and a city that was joyous can be quickly changed. The palaces shall be forgotten, the multitude of the people who lived in the city have fled, the forts and the towers will be as empty dens forever and the conditions of the land will be a joy only for wild asses and a pasture for flocks as it quickly becomes a wasteland because no one will care for the land. This condition will last until the spirit of the LORD be poured upon the people from on high. The LORD is constantly pouring His spirit from on high but the people are out of position to receive the blessing of the spirit which will change the wilderness to a fruitful field, and the fruitful field into a forest like the cedars of Lebanon.

16 Then judgment shall dwell in the wilderness, and righteousness remain in the fruitful field.
17 And the work of righteousness shall be peace; and the effect of righteousness quietness and assurance for ever.
18 And my people shall dwell in a peaceable habitation, and in sure dwellings, and in quiet resting places;
19 When it shall hail, coming down on the forest; and the city shall be low in a low place.
20 Blessed are ye that sow beside all waters, that send forth thither the feet of the ox and the ass.

Then the judgment of the law of the LORD shall dwell in the wilderness where nothing was sown or cared for, and the righteousness shall remain in the fruitful field. The work of righteousness shall be peace; the effect of righteousness shall be quietness and assurance forever. This is because the spirit of the LORD is peaceful and quiet and assured and eternal. The LORD's people shall abide in peaceful habitation, in sure dwellings and in quiet resting places because the LORD's people express the LORD's spirit and reap the results on earth. This is true even if it shall hail during difficult times, the city of Jerusalem is brought to the ground and the forest is removed.

Blessed are you that sow the spirit of the LORD through you beside all the waters, the waters that are the symbol of the truth of the spirit of the LORD Who is in every person that you encounter. Then, the seed of the LORD that you have sown will be sent forth from there through the ox and the ass—the symbols of the minds and the physical bodies, of those whom you have served—to range free in the land trusting the creative process of the LORD to work its design in the earth.

CHAPTER 33

1 Woe to thee that spoilest, and thou wast not spoiled; and dealest treacherously, and they dealt not treacherously with thee! when thou shalt cease to spoil, thou shalt be spoiled; and when thou shalt make an end to deal treacherously, they shall deal treacherously with thee.

Isaiah tells his followers that there should be woe experienced by the person who spoils the seed of the LORD, the truth of the LORD's expression, that was planted for them by a person who was in the covenant with the LORD; they were not spoiled by receiving a distortion of a wrong example. Woe to the person who deals treacherously to others by planting the wrong seeds of expression when they were not dealt the wrong seed, the seed that was not of the LORD, from others! Isaiah wants his followers to know and to understand that when they shall make an end, when they cease to deal treacherously with the people around them, then these people, the closest relatives and friends shall deal treacherously with you. A spiritually, treacherous person is one who is disloyal or traitorous to the spirit of the LORD. A person who is involved in spiritual expression is one who expresses the spirit of the LORD; a person who does not behave this way is disloyal, deceitful and traitorous. Families and friends often react negatively to the spirit of the LORD when it is expressed through a person. Families and friends often choose the "comfort" of the familiar, distorted expression rather than accept the newness of spiritual expression.

2 O LORD, be gracious unto us; we have waited for thee: be thou their arm every morning, our salvation also in the time of trouble.
3 At the noise of the tumult the people fled; at the lifting up of thyself the nations were scattered.
4 And your spoil shall be gathered like the gathering of the caterpiller: as the running to and fro of locusts shall he run upon them.
5 The LORD is exalted; for he dwelleth on high: he hath filled Zion with judgment and righteousness.

Isaiah calls upon the spirit of the LORD, as it is coming out of his followers, to be gracious to the body of people who are seeing and hearing the word of the LORD for the first time. We have been served the spirit of the LORD by others and we serve the spirit of the LORD to others. Isaiah calls on the spirit to be their arm, their power every morning and their salvation in time of trouble. This particular time in Jerusalem was a time of trouble. At the noise of the tumult, the chaos and the disturbance of the invasion, the people fled; at the lifting up of thyself, as the spirit of the LORD began to intensify through many people, the nations were scattered. And your spoil, the spoil of the LORD, shall be gathered like the gathering of a caterpillar in the process of being transformed into a butterfly: or, as the running of locusts, the invaders swarm over the property of Jerusalem and pounce on it. The LORD is at work through all of His people. The LORD is exalted by the changes in the fallen state of the earth. The LORD dwells on high: He has filled Zion, the spiritual place, with judgment and righteousness and the effects of judgment and righteousness shall be made manifest in the earth.

6 And wisdom and knowledge shall be the stability of thy times, and strength of salvation: the fear of the LORD is his treasure.
7 Behold, their valiant ones shall cry without: the ambassadors of peace shall weep bitterly.
8 The highways lie waste, the wayfaring man ceaseth: he hath broken the covenant, he hath despised the cities, he regardeth no man.
9 The earth mourneth and languisheth: Lebanon is ashamed and hewn down: Sharon is like a wilderness; and Bashan and Carmel shake off their fruits.

The wisdom and the knowledge of the spirit of the LORD shall be the stability of the times and the circumstances in which people must live and the strength of their salvation: the fear, the awesome power, of the LORD is His treasure. During these times of distress, behold and see that the valiant ones of the people, who are not identified with the spirit, shall cry and wail without their earthly possessions; and the ambassadors of peace shall weep bitterly because there is no peace. The impending invasion of Jerusalem is taking its toll. Highways lie in waste and they are deserted, and there are no travelers on the roads; the invader has broken the covenant of the LORD which is the way of peace, and he has despised the cities where the people lived; he regards no man as having any worth, let alone the repository of the spirit of the LORD.

The result of the invasion by the Assyrians and the lack of leadership by the people of Judah and Israel is that the earth around Jerusalem mourns and languishes: Lebanon is ashamed and its tall cedars are hewn down: Sharon, the beautiful plain along the coast north of Joppa known for its beautiful foliage and superb grazing land, is like a wilderness; and Bashan and Carmel, prosperous cities of renown, have had the fruits of their cities shaken away from them by the invaders. What is the view of the LORD, which should also be the view of His people, during this time of impending defeat for Jerusalem as the Assyrians are at the gates of the city?

10 Now will I rise, saith the LORD; now will I be exalted; now will I lift up myself.
11 Ye shall conceive chaff, ye shall bring forth stubble: your breath, as fire, shall devour you.
12 And the people shall be as the burnings of lime: as thorns cut up shall they be burned in the fire.
13 Hear, ye that are far off, what I have done; and, ye that are near, acknowledge my might.

The LORD is not upset or disturbed by the defeat of Jerusalem and the loss of the treasures from the surrounding cities. The LORD's position is that now He is exalted and He will lift himself up.

The Testimony of the Major Prophets

The people who remain in the city to hear the word of the LORD are told that they will conceive as chaff, bring forth stubble: the breath of your expressions shall devour you. The people shall be as the burning of lime that causes the eyes to tear and water: as thorns cut up and burned in the fire they shall be burned up and removed. The LORD wants the people from far off to hear and to know what He has done; and you, who are near and close by, to acknowledge the might of the LORD through all people and not just to the inhabitants of the invaded lands. The LORD wants the people to know that they will reap what behavior they have sown.

14 The sinners in Zion are afraid; fearfulness hath surprised the hypocrites. Who among us shall dwell with the devouring fire? who among us shall dwell with everlasting burnings?
15 He that walketh righteously, and speaketh uprightly; he that despiseth the gain of oppressions, that shaketh his hands from holding of bribes, that stoppeth his ears from hearing of blood, and shutteth his eyes from seeing evil;
16 He shall dwell on high: his place of defence shall be the munitions of rocks: bread shall be given him; his waters shall be sure.

The sinners who are in Zion are afraid because they have been the closest to the followers of Isaiah; fear has come upon the hypocrites in this day of divine retribution. The question of the people is, Who among us shall dwell in the devouring fire of the LORD that has been manifest through the invaders? and who among us shall dwell with everlasting burning of the spirit of the LORD moving through the consciousness of the people who did not choose the Way of the LORD?

The obvious answer is those who repent and allow the spirit of the LORD to find expression through themselves. They would be the ones who walk righteously, walk in the Way so that the spirit of the LORD can manifest in the affairs of men, and speak uprightly, so that they can influence others to follow the Way of the LORD. He that despises the gains that are made by oppressing other people, that will shake his hands away from the taking and the holding of bribes, that stops his ears from hearing of blood, and shuts his eyes from seeing evil. These are some of the characteristics of a person who has repented and desires to dwell on high, on the plane of spiritual expression: his place of defense shall be the munitions of rocks, not rocks to be thrown, but the spiritual rocks that are available to stand upon in the high place of the spirit: The bread of Life from the LORD shall be given to the person who dwells in the high place and his water, the water of truth, to drink shall be sure; he shall not hunger or thirst in the high place of spiritual orientation to which he has been called during times of adversity.

17 Thine eyes shall see the king in his beauty: they shall behold the land that is very far off.
18 Thine heart shall meditate terror. Where is the scribe? where is the receiver? where is he that counted the towers?
19 Thou shalt not see a fierce people, a people of a deeper speech than thou canst perceive; of a stammering tongue, that thou canst not understand.

The people who accept the invitation to rise up shall see the King in His beauty: they shall behold the land that is very far off, which means that they shall be able to see the long range results of the seeds of the spirit that they shall be planting. In your own heart, you shall meditate on the terror of your former earthly orientation by asking many questions about the former state and the people

The Symbolic Version of Isaiah

who held positions of power in the old system. Where is the scribe who recorded all the activity of the fallen state? where is the receiver of the revenue that was collected? where is he that was the officer in charge of defense and the towers to protect Jerusalem?

In this new land of spiritual orientation, you shall not see a fierce people who are involved in the ferocity of physical combat, a people of a deeper speech that you can perceive, you will be able to understand them; you will not have to listen to people of stammering tongues that you cannot understand because you will understand what they say. Each person is invited to observe and see the new position of spiritual expression, the high place in one's consciousness.

20 Look upon Zion, the city of our solemnities: thine eyes shall see Jerusalem a quiet habitation, a tabernacle that shall not be taken down; not one of the stakes thereof shall ever be removed, neither shall any of the cords thereof be broken.
21 But there the glorious LORD will be unto us a place of broad rivers and streams; wherein shall go no galley with oars, neither shall gallant ship pass thereby.
22 For the LORD is our judge, the LORD is our lawgiver, the LORD is our king; he will save us.
23 Thy tacklings are loosed; they could not well strengthen their mast, they could not spread the sail: then is the prey of a great spoil divided; the lame take the prey.

Look upon Zion, the city of solemnities, the festivals, where we give our solemn service to the LORD that is a celebration: your eyes shall see Jerusalem, the holy city, as a quiet habitation, a tabernacle that shall not be taken down and moved as was the portable tabernacle of the children of Israel in the desert; there is no need to ever remove any of its stakes and neither shall any of the cords be broken because there are no stakes and there are no cords. The city and its surrounding territory is the tabernacle that can be seen with your new vision.

There on this physical ground, the LORD will be unto us a place for broad rivers and streams and there is no need to have a moving ship and a galley with oars that the people must labor to keep it moving and afloat. In this city, the LORD is our judge, lawmaker and King. He is with us always and He will save us. There is no need to sail away to anyplace else. The tackling, the ropes and the rigging, are loosed because they will not be needed. There is no need to strengthen the mast, the occupants of this ship cannot spread the sail to go anywhere that the wind will blow. Jerusalem is home! The inhabitants of the city are home! Then is the prey of the city of Jerusalem divided as a great spoil among Isaiah and his followers after the invasion; the remaining occupants of the city have raised the banner of spiritual awareness, Jehovah-nissi, the LORD our banner. These remaining people who did not flee, the people who are perceived as lame, who trusted in the LORD and will keep the law of the LORD in their living, take the prey, they take **spiritual** possession of the city of Jerusalem. They will let the spirit of the LORD flow through them into the city and let the devastated city become the Holy City, New Jerusalem.

24 And the inhabitant shall not say, I am sick: the people that dwell therein shall be forgiven their iniquity.

The inhabitant of this Holy City is a spiritual inhabitant, an inhabitant whose spirit is the spirit of the LORD. This person shall not say, I am sick. The spiritual people who dwell in the spirit shall be forgiven their previous iniquity. The iniquity was associated with their material bodies which is the clothing of the spirit. Spirit does not get ill or sick. Spirit is well and eternal. Spirit does not say, "I am sick". The spirit says, "I AM". I am an inhabitant of the spiritual city, the Holy City, New Jerusalem. The reference to sickness has application to the human container. The people who dwell within the spirit that is in the container shall be forgiven of all their iniquity.

CHAPTER 34

1 Come near, ye nations, to hear; and hearken, ye people: let the earth hear, and all that is therein; the world, and all things that come forth of it.
2 For the indignation of the LORD is upon all nations, and his fury upon all their armies: he hath utterly destroyed them, he hath delivered them to the slaughter.
3 Their slain also shall be cast out, and their stink shall come up out of their carcases, and the mountains shall be melted with their blood.

Isaiah (by reason of his presence) has established Jerusalem as the spiritual center from which the sword of the LORD, Jehovah, the manifestation of a body of people would reveal the spirit of the LORD in their living. He has offered the vision of a heavenly kingdom to be built by the spirit of the LORD through his followers in Jerusalem. Now he is opening the doors for others to respond to his call to be a part of the New Jerusalem which will be built by the spirit of the LORD through people. Isaiah issues the call for people of all nations to come near, near to the spirit of the LORD that he brings into material focus and hear what he has to say. His vision is to let the earth hear, all the people on earth who will respond to His invitation, let the world and all things that come forth from it, come to him.

Isaiah's message is that the indignation, the anger of the LORD, the destructive cycle of the LORD's power is upon all nations, and His fury is upon their armies: the power of the LORD utilized and applied improperly on earth has utterly destroyed the nations who have used the LORD's power to deliver them to their slaughter, their elimination. In this manner, the slain people who are not true to the LORD's spirit shall be cast out of physical form, and the stench of the disintegration of their bodies shall come up out of their carcases and the mountains shall be melted, soaked, with their blood.

4 And all the host of heaven shall be dissolved, and the heavens shall be rolled together as a scroll: and all their host shall fall down, as the leaf falleth off from the vine, and as a falling fig from the fig tree.

The Testimony of the Major Prophets

5 For my sword shall be bathed in heaven: behold, it shall come down upon Idumea, and upon the people of my curse, to judgment.
6 The sword of the LORD is filled with blood, it is made fat with fatness, and with the blood of lambs and goats, with the fat of the kidneys of rams: for the LORD hath a sacrifice in Bozrah, and a great slaughter in the land of Idumea.

The hosts of heaven are the material forms of the spiritual people on earth who came from heaven. The physical forms of the spirits or beings shall be dissolved, disintegrated and turned to dust, and the heaven, the spiritual substance of the people shall be rolled together as a scroll; they will be preserved. The host of them, the physical coverings of them, shall fall down as a leaf falls off the vine of life and as the fig falls from the fig tree which can produce more figs in another season. The spirit is preserved but the form disintegrates into a new form that can be used again in the creative process.

The sword of the LORD, Jehovah, the people who carry the spirit of the covenant, shall be bathed, made clean, in heaven. The sword, the people who are the LORD's instrument, shall come down upon Idumea, Edom, the land which lies southeast of Jerusalem, and upon the people who dwell there and who do not reveal the spirit of the LORD in their living, will be brought to judgment, the judgment of the working of the law. The sword of truth through the LORD's people will be an example to the people of Idumea. If the people of Idumea do not reveal the blessing of the LORD through their actions and behaviors, then they must experience the curse of the LORD. Blessing or curse, the power is from the LORD but the experience of blessing or cursing from the LORD's power is determined by the individual or the group.

The sword of the LORD, the right use of the LORD's power which is embodied in the word, Jehovah, is filled with life-giving rich blood, which has a prosperous effect on earth. This is symbolized by the growth of everything that is it is made fat with fatness, and with the blood of lambs and goats, with the fat of the kidneys of rams. An example of this creative use of the power of the LORD is the sacrifice in Bozrah. Sacrifice, in its true interpretation, is the creative process which means, "to make sacred", to reveal the sacred use of the power of the LORD. The correct use of the power of the LORD can be seen in Bozrah, a city 25 miles from the Dead Sea that is known as a great sheep-herding center. The misuse of the power of the LORD, the destructive process, is symbolized by the day of the great slaughter in the land of Idumea, the land of Edom. The experience of the people is directly proportional to the presence of the spirit of the LORD, or the absence of the true spirit, which is expressed by them.

7 And the unicorns shall come down with them, and the bullocks with the bulls; and their land shall be soaked with blood, and their dust made fat with fatness.
8 For it is the day of the LORD's vengeance, and the year of recompences for the controversy of Zion.
9 And the streams thereof shall be turned into pitch, and the dust thereof into brimstone, and the land thereof shall become burning pitch.
10 It shall not be quenched night nor day; the smoke thereof shall go up for ever: from generation to generation it shall lie waste; none shall pass through it for ever and ever.

When the unicorns, the mystical symbol of the animal with one horn that is pointed in single-minded service to the LORD, shall come down with the people who represent Jehovah, then prosperity is produced in the land by the correct use of the spirit of the LORD. The creative process is illustrated by the bullocks who will father more cattle, the flow of the blood of life in the land and the dust that is made fat with living things. But the power can also be used destructively!

When the power is used incorrectly for self-centered instead of God-centered purposes, then it is the day of the LORD's vengeance and the year of recompense, just payment and retribution for the controversy of Zion. The controversy of Zion always has application as to whether the people will use the power of spiritual expression in a true or a counterfeit application. The counterfeit, distorted application of the power causes the flow of the streams of the power of the LORD to turn into pitch, and the dust into brimstone. Pitch is a sticky substance and brimstone is a special earth with a distinctive unpleasant odor of sulfur. When the land becomes covered, symbolically, with burning pitch, the conditions of hell are inevitable. It shall not be quenched night or day; it is a continuous action. The smoke from the destructive process shall go up for ever. This condition shall go on for generation to generation as the land lies in waste; none shall pass through it forever and ever. The conditions on the surface of the land shall be unpleasant because of the actions and the behaviors of the people which are produced by the state of consciousness of the people who dwell there. The evil thoughts in the consciousness are symbolized by birds.

11 But the cormorant and the bittern shall possess it; the owl also and the raven shall dwell in it: and he shall stretch out upon it the line of confusion, and the stones of emptiness.

The cormorant and the bittern, birds of a greedy and rapacious nature, shall possess the consciousness; the owl who sees clearly and hunts in the night shall be there and the raven who eats carrion, the dead and decaying flesh, shall dwell in the land filled with circumstances produced by the fallen consciousness of man: and man, by his actions, shall stretch out the "birds", the symbols of the evil thoughts in his consciousness, to produce the line of confusion and the stones of emptiness that manifest on earth in the minds and hearts of people.

12 They shall call the nobles thereof to the kingdom, but none shall be there, and all her princes shall be nothing.
13 And thorns shall come up in her palaces, nettles and brambles in the fortresses thereof: and it shall be an habitation of dragons, and a court for owls.
14 The wild beasts of the desert shall also meet with the wild beasts of the island, and the satyr shall cry to his fellow; the screech owl also shall rest there, and find for herself a place of rest.
15 There shall the great owl make her nest, and lay, and hatch, and gather under her shadow: there shall the vultures also be gathered, every one with her mate.

The self-active fallen state with its hellish conditions shall call nobles to their kingdom, but no truly noble leader will respond to the call to the distorted state. The princes of the fallen state shall be as nothing if they are not being the representative of the LORD. Isaiah has called the truly noble people to become part of the sword and they have responded to his call. The environment of the fallen state covered with thorns that inflict pain that come up and grow in their palaces, while nettles and brambles grow in the fortresses that are built to protect this unholy land; it shall be a

The Testimony of the Major Prophets

habitation for dragons, which symbolize destructive people, and a court for owls, whose eyes are open wide in the night, where the nocturnal hunters search for their prey.

Harmonious life is impossible in the fallen state. Isaiah continues to link the behavior of the fallen people, the fallen angels, to wild beasts whether they live in the desert or on the island, they are all beasts. The satyr, the mythological figure of half-man and half-beast who plays his pipes of the expression of his music, shall cry out to his fellows to join him in the revelry; the screech owl shall make his unpleasant voice heard in the land and she will find rest in a darkened land such as this. This is the land that the great "wise" owl, the leader of the fallen state shall make her nest, and lay eggs to reproduce herself, hatch the eggs to be just like their mother, gather them under her shadow and watch them grow as they are made in the image and likeness of the mother who gave birth to these creatures. The vultures shall also be gathered, with their mates, here in this land where they shall produce more vultures who survive on the dead things of the fallen state of man. Is there any hope for the fallen state?

16 Seek ye out of the book of the LORD, and read: no one of these shall fail, none shall want her mate: for my mouth it hath commanded, and his spirit it hath gathered them.
17 And he hath cast the lot for them, and his hand hath divided it unto them by line: they shall possess it for ever, from generation to generation shall they dwell therein.

The only answer for the people, the "birds", who are in the fallen state is to seek out the book of the LORD, the person who is the living book of the LORD on earth, and read what he has to say! Isaiah writes that all people should be who they really are: man not destructive birds. No one of the people who are a part of the sword, Jehovah, shall fail, and none shall want her mate more than the LORD. It is the LORD who has commanded the mouth of Isaiah to issue the call to the people in the fallen state and it is the LORD's spirit who gathers them.

The LORD has cast the lot for His people by giving them a choice, and the LORD has divided them by a line that reveals their choice. Whatever choice they make, the Risen State or the fallen state, they shall possess it for ever, from generation to generation. They shall dwell in the choice which they have made for themselves. Presently, the people in the nations are in the fallen state; Isaiah offers them the opportunity, the choice, to step over the line and join him in being a member of the sword of the truth of the LORD, Jehovah, the covenant-agreement between man and the LORD. Any place that a member of the body of Jehovah happens to be on earth will be blessed by reason of his or her presence because they release the spirit of the LORD into their environments on a moment-by-moment basis. This contribution does not seem to be very much of an offering to the fallen human mind, but the fallen human mind has produced all of the distorted conditions on earth.

CHAPTER 35

1 The wilderness and the solitary place shall be glad for them; and the desert shall rejoice, and blossom as the rose.
2 It shall blossom abundantly, and rejoice even with joy and singing: the glory of Lebanon shall be given unto it, the excellency of Carmel and Sharon, they shall see the glory of the LORD, and the excellency of our God.

Isaiah states that the wilderness and the solitary place shall be glad for them, the members of the body of Jehovah, to be in the area where they will release the spirit of the LORD into the earth; and the desert, the place where there is an absence of the fruit of the land, shall rejoice when someone is present to inject the creative spirit into those dry circumstances. The release of the spirit into the environment will cause the area to blossom as the rose, a thing of beauty; the area will be more beautiful and have a pleasing odor.

The symbolic desert, the area where the spirit of the LORD has been absent, shall blossom abundantly when the spirit of the LORD puts in an appearance once again. The people in that area can rejoice with joy and singing if they choose to harmonize with the song of the LORD that is coming forth from someone in their area. The working of the law of the LORD, the reaping will be in proportion to that which is sown, shall produce desirable results such as the glory of Lebanon, and the excellency of Carmel and Sharon. These three cities are renowned for their beautiful trees and foliage in manifest form on earth. The people who truly observe can see the glory of the LORD and the excellency of God as these qualities are released by man who is in harmony with the spirit within him. What is the message for those people who are not skilled at radiating or revealing the spirit of the LORD into the human circumstances which reveal a distorted design?

3 Strengthen ye the weak hands, and confirm the feeble knees.
4 Say to them that are of a fearful heart, Be strong, fear not: behold, your God will come with vengeance, even God with a recompence; he will come and save you.

The Testimony of the Major Prophets

The people who state that they are not able to release the spirit of the LORD into the earth are the very ones who need to choose to do this great service for the LORD; all that they need is the desire and some practice. The release of the nature of spirit is the true nature of everyone on earth. The ability to release true nature already exists in the spirit. It is the physical form which needs some practice. The practice of positive spiritual expression of the spirit of the LORD is the exercise that strengthens the weak hands so that they will mature into steady hands with increased control. It is practice which will confirm whether the person has feeble knees, whether or not the person is weak-kneed.

Isaiah tells the people, who have these feelings of inadequacy that bring fear to the heart of a person, to be strong, and to fear not the circumstances in which a person finds one's self. The fearful heart should acknowledge the feeling of fear as being present: but, the person should behold, hold steady and see, your God will come with a vengeance, a retaliation, against the fallen conditions of the world to make a restitution for the distortions that have taken hold. God will deliver a recompense, a payment, **through you** only as the spirit of God flows through you. Trust that the spirit of God will come and save you from your fear as you allow the spirit of God to flow into your world. The flow of spirit will produce results.

5 Then the eyes of the blind shall be opened, and the ears of the deaf shall be unstopped.
6 Then shall the lame man leap as an hart, and the tongue of the dumb sing: for in the wilderness shall waters break out, and streams in the desert.

The eyes of the blind, (your eyes) shall be opened, and the ears of the deaf, (your ears) shall be unstopped and you shall be able to see and hear more clearly than you have ever seen or heard before. The person who was lame, who was unable to walk because of a fearful heart shall leap as a hart, a male deer, as the spirit moves through the physical form. The tongue of the dumb, the tongue of a person who was dumb because of a fearful heart, shall begin to sing. The person, who is redeemed of the spirit of the LORD as the spirit flows through his capacities of expression, is excited and more alive as the waters of the truth of being break out into the wilderness around that person. The increased release of the spirit of the LORD shall produce streams in the desert, not physical water, but streams of the spirit of truth from the LORD that have been absent for generations.

7 And the parched ground shall become a pool, and the thirsty land springs of water: in the habitation of dragons, where each lay, shall be grass with reeds and rushes.
8 And an highway shall be there, and a way, and it shall be called The way of holiness; the unclean shall not pass over it; but it shall be for those: the wayfaring men, though fools, shall not err therein.
9 No lion shall be there, nor any ravenous beast shall go up thereon, it shall not be found there; but the redeemed shall walk there:

The result of the increased flow from the LORD through a person, who allows the process to occur because he or she is a member of the covenant, shall convert the parched ground into a pool, and the thirsty land shall be filled with springs of spiritual substance that flow like water. In the habitation of dragons, in the depths of the heart, in the sub-conscious levels of the mind, the dragons breathe the fire, the hot, negative feelings of the heart such as fear, anger, hatred, jealousy, resentment, etc., which are not the feelings of a LORD of Love. There shall be a change of heart as this area is watered by the activity of the movement of the truth which will change the appearance from a habitation of dragons to be as one which is filled with growing reeds and rushes that have a useful purpose.

There shall be a new highway in the heart, and there is a way to get to this highway that the person will walk as a representative of the LORD. It is a new way, a **high** way, and it shall be called, **The way of holiness.** Since it is a way of holiness, the unclean shall not pass over it; but it shall be there for those who choose to walk in the way of holiness: the wayfaring men, though perceived by their peers as fools, shall not make a mistake, or err, by walking in the way of holiness. No lion, no destructive person, shall be on the way of holiness, nor any ravenous beast, any person with ravenous or beastly characteristics, shall be found there on the clean road to holiness unto the LORD. Only the redeemed of the LORD shall walk in this "secret" place, which is only a secret to those who are unclean and who intend to remain exactly the way they are. These people are not willing to repent. They make a conscious choice.

10 And the ransomed of the LORD shall return, and come to Zion with songs and everlasting joy upon their heads: they shall obtain joy and gladness, and sorrow and sighing shall flee away.

The people who are willing to repent and to walk in the way of holiness to the LORD shall return to the true way of walking on earth as man made in the image and likeness of God, which is man's true nature. If a person is behaving as a counterfeit of the truth that he or she really is, then it is only necessary to let go of the "only human" counterfeit, and to be the truth of one's real self. A person can not find the true self; but a person can be his or her true self. This is the way to come to Zion, the high place of spiritual consciousness, which is a place within one's outer self. Many people can and do literally scale Mount Zion with their unclean hearts and nothing will happen as a result of the physical journey. Mount Zion is a symbol of the holy place which exists within one's outer material self where the true self resides. Mount Zion is a place to be entered into, and, the way in, is the way of spiritual expression, the way of the expression of the spirit of the LORD through the heart, mind and body of one's outer self.

The return to Zion is a return to the place of the covenant-agreement with the LORD, where Jehovah is known. The people who experience the way of holiness come to Zion with songs in their heart and everlasting joy upon their heads. The conscious mind in their heads are aware of the covenant with the LORD and these people are truly the sons of the covenant, the B'nai B'rith, which is a living spiritual organism of a spiritual vine and its spiritual branches, and not a physical organization. These are the people who shall experience joy and gladness unspeakable on earth and the experience of the covenant shall cause the sorrow and sighing to flee away from a son of the covenant of the LORD, male or female.

CHAPTER 36

1 Now it came to pass in the fourteenth year of king Hezekiah, that Sennacherib king of Assyria came up against all the defenced cities of Judah, and took them.
2 And the king of Assyria sent Rabshakeh from Lachish to Jerusalem unto king Hezekiah with a great army. And he stood by the conduit of the upper pool in the highway of the fuller's field.
3 Then came forth unto him Eliakim, Hilkiah's son, which was over the house, and Shebna the scribe, and Joah, Asaph's son, the recorder.

Isaiah gives his readers more details of the invasion and the conquest of Judah. It came to pass in the 14th year of the reign of King Hezekiah in 701 B.C., that Sennacherib, King of Assyria came up against all the defended, fortified cities of Judah and he conquered them. The King of Assyria sent Rabshakeh, his field commander, from Lachish, an important city about 30 miles southwest of Jerusalem to King Hezekiah with a great army which stood by the conduit, the aqueduct, of the upper pool of water in the highway of the fuller's field, the place where clothes were washed in the running water and dried in the sun. The control of water in a desert country is an important strategy of battle. Three people came forth from Jerusalem to speak to Rabshakeh, the leader of the opposing great army from Assyria: they were Eliakim, the palace executive; Shebna, the scribe; and Joah, Asaph's son, the recorder.

4 And Rabshakeh said unto them, Say ye now to Hezekiah, Thus saith the great king, the king of Assyria, What confidence is this wherein thou trustest?
5 I say, sayest thou, (but they are but vain words) I have counsel and strength for war: now on whom dost thou trust, that thou rebellest against me?
6 Lo, thou trustest in the staff of this broken reed, on Egypt; whereon if a man lean, it will go into his hand, and pierce it: so is Pharaoh king of Egypt to all that trust in him.
7 But if thou say to me, We trust in the LORD our God: is it not he, whose high places and whose altars Hezekiah hath taken away, and said to Judah and to Jerusalem, Ye shall worship before this altar?
8 Now therefore give pledges, I pray thee, to my master the king of Assyria, and I will give thee two thousand horses, if thou be able on thy part to set riders upon them.

9 How then wilt thou turn away the face of one captain of the least of my master's servants, and put thy trust on Egypt for chariots and for horsemen?
10 And am I now come up without the LORD against this land to destroy it? the LORD said unto me, Go up against this land, and destroy it.

Rabshakeh has a message for the three envoys to take to King Hezekiah from his king, the great king of Assyria, which begins with a question: You act confidently but on what are you basing this confidence of yours? Hezekiah says that he has the strategy and military strength but he speaks vain and empty words. On whom do you put your trust, Hezekiah that you rebel against me? You have put your trust in Egypt, which is like a an undependable staff of a broken reed led by a weak Pharaoh that will not keep his word. (Hezekiah, king of Judah, had an alliance and a promise of help from Egypt against an attack by the Assyrians.) Rabshekah belittles the alliance of Judah with Egypt. If Hezekiah says that he trusts in the LORD, then, was it not Hezekiah who ordered the altars taken away and who told the people of Jerusalem and Judah that they must worship Hezekiah, the king? Hezekiah is asked to make a bargain with the king of Assyria who is willing to give him 2,000 horses if Hezekiah is able to do his part to set riders on them. (Hezekiah is offered an alliance with Assyria!) How will Hezekiah turn away one captain from Assyria who is on the outskirts of Jerusalem, (the least of his master's servants), and continue to put his trust in Egypt for chariots and for horsemen? Finally, the message to Hezekiah is, has Assyria come to destroy this land of Judah without the LORD's help? It is the LORD who has said to the king of Assyria, Go up against the land of Judah and destroy it! Assyria claims to be on a divine mission and the LORD is on their side.

11 Then said Eliakim and Shebna and Joah unto Rabshakeh, Speak, I pray thee, unto thy servants in the Syrian language; for we understand it: and speak not to us in the Jews' language, in the ears of the people that are on the wall.
12 But Rabshakeh said, Hath my master sent me to thy master and to thee to speak these words? hath he not sent me to the men that sit upon the wall, that they may eat their own dung, and drink their own piss with you?

The three envoys, Eliakim and Shebna and Joah, asked Rabshakeh, the field commander of the Assyrian army to speak to his servants in Aramaic, the Syrian language, because the envoys understand it: they also requested that Rabshakeh not speak to them in Hebrew, the Jews' language, in the ears of the people that are on the wall. The envoys did not want their own people on the wall to hear the details of the negotiations. But Rabshakeh did not heed their request. He wants the Hebrew people to hear his offer and be demoralized.

13 Then Rabshakeh stood, and cried with a loud voice in the Jews' language, and said, Hear ye the words of the great king, the king of Assyria.
14 Thus saith the king, Let not Hezekiah deceive you: for he shall not be able to deliver you.
15 Neither let Hezekiah make you trust in the LORD, saying, The LORD will surely deliver us: this city shall not be delivered into the hand of the king of Assyria.
16 Hearken not to Hezekiah: for thus saith the king of Assyria, Make an agreement with me by a present, and come out to me: and eat ye every one of his vine, and every one of his fig tree, and drink ye every one the waters of his own cistern;

The Testimony of the Major Prophets

17 Until I come and take you away to a land like your own land, a land of corn and wine, a land of bread and vineyards.

Then Rabshakeh stood, and cried with a loud voice in the Jews' language, and said, Hear the words of the great king of Assyria. Let not Hezekiah deceive you: for he shall not be able to deliver you. Neither let Hezekiah make you trust in the LORD, saying, The LORD will surely deliver us: this city shall not be delivered into the hand of the king of Assyria. Do not listen to Hezekiah: Hear the offer of the king of Assyria: Make an agreement with Assyria and you will receive your own vine, fig tree, and water from his own cistern; the people will be taken away to a land of corn and wine, a land of bread and vineyards.

18 Beware lest Hezekiah persuade you, saying, The LORD will deliver us. Hath any of the gods of the nations delivered his land out of the hand of the king of Assyria?
19 Where are the gods of Hamath and Arphad? where are the gods of Sepharvaim? and have they delivered Samaria out of my hand?
20 Who are they among all the gods of these lands, that have delivered their land out of my hand, that the LORD should deliver Jerusalem out of my hand?
21 But they held their peace, and answered him not a word: for the king's commandment was, saying, Answer him not.

Do not let Hezekiah persuade you, saying, that the LORD will deliver you. Has any god of any nation delivered his land out of the hand of the king of Assyria? Where are the gods of Hamath and Arphad, the defeated cities in Syria? where are the gods of Sepharvaim, another fallen city? and have they delivered Samaria out of the hand of Assyria? Who are they among all the gods of these lands, that have delivered their land out of my hand, that the LORD should deliver Jerusalem out of my hand? But the people on the wall held their peace, and answered him not a word: for the king's command was for the people not to answer the Assyrian commander who was attempting to demoralize the people of the city.

22 Then came Eliakim, the son of Hilkiah, that was over the household, and Shebna the scribe, and Joah, the son of Asaph, the recorder, to Hezekiah with their clothes rent, and told him the words of Rabshakeh.

The three envoys of king Hezekiah, returned with their clothes torn, as a symbol of the bad news that they carried from Rabshakeh, the wily field commander of Sennacherib, king of Assyria.

CHAPTER 37

1 And it came to pass, when king Hezekiah heard it, that he rent his clothes, and covered himself with sackcloth, and went into the house of the LORD.
2 And he sent Eliakim, who was over the household, and Shebna the scribe, and the elders of the priests covered with sackcloth, unto Isaiah the prophet the son of Amoz.
3 And they said unto him, Thus saith Hezekiah, This day is a day of trouble, and of rebuke, and of blasphemy: for the children are come to the birth, and there is not strength to bring forth.
4 It may be the LORD thy God will hear the words of Rabshakeh, whom the king of Assyria his master hath sent to reproach the living God, and will reprove the words which the LORD thy God hath heard: wherefore lift up thy prayer for the remnant that is left.
5 So the servants of king Hezekiah came to Isaiah.

When King Hezekiah heard the report of the Assyrian field commander from his three envoys, he tore his clothes and covered himself with sackcloth to demonstrate his sadness and sorrow. He went into the house of the LORD to seek help from the LORD in his time of difficulty. The king's troubles caused him to turn to the LORD for help. As he turned within, turned to seek aid from the LORD, he thought of Isaiah the prophet of the LORD and he sent Eliakim, who was over the household, Shebna the scribe, and the elders of the priests covered with sackcloth to give Isaiah a message from the king. The message is described as a day of trouble, rebuke and blasphemy: the trouble is that a great army is about to enter Jerusalem; the rebuke is that the king's envoys have been rebuked and humiliated; and the blasphemy is that the field commander has used the name of the LORD in such a way to imply that the LORD was with the Assyrians and that the LORD could not save Jerusalem.

The people of Jerusalem are like a woman who has children ready to be delivered and there is not enough strength to deliver, to bring forth, what is needed. What is needed is the delivery of the people in Jerusalem and Judah to repel the invaders who are at the Upper Pool to refresh themselves and their animals. Hezekiah conveys his fear to Isaiah that the LORD his God will hear the words of Rabshakeh, whom the king of Assyria, his master, has sent to reproach the living God,

The Testimony of the Major Prophets

and will reprove the words which the LORD his God has heard. Hezekiah is asking Isaiah to lift up his prayer and to intercede for the remnant of the people who are left in Jerusalem.

6 And Isaiah said unto them, Thus shall ye say unto your master, Thus saith the LORD, Be not afraid of the words that thou hast heard, wherewith the servants of the king of Assyria have blasphemed me.
7 Behold, I will send a blast upon him, and he shall hear a rumour, and return to his own land; and I will cause him to fall by the sword in his own land.

Isaiah tells the three envoys to convey the word of the LORD to their king, Hezekiah, that he should not be afraid that the servants of the king of Assyria have blasphemed the LORD. The LORD will send a blast, a great wind of spirit in action, so that when the king of Assyria hears a rumor, an oral report, he will return to his own land where the LORD will cause him to fall by the sword.

8 So Rabshakeh returned, and found the king of Assyria warring against Libnah: for he had heard that he was departed from Lachish.
9 And he heard say concerning Tirhakah king of Ethiopia, He is come forth to make war with thee. And when he heard it, he sent messengers to Hezekiah, saying,
10 Thus shall ye speak to Hezekiah king of Judah, saying, Let not thy God, in whom thou trustest, deceive thee, saying, Jerusalem shall not be given into the hand of the king of Assyria.
11 Behold, thou hast heard what the kings of Assyria have done to all lands by destroying them utterly; and shalt thou be delivered?
12 Have the gods of the nations delivered them which my fathers have destroyed, as Gozan, and Haran, and Rezeph, and the children of Eden which were in Telassar?
13 Where is the king of Hamath, and the king of Arphad, and the king of the city of Sepharvaim, Hena, and Ivah?

When Rabshakeh returned from Jerusalem, he found that the king of Assyria had departed the city of Lachish, and he was warring against Libnah. He also heard that Tirhakah, king of Ethiopia and a brother of the Pharaoh, has come to make war with the Assyrians. The Pharaoh of Egypt had kept his word and sent an army to aid Hezekiah withstand the invasion by Assyria even though the field commander of the Assyrians said that the Egyptians would not help Hezekiah in time of trouble. Hezekiah is also informed that he should not let God, in whom he trusts, be used by the Assyrian field commander to deceive him. Jerusalem shall not be given into the hand of control of the king of Assyria.

Surely, the field commander of the Assyrian army told Hezekiah that he has heard of the great victories of the Assyrian army and the way in which the kings of Assyria have utterly destroyed many kings and cities, such as Gozan, Haran, Rezeph, the children of Eden in Telassar, Hamath and Arphad, Sepharvaim, Hena and Ivah?! Why should Jerusalem be an exception and not be delivered to Assyria which is on a successful path with its string of victories?

14 And Hezekiah received the letter from the hand of the messengers, and read it: and Hezekiah went up unto the house of the LORD, and spread it before the LORD.
15 And Hezekiah prayed unto the LORD, saying,

The Symbolic Version of Isaiah

16 O LORD of hosts, God of Israel, that dwellest between the cherubims, thou art the God, even thou alone, of all the kingdoms of the earth: thou hast made heaven and earth.
17 Incline thine ear, O LORD, and hear; open thine eyes, O LORD, and see: and hear all the words of Sennacherib, which hath sent to reproach the living God.
18 Of a truth, LORD, the kings of Assyria have laid waste all the nations, and their countries,
19 And have cast their gods into the fire: for they were no gods, but the work of men's hands, wood and stone: therefore they have destroyed them.
20 Now therefore, O LORD our God, save us from his hand, that all the kingdoms of the earth may know that thou art the LORD, even thou only.

When Hezekiah received the letter and read it, he went to the house of the LORD, spread the written messages before the LORD and prayed to the LORD saying, O LORD of hosts, God of Israel, who dwells between the cherubim, you alone are God of all the kingdoms of the earth: you have made heaven and earth. See and hear O LORD, all the words that Sennacherib has sent to reproach the living God. It is true, LORD, that the kings of Assyria have laid waste all the nations, and their countries, they have cast their gods into the fire: for they were no gods, but the work of men's hands made of wood and stone: therefore, they have destroyed the false gods. Now therefore, O LORD, our God, save us from his hand, that all the kingdoms of the earth may know that you are the LORD. Hezekiah has come to realize that Isaiah is the focus of the LORD on earth.

21 Then Isaiah the son of Amoz sent unto Hezekiah, saying, Thus saith the LORD God of Israel, Whereas thou hast prayed to me against Sennacherib king of Assyria:
22 This is the word which the LORD hath spoken concerning him; The virgin, the daughter of Zion, hath despised thee, and laughed thee to scorn; the daughter of Jerusalem hath shaken her head at thee.
23 Whom hast thou reproached and blasphemed? and against whom hast thou exalted thy voice, and lifted up thine eyes on high? even against the Holy One of Israel.
24 By thy servants hast thou reproached the Lord, and hast said, By the multitude of my chariots am I come up to the height of the mountains, to the sides of Lebanon; and I will cut down the tall cedars thereof, and the choice fir trees thereof: and I will enter into the height of his border, and the forest of his Carmel.
25 I have digged, and drunk water; and with the sole of my feet have I dried up all the rivers of the besieged places.
26 Hast thou not heard long ago, how I have done it; and of ancient times, that I have formed it? now have I brought it to pass, that thou shouldest be to lay waste defenced cities into ruinous heaps.
27 Therefore their inhabitants were of small power, they were dismayed and confounded: they were as the grass of the field, and as the green herb, as the grass on the housetops, and as corn blasted before it be grown up

Isaiah sent a message to Hezekiah: The LORD God of Israel said, Since you have prayed to me against Sennacherib, king of Assyria, This is the word concerning him: The virgin, the daughter of Zion, which symbolizes the people of Jerusalem, have despised you, laughed you to scorn and shaken their heads at you in disbelief of your actions. Whom have you reproached and blasphemed? Against whom have you exalted your own voice and lifted up your own eyes on high, with yourself

The Testimony of the Major Prophets

in the high place? even against the Holy One of Israel? By your servants you have reproached the LORD and have said, By a multitude of your chariots, you have come to the mountain tops, to the borders of Lebanon; you will cut down the tall cedars and the choice fir trees; and you will enter into the height of the border and the forest of Carmel. The position of Sennacherib, king of Assyria continues through the message from Isaiah:

Sennacherib has dug wells in foreign lands and drunk the water there; with the sole of his feet he has blocked the flow and dried up the water of the besieged places so that the people would not have water to drink. Have you not heard long ago that the plans for the expansion of Assyria were made long ago and now, the plan has been formed and brought to pass that cities that have been defended will be transformed into ruinous heaps of stones. The inhabitants of these conquered cities were of small power and they were dismayed and confounded: they were as grass in the field, green herb, grass on housetops and corn blasted before it is grown,

28 But I know thy abode, and thy going out, and thy coming in, and thy rage against me.
29 Because thy rage against me, and thy tumult, is come up into mine ears, therefore will I put my hook in thy nose, and my bridle in thy lips, and I will turn thee back by the way by which thou camest.
30 And this shall be a sign unto thee, Ye shall eat this year such as groweth of itself; and the second year that which springeth of the same: and in the third year sow ye, and reap, and plant vineyards, and eat the fruit thereof.
31 And the remnant that is escaped of the house of Judah shall again take root downward, and bear fruit upward:
32 For out of Jerusalem shall go forth a remnant, and they that escape out of mount Zion: the zeal of the LORD of hosts shall do this.

The message of the LORD through Isaiah states that the LORD knows where Sennacherib "lives" in his consciousness, his going out and coming in. The LORD knows his ways and the rage that the king of Assyria has against the LORD. It is because of this rage that the law of the LORD shall work against him. The Assyrians often led away their captives by tying ropes to rings placed in their noses. Therefore, the law of the LORD will turn the Assyrians back the way by which they came.

This shall be a sign to Hezekiah. The first year you will eat the food that grows by itself; the second year, that which grows from the seeds of that; but in the third year, you will begin to sow and reap and plant vineyards and eat the fruit of your efforts.

The remnant of the people who have escaped of the house of Judah, who ran away when they heard that the Assyrians were coming to invade the country, shall again put roots down into the earth and bear fruit upward to the glory of the LORD: and the remnant that goes forth from Jerusalem and they that escape out of Mount Zion who carry the spirit of the LORD shall also bear fruit as they put down their roots in new places. The zeal of the LORD of hosts shall do this. It is the zeal of the LORD to be fruitful and to multiply the spirit of the LORD.

The Symbolic Version of Isaiah

33 Therefore thus saith the LORD concerning the king of Assyria, He shall not come into this city, nor shoot an arrow there, nor come before it with shields, nor cast a bank against it.
34 By the way that he came, by the same shall he return, and shall not come into this city, saith the LORD.
35 For I will defend this city to save it for mine own sake, and for my servant David's sake.

The LORD has said, in regard to the king of Assyria, that he shall not come into the city of Jerusalem, nor shoot an arrow there from outside the walls, nor come before it with shields, nor cast a bank of earth to run battering rams into the walls. By the way they came to Jerusalem is the way that they shall return. They shall not come into the city. The LORD will defend this city to save it for works that are the LORD's plan and for the sake of David, the father of Hezekiah, and a servant of the LORD, whom God has promised an enduring throne in Jerusalem.

36 Then the angel of the LORD went forth, and smote in the camp of the Assyrians a hundred and fourscore and five thousand: and when they arose early in the morning, behold, they were all dead corpses.
37 So Sennacherib king of Assyria departed, and went and returned, and dwelt at Nineveh.
38 And it came to pass, as he was worshipping in the house of Nisroch his god, that Adrammelech and Sharezer his sons smote him with the sword; and they escaped into the land of Armenia: and Esarhaddon his son reigned in his stead.

Then the angel of the LORD, the dark side of the force of the LORD, did put to death 185,000 people in the camp of the Assyrians. The Greek historian, Herodotus, attributed this destruction to a bubonic plague. Sennacherib, king of Assyria, departed and returned to dwell in Nineveh, the capital of Assyria. It came to pass, 20 years later in 681 B.C., that, while he was worshipping in the house of Nisroch his god, his sons, Adrammelech and Sharezer, killed him with the sword. The sons escaped into the land of Armenia. Esarhaddon, the son, reigned after the murder of the king.

CHAPTER 38

1 In those days was Hezekiah sick unto death. And Isaiah the prophet the son of Amoz came unto him, and said unto him, Thus saith the LORD, Set thine house in order: for thou shalt die, and not live.
2 Then Hezekiah turned his face toward the wall, and prayed unto the LORD,
3 And said, Remember now, O LORD, I beseech thee, how I have walked before thee in truth and with a perfect heart, and have done that which is good in thy sight. And Hezekiah wept sore.

Hezekiah was sick and close to death when Isaiah visited him and said that the LORD's message is to set his house in order: he is going to die, and not live. Hezekiah turned his face to the wall of the temple which was nearby and prayed to the LORD. He asked the LORD to remember now, the way that Hezekiah is walking NOW, how he has been walking before the LORD in truth and with a perfect heart, and has done that which is good in the sight of the LORD and not in his own sight as he did previously when he was living in sin, living off-the-mark of the flow from the LORD. Hezekiah wept sorely for the way in which he lived before he learned the way of the LORD in his own expression. Hezekiah has repented and changed to harmonize with the way of the LORD on earth. The change in Hezekiah on earth produces some changes in the physical form of Hezekiah.

4 Then came the word of the LORD to Isaiah, saying,
5 Go, and say to Hezekiah, Thus saith the LORD, the God of David thy father, I have heard thy prayer, I have seen thy tears: behold, I will add unto thy days fifteen years.
6 And I will deliver thee and this city out of the hand of the king of Assyria: and I will defend this city.
7 And this shall be a sign unto thee from the LORD, that the LORD will do this thing that he hath spoken;
8 Behold, I will bring again the shadow of the degrees, which is gone down in the sun dial of Ahaz, ten degrees backward. So the sun returned ten degrees, by which degrees it was gone down.

Then came the word for Isaiah to go and say to Hezekiah that the God of David, his father, has heard his prayer and seen the tears of his remorse and true repentance: Behold, the LORD will add to his days 15 years. The LORD will deliver Hezekiah and the city out of the hand of the king of Assyria: and the LORD will defend this city of Jerusalem especially since Hezekiah has sworn to let the LORD flow through his human capacities to carry out the divine plan of the LORD on earth in the kingdom of Judah.

Isaiah further tells Hezekiah that there shall be a sign from the LORD that can be explained using the sun dial of Ahaz. Ahaz was the twelfth king of Judah who reigned from 735 to 715 B.C. The name Ahaz, means, "one who takes and possesses". During his reign, Ahaz sought help from the king of Assyria when Israel and Syria threatened to take Judah. This alliance was done by Ahaz against the advice of Isaiah. The king of Assyria not only invaded Israel and Syria but he took Judah as well. In symbolism, the sun dial of Ahaz has reference the movement of the shadow across the face of the sun dial to the length of the reign and the death of Ahaz: the sun dial is the symbol of the death of Ahaz when his time on earth is no more.

A sun dial is used to symbolize the LORD's day through a person. Hezekiah was almost at the end of his time on earth due to his illness. Isaiah explains to Hezekiah that his time was running out before he repented and was granted additional time on earth by the LORD. The limited time that Hezekiah had left on earth is illustrated by the shadow of the sun dial going down ten degrees; after Hezekiah repented and Isaiah helped to cure him of his illness, then, the additional time of the king on earth is illustrated by the sun dial of Ahaz going backwards by ten degrees to symbolize the additional 15 years of life that Hezekiah will enjoy. Hezekiah will live longer in service to the LORD. Each person's life is symbolized as one day in the life of the LORD who lives through each person. As the spirit of the LORD is moving more fully through the physical form of Hezekiah, the day of the LORD through Hezekiah is lengthened.

9 The writing of Hezekiah king of Judah, when he had been sick, and was recovered of his sickness:
10 I said in the cutting off of my days, I shall go to the gates of the grave: I am deprived of the residue of my years.
11 I said, I shall not see the LORD, even the LORD, in the land of the living: I shall behold man no more with the inhabitants of the world.
12 Mine age is departed, and is removed from me as a shepherd's tent: I have cut off like a weaver my life: he will cut me off with pining sickness: from day even to night wilt thou make an end of me.
13 I reckoned till morning, that, as a lion, so will he break all my bones: from day even to night wilt thou make an end of me.
14 Like a crane or a swallow, so did I chatter: I did mourn as a dove: mine eyes fail with looking upward: O LORD, I am oppressed; undertake for me.
15 What shall I say? he hath both spoken unto me, and himself hath done it: I shall go softly all my years in the bitterness of my soul.

This is the writing of Hezekiah king of Judah, when he had been sick, was now recovered from his sickness and who is writing retrospectively: In the cutting off of his days, as his life on earth in physical form grows shorter, he shall definitely go to the gates of the grave. In his heart, he felt

The Testimony of the Major Prophets

that he was deprived of the residue of his years because he felt that he was dying sooner than he should. He knew that everybody dies sooner or later and it's just a matter of time. He felt that he was deprived of the full measure of his years on earth. He said that he shall not see the LORD in the land of the living: and he believed that he would behold man no more with the inhabitants of the world.

Hezekiah feels that his age is departed from him and left him. He has used up almost all of his allotted days on earth. It is only a matter of a little time and he thinks in terms of analogies of how little time he has left. He compares the remaining time to the removal of a shepherd's tent that keeps him protected from the weather; the sting in a weaver's cloth which is cut off at the end of a row, the LORD will cut him off with the pining sickness; all day long, from day to night, the LORD will make an end of Hezekiah.

He reckoned until morning that the LORD as a lion would break all of his bones; all that Hezekiah could think of, day and night while he was sick, was when will the LORD make an end of me. Like a crane or a swallow did Hezekiah chatter day and night, all day long, about the amount of time remaining for him on earth: He did mourn constantly as a dove; his eyes began to fail from looking upward so much for answers from the LORD "up there". His constant prayer to the LORD was how oppressed he was about the amount of time that he had remaining on earth. He asks the LORD to undertake, take control of this circumstance which is shortening his life. What more shall Hezekiah say? The LORD has indeed spoken and the decision has been made: he shall go softly and quietly in all the remaining years in the bitterness of this experience in his soul.

16 O Lord, by these things men live, and in all these things is the life of my spirit: so wilt thou recover me, and make me to live.
17 Behold, for peace I had great bitterness: but thou hast in love to my soul delivered it from the pit of corruption: for thou hast cast all my sins behind thy back.
18 For the grave cannot praise thee, death can not celebrate thee: they that go down into the pit cannot hope for thy truth.
19 The living, the living, he shall praise thee, as I do this day: the father to the children shall make known thy truth.

O LORD, by these things about the amount of time remaining and the time of their death, men live in fear and worry: and in all these things is the life of my spirit which is so involved with fear and the time of death: so will the LORD help me to recover from this torment and make me live according to the plan of the LORD for his son. Behold, for the lack of peace, Hezekiah had great bitterness; but the LORD has, in love, delivered me from the state of corruption: The LORD has cast all my sins behind my back and put them into the past.

Hezekiah understands that the grave and the person in it cannot praise the LORD, and death cannot celebrate the LORD: and that those who go down into the grave cannot hope for the truth from the LORD. The living, the living people are the ones who can give praise to the LORD, as Hezekiah, the son of David does this day. This is the answer for man: the father to the son shall make known this truth.

20 The LORD was ready to save me: therefore we will sing my songs to the stringed instruments all the days of our life in the house of the LORD.
21 For Isaiah had said, Let them take a lump of figs, and lay it for a plaister upon the boil, and he shall recover.
22 Hezekiah also had said, What is the sign that I shall go up to the house of the LORD?

Hezekiah has discovered that the LORD was always ready to save him: the problem was that he was not ready to be saved by the LORD. But now he knows! Therefore, we, the LORD and Hezekiah, will sing my songs to the stringed instruments all the days of our life in the house of the LORD. As a person sings praise to the LORD, he knows and experiences the LORD's praise within himself. Hezekiah is on the way to health and wholeness in the spirit of the LORD; the way to forget all the individual worries of the earth; and, to give praise and thanksgiving to the LORD.

Isaiah helped with the physical sickness. He said to let them make a lump of figs and lay it on the boil for a plaster, or a poultice, and he shall recover. Hezekiah also had said, What is the sign that I shall go up into the house of the LORD? There is a desire in the heart of Hezekiah to serve the LORD in the LORD's house, the house of his own Being.

CHAPTER 39

1 At that time Merodach-baladan, the son of Baladan, king of Babylon, sent letters and a present to Hezekiah: for he had heard that he had been sick, and was recovered.
2 And Hezekiah was glad of them, and shewed them the house of his precious things, the silver, and the gold, and the spices, and the precious ointment, and all the house of his armour, and all that was found in his treasures: there was nothing in his house, nor in all his dominion, that Hezekiah shewed them not.
3 Then came Isaiah the prophet unto king Hezekiah, and said unto him, What said these men? and from whence came they unto thee? And Hezekiah said, They are come from a far country unto me, even from Babylon.
4 Then said he, What have they seen in thine house? And Hezekiah answered, All that is in mine house have they seen: there is nothing among my treasures that I have not shewed them.

Hezekiah is a reformed and repentant man who has vowed to serve the LORD in the remaining years of his life now that he has recovered from his illness. At this period of time in his life, the son of the king of Babylon, Merodach-baladan, sent letters and a present to Hezekiah because he heard that he had been sick and recovered. Hezekiah was glad to receive the letters and the present along with the men who brought the things to him. While the men from Babylon were visiting Hezekiah, he showed the visitors the house of his precious things, the gold and the spices, the precious ointment, the house of his armor and all that was found in his treasures. Hezekiah, in his new relationship with the LORD and with the increase of life which he was enjoying, was very honest and open to his visitors; there was nothing in his house, nor in all his dominion, that Hezekiah did not show to them, the visitors from Babylon.

5 Then said Isaiah to Hezekiah, Hear the word of the LORD of hosts:
6 Behold, the days come, that all that is in thine house, and that which thy fathers have laid up in store until this day, shall be carried to Babylon: nothing shall be left, saith the LORD.
7 And of thy sons that shall issue from thee, which thou shalt beget, shall they take away; and they shall be eunuchs in the palace of the king of Babylon.

8 Then said Hezekiah to Isaiah, Good is the word of the LORD which thou hast spoken. He said moreover, For there shall be peace and truth in my days.

Isaiah said to Hezehiah that he should hear the word of the LORD of hosts as it comes to focus through Isaiah. Isaiah is aware that although Hezekiah has repented and is committed to serving the LORD through himself, the other people in the world have not changed the condition of their minds and hearts. They are the way they have been in the past; the way that Hezekiah was when he was in the fallen state. It is very probable that the son of the king of Babylon, the heir to the throne of his father, is thinking of ways to enlarge his kingdom when he comes to power. It is very likely that a king who has been close to death, who has been having trouble with the Assyrians and who is getting old in years would be a good target for a young prince.

Isaiah tells Hezekiah the word of the LORD of hosts: Behold, see what can occur in the days to come, that all the treasures that are in your house, and everything that your fathers have laid up in store for you and your people until this day, shall be carried to Babylon: nothing shall be left, says the LORD. The information of the wealth of Hezekiah has already been carried away in the consciousness of the visitors who came with a present and letters offering friendship and concern. But plans can be made in the future to secure these treasures for the future rulers of Babylon, so that they will have wealth.

Isaiah states that the sons that shall issue from Hezekiah, which he will produce, shall be taken away; and they shall be eunuchs in the palace of the king of Babylon, unable to produce children of their own who might be a future threat to the kingdom of Babylon. The LORD speaking through Isaiah is trying to help Hezekiah to think generationally, over a period of many years, to help his future sons and the people that they will rule. However, Hezekiah misses the message intended for others, including his own sons. Then said Hezekiah to Isaiah, Good is the word of the LORD which you have spoken. He said moreover, for there shall be peace and truth in my days. Hezekiah is thinking only of himself! He has missed the vision. A king with such limited vision and self-centeredness as demonstrated by Hezekiah cannot save his people. A king could have given the orders for all of his subjects to follow so that the subjects of the king could immediately begin to carry out the leadership of the king.

Hezekiah has demonstrated to the visitors from Babylon that his treasures are of the earth and not of the people under his control who look to their king for leadership. This king did not respond when he was told that his own sons would become eunuchs that would end the seed of Hezekiah. Due to the nature of this lack of leadership to help the spirit of the LORD magnify through the people through the order of their king, the LORD will have to work directly with the people to let his spirit be magnified in Jerusalem and Judah. The LORD will have to work through the people to offer His spirit to his children. The message of the LORD must be carried to the people through messengers who know the LORD's plan of salvation. The message can be delivered to the people by the use of songs and psalms that will be sung by the common people rather than decrees from the king.

CHAPTER 40

1 Comfort ye, comfort ye my people, saith your God.
2 Speak ye comfortably to Jerusalem, and cry unto her, that her warfare is accomplished, that her iniquity is pardoned: for she hath received of the LORD's hand double for all her sins.
3 The voice of him that crieth in the wilderness, Prepare ye the way of the LORD, make straight in the desert a highway for our God.

The message of the LORD is a message of comfort, care, love and concern for His people. Comfort from the LORD's spirit is to be offered to the people **who do not know** that the LORD's spirit is flowing through them by those people **who do know** that the spirit of the LORD is moving through the LORD's people. The people with the message are invited to speak comfortably, to speak a message of comfort, through the hearer of the word to others. The message is not that comfort will come to each person from the LORD as a reward that the people should anticipate; the message is that the LORD needs people to offer His comfort, the spirit of comfort, from the LORD through them to others. The message of comfort is to be offered to the people of Jerusalem, and the cry of what needs o be done is offered to her, the daughter that symbolizes Jerusalem, because the message from the LORD is being carried by His son, the people who do carry the LORD's message, the message which is the offspring from the LORD.

This is a good time to carry the message of peace and comfort to others. The warfare of Jerusalem is accomplished and ended, the iniquity of the people has been pardoned by the LORD and the people of Jerusalem have received double for all her sins: she has received the sowing for the wrong which she has done when Jerusalem has not served the LORD's spirit; and she has received effects of the right sowing which was done through Isaiah and his followers who represent the sword of the LORD.

Therefore, what the LORD really needs is for people who will cry out His message in the wilderness that is Jerusalem in the fallen state. The conditions of any place where the LORD is not represented accurately by His people is a wilderness. The message to the people is to Prepare ye, prepare the way of the LORD through the individual and make straight in the desert a highway for our God.

The high way is the way of righteousness, the way contained within the spirit of the LORD. The desert is the symbol of the place where the water of the truth of the LORD's spirit is not flowing on earth. The way is the way that is observable to others when they see the spirit taking form through a person who releases the spirit of the LORD in his or her living. If more and more people would do this, what would be the result?

4 Every valley shall be exalted, and every mountain and hill shall be made low: and the crooked shall be made straight, and the rough places plain:
5 And the glory of the LORD shall be revealed, and all flesh shall see it together: for the mouth of the LORD hath spoken it.
6 The voice said, Cry. And he said, What shall I cry? All flesh is grass, and all the goodliness thereof is as the flower of the field:
7 The grass withereth, the flower fadeth: because the spirit of the LORD bloweth upon it: surely the people is grass.
8 The grass withereth, the flower fadeth: but the word of our God shall stand for ever.
9 O Zion, that bringest good tidings, get thee up into the high mountain; O Jerusalem, that bringest good tidings, lift up thy voice with strength; lift it up, be not afraid; say unto the cities of Judah, Behold your God!

Every valley that the spirit of the LORD is expressed into shall be exalted and lifted up, and every mountain and hill shall be made low. This does not mean that the topography of the mountains and the valleys will change; it means that the people who hear the word of the spirit of the LORD and respond to the message shall change: the people who are in the valley of depression will be raised up and the people with the big egos of the mountain and the hill shall be brought down. The changes are made in the people: the crooked shall be made straight, and the people with rough places, rough edges to their spiritual characters, shall be made plain and smooth.

This is the way that the glory of the LORD shall be revealed, and all flesh (people who reveal the Spirit) shall see it together: for the mouth of the LORD has spoken it when there are people who will speak the word of the LORD. The voice said, Cry. And he who is interested shall ask, What shall I cry? All flesh of all the people is like grass, and all the goodliness thereof, all the good deeds which they do as they allow the spirit of the LORD to manifest, is as the flower of the field. The grass and the flower, which are physical matter, will surely wither and fade: It will whither and fade because the spirit of the LORD blows upon it: surely, the people are as grass. The grass withers, the flower fades: the material form changes and it is gone, but the word of our God, the spirit which we express, shall stand for ever.

9 O Zion, that bringest good tidings, get thee up into the high mountain; O Jerusalem, that bringest good tidings, lift up thy voice with strength; lift it up, be not afraid; say unto the cities of Judah, Behold your God!

The people who cry out the message of the LORD in the wilderness, either at the time of Isaiah, or 700 years later at the time of John, the Baptist, have the same mission. They bring good tidings, good news, the gospel of the kingdom of God on earth. The message is for Zion, the high sacred spiritual place that is represented by the person who brings the message of the presence of the spirit

The Testimony of the Major Prophets

of the LORD; the message is for Jerusalem, the material aspect of a person who senses that the place of peace is available on earth, that the hierarchy of the LORD in spirit is to be made manifest on earth through the earth of the material bodies of the people. The people of Jerusalem are to bring the good tidings, they are to lift up their individual voice with strength. The individual voice is the only voice that a person can lift up. Other voices can harmonize with your voice if you lift up your voice. A person needs to begin, to make a new beginning, to lift the voice to reveal the spirit of the LORD that flows through each person. There is fear and apprehension involved, but the cry is to be not afraid; say to the cities of Judah, the land around Jerusalem, the land around where you stand, to hear your cry into the world, Behold your God! God is constantly being released into the world as the spirit of life finds expression through everyone simultaneously. The question is, Is the spirit that comes forth the truth of God, or a counterfeit? Is the spirit straight, or crooked? Is it smooth, or rough? We do not have to make the LORD; we need to make His path through us straight.

10 Behold, the Lord GOD will come with strong hand, and his arm shall rule for him: behold, his reward is with him, and his work before him.
11 He shall feed his flock like a shepherd: he shall gather the lambs with his arm, and carry them in his bosom, and shall gently lead those that are with young.

Behold, the LORD God will come with a strong hand of right control to us. His arm which has the strength shall rule for Him. The hand of control and the strength to apply the power needed to do whatever shall rule for the LORD. The reward is with Him and His work is before Him. Man is a work of the LORD and man is to do the work of the LORD on earth. The LORD needs people to work through, to take care of, other people like a Shepherd takes care of his flock. The flock in this analogy are other people who are symbolized by sheep that need care. The LORD shall feed his flock like a shepherd; He shall gather the little lambs with His arms and carry them in His bosom, and He shall gently lead those that are with young. The Shepherd shall do this for the little lambs until they too can become shepherds. The purpose of people in the fallen state is to change from sheep to shepherds. There needs to be a shepherd! Who is the Shepherd? For Whom does the Shepherd work? Isaiah will begin to outline some of His characteristics.

12 Who hath measured the waters in the hollow of his hand, and meted out heaven with the span, and comprehended the dust of the earth in a measure, and weighed the mountains in scales, and the hills in a balance?
13 Who hath directed the Spirit of the LORD, or being his counsellor hath taught him?
14 With whom took he counsel, and who instructed him, and taught him in the path of judgment, and taught him knowledge, and shewed to him the way of understanding?
15 Behold, the nations are as a drop of a bucket, and are counted as the small dust of the balance: behold, he taketh up the isles as a very little thing.
16 And Lebanon is not sufficient to burn, nor the beasts thereof sufficient for a burnt offering.
17 All nations before him are as nothing; and they are counted to him less than nothing, and vanity.

In a series of rhetorical questions, Isaiah asks some specific questions which direct our attention to a greater Creator than exists on earth. Who is so great that the waters of the seas are measured in the hollow of His hand? Who can measure out the stars of the heaven with the breadth of His hand?

The Symbolic Version of Isaiah

Who can comprehend how much dust to use to form the earth, weigh the mountains in a scales and the hills in a balance when He formed the earth?

Who has directed the spirit of the LORD as to where it should flow and what it should do among the people, or being His Counselor has taught the LORD of the earth which is greater than His spirit? Who has given the LORD counsel and instructed Him, taught Him the path of judgment. taught Him knowledge and showed Him the way of understanding? Behold, the nations of the earth are as a drop of a bucket, and are counted as small dust for a balance: behold, He takes the isles as a very little thing. The cedars of Lebanon and all the beasts thereof are not sufficient for a burnt offering. All nations before Him are as nothing: they are counted to Him as less than nothing, and vanity, vain thoughts, by people who think otherwise. He indeed is a great God Almighty! Isaiah has attempted to give us an idea of the magnitude of God in mind-boggling examples.

18 To whom then will ye liken God? or what likeness will ye compare unto him?
19 The workman melteth a graven image, and the goldsmith spreadeth it over with gold, and casteth silver chains.
20 He that is so impoverished that he hath no oblation chooseth a tree that will not rot; he seeketh unto him a cunning workman to prepare a graven image, that shall not be moved.
21 Have ye not known? have ye not heard? hath it not been told you from the beginning? have ye not understood from the foundations of the earth?
22 It is he that sitteth upon the circle of the earth, and the inhabitants thereof are as grasshoppers; that stretcheth out the heavens as a curtain, and spreadeth them out as a tent to dwell in:
23 That bringeth the princes to nothing; he maketh the judges of the earth as vanity.
24 Yea, they shall not be planted; yea, they shall not be sown: yea, their stock shall not take root in the earth: and he shall also blow upon them, and they shall wither, and the whirlwind shall take them away as stubble.

Isaiah asks the people to whom will you compare God? or what image on earth will you compare Him to?
The workmen melt an image, engrave it with features, cover it with gold and decorate it with chains of silver to indicate great value. The poor person, who can make no offering, will use a tree that does not rot and he seeks a craftsman to prepare a graven image in the wood as an idol that can not be moved. Have you not known? have you not heard? has it not been told you from the beginning? have you not understood that these are man's futile attempts to illustrate that there is a Cause for the foundations of the earth that we call God?

It is God that is envisioned as the One who sits upon the circle of the earth, and the inhabitants thereof are as grasshoppers; Who stretches out the heavens as a curtain, and spreads the heavens out as a tent to dwell in: Who brings the princes to nothing; and makes all the judges of the earth as men of vanity. Yes, the princes and the judges of the earth that we know shall not be planted, sown, or their stock shall not take root in the earth: and, if they do, He shall blow upon them, and they shall wither, and the whirlwind shall take them away as stubble. How is God to be pictured by a man who desires to be holy? What is a person to do?

25 To whom then will ye liken me, or shall I be equal? saith the Holy One.

The Testimony of the Major Prophets

26 Lift up your eyes on high, and behold who hath created these things, that bringeth out their host by number: he calleth them all by names by the greatness of his might, for that he is strong in power; not one faileth.
27 Why sayest thou, O Jacob, and speakest, O Israel, My way is hid from the LORD, and my judgment is passed over from my God?
28 Hast thou not known? hast thou not heard, that the everlasting God, the LORD, the Creator of the ends of the earth, fainteth not, neither is weary? there is no searching of his understanding.
29 He giveth power to the faint; and to them that have no might he increaseth strength.
30 Even the youths shall faint and be weary, and the young men shall utterly fall:

The Holy One asks the question as to whom or what on earth shall a man liken God as something that he can observe, see, and understand? or, shall I be equal to the spiritual nature of God? It is not that the truth of man can be the **all** of God but he could be made equal, made of the same spirit **of** God. Isaiah instructs his followers to lift up your eyes, your vision, and behold Who has created these things that bring out their host, their Creator, by number: a person who is identified with the spirit of God is able to call out by number all of the physical forms that are observed by names and that they were made by the greatness of His might and that His spirit is strong enough to be in everything that was made, and not one observable item is lacking of the spirit of God. God is everywhere and in everything.

Why do you say Jacob, as though he were a special material person, and speak of Israel as though he were a special spiritual person who changed his name to indicate his spiritual nature? The premise of that Jacob/Israel view is that the person believes that "My way is hid from the LORD, and my judgment is passed over from my God?" The person with that view believes that he has been passed over by God and it is his personal judgment that God is not with him. Have you not known? have you not heard, that the everlasting God, the LORD, the Creator of the ends of the earth, is not faint or weary to be everywhere? There is no need for searching of His understanding because His understanding is with you in spirit He gives power to the faint; and to them that have no might, he increases their strength. Even the youths shall faint and be weary, and the young men shall utterly fall if they believe that they are separate from God.

31 But they that wait upon the LORD shall renew their strength; they shall mount up with wings as eagles; they shall run, and not be weary; and they shall walk, and not faint.

But those who identify with the LORD and begin by assuming that they are already connected to the LORD in spirit and that their function is to release the spirit of the LORD into the earth shall be in the spirit and the flow of the spirit of God which has always been present. If they "wait" upon the LORD, if they **serve** His spirit to others, then the people who do this shall renew their strength because they are connected to the Source of the strength; they shall mount up with wings as eagles that do not have to struggle to fly, they flap their wings to get some altitude to find the wind, and then they just spread and course their wings and let the wind of the spirit move them, and carry them aloft where they can see what they need to do for the LORD. The people who do this shall be invigorated by the spirit, they shall run to do the work of the spirit and not be weary; and they shall walk in agreement with the LORD and not be faint, faint-hearted about releasing the spirit of the LORD into any circumstance.

CHAPTER 41

1 Keep silence before me, O islands; and let the people renew their strength: let them come near; then let them speak: let us come near together to judgment.
2 Who raised up the righteous man from the east, called him to his foot, gave the nations before him, and made him rule over kings? he gave them as the dust to his sword, and as driven stubble to his bow.
3 He pursued them, and passed safely; even by the way that he had not gone with his feet.
4 Who hath wrought and done it, calling the generations from the beginning? I the LORD, the first, and with the last; I am he.

The LORD speaking through Isaiah tells the people, who are in the area to hear Him and whom He refers to as islands in the sea of his environment, to keep silent, to simply be still in mind and heart. This process of being totally quiet will let these people, who are in the presence of the focus of the LORD on earth, renew their strength. There is an order given to let the people come near. This is not an order to come near physically because they are already in His presence; it is an invitation to come near to him **spiritually** and share the same spirit that Isaiah is experiencing, which is the spirit of the LORD. After they have experienced the movement of the spirit of the LORD through themselves, a spirit which has always been present but their minds and hearts were too noisy and cluttered to perceive it, then let them speak: let us come together in one spirit to judge accurately based on their own individual experience.

The spirit of the LORD speaking through the mouth of Isaiah, His prophet—Who are in covenant-agreement—asked the islands of people around Him who are in the ocean of the spirit which surrounds Isaiah, Who is it that raised up the righteous man from the east, the symbol of a new day of the spirit in action in the affairs of righteous men, called the righteous men to his foot, the symbol of understanding of the ways in which Isaiah and the LORD have walked together? Because Isaiah has walked before the LORD, letting the LORD's spirit find expression through Isaiah's heart, mind and body, the LORD gave Isaiah spiritual authority over all the separate nations that were before him, and He made Isaiah rule over the earthly kings? The LORD has given the kings to Isaiah as the dust, the material substance to His sword, the sword which is the truth of

The Testimony of the Major Prophets

the LORD in the body of a person, or, the bodies of people on earth. The sword of the LORD is composed of the people who carry the spirit of the LORD on earth and they are consciously aware of this spiritual connection, which is the covenant. The earthly kings with their physical power are as driven stubble to the bow, the symbol of power, of the LORD. Isaiah walking before the LORD pursued them, the earthly kings who ruled their little islands of authority around each of them, and he passed safely among the people who are symbolized as islands of influence; the LORD has shown Isaiah the spiritual way that Isaiah had not gone before with his own feet. The way that Isaiah walked with his feet of understanding was on the ocean of spirit which went between the islands of the people. The people did not know that they were connected by the invisible ocean of the spirit of the LORD; they thought that they were separate unto themselves because they had separate physical forms. Who has brought about and done this thing, calling the generations of people from the very beginning of people on this planet? I, the LORD, from the first person, and to the last; I am He.

5 The isles saw it, and feared; the ends of the earth were afraid, drew near, and came.
6 They helped every one his neighbour; and every one said to his brother, Be of good courage.
7 So the carpenter encouraged the goldsmith, and he that smootheth with the hammer him that smote the anvil, saying, It is ready for the sodering: and he fastened it with nails, that it should not be moved.

The isles, the people who have seen themselves as separate people, saw and understood what the LORD has said to them through His servant, Isaiah and they feared; the fear which they experienced was a combination of the positive "fear", which is an awe that they are in the presence of the LORD, and a negative fear that they have not been true to the truth of themselves, spiritually, in the way that they had walked on earth in the past. The people who previously were separated, who were the ends of the earth, in their physical identities, came together in oneness of spirit. They drew near to Isaiah and the spirit of the LORD which he represented. They came together in spiritual oneness, through the ocean of the spirit that connects them together where previously the physical forms had held them apart. They understood that the same spirit was the Father of them all. They understood that the spirit was the real Self and the physical island around the spirit was made of the dust of the ground. Their being was the real Self; the human portion of the human being was the clothing of the spirit that is made of the dust.

8 But thou, Israel, art my servant, Jacob whom I have chosen, the seed of Abraham my friend.
9 Thou whom I have taken from the ends of the earth, and called thee from the chief men thereof, and said unto thee, Thou art my servant; I have chosen thee, and not cast thee away.
10 Fear thou not; for I am with thee: be not dismayed; for I am thy God: I will strengthen thee; yea, I will help thee; yea, I will uphold thee with the right hand of my righteousness.

The LORD speaking through Isaiah says, But you, Israel, the spiritual portion of the people are My servant, the spirit is a part of the LORD and should serve the LORD's purpose on earth through the physical form which is symbolized by Jacob. The LORD has chosen Jacob, the human who knew not the LORD. The human form is the seed of Abraham, My friend, the LORD's friend, when Abraham was in physical form on earth. This experience by a person who has become a part of the LORD's sword on earth—which is an instrument composed of a body of people who will do the work of the LORD using the LORD's methods of love, truth and life—is both awe-inspiring and frightening. It is awesome to the spirit and frightening to the form, which includes the feelings of the heart and the thoughts of the mind. The LORD wants the person who has experienced the covenant to not be afraid.

You specific and special people, whom I have taken from the ends of the earth—from your islands of separate identities where you lived in your own little worlds—have been called away from the chief men of the fallen state. The LORD has told them that they are His servants who will serve the LORD's spirit into the fallen world. You have been chosen by the LORD who has not cast you away. "Fear not; for I am with you: be not dismayed; for I am your God: I will strengthen you; I will help you; yes I will uphold you with the right hand of my righteousness".

11 Behold, all they that were incensed against thee shall be ashamed and confounded: they shall be as nothing; and they that strive with thee shall perish.
12 Thou shalt seek them, and shalt not find them, even them that contended with thee: they that war against thee shall be as nothing, and as a thing of nought.
13 For I the LORD thy God will hold thy right hand, saying unto thee, Fear not; I will help thee.

See and observe that all the people who were incensed against you and your righteousness shall be ashamed and confounded because the spirit in them knows who you are and that you are spirit, the same spirit that is within them; but the physical identity, the human self shall be ashamed and confounded because it does not know the truth: their human self shall be as nothing in your view of them because you know that they do not understand. If they strive against you, the real Self, they will perish because you are spirit and they are form. You shall seek them, the spirit in them, and you shall not find them. You shall not find even those who contended with you because they are unreal selves, they do not exist; they are as unreal people in a fictional story. These unreal people that war against you shall be as nothing; as a material thing is nothing but an accumulation of dust. I, the LORD your God, will hold your right hand, the hand of right control, leading you in the way of the LORD, saying to you always, Fear not: I will help you.

14 Fear not, thou worm Jacob, and ye men of Israel; I will help thee, saith the LORD, and thy redeemer, the Holy One of Israel.
15 Behold, I will make thee a new sharp threshing instrument having teeth: thou shalt thresh the mountains, and beat them small, and shalt make the hills as chaff.
16 Thou shalt fan them, and the wind shall carry them away, and the whirlwind shall scatter them: and thou shalt rejoice in the LORD, and shalt glory in the Holy One of Israel.

The LORD speaking through His prophet Isaiah tells all of His followers not to fear and He terms the followers, who are fearful, a worm of Jacob and men of Israel: the symbolism of these labels is that Jacob is as a worm of the ground who crawls in the dirt, while Israel is comprised of the spirits or beings which are referred to as men. It is only the worm portion of man, the human portion of the human being which experiences the fear. The advice of the LORD is to step across the line from the human personality to the Being, the spiritual identity, and the LORD will help the person do this when one is fearful. Once again Isaiah is speaking for the LORD, the Redeemer, the Holy One of Israel, the One who can redeem a person from a human orientation with a worm to the spiritual orientation of men who are beings. The problem with human beings on earth is with their physical orientation; not their spiritual orientation. It is the human portion of a man that is poor and needy; this is the portion that seeks the water of truth, water is the symbol of the spirit of truth that connects everyone and everything.

17 When the poor and needy seek water, and there is none, and their tongue faileth for thirst, I the LORD will hear them, I the God of Israel will not forsake them.
18 I will open rivers in high places, and fountains in the midst of the valleys: I will make the wilderness a pool of water, and the dry land springs of water.
19 I will plant in the wilderness the cedar, the shittah tree, and the myrtle, and the oil tree; I will set in the desert the fir tree, and the pine, and the box tree together:
20 That they may see, and know, and consider, and understand together, that the hand of the LORD hath done this, and the Holy One of Israel hath created it.

When the poor and the needy, the people in human identity who have certain situations to handle which they call "problems", and they seek water, they seek the water of truth on how to get out of the predicament in which they find themselves, and their tongue fails them because of their thirst, the truth to handle that circumstance, and there is no answer for them, the LORD will hear them, "I the God of Israel will not forsake them". This can be done by the LORD because the LORD is with them, the LORD is omnipresent. The LORD will open rivers in high places, and fountains in the midst of the valleys; the water of truth will come from high and low: The LORD will make a wilderness into a pool of water, and the dry land into springs of water; there will be an answer, a correct way for the spirit of truth to handle the "problem", whatever it is.

The LORD working through the individual with the problem will plant in the wilderness what is right and fitting for the particular environment. Isaiah uses the parable of seven different trees that can be planted in the wilderness in different soils, different environments, such as the cedar, the acacia, the myrtle and the olive; and He will plant three different trees in the desert; the fir, pine and the box tree which are suited to that dry terrain: this shall be done so the people with different problems may, see, know, consider and understand together, that the hand of the LORD has done this thing, and the Holy One of Israel has created what was necessary and fitting for different circumstances. The creative forms of the answers that the LORD will give shall be fitting for the particular circumstances in the environment as are the seven trees for their environments.

21 Produce your cause, saith the LORD; bring forth your strong reasons, saith the King of Jacob.
22 Let them bring them forth, and shew us what shall happen: let them shew the former things, what they be, that we may consider them, and know the latter end of them; or declare us things for to come.
23 Shew the things that are to come hereafter, that we may know that ye are gods: yea, do good, or do evil, that we may be dismayed, and behold it together.
24 Behold, ye are of nothing, and your work of nought: an abomination is he that chooseth you.

The word of the LORD through Isaiah to the person, or the people, with problems is to produce your cause from within yourself; bring forth your strong reasons, says the King of Jacob, King of the human state. Let the king of the mind of Jacob bring forth its answers and show us what will happen: let the human nature state show the way of former things, what they might be, so that everyone might consider them and know the latter end, the outcome, or declare the things to come from the human nature suggestion to handle the problem. The people from the king of Jacob, who represent the human nature state, are asked to show the things that are to come hereafter, that it can be seen and known that you are gods of your world: that you have the power to do good and evil, that may be dismayed, astonished or shocked, and behold the answer together. The LORD's view is that the people of Jacob, human nature, are nothing, and whatever they decide, good or evil, is work that is done for nothing and to no avail: an abomination, a wicked person, is he that chooses to follow you, king of Jacob, ruler of the human nature state without the LORD.

25 I have raised up one from the north, and he shall come: from the rising of the sun shall he call upon my name: and he shall come upon princes as upon morter, and as the potter treadeth clay.
26 Who hath declared from the beginning, that we may know? and beforetime, that we may say, He is righteous? yea, there is none that sheweth, yea, there is none that declareth, yea, there is none that heareth your words.

The LORD has raised up one from the north; the north is the symbol of the present moment since the person who looks at a sun dial faces the north to see the shadow of the sun to determine the time of day; and he is the one who shall come: the one who comes shall dwell in the present moment. He shall call upon the name of the LORD from the rising of the sun, from early in the morning, from the very beginning of the day and all day. The person who comes shall come in the name of the LORD because he calls on the name of the LORD and waits on, or serves the LORD's spirit, into his circumstances. He has been raised to stay in the present moment where the spirit of the LORD is always to be found. He shall come upon the princes of the human nature world and tread upon them as if they were upon mortar, and as the potter treads on clay. He will be on top of, above, the circumstances of the world as he comes on the scene.

Who is it that has declared from the beginning that we may know everything with our minds? who said that we should have the power to predict what is going to happen in the future so that other people in the fallen state may say that we are righteous? Yes, there is none that can show the future, there is none that can declare the future, and there is none that can hear your words when you predict the future. This is the work and desire of the serpent, the symbol of the self-active mind that desires to be God and know all things by judging whether the circumstances of the world are good or evil. The one who comes in the name of the LORD will not eat the forbidden fruit; he will stay in the present moment and serve the LORD's spirit into the earth. He will be as an angel who never fell into the earth. The LORD speaking through Isaiah would reward such a person.

27 The first shall say to Zion, Behold, behold them: and I will give to Jerusalem one that bringeth good tidings.
28 For I beheld, and there was no man; even among them, and there was no counsellor, that, when I asked of them, could answer a word.
29 Behold, they are all vanity; their works are nothing: their molten images are wind and confusion.

The Testimony of the Major Prophets

The first person to do this shall say to Zion, the spiritual aspect of the human beings, behold them, see them as they are. Their minds dwell in the past and they try to get into the future which is movement away from the LORD who is always in the present moment and in the present place. The LORD is always in the Now of the present moment and He is always in the Here of the present place. The first person who sees this as the way of the LORD will be rewarded. The LORD will give to Jerusalem one that brings good tidings, the tidings of the LORD in the present moment.

The LORD was observing the people around him through the physical form of Isaiah and He could behold no man among them: there was no counselor among those assembled who could answer a word when the LORD asked, "Who could come in the name of the LORD?" The word was, Here I Am. Behold, look at the people. They are all vanity; they all come in vain; they come in their earthly names which describe the physical clothing that they wear; their works are nothing because they come in their earthly names; they come in their own molten images made of clay which are wind and confusion, the wind of the spirit and the distortion of the clay of the human flesh. Who shall say, Here I am? I am a server of the LORD!

CHAPTER 42

1 Behold my servant, whom I uphold; mine elect, in whom my soul delighteth; I have put my spirit upon him: he shall bring forth judgment to the Gentiles.
2 He shall not cry, nor lift up, nor cause his voice to be heard in the street.

The LORD speaking through his servant, Isaiah, who carries His spirit tells His followers to Behold Isaiah who is upheld as he goes through life by the spirit of the LORD; Isaiah is the LORD's elect because Isaiah elected, chose, to let the Spirit of the LORD live in his body, mind and heart, his soul, and the LORD's soul delights in that offering. The LORD's spirit is upon Isaiah and Isaiah, the LORD's soul, shall bring forth judgment, the judgment of the LORD, to the Gentiles now that the LORD has a means of expression on earth to speak to the Gentiles, the people who do not let the spirit of the LORD move through their souls, their hearts, minds and bodies, so that their souls can be saved. (According to this interpretation, the majority of Jerusalem and Judah were occupied by spiritual Gentiles!)

In order to let the LORD's spirit be made manifest on earth, Isaiah shall not cry out his own desires, nor lift up his own personal opinions, nor cause his human nature voice to be heard in the streets. Isaiah has given up his old life, his old human nature ways that he inherited from his family and friends so that the LORD would have an open channel from the heaven into the earth so that the eternal LORD, who is always alive in heaven could also be alive on earth. Isaiah had to give up his old way of life, he sacrificed his identification with human nature, so that the spirit or being of the LORD could live. Isaiah has successfully done this, he has made this sacrifice of his earthly self, symbolized by a calf or a bullock, so that the heavenly Self could find expression. Isaiah has discovered that the LORD does not impose or force His power or presence upon anyone. The person must make the offering to the LORD, a burnt offering of the human ego, to the LORD who will graciously accept the true offering of man. The LORD can speak through Isaiah because the covenant is in operation in a win-win situation: the LORD is alive on earth through Isaiah who is truly alive on earth. The physical body of Isaiah did not have to die to get to know the LORD: only the false, counterfeit human ego—which is not man—passed away. Isaiah is present with

The Testimony of the Major Prophets

the LORD upholding Him with more power than ever. What shall the LORD do now that He is consciously on earth?

3 A bruised reed shall he not break, and the smoking flax shall he not quench: he shall bring forth judgment unto truth.
4 He shall not fail nor be discouraged, till he have set judgment in the earth: and the isles shall wait for his law.
5 Thus saith God the LORD, he that created the heavens, and stretched them out; he that spread forth the earth, and that which cometh out of it; he that giveth breath unto the people upon it, and spirit to them that walk therein:

The spirit of the LORD working through his servant Isaiah perceives the people who are "only human" as bruised reeds, injured humans who are weak because they do not know the spirit of the LORD that is within themselves, Who would flow through them, uphold them, and make them strong. The LORD Who is everywhere is not restricted or limited to the physical body of Isaiah. The LORD, moving through all people, is like the smoking flax, the wick of a candle, which is giving smoke rather than light. The LORD does not wish to quench the fire and the light; He wants to trim the wick so that the fire will burn cleanly, the light will glow and people will see the glory of the LORD through man, male and female. In this manner, the LORD on earth through Isaiah and others who are in agreement, in the covenant, with Him shall bring judgment into truth, people who judge the LORD's existence in the heaven or in the earth into the knowing of the truth as the LORD's Spirit moves through them in their living. People know what they express! If they express the LORD's spirit, the spirit of Love, Truth and Life, they will know the LORD.

Isaiah shall not fail or be discouraged until he has set this judgment in the earth. The problem is not with the LORD; the problem is with man. Man, men and women, who are as the isles, little islands, separated from each other and separate from the LORD in their own little worlds of their human minds, shall wait for the law of the LORD to work. The law of the LORD is that if they sow the LORD's spirit, they will reap the LORD's spirit in their little island. This is not the word of Isaiah. This is the word of God the LORD, He that created the heavens, and stretched them out; He that spread forth the earth, and everything that comes out of it; He that gives breath to all the people upon the earth, and Whose spirit is given to and shared with everyone who walks on earth without exception. The LORD sees people exactly the way they are; He knows everything that the person has done because His spirit has been present always. The LORD, Who now has a voice on earth, will call the people from wrong function when they did not know what they were doing, to right function, now that He is present through Isaiah, and others who will accept the invitation to join the covenant. This is the sword of the LORD, the instrument of the LORD on earth for the purpose of offering help to the people in the fallen state and who desire to rise up.

6 I the LORD have called thee in righteousness, and will hold thine hand, and will keep thee, and give thee for a covenant of the people, for a light of the Gentiles;
7 To open the blind eyes, to bring out the prisoners from the prison, and them that sit in darkness out of the prison house.

The LORD operating on earth through Isaiah and others have called the people to righteousness, the correct use of their hearts, minds and bodies rather than the uses to which they have been subjecting themselves to produce such ugliness. There will be a process of transition but during the process, the LORD operating through you will hold your hand, keep you and give you for a covenant for other people, so that you will be a light for the Gentiles, the people who do not yet know the LORD. You will love your work as you open the eyes of the blind, not physically blind, but perceptually blind; you shall bring prisoners of beliefs out of their prisons and those who sit in spiritual darkness out of the prison house; they are in a prison and they do not know that the door of their prison is not locked. Their prison house is their earthly identification with their human nature body. The way out of the prison is to identify with the truth of yourself and function out of that identity which is a divine identity. Who are you? What is your true identity? Who is the spirit that moves through your physical form?

8 I am the LORD: that is my name: and my glory will I not give to another, neither my praise to graven images.
9 Behold, the former things are come to pass, and new things do I declare: before they spring forth I tell you of them.
10 Sing unto the LORD a new song, and his praise from the end of the earth, ye that go down to the sea, and all that is therein; the isles, and the inhabitants thereof.
11 Let the wilderness and the cities thereof lift up their voice, the villages that Kedar doth inhabit: let the inhabitants of the rock sing, let them shout from the top of the mountains.
12 Let them give glory unto the LORD, and declare his praise in the islands.

I AM the LORD: that is my name: and I will not give my glory to another, or give my praise to graven images especially the image that is made of the dust of the ground called my human body. I am not my human body! I am not my human mind! I am not my human emotions, my heart! I am the One who operates this instrument, this equipment while I am on earth in the earth of this equipment. The spirit of the LORD is moving through this human equipment. I am **that** I AM! I Am! Behold, the former things of the human stated are come to pass, the human state has passed away, and new things, the things of the spirit, do I declare: before they spring forth from Me through My physical body, I tell you of them so you shall see the spirit as it converted into form through My feelings, My thoughts, My words, and My actions. This is the call for everyone, who is willing, to sing a new song, a song unto the LORD. If we sing it together, it is not **my** song, it is **our** song.

The LORD speaking through the form of Isaiah is asking the people to sing a new song unto the LORD. Then, His praise shall be heard, if the song of the LORD's spirit is sung through you, from the end of the earth, the end of your former earthly expression, which was off-the-mark of the true song, and when the expression is off-the-mark, it is a sin, a fault, not on-the-mark, not in the bull's eye as in archery. This is what must be done by those of you who would go down to the sea, the sea of the spiritual expression of the LORD which is the total expression of all who serve the LORD's spirit which is all, the total that is therein. This is the way that the sea of the spirit of the LORD reaches and surrounds the isles, the people who know not the LORD. The inhabitants of those separate isles, who are prisoners of their human nature, are now surrounded by the sea of spiritual expression that cannot be seen by human nature.

The Testimony of the Major Prophets

Let the wilderness and the cities which have been created by the expression of the people who expressed their human natures lift up their voice in the expression of the spiritual natures, so the villages that Kedar inhabits, a village in the desert where there is very little water, can receive the water of the truth, the spirit of truth. Let the inhabitants of the rock, those who stand on the solid rock of the LORD, sing; let them shout from the top of the mountains. Let them give glory unto the LORD, and declare His praise in the islands. Let everyone, everywhere, sing praises to the LORD. Then the way of the LORD on earth shall indeed be magnified as all His children sing His song.

13 The LORD shall go forth as a mighty man, he shall stir up jealousy like a man of war: he shall cry, yea, roar; he shall prevail against his enemies.
14 I have long time holden my peace; I have been still, and refrained myself: now will I cry like a travailing woman; I will destroy and devour at once.
15 I will make waste mountains and hills, and dry up all their herbs; and I will make the rivers islands, and I will dry up the pools.
16 And I will bring the blind by a way that they knew not; I will lead them in paths that they have not known: I will make darkness light before them, and crooked things straight. These things will I do unto them, and not forsake them.

The LORD moving through a body of people shall go forth in all directions as a mighty man, a man who is mighty and secure in the expression of the spirit of the LORD. There is no need for the mighty man to use physical might to force the ideas of the spirit of the LORD on anyone because the spirit of the LORD must be willingly accepted by each person in order for the covenant with the LORD to be a reality in that person's experience. This does not mean that the spirit of the LORD in action will not have an effect on people. The mighty man of collective spiritual expression shall stir up jealousy like a man of war. The jealousy will not be in the mighty man who serves the LORD of Love; the jealousy is in those people who do not have the truth of love in their expression which they see, and that they desire, because they do not have it. The cry of the mighty man is a cry, a loud expression of love in action on earth, which will become a roar as others join in the expression. The expression of love shall prevail, shall win, over his enemies immediately, because the LORD and His representatives have no enemies. They observe only other spirits of the LORD who are trapped in the prisons of their concepts and beliefs, and whose beliefs prevent them from radiating the spirit of the LORD.

The LORD has held His peace for a long time; He has been still and refrained Himself because He did not have a person or a body on earth but now that He does have a body on earth to express His spirit, He will make a noise like a woman in labor who is in the process of giving birth. In this process, the LORD will destroy and devour at once; the destruction will be of the false gods and the beliefs about them and the people who are devoured by the LORD are those who are changed from human nature to their spiritual nature. This **creative process** as seen by the LORD and His people is viewed as a **destructive process** by human nature. The forms of human nature will change as there are fewer people to support them. The power of the LORD moving through the consciousness of people, human or divine, will produce change. In symbolic language, the changes are described as making waste to what was built by human nature on the mountains and hills; their herbs will be dried up because no one will tend them; the rivers of human nature thought and action will dry up and become islands; and the pools of consciousness where human nature people did congregate in the past will dry up. And the LORD working through his mighty man will bring the blind by a way that they never knew before; the blind will be led in paths that they have not known: the LORD, working through the people who previously have walked in a way of darkness shall walk in a new way, a way of light, which is before them. The light will be the example of the mighty man. The true and correct example shall make crooked things straight; the distortions of the physical forms on earth shall be made straight by the creation of new forms which are straight. These things will the LORD do for them who are not of the LORD. The LORD shall not forsake them because of their sins.

17 They shall be turned back, they shall be greatly ashamed, that trust in graven images, that say to the molten images, Ye are our gods.
18 Hear, ye deaf; and look, ye blind, that ye may see.
19 Who is blind, but my servant? or deaf, as my messenger that I sent? who is blind as he that is perfect, and blind as the LORD's servant?
20 Seeing many things, but thou observest not; opening the ears, but he heareth not.
21 The LORD is well pleased for his righteousness' sake; he will magnify the law, and make it honourable.

The sinners, the people who have been creating distorted expressions and actions of the LORD's spirit, shall be turned back to their true nature and their true expression. When they are, they shall be greatly ashamed at what they did with the spirit of the LORD, which they are. They trusted in the graven images which they worshipped and that they said to these molten images, that "Ye are our gods". The message from the LORD is that the deaf, the people who do not hear the message of the LORD because they are worshipping false gods, should hear; and the people who are blind to the example of the LORD that is before them as a mighty man, should see the example that the LORD has sent to them. Human nature people are blind to the working of the spirit; the mighty man is seemingly blind to the working of the material forms on earth.

Who is blind, but my servant? The LORD admits that His servant is blind to the power and the trappings of the false gods. The LORD's servant is also deaf to the message of the false gods on earth because the servant in covenant-agreement, the messenger that has been sent by the LORD, has heard the voice of the LORD and knows that he has been sent by the LORD. The messenger knows that he carries the perfect message from the LORD and the messenger is blind to all messages that are not of the LORD's spirit coming through the servant to make him a mighty man. The LORD's servant can see many things with his eyes, but he does not observe teachings that are not true to the truth; the ears of the true servant are open, and he hears what has been said, but he does not hear any message that denies that the LORD's spirit comes through the body of man which was created for this purpose. The LORD is well pleased for his righteousness' sake; the mighty man will magnify the law of the LORD, and make the application of the LORD's law on earth an honorable endeavor.

22 But this is a people robbed and spoiled; they are all of them snared in holes, and they are hid in prison houses: they are for a prey, and none delivereth; for a spoil, and none saith, Restore.
23 Who among you will give ear to this? who will hearken and hear for the time to come?

The Testimony of the Major Prophets

24 Who gave Jacob for a spoil, and Israel to the robbers? did not the LORD, he against whom we have sinned? for they would not walk in his ways, neither were they obedient unto his law.
25 Therefore he hath poured upon him the fury of his anger, and the strength of battle: and it hath set him on fire round about, yet he knew not; and it burned him, yet he laid it not to heart.

The people who are presently on earth are seen by the mighty man as robbed and spoiled. They have been robbed of their everlasting spiritual nature and they have been spoiled by the expression of what is called human nature. All of them are snared into holes, and they are in prison houses of the false concepts and beliefs that keep them in prisons or as sheep in separate folds. They are a prey for people who want to keep them in prison, and none deliver them to the LORD who will set them free. They are a spoil, a prize of captivity in a human nature, and none of their captors say, Restore this angel of the LORD to his rightful position on earth. Who among you will listen to the teaching of the LORD through the mighty man? who will hear and do something about it in the time to come, in your future behavior?

Who gave Jacob, the symbol of the human body, for a spoil, and Israel, the spirit that is within the physical body of man, to the robbers? Did not the LORD do this because Jacob and Israel have sinned against His way on earth? They would not walk in His ways, neither were they obedient unto His law.
Therefore the LORD poured upon Jacob, who symbolizes the people in the fallen state, the fury of His anger, His power which is incorrectly used and distorted on earth. Man is going contrary to the Way of the LORD and man cannot win that battle with the LORD. The strength of battle between a rebellious creation called man and the Creator, who is the LORD, is in the hand of the LORD. This is not the plan of the LORD. This is the result of the rebellion of man against the LORD according to the working of the Law of the Lord. It is the misuse and the misapplication of the Law that has placed fallen man, human nature man in his dire straits. His rebellion against the LORD has set him on fire round about, he is burning in the hell of his own creation; yet, man, in his fallen state did not know how he got in this condition; All that man knows is that the fallen state burned him, that it is an uncomfortable experience and that he does not know his purpose on earth. Yet, man in the fallen state has not accepted the responsibility for the conditions in which he lives; he has not taken it to heart; he has not laid the responsibility for the terrible conditions on his own heart. He created a Satan and a Devil to blame it on.

CHAPTER 43

1 But now thus saith the LORD that created thee, O Jacob, and he that formed thee, O Israel, Fear not: for I have redeemed thee, I have called thee by thy name; thou art mine.
2 When thou passest through the waters, I will be with thee; and through the rivers, they shall not overflow thee: when thou walkest through the fire, thou shalt not be burned; neither shall the flame kindle upon thee.

The LORD who created the human material aspect of mankind, male and female, symbolized by Jacob, and the spiritual aspect of mankind with a being in each human form, symbolized by Israel, has a message for the human beings who are in the fallen state of rebellion away from the spirit of the LORD: the message to Israel and Jacob, the spirits in their human capacities, is Fear not. There is to be no fear in all the fallen people on earth who have been in a pattern of rebellion against the LORD since the fall of man. The LORD has redeemed mankind by calling them to come to the LORD by their name; and the LORD has announced that both Jacob and Israel, no matter what their present condition, belong to Him, they belong to the LORD. The LORD accepts the entire body of mankind exactly the way that they are in the fallen state; everybody is accepted exactly as they are. They cannot remain the way that they are in a sinful state; they must return to the LORD which will require a transition to occur in their identity and in their behavior.

When the people in the fallen state pass through the waters, the waters of transition in the consciousness of the people as they begin to return in consciousness to the LORD, I, the LORD, will be with you. The LORD wants everyone to know that they must pass through two transitions which are symbolized by water and fire. Water is the symbol of truth; and fire is the symbol of love. In order to return to the LORD, in order to make the transition from the fallen state to the ascended state, there is the need for each person to experience both truth and love. Truth and love are spirits before the throne of the LORD. Both of these spirits must be experienced before any person can return to the LORD. The truth flows from the LORD in heaven to everyone as a river flows from its source and each person must return through the rivers; the LORD tells his people that the rivers shall not overflow and destroy those who will return to the LORD; the journey will be a safe one. There is also a need to walk through the fire. Everything that takes place happens within the

The Testimony of the Major Prophets

consciousness; the person who comes through the fire of the LORD's love which emanates from its source in heaven, shall not be burned by the fire of God's love. It is not a **physical** fire; it is a warm, vibrational fire of God's power that must move through a person before a person can know what it is, the truth of the LORD's love. It will neither burn the person nor catch fire to the person.

3 For I am the LORD thy God, the Holy One of Israel, thy Saviour: I gave Egypt for thy ransom, Ethiopia and Seba for thee.
4 Since thou wast precious in my sight, thou hast been honourable, and I have loved thee: therefore will I give men for thee, and people for thy life.
5 Fear not: for I am with thee: I will bring thy seed from the east, and gather thee from the west;

Isaiah is delivering this message to the people from the LORD thy God, the Holy One of Israel, your Savior, the one who can offer salvation of the people in the fallen state: this is the LORD who delivered the people, the children of Israel (Jacob), spirit and form from the people of Egypt, Ethiopia (Cush) and Seba who held them in bondage. The children of Israel were delivered from Egypt to the promised land as the LORD worked through His servant, Moses.

Since children of Israel and their descendants were precious in the sight of the LORD, have been honorable, and the LORD has loved them: therefore, the LORD gave this people His spiritual substance through men for them, so that the people shall have life. The LORD tells the people to: Fear not: for the LORD is with them: and the LORD will bring their seed from the east, out of the future, where they will live on earth for a period of time and then they will be gathered from the west when the LORD will harvest His spirit from their bodies at the end of life in form on earth. The two components are spirit and form. Spirit is either in form, or, it is not in form. When spirit is in form, the form has opportunity to be one with the spirit and to extend the works of spirit to all other forms.

6 I will say to the north, Give up; and to the south, Keep not back: bring my sons from far, and my daughters from the ends of the earth;
7 Even every one that is called by my name: for I have created him for my glory, I have formed him; yea, I have made him.
8 Bring forth the blind people that have eyes, and the deaf that have ears.
9 Let all the nations be gathered together, and let the people be assembled: who among them can declare this, and shew us former things? let them bring forth their witnesses, that they may be justified: or let them hear, and say, It is truth.

The LORD will say to the north, the symbol of the people who live in the present, to give up their emotional attachment to their physical substance; and to the south, the source of the sun which is the symbol of the LORD, so that the sun and the shadow, the spirit and the form, can be one on earth. The shadow is the visible effect of the presence of the sun. In symbolic language, the daughter is the symbol of the **effect** and the son is the symbol of the **cause**. Keep not the source of the LORD's power away from the earth. Bring the sons and daughters, the spirits and the forms, of the LORD from the ends of the earth.

Bring every one that is called by the name of the LORD, Whose name is I am, for everyone has been created for the LORD's glory on earth. The LORD has formed all these people; yes, the LORD has a made everyone without exception. Bring forth the blind people who have eyes with which to see but they do not see the Work and the Way of their LORD in their observations; bring the deaf who have ears to hear but they do not hear the Word of the LORD on earth. Invite and call everyone to the experience of the covenant with the LORD who will come when the LORD calls. The LORD's desire is that all the nations be gathered together in His spirit, and all the forms of the people be assembled: who among the people who are being gathered together can declare and show that this has ever occurred before, or when it happened before? Let those who say that they remember this offer ever having been made before, then let them bring forth their witnesses, that they may be justified: or, let them hear this offer, accept it, and say, It is truth because they have experienced the wonder of the spirit and form in covenant-agreement.

10 Ye are my witnesses, saith the LORD, and my servant whom I have chosen: that ye may know and believe me, and understand that I am he: before me there was no God formed, neither shall there be after me.
11 I, even I, am the LORD; and beside me there is no saviour.
12 I have declared, and have saved, and I have shewed, when there was no strange god among you: therefore ye are my witnesses, saith the LORD, that I am God.
13 Yea, before the day was I am he; and there is none that can deliver out of my hand: I will work, and who shall let it?

The LORD says that those who accept His invitation and experience the truth of His offer are the witness and the servant of the LORD. Each of them has been chosen by the LORD to experience the spirit of the LORD within each of their forms so that they will know and believe the LORD and understand that I am He. Before the LORD, there was no god formed and neither shall their be after: there is only One God. The LORD speaking through Isaiah repeats that there is one God, one Savior and no one else. The LORD speaking through Isaiah has declared, saved people, and showed that there were no strange gods among the people: therefore you the people are the witnesses says the LORD speaking through Isaiah that the LORD is God. Before the day was, before there was a day on earth, the LORD was and is; and none shall deliver His people out of His hand or control. The LORD will continue to work through man and who shall let the spirit of the LORD move through him or her so that the truth can be experienced? The actual, realized experience of the LORD eliminates all beliefs in the false gods!

14 Thus saith the LORD, your redeemer, the Holy One of Israel; For your sake I have sent to Babylon, and have brought down all their nobles, and the Chaldeans, whose cry is in the ships.
15 I am the LORD, your Holy One, the creator of Israel, your King.
16 Thus saith the LORD, which maketh a way in the sea, and a path in the mighty waters;
17 Which bringeth forth the chariot and horse, the army and the power; they shall lie down together, they shall not rise: they are extinct, they are quenched as tow.

The LORD speaking through Isaiah, the redeemer of the people, the Holy One of Israel, says that the spirit has been sent to Babylon and it has brought down all their nobles, their leaders, and the Chaldeans, whose pride is in their ships. Who is able to do such a thing? The LORD speaking

The Testimony of the Major Prophets

through His prophet, Isaiah states, "I am the LORD, your Holy One, the Creator of Israel, your King."

The LORD, the One God, is the author of everything that happens on earth. Who makes a way in the sea, and a path in the mighty waters; Who brings forth the chariot and horse, the army and the power; when they, all the physical forms that contain the LORD's spirit, shall lie down together in what we call death, they, the forms, shall not rise: they are extinct, they are quenched, extinguished, as tow, a short piece of hemp or flax used in a candle as a wick. Dead forms are extinguished and snuffed out as a wick in a candle! The LORD wants the people to know that if they identify with their forms and the forms are gone, then, they have passed away. What shall the people do now? The LORD has some advice for them so that they do not return to their fallen ways where they have separated themselves from the LORD's spirit and which is the cause of the fallen state.

18 Remember ye not the former things, neither consider the things of old.
19 Behold, I will do a new thing; now it shall spring forth; shall ye not know it? I will even make a way in the wilderness, and rivers in the desert.
20 The beast of the field shall honour me, the dragons and the owls: because I give waters in the wilderness, and rivers in the desert, to give drink to my people, my chosen.

The people are not to remember the former things of old that led to wars and hatred. Behold, the LORD will do a new thing; it shall spring forth in the present moment, in the now. Shall you not know what it is if you participate in the process? The action of the LORD will even make a new way in the wilderness, and rivers of new spiritual behavior in the desert where it has never been seen before. The beasts of the fields will honor the creation that the LORD shall bring forth through the rivers of consciousness from the LORD as it flows through man, the chosen people, the people who choose to let the spirit of the LORD flow through them, to produce a balanced and harmonious kingdom on earth between man and beast.

21 This people have I formed for myself; they shall shew forth my praise.
22 But thou hast not called upon me, O Jacob; but thou hast been weary of me, O Israel.
23 Thou hast not brought me the small cattle of thy burnt offerings; neither hast thou honoured me with thy sacrifices. I have not caused thee to serve with an offering, nor wearied thee with incense.
24 Thou hast bought me no sweet cane with money, neither hast thou filled me with the fat of thy sacrifices: but thou hast made me to serve with thy sins, thou hast wearied me with thine iniquities.
25 I, even I, am he that blotteth out thy transgressions for mine own sake, and will not remember thy sins.

The LORD has formed this people on earth to bring forth the LORD's glory and praise. The LORD is willing to bring this harmonious and balanced kingdom on earth which would truly be a kingdom from heaven. But, the problem has been that the people, symbolized by Jacob, have not called upon the LORD and offered their services to the LORD to let it happen. They have rebelled against the LORD. Even the spirit of Israel, the symbol of the capacity to let spirit of the LORD come into the earth, has been weary to perform their roles. People have not brought to the LORD their small cattle as burnt offerings; they have not honored the LORD with their sacrifices because they have grown weary of the LORD. The LORD has not made the people serve Him with their burnt offering or the offering of incense to Him. The people have not brought sweet-smelling plants nor have they given the fat, the largest of their animal sacrifices: the only thing that the people have done is to use the power and the spirit of the LORD to serve themselves as they sin, as they live off-the-mark from the LORD's spirit. The people have wearied the LORD with their iniquities. Even with all this rebellion and lack of respect toward the LORD, He is still the One that blots out the transgressions of the people for His own sake, and the LORD will not remember sins because He chooses not to live with their ugliness.

26 Put me in remembrance: let us plead together: declare thou, that thou mayest be justified.
27 Thy first father hath sinned, and thy teachers have transgressed against me.
28 Therefore I have profaned the princes of the sanctuary, and have given Jacob to the curse, and Israel to reproaches.

The LORD speaking through the voice of his servant, Isaiah, asks the people to put Him in their remembrance once again: let the spirit of the LORD and the forms of the people plead together in oneness of action: the people must declare that they will serve the LORD in their living so that the people will be justified, justified by knowing that the spirit of the LORD is what they are using to create the things that they do on earth.

This is not something new. Your first father, Abraham, has also sinned in this regard. Your teachers have transgressed against the LORD. Therefore, the working of the law of the LORD has produced the effects and the conditions that the people can observe in action all around them if they will only observe. The princes of your sanctuary, the priests and the prophets, have been profaned by their own actions which are profane behaviors; they rejoice at being sinners! It is the application of the law of the LORD that has given Jacob, the material form of men and women, the curse of the LORD that they live with, that they die with, and the working of the law of the LORD that leads Israel to reproaches, to dishonor and disapproval, for the actions in which the spirits within the people do not serve the true nature of the LORD their God. If the people rebel and ignore the LORD, they deserve the hell which they created instead of the heaven which He offers. Fallen man is pathetic.

CHAPTER 44

1 Yet now hear, O Jacob my servant; and Israel, whom I have chosen:

The LORD speaking through Isaiah addresses His remarks to Jacob, His servant on earth. Jacob is the symbol for the physical forms of the people who hear the Word of the LORD: the LORD is also addressing his remarks to Israel, the spirit of the people who reside within the body of Jacob. This difference is based on the experience of Jacob who thought that he was an earthly person, a human, who eventually experienced his spirit and changed his name to Israel when he discovered and experienced his spiritual nature. Every person is a human being. More accurately, every person is a Being or a Spirit in a human form. The LORD wants everyone to know that the names of Jacob and Israel do not apply only to a person who lived many years ago; but, that Jacob has a reference to one's physical form, and Israel has a reference to the in-dwelling spirit of that form. The LORD has a command for Jacob and Israel, for "both" of these two people who are, really, one entity of spirit and form.

2 Thus saith the LORD that made thee, and formed thee from the womb, which will help thee; Fear not, O Jacob, my servant; and thou, Jesurun, whom I have chosen.
3 For I will pour water upon him that is thirsty, and floods upon the dry ground: I will pour my spirit upon thy seed, and my blessing upon thine offspring:
4 And they shall spring up as among the grass, as willows by the water courses.
5 One shall say, I am the LORD's; and another shall call himself by the name of Jacob; and another shall subscribe with his hand unto the LORD, and surname himself by the name of Israel.

The LORD who made the entity and formed it from the womb has this to say to His creation in order to be of help to the person who listens, the person who has ears to hear; Fear not, Jacob, the LORD's servant and Jesurun, the upright and righteous spirit which is another name for Israel, whom the LORD has chosen. The LORD will pour the water of His spirit on him, the individual, who is thirsty. Even though the LORD is speaking to "two" people, Jacob and Israel, Isaiah has written the message in the singular as though he is speaking to only one person. The water of the truth of the spirit of the LORD will be of such a quantity that it will flood the dry ground, the place where there is no water of truth, on Jacob, the human capacity. The LORD will pour his spirit upon the seed of Jacob and the spirit of blessing will be upon the offspring of the Israel-Jacob entity, the Being in the human form. Then the offspring shall spring up as grass, and as willows by the water courses, the streams. The spirit of the LORD shall spread and grow on earth. There will be more than two separate divisions of people on the earth; there will now be three divisions or groups: One group shall say that I am the LORD's; another group shall call himself by the name of Jacob, they are "only human"; and another group shall subscribe with his hand by pointing upward and say that they belong to the LORD and they will surname themselves by the name of Israel, which is the spirit that belongs to the LORD above, but the LORD that they point toward, is separate from Israel. They are not of one spirit.

6 Thus saith the LORD the King of Israel, and his redeemer the LORD of hosts; I am the first, and I am the last; and beside me there is no God.
7 And who, as I, shall call, and shall declare it, and set it in order for me, since I appointed the ancient people? and the things that are coming, and shall come, let them shew unto them.
8 Fear ye not, neither be afraid: have not I told thee from that time, and have declared it? ye are even my witnesses. Is there a God beside me? yea, there is no God; I know not any.
9 They that make a graven image are all of them vanity; and their delectable things shall not profit; and they are their own witnesses; they see not, nor know; that they may be ashamed.
10 Who hath formed a god, or molten a graven image that is profitable for nothing?

The LORD who is the King of Israel, the king to whom Israel gave allegiance, and his redeemer the LORD of hosts Who is the Lord over all the host of people on earth in physical form has this very clear instruction for the people; The LORD announces that He is the first and the last, the beginning and the end; and that, except for Him, there is no other God. The LORD wants to know who, as He shall call His people to Him, shall declare that they are indeed the LORD's people and set their environments in order for the LORD to come on earth which is the responsibility and the purpose that the LORD gave to the ancient people? The things that are coming presently, and shall come in the future, from the LORD, the only God who is the source of everything, out of heaven, the place of Cause where the LORD is, into the earth through Israel and Jacob, who represent the people, are gifts from the LORD that should be shown for everyone to see.

The people are instructed not to fear or be afraid that the LORD is moving through His creation to bring gifts into the earth. The LORD has told man and declared this message on earth in the past; the very existence of the people are the witnesses to the LORD. The LORD asks the rhetorical question as to whether there is a LORD or not and He answers immediately by saying that there is no other God; the LORD knows not any. The people who make a graven image are all vain; and their images which they have made and enjoy shall not profit them in the way that they expect; they are their own witnesses that their prayers to these graven images are not answered; they do not, nor do they know the futility of their prayers to the graven images which they have made and worshipped; that they do not know enough to be ashamed that they are using the power that comes from the LORD to them to worship a false god with the power of life that comes from the true God. Who has formed a god, or molten a graven image that is profitable for nothing? The person who has made an image to worship is not doing it for nothing. They are doing it for some benefit

The Testimony of the Major Prophets

for themselves because the LORD has no need, and has forbidden, the worship of graven images, and it is still being done. Who is doing this worship of graven images?

11 Behold, all his fellows shall be ashamed: and the workmen, they are of men: let them all be gathered together, let them stand up; yet they shall fear, and they shall be ashamed together.
12 The smith with the tongs both worketh in the coals, and fashioneth it with hammers, and worketh it with the strength of his arms: yea, he is hungry, and his strength faileth: he drinketh no water, and is faint.

Behold, look around you and see, all the fellows who are working to build the images that are being worshipped. They should be ashamed! The workmen are men who are gathered together in places where they worship images. Let them stand up and be recognized for what they are doing with the spirit of the LORD which comes to them to give them life. Even though they worship the images and idols that they have created, they still fear, and they should be ashamed together. The smith with tongs works in the hot coals and fashions his idols with hammers and works on the metal with the strength in his arms: yes, he is still hungry for the true God and his strength fails him, he gets no water of truth from God and he is weak. His idol and the worship of it does not refresh him. He has done all the work using the strength from the LORD to work on metal that he has fashioned so that he can worship his own creation.

13 The carpenter stretcheth out his rule; he marketh it out with a line; he fitteth it with planes, and he marketh it out with the compass, and maketh it after the figure of a man, according to the beauty of a man; that it may remain in the house.
14 He heweth him down cedars, and taketh the cypress and the oak, which he strengtheneth for himself among the trees of the forest: he planteth an ash, and the rain doth nourish it.
15 Then shall it be for a man to burn: for he will take thereof, and warm himself; yea, he kindleth it, and baketh bread; yea, he maketh a god, and worshippeth it; he maketh it a graven image, and falleth down thereto.
16 He burneth part thereof in the fire; with part thereof he eateth flesh; he roasteth roast, and is satisfied: yea, he warmeth himself, and saith, Aha, I am warm, I have seen the fire:
17 And the residue thereof he maketh a god, even his graven image: he falleth down unto it, and worshippeth it, and prayeth unto it, and saith, Deliver me; for thou art my god.

The carpenter stretches out his rule; marks it out with a line; uses planes and a compass, to make a figure of a man, according to the beauty of a man who was made by the LORD; so that the beautiful image may remain in the house. He cuts down cedars, the cypress and the oak, which he has allowed to grow for his own use for himself among the trees of the forest: he plants an ash, and the rain nourishes it. Then, it shall be for man to burn: he will take the wood and warm himself; he will use it to bake bread; yea, he will use the same wood from the same trees that he warmed himself and cooked with to make a god, and worship it; he made the wood into a graven image, and falls down to worship an inanimate object made of wood which he has harvested.

He has burned part of the wood in the fire; with part of it he used to eat the flesh with an implement made of wood; he roasted roast with the wood he burned, and he is satisfied: yes, he warms himself, and says, "Aha, I am warm, I have seen the fire": And the residue of the wood in his possession, he uses to make a god, his graven image: he falls down to it, worships and prays unto it, and says, Deliver me; for you are my god.

18 They have not known nor understood: for he hath shut their eyes, that they cannot see; and their hearts, that they cannot understand.
19 And none considereth in his heart, neither is there knowledge nor understanding to say, I have burned part of it in the fire; yea, also I have baked bread upon the coals thereof; I have roasted flesh, and eaten it: and shall I make the residue thereof an abomination? shall I fall down to the stock of a tree?
20 He feedeth on ashes: a deceived heart hath turned him aside, that he cannot deliver his soul, nor say, there not a lie in my right hand?

The people who worship these false gods of metal and wood have not known or they have not understood: they have shut their eyes so that they cannot see, they have eyes to see but they cannot see; and with their hearts closed to the truth of themselves, they cannot understand. No one considers in their hearts, nor is there knowledge or understanding to say to themselves that they have burned part of the wood in the fire, baked bread with another part of it, roasted flesh and eaten it, and after the wood has been used for warmth, and food, the remaining wood is used to make an abomination of an idol. Shall a person fall down to the stock of a tree? He tries to get life from the ashes of the wood that is burned in worship and his deceived heart has turned him aside proving that devoted worship does not benefit the idolater. He cannot command his own soul because he is under the influence of a false god; Is not this false belief that is in the right hand of his control a lie?

21 Remember these, O Jacob and Israel; for thou art my servant: I have formed thee; thou art my servant: O Israel, thou shalt not be forgotten of me.
22 I have blotted out, as a thick cloud, thy transgressions, and, as a cloud, thy sins: return unto me; for I have redeemed thee.
23 Sing, O ye heavens; for the LORD hath done it: shout, ye lower parts of the earth: break forth into singing, ye mountains, O forest, and every tree therein: for the LORD hath redeemed Jacob, and glorified himself in Israel.

Remember these examples, O Jacob and Israel, for you are my servant, your flesh and your spirit; the LORD has formed you. You are my servant, Israel, and you shall not be forgotten of the LORD. You have forgotten the LORD your God, but the LORD has not forgotten you. The LORD speaking through Isaiah says that He has blocked out all the transgressions of Jacob and Israel, and, as a cloud, that passes away, the sins. Now is the time to return unto the LORD because the LORD has redeemed you by accepting you as you are, sins and all transgressions. But, the invitation is to return to the LORD to serve the Spirit of the LORD to others. It is a time for rejoicing. It is a time to sing.

Sing, O ye heavens and the people who dwell there; for the LORD has done it: He has accepted all the people on earth as they are, He has forgiven all their transgressions from the way of the LORD and He has accepted them with all their sins so that they can make a new beginning if they choose to serve the LORD. This is a cause for rejoicing and a time to shout to everyone who is classified as

The Testimony of the Major Prophets

an inhabitant of the lower parts of the earth, the part that is farthest away from the LORD, the part that is composed of the worst of the transgressors and sinners. The invitation is also offered and the door is open for other people to break forth into singing. These people are part of the earth but they are not as far away from the LORD. They are symbolized as the mountains, every tree in the forest. This is done because the LORD working through his servant, Isaiah, has redeemed Jacob, has redeemed the fallen state of man and, by so doing, the LORD has glorified Himself in Israel, in Israel, in the place of the spirit on earth.

24 Thus saith the LORD, thy redeemer, and he that formed thee from the womb, I am the LORD that maketh all things; that stretcheth forth the heavens alone; that spreadeth abroad the earth by myself;
25 That frustrateth the tokens of the liars, and maketh diviners mad; that turneth wise men backward, and maketh their knowledge foolish;
26 That confirmeth the word of his servant, and performeth the counsel of his messengers; that saith to Jerusalem, Thou shalt be inhabited; and to the cities of Judah, Ye shall be built, and I will raise up the decayed places thereof:
27 That saith to the deep, Be dry, and I will dry up thy rivers:
28 That saith of Cyrus, He is my shepherd, and shall perform all my pleasure: even saying to Jerusalem, Thou shalt be built; and to the temple, Thy foundation shall be laid.

The LORD, your individual redeemer, and He that formed you in the womb says that He is the LORD that makes all things in the heaven and the earth and He has done this all by Himself. There are no other gods. This statement frustrates the tokens, the counterfeit gods, of the liars, and makes the diviners, the false prophets who try to divine a god out of metal and wood, angry and mad. It is the truth from the LORD who turn wise men of the earth, the false prophets and the diviners, backward when their knowledge is seen as nonsense.

It is the LORD, who confirms the word of His servant, Isaiah, by giving Jacob, or any person in the fallen state, the experience of the spirit of the LORD when Jacob obeys the LORD's direction through His prophet Isaiah. It is the LORD who performs, and follows through, the counsel and advice of his messengers according to working of the law of the LORD; that says to Jerusalem, You shall be inhabited by the offspring of the LORD; that the cities of Judah, with its decayed places, shall be built.

It is the LORD that says to the deep, the deep symbolizes the mass consciousness of the people, Be dry, do not produce the creations of the LORD that flow through you and the LORD will dry up the rivers of spirit that flow to you: that says of Cyrus, He is My shepherd, and he shall perform all the LORD's pleasure: even saying to Jerusalem, You shall be built; and to the temple, Your foundation shall be laid. This, the LORD commanded, through Cyrus. The decree of Cyrus authorized the rebuilding of the temple which would lead to a restored Jerusalem. There is more to learn about Cyrus.

CHAPTER 45

1 Thus saith the LORD to his anointed, to Cyrus, whose right hand I have holden, to subdue nations before him; and I will loose the loins of kings, to open before him the two leaved gates; and the gates shall not be shut;
2 I will go before thee, and make the crooked places straight: I will break in pieces the gates of brass, and cut in sunder the bars of iron:
3 And I will give thee the treasures of darkness, and hidden riches of secret places, that thou mayest know that I, the LORD, which call thee by thy name, am the God of Israel.
4 For Jacob my servant's sake, and Israel mine elect, I have even called thee by thy name: I have surnamed thee, though thou hast not known me.

Isaiah has identified Cyrus as a shepherd of the LORD when he says the LORD has anointed and works through Cyrus, the king of Persia, by holding his right hand, guided the hand of Cyrus, to subdue the nations before him. The LORD is in operation everywhere and He has loosed the loins of kings, caused the kings to open the two-leaved gates, opened the gates wide, for Cyrus to enter in; and the gates shall not be shut. The LORD goes before Cyrus, and makes the crooked places straight; the LORD's power which is in operation everywhere shall break the gates of brass into pieces, and cut the bars of iron; it is the LORD who gives the treasures of darkness, unknown treasures, and hidden riches from secret places, so that the LORD who calls Cyrus by name, is the God of Israel. The LORD has also called Jacob and Israel by name: the LORD has surnamed Jacob-Israel even though they know not the LORD. The LORD's first name is "I am"; the surname can be Jacob, Israel, or Cyrus. The LORD speaking through Isaiah wants everyone to know that He is everywhere, "I am" is everywhere. I am knows the material form in which the LORD dwells, but the physical form, with its heart and mind, does not know the LORD. Why is the LORD making this point over and over again?

5 I am the LORD, and there is none else, there is no God beside me: I girded thee, though thou hast not known me:
6 That they may know from the rising of the sun, and from the west, that there is none beside me. I am the LORD, and there is none else.

The Testimony of the Major Prophets

7 I form the light, and create darkness: I make peace, and create evil: I the LORD do all these things.

The LORD is making the point that there is only one LORD; there is none else, and there is no God beside the true LORD of all. It is the LORD who has upheld, girded, His servants, but they have not acknowledged Him; the people need to know that there is only one God from the rising of the sun in the east, all day long, to the sunset in the west that there is none on earth before the LORD; there is no one else. It is the LORD who forms the light and the darkness, the LORD Who makes peace and creates evil: it is the power of the LORD working through each of us individually and collectively, that does everything that is done on earth. Once again, the people are to know that the only power on earth is the power of God.

8 Drop down, ye heavens, from above, and let the skies pour down righteousness: let the earth open, and let them bring forth salvation, and let righteousness spring up together; I the LORD have created it.
9 Woe unto him that striveth with his Maker! Let the potsherd strive with the potsherds of the earth. Shall the clay say to him that fashioneth it, What makest thou? or thy work, He hath no hands?
10 Woe unto him that saith unto his father, What begettest thou? or to the woman, What hast thou brought forth?

If the LORD is everywhere, what does the LORD send into the earth to the children that carry the LORD's first name, I am, and the surname, the name of the physical form that identifies each individual? The LORD's righteousness that pours down from the skies above as a symbol of heaven, from the place where the LORD is: "let the earth open" is a command to let the earth of the heart, mind and body of the individual open to receive that which the LORD sends into the earth. This process will bring forth the salvation of the LORD on earth and it will let righteousness spring up together because the LORD has created it and it comes through the human form loud and clear. This open earth is the responsibility of a person.

Woe to him that strives with his Maker! Woe to the person who refuses to let his own earth open up to reveal the blessings that the LORD would send into the earth through an open channel. The person would be broken as a potsherd, a broken piece of pottery, by striving with the power of the LORD. The potsherd is the symbol of a broken and partial person. Isaiah says to let the potsherds, the broken people on earth, strive with each other which is striving with the LORD. The physical form of man, the clay, should not strive with his Maker which is exactly what man is doing! Shall the clay say to Him that fashions it, What are you making? or ask about the Maker's work as though He has no hands? Woe to him that says to his father, What are you making? or to the woman, What have you brought forth?

11 Thus saith the LORD, the Holy One of Israel, and his Maker, Ask me of things to come concerning my sons, and concerning the work of my hands command ye me.
12 I have made the earth, and created man upon it: I, even my hands, have stretched out the heavens, and all their host have I commanded.
13 I have raised him up in righteousness, and I will direct all his ways: he shall build my city, and he shall let go my captives, not for price nor reward, saith the LORD of hosts.

The LORD, the Holy One of Israel, and his Maker, say that it is fitting to ask of things to come in regard to the sons, the offspring of the LORD, and the work concerning His hand and the things that are under His control. The LORD has created the earth and man upon it; His hands have stretched out the heavens and all the hosts of people who are under the LORD's command. The LORD has raised His spiritual children in righteousness and He will direct all the ways of His spiritual children: the spiritual offspring of the LORD shall build His spiritual holy city, and His offspring are like their Father in that they shall let go of the LORD's captives, not for a price or a reward, but because they are His sons, says the LORD of hosts. The hosts are the spiritual offspring of the LORD; they represent the LORD on earth.

14 Thus saith the LORD, The labour of Egypt, and merchandise of Ethiopia and of the Sabeans, men of stature, shall come over unto thee, and they shall be thine: they shall come after thee; in chains they shall come over, and they shall fall down unto thee, they shall make supplication unto thee, saying, Surely God is in thee; and there is none else, there is no God.
15 Verily thou art a God that hidest thyself, O God of Israel, the Saviour.
16 They shall be ashamed, and also confounded, all of them: they shall go to confusion together that are makers of idols.
17 But Israel shall be saved in the LORD with an everlasting salvation: ye shall not be ashamed nor confounded world without end.

The LORD explains that men of stature—Egyptians, Ethiopians and Sabeans who have knowledge and wealth of earthly things—shall come to the sons of the LORD with labor and merchandise of the material world and they and their wealth shall be yours to command: they shall come after you in chains, fall down before you, make supplication and say, Surely, God is in you; and there is none else, except the God that is in you. Truly, you are a God that hides yourself, O God of Israel, the Savior. The people who come to worship shall be ashamed and confounded, all of them; they go to confusion together that are the makers of idols. But Israel, the spirit of the LORD in the people, the sons of the LORD who are hidden in human forms, shall be saved in the LORD of which they are a part with an everlasting salvation. The children of the LORD are a part of the LORD with an everlasting salvation. You shall not be ashamed, nor the confounded world without end to the period of confusion.

18 For thus saith the LORD that created the heavens; God himself that formed the earth and made it; he hath established it, he created it not in vain, he formed it to be inhabited: I am the LORD; and there is none else.
19 I have not spoken in secret, in a dark place of the earth: I said not unto the seed of Jacob, Seek ye me in vain: I the LORD speak righteousness, I declare things that are right.
20 Assemble yourselves and come; draw near together, ye that are escaped of the nations: they have no knowledge that set up the wood of their graven image, and pray unto a god that cannot save.

The LORD that created the heavens; God himself that formed the earth and made it; He has established it and created it not in vain but as a place to be inhabited: Once again He states through His prophet, Isaiah, that He is the LORD; and there is none else. The LORD has not spoken in

The Testimony of the Major Prophets

secret, in a dark place of the earth, He has spoken openly: He did not say to the physical seed of Jacob, the symbol of people who know not the LORD to seek Him in vain, without promise of success. The LORD speaks righteousness; He declares things that are right. He directs the people who hear His voice to assemble themselves and come; draw near together, you that are escaped of the nations: the nations that you have escaped from have no knowledge of the LORD if they set up the wood of their graven images, and pray to a god that cannot save them. The LORD will lead His people to a salvation that is not in vain, but, it is true.

21 Tell ye, and bring them near; yea, let them take counsel together: who hath declared this from ancient time? who hath told it from that time? have not I the LORD? and there is no God else beside me; a just God and a Saviour; there is none beside me.
22 Look unto me, and be ye saved, all the ends of the earth: for I am God, and there is none else.
23 I have sworn by myself, the word is gone out of my mouth in righteousness, and shall not return, That unto me every knee shall bow, every tongue shall swear.
24 Surely, shall one say, in the LORD have I righteousness and strength: even to him shall men come; and all that are incensed against him shall be ashamed.
25 In the LORD shall all the seed of Israel be justified, and shall glory.

The LORD speaking through the form of His prophet, Isaiah tells all of His listeners to tell their friends what has been said and bring them near: yes, let them take counsel together among themselves: let them remember Who has declared this message from ancient times? Who told it from that time? Has it not been the LORD? There is no God beside the LORD who is coming forth through Isaiah; a just God and a Savior; there is none beside the LORD as revealed through Isaiah. Isaiah has a very clear message for his listeners as he reveals the LORD to them.

Look to the example of Isaiah as he reveals the LORD for them to see and they too can be saved if they follow the example he sets for everyone to the ends of the earth: for the God that comes forth accurately through a person is the true God and there is none else. Isaiah has sworn for himself that the word of the LORD that has gone out of his mouth in righteousness and shall not return; therefore, the word must go forth rightly. It will produce a result to those who hear the word of the LORD and respond to it. It is the word of the LORD that goes forth. Every knee that returns to Isaiah shall bow to the LORD Who Isaiah represents, every tongue shall swear to the LORD in covenant with Isaiah. Surely, one shall say, that in the LORD's spirit, Isaiah has righteousness and strength: even to him shall men shall come to Isaiah and they will come to the LORD because Isaiah is representing the LORD's spirit; all that are incensed against Isaiah shall be ashamed. In the LORD that Isaiah represents to his followers shall all the seed of Israel, the spirit that is within each person be justified, and shall glory in his presence. The people who come to Isaiah and therefore come to the LORD whom he represents, shall experience the transition from Jacob to Israel, from "only human" to spiritual identity.

CHAPTER 46

1 Bel boweth down, Nebo stoopeth, their idols were upon the beasts, and upon the cattle: your carriages were heavy loaden; they are a burden to the weary beast.
2 They stoop, they bow down together; they could not deliver the burden, but themselves are gone into captivity.
3 Hearken unto me, O house of Jacob, and all the remnant of the house of Israel, which are borne by me from the belly, which are carried from the womb:
4 And even to your old age I am he; and even to hoar hairs will I carry you: I have made, and I will bear; even I will carry, and will deliver you.

Bel, another name for Marduk, the chief deity of Babylon, and Nebo (Nabu), the son of Marduk, was the god of learning and writing, whose idols were being carried by the beasts and cattle: the carriages were loaded too heavily; they were a burden to the weary beasts who were brought low and bowed down under the weight so that they could not deliver the burden of the gods that they were pulling with their own power. The gods were not able to rescue themselves or the beasts who were transporting them from one place to another. Isaiah is making the point that these false gods and idols do not have the power to save their own images or the beasts that carry them from place to place. They were totally helpless and they were gone into captivity of their misfortune and could not save themselves.

The LORD speaking through Isaiah says that the house of Jacob, the house of the physical, human, "animal" aspect of man, as well as the small remnant of the house of Israel, the spiritual or Being aspect of man, should listen to the message. The LORD has carried all people from the time of conception in the belly of a woman, carried from the womb to your old age when your hairs are white with old age. The LORD has made each of you. He has been carrying you and He will deliver you to your destination which was not accomplished by the beasts who were pulling the idols of Bel and Nebo. Isaiah has made a vivid comparison between an idol, a false god and the true God; the form and the spirit Who is with His creation, always.

5 To whom will ye liken me, and make me equal, and compare me, that we may be like?

The Testimony of the Major Prophets

6 They lavish gold out of the bag, and weigh silver in the balance, and hire a goldsmith; and he maketh it a god: they fall down, yea, they worship.
7 They bear him upon the shoulder, they carry him, and set him in his place, and he standeth; from his place shall he not remove: yea, one shall cry unto him, yet can he not answer, nor save him out of his trouble.
8 Remember this, and shew yourselves men: bring it again to mind, O ye transgressors.

The LORD speaking through Isaiah wants to know to whom will a person compare Him and make Him equal so that the two of them, the LORD moving through the form of Isaiah and the person who is doing the observation, may be alike? The LORD is inviting the person who is watching the spiritual expression of the LORD through Isaiah to do the same thing that Isaiah is doing. Isaiah is **serving** the LORD's spirit; the person is **observing** the process. The invitation to all people who have ears to hear and eyes to see is to change from an **ob**server of the spirit of the LORD being released into the earth to a server of the LORD's spirit being released into the earth through one's own heart, mind and body which is the only way that a person can assume the responsibility for serving the LORD in spirit and in truth. People try to serve the LORD in many other ways than this!

People lavish gold from a bag, weigh silver on a scale, and hire a goldsmith to make this metal into a god which they fall down and worship. Then, they bear this idol made of metal up on their shoulder, carry him, and set him in a place where it remains stationary; the idol shall not move from this place: yes, people shall cry aloud and pray to him, yet he can not answer, nor save that person out of his trouble, whatever it is. Remember this, that an idol has no life or power like the LORD. Show yourselves as men, whom the spirit of the LORD is moving through: bring this again to mind, when you are transgressors.

9 Remember the former things of old: for I am God, and there is none else; I am God, and there is none like me,
10 Declaring the end from the beginning, and from ancient times the things that are not yet done, saying, My counsel shall stand, and I will do all my pleasure:
11 Calling a ravenous bird from the east, the man that executeth my counsel from a far country: yea, I have spoken it, I will also bring it to pass; I have purposed it, I will also do it.
12 Hearken unto me, ye stouthearted, that are far from righteousness:
13 I bring near my righteousness; it shall not be far off, and my salvation shall not tarry: and I will place salvation in Zion for Israel my glory.

Remember, when you are a transgressor from the only way that the power of the LORD can come into the earth, the things of old, the teachings that say that the LORD's name is I AM. There is none else or no other way for God to be known except to say, I am that I AM, and let the spirit flow from God through you into the earth declaring that the end result that appears on earth are from its beginning in spirit of the LORD. This has been the way that the spirit of God and the things of God get into the earth since ancient times and what the LORD will bring into the earth has not been done yet. The counsel of the LORD shall stand on earth because it is true, and the LORD will always do what is pleasurable to the LORD: the problem has been that the selfish thoughts contained within the human self, which is symbolized by a ravenous bird that comes out of the east, are contained within a person who is a stranger to the LORD. The stranger to the LORD who knows not the ways of the LORD tries to execute the LORD's counsel through his impure heart and mind and produces a distortion of the LORD's spirit.

The LORD has spoken truly in the realm of spirit; The LORD will bring the blessings of His spirit to pass; the LORD has purpose in His spirit and the LORD will do His part in the creative process. People have been out of position to receive the spirit of the LORD without distorting the blessings that the LORD sends continually. People destroy and distort the blessings and they appear on earth as a cursing from the LORD. The LORD is looking for people who will not distort His blessings as they flow through man who was designed to deliver the spiritual blessing from the LORD into the earth. These would be people who would admit that they have not been serving the LORD's spirit, and that they would be willing to begin to do it. These are the stouthearted people who were far from righteousness, the right-use-ness of their hearts, minds, and bodies but who are willing to repent and serve the spirit of the LORD. The LORD brings forth His righteousness through His prophet, Isaiah, who lets the LORD's spirit flow through him which is the act of prophesying the LORD.

The righteousness of the spirit of the LORD delivered on earth through Isaiah shall not be far off; the spirit of the LORD has been expressed on earth through Isaiah and it is out of heaven and into the earth where it is available to be observed by the followers of Isaiah. The LORD's salvation shall not tarry in its action once that it is on earth to be seen and felt. The LORD will place the spirit that has been expressed into the earth into a special place where it will be available on earth for those who desire and long for the spirit of the LORD. The high place where the spirit of the LORD dwells on earth, where salvation dwells on earth, is called Zion. It is a place of the spirit of the LORD on earth that is available within everyone who hears the word of the LORD. The people who desire to step up into the high place of Zion are called Israel. Israel, the people who express the spirit of the LORD on earth are the means to release the glory of the LORD on earth

CHAPTER 47

1 Come down, and sit in the dust, O virgin daughter of Babylon, sit on the ground: there is no throne, O daughter of the Chaldeans: for thou shalt no more be called tender and delicate.
2 Take the millstones, and grind meal: uncover thy locks, make bare the leg, uncover the thigh, pass over the rivers.
3 Thy nakedness shall be uncovered, yea, thy shame shall be seen: I will take vengeance, and I will not meet thee as a man.

The LORD speaking through His prophet, Isaiah, invites people who do not know the LORD within themselves to come and have the opportunity to learn about the LORD. The people who do not know the LORD, the people who are not Man on earth, made in the image and likeness of God, are classified as women. From their point of view, the point of view of their conscious minds, the spirit of the LORD has not entered into them and they are considered as spiritual virgins. The fact that they are in the fallen state is symbolized by classifying them as opponents of Jerusalem. The people who are invited to hear the word of the LORD through Isaiah are symbolized by the virgin daughters of Babylon and Chaldea. Isaiah invites the people—who do not know the LORD, who are opponents, not in the place of the LORD, who know that they are not Man—to come to Him that he represents on earth.

The people who are invited are asked to come and sit in the dust because there is no throne available on earth where one person is better than another if the spirit of the LORD is to flow simultaneously through everyone. The virgin daughters of Babylon, the new followers of Isaiah who can come from everywhere, are not to be considered tender and delicate. They are strong as the spirit of the LORD increases through them consciously which shall produce a change from weakness to strength. A new beginning is being made in the experience of the new followers, the daughters of Babylon. The experience is not new to Isaiah who is the leader and who knows where he is leading his new flock.

Isaiah advised the people to assume responsibility to take the millstones, and grind meal; they are to be a part of what is doing the grinding and not a part of what is being ground, a victor rather

The Symbolic Version of Isaiah

than a victim: uncover the locks so that you can see and deal with the places in the mind that have been locked and you have been denied access to change your old habitual ways: make bare the leg, uncover the thigh, pass over the rivers. This is an invitation to remove the shoes of understanding of the way that you walked through life with the concepts and beliefs inherited from the past, uncover the thigh and pass over rivers which is symbolism for walking through new waters which is quite deep. Your individual nakedness of the previous behavior of the fallen state shall be uncovered and, yea, the shame which a person has because they walked not in the way of righteousness shall be seen: The LORD will take vengeance on these unrighteous qualities, by eliminating them from the person's expression of life. Isaiah states that he will not meet his followers as a man: he will meet them as a server of the LORD. Isaiah will redeem them.

4 As for our redeemer, the LORD of hosts is his name, the Holy One of Israel.
5 Sit thou silent, and get thee into darkness, O daughter of the Chaldeans: for thou shalt no more be called, The lady of kingdoms.

As for the redeemer, his name is the LORD of hosts, He is the LORD of all the hosts of the people on earth, the Holy One of Israel. This is the spirit that is being expressed through Isaiah. The followers of Isaiah are instructed to sit silently and listen in the spiritual darkness in which they find themselves. They sit as a symbolic daughter of the Chaldeans who is in a strange new land. Their old ways must pass away and they shall no more be called the lady of individual kingdoms, wherein they are the center of their individual worlds. (Years later, the Beloved Disciple, John, referred to this state as the great whore of Babylon.) The people who are in the fallen state must begin to see what they, collectively, have done to the LORD's earth. People who are in the fallen state must see how their actions have produced the conditions on earth due to the working of the law of the LORD.

6 I was wroth with my people, I have polluted mine inheritance, and given them into thine hand: thou didst shew them no mercy; upon the ancient hast thou very heavily laid thy yoke.
7 And thou saidst, I shall be a lady for ever: so that thou didst not lay these things to thy heart, neither didst remember the latter end of it.
8 Therefore hear now this, thou that art given to pleasures, that dwellest carelessly, that sayest in thine heart, I am, and none else beside me; I shall not sit as a widow, neither shall I know the loss of children:
9 But these two things shall come to thee in a moment in one day, the loss of children, and widowhood: they shall come upon thee in their perfection for the multitude of thy sorceries, and for the great abundance of thine enchantments.

Due to the working of the law of the LORD, He has presently, and in the past, been angry with His people, polluted the land of their inheritance, given them into the hand of control of man in the fallen state: Fallen man, symbolized by Jacob, did not show mercy to their brothers and sisters; they blamed conditions on the ancients, the people who lived many years before and laid the yoke of responsibility on the past generations who went before them. And the people who were raised in the fallen state said, this is the way I am, I shall be a lady, one who receives and not one who gives, for ever: so these things were not taken to heart, nor did anyone remember the latter end, how things ended up this way.

The Testimony of the Major Prophets

Therefore, Isaiah asks those who would be his followers to hear that people in the fallen state are given to pleasures, they live carelessly, they say in their heart, I am the only one who is important, and there is no one else in the world who is important beside me; as long as I am alone and unmarried; if I remain a virgin and unmarried, then, I shall not have to sit as a widow, or to know the loss of children, the loss of love. But these two things shall come to a person who is in the fallen darkened state in a moment, in one day, the loss of children, and widowhood: Isaiah is speaking about the death of the physical form where everything is lost to the person identified with the material form of the earth and earthly connections. A person must give love in order to know love; this is known by women who love their husband and love their children. A greedy self-centered person does not give love, they do not express love, they seek happiness by greed and by getting feelings and things of the earth. They will surely reap the greed and selfishness which they have sown. The results of their sowing shall come upon them in the perfection of the working of the law for the multitude of the sorceries, and the great abundance of the enchantments which the person expressed in the fallen state.

10 For thou hast trusted in thy wickedness: thou hast said, None seeth me. Thy wisdom and thy knowledge, it hath perverted thee; and thou hast said in thine heart, I am, and none else beside me.
11 Therefore shall evil come upon thee; thou shalt not know from whence it riseth: and mischief shall fall upon thee; thou shalt not be able to put it off: and desolation shall come upon thee suddenly, which thou shalt not know.
12 Stand now with thine enchantments, and with the multitude of thy sorceries, wherein thou hast laboured from thy youth; if so be thou shalt be able to profit, if so be thou mayest prevail.
13 Thou art wearied in the multitude of thy counsels. Let now the astrologers, the stargazers, the monthly prognosticators, stand up, and save thee from these things that shall come upon thee.
14 Behold, they shall be as stubble; the fire shall burn them; they shall not deliver themselves from the power of the flame: there shall not be a coal to warm at, nor fire to sit before it.
15 Thus shall they be unto thee with whom thou hast laboured, even thy merchants, from thy youth: they shall wander every one to his quarter; none shall save thee.

Persons in the fallen state trust in their wickedness which they call "normal": they say to themselves that no one has seen what they do in private and they conclude that they will not get caught. The wisdom and knowledge of the wicked used in selfishness has perverted the way of the LORD. You have said in your heart that this is the way I am and there is no one else beside me. Therefore evil shall come upon you and you will not know from where it did arise; mischief shall fall upon you; you shall not be able to put it away from you; and desolation shall come upon you suddenly, and you shall not know the cause of it.

Isaiah advises his followers to stand up and look at their sins and faults which the fallen people see as their enchantments and sorceries which they use to take advantage of other people. These habit patterns have been with you from your youth. If you do look at these faults, you can profit by the experience, and you are in a position to choose not to do these things; you will prevail and have the victory over them if you take responsibility for your expressions into the earth. Isaiah knows that people, who have problems and circumstances with which they have to deal, turn to others to help them to get away from their troubles from a variety of sources. People are wearied in the multitude of the counsel and advice that they get from conflicting sources. People may have offered their "good" advice and predictions to others in their attempts to be helpful.

Isaiah calls for the astrologers, the stargazers, the monthly prognosticators, stand up now, and save you from these things that shall come upon you as a result of the working of the law. Behold, they shall fail in their attempts, they shall be as useless stubble that shall be burned in the fire. The false prophets who believe that they can set aside the working of the law of the LORD shall not be able to deliver themselves from the power of the flame of the fire of the LORD. They shall not have the comfort that they seek because there is no comfort except in the proper application of the law; they shall not find a coal to warm at, or a fire to sit before it. This is the application of the working of the law and it shall work unto you according to your expressions with the people with whom you have labored in the LORD's vineyard. This is the working of the law, even from the merchants, what went forth from you from your youth: every expression, every behavior, shall wander and move to its own place, its own quarter, according to the working of the law and no one, no false prophet, shall save you from the LORD's law of cause and effect; as you sow, so shall you reap. Isaiah's message to his new followers, symbolized by the daughters of Babylon, is to be very aware of the working of the law of the LORD.

CHAPTER 48

1 Hear ye this, O house of Jacob, which are called by the name of Israel, and are come forth out of the waters of Judah, which swear by the name of the LORD, and make mention of the God of Israel, but not in truth, nor in righteousness.
2 For they call themselves of the holy city, and stay themselves upon the God of Israel; The LORD of hosts is his name.

Isaiah tells the house of Jacob, the symbol of the physical forms of people in the fallen state, who call themselves by the name Israel, which is the name for those who are identified with the spirit within themselves, who have come forth out of the waters, the symbol for the consciousness, of the people who are living in the land of Judah. These fallen people swear by the name of the LORD, and they make mention of the God of Israel, the God of the spiritual aspect of man, but they do not do it in truth or righteousness. Isaiah has called them liars and hypocrites because they have used the name of the LORD in vain. They have not released the spirit of the LORD in their living. They call themselves of the holy city, and they stay themselves, they fix their minds on the idea and the concept of a God of Israel: whose name is the LORD of hosts. This is the divine position that is represented by Isaiah for the house of Jacob and the people of Judah but they are not hearing his teachings.

3 I have declared the former things from the beginning; and they went forth out of my mouth, and I shewed them; I did them suddenly, and they came to pass.
4 Because I knew that thou art obstinate, and thy neck is an iron sinew, and thy brow brass;
5 I have even from the beginning declared it to thee; before it came to pass I shewed it thee: lest thou shouldest say, Mine idol hath done them, and my graven image, and my molten image, hath commanded them.

Isaiah has declared these teachings from the beginning of the LORD's ministry, His ministry, and they did go forth from the mouth, the expressions and the behaviors of Isaiah who showed them; Isaiah did these things quickly and they came to pass according to the working of the law. Isaiah knows that fallen nature, human nature, is obstinate and people, trapped in the behaviors of human

The Symbolic Version of Isaiah

nature, are very reluctant to change; their necks, the symbol of turning to see a new direction, is like an iron sinew because they are a stiff-necked people who are very resistant to change. Their brow, where true thinking should take place, is like shining brass because it reflects the behaviors of the people around them. Brass is a metal that tarnishes easily and must be regularly polished to keep its shine. Isaiah has told these reluctant people what he was going to do in advance, before it came to pass in physical form, so that they would not say that Isaiah's idols, graven images or molten images have commanded certain things to come to pass.

6 Thou hast heard, see all this; and will not ye declare it? I have shewed thee new things from this time, even hidden things, and thou didst not know them.
7 They are created now, and not from the beginning; even before the day when thou heardest them not; lest thou shouldest say, Behold, I knew them.
8 Yea, thou heardest not; yea, thou knewest not; yea, from that time that thine ear was not opened: for I knew that thou wouldest deal very treacherously, and wast called a transgressor from the womb.
9 For my name's sake will I defer mine anger, and for my praise will I refrain for thee, that I cut thee not off.

The people of Judah have seen and heard all of this but, will they declare the teaching of Isaiah in their own expressions? Isaiah has shown them new things from this time, the present moment, as he revealed the spirit of the LORD in his personal representation of the LORD's spirit; even things which were hidden from them which they did not know before Isaiah told them. Now, new things are created in physical form through Isaiah where in the beginning there was nothing in form until Isaiah brought the spirit of the LORD into form; even before the day when the people did not hear what Isaiah would bring forth in spiritual expression, the people could say, that they knew beforehand what Isaiah would bring forth. All people are spiritual people and spirit within the human people hear the spirit when it is expressed.

The people of Judah did not hear; they did not know; and from that time their ears were not opened to the word of Isaiah, who knew that the people would deal treacherously with what Isaiah had to say. Isaiah would be called a transgressor from the time of his birth. For Isaiah's names sake, (I am!), Isaiah will defer his anger, and because of his mission to praise the LORD and influence everyone to praise the LORD, Isaiah will refrain from retaliating in like kind, and he will not cut them off from the word of the LORD.

10 Behold, I have refined thee, but not with silver; I have chosen thee in the furnace of affliction.
11 For mine own sake, even for mine own sake, will I do it: for how should my name be polluted? and I will not give my glory unto another.
12 Hearken unto me, O Jacob and Israel, my called; I am he; I am the first, I also am the last.
13 Mine hand also hath laid the foundation of the earth, and my right hand hath spanned the heavens: when I call unto them, they stand up together.

Isaiah tells the people that He has refined them but not with silver, silver is the symbol of truth. Silver, like fallen people, are tarnished with a black dross on the silver which can be polished away to result once again in a shiny metal. Isaiah has chosen people who are in the furnace of affliction

The Testimony of the Major Prophets

from the working of the law. People have expressed their faults and sins and reaped the results of their own behavior. Isaiah will help the afflicted for his own sake, even for his own sake will he do it: shall the LORD speaking through Isaiah allow his own name, I Am, be polluted? Isaiah will not give his glory, the glory of expressing the spirit of the LORD in momentary living, to another person which will cause Isaiah to cease praising the LORD. Isaiah can only express the spirit of the LORD through himself.

Isaiah once again calls the people of Jacob and Israel, to listen to him as he repeats that I am He; I am the first and the last; the all that is; I Am a focus of the Spirit. The LORD has used His control to lay the foundations of the earth, and His right hand has spanned the heavens: when the LORD calls out to the heavens, they stand up together. When the LORD speaks to the people who have both a spirit and a form, the spirit within them listens, but the form can use the self-active mind to choose to ignore the LORD. Isaiah speaks to the spirits of the people.

14 All ye, assemble yourselves, and hear; which among them hath declared these things? The LORD hath loved him: he will do his pleasure on Babylon, and his arm shall be on the Chaldeans.
15 I, even I, have spoken; yea, I have called him: I have brought him, and he shall make his way prosperous.

All who hear the voice of Isaiah are called to assemble themselves and hear the spiritual message in the teaching of Isaiah who asks which among you have declared the things that Isaiah has declared? Who has emulated the example of Isaiah? The LORD loves him; His creation of man. The people who follow the example of Isaiah will do His pleasure, the pleasure of the LORD to give life in Babylon, and His arm, the might of the LORD, shall be on the Chaldeans. The LORD has spoken to them, also. Yes, the LORD has called to the Chaldeans. The Chaldeans have responded and the power of the LORD, moving through the Chaldeans, shall prosper to the extent that they harmonize with the spirit of the LORD.

16 Come ye near unto me, hear ye this; I have not spoken in secret from the beginning; from the time that it was, there am I: and now the Lord GOD, and his Spirit, hath sent me.
17 Thus saith the LORD, thy Redeemer, the Holy One of Israel; I am the LORD thy God which teacheth thee to profit, which leadeth thee by the way that thou shouldest go.
18 O that thou hadst hearkened to my commandments! then had thy peace been as a river, and thy righteousness as the waves of the sea:
19 Thy seed also had been as the sand, and the offspring of thy bowels like the gravel thereof; his name should not have been cut off nor destroyed from before me.

Isaiah invites everyone near to hear what he has to say; he has not spoken in secret from the very beginning; from the time when it was in the past, there is the spirit of the LORD that was in the past. Now, in the present time, the LORD God has sent Isaiah forth on the LORD's mission with a message. The message from the LORD, your Redeemer, the Holy One of Israel is: I am the LORD your God which teaches you to profit, which leads you by the way that you should go. Isaiah has a way of life from the LORD for people to live on earth that can be very valuable. O, if people had only listened to the word of the LORD and kept His commandments! Then peace would have been as a river and the righteousness of man would have been coming into the earth as the waves of the sea. People are the problem, not the LORD.

The seed of peaceful men also would have been as plentiful as the grains of sand of the sea and the offspring that came forth from your bowels, your descendants, like the gravel thereof; larger in size and strength. If man would have listened to the word of the LORD, His name, I am, should not have been cut off from man, or His blessings destroyed from before the LORD as they are distorted into cursings by man.

20 Go ye forth of Babylon, flee ye from the Chaldeans, with a voice of singing declare ye, tell this, utter it even to the end of the earth; say ye, The LORD hath redeemed his servant Jacob.
21 And they thirsted not when he led them through the deserts: he caused the waters to flow out of the rock for them: he clave the rock also, and the waters gushed out.
22 There is no peace, saith the LORD, unto the wicked.

The message of Isaiah is for the people, all people to go forth from Babylon, the symbol of the fallen state, to flee from the ways of the Chaldeans with a voice of singing and declare to everyone, tell this message, utter it even to the end of the earth: say, the LORD is on earth and has redeemed his fallen servant, Jacob. Jacob can become Israel. And the people who hear the message and put it into practice in their living shall have the water of truth from the LORD. The people who followed the LORD had the water of truth from the LORD in the desert and they did not thirst; The LORD caused the water to flow out of a rock for them: He clave the rock of Jacob, of fallen human nature, and the waters gushed out. The blessing of the water that comes forth is for those who follow the LORD and express His spirit. There is no peace to the wicked, the people who do not express the spirit of the LORD.

CHAPTER 49

1 Listen, O isles, unto me; and hearken, ye people, from far; The LORD hath called me from the womb; from the bowels of my mother hath he made mention of my name.
2 And he hath made my mouth like a sharp sword; in the shadow of his hand hath he hid me, and made me a polished shaft; in his quiver hath he hid me;
3 And said unto me, Thou art my servant, O Israel, in whom I will be glorified.

Isaiah calls to the little isles, the symbols of separate pieces of land which represent the separated people, people in the fallen state, the people who compose the body of Jacob, to come to him; these are the people who are immediately around him in his environment; he also wants the people from afar to hear what he has to say because the LORD is the LORD of all, the LORD of hosts. Isaiah states that the LORD has called him from his mother's womb; while he was still within his mother, the LORD made mention of His name; I am here. The LORD's spirit flowing through the form of Isaiah has made his mouth of expression as a sharp sword of truth; in the shadow of His hand, the LORD has hidden Isaiah and made him into a polished shaft which the LORD hid in His quiver until the LORD wanted to shoot the arrow. The LORD said to Isaiah that he is the servant of the LORD, called him Israel, the focus of spirit, in whom the LORD will be glorified.

4 Then I said, I have laboured in vain, I have spent my strength for nought, and in vain: yet surely my judgment is with the LORD, and my work with my God.
5 And now, saith the LORD that formed me from the womb to be his servant, to bring Jacob again to him, Though Israel be not gathered, yet shall I be glorious in the eyes of the LORD, and my God shall be my strength.
6 And he said, It is a light thing that thou shouldest be my servant to raise up the tribes of Jacob, and to restore the preserved of Israel: I will also give thee for a light to the Gentiles, that thou mayest be my salvation unto the end of the earth.

Isaiah has felt and said that he has labored in vain, he has spent his strength for nothing, without any results, in vain. Yet, all the time, Isaiah believed upon reflection that his judgment was always with the LORD, and that his work was with his God. And now, the LORD that formed Isaiah from the womb to be His servant, said to bring Jacob, those people who do not know the LORD, to Him again. Although Israel, the spirits from the LORD who dwell within the physical forms on earth, have not been gathered, yet Isaiah shall be glorious in the eyes of the LORD, and God shall be Isaiah's strength. The LORD said that it is a **light** thing that you should be my servant to raise up the tribes of Jacob, and to restore the preserved of Israel: the word, light, has reference to a light of understanding and leading the way to the LORD by letting the LORD's light shine through Isaiah. The LORD will also give Isaiah for a light to the Gentiles, so that he may also be the LORD's salvation to the end of the earth.

7 Thus saith the LORD, the Redeemer of Israel, and his Holy One, to him whom man despiseth, to him whom the nation abhorreth, to a servant of rulers, Kings shall see and arise, princes also shall worship, because of the LORD that is faithful, and the Holy One of Israel, and he shall choose thee.
8 Thus saith the LORD, In an acceptable time have I heard thee, and in a day of salvation have I helped thee: and I will preserve thee, and give thee for a covenant of the people, to establish the earth, to cause to inherit the desolate heritages;
9 That thou mayest say to the prisoners, Go forth; to them that are in darkness, Shew yourselves. They shall feed in the ways, and their pastures shall be in all high places.
10 They shall not hunger nor thirst; neither shall the heat nor sun smite them: for he that hath mercy on them shall lead them, even by the springs of water shall he guide them.
11 And I will make all my mountains a way, and my highways shall be exalted.

The LORD, the Redeemer, and his Holy One, has said to Isaiah whom man despises, to him who is abhorred by nations of people, to a servant of rulers, that the time will come when kings shall see and arise, princes shall worship because of the LORD that is faithful, and the Holy One of Israel shall choose to reveal Himself through you. In an acceptable time, the LORD shall hear you and help you in a day of salvation for His people. The LORD will preserve you and give <u>you</u> for a covenant of the people, to establish the divine design earth, and to inherit the desolate heritages of a people who have spent generations in the fallen state of darkness. You may say to the prisoners that you will find incarcerated in the prisons of false beliefs, Go forth; Go to the people who are in darkness, Show yourselves. Be a light to others. They shall feed in the ways of the LORD that is offered by your steadfast example, and their pastures, the spiritual things that they take into themselves, shall be in all high places that will be pleasing to the LORD. The people who truly desire to find the LORD shall not hunger nor thirst; they will be satisfied and fulfilled; the heat nor sun hurt them in their quest: for the LORD that has mercy on them shall lead them, and guide them by the springs of water, so that they will not be thirsty along the way. The LORD will make all His mountains a way, and His highways shall be exalted, which illustrates that the way will be made easy.

12 Behold, these shall come from far: and, lo, these from the north and from the west; and these from the land of Sinim.
13 Sing, O heavens; and be joyful, O earth; and break forth into singing, O mountains: for the LORD hath comforted his people, and will have mercy upon his afflicted.
14 But Zion said, The LORD hath forsaken me, and my Lord hath forgotten me.

The Testimony of the Major Prophets

15 Can a woman forget her sucking child, that she should not have compassion on the son of her womb? yea, they may forget, yet will I not forget thee.
16 Behold, I have graven thee upon the palms of my hands; thy walls are continually before me.
17 Thy children shall make haste; thy destroyers and they that made thee waste shall go forth of thee.

Behold, people shall come from far away: from the north, the west and as far south as Sinim, Aswan in southern Egypt. This is a joyous time and the heavens and the earth, the place of the spirit and the form, for the people everywhere to break forth into singing the praises of the LORD who has comforted the people once again with His spirit on earth and will have mercy on His afflicted people. There is a great amount of singing among the people wherever they happen to be.

But Zion, the holy place of high spiritual expression atop Mount Zion and where the heart within a person receives inspiration from the LORD, said, the LORD has forsaken me, and my Lord has forgotten me. There is spiritual activity elsewhere other than Zion. The immediate reply is, Can a woman forget her sucking child, that she should not have compassion on the son of her womb? It is possible for people to praise the LORD by letting the spirit of the LORD find expression in more than one place.

Yes, some of the people may forget the holy place of Mount Zion, but, the LORD will not forget. Behold, I have graven you upon the palms of my hands; the names of the 12 tribes are engraved on the 12 stones, jewels, worn on the ephod of the high priest; the walls of the holy place of Zion are continually before me. The children shall make haste; the destroyers and they that made waste shall go forth from you.

18 Lift up thine eyes round about, and behold: all these gather themselves together, and come to thee. As I live, saith the LORD, thou shalt surely clothe thee with them all, as with an ornament, and bind them on thee, as a bride doeth.
19 For thy waste and thy desolate places, and the land of thy destruction, shall even now be too narrow by reason of the inhabitants, and they that swallowed thee up shall be far away.
20 The children which thou shalt have, after thou hast lost the other, shall say again in thine ears, The place is too strait for me: give place to me that I may dwell.
21 Then shalt thou say in thine heart, Who hath begotten me these, seeing I have lost my children, and am desolate, a captive, and removing to and fro? and who hath brought up these? Behold, I was left alone; these, where had they been?

Isaiah is commanded by the LORD to lift up his eyes round about in every direction, to see with high spiritual vision and behold all these people who gather themselves together and come to you in crowds. As the spirit of the LORD lives through more and more people, then Isaiah shall surely be clothed with all of them, as ornaments, that will be bound to you, as a bride places ornaments on herself on her wedding day. In symbolism, the LORD would be the bridegroom; Isaiah would be the bride, the person that the LORD comes through, and the ornaments would represent the gifts, gifts composed of people who have come to serve the LORD through Isaiah, the focus of His spirit.

The land of the fallen state that was covered with waste, desolation and destruction is now too small and narrow to hold the inhabitants that have be drawn and attracted to the spirit of God. The people that swallowed you up, previously, and who learned to serve the LORD and were sent out to spread the word to others are now far away. The spiritual children which you shall have around you, after you had lost the others, shall say again in your ears, The place is too small for me: give a place to me that I may dwell and let my light shine. Then you shall say in your heart, Who has begotten me all these spiritual children who are the offspring of the LORD and Isaiah, the bridegroom and the bride, the LORD and His prophet, seeing I have lost my children, and am desolate, a captive, and removing to and fro? and who has brought up these? Behold, I was left alone; these offspring are new, where had they been?

22 Thus saith the Lord GOD, Behold, I will lift up mine hand to the Gentiles, and set up my standard to the people: and they shall bring thy sons in their arms, and thy daughters shall be carried upon their shoulders.
23 And kings shall be thy nursing fathers, and their queens thy nursing mothers: they shall bow down to thee with their face toward the earth, and lick up the dust of thy feet; and thou shalt know that I am the LORD: for they shall not be ashamed that wait for me.
24 Shall the prey be taken from the mighty, or the lawful captive delivered?

The LORD says to behold and see the results as He will lift up the hand of welcome into the covenant to the Gentiles. He shall set up the standard, the banner of the LORD, Jehovah-nissi, as an invitation to the people to join the covenant and to be a part of the sword of the LORD on earth to the people who do not know the LORD: and the Gentiles shall bring their sons, their positive expressions, in their arms and their daughters, their negative faults and sins, shall be carried upon their shoulders.

And kings who represent the spiritual aspect of the earth with great power, and people who are under their control shall come to Isaiah, and they shall be as your nursing fathers who desire the milk of the LORD; their queens, their physical forms, shall be as your nursing mothers: they, the physical forms, shall bow down to you with their faces toward the earth, and lick up the dust of your feet because they want to know the way that you walk through life; and the ones who shall know that I am the LORD: for they shall not be ashamed that wait for me, that serve the spirit of the LORD. What shall be done with this prey that has been captured from the fallen state and drawn into the kingdom of the LORD by the attractiveness of the spirit of the LORD? Shall the prey be taken from the mighty LORD, or the lawful captive delivered?

25 But thus saith the LORD, Even the captives of the mighty shall be taken away, and the prey of the terrible shall be delivered: for I will contend with him that contendeth with thee, and I will save thy children.
26 And I will feed them that oppress thee with their own flesh; and they shall be drunken with their own blood, as with sweet wine: and all flesh shall know that I the LORD am thy Saviour and thy Redeemer, the mighty One of Jacob.

The LORD says that the captives of the mighty shall be taken away, and the prey, the captives taken by the LORD's spirit shall be delivered. The LORD is the deliverer who delivers the people into

The Testimony of the Major Prophets

the LORD's service so that they are a part of the LORD's spiritual body on earth. The LORD will contend with him, any person in the fallen state, who contends for one of the LORD's children. The LORD will save and deliver His spiritual children; the physical form of the person that will not release the spiritual child to return to his LORD shall suffer the pains of contending with the LORD.

And the LORD will feed them, the spiritual children, the true children of Israel, the Beings, that oppress you with their own flesh, the human aspect of their beings, the offspring or the body of Jacob; and they, the physical human forms, shall be drunken with their own blood, not physical blood but the stream of life from the LORD, as with sweet wine: and all flesh, the emotions, the mind and the physical form, shall know that I, the LORD Who is everywhere, am the Savior and the Redeemer, of the human form, the mighty One of Jacob.

CHAPTER 50

1 Thus saith the LORD, Where is the bill of your mother's divorcement, whom I have put away? or which of my creditors is it to whom I have sold you? Behold, for your iniquities have ye sold yourselves, and for your transgressions is your mother put away.

The LORD who is the bridegroom to the "bride" of his prophet, Isaiah, (symbol of the covenant) has produced many spiritual children and the LORD is the Father to these children of the spirit. The spirits on the earth are the sons of their Father, the LORD. Spiritual man is symbolized by Israel. The physical forms in which the sons reside on earth are the daughters of God. Material mankind is symbolized by Jacob. The spiritual nature of a human being, the son, comes from the Father, the LORD God; the physical nature of a human being is a daughter of God who is patterned after Isaiah. Isaiah represents the "Father" spirit and also the visible "mother" to many males and females, sons and daughters, on earth. Mother earth is the physical substance of atoms and molecules which constitutes the dust. The LORD has some questions for His sons and daughters on earth.

The LORD asks his sons and daughters who are no longer a part of His household, who do not live in their Father's house from their distorted point of view, Where is the bill of your mother's divorcement, whom I have put away? The LORD has not "divorced" Himself from the earth but the children behave as though He has! The LORD speaking through Isaiah asks, Which of my creditors is it to whom I have sold you? The LORD has not sold, or relinquished His ownership, on his children and the children can see immediately that they have not been sold to another owner. The LORD gives his children the answer to their separation from consciously knowing their Father. Behold, for your iniquities, for your sin and fault of not letting the LORD's spirit flow through them, you have sold yourselves into an identification with the dust of the ground, with its fallen mind and impure heart. It is because of these transgressions on your part that your mother, the earthly portion of you has been put away, separated from the spiritual portion of you, which is the LORD's spirit.

The Testimony of the Major Prophets

2 Wherefore, when I came, was there no man? when I called, was there none to answer? my hand shortened at all, that it cannot redeem? or have I no power to deliver? behold, at my rebuke I dry up the sea, I make the rivers a wilderness: their fish stinketh, because there is no water, and dieth for thirst.
3 I clothe the heavens with blackness, and I make sackcloth their covering.

The LORD speaking through Isaiah states that this is the reason that when the LORD came and called to man, why was there no man, why was there no spiritual man who knew that his true identity was spirit? when the LORD called, there was no one to answer? Man created as a spirit had descended or fallen into an identification in physical form and he has forgotten his true identity, his divine identity, the truth that he is a spirit of the LORD. The LORD, speaking through Isaiah, asks His fallen children if His hand is shortened at all so that the LORD cannot redeem them from the condition into which they have fallen? or does the LORD have no power to deliver his children from their fallen state? behold, and be aware of my rebuke of you! As you move away from identification with the spirit of the LORD, the sea of awareness in the consciousness of mankind is dried up; no water of truth, no conscious awareness. The movement away from the LORD makes the rivers of water of the spirit of truth that flow from the LORD diminish in quantity and that produces a wilderness: their fish, the living food that would feed man and be a blessing to him from the LORD, stinks because there is no water, and the blessings die because of their thirst; they are not being watered from the spiritual Source, the garden of the LORD. The inevitable result of this separation from your Father, caused by your movement away from Him, is that, due to the working of the law, He clothed the heavens with blackness, and made sackcloth their covering, a veil has been placed to cloud your vision which has produced the sad conditions experienced by mankind.

4 The Lord GOD hath given me the tongue of the learned, that I should know how to speak a word in season to him that is weary: he wakeneth morning by morning, he wakeneth mine ear to hear as the learned.
5 The Lord GOD hath opened mine ear, and I was not rebellious, neither turned away back.
6 I gave my back to the smiters, and my cheeks to them that plucked off the hair: I hid not my face from shame and spitting.
7 For the Lord GOD will help me; therefore shall I not be confounded: therefore have I set my face like a flint, and I know that I shall not be ashamed.
8 He is near that justifieth me; who will contend with me? let us stand together: who is mine adversary? let him come near to me.

Isaiah states the Lord GOD has given him the tongue of a learned man so that Isaiah can speak in season, when it is fitting, to a person who is weary of the state to which he has fallen in separation from knowing the LORD. Isaiah is being instructed during his sleep, when his conscious mind is asleep, and morning by morning, with each passing day, Isaiah has learned. Isaiah did not rebel against this process of instruction, neither did he turn back from the responsibilities inherent in the enlightened state to preach to others. Many people did not want to hear the word of the LORD through Isaiah who gave his back to those who would physically strike him since beatings were for fools and criminals. He gave his cheeks toward the people who would pluck the hair from his beard as sign of disrespect and contempt. Neither did Isaiah hide his face from the shame, the mocking and the spitting which he had to endure as he served the message from the LORD to the people in the fallen state who behaved in terrible ways.

This treatment could be endured because the LORD Who is near justifies the actions of Isaiah toward the self-righteous people who will not listen to the righteousness of the LORD spoken through the mouth of Isaiah. Who will contend with the truth of Isaiah's words on the basis of the truth? Let us stand together and reason together: Isaiah is looking for an adversary who will truly reason with him. Who is this adversary who will listen and reason without beating, and spitting? Let that person in the fallen state come to Isaiah. Isaiah is searching for such a person.

9 Behold, the Lord GOD will help me; who is he that shall condemn me? lo, they all shall wax old as a garment; the moth shall eat them up.
10 Who is among you that feareth the LORD, that obeyeth the voice of his servant, that walketh in darkness, and hath no light? let him trust in the name of the LORD, and stay upon his God.
11 Behold, all ye that kindle a fire, that compass yourselves about with sparks: walk in the light of your fire, and in the sparks that ye have kindled. This shall ye have of mine hand; ye shall lie down in sorrow.

Isaiah states that the Lord GOD will help him; and he wants to know who will condemn him and what he has to say in the name of the LORD because this is the working of the law: people will either respond favorably to the message or they will react unfavorably. They are only the material forms that clothe the spirits of the LORD which will grow old as a garment grows old to be consumed and eaten by the moths just as the physical forms of the fallen people will be eaten by worms. Isaiah is looking for favorable response to lead these people to the LORD. He endures all the abuses of fallen man to find these people; he is willing to sift through a lot of dirt to find the gold.

Who is among you that fears the LORD, that obeys the voice of His servant, that walks in darkness, and will admit that he has no light? let that person trust in the name of the LORD, and stay focused and fixed upon His God. A person who wants to "find" the LORD (the LORD isn't lost!), must let the fire of the LORD's spirit burn as a candle within themselves and through their hearts, minds and bodies. Behold, all of you that kindle a fire, those who truly desire to let the fire of the LORD's spirit burn within you, and you have some experience of this process of which Isaiah speaks as you have been aware of the sparks of the LORD's fire that come out around you from time to time. But, they are only sparks because the process is not a consistent one; it is intermittent. Isaiah's advice to you is to walk in the light of your fire, and in the sparks, the way of the LORD that you have known in your past experience, which you have kindled as you walked partially in the Way. This example of the steady burning of the fire, which is serving the LORD, you shall have before you from my hand of right control; however, if you do not let the fire of the LORD burn in you, you should certainly expect to lie down in sorrow. Joy is in the spirit of the LORD, the LORD Who is joyous!

CHAPTER 51

1 Hearken to me, ye that follow after righteousness, ye that seek the LORD: look unto the rock whence ye are hewn, and to the hole of the pit whence ye are digged.
2 Look unto Abraham your father, and unto Sarah that bare you: for I called him alone, and blessed him, and increased him.
3 For the LORD shall comfort Zion: he will comfort all her waste places; and he will make her wilderness like Eden, and her desert like the garden of the LORD; joy and gladness shall be found therein, thanksgiving, and the voice of melody.

Isaiah instructs his followers to listen to the spirit of the LORD, that is contained in his words, with the spirit of the LORD that is within each of them. Listen with spiritual perception because your spirit is present within you or you would not be alive. Life comes from the Lord God. Isaiah advises that those who seek the LORD should follow after righteousness: one way to do this is to look to the rock of God, the spirit from which you are hewn: you are a piece of the total spirit of the Rock. Look also to the hole, the missing piece of the rock, which has fallen from the rock, which was dug away from the rock by fallen man. to produce your sense of separation.

Look to Abraham and Sarah, the symbols for your spiritual Father and your spiritual earth-mother, as a comprehensible illustration for your mind to understand. The LORD called him, Abraham, alone, and blessed him, and increased him, and you are a part of the spirit of Abraham the Father.

The LORD shall comfort Zion, the earthly kingdom of the spirit: it is not as if Zion is totally absent; Zion is present as a distortion, or an abstraction, of the true design that the LORD is bringing on earth. The abstraction is due to the fact that the LORD must bring the design through His creation, Man, who is not all there. He is a partial creature rather than a whole man. Zion, the spiritual kingdom on earth, needs to be comforted by the LORD in all of her waste places, the places on earth which are wasted because man in the fallen state has distorted the design of the earthly kingdom, the kingdom of heaven that is to come on earth. The LORD, flowing through His people, will make the wilderness like Eden, and her desert like the garden of the LORD; joy and gladness shall be found in the service of the LORD in the building of His kingdom. There is thanksgiving, the giving of thanks for the opportunity to be in the LORD's service, and the voice of melody will be heard everywhere as people sing praises to the LORD.

4 Hearken unto me, my people; and give ear unto me, O my nation: for a law shall proceed from me, and I will make my judgment to rest for a light of the people.
5 My righteousness is near; my salvation is gone forth, and mine arms shall judge the people; the isles shall wait upon me, and on mine arm shall they trust.
6 Lift up your eyes to the heavens, and look upon the earth beneath: for the heavens shall vanish away like smoke, and the earth shall wax old like a garment, and they that dwell therein shall die in like manner: but my salvation shall be for ever, and my righteousness shall not be abolished.

Isaiah increases the call of the LORD for His people, the people who rightfully belong to His nation, to return home to Him. The people with ears to hear are of the law that proceeds from the LORD and that the working of this law, the law of sowing and reaping, will be the judgment of the people based upon their expressions and behaviors. The working of this law shall be seen as a light, a beacon, for the people to understand how the power of the LORD works on earth through man.

The righteousness of the LORD is near to every person as the spirit within the person; the salvation of the LORD is gone forth through man to produce a kingdom of beauty unless man distorts the design which would distort the design into ugliness; the arms of the LORD, his strength and power, shall judge the people as they observe in physical manifestation that has been created by man; the isles who were separated from the LORD shall now wait upon, serve, the LORD and trust His power and strength.

The LORD's people are directed by Isaiah to lift up their vision to the heavens, to the place of spirit, and to look upon the earth beneath as a place of dust that surrounds the spiritual pattern: When this is done, the person who does it steps across a dividing line into the world of spirit and the idea of heaven as a separate place shall vanish like smoke, and the earth shall grow old, like a garment that is clothing for the spirit. The people who dwell in the earth shall die in the process of disintegration and rearrangement of the dust: but the salvation of the LORD in the world of the spirit shall be forever, and My righteousness shall not be abolished ever, because the spirit does not perish..

7 Hearken unto me, ye that know righteousness, the people in whose heart is my law; fear ye not the reproach of men, neither be ye afraid of their revilings.
8 For the moth shall eat them up like a garment, and the worm shall eat them like wool: but my righteousness shall be for ever, and my salvation from generation to generation.
9 Awake, awake, put on strength, O arm of the LORD; awake, as in the ancient days, in the generations of old. Art thou not it that hath cut Rahab, and wounded the dragon?
10 Art thou not it which hath dried the sea, the waters of the great deep; that hath made the depths of the sea a way for the ransomed to pass over?

Isaiah instructs the people who have and know righteousness, the people in whose heart is the law of the LORD and who are willing to abide by it, to not fear the reproach of men; nor be afraid of their behavior when they revile you. Simply, observe the antics of the dust surrounding a fallen

The Testimony of the Major Prophets

spirit, be aware of the circumstance and do what is fitting for the spirit to do in the moment. Remember that the moth shall eat them up like a garment, and the worm shall eat them like wool; but the righteousness of the LORD shall be forever, and the salvation of the LORD transcends time and is from generation to generation.

The call of Isaiah is for the people who are in the fallen state to awake, wake up, put on the strength of the power of the LORD which is in spirit; awake as in ancient days, in the generations of old when the people on earth knew that they were spirits who were in forms. In reality, are you not the spirit of victory who has cut Rahab, the monster, and wounded the dragon, of the self-active fallen mind that directs the monster of human nature? In reality of spirit, are you not the spirit that has dried the sea, the consciousness of the fallen state that knows not the LORD, the waters of the great deep, the waters of the truth of spirit which is in the darkened state of the great deep that symbolizes the place where light is absent from the consciousness of fallen man; who has made a way from the darkened depths of the sea to the light on the surface for the ransomed people, the people who paid the price of choosing to serve the LORD, to pass over? Where will they pass to?

11 Therefore the redeemed of the LORD shall return, and come with singing unto Zion; and everlasting joy shall be upon their head: they shall obtain gladness and joy; and sorrow and mourning shall flee away.
12 I, even I, am he that comforteth you: who art thou, that thou shouldest be afraid of a man that shall die, and of the son of man which shall be made as grass;
13 And forgettest the LORD thy maker, that hath stretched forth the heavens, and laid the foundations of the earth; and hast feared continually every day because of the fury of the oppressor, as if he were ready to destroy? and where is the fury of the oppressor?

The redeemed of the LORD shall return, and come with singing, expressing the song of the LORD, to Zion, the place of the heavenly kingdom on earth; everlasting joy shall be in the heads, in the minds of those who experience the covenant with the LORD. In this process of coming home, the people who have the experience of victory over the fallen state by leaving it, shall experience gladness and joy of the covenant; the sorrow and the mourning shall flee away from them.

The LORD is the One who comforts you: in the covenant there is agreement, the piece of the rock that has fallen from the Rock has returned to the Rock from which it fell. Who are you now that you have returned to your true position? Should you be afraid of an earthly man that shall die, and of the son of man which shall be made of grass; these manifestations of the spirit are temporary creations that were used in the service of the LORD. The son of man, the creation, has forgotten the LORD who was his Maker, Who stretched forth the heavens and laid the foundations of the earth; the fallen creation who has feared every day because of the fury of oppressor, the LORD Who was oppressing the person in the fallen state, as if the LORD were ready to destroy the creation? Well, now that the piece of the Rock has returned to the Rock, where is the fury of the oppressor against the creation of earthly man? There is no fury of the oppressor! There is no oppressor! There is only the LORD!

14 The captive exile hasteneth that he may be loosed, and that he should not die in the pit, nor that his bread should fail.

15 But I am the LORD thy God, that divided the sea, whose waves roared: The LORD of hosts is his name.
16 And I have put my words in thy mouth, and I have covered thee in the shadow of mine hand, that I may plant the heavens, and lay the foundations of the earth, and say unto Zion, Thou art my people.

People in the fallen state that Isaiah calls captive exiles, because they are held captive in the fallen state and they are exiles from the Rock of the LORD's kingdom, hasten, they are in a hurry, to be loosed and set free from their bondage and captivity. They do not want to die in the pit, in the earth and remain buried there. Nor do they want their bread of life to fail to reach them and they will die without their daily bread of life from the LORD. But in true identity, I am the LORD your God, that divided the sea of consciousness, whose waves roared into the earth, to water the earth: The LORD of hosts, the LORD of all the hosts of people who are on the earth, is the name of the LORD. It is the LORD who has put the words into the mouth of the earthly creations, and who has covered you with the shadow of the hand of the LORD, so that the LORD could plant the heavens and lay the foundations of the earth, to use the spiritual substance and the earthly substance needed for the creation, and say to Zion, You are my people!

17 Awake, awake, stand up, O Jerusalem, which hast drunk at the hand of the LORD the cup of his fury; thou hast drunken the dregs of the cup of trembling, and wrung them out.
18 There is none to guide her among all the sons whom she hath brought forth; neither is there any that taketh her by the hand of all the sons that she hath brought up.
19 These two things are come unto thee; who shall be sorry for thee? desolation, and destruction, and the famine, and the sword: by whom shall I comfort thee?
20 Thy sons have fainted, they lie at the head of all the streets, as a wild bull in a net: they are full of the fury of the LORD, the rebuke of thy God.

The call to people everywhere, who are the hosts of the LORD and do not know it, is to wake up! Awake, awake, stand up, O people of Jerusalem. In the experience of the fallen state, you have drunk from the cup of the LORD's fury; you have drunken the dregs of the cup of fear and trembling, and you have wrung them out through you in your experience of living on earth. This has happened to the people in the fallen state, symbolized by a woman, because there is no one to provide the proper guidance to all the sons whom she brought forth; neither is there any that takes her by the hand and shows her the error of her ways. She, the fallen people, are not to be blamed because they did not know. But now there are two choices placed before the people.

These two choices are now placed before the people; who shall be sorry for you any more when you are allowed to choose which way you will walk on earth? You may choose desolation, destruction, and the famine which you have known in your experience heretofore: or the sword, the sword of the LORD, the covenant with the LORD, Jehovah, the LORD in action on earth through people. These are the two choices: human nature which you have known in your experience; or, the "new" nature of the sword of the LORD. By which choice will the LORD comfort you? Is there really a choice? Your sons, your expressions of the human nature state have fainted, they have not had the strength to do what was needed; they lie in the streets as a wild bull in a net: they are full of the fury of the LORD, the rebuke of your God. Their failure is available to be seen everywhere.

The Testimony of the Major Prophets

21 Therefore hear now this, thou afflicted, and drunken, but not with wine:
22 Thus saith thy Lord the LORD, and thy God that pleadeth the cause of his people, Behold, I have taken out of thine hand the cup of trembling, even the dregs of the cup of my fury; thou shalt no more drink it again:
23 But I will put it into the hand of them that afflict thee; which have said to thy soul, Bow down, that we may go over: and thou hast laid thy body as the ground, and as the street, to them that went over.

Therefore, people in the fallen state, hear this, you who are afflicted and drunken, but not with wine: The LORD your God pleads the cause of His people: Behold, the cup of trembling and fear, even the dregs of the fury of the LORD have been taken from your hand: you need not drink it again. You need not be afraid or fearful. Let the people who have taught you to fear and tremble at your LORD do all the trembling. Isaiah has taken the cup of fear of the LORD from the children of the LORD. But I will put the cup of trembling into the hand of the people in the fallen state who will afflict you with their fear; those people who have said to you, Bow down before us so that we may use you as a street to walk all over you for our humanly devised purposes.

CHAPTER 52

1 Awake, awake; put on thy strength, O Zion; put on thy beautiful garments, O Jerusalem, the holy city: for henceforth there shall no more come into thee the uncircumcised and the unclean.
2 Shake thyself from the dust; arise, and sit down, O Jerusalem: loose thyself from the bands of thy neck, O captive daughter of Zion.
3 For thus saith the LORD, Ye have sold yourselves for nought; and ye shall be redeemed without money.

Isaiah calls to those people who desire to dwell in the Holy Place, symbolized by the word, Zion, to Awake, awake and put on your spiritual strength that comes from within you. Put on your beautiful garments, the clothing of divine state of the spirit of the LORD, the risen state, the glory of the true nature of man before the fall, O Jerusalem, the people of the city that should be and can be a Holy City if they reveal the glory of the LORD's spiritual garments. The true nature of each person is that they are a spiritual being, an individual piece of the God. In order to be this spiritual person, a change needs to be made in the behavior of the inhabitants of the city. The change in behavior is described as the spiritual person shall no more allow the fallen ways of the uncircumcised, those who have not cut away their wrong behavior from the expression of life through them to let the spirit of the LORD flow through them. If the spirit does not flow through the forms of the people, the unclean behaviors, the sins of the people in the fallen state will flow into them from the sinful environment and produce a distorted expression of life. The people of Jerusalem have been called by Isaiah to shake their spiritual Selves from the dust, the earthly identity of the fallen state, and, Arise.

They are to arise from the fallen identity to the ascended identity of their Spirits which have always been present with them, but heretofore, unexpressed. As they arise from the dust, they are directed to sit down. It is not necessary to arise to a standing position and totally function in the fullness of the spirit immediately. The direction is to sit down and remove the bands of earthly habits of the fallen state from your neck which have been holding each person as a captive, as a daughter of Zion, who does the bidding of the peers of the earth, rather than a son of Zion who would represent the LORD, the Father. The LORD has said that you have sold yourselves for naught, for the nothingness of the fallen state which is dust and distortion; and you shall be redeemed from that fallen state without the payment of money to anyone because there is nothing holding the captive to that fallen state of nothingness except inanimate dust.

4 For thus saith the Lord GOD, My people went down aforetime into Egypt to sojourn there; and the Assyrian oppressed them without cause.
5 Now therefore, what have I here, saith the LORD, that my people is taken away for nought? they that rule over them make them to howl, saith the LORD; and my name continually every day is blasphemed.
6 Therefore my people shall know my name: therefore they shall know in that day that I am he that doth speak: behold, it is I.
7 How beautiful upon the mountains are the feet of him that bringeth good tidings, that publisheth peace; that bringeth good tidings of good, that publisheth salvation; that saith unto Zion, Thy God reigneth!
8 Thy watchmen shall lift up the voice; with the voice together shall they sing: for they shall see eye to eye, when the LORD shall bring again Zion.

Isaiah states that the Lord GOD has said that His people went down to Egypt in a past time period to sojourn, spend some time in that place, and they were held in bondage until the time of Moses; and lately, the Assyrians have oppressed His people without any reason, without just cause. Now, in this present time, what the LORD has to deal with here is that His people have been taken away from Him for no reason that the LORD has done; His people have been taken into custody and ruled over by an enemy who has made them howl with their mistreatment and pain. This "invisible enemy" is the fallen human nature of man who uses the name of the LORD, I AM, continually every day and blasphemes the LORD with an untrue nature. The expression of any untrue nature, human nature, is blasphemy and we have been born into a world of blasphemy. This maltreatment has gone on long enough and a stop must be put to the blasphemy of a people using the LORD's name, I AM, in vain, in the application of I AM to a wrong function that is not the true nature of who I Am. Therefore, the people shall know in the day that the spirit of the LORD, I Am, speaks through the physical form of a human being such as Isaiah, then Isaiah, speaking the word of the spirit of the LORD can say, It is I, the LORD who speaks. This would be a glorious day when the LORD "returns" to the earth once more in a human body that is conscious of its True Occupant, the spirit of the LORD. The LORD's message is, All is forgiven. Arise.

How beautiful upon the mountains, the high spiritual vision, are the feet, the understanding, of Him, the LORD, that brings good tidings, that publishes peace; the LORD that brings good tidings, that publishes salvation to the human nature people on earth who are in the fallen state which will give them the invitation to rise up to the spiritual mountaintop from which they have fallen so long ago that no one remembers the ascended state; the spiritual person in covenant-agreement with the LORD shall say to Zion, the place where the people with spiritual understanding dwell, Your God reigns on earth once again!

The LORD shall lift up your watchmen, your thoughts, who shall lift up the voice, your voice, which will cry out the good news; all the people who see this shall sing together with the combined voices of others who will do likewise: the people can do this for they shall see eye to eye, they are

The Symbolic Version of Isaiah

in spiritual agreement, when the LORD shall bring Zion, the place where the holy spirits dwell together on earth in agreement.

9 Break forth into joy, sing together, ye waste places of Jerusalem: for the LORD hath comforted his people, he hath redeemed Jerusalem.
10 The LORD hath made bare his holy arm in the eyes of all the nations; and all the ends of the earth shall see the salvation of our God.

How do people experience the in-dwelling spirit of the LORD, Who is the spiritual occupant of the human form? People must express their spiritual nature to receive the experience of it in their hearts, minds and bodies. People must acknowledge their present starting point, that their prior human experience has been a waste place of Jerusalem, that their prior experience has been worthless except that it brought you to the present moment. A new beginning must be made as a spiritual being who will break forth, express, the joy of life, and sing together in joy. The LORD, who is in operation through the physical form of Isaiah, has made bare, exposed, His holy arm, the holy power of the spirit of the LORD through—in the eyes of all the nations who have eyes to see—the example that has been set by Isaiah. This spirit shall be observed and replicated by more and more people singing together with the result that all the fallen people from all the ends of the earth shall see the salvation of God that has been extended to them.

11 Depart ye, depart ye, go ye out from thence, touch no unclean thing; go ye out of the midst of her; be ye clean, that bear the vessels of the LORD.
12 For ye shall not go out with haste, nor go by flight: for the LORD will go before you; and the God of Israel will be your rere-ward.
13 Behold, my servant shall deal prudently, he shall be exalted and extolled, and be very high.
14 As many were astonied at thee; his visage was so marred more than any man, and his form more than the sons of men:
15 So shall he sprinkle many nations; the kings shall shut their mouths at him: for that which had not been told them shall they see; and that which they had not heard shall they consider.

The people in the fallen human nature state who do not know the LORD are specifically called to depart out of this state of identification with the physical form and the environment which it collectively has created. On the way out of this distorted, fallen, twisted state, the person is cautioned to touch no unclean thing, to take none of the sins of the fallen state into themselves; the people who want to leave the unclean state must personally go out of the midst of her, the distorted state created by the desires of fallen human nature. Be clean; be a person who bears, carries, the blessings of the LORD to others in your area of influence.

A person shall not leave the fallen state with haste, immediately, by running away from this state which exists within their own consciousness just because that is their desire. A person cannot fly away or be extracted from the fallen state of one's own mind and heart. The spirit of the LORD will go before a person as it flows through the heart, mind and body and leads you out of the fallen state; the spirit of the God of Israel as it flows through shall be your rere-guard, your rear guard, also. The spirit of the LORD is before you and behind you as you express it.

The Testimony of the Major Prophets

Behold, my servant, Isaiah, shall deal prudently with you as you exit from your identification with the fallen state that is filled with the distortions, faults and sins. The living example of the LORD's servant, Isaiah, shall be exalted and extolled, and be very high as he acts very wisely. As many people who were astonished at the transformation of you from the fallen state to the ascended state, the visage, the countenance of Isaiah, was marred more than any man, and his form more than the sons of men because he has observed many people make the transition from the fallen state to the ascended, true state. Isaiah will have many followers who will pass on the call, the word to others.

So shall Isaiah sprinkle many nations with people who have experienced the transition to the new spiritual state; it is like adding leaven into the lump of the body of mankind. The kings of the earth of the fallen state shall shut their mouths at the living example of true identity: for the living example of a spirit of the LORD on earth that has not been told to them shall be seen by those with eyes to see once the living example has been expressed. When they see the spiritual expression, which had not been heard previously, it shall be considered by those with ears to hear. The responsibility of the servant of the LORD is to express the LORD's nature on earth.

CHAPTER 53

1 Who hath believed our report? and to whom is the arm of the LORD revealed?
2 For he shall grow up before him as a tender plant, and as a root out of a dry ground: he hath no form nor comeliness; and when we shall see him, there is no beauty that we should desire him.
3 He is despised and rejected of men; a man of sorrows, and acquainted with grief: and we hid as it were our faces from him; he was despised, and we esteemed him not.
4 Surely he hath borne our griefs, and carried our sorrows: yet we did esteem him stricken, smitten of God, and afflicted.

Isaiah has related his experience from a fallen, human identity to an ascended, true identity to his followers. He asks, Who has believed his report that such a transition was possible from a material identity, in which a person is identified with the outer physical form, to a spiritual identity, in which a person would be identified with the spirit of the LORD of hosts? After Isaiah offered his experience to others, he wanted to know by whom the arm, the symbol of the extension of the power, of the LORD's spirit has been received and revealed by the people to whom it was offered? As Isaiah offers the spirit which he represents, to other people, the people who accept the invitation to express the spirit shall grow up before Isaiah as a tender plant is watered. Isaiah will be able to watch the unfoldment and transition of a person from the human expression toward the divine expression.

The person in the human nature state does not have an expression, or an atmosphere around him that is consistently desirable and attractive from a spiritual point of view; and when we see that person and his behavior, there is no beauty being expressed consistently so that other people would desire to be around that individual at all times. A person in the fallen state is despised and rejected by other people who observe him; the person in the fallen state is a man of sorrows, who is well-acquainted with grief: and we hid, as it were, our faces from him; he was despised, and we esteemed him not, because he was not distinguished in our eyes. Surely, the person who serves as a mentor or a teacher has borne the grief, and carried the sorrows of the student or follower who was expressing his undesirable human nature behaviors and faults: yet the teachers and the mentors did esteem him stricken, smitten of God, and afflicted by the movement of the power of God flowing

The Testimony of the Major Prophets

in a distorted pattern through the student or disciple. The human nature person is to be loved because that person in reality is a spirit of the LORD. It is this wrong behavior pattern that is the punishment from the LORD. A person is punished **by** his sin when he is off-the-mark. There is no need for a spiritual person to add to the punishment that has already been given by the LORD.

5 But he was wounded for our transgressions, he was bruised for our iniquities: the chastisement of our peace was upon him; and with his stripes we are healed.
6 All we like sheep have gone astray; we have turned every one to his own way; and the LORD hath laid on him the iniquity of us all.
7 He was oppressed, and he was afflicted, yet he opened not his mouth: he is brought as a lamb to the slaughter, and as a sheep before her shearers is dumb, so he openeth not his mouth.
8 He was taken from prison and from judgment: and who shall declare his generation? for he was cut off out of the land of the living: for the transgression of my people was he stricken.

Generally speaking, the younger people, or students, have been wounded by the behaviors and faults generated and produced by the previous generations. The younger people were bruised and spoiled by the iniquities of the older people; the sins of the fathers were visited upon the children: when the older generation did find and experience peace, a behavior that was in alignment or agreement with the true design of man, they chastised, punished and scolded the younger generation if the offspring did not live up to the ways of peace. It is by these stripes and wounds, the punishment inflicted on and experienced by the offspring, that were the lessons learned to provide healing to the body of mankind.

All the people in the fallen state are like sheep that have gone astray and all the sheep are going their own ways, in their own directions, without the benefit of a shepherd to hold them together; this condition of separateness can cause the working of the law of the LORD to result in iniquity upon everybody. The people of the younger generation were oppressed and afflicted by the behavior and the example set by their elders, and yet they did not open their mouths to complain about it because they do not have any basis for comparison: they deem the nature of the expression of the inherited behavior as "normal" as it applies to each of them because that is the way it was when they grew up. The person who grows up in these conditions is like a lamb who is brought to the slaughter; and the reason that a sheep, which is brought before her shearers, is dumb because they don't know what is going to happen to them.

So, the person who is symbolized by the sheep does not open not his mouth. He was taken from the prison of his isolated experience and from the judgment that has been learned in his isolation: and who shall declare, who shall judge the generation, the expression and the behavior, that comes forth from the person who has been raised in this environment which is out of the land of the living, out of the land of the true state, where people are truly alive. The person who has been raised in an environment of the fallen state has been stricken and afflicted by the people who created the distorted conditions in which the younger generations of people were raised. This fallen state is a dying state that leads toward the grave and not toward life. We do not need to add to their misery.

9 And he made his grave with the wicked, and with the rich in his death; because he had done no violence, neither was any deceit in his mouth.

The Symbolic Version of Isaiah

10 Yet it pleased the LORD to bruise him; he hath put him to grief: when thou shalt make his soul an offering for sin, he shall see his seed, he shall prolong his days, and the pleasure of the LORD shall prosper in his hand.

The people observed and copied the incorrect learned behaviors from the older generation make their grave in a dying environment with the wicked, and with the actions of the rich because they are following the example of successful people in a materialistic world. The fact that a young person is with the group of the older generation in an environment which is characterized by the fact that it is a distorted environment, does not make that person evil. A person does not live in sin because of their location. A person is judged by the nature of his or her expression, by what comes forth through his or her capacities. If the person does not do any violence, or utter any deceit from his mouth, he will produce a beautiful environment around himself which will have its effect on the world according to the working of the law.

Yet, it pleased the LORD to bruise him, bruise the person who does wrong, because the LORD delights in the working of the law of the LORD. It is the LORD and the working of the law that has put the person to grief. The time will come when the wrong behavior expressed through the younger generation that the soul—the body, mind and heart—shall be an offering for the sins, the faults, that they had expressed in their living. The material form of the person who functions outside the parameters of the divine design, a person who does not express the LORD's nature, shall result in distortions in the material body. The soul of the material form becomes as an offering for the sinful behavior. This shall be done so that a person can see his seed, that which is being generated through his body, and consequently change his behavior thereby prolonging his days on earth. It is possible for a person to comprehend and learn from the cause-effect relationship which is the operation of the Law. It is this small change in the behavior which can help the next generation if they learn from the "sins of the fathers". If a person understands the cause-effect relationship, then the pleasure of the LORD, which is the working of the law of the LORD, shall produce beautiful and glorious results. The pleasure of the LORD rather than the wrath of the LORD shall prosper in the hand, in the control, of any person who is wise enough to take control of his expression.

11 He shall see of the travail of his soul, and shall be satisfied: by his knowledge shall my righteous servant justify many; for he shall bear their iniquities.
12 Therefore will I divide him a portion with the great, and he shall divide the spoil with the strong; because he hath poured out his soul unto death: and he was numbered with the transgressors; and he bare the sin of many, and made intercession for the transgressors.

The person who is in a position to see the operation of the law of the LORD which has produced the difficulties that have been experienced by one's own physical form shall be satisfied. He shall be satisfied because he will harmonize **with** the working of the law instead of functioning **against** the operation of it. He gets wisdom from the working of the law of the LORD and satisfied with the knowledge of how it works and that it is absolutely fair in its application. The working of the Law of the LORD through a person who uses it correctly can justify many, can help many people behave in such a way that their lives will be a blessing to many others. The person who uses the law correctly will be a mentor and a teacher of the law to others and, in this manner, they bear with the iniquities that befall their students or the people who are willing to follow their example.

The Testimony of the Major Prophets

Therefore, according to the working of the law of the LORD, cause and effect, the flowing power of the LORD shall be divided, distributed, to all the people depending on whether they harmonize with or rebel against the divine design of the LORD. It is LORD's desire that all things shall work together to perfection and that the design will be creative and harmonious. The design originates in the LORD and the power from the LORD distributes it through his creation, man, who will be great, be increased by the spirit that flows through him. As man receives the spirit, he shall divide the spoil, the spirit, with the strong, the people with the spiritual strength, to pour out from their soul—the heart, mind and body—the wants and desires of human nature to let the spirit of the LORD fill the soul. **This will be the death of human nature and the birth of spiritual nature within a person, that results in the person being "born again" of the spirit.**

The identities of the human nature people are numbered with the transgressors, the offenders, the sinners, the violators, of the law of the LORD. The transgressor bears the sins of many because in the fallen state the sinner is carrying the sins of many people from the present and previous generations. It is necessary for some one to intercede in the affairs of men to reverse this process which produces sinners from one generation to the next. This person who intercedes with the transgressor of the law, who intercedes with the sinner, is an intercessor. The intercessor is the teacher or the mentor for the followers or the students.

CHAPTER 54

1 Sing, O barren, thou that didst not bear; break forth into singing, and cry aloud, thou that didst not travail with child: for more are the children of the desolate than the children of the married wife, saith the LORD.
2 Enlarge the place of thy tent, and let them stretch forth the curtains of thine habitations: spare not, lengthen thy cords, and strengthen thy stakes;
3 For thou shalt break forth on the right hand and on the left; and thy seed shall inherit the Gentiles, and make the desolate cities to be inhabited.

Isaiah tells the people who are willing to listen to him and be his followers to sing, and make a joyful noise, in the living of life. He is addressing the people who are barren. Barrenness refers to the people who have not experienced the birth of the spiritual child within them, the experience of being "born again", the spirit of the LORD finding expression on earth through their hearts, minds and bodies. If the spirit of the LORD is truly within the person who believes himself to be a physical entity, the only way to experience the spiritual entity is to let the spirit break forth into singing and let the spirit cry aloud, let the indwelling spirit express itself loudly. The person who expresses the nature of the spirit of the LORD will know what it is: a person knows what he expresses. A person who expresses anger, knows anger; a person who expresses love, knows love.

This message is addressed to the people who did not give birth to the spiritual child within them. The majority of the people, then or now, do not give birth to this spiritual child because there are more people on earth who are the children of the desolate, people who are in the earthly identity of the fallen state, than there are children of the married wife, which is the symbol for any person on earth, male or female, who is married to, in oneness with, in a spiritual covenant-agreement, with the LORD. There is a need for people to enlarge the place of your tent, to increase the space available for the spirit of the LORD within everyone. This will take a little effort on the part of a person who wants to do this. This process is described as stretching forth the curtains of your habitations, or letting the borders of your tent, the expansion of the mind and the heart to accommodate the expanding presence of the spirit of the LORD: spare not, do not hesitate to let the spirit of the LORD occupy the heart and mind of His crowning creation.

The person is encouraged to aid in the process of expansion of one's consciousness; this teaching is exemplified in the instruction to lengthen the cords, and strengthen the stakes which expands the tent of one's spiritual awareness. The lengthening cords represent the expansion of the mind and the heart to accommodate the increased flow of spiritual expression. The expansion of the spirit within a person will flow through and out of a person with the result that the spirit, you, shall break forth on the right hand and on the left in the process of expansion; and your seed, the seed of the spirit shall grow and it shall inherit the Gentiles, and make the desolate cities be inhabited by the spirit that flows through you.

4 Fear not; for thou shalt not be ashamed: neither be thou confounded; for thou shalt not be put to shame: for thou shalt forget the shame of thy youth, and shalt not remember the reproach of thy widowhood any more.
5 For thy Maker is thine husband; the LORD of hosts is his name; and thy Redeemer the Holy One of Israel; The God of the whole earth shall he be called.
6 For the LORD hath called thee as a woman forsaken and grieved in spirit, and a wife of youth, when thou wast refused, saith thy God.
7 For a small moment have I forsaken thee; but with great mercies will I gather thee.
8 In a little wrath I hid my face from thee for a moment; but with everlasting kindness will I have mercy on thee, saith the LORD thy Redeemer.

Isaiah tells all the people who are in the fallen state of human nature to Fear not. He understands that people are afraid and experience fear at the thought of making an approach to the LORD. People know that they have been less than they were created to be and they are ashamed of their fallen behavior while they are in the fallen state. It is the advice of the LORD through Isaiah to not be afraid, not to be ashamed and not to be confounded, confused or bewildered for the faults and the sins that they committed in the past experiences of their lives if they truly desire to return to and serve the LORD. The repentant person will not be put to shame: the person should forget the shame of his youth, and everyone's behavior and expression is as a child, childish, and has not matured into the spiritual behavior which is the available potential. A person who has not experienced the covenant-agreement with the LORD is like a woman without a husband; she is as a widow. Isaiah says that the "widow" should not reproach herself anymore; in other words, forget all past behaviors and begin anew. Begin anew with your Maker. Isaiah specifically identifies the Maker by the use of some of His many names.

For your Maker is your husband; the LORD of hosts is His name; and your Redeemer the Holy One of Israel; He shall be called the God of the whole earth. God, or the LORD has called you as a woman who has been forsaken and grieved in spirit, and a wife of youth, when you were refused and another has been chosen leaving you forsaken, alone and abandoned. Your experience will be akin to that. Consider that the LORD has abandoned or forsaken you for a small moment; but with great mercies will the LORD gather you regardless of your past behaviors. From your point of view, it is in a little wrath that the LORD hid his face from you for a moment; but with everlasting kindness, the LORD, your Redeemer, says, He shall have mercy on you.

9 For this is as the waters of Noah unto me: for as I have sworn that the waters of Noah should no more go over the earth; so have I sworn that I would not be wroth with thee, nor rebuke thee.
10 For the mountains shall depart, and the hills be removed; but my kindness shall not depart from thee, neither shall the covenant of my peace be removed, saith the LORD that hath mercy on thee.
11 O thou afflicted, tossed with tempest, and not comforted, behold, I will lay thy stones with fair colours, and lay thy foundations with sapphires.
12 And I will make thy windows of agates, and thy gates of carbuncles, and all thy borders of pleasant stones.

This absolute forgiveness and redemption of you, regardless of your past behavior, is akin to the LORD's forgiveness of Noah: The LORD has sworn that the waters of Noah should go over the earth no more to destroy all recollection of wrong behaviors and sins. The LORD will not be angry with you or rebuke you for what you have done in the fallen state. All of the mountains and hills of your worst sins shall depart from you and be removed from troubling your heart; but the kindness of the LORD shall not depart from you, nor the covenant of the peace be removed from you says the LORD, who has mercy on you.

O, you people who have been afflicted, tossed by the tempest of the fallen state and not comforted because of the fallen state in which you have been living, behold, the LORD will lay the stones of a new path for you to walk upon. You will walk on a new path with fair colors that will make you want to walk in the new way because it will be a pleasant and enjoyable path. It is also a valuable path that the foundations of it will be of laid with precious sapphires. The LORD will make your windows of agates, you will view your world through gemstones, you will see value wherever you look; your gates that you walk through shall be as carbuncles, precious stones, and the borders of your observable environment will be of precious stones. The gems are used as symbols to portray that the person who has been forgiven, who comes to the LORD, who walks in a new path of the LORD shall see value everywhere. This new path, the new way that you will walk through life, on stones of fair colors, stones that you will walk upon, stones of love, truth and life, are not for you alone.

13 And all thy children shall be taught of the LORD; and great shall be the peace of thy children.
14 In righteousness shalt thou be established: thou shalt be far from oppression; for thou shalt not fear: and from terror; for it shall not come near thee.
15 Behold, they shall surely gather together, but not by me: whosoever shall gather together against thee shall fall for thy sake.

All your children shall be taught of the way of the LORD, to walk on the stones of love, truth and life; and when this is learned, then great shall be the peace of your children. If you walk in righteousness, which is on the stones of love, truth and life, then in righteousness you shall be established: you shall be far from oppression; for you shall not fear: and terror shall not come near to you. Behold, look around you and see as you walk on the stones of a firm foundation, that fear, oppression and terror shall surely gather together, but they will not be gathered by the LORD: whosoever shall gather together fear, oppression and terror against you shall fall for your

The Testimony of the Major Prophets

sake, because you are present walking in the example of love, truth and life, which is the way, the working of the law of the LORD.

16 Behold, I have created the smith that bloweth the coals in the fire, and that bringeth forth an instrument for his work; and I have created the waster to destroy.
17 No weapon that is formed against thee shall prosper; and every tongue that shall rise against thee in judgment thou shalt condemn. This is the heritage of the servants of the LORD, and their righteousness is of me, saith the LORD.

The LORD speaking through the mouth of Isaiah tells His followers that He has created the smith, the worker who blows, supplies, the air by using a fan, wind or bellows to heat the coals of the fire to provide the necessary heat which is needed to build an instrument or an implement to do what it was designed to do to take care of the things on earth; the LORD also created the waster to destroy the physical forms on earth which must be removed to make space for an additional physical manifestation. It is necessary that there be a creative cycle and a destructive cycle on earth to bring about changes in the physical forms of things which are designed to change. But man is a spirit and not the material form in which he resides. The spirit can shape matter; but matter can not harm the spirit.

This is the reason that, if man identifies with the spirit which he is, then no material weapon that can be formed against man can prosper, be successful, in harming the spiritual man. Spirit is designed to shape matter in an integrative, creative manner; but matter is unable to harm the spirit which has dominion over all forms on earth. Every tongue that rises up against the dominion of spiritual man and declares in judgment as to the absolute accuracy of this statement shall be put down and condemned for the inaccuracy of his statement. Victory and supremacy of the spirit is the heritage of the servants of the LORD, the servants who serve and extend the spirit of the LORD through the physical forms under its dominion. The LORD has said that the righteousness of the spiritual servants is of the LORD because there is no other power except the power of the LORD. The LORD's power is behind every action on earth whether the action is creative or destructive. The power is the power of the LORD; the creativeness or the destructiveness that is produced in the physical earth is the responsibility of man.

CHAPTER 55

1 Ho, every one that thirsteth, come ye to the waters, and he that hath no money; come ye, buy, and eat; yea, come, buy wine and milk without money and without price.
2 Wherefore do ye spend money for that which is not bread? and your labour for that which satisfieth not? hearken diligently unto me, and eat ye that which is good, and let your soul delight itself in fatness.
3 Incline your ear, and come unto me: hear, and your soul shall live; and I will make an everlasting covenant with you, even the sure mercies of David.

There are some people in the fallen state who are ready to experience something other than the familiar human nature state which has produced the distortions in the environment. The fallen-state people thirst for something they sense is missing; there must be a better way on earth to produce creative action instead of destruction. It is to these people that Isaiah issues the invitation from the LORD to come to the waters. The waters are not the waters that a person drinks from a well or a spring. These particular waters are the waters which symbolize the truth of the spirit that flows into the earth to water the earth of the people, the human nature state. The people who have no money are invited because the LORD does not refuse anyone entrance to the kingdom. The people are invited to come and buy and eat of the spirit from the LORD which Isaiah is offering to the children of men. The spirit which Isaiah is offering to the people, the wine of life and the milk of divine kindness, is available to all without money and without price.

The LORD asks the people why they spend money for that which is not bread, that which will not sustain them? Why do the people labor so hard for that which does not satisfy the inner hunger of a human being? Isaiah is asking the people to listen diligently to what he has to say and to eat that which is truly good from the perspective of the spirit and then, when that is done, your soul shall delight itself in fatness, your soul shall be satisfied and the spiritual hunger will be gone. Isaiah, the servant of the LORD, asks the people to incline your ears, and come to him: hear the word, which is the water of the truth of spirit or being from the LORD, and your soul shall live; and the LORD will make an everlasting covenant with you, even as the sure mercies of love from the

The Testimony of the Major Prophets

LORD were given to David. David had been promised an unending dynasty and Jerusalem is the city of David.

4 Behold, I have given him for a witness to the people, a leader and commander to the people.
5 Behold, thou shalt call a nation that thou knowest not, and nations that knew not thee shall run unto thee because of the LORD thy God, and for the Holy One of Israel; for he hath glorified thee.

Behold, the LORD has given David for a witness to the people, a leader and a commander to the people of Jerusalem and Judah which can spread further out. The people who respond to the call of the LORD through Isaiah shall call together a nation of people, and the people who are called will not know the people who will respond to the invitation of the LORD. People who are unknown to you will answer the call from the LORD and therefore be drawn to the LORD and run into you. This is because all the people who are drawn to the LORD through the word of Isaiah are being drawn to the central spot where Isaiah stands. The invitation is from the LORD your God, and from the Holy One of Israel. It is the LORD and the Holy One who will glorify the people who respond to the LORD. Isaiah states that the LORD will glorify the people who come to be a part of the body of the LORD on earth and they will come to know that they are a part of the LORD's body.

6 Seek ye the LORD while he may be found, call ye upon him while he is near:
7 Let the wicked forsake his way, and the unrighteous man his thoughts: and let him return unto the LORD, and he will have mercy upon him; and to our God, for he will abundantly pardon.
8 For my thoughts are not your thoughts, neither are your ways my ways, saith the LORD.
9 For as the heavens are higher than the earth, so are my ways higher than your ways, and my thoughts than your thoughts.
10 For as the rain cometh down, and the snow from heaven, and returneth not thither, but watereth the earth, and maketh it bring forth and bud, that it may give seed to the sower, and bread to the eater:

Isaiah is advising people to seek the LORD while He may be found, and to call upon Him while He is near. The implication of the invitation is that the seeker does not have to die to find the LORD and that there is a way for the people who truly desire to know the LORD to find the LORD. What is this way? Isaiah tells the people who are interested that those who are wicked must forsake, give up, relinquish, the ways of wickedness, and the unrighteous man must relinquish his unrighteous thoughts. The interested person must return to the LORD. This is not a simple physical relocation to the LORD; it is a return to the Way of the LORD, the way of the personal expression of the LORD's spirit of love, truth and life which descends from the LORD to man and man has the responsibility of taking the LORD's spirit and letting the spirit of the LORD be magnified on earth. If man, any man or woman, will do this, then the LORD will have mercy on that person. God will abundantly pardon the person regardless of his many transitions. Human beings in the fallen state are not as loving and forgiving as the LORD.

For my thoughts are not your thoughts, neither are your ways my ways, says the LORD. If man is in the fallen state, and the LORD is in the ascended state, from which man has fallen, then it should be obvious that there is a difference in the thoughts and ways of a man as contrasted with the thoughts and ways of the LORD. It is this difference between the consciousness, the content of the minds and the hearts, of the LORD, and the minds and the hearts of the fallen people in the environment that prevents man from harmonizing with God to achieve a unity consciousness or to experience the covenant-agreement with the LORD. The LORD wants the people to see that there is a difference in the minds and hearts of the LORD and this difference must be repaired.

For as the heavens are higher than the earth, so are the ways of the LORD higher than the ways of fallen man, and the thoughts of the LORD are higher than the thoughts of man. The higher thoughts of the LORD are designed to descend as the rain comes down from on high. As the rain comes down from the higher levels, and as the snow comes down from heaven, it is a one-way movement. The falling water and snow do not return to the heavens, but the water from heaven is to water the entire earth for the purpose of making the earth bring forth buds, that it may give seed to the sower, and bread to the eater: Living material things are supposed to grow.

11 So shall my word be that goeth forth out of my mouth: it shall not return unto me void, but it shall accomplish that which I please, and it shall prosper in the thing whereto I sent it.
12 For ye shall go out with joy, and be led forth with peace: the mountains and the hills shall break forth before you into singing, and all the trees of the field shall clap their hands.
13 Instead of the thorn shall come up the fir tree, and instead of the brier shall come up the myrtle tree: and it shall be to the LORD for a name, for an everlasting sign that shall not be cut off.

The LORD has used this analogy of the water from heaven to produce buds and seeds on the earth to explain the purpose of the spirit of the LORD that falls from heaven goes out of the mouth of the LORD and it also shall go forth, and it shall not return void, with nothing. The spirit which has dominion over matter shall accomplish what the LORD pleases because the design is in the spirit and it shall prosper in the earth to do what the LORD, Who sent the spirit into the earth, intended it to do. Man is designed to carry the spirit of the LORD into the earth. Man is to go out into the world carrying the spirit of the LORD, a spirit of love, truth and life, with joy, and to be led with peace: the mountains and the hills shall break forth before you into singing, and all the trees of the field shall clap their hands. This is symbolic language that simply says that the material earth must respond to the spirit. It is man's responsibility to carry the spirit of the LORD; the material earth will gladly respond to the one who carries the spirit of the LORD. The environment, which has been desecrated by the thoughts and ways of human nature, will be restored rapidly when the people carry the spirit of the LORD. Instead of the environment being filled with thorns, there shall come up a fir tree and instead of a briar, there shall come up a myrtle tree: this process shall be to the glory of the LORD for an everlasting sign. When the people carry the spirit of the LORD, beauty shall be born into the earth.

CHAPTER 56

1 Thus saith the LORD, Keep ye judgment, and do justice: for my salvation is near to come, and my righteousness to be revealed.
2 Blessed is the man that doeth this, and the son of man that layeth hold on it; that keepeth the sabbath from polluting it, and keepeth his hand from doing any evil.

The spirit of the LORD moving through the physical form of Isaiah tells his followers that they, individually and collectively, should keep the judgment, the discernment and the understanding, that it is the spirit of the LORD that moves through each of them that should be the cause of each person's actions and behaviors. This is the only requirement for everyone who wants to do justice, who desires to serve the LORD equitably to fulfill the purpose of his Maker. This is the only way that the salvation of the LORD can come into the earth. The LORD's salvation is always near to come into the earth but the spirit of the LORD must emerge through man for the righteousness of the LORD to be revealed on earth.

Blessed is the man who does this, who lets the spirit from an invisible LORD be made visible through one's own body, which not only produces a blessing to the heart, mind and body of the person who lets the spirit flow through one's self so that the spirit can be seen by others, but also the spirit of the LORD has been made visible on earth to be observed and a blessing to others. The person who observes the blessing of the LORD coming through the form of the one who is making the invisible spirit become visible is the son of man, the extension of the spirit of the LORD that has occurred because of the man who has served the LORD's spirit to them so that it can be followed, so that he can lay hold on the spirit and follow it. This spirit is a holy spirit if it comes through the form of man accurately. The responsibility of man is to let the spirit of the LORD come through him accurately at all times! This is serving the LORD; this is keeping the Sabbath; this is not polluting the spirit of the LORD with the distorted spirits of the earth; this is the way that man can keep his hand, his control, from doing any evil. Evil is the distortion of the spirit of the LORD; evil is anything that is not of love, truth and life. The person who follows the example of this man is the son of man.

3 Neither let the son of the stranger, that hath joined himself to the LORD, speak, saying, The LORD hath utterly separated me from his people: neither let the eunuch say, Behold, I am a dry tree.
4 For thus saith the LORD unto the eunuchs that keep my sabbaths, and choose the things that please me, and take hold of my covenant;
5 Even unto them will I give in mine house and within my walls a place and a name better than of sons and of daughters: I will give them an everlasting name, that shall not be cut off.

The son of the stranger is the expression of a spirit that is not the spirit of the LORD which appears through people who are strangers to the spirit of the LORD; these people carry the evil spirits of anger resentment, jealousy, hate, greed, etc. The spirit of the LORD is always present with you and with everyone; the expression of the evil spirit is the distorted spirit carried by the son of the stranger, who can join himself to the servers of the LORD and say that the LORD has utterly separated him from His people. Never let the son of the stranger say that you are separated from the spirit of the LORD because you are **never** separated from the LORD's spirit. If you say that you are separated from the LORD's spirit, you have identified with the person who carries the evil spirit and your focus has descended to the evil spirit instead of the spirit of the LORD which is present. This is analogous to the eunuch who says that he is a dry tree, unable to reproduce himself. The eunuch is speaking of physical offspring and not the offspring of the spirit of the LORD which is always available in form as long as the form has life that comes from the LORD.

The word of the LORD to the eunuchs who keep His Sabbaths is that the eunuchs should choose the expressions that please the LORD, which is the release and the magnification of the LORD's spirit which will keep the spiritual covenant between the eunuch and the LORD. Isaiah is pointing out that the spiritual seed from the LORD is more important that the physical seed from the form of the eunuch. The people, symbolized as eunuchs, who use their freedom of choice to choose to serve the spirit of the LORD shall receive a reward from the LORD. The reward from the LORD is something better than the physical sons and daughters; the LORD will give to them a place in the house of the LORD and within His walls and a name, an everlasting name, a spiritual name that will not be cut off or ended as is the case when death occurs to the physical form. The spiritual name is a name that has everlasting life with the LORD and in the LORD's house. It is the LORD's name: I AM.

6 Also the sons of the stranger, that join themselves to the LORD, to serve him, and to love the name of the LORD, to be his servants, every one that keepeth the sabbath from polluting it, and taketh hold of my covenant;
7 Even them will I bring to my holy mountain, and make them joyful in my house of prayer: their burnt offerings and their sacrifices shall be accepted upon mine altar; for mine house shall be called an house of prayer for all people.

The sons of the stranger are those people who do not know the LORD, who join themselves with those who do serve the LORD with the desire to serve Him to others and who want to identify with the LORD's spirit. They desire to love the name of the LORD and be His servants; everyone keeps the Sabbath and does not pollute the spirit of the LORD as it flows through them; this is the way that a son of the stranger takes hold and becomes one with the covenant of the spirit which is

The Testimony of the Major Prophets

available to everyone who does the things that are required to receive a just reward for their devoted service. They will be brought by the LORD to His holy mountain, and they will be made joyful in His house of prayer, a house where everyone prays, releases, the spirit of the LORD through their forms simultaneously and continuously while they are still alive in human forms. Their behaviors and prayers, as they release the spirit of the LORD, are the burnt offerings and their sacrifices, the things that they make sacred by the way that they handle them, which are acceptable upon the altar of the LORD. In this manner, the house of the LORD in material form on earth shall be called the house of prayer for all people. In its true condition, the earth should be a house of prayer for everyone and the kingdom of the Father, the kingdom of heaven would be on earth. Of course, in its present fallen state, the earth is not this way and the Lord GOD must work with the people the way that they are presently.

8 The Lord GOD which gathereth the outcasts of Israel saith, Yet will I gather others to him, beside those that are gathered unto him.
9 All ye beasts of the field, come to devour, yea, all ye beasts in the forest.
10 His watchmen are blind: they are all ignorant, they are all dumb dogs, they cannot bark; sleeping, lying down, loving to slumber.
11 Yea, they are greedy dogs which can never have enough, and they are shepherds that cannot understand: they all look to their own way, every one for his gain, from his quarter.
12 Come ye, say they, I will fetch wine, and we will fill ourselves with strong drink; and to morrow shall be as this day, and much more abundant.

The purpose of the Lord GOD at this time is to gather the outcasts of Israel, the people who have been cast out of the spiritual pattern of Israel and who are functioning in the material pattern of Jacob. The physical bodies are there but they are not releasing the spirit of the LORD. Isaiah and his followers, who have offered their own bodies in service to the LORD, will gather others to Him besides those who are gathered to him already. These others, the other people, who will be gathered are compared to **beasts of the field** who believe that they have come on earth to devour, to get material treasures, to satisfy their hunger as beasts in the forest. The leaders of these people are compared to watchmen who are blind: they are ignorant as dumb dogs that cannot bark to warn of danger; they love to sleep, or lying down, they love to slumber and they do not love to work and be creative. Yes, these people are compared to greedy dogs who can never have enough, while in reality, they are shepherds who cannot understand their purpose on earth. They look to their own way with everyone seeking their own gain from their own small area of control. Their wanton behavior, characterized by what they say and what comes forth from their mouths, reveals their thoughts: they will fetch wine, fill themselves with strong drink; and they believe that tomorrow will be more of the same as today, only much "better" even though they have made no changes in their habits.

CHAPTER 57

1 The righteous perisheth, and no man layeth it to heart: and merciful men are taken away, none considering that the righteous is taken away from the evil to come.
2 He shall enter into peace: they shall rest in their beds, each one walking in his uprightness.

Isaiah speaking the words of the LORD tells his followers that the righteous spirits who have incarnated in human forms on earth perish in the fallen state, and no man, no one is taking this waste to heart to the extent that they will do something to change this situation. Merciful men, spirits of the LORD who are full of mercy to be expressed into the earth, are taken away from their appointed tasks because they have been usurped by the rebellion of the human creatures who are using the LORD's spirits for their own self-centered pleasure. The righteous ones who incarnate on earth have been taken away by the evil identities who use the spirit of the LORD to allow evil to come on earth. The righteous spirits enter into the peace which exists deep within the human form: they rest in their beds as though they are asleep but each one is walking in their uprightness, where these spirits are still in agreement with the LORD, but the physical forms, under the control of the fallen, self-active minds, rebel against the spirit of the LORD and proclaim that they will live their own lives, separate from the LORD. However, now that Isaiah is present, a person who is in covenant-agreement with the LORD, who is in the true state of man, he can chastise the usurper who has taken control of the LORD's instrument of action on earth called man; the usurper who turned man, made in the image and likeness of God, into something that is very distorted.

3 But draw near hither, ye sons of the sorceress, the seed of the adulterer and the whore.
4 Against whom do ye sport yourselves? against whom make ye a wide mouth, and draw out the tongue? are ye not children of transgression, a seed of falsehood,
5 Enflaming yourselves with idols under every green tree, slaying the children in the valleys under the clifts of the rocks?

Isaiah, the prophet or representative of the LORD, calls upon the people in the fallen state who will listen (most people will not!) to draw near to him. Isaiah correctly calls them for what they are: you sons of the sorceress, the seed of the adulterer and the whore; these three descriptions are

The Testimony of the Major Prophets

not three separate people; they are different names for the same entity, any person who represents the fallen state on earth, man in the fallen state, the son of perdition. Mankind in the fallen state is the son of the sorceress because the human form is symbolized as a woman who should be a bride to the Bridegroom, the LORD. This woman has removed herself from spiritual expression of the LORD and she is in agreement with the person in the environment, the son of perdition, who is having an illicit affair with her. The distortion of man in the fallen state is the seed, the offspring of the adulterer and the whore, the human form, who has left the spirit of the LORD and is having an affair with fallen man. Isaiah, who is the bride to the Bridegroom and therefore understands the true connection of the covenant continues to chastise the distortions of the LORD's people who have been jeering at him for representing the LORD on earth.

Isaiah chastises their actions by asking them if they really know who it is that they ridicule when they ridicule and make sport of Isaiah? Against whom do they make faces and stick out their tongues in ridicule of the message of Isaiah? Isaiah asks them if they are not children of transgression, those who have transgressed from the way of the LORD? Are they not a seed of falsehood because they are not a representation of the seed of truth that comes from the LORD? Are they not emotionally inflaming themselves with man-made idols that appear under every green tree, slaying the children of the LORD in the valleys of the shadow of death where they dwell in darkness under the clefts of the rocks where they are hidden from the light of the LORD?

6 Among the smooth stones of the stream is thy portion; they, they are thy lot: even to them hast thou poured a drink offering, thou hast offered a meat offering. Should I receive comfort in these?
7 Upon a lofty and high mountain hast thou set thy bed: even thither wentest thou up to offer sacrifice.
8 Behind the doors also and the posts hast thou set up thy remembrance: for thou hast discovered thyself to another than me, and art gone up; thou hast enlarged thy bed, and made thee a covenant with them; thou lovedst their bed where thou sawest it.
9 And thou wentest to the king with ointment, and didst increase thy perfumes, and didst send thy messengers far off, and didst debase thyself even unto hell.

The children, the offspring of the LORD do not belong in the clefts of a valley; their portion, their place is among the smooth stones of the stream which carries the water of truth that flows from the LORD to nurture the earth. This is the true position of everyone, including the sons of the sorceress, who are using the water of truth as it comes from the LORD to distort the human condition. The LORD has offered a **drink-offering** of the water, which symbolizes the flow of His spirit, but the sons of the sorceress have offered a **meat-offering**, a material offering into the material world. Should the spirit of the LORD take comfort in the offerings of the sons of the sorceress, the spiritual people who are trapped in the body of the son of perdition?

The sons of the sorceress have set their beds upon a lofty and high mountain in the material world; they even go to worship in a high place to offer their sacrifices to the LORD. Man in the fallen state has set up his remembrances to the LORD to give glory to those idols that man has formed to pay homage and obeisance to those idols that are different than the LORD. The sons of the sorceress have enlarged their bed, the area of their responsibility where they rule in a self-induced dream state and they have made a covenant with the material world instead of making a covenant with the spirit of the LORD. Man in the fallen state loves the bed, the place where they dream their dreams that there is no LORD to whom they are accountable and therefore they can take control of "their" world which they believe does not belong to the LORD. They go to the kings of the world with gifts of ointment and perfumes through his messengers to far-off places, and by doing these things, man in the fallen state has debased himself and his environment, adulterated and cheapened to a condition called hell. Man in the fallen state, and no one else, has created a hell on earth.

10 Thou art wearied in the greatness of thy way; yet saidst thou not, There is no hope: thou hast found the life of thine hand; therefore thou wast not grieved.
11 And of whom hast thou been afraid or feared, that thou hast lied, and hast not remembered me, nor laid it to thy heart? have not I held my peace even of old, and thou fearest me not?
12 I will declare thy righteousness, and thy works; for they shall not profit thee.
13 When thou criest, let thy companies deliver thee; but the wind shall carry them all away; vanity shall take them: but he that putteth his trust in me shall possess the land, and shall inherit my holy mountain;

The person who dwells in the fallen state is weary in the "greatness" of the way that he has created for himself; yet he would not say that there is no hope: you do say that you have found the life for you that is just right for your hand of control; therefore deceiving yourself into thinking that you were not grieved by your circumstances, but you are. During all this time of rebellion of man from the LORD, then of whom has fallen man been afraid, feared, lied and not remembered nor considered it in his heart? Has the LORD not kept His peace even of old times long ago, when the person did not fear the LORD?

The LORD will declare or acknowledge the righteousness that man in the fallen state performs, and the works of his righteousness; the behavior of man in the fallen state is not all wrong; but these righteous works will not profit or benefit man in the fallen state because they rightfully belong to the LORD, Who is the Author of the true state. When fallen man cries aloud for the companies of his many idols to deliver him in his time of trouble, the wind, the spirit of the true design of the LORD shall take them all away; the vanity with which they were built shall take them. But he that puts his trust in the LORD shall possess the land and shall inherit the holy mountain of the LORD.

14 And shall say, Cast ye up, cast ye up, prepare the way, take up the stumblingblock out of the way of my people.
15 For thus saith the high and lofty One that inhabiteth eternity, whose name is Holy; I dwell in the high and holy place, with him also that is of a contrite and humble spirit, to revive the spirit of the humble, and to revive the heart of the contrite ones.
16 For I will not contend for ever, neither will I be always wroth: for the spirit should fail before me, and the souls which I have made.

The person who trusts the LORD shall say, Cast yourself up, lift up the people out of the hell of their environment into a higher state. Prepare the way of the LORD on earth, take the stumbling blocks out of the way of the LORD's people. The stumbling blocks in the way are in the consciousness of man. Thus speaks the high and the lofty One that inhabits eternity, whose name is Holy. It is

The Testimony of the Major Prophets

the LORD who dwells in the high and holy place, and with Him is the person who is of a contrite and humble spirit. It takes someone of integrity who can speak from experience to revive the spirit of the humble and to revive the heart of the contrite ones. The LORD will not contend with His creation forever and neither will the experience of the LORD in man be wroth, filled with anger: the spirit of wrath should fade before the moving spirit of the LORD and it should also pass away from the souls, the human creatures which the LORD has made. The spirit of the LORD shall prevail.

17 For the iniquity of his covetousness was I wroth, and smote him: I hid me, and was wroth, and he went on frowardly in the way of his heart.
18 I have seen his ways, and will heal him: I will lead him also, and restore comforts unto him and to his mourners.
19 I create the fruit of the lips; Peace, peace to him that is far off, and to him that is near, saith the LORD; and I will heal him.
20 But the wicked are like the troubled sea, when it cannot rest, whose waters cast up mire and dirt.
21 There is no peace, saith my God, to the wicked.

The LORD speaking through Isaiah states that the iniquity of the covetousness, the greed of His creation, man, is the reason that the LORD smote man, punished man with a reprimand: the LORD hid Himself from man so that man lost his conscious awareness of the presence of the LORD. The awareness of the LORD was perceived as anger instead of love. Man continued to go forth in his fallen way of the desires of his heart for the pleasures of the material world. The LORD through Isaiah has seen the fallen ways of man and the misery that these ways have produced and the LORD shall heal man: the LORD will also lead him, and restore comforts unto him and to his mourners if man chooses to return to the way of the LORD.

The LORD is the creator of the fruit of the lips, the expressions that come forth through man. Peace is the word on the lips; peace to him that is far off and peace to him that is near is the word of the LORD; and the LORD will heal man from his transgression. But the wicked men in the world are like the troubled sea, when it cannot rest, whose waters cast up mire and dirt. The experience of the consciousness of man in the fallen state is like the turbulent sea that produces the stormy materialistic conditions of human nature. The sea will calm down, in time, to a sea of glass, clear as crystal, when the mire and the dirt of human nature settles to the bottom. This cannot occur as long as man remains wicked. There is no peace on earth for the people who are wicked, says the God of Isaiah.

CHAPTER 58

1 Cry aloud, spare not, lift up thy voice like a trumpet, and shew my people their transgression, and the house of Jacob their sins.
2 Yet they seek me daily, and delight to know my ways, as a nation that did righteousness, and forsook not the ordinance of their God: they ask of me the ordinances of justice; they take delight in approaching to God.

The LORD speaking through Isaiah tells his followers to cry aloud so that their message can be heard, spare not and do not hold back the message that you carry. Lift up your voice as a trumpet so that you can be heard in the land as you tell the LORD's people of their transgressions from His ways to the fallen ways of human nature. The body of people in the fallen state are symbolized by the house of Jacob and the people in this house carry the sins that keep them away from the covenant with the spirit of the LORD. The people in the house of Jacob, the fallen state, seek the LORD daily in their rituals and they delight in knowing the ways of the LORD as a nation that does righteousness and did not forsake the ordinance of their God as the ordinance was taught to them by their teachers: the people ask the LORD the ordinances of justice because they delight in their approaches to God

3 Wherefore have we fasted, say they, and thou seest not? wherefore have we afflicted our soul, and thou takest no knowledge? Behold, in the day of your fast ye find pleasure, and exact all your labours.
4 Behold, ye fast for strife and debate, and to smite with the fist of wickedness: ye shall not fast as ye do this day, to make your voice to be heard on high.
5 Is it such a fast that I have chosen? a day for a man to afflict his soul? is it to bow down his head as a bulrush, and to spread sackcloth and ashes under him? wilt thou call this a fast, and an acceptable day to the LORD?
6 Is not this the fast that I have chosen? to loose the bands of wickedness, to undo the heavy burdens, and to let the oppressed go free, and that ye break every yoke?

The Testimony of the Major Prophets

7 Is it not to deal thy bread to the hungry, and that thou bring the poor that are cast out to thy house? when thou seest the naked, that thou cover him; and that thou hide not thyself from thine own flesh?

The people want to know why after they have done as they have been told, they say they have fasted, and the LORD apparently does not see? The people have afflicted their souls, their hearts, minds and bodies, and seemingly, the LORD takes no knowledge of their efforts? The LORD speaking through Isaiah tells the people who are asking the questions that, in the day of their fast, they experienced the pleasure of worshipping the LORD. Symbolically, a fast is a deliberately measured release of the expression of the spirit. Therefore, they exacted what they should from the LORD for the labors that they have exerted to bring about the LORD's kingdom. Behold, you who pray to the LORD, you fast for strife and debate and to hurt other people with the fist of wickedness: if the people continue to fast as they do in this day, then their voice will not be heard on high.

Is this the kind of a fast that the LORD has chosen? a single day of the week for man to afflict his soul? Is it the LORD's desire for man to bow down his head as a bulrush, and to spread sackcloth and ashes under him? Would you call this form of worship a fast and an acceptable day for man in the sight of the LORD? Or, is this not the fast that the LORD has chosen? to loose that bands of wickedness, to undo the heavy burdens that have been placed upon them, to let the oppressed go free and to break every yoke that keeps the LORD's people tied to the earth? Is not the fast and the worship of the LORD to share their bread with the hungry, to bring the poor who are cast out to your own house? when you see the naked, that you cover him; and that you hide not yourself, the spirit of you, from your own flesh so that your spirit shines through your own flesh?

8 Then shall thy light break forth as the morning, and thine health shall spring forth speedily: and thy righteousness shall go before thee; the glory of the LORD shall be thy rereward.
9 Then shalt thou call, and the LORD shall answer; thou shalt cry, and he shall say, Here I am. If thou take away from the midst of thee the yoke, the putting forth of the finger, and speaking vanity;
10 And if thou draw out thy soul to the hungry, and satisfy the afflicted soul; then shall thy light rise in obscurity, and thy darkness be as the noonday:
11 And the LORD shall guide thee continually, and satisfy thy soul in drought, and make fat thy bones: and thou shalt be like a watered garden, and like a spring of water, whose waters fail not.

Isaiah tells the people, and he encourages other people to do the same, that their spiritual light shall break forth as the morning shines in the darkness of the night, and your health shall spring forth speedily as the spirit comes forth: as this is done, your righteousness shall go forth before you if you let the spirit find expression on earth. The glory of the LORD that you expressed will be your rear guard as you allow the spirit to come forth. If the people fast and pray in this manner, then, when you call, the LORD shall answer; you shall cry to the LORD and the LORD shall say, Here I am. This can occur because you are letting the LORD's spirit flow through you which is the requirement of the covenant. By the same token, Here I Am, is the attitude man—male and female—needs to represent the LORD.

Isaiah tells the people that if they take away from the midst of them the yoke of wanting the things of the material world, the putting forth of the finger of accusation and blame toward others because you believe them to be wrong always, and the speaking of vanity from one's own heart to others; if you take care of the hungry, and satisfy the afflicted soul; then your light that is in you shall rise from obscurity, and your spiritual darkness shall be as noonday. The LORD shall guide you continuously and satisfy your soul in times of drought, and make your bodies fat: and you shall be as a watered garden in the desert, like a spring of water that is flowing consistently, whose waters never fail. The waters of which Isaiah is speaking are the waters of the LORD's spirit of truth because His spirit flows like water to each of His children.

12 And they that shall be of thee shall build the old waste places: thou shalt raise up the foundations of many generations; and thou shalt be called, The repairer of the breach, The restorer of paths to dwell in.
13 If thou turn away thy foot from the sabbath, from doing thy pleasure on my holy day; and call the sabbath a delight, the holy of the LORD, honourable; and shalt honour him, not doing thine own ways, nor finding thine own pleasure, nor speaking thine own words:
14 Then shalt thou delight thyself in the LORD; and I will cause thee to ride upon the high places of the earth, and feed thee with the heritage of Jacob thy father: for the mouth of the LORD hath spoken it.

The people who are watered by you with the spirit that flows from the LORD through you to them shall build the old waste places because they will know to let the spirit flow through them and let their light shine. The people who let the spirit of the LORD flow through them shall raise up the foundations of the waste of many generations; and, when you as an individual actually do this, you shall be called, "The repairer of the breach", because there has been a breach when the people of the LORD were not in position to let the spirit of the LORD flow through them to build the LORD's kingdom. You shall also be called, "The restorer of paths to dwell in" because people who see your example of the shining of the light shall have a path, a light, to follow which is vital to the restoration.

If you turn away your foot, the way that you walk on earth doing your own pleasure on the holy day of the LORD; if you call the Sabbath, the holiness of doing the LORD's pleasure on earth on His holy day a delight; and call the Sabbath a delight, the holy of the LORD, honorable; and you shall honor the LORD, not doing your own ways, nor finding your own pleasure, nor speaking your own words: then you shall delight yourself in the service of the LORD; and the LORD will cause you to ride upon the high places of the earth, and feed you with the heritage of Jacob your father.

The heritage of Jacob is Israel and it is Israel who experiences oneness with the LORD: for the mouth of the LORD through Isaiah has spoken the way to oneness with the LORD.

CHAPTER 59

1 Behold, the LORD's hand is not shortened, that it cannot save; neither his ear heavy, that it cannot hear:
2 But your iniquities have separated between you and your God, and your sins have hid his face from you, that he will not hear.
3 For your hands are defiled with blood, and your fingers with iniquity; your lips have spoken lies, your tongue hath muttered perverseness.
4 None calleth for justice, nor any pleadeth for truth: they trust in vanity, and speak lies; they conceive mischief, and bring forth iniquity.

Isaiah tells his followers that the problem that a person has who worships the LORD and receives no answer is not with the LORD: the hand of the LORD is not shortened that it cannot reach you wherever you are because the spirit of God is everywhere and there is not a place on earth where the spirit is not present and unable to save the person who calls for the LORD to be with him. Neither is the ear of the LORD heavy, with the requests of many, that He cannot hear your prayer to be in oneness with the LORD's spirit. But the person who cries for oneness with the LORD should know that it is the iniquities — the faults, evils and weaknesses—that have resulted in the separation between you and your God. It is not that God has abandoned you, God is everywhere; the problem is that your sins have hid His face from you so that you are not consciously aware of His presence within you and within every living thing. This is the reason that it appears that God does not hear you: there is too much clutter in your consciousness, in your own mind and heart, that you cannot perceive what has always been present.

Isaiah becomes even more specific when he tells his followers that their hands are defiled with the blood of destroying things, your fingers are defiled with iniquity such as blaming and accusing others, your lips have spoken lies about God, one's self and one's neighbors, and your tongue has muttered wicked things to others in gossip that degrades your fellow man. None calls for true justice, nor pleads for truth that man should reveal God's spirit on earth: they trust in the vanity of the false counterfeit self which they believe that they are, and they speak lies based upon the human self, that they **believe** they are, instead of the spirit in human form which they **really** are;

they conceive mischief when functioning from this false identity, and this error in identity brings forth iniquity and evil in many forms.

5 They hatch cockatrice' eggs, and weave the spider's web: he that eateth of their eggs dieth, and that which is crushed breaketh out into a viper.
6 Their webs shall not become garments, neither shall they cover themselves with their works: their works are works of iniquity, and the act of violence is in their hands.
7 Their feet run to evil, and they make haste to shed innocent blood: their thoughts are thoughts of iniquity; wasting and destruction are in their paths.

The false self, which is a distortion of the truth of man, hatches the eggs of the cockatrice. The cockatrice is a mythical serpent that hatches from an egg and is deadly to anyone who feels its breath on them or sees its glance. (It can be compared to the serpent in the garden of Eden who caused the trouble for Adam and Eve!) The false self, the human identity, also weaves the spider's web to trap and ensnare others to its selfish purposes. Isaiah uses these illustrations to depict the end result of the human ego state: a person who eats of the cockatrice's eggs shall die and the egg that is crushed, broken open and released shall break out of the egg into a viper. This poisonous viper is the destructive distortion of man in the fallen state. Their webs are not physical garments that can be seen and observed; neither will the people who do these things cover themselves with their works that can be easily seen on their person: their works are works of iniquity, and the act of violence is in their hand of control which springs from an inner source of evil. Their feet run to do evil and they make haste to shed innocent blood because this is the nature of the selfish state that will do anything to get the treasures that they want; the thoughts of the false self are thoughts of iniquity; wasting and destruction are in their paths, the paths that they leave behind them as a trail, because they generate destruction and waste based upon their destructive thoughts that they call "good" thoughts. The thoughts of fallen man and the thoughts of the LORD are not the same thoughts.

8 The way of peace they know not; and there is no judgment in their goings: they have made them crooked paths: whosoever goeth therein shall not know peace.
9 Therefore is judgment far from us, neither doth justice overtake us: we wait for light, but behold obscurity; for brightness, but we walk in darkness.

The people who are in the fallen state do not know the way of peace which is offered by the spirit of the LORD. There is no true judgment in the way that they are going through life, doing the things that they do; they are "normal" people. They have made crooked paths in the way that they have walked on earth: and whosoever goes on that crooked path shall never know peace, the peace that passes all understanding. There is no need to enter into judgment because we can see the reasons why man is in the fallen state, and why there is no need to blame them for what they are doing. They do not know what they are doing; they only know one state which we call the fallen state. If we can begin to see the conditions of the fallen state, then we are in the process of separating ourselves from it. There is no need for some false sense of justice to overtake us and to fight against this distortion that fallen man, in his ignorance, has created. We wait for light, we serve the light into the condition which we behold as obscurity, vagueness and dimness of the light that has not emerged brightly through man in his fallen state. We can begin to understand that our role with the

The Testimony of the Major Prophets

LORD is to walk in brightness, letting our lights shine, but we walk in an environment of darkness and let our lights shine into the dark and our material environment will begin to reflect our light.

10 We grope for the wall like the blind, and we grope as if we had no eyes: we stumble at noonday as in the night; we are in desolate places as dead men.
11 We roar all like bears, and mourn sore like doves: we look for judgment, but there is none; for salvation, but it is far off from us.

Isaiah teaches his followers that they are not to condemn, blame or chastise anyone who is in the fallen state because we have all been born into it and we know what it is like to exist in such an environment. We grope for a wall as the blind do to help them walk in their darkness, and in our perceptual blindness we have groped as if we had no eyes: except we stumble through life at noonday when there is a maximum of light as if it were the night when it is dark. We know what it is like to be in desolate places as dead men who do not have the life from the LORD. In the fallen state, we have roared and growled like bears when we did not get what we want immediately to display the anger within us, and we have mourned like doves to display our sadness when we did not get what we wanted. In the fallen state, we look for judgment in the conditions of the world, but there is none that we can see. We look for salvation and deliverance in the world of the fallen state, but it is far off from us. It seems that there is no justice and no salvation for us on earth. But there is justice in the working of the law of the LORD!

12 For our transgressions are multiplied before thee, and our sins testify against us: for our transgressions are with us; and as for our iniquities, we know them;
13 In transgressing and lying against the LORD, and departing away from our God, speaking oppression and revolt, conceiving and uttering from the heart words of falsehood.
14 And judgment is turned away backward, and justice standeth afar off: for truth is fallen in the street, and equity cannot enter.
15 Yea, truth faileth; and he that departeth from evil maketh himself a prey: and the LORD saw it, and it displeased him that there was no judgment.

Isaiah teaches us that we can begin to see our transgressions multiplied before us, and the sins that we and our forefathers have committed testify against our behaviors because they appear in form before our eyes. The only way that the transgressions appear in the environment is as they were expressed through people. Our transgressions as a people, mankind, are with us; and as for our particular contributions to the chaos around us, we know them because we put our share into the environment. Isaiah tells us that we have done this by transgressing and lying against the LORD, not expressing the way of the LORD which is man's mission on earth. The truth of the LORD is with us but we have been expressing something else of our own: lies. We have departed away from the way of our God, speaking oppression and revolt against the LORD, conceiving and uttering words of falsehood from our hearts. All of this is a smoke screen to keep us from serving the nature of the LORD on earth which would eliminate and correct all the "problems" that we fight against and try to correct by our frenzied activity.

True judgment is turned away backward, it is reversed in our observation. We are getting exactly what we made and what we deserve according to the working of the law and yet we believe that the law is unfair and that true justice, justice that would be pleasing to man in the fallen state, is far away. The truth of the distorted state that man has created over the past generations is fallen in the street for us to observe, and the true equity from the LORD cannot enter and appear before us because we have made these horrible distortions instead of making visible the truth from the LORD. Yes the truth from the LORD which the LORD has sent to man has failed to be expressed into the earth where it can be observed because man did not do his job. If any person began to see what was transpiring on earth and he departed from the evil that was being produced by himself and his fellow man, he made himself a prey for the people who resented and objected to the change. The LORD saw this, and it displeased Him that there was no judgment, no decision on the part of fallen man to serve the LORD and bring the true design of heaven on earth.

16 And he saw that there was no man, and wondered that there was no intercessor: therefore his arm brought salvation unto him; and his righteousness, it sustained him.
17 For he put on righteousness as a breastplate, and an helmet of salvation upon his head; and he put on the garments of vengeance for clothing, and was clad with zeal as a cloke.

Isaiah saw what was transpiring on earth and that there was no man, no man made in the image of the LORD, no example of the true state for fallen man to follow as a true pattern. There was no intercessor, no person who would represent the true state and intercede on behalf of his fellow men on earth. Isaiah decided to be this true pattern on earth. Therefore, his arm, his power and might would be used to provide this right pattern and it brought salvation to him; his righteousness sustained him. Isaiah donned the clothing of a true representative of the LORD on earth, he would re-present the spirit of the LORD to others. Isaiah would make the invisible spirit of the LORD visible by letting the spirit flow through his heart, his mind and his body He put on righteousness as a breastplate, and a helmet of salvation upon his own head; and he put on the garments of vengeance against the fallen state for clothing, and was clad with zeal as a cloak for his entire body. Isaiah would be as a sword for the LORD on earth to deal with the people in the same manner as the LORD would deal with people according to the working of the law.

18 According to their deeds, accordingly he will repay, fury to his adversaries, recompence to his enemies; to the islands he will repay recompence.
19 So shall they fear the name of the LORD from the west, and his glory from the rising of the sun. When the enemy shall come in like a flood, the Spirit of the LORD shall lift up a standard against him.
20 And the Redeemer shall come to Zion, and unto them that turn from transgression in Jacob, saith the LORD.
21 As for me, this is my covenant with them, saith the LORD; My spirit that is upon thee, and my words which I have put in thy mouth, shall not depart out of thy mouth, nor out of the mouth of thy seed, nor out of the mouth of thy seed's seed, saith the LORD, from henceforth and for ever.

Isaiah is in the midst of the people and he treated the people around him in a way that was different than he treated them before he decided to repay people according to the law. According to their deeds, accordingly he will repay them: fury to his adversaries, recompense, payment and compensation in kind, to his enemies; to the islands, the people who are far away from him, he will repay recompense by leaving them alone and maintaining his distance. So, in this manner,

The Testimony of the Major Prophets

the people who had direct dealings with Isaiah came to fear the name of the LORD from the west, from the result of his day's actions and expressions, and his glory from the rising of the sun, from the beginning of each day when he vowed to let the LORD manifest on earth through him. Isaiah did not aggressively wage war or use excessive power or force to get what he wanted. However, Isaiah was not a door mat for those who were aggressive to him. When the enemy came in like a flood, the Spirit of the LORD shall lift up a standard against the invader and protect itself.

And, in this manner, the Redeemer from the LORD shall come to Zion, the place of those who reside in the spiritual consciousness of the LORD, and this holy place on earth is available, to them that turn from transgression in Jacob, the symbol of the body of mankind in the fallen state, to another state, a spiritual state on earth, a choice for those who desire to leave identification with Jacob and dwell in Zion. Isaiah tells us that this is the word of the LORD

As for the position of the LORD, this is the LORD's covenant with the people to prove that He will be with man in His continuing agreement in the covenant, says the LORD. The LORD's spirit that is upon you, and the words of the LORD which have been put in your mouth, shall not depart out of your mouth, nor out of the mouth of your seed, your children, nor out of the mouth of your seed's seed, your grandchildren, etc., says the LORD, from henceforth and for ever. Isaiah has provided a visible light on earth in representation of the LORD. He has assumed the position of the High Priest exactly where he happens to be twenty four hours of the day. He will offer the LORD's light to everyone. He will ask everyone to let his or her light shine. As the High Priest, Isaiah shall represent the LORD to the people and the people to the LORD so that the vertical line of connection is in operation and this covenant-agreement will provide a visible point of orientation for others.

CHAPTER 60

1 Arise, shine; for thy light is come, and the glory of the LORD is risen upon thee.
2 For, behold, the darkness shall cover the earth, and gross darkness the people: but the LORD shall arise upon thee, and his glory shall be seen upon thee.
3 And the Gentiles shall come to thy light, and kings to the brightness of thy rising.

Isaiah, who is in position to represent the LORD to the people and the people to the LORD, as a visible intercessor, a visible light on earth for people to follow, calls for his followers to Arise, rise up above identification with their earthly heredity, and shine, let the indwelling spirit shine; Isaiah can say this to them because he is their light to show them the Way of the LORD on earth. The glory of the LORD, the radiance of the spirit of the LORD, is risen and shining upon the followers who have been listening to the teachings of Isaiah. The followers are being called to let their lights shine in concerted action with the light that is shining through Isaiah. There is plenty of room for the shining of the light, spiritual light, not physical light, on earth.

The people are instructed by Isaiah to behold, to see, that the darkness shall cover the earth, and gross darkness the people; as people get further and further away from the source of the light within them, then there is less and less light on the earth with the result that darkness shall cover the whole earth and gross darkness, the lack of radiance of light will cover the people who have very little spiritual light in them. But the LORD and His spirit shall rise upon the spirits of Isaiah and his followers and the glory of the LORD shall be seen upon those who let the spirit of the LORD shine on earth as their teacher Isaiah is indeed doing. The followers who do this shall become points of light, who, in turn, shall become guiding lights for others. The lights on earth will continue to grow in both number and the quantity of light in the system so that the example of light would be available for others. And the Gentiles shall come to your light, and the kings of far-away places shall be attracted to the brightness of your rising. The followers of Isaiah have been changing and expressing more light, spiritual light, than they themselves are aware of the change. The shining of the light causes people to rise up.

The Testimony of the Major Prophets

4 Lift up thine eyes round about, and see: all they gather themselves together, they come to thee: thy sons shall come from far, and thy daughters shall be nursed at thy side.
5 Then thou shalt see, and flow together, and thine heart shall fear, and be enlarged; because the abundance of the sea shall be converted unto thee, the forces of the Gentiles shall come unto thee.

Isaiah directs his followers to lift up their eyes round about, and see what is in their environment. They are to see all those who gather themselves together. The people are gathering to come to the person, follower or disciple; these are your potential spiritual sons who have come from afar. The sons are the symbols for the offspring who carry the positive spirit of the LORD; and the daughters are the symbols of the people who are attracted to a point of light but they have not yet made a "spiritual marriage", and they are nursed at the side of the person who is providing the nourishment. Then, the followers shall see the response that is drawn to the shining of the light, like water or lighted candles, they shall flow together into oneness and your heart will fear and be enlarged; because the abundance of the sea shall be converted to you, so that you will be a light to them, a lamp that is a point of orientation for them. Even the forces of the Gentiles shall come to you because they are drawn to the light; the response to the light will continue and grow. The light is the light of the LORD.

6 The multitude of camels shall cover thee, the dromedaries of Midian and Ephah; all they from Sheba shall come: they shall bring gold and incense; and they shall shew forth the praises of the LORD.
7 All the flocks of Kedar shall be gathered together unto thee, the rams of Nebaioth shall minister unto thee: they shall come up with acceptance on mine altar, and I will glorify the house of my glory.
8 Who are these that fly as a cloud, and as the doves to their windows?

Camels and dromedaries shall come from Midian, Ephah, and Sheba bringing gold and incense to demonstrate their praises of the LORD. The finest flocks of Kedar and the famous rams of Nebaioth shall minister to you to produce a flock of such quality that the offspring will be pleasing to the LORD and accepted at His altar. The house of the LORD on earth will be glorified as the radiance of the light through the LORD's people builds a totally new state on earth of people and animals. Who are these people that are so attracted by the light that they fly toward you as peaceful as a cloud, and as doves to the windows, the source of the shining of the light from a person? The person who is attracted to the light is the **window** of the LORD and Isaiah is the **door** (a larger opening) of the LORD. More light and air of the spirit goes forth from an open door than through an open window.

9 Surely the isles shall wait for me, and the ships of Tarshish first, to bring thy sons from far, their silver and their gold with them, unto the name of the LORD thy God, and to the Holy One of Israel, because he hath glorified thee.
10 And the sons of strangers shall build up thy walls, and their kings shall minister unto thee: for in my wrath I smote thee, but in my favour have I had mercy on thee.
11 Therefore thy gates shall be open continually; they shall not be shut day nor night; that men may bring unto thee the forces of the Gentiles, and that their kings may be brought.

12 For the nation and kingdom that will not serve thee shall perish; yea, those nations shall be utterly wasted.

Isaiah sees the spread of the LORD's light to far away places which are symbolized by the isles, the small pieces of land that represent isolated pockets which the spirit needs to bring forth into light. The large ships of Tarshish which sail the great sea of the Mediterranean shall bring their gold and silver, the symbols of love and truth to the name of the LORD your GOD, and to the Holy One of Israel, because he has glorified you. Isaiah has identified the spirit within each of followers as the LORD your God and to himself as the Holy One of Israel because he is the one who has glorified you. Many people will be drawn by the light, the spiritual light, who will offer and desire to build the LORD's kingdom,

And the sons of strangers shall build up your walls, and their kings shall minister to you: the law of the LORD is explained when Isaiah, speaking the word of the LORD, says that in the LORD's wrath, the experience was one of being smitten, but, when the creation of man is in harmony with the LORD, when man is in favor, then the LORD has shown His mercy on those who do His service and bidding. Therefore your gates to the source of the light shall be open continually; they shall not be shut day nor night; that men may bring unto you the forces of the Gentiles who are attracted by the shining of the light of the LORD, and that their kings may be brought so that they can order their kingdoms to make changes in the name of the LORD. The spirit of the LORD shall proliferate quickly on earth with the result that the nation and kingdom that will not serve the LORD shall perish; yes indeed, those nations shall be utterly wasted by the working of the law. Since the earth belongs to the LORD, then the treasures of the earth shall return to the LORD and His people when the LORD has a home on earth once again.

13 The glory of Lebanon shall come unto thee, the fir tree, the pine tree, and the box together, to beautify the place of my sanctuary; and I will make the place of my feet glorious.
14 The sons also of them that afflicted thee shall come bending unto thee; and all they that despised thee shall bow themselves down at the soles of thy feet; and they shall call thee, The city of the LORD, The Zion of the Holy One of Israel.
15 Whereas thou hast been forsaken and hated, so that no man went through thee, I will make thee an eternal excellency, a joy of many generations.
16 Thou shalt also suck the milk of the Gentiles, and shalt suck the breast of kings: and thou shalt know that I the LORD am thy Saviour and thy Redeemer, the mighty One of Jacob.
17 For brass I will bring gold, and for iron I will bring silver, and for wood brass, and for stones iron: I will also make thy officers peace, and thine exactors righteousness.
18 Violence shall no more be heard in thy land, wasting nor destruction within thy borders; but thou shalt call thy walls Salvation, and thy gates Praise.

The glory of Lebanon shall come to you without asking for them, the fir tree, the pine tree, and the box tree together, to beautify the place of my sanctuary; and the LORD working through His people will make the place of His feet on earth glorious. Everywhere that the LORD walks consciously shall be made beautiful. The sons also of them that afflicted you shall come bending and bowing to you and all they that despised you shall bow themselves down at the soles of your

The Testimony of the Major Prophets

feet; and they shall call you, The city of the LORD, the Zion of the Holy One of Israel to show that they know that the LORD dwells in the consciousness of Isaiah.

Whereas you have been forsaken and hated, so that no man went through you, through the open door which you have been for others, I, the LORD, will make you an eternal excellency, a joy of many generations. You shall also suck the milk of the Gentiles, and shall suck the breast of kings which is symbolic language that you shall enjoy the treasures of the earth: and you shall know that I, the LORD, am your Savior and your Redeemer, the mighty One of Jacob. Jacob, who was the symbol for the fallen state of man, is in the process of being resurrected and returned to the LORD from whom he had fallen and become separated. The transition will produce change, but the changes will be productive for those who serve the LORD. For brass, I will bring gold, and for iron, I will bring silver, and for wood, brass, and for stones, iron: I will also make your officers peace, and your exactors righteousness. Violence shall no more be heard in your land, the land of your physical form, wasting nor destruction within your borders; but you shall call your walls, Salvation, and your gates, Praise. The walls are the boundaries of your city, the gates are the people who can open their doors to let other people enter. Salvation shall be offered to everyone who compose the walls of the new city that the LORD will build on earth, and praise shall be given to the LORD by those who accept the LORD's spirit as their own.

19 The sun shall be no more thy light by day; neither for brightness shall the moon give light unto thee: but the LORD shall be unto thee an everlasting light, and thy God thy glory.
20 Thy sun shall no more go down; neither shall thy moon withdraw itself: for the LORD shall be thine everlasting light, and the days of thy mourning shall be ended.
21 Thy people also shall be all righteous: they shall inherit the land for ever, the branch of my planting, the work of my hands, that I may be glorified.
22 A little one shall become a thousand, and a small one a strong nation: I the LORD will hasten it in his time.

The sun shall be no more your source of light by day; neither for brightness shall the moon give light to you: but the LORD shall be unto you as an everlasting internal light, and your God shall be your glory. Your sun shall no more go down; neither shall your moon withdraw itself: for the LORD shall be your everlasting light, and the days of your mourning shall be ended. Your people also shall be all righteous: they shall inherit the land for ever, the branch of the LORD's planting, the work of His hands, so that the LORD may be glorified. A little one who is in covenant-agreement with the LORD shall become a thousand, and a small one a strong nation: the LORD will hasten this transition from human control to divine control in His time. The spiritual light of the LORD which is eternal is the same light that is in Isaiah and his followers who serve the LORD's spirit to others. There is only One Light.

CHAPTER 61

1 The Spirit of the Lord GOD is upon me; because the LORD hath anointed me to preach good tidings unto the meek; he hath sent me to bind up the brokenhearted, to proclaim liberty to the captives, and the opening of the prison to them that are bound;
2 To proclaim the acceptable year of the LORD, and the day of vengeance of our God; to comfort all that mourn;
3 To appoint unto them that mourn in Zion, to give unto them beauty for ashes, the oil of joy for mourning, the garment of praise for the spirit of heaviness; that they might be called trees of righteousness, the planting of the LORD, that he might be glorified.

Isaiah tells his followers very plainly that the spirit of the Lord GOD is upon him: his mission, and their mission if they choose to join with him, is the LORD has anointed him to preach good tidings to the meek; God has sent Isaiah to bind up, to heal, the brokenhearted whose hearts are broken because of some earthly relationship or treasure, which is evidence that the person's heart is not where it should be; to proclaim liberty to the captives, the captives who are being held in any configuration of men which keeps a person tied to the earth instead of being free to return to the spirit of the LORD Who will make him a king of the earth; and the opening of the prison to them that are bound. The greatest prison is that a person is restricted and bound to a human body or a human organization instead of being a part of the living organism which is the spiritual body of the LORD on earth.

Isaiah is to proclaim the acceptable year of the LORD which is while Isaiah is in form on earth to speak the word of the LORD through human lips. The time is now; the place is here. From the LORD's point of view, the time has always been, **Now**, and the place has always been, **Here**. The difference in 700 BC was that the LORD had Isaiah to speak the word of the LORD on earth. As Isaiah releases the spirit of the LORD in his moment by moment living, then the day that he performs this service for the LORD is the day of vengeance for the LORD because Isaiah has given the LORD a voice, his voice, through which the LORD can and does speak. The spirit is the LORD's; the voice is Isaiah's. The LORD is not going to condemn man for all the trouble on earth

The Testimony of the Major Prophets

that man has made; the LORD will comfort those that mourn and offer them the opportunity to become a part of His kingdom.

The LORD will appoint to them that mourn for the LORD's spirit a place in Zion, the place of the spirit, where the LORD will give to them that will serve Him beauty for ashes, the oil of joy for mourning, the garment of praise for the spirit of heaviness; that they might be called trees of righteousness, the planting of the LORD, so that the LORD might be glorified on earth. The LORD offers them light for darkness and joy for sadness.

4 And they shall build the old wastes, they shall raise up the former desolations, and they shall repair the waste cities, the desolations of many generations.
5 And strangers shall stand and feed your flocks, and the sons of the alien shall be your plowmen and your vinedressers.
6 But ye shall be named the Priests of the LORD: men shall call you the Ministers of our God: ye shall eat the riches of the Gentiles, and in their glory shall ye boast yourselves.
7 For your shame ye shall have double; and for confusion they shall rejoice in their portion: therefore in their land they shall possess the double: everlasting joy shall be unto them.

The people who offer to serve the LORD on earth are called trees of righteousness. These are the ones who shall build the old wastes, raise up the former desolations that have been made desolate by fallen man and they shall repair the waste cities, the desolations that have occurred over many past generations. Many new people from near and far will join and be drawn by the spirit of the LORD which is now in the earth. Strangers shall stand and feed your flocks, and the sons of the alien in times past, shall be your plowmen and your vine-dressers. Response to the spirit of the LORD in action on earth through man comes from all quarters.

But you who choose to serve the LORD shall be named the Priests of the LORD: men shall call you the Ministers of our God: you shall eat the riches of the Gentiles, and in your glory, as the LORD shines through you, you shall boast yourselves and be glad for them because you represent the spirit of the LORD which is with them and that has done the work. For your shame that you experience as a priest of the LORD, you shall have double, shame for yourself and shame for your flock as you remove their shame from them and forgive them in the name of the LORD; and for confusion, they shall rejoice in their portion because confusion is a temporary condition on earth: therefore in their land they shall possess the double; they shall possess the positive spirit in the heaven and also the positive form in the earth: everlasting joy shall be unto them.

8 For I the LORD love judgment, I hate robbery for burnt offering; and I will direct their work in truth, and I will make an everlasting covenant with them.
9 And their seed shall be known among the Gentiles, and their offspring among the people: all that see them shall acknowledge them, that they are the seed which the LORD hath blessed.
10 I will greatly rejoice in the LORD, my soul shall be joyful in my God; for he hath clothed me with the garments of salvation, he hath covered me with the robe of righteousness, as a bridegroom decketh himself with ornaments, and as a bride adorneth herself with her jewels.

11 For as the earth bringeth forth her bud, and as the garden causeth the things that are sown in it to spring forth; so the Lord GOD will cause righteousness and praise to spring forth before all the nations.

The LORD loves the law of His judgment because it is so consistent; the LORD hates robbery for a burnt offering because the person steals the LORD's property and offers it to the LORD instead of offering the person who is the thief; if the person repents and offers himself, then the LORD will direct his work in truth and the LORD will make an everlasting covenant with him. The covenant on earth has to do with the planting of the LORD's seeds of behavior. As a person sows, so shall he reap. The LORD blesses all seeds of expression, righteous or wicked, that are made by man: both will grow. And their seed shall be known among the Gentiles, and their offspring among the people: all that see them shall acknowledge them that they are the seed which the LORD has blessed. The covenant of the LORD in this regard is that the law of sowing and reaping will always work.

Isaiah will greatly rejoice in the LORD and the soul—the heart, mind and body—of Isaiah shall be joyful in the spirit of My God; for the LORD has clothed Isaiah with the garments of salvation, He has covered Isaiah with the robe of righteousness, as a bridegroom decks himself with ornaments, and as a bride adorns herself with her jewels. For as the earth brings forth her bud, and as the garden causes the things that are sown in it to spring forth; so the Lord GOD will cause righteousness and praise to spring forth before all the nations. The LORD is the sower of the seeds of righteousness and praise; man in the fallen state is the sower of the seeds of iniquity. The fault is always with man. If man sows the good seed, the LORD will surely see that they are reaped in the earth. This law guarantees that the divine design can return to the earth if we, as a people, plant the right seed of the spirit through human form.

CHAPTER 62

1 For Zion's sake will I not hold my peace, and for Jerusalem's sake I will not rest, until the righteousness thereof go forth as brightness, and the salvation thereof as a lamp that burneth.
2 And the Gentiles shall see thy righteousness, and all kings thy glory: and thou shalt be called by a new name, which the mouth of the LORD shall name.
3 Thou shalt also be a crown of glory in the hand of the LORD, and a royal diadem in the hand of thy God.
4 Thou shalt no more be termed Forsaken; neither shall thy land any more be termed Desolate: but thou shalt be called Hephzibah, and thy land Beulah: for the LORD delighteth in thee, and thy land shall be married.

Isaiah tells his followers that for the sake of Zion, for the sake of a spiritual place within an individual on earth where the LORD may rest His head and call it His home, Isaiah will not hold his peace in quiet and keep the knowledge to himself that the LORD comes on earth through the consciousness of man. He will share this knowledge with others so that they can experience what Isaiah has experienced: oneness in spirit with the LORD. Isaiah will not hold his peace for the sake of Jerusalem. He will not rest until the righteousness of the people of Jerusalem, who should carry and reveal the spirit of the LORD, should go forth in brightness, and the salvation that will result from this action shall be as a lamp that burns on the hill that everyone can see. The light of the LORD manifesting through the people of Jerusalem shall make the city and its surrounding areas strong with the strength and wisdom of the spirit of the LORD.

As the light of Isaiah's followers and the people of Jerusalem shines brightly through the people, they will truly be the LORD's people and achieve what the LORD has promised them. What has been missing is the shining of the light from the LORD. The Gentiles shall see the righteousness of the shining of the light through the people if it is shining. All the kings shall see the glory of Jerusalem if the light shines through the people: and you shall be called by a new name, which the mouth of the LORD shall name in your ear when you experience the covenant. You shall not be alone. You shall also be a crown of glory in the hand of the LORD, and a royal diadem, a royal headdress, in the hand of your God. When the LORD is with you, you shall no more be termed,

Forsaken; neither shall your land any more be termed, Desolate: but you shall be called Hephzibah, which means, "pleasure and delight", and your land, Beulah, which means, "marriage": for the LORD delights in you when you are in the covenant with Him, and the land of your individual bodies and your city, your consciousness, shall be married to the LORD: the daughter of Jerusalem, the entire population of the city should rightly be the bride of the LORD.

5 For as a young man marrieth a virgin, so shall thy sons marry thee: and as the bridegroom rejoiceth over the bride, so shall thy God rejoice over thee.
6 I have set watchmen upon thy walls, O Jerusalem, which shall never hold their peace day nor night: ye that make mention of the LORD, keep not silence,
7 And give him no rest, till he establish, and till he make Jerusalem a praise in the earth.
8 The LORD hath sworn by his right hand, and by the arm of his strength, Surely I will no more give thy corn to be meat for thine enemies; and the sons of the stranger shall not drink thy wine, for the which thou hast laboured:

Isaiah tells his followers that people will respond to the shining of the light from the LORD with strong feelings of the heart. Isaiah is using a physical analogy to give some understanding to the feeling of love, the love connection, in a spiritual connection between the bridegroom and the LORD. As a young man marries a virgin, so shall your spiritual sons "marry" you; and as a bridegroom rejoices over the bride, so shall God rejoice over you. The feelings of love and devotion are intense and deep but they are on a high spiritual plane of mutual respect.

Isaiah has set watchmen on the walls of Jerusalem, as he speaks to a material city which should be a spiritual city; the watchmen, who shall never hold their peace day nor night: the watchmen are searching for the people that the LORD has attracted and drawn to Jerusalem to be His servers. You that make mention of the LORD, that desire to find the LORD and his people, keep not silent about your goal. And give the watchman no rest, until he establishes contact with you, and until he makes Jerusalem a praise for you in the earth that you have found the LORD's people who have a covenant with the LORD and you have found the covenant with the LORD that has drawn you to Jerusalem. This is the way that you will come to know the LORD.

The LORD has sworn by his right hand, by everything that is under His control, and by the arm of his strength, Surely, the LORD will no more give your corn, the food from the LORD that is intended specifically for you, to be meat for your enemies; and the sons of the stranger, the people who know not the LORD and who are not willing to serve the LORD, shall not drink your wine, the wine of life that the LORD has intended for you, for which you have labored.

9 But they that have gathered it shall eat it, and praise the LORD; and they that have brought it together shall drink it in the courts of my holiness.
10 Go through, go through the gates; prepare ye the way of the people; cast up, cast up the highway; gather out the stones; lift up a standard for the people.
11 Behold, the LORD hath proclaimed unto the end of the world, Say ye to the daughter of Zion, Behold, thy salvation cometh; behold, his reward is with him, and his work before him.
12 And they shall call them, The holy people, The redeemed of the LORD: and thou shalt be called, Sought out, A city not forsaken.

The Testimony of the Major Prophets

Isaiah tells his followers that they have gathered the spiritual substance in service to the LORD and shall eat it, not physically eat a spiritual substance, but the behavior becomes a part of their physical forms, and it is this spiritual substance that allows a person to truly praise the LORD. The people who have brought together the dedicated ones who have a common spiritual unity, a spiritual community of Zion that overflows into Jerusalem, shall drink in the courts of the LORD's holiness. The gates to Zion are open and the people with spiritual discernment can go through the spiritual gates. Prepare the way of the people so that others can see the way of the LORD. Let your actions cast up, cast up a spiritual highway for people to walk upon in the spirit of the LORD; gather out the stones that are needed to build the highway; lift up a standard, a spiritual standard of the LORD in action on earth through His people.

Isaiah writes, Behold, the LORD has proclaimed this until the end of the world that you should issue this invitation. You, who have discovered the spiritual place that Isaiah calls Zion, should say to the daughter of Zion, the person who is not yet married to the LORD but desires to reside in Zion, Behold, your salvation comes from the LORD; behold, His reward is with Him, and His work before Him. His reward is that he shall become aware of the covenant; his work that is before him is to rebuild the city, the consciousness of the people, that has broken down and extend the covenant to others. The two jobs that need to be done are to rebuild the city and to bring new citizens into the kingdom of the spirit. The spirit is everywhere! The physical kingdom of the LORD that is broken down is everywhere! The people who volunteer for this work are a very special people. Even though everyone has the potential, even though the invitation is extended to all, even though many are called, few are chosen, relatively few choose to truly serve the Lord's spirit on earth to others so that they may have a choice to observe the spirit in action.

And the people who are truly interested in spiritual things shall call the people who radiate the LORD's spirit, The holy people, The redeemed of the LORD: and you who are interested in Zion shall be called, "Sought out", and, "A city not forsaken". These two groups of people are searching for each other on earth. Isaiah has provided a place for them to find each other in Jerusalem.

CHAPTER 63

1 Who is this that cometh from Edom, with dyed garments from Bozrah? this that is glorious in his apparel, travelling in the greatness of his strength? I that speak in righteousness, mighty to save.
2 Wherefore art thou red in thine apparel, and thy garments like him that treadeth in the winefat?
3 I have trodden the winepress alone; and of the people there was none with me: for I will tread them in mine anger, and trample them in my fury; and their blood shall be sprinkled upon my garments, and I will stain all my raiment.

Isaiah sees a person approaching Jerusalem from the direction of Edom, with dyed garments from Bozrah. The country of Edom and the Edomites are symbolic of all the enemies of God; and Bozrah is an important city, a sheep-herding center, in Edom located about 25 miles southeast of the southern end of the Dead Sea. The name Bozrah means, "grape gathering". Isaiah asks, Who is this person that is coming from the land of enemies of Jerusalem dressed in garments dyed red that will call attention to himself? (Red is the color that symbolizes the materialistic portion of the color spectrum.) Isaiah who speaks in righteousness as a representative and prophet of the LORD is mighty to save even this "enemy" of Jerusalem. Isaiah realizes that the Edomites are the descendants of Esau, the first born of Isaac, son of Abraham. Esau, a founder of Edom, was a brother to Jacob, who became Israel. Although, Esau was the first-born of Isaac, Jacob and his mother schemed to take the birthright and the blessing from Esau. Eventually, Esau and Jacob were reunited. (See *The Symbolic Version of Genesis*.) The point is that Isaiah has the door open for a person who is perceived as an "enemy" by the inhabitants of Jerusalem based on the fact that, in the past, the Edomites rejoiced at the destruction of Jerusalem.

Isaiah asks the Edomite why he is clothed in apparel that is dyed red as a person who treads grapes in a winepress and gets the stain of the grapes on his clothing? The Edomite replies that he has trodden the winepress alone, which symbolizes that he has gone among the people of Edom and Bozrah preaching the word of the LORD in clothing that was dyed red, the symbol of power, to attract attention to his message; and of the people to whom he spoke, there was none with him in the spirit of the LORD that he was preaching: the person in red clothing did tread the people of Edom in his anger and trampled them in his fury; the red color in his garment is the symbol of their

The Testimony of the Major Prophets

blood, the blood of the Edomites, that was sprinkled upon his garments to illustrate that he had assumed the responsibility for preaching the word of the LORD to the people of Edom. He tells Isaiah that he will stain all his raiment so that people will see him coming and know his message by the color of his raiment.

4 For the day of vengeance is in mine heart, and the year of my redeemed is come.
5 And I looked, and there was none to help; and I wondered that there was none to uphold: therefore mine own arm brought salvation unto me; and my fury, it upheld me.
6 And I will tread down the people in mine anger, and make them drunk in my fury, and I will bring down their strength to the earth.

The person in the red clothing continues to tell Isaiah that the day of the vengeance of the LORD is in his heart and that the year that the LORD will redeem His people is come because he is willing and working to do something about the circumstances of his environment into which he was born. He looked around to find someone to agree with him in his mission to redeem the people of Edom and there was no one to help him; he wondered why there was no one to uphold the way of the LORD that he could find, and he did look for them; therefore he did what he felt was right in his heart using the power of his own arm, his own power that was available to him, and that brought salvation to him if no one else in Edom; the fury, that he had within himself that no one would stand up for the LORD, upheld him and kept him going. The person tells Isaiah that he will continue to tread down, to berate, the people in his anger at them for the way that they are ignoring the LORD; and he will make them drunk, he will make their minds spin, with thoughts of God delivered to them in his fury, his fiery zeal to serve the LORD; and he will bring down their strength to the earth as he tells them that the heaven and the earth belong to the LORD.

7 I will mention the lovingkindness of the LORD, and the praises of the LORD, according to all that the LORD hath bestowed on us, and the great goodness toward the house of Israel, which he hath bestowed on them according to his mercies, and according to the multitude of his lovingkindness.
8 For he said, Surely they are my people, children that will not lie: so he was their Saviour.
9 In all their affliction he was afflicted, and the angel of his presence saved them: in his love and in his pity he redeemed them; and he bare them, and carried them all the days of old.

The man in the red garment tells Isaiah further that he will mention the loving kindness and the praises of the LORD, according to all that the LORD has bestowed on us, and the great goodness that the LORD has shown toward the house of Israel. The LORD has bestowed on the house of Israel, the house of spiritual expression of the LORD, according to the mercies expressed by the people of Israel, and according to the multitude of the loving kindness demonstrated by the people. The LORD **gives** blessings and mercies to the people who **express** blessings and mercies.

For the man in the red garment said, Surely they, the people of the house of Israel, are my people even though he was an Edomite; the house of Israel are children of the LORD who will not lie: so, in like manner, the man in the red garment was the Savior for the people of Edom. After all, Esau and Jacob, who became Israel, are half-brothers since both are the sons of Abraham. In order to do this, he had to assume responsibility for the body of the Edomites and hold them in his consciousness as a burden. In all their affliction, he was afflicted, and the angel of his presence

The Symbolic Version of Isaiah

saved them: in his love and in his pity, he redeemed them; and he bare them, and carried them all the days of old. This was the experience in the consciousness of the man in the red garment; it was not the experience of the people of Edom. They acted in a totally different way.

10 But they rebelled, and vexed his holy Spirit: therefore he was turned to be their enemy, and he fought against them.
11 Then he remembered the days of old, Moses, and his people, saying, Where is he that brought them up out of the sea with the shepherd of his flock? where is he that put his holy Spirit within him?
12 That led them by the right hand of Moses with his glorious arm, dividing the water before them, to make himself an everlasting name?
13 That led them through the deep, as an horse in the wilderness, that they should not stumble?

The people of Edom rebelled against his teaching and vexed his Holy Spirit with the result that he was considered to be their enemy. He fought against the beliefs and the hatreds of his people. Then he remembered the days of Moses and how Moses had to deal with his own people who said, Where is He who brought them up out of the sea with the shepherd of His flock? Where is He, the LORD, that put His Holy Spirit within Moses? Where is He that led the children of Israel by the right hand, the right control, of Moses with his glorious arm, his glorious power, dividing the water before them to make the name of Moses an everlasting name? Where is He that led the children of Israel through the deep of the unknown, as a horse is led in the wilderness, that the children of Israel did not stumble? The people of Edom asked the man in the red garment, as the children of Israel asked Moses, to let them see the LORD. People in the fallen state want to see the LORD with their eyes before they follow Him; Moses and the man in the red garment let the LORD's spirit move through their hearts in faith and trust.

14 As a beast goeth down into the valley, the Spirit of the LORD caused him to rest: so didst thou lead thy people, to make thyself a glorious name.
15 Look down from heaven, and behold from the habitation of thy holiness and of thy glory: where is thy zeal and thy strength, the sounding of thy bowels and of thy mercies toward me? are they restrained?

As a beast goes down into a valley in faith and trust led by its owner, it is the Spirit of the LORD that caused the beast to rest in trust during the journey into the unknown valley. In like manner, the Spirit of the LORD within Moses led the LORD's people out of Egypt to the promised land to make a glorious name for himself. Moses did not do what he did to make a glorious name for himself in the eyes of the people in the fallen state; Moses received glory because he represented the LORD for the LORD's purpose and not his own purpose. Moses was a servant of the LORD because he served the LORD's spirit to others.

Moses was able to do this because he looked down from heaven, the place of the LORD, to see with the LORD's vision and what the LORD instructed him to do on earth. From the vantage point of the heaven, it was possible to behold, to see, from the habitation of the LORD's holiness and the LORD's glory, the conditions on the earth because they are connected to each other: heaven and earth are one. Where is the LORD's zeal, His strength, the sounding of His bowels and the

The Testimony of the Major Prophets

LORD's mercies toward the person in the fallen state? They are in the body of the people who carry the spirit of the LORD on earth. Are the people restrained from releasing the power of the LORD from heaven into the earth? There is no restraint from the heavenly point of view. The people must release the power of the LORD on earth if it is to be released, automatically, from the heaven. There is no restraint of power by the LORD.

16 Doubtless thou art our father, though Abraham be ignorant of us, and Israel acknowledge us not:
thou, O LORD, art our father, our redeemer; thy name is from everlasting.
17 O LORD, why hast thou made us to err from thy ways, and hardened our heart from thy fear? Return for thy servants' sake, the tribes of thine inheritance.
18 The people of thy holiness have possessed it but a little while: our adversaries have trodden down thy sanctuary.
19 We are thine: thou never barest rule over them; they were not called by thy name.

In this day and age due to the LORD's Prayer, there is a mental awareness that the LORD is our Father, who dwells in the heaven always and eternally. There have been physical forms on earth who have been aware of the spirit of the LORD, people such as Abraham, who is spoken of as the father of the many tribes of people, but Abraham is ignorant of us as a people who live today; and Israel, the enlightened state of Jacob does not acknowledge us as a people. The LORD who dwells in the heaven is Our Father, Our Redeemer: Your name is from everlasting and from generation to generation.

O LORD, why have You made us to err from Your ways, and hardened our heart from Your fear, Your awesomeness? Return to us for Your servants' sake; we are the tribes of Your inheritance. We desire Your Spirit to be with us. The few people who were consciously aware of Your holiness have possessed Your Spirit for only a little while: our adversaries, the people who do not carry Your Spirit have trodden down Your sanctuary, the earth which is Yours. We acknowledge that we are Your people: You have barely ruled over them because of their rebelliousness; they were not called by Your name; they are not called the people of the LORD, the children of the LORD, the sons and daughters of the LORD.

CHAPTER 64

1 Oh that thou wouldest rend the heavens, that thou wouldest come down, that the mountains might flow down at thy presence,
2 As when the melting fire burneth, the fire causeth the waters to boil, to make thy name known to thine adversaries, that the nations may tremble at thy presence!
3 When thou didst terrible things which we looked not for, thou camest down, the mountains flowed down at thy presence.
4 For since the beginning of the world men have not heard, nor perceived by the ear, neither hath the eye seen, O God, beside thee, what he hath prepared for him that waiteth for him.

The man in the red garment from Edom prays to the LORD for help. Oh LORD, the prayer of Your people on earth who carry Your Spirit is that You would open the heavens and You would come down into the earth, that the mountains of Your Substance might flow down with You as when the melting fire burns—the hot fire that melts metal and that causes the water to boil—to make Your Name known to Your adversaries, that the separate nations of the earth who have rebelled against You may tremble at Your Presence. (Isaiah, who is listening to the Edomite, is aware that fire is the symbol of God's love and water is the symbol for the truth that is in the earth; fire that is applied to water will make steam, the symbol of water in the ascended state. In the ascended state, the water, which symbolizes the people who are not aware of the LORD, becomes steam, a higher form of water, that knows the LORD.) As the LORD's people appear on earth, the adversaries begin to tremble, to be shaken, by the presence of the people who represent the LORD. The Edomites were shaken up by the "different" man in the red garment.

When the LORD did terrible things on earth, which the people did not look for or anticipate and called them acts of God, the man in the red garment believed that the LORD came down to do destructive things and the mountains of the LORD's Power flowed down from the heavens to do these destructive things. But what of the creative and the beautiful things that the LORD's power could produce on earth if the power were used for His purposes? Since the beginning of the world, men have not heard with the ear, nor has the eye seen, what God has prepared for the people that serve the LORD in a creative way.

The Testimony of the Major Prophets

5 Thou meetest him that rejoiceth and worketh righteousness, those that remember thee in thy ways: behold, thou art wroth; for we have sinned: in those is continuance, and we shall be saved.
6 But we are all as an unclean thing, and all our righteousnesses are as filthy rags; and we all do fade as a leaf; and our iniquities, like the wind, have taken us away.
7 And there is none that calleth upon thy name, that stirreth up himself to take hold of thee: for thou hast hid thy face from us, and hast consumed us, because of our iniquities.
8 But now, O LORD, thou art our father; we are the clay, and thou our potter; and we all are the work of thy hand.

The man in the red garment believes that the LORD meets the people who rejoice and work righteousness, those that remember the LORD, who remember the LORD in their own daily actions and behaviors. The people understand the working of the law to the extent that the LORD is angry when the people have sinned: love is turned into anger by the people who are off-the-mark and not carrying out the LORD's purpose. If the people who want to truly be the children of the LORD, and continue to express the LORD's spirit of love, then they shall be saved. The people of the LORD are just beginning to see these things.

But the man in red sees that the problem is that all the people are as an unclean thing, and our self-righteous behaviors are as filthy rags; and we all do fade as a leaf; and our iniquities, like the wind, have taken us away from the tree which gives us life. And there is no one that calls upon the LORD's name, that stirs up himself to take hold of the LORD and His ways on earth: for the LORD has hid His face, the conscious awareness of what the LORD expects from us as a people and the lack of this knowledge has consumed us because of our own behaviors and iniquities. But now, O LORD, You are Our Father; we are the clay, and You are our Potter; and we all are the work of Your hand. We have repented and we are ready to allow you to reshape us as a potter molds his clay.

9 Be not wroth very sore, O LORD, neither remember iniquity for ever: behold, see, we beseech thee, we are all thy people.
10 Thy holy cities are a wilderness, Zion is a wilderness, Jerusalem a desolation.
11 Our holy and our beautiful house, where our fathers praised thee, is burned up with fire: and all our pleasant things are laid waste.
12 Wilt thou refrain thyself for these things, O LORD? wilt thou hold thy peace, and afflict us very sore?

The man in red speaking to Isaiah pleads for the LORD to not be sore and angry at the iniquities of His people forever. Instead, he asks the LORD to remember that all of us are His people and some of the people now realize what they have done. The holy cities are a wilderness; Zion is a wilderness; and Jerusalem is a desolation. Our holy and our beautiful house, where our fathers praised the LORD, is burned up with fire: and all our pleasant things are laid waste. The man in the red garment has seen the abomination of desolation that is in the holy place!

The questions that the man in the red garment voices to Isaiah are, Will the LORD refrain Himself from seeking retribution from the people who did these things? will the LORD hold His peace, or afflict us very painfully for the iniquities which we have done?

CHAPTER 65

1 I am sought of them that asked not for me; I am found of them that sought me not: I said, Behold me, behold me, unto a nation that was not called by my name.

Isaiah has something to say to the man in the red garment who came from Edom, the land of the "enemies", but, who was interested in knowing and serving the LORD. This made him very different from the usual behaviors and culture of the Edomites: THE MAN IN THE RED GARMENT REPRESENTS AND SYMBOLIZES ANYONE WHO IS INTERESTED IN FINDING THE LORD. Isaiah, speaking the word of the LORD, tells the man in the red garment that the LORD is sought and revealed to those people who did not ask or seek Him: the LORD is invisible and all powerful and cannot be seen directly by those who want to see Him. However, the LORD can be seen in human form if the LORD is in action on earth through a human form: this would not be God Almighty, but Jehovah, God in action on earth through man. Isaiah is in this position to represent the LORD on earth, which gives him the authority to say, through his human form, Behold me, Behold me, to a nation that was not called by the name of Isaiah. If the followers of Isaiah, truly see the spirit that Isaiah has been exemplifying for them, then they have seen and heard the LORD through the physical form of Isaiah. Isaiah has much experience in representing the LORD to many people.

2 I have spread out my hands all the day unto a rebellious people, which walketh in a way that was not good, after their own thoughts;
3 A people that provoketh me to anger continually to my face; that sacrificeth in gardens, and burneth incense upon altars of brick;
4 Which remain among the graves, and lodge in the monuments, which eat swine's flesh, and broth of abominable things is in their vessels;
5 Which say, Stand by thyself, come not near to me; for I am holier than thou. These are a smoke in my nose, a fire that burneth all the day.

Isaiah has spread out his hands, not literally, but open-heartedly to receive those who were interested, all the day, every day. Isaiah has been an open door to a rebellious people who walked in a way that was not good, a way after their own thoughts, the way of human nature. These rebellious people provoked Isaiah continually to anger to his face because they did not know that the spirit of the LORD was in Isaiah. The rebellious people performed their sacrifices in gardens, and burned incense upon altars of brick; a people who remain among the graves where the bodies of the dead are buried to pray to a living God; a people who lodge, who spend their nights, in vigil to memorials to the dead, to monuments; who eat the flesh of swine which is against their beliefs, and broth filled with unclean things in their cooking vessels; a people who say, Stand away by yourself, come not near to me because they are holier than you. These actions and behaviors are like a smoke in the nose of Isaiah, a fire of behaviors and actions that burns all day in the view of Isaiah, the representative of the LORD. Isaiah sees these behaviors, these offerings to the LORD, day after day.

6 Behold, it is written before me: I will not keep silence, but will recompense, even recompense into their bosom,
7 Your iniquities, and the iniquities of your fathers together, saith the LORD, which have burned incense upon the mountains, and blasphemed me upon the hills: therefore will I measure their former work into their bosom.
8 Thus saith the LORD, As the new wine is found in the cluster, and one saith, Destroy it not; for a blessing is in it: so will I do for my servants' sakes, that I may not destroy them all.
9 And I will bring forth a seed out of Jacob, and out of Judah an inheritor of my mountains: and mine elect shall inherit it, and my servants shall dwell there.
10 And Sharon shall be a fold of flocks, and the valley of Achor a place for the herds to lie down in, for my people that have sought me.

Behold and see, the behaviors, the offerings of the people, are written in their actions as they stand before Isaiah, the servant of the LORD. Isaiah represents the LORD to the people and the people to the LORD. The LORD will not keep silence, but He will recompense, compensate the people individually, for their own iniquities and the sins of their fathers which they inherited from previous generations. The burning of incense upon the high places of the mountains and the blasphemy of the LORD's name, I Am, which has a been used in vain, in vanity by human nature people, shall be subject to the working of the law of the LORD. All behaviors, past and present, are subject to the working of the law and the results of the law must be applied to the bosom, the physical self, of the person who committed the sins.

The LORD speaking through Isaiah states that as a new vine is found in a cluster of vines, and a person says, Do not destroy the cluster because there might be a blessing in one of the vines, then the LORD shall do likewise for the sake of His servants so the person who is the blessing among the cluster will not be destroyed. The LORD will bring forth a seed out of Jacob, the symbol of the fallen state of man, and out of Judah, the country in which the followers dwell. The seed will be an inheritor of the spiritual mountains and high places that Isaiah dwells with the LORD: and the elect, the people who elect to be a part of Isaiah's spiritual body, shall inherit it, and the servants of the LORD shall dwell there. The place where the people shall dwell is from the western edge of the land, Sharon, to the eastern edge of the land, the valley of Achor, which symbolically represents the whole country. This land shall be a fold of flocks and a place for the herds to lie down in for the people that have sought the LORD.

The Testimony of the Major Prophets

11 But ye are they that forsake the LORD, that forget my holy mountain, that prepare a table for that troop, and that furnish the drink offering unto that number.

What is the fate of the people who have not sought the LORD? Isaiah contrasts the difference between those who sought and those who did forsake the LORD. The LORD speaking through Isaiah, the LORD Jehovah, speaks to those people and identifies them as the ones who forgot the holy mountain of the LORD, from which they came, into the earth. These forgetful people who forgot the holy mountain of the LORD have turned to earthly deities to offer to two of them a table of food and drink. The rebellious people have prepared a table for that troop, whose name, Gad means, Fortune; and that furnish the drink offering for that number, which means, Destiny or Fate. The people who turn from the LORD and the working of the law worship the two pagan gods of Fortune and Destiny. The contrast is between the LORD on one side of the dividing line, and Fortune and Destiny on the other.

12 Therefore will I number you to the sword, and ye shall all bow down to the slaughter: because when I called, ye did not answer; when I spake, ye did not hear; but did evil before mine eyes, and did choose that wherein I delighted not.
13 Therefore thus saith the Lord GOD, Behold, my servants shall eat, but ye shall be hungry: behold, my servants shall drink, but ye shall be thirsty: behold, my servants shall rejoice, but ye shall be ashamed:
14 Behold, my servants shall sing for joy of heart, but ye shall cry for sorrow of heart, and shall howl for vexation of spirit.

On one side of the dividing line is the sword, not a literal sword, but the sword of truth on earth which is the body of Jehovah. Isaiah has been inviting individuals to join the body of people who will represent the LORD on earth: some have accepted but most people have refused. The people who refused shall bow down to the slaughter, they will not experience salvation and they will experience death without knowing the LORD. There is no mystery to this outcome: When Jehovah called, you did not answer; when Jehovah spoke, you did not hear; you continued to do evil before His eyes and chose to do the things, the sins, that Jehovah did not delight in seeing. The true experience of living on earth is totally different from this.

Therefore, the Lord GOD has said, Behold, my servants shall eat, but you shall be hungry: behold, my servants shall drink, but you shall be thirsty: behold, my servants shall rejoice, but you shall be ashamed.
Behold, my servants shall sing for joy of heart, but you shall cry for sorrow of heart, and shall howl for vexation and irritation of the spirit as it moves through a pattern of the distorted use of the human form.

15 And ye shall leave your name for a curse unto my chosen: for the Lord GOD shall slay thee, and call his servants by another name:
16 That he who blesseth himself in the earth shall bless himself in the God of truth; and he that sweareth in the earth shall swear by the God of truth; because the former troubles are forgotten, and because they are hid from mine eyes.

17 For, behold, I create new heavens and a new earth: and the former shall not be remembered, nor come into mind.
18 But be ye glad and rejoice for ever in that which I create: for, behold, I create Jerusalem a rejoicing, and her people a joy.

The people who are not a part of the sword of the LORD, Jehovah, are a curse to the people who are a blessing of the LORD: one group is slain; the other is saved. The Lord GOD shall slay the identity of the person who is a curse, and God will call His servants by another name that will survive what is known as the second death. The person who desires to bless himself on earth shall bless himself in the spirit of the God of truth; he that swears on earth shall swear by the God of truth; because the former troubles, the sins, are forgotten by the God of truth and there is a nullification of the working of the law. The sins are hidden from the eyes, forgotten and forgiven. This allows for a totally new experience to begin.

Behold, the God of truth shall create new heavens, new creative causes in the heavens, and a new earth, new physical forms that are true to the truth: and the former things, the distortions, shall not be remembered or come into the person's mind. The people of the body of the sword, are to be glad and rejoice forever in that which the LORD creates: for the LORD creates Jerusalem rejoicing and her people are a joy.

19 And I will rejoice in Jerusalem, and joy in my people: and the voice of weeping shall be no more heard in her, nor the voice of crying.
20 There shall be no more thence an infant of days, nor an old man that hath not filled his days: for the child shall die an hundred years old; but the sinner being an hundred years old shall be accursed.
21 And they shall build houses, and inhabit them; and they shall plant vineyards, and eat the fruit of them.
22 They shall not build, and another inhabit; they shall not plant, and another eat: for as the days of a tree are the days of my people, and mine elect shall long enjoy the work of their hands.

The LORD will rejoice in Jerusalem, and there will be joy in His people: Jerusalem during the time of Isaiah was the city in which he dwelled; Isaiah could rejoice in Jerusalem because the spirit of the LORD was in the city and His people were joyful. The voice of weeping and the voice of crying were not heard in the people who lived in the **spiritual** Jerusalem. In the spiritual Jerusalem, there is no age in the eternal spiritual city because it exists above the world of time, in the timelessness of time, where it is always, **Now**.

The children of the LORD are spiritual children who are not ravaged by time as the human material body ages. There shall be no more in the spiritual Jerusalem an infant who has not achieved his days or an old man who has not fulfilled his days because infant and the old man are material descriptions of the spirit who dwells within the forms. The spiritual child shall die a hundred years old but the sinner being a hundred years shall be accursed. The spiritual children of the LORD shall build houses and inhabit them; they shall plant vineyards and eat the fruit of them on earth because they are spirits in forms on earth. They shall not build on earth and another shall inhabit what they have built; they shall not plant, and another will do the eating. As the days of a tree, the

The Testimony of the Major Prophets

Tree of Life, are the days of the LORD's people, and the LORD's elect, the ones who elect to serve the LORD, shall enjoy the work of their spiritual hands.

23 They shall not labour in vain, nor bring forth for trouble; for they are the seed of the blessed of the LORD, and their offspring with them.
24 And it shall come to pass, that before they call, I will answer; and while they are yet speaking, I will hear.
25 The wolf and the lamb shall feed together, and the lion shall eat straw like the bullock: and dust shall be the serpent's meat. They shall not hurt nor destroy in all my holy mountain, saith the LORD.

The people who choose to serve the LORD shall not labor in vain, in their own vanity of self-centeredness, nor bring forth trouble; for they are the seed of the blessed of the LORD, and their offspring, the expressions that come forth from the seed, with them. It shall come to pass, that before they call, the LORD will answer; and while they are yet speaking, the LORD will hear. The LORD will be close to the offspring, the expressions, that come forth from the blessed of the LORD.

In the spiritual world of the LORD, all is in harmony. Heaven is a harmonious place. The people in the fallen state who once were symbolized as a wolf and a lamb shall feed together, and the person who was as a destructive lion shall eat straw like the bullock: and the dust of the material earth shall be the serpent's meat, the meat of the mind. The spiritual people shall not hurt nor destroy anything in all my holy spiritual mountain, says the LORD.

CHAPTER 66

1 Thus saith the LORD, The heaven is my throne, and the earth is my footstool: where is the house that ye build unto me? and where is the place of my rest?
2 For all those things hath mine hand made, and all those things have been, saith the LORD: but to this man will I look, even to him that is poor and of a contrite spirit, and trembleth at my word.

Isaiah tells his followers that the LORD has said that the heaven, the place where He and all of the community of spirits dwell, is His throne; and the earth is His footstool: the footstool is a very small physical place where a portion of His body, His feet, can find rest. The LORD is the Master of the heaven and the earth. He would like to know, where is the house that the people, the individuals and the entire body of mankind, have built in honor of the One who created the heaven and the earth? and where is the place on earth that He can find rest because His creation is doing His work on earth?

The LORD has made all the material things on earth with His own hand according to His design, and all those things have been on earth as building blocks for man to build a house, a place for the LORD to dwell, that would give praise to the LORD. The LORD says that He will look to man, mankind, who was made in the image and likeness of God, to create a living altar to Him that would be praiseworthy. Man, as a Co-creator with the LORD on the planet Earth, should create praiseworthy things from the material building blocks which the LORD has given for His spiritual children to use their divine creativity to create objects that give glory to the LORD. In order for man to perform his role on earth, the LORD will look to man to fulfill this responsibility which he has to his Creator. The LORD will look to man, mankind, that is poor in wanting the things of the earth for himself which will prevent him from building the house for the LORD; the man must be contrite, humble, that he is here to serve the LORD and not himself; and he should tremble, shake and move, in harmony with the word of the LORD as it comes to him directly from the spirit of the LORD in heaven so that he is the means for the work of the LORD on earth. Man was created to do the work of the LORD on earth to build the kingdom of heaven on earth using the spirit of the LORD to build the material forms. Man has fallen from his true purpose, and what kind of a

The Testimony of the Major Prophets

house is he building for the LORD? He has devised some foolish rituals of sacrifice to replace his true purpose.

3 He that killeth an ox is as if he slew a man; he that sacrificeth a lamb, as if he cut off a dog's neck; he that offereth an oblation, as if he offered swine's blood; he that burneth incense, as if he blessed an idol. Yea, they have chosen their own ways, and their soul delighteth in their abominations.
4 I also will choose their delusions, and will bring their fears upon them; because when I called, none did answer; when I spake, they did not hear: but they did evil before mine eyes, and chose that in which I delighted not.

Fallen man kills an ox, the symbol for a self-centered fallen man who will not do the will of the LORD, instead of destroying the counterfeit man who has usurped the LORD's creation; fallen man sacrifices a lamb,(the symbol of man in his true state as a lamb of God who will follow the Good Shepherd), as though he has cut off a dog's neck, (the symbol of the dog is an unclean thing that was never used in sacrifices,) the dog is the symbol of the counterfeit man in the fallen state; fallen man offers an oblation, a drink, to the LORD that is as if he offered a swine's blood, the liquid symbol of the unclean pig which was forbidden to eat; he burns incense to his Creator, as if he were worshipping an idol, a false god of the earth. Yes, fallen men have chosen their own ways where they offer a form of unacceptable sacrifice to their concept of the LORD so that they can maintain their rebellion against their Creator. And their soul, the distorted fallen self that has descended so far from the true purpose for which they were created, delights itself in its abominations.

The LORD says that He will choose their delusions, their hallucinations while they are in this nightmare which they have created for themselves and the LORD will bring fears upon them; this action was taken by the LORD because when He called to them, directly from His spirit to them, and through His prophets,
none did answer; when the LORD spoke, they did not hear because they tuned Him out: but they continued to do evil before the LORD's eyes, while acknowledging that He is present, through their foolish sacrificial rituals, and they chose to do the things that did not delight the LORD.

5 Hear the word of the LORD, ye that tremble at his word; Your brethren that hated you, that cast you out for my name's sake, said, Let the LORD be glorified: but he shall appear to your joy, and they shall be ashamed.
6 A voice of noise from the city, a voice from the temple, a voice of the LORD that rendereth recompence to his enemies.

The LORD has some instruction for those who want to hear the word of the LORD, the people who will tremble, be moved into action, by His word. In order to be moved by the word of the LORD, the people who were willing to listen were not like the people who were self-satisfied and they were harassed by their brethren for being different. The brethren that hated you, that cast you out from their temples into the city because you tried to do the right thing, said that they were taking the action that they did for the glory of the LORD, to perpetuate their concepts and rituals about the LORD that they did not know: but He shall appear to you to your joy, and they shall be ashamed. The voice of the LORD is in operation everywhere! It manifests as the distorted, discordant noise from the people who live in the city who give little thought to the LORD; the voice from the temple that gives much thought to the LORD through their beliefs and rituals which is less noisy; a voice of the LORD that will render recompense to the LORD's enemies. The voice of Isaiah, the voice of the LORD in action on earth through Isaiah, Jehovah, the sword of the LORD, is the person whose tongue is like a sword that will bring recompense to the enemies of the LORD with the sword of truth. The LORD desires the truth of His love to be born on earth once again. Isaiah explains this using the analogy of childbirth.

7 Before she travailed, she brought forth; before her pain came, she was delivered of a man child.
8 Who hath heard such a thing? who hath seen such things? Shall the earth be made to bring forth in one day? or shall a nation be born at once? for as soon as Zion travailed, she brought forth her children.
9 Shall I bring to the birth, and not cause to bring forth? saith the LORD: shall I cause to bring forth, and shut the womb? saith thy God.

Isaiah tells his followers that before a woman travailed, works hard, in the final stage of labor, she was in the process of bringing forth to the point of delivery; before her pain came, she was delivered of a man child, a spirit from the LORD, a spirit of the Father, that would be clothed with the physical form from its earthly parents who provided the physical matter, the earth from the Mother, to form a spiritual-material child months before the delivery of the finished Being in a human form. The delivery of the spirit of the LORD, the spiritual child, which has been present since the moment of conception, is analogous to the birth of a physical child.

Who has heard such a thing? who has seen such things? The earth is the place where the LORD's spiritual children are to be born and to live. Shall the earth be made to bring forth all the spiritual children in one day or is it a creative process? or shall a nation be born at once? A spiritual child, a follower of Isaiah is like a spiritual child who is growing in a spiritual place within himself called Zion. For as soon as Zion travailed, when the time was right for the spiritual child of the LORD to be born, she, the earth Mother, man, male or female, brought forth her spiritual children. Shall the LORD bring His spirit to the birth, and not cause His offspring to bring forth on earth? says the LORD: shall the LORD cause and create this process to bring forth on earth, and shut the womb of the earth so that the spirit can not be born through you on earth? says the God that is in your physical form. What will the spiritual child do after it is born again on the earth and discovers its Self in a human form in the city of Jerusalem?

10 Rejoice ye with Jerusalem, and be glad with her, all ye that love her: rejoice for joy with her, all ye that mourn for her:
11 That ye may suck, and be satisfied with the breasts of her consolations; that ye may milk out, and be delighted with the abundance of her glory.

Isaiah tells his followers to rejoice where they are spiritually born in the city of Jerusalem, or any city, and be glad with her, the mother earth, wherever you happen to be, all who love her: rejoice for joy with your environment, all you who mourn her. The mourning must turn to joy because the spirit is joyful while the counterfeit self that has not been born of the spirit mourns. The spiritual child sucks, nurses, and lives with the mother, in harmony with the environment, in which He finds

The Testimony of the Major Prophets

its Self and He is satisfied with the breasts of her consolations, her comforts; that the spiritual child may nurse and be delighted with the abundance of her glory. The glory is present and available to be seen by the spiritual child who is joyful and who does not mourn his location.

12 For thus saith the LORD, Behold, I will extend peace to her like a river, and the glory of the Gentiles like a flowing stream: then shall ye suck, ye shall be borne upon her sides, and be dandled upon her knees.
13 As one whom his mother comforteth, so will I comfort you; and ye shall be comforted in Jerusalem.
14 And when ye see this, your heart shall rejoice, and your bones shall flourish like an herb: and the hand of the LORD shall be known toward his servants, and his indignation toward his enemies.

The LORD says that He will extend peace to her, Jerusalem, the environment, like a river as the spirit flows through His child into the city. The spirit shall also overflow to the Gentiles like a flowing stream as it pours forth in abundance. Then shall you, the spiritual child, nurse even more. You, like a young child, shall be lifted up upon her sides and dandled, to be moved up and down lightly, upon her knees; the environment will be an uplifting experience because of your presence. The spiritual child will not be alone in the environment of its mother earth.

As one whom his mother comforts, the LORD will comfort you; and you will be comforted in Jerusalem. When you see this, when you experience what has been described to you in words, your heart will rejoice, and your bones, your physical body, shall flourish as an herb which emits fragrant aromas and add spice to food. Since the person knows that the Father is with him, then the hand of the LORD is extended through the child and the spirit of the LORD will be known to his servants as a joy; but the LORD's indignation will be experienced by His enemies. It is the same spirit of the LORD which produces joy or indignation depending upon whether the person is **<u>with</u>** the moving spirit, or **<u>against</u>** it. The LORD's spirit in action on earth, Jehovah, will have an effect.

15 For, behold, the LORD will come with fire, and with his chariots like a whirlwind, to render his anger with fury, and his rebuke with flames of fire.
16 For by fire and by his sword will the LORD plead with all flesh: and the slain of the LORD shall be many.
17 They that sanctify themselves, and purify themselves in the gardens behind one tree in the midst, eating swine's flesh, and the abomination, and the mouse, shall be consumed together, saith the LORD.

Isaiah tells his disciples, his followers who were willing to be disciplined by his teaching, that the LORD comes with power that he symbolizes by fire and by chariots that move with such power and speed that they create a whirlwind. The purpose of the power on earth is to render His anger with fury over the idols to Him that have been created by man in his fallen state. His rebuke with flames of fire, the power of the LORD on earth, will cause the destruction of the forms which are false and a warm glow to the true forms. Fire can either burn or warm depending on its degree of intensity. The fire of Love needs to be controlled by the Truth.

The LORD shall use His power of Love, symbolized by fire, and His Truth, symbolized by the sword, to plead with all flesh of fallen human beings to return to the spirit of the LORD which is flowing through the flesh continuously, and continually being ignored. This is the action of the flaming sword which is in operation. The flesh that ignores the LORD's spirit shall be slain and there shall be many who are called and few who choose to let the LORD's spirit, His child that is within them, to move through the flesh which they believe to be their own.

Many will continue to practice the ways that they and their fathers have devised over many generations. They sanctify themselves, and purify themselves behind one tree, one source of belief that has been growing for many years. As they purify and sanctify themselves, they are not being purified and sanctified by the spirit of the LORD which is moving through them. As they remain unchanged, they remain spiritually unclean, symbolized by familiar unclean objects to them such as swine's blood, the abomination of idolatry and the mouse which brings uncleanness into their homes. All unclean flesh shall be consumed and destroyed together says the LORD.

18 For I know their works and their thoughts: it shall come, that I will gather all nations and tongues; and they shall come, and see my glory.
19 And I will set a sign among them, and I will send those that escape of them unto the nations, to Tarshish, Pul, and Lud, that draw the bow, to Tubal, and Javan, to the isles afar off, that have not heard my fame, neither have seen my glory; and they shall declare my glory among the Gentiles.

The LORD has been with all flesh that has refused His call to them and therefore, He knows their thoughts and their works; the flesh, with its earthly mind that is separated from the LORD, does not know that the LORD has been present in the flesh all along since the moment of conception individually and on the entire planet which is His footstool. The LORD, being eternal, has time on His side. All flesh shall come to Him, the true design shall return, the LORD will gather all nations and tongues together in the simultaneous operation of His spirit and they shall see His glory in operation.

The LORD will set a sign among them, the sign shall be the people who have the victory over the flesh and let the spirit of the LORD shine through their flesh. The LORD will send those people who have escaped from the world of the flesh to the world of the spirit within the flesh to all nations far and wide. Isaiah mentions some nations as Tarshish, Pul, and Lud, that draw the bow (archers), to Tubal, and Javan, to the isles afar off, that have not heard of the LORD's fame, nor seen His glory; and the LORD's emissaries, the signs, the people who carry the LORD's spirit, shall declare His glory among the Gentiles, the people who have never heard of the One God. What is the responsibility of the people who carry the LORD's spirit?

20 And they shall bring all your brethren for an offering unto the LORD out of all nations upon horses, and in chariots, and in litters, and upon mules, and upon swift beasts, to my holy mountain Jerusalem, saith the LORD, as the children of Israel bring an offering in a clean vessel into the house of the LORD.
21 And I will also take of them for priests and for Levites, saith the LORD.

The Testimony of the Major Prophets

The emissaries or envoys of the LORD, the people who carry the LORD's spirit, shall bring all your brethren, male and female, who want to offer their flesh to the LORD out of all the nations to which they journey upon horses, in chariots, litters, upon mules and swift beasts to the LORD's holy mountain, Jerusalem, says the LORD, as the children of Israel bring an offering in a clean vessel into the house of the LORD. Isaiah has made a comparison between the liquid offering of the children of Israel in a clean vessel, and his teaching that the individuals who are willing to let their flesh be used for the flow of the spirit of the LORD should come to him. Isaiah will take them for priests and for Levites, who were the tribe that assumed the permanent responsibility for the priesthood. Isaiah was looking for the people who would let the spirit of the LORD, the Word, be made flesh. As the spirit of the LORD flows through the flesh, something wonderful transpires

22 For as the new heavens and the new earth, which I will make, shall remain before me, saith the LORD, so shall your seed and your name remain.
23 And it shall come to pass, that from one new moon to another, and from one sabbath to another, shall all flesh come to worship before me, saith the LORD.
24 And they shall go forth, and look upon the carcases of the men that have transgressed against me: for their worm shall not die, neither shall their fire be quenched; and they shall be an abhorring unto all flesh.

The spirit of the LORD, when allowed to move through the flesh of people, moves also through the consciousness of the people who allow it to happen. They become aware of a new heaven and a new earth, a divinely inspired cause and its earthly effect, are created that would be in harmony with the Way of the LORD, and which would bring Him delight as He brings the Kingdom of Heaven on earth in fulfillment of the LORD's prayer. The new heavens and the new earth are made by the LORD and shall remain before Him, and so shall your seed and your name remain because you and your LORD are one in the covenant-agreement which has been available from the LORD always. The flesh of man in the fallen state ruled by his self-active rebellious mind has refused the covenant-agreement and consequently, he has experienced all the misery that his refusal and rebellion have produced.

And it shall come to pass, that from one new moon to another, and from one Sabbath to another, all flesh shall come to worship before the LORD to experience the reality of the covenant. The LORD has unlimited time!

And when the people do experience for themselves that the covenant is real and available on this side of the grave, then, they, too, shall go forth, as Isaiah did, and look upon the carcasses of the men and women who have transgressed against the LORD. If they can be brought to the LORD, well and good. If not, they will be slain, they will die, not knowing that the LORD has been with them. But, their worm shall not die, the worm that was created to consume the slain flesh. The worm is the symbol for the destroyer of the flesh that is reduced to dust. The fire, the power of the LORD, that is in the worm will not be quenched; its purpose is to abhor the slain flesh, to recycle the flesh into components that can be used in the creative processes of the LORD on earth.

Isaiah has given each fallen person a choice of the heavenly inheritance of the covenant-agreement of everlasting life in oneness with the LORD; or the person may choose the earthly inheritance of the destructive cycle by the worm of the dust. There is a choice!

Anthony John Monaco   **August 7, 1997**

The Symbolic Version of
Ezekiel

Anthony John Monaco
A Stars of the Scriptures Series

FOREWORD

The name, Ezekiel, means, "the strength of God" or "God is my strength". The meaning which is inherent in the name Ezekiel relates to the fact that there is a relationship between God and Ezekiel and that the relationship conveys strength from God to Ezekiel. This relationship has been called "the covenant with the LORD". The covenant relationship gives Ezekiel the spiritual strength to speak out and to be heard by those who have not had the covenant-experience which results in authority. The actual proof of the relationship between God and Ezekiel would be for a person to have the conscious experience with God in an individual covenant experience.

As the book begins, Ezekiel was among the Jews who were exiled to Babylon by Nebuchadnezzar in 597 BC He was away from Jerusalem, the city of David, when Nebuchadnezzar sent the Babylonians to lay siege to the city in 588 when the walls were breached and the city was plundered. On August 14, 586 BC, the city of Jerusalem and the temple were burned. Israel's monarchy was ended. The City of David and the temple no longer existed. Babylon dominated the entire area until it was crushed by Cyrus the Persian in 539.

Ezekiel was a member of a priestly family and therefore, he was eligible to serve as a priest. He was an exiled priest in a strange land and far removed from the temple in Jerusalem with its sacrifices, rituals and ceremonies. As Ezekiel—married and living in a house of his own—lived among his fellow exiles, he received the call, he experienced the covenant, to become a prophet in July, 593 BC

Ezekiel was able to see the events of the times exactly as they were. While others in exile had hopes of expectations to return to an undamaged Jerusalem and an unblemished temple, Ezekiel faithfully relayed the factual information to his fellow Jews that Jerusalem would eventually (and actually did) fall to the Babylonians. The only hope that the prophet was authorized to extend to his listeners was that they should live at peace with themselves during their exile from Jerusalem, their native land. Once the news was received that Jerusalem had fallen and the temple had been destroyed, Ezekiel's message from the LORD to his people was that they should experience revival, restoration and a glorious future exactly where they were as the kingdom of God comes into the world through them.

The Symbolic Version of Ezekiel will bring to focus the fact that the spirit of the Lord did come to focus in a person far away from the physical temple in Jerusalem seven years before its destruction and the spirit survived in that person for another 15 years after the destruction of the temple building. The covenant-agreement between the LORD and Ezekiel occurred far away from Jerusalem and the temple which gives emphasis to the fact that the relationship between man and God is a personal one which occurs wherever man happens to be.

The Book of Ezekiel is rich in symbolism that explains the relationship of the LORD to the body of mankind in varying degrees as explained through His servant, Ezekiel. Let us consider The Symbolic Version of Ezekiel to determine whether this book of the Holy Bible has specific and individual application today for those who desire a personal experience of the covenant-agreement with the LORD.

CHAPTER 1

1 Now it came to pass in the thirtieth year, in the fourth month, in the fifth day of the month, as I was among the captives by the river of Chebar, that the heavens were opened, and I saw visions of God.
2 In the fifth day of the month, which was the fifth year of king Jehoiachin's captivity,
3 The word of the LORD came expressly unto Ezekiel the priest, the son of Buzi, in the land of the Chaldeans by the river Chebar; and the hand of the LORD was there upon him.

The Book of Ezekiel begins with the actual covenant-experience between Ezekiel and the LORD which is specifically identified as occurring on the fifth day of the fourth month in the thirtieth year of the life of Ezekiel while he was among his fellow captives by the river of Chebar, which is a branch of the Euphrates River near the city of Nippur. Ezekiel is stating in very clear language that he precisely knows where he was and when the spiritual experience with the LORD transpired. Ezekiel describes this spiritual experience and the vision which he acquired as the opening of the heavens so that he could see, in his own consciousness, new visions which he attributes to the action of God on earth through him. Ezekiel further describes this particular time of his revelation with God as the fifth day of the month which was the fifth year since king Jehoiachin of Judah—along with 10,000 Jews, including Ezekiel—was captured. The scripture emphasizes once again that the word of the LORD came expressly to Ezekiel the priest, the son of Buzi, in the land of the Chaldeans by the river Chebar; and the hand, the symbol of control, of the LORD was there upon him. Ezekiel knows exactly the time and the place of his covenant-experience which gave him strength and vision. Ezekiel is in the process of describing his spiritual experience with the LORD in symbolic language, because material symbols must be used to describe a spiritual experience in which the invisible hand of the LORD has had an effect within a person.

4 And I looked, and, behold, a whirlwind came out of the north, a great cloud, and a fire infolding itself, and a brightness was about it, and out of the midst thereof as the colour of amber, out of the midst of the fire.

As Ezekiel looked into the heavens which have been opened within his consciousness, behold, he saw a whirlwind come out of the north. Air is the symbol of the movement of the spirit and a whirlwind is the experience of a great activity of spirit. The movement of the spirit is described in material terms as coming out of the north, the symbol that carries an invigorating coldness in the air in the present moment. The whirlwind of the spirit is described as a great cloud, which symbolizes that moisture is present. Water and moisture are symbols of the visible truth that is contained and moved by the wind of the spirit. Fire symbolizes the warmth of God's love enfolding itself and emanating from God. As the heavens are opened, then the view in the consciousness of Ezekiel is one of love, truth and life which are symbolized by the fire of love, the cloud of truth and the whirlwind of life. These three visible attributes of fire, water and the movement of air reveal as the radiant brightness that proceeded outward from the fire. The brightness is the radiance of the LORD. Out of the midst of the brightness, there came a golden-yellow, flowing substance, like amber, which symbolizes the presence of a flowing spiritual substance that proceeds from the fire like a river. The amber-like, flowing, spiritual substance that comes forth from the fire begins to take shape.

The Testimony of the Major Prophets

5 Also out of the midst thereof came the likeness of four living creatures. And this was their appearance; they had the likeness of a man.
6 And every one had four faces, and every one had four wings.

Ezekiel's vision continues as the flowing spiritual substance assumes shapes with the likenesses of four living creatures and this was their appearance; they, the four living creatures, all had the likeness of a man. Every one had four faces and every one of them had four wings. The faces give them, the men, separate and distinct identities and the wings symbolize the ability of the men to fly through the air like birds. The four wings, two pair of wings, symbolize the thoughts which fly through the mind, and the feelings which fly through the heart of the physical forms of the men in the vision.

7 And their feet were straight feet; and the sole of their feet was like the sole of a calf's foot: and they sparkled like the colour of burnished brass.
8 And they had the hands of a man under their wings on their four sides; and they four had their faces and their wings.
9 Their wings were joined one to another; they turned not when they went; they went every one straight forward.

The feet, the symbol of the personal understanding of the men, were straight feet as seen from each of them from above, but the sole of their feet was crooked, like the sole of a calf's foot. Each foot appears to be going straight but it leaves a crooked imprint in the ground. The vision reveals that the men think that they are walking a straight path in their own eyes, in their own view of things, but their path is in fact crooked. The way that a person in the fallen state walked in his crooked way was shiny, like the color of burnished brass. The shiny brass symbolizes that the person with the shiny foot believes his path to be correct in his own eyes, in his own vision, like gold, but, eventually the shiny brass would soon tarnish after some use. This is the way of the viewpoint of the fallen state: it is a tarnished view of the situation or circumstance: it is brass, not gold.

The creatures in Ezekiel's vision had the hands of a man under their wings on their four sides to demonstrate that the control of the wings of the mind and the feelings of the heart are under man's control. Man has the ability to power the wings of the living creatures; and each of the four creatures had their faces and their wings. Their wings were joined one to another to demonstrate and symbolize that they were and are connected in mind and heart even though they are separated by their physical forms and actions. The flying creatures, the four men with wings, did not turn when they went; each of them went straight forward as a single body of mankind which is connected in mind and heart where the feelings and the thoughts have an effect on the one body. There is one body of mankind but it appears that there are four faces to the four men with wings.

10 As for the likeness of their faces, they four had the face of a man, and the face of a lion, on the right side: and they four had the face of an ox on the left side; they four also had the face of an eagle.

As for the likeness of their faces, the four creatures had totally different countenances: each of the four creatures had the face of a man and the face of a lion on the right side of the body of each man in the vision: and the four had the face of an ox on the left side and the face of an eagle. It appears that the single body of mankind has four different faces and that there are four different men. Let us take a closer look at an overview of the four faces.

In the language of symbolism, the lion represents a powerful destructive nature of the physical body; the right side symbolizes that the right side has more strength than the weaker left side, due to a lifetime of use by the majority of people. The face of a man symbolizes the condition of man in the fallen state whose face reveals the negative emotions of harmful feelings which reveal themselves on the face of man. The lion and the man on the right side of the creature symbolizes that the powerful side of man in the fallen state governed by his negative emotions is as destructive as a lion.

The ox, a strong and temperamental beast, symbolizes the self-active human mind which has the potential to lead the out-of-control physical form in a direction to do damage. The eagle is the symbol of the highest vision possible for an earthly creature to see clearly. True vision is not possible as long as man remains in the fallen state of mankind. The ox

The Symbolic Version of Ezekiel

and the eagle of man in the fallen state are pictured in the vision on the left side, the fallen side, of the living creature. The left side symbolizes the unclean, sinister, wrong side of man who keeps himself in the fallen state by reason of his distorted vision that results from the ox-like self-activity of his fallen human consciousness.

The creatures in the vision symbolize the various aspects of any person as he or she knows himself on earth as a powerful physical person (lion); a strong mental person (ox); a person who uses the body and the mind to get what he or she wants in self-satisfaction for one's feelings. The feelings of man are seen and observed on his face (man); and finally, the face of the eagle which senses the highest vision of the spiritual expression plane of man to rise up toward the restored or ascended state from which man fell to the earth from the position of the covenant with God by using the capacity to express the spirit of God which is present with each one. Each person can rotate through his four faces from the physical to the mental to the emotional to the spiritual expression of a distorted sense of self.

11 Thus were their faces: and their wings were stretched upward; two wings of every one were joined one to another, and two covered their bodies.
12 And they went every one straight forward: whither the spirit was to go, they went; and they turned not when they went.

Thus were the faces in Ezekiel's vision of the various stages of man in the fallen state in varying degrees of separation from the LORD from the lowest to the highest: from the lion to the ox to the man to the eagle. A beautiful symbolic picture of mankind in the fallen state. All four categories have their wings stretched upward in the longing of their hearts to return to the position from which they fell, and each category wants to use their particular means, the face of their identities, to return to the true state which is symbolized by the Garden of Eden.

The wings of each creature were joined one to another to demonstrate that they do have wings that are wings of connection in the realm of **spirit**, and two wings covered their physical bodies to demonstrate that they are wings of separation in the realm of **form** on earth. Each creature went straight forward when they were under the control of the wings of the spirit moving in the direction in which the spirit of the LORD was moving; as they moved under the impulse of the spirit from the heaven, they turned not when they went forth under spiritual control. In other words, they—the body, the mind, the feelings and the capacity for spiritual expression—flew in formation. The four creatures were living creatures that were moving with the spirit. It is possible for mankind under the control of spirit to "fly" together in harmony without bumping into each other as we observe when birds land on the ground or fly into the air. It should be obvious, by observation, that man in the fallen state, is not under the control of the wings of the spiritual control from the LORD.

13 As for the likeness of the living creatures, their appearance was like burning coals of fire, and like the appearance of lamps: it went up and down among the living creatures; and the fire was bright, and out of the fire went forth lightning.
14 And the living creatures ran and returned as the appearance of a flash of lightning.

As for the likeness of the living creatures, their appearance was like burning coals of fire and the appearance of lamps: these items of the fire of heat and the shining of the light symbolize the radiant energy of love and truth from the divine spiritual source, the LORD. This radiant energy went up and down among the living creatures of the human equipment of body, mind and heart which are being used by the spirit. Radiant energy from the LORD is burning bright as a fire in the creatures of the LORD. The fire was bright and from out of the fire came lightning, which contains both power and sound for the eye to see and the ear to hear. The living creatures in Ezekiel's vision symbolize the four stages of fallen mankind who are in the process of returning to or moving farther away from, the spirit of the LORD. Living creatures have the opportunity to run and return as the appearance of the flash of lightning, the symbol of the radiant energy from the LORD, puts in an appearance.

15 Now as I beheld the living creatures, behold one wheel upon the earth by the living creatures, with his four faces.
16 The appearance of the wheels and their work was like unto the colour of a beryl: and they four had one likeness: and their appearance and their work was as it were a wheel in the middle of a wheel.

The Testimony of the Major Prophets

Now as Ezekiel beheld the four living creatures that symbolize the four various stages of mankind, he saw one wheel upon the earth by the living creatures with his four faces. The one wheel is the one body of mankind. It appears that there are four different "men", four different wheels, but it is only one wheel that appears to be four different distortions. This one wheel of the body of mankind in the fallen state is the wheel of the "gods", the wheel of the LORD, which grinds the conditions on earth exceedingly fine. The appearance of the four separate wheels and their work was like the color of beryl: beryl is a vitreous mixture of colors ranging from green, blue, pink and white as contrasted to the flow of the golden-yellow, clear amber.

The four seemingly separate wheels moving together had one likeness and they produce a mixture of colors: and their appearance and their work was as it were a wheel in the middle of a wheel making different tracks of distortion. All the power of the four wheels, like the four men with four different faces that have the same likeness whether they represent the physical, mental, emotional or spiritual, is being transferred into one large wheel through the body of mankind on earth. There are not really four wheels; there is only one wheel of the body of mankind from the viewpoint of the LORD. The "four" wheels of the physical, mental, emotional and spiritual aspects are all contained within one wheel that makes one track: the action of the body of mankind on earth.

17 When they went, they went upon their four sides: and they turned not when they went.
18 As for their rings, they were so high that they were dreadful; and their rings were full of eyes round about them four.
19 And when the living creatures went, the wheels went by them: and when the living creatures were lifted up from the earth, the wheels were lifted up.
20 Whithersoever the spirit was to go, they went, thither was their spirit to go; and the wheels were lifted up over against them: for the spirit of the living creature was in the wheels.

When the four wheels go separately without the coordination of the wings of the spirit which are all joined to produce harmonious action, the wheels fall over on their four sides and they do not turn where and when they want to go due to the fallen position in which they find themselves. The fallen wheels rotate on their hubs and not on their rims. The motion is horizontal and not vertical. Vertical, upright wheels are powered by the spirit of the LORD to produce the machinery of the divine design. Horizontal, fallen wheels are being influenced and controlled by the things of the earth.

As for their rings, the symbols that control the movement of the wheels, they are so high that they are dreadful because they can't control anything. The rings of control are full of eyes in which everyone wants to be in charge, in control, which only brings chaos to the operation of the divine machinery of the LORD called mankind.

The material wheels by which things are done on earth are connected to living spiritual creatures. When the living creatures went up, rise up, in service to the LORD, the wheels go with them. The wheels and the living creatures are connected. When the spiritual machinery of the living creatures are lifted up from the earth, the wheels are lifted up also. Wherever the spirit was to go, the wheels of the spiritual machinery move with the spirit. The spirit is in control. Wherever the spirit goes, the living creatures go. The wheels, the spiritual machinery, are always over against the living creatures: for the spirit of the living creatures is in the wheels, the machinery of the spirit. The spirit and the machinery of the spirit (the wheels) are interconnected.

21 When those went, these went; and when those stood, these stood; and when those were lifted up from the earth, the wheels were lifted up over against them: for the spirit of the living creature was in the wheels.
22 And the likeness of the firmament upon the heads of the living creature was as the colour of the terrible crystal, stretched forth over their heads above.
23 And under the firmament were their wings straight, the one toward the other: every one had two, which covered on this side, and every one had two, which covered on that side, their bodies.

When the spirit moves, the machinery moves; when the spirit stands still, the machinery stands still; when the living creatures were lifted up from the earth, the wheels of the spiritual machinery were moved up also because the spirit of the living creature is in the wheels. The wheels are powered by the spirit. There is no other power except the spiritual power from the LORD.

The Symbolic Version of Ezekiel

The likeness of the firmament, the spiritual substance of connection, upon the heads of the living creature was as the color of the terrible (awesome) crystal, that is stretched forth over the heads of the living creatures to give forth its terrible light. And under this firmament of darkness, the wings were straight to guide the living creatures in the direction of the darkness to influence the direction of darkness and light, wrong or right. Each creature has two wings on each side, right or wrong, clean or dirty, to cover their bodies to lead them in the direction of the light or the darkness. The direction and the control is within each one; the hands of man control the wings of the mind and the heart (the feelings). Man can produce either beauty or noise.

24 And when they went, I heard the noise of their wings, like the noise of great waters, as the voice of the Almighty, the voice of speech, as the noise of an host: when they stood, they let down their wings.
25 And there was a voice from the firmament that was over their heads, when they stood, and had let down their wings.

And when the living creatures with the four faces moved, Ezekiel heard the noise of the movement of their wings, like the noise of great waters which is the evidence of the voice of the Almighty, the voice of speech that comes from the Almighty, as the noise of the host. Mankind in the fallen state is making noise, not music! The great waters of truth that flow from God out of heaven are distorted from heavenly strains of music into noise as the voice of the Almighty is distorted, by man in the fallen state, into a voice of distortion. The distortion is caused as the self-active minds and hearts of a fallen people who attempt to get what they want by controlling their own wings instead of letting the spirit of the LORD move their wings that control the thoughts of the mind and the meditations of the heart. It is possible for man in the fallen state to let down their wings, let go of their wings by standing up in oneness with the spirit of God which is coming down from God out of heaven into the earth.

When men in the fallen state stood, they let down their wings and let the spirit of God flow through the human equipment. When man stands up to reveal the spirit of the LORD, fallen man lets go of, lets down, his wings. Fallen man dose not use his wings to do what the thoughts of his mind and the feelings of his heart desire to do. When fallen man voluntarily lets down his wings, the spirit of the LORD powers the heart, mind and body.

26 And above the firmament that was over their heads was the likeness of a throne, as the appearance of a sapphire stone: and upon the likeness of the throne was the likeness as the appearance of a man above upon it.
27 And I saw as the colour of amber, as the appearance of fire round about within it, from the appearance of his loins even upward, and from the appearance of his loins even downward, I saw as it were the appearance of fire, and it had brightness round about.

And above the firmament, the firmament is the connecting substance that connects the heaven with the earth, that was over their heads, the heads of men and women in the fallen state, there was the likeness of a throne. The throne is the place upon which sits the occupant of the heaven. The appearance of the throne is described as the appearance of a sapphire stone. A sapphire is blue and the color blue is the symbol of truth. Upon the likeness of the throne was the likeness as the appearance of a true man upon and above it. This man is spiritual man: man made in the image and likeness of God, the truth of man.

Ezekiel in his vision saw the color of amber, as the appearance of fire round about within it, from the appearance of his loins even upward, and from the appearance of his loins even downward, I saw as it were the appearance of fire, and it had brightness round about.

28 As the appearance of the bow that is in the cloud in the day of rain, so was the appearance of the brightness round about. This was the appearance of the likeness of the glory of the LORD. And when I saw it, I fell upon my face, and I heard a voice of one that spake.

Ezekiel describes the appearance of the glory of the LORD to him as the appearance of the brightness round about that can be compared to the appearance of a rainbow that is in the cloud in the day of rain. A rainbow has the seven colors of the spectrum in it. And when Ezekiel saw the brightness which is the radiance of the spirit of the LORD, he states that he fell upon his face, and he heard a voice of one that spoke. The one that spoke to him was the LORD. Ezekiel has achieved the covenant by letting the spirit of the LORD move through him, and he has received the spiritual strength from God.

CHAPTER 2

1 And he said unto me, Son of man, stand upon thy feet, and I will speak unto thee.
2 And the spirit entered into me when he spake unto me, and set me upon my feet, that I heard him that spake unto me.
3 And he said unto me, Son of man, I send thee to the children of Israel, to a rebellious nation that hath rebelled against me: they and their fathers have transgressed against me, even unto this very day.
4 For they are impudent children and stiffhearted. I do send thee unto them; and thou shalt say unto them, Thus saith the Lord GOD.

And God, the Father, said to Ezekiel, a spiritual Son in the body of mankind, Son of man, stand upon your feet and God will speak to you. Every person in the body of mankind, male or female, is included in the spiritual Son of the Father: the Son has reference to the spirit or the being in the Son; man has reference to the human or material creation in which the spirit inhabits. The command of God to Ezekiel is to stand up on his feet. This can be interpreted to mean the feet of his spiritual understanding that the spirit of all living forms comes from Almighty God; or, it can mean to stand on the feet as a man to hear what God has to say to Ezekiel. If Ezekiel is not on his feet, as a man, to hear what God will say to him, then Ezekiel could be on his knees or laying prostrate with his face to the ground in fear. God wants his Son to rise up, stand up, to receive the word of divine instruction.

Ezekiel describes the event of God speaking to him as the spirit of God entering into his human equipment which set him upon his feet so that Ezekiel could hear the word that was spoken to him. God gave Ezekiel a commission to go to the children of Israel who were described as a rebellious nation that had rebelled against God. This was not a recent rebellion but a rebellion of a long-standing nature described as a transgression by the present children of Israel and their fathers before them. The rebellion continues to this very day. The children of Israel are described by God as impudent and stiff-hearted: impudent because they are insolent and disrespectful to God; and, stiff-hearted because their hearts are not moved by the impulse of the spirit which God is constantly sending to all members of the body of the Son of man on earth. Now that God has the attention of a spokesman to carry His word to the rebellious children of Israel, then Ezekiel can quote the Lord GOD that the words are the words of God; thus says the Lord GOD. Ezekiel has heard the word of God and he has been commissioned by God to deliver the word to the people. Will the people hear and listen to the word of God through Ezekiel who is a captive in a strange land and not in a temple in Jerusalem?!

5 And they, whether they will hear, or whether they will forbear, (for they are a rebellious house,) yet shall know that there hath been a prophet among them.
6 And thou, son of man, be not afraid of them, neither be afraid of their words, though briers and thorns be with thee, and thou dost dwell among scorpions: be not afraid of their words, nor be dismayed at their looks, though they be a rebellious house.
7 And thou shalt speak my words unto them, whether they will hear, or whether they will forbear: for they are most rebellious.

The Symbolic Version of Ezekiel

8 But thou, son of man, hear what I say unto thee; Be not thou rebellious like that rebellious house: open thy mouth, and eat that I give thee.

Whether the people hear the message or whether they will refrain, (for God knows that they have been a rebellious house of people), then whether they accept or reject the word of God through Ezekiel, the people shall know that there has been a prophet of God among them. Ezekiel, the son of man, a member of the fallen state, is counseled that he should not be afraid of the people or their words. God understands that briers and thorns that symbolize a new and unpleasant task will be the experience of Ezekiel as he dwells among the people who compared to scorpions with a poisonous sting. God cautions Ezekiel to not be afraid of the words of the rebellious people, nor be dismayed by their looks because they are a rebellious house of people who have rebelled against the commandments of God. They are outside the covenant.

In any event, whether they respond favorably or react violently, Ezekiel shall speak the words of God to the children of Israel whether they will hear or whether they will refrain from hearing: God knows that they are a rebellious people. Their unfavorable reaction or favorable response is the choice of the hearers of the word of God, but, Ezekiel, the son of man, shall hear what God has said to him. God has cautioned Ezekiel that he, or anyone who desires to depart from the fallen position of the son of man, should not be rebellious like those who have the past experience of being a member of the body of a rebellious house of people on earth. The rebellious people have ignored the word of God as though it had never been spoken through Moses, David, Solomon and Isaiah. The rebellious people believed that the word of God was for the special prophets who carried the message instead of instruction that is available for all the people. Ezekiel, the representative of the son of man, is instructed by God to hear what is said to him as an individual; Ezekiel is instructed not to be rebellious like that rebellious house who call themselves the children of Israel. Ezekiel is instructed to open his mouth, the mouth of his emotional realm so that God can feed him the spiritual food that will nourish and sustain him while he is on his mission for God.

9 And when I looked, behold, an hand was sent unto me; and, lo, a roll of a book was therein;
10 And he spread it before me; and it was written within and without: and there was written therein lamentations, and mourning, and woe.

When Ezekiel looked to behold what God wanted him to do, the consciousness of Ezekiel was aware what the consciousness of God expected him to do. This understanding of mission was symbolized in material terms as a hand that was sent to him with the roll of a book contained within the hand. God spread the roll before Ezekiel and it was written within and without, on both sides, the lamentations, mourning and woes that Ezekiel would encounter from listeners as he delivers the word of God.

CHAPTER 3

1 Moreover he said unto me, Son of man, eat that thou findest; eat this roll, and go speak unto the house of Israel.
2 So I opened my mouth, and he caused me to eat that roll.
3 And he said unto me, Son of man, cause thy belly to eat, and fill thy bowels with this roll that I give thee. Then did I eat it; and it was in my mouth as honey for sweetness.

Ezekiel continues to describe that God said to him in the position of the Son of man, in the position as a focus point of the body of mankind in the restored state, that he should eat the roll, the roll that he saw in his consciousness that was written within and without, not literally but symbolically so that he digests the contents and the message of God becomes a part of him. After that occurs, then Ezekiel should go speak to the house of Israel who proclaim that they are interested in the word of God. So, Ezekiel opened his mouth, the mouth of his heart because he was willing that it should be so, and God caused him to eat the roll of divine instruction. God would never force anyone to accept his spirit or his instruction which is offered freely to those who are willing.

God said, Son of man, you cause your belly to eat, you willingly receive the spiritual nourishment into your heart and mind, and fill your bowels with the instruction which is available to you from God. Then Ezekiel did "eat", sup, commune with the spirit of God; and it was as sweet in his mouth as honey. The spiritual food from a God of love should be a lovely experience. God did not give the food to Ezekiel so that Ezekiel should keep it all to himself. God has been waiting a long time for a person to "make contact" to receive the invisible word of God in covenant-agreement, as between God and Ezekiel. Now, the word of God can be spoken to others through the human voice of Ezekiel to people who are waiting to hear from their God.

4 And he said unto me, Son of man, go, get thee unto the house of Israel, and speak with my words unto them.
5 For thou art not sent to a people of a strange speech and of an hard language, but to the house of Israel;
6 Not to many people of a strange speech and of an hard language, whose words thou canst not understand. Surely, had I sent thee to them, they would have hearkened unto thee.
7 But the house of Israel will not hearken unto thee; for they will not hearken unto me: for all the house of Israel are impudent and hardhearted.

Son of man, Ezekiel, go, get yourself to the house of Israel and speak the words of God to them. You are not being sent to a people of strange speech and of a hard foreign language which is difficult to understand; you are being sent to the house of Israel. Ezekiel is not being sent to many people of a strange speech and a hard language whose words he is not able to understand. God tells Ezekiel that if he were sent to a strange people they would have listened to him. But the house of Israel will not hearken, they will not listen and respond, because all the members of the house of Israel are impudent and hardhearted.

8 Behold, I have made thy face strong against their faces, and thy forehead strong against their foreheads.

9 As an adamant harder than flint have I made thy forehead: fear them not, neither be dismayed at their looks, though they be a rebellious house.

Behold, the covenant experience which you have with God makes your face strong against the faces of the people in the house of Israel and your forehead, your conscious awareness of your relationship with God, is stronger than the beliefs, the knowledge and awareness of God of the house of Israel who do not know the LORD their God. As a firm foundation harder than flint, your forehead, the symbol of determination and courage, has been made firm and steadfast. Ezekiel is not to fear the people of the house of Israel, nor be dismayed at their looks, even though they have been a rebellious people descended from the house of Israel.

10 Moreover he said unto me, Son of man, all my words that I shall speak unto thee receive in thine heart, and hear with thine ears.
11 And go, get thee to them of the captivity, unto the children of thy people, and speak unto them, and tell them, Thus saith the Lord GOD; whether they will hear, or whether they will forbear.

Moreover, God said to the Son of man, that all the words of God that have been spoken to Ezekiel shall be received in his heart and heard in his ears. The word of God is to be taken to the people in captivity, the children of your own people, and speak to them and tell them that the message is from God. Let the people who hear decide for themselves whether they will hear and respond favorably or whether they will react and forbear the word which Ezekiel brings to them.

12 Then the spirit took me up, and I heard behind me a voice of a great rushing, saying, Blessed be the glory of the LORD from his place.
13 I heard also the noise of the wings of the living creatures that touched one another, and the noise of the wheels over against them, and a noise of a great rushing.
14 So the spirit lifted me up, and took me away, and I went in bitterness, in the heat of my spirit; but the hand of the LORD was strong upon me.
15 Then I came to them of the captivity at Telabib, that dwelt by the river of Chebar, and I sat where they sat, and remained there astonished among them seven days.

When Ezekiel was willing to accept the divine commission from the LORD, the spirit lifted him up and he heard a voice of the spirit, a voice of great rushing of spirit, saying, Blessed be the glory of the LORD from his place, the place in heaven where the LORD resides. Ezekiel also heard the noise of the wings of the living creatures that touched one another at the level of the spirit since all the children of the Father, all the members of the body of the Son of man, touch each other at the level of the spirit. The spirit moves through and connects everything. The noise of the wheels, the machinery of spiritual reality, are in operation at the level of spiritual expression and there is a noise of great rushing, great movement, from the place of the LORD which is the place of cause.

So the spirit lifted Ezekiel up, and took him away, and Ezekiel went in bitterness, in the heat of his spirit because Ezekiel saw what man in the rebellious state has done to cause the distortion of the kingdom of the spirit in the holy place of heaven; but the hand of the LORD was strong upon Ezekiel to prevent foolish actions that the people of the house of Israel could not comprehend. Then Ezekiel came to the people who were held in captivity at Telabib, that dwelt by the river of Chebar. Ezekiel sat where they sat, and remained there among them for seven days astonished and in a state of spiritual shock due to his encounter with God in the covenant-agreement. Ezekiel needs some time to settle down from his being lifted up from a state of material orientation to a new state of spiritual orientation which is the result of the covenant with the LORD.

16 And it came to pass at the end of seven days, that the word of the LORD came unto me, saying,
17 Son of man, I have made thee a watchman unto the house of Israel: therefore hear the word at my mouth, and give them warning from me.
18 When I say unto the wicked, Thou shalt surely die; and thou givest him not warning, nor speakest to warn the wicked from his wicked way, to save his life; the same wicked man shall die in his iniquity; but his blood will I require at thine hand.

The Testimony of the Major Prophets

19 Yet if thou warn the wicked, and he turn not from his wickedness, nor from his wicked way, he shall die in his iniquity; but thou hast delivered thy soul.

At the end of the seven day period, after Ezekiel settled down from his uplifting spiritual experience, the word of the LORD came to him again saying, Son of man, I have made you a watchman over the house of Israel, a point of orientation, of one who knows the way of the LORD. Therefore, you are in a position to hear the word of God and give the house of Israel proper warning from God when the people from the house of Israel stray away from righteousness. God will have a watchman, a spokesman, who will make the people aware of the working of the law of God on earth and when they are breaking the law.

When God says to the wicked, You shall surely die because of your aberrant behavior; and you, the watchman, do not give the wicked warning, nor speak to warn the wicked from his wicked way, to save his life, then, the same wicked man shall die in his iniquity; but his blood will be required at your hand. Yet, if you warn the wicked, and he chooses not to turn from his wickedness, nor from his wicked way, he shall surely die in his iniquity; but you have delivered your soul because the fault is not yours. The LORD is teaching Ezekiel the rudiments of being a watchman, or a priest of the LORD, to care for the people, the flock. A priest of the LORD provides a living example of how the blood, the life force from the LORD, operates in harmony with the law.

20 Again, When a righteous man doth turn from his righteousness, and commit iniquity, and I lay a stumblingblock before him, he shall die: because thou hast not given him warning, he shall die in his sin, and his righteousness which he hath done shall not be remembered; but his blood will I require at thine hand.
21 Nevertheless if thou warn the righteous man, that the righteous sin not, and he doth not sin, he shall surely live, because he is warned; also thou hast delivered thy soul.
22 And the hand of the LORD was there upon me; and he said unto me, Arise, go forth into the plain, and I will there talk with thee.

Again, when a righteous man, which every person is in spiritual identity, does turn away from his true path of righteousness to commit iniquity, then the LORD shall lay a stumbling block before him, and he shall die. It should be expected that the LORD shall lay stumbling blocks on the paths of the people who stray from righteousness to influence them back to the true path. Because you have not given him warning, he shall die in his sin, and the righteousness which he has done shall not be remembered; but the LORD shall require his blood at your hand. Nevertheless if you warn the righteous man, so that the righteous does not sin, he shall surely live, because he was warned; also you have delivered his soul into righteousness.

And the hand of the LORD was there upon Ezekiel; the LORD said to him, Arise, go forth into the plain, where people dwell, and I will talk with you there.

23 Then I arose, and went forth into the plain: and, behold, the glory of the LORD stood there, as the glory which I saw by the river of Chebar: and I fell on my face.
24 Then the spirit entered into me, and set me upon my feet, and spake with me, and said unto me, Go, shut thyself within thine house.
25 But thou, O son of man, behold, they shall put bands upon thee, and shall bind thee with them, and thou shalt not go out among them:
26 And I will make thy tongue cleave to the roof of thy mouth, that thou shalt be dumb, and shalt not be to them a reprover: for they are a rebellious house.
27 But when I speak with thee, I will open thy mouth, and thou shalt say unto them, Thus saith the Lord GOD; He that heareth, let him hear; and he that forbeareth, let him forbear: for they are a rebellious house.

Then Ezekiel arose and went forth into the plain: and behold, the glory of the LORD was there in the plain as the glory was seen by Ezekiel by the river Chebar: and Ezekiel fell upon his face when he became aware that the glory of the LORD was everywhere and not at a specific place where the person first becomes aware of the spirit of the LORD. Then the spirit entered into Ezekiel, and the moving spirit set him upon his feet, caused him to stand before the LORD, spoke with him, and said, Go, shut yourself within your house. The spirit of the LORD is with you everywhere and always.

The Symbolic Version of Ezekiel

But you, O son of man, who does not allow the spirit of the LORD to flow through the human capacities, behold, the people in the fallen state shall put bands upon you, and shall bind you with them, and you shall not go out from among them. And the spirit of the LORD that is not moving through you according to the divine design of the LORD will make your tongue cleave to the roof of your mouth so that you can not speak properly with the result that you shall be dumb. In this way, you shall not be to them a reprover, a blamer, an accuser, for they are a rebellious house who are functioning incorrectly and you would be blaming them for their actions constantly.

But when the LORD speaks with you, the LORD will open your mouth, and you shall say unto them, Thus says the Lord GOD. He that hears, let him hear and carry out the impulse of the spirit; and he that forbears, let him forbear, refrain, abstain from wrong behavior: for they are a rebellious house. In any moment, a person can be in alignment with, the spirit of the LORD to produce a holy house; or in disagreement with the spirit of the LORD to produce a rebellious house.

CHAPTER 4

1 Thou also, son of man, take thee a tile, and lay it before thee, and portray upon it the city, even Jerusalem:
2 And lay siege against it, and build a fort against it, and cast a mount against it; set the camp also against it, and set battering rams against it round about.

The spirit of the LORD God is working through the body of Ezekiel to inform him as one man about a pattern or prototype of what is required for all men and women in the fallen state. Ezekiel is a captive in exile and under the control of a foreign king. His individual body is likened to the city of Jerusalem which is held under siege by the invaders. God wants Ezekiel to see the parallel between his individual position in captivity and the captivity of the holy city of Jerusalem.

Ezekiel, the son of man who has arisen from the fallen state of mankind, is instructed to take a soft tile, a blank clay tablet, lay it before him and draw on it an outline of the city of Jerusalem. The illustration drawn by Ezekiel is to picture the city under siege from the enemy who uses forts to protect themselves, ramps to approach the walls, camps of the enemy holding the city under siege and battering rams to break down the walls. This illustration of the city of Jerusalem under siege is to be used as a sign to the house of Israel. The house of Israel is the spiritual house of the LORD that is within the human physical body of each person as the spirit of Israel was contained within the physical form of Jacob. As Ezekiel observes the fate of Jerusalem from far away Babylon, he is able to see the circumstance of the temple in the city surrounded by the enemies who want to destroy the LORD's temple and the city which the LORD is trying to build on earth, the house of Israel. The house of Israel needs to be protected.

3 Moreover take thou unto thee an iron pan, and set it for a wall of iron between thee and the city: and set thy face against it, and it shall be besieged, and thou shalt lay siege against it. This shall be a sign to the house of Israel.
4 Lie thou also upon thy left side, and lay the iniquity of the house of Israel upon it: according to the number of the days that thou shalt lie upon it thou shalt bear their iniquity.
5 For I have laid upon thee the years of their iniquity, according to the number of the days, three hundred and ninety days: so shalt thou bear the iniquity of the house of Israel.

Moreover, Ezekiel is instructed to take an iron pan and set it as a barrier of a wall of iron between Ezekiel, the spiritual representation of the son of man and the city of Jerusalem. Ezekiel is to set his face, he is to face the wall of iron so that the city of Jerusalem is enclosed in a wall of iron and under siege. This illustration is to be a sign to the house of Israel that the spirit is under siege from the invaders who are determined to destroy the holy city.

Ezekiel is instructed to lie on his left side, symbolizing the northern side of the city, the northern kingdom of Israel, and lay the iniquity and the evil of the house of Israel upon it. As long as the person who represents the house of Israel lies on his left side, behaving in an evil manner, then according to the number of days that the person who symbolizes the son of man is in the unclean position, the physical form of the son of man, mankind, shall bear the iniquity. For the

The Symbolic Version of Ezekiel

LORD has laid upon the son of man, mankind, the years of their iniquity and sinful behavior, according to the number of the days that mankind has been in the sinful state. The LORD is telling Ezekiel that he and mankind shall bear the iniquity of the house of Israel for as many days as they remain sinful, three hundred and ninety days that represent three hundred and ninety years since the division of Solomon's kingdom until the fall of Jerusalem.

6 And when thou hast accomplished them, lie again on thy right side, and thou shalt bear the iniquity of the house of Judah forty days: I have appointed thee each day for a year.
7 Therefore thou shalt set thy face toward the siege of Jerusalem, and thine arm shall be uncovered, and thou shalt prophesy against it.

After you have accomplished the payment for the working of the Law of Sowing and Reaping based upon the behavior symbolized by lying on the left side, then lie down again on the right side. The right side symbolizes the southern kingdom of Judah. Ezekiel, as one body, the son of man, the body of mankind shall bear the iniquity of Judah for forty days. The LORD has appointed one day for each year. The atonement of forty days represents the period of forty years. Therefore, Ezekiel shall set his face, shall focus his attention so that he can see and understand the siege of Jerusalem as the result of the division between the people of Israel and the people of Judah who are symbolized as lying down instead of standing upright in representation of the LORD their God. Ezekiel's arm shall be uncovered so that he can have the power to prophesy against the people of the house of Israel and the house of Judah who rebelled against the LORD by going their own ways, left and right, instead of the upright way of the LORD.

8 And, behold, I will lay bands upon thee, and thou shalt not turn thee from one side to another, till thou hast ended the days of thy siege.

Ezekiel, speaking the word of the LORD, tells the people of Jerusalem under siege that the LORD will lay bands upon them so that they shall not turn from side to side in separate camps of a divided people until they have ended the days of their siege, their rebellion, against the LORD. The divided people must learn that they shall reap the behavior that they have sown just as surely as they must eat the crops that they have grown. What was available as material substance must be used. There is no other material substance available.

9 Take thou also unto thee wheat, and barley, and beans, and lentiles, and millet, and fitches, and put them in one vessel, and make thee bread thereof, according to the number of the days that thou shalt lie upon thy side, three hundred and ninety days shalt thou eat thereof.
10 And thy meat which thou shalt eat shall be by weight, twenty shekels a day: from time to time shalt thou eat it.
11 Thou shalt drink also water by measure, the sixth part of an hin: from time to time shalt thou drink.
12 And thou shalt eat it as barley cakes, and thou shalt bake it with dung that cometh out of man, in their sight.

The LORD is informing Ezekiel that the body of the son of man had to live on the crops available for the people according to the working of divine law over the period of time of three hundred ninety years that was symbolized by three hundred ninety days. In symbolic language, the people had to eat the "bread" which they had made from the combined fallen behavior that was symbolized by the grains, the fruit of their expression, that was placed in one vessel for them to eat. They shall also have meat to eat, the meat from the LORD which is more preferable, but it will be available to them only from time to time. The meat from the LORD shall be available by weight, and the weight is determined by their own behavior on how well they represent the LORD as the LORD's people. They shall have water to drink—water is the symbol of the truth of spirit—and it too will be available from time to time. The food available to them shall be eaten as barley cakes cooked with the waste that comes out of man. Dung was used as fuel to burn to create heat for cooking. Fallen man shall see and know that the waste products of their behavior must be used as fuel for their own source of fire.

13 And the LORD said, Even thus shall the children of Israel eat their defiled bread among the Gentiles, whither I will drive them.
14 Then said I, Ah Lord GOD! behold, my soul hath not been polluted: for from my youth up even till now have I not eaten of that which dieth of itself, or is torn in pieces; neither came there abominable flesh into my mouth.
15 Then he said unto me, Lo, I have given thee cow's dung for man's dung, and thou shalt prepare thy bread therewith.

The Testimony of the Major Prophets

The LORD said that the children of Israel must eat their defiled bread among the Gentiles where the LORD will drive them by the working of the Law of Sowing and Reaping. Ezekiel said to the Lord GOD that his own soul has not been polluted from his youth until the present time. He has not eaten food which died of its own accord from sickness, nor food which was torn in pieces: abominable flesh has not come into his mouth. The LORD allowed some mercy to Ezekiel when he allows Ezekiel to use cow's dung for fuel instead of man's dung to prepare his bread which indicates an amelioration of the working of the law for those who are not defiled. There is a cleaner way to those who look for it.

16 Moreover he said unto me, Son of man, behold, I will break the staff of bread in Jerusalem: and they shall eat bread by weight, and with care; and they shall drink water by measure, and with astonishment:
17 That they may want bread and water, and be astonied one with another, and consume away for their iniquity.

Moreover, the LORD said to Ezekiel, Son of man, the representative of the LORD's spiritual son among fallen man on earth, that the LORD will break the staff of bread in Jerusalem. The staff of bread has reference to the bread of life from the LORD that has been available to feed the spiritual needs of the people through the temple in Jerusalem. The LORD will break the provision of spiritual bread. The people will learn to eat their bread of life from the LORD with care; and they shall drink the water of truth by measuring very carefully how they use the water that symbolizes the truth of the spirit of the LORD with astonishment. The people will want the bread of life and the water of truth which comes from the LORD through his people, and they will be astonished one with another as they begin to observe the effect of the rationing of the LORD's spirit. The distorted results occur and they are appalled by the sight of each other without the LORD's spirit and the way in which they are consumed by their iniquity and their sin brought about by the absence of the LORD's spirit.

CHAPTER 5

1 And thou, son of man, take thee a sharp knife, take thee a barber's rasor, and cause it to pass upon thine head and upon thy beard: then take thee balances to weigh, and divide the hair.

Hair is a growth of substance that proceeds outward from the physical body: it is soft and fine on the head of a baby; and it is coarse and brittle as it appears on an aged person. Hair is a visible symbol of expression; that which comes forth from a person. As hair is used as a symbol of total expression that comes forth from a human being, then hair that grows wild and unruly needs to be groomed and cared for to present an attractive appearance. The LORD continues in his instruction to the people of the world who are in the fallen state in any generation and who are referred to as the son of man. The entire body of the son of man is brought to focus in the physical form of one person, Ezekiel, but the teaching is available for everyone. The son of man has reference to the body of mankind in the fallen state; the Son of man has reference to the body of mankind in its restored state.

2 Thou shalt burn with fire a third part in the midst of the city, when the days of the siege are fulfilled: and thou shalt take a third part, and smite about it with a knife: and a third part thou shalt scatter in the wind; and I will draw out a sword after them.

The LORD tells Ezekiel, the focus of the **son** of man, the focus of mankind in the fallen state as well as the focus of the **Son** of man, mankind in the restored state, that he should take a sharp knife, or take
a barber's razor, and cause it to pass on the head and on the beard to trim away the excess hair. Then take away the hair that has been removed, weigh it in the balances, and divide the hair into three parts. Since man is in the fallen state, the hair that symbolizes the fallen and distorted expressions that appear through the physical body, the mind and the emotions are removed. This hair shall be subjected to the fire that symbolizes the power of love from God, to the knife which symbolizes the instrument that cuts away that which is not of the truth, and to the wind, which symbolizes the movement of life in the invisible realm which can only be known because of the movement of visible material substance. The hair must be burned with fire in the midst of the city of Jerusalem when the days of the siege are fulfilled. The city of Jerusalem is a symbol of the state of consciousness of the people who live in the holy city. The people have developed a "siege mentality" which is a severe form of the fallen state of the people. The fire of the power of love is required to burn away the negative emotions of the fallen state.

There is also a second part of hair, distorted expressions of the mind which must be cut away, symbolically, with a knife or a razor because true healing and the return to the true state cannot be achieved with the memory of the expressions of the fallen mind that cause destruction. The third part of the hair, the physical aspects of the distortions of the true state, can not be thrown to the winds for elimination from the experience of a person until the person is willing to let the wrong behaviors pass away from their fallen and distorted character. These three aspects of the destruction of the emotional, mental and physical which are wrong must transpire before the fourth aspect of man can put in an appearance. The fourth aspect is called the sword, the sword of the truth of man, which was described by Isaiah as a

The Testimony of the Major Prophets

group of people who will let the spirit of the LORD find expression through each one as a group to compose the sword of truth, the truth of man made in the image and likeness of God. The LORD can not draw out the sword of man until man in the fallen state is willing to let his distortions pass away as distorted and discarded hair that symbolizes the distorted expression of man. No one is expected to eliminate all of their distortions, all of their wild hair, at one time. It is an ongoing process.

3 Thou shalt also take thereof a few in number, and bind them in thy skirts.
4 Then take of them again, and cast them into the midst of the fire, and burn them in the fire; for thereof shall a fire come forth into all the house of Israel.
5 Thus saith the Lord GOD; This is Jerusalem: I have set it in the midst of the nations and countries that are round about her.
6 And she hath changed my judgments into wickedness more than the nations, and my statutes more than the countries that are round about her: for they have refused my judgments and my statutes, they have not walked in them.

A person is to take only a few of the distortions of the spirit, sins, in number and bind them in the skirts, the clothing of the day, and then take them each day and cast the wrong behaviors into the midst of the fire that comes from God in heaven constantly and burn them. In this manner, the true fire from God in heaven shall come forth from the whole house of Israel.

Then the Lord GOD shall say, This is Jerusalem, the true spiritual city of peace, which the LORD has set in the midst of the nations and the countries round about. This is the new Jerusalem that is always available to rise up out of the ashes of the old Jerusalem. The LORD is always sending the New Jerusalem to replace the distortions of the old Jerusalem which has been produced by the sins of the fathers. The distortions are referred to as a fallen woman, a whore, the symbol of who has brought forth the fallen son of man. The whore, the material woman of the fallen state, has changed the true judgments of the LORD into the fallen state, into wickedness that is more than the nations and the countries which are round about the city of Jerusalem. This worldwide distortion has occurred because the people have refused the judgments and the statutes of the LORD which the LORD has constantly sent to the Son of man from the beginning. The LORD has sent man the correct judgments but the people have not walked in the LORD's statutes; they have walked in their own distorted paths doing their own distorted things.

7 Therefore thus saith the Lord GOD; Because ye multiplied more than the nations that are round about you, and have not walked in my statutes, neither have kept my judgments, neither have done according to the judgments of the nations that are round about you;
8 Therefore thus saith the Lord GOD; Behold, I, even I, am against thee, and will execute judgments in the midst of thee in the sight of the nations.
9 And I will do in thee that which I have not done, and whereunto I will not do any more the like, because of all thine abominations.

Therefore, the Lord GOD has said that because of the fallen nature of what man has sown on earth, because he has multiplied other than the judgments and statutes of the LORD, then even the Lord GOD is against the people of Jerusalem and the children of Israel because of the abominations that they have expressed in their living. What is being done in and through the fallen people are things that the Lord GOD would not do because they are abominations produced from the rebellion of the people who are in the fallen state. The distorted and abominable wrong behaviors of the sons are mingled with the wrong behaviors of the fathers and the wrong behaviors multiply.

10 Therefore the fathers shall eat the sons in the midst of thee, and the sons shall eat their fathers; and I will execute judgments in thee, and the whole remnant of thee will I scatter into all the winds.
11 Wherefore, as I live, saith the Lord GOD; Surely, because thou hast defiled my sanctuary with all thy detestable things, and with all thine abominations, therefore will I also diminish thee; neither shall mine eye spare, neither will I have any pity.

Therefore the fathers will "eat", assimilate, the wrong behaviors of their sons and the sons shall "eat", ingest the wrong behaviors of the fathers: and the power of the LORD working through the fallen consciousness of the people shall execute judgments that will produce distorted conditions in the environment which the Lord GOD shall surely scatter to the winds.

Wherefore, as the Lord GOD lives through and in his people, the people have defiled the sanctuary of the LORD with all detestable things and abominations that erupt from the fallen consciousness of man. Therefore, the LORD will diminish man from his divine stature and reduce him to a fallen stature from which fallen man will generate the terrible conditions in which he must live. The eye of the LORD shall not spare man from his self-created environment and the LORD shall have no pity on fallen man who will suffer diseases, famine, pestilence and death.

12 A third part of thee shall die with the pestilence, and with famine shall they be consumed in the midst of thee: and a third part shall fall by the sword round about thee; and I will scatter a third part into all the winds, and I will draw out a sword after them.
13 Thus shall mine anger be accomplished, and I will cause my fury to rest upon them, and I will be comforted: and they shall know that I the LORD have spoken it in my zeal, when I have accomplished my fury in them.
14 Moreover I will make thee waste, and a reproach among the nations that are round about thee, in the sight of all that pass by.

The Lord GOD describes how people in the fallen state who are in your midst and who have rebelled against the LORD shall die with pestilence and with famine: instead of the glory of the LORD coming through the people, the anger of the LORD shall be applied to the rebellious people as the same power is used against them because they are in the wrong position. War, and anger and fury shall come to rest upon the people and the LORD will be satisfied because of the working of the law. The working of the law of the LORD shall comfort the LORD and the people shall know that the fury of the LORD has been accomplished in them. In addition, waste and reproach shall be among the nations that are round about the people in the sight of all who pass by.

15 So it shall be a reproach and a taunt, an instruction and an astonishment unto the nations that are round about thee, when I shall execute judgments in thee in anger and in fury and in furious rebukes. I the LORD have spoken it.
16 When I shall send upon them the evil arrows of famine, which shall be for their destruction, and which I will send to destroy you: and I will increase the famine upon you, and will break your staff of bread:
17 So will I send upon you famine and evil beasts, and they shall bereave thee; and pestilence and blood shall pass through thee; and I will bring the sword upon thee. I the LORD have spoken it.

The LORD has spoken that His power shall be a reproach and a taunt, and nations round about shall be astonished when the LORD executes judgments of fury and anger in his people. The LORD has set the punishment for the rebellious people: it is famine from the heavenly bread of the spirit of the LORD which shall result in physical famine; and evil beasts of people that shall cause much grief. Pestilence and blood shall pass through the son of man as the destructive aspect of the sword brings certain damage.

CHAPTER 6

1 And the word of the LORD came unto me, saying,
2 Son of man, set thy face toward the mountains of Israel, and prophesy against them,
3 And say, Ye mountains of Israel, hear the word of the Lord GOD; Thus saith the Lord GOD to the mountains, and to the hills, to the rivers, and to the valleys; Behold, I, even I, will bring a sword upon you, and I will destroy your high places.
4 And your altars shall be desolate, and your images shall be broken: and I will cast down your slain men before your idols.
5 And I will lay the dead carcases of the children of Israel before their idols; and I will scatter your bones round about your altars.

The word of the LORD came to Ezekiel, who is addressed as the Son of man, the focalization of the spiritual offspring, the Son of man, who is a pattern for any individual in the body of mankind. The Son of man is the true identity in the restored or ascended state; the position from which man fell in his separation from the LORD. The Son of man, Ezekiel, is commanded to set his face toward the mountains of Israel, the present leaders of Israel in the fallen state, and prophesy against them, against the position in the fallen state which they advocate. Ezekiel is to tell the leaders, the mountains, that carry the responsibility of the people, as well as the hills, who are people in reduced positions of leadership, whose authority flows out to the masses as water flows from the high places through the rivers and the valleys, that a change is coming. The LORD will bring a sword upon the existing power structure of the fallen state and the sword will destroy the high places which they presently occupy in their self-centered ways.

The altars that they have built to their false gods shall be made desolate, and the images that they have made shall be broken by the spiritual sword of truth which comes from the LORD. The sword is the spirit of the LORD moving through the physical forms of the LORD's people. The moving spirit will destroy and cast down the men of the fallen state before their idols which are made of material objects. The moving spirit of the LORD will lay dead the carcasses, remove the life from the false beliefs of the children of Israel before their idols; the bones, the structures which hold the false patterns of organizations together, will be scattered around their altars. The living spirit of the LORD moving through the people will destroy the false forms and replace the old forms with new forms that are shaped by the spirit of the LORD.

6 In all your dwellingplaces the cities shall be laid waste, and the high places shall be desolate; that your altars may be laid waste and made desolate, and your idols may be broken and cease, and your images may be cut down, and your works may be abolished.
7 And the slain shall fall in the midst of you, and ye shall know that I am the LORD.

Since almost all of mankind is in the fallen state, the forms of mankind are distortions of the true state. All of the dwelling places of the cities shall be laid to waste as the divine pattern of the LORD replaces the cities created by human nature. The altars of human nature shall be laid waste and made desolate, the idols which human nature worships shall be broken, the images of human nature may be cut down, and the works of sinful man may be abolished. These changes will occur automatically as people begin to accept the moving spirit of the LORD, which is the sword of the LORD. As this is done, the false creature, the counterfeit human self, shall fall in the midst of you and the person who accepts the moving spirit of the LORD as his or her own shall know the reality of the identity, the I Am, that is the LORD. This acceptance of the spirit of the LORD does not happen unless each person accepts the spiritual sword of the LORD's spirit as one's own. There will be a transition from human nature to the original divine nature of man made in the image and likeness of God. The spirit of the LORD must come to individual focus within each person.

8 Yet will I leave a remnant, that ye may have some that shall escape the sword among the nations, when ye shall be scattered through the countries.
9 And they that escape of you shall remember me among the nations whither they shall be carried captives, because I am broken with their whorish heart, which hath departed from me, and with their eyes, which go a whoring after their idols: and they shall lothe themselves for the evils which they have committed in all their abominations.
10 And they shall know that I am the LORD, and that I have not said in vain that I would do this evil unto them.

A remnant, a residue of the fallen state, shall escape the spiritual sword, that is flowing through everyone who is alive. The people who refuse to accept the sword shall escape the living sword and be scattered among the nations and the countries which do not know the LORD. The people who are scattered do not carry the spirit of the LORD, the sword, in their hearts: they are not part of the sword. They that escape the conscious participation with the spirit of the LORD shall remember the LORD wherever they are carried as captives of the material world because they do not know the LORD in their own hearts. The covenant, the connection with the LORD is broken by a whorish heart, a heart that has departed from the spirit of the LORD to find solace in worshipping the idols of the material things of the world. A person must go whoring after material idols with their eyes trying to seek the treasures of the environment: and they loathe themselves because they have forsaken the LORD for the atoms and the molecules of the things in the environment, the evils that they seek, which are an abomination in the sight of the LORD because they are distortions of the true design. The LORD shall allow the people who seek the evils to reap them and to forsake the experience of the LORD. The fact that they are not one with the LORD is proof that they do not know the LORD. The LORD has not said in vain when He has allowed the Law of Sowing and Reaping to bring this evil consequence upon them.

11 Thus saith the Lord GOD; Smite with thine hand, and stamp with thy foot, and say, Alas for all the evil abominations of the house of Israel! for they shall fall by the sword, by the famine, and by the pestilence.

The LORD has given to the people through Ezekiel the formula for knowing the divine spirit. The person must make a commitment that is symbolized by smiting with one's hand and stamping one's foot in a gesture of authority that they will turn away from all the material controls, the evil abominations of the house of Israel which have been placed above the LORD! Once this act of authority is done, the idols and all material controls made of atoms and molecules shall fall by the acceptance of the spiritual sword and famine and pestilence shall result to cause the deterioration of the false patterns which cannot survive when the person ceases to give the material things their life force which comes from God. When the sword of the LORD is represented on earth, changes come quickly in two ways.

12 He that is far off shall die of the pestilence; and he that is near shall fall by the sword; and he that remaineth and is besieged shall die by the famine: thus will I accomplish my fury upon them.

He that is far off from the focus of the spirit, the sword, shall die of pestilence, the sickness which comes when the spirit of life is absent. There is no need to fight against the abominations and evil because they will naturally pass away. He that is near to the sword shall fall by the sword as he accepts the sword, the spirit of the LORD, as his own, then the false self is slain by the spirit which he has accepted. The people who remain, uncommitted, shall die by the famine as less spiritual nourishment is received by them. The absence of the spirit of the LORD is the means by which the LORD accomplishes his fury upon the people who do not accept his spirit.

13 Then shall ye know that I am the LORD, when their slain men shall be among their idols round about their altars, upon every high hill, in all the tops of the mountains, and under every green tree, and under every thick oak, the place where they did offer sweet savour to all their idols.

The Testimony of the Major Prophets

14 So will I stretch out my hand upon them, and make the land desolate, yea, more desolate than the wilderness toward Diblath, in all their habitations: and they shall know that I am the LORD

The people who desire the living and moving spirit of the LORD shall know that there is a living and moving spirit when they shall see slain men worshipped as idols round about their altars which are constructed upon every high hill, mountain top, green tree, and the places where they offer sweet savor and worship to their idols. When this is seen, the person should remember that the LORD is within them.

Then the person who is alive by means of the spirit of the LORD shall stretch out his hand of spiritual control upon the people who worship idols and make their land more desolate than the wilderness toward Diblath in Moab. The people who do this and represent the LORD shall know the reality of the LORD in their own experience.

CHAPTER 7

1 Moreover the word of the LORD came unto me, saying,
2 Also, thou son of man, thus saith the Lord GOD unto the land of Israel; An end, the end is come upon the four corners of the land.
3 Now is the end come upon thee, and I will send mine anger upon thee, and will judge thee according to thy ways, and will recompense upon thee all thine abominations.
4 And mine eye shall not spare thee, neither will I have pity: but I will recompense thy ways upon thee, and thine abominations shall be in the midst of thee: and ye shall know that I am the LORD.

The word of the LORD came to Ezekiel, who was a revelation of the spiritual strength of God on earth, with this instruction for the son of man, mankind in the fallen state, which is to be delivered to the house of Israel, who are the people who state that they are interested in the way of the LORD on earth. The message is that an end is come to the four corners of the land of the fallen state of affairs on earth. The end is come to the fallen state because the LORD has a true pattern in the person of Ezekiel to reveal the truth of man as compared with the distortion that mankind has become since he fell from grace, the divine estate, when man revealed the image and likeness of God.

Now, in the present time, which is any time that the LORD can reveal his spirit accurately through a person, the end of the distorted, deviled state when the true state can reveal itself. When this occurs, then the LORD can send his anger upon mankind because there is a true pattern to which fallen man can orient himself. The law of the LORD, the Law of Sowing and Reaping, will "reward" man consciously according to his behaviors. Mankind shall know that he shall be recompensed for his abominations. The eye of the LORD will not spare man, nor will the LORD have pity on man because the true representative of the LORD on earth will make fallen man know the implications and the ramifications of the working of the law and that man's behavior produces the results of his behavior. The abominations of man's behavior produces conditions in which man must abide. This is the working of the Law. And the people who see the operation of the Law of the LORD shall know that if the law of the LORD is at work then the LORD is present and alive in the affairs of men.

5 Thus saith the Lord GOD; An evil, an only evil, behold, is come.
6 An end is come, the end is come: it watcheth for thee; behold, it is come.
7 The morning is come unto thee, O thou that dwellest in the land: the time is come, the day of trouble is near, and not the sounding again of the mountains.
8 Now will I shortly pour out my fury upon thee, and accomplish mine anger upon thee: and I will judge thee according to thy ways, and will recompense thee for all thine abominations.
9 And mine eye shall not spare, neither will I have pity: I will recompense thee according to thy ways and thine abominations that are in the midst of thee; and ye shall know that I am the LORD that smiteth.

The Testimony of the Major Prophets

Ezekiel delivers the message of the LORD; Behold and observe the evil conditions that have come on earth which are the results of the vision and behaviors of fallen man. The material conditions of the environment made of atoms and molecules are the end result of the spiritual expression—accurate or distorted—which occurs as the spirit of the LORD creates conditions through the consciousness of men and women. The end of this creative process is come. It, the material world, watches for the nature of the expression of the people to produce the results in observable forms. Behold, observe, this is how the nature of conditions become the way that they are and the way that they will be.

The morning, the dawning of the light, as to how the LORD makes conditions on earth, has come to those who will observe and see. This is the working of the Law. A person who dwells in the land shall see that the time has come for them to know how the day of trouble arrives on earth. The day of trouble is as near as the condition of one's own consciousness and the troubled conditions do not come from the mountains, the high leaders of the world. The LORD will pour out his fury upon mankind and accomplish his anger upon man according to the Law of Sowing and Reaping. According to this law, which is never repealed, the LORD judges what appears in form based upon the conditions which exist in the consciousness of man. People are recompensed according to their own abominations. The eye of the LORD will not spare anyone from the operation of the law, nor will the LORD have pity on anyone. The Law must be dependable and the Law must work. The LORD will recompense mankind according to his ways and his abominations that are in the midst of his heart and mind, his own consciousness; as people observe the working of the law then they shall know and you shall know that it is the LORD that smites them based upon their own behavior.

10 Behold the day, behold, it is come: the morning is gone forth; the rod hath blossomed, pride hath budded.
11 Violence is risen up into a rod of wickedness: none of them shall remain, nor of their multitude, nor of any of theirs: neither shall there be wailing for them.

Behold the day of the LORD at work on earth is come. The morning awareness has gone forth as to how things become the way that they do. The rod, the control of conditions through people, has blossomed, and pride had budded on earth due to the working of the Law. Violence within the hearts of the people has risen up out of the rod, the person who is wicked. None of the violent people shall remain, nor of their multitudes, nor any like them; neither shall their be any wailing for the violent people because the person begins to see and understand that the kingdom of the LORD cannot come through violent and wicked people. People who love the LORD begin to see the operation of the Law in the present time in the interactions between men and women who compose one body of inter-connected people. These inter-connected people are referred to as the buyer and the seller.

12 The time is come, the day draweth near: let not the buyer rejoice, nor the seller mourn: for wrath is upon all the multitude thereof.
13 For the seller shall not return to that which is sold, although they were yet alive: for the vision is touching the whole multitude thereof, which shall not return; neither shall any strengthen himself in the iniquity of his life.

The time is come and the day is here for people to see and understand that the buyer cannot rejoice nor the seller mourn in the event of a bad bargain: the wrath of the result of a bad bargain is upon the whole multitude of the people. The seller is the person who expresses the spirit of the LORD through his own state of consciousness. Once a behavior is "sold", or expressed, the seller cannot return the behavior which has been expressed to the past as though the past is still alive. Life and the power of the LORD is always in the present. The true vision is to be able to see that what is expressed touches the whole multitude of the people and that no behavior can ever be returned to the past. Neither shall any person ever strengthen himself by iniquity, evil, sin, abomination or wrong function which poisons the body of mankind. It is impossible to fight against iniquity and evil which has been expressed in the past.

14 They have blown the trumpet, even to make all ready; but none goeth to the battle: for my wrath is upon all the multitude thereof.
15 The sword is without, and the pestilence and the famine within: he that is in the field shall die with the sword; and he that is in the city, famine and pestilence shall devour him.
16 But they that escape of them shall escape, and shall be on the mountains like doves of the valleys, all of them mourning, every one for his iniquity.
17 All hands shall be feeble, and all knees shall be weak as water.

18 They shall also gird themselves with sackcloth, and horror shall cover them; and shame shall be upon all faces, and baldness upon all their heads.

There are those who try to fight against the evil in the material world as they blow the trumpet to make ready to do battle against evil; but no one goes to the battle against evil which was expressed in the past when the evil is already growing in the multitude of the body of mankind. The sword of the truth is without, outside of, the body of mankind in the realm of spirit, and the pestilence and the famine are within the physical body of mankind. He who is in the field of the material body of mankind shall die by means of the spiritual sword which is spirit; and he that is in the material city, the forms of the earth, shall be devoured by the famine and pestilence which have been expressed into the material body of mankind. The only hope for fallen man is to rise up out of identification with the physical body and escape from it.

But the people who escape out of the control of the material body shall escape from the famine and the pestilence that exists in the physical form. The individual may escape from the valley of the material form to the mountain of the spiritual substance. The person who escapes from the material world to the spiritual world shall be positioned on the mountains like doves are in the valleys, all of them mourning, every one for the iniquity that he has contributed by his own expression into the body of mankind. This mourning with regard to wrong behavior accomplishes nothing constructive. Ezekiel describes the people who mourn with hands that are feeble, and knees as weak as water; useless hands and weak-kneed in the present expression of spirit. The useless and weak-kneed people shall also gird themselves with sackcloth, and horror shall cover them; and shame shall be upon all faces, and baldness upon all their heads. They are wasting their spiritual expression from the LORD which is symbolized as silver and gold that represent the spirit of truth and the spirit of love from the LORD.

19 They shall cast their silver in the streets, and their gold shall be removed: their silver and their gold shall not be able to deliver them in the day of the wrath of the LORD: they shall not satisfy their souls, neither fill their bowels: because it is the stumblingblock of their iniquity.
20 As for the beauty of his ornament, he set it in majesty: but they made the images of their abominations and of their detestable things therein: therefore have I set it far from them.
21 And I will give it into the hands of the strangers for a prey, and to the wicked of the earth for a spoil; and they shall pollute it.

The people who continue to mourn are like those who cast their silver in the streets and their gold is removed from them; they are wasting their spiritual treasures of truth and love, symbolized by silver and gold, that should be expressed into the ailing physical body. Material silver and gold shall not deliver them in the day of the wrath of the LORD which had its source in another time, in the past. The people who mourn because of their past behavior shall not satisfy their souls or fill the emptiness of their emotional bowels because what they are doing is the stumbling block of their iniquity. They continue to sin by their complaint and mournful expression. There is another expression that is totally different from the wrath of the LORD.

It is the divine expression from the LORD which is the beauty of his ornament, that is set in the majesty of the LORD. But the sinners have made images of the gift of beauty in their abominable behaviors and the detestable things that they have created with the gifts from the LORD. Therefore, the LORD has set beauty far from the sinners so that the beauty of the LORD is not available to those who continue to mourn and repeat the fallen behavior of mankind. The gift from the LORD—the pure spirit of love, truth and life—is given into the hands of strangers to prey upon, and to the wicked of the earth as a spoil and the wicked people shall pollute the gift from the LORD. The LORD who is present will not be with the people consciously because the people are not one with the spirit of the LORD.

22 My face will I turn also from them, and they shall pollute my secret place: for the robbers shall enter into it, and defile it.
23 Make a chain: for the land is full of bloody crimes, and the city is full of violence.
24 Wherefore I will bring the worst of the heathen, and they shall possess their houses: I will also make the pomp of the strong to cease; and their holy places shall be defiled.
25 Destruction cometh; and they shall seek peace, and there shall be none.

The Testimony of the Major Prophets

26 Mischief shall come upon mischief, and rumour shall be upon rumour; then shall they seek a vision of the prophet; but the law shall perish from the priest, and counsel from the ancients.
27 The king shall mourn, and the prince shall be clothed with desolation, and the hands of the people of the land shall be troubled: I will do unto them after their way, and according to their deserts will I judge them; and they shall know that I am the LORD.

The face of the LORD, which is always present, is turned away from the people who are behaving abominably. Abominable behavior pollutes the secret place of the LORD within themselves. The sinners who do not serve the LORD are as robbers who steal the gift of life for themselves and they defile the gift when they do not use it to build the kingdom of the LORD. The life force from the LORD is used to make a chain for the robbers who have made a land that is filled with bloody crimes and the city that is full of violence. Man in the fallen state makes the chains of behaviors which bind him to the fallen state. The power of the LORD is used to create the worst that the heathen can bring and the distortions shall possess their houses: The LORD will make the pomp of the strong to cease and their holy places shall be defiled when they do not reveal the sprit of the LORD.

It is understandable that destruction will come upon them because they rebelled against the spirit of the LORD and they shall desire to seek peace which they sense is available and there shall be no peace for them as long as they are separate from the LORD. Mischief shall come upon mischief, and rumor upon rumor as they continue in their fallen ways. Then they, in the misery which they have created, shall seek the vision of a prophet, but the understanding of the universal application law of Sowing and Reaping shall perish from the teaching of a priest and the counsel of the ancients shall be forgotten.

The king, the fallen human ego, of their fallen state shall mourn, and the prince, the expression and offspring of the king, his earthly father, shall be clothed with desolation, and the hands, the creations, of the people of the land shall be troubled. The working of the Law of the LORD will do unto them after their way according to their behaviors which are sown as seeds, and according to their deserts, the dry conditions which they have created, will the LORD judge them; and they shall know that the LORD is with them as his law works.

CHAPTER 8

1 And it came to pass in the sixth year, in the sixth month, in the fifth day of the month, as I sat in mine house, and the elders of Judah sat before me, that the hand of the Lord GOD fell there upon me.
2 Then I beheld, and lo a likeness as the appearance of fire: from the appearance of his loins even downward, fire; and from his loins even upward, as the appearance of brightness, as the colour of amber.

Ezekiel describes another encounter which he has with the Lord God. This second encounter occurs one year and two months after his first encounter with the LORD that is recorded in Chapter 1 when he was 30 years of age. Ezekiel is very specific about the dates of his experiences with the LORD which would be very memorable and unforgettable to the person who had the divine encounter. When the hand of the Lord GOD descended upon Ezekiel to produce a vision in his consciousness, the elders of Judah were with him in his house.

Ezekiel state that he beheld a likeness which had the appearance of fire. It was not fire but it had the appearance of fire. Fire is the symbol of love that illustrates the presence of God. Ezekiel describes the appearance as fire from the loins downward as fire, and from the appearance of the loins upward as brightness, as the color of amber which is golden-yellow. The brightness of the light that symbolizes truth and the appearance of fire that symbolizes the power of love is an illustration of deity in the consciousness of Ezekiel.

3 And he put forth the form of an hand, and took me by a lock of mine head; and the spirit lifted me up between the earth and the heaven, and brought me in the visions of God to Jerusalem, to the door of the inner gate that looketh toward the north; where was the seat of the image of jealousy, which provoketh to jealousy.
4 And, behold, the glory of the God of Israel was there, according to the vision that I saw in the plain.

Ezekiel describes the action of God lifting up his consciousness in material terms as putting forth his hand and lifting him up by a lock of the hair of his head to a position between the earth and the heaven, which is the connecting point between heaven and earth in the place of the covenant. It is at this point that Ezekiel experiences visions of Jerusalem to the door of the inner gate that looks to the north. It is at this point where the seat of the image of jealousy is located. A person who sits in this seat is provoked to be jealous. Ezekiel further describes that the glory of the God of Israel was there, according to the vision that Ezekiel saw in the plain. It is the God of Israel who speaks to Ezekiel.

5 Then said he unto me, Son of man, lift up thine eyes now the way toward the north. So I lifted up mine eyes the way toward the north, and behold northward at the gate of the altar this image of jealousy in the entry.
6 He said furthermore unto me, Son of man, seest thou what they do? even the great abominations that the house of Israel committeth here, that I should go far off from my sanctuary? but turn thee yet again, and thou shalt see greater abominations.

The Testimony of the Major Prophets

God addresses Ezekiel as the focus point of the spirit of God that is with man, the Son of man, and instructs him to lift up his eyes toward the north to see the image of jealousy at the entry place of the gate. Ezekiel is shown in the vision that jealousy is in the way between Jerusalem (the form) and Israel (the spirit). Furthermore, God asks the Son of man, the spiritual person to whom He is speaking, Ezekiel, if he sees what they do? Does the Son of man see the great abominations that the house of Israel, the people who inhabit the land to the north, are committing by their actions and behaviors which cause God to go afar off, to leave, His sanctuary which is within the people of Israel? God cannot dwell where there are abominations: the abominations would be repelled away from God as Adam and Eve were repelled from the Garden of Eden. Jealousy is not the only abomination that God desires to show Ezekiel: turn again and see even greater abominations than jealousy.

7 And he brought me to the door of the court; and when I looked, behold a hole in the wall.
8 Then said he unto me, Son of man, dig now in the wall: and when I had digged in the wall, behold a door.
9 And he said unto me, Go in, and behold the wicked abominations that they do here.
10 So I went in and saw; and behold every form of creeping things, and abominable beasts, and all the idols of the house of Israel, portrayed upon the wall round about.

God brought the consciousness of Ezekiel to the door of the court in Jerusalem; and when Ezekiel, the Son of man, looked, he saw a hole in the wall. The Son of man was instructed by God to dig in the wall where the hole was seen and the hole became a door, the enlargement of the small hole. Ezekiel is encouraged to go in through the door and observe the people of the house of Israel to behold with his own eyes the abominations that the people of the house of Israel actually do in their living. God has been aware of the abominations and He is making Ezekiel aware of the view that God has known all along. The Son of man did go in and he saw the behaviors of the people who comprise the house of Israel, These distorted behaviors, sinful behaviors, took every form of creeping things and abominable beasts that man made in the image and likeness of God had become. Ezekiel saw all of these idols, all of the behaviors that the people of the house of Israel were worshipping, portrayed on the wall of his consciousness round about, everywhere that he looked. God is sharing His vision with Ezekiel so that the Father and the Son of man can see the conditions of seventy leaders of the house of Israel with the same divine vision.

11 And there stood before them seventy men of the ancients of the house of Israel, and in the midst of them stood Jaazaniah the son of Shaphan, with every man his censer in his hand; and a thick cloud of incense went up.
12 Then said he unto me, Son of man, hast thou seen what the ancients of the house of Israel do in the dark, every man in the chambers of his imagery? for they say, The LORD seeth us not; the LORD hath forsaken the earth.

In the vision, there stood before God and Ezekiel, seventy men of the ancients, the wisest leaders of the house of Israel, every man with his censer in his hand. The censer is the symbol of the human equipment that a person uses to make an offering to the LORD and the thick cloud of incense is the offering of individual behavior that rises up from the censer to the glory of God. In the midst of the seventy leaders stood Jaazaniah, which means, "whom the LORD will hear". He is the son, the offspring of Shaphan, whose name means, "a wild rat".

The God said to Ezekiel, the Son of man, Have you seen what the ancients of the house of Israel do in the dark, every man in the chambers of his imagery where he creates the images of his fallen, abominable behavior? The leaders of the house of Israel say, that the LORD does not see us and what we do; The leaders say that the LORD has forsaken the earth and that He is not present.

13 He said also unto me, Turn thee yet again, and thou shalt see greater abominations that they do.
14 Then he brought me to the door of the gate of the LORD's house which was toward the north; and, behold, there sat women weeping for Tammuz.

God wants to share even more with the Son of man and asks him to turn again and see even greater abominations that are done by the ancients, the leaders of the house of Israel. God brought Ezekiel to the door of the gate of the LORD's house which is toward the north, toward Israel. There are other gates in other directions because the earth is the LORD's in every direction. Behold, there sat women weeping for Tammuz. Tammuz was the Babylonian god of fertility. The women were weeping because they sensed that better conditions were available and since the conditions did not improve under the leadership of the ancients of the house of Israel and their abominable behavior, the women were praying to the fertility god of Babylon to produce results.

15 Then said he unto me, Hast thou seen this, O son of man? turn thee yet again, and thou shalt see greater abominations than these.
16 And he brought me into the inner court of the LORD's house, and, behold, at the door of the temple of the LORD, between the porch and the altar, were about five and twenty men, with their backs toward the temple of the LORD, and their faces toward the east; and they worshipped the sun toward the east.

Then God asked Ezekiel if the Son of man has seen this abomination? Turn again and see these greater abominations to the God of Israel. God brought Ezekiel to the inner court of the LORD's house and showed him at the door of the temple, between the porch and the altar, about twenty-five men with their backs toward the temple of the LORD and their faces were toward the east. Ezekiel could see that the men who should be serving the LORD had their backs toward the LORD and their faces were toward the east, to Babylon, to the material wealth of the kingdom toward the east where they worshipped the material success of Babylon.

17 Then he said unto me, Hast thou seen this, O son of man? Is it a light thing to the house of Judah that they commit the abominations which they commit here? for they have filled the land with violence, and have returned to provoke me to anger: and, lo, they put the branch to their nose.
18 Therefore will I also deal in fury: mine eye shall not spare, neither will I have pity: and though they cry in mine ears with a loud voice, yet will I not hear them.

Then God said to Ezekiel, the son of man who also represented mankind in the fallen state, if he has seen this vision previously? Is it a light thing to the house of Judah that the house of Israel commits the abominations which they commit here? The house of Israel has filled the land with violence and they have returned to provoke the LORD to anger as they put the branch to their nose, as they put the branch of the LORD's tree, which they should represent, to their nose to smell how much they can get away with in rebellion against the LORD while taking the name of the LORD in vain, in their own vanity.

Therefore, because of their wicked and abominable behavior, which is not the acceptable worship of the LORD, the rebellious people shall be dealt with in fury and wrath which is the result of rebelling against the spirit of the LORD. The eye of the LORD shall not spare or have pity on them, the people who rebel against the spirit of the LORD: and though they cry in the ears of the LORD with a loud voice, the LORD will not hear them.

CHAPTER 9

1 He cried also in mine ears with a loud voice, saying, Cause them that have charge over the city to draw near, even every man with his destroying weapon in his hand.
2 And, behold, six men came from the way of the higher gate, which lieth toward the north, and every man a slaughter weapon in his hand; and one man among them was clothed with linen, with a writer's inkhorn by his side: and they went in, and stood beside the brasen altar.

The vision continues as the Lord GOD loudly calls into the ears of Ezekiel, into the consciousness of Ezekiel, who is willing to hear the word of the spirit of the LORD, the message to rally the people to take charge over the city of Jerusalem. The people are to draw near and every man should have a destroying weapon in his hand. In the vision, six men came from the northern gate that opened toward Israel that was to the north, and every man had a slaughter weapon in his hand which indicated that they carried instruments of destruction. One man among them was clothed with linen with a writer's inkhorn, a writing kit, at his side to record the activities of the group. The six armed men went in to the bronze altar.

3 And the glory of the God of Israel was gone up from the cherub, whereupon he was, to the threshold of the house. And he called to the man clothed with linen, which had the writer's inkhorn by his side;
4 And the LORD said unto him, Go through the midst of the city, through the midst of Jerusalem, and set a mark upon the foreheads of the men that sigh and that cry for all the abominations that be done in the midst thereof.

The glory of the God of Israel went up from the cherub, the heavenly spirit which must proceed from an angel of God, to the threshold, the door sill of the entrance to the house where the glory of the LORD is located. The LORD called the man clothed with linen with the inkhorn by his side and instructed him to go through the midst of the city, the midst of Jerusalem, and set a mark upon the foreheads of the men who sigh and cry, who long for a change to occur so that all the abominations be ended in the city. The LORD is interested in placing a mark on those people who desire for the abominations in the people to come to an end.

5 And to the others he said in mine hearing, Go ye after him through the city, and smite: let not your eye spare, neither have ye pity:
6 Slay utterly old and young, both maids, and little children, and women: but come not near any man upon whom is the mark; and begin at my sanctuary. Then they began at the ancient men which were before the house.
7 And he said unto them, Defile the house, and fill the courts with the slain: go ye forth. And they went forth, and slew in the city.

Ezekiel heard the LORD tell the others to go after the man in linen and destroy, without exception and without pity, everyone who does not have the mark. This includes the young and old, the maids, children and women. And the destruction is to begin at the door to the sanctuary. The destruction began by the men with their weapons of destruction at the ancient men, the leaders with their ideas from the past, which were before the house where the LORD resides. The LORD has authorized the destruction of the people who did not want to bring about the end of abominations. Their destruction would defile the house and fill the courts with the people who were slain. In symbolic images, the destructive forces with their weapons went forth and did slay the people in the city who did not have the mark upon them according to the working of the Law.

8 And it came to pass, while they were slaying them, and I was left, that I fell upon my face, and cried, and said, Ah Lord GOD! wilt thou destroy all the residue of Israel in thy pouring out of thy fury upon Jerusalem?
9 Then said he unto me, The iniquity of the house of Israel and Judah is exceeding great, and the land is full of blood, and the city full of perverseness: for they say, The LORD hath forsaken the earth, and the LORD seeth not.
10 And as for me also, mine eye shall not spare, neither will I have pity, but I will recompense their way upon their head.
11 And, behold, the man clothed with linen, which had the inkhorn by his side, reported the matter, saying, I have done as thou hast commanded me.

While the destruction of the workers of abomination was taking place, Ezekiel fell upon his face in a gesture that he did not want to see the slaying of the people and he asked if the Lord GOD would destroy all of Israel in the pouring out of the fury which is being heaped upon Jerusalem? The LORD instructed Ezekiel that the iniquity of the house of Israel and Judah is exceedingly great, the land is full of blood and the city is full of perverse behavior: the wicked people say that the LORD has forsaken the earth and that the LORD does not see what is transpiring. The LORD is being blamed for the wickedness of the people. The LORD declares that the people will be recompensed according to their deeds without exception or pity.

The vision of Ezekiel reveals that the man clothed with linen and with the writing kit reported that he had done what the LORD had commanded. In symbolic language, the vision of Ezekiel teaches in language that the people can understand, that the sins of the fathers, the abominations of the people, shall result in death and the people who long for the absence of abominations shall live. The vision offers life or death to the people based upon their individual behavior and choice. This is the working of the Law. However, the mere survival of those who desire an end to the abominations is not the goal, the divine plan of the LORD.

CHAPTER 10

1 Then I looked, and, behold, in the firmament that was above the head of the cherubims there appeared over them as it were a sapphire stone, as the appearance of the likeness of a throne.
2 And he spake unto the man clothed with linen, and said, Go in between the wheels, even under the cherub, and fill thine hand with coals of fire from between the cherubims, and scatter them over the city. And he went in in my sight.

Once Ezekiel, the son of man, accepted the working of the Law of the LORD in the affairs of men, then he was able to observe more of the vision. In the firmament of the heaven that was above the head of the cherubim, the angels who bring the radiance of the LORD to the earth, there appeared over the cherubim a sapphire stone that had the appearance of the likeness of a throne. The blue sapphire is the symbol of the truth which is symbolized as a precious stone. The fact that it is in the shape of a throne symbolizes divine authority that is higher than the cherubim, the angels.

The LORD spoke to the man clothed with linen, the man who was interested in saving the people who were interested in the end of the abominations, and instructed him to go in between the wheels, the symbols of the divine machinery which are the people who desire to serve the spirit of the LORD on earth, below the place of the cherub, the heavenly spirit which everyone is, and fill his hand with the heavenly coals of fire, the symbol of divine behavior from the LORD, and scatter the coals of divine behavior, coals of warmth and light, over the city to spread the word of the LORD to the people in the fallen state who are willing to serve the LORD and live. And Ezekiel saw the man in linen as he went among the cherubim and did the command of the LORD.

3 Now the cherubims stood on the right side of the house, when the man went in; and the cloud filled the inner court.
4 Then the glory of the LORD went up from the cherub, and stood over the threshold of the house; and the house was filled with the cloud, and the court was full of the brightness of the LORD's glory.
5 And the sound of the cherubims' wings was heard even to the outer court, as the voice of the Almighty God when he speaketh.

As the man in linen, any man who is willing to do the command of the LORD, went in to the place where the cherubim reside on the right side, the clean side, of the house of the LORD, a cloud of glory filled the inner court. Then the glory of the LORD went up from the cherub, and stood over the threshold of the house; and the house was filled with the cloud of glory and the court was filled with the brightness of the LORD's glory. The glory of the LORD is magnified when a man in linen, a man from outside the gate, goes among the cherubim to gather coals of fire to help the people. When the man in linen, any man who does this service, he shall hear the sound of the wings of the cherubim even to the outer court as the voice of Almighty God when he speaks. The voice of the LORD is magnified on earth by the men and women dressed in linen who are willing to serve the word of God.

6 And it came to pass, that when he had commanded the man clothed with linen, saying, Take fire from between the wheels, from between the cherubims; then he went in, and stood beside the wheels.

7 And one cherub stretched forth his hand from between the cherubims unto the fire that was between the cherubims, and took thereof, and put it into the hands of him that was clothed with linen: who took it, and went out.
8 And there appeared in the cherubims the form of a man's hand under their wings.
9 And when I looked, behold the four wheels by the cherubims, one wheel by one cherub, and another wheel by another cherub: and the appearance of the wheels was as the colour of a beryl stone.

In Ezekiel's vision of the way that the power and light come from God to the people, it came to pass that God commanded the man clothed with linen to take fire from between the wheels of the cherubim, the divine machinery of beings in human forms, and the man in linen did go in and take his place beside the wheels as a part of the divine machinery. One cherub, a spiritual being, stretched forth his hand from between the cherubim to the fire that was between them, took some of the heavenly fire, and put it into the hands of the man that was clothed with linen. The man clothed with linen took the fire of God's love and went out to deliver it to the people in the fallen state. The man in linen will bring the heavenly fire into the earth.

There appeared in the cherubim the form of a man's hand, the man in linen, under their wings as a symbol that the hand of physical man has reached the level of the angel's wings. When Ezekiel looked, behold, he saw the four wheels of the cherubim, one wheel by each cherub, one human form to each cherub. The appearance of the earthly wheels, the physical machinery of the cherub, was as the color of beryl, multicolored to indicate physical diversity. But in their physical diversity, there was unity.

10 And as for their appearances, they four had one likeness, as if a wheel had been in the midst of a wheel.
11 When they went, they went upon their four sides; they turned not as they went, but to the place whither the head looked they followed it; they turned not as they went.
12 And their whole body, and their backs, and their hands, and their wings, and the wheels, were full of eyes round about, even the wheels that they four had.
13 As for the wheels, it was cried unto them in my hearing, O wheel.

As for their physical appearances, the four had one likeness, one spiritual likeness, as though each physical wheel had been in the midst of one spiritual wheel. When they, the four physical wheels, went they went upon their four separated physical sides, but they turned not, in different directions, as they went, they all moved together in oneness. They, the wheels, moved in the coordinated direction that the spiritual head looked and the wheels followed the spiritual head, the spiritual wheel which is the wheel that encompasses the physical wheels. The spirit and the forms are connected; they are one. Their whole body, their backs, their hands, their wings and the wheels were full of eyes to see in every direction and to see everything the same as it is. Even the physical wheels see everything the same because they see with spiritual vision. As for the four wheels, that symbolized the four people, Ezekiel heard the cry, O wheel, to indicate that the four wheels were one spiritual wheel available to the LORD as machinery of beings in human forms for the LORD's purpose.

14 And every one had four faces: the first face was the face of a cherub, and the second face was the face of a man, and the third the face of a lion, and the fourth the face of an eagle.
15 And the cherubims were lifted up. This is the living creature that I saw by the river of Chebar.
16 And when the cherubims went, the wheels went by them: and when the cherubims lifted up their wings to mount up from the earth, the same wheels also turned not from beside them.
17 When they stood, these stood; and when they were lifted up, these lifted up themselves also: for the spirit of the living creature was in them.

Every wheel, every person, had four faces: the first face was the face of an angelic, spiritual cherub, instead of an ox that symbolized an animalistic human mind; and the second face was the face of a man that could reveal positive emotions, and the third the face of a lion with physical strength under spiritual control, and the fourth the face of an eagle with divine vision. And the cherubim were lifted up in service toward the LORD. This is the living creature that Ezekiel saw by the river of Chebar, the river of power, except for the face of the ox which was replaced by the face of a cherub. The difference between the two creatures was that in one creature man thinks that he is an animal rather than a cherub, a spiritual being, in a human form!

The Testimony of the Major Prophets

18 Then the glory of the LORD departed from off the threshold of the house, and stood over the cherubims.
19 And the cherubims lifted up their wings, and mounted up from the earth in my sight: when they went out, the wheels also were beside them, and every one stood at the door of the east gate of the LORD's house; and the glory of the God of Israel was over them above.
20 This is the living creature that I saw under the God of Israel by the river of Chebar; and I knew that they were the cherubims.
21 Every one had four faces apiece, and every one four wings; and the likeness of the hands of a man was under their wings.
22 And the likeness of their faces was the same faces which I saw by the river of Chebar, their appearances and themselves: they went every one straight forward.

Then the glory of the LORD departed from off the threshold of the house of the LORD and stood over the cherubim who lifted up their wings and mounted up from the earth in Ezekiel's sight. The cherubim of the LORD can fly on earth in human bodies: the wheels are with the cherubim, and every one stood at the east gate of the LORD's house, the direction of the future symbolized by the rising sun. The glory of God was above and over them.

This is the living creature that Ezekiel saw under the God of Israel by the river of Chebar; and he knew that they were the cherubim of God. Every one had four faces apiece, and every one four wings; and the likeness of the hands of a man was under their wings to indicate man's true responsibility on earth is to reveal the cherubim. The likeness of their faces was the same faces which he saw by the river of Chebar, their appearances and themselves: they went every one straight forward in service to the LORD.

CHAPTER 11

1 Moreover the spirit lifted me up, and brought me unto the east gate of the LORD's house, which looketh eastward: and behold at the door of the gate five and twenty men; among whom I saw Jaazaniah the son of Azur, and Pelatiah the son of Benaiah, princes of the people.

Ezekiel describes the vision, which occurred in his consciousness, as the spirit of the LORD lifting him up to a place where he was brought to the east gate of the LORD's house which looked eastward. Ezekiel is in the LORD's house, the place where the LORD lives and where the LORD sees things, looking outward where he observes twenty-five men at the door of the gate. These twenty-five men are in a position to be seen by Ezekiel, but they are outside the gate rather than inside the gate. They are very close to the entrance to the LORD's house but they are not inside. Among the men who are very close to the entry to the LORD's house, the house of the spirit, are Jaazaniah, which means, "whom the LORD will hear", the son of Azur, which means "he that assists"; and Pelatiah, which means, "let the LORD deliver", son of Benaiah, which means, "the son, or the building of the LORD". They are princes of the people who are outside the LORD's house.

The entrance to the LORD's house is always available to those who will serve the spirit of the LORD and the LORD will do his part to assist his children to reach the covenant of the house of the LORD. The entrance is always open to those people who will let the LORD's spirit deliver them into the entrance of the LORD's house as the spirit of the Father is allowed to flow through the son or the material building, the human person. However, these two people are outside the house of the LORD. They have the potential to let the spirit of the LORD flow through them on a consistent basis but they have not allowed it to be so. The LORD has some words of instruction to the person who desires to enter the house of the LORD, the covenant.

2 Then said he unto me, Son of man, these are the men that devise mischief, and give wicked counsel in this city:
3 Which say, It is not near; let us build houses: this city is the caldron, and we be the flesh.
4 Therefore prophesy against them, prophesy, O son of man.

The LORD informs the Son of man, the focus of the LORD's spirit on earth, Ezekiel, tat these two men are examples of the men who devise mischief and give wicked counsel in this city; their wicked counsel is that the LORD's house is not near; it is far away (on the other side of the grave); so since the LORD's house is so far away then let us build houses to the LORD to honor Him, This city, any fallen city, is the cauldron and the people are the flesh in the cauldron who are doing their best to build their houses without the LORD who is far away. The LORD instructs Ezekiel, a member of the body of the son of man, who is one of them on a material basis, to prophesy against the people who are outside the LORD's house and who speak falsely in the name of the LORD. Ezekiel can do this truly because he is a member of the spiritual body of the Son of man in addition to being a physical member of the body of the son of man. Ezekiel sees his purpose and what he is to do for the LORD.

The Testimony of the Major Prophets

5 And the Spirit of the LORD fell upon me, and said unto me, Speak; Thus saith the LORD; Thus have ye said, O house of Israel: for I know the things that come into your mind, every one of them.
6 Ye have multiplied your slain in this city, and ye have filled the streets thereof with the slain.

When Ezekiel sees his responsibility as a member of the body of the Son of man, then the spirit of the LORD fell upon him and commanded him to speak in the name, in the authority, of the LORD's spirit. Thus says the LORD, because Ezekiel is in the LORD's house and the twenty-five are outside the gate. Ezekiel is instructed to tell the people, the house of Israel, that the LORD is aware of everything that comes into their minds, each and every one of them. They have multiplied the people who have been slain in the city and they have filled the streets with the slain. Their teaching and leadership has led to death not to life.

7 Therefore thus saith the Lord GOD; Your slain whom ye have laid in the midst of it, they are the flesh, and this city is the caldron: but I will bring you forth out of the midst of it.
8 Ye have feared the sword; and I will bring a sword upon you, saith the Lord GOD.
9 And I will bring you out of the midst thereof, and deliver you into the hands of strangers, and will execute judgments among you.
10 Ye shall fall by the sword; I will judge you in the border of Israel; and ye shall know that I am the LORD.

The LORD explains through Ezekiel that the slain whom are laid in the midst of the city are the flesh and the city in which they dwell is the cauldron where death occurs in their consciousness. The LORD will bring you out of the midst of the cauldron in which you find yourselves. The people in the fallen state have feared the sword of death but the Lord GOD will bring a sword of truth upon you. The Lord GOD will bring the people in the fallen state out of the midst of it and deliver them into the hands of strangers, strangers that you have not known in the fallen state, because they are not in the fallen state. The Lord GOD will execute true judgments among you. You shall fall by the spiritual sword of truth and you shall be judged in the border, the point of connection, the covenant, between the LORD and Israel; and when the person experiences the covenant, then the person shall know the LORD in a new city, in his or her own experience.

11 This city shall not be your caldron, neither shall ye be the flesh in the midst thereof; but I will judge you in the border of Israel:
12 And ye shall know that I am the LORD: for ye have not walked in my statutes, neither executed my judgments, but have done after the manners of the heathen that are round about you.

The new spiritual city, the city of the LORD, shall not be the cauldron with which you have been familiar, and you shall no longer be the flesh in the midst of the city. The LORD will judge you in a new spiritual place which is at the border of material Israel: and you shall know that the person who speaks with the spiritual authority of the LORD is the LORD. If you do not know the LORD in your own experience, then you have not walked in the statutes of the LORD, nor executed the judgments of the LORD, but rather, you have done after the manners of the heathen, the normal people of the fallen state, that are round about you in your environment.

13 And it came to pass, when I prophesied, that Pelatiah the son of Benaiah died. Then fell I down upon my face, and cried with a loud voice, and said, Ah Lord GOD! wilt thou make a full end of the remnant of Israel?

And it came to pass that when Ezekiel prophesied, that Pelatiah, the one who let the LORD deliver, the one who was the building of the LORD, died. Ezekiel fell down on his face and cried with a loud voice to the Lord GOD, Will you make a full end to the remnant of Israel that remains?

14 Again the word of the LORD came unto me, saying,
15 Son of man, thy brethren, even thy brethren, the men of thy kindred, and all the house of Israel wholly, are they unto whom the inhabitants of Jerusalem have said, Get you far from the LORD: unto us is this land given in possession.
16 Therefore say, Thus saith the Lord GOD; Although I have cast them far off among the heathen, and although I have scattered them among the countries, yet will I be to them as a little sanctuary in the countries where they shall come.

The Symbolic Version of Ezekiel

Again the word of the LORD came to Ezekiel, the representative of the Son of man, saying, that Ezekiel's material brethren, the flesh members of his kindred, and all the house of Israel who are in the fallen state, are the ones to whom the inhabitants of Jerusalem have said, Get yourselves far away from the LORD. The land is not the LORD's land: it is the possession of the people who do not know the LORD.

Ezekiel is instructed to say on behalf of the Lord GOD that although the action of the LORD has cast the people afar off among the heathen, and although they have been scattered among the countries of the earth, yet the LORD will be to each one of them as a little sanctuary in the countries where they shall come. They will be all alone but the spirit of the LORD shall be with them. The spirit of the LORD shall always be connected to them wherever they are.

17 Therefore say, Thus saith the Lord GOD; I will even gather you from the people, and assemble you out of the countries where ye have been scattered, and I will give you the land of Israel.
18 And they shall come thither, and they shall take away all the detestable things thereof and all the abominations thereof from thence.
19 And I will give them one heart, and I will put a new spirit within you; and I will take the stony heart out of their flesh, and will give them an heart of flesh:
20 That they may walk in my statutes, and keep mine ordinances, and do them: and they shall be my people, and I will be their God.

Since the spirit of the Lord GOD is with all the people, then the LORD will gather you from the people and assemble you out of the countries where you have been scattered and will give you the land of Israel, which is the spiritual land of the spirit of God. The people shall come there to the spiritual place where they shall take away all the detestable things and all the abominations from there.

The LORD will give them one heart, and put a new spirit within you; the LORD will take the stony heart out of their flesh and give them a heart made of the LORD's spiritual flesh. It is with this new spirit and heart that the people may walk in the LORD's statutes, keep the LORD's ordinances and do them. Then, they shall be the LORD's people and the LORD will be their God if they walk in the LORD's spirit and in the heart of the LORD.

21 But as for them whose heart walketh after the heart of their detestable things and their abominations, I will recompense their way upon their own heads, saith the Lord GOD.

The heart is the key to the kingdom of the LORD. The people who walk after the heart's desire of detestable things and their abominations will be recompensed as the way of their evil comes upon their own heads by the working of the law of the LORD.

22 Then did the cherubims lift up their wings, and the wheels beside them; and the glory of the God of Israel was over them above.
23 And the glory of the LORD went up from the midst of the city, and stood upon the mountain which is on the east side of the city.

Then the cherubim did lift up their wings and fly, act, with their wheels, the human flesh bodies, beside them and the glory of Israel was above them because the God of Israel was above them. This results in the glory of the LORD going up over the midst of the city and the glory of the LORD stood upon the mountain which is on the east of the city. The east is the symbol for the future and the glorious future described will come to any city if the people release the spirit of God.

24 Afterwards the spirit took me up, and brought me in a vision by the Spirit of God into Chaldea, to them of the captivity. So the vision that I had seen went up from me.
25 Then I spake unto them of the captivity all the things that the LORD had shewed me.

Ezekiel states that afterward, the spirit took him up and brought him in a vision by the Spirit of God into Chaldea, to the people who were in captivity there. The vision that Ezekiel had seen applied to them. Ezekiel spoke to those captives of all things that the LORD had shown him.

CHAPTER 12

1 The word of the LORD also came unto me, saying,
2 Son of man, thou dwellest in the midst of a rebellious house, which have eyes to see, and see not; they have ears to hear, and hear not: for they are a rebellious house.

Ezekiel, who is in the spirit of the covenant-agreement with the LORD, declares that the word of the LORD came to him saying, Son of man, the offspring of the Father in the body of man, you dwell in the midst of a rebellious house. The rebellious house has reference to the rebellious people, the people who have rebelled against the spirit of the LORD, the people in the fallen state of mankind. These fallen people have eyes to see and they do not see the action and beauty of the LORD on earth in physical form; they have ears to hear the vibrations of sound that all originate from the LORD but they do not hear the true sound. They do not see and hear the divine design because they are a rebellious house of people who have rebelled against the spirit of the LORD which is their true path. The LORD must have some advice to help Ezekiel move the rebellious people to return to a people who would be obedient to the word of the LORD.

3 Therefore, thou son of man, prepare thee stuff for removing, and remove by day in their sight; and thou shalt remove from thy place to another place in their sight: it may be they will consider, though they be a rebellious house.
4 Then shalt thou bring forth thy stuff by day in their sight, as stuff for removing: and thou shalt go forth at even in their sight, as they that go forth into captivity.

There is contamination and distortion of stuff contained in the divine design and the son of man is advised to prepare the true stuff, the true spiritual substance, that will remove the distortions from the sight of the rebellious people by day, when they can see the true spiritual stuff that Ezekiel will release into the world. This will be a contrast to what has been produced by a rebellious people. If they see the true material substance produced by the spirit of the LORD through Ezekiel then the people in the fallen state might consider the example even though they are a rebellious house of people.

This is the responsibility of Ezekiel and the people who compose the body of the Son of man. They are to bring forth the spirit of the LORD in manifest earthly form, stuff, by day so that it can be seen as stuff that will remove the wrong stuff that is made by people in the fallen state, who are a rebellious people. At the end of the day, at even time, Ezekiel shall go forth freely in their sight, because he is free of all material things while he is under the control of the spirit of the LORD, while they, the rebellious house, go forth in their captivity to the material world.

5 Dig thou through the wall in their sight, and carry out thereby.
6 In their sight shalt thou bear it upon thy shoulders, and carry it forth in the twilight: thou shalt cover thy face, that thou see not the ground: for I have set thee for a sign unto the house of Israel.

The Symbolic Version of Ezekiel

Ezekiel is instructed to dig through the wall that separates the people in the fallen state from the spiritual source of the LORD and carry out the responsibility of spiritual expression, the expression of the spirit into the world of form which is the sole purpose of a person who is not rebellious. In the sight of the rebellious people, Ezekiel, and anyone who will follow him, shall bear the responsibility of the expression of the spirit of the LORD on earth on one's shoulders and carry it forth into the twilight, into the time when the light of life fades from human expression. The role and function of Ezekiel is to cover his face from the judgment of the physical form of things in the material world so that he does not look at the ground to judge the forms. The LORD has set Ezekiel as a living example for a sign to the people, the house of Israel, of what a child of Israel should be doing on earth to express the spirit of the LORD.

7 And I did so as I was commanded: I brought forth my stuff by day, as stuff for captivity, and in the even I digged through the wall with mine hand; I brought it forth in the twilight, and I bare it upon my shoulder in their sight.

Ezekiel did as he was commanded. He brought forth his spiritual stuff by day when people could see that he brought forth the right stuff as stuff for comparison to the stuff that was brought forth by the rebellious people who were in captivity to the things and conditions of the material world. At the end of the day, Ezekiel, with his own hand of control, dug through the wall of distortion which had been made by the fallen people. Ezekiel brought forth the true design of spirit in the twilight of the day, and he shouldered the responsibility of bringing forth the evidence of spiritual expression in their sight. Ezekiel does this, he serves the spirit of the LORD, for one day.

8 And in the morning came the word of the LORD unto me, saying,
9 Son of man, hath not the house of Israel, the rebellious house, said unto thee, What doest thou?
10 Say thou unto them, Thus saith the Lord GOD; This burden concerneth the prince in Jerusalem, and all the house of Israel that are among them.
11 Say, I am your sign: like as I have done, so shall it be done unto them: they shall remove and go into captivity.
12 And the prince that is among them shall bear upon his shoulder in the twilight, and shall go forth: they shall dig through the wall to carry out thereby: he shall cover his face, that he see not the ground with his eyes.

In the morning, the word of the LORD came to Ezekiel, saying, Son of man, have not the rebellious people of the house of Israel said, What are you doing? and, Why are you doing things differently than us? Ezekiel is instructed to answer them with the authority of the Lord GOD; This burden of spiritual expression concerns the prince in Jerusalem, the prince is the son of the King, and all the house of Israel that are among those who would be a member of the body of the Son of the King, The Son of the Father and the Son of man. The LORD instructs Ezekiel to say, I am your sign. As I have done in the expression of the spirit of the King, the Father, so shall it be done by you to them, those who are fallen members of the house of Israel. The people who see your sign of spiritual expression shall either respond to your sign or they will go into the captivity of emotional involvement with the material world.

The prince, the son of the King, who is among you shall bear the spirit and the authority upon his shoulder as he goes into the twilight of his life as he goes forth in the covenant with the LORD. Then, he too, shall dig through the wall of distortion to carry out his responsibility on earth. He also shall cover his face and not judge the conditions of the ground with his eyes because the earth will portray the material pattern that is created from the consciousness of man.

13 My net also will I spread upon him, and he shall be taken in my snare: and I will bring him to Babylon to the land of the Chaldeans; yet shall he not see it, though he shall die there.
14 And I will scatter toward every wind all that are about him to help him, and all his bands; and I will draw out the sword after them.
15 And they shall know that I am the LORD, when I shall scatter them among the nations, and disperse them in the countries.
16 But I will leave a few men of them from the sword, from the famine, and from the pestilence; that they may declare all their abominations among the heathen whither they come; and they shall know that I am the LORD.

The large net of the LORD will be spread upon him who expresses the spirit of the LORD and he shall be taken, included within, the snare of the LORD. The LORD will bring him to Babylon to the land of the Chaldeans which is the evidence of the material distortions made by the people who rebelled against the spirit of the LORD to create the

The Testimony of the Major Prophets

distorted fallen world. Yet, he who is caught in the LORD's net shall not see the fallen world though he shall die there. (He shall see the earth that is the LORD's.) The LORD will scatter the spiritual expression of the prince, the Son of man, toward every wind that is about him to help him and all his bands that surround him. In this manner, the LORD will draw out the constructive edge of the sword of the covenant against the rebellious people of Babylon. And they shall know that it is the LORD who shall scatter them among the nations, and disperse them in the countries to express the spirit of the LORD in their living.

But the LORD will leave a few men of them from the destructive aspect of the sword, from the famine, and from the pestilence; that they may declare all their abominations among the heathen whither they come; and they shall know that I am the LORD.

17 Moreover the word of the LORD came to me, saying,
18 Son of man, eat thy bread with quaking, and drink thy water with trembling and with carefulness;
19 And say unto the people of the land, Thus saith the Lord GOD of the inhabitants of Jerusalem, and of the land of Israel; They shall eat their bread with carefulness, and drink their water with astonishment, that her land may be desolate from all that is therein, because of the violence of all them that dwell therein.
20 And the cities that are inhabited shall be laid waste, and the land shall be desolate; and ye shall know that I am the LORD.

Ezekiel has declared the word of the LORD by saying that the Son of man, the representatives of the LORD on earth through man, should eat their daily bread of the spirit from the LORD quaking with the impulse of the LORD's spirit and drink the water of his truth with trembling and with carefulness befitting a person who comprehends that it is the spirit of the LORD that flows through man. Tell the people of the land that the Lord GOD of the inhabitants of Jerusalem and of the land of Israel that they should eat their bread of life from the LORD with carefulness, and drink their water of truth from the LORD with astonishment so that the land of distortion which they have made in rebellion against the spirit shall become desolate. The distortions were produced by their violence because they were not careful of their own relationship with the LORD. For this reason, the cities that are inhabited by rebellious people are laid waste and the land shall be desolate. This is the working of the law of the LORD and the people will know by the desolation that the LORD is with them and that their rebellion has caused the desolation.

21 And the word of the LORD came unto me, saying,
22 Son of man, what is that proverb that ye have in the land of Israel, saying, The days are prolonged, and every vision faileth?
23 Tell them therefore, Thus saith the Lord GOD; I will make this proverb to cease, and they shall no more use it as a proverb in Israel; but say unto them, The days are at hand, and the effect of every vision.
24 For there shall be no more any vain vision nor flattering divination within the house of Israel.
25 For I am the LORD: I will speak, and the word that I shall speak shall come to pass; it shall be no more prolonged: for in your days, O rebellious house, will I say the word, and will perform it, saith the Lord GOD.

The instruction of the LORD came to Ezekiel saying, Son of man, the focus of spirit in the body of mankind, What is that proverb that you have in the land of Israel that says, The days of the coming of the LORD are prolonged and every vision of his coming fails? Tell those people who do not understand this proverb that the Lord GOD will make this proverb cease and they shall use it no more as a proverb in Israel. Say to them, The days of the LORD are at hand, and the effect of every vision in the consciousness of man shall be fulfilled in manifest form according to the working of the law. As people express the spirit of the LORD, they shall reap the kingdom of the LORD on earth.

There shall be no more any vain vision, visions of vanity, nor flattering divination within the house of Israel. The LORD will speak and the word that the LORD speaks shall come to pass. The word of the LORD shall be no more prolonged but it will happen quickly. In your days, people of the rebellious house, when the LORD says the word, it shall be performed immediately says the Lord GOD. The word, the effect of the speaking of the LORD, shall have an effect exactly consistent with the consciousness of man.

26 Again the word of the LORD came to me, saying,

27 Son of man, behold, they of the house of Israel say, The vision that he seeth is for many days to come, and he prophesieth of the times that are far off.
28 Therefore say unto them, Thus saith the Lord GOD; There shall none of my words be prolonged any more, but the word which I have spoken shall be done, saith the Lord GOD.

The LORD said to Ezekiel as the connecting link to the true state of mankind, the Son of man, behold, the people of the house of Israel say that the vision that he sees is for many days to come and he prophesies of times that are far off into the future. Therefore, say to them, with the authority of the Lord GOD, that none of the power of the words of the LORD shall be prolonged or withheld any more. The words, the power of the LORD which have been spoken by the LORD through the Son of man, through all of mankind in the divine state, shall be done as the LORD fulfills his responsibility in the covenant agreement with mankind. Man shall reap what he sows through his consciousness. Mankind can choose to be the Son of man or the fallen son of man. The glory or the desolation which man produces is his responsibility. This is the working of the law. This simple and clear instruction is not being taught to the people by the false prophets.

CHAPTER 13

1 And the word of the LORD came unto me, saying,
2 Son of man, prophesy against the prophets of Israel that prophesy, and say thou unto them that prophesy out of their own hearts, Hear ye the word of the LORD;
3 Thus saith the Lord GOD; Woe unto the foolish prophets, that follow their own spirit, and have seen nothing!
4 O Israel, thy prophets are like the foxes in the deserts.
5 Ye have not gone up into the gaps, neither made up the hedge for the house of Israel to stand in the battle in the day of the LORD.
6 They have seen vanity and lying divination, saying, The LORD saith: and the LORD hath not sent them: and they have made others to hope that they would confirm the word.
7 Have ye not seen a vain vision, and have ye not spoken a lying divination, whereas ye say, The LORD saith it; albeit I have not spoken?

The word of the LORD came to Ezekiel saying that the Son of man should prophesy against the prophets of Israel, who are prophesying out of their own impure hearts, that that they should hear the word of the LORD. The LORD says that woe shall come unto the foolish prophets that follow their own spirit instead of the spirit of the LORD and consequently they have seen nothing of the glory and the majesty which the LORD would bring on earth. The false prophets are compared to foxes in the desert, jackals among the ruins of the divine design of the LORD.

The foolish prophets have not gone up into the gaps, the empty positions of responsibility, that must be filled with servants of the LORD to deliver the LORD's spirit of love, truth and life into the earth; neither have they made the hedge of protection for the LORD's spirit to survive and stand in the battle between divine nature that comes from the LORD and human nature which comes from the impure and fallen hearts of man in his selfishness and rebellion from God. The false prophets have seen their own vanity and lying divination, a false expression of the divine behavior, as they say that the LORD has sent them and their message, but the LORD has not sent them. The false prophets and their false prophesy have made others to hope that the false prophets, the leaders of the son of man, would confirm the word of the LORD. Have the false prophets not seen the vain vision that they are preaching and have they not seen the lying divination of the spirit which they claim is from the LORD but which is not the word of the LORD? The results on earth from the false prophets are not the design of the LORD; they are not the evidence of the spirit of the LORD in action on earth; the results are the working of the law through the impure hearts and vanity of the foolish prophets. The false prophets must pay for their false representation.

8 Therefore thus saith the Lord GOD; Because ye have spoken vanity, and seen lies, therefore, behold, I am against you, saith the Lord GOD.
9 And mine hand shall be upon the prophets that see vanity, and that divine lies: they shall not be in the assembly of my people, neither shall they be written in the writing of the house of Israel, neither shall they enter into the land of Israel; and ye shall know that I am the Lord GOD.

10 Because, even because they have seduced my people, saying, Peace; and there was no peace; and one built up a wall, and, lo, others daubed it with untempered morter:
11 Say unto them which daub it with untempered morter, that it shall fall: there shall be an overflowing shower; and ye, O great hailstones, shall fall; and a stormy wind shall rend it.
12 Lo, when the wall is fallen, shall it not be said unto you, Where is the daubing wherewith ye have daubed it?

Therefore, the Lord GOD declares through Ezekiel that because the foolish prophets have spoken vanity and seen the results of their lies made manifest in conditions on earth, behold, the Lord GOD is against them. The hand of the LORD, through the working of the Law of spirit into the world of form shall be upon the false prophets who see their vanity and divine lies. The false prophets shall not be in the assembly of the LORD's people, the Son of man on earth, and neither shall they be written as members in the house of Israel nor shall they enter into the spiritual land of Israel, the covenant. Since they are not in the spiritual covenant which is available to them if they were not vain, they shall know that the Lord GOD is not with them as they prophesy.

Since the false prophets have seduced the LORD's people by saying Peace, and there was no peace; and one false prophet attempts to build a wall of the house of the LORD and others daub it with untempered mortar, whitewash which will not hold, then tell those who are using the whitewash to give an appearance of cleanliness and strength that what they are trying to build shall fall. A shower of the truth from the LORD shall come and a stormy wind of the true spirit shall blow and break what you have tried to build. The false prophets are called hailstones, frozen water containing their crystallized beliefs which will melt as the suns shines on them. When their wall is fallen, because it cannot stand when the truth is present, then shall it not be said of you, foolish prophets, where is the whitewash, the surface daubing, that you used to try to hold your wall of vanity together? Ezekiel describes the destruction of the wall of the false prophets, the counterfeit son of man, human nature, in more detail.

13 Therefore thus saith the Lord GOD; I will even rend it with a stormy wind in my fury; and there shall be an overflowing shower in mine anger, and great hailstones in my fury to consume it.
14 So will I break down the wall that ye have daubed with untempered morter, and bring it down to the ground, so that the foundation thereof shall be discovered, and it shall fall, and ye shall be consumed in the midst thereof: and ye shall know that I am the LORD.
15 Thus will I accomplish my wrath upon the wall, and upon them that have daubed it with untempered morter, and will say unto you, The wall is no more, neither they that daubed it;
16 To wit, the prophets of Israel which prophesy concerning Jerusalem, and which see visions of peace for her, and there is no peace, saith the Lord GOD.

As the truth of the spirit of the LORD is expressed on earth through the people who compose the Son of man, the false wall of the counterfeit building which does not contain the mortar of the LORD's spirit shall be broken down in the fury, the destructive power, described in the symbolism of the overflowing shower of the anger of the LORD, the stormy wind and the hailstones. The wall of the false design of the LORD's church, the son of man, shall be brought down to the ground because it has been built with untempered mortar, the whitewash, that does not hold it together. The foundation of falsity and vanity shall be discovered and it shall fall and the false prophets shall be consumed in the midst of its disintegration and they shall know that the LORD has been the cause of the destruction.

In this manner, the LORD shall accomplish his wrath against the wall that the false prophets have built and upon them who daubed the false wall with the untempered mortar, the whitewash. The LORD will say to them, The wall is no more, neither they, the false prophets, who daubed it; specifically, the prophets of Israel who prophesy concerning Jerusalem and see visions of peace for Jerusalem and there is no peace possible in the fallen state of the son of man, says the Lord GOD.

17 Likewise, thou son of man, set thy face against the daughters of thy people, which prophesy out of their own heart; and prophesy thou against them,
18 And say, Thus saith the Lord GOD; Woe to the women that sew pillows to all armholes, and make kerchiefs upon the head of every stature to hunt souls! Will ye hunt the souls of my people, and will ye save the souls alive that come unto you?

The Testimony of the Major Prophets

19 And will ye pollute me among my people for handfuls of barley and for pieces of bread, to slay the souls that should not die, and to save the souls alive that should not live, by your lying to my people that hear your lies?

The son of man, man in the fallen state must change. They are advised and instructed to set their face against the daughters of the people, to turn their face of response away from the alluring daughters that have been attractive to them. The daughters are symbols of the attractions in the environment who compete with the spiritual beauty of the LORD. These "daughters" prophesy out of their own heart, their own feelings; and the son of man is instructed to prophesy against them, and say, Thus says the Lord GOD; Woe to the women that sew pillows to armholes to give the appearance of broad shoulders that make the wearer of the garment appear to be more than he is! Woe to the women who make kerchiefs, headdresses for the heads of every stature, to hunt for souls, for people to make a part of their wall! The LORD speaking through Ezekiel asks the women if they hunt for the souls of the LORD's people to bring them to the LORD, and will they save the souls alive, that come to them with life from the LORD? Will they lead the people to an experience with the LORD while they are still alive?

And will they pollute the LORD among his people for handfuls of barley and for pieces of bread that they collect, as they promise to slay the people who should not die, and try to save the people alive that should not live, by lying to the people that hear your lies as you prophesy in the name of the LORD falsely? The LORD will state his position with regard to the false and foolish prophets who prophesy in the name of the LORD.

20 Wherefore thus saith the Lord GOD; Behold, I am against your pillows, wherewith ye there hunt the souls to make them fly, and I will tear them from your arms, and will let the souls go, even the souls that ye hunt to make them fly. 21 Your kerchiefs also will I tear, and deliver my people out of your hand, and they shall be no more in your hand to be hunted; and ye shall know that I am the LORD.

The Lord God is against the pillows, the symbols of soft whisperings that entice people into the armholes of those who would capture and ensnare the people for their own use by using the name of the LORD in vain, in vanity by making the people fly to them. The LORD will tear them from the arms of your control and he will let the people go free, even the people that you hunt to make them fly to you instead of the LORD. The LORD will tear your kerchiefs, the coverings that you wear on your heads as symbols of authority, to deliver the people out of your hands so that they will be in the hand of your control no longer to be hunted and snared by you for your false purposes; then you shall know that the one who speaks through the form of Ezekiel is the LORD.

*22 Because with lies ye have made the heart of the righteous sad, whom I have not made sad; and strengthened the hands of the wicked, that he should not return from his wicked way, by promising him life:
23 Therefore ye shall see no more vanity, nor divine divinations: for I will deliver my people out of your hand: and ye shall know that I am the LORD.*

The lies expressed by you, the false prophets, have made the heart of the righteous people sad; the righteous people have not been made sad by the LORD. You have strengthened the hands of the wicked so that he should not repent and return from his wicked way, by promising him life. Therefore you shall see no more vanity nor divine revelations: for the LORD shall deliver his people out of the hand of your control; and you shall know the LORD is the cause of all the changes that return the spirit of the LORD directly through the people to the state of the Son of man.

CHAPTER 14

1 Then came certain of the elders of Israel unto me, and sat before me.
2 And the word of the LORD came unto me, saying,
3 Son of man, these men have set up their idols in their heart, and put the stumblingblock of their iniquity before their face: should I be inquired of at all by them?
4 Therefore speak unto them, and say unto them, Thus saith the Lord GOD; Every man of the house of Israel that setteth up his idols in his heart, and putteth the stumblingblock of his iniquity before his face, and cometh to the prophet; I the LORD will answer him that cometh according to the multitude of his idols;
5 That I may take the house of Israel in their own heart, because they are all estranged from me through their idols.

Ezekiel relates the time when certain elders of Israel came and sat before him. The word of the LORD came to him saying, Son of man, these men of Israel have set up idols in their heart, and put a stumbling block of their iniquity between themselves and the focus of the LORD in the person of Ezekiel. The LORD asks if he should be open for inquiry at all by those who have iniquity in their hearts?

The LORD speaks to Ezekiel, the focus of the Son of man, a person who does not bring iniquity and sin before the LORD, to tell the elders of Israel, who have set up idols of worship in their hearts, that when they come to the prophet of the LORD with idols, then the LORD must speak to the elders through the multitude of idols which they have placed before the LORD. It is the idols that they have set between them and the LORD which keep them estranged from knowing the LORD. The idols which they worship are the barrier to the covenant.

6 Therefore say unto the house of Israel, Thus saith the Lord GOD; Repent, and turn yourselves from your idols; and turn away your faces from all your abominations.
7 For every one of the house of Israel, or of the stranger that sojourneth in Israel, which separateth himself from me, and setteth up his idols in his heart, and putteth the stumblingblock of his iniquity before his face, and cometh to a prophet to inquire of him concerning me; I the LORD will answer him by myself:
8 And I will set my face against that man, and will make him a sign and a proverb, and I will cut him off from the midst of my people; and ye shall know that I am the LORD.

The LORD speaking through Ezekiel tells the elders of Israel to repent by turning themselves away from their idols; and turn their faces of response and worship away from the idols which are abominations to the LORD. The LORD requires each person to come to him naked and unashamed, without any idols in their consciousness to separate themselves from the LORD. Every one of the house of Israel, or a stranger who travels in Israel, who puts idols and stumbling blocks of evil that separate themselves from LORD shall be cut off from the midst of the LORD's people who have a direct connection with the LORD their God. The fact that the LORD's face is not known by the elders of Israel is a sign and a proverb that they are worshipping idols and they shall not know that the LORD is their God and that they are not in covenant-agreement with the LORD. Their faces, the face of the LORD and the face of the elder of

The Testimony of the Major Prophets

Israel, are not seeing each other directly. The idols and the iniquities are the stumbling blocks that are in the way. Each person in covenant-agreement with the LORD knows the LORD and he is a prophet of the LORD; he is, like Ezekiel, a member of the body of the Son of man. The true nature of man is to be a prophet of the LORD and let the LORD's spirit find expression directly through each one's heart, mind and body to reveal the truth of the LORD.

9 And if the prophet be deceived when he hath spoken a thing, I the LORD have deceived that prophet, and I will stretch out my hand upon him, and will destroy him from the midst of my people Israel.
10 And they shall bear the punishment of their iniquity: the punishment of the prophet shall be even as the punishment of him that seeketh unto him;
11 That the house of Israel may go no more astray from me, neither be polluted any more with all their transgressions; but that they may be my people, and I may be their God, saith the Lord GOD.

If a prophet be deceived when he has spoken a thing, expressed anything that is not the nature of the LORD, then the LORD has deceived that prophet and the direct control of the hand of the LORD on that person will destroy him from the midst of the LORD's people. The LORD's people obey the LORD and release the LORD's spirit and nature. The LORD's people who release the spirit of the LORD are Israel. Israel is not a material place; it is a spiritual place where the spirit of the LORD and the spirit of Israel are the same spirit. A person who does not reveal the spirit of the LORD shall bear the punishment of their iniquity as the presence of their iniquity or sin causes that person to be repelled away from the presence of the LORD. The punishment of the prophet is the punishment of the iniquity that the person brings to the LORD. This is done so that the house of Israel may not go astray from the LORD nor be polluted by their transgressions. If evil and sin, the idols that people worship, push people away from the LORD, then the relinquishment of all idols will cause everyone to be in the LORD's spirit and therefore, be the LORD's people and the LORD will be their God on a one-to-one basis.

12 The word of the LORD came again to me, saying,
13 Son of man, when the land sinneth against me by trespassing grievously, then will I stretch out mine hand upon it, and will break the staff of the bread thereof, and will send famine upon it, and will cut off man and beast from it:
14 Though these three men, Noah, Daniel, and Job, were in it, they should deliver but their own souls by their righteousness, saith the Lord GOD.

Ezekiel relates to the elders of Israel, the people who are old and wise enough to hear the word of the LORD, that the people in the land who trespass against the spirit of the LORD by expressing some other spirit, then the LORD shall break the staff of the bread of the spirit of love, truth and life, which is provided in the covenant, and the break in spirit will cause famine in the land of material form. Man and beast shall be cut off from connection with the LORD and the material forms of man and beast shall experience the famine of the fall of man. The absence of the LORD's blessing will be known in the land of Israel instead of the blessing of the spirit of the LORD. Noah, Daniel and Job were in the spirit of the LORD, so that they should deliver their own souls, their own individual bodies, minds and hearts by their own righteousness, the righteous behavior inherent in the spirit of the LORD.

15 If I cause noisome beasts to pass through the land, and they spoil it, so that it be desolate, that no man may pass through because of the beasts:
16 Though these three men were in it, as I live, saith the Lord GOD, they shall deliver neither sons nor daughters; they only shall be delivered, but the land shall be desolate.
17 Or if I bring a sword upon that land, and say, Sword, go through the land; so that I cut off man and beast from it:
18 Though these three men were in it, as I live, saith the Lord GOD, they shall deliver neither sons nor daughters, but they only shall be delivered themselves.
19 Or if I send a pestilence into that land, and pour out my fury upon it in blood, to cut off from it man and beast:
20 Though Noah, Daniel, and Job, were in it, as I live, saith the Lord GOD, they shall deliver neither son nor daughter; they shall but deliver their own souls by their righteousness.

The LORD is the cause of everything! If the LORD causes noisome beasts, distortions of the true design, to pass through the land and they spoil it to cause desolation even if these three men were in it, they shall have no sons or daughters, no offspring; only they shall be delivered because they are in the spirit of the LORD. The land around them shall be desolate because the spirit of the LORD works directly through their human forms.

The Symbolic Version of Ezekiel

If the LORD brings his sword of the truth of his spirit through the land so that man and beast shall be separated from the land; though these three men were in the land at the same time, they would be saved themselves but not their sons and daughters. This reveals that the LORD is God of everyone individually and the conscious awareness of the spirit of God does not flow physically through the families of great men as a physical inheritance.

If the LORD sends pestilence through the land, pouring out his fury in blood to cut off man and beast, though the three men of Noah, Daniel and Job be present in the spirit, they could not deliver their own sons and daughters, but only their own souls by their own righteousness. The covenant with the LORD is very personal.

21 For thus saith the Lord GOD; How much more when I send my four sore judgments upon Jerusalem, the sword, and the famine, and the noisome beast, and the pestilence, to cut off from it man and beast?
22 Yet, behold, therein shall be left a remnant that shall be brought forth, both sons and daughters: behold, they shall come forth unto you, and ye shall see their way and their doings: and ye shall be comforted concerning the evil that I have brought upon Jerusalem, even concerning all that I have brought upon it.
23 And they shall comfort you, when ye see their ways and their doings: and ye shall know that I have not done without cause all that I have done in it, saith the Lord GOD.

The Lord GOD says; How much more will the desolation be when he sends his four sore judgments upon Jerusalem to cut it off from man and beast: the sword of disintegration and devastation, the famine from the absence of the LORD's spirit, the noisome beast which is the distortion caused as the spirit of the LORD passes through the iniquities in the consciousness of the people in the fallen state and the pestilence and disease which come from not wholly serving the LORD.

Yet, in all the devastation, there shall be left a remnant that shall come forth from the sons and daughters. The remnant is that a portion of the LORD's spirit shall always be present in the devastation because the power of the LORD is the cause of the devastation. You shall see their way and their doings, some evidence of the true design, and this shall be a comfort concerning the evil that is brought to you. If the law works to produce the evil and the distortions, then the law will work to produce harmony and beauty on earth if man will learn to plant those seeds of quality. If you see these things, they shall comfort you when you see the ways and the doings of the working of the law: the LORD has not made these particular conditions on earth without cause and the cause is the state of consciousness of man.

CHAPTER 15

1 And the word of the LORD came unto me, saying,
2 Son of man, What is the vine tree more than any tree, or than a branch which is among the trees of the forest?
3 Shall wood be taken thereof to do any work? or will men take a pin of it to hang any vessel thereon?
4 Behold, it is cast into the fire for fuel; the fire devoureth both the ends of it, and the midst of it is burned. Is it meet for any work?
5 Behold, when it was whole, it was meet for no work: how much less shall it be meet yet for any work, when the fire hath devoured it, and it is burned?

The word, the radiance, of the LORD came to Ezekiel, saying, Son of man—the focus of the LORD in a man, specifically and available in all mankind generally—and asking rhetorical questions to aid the spiritual understanding of the house of Israel. What is the <u>spiritual</u> vine tree, or a spiritual branch of the vine that is among all the <u>material</u> trees of the forest? The spiritual vine symbolizes the connection in spirit which is everywhere, while the trees of the forest symbolize the material forms of living people and things. Shall wood be taken from the spiritual tree to do any work? The spirit which is not moving through form cannot do any work otherwise the spirit of the LORD would have made changes to bring the divine design to earth centuries ago. The spirit needs willing and available physical forms to do the work of spirit. Material wood cannot be taken from the spiritual vine to do any work. Will men take a pin out of the spiritual tree to hang a vessel on it? No, material things cannot hang on a spiritual pin or peg but the material vessel can be filled with the spirit to contain living spirit, to be guided by its radiance and do the work of spirit.

Behold, the invisible, spiritual vine of life is cast into the fire of the LORD's power for fuel; the spiritual fire which burns and warms all living things connects material things as symbolized by the vine that connects trees in the forest. The fire of the power of spirit consumes both ends of the material things through which life flows, and in the midst of the material thing, it is burned also. The spiritual power symbolized by fire burns in all living things. Is it, invisible life, meet or present for any work? Behold, when it was whole, when it was only spirit not moving through form, it was fitting for no work: how much less shall it be present for any work when the fire has devoured it and it is burned into nothingness? When the form is consumed by the spirit, there is no form available for the spirit to act on earth. Spirit needs form to reveal itself. The death of a human form removes the vessel or the vehicle which is needed for the action of spirit which reveals itself through form. The invisible spirit has eternal energy and power while the material substance is consumed, burned and is no more. The action of spirit in man requires human forms to do the work of the LORD on earth.

6 Therefore thus saith the Lord GOD; As the vine tree among the trees of the forest, which I have given to the fire for fuel, so will I give the inhabitants of Jerusalem.
7 And I will set my face against them; they shall go out from one fire, and another fire shall devour them; and ye shall know that I am the LORD, when I set my face against them.
8 And I will make the land desolate, because they have committed a trespass, saith the Lord GOD.

Therefore, the Lord GOD says, As the vine tree, the symbol of the invisible spirit of the vine moving through a visible tree, is among the trees of the forest, which the LORD has given to the fire for fuel, so also will the LORD give the inhabitants of Jerusalem, the living vine tree to the people in the body of mankind who do not know the LORD. The people who are in the fire of the spirit of the LORD shall be used by the LORD as a living vine to carry the LORD's spirit to others, symbolized by the trees in the forest. These people are in covenant-agreement with the LORD and they face the LORD to do his will.

The LORD will set his face against the people of Jerusalem and they shall go out from one fire, the integrative fire of the spirit, and another fire, the disintegrative fire of the same spirit, shall devour them. A person who truly observes the way in which material things are consumed when the face of the LORD is against them shall know that the LORD is at work. It is the LORD who will make the land desolate when the people who should be revealing the LORD have committed a trespass against the LORD. The trespasses against the LORD produce the devastation because the people are not one with the LORD; they are against the spirit of the LORD.

CHAPTER 16

1 Again the word of the LORD came unto me, saying,
2 Son of man, cause Jerusalem to know her abominations,
3 And say, Thus saith the Lord GOD unto Jerusalem; Thy birth and thy nativity is of the land of Canaan; thy father was an Amorite, and thy mother an Hittite.
4 And as for thy nativity, in the day thou wast born thy navel was not cut, neither wast thou washed in water to supple thee; thou wast not salted at all, nor swaddled at all.
5 None eye pitied thee, to do any of these unto thee, to have compassion upon thee; but thou wast cast out in the open field, to the loathing of thy person, in the day that thou wast born.

The word of the LORD has come to Ezekiel so that he can cause the people who live in the "holy city" of Jerusalem to know and become aware of her abominations, her behaviors which are sinful and which do not reveal the spirit of the LORD. The Lord GOD says to the people of Jerusalem that their physical birth into the earthly land is of Canaan; the father was an Amorite, and the mother is a Hittite. This statement indicates that their earthly parents are from the fallen state and they have no point of reference to the spiritual state, the divine state, from their heavenly parents of Father God and Mother Earth.

The LORD states that the nativity of the fallen people, the sinners, of Jerusalem, from the day that they were born into the earth, the Son of man was not cared for in a manner to teach the child of its heavenly heritage. Instead the newborn angels of the LORD did not have divine orientation: their connection to the earth, their navel, was not cut, neither were they washed in the water of the truth of spirit to supple them to make them flexible and pliable to the impulse of spirit from the Father; they were not salted at all with their spiritual heritage, nor swaddled, wrapped in the origins of their spiritual beginnings at all.
Since all memory of the spiritual state had been forgotten, there was no one with the eye, the vision, to pity the newborn children, to do any of these things to show compassion upon the spiritual beings in human forms. Instead, each newborn spirit from the LORD was cast out in the open field, to the loathing of each person, who knew that they were not the true spiritual self from the day that they were born.

6 And when I passed by thee, and saw thee polluted in thine own blood, I said unto thee when thou wast in thy blood, Live; yea, I said unto thee when thou wast in thy blood, Live.
7 I have caused thee to multiply as the bud of the field, and thou hast increased and waxen great, and thou art come to excellent ornaments: thy breasts are fashioned, and thine hair is grown, whereas thou wast naked and bare.

And when the LORD passed by each person, as the LORD does pass through every living form, and saw each of his children polluted in their own blood, the LORD said to each of his children, Live. The LORD has constantly said to all of the divine offspring, who are in a polluted state of the blood of fallen human nature, Live. It is the presence of the

LORD moving through each one that causes the offspring to multiply as the buds in the field, and the people on earth have increased in numbers and grown great. They have come into excellent ornaments, excellent physical specimens. They have physically matured as indicated by the shape of their breasts and the growth of hair, whereas they were naked and bare at the time of their nativity.

8 Now when I passed by thee, and looked upon thee, behold, thy time was the time of love; and I spread my skirt over thee, and covered thy nakedness: yea, I sware unto thee, and entered into a covenant with thee, saith the Lord GOD, and thou becamest mine.
9 Then washed I thee with water; yea, I throughly washed away thy blood from thee, and I anointed thee with oil.
10 I clothed thee also with broidered work, and shod thee with badgers' skin, and I girded thee about with fine linen, and I covered thee with silk.
11 I decked thee also with ornaments, and I put bracelets upon thy hands, and a chain on thy neck.
12 And I put a jewel on thy forehead, and earrings in thine ears, and a beautiful crown upon thine head.
13 Thus wast thou decked with gold and silver; and thy raiment was of fine linen, and silk, and broidered work; thou didst eat fine flour, and honey, and oil: and thou wast exceeding beautiful, and thou didst prosper into a kingdom.
14 And thy renown went forth among the heathen for thy beauty: for it was perfect through my comeliness, which I had put upon thee, saith the Lord GOD.

Now when the spirit of the LORD passed over each child, behold, the time which was experienced was a time of love because the LORD was present. The LORD spread a skirt over the child and covered his nakedness of the fallen state. The LORD swore a covenant with the fallen child and the LORD accepted each one into a covenant and the newborn child became the LORD's. From that time forward, the LORD, whose spirit is flowing through all of his children simultaneously, washed each child with the water of truth; The LORD thoroughly washed away the polluted blood from you, and each person was anointed with the oil of God's love. The spirit of each person is unpolluted and clean. The divine design for man is available in spirit and it needs to come into form.

Since the design for the Son of man is in spirit and awaits man to bring it into form, the Lord GOD can say that He clothed man with everything in material form necessary for life on earth. Man must create the things which he needs with his innate intelligence. Man must be a co-creator with the LORD to produce what is needed. These things are illustrated by embroidered work, sandals made from badger's skins, linens and silks.

The LORD decked man with ornaments, bracelets upon his hands, and a chain on his neck; put a jewel on his forehead, earrings in his ears, and a beautiful crown upon his head. He was decked with gold and silver; and his raiment was of fine linen, and silk, and embroidered work; he ate fine flour, honey, and oil: and he was created to be exceedingly beautiful and to prosper into a kingdom. The renown of the Son of man went forth among the heathen as sign of beauty: for it was perfect through the comeliness, which the Lord GOD had put upon his crowning creation. However, man did not accept the perfection of the divine design that the LORD endowed.

15 But thou didst trust in thine own beauty, and playedst the harlot because of thy renown, and pouredst out thy fornications on every one that passed by; his it was.
16 And of thy garments thou didst take, and deckedst thy high places with divers colours, and playedst the harlot thereupon: the like things shall not come, neither shall it be so.
17 Thou hast also taken thy fair jewels of my gold and of my silver, which I had given thee, and madest to thyself images of men, and didst commit whoredom with them,
18 And tookest thy broidered garments, and coveredst them: and thou hast set mine oil and mine incense before them.
19 My meat also which I gave thee, fine flour, and oil, and honey, wherewith I fed thee, thou hast even set it before them for a sweet savour: and thus it was, saith the Lord GOD.

Man in the fallen state trusted his own self-centered beauty, and played the harlot by expressing desire to everyone that passed by in the environment instead of being true to the spirit of the LORD, who was the true bridegroom. The fornication of the harlot is not restricted to a physical relationship, but rather, to a merging and a blending with the physical forms of the material world instead of a monogamous relationship with the spirit of the LORD. Fallen man who had become the harlot took the garments, the earthly coverings of the spirit to decorate high places in the human

The Testimony of the Major Prophets

nature world to play the harlot. The things that the harlot hoped to obtain to make her happy will not come to her, and will never come to her. Happiness is impossible while ignoring the presence of the LORD.

The harlot has taken the jewels of the LORD's gold and silver, the symbols of love and truth, which were given to the woman by the LORD who made images of men, and committed whoredom with the images which she had created. The woman who symbolized Jerusalem took her embroidered garments and covered them: and the woman, the symbol of Jerusalem, who had become a whore, took the oil of love from the LORD and his incense before the people who were adulterers. The gifts from the LORD which were given to Jerusalem, fine flour, oil and honey, has been set before the heathen, who were given the blessings from the LORD without worshipping the LORD.

20 Moreover thou hast taken thy sons and thy daughters, whom thou hast borne unto me, and these hast thou sacrificed unto them to be devoured. Is this of thy whoredoms a small matter,
21 That thou hast slain my children, and delivered them to cause them to pass through the fire for them?
22 And in all thine abominations and thy whoredoms thou hast not remembered the days of thy youth, when thou wast naked and bare, and wast polluted in thy blood.

The inhabitants of Jerusalem, symbolized by the woman who had become a harlot, has taken her sons and daughters, who were borne to the LORD, have been sacrificed to be devoured by the sinners, the unholy people. Is this result of the whoredom of Jerusalem a small matter, that the offspring of the LORD, the creations of the LORD which have come through the fire of the LORD, and the woman who symbolizes Jerusalem have been slain for the people in the fallen state? In all the abominations created by the people of Jerusalem and her whoredom. has the woman not remembered when she was naked and bare and was polluted in the blood of the fallen world?

23 And it came to pass after all thy wickedness, (woe, woe unto thee! saith the Lord GOD;)
24 That thou hast also built unto thee an eminent place, and hast made thee an high place in every street.
25 Thou hast built thy high place at every head of the way, and hast made thy beauty to be abhorred, and hast opened thy feet to every one that passed by, and multiplied thy whoredoms.
26 Thou hast also committed fornication with the Egyptians thy neighbours, great of flesh; and hast increased thy whoredoms, to provoke me to anger.
27 Behold, therefore I have stretched out my hand over thee, and have diminished thine ordinary food, and delivered thee unto the will of them that hate thee, the daughters of the Philistines, which are ashamed of thy lewd way.
28 Thou hast played the whore also with the Assyrians, because thou wast unsatiable; yea, thou hast played the harlot with them, and yet couldest not be satisfied.
29 Thou hast moreover multiplied thy fornication in the land of Canaan unto Chaldea; and yet thou wast not satisfied herewith.

It came to pass after all the wickedness of the harlot, the symbol of the people living in Jerusalem in the fallen state, (woe, woe to you says the Lord GOD because wicked behavior brings woe according to the working of the law), the people have built an eminent place of Jerusalem and has made a high place in every street of the city. The city of Jerusalem with its sinful, fallen inhabitants have built a culture that the place of the fallen individual is exalted and that the true beauty of the divine creation is to be abhorred. The understanding of the divine feet have been opened to everyone that passes by and the whoredom that Jerusalem has become has been multiplied due to its wrong example. This situation has the whoredom of the relationship which provokes the LORD to anger. The fallen and sinful nature of the world is proliferating due to the relationship. The city of Jerusalem has committed fornication with the Egyptians, who are great in their worship of the flesh.

Therefore, the LORD has stretched forth the hand of His control over the people of Jerusalem and diminished their food and delivered them into the hands of the enemy who hate them, the daughters of the Philistines, who are afraid of your lewd ways. The woman, who symbolizes the city of Jerusalem, has played the whore also with the Assyrians, because she was insatiable in her appetite to get what she wants and she cannot be satisfied. Moreover, the city of Jerusalem (as the fallen harlot) has multiplied her fornication—her abandonment of the way of the LORD for the ways of other people who know not the LORD—from the land of Canaan to the people of Chaldea; and still, the people of Jerusalem were not satisfied.

30 How weak is thine heart, saith the Lord GOD, seeing thou doest all these things, the work of an dimperious whorish woman;
31 In that thou buildest thine eminent place in the head of every way, and makest thine high place in every street; and hast not been as an harlot, in that thou scornest hire;
32 But as a wife that committeth adultery, which taketh strangers instead of her husband!
33 They give gifts to all whores: but thou givest thy gifts to all thy lovers, and hirest them, that they may come unto thee on every side for thy whoredom.
34 And the contrary is in thee from other women in thy whoredoms, whereas none followeth thee to commit whoredoms: and in that thou givest a reward, and no reward is given unto thee, therefore thou art contrary.

The LORD knows immediately that the problem is the condition of the heart, the emotional realm that wants happiness and satisfaction from an external source, of the whore. Her whoredom is an effect of the fact that she wants the things of the world. This is the reason that she builds for herself an eminent place at the head of every way and makes a high place for herself in every street. She wants to be adored and wanted. She scorns putting herself out for hire as a harlot does for money; she is as a wife who commits adultery with strangers instead of loving her husband.

The men who use whores give gifts to all whores for the pleasures which they receive. But the whore who symbolizes the fallen state of Jerusalem gives gifts to all her lovers, and hires them that they may come to her for her favors and pleasure. Contrary to other women engaged in whoredom, no one follows the example of the harlot that is Jerusalem, in that Jerusalem gives a reward and no reward is given to Jerusalem. The people of Jerusalem have been classified as a very different kind of harlot that is worse than the usual harlot. The LORD has particular words for the people of Jerusalem, who is supposed to be a holy city, and who are characterized as worse than a harlot.

35 Wherefore, O harlot, hear the word of the LORD:
36 Thus saith the Lord GOD; Because thy filthiness was poured out, and thy nakedness discovered through thy whoredoms with thy lovers, and with all the idols of thy abominations, and by the blood of thy children, which thou didst give unto them;
37 Behold, therefore I will gather all thy lovers, with whom thou hast taken pleasure, and all them that thou hast loved, with all them that thou hast hated; I will even gather them round about against thee, and will discover thy nakedness unto them, that they may see all thy nakedness.

The Lord GOD declares that because the filthiness of the people in Jerusalem was poured out in their expressions of living and their nakedness was discovered through the whoredom with their lovers and all the idols of their abominations, and the blood of the children, the offspring, which were given to their lovers, behold, the LORD will gather the lovers of Jerusalem with whom the people have taken pleasure or hated while they have ignored the LORD. The LORD will gather them all round about the people in the city of Jerusalem so that everyone can see the nakedness of the city of Jerusalem.

38 And I will judge thee, as women that break wedlock and shed blood are judged; and I will give thee blood in fury and jealousy.
39 And I will also give thee into their hand, and they shall throw down thine eminent place, and shall break down thy high places: they shall strip thee also of thy clothes, and shall take thy fair jewels, and leave thee naked and bare.
40 They shall also bring up a company against thee, and they shall stone thee with stones, and thrust thee through with their swords.
41 And they shall burn thine houses with fire, and execute judgments upon thee in the sight of many women: and I will cause thee to cease from playing the harlot, and thou also shalt give no hire any more.
42 So will I make my fury toward thee to rest, and my jealousy shall depart from thee, and I will be quiet, and will be no more angry.
43 Because thou hast not remembered the days of thy youth, but hast fretted me in all these things; behold, therefore I also will recompense thy way upon thine head, saith the Lord GOD: and thou shalt not commit this lewdness above all thine abominations.

The people of the city of Jerusalem shall be judged as women that break their vows of wedlock; they will be given the blood of the spirit of the LORD through people filled with fury and jealousy. The people of Jerusalem will be given

The Testimony of the Major Prophets

into the hand of their enemies who shall throw them down from their eminent place and break down their high places which they have built for themselves: the enemies shall strip the harlots of their clothes, take their jewels and leave them naked and bare. The people of Jerusalem, like an unfaithful whore, shall be stoned with stones and thrust through with swords. Their houses will be burned with fire and judgments shall be executed upon the people according to the working of the law, and the LORD will cause the woman to cease to play the harlot and give no hire any more. In this manner of retribution by means of the working of the law, the LORD's fury shall come to rest, and the jealousy shall depart from the people of Jerusalem. The LORD moving through the people shall be quiet and angry no more.

These things will transpire because the people of Jerusalem have not remembered the days of their youth and their proper relationship with the LORD, but instead, the people have fretted the LORD in all their distorted behaviors. Therefore the LORD will recompense the people according to the working of the Law as their way is returned to your head, the consciousness which originated the distortion. The people will not commit this lewdness, the expression of the evils in their own consciousness, above all their abominations.

44 Behold, every one that useth proverbs shall use this proverb against thee, saying, As is the mother, so is her daughter.
45 Thou art thy mother's daughter, that loatheth her husband and her children; and thou art the sister of thy sisters, which loathed their husbands and their children: your mother was an Hittite, and your father an Amorite.
46 And thine elder sister is Samaria, she and her daughters that dwell at thy left hand: and thy younger sister, that dwelleth at thy right hand, is Sodom and her daughters.
47 Yet hast thou not walked after their ways, nor done after their abominations: but, as if that were a very little thing, thou wast corrupted more than they in all thy ways.

All people who use proverbs and understand the inherent wisdom in them shall say of the wickedness of Jerusalem, as is the mother, so is the daughter. If the mother is a harlot, so is her daughter. You, harlot of Jerusalem are your mother's daughter that loathes your husband, the LORD, and her children; you are also the sister of your sisters, which loathed their husbands and their children. Your mother was an Hittite, whose name means, "fear", and, your father was an Amorite, whose name means, a "rebel". The people of Jerusalem have become rebellious and fearful instead of revealing the love and the truth of the LORD.

The elder sister of the harlot, who symbolizes Jerusalem, is Samaria, a city whose name means "prison" and Sodom, whose name means, "secret". The harlot has been living in a prison of her own making and has kept this way of existing in prison a secret from everyone but the LORD. Yet, Jerusalem has not walked after the ways of her sisters, satellite cities, nor done after their abominations. But, if one considers that to be a little thing, Jerusalem was corrupted more than Samaria and Sodom.

48 As I live, saith the Lord GOD, Sodom thy sister hath not done, she nor her daughters, as thou hast done, thou and thy daughters.
49 Behold, this was the iniquity of thy sister Sodom, pride, fulness of bread, and abundance of idleness was in her and in her daughters, neither did she strengthen the hand of the poor and needy.
50 And they were haughty, and committed abomination before me: therefore I took them away as I saw good.
51 Neither hath Samaria committed half of thy sins; but thou hast multiplied thine abominations more than they, and hast justified thy sisters in all thine abominations which thou hast done.
52 Thou also, which hast judged thy sisters, bear thine own shame for thy sins that thou hast committed more abominable than they: they are more righteous than thou: yea, be thou confounded also, and bear thy shame, in that thou hast justified thy sisters.
53 When I shall bring again their captivity, the captivity of Sodom and her daughters, and the captivity of Samaria and her daughters, then will I bring again the captivity of thy captives in the midst of them:
54 That thou mayest bear thine own shame, and mayest be confounded in all that thou hast done, in that thou art a comfort unto them.

The Lord GOD declares that Sodom, the sister to Jerusalem has not done what Jerusalem has done. The iniquity of Sodom was pride, much bread and idleness. She did not strengthen the hand of the poor and the needy. The people of Sodom were haughty and committed abominations before the LORD: therefore. they were taken away by the LORD as he saw the good in doing so. Neither has Samaria committed half the sins that Jerusalem has done. Yet, Jerusalem has judged her "sisters" while she should have borne the shame of her own sins which were more abominable. The two sister cities are more righteous than Jerusalem who should bear its own shame.

When the LORD brings the captivity of the two sister-cities and Jerusalem, then the captivity of all the cities shall be combined together so that the people can be confounded by and bear their own shame in everything that they have done and this will be a comfort to the people in the sister-cities.

55 When thy sisters, Sodom and her daughters, shall return to their former estate, and Samaria and her daughters shall return to their former estate, then thou and thy daughters shall return to your former estate.
56 For thy sister Sodom was not mentioned by thy mouth in the day of thy pride,
57 Before thy wickedness was discovered, as at the time of thy reproach of the daughters of Syria, and all that are round about her, the daughters of the Philistines, which despise thee round about.
58 Thou hast borne thy lewdness and thine abominations, saith the LORD.

When Sodom and Samaria return to their former places in which they are no longer held captives in Babylon, then the people of Jerusalem can no longer look with disdain at the people of Sodom as though the people of Jerusalem are better than they. The wickedness of the people of Jerusalem has been discovered and compared to the harlot; she has been seen for her own abominations and the people of Jerusalem are not the holy people who were looked up to at the time of David and Solomon.

59 For thus saith the Lord GOD; I will even deal with thee as thou hast done, which hast despised the oath in breaking the covenant.
60 Nevertheless I will remember my covenant with thee in the days of thy youth, and I will establish unto thee an everlasting covenant.
61 Then thou shalt remember thy ways, and be ashamed, when thou shalt receive thy sisters, thine elder and thy younger: and I will give them unto thee for daughters, but not by thy covenant.
62 And I will establish my covenant with thee; and thou shalt know that I am the LORD:
63 That thou mayest remember, and be confounded, and never open thy mouth any more because of thy shame, when I am pacified toward thee for all that thou hast done, saith the Lord GOD.

The Lord GOD will deal with the people of Jerusalem as they have done as they broke the oath of the covenant. Nevertheless, the LORD shall keep and remember his everlasting covenant with the people. Then, the people of Jerusalem shall remember their ways and the people will be ashamed because they will receive the two sisters as daughters to care for but not at their own request, not by their own covenant. The LORD has put together the people and the people shall know that the LORD is God. Then the people shall remember and be confounded and never open their mouth any more because of their own history of shameful behavior. When the LORD is pacified toward Jerusalem for all that they have done, they should not open their mouths any more because of their shameful behavior.

CHAPTER 17

1 And the word of the LORD came unto me, saying,
2 Son of man, put forth a riddle, and speak a parable unto the house of Israel;
3 And say, Thus saith the Lord GOD; A great eagle with great wings, longwinged, full of feathers, which had divers colours, came unto Lebanon, and took the highest branch of the cedar:
4 He cropped off the top of his young twigs, and carried it into a land of traffick; he set it in a city of merchants.
5 He took also of the seed of the land, and planted it in a fruitful field; he placed it by great waters, and set it as a willow tree.
6 And it grew, and became a spreading vine of low stature, whose branches turned toward him, and the roots thereof were under him: so it became a vine, and brought forth branches, and shot forth sprigs.

The word of the LORD came to Ezekiel, the focus of the Son of man, who is the prototype for the spirit of the Son of the LORD within the body of mankind, to put forth a riddle and speak a parable to the house of Israel. The parable, or riddle, is from the Lord GOD. In the parable, a great eagle with great wings, long wings, full of feathers which had diverse colors came to Lebanon and took the highest branch of the cedar. The eagle symbolizes a great leader of the human state with great vision. This eagle not only has great vision but he is full of feathers which can take him higher than eagles with smaller and lesser wings. The fact that the feathers have diverse colors means that the eagle is able to bring together the people of many shades of belief and different colors; he wants to be the leader of many people and nations. This particular eagle landed atop the highest branch of a cedar of Lebanon. The eagle has landed on a high place which symbolizes the highest point of Lebanon which is located in the kingdom of Israel. This eagle symbolizes the king of Babylon who has come to Israel.

The great eagle cropped off the top of the young twigs, the king of Israel and carried it into the land of traffic, a land of many people and he offered the young twigs, the princes of Israel, for sale in a city of merchants, which is Babylon. The eagle also took the seed of the land, the person of Ezekiel, and planted it in a fruitful field; he placed it by great waters and set it to receive water as a willow tree. The seed of the land, Ezekiel, grew and became a spreading vine of low stature, whose branches turned toward him and the roots of the vine were under him: so the roots of the spiritual vine of life were under the eagle as Ezekiel is a captive in Babylon. So it became a vine that brought forth branches and shot forth sprigs to attach themselves to other living things as they entwine around the other earthly growth. This vine which is growing on earth is the spiritual vine in captivity brought by a man who symbolizes the angel of the LORD with great vision that needs to be accepted and magnified on earth.

7 There was also another great eagle with great wings and many feathers: and, behold, this vine did bend her roots toward him, and shot forth her branches toward him, that he might water it by the furrows of her plantation.
8 It was planted in a good soil by great waters, that it might bring forth branches, and that it might bear fruit, that it might be a goodly vine.

The Symbolic Version of Ezekiel

9 Say thou, Thus saith the Lord GOD; Shall it prosper? shall he not pull up the roots thereof, and cut off the fruit thereof, that it wither? it shall wither in all the leaves of her spring, even without great power or many people to pluck it up by the roots thereof.
10 Yea, behold, being planted, shall it prosper? shall it not utterly wither, when the east wind toucheth it? it shall wither in the furrows where it grew.

In the parable, there is another eagle with great wings and many feathers and behold, this vine did bend her roots toward him and shot forth her branches toward him so that he might water it by the furrows of her plantation. This vine was planted in good soil by great waters so it will bear fruit and be a goodly vine.

The Lord GOD has instructed Ezekiel to ask if the vine shall prosper? shall he not pull up the roots of the vine and cut off the fruit thereof so that it shall wither? it shall wither in all the years of her spring, even without great power or many people to pluck the vine up by its roots. Shall the vine being planted prosper? shall it wither when the east wind touches it? it shall wither in the furrows where it grew.

11 Moreover the word of the LORD came unto me, saying,
12 Say now to the rebellious house, Know ye not what these things mean? tell them, Behold, the king of Babylon is come to Jerusalem, and hath taken the king thereof, and the princes thereof, and led them with him to Babylon;
13 And hath taken of the king's seed, and made a covenant with him, and hath taken an oath of him: he hath also taken the mighty of the land:
14 That the kingdom might be base, that it might not lift itself up, but that by keeping of his covenant it might stand.
15 But he rebelled against him in sending his ambassadors into Egypt, that they might give him horses and much people. Shall he prosper? shall he escape that doeth such things? or shall he break the covenant, and be delivered?

Moreover, the word of the LORD came to Ezekiel, saying, Say now to the rebellious house, Know you not what these things mean? Tell them that the king of Babylon has come to Jerusalem, and has taken the king and the princes thereof and led them with him to Babylon; and he has taken king's seed and made a covenant with him, and taken an oath with him. There is an earthly agreement between Babylon and Israel. The king of Babylon has also taken the mighty of the land, the leadership of Israel away from the people, so that the defeated kingdom of Israel might become base, lowered and fallen so that it cannot lift itself up, but by the keeping of his covenant it might stand. But the leaders of Jerusalem rebelled against the king of Babylon by sending ambassadors to Egypt, that the Egyptians might give them horses and people to defend themselves from Babylon. The questions to be answered are these: Shall the king of Israel prosper? shall he escape that does such things? or, shall he break the covenant with Babylon and be delivered?

16 As I live, saith the Lord GOD, surely in the place where the king dwelleth that made him king, whose oath he despised, and whose covenant he brake, even with him in the midst of Babylon he shall die.
17 Neither shall Pharaoh with his mighty army and great company make for him in the war, by casting up mounts, and building forts, to cut off many persons:
18 Seeing he despised the oath by breaking the covenant, when, lo, he had given his hand, and hath done all these things, he shall not escape.

The Lord GOD says that as surely as he lives, the place where the king dwells among the people that made him king, surely in the place where the king dwelt that made him king, whose oath he despised, and whose covenant he broke, even with him in the midst of Babylon, he shall die. Pharaoh with his mighty army and great company will not give the king of Israel mounts, horses with which to fight, and building forts, to stop many persons. Pharaoh can see that the king of Israel despised the oath he made with the king of Babylon by breaking the covenant. The king of Israel shall not escape the things which he has done. The king of Israel has broken the covenant that has made with the earthly kings of Babylon and Egypt.

19 Therefore thus saith the Lord GOD; As I live, surely mine oath that he hath despised, and my covenant that he hath broken, even it will I recompense upon his own head.
20 And I will spread my net upon him, and he shall be taken in my snare, and I will bring him to Babylon, and will plead with him there for his trespass that he hath trespassed against me.

The Testimony of the Major Prophets

21 And all his fugitives with all his bands shall fall by the sword, and they that remain shall be scattered toward all winds: and ye shall know that I the LORD have spoken it.

Therefore the Lord GOD says, that the king of Israel has despised the oath of the covenant with the LORD, and since the king of Israel has broken the covenant with the LORD, then the LORD will recompense Israel for breaking the covenant. The LORD's net will be spread over the king of Israel and he shall be taken in the LORD's snare, brought to Babylon as a captive there he shall pay for breaking the covenant with the LORD by trespassing against him. All his fugitives and his bands of men shall fall by the sword, and they that remain shall be scattered in all directions, toward all the winds. When you see this event come to pass then you shall know that the LORD has spoken these things.

22 Thus saith the Lord GOD; I will also take of the highest branch of the high cedar, and will set it; I will crop off from the top of his young twigs a tender one, and will plant it upon an high mountain and eminent:
23 In the mountain of the height of Israel will I plant it: and it shall bring forth boughs, and bear fruit, and be a goodly cedar: and under it shall dwell all fowl of every wing; in the shadow of the branches thereof shall they dwell.
24 And all the trees of the field shall know that I the LORD have brought down the high tree, have exalted the low tree, have dried up the green tree, and have made the dry tree to flourish: I the LORD have spoken and have done it.

The Lord GOD says that he will take the highest branch of the high cedar, which symbolizes a person, and will set it in the position of leadership; the LORD will crop off from the top of his young twigs a tender person that will grow and plant it on a high and eminent mountain, a position of leadership, in Israel. The spiritual leader shall bring forth boughs and bear fruit and be a goodly cedar, which symbolize other spiritual people in agreement with the leader, to create the symbol of a tree of life, which represents people who are a part of the living organism on earth which is the tree of life in manifest form. Under the tree of life shall dwell all fowl of every wing; fowl and birds are the symbols of divine thoughts that fly through the air of the spirit where they will dwell in the shadow of the branches, in the living consciousness of the tree of life. And all the trees of the field, which symbolize people, shall know that the LORD has brought down the high tree, the king of Israel, and has exalted the low tree, the person that the LORD has planted. The LORD has dried up the tree that appeared green in the eyes of men, and made the seemingly dry tree to flourish. The spirit of the LORD moving through the affairs of men has spoken and has done it. The king of Israel has fallen and the head of the spiritual tree of life, the representative of the LORD, Ezekiel, has been raised up for those with eyes to see.

CHAPTER 18

1 The word of the LORD came unto me again, saying,
2 What mean ye, that ye use this proverb concerning the land of Israel, saying, The fathers have eaten sour grapes, and the children's teeth are set on edge?
3 As I live, saith the Lord GOD, ye shall not have occasion any more to use this proverb in Israel.
4 Behold, all souls are mine; as the soul of the father, so also the soul of the son is mine: the soul that sinneth, it shall die.

The word of the LORD came once again to Ezekiel, the focus of the Son of man on earth, saying what is the meaning of this proverb that you will use concerning the land of Israel when it is said, The fathers have eaten sour grapes, and the children's teeth are set on edge? The fathers who represent the consciousness of the way things were when there was a visible earthly king who ruled an earthly kingdom. This period of time is over. The countenance of the fathers who hear this news is as though they have eaten sour grapes and their faces reveal the sourness of the message comparable to when they eat sour grapes, and the teeth of their children are set on edge in anticipation of what will become of them as a result of this drastic change.

The Lord GOD states that the fathers and the children of Israel shall no more use this proverb in Israel that has reference to an earthly king who will rule the people. The Lord GOD declares that all souls, all the people are his people: this includes the physical soul with its mind and heart of the father and also the soul of the son. The human souls who acknowledge that they are the children of the LORD, the heavenly Father and King, shall live. The human soul that sins, the person who is "off the mark", who ignores the moving spirit of the LORD and continues to worship earthly idols, shall die. The LORD offers the people who are in agreement with His spirit, life; the people who are attracted to form, death. A person who has sinned in the past is not condemned; there is an opportunity for the person to change while they are alive.

5 But if a man be just, and do that which is lawful and right,
6 And hath not eaten upon the mountains, neither hath lifted up his eyes to the idols of the house of Israel, neither hath defiled his neighbour's wife, neither hath come near to a menstruous woman,
7 And hath not oppressed any, but hath restored to the debtor his pledge, hath spoiled none by violence, hath given his bread to the hungry, and hath covered the naked with a garment;
8 He that hath not given forth upon usury, neither hath taken any increase, that hath withdrawn his hand from iniquity, hath executed true judgment between man and man,
9 Hath walked in my statutes, and hath kept my judgments, to deal truly; he is just, he shall surely live, saith the Lord GOD.

If a man, who did worship material kings and idols in the past, behaves in the present moment in a way that is just, and does what is lawful and right, which means the person must walk in the statutes of the LORD and keeps the LORD's

The Testimony of the Major Prophets

judgments to deal truly with people to prove that he is just, then, the person shall live in agreement with the LORD. There are a list of cautions that people have been doing in their past behavior that are called to their attention so that the sinners will cease the actions which makes them sinners. They should not consider themselves as superior to the other children of the LORD which is symbolized in the expression of eating upon the mountains which are higher than others; nor worshipped idols of material forms of the house of Israel; nor defiled his neighbor's wife; nor come near a menstruous woman; or oppressed any one who is in debt to him but, rather, restored the person's pledge to repay the debt; nor harmed anyone by violence, has given bread to the hungry and clothed the naked with a garment which are evidences of a kind spirit; nor participated in usury, or taken any increase in punishment from a person who has withdrawn from the control of iniquity; and who has executed the true judgment of the LORD's spirit working through each person when dealing with men everywhere. Each individual person is responsible directly to the spirit of the LORD who is connected directly with each one. Since all souls belong to the Lord GOD, then what of the relationship between the father and his son?

10 If he beget a son that is a robber, a shedder of blood, and that doeth the like to any one of these things,
11 And that doeth not any of those duties, but even hath eaten upon the mountains, and defiled his neighbour's wife,
12 Hath oppressed the poor and needy, hath spoiled by violence, hath not restored the pledge, and hath lifted up his eyes to the idols, hath committed abomination,
13 Hath given forth upon usury, and hath taken increase: shall he then live? he shall not live: he hath done all these abominations; he shall surely die; his blood shall be upon him.

If an earthly father begets a son that is a robber, a person who harms or slays another, a son that does not do the right behaviors, but does the sinful behaviors, such as vanity (eating upon the mountains), defiling a neighbor's wife, oppressing the poor and needy, spoiled other people and things by violence, has not restored the pledge to debtors to assume responsibility for their own debts, worshipped idols, committed abominations, participated in usury and take increased advantage of his fellow man, then shall that person live in the kingdom of God? He shall not live in the kingdom of God because he has done and will not cease from doing all these abominations and he shall surely die as he moves away from the spirit of the LORD. The blood of his death is upon him because of his own behavior; it is not upon the father.

14 Now, lo, if he beget a son, that seeth all his father's sins which he hath done, and considereth, and doeth not such like,
15 That hath not eaten upon the mountains, neither hath lifted up his eyes to the idols of the house of Israel, hath not defiled his neighbour's wife,
16 Neither hath oppressed any, hath not withholden the pledge, neither hath spoiled by violence, but hath given his bread to the hungry, and hath covered the naked with a garment,
17 That hath taken off his hand from the poor, that hath not received usury nor increase, hath executed my judgments, hath walked in my statutes; he shall not die for the iniquity of his father, he shall surely live.

Now if the son sees all the sins that his father has done, considers the wrong actions, and he does not do likewise by the sins of vanity, idolatry, defilement of women, oppressing others, being violent to his fellowman instead of feeding and clothing the poor, who does not practice usury, then that son has walked in the footsteps of the statutes and the judgments of the LORD, then, that son shall not die even if he has a father who is a sinner and continues to live in iniquity. The father will not escape the law of the LORD.

18 As for his father, because he cruelly oppressed, spoiled his brother by violence, and did that which is not good among his people, lo, even he shall die in his iniquity.
19 Yet say ye, Why? doth not the son bear the iniquity of the father? When the son hath done that which is lawful and right, and hath kept all my statutes, and hath done them, he shall surely live.

The father will die in his iniquity according to the law of the LORD. Yet, you may ask why does the father die and the son live? Does not the son bear the iniquity of the father? The LORD answers that when the son has done that which is lawful and right, kept and done the statutes, he shall surely live.

20 The soul that sinneth, it shall die. The son shall not bear the iniquity of the father, neither shall the father bear the iniquity of the son: the righteousness of the righteous shall be upon him, and the wickedness of the wicked shall be upon him.
21 But if the wicked will turn from all his sins that he hath committed, and keep all my statutes, and do that which is lawful and right, he shall surely live, he shall not die.

The soul, the person, that sins shall die. The son shall not bear the iniquity of the father, neither shall the father bear the iniquity of the son: the law of the LORD is that the righteousness of the righteous shall be upon him, and the wickedness of the wicked shall be upon him. But if the wicked will repent and turn away from all his sins, then he shall surely live and not die because life is in the spirit of the LORD.

22 All his transgressions that he hath committed, they shall not be mentioned unto him: in his righteousness that he hath done he shall live.
23 Have I any pleasure at all that the wicked should die? saith the Lord GOD: and not that he should return from his ways, and live?
24 But when the righteous turneth away from his righteousness, and committeth iniquity, and doeth according to all the abominations that the wicked man doeth, shall he live? All his righteousness that he hath done shall not be mentioned: in his trespass that he hath trespassed, and in his sin that he hath sinned, in them shall he die.

All his transgressions that he has committed in the past shall not be mentioned to him: in the righteousness—the right-use-ness of his earthly equipment— the behaviors that he has done, he shall live. Have I any pleasure at all that the wicked should die? asks the Lord GOD: and should not a sinner return from his ways, and live? But when the righteous turns away from his righteousness, and commits iniquity, and behaves according to all the abominations that the wicked man does, shall he live? All his righteousness that he has done in the past shall not be mentioned: a person shall die by the trespasses and sins away from the statutes of the LORD in the behaviors and actions of the person. In the past, people have said that the way of the LORD is not equal.

25 Yet ye say, The way of the Lord is not equal. Hear now, O house of Israel; Is not my way equal? are not your ways unequal?
26 When a righteous man turneth away from his righteousness, and committeth iniquity, and dieth in them; for his iniquity that he hath done shall he die.
27 Again, when the wicked man turneth away from his wickedness that he hath committed, and doeth that which is lawful and right, he shall save his soul alive.
28 Because he considereth, and turneth away from all his transgressions that he hath committed, he shall surely live, he shall not die.

Ezekiel, as the spokesperson for the Son of man on earth, declares that the house of Israel should hear the voice of the LORD: Is not my way equal? are not your ways unequal? The reward and punishment should be obvious and immediate. When a righteous man turns away from his righteousness, and commits iniquity, and dies in them; for his iniquity that he has done, he shall die. Dying is moving away from the spirit of the LORD. Again, when the wicked man turns away from his wickedness that he has committed, and does that which is lawful and right, he shall save his soul alive as he moves toward, and expresses, the spirit of the LORD. Because he considers, and turns away from all his transgressions that he has committed, he shall surely live; he shall not die if he is in the spirit of the LORD because the LORD does not die.

29 Yet saith the house of Israel, The way of the Lord is not equal. O house of Israel, are not my ways equal? are not your ways unequal?
30 Therefore I will judge you, O house of Israel, every one according to his ways, saith the Lord GOD. Repent, and turn yourselves from all your transgressions; so iniquity shall not be your ruin.
31 Cast away from you all your transgressions, whereby ye have transgressed; and make you a new heart and a new spirit: for why will ye die, O house of Israel?
32 For I have no pleasure in the death of him that dieth, saith the Lord GOD: wherefore turn yourselves, and live ye.

The Testimony of the Major Prophets

Yet, the house of Israel, in its fallen state, says, The way of the Lord is not equal. O house of Israel, are not my ways equal? are not your ways unequal? Therefore, the LORD will judge the house of Israel, the people who represent Israel in the fallen state, according to your ways, your actions and behaviors. The house of Israel, the people in the fallen state, are advised to repent and turn away from their transgressions from the way of the LORD, so that iniquity will not be their ruin.

Cast away from you all your transgressions, whereby you have transgressed; and make you a new heart and a new spirit: for why will you die, O house of Israel? I have no pleasure in the death of him that dies, declares the Lord GOD: wherefore, turn yourselves, repent from your ways of iniquity and live in the moving spirit of the LORD by being true to the spirit of the LORD.

CHAPTER 19

1 Moreover take thou up a lamentation for the princes of Israel,
2 And say, What is thy mother? A lioness: she lay down among lions, she nourished her whelps among young lions.
3 And she brought up one of her whelps: it became a young lion, and it learned to catch the prey; it devoured men.
4 The nations also heard of him; he was taken in their pit, and they brought him with chains unto the land of Egypt.

Ezekiel instructs those who will listen and respond to his teachings that it is time for them to lament. A lament is a metered chant of three beats followed by two beats usually composed for funerals of fallen leaders. A lament was often used by prophets in the Old Testament to predict the death of a nation. This lamentation describes, in allegorical terms, the recent fate of Israel through the experience of the princes of Israel. The princes of Israel were Jehoahaz and Jehoiachin: each of the princes reigned only three months.

The lioness is the symbol of the nation of Israel, Judah and Jerusalem who nurtured her young lions to become leaders. One of her cubs, Jehoahaz, learned to catch prey and devoured men, which is symbolic language for his oppressive policies. The nations around Israel heard of him, eventually captured him, and took him in chains to the land of Egypt. This leader, symbolized by a young lion, did not stay in power for very long.

5 Now when she saw that she had waited, and her hope was lost, then she took another of her whelps, and made him a young lion.
6 And he went up and down among the lions, he became a young lion, and learned to catch the prey, and devoured men.
7 And he knew their desolate palaces, and he laid waste their cities; and the land was desolate, and the fulness thereof, by the noise of his roaring.
8 Then the nations set against him on every side from the provinces, and spread their net over him: he was taken in their pit.
9 And they put him in ward in chains, and brought him to the king of Babylon: they brought him into holds, that his voice should no more be heard upon the mountains of Israel.

Now when the lioness, who symbolizes the mother of the people of Israel, saw what had happened to the young lion, the prince who tried to lead Israel, she took another of her whelps and made him a young lion, a young leader and he went down among the lions and devoured men, advocated oppressive policies. He knew their desolate palaces, the lions lived in places that were desolate of the spirit of the LORD, and he laid waste to their cities. The land, without the spirit of the LORD, would become desolate in the fullness, throughout the land as the desolation in the men revealed itself in the environment created by desolate people

Then the nations set against him, they did not follow their leader, and he was captured in their net, put in chains and brought to the king of Babylon. His voice was heard no more in the mountains of Israel, which are the symbols for the

The Testimony of the Major Prophets

consciousness of the leadership of Israel. The reason for the lamentation by Ezekiel is that Israel is leaderless since the two princes have been taken captives by Egypt and Babylon respectively.

10 Thy mother is like a vine in thy blood, planted by the waters: she was fruitful and full of branches by reason of many waters.
11 And she had strong rods for the sceptres of them that bare rule, and her stature was exalted among the thick branches, and she appeared in her height with the multitude of her branches.
12 But she was plucked up in fury, she was cast down to the ground, and the east wind dried up her fruit: her strong rods were broken and withered; the fire consumed them.
13 And now she is planted in the wilderness, in a dry and thirsty ground.
14 And fire is gone out of a rod of her branches, which hath devoured her fruit, so that she hath no strong rod to be a sceptre to rule. This is a lamentation, and shall be for a lamentation.

Ezekiel is making the point that the problem is not with the lioness, the mother of the young princes who were leaders for a short period of time. The lioness brings forth young lions to lead the people. She is like a vine in your blood planted by waters so that she will bear quantities of fruit. She is fruitful and full of branches by reason of the many waters, the spirit of truth from the LORD which is flowing through the body of mankind. She had strong rods, symbols of direction and authority, for them who would rule. Her stature was exalted among the thick branches which are symbols of the stronger people within the living vine. The vine, the mother of the young lions, is growing and she is seen in her height with her many branches. People are available everywhere in quantity; there is no shortage of human beings.

But the people of Israel were plucked up in the fury by the people around her, and she was cast down to the ground and not allowed to multiply and grow. The east wind, the wind that came out of the east, the symbol of the future, and also the location of the direction of Babylon, dried up her fruit, dried up the leadership and the people. Her strong rods, her leadership, were broken and withered; the fire, the power of the people of Babylon, consumed them.

Now she, the vine of the people of Israel, is planted in the wilderness, in a dry and thirsty ground And fire, the spiritual fire, is gone out of a rod of her branches, which has devoured her fruit, so that she has no strong rod to be a scepter to rule. This is a lamentation that Ezekiel is calling to the attention of his listeners, and, it shall be a lamentation until some one, some people, will assume the responsibility to nurture the vine of life by letting the power of the spirit of the LORD, the creative fire, find increased expression through the vine of life.

CHAPTER 20

1 And it came to pass in the seventh year, in the fifth month, the tenth day of the month, that certain of the elders of Israel came to inquire of the LORD, and sat before me.
2 Then came the word of the LORD unto me, saying,
3 Son of man, speak unto the elders of Israel, and say unto them, Thus saith the Lord GOD; Are ye come to inquire of me? As I live, saith the Lord GOD, I will not be inquired of by you.

Certain elders of Israel, the religious hierarchy of the time, came to Ezekiel to inquire of the LORD and they sat before him. There was a recognition by these particular elders that Ezekiel had a special relationship with the LORD that they did not possess. The fact that they came to Ezekiel to inquire of the LORD is a significant event as they sensed that they could inquire of the LORD through the person of Ezekiel.

Then came the word of the LORD to Ezekiel saying, Son of man, the spiritual focus of mankind who receives the word of the LORD, speak to the elders of Israel and say to them with the authority of the Lord GOD; Are you come to inquire of the LORD? The Lord GOD speaking through Ezekiel states that the LORD will not be questioned by the elders of Israel. The true position of fallen man to the LORD is not to **question** the LORD but rather to **serve** the LORD. The approach of the elders of Israel is not harmonious to a covenant-agreement with the LORD which would move them toward the restored state as a member of the body of the Son of man; their approach will keep them in the fallen state as a member of the fallen body of the son of man, mankind in the fallen state. The LORD asks Ezekiel to intercede for them and make them aware of their sin.

4 Wilt thou judge them, son of man, wilt thou judge them? cause them to know the abominations of their fathers:
5 And say unto them, Thus saith the Lord GOD; In the day when I chose Israel, and lifted up mine hand unto the seed of the house of Jacob, and made myself known unto them in the land of Egypt, when I lifted up mine hand unto them, saying, I am the LORD your God;
6 In the day that I lifted up mine hand unto them, to bring them forth of the land of Egypt into a land that I had espied for them, flowing with milk and honey, which is the glory of all lands:
7 Then said I unto them, Cast ye away every man the abominations of his eyes, and defile not yourselves with the idols of Egypt: I am the LORD your God.

Ezekiel, who is a member of the body of the Son of man, is asked to put himself in their fallen position, the son of man, and judge them by making the elders aware of their sin, the abominations of their fathers who turned themselves away from the LORD. The LORD instructs Ezekiel to remind the elders of the day when the LORD chose Israel, the spiritual expression of the LORD through a people, which began when the LORD lifted up his hand to offer the seed, the offspring of the house of Jacob (who became Israel), saying, I am the LORD your God. This reminder is necessary to indicate to a people who had forgotten that the LORD had chosen them to let His spirit find manifestation into the earth. If the people, the children of Israel, would do this, then, they would be brought forth from the land of Egypt

The Testimony of the Major Prophets

into a land seen by God that would be flowing with milk and honey, a land that would be blessed by the spirit of God released through God's people into the earth, which is the glory of the LORD available to all lands.

Then, Ezekiel said to the elders of Israel, that they are to cast away all abominations from their eyes which keep them attached to the fallen state. The elders are not to defile themselves with these earthy treasures, the material idols that are symbolized as the false gods of Egypt: I am the LORD your God. Would the elders of Israel listen to the word of the LORD as spoken through Ezekiel?

8 But they rebelled against me, and would not hearken unto me: they did not every man cast away the abominations of their eyes, neither did they forsake the idols of Egypt: then I said, I will pour out my fury upon them, to accomplish my anger against them in the midst of the land of Egypt.

The elders of Israel behaved in the ways of their fathers: they rebelled against the word of the LORD and they would not listen to the admonition of Ezekiel. The elders did not cast away their abominations, their abominable behaviors, and neither did they forsake the idols of Egypt, the material treasures of the earth which they worshipped. Since the elders would not repent and change their ways, the LORD pours out his fury upon them as punishment to those who remain in the midst of Egypt, the symbol of the materialistic state which has been chosen instead of the spiritual state of serving the LORD. The distortions of the true design would appear on earth instead of the kingdom of God. The people were captives in Egypt and they had forgotten that their mission was and is to bring the kingdom of God into the earth. God could not allow this distortion to continue.

9 But I wrought for my name's sake, that it should not be polluted before the heathen, among whom they were, in whose sight I made myself known unto them, in bringing them forth out of the land of Egypt.
10 Wherefore I caused them to go forth out of the land of Egypt, and brought them into the wilderness.
11 And I gave them my statutes, and shewed them my judgments, which if a man do, he shall even live in them.
12 Moreover also I gave them my sabbaths, to be a sign between me and them, that they might know that I am the LORD that sanctify them.

The spirit of the LORD working through a few of his servants wrought, brought about, the exodus from Egypt so that the LORD's kingdom would not remain polluted and distorted in Egypt. It was the LORD who brought the children of Israel from Egypt into the wilderness where they received the LORD's statutes and Judgments. If the children of Israel do these things, they shall live. The LORD would give them the Sabbaths, the holy days, that come from the LORD as a sign between the LORD and his people so that they might know that it is the LORD that sanctifies them. The children of Israel can only know this experience if they are in the covenant-agreement with the LORD. Did the elders of Israel accept the invitation, instruction and statutes of the LORD?

13 But the house of Israel rebelled against me in the wilderness: they walked not in my statutes, and they despised my judgments, which if a man do, he shall even live in them; and my sabbaths they greatly polluted: then I said, I would pour out my fury upon them in the wilderness, to consume them.
14 But I wrought for my name's sake, that it should not be polluted before the heathen, in whose sight I brought them out.
15 Yet also I lifted up my hand unto them in the wilderness, that I would not bring them into the land which I had given them, flowing with milk and honey, which is the glory of all lands;
16 Because they despised my judgments, and walked not in my statutes, but polluted my sabbaths: for their heart went after their idols.

The house of Israel did not obey the LORD. They rebelled against the word of the LORD. They did not walk in the statutes; they despised the judgments which, if they lived in them, they would live. They polluted the Sabbaths, the holy days, which the LORD gave them. It is because of the rebellion of the people who did not reveal the spirit of the LORD that the people experienced the fury of the LORD in the wilderness. The spirit of the LORD was always offered to the people but it was the people who polluted the name of the LORD, I AM, which each of them carries. The land flowing with milk an honey, the symbol of the manifest kingdom of God on earth, has always been available for the people who live and reveal the LORD's spirit which would produce the glory of the LORD. The people chose to

The Symbolic Version of Ezekiel

despise the LORD's judgments, not walk in His statures and pollute the Sabbath days because their hearts went after their idols, their own earthly treasures, instead of serving the spirit of the LORD on earth.

17 Nevertheless mine eye spared them from destroying them, neither did I make an end of them in the wilderness.
18 But I said unto their children in the wilderness, Walk ye not in the statutes of your fathers, neither observe their judgments, nor defile yourselves with their idols:
19 I am the LORD your God; walk in my statutes, and keep my judgments, and do them;
20 And hallow my sabbaths; and they shall be a sign between me and you, that ye may know that I am the LORD your God.

Nevertheless, the vision of the LORD spared the children of Israel from destruction in the wilderness. But the LORD did command the fallen people to not walk in the ways and statutes of their earthly fathers, observe their judgments as to what was right or defile themselves by worshipping the idols which their fathers were worshipping. The LORD's spirit is with each one of them individually. This is the reason that the LORD can say, "I am the LORD your God; walk in my statutes, and keep my judgments, and do them; And hallow my Sabbaths; and they shall be a sign between me and you, that you may know that I am the LORD your God." If a person **expresses** the spirit of the LORD, the person will **know** the spirit of the LORD which is flowing through the human capacities.

21 Notwithstanding the children rebelled against me: they walked not in my statutes, neither kept my judgments to do them, which if a man do, he shall even live in them; they polluted my sabbaths: then I said, I would pour out my fury upon them, to accomplish my anger against them in the wilderness.
22 Nevertheless I withdrew mine hand, and wrought for my name's sake, that it should not be polluted in the sight of the heathen, in whose sight I brought them forth.
23 I lifted up mine hand unto them also in the wilderness, that I would scatter them among the heathen, and disperse them through the countries;
24 Because they had not executed my judgments, but had despised my statutes, and had polluted my sabbaths, and their eyes were after their fathers' idols.

The LORD is aware that the children of Israel, then and now, rebel against His spirit which is flowing through everyone in every generation. Fallen people do not walk in the LORD's statutes or keep His judgments, which if man did, he shall live in the spirit of the LORD. Since, man does not walk in the spirit of the LORD, he pollutes the Sabbaths, the potential holy days, and the fury of the LORD is poured upon the people instead of the blessings.

Nevertheless, the LORD withdrew his hand, his conscious control and participation, from people in the fallen state so that the name of the LORD, I AM, is not polluted in the sight of the heathen, the sinners and the fallen people, whom the LORD had brought forth from Egypt. The result without the cohesive spirit of the LORD to hold them together was that the children of Israel would be scattered among the heathen and dispersed throughout the countries of the heathen. This is the direct, predictable result when the people ignore the statutes, pollute the Sabbaths and lust after the idols of the material world by ignoring the spirit of the LORD which is everywhere and in all things. As the spirit of the LORD is ignored, the LORD gives a different set of circumstances which are not heavenly.

25 Wherefore I gave them also statutes that were not good, and judgments whereby they should not live;
26 And I polluted them in their own gifts, in that they caused to pass through the fire all that openeth the womb, that I might make them desolate, to the end that they might know that I am the LORD.
27 Therefore, son of man, speak unto the house of Israel, and say unto them, Thus saith the Lord GOD; Yet in this your fathers have blasphemed me, in that they have committed a trespass against me.
28 For when I had brought them into the land, for the which I lifted up mine hand to give it to them, then they saw every high hill, and all the thick trees, and they offered there their sacrifices, and there they presented the provocation of their offering: there also they made their sweet savour, and poured out there their drink offerings.

The LORD, whose spirit is everywhere, gives to fallen man statutes which are not good and judgments whereby they shall not live, but would lead to death. The heavenly gifts which the LORD gives are polluted by man because man is fallen; he is out of position to receive the heavenly fire which warms the soul and he receives the hell-fire which burns the soul. It is all fire, the power, of the LORD which brings comfort or desolation to the end that the people shall know

The Testimony of the Major Prophets

that there is only one LORD who does everything and who is everywhere. The unpleasant experience of the burning of the fire can be seen as a warning for man to change his ways.

29 Then I said unto them, What is the high place whereunto ye go? And the name thereof is called Bamah unto this day.
30 Wherefore say unto the house of Israel, Thus saith the Lord GOD; Are ye polluted after the manner of your fathers? and commit ye whoredom after their abominations?
31 For when ye offer your gifts, when ye make your sons to pass through the fire, ye pollute yourselves with all your idols, even unto this day: and shall I be inquired of by you, O house of Israel? As I live, saith the Lord GOD, I will not be inquired of by you.
32 And that which cometh into your mind shall not be at all, that ye say, We will be as the heathen, as the families of the countries, to serve wood and stone.

Then Ezekiel said to the elders of Israel, What is the high place to which you aspire to go? And the name of this place is called Bamah, which means, "an eminence", or, "high place", which can be seen as a heavenly place or a place of the covenant-agreement with the LORD. Ezekiel is commanded to speak for the Lord GOD as he asks the elders of Israel if they are polluted after the manner of their fathers? and do they commit whoredom by lusting after the abominations of the material world that their fathers were guilty of lusting after? When the fathers teach their sons to walk in the wicked, fallen ways by which the fathers have polluted themselves as they worship the idols of the environment, they make their sons walk through the same fire of the wrong experience. The fathers must see themselves as sinners against the way of the LORD. Shall the LORD be questioned by the sinners of the house of Israel? The Lord GOD states that he will not be inquired of, he will not answer, a people who are not his servants. The LORD declares through Ezekiel that the divine things from God which come into the minds of man shall not come to pass for those who will live as the heathen do when they worship their idols of wood and stone, the material things of the world. There is no success possible for man as long as he remains in the fallen state.

33 As I live, saith the Lord GOD, surely with a mighty hand, and with a stretched out arm, and with fury poured out, will I rule over you:
34 And I will bring you out from the people, and will gather you out of the countries wherein ye are scattered, with a mighty hand, and with a stretched out arm, and with fury poured out.
35 And I will bring you into the wilderness of the people, and there will I plead with you face to face.
36 Like as I pleaded with your fathers in the wilderness of the land of Egypt, so will I plead with you, saith the Lord GOD.
37 And I will cause you to pass under the rod, and I will bring you into the bond of the covenant:
38 And I will purge out from among you the rebels, and them that transgress against me: I will bring them forth out of the country where they sojourn, and they shall not enter into the land of Israel: and ye shall know that I am the LORD.

The eternal Lord God states, through Ezekiel, that as He lives, He shall rule with a mighty hand and with a stretched out arm that holds man away from the LORD with fury. The LORD will bring each person into a wilderness, a place which is barren of the blessings of the LORD, to plead with each person face to face as the LORD pleaded with their fathers in the wilderness of the land of Egypt.

The purpose of the fury of the LORD is not punishment! The purpose of the LORD is to have the individual pass under the rod of discipline and control to accept the spirit of the LORD so that the person can be brought into the bond of the covenant, a close bond of association with the LORD. In the covenant, the LORD will purge away from you the rebels, rebellious people with rebellious thoughts, that transgress against the spirit of the LORD. The LORD can bring the people who are willing to express the LORD's spirit out of the country where they sojourn in the fallen state, and the people who are not willing to follow shall not enter the promised land of spiritual Israel. A separation will occur between the followers of the LORD's spirit into the covenant and the rebels who will not enter into the covenant. In the place of the covenant, the person shall know the LORD. The elders of Israel are not in oneness, in agreement, in the covenant with the spirit of the LORD.

39 As for you, O house of Israel, thus saith the Lord GOD; Go ye, serve ye every one his idols, and hereafter also, if ye will not hearken unto me: but pollute ye my holy name no more with your gifts, and with your idols.
40 For in mine holy mountain, in the mountain of the height of Israel, saith the Lord GOD, there shall all the house of Israel, all of them in the land, serve me: there will I accept them, and there will I require your offerings, and the firstfruits of your oblations, with all your holy things.

The word of the LORD spoken through Ezekiel tells the house of Israel to go their way presently and hereafter, as they serve their idols, their behaviors, which they have inherited from their fathers from the past. If the house of Israel chooses not to listen to the word of the LORD, they can go their own way but they are told not to pollute the LORD's holy name with their gifts and their idols. The elders of Israel have been told that the LORD will accept all who will serve the LORD by serving the LORD's spirit, by letting the spirit of the LORD flow through them. These are the people who are in the holy mountain of the LORD, the holy place in spiritual consciousness, where the LORD and his people are one. It is in this holy place that the LORD will require the holy offerings of a people who are willing to serve the LORD's spirit in all that they do, all their offerings and oblations, which are holy things. This is the place of acceptance by the LORD of His restored people.

41 I will accept you with your sweet savour, when I bring you out from the people, and gather you out of the countries wherein ye have been scattered; and I will be sanctified in you before the heathen.
42 And ye shall know that I am the LORD, when I shall bring you into the land of Israel, into the country for the which I lifted up mine hand to give it to your fathers.
43 And there shall ye remember your ways, and all your doings, wherein ye have been defiled; and ye shall lothe yourselves in your own sight for all your evils that ye have committed.
44 And ye shall know that I am the LORD, when I have wrought with you for my name's sake, not according to your wicked ways, nor according to your corrupt doings, O ye house of Israel, saith the Lord GOD.

This is the spiritual place of acceptance which is available to each person. In this place the LORD will accept each person who expresses the sweet savor of the LORD's spirit as it is expressed through each one. The LORD will bring the person who does this out from the fallen people and gather them from the places to which them have been scattered. This can only occur as the LORD's spirit is sanctified in the individual before, in the sight of, the heathen, the people who do not know the LORD. In this holy place, the person shall know the LORD who has brought them into the land of Israel, into the spiritual place where the fallen Jacob became Israel. This is the place that the LORD gave to your forefathers. In this holy place, you shall remember your ways, all your distorted and polluted doings, where you have defiled yourselves by your behaviors. You shall loathe yourself in your own vision and viewpoint for all the evils that you have committed. In the holy place of the covenant with the LORD, you shall know that it is the LORD who has brought you out of the fallen state for His own sake and not because of your wicked ways or your corrupt behaviors, you members of the body of people called the house of Israel

45 Moreover the word of the LORD came unto me, saying,
46 Son of man, set thy face toward the south, and drop thy word toward the south, and prophesy against the forest of the south field;
47 And say to the forest of the south, Hear the word of the LORD; Thus saith the Lord GOD; Behold, I will kindle a fire in thee, and it shall devour every green tree in thee, and every dry tree: the flaming flame shall not be quenched, and all faces from the south to the north shall be burned therein.
48 And all flesh shall see that I the LORD have kindled it: it shall not be quenched.
49 Then said I, Ah Lord GOD! they say of me, Doth he not speak parables?

Ezekiel had been commanded by his LORD, who addresses the Son of man, Ezekiel and all who hear and do his words, with their mission on earth for the LORD. They are to set their faces to the south, the symbol of the present time, and prophesy, to the people in the fallen state who are willing to listen, who are symbolized as the forest of the south, to hear the word of the LORD as they have heard the word of the LORD. It is not the word of the fallen person who speaks but the word of the LORD carried by a restored person, a member of the body of the Son of man.

Behold, the LORD will kindle a fire in you who listen and respond, and it shall devour every green tree in you, and every dry tree, which are the symbols of the trees of hope for the future and the disbelief caused by the failures of

The Testimony of the Major Prophets

the past. The flaming flame of the spirit of the LORD shall not be quenched, and all faces of the people who hear the words of fire from the south to the north shall be burned in the light and heat of the words. And all flesh shall see that the LORD has kindled this heavenly fire and it shall not be quenched.

Then said Ezekiel, Oh Lord GOD! they say of me, Does he not speak parables? If a person can not truly understand until he experiences the reality of the spirit of the LORD for himself, the reality of the covenant-agreement, then he who does not yet understand thinks that Ezekiel speaks in parables. But parables are words used to lead a person who does not know to the truth in one's own experience.

CHAPTER 21

1 And the word of the LORD came unto me, saying,
2 Son of man, set thy face toward Jerusalem, and drop thy word toward the holy places, and prophesy against the land of Israel,
3 And say to the land of Israel, Thus saith the LORD; Behold, I am against thee, and will draw forth my sword out of his sheath, and will cut off from thee the righteous and the wicked.

The expression of the spirit from the LORD came to Ezekiel saying, Son of man, the spirit of the LORD coming to focus in the flesh of man, set the face of your attention toward Jerusalem, the center of the power structure of the religious world and deliver your message toward the holy places which are in Jerusalem. In your message, you should prophesy against the land of Israel by delivering this message from the LORD: Behold, inhabitants of Jerusalem, the LORD is against you and He will draw forth his sword out of his sheath and cut off the righteous and the wicked. The sword is the symbol of the spirit of the LORD and the sheath in which it is enclosed is flesh body of mankind.

As long as the spiritual sword of the LORD is in the sheath, the sword is not available to do the work of the LORD. But, as soon as there is someone who is available to wield the sword of the LORD, then the sword of the spirit can be used to shape that which is of the LORD and destroy that which is not of the LORD. The spiritual sword can be used to shape the righteous and destroy the wicked. Ezekiel, a member of the body of the Son of man, can use the sword of truth to prophesy against the land of Israel. Ezekiel, a Son of man, can wield the spiritual sword for the LORD. The LORD has a prophet in the person of Ezekiel to prophesy, to speak for the LORD, to the fallen people of Israel.

4 Seeing then that I will cut off from thee the righteous and the wicked, therefore shall my sword go forth out of his sheath against all flesh from the south to the north:
5 That all flesh may know that I the LORD have drawn forth my sword out of his sheath: it shall not return any more.

The LORD uses Ezekiel to release His spirit into the earth to cut off from the people who live in the land of Israel into two groups: the righteous and the wicked. This separation could not have occurred unless the sword of the spirit of the LORD is out of the sheath and wielded by someone. The sword, which is the focus of the spirit of truth from the LORD, is used against all flesh from the south to the north, in the present time, as contrasted with the east of the future and the west of the past. The purpose for wielding the sword of the LORD is to let people know that the sword has been drawn by the LORD working through the physical capacities of Ezekiel, whose name means, "the strength of God". Once the sword is out of the sheath, once Ezekiel knows that he is an individual aspect of the spirit of the LORD on earth, then, the sword shall not return anymore to the sheath and be hidden by the sheath of the human equipment. The human equipment which does not know that the sword is within the sheath is known as the son of man; the sword which knows from whence it came is the Son of man.

6 Sigh therefore, thou son of man, with the breaking of thy loins; and with bitterness sigh before their eyes.

The Testimony of the Major Prophets

7 And it shall be, when they say unto thee, Wherefore sighest thou? that thou shalt answer, For the tidings; because it cometh: and every heart shall melt, and all hands shall be feeble, and every spirit shall faint, and all knees shall be weak as water: behold, it cometh, and shall be brought to pass, saith the Lord GOD.

The son of man, the people who dwell in the land of Israel in the fallen state, should sigh in sadness therefore, because the son of man does not know the LORD; it is with bitterness of experience that the son of man sighs before the eyes of his peers who make up the body of the fallen son of man. When the son of man, the people in the fallen state, are asked, Why do you sigh in sadness? The person answers, It is because of the tidings, the message of the spirit of the LORD is within each one. Every spirit of the son of man in the fallen state shall melt and all hands shall be feeble; every spirit from the fallen state shall faint, and all knees shall be as weak as water. Behold, the good tidings from the LORD comes to tell the people that the sword of the LORD is within everyone and it comes through each person and it shall be brought to pass through the people who let it be so.

8 Again the word of the LORD came unto me, saying,
9 Son of man, prophesy, and say, Thus saith the LORD; Say, A sword, a sword is sharpened, and also furbished:
10 It is sharpened to make a sore slaughter; it is furbished that it may glitter: should we then make mirth? it contemneth the rod of my son, as every tree.
11 And he hath given it to be furbished, that it may be handled: this sword is sharpened, and it is furbished, to give it into the hand of the slayer.
12 Cry and howl, son of man: for it shall be upon my people, it shall be upon all the princes of Israel: terrors by reason of the sword shall be upon my people: smite therefore upon thy thigh.
13 Because it is a trial, and what if the sword contemn even the rod? it shall be no more, saith the Lord GOD.

Again, the word of the LORD came to Ezekiel saying, Son of man, prophesy to the people the way that the spirit of the LORD works on earth through man. Say, a sword is sharpened and also furbished, polished, ready for use. The sword of the truth of being is to be used on one's false self and not on others. The sword already exists within each person, sharpened and ready to be used to slaughter the human usurper, the fallen identity, of the power of the LORD on earth. Should the people make mirth and be happy at the terrible conditions which mankind has made on earth? The fallen state of man has condemned the rod, the straight rod of right control, which has been present, but hidden in every single man, male or female, who is symbolized as a tree in the forest.

The spiritual sword of the LORD has been given to every man to be polished and handled rightly by each person. This spiritual sword is sharpened and polished; it is ready to be given into the hand of the slayer. The slayer is the Son of man within each person and the one to be slain is the human self, the son of man, in the fallen state. The fallen son of man must be destroyed by the restored Son of man. It is understandable that the son of man, the fallen self, will cry and howl: it is scheduled for extinction. The death of the son of man and the rising of the Son of man shall be upon all of the LORD's people while they are alive on earth. It shall be upon all the princes of Israel who are the sons of the spiritual King of Israel. The people shall experience terrors by reason of the spiritual sword which is present with all people. The sword of truth must be applied to one's self; each person must smite his own thigh. Each person must do this because it is a trial in which the person must choose himself in the fallen state or the spirit of the LORD which is the sword. Which will survive: the spiritual sword or the rod of the fallen human state?

14 Thou therefore, son of man, prophesy, and smite thine hands together, and let the sword be doubled the third time, the sword of the slain: it is the sword of the great men that are slain, which entereth into their privy chambers.
15 I have set the point of the sword against all their gates, that their heart may faint, and their ruins be multiplied: ah! it is made bright, it is wrapped up for the slaughter.
16 Go thee one way or other, either on the right hand, or on the left, whithersoever thy face is set.
17 I will also smite mine hands together, and I will cause my fury to rest: I the LORD have said it.

Each person, each focus point of the son of man in the fallen state, must prophesy, must express, the truth of man, the truth of the sword of the spirit of the LORD. The person must strike his hands together in agreement so that the sword can be doubled the third time: the first time is the LORD; the second time is Ezekiel, who represents the invisible spirit of the LORD; and the third time is the person who will agree with Ezekiel to become a member of the spiritual body

The Symbolic Version of Ezekiel

of mankind made flesh. The sword is the symbol of the spirit of truth on earth. It is by this spiritual sword that great men are slain in the spirit of the LORD which enters into their private chambers.

The LORD has set the point of His sword against all the gates of His people so that their human hearts may faint, and the ruins of the fallen state be multiplied. it is by this process that the human equipment is made bright and wrapped up for the slaughter of the false self. Each person has a choice to make whether he will serve the LORD or not. Each person must go one way or the other, either on the right hand, the clean hand, or the left hand, which is the hand of the sinner. The choice is up to each one; however he sets his face, however he focuses his attention, that is the way that he will go. If a person chooses the word of Ezekiel who is in agreement with the LORD, then, the LORD will cause his fury to rest in the experience of the person who chooses the LORD. This is the covenant and the LORD, speaking through Ezekiel, has said it.

18 The word of the LORD came unto me again, saying,
19 Also, thou son of man, appoint thee two ways, that the sword of the king of Babylon may come: both twain shall come forth out of one land: and choose thou a place, choose it at the head of the way to the city.
20 Appoint a way, that the sword may come to Rabbath of the Ammonites, and to Judah in Jerusalem the defenced.
21 For the king of Babylon stood at the parting of the way, at the head of the two ways, to use divination: he made his arrows bright, he consulted with images, he looked in the liver.

The word of the LORD came to Ezekiel, the focus of the Son of man, saying that the son of man, man in the fallen state, should mark two ways for the earthly power and authority, the sword, of the king of Babylon to take. The two ways that come forth out of one land are the way of the mind and the way of the heart which come forth from the king of Babylon. The son of man, the people who desire to build an earthly kingdom without the spirit of the LORD, the people in the fallen state, come to focus in the people of Babylon. The king of Babylon must choose a place, a direction, for the Babylonians to travel to reach the city that they will conquer. A decision needs to be made to bring the sword of Babylon to one of two places: Rabbath of the Ammonites and Judah in Jerusalem.

The king of Babylon stood at the parting of the way, at the head of the two ways to travel. Instead of calling on the LORD, he uses the ways of divination by using arrows, images and looking at the color and shape of livers of sheep to foretell the future. Arrows, marked with the names of Rabbath and Jerusalem were placed in a quiver, then drawn out with each hand to make the decision as to which way to go. The arrow selected by the right hand selection was seen as a good omen.

22 At his right hand was the divination for Jerusalem, to appoint captains, to open the mouth in the slaughter, to lift up the voice with shouting, to appoint battering rams against the gates, to cast a mount, and to build a fort.
23 And it shall be unto them as a false divination in their sight, to them that have sworn oaths: but he will call to remembrance the iniquity, that they may be taken.

In the right hand of the king of Babylon was the arrow with the name of Jerusalem which was used to mount the campaign in that direction. Captains were appointed to lead the people into war, slaughter and the shouting of anger to provide power for the battering rams and the tools of war. These preparations for war will seem to be a false divination to the people but they have sworn their oaths to an earthly king who will remind them of the iniquity of not following their king and they will be taken with the decision to make war.

24 Therefore thus saith the Lord GOD; Because ye have made your iniquity to be remembered, in that your transgressions are discovered, so that in all your doings your sins do appear; because, I say, that ye are come to remembrance, ye shall be taken with the hand.
25 And thou, profane wicked prince of Israel, whose day is come, when iniquity shall have an end,
26 Thus saith the Lord GOD; Remove the diadem, and take off the crown: this shall not be the same: exalt him that is low, and abase him that is high.
27 I will overturn, overturn, overturn, it: and it shall be no more, until he come whose right it is; and I will give it him.

The Testimony of the Major Prophets

Therefore the Lord GOD said that because of the iniquity and the transgressions which are discovered by your behaviors, and your sins are revealed in your expressions; the people who commit the sins are called to the remembrance of the LORD and you shall be taken with the hand of the invading Babylonians. The LORD will use the sword from Babylon to remove the wicked prince of Israel whose day is come for his reign of iniquity to end. The Lord GOD will remove the diadem, the crown of authority, from the prince of Israel, so that things will not remain the same. In this manner, the LORD who was perceived as being low is exalted, and the prince of Israel who was on high is abased, degraded and humiliated. The action of the LORD overturns all patterns in material form that are not the true design of the LORD. The false pattern shall be no more in Israel until the person comes to lead who has the right to lead. The LORD will give that person the right.

28 And thou, son of man, prophesy and say, Thus saith the Lord GOD concerning the Ammonites, and concerning their reproach; even say thou, The sword, the sword is drawn: for the slaughter it is furbished, to consume because of the glittering:
29 Whiles they see vanity unto thee, whiles they divine a lie unto thee, to bring thee upon the necks of them that are slain, of the wicked, whose day is come, when their iniquity shall have an end.
30 Shall I cause it to return into his sheath? I will judge thee in the place where thou wast created, in the land of thy nativity.
31 And I will pour out mine indignation upon thee, I will blow against thee in the fire of my wrath, and deliver thee into the hand of brutish men, and skilful to destroy.
32 Thou shalt be for fuel to the fire; thy blood shall be in the midst of the land; thou shalt be no more remembered: for I the LORD have spoken it.

The son of man, man in the fallen state, shall see these things, prophesy and say that the Lord GOD has a message for the Ammonites concerning their reproach: They are not exempt from the sword of the Babylonians because Jerusalem was attacked first. The sword of Babylon is drawn, it has been used successfully, and it will be used on them also.

Shall the LORD cause the sword to return to its sheath? The LORD will judge the people in the place where they were created, in the human forms that they inhabit, based upon the decisions that they make. If the people choose a way which is not the spirit of the LORD, then the LORD will pour out his indignation upon the people, the fire of the wrath of the LORD, and deliver the people into the hands of brutish men who are skillful at destroying the people with whom they come into contact. The people of Israel shall be fuel for the fires of war and destruction; their blood shall be in the midst of the land and they shall be remembered no more. This is the fate of those who do not let the spirit of the LORD shine forth through them. The LORD has spoken to reveal the operation of his Law of Sowing and Reaping.

CHAPTER 22

1 Moreover the word of the LORD came unto me, saying,
2 Now, thou son of man, wilt thou judge, wilt thou judge the bloody city? yea, thou shalt shew her all her abominations.
3 Then say thou, Thus saith the Lord GOD, The city sheddeth blood in the midst of it, that her time may come, and maketh idols against herself to defile herself.
4 Thou art become guilty in thy blood that thou hast shed; and hast defiled thyself in thine idols which thou hast made; and thou hast caused thy days to draw near, and art come even unto thy years: therefore have I made thee a reproach unto the heathen, and a mocking to all countries.
5 Those that be near, and those that be far from thee, shall mock thee, which art infamous and much vexed.

The word of the LORD came to Ezekiel asking whether the son of man, man in the fallen state, is able to judge the bloody city? Ezekiel is in position as a Son of man to show the people in the fallen state all of her abominations that led to the manifestation of the bloody city. Ezekiel is to say, thus says the LORD, The city sheds blood, the evidence of destruction, in the midst of the city so that her time of self-destruction shall come to an end which was the end result of the practice of making idols of material things which were used to defile herself. The people in the city have become guilty in the blood that they have shed, by their own expression of abominations; she has defiled herself in the idols that she has made; this is what has caused the end of her days and her years to draw near. The abominable behavior is what has made the people of the city a reproach to the heathen and a mockery to all countries. People from near and far shall mock the person who has become disreputable and troubled by one's own behavior.

6 Behold, the princes of Israel, every one were in thee to their power to shed blood.
7 In thee have they set light by father and mother: in the midst of thee have they dealt by oppression with the stranger: in thee have they vexed the fatherless and the widow.
8 Thou hast despised mine holy things, and hast profaned my sabbaths.
9 In thee are men that carry tales to shed blood: and in thee they eat upon the mountains: in the midst of thee they commit lewdness.
10 In thee have they discovered their fathers' nakedness: in thee have they humbled her that was set apart for pollution.
11 And one hath committed abomination with his neighbour's wife; and another hath lewdly defiled his daughter in law; and another in thee hath humbled his sister, his father's daughter.
12 In thee have they taken gifts to shed blood; thou hast taken usury and increase, and thou hast greedily gained of thy neighbours by extortion, and hast forgotten me, saith the Lord GOD.

The LORD tells Ezekiel, the focus point of the Son of man, to behold the princes of Israel. The princes of Israel are the sons of the King of Israel, the LORD. Every one of them is in the body of the Son of man on earth and the Son of man is the source of the spiritual power. Fallen man, the son of man, usurps this power and uses the power for his own

The Testimony of the Major Prophets

self-centered purposes to shed blood, to express their destructive ways. In the spiritual body of the Son of man, the people in the fallen state have set their light of understanding by their earthy father and mother. In the distorted spirit of the son of man, they dealt with the stranger by oppression; using the spiritual power usurped from the Son, they have vexed the fatherless and the widow. They have despised the holy things from the LORD and profaned the holy days of the Sabbaths of the LORD, which is every day.

The LORD continues to tell Ezekiel, the spiritual focus of the Son of man, that within his earthly flesh body of the fallen son of man, men carry tales to shed blood and do destructive things: they eat upon the mountains as they receive the spirit of life from the LORD and they commit acts of lewdness. They have discovered the nakedness of their fathers; they have humbled her who was set apart for pollution. The people in the fallen state have committed abomination with the neighbor's wife; and another has lewdly defiled his daughter-in-law; while another has humbled his sister. By using your divine spirit, the fallen son of man has accepted gifts, bribes, to do terrible things; he has accepted usury and excessive interest to greedily gain from neighbor's by extortion They have forgotten the way of the LORD.

13 Behold, therefore I have smitten mine hand at thy dishonest gain which thou hast made, and at thy blood which hath been in the midst of thee.
14 Can thine heart endure, or can thine hands be strong, in the days that I shall deal with thee? I the LORD have spoken it, and will do it.
15 And I will scatter thee among the heathen, and disperse thee in the countries, and will consume thy filthiness out of thee.
16 And thou shalt take thine inheritance in thyself in the sight of the heathen, and thou shalt know that I am the LORD.

Ezekiel, the focus of the Son of man, is urged to behold and see that the LORD has used the power of his hand at the dishonest gain which has been made by man in the distorted, fallen state which takes place within the spiritual body of the Son of man, the true house of Israel. Ezekiel is asked if his heart can endure and his hands be strong in the days that the LORD shall deal with the body of the fallen son of man? The LORD has spoken that He will do it. The action of the LORD will scatter the members of the body among the heathen, and disperse them into countries; this process will consume the filthiness out of the members of the body of the son of man. Ezekiel must take his total inheritance within himself in the sight of the heathen, who do not know the LORD. It is within the fallen body of mankind that Ezekiel is to know the presence of the LORD

17 And the word of the LORD came unto me, saying,
18 Son of man, the house of Israel is to me become dross: all they are brass, and tin, and iron, and lead, in the midst of the furnace; they are even the dross of silver.
19 Therefore thus saith the Lord GOD; Because ye are all become dross, behold, therefore I will gather you into the midst of Jerusalem.
20 As they gather silver, and brass, and iron, and lead, and tin, into the midst of the furnace, to blow the fire upon it, to melt it; so will I gather you in mine anger and in my fury, and I will leave you there, and melt you.
21 Yea, I will gather you, and blow upon you in the fire of my wrath, and ye shall be melted in the midst thereof.
22 As silver is melted in the midst of the furnace, so shall ye be melted in the midst thereof; and ye shall know that I the LORD have poured out my fury upon you.

The LORD explains to Ezekiel that the house of Israel has become dross, covered with blackness and pollution, in the vision of the LORD. Ezekiel, the focus of the Son of man, shall see these polluted things also. The house of Israel who think of themselves as a chosen people are like brass, tin iron and lead: they are all like the dross on the silver. The people of the house of Israel are only distortions of what they could be. Therefore, the Lord GOD says that because all of you have become dross, then everyone will be gathered together as silver, brass, iron, lead and tin are placed in the midst of a furnace to blow fire on the metals to melt them for the purpose of purification. The LORD will leave the people there and melt them with the fire of his wrath. As silver is melted in the midst of the furnace to purify it from the dross, so shall man in the fallen state be melted by the fire of God's love to reveal the truth of man, the silver which has been present under the dross. In this process of purification, the person shall know that the LORD has poured His fury over man to help man.

23 And the word of the LORD came unto me, saying,
24 Son of man, say unto her, Thou art the land that is not cleansed, nor rained upon in the day of indignation.
25 There is a conspiracy of her prophets in the midst thereof, like a roaring lion ravening the prey; they have devoured souls; they have taken the treasure and precious things; they have made her many widows in the midst thereof.
26 Her priests have violated my law, and have profaned mine holy things: they have put no difference between the holy and profane, neither have they shewed difference between the unclean and the clean, and have hid their eyes from my sabbaths, and I am profaned among them.
27 Her princes in the midst thereof are like wolves ravening the prey, to shed blood, and to destroy souls, to get dishonest gain.
28 And her prophets have daubed them with untempered morter, seeing vanity, and divining lies unto them, saying, Thus saith the Lord GOD, when the LORD hath not spoken.

The word of the LORD came to Ezekiel saying that the spiritual Son of man is to say to her, the woman who symbolizes the fallen state, that she is like the land that is not cleansed, nor rained upon in the day of indignation. There is within the woman, who symbolizes mankind in the fallen state, a conspiracy of many prophets who are like a roaring lion ravenously devouring their prey. The false prophets have devoured many souls; they have taken treasure and precious things; they have made many widows by the destructiveness of their policies.

The priests have violated the law of the LORD and they have profaned many holy things with their unholy hands. The people who call themselves priests of the LORD have put no difference between the holy and the profane, nor shown any difference between the unclean and the clean. The "priests" have hid themselves from the Sabbaths which are the days of the LORD and the LORD is profaned when He is in their presence. The princes within the woman, who symbolizes the fallen body of mankind, are like wolves who are ravenous to seek their prey, to shed blood to destroy souls to get their dishonest gain. The prophets, so called, of the fallen state have daubed them with untempered mortar seeing the vanity that is present in them and yet divining lies into them, using the name of the Lord GOD, when the LORD has not spoken to them at all.

29 The people of the land have used oppression, and exercised robbery, and have vexed the poor and needy: yea, they have oppressed the stranger wrongfully.
30 And I sought for a man among them, that should make up the hedge, and stand in the gap before me for the land, that I should not destroy it: but I found none.
31 Therefore have I poured out mine indignation upon them; I have consumed them with the fire of my wrath: their own way have I recompensed upon their heads, saith the Lord GOD.

The people who live in the land of the fallen state have used oppression, robbery, vexed the poor and needy, and oppressed the stranger wrongfully. The LORD sought for a man among them that would make a hedge, and stand in the gap, between the LORD and the land so that the land would not be destroyed; but the LORD found no one to accept that responsibility. Therefore, the LORD has poured out His indignation upon them, consumed them with the fire of His wrath that destroys patterns that are not of the LORD's design. The LORD has recompensed them with the behaviors which the people in the fallen state generated through their own heads, through their polluted and impure states of consciousness.

CHAPTER 23

1 The word of the LORD came again unto me, saying,
2 Son of man, there were two women, the daughters of one mother:
3 And they committed whoredoms in Egypt; they committed whoredoms in their youth: there were their breasts pressed, and there they bruised the teats of their virginity.
4 And the names of them were Aholah the elder, and Aholibah her sister: and they were mine, and they bare sons and daughters. Thus were their names; Samaria is Aholah, and Jerusalem Aholibah.

The word of the LORD came to Ezekiel, saying to Ezekiel in a parable, Son of man, there were two women, who were the daughters of one mother, mother Earth, that committed whoredoms in Egypt, the symbolic place of the fallen state; the two daughters committed whoredoms in their youth: there in Egypt were their breasts pressed, their teats bruised of their virginity. Their names were Aholah the elder, and Aholibah her sister: Aholah means, "**his** tabernacle or tent"; Aholibah means, "**my** tabernacle or tent". Aholibah is closer to the LORD and His spirit than is Aholah, who is closer to someone else who is separate from the spirit of the LORD. The LORD declares that both of the two women were his, and they bare sons and daughters. Thus were their names; in the parable, Samaria is Aholah, and Jerusalem Aholibah. Both of them have behaved as whores who sold themselves for material goods or money.

5 And Aholah played the harlot when she was mine; and she doted on her lovers, on the Assyrians her neighbours,
6 Which were clothed with blue, captains and rulers, all of them desirable young men, horsemen riding upon horses.
7 Thus she committed her whoredoms with them, with all them that were the chosen men of Assyria, and with all on whom she doted: with all their idols she defiled herself.
8 Neither left she her whoredoms brought from Egypt: for in her youth they lay with her, and they bruised the breasts of her virginity, and poured their whoredom upon her.
9 Wherefore I have delivered her into the hand of her lovers, into the hand of the Assyrians, upon whom she doted.
10 These discovered her nakedness: they took her sons and her daughters, and slew her with the sword: and she became famous among women; for they had executed judgment upon her.

Aholah, who represents Samaria in the parable, played the harlot even though she belongs to the LORD. She doted on her lovers who are identified as the Assyrians, who were her neighbors, clothed in blue, captains and rulers, desirable, wealthy, young men as they ride on their horses. The Samarians, who are symbolized in the parable by Aholah, committed her whoredom, her alliance for political and financial gain, with the leaders, the chosen men, of the Assyrians upon whom she doted and defiled herself with their idols, the symbols of their materialistic values.

Aholah did not cease the whoredoms, the mixing and the blending with the ways of the fallen world which she brought with her from Egypt, the place where she learned these behaviors in her youth where she learned the behaviors perceived as "normal" and "acceptable" in Egypt. Based upon this background, the LORD, who is the source of all power and functions according to the working of the Law of Sowing and Reaping, has delivered her into the hand of her lovers, the Assyrians, upon whom she doted and was attracted to them. The Assyrians, in close association with Aholah who represents Samaria, discovered her nakedness and destroyed her with a sword. She, Samaria, became famous as the Assyrians had executed judgment upon her.

11 And when her sister Aholibah saw this, she was more corrupt in her inordinate love than she, and in her whoredoms more than her sister in her whoredoms.
12 She doted upon the Assyrians her neighbours, captains and rulers clothed most gorgeously, horsemen riding upon horses, all of them desirable young men.
13 Then I saw that she was defiled, that they took both one way,
14 And that she increased her whoredoms: for when she saw men portrayed upon the wall, the images of the Chaldeans portrayed with vermilion,
15 Girded with girdles upon their loins, exceeding in dyed attire upon their heads, all of them princes to look to, after the manner of the Babylonians of Chaldea, the land of their nativity:
16 And as soon as she saw them with her eyes, she doted upon them, and sent messengers unto them into Chaldea.

When her sister, Aholibah, who represents Jerusalem in the parable, saw what had happened to Samaria, she was more corrupt in her whoredoms, her wicked ways, than her sister. She, Jerusalem, also doted upon the Assyrians, their leaders clothed in gorgeous dress and riding the horses that symbolize power and wealth. Ezekiel saw that Jerusalem was defiled, as was Samaria, by the Assyrians. The leaders of Jerusalem, symbolized by Aholibah, increased her whoredoms, her trade and commerce, with Assyria. She saw men portrayed upon the walls in scarlet color, girded with girdles and dyed attire upon their heads to give them the appearance of princes of the world after the manner of the Babylonians, the land of their nativity. As soon as she, the harlot of Jerusalem, saw them, she doted upon them and sent messengers to Chaldea. Jerusalem has been attracted to and impressed by the Babylonians.

17 And the Babylonians came to her into the bed of love, and they defiled her with their whoredom, and she was polluted with them, and her mind was alienated from them.
18 So she discovered her whoredoms, and discovered her nakedness: then my mind was alienated from her, like as my mind was alienated from her sister.
19 Yet she multiplied her whoredoms, in calling to remembrance the days of her youth, wherein she had played the harlot in the land of Egypt.

The Babylonians came to Aholibah—the symbol of the harlot that Jerusalem had become—to the bed of love and they defiled her with their manner of whoredom, their distortions from the way of the LORD, and she, Jerusalem, was polluted by the Babylonians and her mind was alienated from them as she came to see their pollution for what it was. She discovered her whoredom, her wrong doing, and she became aware of her nakedness. Then, the mind of Ezekiel and the LORD were alienated from Jerusalem as the mind was alienated from her sister, Samaria. Yet, she multiplied her whoredoms, her wrong doings, by calling to remembrance the days of her youth where she learned to be a harlot in the land of Egypt.

20 For she doted upon their paramours, whose flesh is as the flesh of asses, and whose issue is like the issue of horses.
21 Thus thou calledst to remembrance the lewdness of thy youth, in bruising thy teats by the Egyptians for the paps of thy youth.
22 Therefore, O Aholibah, thus saith the Lord GOD; Behold, I will raise up thy lovers against thee, from whom thy mind is alienated, and I will bring them against thee on every side;
23 The Babylonians, and all the Chaldeans, Pekod, and Shoa, and Koa, and all the Assyrians with them: all of them desirable young men, captains and rulers, great lords and renowned, all of them riding upon horses.
24 And they shall come against thee with chariots, wagons, and wheels, and with an assembly of people, which shall set against thee buckler and shield and helmet round about: and I will set judgment before them, and they shall judge thee according to their judgments.

The harlot that Jerusalem had become doted on her lovers whose genitals were as the large flesh of donkeys and whose issue had the smell of horses. The people of Jerusalem blamed their deviation from the way of the LORD upon the lewdness of their youth in Egypt where they learned these behaviors.

The Testimony of the Major Prophets

Therefore, the Lord GOD said to Aholibah, the people of Jerusalem who had become as harlots, that He will raise her lovers against the people whose mind has become alienated from the LORD with the result that enemies surround Jerusalem from every side: Babylonians and all the Chaldeans (often identified with Babylonians), Pekod (Aramaic people located east of Babylon), Shoa and Koa, (Babylonian allies of uncertain location) and all the Assyrians. They have all been seen as desirable young men by the harlot of Jerusalem They shall all come against Jerusalem as an assembly of people and their equipment to wage war. The LORD will set judgment before the invaders, and the enemy shall judge the people of Jerusalem according to their judgments.

25 And I will set my jealousy against thee, and they shall deal furiously with thee: they shall take away thy nose and thine ears; and thy remnant shall fall by the sword: they shall take thy sons and thy daughters; and thy residue shall be devoured by the fire.
26 They shall also strip thee out of thy clothes, and take away thy fair jewels.
27 Thus will I make thy lewdness to cease from thee, and thy whoredom brought from the land of Egypt: so that thou shalt not lift up thine eyes unto them, nor remember Egypt any more.

According to the working of the Law, the LORD will set His jealousy against the people of Jerusalem who have worshipped false gods and the invaders will deal furiously with them according to their customs. They shall cut off your nose and ears and those who remain shall fall by the sword. Your sons and daughters will be taken captive and those who are not desirable will be consumed by fire. They will strip you of your clothes and jewels. In this manner, the LORD will make your lewdness and the whoredom which you brought from the land of Egypt cease to come forth from you so that you will not lift up your eyes to worship them or remember Egypt any more.

28 For thus saith the Lord GOD; Behold, I will deliver thee into the hand of them whom thou hatest, into the hand of them from whom thy mind is alienated:
29 And they shall deal with thee hatefully, and shall take away all thy labour, and shall leave thee naked and bare: and the nakedness of thy whoredoms shall be discovered, both thy lewdness and thy whoredoms.
30 I will do these things unto thee, because thou hast gone a whoring after the heathen, and because thou art polluted with their idols.
31 Thou hast walked in the way of thy sister; therefore will I give her cup into thine hand.

Ezekiel delivers the message from the Lord GOD that the people are to Behold, that it is the power of the LORD that will deliver the people of Jerusalem who have played the harlot into the hands of the people that they hated and into the hands of them from whom their minds were alienated. The invaders shall deal hatefully with the people of Jerusalem. They will take away everything for which the people of Jerusalem labored and leave them naked and bare. The nakedness of your wrong behavior, your whoredom and your lewdness, has been discovered.

The LORD will do these things to you because you have gone a-whoring after the heathen, and because you are polluted with their idols. You have walked in the way of your sister, who symbolized the people of Samaria; therefore will I give the cup of judgment which she has received into your hand.

32 Thus saith the Lord GOD; Thou shalt drink of thy sister's cup deep and large: thou shalt be laughed to scorn and had in derision; it containeth much.
33 Thou shalt be filled with drunkenness and sorrow, with the cup of astonishment and desolation, with the cup of thy sister Samaria.
34 Thou shalt even drink it and suck it out, and thou shalt break the sherds thereof, and pluck off thine own breasts: for I have spoken it, saith the Lord GOD.
35 Therefore thus saith the Lord GOD; Because thou hast forgotten me, and cast me behind thy back, therefore bear thou also thy lewdness and thy whoredoms.

The working of the Law of the LORD shall result in the people of Jerusalem drinking the cup of her harlot sister to receive a similar punishment. The cup of retribution is deep and large; it contains much. The people shall be laughed to scorn and derision; they shall be filled with drunkenness and sorrow, astonishment and desolation when they suffer the same fate as Samaria, the sister who also played the harlot. The people of Jerusalem shall drink every bit of the cup which they have brewed by their own behavior and when it is all gone, they shall break the cup which contained the memory of the desires of the days in Egypt, the fallen state. The broken cup will intensify their sense of emptiness. This is the word of the Lord GOD as spoken through Ezekiel because the people of Jerusalem have forgotten the LORD, their God, and cast Him behind their back, so, therefore, they must bear the fruit of their lewdness and their whoredom.

36 The LORD said moreover unto me; Son of man, wilt thou judge Aholah and Aholibah? yea, declare unto them their abominations;
37 That they have committed adultery, and blood is in their hands, and with their idols have they committed adultery, and have also caused their sons, whom they bare unto me, to pass for them through the fire, to devour them.

The LORD has shared His vision and his Word with Ezekiel and asks him, as the focus of the Son of man, if he will judge Aholah and Aholibah, Samaria and Jerusalem, in the same manner? Yes, declare their abominations to them that they have committed adultery by harmonizing and blending with the evil cultures of a fallen people who did not know the LORD. The blood of their behavior is on their hands and with the idols that they have committed adultery. Not only did they sin for themselves, but their behavior has caused their sons, which were offered to the LORD, to walk through the fire to destroy them also .

38 Moreover this they have done unto me: they have defiled my sanctuary in the same day, and have profaned my sabbaths.
39 For when they had slain their children to their idols, then they came the same day into my sanctuary to profane it; and, lo, thus have they done in the midst of mine house.
40 And furthermore, that ye have sent for men to come from far, unto whom a messenger was sent; and, lo, they came: for whom thou didst wash thyself, paintedst thy eyes, and deckedst thyself with ornaments,
41 And satest upon a stately bed, and a table prepared before it, whereupon thou hast set mine incense and mine oil.
42 And a voice of a multitude being at ease was with her: and with the men of the common sort were brought Sabeans from the wilderness, which put bracelets upon their hands, and beautiful crowns upon their heads.

The people of Jerusalem who thought of themselves as so good and holy must consider what they have done to the LORD. They have defiled the LORD's sanctuary and profaned His sabbaths. When they had slain their children to their idols by their fallen behavior, then they came the same day into the LORD's sanctuary to profane it; and, lo, thus have they done in the midst of mine house, the house of the LORD's dwelling which is the people of Jerusalem.

Furthermore, you have sent a messenger for the Babylonians to come from far away, and, lo, they came: you did wash yourself, painted your eyes, and decked yourself with ornaments to please them, sat on a stately bed, and a table prepared before it, whereupon you set incense and oil that belonged to the LORD. The voice of a multitude, people of a common sort and Sabeans from the wilderness, were brought into the holy city of Jerusalem which put bracelets upon their hands, and beautiful crowns upon their heads in relationships which were not of the LORD. They were adulterous relationships that forgot the LORD.

43 Then said I unto her that was old in adulteries, Will they now commit whoredoms with her, and she with them?
44 Yet they went in unto her, as they go in unto a woman that playeth the harlot: so went they in unto Aholah and unto Aholibah, the lewd women.
45 And the righteous men, they shall judge them after the manner of adulteresses, and after the manner of women that shed blood; because they are adulteresses, and blood is in their hands.

Ezekiel asked if the strangers to the holy city of Jerusalem will commit whoredoms with the inhabitants, and they with them? The answer was that the invaders did go into the woman that played the harlot, Aholah and Aholibah, Samaria and Jerusalem. Righteous men shall judge the behavior of the two sisters after the manner of adulteresses and women with the blood of their own wrong behavior on their hands.

46 For thus saith the Lord GOD; I will bring up a company upon them, and will give them to be removed and spoiled.

The Testimony of the Major Prophets

47 And the company shall stone them with stones, and dispatch them with their swords; they shall slay their sons and their daughters, and burn up their houses with fire.
48 Thus will I cause lewdness to cease out of the land, that all women may be taught not to do after your lewdness.
49 And they shall recompense your lewdness upon you, and ye shall bear the sins of your idols: and ye shall know that I am the Lord GOD.

The Lord GOD declared that He will bring a company of people upon the people of Samaria and Jerusalem who will be removed and spoiled. The company of people will stone them and dispatch them with swords; their sons and daughters will be slain and their houses will be burned with fire. In this manner, the LORD will cause lewdness to come out of the land, and women, the symbol of the earthly capacities of body, mind and heart, will be taught not to do the ways of lewdness. The Law of the LORD will function and the lewdness of your behavior shall be brought to bear upon you so that you will bear the sins of your idols. Then, you shall know that the LORD is with you and he is your God.

CHAPTER 24

1 Again in the ninth year, in the tenth month, in the tenth day of the month, the word of the LORD came unto me, saying,
2 Son of man, write thee the name of the day, even of this same day: the king of Babylon set himself against Jerusalem this same day.
3 And utter a parable unto the rebellious house, and say unto them, Thus saith the Lord GOD; Set on a pot, set it on, and also pour water into it:
4 Gather the pieces thereof into it, even every good piece, the thigh, and the shoulder; fill it with the choice bones.
5 Take the choice of the flock, and burn also the bones under it, and make it boil well, and let them seethe the bones of it therein.

Ezekiel is very specific about the exact date that the word of the LORD came to him on the tenth day of the tenth month in the ninth year of his captivity by the Babylonians. The LORD tells Ezekiel, the focus point for the Son of man, that the king of Babylon has laid siege against Jerusalem on this day. In order to explain what is happening to Jerusalem from the divine standpoint, the Lord GOD gives Ezekiel a parable to deliver to the rebellious house of Israel, the people who have rebelled against the LORD. In the parable the LORD compares Jerusalem to a cooking pot which has been set on a fire, water poured into it, and good pieces of meat, the thigh and the shoulder which symbolize the people who do the work of the LORD; fill it with bones which give structure and support to the body. The material in the cooking pot is to be brought to a boil wherein the ingredients are to cook and seethe. This is the condition of Jerusalem under siege.

6 Wherefore thus saith the Lord GOD; Woe to the bloody city, to the pot whose scum is therein, and whose scum is not gone out of it! bring it out piece by piece; let no lot fall upon it.
7 For her blood is in the midst of her; she set it upon the top of a rock; she poured it not upon the ground, to cover it with dust;
8 That it might cause fury to come up to take vengeance; I have set her blood upon the top of a rock, that it should not be covered.

The Lord GOD says, Woe to the city of Jerusalem which is a bloody city that has been torn asunder, and to the pot which has the scum of wrong behavior of the people and that scum has not gone out of the city which was supposed to be a holy place for the LORD's glory. The scum is to be brought out piece by piece during the cooking process, the creative process by which the LORD will purify his people. There should be no identification with the removal of the scum.

The spiritual blood of the people of Jerusalem is in the midst of her, the true design is in spirit; she set it upon the top of a rock as though the spirit were separate from her; she did not pour it upon the ground to cover it with dust so that the spirit of the LORD would grow; the growth of the spiritual blood of the LORD would cause fury to come up to

The Testimony of the Major Prophets

take vengeance on a rebellious people. The LORD has set the spiritual blood of the people of Jerusalem on the top of a rock that it should not be covered. The spirit of the LORD is meant to be seen.

9 Therefore thus saith the Lord GOD; Woe to the bloody city! I will even make the pile for fire great.
10 Heap on wood, kindle the fire, consume the flesh, and spice it well, and let the bones be burned.
11 Then set it empty upon the coals thereof, that the brass of it may be hot, and may burn, and that the filthiness of it may be molten in it, that the scum of it may be consumed.
12 She hath wearied herself with lies, and her great scum went not forth out of her: her scum shall be in the fire.
13 In thy filthiness is lewdness: because I have purged thee, and thou wast not purged, thou shalt not be purged from thy filthiness any more, till I have caused my fury to rest upon thee.
14 I the LORD have spoken it: it shall come to pass, and I will do it; I will not go back, neither will I spare, neither will I repent; according to thy ways, and according to thy doings, shall they judge thee, saith the Lord GOD.

Therefore, since Jerusalem has not been a holy city, the Lord GOD says, Woe to the bloody city. The LORD will make the fire great to increase the heat that is used for the purification of the city in the cooking pot. In the parable, the LORD states that the wood should be heaped on, the fire kindled and the flesh of the fallen people should be consumed. The "stew" in the pot should be spiced well, to increase its taste; let the bones of the old structure of a sinful past be burned away. In symbolic language, the old fallen and sinful Jerusalem must be consumed.

The cooking pot of the parable, which is the city of Jerusalem, should be set empty upon the coals of the fire to raise the temperature of the brass so that the filthiness of the city may become molten and the scum of it be consumed. The city of Jerusalem has wearied herself with lies, and her great scum did not leave her. Her scum must be in the fire to eliminate the encrusted wrong behavior of the people from the city.

In the filthiness of the city is lewdness of behavior. The LORD's spirit flowing through the people constantly had the potential of purging the people from their lewdness but the people have rebelled against the spirit of the LORD and have not been purged by gentle and loving means. Now the time has come for the fury of the LORD to come to bear upon the people of Jerusalem. The LORD has spoken and it shall come to pass. The Lord GOD will do it and not go back. The LORD will not spare, or repent; the people of Jerusalem will be judged according to their behaviors as they reap what they have sown.

15 Also the word of the LORD came unto me, saying,
16 Son of man, behold, I take away from thee the desire of thine eyes with a stroke: yet neither shalt thou mourn nor weep, neither shall thy tears run down.
17 Forbear to cry, make no mourning for the dead, bind the tire of thine head upon thee, and put on thy shoes upon thy feet, and cover not thy lips, and eat not the bread of men.
18 So I spake unto the people in the morning: and at even my wife died; and I did in the morning as I was commanded.

The word of the LORD came to Ezekiel saying, Son of man, Behold that the desire of your eyes to receive what you think that the LORD should do to make Jerusalem a beautiful city has been removed from you with a stroke from the spirit of the LORD. You shall not mourn or weep, nor tears run down your face, at the plight of Jerusalem because you see and understand the working of the spirit of the Law of Sowing and Reaping. Do not cry or mourn for the dead by removing your turban and putting dust on your head as others do. Put your shoes on your feet and walk in the spirit of the LORD. Do not cover your face and eat the customary bread of mourners. So, Ezekiel spoke to the people in the morning of the word of the LORD: in the evening, the wife, the physical self of sadness and mourning with which Ezekiel had been identified, passed away, died, and Ezekiel did as he was commanded by the LORD and he did not mourn over the fate of Jerusalem. Of course, the "normal" people did not understand the way of Ezekiel.

19 And the people said unto me, Wilt thou not tell us what these things are to us, that thou doest so?
20 Then I answered them, The word of the LORD came unto me, saying,
21 Speak unto the house of Israel, Thus saith the Lord GOD; Behold, I will profane my sanctuary, the excellency of your strength, the desire of your eyes, and that which your soul pitieth; and your sons and your daughters whom ye have left shall fall by the sword.

The Symbolic Version of Ezekiel

22 And ye shall do as I have done: ye shall not cover your lips, nor eat the bread of men.
23 And your tires shall be upon your heads, and your shoes upon your feet: ye shall not mourn nor weep; but ye shall pine away for your iniquities, and mourn one toward another.
24 Thus Ezekiel is unto you a sign: according to all that he hath done shall ye do: and when this cometh, ye shall know that I am the Lord GOD.

When the people inquired as to what these things mean to them, Ezekiel explains that the word of the LORD came to him to speak to the house of Israel, to those who desire to enter into the covenant with the LORD that Israel experienced. Ezekiel explains that the sanctuary of the LORD will be profaned by many changes that have been near and dear to them. Their hearts are not to be troubled as the external arrangements which gave them strength, the desire of their eyes, the things that they would normally pity, and the sons and daughters which they left in Jerusalem would fall by the sword of the invaders.

The people are to do as Ezekiel has done as he obeyed the command of the LORD. The people are not to cover their faces and eat the bread of a mourner or victim; they are not to remove the coverings from their heads and put dust on them; they should keep their shoes on their feet and go about their daily affairs; and they should not mourn or weep about the things that have happened. But they should pine to change their own iniquities in the sight of the LORD and help one another to do the same. Ezekiel has done this to become a focus of the Son of man and he is to be a sign to them that it can be done. According to what Ezekiel has done, the people who have observed him can do it also. When the people have let the spirit that flows through Ezekiel flow through them also, then they shall know the Lord GOD.

25 Also, thou son of man, shall it not be in the day when I take from them their strength, the joy of their glory, the desire of their eyes, and that whereupon they set their minds, their sons and their daughters,
26 That he that escapeth in that day shall come unto thee, to cause thee to hear it with thine ears?
27 In that day shall thy mouth be opened to him which is escaped, and thou shalt speak, and be no more dumb: and thou shalt be a sign unto them; and they shall know that I am the LORD.

Also son of man, man in the fallen state, shall it not be so that when the LORD removes the strength, joy, desire and glory from the fallen son of man, that in that day, the person who escapes from the body of the son of man shall hear with his own ears the spirit of the Son of man which comes from the LORD? In that day, when that occurs to you in your own experience, you shall be dumb no more about the way of the LORD. You shall be a sign to those who seek the LORD and they shall know the LORD as they express His spirit.

CHAPTER 25

1 The word of the LORD came again unto me, saying,
2 Son of man, set thy face against the Ammonites, and prophesy against them;
3 And say unto the Ammonites, Hear the word of the Lord GOD; Thus saith the Lord GOD; Because thou saidst, Aha, against my sanctuary, when it was profaned; and against the land of Israel, when it was desolate; and against the house of Judah, when they went into captivity;
4 Behold, therefore I will deliver thee to the men of the east for a possession, and they shall set their palaces in thee, and make their dwellings in thee: they shall eat thy fruit, and they shall drink thy milk.
5 And I will make Rabbah a stable for camels, and the Ammonites a couchingplace for flocks: and ye shall know that I am the LORD.

Ezekiel states that the word of the LORD came to him saying, Son of man, set the face of your attention toward the Ammonites and prophesy, express, the spirit of the LORD to them which will be against what they are doing in the fallen state in which they find themselves. The Ammonites do not consider themselves to be in the fallen state; from their point of view their experience is a normal, familiar state. The word Ammonite, means, "the son of my people".

6 For thus saith the Lord GOD; Because thou hast clapped thine hands, and stamped with the feet, and rejoiced in heart with all thy despite against the land of Israel;
7 Behold, therefore I will stretch out mine hand upon thee, and will deliver thee for a spoil to the heathen; and I will cut thee off from the people, and I will cause thee to perish out of the countries: I will destroy thee; and thou shalt know that I am the LORD.

The Ammonites had been rejoicing over the dire circumstances which had befallen the land of Israel which they displayed as they clapped their hands, stamped their feet and rejoiced in their hearts. The Lord GOD said to Ezekiel to tell the Ammonites that they would be delivered as a spoil of war, as a captive prize, to the heathen, the Babylonians who had previously captured Israel. The Ammonites would suffer a similar fate as they would be cut off from their countrymen, taken away and perish in a strange land. The Ammonites will be destroyed and they shall know when these things come to pass that the LORD foretold what would befall them.

8 Thus saith the Lord GOD; Because that Moab and Seir do say, Behold, the house of Judah is like unto all the heathen;
9 Therefore, behold, I will open the side of Moab from the cities, from his cities which are on his frontiers, the glory of the country, Beth-jeshimoth, Baalmeon, and Kiriathaim,
10 Unto the men of the east with the Ammonites, and will give them in possession, that the Ammonites may not be remembered among the nations.
11 And I will execute judgments upon Moab; and they shall know that I am the LORD.

The Lord GOD declared, through Ezekiel, that because the people of Moab and Seir said that the house of Judah is no different than other people and that they are like the heathen, therefore, the frontier boundaries of Moab shall be opened and the frontier towns of Beth-jeshimoth, Baalmeon and Kiriathaim shall be taken by the men of the army of the east, the Babylonians. The Ammonites will be taken in possession by the Babylonians and the Ammonites will no longer be remembered as a separate people. This is the judgment of the LORD upon Moab; and when it comes to pass they shall know that the LORD foretold their fate.

12 Thus saith the Lord GOD; Because that Edom hath dealt against the house of Judah by taking vengeance, and hath greatly offended, and revenged himself upon them;
13 Therefore thus saith the Lord GOD; I will also stretch out mine hand upon Edom, and will cut off man and beast from it; and I will make it desolate from Teman; and they of Dedan shall fall by the sword.
14 And I will lay my vengeance upon Edom by the hand of my people Israel: and they shall do in Edom according to mine anger and according to my fury; and they shall know my vengeance, saith the Lord GOD.

Ezekiel continues with the word of the Lord GOD who declared through him that because Edom has taken revenge against the house of Judah, they have greatly offended and planted the seeds which will come to harvest against them according to the Law of Sowing and Reaping. In retribution, the working of the Law will be seen as the LORD stretching out his hand upon Edom to cut off man and beast from the spirit of the LORD. The land will be made desolate from Teman, a district near Petra in southern Edom, to Dedan, a territory in southern Edom, as they fall by the sword of the invader. The LORD will lay vengeance upon Edom by His people, Israel. Israel is the name of the spiritual children of the LORD who are incarnate in the forms of men. They, the spiritual children of the LORD, shall do in Edom according to the anger and the fury of the LORD against those who do not do the works of the LORD on earth.

15 Thus saith the Lord GOD; Because the Philistines have dealt by revenge, and have taken vengeance with a despiteful heart, to destroy it for the old hatred;
16 Therefore thus saith the Lord GOD; Behold, I will stretch out mine hand upon the Philistines, and I will cut off the Cherethims, and destroy the remnant of the sea coast.
17 And I will execute great vengeance upon them with furious rebukes; and they shall know that I am the LORD, when I shall lay my vengeance upon them.

The Lord GOD said that because the Philistines, the inhabitants of the coastal plain west of Judah along the Mediterranean Sea, have sown revenge, and taken revenge to destroy because of old hatreds with Israel, therefore, the LORD will stretch out His hand upon the Philistines, cut off the Cherethims, close allies of the Philistines, and destroy the people remaining along the sea coast. As the people express hatred and revenge in their ways, the LORD will execute a great vengeance upon them with furious rebukes as the people refuse to accept the spirit of the LORD as their own.

CHAPTER 26

1 And it came to pass in the eleventh year, in the first day of the month, that the word of the LORD came unto me, saying,
2 Son of man, because that Tyrus hath said against Jerusalem, Aha, she is broken that was the gates of the people: she is turned unto me: I shall be replenished, now she is laid waste:
3 Therefore thus saith the Lord GOD; Behold, I am against thee, O Tyrus, and will cause many nations to come up against thee, as the sea causeth his waves to come up.
4 And they shall destroy the walls of Tyrus, and break down her towers: I will also scrape her dust from her, and make her like the top of a rock.
5 It shall be a place for the spreading of nets in the midst of the sea: for I have spoken it, saith the Lord GOD: and it shall become a spoil to the nations.
6 And her daughters which are in the field shall be slain by the sword; and they shall know that I am the LORD.

In the eleventh year, in the first day of the month, of the captivity of Ezekiel, the word of the LORD came to him, saying, Son of man, the focus of the LORD in the body of mankind, with this message. Tyrus, or Tyre, the island-capital of Phoenicia, which is present-day Lebanon, has spoken against Jerusalem. The people have said, Aha, which is a cry of malicious joy through which they express pleasure at the misfortune of Jerusalem. The people of Tyre recognized that Jerusalem was the gate of the LORD moving through His people and now the gate of entry of the spirit of the LORD is broken. The spirit has turned back to the LORD, who will be replenished with spirit that needs to find expression into the earth now that Jerusalem is laid waste. As the influence of the spirit of the LORD through Jerusalem to Tyre has ceased to flow, then the LORD declares that the spirit of the LORD will work against Tyre.

Many nations will come up against Tyre as the waves of the sea come upon its shores. The nations who invade Tyre will destroy its walls and break down her towers. The power of the spirit of the LORD shall scrape the dust of destruction away from Tyre to make her like a bare rock. Tyre, a port of international trade, shall become a barren place for the spreading of nets to dry in the sun. The LORD has spoken this fate for Tyre which will become a spoil to the invading nations. Her daughters which are in the field, the inhabitants of Tyre, shall be slain by the sword, the spiritual power of the LORD moving through all people, and an end will come to the activities in Tyre. When this occurs, the people will know that the LORD foretold the fate of Tyre through Ezekiel and that the LORD does exist.

7 For thus saith the Lord GOD; Behold, I will bring upon Tyrus Nebuchadrezzar king of Babylon, a king of kings, from the north, with horses, and with chariots, and with horsemen, and companies, and much people.
8 He shall slay with the sword thy daughters in the field: and he shall make a fort against thee, and cast a mount against thee, and lift up the buckler against thee.
9 And he shall set engines of war against thy walls, and with his axes he shall break down thy towers.

The Symbolic Version of Ezekiel

10 By reason of the abundance of his horses their dust shall cover thee: thy walls shall shake at the noise of the horsemen, and of the wheels, and of the chariots, when he shall enter into thy gates, as men enter into a city wherein is made a breach.
11 With the hoofs of his horses shall he tread down all thy streets: he shall slay thy people by the sword, and thy strong garrisons shall go down to the ground.
12 And they shall make a spoil of thy riches, and make a prey of thy merchandise: and they shall break down thy walls, and destroy thy pleasant houses: and they shall lay thy stones and thy timber and thy dust in the midst of the water.
13 And I will cause the noise of thy songs to cease; and the sound of thy harps shall be no more heard.
14 And I will make thee like the top of a rock: thou shalt be a place to spread nets upon; thou shalt be built no more: for I the LORD have spoken it, saith the Lord GOD.

The LORD speaking through Ezekiel, His prophet, identifies Nebuchadrezzar king of Babylon, a king of kings of the fallen world, would come from the north with horses, chariots and companies of people. He shall use the power which is under his control to slay the people of Tyre in the field; he will make a fort and use his shield as he sets the engines of war against the walls of the city and his axes will break their towers. An abundance of his horses will make dust that will cover Tyre and the walls will shake at the noise of the horsemen, and the wheels and the chariots. The king shall enter into Tyre as he enters into the gates of city when there is a breach in the walls of defense.

The hoofs of his horses shall be heard as he treads down the streets: he shall slay the people of Tyre and the garrisons of the city shall go down to the ground. The Babylonians will take in spoils of war your riches and merchandise; your houses will be destroyed and the stones and timbers will be cast into the sea. The LORD will cause the noise of the songs that Tyre was singing to cease and the sound of the harps shall be heard no more. Tyre will be reduced to a barren rock and it will be used as a place to spread nets upon it. It shall not be an important place of trade. The LORD has spoken it on earth through the voice of Ezekiel and the message came from the Lord GOD.

15 Thus saith the Lord GOD to Tyrus; Shall not the isles shake at the sound of thy fall, when the wounded cry, when the slaughter is made in the midst of thee?
16 Then all the princes of the sea shall come down from their thrones, and lay away their robes, and put off their broidered garments: they shall clothe themselves with trembling; they shall sit upon the ground, and shall tremble at every moment, and be astonished at thee.
17 And they shall take up a lamentation for thee, and say to thee, How art thou destroyed, that wast inhabited of seafaring men, the renowned city, which wast strong in the sea, she and her inhabitants, which cause their terror to be on all that haunt it!
18 Now shall the isles tremble in the day of thy fall; yea, the isles that are in the sea shall be troubled at thy departure.

The Lord GOD asks, Shall not the isles of Tyre shake at the sound of your fall, when the wounded cry and a slaughter is made in the midst of the city? The princes of the sea, the princes of Tyre, who rejoiced at the fall of Jerusalem shall lay away their fine robes and embroidered garments as a defeated nation; they shall clothe themselves with trembling, sit upon the ground and tremble at every moment and be astonished at the power that caused the destruction that they did not foresee for their city.

The defeated people shall lament for the loss of their city. They will ask, How can a renowned city, strong in the sea, and her inhabitants of seafaring men be destroyed? Terror is in the hearts of all who remain on it. The isles tremble in the day of the fall of Tyre. Yes, the isles that are in the sea shall be troubled at the departure of the glory that was Tyre.

19 For thus saith the Lord GOD; When I shall make thee a desolate city, like the cities that are not inhabited; when I shall bring up the deep upon thee, and great waters shall cover thee;
20 When I shall bring thee down with them that descend into the pit, with the people of old time, and shall set thee in the low parts of the earth, in places desolate of old, with them that go down to the pit, that thou be not inhabited; and I shall set glory in the land of the living;
21 I will make thee a terror, and thou shalt be no more: though thou be sought for, yet shalt thou never be found again, saith the Lord GOD.

The Testimony of the Major Prophets

The Lord GOD says that when Tyre is made a desolate city like cities that are not inhabited; when the LORD shall bring the deep of despair upon you and great waters of invading armies have covered you, then you shall know what it was like when people of old were thrown into a pit and became desolate and were brought low in the earth of their circumstances. When the time comes that they are no longer inhabited by the invaders, then the LORD shall set the glory of being in the land of the living, in the land that belongs to the living God.

The LORD has moved in such a way to make the people of Tyre a people of terror so that they can choose not to live in terror. They can choose to be people of the LORD. Then, they, the sinners of old, shall be sought for and yet they will be no more. They shall not be found again, says the Lord GOD, because they will have repented and become His people.

CHAPTER 27

1 The word of the LORD came again unto me, saying,
2 Now, thou son of man, take up a lamentation for Tyrus;
3 And say unto Tyrus, O thou that art situate at the entry of the sea, which art a merchant of the people for many isles, Thus saith the Lord GOD; O Tyrus, thou hast said, I am of perfect beauty.
4 Thy borders are in the midst of the seas, thy builders have perfected thy beauty.

The word of the LORD came to Ezekiel, the focus point of the spiritual Son of man, saying, Now, the fallen, materialistic son of man will lament for the fate that has befallen Tyre as it was invaded and made desolate by the Babylonian invaders. Ezekiel is instructed by the LORD to say to the people of Tyre and to those who have become aware of her fate that they are beautifully situated at the entry of the sea and they are a merchant of the people for many isles. The inhabitants of Tyre were aware that as a city and as a choice location to communicate with many people, Tyre was a perfect beauty; her borders are in the midst of the seas and the builders perfected the beauty of her location. Only the best from the material world were used by the builders in the construction of Tyre as a center of commerce and trade.

5 They have made all thy ship boards of fir trees of Senir: they have taken cedars from Lebanon to make masts for thee.
6 Of the oaks of Bashan have they made thine oars; the company of the Ashurites have made thy benches of ivory, brought out of the isles of Chittim.
7 Fine linen with broidered work from Egypt was that which thou spreadest forth to be thy sail; blue and purple from the isles of Elishah was that which covered thee.
8 The inhabitants of Zidon and Arvad were thy mariners: thy wise men, O Tyrus, that were in thee, were thy pilots.
9 The ancients of Gebal and the wise men thereof were in thee thy calkers: all the ships of the sea with their mariners were in thee to occupy thy merchandise.
10 They of Persia and of Lud and of Phut were in thine army, thy men of war: they hanged the shield and helmet in thee; they set forth thy comeliness.
11 The men of Arvad with thine army were upon thy walls round about, and the Gammadims were in thy towers: they hanged their shields upon thy walls round about; they have made thy beauty perfect.

The boards of the ships were made from the fir trees of Senir, the Amorite name for Hermon; the cedars of Lebanon were used to make the masts. The oaks of Bashan, the rich land east of the Sea of Galilee, were used to make the oars; The Ashurites made her benches, inlaid with ivory, in the cedar brought from the isles of Chittim, a town in southern Cyprus. Your sails were made of fine linen from Egypt; and blue and purple awnings from the isles of Elishah, a city on the east side of Cyprus, covered you.

The Testimony of the Major Prophets

The inhabitants of Zidon and Arvad, two harbor cities north of Tyre, were skilled mariners who manned your ships; the wise men of Tyre were the pilots of your ships. The ancient craftsmen of Gebal, a city on the coast between Sidon and Arvad, caulked the seams of your ships: all the ships of the sea with their mariners came to Tyre to trade for her merchandise. Men from Persia, Lud (Asia minor) and Phut (North Africa) were in the army of people who came to you and hanged their helmets and shields in peace as they visited you and appreciated your splendor. The men of Arvad with their army were upon your walls round about to protect you, and the Gammadims, the men of Gammad, a coastal town near Arvad, were in your towers to watch over you. They hanged their shields upon your walls in peace; they have made your beauty perfect. Tyre had become a center for international trade from the western Mediterranean Sea to the east.

12 Tarshish was thy merchant by reason of the multitude of all kind of riches; with silver, iron, tin, and lead, they traded in thy fairs.
13 Javan, Tubal, and Meshech, they were thy merchants: they traded the persons of men and vessels of brass in thy market.
14 They of the house of Togarmah traded in thy fairs with horses and horsemen and mules.
15 The men of Dedan were thy merchants; many isles were the merchandise of thine hand: they brought thee for a present horns of ivory and ebony.
16 Syria was thy merchant by reason of the multitude of the wares of thy making: they occupied in thy fairs with emeralds, purple, and broidered work, and fine linen, and coral, and agate.
17 Judah, and the land of Israel, they were thy merchants: they traded in thy market wheat of Minnith, and Pannag, and honey, and oil, and balm.

The silver, iron, tin, and lead from Tarshish in Spain were traded for the great wealth of goods contained in Tyre. Merchants from Javan, Tubal and Meshech, from Greece and Asia Minor, traded slaves and brass vessels for your wares. The people of the house of Togarmah in eastern Asia Minor, present day Armenia, traded their horses, horsemen and mules. The men of Dedan, a tribe in southern Edom, traded with Tyre; many islands brought their goods to be sold in Tyre: such as ivory tusks and ebony.

The merchandise of trade also came to Tyre by land. Syria brought a multitude of wares such as emeralds, coral, agate, embroidered work and fine linen. Judah and the land of Israel traded as merchants in your city: they traded in the wheat from Pannag and Minnith, an Ammonite town known for its superior quality of wheat; and honey, oil and balm from Gilead.

18 Damascus was thy merchant in the multitude of the wares of thy making, for the multitude of all riches; in the wine of Helbon, and white wool.
19 Dan also and Javan going to and fro occupied in thy fairs: bright iron, cassia, and calamus, were in thy market.
20 Dedan was thy merchant in precious clothes for chariots.
21 Arabia, and all the princes of Kedar, they occupied with thee in lambs, and rams, and goats: in these were they thy merchants.
22 The merchants of Sheba and Raamah, they were thy merchants: they occupied in thy fairs with chief of all spices, and with all precious stones, and gold.
23 Haran, and Canneh, and Eden, the merchants of Sheba, Asshur, and Chilmad, were thy merchants.
24 These were thy merchants in all sorts of things, in blue clothes, and broidered work, and in chests of rich apparel, bound with cords, and made of cedar, among thy merchandise.

Damascus, the capital of Syria, came to trade the wine of Helbon, a town north of Damascus still in existence as a wine making center, and white wool because of the multitude of goods which were available in Tyre. Bright iron, and the spices of cassia and calamus were brought to Tyre from Dan and Javan. Precious clothes for chariots came from Dedan. Arabia and all the princes of Kedar, a general name for the Bedouin tribes from Aram to the Arabian Desert, traded their lambs, rams and goats. Merchants from Sheba, southern Yemen, and Raamah, a city in southern Arabia, traded their spices, precious stones and gold. Merchants from Haran, the city in eastern Turkey which Abraham left to go to Canaan, and other cities in the region traded all sorts of things as clothes, embroidered work, and chests made of cedar.

The Symbolic Version of Ezekiel

Tyre had indeed become famous as a center of trade.

25 The ships of Tarshish did sing of thee in thy market: and thou wast replenished, and made very glorious in the midst of the seas.
26 Thy rowers have brought thee into great waters: the east wind hath broken thee in the midst of the seas.
27 Thy riches, and thy fairs, thy merchandise, thy mariners, and thy pilots, thy calkers, and the occupiers of thy merchandise, and all thy men of war, that are in thee, and in all thy company which is in the midst of thee, shall fall into the midst of the seas in the day of thy ruin.

The ships from as far away as Tarshish in Spain sang the praises of Tyre, as a symbol of a ship of trade, which was a famous merchant city in the marketplace of the sea. Tyre had been constantly replenished with goods for sale and trade which had been made her glorious in the midst of the seas. The rowers, the leaders, have steered Tyre into great waters in the commerce of trade: but the wind from the east, the invasion by the Babylonians, have broken Tyre in the midst of the seas which surround her.

The riches of Tyre, the trading fairs, the mariners and the pilots of ships, the caulkers who repair the ships, the merchants and the men of war who guard the city shall fall into the sea in the day of the ruin of Tyre. The fall and the destruction of Tyre will affect many people who will mourn at its destruction and the mourning and lamentation will be heard round about the city.

28 The suburbs shall shake at the sound of the cry of thy pilots.
29 And all that handle the oar, the mariners, and all the pilots of the sea, shall come down from their ships, they shall stand upon the land;
30 And shall cause their voice to be heard against thee, and shall cry bitterly, and shall cast up dust upon their heads, they shall wallow themselves in the ashes:
31 And they shall make themselves utterly bald for thee, and gird them with sackcloth, and they shall weep for thee with bitterness of heart and bitter wailing.
32 And in their wailing they shall take up a lamentation for thee, and lament over thee, saying, What city is like Tyrus, like the destroyed in the midst of the sea?

The suburbs around the city shall shake at the cry of the pilots of the ships that came into Tyre; as well as those that handled the oars, the mariners and all the pilots of the sea shall come down from their ships and stand upon the land; their voices shall be heard as they cry bitterly, cast dust upon their heads to symbolize their grief, and wallow in ashes; they shall make themselves bald as they pull out their hair because of the loss, and wrap themselves with sackcloth as they weep with bitterness of heart and bitter wailing. The wailing shall lead to lamenting for the destruction of Tyre as they cry with grief for the loss of Tyre as they ask, What city like Tyre has ever been destroyed in the midst of the sea?

33 When thy wares went forth out of the seas, thou filledst many people; thou didst enrich the kings of the earth with the multitude of thy riches and of thy merchandise.
34 In the time when thou shalt be broken by the seas in the depths of the waters thy merchandise and all thy company in the midst of thee shall fall.
35 All the inhabitants of the isles shall be astonished at thee, and their kings shall be sore afraid, they shall be troubled in their countenance.
36 The merchants among the people shall hiss at thee; thou shalt be a terror, and never shalt be any more.

When the wares went forth from Tyre, many people were filled with the material goods which were traded and sold; Tyre did enrich the kings of the earth with a multitude of material riches and merchandise. In the time when Tyre is broken by the seas in the midst of the waters, the merchandise and all the people involved in the midst of her shall fall also.

All the inhabitants of the isles shall be astonished at the destruction and the fall of Tyre, and their kings shall be sore afraid. They earthly kings shall be troubled in their countenance and their troubled faces will reveal their worry. The merchants among the people who have lost their lucrative livelihood shall hiss at the destruction of Tyre, and the story of the fall and destruction of Tyre shall be a terror to those who hear the story. The city and the glory that was Tyre shall never be any more.

CHAPTER 28

1 The word of the LORD came again unto me, saying,
2 Son of man, say unto the prince of Tyrus, Thus saith the Lord GOD; Because thine heart is lifted up, and thou hast said, I am a God, I sit in the seat of God, in the midst of the seas; yet thou art a man, and not God, though thou set thine heart as the heart of God:
3 Behold, thou art wiser than Daniel; there is no secret that they can hide from thee:
4 With thy wisdom and with thine understanding thou hast gotten thee riches, and hast gotten gold and silver into thy treasures:
5 By thy great wisdom and by thy traffick hast thou increased thy riches, and thine heart is lifted up because of thy riches:
6 Therefore thus saith the Lord GOD; Because thou hast set thine heart as the heart of God;
7 Behold, therefore I will bring strangers upon thee, the terrible of the nations: and they shall draw their swords against the beauty of thy wisdom, and they shall defile thy brightness.

The word of the LORD came to Ezekiel, the focus point of the Son of man, instructing him to give this message to the prince of Tyre: Because your heart is lifted up to the position where you have said, I am a God, I sit in the seat of God, in the midst of the seas in the city of Tyre; but you are a man, and not God, even though you set your heart as the heart of God: Behold, you believe that you are wiser than Daniel, which means, "the judgment of God"; you believe there is no secret about man in his relationship to God that people can hide from you. By means of your great wisdom and understanding, you have obtained riches of gold and silver into your treasures: by your wisdom, the traffic through Tyre has increased your riches, and your heart has been lifted up because of your material riches.

Therefore, says the Lord GOD through Ezekiel, because you have set your heart as the heart of God, the LORD will bring strangers upon you, the terrible invaders of nations who will draw their sword of destructive power against the beauty of your materialistic wisdom, and they shall defile the brightness of the shining success of Tyre.

8 They shall bring thee down to the pit, and thou shalt die the deaths of them that are slain in the midst of the seas.
9 Wilt thou yet say before him that slayeth thee, I am God? but thou shalt be a man, and no God, in the hand of him that slayeth thee.
10 Thou shalt die the deaths of the uncircumcised by the hand of strangers: for I have spoken it, saith the Lord GOD.

The invaders of Tyre shall bring you down into the pit where things deteriorate and decompose, and the people of Tyre shall die the deaths of them that are slain in the midst of the seas. Under these conditions of the destruction of Tyre, will you continue to say before the him that slays you, I am God? You will be a human man, and no God, in the hand of the one that slays you. You shall die the deaths of the uncircumcised, the people who do not know the reality of the

The Testimony of the Major Prophets

covenant with God, under the yoke of the strangers who have invaded "your" kingdom of wealth. The Lord GOD has spoken to the prince of Tyre.

11 Moreover the word of the LORD came unto me, saying,
12 Son of man, take up a lamentation upon the king of Tyrus, and say unto him, Thus saith the Lord GOD; Thou sealest up the sum, full of wisdom, and perfect in beauty.
13 Thou hast been in Eden the garden of God; every precious stone was thy covering, the sardius, topaz, and the diamond, the beryl, the onyx, and the jasper, the sapphire, the emerald, and the carbuncle, and gold: the workmanship of thy tabrets and of thy pipes was prepared in thee in the day that thou wast created.
14 Thou art the anointed cherub that covereth; and I have set thee so: thou wast upon the holy mountain of God; thou hast walked up and down in the midst of the stones of fire.

Moreover, the word of the LORD came to Ezekiel, the true servant of God, saying, Son of man, Take a lamentation, an expression of sorrow, to the king of Tyre with this message from the Lord GOD; You have sealed up the sum, the addition that God would bring on earth through you, which would reveal the nature of God on earth that would be full of wisdom and perfect in beauty. You have been in Eden, the garden of God; every precious stone was yours to wear as a covering— the sardius, topaz, and the diamond, the beryl, the onyx, and the jasper, the sapphire, the emerald, and the carbuncle, and gold. Gold is the symbol of the **spirit** of love from God; the nine precious stones which man wore as a garment symbolize his earthly clothing in the garden of God on earth. The workmanship of your tabrets, the tabular registry and chronology of what you were to do on earth, and of your pipes, the way that you would bring these plans into fruition, was prepared in you in the day that you were created by the LORD. You are the anointed cherub, spiritual offspring, that covers the earth: The LORD has set you in that position to serve the LORD, not your fallen self. You were upon the holy mountain of God. You have walked up and down in the midst of stones of spiritual fire that come from the LORD. The king of Tyre would understand his LORD and King; the prince of Tyre, the one who would be an earthly king, would not understand the way of the LORD.

15 Thou wast perfect in thy ways from the day that thou wast created, till iniquity was found in thee.
16 By the multitude of thy merchandise they have filled the midst of thee with violence, and thou hast sinned: therefore I will cast thee as profane out of the mountain of God: and I will destroy thee, O covering cherub, from the midst of the stones of fire.
17 Thine heart was lifted up because of thy beauty, thou hast corrupted thy wisdom by reason of thy brightness: I will cast thee to the ground, I will lay thee before kings, that they may behold thee.
18 Thou hast defiled thy sanctuaries by the multitude of thine iniquities, by the iniquity of thy traffick; therefore will I bring forth a fire from the midst of thee, it shall devour thee, and I will bring thee to ashes upon the earth in the sight of all them that behold thee.
19 All they that know thee among the people shall be astonished at thee: thou shalt be a terror, and never shalt thou be any more.

The LORD speaking through Ezekiel declares that the spiritual king of Tyre was perfect from the day that he was created until iniquity and sin were found in him and he acted like an earthly prince instead of a spiritual king. By the multitude of the material wealth of merchandise, these material things have filled the midst of you with violence and you have sinned as the material goods became more important to you than the spiritual kingdom of the LORD. Therefore, the LORD will cast you out of His garden, the spiritual mountain of God, as profane. The LORD will destroy you, the false covering of the cherub, from the midst of the stones of fire that destroy everything which is not of the divine design of God.

Your heart was lifted up because of your spiritual beauty which comes from God, but you have corrupted your wisdom by reason of your material success. The material treasures became more important to you than the LORD your God. The action and the law of the LORD will cast you to the ground, lay you before the true kings of the earth, so that they may behold you in your punishment. You have defiled your sanctuaries by the multitude of your iniquities and sins; by the iniquities, the distortions of the traffic that went through Tyre. Therefore, the LORD will bring forth a destructive fire from the midst of you which shall devour you and bring you to ashes upon the earth in the sight of all who see you. All the people who know you shall be astonished at your fate: you shall be a terror of what could happen to them; and you shall never be any more.

The Symbolic Version of Ezekiel

20 Again the word of the LORD came unto me, saying,
21 Son of man, set thy face against Zidon, and prophesy against it,
22 And say, Thus saith the Lord GOD; Behold, I am against thee, O Zidon; and I will be glorified in the midst of thee: and they shall know that I am the LORD, when I shall have executed judgments in her, and shall be sanctified in her.
23 For I will send into her pestilence, and blood into her streets; and the wounded shall be judged in the midst of her by the sword upon her on every side; and they shall know that I am the LORD.
24 And there shall be no more a pricking brier unto the house of Israel, nor any grieving thorn of all that are round about them, that despised them; and they shall know that I am the Lord GOD.

Again the word of the LORD came to Ezekiel, the person in the true position of the Son of man, to set the face of his attention toward Sidon, and prophesy against the people in that city because their behavior is like the people of Tyre. The LORD will be glorified in the midst of the people of Sidon, within their hearts, minds and bodies. Then they shall know that the LORD who is finding expression through the people who execute the LORD's judgments within them and the LORD shall be sanctified in the people who serve the LORD's spirit.

If the people of Sidon refuse, then, the LORD will send pestilence and blood in the streets; the wounded shall be judged in the midst of the city by the sword, the destructive power of the LORD, which shall appear on every side as it is expressed through the people who distort the beauty of the LORD. Then, the people shall know that the LORD has been with them and that He is the LORD. As they are destroyed, they shall not be as a pricking briar, a thorn, in the house of Israel, the spiritual house of the LORD, which was known by the fallen, material Jacob who became the ascended spiritual person, Israel. There shall be the absence of grieving thorns, the fallen people, who despised the people in the house of Israel. Then the people who repent and know that it is the LORD's true spirit as it moves through them and they shall know the Lord GOD as they express His spirit.

25 Thus saith the Lord GOD; When I shall have gathered the house of Israel from the people among whom they are scattered, and shall be sanctified in them in the sight of the heathen, then shall they dwell in their land that I have given to my servant Jacob.
26 And they shall dwell safely therein, and shall build houses, and plant vineyards; yea, they shall dwell with confidence, when I have executed judgments upon all those that despise them round about them; and they shall know that I am the LORD their God.

This is the message of the Lord GOD. When He has gathered the house of Israel, the restored spiritual people, from the fallen people among whom they were scattered, and when the LORD is sanctified in them, the heathen who have rebelled against God, then they shall dwell in the land, the place on earth that the LORD has given to his servant, Jacob. But Jacob, the fallen person, must become Israel, the restored person.

And the people shall dwell safely in this land on earth. They shall build their houses and plant vineyards. They shall dwell with confidence as the spirit of the LORD executes his judgments through all those people round about who have despised those who serve the spirit of the LORD. The spirit of the LORD is moving through all of his people simultaneously. Then they shall know the LORD their God because they are in the covenant of the LORD which has always been available to be experienced. The **son of man** will not have the experience of the covenant: The **Son of man** will have the experience of the covenant. Ezekiel is the focus point of the Son of man.

CHAPTER 29

1 In the tenth year, in the tenth month, in the twelfth day of the month, the word of the LORD came unto me, saying,
2 Son of man, set thy face against Pharaoh king of Egypt, and prophesy against him, and against all Egypt:
3 Speak, and say, Thus saith the Lord GOD; Behold, I am against thee, Pharaoh king of Egypt, the great dragon that lieth in the midst of his rivers, which hath said, My river is mine own, and I have made it for myself.

In the tenth year on the twelfth day of the tenth month of the captivity of Ezekiel, the word of the LORD came to Ezekiel, saying, Son of man, the true representation of the spirit of the LORD through man on earth, set your face, give your full attention, to Pharaoh, the earthly king of Egypt, and prophesy against him and all of the inhabitants of the great country of Egypt. Ezekiel is to speak with the message of the Lord GOD declaring that the LORD is against Pharaoh, king of Egypt who is described as a great dragon that lies in the midst of his rivers, the symbol of the flowing spirit that is contained in his people. Pharaoh has said that the river of people who represent Egypt belong to Pharaoh. The river is his property and possession, and he has made it for himself. Pharaoh has stated that the people are his own and they do not belong to the LORD. Pharaoh does not know the LORD. The LORD, who is the rightful owner of the people and the earth upon which they walk, has a message for Pharaoh through Ezekiel.

4 But I will put hooks in thy jaws, and I will cause the fish of thy rivers to stick unto thy scales, and I will bring thee up out of the midst of thy rivers, and all the fish of thy rivers shall stick unto thy scales.
5 And I will leave thee thrown into the wilderness, thee and all the fish of thy rivers: thou shalt fall upon the open fields; thou shalt not be brought together, nor gathered: I have given thee for meat to the beasts of the field and to the fowls of the heaven.
6 And all the inhabitants of Egypt shall know that I am the LORD, because they have been a staff of reed to the house of Israel.
7 When they took hold of thee by thy hand, thou didst break, and rend all their shoulder: and when they leaned upon thee, thou brakest, and madest all their loins to be at a stand.

The LORD has a message for Pharaoh. The LORD will put a hook in the jaws of Pharaoh and catch him like a fish. The LORD will cause the fish, the people, in the rivers, to stick to the scales of Pharaoh as one large dragon with all the fish that symbolize the Egyptian people sticking to the scales of the dragon who is Pharaoh. The LORD will remove Pharaoh from the familiar river in which he has been swimming and Pharaoh will be thrown into the wilderness along with all his fish, his people. Pharaoh shall fall upon the open fields where they shall not be brought together, nor gathered together to be saved by the LORD. Instead, the LORD has given the Egyptians for meat to the beasts of the field and to the fowls of heaven who will consume the Egyptians. When this event occurs, then all the inhabitants of Egypt shall know that the LORD, who foretold their misfortune, is indeed the LORD their God when the Egyptians discover that they are indeed like a staff of material reed that has covered the spiritual clothing of the spiritual house of Israel. All people, including the Egyptians, belong to the LORD. When the house of Israel, the spiritual beings within each human form, takes hold of the material forms by their hands, then the people in the fallen state, the Egyptians, shall break their shoulders, break their ability to do work for the LORD. When the spirits of the LORD lean upon the human capacities of heart, mind and body, the human capacities will break and all the loins of the spiritual people will be at a stand, upright, in reverence to the LORD.

8 Therefore thus saith the Lord GOD; Behold, I will bring a sword upon thee, and cut off man and beast out of thee.
9 And the land of Egypt shall be desolate and waste; and they shall know that I am the LORD: because he hath said, The river is mine, and I have made it.
10 Behold, therefore I am against thee, and against thy rivers, and I will make the land of Egypt utterly waste and desolate, from the tower of Syene even unto the border of Ethiopia.
11 No foot of man shall pass through it, nor foot of beast shall pass through it, neither shall it be inhabited forty years.
12 And I will make the land of Egypt desolate in the midst of the countries that are desolate, and her cities among the cities that are laid waste shall be desolate forty years: and I will scatter the Egyptians among the nations, and will disperse them through the countries.

Therefore, the Lord GOD will bring a sword of His power upon the Pharaoh of Egypt to cut off man and beast away from the dragon which Pharaoh and his people have become. The land of Egypt shall be desolate and laid waste because Pharaoh and his people have said that the river of spirit which is in Egypt belongs to Pharaoh and that Pharaoh has made it. Behold, see, that the LORD is against Pharaoh and his rivers of people. The LORD will make the land of Egypt utterly desolate and waste from the tower of Syene, which was once an important city in Egypt, to the border of Ethiopia, where many tribes lived in the wilderness.

No foot of man or beast shall pass through it for forty years. The LORD will make the land of Egypt desolate in the midst of countries which are desolate, and her cities among the cities that are laid waste for forty years. The Egyptians shall be scattered among the nations and dispersed through the countries because they have denied the spirit of the LORD.

13 Yet thus saith the Lord GOD; At the end of forty years will I gather the Egyptians from the people whither they were scattered:
14 And I will bring again the captivity of Egypt, and will cause them to return into the land of Pathros, into the land of their habitation; and they shall be there a base kingdom.
15 It shall be the basest of the kingdoms; neither shall it exalt itself any more above the nations: for I will diminish them, that they shall no more rule over the nations.
16 And it shall be no more the confidence of the house of Israel, which bringeth their iniquity to remembrance, when they shall look after them: but they shall know that I am the Lord GOD.

Yet, the Lord GOD says that He will gather the Egyptians together from the people where they were scattered; and the LORD will bring again the captivity of Egypt and cause them to return to the land of Pathros, the land of Southern Egypt, which shall be a base kingdom, a kingdom that is sordid and degraded. This basest of kingdoms shall not exalt itself any more above other nations for the LORD will diminish them among the nations and they shall rule no more. And the kingdom of the fallen state shall be no more, or have the confidence of the house of Israel, the confidence which comes from the covenant with the LORD, when the people who love the LORD look after the people. Then they shall know that the LORD is God over all.

17 And it came to pass in the seven and twentieth year, in the first month, in the first day of the month, the word of the LORD came unto me, saying,
18 Son of man, Nebuchadrezzar king of Babylon caused his army to serve a great service against Tyrus: every head was made bald, and every shoulder was peeled: yet had he no wages, nor his army, for Tyrus, for the service that he had served against it:
19 Therefore thus saith the Lord GOD; Behold, I will give the land of Egypt unto Nebuchadrezzar king of Babylon; and he shall take her multitude, and take her spoil, and take her prey; and it shall be the wages for his army.
20 I have given him the land of Egypt for his labour wherewith he served against it, because they wrought for me, saith the Lord GOD.

The Testimony of the Major Prophets

21 In that day will I cause the horn of the house of Israel to bud forth, and I will give thee the opening of the mouth in the midst of them; and they shall know that I am the LORD.

And it came to pass in the twenty-seventh year on the first day of the first month of the captivity of Ezekiel that the word of the LORD came to Ezekiel saying, Son of man, Nebuchadrezzar, king of Babylon, caused his army to serve a great service against Tyre. Every head was made bald and every shoulder was peeled: yet he had no wages or army for Tyre for the service that he had served against it. Therefore the Lord GOD said that he will give the land of Egypt to Nebuchadrezzar, king of Babylon as a prey and a spoil; Egypt shall be given as wages to the army of Nebuchadrezzar.

The power of the LORD working through the Babylonians has given the land of Egypt to them for their service that they wrought for the LORD. In that day, the LORD will cause the horn of the house of Israel to bud forth and the LORD will give the house of Israel an opening of the mouth, a spokesman for the LORD, in the midst of the Egyptians; and they shall know that the LORD is God.

CHAPTER 30

1 The word of the LORD came again unto me, saying,
2 Son of man, prophesy and say, Thus saith the Lord GOD; Howl ye, Woe worth the day!
3 For the day is near, even the day of the LORD is near, a cloudy day; it shall be the time of the heathen.
4 And the sword shall come upon Egypt, and great pain shall be in Ethiopia, when the slain shall fall in Egypt, and they shall take away her multitude, and her foundations shall be broken down.
5 Ethiopia, and Libya, and Lydia, and all the mingled people, and Chub, and the men of the land that is in league, shall fall with them by the sword.

The word of the LORD came to Ezekiel, saying, Son of man, all people who wish to identify with the body of the Son of the Lord GOD on earth, must prophesy, speak and express the spirit of the LORD, through each of them individually. The chosen body of people, the people who choose to express the spirit of the LORD in their living, must howl, must express a long bellow of the spirit of the LORD in their individual experience consistently, day by day. This is the only way that the spirit of the LORD is magnified on earth through His people. The people who do this will experience a woe, an experience of sorrow and pain, as their old and fallen sense of self passes away to be replaced by a new Self which carries the spirit of the LORD. But the transition is well worth the discomfort of the day!

For the day is near, even the day of the LORD is near, and it will be a cloudy day where the people who participate in the process will not see the whole picture clearly. But it shall be the time of the heathen returning to the place from which the heathen fell before they were heathens. And the sword of the LORD's power shall come upon Egypt through the armies of Nebuchadrezzar, to the people of Egypt, the people who are in the darkened fallen state. Great pain shall be in the multitude of people who comprise Africa, south of Egypt in Ethiopia, Lydia and Chub, and the land west of Egypt, Libya, as the foundations of the kingdom of Egypt are broken down.

6 Thus saith the LORD; They also that uphold Egypt shall fall; and the pride of her power shall come down: from the tower of Syene shall they fall in it by the sword, saith the Lord GOD.
7 And they shall be desolate in the midst of the countries that are desolate, and her cities shall be in the midst of the cities that are wasted.
8 And they shall know that I am the LORD, when I have set a fire in Egypt, and when all her helpers shall be destroyed.
9 In that day shall messengers go forth from me in ships to make the careless Ethiopians afraid, and great pain shall come upon them, as in the day of Egypt: for, lo, it cometh.

Egypt is a representative of the fallen state, the distorted state of man, on earth. The people who uphold Egypt and the pride of her power shall fall from the tower of Syene, which is the tower of enmity, animosity, anger and loathing that shall fall by the moving power of the spirit of the Lord GOD moving through His people. The people shall be desolate in the midst of the countries that are desolate, and the cities built by fallen people shall be in the midst of the cities

The Testimony of the Major Prophets

that are wasted. The people will know that the LORD is God when He has set a fire in Egypt and all her helpers are destroyed. In that day, messengers shall go forth in ships, to make the careless Ethiopians afraid as great pain comes upon Egypt.

10 Thus saith the Lord GOD; I will also make the multitude of Egypt to cease by the hand of Nebuchadrezzar king of Babylon.
11 He and his people with him, the terrible of the nations, shall be brought to destroy the land: and they shall draw their swords against Egypt, and fill the land with the slain.
12 And I will make the rivers dry, and sell the land into the hand of the wicked: and I will make the land waste, and all that is therein, by the hand of strangers: I the LORD have spoken it.

The action of the Lord GOD will make the multitude of the people in Egypt to cease by the hand of Nebuchadrezzar, king of Babylon, who will come to Egypt with his people, the terrible of nations, to draw their swords against Egypt and destroy the people. The rivers will become dry and the land shall be sold to the wicked. The land will be made waste and all the people who dwell therein. The word is spoken by the LORD through Ezekiel.

13 Thus saith the Lord GOD; I will also destroy the idols, and I will cause their images to cease out of Noph; and there shall be no more a prince of the land of Egypt: and I will put a fear in the land of Egypt.
14 And I will make Pathros desolate, and will set fire in Zoan, and will execute judgments in No.
15 And I will pour my fury upon Sin, the strength of Egypt; and I will cut off the multitude of No.
16 And I will set fire in Egypt: Sin shall have great pain, and No shall be rent asunder, and Noph shall have distresses daily.
17 The young men of Aven and of Pibeseth shall fall by the sword: and these cities shall go into captivity.
18 At Tehaphnehes also the day shall be darkened, when I shall break there the yokes of Egypt: and the pomp of her strength shall cease in her: as for her, a cloud shall cover her, and her daughters shall go into captivity.
19 Thus will I execute judgments in Egypt: and they shall know that I am the LORD.

Moreover, the Lord GOD says that He will destroy the idols and cause their images to cease out of Noph; there will no longer be a prince in the land of Egypt and fear will spread throughout the land. The cities of Egypt will experience the desolation, fire, judgments, desolation, pain and fury of the destructive cycles that occur when the people do not serve the spirit of the LORD. The young men of the invaded cities will be slain by the sword and the cities will go into captivity. It will be a dark and destructive day when the law of the LORD breaks the yoke that Egypt had over the people when the country was powerful; but the pomp of her strength shall cease to be as the cloud covers her when her daughters, who symbolize the Egyptian people, are taken in captivity. When these judgments occur in Egypt then the people shall know that the LORD has foretold the events before they happened.

20 And it came to pass in the eleventh year, in the first month, in the seventh day of the month, that the word of the LORD came unto me, saying,
21 Son of man, I have broken the arm of Pharaoh king of Egypt; and, lo, it shall not be bound up to be healed, to put a roller to bind it, to make it strong to hold the sword.
22 Therefore thus saith the Lord GOD; Behold, I am against Pharaoh king of Egypt, and will break his arms, the strong, and that which was broken; and I will cause the sword to fall out of his hand.
23 And I will scatter the Egyptians among the nations, and will disperse them through the countries.
24 And I will strengthen the arms of the king of Babylon, and put my sword in his hand: but I will break Pharaoh's arms, and he shall groan before him with the groanings of a deadly wounded man.
25 But I will strengthen the arms of the king of Babylon, and the arms of Pharaoh shall fall down; and they shall know that I am the LORD, when I shall put my sword into the hand of the king of Babylon, and he shall stretch it out upon the land of Egypt.
26 And I will scatter the Egyptians among the nations, and disperse them among the countries; and they shall know that I am the LORD.

Ezekiel states that it was on the seventh day of the first month in the eleventh year of his captivity that the word of the LORD came to him saying, Son of man, the LORD has broken the arm of Pharaoh, king of Egypt; the arm shall not be bound so that it might be healed; and the LORD will cause the sword of power to fall out of the hand of Pharaoh. The

Egyptians will be scattered among the nations and dispersed among their people as the law of the LORD strengthens the arms of the king of Babylon as the power from the LORD is placed in the hand of the king of Babylon who will use the power to destroy the dominion of Egypt. The king of Babylon will stretch forth his sword in a show of victory over the land of Egypt. The Egyptians will be scattered by the power of the LORD among the nations and the people will be dispersed among other countries. When these things come to pass as they were foretold, then the people who are dispersed through many countries shall know that the power of the LORD has been used to bring these things to pass.

CHAPTER 31

1 And it came to pass in the eleventh year, in the third month, in the first day of the month, that the word of the LORD came unto me, saying,
2 Son of man, speak unto Pharaoh king of Egypt, and to his multitude; Whom art thou like in thy greatness?
3 Behold, the Assyrian was a cedar in Lebanon with fair branches, and with a shadowing shroud, and of an high stature; and his top was among the thick boughs.
4 The waters made him great, the deep set him up on high with her rivers running round about his plants, and sent out her little rivers unto all the trees of the field.
5 Therefore his height was exalted above all the trees of the field, and his boughs were multiplied, and his branches became long because of the multitude of waters, when he shot forth.

In the eleventh year of the captivity of Ezekiel by the Babylonians, in the third month on the first day of the month, the word of the LORD said, Son of man, the spirit of the Son of the spirit of the LORD and his body on earth, speak to the king of Egypt and to his multitude, who represent the fallen son of man and his body and ask him this question: Whom are you like in your greatness? The LORD will provide the king of Egypt a parable about Assyria with which to compare his earthly greatness.

The kingdom of Assyria was like a cedar of Lebanon with fair branches that cast its shadow over the other trees in the forest because of its high stature and thick boughs. The waters which fell from the sky symbolized the blessing from heaven which made the cedar tree and Assyria great. As rivers of water flowed from the heights of the cedar of Lebanon to form little rivers that nourished other smaller trees in the field, so did Assyria have its tributaries which were nourished by its kingdom and power. The height of the cedar tree was exalted above all the trees of the field, its boughs were multiplied, and its branches became long because of the multitude of waters which caused it to grow. Assyria was a great nation and it grew in the manner of the cedar of Lebanon to the benefit of all the people in its immediate environment.

6 All the fowls of heaven made their nests in his boughs, and under his branches did all the beasts of the field bring forth their young, and under his shadow dwelt all great nations.
7 Thus was he fair in his greatness, in the length of his branches: for his root was by great waters.
8 The cedars in the garden of God could not hide him: the fir trees were not like his boughs, and the chestnut trees were not like his branches; nor any tree in the garden of God was like unto him in his beauty.
9 I have made him fair by the multitude of his branches: so that all the trees of Eden, that were in the garden of God, envied him.

All the fowls of heaven made their nests in the boughs of the tall cedar that symbolized Assyria. Birds symbolize thoughts in the consciousness of the Assyrian leadership. All the beasts of the field, the symbols of earthly effects, brought forth their young, and under the shadow of this tree dwelt great nations. In its growth and beauty, there was greatness which came because the root of the tree was nourished from the waters which fell from heaven, the spirit of truth which originates in heaven, the place of cause.

The cedars in the garden of God could not hide the presence and the power of God: but the fir trees were not like the branches from God; nor was any tree in the garden of God like God in His beauty. The cedar tree was made beautiful by its growth and the multitude of its branches. So all the trees of Eden, which symbolize the people in the garden of God, envied the tall cedar. The tall cedar symbolized Assyria which had grown in size and self-centeredness.

10 Therefore thus saith the Lord GOD; Because thou hast lifted up thyself in height, and he hath shot up his top among the thick boughs, and his heart is lifted up in his height;
11 I have therefore delivered him into the hand of the mighty one of the heathen; he shall surely deal with him: I have driven him out for his wickedness.
12 And strangers, the terrible of the nations, have cut him off, and have left him: upon the mountains and in all the valleys his branches are fallen, and his boughs are broken by all the rivers of the land; and all the people of the earth are gone down from his shadow, and have left him.
13 Upon his ruin shall all the fowls of the heaven remain, and all the beasts of the field shall be upon his branches:
14 To the end that none of all the trees by the waters exalt themselves for their height, neither shoot up their top among the thick boughs, neither their trees stand up in their height, all that drink water: for they are all delivered unto death, to the nether parts of the earth, in the midst of the children of men, with them that go down to the pit.

Therefore, the Lord GOD said, Because Assyria had lifted itself in height, and grown high among the thick boughs, and his heart was lifted up in his height and growth to love itself and its physical size and growth, therefore, the LORD has delivered Assyria into the hand of the heathen. The heathen were the Babylonians who attacked the Assyrians and Assyria passed from history. Babylon surely dealt with the Assyrians and the LORD dealt with the Assyrians in this manner for her wickedness. Assyria would disintegrate and come apart as a great nation as the strangers, the terrible Babylonians, have cut off and left the Assyrians desolate in the mountains and the valleys, the branches are fallen and the boughs are broken by the rivers of the land. All the people of Assyria are gone down from its shadow and have left the kingdom called Assyria. Upon the ruin of Assyria, the fowls of the heaven, the thoughts of the beautiful design of the heaven, shall remain on the ruin of Assyria, and all the beasts of the field, the fallen people, shall be upon his branches. The result of the defeat is that none of all the trees, which symbolize the people in the fallen state, shall exalt themselves because of their growth in physical height. They shall not shoot up their top, their high opinion of themselves, among the thick boughs of the earthly kingdom. The trees shall not stand up and grow. They shall be delivered unto death, to the nether parts of the earth, in the midst of the children of men, with those who go down into the pit of death of the material form.

15 Thus saith the Lord GOD; In the day when he went down to the grave I caused a mourning: I covered the deep for him, and I restrained the floods thereof, and the great waters were stayed: and I caused Lebanon to mourn for him, and all the trees of the field fainted for him.
16 I made the nations to shake at the sound of his fall, when I cast him down to hell with them that descend into the pit: and all the trees of Eden, the choice and best of Lebanon, all that drink water, shall be comforted in the nether parts of the earth.
17 They also went down into hell with him unto them that be slain with the sword; and they that were his arm, that dwelt under his shadow in the midst of the heathen.
18 To whom art thou thus like in glory and in greatness among the trees of Eden? yet shalt thou be brought down with the trees of Eden unto the nether parts of the earth: thou shalt lie in the midst of the uncircumcised with them that be slain by the sword. This is Pharaoh and all his multitude, saith the Lord GOD.

Thus said the Lord GOD; In the day when he went down into the grave, the LORD caused a mourning and sadness for the fate of the Assyrians as the LORD withheld the flood from heaven and the waters were stopped from flowing: The LORD caused Lebanon to mourn for the passing of Assyria. The LORD made other nations shudder at the sound of the fall of Assyria, when Assyria was cast down into the material hell with them that descend into the pit to decompose. All the trees of Eden, the choice and best of Lebanon, all that drink the water of truth which comes from the LORD, shall be comforted in the nether parts of the earth where the destruction is taking place.

The Testimony of the Major Prophets

The people, who were the followers of Assyria, also went down into the hell of material disintegration with him unto them that be slain with the sword of the power of the LORD which destroys the forms that are not of the true design; and they that were his arm, the people who gave the power to Assyria, that dwell under the shadow of Assyria in the midst of the heathen shall also be slain.

Once again the LORD asks Egypt, To whom are they like in glory and in greatness among the trees of Eden? Are they not like the Assyrians? Yet, Egypt shall be brought down with the trees of Eden unto the nether parts of the earth. Egypt is described as a tree in Eden and its people are described as fruit on that tree. The tree of Egypt will be brought down and disintegrate. The Egyptians shall lie in the midst of the uncircumcised, the unclean, with them, the Assyrians, who were slain by the sword that symbolizes the spirit of truth that destroys the people who are not true to the spirit of the LORD. . This is the true view of the outworking that shall come to pass for Pharaoh and all his multitude of people who are lost in the fallen state, said the Lord GOD.

CHAPTER 32

1 And it came to pass in the twelfth year, in the twelfth month, in the first day of the month, that the word of the LORD came unto me, saying,
2 Son of man, take up a lamentation for Pharaoh king of Egypt, and say unto him, Thou art like a young lion of the nations, and thou art as a whale in the seas: and thou camest forth with thy rivers, and troubledst the waters with thy feet, and fouledst their rivers.
3 Thus saith the Lord GOD; I will therefore spread out my net over thee with a company of many people; and they shall bring thee up in my net.
4 Then will I leave thee upon the land, I will cast thee forth upon the open field, and will cause all the fowls of the heaven to remain upon thee, and I will fill the beasts of the whole earth with thee.
5 And I will lay thy flesh upon the mountains, and fill the valleys with thy height.

It came to pass in the twelfth year of the captivity of Ezekiel, on the first day of the twelfth month, that the word of the LORD came, saying, Son of man, take up a lamentation, an expression of sorrow, for Pharaoh, king of Egypt. Say to Pharaoh that he is like an immature young lion of the nations, and he is very large, like a whale in the seas. Pharaoh has come forth with rivers of people and power that trouble the traditional waters of consciousness with the feet of your limited fallen understanding and you have fouled their waters, the waters of the consciousness of the people that you lead. Pharaoh is leading the people in a materialistic way that is contrary to the spirit of the LORD.

The Lord GOD will spread out His net over Pharaoh and his people with a company of many people and they shall bring up, lift up to a higher level, the lion, that symbolizes Pharaoh, with the net of the LORD. Then, the captured Pharaoh will be left upon the land, cast into an open field, where the LORD will cause all the fowls, the symbols of thoughts, of heaven to remain upon Pharaoh where the beasts of the earth, the people in the fallen state, will be with him. The LORD will lay the flesh of Pharaoh, the physical bodies who are subjects of Pharaoh, upon the mountains and fill the valleys with the height, the high image that Pharaoh has of himself. The people under the control of Pharaoh will follow their king.

6 I will also water with thy blood the land wherein thou swimmest, even to the mountains; and the rivers shall be full of thee.
7 And when I shall put thee out, I will cover the heaven, and make the stars thereof dark; I will cover the sun with a cloud, and the moon shall not give her light.
8 All the bright lights of heaven will I make dark over thee, and set darkness upon thy land, saith the Lord GOD.

The LORD will water with the blood of Pharaoh, not physical blood but rather the expression that comes forth from Pharaoh, the land wherein Pharaoh swims, where Pharaoh has authority, even to the mountains; the rivers of consciousness in the people shall be full of your blood of the fallen state that you represent. When the LORD shall put out the false human ego light of Pharaoh, the expression of the fallen and distorted state that Pharaoh represents, as

The Testimony of the Major Prophets

the spirit of the LORD flows through Pharaoh and his people, then the glory of the LORD will cover the heaven and make the stars of the fallen state dark. The LORD will cover the sun of the conscious mind of the fallen state with a cloud that will diminish the human state, and the moon, the reflection of the light that comes from the distorted light of the fallen state, shall not give her light, the reflection of the sins of distortion. The Lord GOD says that if Pharaoh does not serve the light of the LORD, then, all the bright lights of heaven will be made dark, and the darkness of the fallen state shall be set upon the land under Pharaoh's control. This will be a destructive cycle of Pharaoh's making, and not the lighting, the blessing from the LORD.

9 I will also vex the hearts of many people, when I shall bring thy destruction among the nations, into the countries which thou hast not known.
10 Yea, I will make many people amazed at thee, and their kings shall be horribly afraid for thee, when I shall brandish my sword before them; and they shall tremble at every moment, every man for his own life, in the day of thy fall.
11 For thus saith the Lord GOD; The sword of the king of Babylon shall come upon thee.

The LORD will vex, will plague, the hearts of many people when the power of the LORD, used in a distorted manner, brings destruction among the nations which will expand into countries that Pharaoh has not known. Yes, the power of the LORD moving outward from Egypt will make many people amazed at Pharaoh when the sword of the LORD, the power of the LORD moving through Pharaoh, is brandished before them; they shall tremble at every moment, every man for his own life, in the day of the fall of Pharaoh. The Lord GOD declares that the sword, the power, of the king of Babylon shall come upon Pharaoh.

12 By the swords of the mighty will I cause thy multitude to fall, the terrible of the nations, all of them: and they shall spoil the pomp of Egypt, and all the multitude thereof shall be destroyed.
13 I will destroy also all the beasts thereof from beside the great waters; neither shall the foot of man trouble them any more, nor the hoofs of beasts trouble them.
14 Then will I make their waters deep, and cause their rivers to run like oil, saith the Lord GOD.

By the swords of the mighty of the fallen state, the LORD will cause the multitude of people in the fallen state, the terrible of nations, all of them, to fall: the invaders who wage war shall spoil the pomp of Egypt, the ego and the psyche of Egypt, and all the multitude shall be destroyed. The LORD moving through the distorted state of consciousness of fallen human nature will destroy all the beasts from around the great waters that symbolizes the consciousness of the invaders. The foot of man and the hoofs of beasts will trouble them no more. The LORD says that the waters of consciousness of the invaders will become deep and their rivers will run like oil which is burning and destructive.

15 When I shall make the land of Egypt desolate, and the country shall be destitute of that whereof it was full, when I shall smite all them that dwell therein, then shall they know that I am the LORD.
16 This is the lamentation wherewith they shall lament her: the daughters of the nations shall lament her: they shall lament for her, even for Egypt, and for all her multitude, saith the Lord GOD.

It is always the power of the LORD which is used or misused: there is no other power. The invaders shall make the land of Egypt desolate, and the country shall be destitute of the material plenty with which it was formerly full. The power of the LORD shall smite all of them who dwell in the land and they shall know that the Lord is GOD and victorious as the Law of the LORD works.

17 It came to pass also in the twelfth year, in the fifteenth day of the month, that the word of the LORD came unto me, saying,
18 Son of man, wail for the multitude of Egypt, and cast them down, even her, and the daughters of the famous nations, unto the nether parts of the earth, with them that go down into the pit.
19 Whom dost thou pass in beauty? go down, and be thou laid with the uncircumcised.
20 They shall fall in the midst of them that are slain by the sword: she is delivered to the sword: draw her and all her multitudes.
21 The strong among the mighty shall speak to him out of the midst of hell with them that help him: they are gone down, they lie uncircumcised, slain by the sword.

The Symbolic Version of Ezekiel

It came to pass in the twelfth year of the captivity of Ezekiel, on the fifteenth day of the month, that the word of the LORD came, saying, Son of man, wail your sorrow for the multitude of Egypt—who are spiritual beings in captivity of fallen human nature—and cast them down into the earthly disintegration which occurs with everyone who goes down into the pit of death and decay.

The LORD asks Ezekiel, the focus point of the Son of man, whom does he pass in beauty? All spiritual beings from the LORD are the same; they are focus points of spirit in the body of the Son of man. If people are not in the body of the Son of man, then they shall be laid with the uncircumcised who are the fallen members of the son of man; while the circumcised, the people who have the distortions of human nature removed from them and are open, free-flowing channels of the LORD's spirit, are the members of the body of the Son of man. The Son of man is to deliver all people to the sword, the power of the LORD, which is brought to focus in the Son of man on earth. The people will be either slain by the sword or saved by the sword, the power of the LORD on earth that appears through the spiritual body, the Son, of the LORD. The Son is strong in representation of the spirit of the LORD! The strong shall speak to the fallen people out of the midst of hell, the conditions of distortion, where they are gone down, where they have descended into the fallen state, and lie with the uncircumcised, wounded and slain by the power of the sword which is the LORD's power.

22 Asshur is there and all her company: his graves are about him: all of them slain, fallen by the sword:
23 Whose graves are set in the sides of the pit, and her company is round about her grave: all of them slain, fallen by the sword, which caused terror in the land of the living.
24 There is Elam and all her multitude round about her grave, all of them slain, fallen by the sword, which are gone down uncircumcised into the nether parts of the earth, which caused their terror in the land of the living; yet have they borne their shame with them that go down to the pit.

Asshur, the city north of Babylon in Assyria, is there and all her people, in graves everywhere; all of them slain and fallen—their graves are set in the sides of the pit—by the power of the sword of the LORD which used incorrectly caused terror in the land of the living. Elam, a country east of Assyria in present day Iran, is there in all her multitude, all of them slain and fallen by the sword, which are gone down uncircumcised into the nether parts of the earth because they caused their share of terror in the land of the living while they were alive; they have taken their shame with them that die and go into the pit of death.

25 They have set her a bed in the midst of the slain with all her multitude: her graves are round about him: all of them uncircumcised, slain by the sword: though their terror was caused in the land of the living, yet have they borne their shame with them that go down to the pit: he is put in the midst of them that be slain.
26 There is Meshech, Tubal, and all her multitude: her graves are round about him: all of them uncircumcised, slain by the sword, though they caused their terror in the land of the living.
27 And they shall not lie with the mighty that are fallen of the uncircumcised, which are gone down to hell with their weapons of war: and they have laid their swords under their heads, but their iniquities shall be upon their bones, though they were the terror of the mighty in the land of the living.
28 Yea, thou shalt be broken in the midst of the uncircumcised, and shalt lie with them that are slain with the sword.

The people of Assyria and Elam have made their bed in the midst of the slain and her multitude: the graves are all around the Son of man. All of them are uncircumcised and slain by the sword, the power of the LORD at work: they are not members of the body of the Son of man who is alive. The terror which they created was caused in the land of the living and they have borne their shame with them who go down into the pit of disintegration and decay of those who have been slain.

Meshech and Tubal, people of Asia minor, who have followed the path to the distortion of earthly glory, and her multitudes are also in the pit. Her graves are round about the Son of man who is alive and living. All of them in the pit who are uncircumcised—those who have not had the distortions of human nature cut away from them—have been slain by the sword of the LORD. The terror which they created was in the land of the living, the land on earth in which the body of the Son of man dwells.

The Testimony of the Major Prophets

29 There is Edom, her kings, and all her princes, which with their might are laid by them that were slain by the sword: they shall lie with the uncircumcised, and with them that go down to the pit.

There is Edom, the land southeast of the Dead Sea, with her kings and princes, which with their might applied in wrong causes are laid by them who were slain with the sword: they, too, shall lie in the pit with the uncircumcised, and with them that go down into the pit of disintegration and death.

30 There be the princes of the north, all of them, and all the Zidonians, which are gone down with the slain; with their terror they are ashamed of their might; and they lie uncircumcised with them that be slain by the sword, and bear their shame with them that go down to the pit.
31 Pharaoh shall see them, and shall be comforted over all his multitude, even Pharaoh and all his army slain by the sword, saith the Lord GOD.
32 For I have caused my terror in the land of the living: and he shall be laid in the midst of the uncircumcised with them that are slain with the sword, even Pharaoh and all his multitude, saith the Lord GOD.

There are also the princes of the north, all of them in the fallen state, and all the Sidonians who lived north of Tyre in Phoenicia, have gone down with the slain; in the terror of their ways, they were ashamed of their might which was not used for the glory of the LORD; they lie uncircumcised, unclean, with them that were slain by the sword of the LORD instead of having their uncleanness cut away by the power of the sword. They bear the shame of those who go down to the pit of death.

Pharaoh shall see them, and he shall be comforted by all of his multitude, even though Pharaoh and his army were slain by the sword of the Lord GOD. Pharaoh has gone the way into the pit as did the Assyrians, the people of Elam and Edom, and he foolishly takes comfort in the fact that he has gone the wrong direction of many others.

The Lord GOD speaking through Ezekiel, his prophet, states that He has caused terror in the land of the living for those who do not serve the spirit of the LORD. Pharaoh shall be laid in the midst of the uncircumcised, the unclean, who have not accepted the spirit of the sword of the LORD to cut away the uncleanness from their expressions on earth while they are alive. The Lord GOD has said that Pharaoh and his multitude of subjects have chosen to be slain by the sword to receive the fate of the body of the fallen **son** of man. The body of the cleansed and circumcised **Son** of man was also available to them.

CHAPTER 33

1 Again the word of the LORD came unto me, saying,
2 Son of man, speak to the children of thy people, and say unto them, When I bring the sword upon a land, if the people of the land take a man of their coasts, and set him for their watchman:
3 If when he seeth the sword come upon the land, he blow the trumpet, and warn the people;
4 Then whosoever heareth the sound of the trumpet, and taketh not warning; if the sword come, and take him away, his blood shall be upon his own head.
5 He heard the sound of the trumpet, and took not warning; his blood shall be upon him. But he that taketh warning shall deliver his soul.
6 But if the watchman see the sword come, and blow not the trumpet, and the people be not warned; if the sword come, and take any person from among them, he is taken away in his iniquity; but his blood will I require at the watchman's hand.

Again the word of the LORD came to Ezekiel, saying, Son of man, speak to the children of the people who will listen to you and give them this message: When the LORD brings a sword of power upon the land, and if the people take a man of their coasts, a man who stands at the boundary of the physical land and the water which symbolizes the spirit of truth, and sets him for their watchman, for their leader who will look after their spiritual welfare because he looks out for his own spiritual welfare in the sight of the LORD. If the watchman sees the word of the LORD come upon the land, he will blow the trumpet and warn the people. Then, whoever hears the sound of the trumpet and does not take the warning of the watchman, then the person who ignored the warning will have his own blood on his own head. But he that hears the warning shall deliver his soul—his heart, mind and body—to the service of the sword of the LORD. But if the watchman sees the sword of the LORD come, and he does not blow the trumpet to sound a warning to his people, then the person who is taken away in his iniquity, his separation from the spirit of the LORD, by the sword without being warned, then the blood of that person is on the head, is the conscious responsibility of the watchman who did not warn his brethren. A watchman should warn the people that he watches over.

7 So thou, O son of man, I have set thee a watchman unto the house of Israel; therefore thou shalt hear the word at my mouth, and warn them from me.
8 When I say unto the wicked, O wicked man, thou shalt surely die; if thou dost not speak to warn the wicked from his way, that wicked man shall die in his iniquity; but his blood will I require at thine hand.
9 Nevertheless, if thou warn the wicked of his way to turn from it; if he do not turn from his way, he shall die in his iniquity; but thou hast delivered thy soul.

The LORD declares through Ezekiel that the son of man, a person in the fallen state who takes responsibility for his fellow men, is a watchman to the house of Israel, the representative of the house of the LORD on earth, the Son of man; therefore the son of man, a person in the fallen state who hears the word of the LORD through a mouth that knows the LORD has the responsibility to make the LORD's presence known to others.

The Testimony of the Major Prophets

When the LORD says to the wicked, Oh wicked one, you shall surely die if you do not speak to warn the wicked from his fallen way that will surely lead that person to die in his iniquity. If this occurs, the LORD will hold the person responsible who did not warn his colleague and friend. Nevertheless, if you warn the wicked to turn from his way, and the wicked person does not do so, he shall die in his iniquity; but the person who warned the wicked has delivered his own soul by his correct behavior.

10 Therefore, O thou son of man, speak unto the house of Israel; Thus ye speak, saying, If our transgressions and our sins be upon us, and we pine away in them, how should we then live?
11 Say unto them, As I live, saith the Lord GOD, I have no pleasure in the death of the wicked; but that the wicked turn from his way and live: turn ye, turn ye from your evil ways; for why will ye die, O house of Israel?

Therefore, it is prudent for the fallen son of man to speak to the house of Israel, the house of spirit of the LORD in the body of human flesh. The person in the fallen state is advised to speak to others as though they are members of the house of Israel, the body of the Son of man, which includes everyone in the true state of man on earth. The one who speaks for the LORD must say, If our transgressions and our sins are upon us, and we pine away in what we have done wrong, how should we then live in the true state? The Lord GOD says that as He lives, the LORD has no pleasure in the death of the wicked; it is the LORD's desire that the wicked turn from his way that leads to death and live. Turn away from your evil ways; for why would you want to die, O house of Israel?

12 Therefore, thou son of man, say unto the children of thy people, The righteousness of the righteous shall not deliver him in the day of his transgression: as for the wickedness of the wicked, he shall not fall thereby in the day that he turneth from his wickedness; neither shall the righteous be able to live for his righteousness in the day that he sinneth.
13 When I shall say to the righteous, that he shall surely live; if he trust to his own righteousness, and commit iniquity, all his righteousnesses shall not be remembered; but for his iniquity that he hath committed, he shall die for it.
14 Again, when I say unto the wicked, Thou shalt surely die; if he turn from his sin, and do that which is lawful and right;
15 If the wicked restore the pledge, give again that he had robbed, walk in the statutes of life, without committing iniquity; he shall surely live, he shall not die.
16 None of his sins that he hath committed shall be mentioned unto him: he hath done that which is lawful and right; he shall surely live.
17 Yet the children of thy people say, The way of the Lord is not equal: but as for them, their way is not equal.

Therefore son of man, you as an individual in the fallen state, say to the children of your people that the righteousness of the righteous person shall not deliver him in the day of his transgression from the spirit of the LORD; neither shall the righteous person be able to live because of his past righteousness in the day that he sins in the present time. When the LORD says to the righteous that he shall surely live if he follows the righteousness of the LORD, it shall be so. But if he trusts his own sense of righteousness from the fallen state and commits iniquity, all of his righteousness, his right behavior, shall not be remembered: but for the iniquity which he has committed, he shall die for it. As for the wickedness of the wicked, he shall not fall in the day that he repents and turns away from his wicked behavior.

18 When the righteous turneth from his righteousness, and committeth iniquity, he shall even die thereby.
19 But if the wicked turn from his wickedness, and do that which is lawful and right, he shall live thereby.
20 Yet ye say, The way of the Lord is not equal. O ye house of Israel, I will judge you every one after his ways.

When the righteous person turns away from righteousness, and commits iniquity, he shall die thereby. But if the wicked turns from his wickedness and does that which is lawful and right, he shall live by that behavior. Yet, man, in the fallen state, says that the way of the Lord is not equal. O you member of the house of Israel, the LORD will judge each of you after the ways of your expressions and behaviors according to the Law of Sowing and Reaping.

21 And it came to pass in the twelfth year of our captivity, in the tenth month, in the fifth day of the month, that one that had escaped out of Jerusalem came unto me, saying, The city is smitten.

22 Now the hand of the LORD was upon me in the evening, afore he that was escaped came; and had opened my mouth, until he came to me in the morning; and my mouth was opened, and I was no more dumb.
23 Then the word of the LORD came unto me, saying,
24 Son of man, they that inhabit those wastes of the land of Israel speak, saying, Abraham was one, and he inherited the land: but we are many; the land is given us for inheritance.
25 Wherefore say unto them, Thus saith the Lord GOD; Ye eat with the blood, and lift up your eyes toward your idols, and shed blood: and shall ye possess the land?
26 Ye stand upon your sword, ye work abomination, and ye defile every one his neighbour's wife: and shall ye possess the land?

It came to pass in the twelfth year of the captivity of Ezekiel, in the tenth month and the fifth day of the month, that a person who had escaped from Jerusalem came and said, the city of Jerusalem has fallen. Now, the evening before the man arrived, the hand of the LORD was upon Ezekiel and opened the mouth of Ezekiel, and in the morning, the mouth of Ezekiel was no longer dumb. Ezekiel could speak the word of the LORD.

The word of the LORD came to Ezekiel saying, Son of man, the people who inhabit the wastes of the land of Israel speak and they say that Abraham was one with the LORD, and he inherited the land: we are many people and the land is given to us for an inheritance. Wherefore Ezekiel has been instructed to say to them, Thus says the Lord GOD: You have eaten with the blood and lifted up your eyes to idols and expressed your beliefs, your blood: and shall you possess the land? You stand upon your sword, your power, and you work abomination; you defile everyone the neighbor's wife, and shall you in your sin, possess the land in the name of the LORD?

27 Say thou thus unto them, Thus saith the Lord GOD; As I live, surely they that are in the wastes shall fall by the sword, and him that is in the open field will I give to the beasts to be devoured, and they that be in the forts and in the caves shall die of the pestilence.
28 For I will lay the land most desolate, and the pomp of her strength shall cease; and the mountains of Israel shall be desolate, that none shall pass through.
29 Then shall they know that I am the LORD, when I have laid the land most desolate because of all their abominations which they have committed.

Say this to them in the name of the Lord GOD who lives. Surely, the people who are in the wastes shall fall by the sword, and he who is in the open field will be given to live with the beasts to be devoured, and they who live in forts and in the caves shall die of pestilence. The sword of the LORD will lay the land most desolate, and the pomp of her strength which she once had will cease. The mountains of Israel shall be desolate that none shall pass through. When these conditions occur, then the people shall know that the LORD is present to bring about the conditions from within the people as the land became desolate due to the abominations committed by the people.

30 Also, thou son of man, the children of thy people still are talking against thee by the walls and in the doors of the houses, and speak one to another, every one to his brother, saying, Come, I pray you, and hear what is the word that cometh forth from the LORD.
31 And they come unto thee as the people cometh, and they sit before thee as my people, and they hear thy words, but they will not do them: for with their mouth they shew much love, but their heart goeth after their covetousness.
32 And, lo, thou art unto them as a very lovely song of one that hath a pleasant voice, and can play well on an instrument: for they hear thy words, but they do them not.
33 And when this cometh to pass, (lo, it will come,) then shall they know that a prophet hath been among them.

Also, you, the individual fallen son of man, the children of your people are talking against you by the walls and in the doors of your houses. They speak every one to another, and every one to his brother, saying, Come, I pray you, and hear what is the word that comes forth from the LORD. They come to you as the people come and sit before you as the people of the LORD. They hear the words but they will not do them. For with their mouths, they show much love, but their heart goes after what they covet.

And lo, you are to them as a lovely song of one who has a pleasant voice, and can play well on an instrument to entertain them: they hear your words, but they do not do them. When this comes to pass, (and it will come,) then they shall know that a prophet has been among them to represent the view and the word of the LORD in regard to their fallen behavior.

CHAPTER 34

1 And the word of the LORD came unto me, saying,
2 Son of man, prophesy against the shepherds of Israel, prophesy, and say unto them, Thus saith the Lord GOD unto the shepherds; Woe be to the shepherds of Israel that do feed themselves! should not the shepherds feed the flocks?
3 Ye eat the fat, and ye clothe you with the wool, ye kill them that are fed: but ye feed not the flock.
4 The diseased have ye not strengthened, neither have ye healed that which was sick, neither have ye bound up that which was broken, neither have ye brought again that which was driven away, neither have ye sought that which was lost; but with force and with cruelty have ye ruled them.
5 And they were scattered, because there is no shepherd: and they became meat to all the beasts of the field, when they were scattered.
6 My sheep wandered through all the mountains, and upon every high hill: yea, my flock was scattered upon all the face of the earth, and none did search or seek after them.

The word of the LORD came to Ezekiel, saying, Son of man, the truth of man on earth in a covenant relationship to the LORD, prophesy, speak the truth of the LORD to the shepherds of Israel, the religious leaders who say that they are the leaders of the flock of people who look to them for guidance. Say to them that the Lord GOD has this to say to the shepherds of the flock: Woe to the shepherds that feed themselves! Should not the shepherds feed the flocks? The religious leaders eat the fat and clothe themselves with the wool from the flocks as you kill them that are fed: but you do not feed the flock.

You have not strengthened the people afflicted with disease, nor healed the sick; you have not bound that which was broken, nor brought back again those who were driven away from the LORD; you have not sought the sheep that were lost, but you have ruled the flock with force and with cruelty. The flock of people were scattered because there was no true shepherd for them: and they became meat to all the fallen and lowly beasts of the field when they were scattered. The LORD's sheep wandered through all the mountains, and upon every high hill: yes, the LORD's flock was scattered upon the face of the earth, and none, who say that they are shepherds, did search or seek after them.

7 Therefore, ye shepherds, hear the word of the LORD;
8 As I live, saith the Lord GOD, surely because my flock became a prey, and my flock became meat to every beast of the field, because there was no shepherd, neither did my shepherds search for my flock, but the shepherds fed themselves, and fed not my flock;
9 Therefore, O ye shepherds, hear the word of the LORD;
10 Thus saith the Lord GOD; Behold, I am against the shepherds; and I will require my flock at their hand, and cause them to cease from feeding the flock; neither shall the shepherds feed themselves any more; for I will deliver my flock from their mouth, that they may not be meat for them.

The Testimony of the Major Prophets

Therefore, you shepherds, hear the word of the LORD; As the Lord GOD lives to speak his word through Ezekiel, surely, it can be seen that His flock has become a prey for human predators of the fallen state and meat for every beast of the field because there was no shepherd. The people who said they were shepherds did not search for the flock, the LORD's people, but rather the shepherds fed themselves and did not feed the flock. Therefore, the Lord GOD says that He is against the shepherds; the LORD will require His people from the hand of control of the shepherds. The LORD will cause the shepherds to cease from feeding the flock; neither shall the shepherds feed themselves anymore; for the LORD will deliver His flock from their mouth of wrong expression so that the flock will no longer be meat for the religious leaders.

11 For thus saith the Lord GOD; Behold, I, even I, will both search my sheep, and seek them out.
12 As a shepherd seeketh out his flock in the day that he is among his sheep that are scattered; so will I seek out my sheep, and will deliver them out of all places where they have been scattered in the cloudy and dark day.
13 And I will bring them out from the people, and gather them from the countries, and will bring them to their own land, and feed them upon the mountains of Israel by the rivers, and in all the inhabited places of the country.
14 I will feed them in a good pasture, and upon the high mountains of Israel shall their fold be: there shall they lie in a good fold, and in a fat pasture shall they feed upon the mountains of Israel.
15 I will feed my flock, and I will cause them to lie down, saith the Lord GOD.
16 I will seek that which was lost, and bring again that which was driven away, and will bind up that which was broken, and will strengthen that which was sick: but I will destroy the fat and the strong; I will feed them with judgment.

The Lord GOD says, Behold, I will search for My sheep and seek them out. As the shepherd seeks out his flock in the day that he is among the sheep that are scattered; so will the spiritual shepherd seek out the sheep of the LORD and deliver them out of all places where they have been scattered in the cloudy and dark day where there is little or no spiritual light. The LORD will bring His sheep, the people who are willing to follow Him, out from the people in the fallen state who are separated from the spirit of the LORD. The LORD will gather them from the countries where they have been scattered and bring them to their own land to be fed upon the spiritual mountains of Israel by the rivers of spirit that flow from the LORD and in all inhabited places of the country where people dwell.

The LORD will feed His sheep in a good pasture and the high spiritual mountains of Israel shall be their fold, their dwelling place. In the spiritual fold of the covenant, they shall lie in a good fold, and in a fat pasture shall they feed upon the mountains of Israel. The Lord GOD will feed his spiritual flock and cause them to lie down in safety. The LORD will seek that which was lost and bring again that which was driven away; He will bind up that which was broken and strengthen that which was sick, which is the result of the covenant with the LORD. But the LORD, speaking through Ezekiel, will destroy the fat and the strong of the fallen state: the LORD will feed them with true judgment which is inherent in His spirit.

17 And as for you, O my flock, thus saith the Lord GOD; Behold, I judge between cattle and cattle, between the rams and the he goats.
18 Seemeth it a small thing unto you to have eaten up the good pasture, but ye must tread down with your feet the residue of your pastures? and to have drunk of the deep waters, but ye must foul the residue with your feet?
19 And as for my flock, they eat that which ye have trodden with your feet; and they drink that which ye have fouled with your feet.

The Lord GOD speaks to His flock of people on earth who claim to be shepherds. He tells them to Behold that the LORD can judge between the cattle in the true state and the cattle of the fallen state, between the rams of the restored state and the he-goats of the fallen state. These animals represent people who know their LORD and those who do not. Does it seem like a small thing to you to have eaten up good pasture for yourselves, but at the same time you tread down with your feet the residue of your pastures so that others can not eat? and to have drunk of the deep waters of the spirit, but, in the process you must foul the residue with your feet so that others cannot drink what you have spoiled? As for the flock of the LORD, they eat that which you have trodden with your feet; and they drink what you have fouled with your feet. The feet are the symbols of the way that people have walked through life as given evidence by their behaviors.

The Symbolic Version of Ezekiel

20 Therefore thus saith the Lord GOD unto them; Behold, I, even I, will judge between the fat cattle and between the lean cattle.
21 Because ye have thrust with side and with shoulder, and pushed all the diseased with your horns, till ye have scattered them abroad;
22 Therefore will I save my flock, and they shall no more be a prey; and I will judge between cattle and cattle.
23 And I will set up one shepherd over them, and he shall feed them, even my servant David; he shall feed them, and he shall be their shepherd.
24 And I the LORD will be their God, and my servant David a prince among them; I the LORD have spoken it.

Therefore the Lord GOD says to them, Behold, I will judge between the fat cattle and the lean cattle, the people who are rich and poor in the spirit of the LORD. Because you, the shepherds and religious leaders have thrust away from you, with side and with shoulder, and pushed all the diseased with your horns, you have scattered them abroad. Therefore, the LORD will save His flock by bringing them to Himself and they shall no more be a prey; and the LORD will judge between spiritual "cattle" and material "cattle".

The LORD will set one shepherd over them, and He shall feed them, even the LORD's servant David; the one shepherd shall feed them with his many psalms and he shall be their shepherd. And the LORD, speaking through His prophet, Ezekiel, will be their God, and David will be a prince among the people. The LORD has spoken it.

25 And I will make with them a covenant of peace, and will cause the evil beasts to cease out of the land: and they shall dwell safely in the wilderness, and sleep in the woods.
26 And I will make them and the places round about my hill a blessing; and I will cause the shower to come down in his season; there shall be showers of blessing.
27 And the tree of the field shall yield her fruit, and the earth shall yield her increase, and they shall be safe in their land, and shall know that I am the LORD, when I have broken the bands of their yoke, and delivered them out of the hand of those that served themselves of them.

The spirit of the LORD will be the covenant of peace with each individual who desires to be in the covenant. The covenant will cause the beasts to cease to come out of the land: the people shall dwell safely in the wilderness and sleep in the woods without fear. The spirit of the LORD moving through the people and the places round about the hill of the LORD creates a blessing; and the LORD will cause the spirit of the LORD to come down in season; there will be showers of blessing that come on earth through the people who love and serve the spirit of the LORD. The result will be that the spiritual design of the tree of the field, the tree of life, shall yield her fruit, and the earth shall yield her increase, and the people shall be safe in their land, and they shall know that I am the LORD, when I have broken the bands of their yoke to the fallen state, and they have been delivered out of the hand of those religious leaders that served themselves from the efforts of the people.

28 And they shall no more be a prey to the heathen, neither shall the beast of the land devour them; but they shall dwell safely, and none shall make them afraid.
29 And I will raise up for them a plant of renown, and they shall be no more consumed with hunger in the land, neither bear the shame of the heathen any more.
30 Thus shall they know that I the LORD their God am with them, and that they, even the house of Israel, are my people, saith the Lord GOD.
31 And ye my flock, the flock of my pasture, are men, and I am your God, saith the Lord GOD.

The people of the LORD, the flock who are in covenant with the LORD, shall no more be a prey to the heathen who are not of God, and the human beasts of the field shall not devour them; the flock shall dwell safely and none shall make them afraid. The LORD will raise up for them a plant of renown, the true design for man on earth, and they shall no more be consumed with hunger of the LORD in the land, nor bear the shame of the heathen who do not know the LORD. They shall know that the LORD their God is with them, and that they, the house of Israel, the people who let the spirit of the LORD flow through them, are the people of the Lord GOD and the people are His flock. The people on earth are the flock of His pasture on earth and the people belong to the Lord GOD.

CHAPTER 35

1 Moreover the word of the LORD came unto me, saying,
2 Son of man, set thy face against mount Seir, and prophesy against it,
3 And say unto it, Thus saith the Lord GOD; Behold, O mount Seir, I am against thee, and I will stretch out mine hand against thee, and I will make thee most desolate.
4 I will lay thy cities waste, and thou shalt be desolate, and thou shalt know that I am the LORD.
5 Because thou hast had a perpetual hatred, and hast shed the blood of the children of Israel by the force of the sword in the time of their calamity, in the time that their iniquity had an end:
6 Therefore, as I live, saith the Lord GOD, I will prepare thee unto blood, and blood shall pursue thee: since thou hast not hated blood, even blood shall pursue thee.

Moreover the word of the LORD came to Ezekiel saying, Son of man, set your face, direct your attention against mount Seir and prophesy, express the truth of the LORD, against it. The word, Seir, means, "demon" or "tempest". The LORD would not direct Ezekiel to prophesy against a piece of real estate in the shape of a mountain of dirt and stone: but the LORD would direct Ezekiel to prophesy against the source of all the so-called problems of the world, the fallen human consciousness which is the source of the tempest and the demons that manifest in the environment.

Ezekiel is instructed by the Lord GOD to declare through himself, and all who wish to be a part of the body of the Son of man on earth, to prophesy against mount Seir which is the source of distortion in the world by emphatically declaring that, individually and collectively, I am against you. I will stretch out my hand of control against you as you are present in my consciousness and I will make you most desolate. This is the way to lay the cities of distortion to waste and the way that the demon of mount Seir to become desolate and destroyed. Then the individual who does this will know the LORD in one's own experience as the spirit of the LORD replaces the spirit of the demon.

It is because the mount Seir within each person has had a perpetual hatred over the generations of the fallen state, and the expression, the blood of the immature children of Israel, has entered the environment by the force of the power of the sword which comes from the LORD, in the time of the calamity and the iniquity within the consciousness had an end in observable material forms. Therefore, as the spirit of the Lord GOD is allowed to flow through each person's consciousness, the LORD will prepare a new expression, new blood, that will be inserted into the material world where it can be observed: since you have not hated the blood of the spirit of the LORD, then the spirit, the blood, of the LORD will pursue you into the environment to produce beauty.

7 Thus will I make mount Seir most desolate, and cut off from it him that passeth out and him that returneth.
8 And I will fill his mountains with his slain men: in thy hills, and in thy valleys, and in all thy rivers, shall they fall that are slain with the sword.
9 I will make thee perpetual desolations, and thy cities shall not return: and ye shall know that I am the LORD.

The Symbolic Version of Ezekiel

The flow of the spirit of the LORD through the consciousness of fallen man s will make mount Seir, the distorted demon within the consciousness of man, desolate and cut off from the flow of the spirit of the LORD that which passes out, is expressed, and that which returns from the distortions of the fallen conditions of the world. The spirit of the LORD will fill the mountains of the demons with his slain men: in the hills and in the valleys and in all your rivers of expression, they, the false distortions shall fall when they are slain by the power of the sword of the LORD as it flows though each person. The constant flow of the spirit of the LORD will make the demon in you a perpetual desolation and the cities of wickedness will not return: the people who do this will know the spirit of the LORD as it flows through them.

10 Because thou hast said, These two nations and these two countries shall be mine, and we will possess it; whereas the LORD was there:
11 Therefore, as I live, saith the Lord GOD, I will even do according to thine anger, and according to thine envy which thou hast used out of thy hatred against them; and I will make myself known among them, when I have judged thee.
12 And thou shalt know that I am the LORD, and that I have heard all thy blasphemies which thou hast spoken against the mountains of Israel, saying, They are laid desolate, they are given us to consume.

The problem with man in the fallen state has been continued because fallen man has said that two nations—both the divine from the LORD and the wickedness from mount Seir—shall live within the consciousness. The problem is the belief that both fallen man and the LORD shall inhabit the space and the place where the LORD should rule. Therefore, as the LORD lives within the consciousness of man, the power of the LORD will create conditions according to the anger, the envy, the hatred which is present in consciousness. The LORD moving through the distortions in consciousness creates distorted expressions in the environment where they can be seen by your fellow men. It is the power of the spirit of the LORD moving through the individual consciousness which judges each person and reveals what is present in consciousness by what is expressed by the individual. By their expressions, by their fruits, you will know the condition of the consciousness. When a person understands the creative process of the spirit of the LORD at work within each individual, they will know the LORD is present and the LORD has heard all the blasphemies which were spoken against the mountains of Israel, saying, They, the distortions are laid desolate, and they are to be consumed.

13 Thus with your mouth ye have boasted against me, and have multiplied your words against me: I have heard them.
14 Thus saith the Lord GOD; When the whole earth rejoiceth, I will make thee desolate.
15 As thou didst rejoice at the inheritance of the house of Israel, because it was desolate, so will I do unto thee: thou shalt be desolate, O mount Seir, and all Idumea, even all of it: and they shall know that I am the LORD.

In this manner, man in the fallen state has boasted with the mouth of his expression against the spirit of the LORD which has been present, and multiplied the distortions contained in his words: The LORD has heard every one of every expression because the LORD has always been present. It is fallen man who is unaware of the presence of the Lord GOD. The Lord GOD says, when the whole earth rejoices at His presence, the LORD will make the place where fallen man lives desolate. As you rejoiced at the inheritance of the house of Israel, because it was desolate of the distortions, so will the LORD do to you who are in the fallen state and who is symbolized by mount Seir, the focus point of the demon within, and all Idumea, the land south of the Dead Sea where the effects of desolation can be seen. The people who compose the body of the son of man, who rejoice in the creative process of the LORD, shall come to know the LORD in personal experience. They, like Ezekiel, are members of the body of the Son of man.

CHAPTER 36

1 Also, thou son of man, prophesy unto the mountains of Israel, and say, Ye mountains of Israel, hear the word of the LORD:
2 Thus saith the Lord GOD; Because the enemy hath said against you, Aha, even the ancient high places are ours in possession:

The son of man, the people who are lost in the fallen state and desire to find their way to the restored state on this side of the grave must prophesy to the mountains of Israel. The mountains of Israel are the symbols for the consciousness of man, men and women in the restored state, the Son of man. The mountains of Israel are present as surely as mount Seir, the distortion of the demon, is present. The Lord GOD speaking through Ezekiel says that the enemy, the demon within (which is the false self who has usurped the true position of man made in the image and likeness of God,) has spoken against the presence of you, the true Self, a piece of God, that is present with each one. The enemy has said, Aha, an expression of malicious joy, that the ancient high places of worship are under the control and possession of the enemy, the false leaders. The mountains of Israel, the people who are willing to rise up to speak for the LORD, are instructed to prophesy, to express the spirit of the LORD.

3 Therefore prophesy and say, Thus saith the Lord GOD; Because they have made you desolate, and swallowed you up on every side, that ye might be a possession unto the residue of the heathen, and ye are taken up in the lips of talkers, and are an infamy of the people:
4 Therefore, ye mountains of Israel, hear the word of the Lord GOD; Thus saith the Lord GOD to the mountains, and to the hills, to the rivers, and to the valleys, to the desolate wastes, and to the cities that are forsaken, which became a prey and derision to the residue of the heathen that are round about;
5 Therefore thus saith the Lord GOD; Surely in the fire of my jealousy have I spoken against the residue of the heathen, and against all Idumea, which have appointed my land into their possession with the joy of all their heart, with despiteful minds, to cast it out for a prey.

The Lord GOD wants his people to know that because the enemy, the distortions of the false self who compose the body of the son of man, have made you desolate, and swallowed you up on every side so that you might be a possession of the heathen, the people who do not know the LORD, and you are taken up by the words that come from the lips of talkers who are an infamy to the people: Therefore, they must be willing to hear the word of the LORD which is spoken to His people who have become a prey to the heathen. The LORD's people are everywhere as symbolized by the mountains to the hills, to the rivers and the valleys where the desolate waste and the cities reveal that they have been forsaken.

The Lord GOD, who is a jealous God that wants no false gods before Him, speaks in the fire of His love, the truth which is against what the residue of the heathen, the people who are against the spirit of the LORD. The LORD speaks against Idumea, the symbol of desolation, and the people who have taken the LORD's land into their possession with the joy of their impure hearts, with despiteful minds, to be used to capture the LORD's flock as a prey.

6 Prophesy therefore concerning the land of Israel, and say unto the mountains, and to the hills, to the rivers, and to the valleys, Thus saith the Lord GOD; Behold, I have spoken in my jealousy and in my fury, because ye have borne the shame of the heathen:
7 Therefore thus saith the Lord GOD; I have lifted up mine hand, Surely the heathen that are about you, they shall bear their shame.

Ezekiel states that he has spoken and that others should prophesy concerning the land that Israel should be as promised by the Lord GOD. The LORD has spoken in His jealousy and fury because the heathen have borne and endured the shame of the heathen. Therefore, the LORD will lift up His hand and declare that the heathen who are round about you shall bear the shame for what they have done.

8 But ye, O mountains of Israel, ye shall shoot forth your branches, and yield your fruit to my people of Israel; for they are at hand to come.
9 For, behold, I am for you, and I will turn unto you, and ye shall be tilled and sown:
10 And I will multiply men upon you, all the house of Israel, even all of it: and the cities shall be inhabited, and the wastes shall be builded:
11 And I will multiply upon you man and beast; and they shall increase and bring fruit: and I will settle you after your old estates, and will do better unto you than at your beginnings: and ye shall know that I am the LORD.

But you, the mountains of Israel, the ones who will stand up to be seen, shall shoot forth your branches and yield the fruit of your efforts and you express the spirit of the LORD to the LORD's people of Israel who are at hand, available, to come as you speak the word of the LORD. Behold, the LORD is with you and will turn to you as you are tilled and sown by the spirit of the LORD moving through you. You will be multiplied in your efforts by all the house of Israel: the cities shall be inhabited and the divine plan that was wasted shall be built. The spirit of the LORD moving through you will multiply your efforts with man and beast that shall increase and bring fruit. The LORD will settle you after your old estates, your old fallen ways, and you will do better as you continually express the LORD's spirit than you experienced at the beginning of spiritual expression. As you express the spirit of the LORD, you shall know the LORD's spirit that you express in momentary living.

12 Yea, I will cause men to walk upon you, even my people Israel; and they shall possess thee, and thou shalt be their inheritance, and thou shalt no more henceforth bereave them of men.
13 Thus saith the Lord GOD; Because they say unto you, Thou land devourest up men, and hast bereaved thy nations;
14 Therefore thou shalt devour men no more, neither bereave thy nations any more, saith the Lord GOD.
15 Neither will I cause men to hear in thee the shame of the heathen any more, neither shalt thou bear the reproach of the people any more, neither shalt thou cause thy nations to fall any more, saith the Lord GOD.

Yes, I will cause men to walk upon you, to follow your example, even my people, Israel, the people who express the spirit of the LORD, as you express the spirit of the LORD in your living. The people who follow your example shall possess you, the spirit that you express, the spirit that you are, and your spirit shall be their inheritance and you shall henceforth, from the time that you express the spirit of the LORD, bereave them anymore.

The Lord GOD says that because they say to you, the spiritual land that you offer devours men and bereaves nations; you shall reply to them that they are to devour men no more as they have in the past and bereave men no more. The Lord GOD says that His spirit moving through His people will not cause other men to hear the shame of the heathen come forth from you any more, and you will not cause the LORD's spiritual nation to fall any more by your actions which is each person's first responsibility.

16 Moreover the word of the LORD came unto me, saying,
17 Son of man, when the house of Israel dwelt in their own land, they defiled it by their own way and by their doings: their way was before me as the uncleanness of a removed woman.

The Testimony of the Major Prophets

18 Wherefore I poured my fury upon them for the blood that they had shed upon the land, and for their idols wherewith they had polluted it:
19 And I scattered them among the heathen, and they were dispersed through the countries: according to their way and according to their doings I judged them.
20 And when they entered unto the heathen, whither they went, they profaned my holy name, when they said to them, These are the people of the LORD, and are gone forth out of his land.
21 But I had pity for mine holy name, which the house of Israel had profaned among the heathen, whither they went.

Moreover the word of he LORD came to Ezekiel saying, Son of man, when the house of Israel dwelt in their own land, they defiled the land by their own ways and by their own behaviors: their ways were before the LORD as the uncleanness of a woman who has been removed for her unclean actions. Where fore the people received the fury of the LORD, instead of the blessings of the LORD, because of the blood, the symbol for the expression of spirit, which they shed upon the land as they pursued their idols and polluted their environments. This scattered and dispersed the heathen based upon their own behaviors which is the working of the Law of the LORD and the way that the LORD judges them.

When they, the LORD's spiritual people, entered into the heathen, where they did indeed go, they profaned the holy name of the LORD when they said that they were the people of the LORD but they did not express the LORD's spirit. But they said that they were from the LORD and came forth from His land. The LORD had pity for the holy name of the LORD, I AM, which the house of Israel had profaned among the heathen which is where they went when the left the presence of the LORD. This situation cannot go unpunished and unresolved.

22 Therefore say unto the house of Israel, Thus saith the Lord GOD; I do not this for your sakes, O house of Israel, but for mine holy name's sake, which ye have profaned among the heathen, whither ye went.
23 And I will sanctify my great name, which was profaned among the heathen, which ye have profaned in the midst of them; and the heathen shall know that I am the LORD, saith the Lord GOD, when I shall be sanctified in you before their eyes.
24 For I will take you from among the heathen, and gather you out of all countries, and will bring you into your own land.
25 Then will I sprinkle clean water upon you, and ye shall be clean: from all your filthiness, and from all your idols, will I cleanse you.
26 A new heart also will I give you, and a new spirit will I put within you: and I will take away the stony heart out of your flesh, and I will give you an heart of flesh.
27 And I will put my spirit within you, and cause you to walk in my statutes, and ye shall keep my judgments, and do them.
28 And ye shall dwell in the land that I gave to your fathers; and ye shall be my people, and I will be your God.

Therefore, say to the house of Israel, that the Lord GOD does not do this for your sake but for the sake of the LORD's name which you have profaned among the heathen where you went. The LORD will sanctify His great name which was profaned and the heathen will know that the LORD is present when the spirit of the LORD is sanctified in you before the eyes of the heathen. As you express the spirit of the LORD, the LORD will take you from among the heathen and gather you from all the countries to bring you to your own land. The clean water of truth from the LORD's spirit flowing through you will make you clean from all your filthiness and all your idols. The spirit will cleanse you.

The LORD will give you a new heart and a new spirit will be put in you: and the LORD will take away the stony heart out of your flesh and the LORD will give you a heart of flesh, put His spirit in you and cause you to walk in the LORD's statutes, keep His judgment and do them. You shall dwell in the land that the LORD gave to your fathers; and you shall be the people of the LORD and the LORD will be your God.

29 I will also save you from all your uncleannesses: and I will call for the corn, and will increase it, and lay no famine upon you.
30 And I will multiply the fruit of the tree, and the increase of the field, that ye shall receive no more reproach of famine among the heathen.

31 Then shall ye remember your own evil ways, and your doings that were not good, and shall loathe yourselves in your own sight for your iniquities and for your abominations.
32 Not for your sakes do I this, saith the Lord GOD, be it known unto you: be ashamed and confounded for your own ways, O house of Israel.

The LORD speaking through Ezekiel says, I will save you from all your uncleanness: and I will call for the corn (of cleanness) and will increase it, and lay no famine (of cleanness) upon you. The fruit of the tree of life and the increase of the field will multiply so that you will receive no more the reproach of famine, the desire for wanting more and more, which comes from the heathen. Then you shall remember your evil ways and your actions which were not good. You shall loathe yourselves in your own vision for your iniquities and abominations. The LORD says that it should be known to you that He does not do this for your sake: you are ashamed and confounded for your own ways and behaviors, as a house of Israel. The LORD loves His people and frees them from abominations and iniquities.

33 Thus saith the Lord GOD; In the day that I shall have cleansed you from all your iniquities I will also cause you to dwell in the cities, and the wastes shall be builded.
34 And the desolate land shall be tilled, whereas it lay desolate in the sight of all that passed by.
35 And they shall say, This land that was desolate is become like the garden of Eden; and the waste and desolate and ruined cities are become fenced, and are inhabited.
36 Then the heathen that are left round about you shall know that I the LORD build the ruined places, and plant that that was desolate: I the LORD have spoken it, and I will do it.

The Lord GOD says that in the day when He has cleansed you from your iniquities, then you shall dwell consciously in the cities and the wastes in those cities will be built because you are there to build them with the spirit of the LORD. The desolate land shall be tilled whereas before it lay desolate before the sight of all who passed by. The observers will say that the land that was desolate is become like the garden of Eden, the return to the true design; and the waste, desolate and ruined cities have become fenced and inhabited. Then the heathen that are left, that remain, shall know that the LORD has built the ruined places and planted where there was desolation. The LORD has spoken and will do it.

37 Thus saith the Lord GOD; I will yet for this be inquired of by the house of Israel, to do it for them; I will increase them with men like a flock.
38 As the holy flock, as the flock of Jerusalem in her solemn feasts; so shall the waste cities be filled with flocks of men: and they shall know that I am the LORD.

The Lord GOD says that divine action will be inquired of by the house of Israel to do more for them; and the LORD will increase them with more men like a flock. As a holy flock, as the flock of Jerusalem in her solemn feasts, the wasted cities shall be filled with flocks of man who want to serve the spirit of the LORD. These men shall know that I Am the LORD as they release the LORD's spirit.

CHAPTER 37

1 The hand of the LORD was upon me, and carried me out in the spirit of the LORD, and set me down in the midst of the valley which was full of bones,
2 And caused me to pass by them round about: and, behold, there were very many in the open valley; and, lo, they were very dry.
3 And he said unto me, Son of man, can these bones live? And I answered, O Lord GOD, thou knowest.

The hand of the LORD, the symbol of spiritual control by the LORD, was on Ezekiel and carried him out in the spirit of the LORD, and set him down in a place in Ezekiel's consciousness described as the midst of a valley that was filled with dry bones. The spirit of the LORD moving through the consciousness of Ezekiel caused him to pass by the bones which were round about him. There were very many bones in the open valley, and lo, they were very dry. The LORD said to Ezekiel, Son of man, a man on earth through whom the spirit of the LORD flows, can these bones live? Ezekiel answered, O Lord GOD, only you know the answer to that question because Ezekiel did not know the significance of the parable that the LORD was using to teach a lesson. Ezekiel's heart and mind were centered in the spirit of the LORD which put him in position to be a Son of man.

4 Again he said unto me, Prophesy upon these bones, and say unto them, O ye dry bones, hear the word of the LORD.
5 Thus saith the Lord GOD unto these bones; Behold, I will cause breath to enter into you, and ye shall live:
6 And I will lay sinews upon you, and will bring up flesh upon you, and cover you with skin, and put breath in you, and ye shall live; and ye shall know that I am the LORD.
7 So I prophesied as I was commanded: and as I prophesied, there was a noise, and behold a shaking, and the bones came together, bone to his bone.
8 And when I beheld, lo, the sinews and the flesh came up upon them, and the skin covered them above: but there was no breath in them.

Again the LORD said to Ezekiel, Prophesy upon these bones, and say unto them, O you individual dry bone, hear the word of the LORD that will be articulated through Ezekiel. The message of the Lord God, spoken through his prophet, Ezekiel, was, Behold, dry bones, the LORD will cause the breath of life to enter into you, and you shall live. And the LORD will lay sinews upon you, and will bring up flesh upon you, and cover you with skin, and put breath in you, and you shall live; and you shall know that I AM the LORD.

So Ezekiel prophesied as he was commanded: and as he prophesied, there was a noise, and behold a shaking, and the bones came together, bone to his bone. And when Ezekiel beheld the movement of the bones, sinews and flesh came up upon them, and the skin covered them above: but there was no breath in neither the bones, nor in the sinews of flesh, which were covered with skin. Ezekiel began to see a lifeless body which had all the physical equipment to represent man, a body of men and women, but there was no life in this body which symbolized the formation of the Son of man on earth which has not yet come together with life moving through it. The body of the Son of man was lifeless.

9 Then said he unto me, Prophesy unto the wind, prophesy, son of man, and say to the wind, Thus saith the Lord GOD; Come from the four winds, O breath, and breathe upon these slain, that they may live.
10 So I prophesied as he commanded me, and the breath came into them, and they lived, and stood up upon their feet, an exceeding great army.
11 Then he said unto me, Son of man, these bones are the whole house of Israel: behold, they say, Our bones are dried, and our hope is lost: we are cut off for our parts.

Then the LORD said to Ezekiel, the focus point of the Son of man on earth who would be the pattern for the living body of the Son of man, prophesy to the wind, the symbol of the spirit which is enfolding and blowing over the people who have bones, flesh and skin, the people who compose the fallen son of man who dwells in the valley of the shadow of death. Ezekiel, a Son of man, has been commanded by the Lord GOD, God who moves through every living thing, to speak to the son of man, the people who do not know the LORD, with this message: Come from the four winds, from all directions of spirit, the breath of life which comes from GOD and breathe the breath of life upon all these slain people, who are spiritually dead, that they may live and know the LORD their God.

So, Ezekiel prophesied, he expressed the spirit of the LORD which was upon him, as the LORD commanded, and the breath of life came to the dry bones of the son of man, and they lived, stood up upon their feet, an exceeding great army of people, who were filled with the living spirit that transformed them from the fallen son of man into the Son of man who represents the LORD on earth because they carry and express the spirit of the LORD.

Then the Lord GOD said to Ezekiel, Son of man, these bones are the whole house of Israel: these bones in the parable are the symbols of the spiritual beings of the LORD in human forms who are the real house of Israel, the ascended and restored man on earth as he was created by God. Behold, Ezekiel, the fallen son of man will say, Our bones are dried because they have no spirit, and our hope for spirit on earth is lost: we who are in the fallen state are cut off for our parts that would make us a whole people.

12 Therefore prophesy and say unto them, Thus saith the Lord GOD; Behold, O my people, I will open your graves, and cause you to come up out of your graves, and bring you into the land of Israel.
13 And ye shall know that I am the LORD, when I have opened your graves, O my people, and brought you up out of your graves,
14 And shall put my spirit in you, and ye shall live, and I shall place you in your own land: then shall ye know that I the LORD have spoken it, and performed it, saith the LORD.

Ezekiel is commanded to prophesy, express the spirit of the LORD which is upon him, and say to the bones of the son of man to behold as the Lord GOD opens your graves, the graves to which you descended and fell into, and cause you to come out of your graves, and bring you into the spiritual land of Israel, the spiritual land to which Jacob ascended that caused him to change his name to Israel, which means, "a prince of God". You shall know the LORD is your God when He opens your graves and you will know that you are indeed the LORD's people because He brought you out of the rut of the world of material identification with your physical dry bones to the land of the living spirit of the LORD. In the land of Israel, the LORD shall put His spirit in you and you shall live in the body of the LORD, the body of the Son of man, and the LORD will put you into your own land of living flesh. Then you shall know that the LORD has spoken these things to you in your own experience and the LORD has performed this great feat.

15 The word of the LORD came again unto me, saying,
16 Moreover, thou son of man, take thee one stick, and write upon it, For Judah, and for the children of Israel his companions: then take another stick, and write upon it, For Joseph, the stick of Ephraim, and for all the house of Israel his companions:
17 And join them one to another into one stick; and they shall become one in thine hand.

The word of the LORD came again to Ezekiel in a parable saying that the son of man, a man in the fallen state, should take one stick, the symbol of his own human body, mind and heart, and write upon it with the spirit of the LORD that

The Testimony of the Major Prophets

is flowing to him from the LORD. The writing shall say that this stick is for Judah, one of the twelve tribes, and for the children of Israel, who desire to enter the spiritual land of Israel to be with your companions in spirit. Take another stick and write upon it, for Joseph, the stick of Ephraim, which means, "to bring forth fruit and grow" with all his companions in the house of Israel.

The sticks are to be joined together, one to another, until they become one stick, in your hand which represents the control of the LORD moving through all sticks simultaneously to give the twelve tribes the strength of the spirit of the LORD, which is Israel.

18 And when the children of thy people shall speak unto thee, saying, Wilt thou not shew us what thou meanest by these?
19 Say unto them, Thus saith the Lord GOD; Behold, I will take the stick of Joseph, which is in the hand of Ephraim, and the tribes of Israel his fellows, and will put them with him, even with the stick of Judah, and make them one stick, and they shall be one in mine hand.
20 And the sticks whereon thou writest shall be in thine hand before their eyes.

When the children of your people, the son of man—who are scattered and not in the spiritual agreement of oneness with the LORD—speak to you and say, Will you not show us what you mean by this parable? The Lord GOD has said that He will take the sticks, that represent the separate people in the separate tribes, beginning with Joseph who served the LORD while in captivity, and Ephraim, his fruitful son, plus all the tribes of Israel and put them together with the stick of Judah and make them one stick which will be in the control of the LORD. While it will appear that the sticks upon which you write, your individual actions and behaviors, will be in your own hand before the eyes of those who observe your actions they will not be able to see the control of the invisible God whose spirit is the connecting substance that holds the people together.

21 And say unto them, Thus saith the Lord GOD; Behold, I will take the children of Israel from among the heathen, whither they be gone, and will gather them on every side, and bring them into their own land:
22 And I will make them one nation in the land upon the mountains of Israel; and one king shall be king to them all: and they shall be no more two nations, neither shall they be divided into two kingdoms any more at all:
23 Neither shall they defile themselves any more with their idols, nor with their detestable things, nor with any of their transgressions: but I will save them out of all their dwellingplaces, wherein they have sinned, and will cleanse them: so shall they be my people, and I will be their God.

Ezekiel is to say that the Lord GOD will take the children of Israel from among the heathen, where they have gone when they left the spirit of the LORD, and the children of Israel will be gathered together and brought to their own land. The spirit of the LORD moving through them will make them one nation upon the spiritual mountains of Israel; and one king shall be the king to all the tribes. The king on earth will be a representative of the King in heaven. Heaven and earth are one. There shall no longer be two nations and two kingdoms any more at all. The people shall no more defile themselves with their idols, their detestable things and any of their transgressions which have caused the separation of the nation. The spirit of the LORD will save them out of their dwelling places, where they have sinned, and cleanse them. The people must be cleansed so that they shall be the LORD's people and the LORD will be their God.

24 And David my servant shall be king over them; and they all shall have one shepherd: they shall also walk in my judgments, and observe my statutes, and do them.
25 And they shall dwell in the land that I have given unto Jacob my servant, wherein your fathers have dwelt; and they shall dwell therein, even they, and their children, and their children's children for ever: and my servant David shall be their prince for ever.

The Lord GOD says through Ezekiel, His prophet, that the spirit moving through His servant David shall be king over them; and they shall have one shepherd. The LORD has identified a king for the people: but the people must walk in the judgments and observe the statutes of the LORD, and do them. Then, they shall dwell in the spiritual land that the LORD has given to Jacob, His servant, the land where their fathers have dwelt. As the people express the spirit of the

LORD in their living, they may dwell in the land of the spirit with their children and grandchildren forever: and the LORD's servant David shall be their prince forever. They will be spiritual sons of David.

26 Moreover I will make a covenant of peace with them; it shall be an everlasting covenant with them: and I will place them, and multiply them, and will set my sanctuary in the midst of them for evermore.
27 My tabernacle also shall be with them: yea, I will be their God, and they shall be my people.
28 And the heathen shall know that I the LORD do sanctify Israel, when my sanctuary shall be in the midst of them for evermore.

Moreover, the LORD will make a covenant of peace with the people who have been cleansed and He will place them where they will serve the spirit of the LORD, multiply them and set the sanctuary of the LORD in the midst of each person for evermore. The tabernacle of the LORD shall be with His people and the LORD shall be their God in the covenant between God and the people who dwell together in holiness. The heathen shall know that the LORD has sanctified Israel, when the sanctuary will be in the midst of them. The heathen, the people who are separated from God, are as the dry bones in the valley which have come together under the spirit of the Lord GOD to form the living body of the Son of man on earth. The plan of salvation for the body of people who compose the fallen son of man is to repent and become the body of the Son of man by the expression of the spirit of the LORD through each person.

CHAPTER 38

1 And the word of the LORD came unto me, saying,
2 Son of man, set thy face against Gog, the land of Magog, the chief prince of Meshech and Tubal, and prophesy against him,

The word of the LORD came to Ezekiel, saying, Son of man, set your face, direct your attention against Gog, the land of Magog. Gog is the enemy of God, the spirit of God which is distorted as it moves through the fallen state of consciousness. Gog is distorted cause. Magog is the material land of Gog in which the distortion appears in a form that is observable by the senses. Magog is the name for distorted effects. Magog means, "that which covers or dissolves" as material things, thoughts and feelings dissolve and disintegrate. The distortions of wrong cause and wrong effect are revealed in the chief prince of Meshech and Tubal. Meshech means, "one who is drawn or surrounded" by wrong cause; and Tubal means, "the world or confusion" that is observed as wrong effects. The Son of man is to prophesy against the distortions of the spirit of God, Gog, and the visible effects of the distortion, Magog, which appears through the chief prince, people, who are drawn by the distortions.

3 And say, Thus saith the Lord GOD; Behold, I am against thee, O Gog, the chief prince of Meshech and Tubal:
4 And I will turn thee back, and put hooks into thy jaws, and I will bring thee forth, and all thine army, horses and horsemen, all of them clothed with all sorts of armour, even a great company with bucklers and shields, all of them handling swords:
5 Persia, Ethiopia, and Libya with them; all of them with shield and helmet:
6 Gomer, and all his bands; the house of Togarmah of the north quarters, and all his bands: and many people with thee.

The Lord GOD is against Gog, the distortion of the spirit of God, which comes forth as wrong cause and wrong effect, sins, from Meshech and Tubal, the people who reveal the distortions of the spirit of God. It should be expected that the spirit of God should turn back the distortions of spirit represented by Gog. The spirit of God will put hooks in the jaws of Gog, as a beast is controlled by a chain, and bring him forth with all his army, horses, horsemen, all clothed with armor, with bucklers, shields and swords ready to wage war against places from all directions to expand their distorted control, which is not of the LORD: Persia to the east, Ethiopia to the south, and Libya, Gomer and Togarmah to the north and west.

7 Be thou prepared, and prepare for thyself, thou, and all thy company that are assembled unto thee, and be thou a guard unto them.
8 After many days thou shalt be visited: in the latter years thou shalt come into the land that is brought back from the sword, and is gathered out of many people, against the mountains of Israel, which have been always waste: but it is brought forth out of the nations, and they shall dwell safely all of them.

The Symbolic Version of Ezekiel

9 Thou shalt ascend and come like a storm, thou shalt be like a cloud to cover the land, thou, and all thy bands, and many people with thee.

The people who hear the word of he LORD must be prepared and be on guard from invasion by those who are ravenous in nature, and prepare yourself, so that you, and the company of people who are assembled around you, do not become aggressors and oppressors. After many days of peaceful living with the spirit of the LORD, you shall be visited: in the latter years, you shall come into the land that has been brought back into the control of the sword of the spirit of the LORD. This land has been gathered from many people, who were against the spiritual mountains of Israel, which have always been wasteland. But the land was not conquered with force; it was brought forth out of the nations, and all of them shall dwell safely in the expanding spirit and multiplication of the spirit of God. The house of Israel shall ascend and come like a storm, and the body of the Son of man shall be like a cloud to cover the land, and the many people who are with you.

10 Thus saith the Lord GOD; It shall also come to pass, that at the same time shall things come into thy mind, and thou shalt think an evil thought:
11 And thou shalt say, I will go up to the land of unwalled villages; I will go to them that are at rest, that dwell safely, all of them dwelling without walls, and having neither bars nor gates,
12 To take a spoil, and to take a prey; to turn thine hand upon the desolate places that are now inhabited, and upon the people that are gathered out of the nations, which have gotten cattle and goods, that dwell in the midst of the land.
13 Sheba, and Dedan, and the merchants of Tarshish, with all the young lions thereof, shall say unto thee, Art thou come to take a spoil? hast thou gathered thy company to take a prey? to carry away silver and gold, to take away cattle and goods, to take a great spoil?

The Lord GOD says that it shall come to pass that at the time of the success of expansion, things shall come into your mind and you shall think an evil thought: you shall say, I will go up to the land of the unwalled villages; I will go to them who are at rest and dwell safely in the land without walls, having neither bars or gates. You may think to take spoil and prey; to use your superior control against desolate places which are now inhabited, and you may think to prey upon the people that dwell in the land who have gathered out of the nations, and who now have possessions of cattle and goods.

The traders of the south, Sheba, and Dedan, and the merchants of Tarshish across the Mediterranean, with all the young lions thereof, shall say to you, Are you come to take a spoil? have you gathered your company of people to take an easy prey? to carry away silver and gold, to take away cattle and goods, to take a great spoil? They will say that it will be very easy to conquer and take whatever spoil that you want.

14 Therefore, son of man, prophesy and say unto Gog, Thus saith the Lord GOD; In that day when my people of Israel dwelleth safely, shalt thou not know it?
15 And thou shalt come from thy place out of the north parts, thou, and many people with thee, all of them riding upon horses, a great company, and a mighty army:
16 And thou shalt come up against my people of Israel, as a cloud to cover the land; it shall be in the latter days, and I will bring thee against my land, that the heathen may know me, when I shall be sanctified in thee, O Gog, before their eyes.

Therefore, son of man, who has already entered the fallen state if these materialistic thoughts have come into his mind, prophesy, express the spirit of the LORD, and say to Gog, that the Lord GOD says, in the day that the people of Israel, the spiritual people of the LORD, dwell safely, shall you not know it? And Gog, the distortion of the spirit of God, shall come from the north with their people, horses and army to come against the people of Israel to invade and cover the land with their wickedness. It shall be in the latter days when people have forgotten the value of peace on earth which came by expressing the LORD's spirit. The power of the LORD should be used by wicked people so that the heathen shall know the truth of the LORD who will be sanctified in Gog before the eyes of the invaders as the heathen express the true spirit of the LORD without distorting it.

17 Thus saith the Lord GOD; Art thou he of whom I have spoken in old time by my servants the prophets of Israel, which prophesied in those days many years that I would bring thee against them?

The Testimony of the Major Prophets

18 And it shall come to pass at the same time when Gog shall come against the land of Israel, saith the Lord GOD, that my fury shall come up in my face.
19 For in my jealousy and in the fire of my wrath have I spoken, Surely in that day there shall be a great shaking in the land of Israel;
20 So that the fishes of the sea, and the fowls of the heaven, and the beasts of the field, and all creeping things that creep upon the earth, and all the men that are upon the face of the earth, shall shake at my presence, and the mountains shall be thrown down, and the steep places shall fall, and every wall shall fall to the ground.

The Lord GOD says; Are you the he, Gog, the distortion of the LORD, that the LORD has spoken to in times of old by the servants of the spirit of the LORD, who are the prophets of Israel that prophesied the distortions of Gog in a battle that is caused by Gog. The truth of man is to be peaceful; the distortion of man is to make war to gather material things which are idols of Gog. When Gog comes against the land of Israel, the fury of the LORD shall rise up in the face of the LORD. In that day of conflict between God and Gog, the true state and the counterfeit state, there shall be a great shaking in the land of Israel so that the fishes of the sea, and the fowls of the heaven, and the beasts of the field, and all creeping things that creep upon the earth, and all the men that are upon the face of the earth, shall shake at the presence of the LORD who will always be against the distortions of Gog. The mountains of belief shall be thrown down, and the steep places of false ego shall fall, and every wall of separation shall fall to the ground as the Son of man battles the fallen son of man within a person's consciousness.

21 And I will call for a sword against him throughout all my mountains, saith the Lord GOD: every man's sword shall be against his brother.
22 And I will plead against him with pestilence and with blood; and I will rain upon him, and upon his bands, and upon the many people that are with him, an overflowing rain, and great hailstones, fire, and brimstone.
23 Thus will I magnify myself, and sanctify myself; and I will be known in the eyes of many nations, and they shall know that I am the LORD.

The Lord GOD will call for the fury of the LORD to manifest through all of His mountains: every man's sword shall be against his brother. The LORD will plead against Gog with pestilence and with blood; the LORD will rain against Gog, the symbol of the distortion of man, and against his bands of people who will experience the rain, hailstones, fire, and brimstone. This is the way that the LORD will magnify himself and sanctify himself; the LORD will be known in the eyes of many nations by the destructive power that is released through the distortions. The distortions are evidence that the LORD is present, but ignored.

CHAPTER 39

1 Therefore, thou son of man, prophesy against Gog, and say, Thus saith the Lord GOD; Behold, I am against thee, O Gog, the chief prince of Meshech and Tubal:
2 And I will turn thee back, and leave but the sixth part of thee, and will cause thee to come up from the north parts, and will bring thee upon the mountains of Israel:
3 And I will smite thy bow out of thy left hand, and will cause thine arrows to fall out of thy right hand.
4 Thou shalt fall upon the mountains of Israel, thou, and all thy bands, and the people that is with thee: I will give thee unto the ravenous birds of every sort, and to the beasts of the field to be devoured.
5 Thou shalt fall upon the open field: for I have spoken it, saith the Lord GOD.

Therefore, the Lord GOD declares that the fallen son of man, the people who think and believe that they are only human, must prophesy against Gog, the distortion of cause, that is expressed through the human consciousness. The Lord GOD is against the false god, called Gog, who is the chief prince of Meshech and Tubal, the symbolic people who represent the distortion of power and confusion caused by false cause. The Lord GOD will turn Gog, the spirit in the fallen state, back to his true state from which he fell. The LORD will leave only the sixth part of Gog—the number six is the symbol of the expression that comes forth through the human equipment. (See the symbolism of numbers in the Symbolic Version of Revelation) This sixth part, the expression that comes forth, is all that will remain of Gog, who is a distortion of the spirit of God, when the LORD causes Gog to come in from the cold, from the north parts, and bring him back to the true spiritual place from which he fell that is symbolized by the mountains of Israel.

The LORD will disarm the usurper of His power as He smites the bow from Gog's left hand and the arrows from his right hand. The victory of the Lord GOD over Gog is inevitable. Gog, his bands and his people, shall fall upon the mountains of Israel, the people who have restored to the ascended and restored state of man, made in the image and likeness of God. The remains of Gog will be given to the ravenous birds and the beasts of he field to be devoured, which is the symbolism of the disintegrative process, as Gog falls upon the open field which is open to receive the undistorted spirit of the LORD.

6 And I will send a fire on Magog, and among them that dwell carelessly in the isles: and they shall know that I am the LORD.
7 So will I make my holy name known in the midst of my people Israel; and I will not let them pollute my holy name any more: and the heathen shall know that I am the LORD, the Holy One in Israel.

As Gog, the symbol of the distortion of **cause** is devoured and destroyed, then the **effects** of the wrong cause, Magog, will be destroyed by fire, the creative power of love from the spirit of the LORD. Distorted effects have appeared on earth because of the fallen people who dwell carelessly in the isles of their particular areas of responsibility. As they fallen people express the spirit of God, they shall come to know the LORD because people know what they express. The expression of the spirit of the LORD is the only way that the holy name of the LORD, I AM, can be known in the

The Testimony of the Major Prophets

midst of the LORD's restored people, Israel. People must repent and change from Gog to the spirit of God in order to experience the transition that Jacob experienced as he transformed into Israel. The outward appearance of the physical body of Jacob did not change; the expression through it changed to reveal the spirit of the LORD. As this occurs, the LORD will not let that person pollute his holy name, I AM, any more. In this way, the heathen, symbolized by Gog and Magog, shall know that I am the LORD, the Holy One in Israel when the spirit of the LORD is expressed through the heart, mind and body of an individual. This is the only way that the individual can know for himself or herself.

8 Behold, it is come, and it is done, saith the Lord GOD; this is the day whereof I have spoken.
9 And they that dwell in the cities of Israel shall go forth, and shall set on fire and burn the weapons, both the shields and the bucklers, the bows and the arrows, and the handstaves, and the spears, and they shall burn them with fire seven years:
10 So that they shall take no wood out of the field, neither cut down any out of the forests; for they shall burn the weapons with fire: and they shall spoil those that spoiled them, and rob those that robbed them, saith the Lord GOD.

Behold that when the spirit of the LORD, the spirit of love, truth and life, is expressed through the equipment of the heart, mind and body, then the spirit which has always been flowing, has come to the human equipment of the body, mind and heart which have not known heretofore the spirit of the LORD. It is done, says the Lord GOD; this is the day whereof I have spoken. The person must express God's spirit to know God's spirit. There is not a battle or a war; simply the fitting expression of the spirit of the LORD through a person into the environment.

The predictable result is that they who dwell in the cities of Israel, in the spiritual, heavenly places where each one is, in spirit, then they shall go forth, and shall set on fire and burn the weapons, both the shields and the bucklers, the bows and the arrows, and the handstaves, and the spears, and they shall burn them with the fire of the spirit of the LORD within their own consciousness for seven years, the symbol for the completion of the process. During this time, the people shall take no wood out of the field of their environments, neither cut down any out of the forests which is symbolic language to take nothing from the distorted material environment into one's consciousness as an idol to worship; let the spirit of the LORD burn the weapons that exist in your consciousness with the fire of His love. In this manner, the person shall spoil those weapons of feelings and thoughts in one's heart and mind that spoiled them and robbed them of their divine inheritance, said the Lord GOD.

11 And it shall come to pass in that day, that I will give unto Gog a place there of graves in Israel, the valley of the passengers on the east of the sea: and it shall stop the noses of the passengers: and there shall they bury Gog and all his multitude: and they shall call it The valley of Hamongog.

It shall come to pass in that day when the spirit of the LORD moves clearly and cleanly through the consciousness of a person, the LORD will give Gog, the distorted expression of man, a place in the graves of Israel, which is the end of the passengers on the east of the sea who have arrived at their destination after a long voyage. The graves of Israel can be seen as the end of the voyage for the continuation of the fallen state of man on earth which has produced a terrible stench that shall stop the noses of the passengers with the horrible odor produced by the fallen human expression. When this low point in the valley is seen, it is there that they shall bury Gog and all his multitude of wrong function which has defiled the true nature of man on earth. This place, this graveyard where the death of evil is buried is called Hamongog, which means, "a multitude of Gog", a multitude of distortions, sinners and devils.

12 And seven months shall the house of Israel be burying of them, that they may cleanse the land.
13 Yea, all the people of the land shall bury them; and it shall be to them a renown the day that I shall be glorified, saith the Lord GOD.
14 And they shall sever out men of continual employment, passing through the land to bury with the passengers those that remain upon the face of the earth, to cleanse it: after the end of seven months shall they search.
15 And the passengers that pass through the land, when any seeth a man's bone, then shall he set up a sign by it, till the buriers have buried it in the valley of Hamongog.
16 And also the name of the city shall be Hamonah. Thus shall they cleanse the land.

The restored spiritual people, who are the house of Israel, shall be burying the distorted people, who are the multitude of Gog, and thereby cleanse the land. Yes, all the living spiritual people of the land shall bury their fallen selves, their counterfeit expressions; and it shall be to those victorious people a day of renown when the LORD shall be glorified on earth through themselves. This event can occur after a period of time, symbolized by seven months, and the number seven is the completion of the creative cycle as the spirit finds expression through the impure heart, mind and body of man. These people are the servers of the spirit of the LORD who will have continual employment as they pass through the land to bury the false selves that remain on the earth, to cleanse the earth in the only way that it can be cleansed as others go through the creative process of cleansing their impure hearts and unclean thoughts. The spiritual passengers who pass through the land will, when he observes a person in the fallen state, a dry bone which is the symbol of fallen man in the valley of the dry bones, shall set up a sign by it, until the buriers have buried it in the valley of Hamongog, which is the valley of the dead where the distortions are buried. Also the name of the city shall be Hamonah, which means, "a multitude of the LORD's people", who are the ones that live in the city and who have accepted the responsibility to cleanse the land by cleansing themselves.

17 And, thou son of man, thus saith the Lord GOD; Speak unto every feathered fowl, and to every beast of the field, Assemble yourselves, and come; gather yourselves on every side to my sacrifice that I do sacrifice for you, even a great sacrifice upon the mountains of Israel, that ye may eat flesh, and drink blood.
18 Ye shall eat the flesh of the mighty, and drink the blood of the princes of the earth, of rams, of lambs, and of goats, of bullocks, all of them fatlings of Bashan.
19 And ye shall eat fat till ye be full, and drink blood till ye be drunken, of my sacrifice which I have sacrificed for you.
20 Thus ye shall be filled at my table with horses and chariots, with mighty men, and with all men of war, saith the Lord GOD.

The Lord GOD commands the individual son of man to speak to every feathered fowl, to every evil and veiled thought, and to every beast of the field which symbolizes each person's beastly expressions, to assemble themselves and come to the sacrifice that the fallen son of man will make for his fellow men. This sacrifice of the false self to reveal the coming of the true Self, is a great sacrifice which is made on the mountains of Israel, the highest places in spiritual consciousness. This is the way that the observer may eat of the flesh of a true example and drink the blood of a true expression. A person in the fallen state, a member of the body of the son of man, who is in the company of the restored mountains of Israel, the people who have learned to express their spiritual nature, shall eat the flesh of the mighty and drink the blood of the princes of the earth as they lead the good life as they are rewarded with the fruits of the right expressions of the people who reveal the spirit of the LORD in their living. These people are fortunate to have been filled at the table of the LORD with the items which are fitting for a prince, who is a child of the King, says the LORD.

21 And I will set my glory among the heathen, and all the heathen shall see my judgment that I have executed, and my hand that I have laid upon them.
22 So the house of Israel shall know that I am the LORD their God from that day and forward.
23 And the heathen shall know that the house of Israel went into captivity for their iniquity: because they trespassed against me, therefore hid I my face from them, and gave them into the hand of their enemies: so fell they all by the sword.
24 According to their uncleanness and according to their transgressions have I done unto them, and hid my face from them.
25 Therefore thus saith the Lord GOD; Now will I bring again the captivity of Jacob, and have mercy upon the whole house of Israel, and will be jealous for my holy name;
26 After that they have borne their shame, and all their trespasses whereby they have trespassed against me, when they dwelt safely in their land, and none made them afraid.
27 When I have brought them again from the people, and gathered them out of their enemies' lands, and am sanctified in them in the sight of many nations;
28 Then shall they know that I am the LORD their God, which caused them to be led into captivity among the heathen: but I have gathered them unto their own land, and have left none of them any more there.
29 Neither will I hide my face any more from them: for I have poured out my spirit upon the house of Israel, saith the Lord GOD.

The Testimony of the Major Prophets

The Lord GOD declares that He will bring the captivity of Jacob in his fallen human state to the understanding of willing people in the fallen state so that the mercy of the LORD can be extended to the whole house of Israel, which is the restored state of man on earth, and the LORD will be revealed by his people through the name of the LORD which is I Am. The LORD is jealous o His name and He wants only His people to use His name after they have borne their shame and their trespasses against the name of the LORD. People in the fallen state have taken the name of the LORD, I AM, in vain, in vanity and sinfulness, while they did not let the spirit of the LORD flow through them in their land where they dwelled safely and were not afraid as they were separated from the spirit of the LORD.

When the LORD has brought the fallen people out of their enemies' lands, the lands of Gog, because the spirit of the LORD is moving through the fallen people which will sanctify them in the sight of many others, many nations; then, they shall know that it is the Lord GOD which caused them to be led into captivity among the heathen because they rebelled against the LORD their God. The spirit of the LORD moving through the individual gathers the LORD's people back to the land of the LORD and no one is left separated from the LORD any more. The Lord GOD has never hid his face from the people in the fallen state because the LORD has poured out His spirit upon the house of Israel always. It is the people who have turned their faces away from the constantly moving spirit of the LORD.

CHAPTER 40

1 In the five and twentieth year of our captivity, in the beginning of the year, in the tenth day of the month, in the fourteenth year after that the city was smitten, in the selfsame day the hand of the LORD was upon me, and brought me thither.
2 In the visions of God brought he me into the land of Israel, and set me upon a very high mountain, by which was as the frame of a city on the south.
3 And he brought me thither, and, behold, there was a man, whose appearance was like the appearance of brass, with a line of flax in his hand, and a measuring reed; and he stood in the gate.
4 And the man said unto me, Son of man, behold with thine eyes, and hear with thine ears, and set thine heart upon all that I shall shew thee; for to the intent that I might shew them unto thee art thou brought hither: declare all that thou seest to the house of Israel.

On the tenth day of the month in the beginning of the twenty fifth year of the captivity of Ezekiel, since he was taken to Babylon from Jerusalem, which was fourteen years after the fall of the city of Jerusalem, in that very day, the hand of the LORD was upon Ezekiel and brought him there in consciousness to the city. In the visions of God, Ezekiel was brought into the land of Israel, into the land of the spirit and set upon a high mountain where Ezekiel could see the frame of city from the south. The south is the symbolic direction of the present moment which can be seen from the direction of the sun which is located in the south. The spirit of the LORD brought Ezekiel to the city where he observed a man in the gate to the city, whose appearance was shiny and polished like brass. Brass is the symbol of human flesh which loses its luster, while gold is the symbol of spirit which remains the same and does not darken or deteriorate with age. This man is another spirit in a human form who is enlightened about the way into the dwelling place within the wall. The man with the appearance of brass had a line of flax, a linen cord, in his hand and a measuring reed; these two items symbolized the fact that the man has the tools, and knows how to use them, to measure his way as he goes through life. The man has a measured approach.

The man addressed Ezekiel as the Son of man, which indicates that the man in brass knows that Ezekiel was the focus of the spirit of the LORD, and he told Ezekiel to behold with his eyes, hear with his own ears and set his heart upon all that the man would show to him so that he would remember what was said. Ezekiel was brought to the man for the purpose and intent to be shown a divine vision of what is to be declared by Ezekiel to the whole house of Israel, to all the spirits in form on earth.

5 And behold a wall on the outside of the house round about, and in the man's hand a measuring reed of six cubits long by the cubit and an hand breadth: so he measured the breadth of the building, one reed; and the height, one reed.
6 Then came he unto the gate which looketh toward the east, and went up the stairs thereof, and measured the threshold of the gate, which was one reed broad; and the other threshold of the gate, which was one reed broad.

The Testimony of the Major Prophets

In the vision, Ezekiel saw a wall that was built surrounding the outside of a house. There is a house available to be lived in but this dwelling place is surrounded by a wall that has been built by someone. Ezekiel saw the man with a measuring reed six cubits long and a hand's breadth: this "longer" cubit is about twenty-one inches compared to the shorter cubit of eighteen inches. The man who is teaching Ezekiel can handle a measuring implement that is a little larger than normally used by normal humans of the day. The man measured the breadth and the height of the building, the wall that surrounds the dwelling place within, as one reed thick and one reed high. The reed is about ten feet four inches. This symbolizes that the man knows the thickness of the wall around the dwelling place within. There are gates in the wall to allow entrance through the wall and the wall can only be measured in the opening of the gate. The length of the wall can be measured from the outside but the thickness of the way into and through the wall can only be measured in the opening of the gate. This symbolizes that you must go through the gate to measure how thick the wall really is!

The man in Ezekiel's vision came to the gate which looked toward the east, the symbolic direction for the future, and he went up the stairs, he ascended higher, and measured the threshold, the entrance into the gate. The threshold is at a higher level and the man had to rise up to go through the entry in the wall. The person who desires to go through the wall must step over the threshold. In the gate, the portal of entry, the thickness of the wall can be measured, and it was one reed, ten feet, thick. On the inside of the wall, the man and Ezekiel can see small chambers in which people live in separate compartments.

7 And every little chamber was one reed long, and one reed broad; and between the little chambers were five cubits; and the threshold of the gate by the porch of the gate within was one reed.
8 He measured also the porch of the gate within, one reed.
9 Then measured he the porch of the gate, eight cubits; and the posts thereof, two cubits; and the porch of the gate was inward.

Every little chamber was one reed long and one reed wide (10 feet by 10 feet) and, between the little chambers were five cubits (approximately 10 feet). Each chamber is large enough to accommodate one person who is a part of the wall that surrounds the dwelling place. The threshold of the gate by the porch was one reed (10 feet) and the porch of the gate within was one reed, which is the same measurement of the chamber. Symbolically, this means that man can be either a gate, an entry through the wall or a part of the wall. The wall is closed and the gate is open. Then, the man measured the porch of the gate as eight cubits (14 feet), the size of the porch upon which man stands increased by four feet. The place upon which he stands has become larger. The posts of the gate, the jambs that indicate thickness, were two cubits (3 ½ feet) which symbolizes that the wall has become thinner; the porch of the gate was inward toward the dwelling place.

10 And the little chambers of the gate eastward were three on this side, and three on that side; they three were of one measure: and the posts had one measure on this side and on that side.
11 And he measured the breadth of the entry of the gate, ten cubits; and the length of the gate, thirteen cubits.
12 The space also before the little chambers was one cubit on this side, and the space was one cubit on that side: and the little chambers were six cubits on this side, and six cubits on that side.
13 He measured then the gate from the roof of one little chamber to the roof of another: the breadth was five and twenty cubits, door against door.

The little chambers of the gate eastward toward the future, were three on this side and three on that side; the three were of one measure and they could be measured as a unit, The three chambers on this side from which the man and Ezekiel are entering inward are **material**; and the three chambers on that side to which they are going are **spiritual**. The posts had one measure on this side and that side. The posts have the same thickness; the spirit and the form have the same measure because they are made for each other to be joined together at the interface of the spiritual post and the material post by the lintel that connects them above the threshold of the gate, or door. In the gate, Ezekiel can be seen as the threshold and the man in brass as the lintel who is above the threshold. The lintel is at a higher level than the threshold which illustrates in symbolism that the vision of the man in brass is higher than the vision of Ezekiel.

The Symbolic Version of Ezekiel

The man measured the entry of the gate at 10 cubits on the material side of the gate and the length of the gate as 13 cubits on the spiritual side of the gate. The entry of the gate has increased in size on the spiritual side of the gate to indicate that the spirit would be pleased to have larger gates or openings in the wall.

The space before the little chambers was one cubit on this material side, and the space was one cubit on that spiritual side which symbolizes the fact that the entrance to the little chambers is only a cubit, only one step away, for a person to enter into the rooms which are symbolized by the chambers. The little chambers were six cubits on this material side, and six cubits on that spiritual side. The number six is the symbol of expression, the coming forth, into the world through a spiritual man. The two little chambers are to be occupied by the spirit of the man and physical form of Ezekiel as they move towards the east of the future. Then the man measured the gate from the roof of one little chamber to the roof of another: the breadth was five and twenty cubits, door against door, as the chamber of spirit and the chamber of form, the chamber of Being and the chamber of human form, are joined together, door to door, to make a real being in human form.

14 He made also posts of threescore cubits, even unto the post of the court round about the gate.
15 And from the face of the gate of the entrance unto the face of the porch of the inner gate were fifty cubits.
16 And there were narrow windows to the little chambers, and to their posts within the gate round about, and likewise to the arches: and windows were round about inward: and upon each post were palm trees.

The man who knew the way through the wall by way of an open gate into the chambers which were ready and waiting for him and his guest also made posts of sixty cubits, even to the post of the court round about the gate. The court is on the inside of the wall, the wall which **separates** the world of spirit from the world of form, when viewed from the world of form. However, from the court, the wall is seen as the wall that **connects** the world of spirit to the world of form when viewed from the world of spirit inside the court.

And from the face of the gate of the entrance of the world of form into the face of the porch of the inner gate of the world of spirit were fifty cubits. And there were narrow windows to the little chambers, through which it is possible to look out into the world of spirit with a limited point of view. There are posts within the gate round about to support the gate in the wall and likewise, the arches: and windows were round about inward and facing inward into the world of the spirit for spiritual insight: and upon each post were palm trees to symbolize the living nature of everything in the world of spirit.

17 Then brought he me into the outward court, and, lo, there were chambers, and a pavement made for the court round about: thirty chambers were upon the pavement.
18 And the pavement by the side of the gates over against the length of the gates was the lower pavement.
19 Then he measured the breadth from the forefront of the lower gate unto the forefront of the inner court without, an hundred cubits eastward and northward.
20 And the gate of the outward court that looked toward the north, he measured the length thereof, and the breadth thereof.

Then, the man, who knew his way around the spiritual courtyard, brought Ezekiel into the outer court of the spiritual courtyard, which is within the wall; and, lo, there were thirty chambers to be inhabited and a pavement made for the court: thirty chambers were upon the pavement. The pavement by the side of the gates over against the length of the gates was the lower pavement. The pavement sloped downward from the higher point of the wall to the outer court to the inner court. This symbolizes that once the person gets through the wall, the symbol of the separation of the material world form the spiritual world, the path is easier on a down slope.

Then the man measured the breadth from the forefront of the lower gate to the forefront of the inner court which was a hundred cubits eastward and northward. He also measured the length and the breadth from the gate of the outward court that looked toward the north. It is obvious to him that while the wall from the material side appears stark and barren, appears as a plain wall of separation, from the inside of the wall, the spiritual side of the wall, there is an orderly design that has been cared for, with pavements and chambers for visitors to dwell.

The Testimony of the Major Prophets

21 And the little chambers thereof were three on this side and three on that side; and the posts thereof and the arches thereof were after the measure of the first gate: the length thereof was fifty cubits, and the breadth five and twenty cubits.
22 And their windows, and their arches, and their palm trees, were after the measure of the gate that looketh toward the east; and they went up unto it by seven steps; and the arches thereof were before them.
23 And the gate of the inner court was over against the gate toward the north, and toward the east; and he measured from gate to gate an hundred cubits.

The little chambers were three on this side, the material side, to contain the material equipment of physical body, mind and heart, and three on the spiritual side to house the triune spiritual aspects of life, truth and love. This illustrates that there is provision for the physical equipment in the area of spirit. Ezekiel is not a disembodied spirit. The posts, the jambs, of the chambers and the arches were after the measure of the first gate through the wall, which symbolizes that they have both a material and a spiritual component: the length was fifty cubits and the breadth was half that amount, twenty-five cubits.

The windows through which a person can observe is to illustrate that the spirit of truth is present, the arches which connect the openings of the gates illustrates that the spirit of love is present, and the palm tree illustrates that the spirit of life is present. These three spirits are needed to look toward the east, the symbol of the future. Ezekiel and the man, who is showing him the way, went up into it by seven steps; the seven steps lead to something which is presently unknown, and that something can only be known by walking up the seven steps. The steps are not blocked by a wall. There are arches before Ezekiel and the man through which to enter the area at the top of the seven steps. The way to the gate toward the north is to look to the east, the future, rather than the west, the symbol of the past. There is no entry from the west, the past. The man measured the distance from gate to gate and it was a hundred cubits. It is measurable to get to the north entrance through the reflection of spirit in the present moment through someone else.

The gate to the inner court was over against the gate in the wall toward the north, the symbol of the present moment which is opposite from the radiation of the present moment from the sun which is in the south. The north is the reflection in material form of the radiation of the spirit that is symbolized by the sun in the south. The individual cannot get into the place of the spiritual destination through the observed reflection of someone else who knows the way, symbolized by the direction of north, but through one's own radiation of the spirit which is symbolized in the present moment of the south.

24 After that he brought me toward the south, and behold a gate toward the south: and he measured the posts thereof and the arches thereof according to these measures.
25 And there were windows in it and in the arches thereof round about, like those windows: the length was fifty cubits, and the breadth five and twenty cubits.
26 And there were seven steps to go up to it, and the arches thereof were before them: and it had palm trees, one on this side, and another on that side, upon the posts thereof.

After Ezekiel realizes that way to spiritual fulfillment is through his own expression and not through the expression of someone else, someone who knows the way because he has been there, the man, Ezekiel's spiritual guide in the vision, brought him back to the south, and behold there is a gate toward the south, available in the present moment. He measured the posts and the arches of the entrance and the exit which are the same. There were windows and arches of the same dimensions in the south, within his own present experience, as was shown to him in the east of the future and in the north, that was reflected to him by someone else. There were seven steps to go up into it and the arches were before them, the man and Ezekiel, the Son of man. There were two palm trees that symbolize the spirit of life, one on this side and one on that side, upon the posts, the jambs, that lead into the way of life. There is a gate to the spirit of life symbolized by a tree of life.

27 And there was a gate in the inner court toward the south: and he measured from gate to gate toward the south an hundred cubits.
28 And he brought me to the inner court by the south gate: and he measured the south gate according to these measures;

29 And the little chambers thereof, and the posts thereof, and the arches thereof, according to these measures: and there were windows in it and in the arches thereof round about: it was fifty cubits long, and five and twenty cubits broad.
30 And the arches round about were five and twenty cubits long, and five cubits broad.
31 And the arches thereof were toward the outer court; and palm trees were upon the posts thereof: and the going up to it had eight steps.

There was a gate to the inner court toward the south, in the present moment: and the man measured the distance from gate to gate as a hundred cubits, the symbol of a total commitment. The man brought Ezekiel to the inner court toward the south gate and measured the south gate, the little chambers thereof and the posts thereof: there were windows to let his own spirit of truth look through into the world, the arches of the spirit of love, and the measurements of the south were the same as he had been shown in the measurements of the east. Ezekiel understood that his future had become his present as they moved from the east to the south. The qualities and characteristics which he had observed in the man are also available in himself. Ezekiel notices that when he looked at the arches and the palm trees on the posts, they opened to the **outer** court which means that Ezekiel was through the gate and on the **inside**. There was only one difference: the going up to the top of his journey had eight steps, not seven.

32 And he brought me into the inner court toward the east: and he measured the gate according to these measures.
33 And the little chambers thereof, and the posts thereof, and the arches thereof, were according to these measures: and there were windows therein and in the arches thereof round about: it was fifty cubits long, and five and twenty cubits broad.
34 And the arches thereof were toward the outward court; and palm trees were upon the posts thereof, on this side, and on that side: and the going up to it had eight steps.
35 And he brought me to the north gate, and measured it according to these measures;
36 The little chambers thereof, the posts thereof, and the arches thereof, and the windows to it round about: the length was fifty cubits, and the breadth five and twenty cubits.
37 And the posts thereof were toward the outer court; and palm trees were upon the posts thereof, on this side, and on that side: and the going up to it had eight steps.

The man brought Ezekiel into the inner court toward the east, toward the future: and he measured the gate according to these measures. The little chambers which contain the heart mind and physical body are there, the posts and the arches which allow the person to walk through the opening are there according to measures that allow a person who measures up to pass through. The windows to observe with the eyes of truth and the arches that are connected with love. The arches of love are toward the outer court which symbolize that Ezekiel is inside the outer court which he can observe. The palm trees that symbolize life were upon the posts, on this side, the spiritual side and that side, the material side. The steps that ascend higher had eight steps.

The man brought Ezekiel to the north gate, the symbol of the example that he is showing Ezekiel through his own behavior, and measured it according to the measures that are required to enter the spiritual destination. The little chambers that house the human equipment of body, mind and heart, the posts which are the open door to the spirit, the arches that symbolize the connectedness of love, and the windows through which the truth is seen. The measures of length and breadth fifty by twenty-five cubits, and the posts open to the outer courts which mean that the person is inside the gate in the realm of the spirit. The palm trees symbolize the spirit of life is on the posts on both the spiritual side and the material side. And the way up, the ascension to the realm of spirit, had eight steps. Ezekiel is able to see and observe more clearly.

38 And the chambers and the entries thereof were by the posts of the gates, where they washed the burnt offering.
39 And in the porch of the gate were two tables on this side, and two tables on that side, to slay thereon the burnt offering and the sin offering and the trespass offering.
40 And at the side without, as one goeth up to the entry of the north gate, were two tables; and on the other side, which was at the porch of the gate, were two tables.
41 Four tables were on this side, and four tables on that side, by the side of the gate; eight tables, whereupon they slew their sacrifices.

42 And the four tables were of hewn stone for the burnt offering, of a cubit and an half long, and a cubit and an half broad, and one cubit high: whereupon also they laid the instruments wherewith they slew the burnt offering and the sacrifice.
43 And within were hooks, an hand broad, fastened round about: and upon the tables was the flesh of the offering.

He saw the chambers and the entries were the posts and the gates that enter into the area where they washed the burnt offering. In the porch of the gate were two tables on this side, the material side, and two tables on the spiritual side, to slay the burnt offering, the sin offering and the trespass offering. Ezekiel does not know the nature of these offerings so he must see them through the example of the man, his spiritual guide, as they go to the north gate, the gate through which he sees what he needs to observe through someone else.

Ezekiel must enter the north gate from the side without, the outside, the material side, with which he is familiar, and he goes to enter the north gate where he sees two tables. There are two tables on the other side, the spiritual side, on the porch of the gate, the other side of the gate. Since the man is with Ezekiel, there are four tables on the material side and four tables on the spiritual side of the gate for a total of eight tables where upon the two men did slay their sacrifices. The four tables were hewn of stone for a burnt offering; the dimensions of the stone were one and a half cubits long and wide with a height of one cubit. Also present were the instruments with which they slew the burnt offering and the sacrifice. And within the room were hooks, as broad as a hand, fastened round about: and upon the tables was the flesh of the offering to be sacrificed.

44 And without the inner gate were the chambers of the singers in the inner court, which was at the side of the north gate; and their prospect was toward the south: one at the side of the east gate having the prospect toward the north.
45 And he said unto me, This chamber, whose prospect is toward the south, is for the priests, the keepers of the charge of the house.
46 And the chamber whose prospect is toward the north is for the priests, the keepers of the charge of the altar: these are the sons of Zadok among the sons of Levi, which come near to the LORD to minister unto him.

Outside the inner gate were the chambers of the singers in the inner court which was at the side of the north gate; and their prospect (view) was toward the south, toward the present time, when they could become singers of the present. There is also one singer at the east gate, one who is looking to the future having a prospect, a look ahead, at seeing a person who was actually singing. This person said to Ezekiel, This chamber, whose prospect is toward the south that symbolizes the present moment, is for the priests who are the keepers in charge of the house. The chamber whose prospect is toward the north, symbolizes the priests who are in charge of the altar. These priests are the sons of Zadok who are among the sons of Levi, the tribe which has dedicated their service and allegiance to the LORD to minister to Him.

47 So he measured the court, an hundred cubits long, and an hundred cubits broad, foursquare; and the altar that was before the house.
48 And he brought me to the porch of the house, and measured each post of the porch, five cubits on this side, and five cubits on that side: and the breadth of the gate was three cubits on this side, and three cubits on that side.
49 The length of the porch was twenty cubits, and the breadth eleven cubits; and he brought me by the steps whereby they went up to it: and there were pillars by the posts, one on this side, and another on that side.

The man measured the court and it was a hundred cubits long and a hundred cubits broad; it was four square and the altar was before the house. The man was in position to see the entire court upon which the altar was standing before a house. The man brought Ezekiel to the porch of the house, and measured each post of the porch upon which they were standing. It was five cubits on this material side and five cubits on that spiritual side. The breadth of the gate was three cubits on this side and three cubits on that side. The length of the porch was twenty cubits and the breadth eleven cubits.

The man brought Ezekiel by the steps that went up to it: and there were pillars by the posts, one on this side and another on that side. Ezekiel could see the steps that went up to it, and he could see the two pillars by the posts, one on this side and one on the other side. But Ezekiel did not know what **it** was.

CHAPTER 41

1 Afterward he brought me to the temple, and measured the posts, six cubits broad on the one side, and six cubits broad on the other side, which was the breadth of the tabernacle.
2 And the breadth of the door was ten cubits; and the sides of the door were five cubits on the one side, and five cubits on the other side: and he measured the length thereof, forty cubits: and the breadth, twenty cubits.
3 Then went he inward, and measured the post of the door, two cubits; and the door, six cubits; and the breadth of the door, seven cubits.
4 So he measured the length thereof, twenty cubits; and the breadth, twenty cubits, before the temple: and he said unto me, This is the most holy place.

Afterward the man brought Ezekiel to the temple, and measured the posts of the entrance to the temple to demonstrate that the way in to the temple was measurable and discernible to a person who knows the way to show the way to another person. The posts were six cubits broad on the one side, the material side, and six cubits broad on the other side, the spiritual side, which was the breadth of the tabernacle. Ezekiel has become aware that **it** was a temple and that there was a tabernacle in the temple. And the breadth of the door was ten cubits, which was twice as wide as the sides of the door jambs; and the sides of the door, the projecting walls, were five cubits on the one side, the material side, and five cubits on the other side, the spiritual side: and the man, the spiritual guide of Ezekiel, measured the length of the outer sanctuary as forty cubits: and the breadth was twenty cubits.

Then went the man went inward, and measured the post of the door, two cubits; and the door, six cubits; and the breadth of the door, seven cubits. So he measured the length thereof, twenty cubits; and the breadth, twenty cubits, before the temple: and he said unto me, This is the most holy place. The man who was measuring everything, material and spiritual, is symbolically indicating that it is possible to "measure" spiritual things while a person is in material form of a human body. He also states to Ezekiel that these measurements have led them to "The Most Holy Place".

5 After he measured the wall of the house, six cubits; and the breadth of every side chamber, four cubits, round about the house on every side.
6 And the side chambers were three, one over another, and thirty in order; and they entered into the wall which was of the house for the side chambers round about, that they might have hold, but they had not hold in the wall of the house.
7 And there was an enlarging, and a winding about still upward to the side chambers: for the winding about of the house went still upward round about the house: therefore the breadth of the house was still upward, and so increased from the lowest chamber to the highest by the midst.

After the man measured the wall of the house as six cubits; and the breadth of every side chamber, or room, was four cubits wide round about the house on every side. The side rooms were on three levels, one above another, thirty rooms on each of the three levels. The man and Ezekiel entered into the wall which was of the house, a ledge, which

The Testimony of the Major Prophets

illustrated the spiritual place to walk for the rooms, but the wall did not extend into the material wall of the house. In the temple, the people who dwell there can walk in the spirit which is separated from the form. The side rooms all around the temple were wider and larger as they went upward, connected by a winding stairway from the lower floor to the top floor. This symbolized that the higher rooms, and the people who occupied the rooms, held more spirit than the lower rooms but all the rooms in the temple are connected, not separated, as a part of one temple.

8 I saw also the height of the house round about: the foundations of the side chambers were a full reed of six great cubits.
9 The thickness of the wall, which was for the side chamber without, was five cubits: and that which was left was the place of the side chambers that were within.
10 And between the chambers was the wideness of twenty cubits round about the house on every side.
11 And the doors of the side chambers were toward the place that was left, one door toward the north, and another door toward the south: and the breadth of the place that was left was five cubits round about.

Ezekiel also saw that the height of the temple was a raised base round about, forming a foundation for the side rooms which were a full reed, six great cubits, ten and a half feet. The thickness of the outer wall for a side room, a material room, was five cubits thick. The space which was left was the place for the rooms that were within, the spiritual rooms. And between the chambers was the space of twenty cubits round about the house on every side. The doors of the rooms were toward the space that was left, one door toward the north, the direction that symbolizes the reflection of the spirit, and another door toward the south, the direction that symbolizes the radiation or the source of the spirit: the breadth of the space in between was five cubits round about.

12 Now the building that was before the separate place at the end toward the west was seventy cubits broad; and the wall of the building was five cubits thick round about, and the length thereof ninety cubits.
13 So he measured the house, an hundred cubits long; and the separate place, and the building, with the walls thereof, an hundred cubits long;
14 Also the breadth of the face of the house, and of the separate place toward the east, an hundred cubits.
15 And he measured the length of the building over against the separate place which was behind it, and the galleries thereof on the one side and on the other side, an hundred cubits, with the inner temple, and the porches of the court;
16 The door posts, and the narrow windows, and the galleries round about on their three stories, over against the door, cieled with wood round about, and from the ground up to the windows, and the windows were covered;
17 To that above the door, even unto the inner house, and without, and by all the wall round about within and without, by measure.

The building that was before the separate place at the end toward the west, the symbolic direction for the past, was seventy cubits wide and the wall of the building was five cubits thick all around. The length of the building was ninety cubits. So the man measured the temple, which was a hundred cubits in length; the temple courtyard with its building and its walls, the front of the temple, were also a hundred cubits long.

Then the man measured the length of the building facing the courtyard at the rear of the temple, the west side which symbolizes the direction for the past, including its galleries, the place where things are seen, on the one side, the material side, and the other side, the spiritual side, to illustrate that both the spirit and the form were present in the creation of one's own past; and it was a hundred cubits. The building is connected to the inner temple and the porches of the court.

The door posts, the entrance into the inner temple, and the narrow windows through which people get a glimpse into the inner temple, and the galleries through which things are shown from the inner temple through the three stories of rooms over against the door, covered with wood round about, and from the ground up to the windows, and the windows were covered so that nothing can be seen into the inner temple. Nothing can be seen through the closed door into the inner temple, as a wall round about that cannot be measured within and without.

18 And it was made with cherubims and palm trees, so that a palm tree was between a cherub and a cherub; and every cherub had two faces;

19 So that the face of a man was toward the palm tree on the one side, and the face of a young lion toward the palm tree on the other side: it was made through all the house round about.
20 From the ground unto above the door were cherubims and palm trees made, and on the wall of the temple.

The wall to the inner temple was made with cherubim, angels from God, and palm trees to symbolize everlasting life. A palm tree was between each cherub, or spirit from God. Each cherub had two faces. The cherub had the face of a man, which symbolized the truth of man made in the image and likeness of God, toward the palm tree that symbolized the spiritual side, and the face of a young lion, the symbol of the potential destructive side, that was toward the material side, the other side which can be contaminated. The cherubim with two faces and the palm trees were carved on the wall of the temple.

21 The posts of the temple were squared, and the face of the sanctuary; the appearance of the one as the appearance of the other.
22 The altar of wood was three cubits high, and the length thereof two cubits; and the corners thereof, and the length thereof, and the walls thereof, were of wood: and he said unto me, This is the table that is before the LORD.

The posts, the jambs, of the temple were squared, to allow equal egress of spirit from the temple through the wall of the face of the sanctuary; the appearance of one was as the appearance of another. The altar of wood was three cubits high and the length of two cubits. The corners, length and the walls were all made of wood which is symbolic that the altar could be totally burned, or consumed, The man said to Ezekiel that, This is the table that is before the LORD. The table before the LORD is the offering which will be burned and consumed as an offering to the LORD. As Ezekiel understood the total offering that was required, he was able to see that there was an opening into the temple.

23 And the temple and the sanctuary had two doors.
24 And the doors had two leaves apiece, two turning leaves; two leaves for the one door, and two leaves for the other door.
25 And there were made on them, on the doors of the temple, cherubims and palm trees, like as were made upon the walls; and there were thick planks upon the face of the porch without.
26 And there were narrow windows and palm trees on the one side and on the other side, on the sides of the porch, and upon the side chambers of the house, and thick planks.

The temple and the sanctuary had two doors: one door was for the man and the other door was for Ezekiel. The doors had two turning leaves apiece that allowed entrance and exit into the temple and the sanctuary. On the doors of the temple were carved cherubim and palm trees as were carved on the walls. There were thick planks on the face of the porch which provided the entrance into the temple. There were narrow windows, a limited vision, into the temple and palm trees, to symbolize the life which was available to be experienced on the material side and the spiritual side of the windows. The form and the spirit are connected through the narrow windows, the sides of the porch, and the rooms of the house and the thick planks upon which the man and Ezekiel were standing. Ezekiel has become aware that a realized experience with the LORD is available to him through the leadership of the spiritual man.

CHAPTER 42

1 Then he brought me forth into the outer court, the way toward the north: and he brought me into the chamber that was over against the separate place, and which was before the building toward the north.
2 Before the length of an hundred cubits was the north door, and the breadth was fifty cubits.
3 Over against the twenty cubits which were for the inner court, and over against the pavement which was for the utter court, was gallery against gallery in three stories.
4 And before the chambers was a walk of ten cubits breadth inward, a way of one cubit; and their doors toward the north.

The spiritual man brought Ezekiel into the outer court, the way toward the north, the symbolic direction of the reflection of spirit through the form of another person. The man brought him into the chamber of the outer court that was over against the separate place which was before the building toward the north. The north door was a hundred cubits in length and fifty cubits in width away.

5 Now the upper chambers were shorter: for the galleries were higher than these, than the lower, and than the middlemost of the building.
6 For they were in three stories, but had not pillars as the pillars of the courts: therefore the building was straitened more than the lowest and the middlemost from the ground.
7 And the wall that was without over against the chambers, toward the outer court on the forepart of the chambers, the length thereof was fifty cubits.
8 For the length of the chambers that were in the utter court was fifty cubits: and, lo, before the temple were an hundred cubits.
9 And from under these chambers was the entry on the east side, as one goeth into them from the outer court.
10 The chambers were in the thickness of the wall of the court toward the east, over against the separate place, and over against the building.

Now the upper rooms were narrower for the galleries were higher than the lower, and the middle floors of the building. The rooms on the third floor had no pillars as the courts had: therefore the building was
more limited than the lowest and the middle floors from the ground. There was an outer wall parallel to the rooms and the outer court with a length of fifty cubits. The length of the rooms in the outer court was fifty cubits and the row of rooms on the side nearest the sanctuary was a hundred cubits. From under these rooms, there was an entry from the east side as one enters them from the outer court. The rooms were in the thickness of the wall of the court toward the east, over against the separate place, and over against the building.

11 And the way before them was like the appearance of the chambers which were toward the north, as long as they, and as broad as they: and all their goings out were both according to their fashions, and according to their doors.

12 And according to the doors of the chambers that were toward the south was a door in the head of the way, even the way directly before the wall toward the east, as one entereth into them.
13 Then said he unto me, The north chambers and the south chambers, which are before the separate place, they be holy chambers, where the priests that approach unto the LORD shall eat the most holy things: there shall they lay the most holy things, and the meat offering, and the sin offering, and the trespass offering; for the place is holy.

The way before the man and Ezekiel was like the appearance of the rooms which were before the north as long as they and as broad as they: all their goings on, all their expressions, were according to their fashions and according to their doors, whatever is fitting for them to let flow through their doors.

And according to the doors of the rooms that were toward the south, toward the south which symbolizes the source of the radiation, was a door in the head of the way, even the way directly before the wall toward the east, the east that symbolizes the future, as one enters into them. Then, the man said to Ezekiel, The north rooms, which symbolize the reflection of the spirit and the south rooms, which symbolize the radiation and outward flow of the spirit which are before the temple, are holy rooms, where the priests that approach the LORD shall eat the most holy things: there shall they lay the most holy things in service to the LORD, as well as the meat offering of one's own physical form, and the sin offering, and the trespass offering which are distortions of the spirit of the LORD; all sin and trespasses must be left on the outside because the place to which the man and Ezekiel are about to enter is holy.

14 When the priests enter therein, then shall they not go out of the holy place into the outer court, but there they shall lay their garments wherein they minister; for they are holy; and shall put on other garments, and shall approach to those things which are for the people.
15 Now when he had made an end of measuring the inner house, he brought me forth toward the gate whose prospect is toward the east, and measured it round about.
16 He measured the east side with the measuring reed, five hundred reeds, with the measuring reed round about.
17 He measured the north side, five hundred reeds, with the measuring reed round about.
18 He measured the south side, five hundred reeds, with the measuring reed.
19 He turned about to the west side, and measured five hundred reeds with the measuring reed.
20 He measured it by the four sides: it had a wall round about, five hundred reeds long, and five hundred broad, to make a separation between the sanctuary and the profane place.

When the priests enter into the place where the LORD dwells, then they shall not go out of the holy place into the outer court, but there they shall lay their garments wherein they minister; for they are holy; and they shall put on other garments, and shall approach to those things from the LORD which are for the people. The priests are in the position to receive the blessings from the LORD to be delivered to the people.

Now when the man had made an end of measuring the inner house, he brought Ezekiel forth toward the gate whose prospect is toward the east, toward the future, and measured it round about for a distance of five hundred reeds. The measurement of the north, the symbol for the direction of the reflection of spirit was five hundred reeds. The measurement of the south, the symbol for the direction of the radiation of the spirit was five hundred reeds. The measurement of the west, the symbol for the direction of the past was five hundred reeds. The spiritual man measured it by four sides in each direction and there was a wall five hundred reeds long in each direction. The purpose of this wall was to make a separation between the sanctuary, the holy place and the profane place which must remain outside the temple of the LORD.

CHAPTER 43

1 Afterward he brought me to the gate, even the gate that looketh toward the east:
2 And, behold, the glory of the God of Israel came from the way of the east: and his voice was like a noise of many waters: and the earth shined with his glory.
3 And it was according to the appearance of the vision which I saw, even according to the vision that I saw when I came to destroy the city: and the visions were like the vision that I saw by the river Chebar; and I fell upon my face.

Afterward, after Ezekiel saw and comprehended that the profane can not be brought into the holy place within oneself, then, the spiritual man brought him to the gate that looked toward the east, the symbolic direction of the rising sun that symbolizes the future. Behold, the God of Israel came from the way of the east, from the direction of the future: and His voice was like a noise of many waters, many different aspects of the truth: and the earth did shine with the glory of the LORD as the waters, the symbol of the truth falling from the LORD, did fall upon the earth to produce divine radiant glory. The glory of God was according to the appearance of the vision which Ezekiel saw when the LORD came to destroy the city: the visions were like the vision that Ezekiel saw by the river, Chebar; Ezekiel fell upon his face in awe and shock at hearing and seeing the voice of the LORD.

4 And the glory of the LORD came into the house by the way of the gate whose prospect is toward the east.
5 So the spirit took me up, and brought me into the inner court; and, behold, the glory of the LORD filled the house.
6 And I heard him speaking unto me out of the house; and the man stood by me.
7 And he said unto me, Son of man, the place of my throne, and the place of the soles of my feet, where I will dwell in the midst of the children of Israel for ever, and my holy name, shall the house of Israel no more defile, neither they, nor their kings, by their whoredom, nor by the carcases of their kings in their high places.
8 In their setting of their threshold by my thresholds, and their post by my posts, and the wall between me and them, they have even defiled my holy name by their abominations that they have committed: wherefore I have consumed them in mine anger.

Ezekiel states that the glory of the LORD came into the house by way of the gate whose view is to the future. So the spirit took him up into the inner court; and behold, the glory of the LORD filled the house. Ezekiel heard the LORD speaking to him as he stood outside the house and the spiritual man stood by him.

The spiritual man who had shown Ezekiel the way, said, Son of man, the place of my throne, and the place of the soles of my feet, where I will dwell in the midst of the children of Israel for ever, and my holy name, shall the house of Israel no more defile, neither they, nor their kings, by their whoredom, nor by the carcasses of their kings in their high places. In their setting of their threshold by my thresholds, and their post by my posts, and the wall between me and them, they have even defiled My holy name by the abominations that they have committed: wherefore I have consumed them in My anger. I have allowed the Law of Sowing and Reaping to operate with absolute precision.

The Symbolic Version of Ezekiel

9 Now let them put away their whoredom, and the carcases of their kings, far from me, and I will dwell in the midst of them for ever.
10 Thou son of man, shew the house to the house of Israel, that they may be ashamed of their iniquities: and let them measure the pattern.
11 And if they be ashamed of all that they have done, shew them the form of the house, and the fashion thereof, and the goings out thereof, and the comings in thereof, and all the forms thereof, and all the ordinances thereof, and all the forms thereof, and all the laws thereof: and write it in their sight, that they may keep the whole form thereof, and all the ordinances thereof, and do them.

Now, in the present moment, let them put away their whoredoms and the carcases of their kings, far from the man who led Ezekiel. This spiritual man in the vision of Ezekiel is the symbol of the LORD. The LORD will dwell in the midst of man forever. The son of man is to show the house to the house of Israel so that they may be ashamed of their iniquities; and let them measure the patterns of their iniquities and sins. If they are ashamed of all that they have done, show them the form of the house, the house of the LORD, the fashion of it, the expressions that go forth and the coming in of the expressions from others. The ordinances, laws, and material forms of the kingdom of the LORD should be known by the people. Ezekiel is to write it in their sight so that they will come to know the laws and ordinances of heaven and consequently, do them.

12 This is the law of the house; Upon the top of the mountain the whole limit thereof round about shall be most holy. Behold, this is the law of the house.
13 And these are the measures of the altar after the cubits: The cubit is a cubit and an hand breadth; even the bottom shall be a cubit, and the breadth a cubit, and the border thereof by the edge thereof round about shall be a span: and this shall be the higher place of the altar.
14 And from the bottom upon the ground even to the lower settle shall be two cubits, and the breadth one cubit; and from the lesser settle even to the greater settle shall be four cubits, and the breadth one cubit.
15 So the altar shall be four cubits; and from the altar and upward shall be four horns.
16 And the altar shall be twelve cubits long, twelve broad, square in the four squares thereof.
17 And the settle shall be fourteen cubits long and fourteen broad in the four squares thereof; and the border about it shall be half a cubit; and the bottom thereof shall be a cubit about; and his stairs shall look toward the east.

This is the law of the house of the LORD; Upon the top of the spiritual mountain of consciousness of man, the whole limit round about, shall be most holy. Behold, this is the law of the house of the LORD that the consciousness of man must be holy.

And these are the measures of the altar after the cubits: The cubit is a cubit and an hand breadth; even the bottom shall be a cubit, and the breadth a cubit, and the border thereof by the edge thereof round about shall be a span: and this shall be the higher place of the altar.

And from the bottom upon the ground even to the lower settle shall be two cubits, and the breadth one cubit; and from the lesser settle even to the greater settle shall be four cubits, and the breadth one cubit.
So the altar shall be four cubits; and from the altar and upward shall be four horns.
And the altar shall be twelve cubits long, twelve broad, square in the four squares thereof.
And the settle shall be fourteen cubits long and fourteen broad in the four squares thereof; and the border about it shall be half a cubit; and the bottom thereof shall be a cubit about; and his stairs shall look toward the east.

18 And he said unto me, Son of man, thus saith the Lord GOD; These are the ordinances of the altar in the day when they shall make it, to offer burnt offerings thereon, and to sprinkle blood thereon.
19 And thou shalt give to the priests the Levites that be of the seed of Zadok, which approach unto me, to minister unto me, saith the Lord GOD, a young bullock for a sin offering.
20 And thou shalt take of the blood thereof, and put it on the four horns of it, and on the four corners of the settle, and upon the border round about: thus shalt thou cleanse and purge it.
21 Thou shalt take the bullock also of the sin offering, and he shall burn it in the appointed place of the house, without the sanctuary.

The Testimony of the Major Prophets

22 And on the second day thou shalt offer a kid of the goats without blemish for a sin offering; and they shall cleanse the altar, as they did cleanse it with the bullock.
23 When thou hast made an end of cleansing it, thou shalt offer a young bullock without blemish, and a ram out of the flock without blemish.

The man who spoke for the LORD, the word of the LORD, said to Ezekiel, Son of man, this is the message from the Lord GOD. These are the ordinances of the altar in the day when they shall make it, to offer burnt offerings on the altar and to sprinkle the blood of their expression on the altar of the LORD. You shall give to the priests, the Levites who are the seed of Zadok, who approach the LORD to be ministers of the LORD a young bullock for a sin offering. The young bullock is the symbol of the false human ego state that is to be offered to the LORD as a sin offering.

The blood of the bullock is to be put on the four horns of the altar and the four corners of the settle, the upper ledge, and upon the border round about: in this manner, the human ego and its sins shall be cleansed and purged. The sins of the bullock shall be burned in the appointed place outside the sanctuary. On the second day, the person who seeks salvation shall offer a kid of the goats without blemish for a sin offering, and they shall cleanse the altar, as they did cleanse it with the bullock. When you have made an end of cleansing it, you shall offer a young bullock without blemish, and a ram out of the flock without blemish. The offering is not to be the obvious visible flaw or the blemish; the offering is to be the flames without blemish.

24 And thou shalt offer them before the LORD, and the priests shall cast salt upon them, and they shall offer them up for a burnt offering unto the LORD.
25 Seven days shalt thou prepare every day a goat for a sin offering: they shall also prepare a young bullock, and a ram out of the flock, without blemish.
26 Seven days shall they purge the altar and purify it; and they shall consecrate themselves.
27 And when these days are expired, it shall be, that upon the eighth day, and so forward, the priests shall make your burnt offerings upon the altar, and your peace offerings; and I will accept you, saith the Lord GOD.

These offerings from the aspiring individual shall be offered to the LORD, and the priests shall cast salt upon them to bring out their flavor. They shall be offered as a burnt offering to the LORD as a symbol of their total devotion to the LORD. Seven days shall you prepare every day a goat for a sin offering: they shall also prepare a young bullock, and a ram out of the flock, without blemish. They shall purge the altar for seven days and purify it and they shall consecrate themselves in the same manner. When these days are expired, it shall be, that upon the eighth day, and so forward, the priests shall make your burnt offerings upon the altar, and your peace offerings; and I will accept you, says the Lord GOD.

CHAPTER 44

1 Then he brought me back the way of the gate of the outward sanctuary which looketh toward the east; and it was shut.
2 Then said the LORD unto me; This gate shall be shut, it shall not be opened, and no man shall enter in by it; because the LORD, the God of Israel, hath entered in by it, therefore it shall be shut.
3 It is for the prince; the prince, he shall sit in it to eat bread before the LORD; he shall enter by the way of the porch of that gate, and shall go out by the way of the same.
4 Then brought he me the way of the north gate before the house: and I looked, and, behold, the glory of the LORD filled the house of the LORD: and I fell upon my face.

Then the man brought Ezekiel back to the way of the gate of the outward sanctuary which looks toward the east, the place from which the future comes; and that gate was shut. The LORD said to Ezekiel that the gate to the future shall not be opened, and no man shall enter into it. The Lord GOD of Israel enters into this gate, and therefore it shall remain shut. This gate is for the prince, the offspring of the king. The prince can sit in the east gate, and eat bread, before the Lord GOD. The prince shall enter by way of the porch that leads to the gate and he shall go out by the way of the same gate. The LORD brought Ezekiel by the way of the north gate before the house, the gate in which the spirit is being reflected by the man who has led Ezekiel. Ezekiel has looked and seen the glory of the LORD fill the house of the LORD through the man who had led Ezekiel. Ezekiel fell upon his face in reverence to the man who was in the position of the prince.

5 And the LORD said unto me, Son of man, mark well, and behold with thine eyes, and hear with thine ears all that I say unto thee concerning all the ordinances of the house of the LORD, and all the laws thereof; and mark well the entering in of the house, with every going forth of the sanctuary.
6 And thou shalt say to the rebellious, even to the house of Israel, Thus saith the Lord GOD; O ye house of Israel, let it suffice you of all your abominations,
7 In that ye have brought into my sanctuary strangers, uncircumcised in heart, and uncircumcised in flesh, to be in my sanctuary, to pollute it, even my house, when ye offer my bread, the fat and the blood, and they have broken my covenant because of all your abominations.
8 And ye have not kept the charge of mine holy things: but ye have set keepers of my charge in my sanctuary for yourselves.

The LORD said to Ezekiel, Son of man, mark well and behold with your eyes, and hear with your ears all that I say to you concerning the ordinances of the house of the LORD, the temple and all its laws. Mark well the entering in and the going forth of the sanctuary. Ezekiel is to say to the rebellious, the people who have rebelled against the spirit of the LORD, including the house of Israel, to let it be enough of all the abominations that you have brought into my sanctuary—strangers, uncircumcised in heart and uncircumcised in flesh—to pollute the house of the LORD

The Testimony of the Major Prophets

by offering the bread, the fat and the blood while they have broken the covenant of the LORD by their abominable behavior. You have not kept charge of the LORD's holy things: you have put others in charge of my sanctuary.

9 Thus saith the Lord GOD; No stranger, uncircumcised in heart, nor uncircumcised in flesh, shall enter into my sanctuary, of any stranger that is among the children of Israel.
10 And the Levites that are gone away far from me, when Israel went astray, which went astray away from me after their idols; they shall even bear their iniquity.
11 Yet they shall be ministers in my sanctuary, having charge at the gates of the house, and ministering to the house: they shall slay the burnt offering and the sacrifice for the people, and they shall stand before them to minister unto them.
12 Because they ministered unto them before their idols, and caused the house of Israel to fall into iniquity; therefore have I lifted up mine hand against them, saith the Lord GOD, and they shall bear their iniquity.
13 And they shall not come near unto me, to do the office of a priest unto me, nor to come near to any of my holy things, in the most holy place: but they shall bear their shame, and their abominations which they have committed.
14 But I will make them keepers of the charge of the house, for all the service thereof, and for all that shall be done therein.

The Lord GOD declares that no stranger who is uncircumcised and unclean in heart and flesh— because they do not radiate the spirit of the LORD which will cause a circumcised heart and circumcised flesh as the distortions are cut away—enter into His sanctuary. The true children of Israel are those who keep the covenant of the LORD; those who do not keep the covenant are strangers. The Levites, who should have remained the priesthood, and went away after their idols, shall bear their iniquity.

Yet the Levites shall be ministers in the sanctuary, having charge at the gates of the house, and ministering to the house: they shall slay the burnt offering and the sacrifice for the people, and they shall stand before them to minister unto them. The Levites, who ministered to the idols, caused the house of Israel to fall into iniquity because there was no one in position to represent the spirit of the LORD; therefore, the LORD lifted up His hand against them. While they are worshipping the idols of the material environment, they shall not come near to do the office of a priest unto the LORD, nor come near any holy things in the most holy place: but they shall bear their shame, and their abominations which they have committed. But the LORD's spirit will make them keepers of the charge of the house, for all the service thereof, and for all that shall be done.

15 But the priests the Levites, the sons of Zadok, that kept the charge of my sanctuary when the children of Israel went astray from me, they shall come near to me to minister unto me, and they shall stand before me to offer unto me the fat and the blood, saith the Lord GOD:
16 They shall enter into my sanctuary, and they shall come near to my table, to minister unto me, and they shall keep my charge.

But there were priests of the Levites, the sons of Zadok, who did keep charge of the sanctuary when the children of Israel went astray from the spirit of the LORD and began to worship the material idols of the environment. Zadok could trace his Levitical heritage back to Aaron, brother of Moses. The priests of Zadok understood that the spirit of the LORD must be represented on earth through a priesthood which is dedicated to the spirit of the LORD and who are committed to minister to the LORD. They shall keep the charge, the commandment of the LORD.

17 And it shall come to pass, that when they enter in at the gates of the inner court, they shall be clothed with linen garments; and no wool shall come upon them, whiles they minister in the gates of the inner court, and within.
18 They shall have linen bonnets upon their heads, and shall have linen breeches upon their loins; they shall not gird themselves with any thing that causeth sweat.
19 And when they go forth into the outer court, even into the outer court to the people, they shall put off their garments wherein they ministered, and lay them in the holy chambers, and they shall put on other garments; and they shall not sanctify the people with their garments.
20 Neither shall they shave their heads, nor suffer their locks to grow long; they shall only poll their heads.

The Symbolic Version of Ezekiel

And it shall come to pass that the priests of Zadok will clothe themselves with linen, the symbol of cleanliness and godliness, when they enter into the gates of the inner court as they minister to the LORD. The linen bonnets on their heads and the linen breeches symbolized a total covering of cleanliness in the service of the spirit of the LORD. They shall not gird themselves with anything, any emotional connection with the material idols of the environment, which will cause sweat. Linen is the symbol of spiritual covering in the presence and service of the LORD. When the priests go forth into the outer court, to the people, they shall put off the garments in which they ministered and they shall put on other garments, similar to the garments of the people to whom they will represent the spirit of the LORD at the level where the people are in their fallen state. They shall not shave their heads, nor cause their hair to grow long, to appear different from the people and unacceptable to them.

21 Neither shall any priest drink wine, when they enter into the inner court.
22 Neither shall they take for their wives a widow, nor her that is put away: but they shall take maidens of the seed of the house of Israel, or a widow that had a priest before.
23 And they shall teach my people the difference between the holy and profane, and cause them to discern between the unclean and the clean.
24 And in controversy they shall stand in judgment; and they shall judge it according to my judgments: and they shall keep my laws and my statutes in all mine assemblies; and they shall hallow my sabbaths.
25 And they shall come at no dead person to defile themselves: but for father, or for mother, or for son, or for daughter, for brother, or for sister that hath had no husband, they may defile themselves.
26 And after he is cleansed, they shall reckon unto him seven days.

A priest in service to the LORD on earth shall not drink any wine to affect his consciousness when he enters into the inner court to receive the spirit of the LORD. They shall not take for their wives a widow, a grieving woman, which is the symbol of the bereaved human self, nor a woman who has been put away for her sinfulness. They shall take maidens of the seed of Israel, human containers of body, mind and heart, which are willing to receive the spirit of the LORD, or a woman, who had been married to a priest before. The priest has reference to the spiritual nature of man and the woman has reference to the material nature of man, male or female.

The priesthood of the LORD shall teach the people the difference between the holy and the profane, the holy which reveals the sprit of the LORD on earth and the profane which reveals a distortion of the spirit of the LORD through human form which can be discerned as clean or an unclean behavior. The clean and the unclean, the holy and the profane, shall stand in judgment before the LORD and the priests can discern the condition of the people according to the judgments of the LORD's spirit moving through the consciousness and the forms of the people. the LORD's people shall keep the laws and the statutes everywhere and honor the sabbaths of the LORD which is every day.

And the people who love the LORD shall blame no dead person to defile themselves because blame defiles each person who blames. The wrong behavior of the father, or for mother, for son or for daughter, brother, or for sister that has had no husband, defile themselves by their own behavior. And after the individual person is cleansed, they shall reckon with the cleansed person, the servant of the LORD, for the seven symbolic days that they must pass through until they too become servants of the LORD.

27 And in the day that he goeth into the sanctuary, unto the inner court, to minister in the sanctuary, he shall offer his sin offering, saith the Lord GOD.
28 And it shall be unto them for an inheritance: I am their inheritance: and ye shall give them no possession in Israel: I am their possession.
29 They shall eat the meat offering, and the sin offering, and the trespass offering; and every dedicated thing in Israel shall be theirs.
30 And the first of all the firstfruits of all things, and every oblation of all, of every sort of your oblations, shall be the priest's: ye shall also give unto the priest the first of your dough, that he may cause the blessing to rest in thine house.
31 The priests shall not eat of any thing that is dead of itself, or torn, whether it be fowl or beast.

In the day that any sinful person goes into the sanctuary of the LORD within himself, to minister in the sanctuary, the person must offer his sin offering, to depart from his own sinful behaviors, says the Lord GOD. The offering to depart

The Testimony of the Major Prophets

from sin, to become holy and clean, is the inheritance from the LORD which comes from the LORD. The LORD is the inheritance of the people. A person shall give others no other possession in Israel: the LORD is their possession.

The people who are clothed in the spirit of the LORD shall eat, take into themselves to be aware of, the sinful actions of others symbolized by the meat offering which is acceptable and the sin offering and the trespass offering which are distortions of the true offering from the LORD; every dedicated thing in Israel shall be theirs. The first fruits of all things and every oblation of every sort shall be the priest's environment with which he must handle in the sprit of the LORD. Each person who desires to "find" the LORD must give to the priest the very best of their behavior, the first of your dough, that he may cause the blessing to rest in your house, the house of your being. The priest shall not eat of any thing, any behavior, that is dead of itself, that does not reveal the sprit of the LORD in expression through a person whether it be fowl or beast, the symbols of thoughts which fly through the air of the consciousness or physical deeds that do the work of thoughts. The spirit of the LORD moves through the fowl that fly through the air and the beasts of burden who move the earth. In like manner, the spirit of the LORD should also move through the thoughts and the deeds in the consciousness of man, men and women, in every generation so that the spirit shall take form on earth through man to bring the kingdom of the LORD on earth.

CHAPTER 45

1 Moreover, when ye shall divide by lot the land for inheritance, ye shall offer an oblation unto the LORD, an holy portion of the land: the length shall be the length of five and twenty thousand reeds, and the breadth shall be ten thousand. This shall be holy in all the borders thereof round about.

The design of the LORD's kingdom exists in the realm of the spirit that comes from the LORD. The design of the kingdom on earth must come through man who will build the spiritual kingdom using the spirit of the LORD. When man begins to build the LORD's kingdom as an inheritance for the LORD, man must use the LORD's spirit which is the offering to the LORD. All building must utilize the spirit of the LORD which is the holy portion of the land. The area of holy land to be built is described in Ezekiel's vision as a length of 25,000 reeds and a width of 10,000 reeds. A reed is equivalent to six cubits, which is approximately 120 inches or 10 feet. A length of 25,000 reeds would be 250,000 feet, or, approximately 50 miles. The width of 10,000 reeds would be 100,000 feet or approximately 20 miles. Symbolically a reed is greater and beyond the reach of a physical man: a cubit, is described as the length of the forearm, or 18 to 20 inches; a reed is 6 cubits or 6 times the length of the forearm symbolizing that the spiritual reach of man is greater than the physical reach of man.

This area of land shall be holy in all the borders of it which means that all the people who work within the borders of the holy land must be whole and holy people.

2 Of this there shall be for the sanctuary five hundred in length, with five hundred in breadth, square round about; and fifty cubits round about for the suburbs thereof.
3 And of this measure shalt thou measure the length of five and twenty thousand, and the breadth of ten thousand: and in it shall be the sanctuary and the most holy place.

Within the borders of the holy land, there shall be a sanctuary in the form of a square that is 500 cubits in length and breadth. There will be a perimeter around the holy square of 50 cubits in width. The sanctuary shall be within the area of 25,000 reeds in length and 10,000 reeds in width which is the area that contains the sanctuary and the most holy place within the sanctuary.

4 The holy portion of the land shall be for the priests the ministers of the sanctuary, which shall come near to minister unto the LORD: and it shall be a place for their houses, and an holy place for the sanctuary.
5 And the five and twenty thousand of length, and the ten thousand of breadth, shall also the Levites, the ministers of the house, have for themselves, for a possession for twenty chambers.
6 And ye shall appoint the possession of the city five thousand broad, and five and twenty thousand long, over against the oblation of the holy portion: it shall be for the whole house of Israel.

The Testimony of the Major Prophets

The holy portion of the spiritual kingdom that is to be built on earth on land that is to be occupied by the priests who are to be ministers of the sanctuary. These are the people who have come to minister to the LORD. The land is for their houses and for the sanctuary that reminds them of their purpose. This holy land, 25,000 reeds in length and 10,000 reeds in width, is to be occupied by the Levites who will dwell in the twenty chambers that they build on the land. The purpose of the Levites is to expand the holy place through their holy efforts and example. The Levites are to build the city described as 25,000 reeds in length and 5,000 reeds in width contiguous with the holy land upon which they dwell. This expansion shall be intended for the whole house of Israel.

7 And a portion shall be for the prince on the one side and on the other side of the oblation of the holy portion, and of the possession of the city, before the oblation of the holy portion, and before the possession of the city, from the west side westward, and from the east side eastward: and the length shall be over against one of the portions, from the west border unto the east border.
7 And a portion shall be for the prince on the one side and on the other side of the oblation of the holy portion, and of the possession of the city, before the oblation of the holy portion, and before the possession of the city, from the west side westward, and from the east side eastward: and the length shall be over against one of the portions, from the west border unto the east border.
8 In the land shall be his possession in Israel: and my princes shall no more oppress my people; and the rest of the land shall they give to the house of Israel according to their tribes.

A portion of this strip of land shall be for the prince on the one side, the side of the holy land, who shall offer the spirit of the LORD through themselves to the people on the other side who are not expressing the spirit of the LORD as their offering to the LORD. The land which should reveal the spirit of the LORD is to be expanded eastward from the east side and westward from the west side as the borders expand from east to west. The princes who represent their King, the LORD, shall no more oppress the LORD's people, who are all the people on earth. The expansion of the land that reveals the spirit of the LORD will take place through the house of Israel according to their twelve tribes who will use the spirit of the LORD in the building of the kingdom.

9 Thus saith the Lord GOD; Let it suffice you, O princes of Israel: remove violence and spoil, and execute judgment and justice, take away your exactions from my people, saith the Lord GOD.
10 Ye shall have just balances, and a just ephah, and a just bath.
11 The ephah and the bath shall be of one measure, that the bath may contain the tenth part of an homer, and the ephah the tenth part of an homer: the measure thereof shall be after the homer.
12 And the shekel shall be twenty gerahs: twenty shekels, five and twenty shekels, fifteen shekels, shall be your maneh.
13 This is the oblation that ye shall offer; the sixth part of an ephah of an homer of wheat, and ye shall give the sixth part of an ephah of an homer of barley:
14 Concerning the ordinance of oil, the bath of oil, ye shall offer the tenth part of a bath out of the cor, which is an homer of ten baths; for ten baths are an homer:
15 And one lamb out of the flock, out of two hundred, out of the fat pastures of Israel; for a meat offering, and for a burnt offering, and for peace offerings, to make reconciliation for them, saith the Lord GOD.

The Lord GOD advises His princes, the princes of Israel who shall return the earth to the LORD, to remove violence and spoil from their fallen natures and behaviors and execute judgment and justice that is inherent in the spirit of the LORD. The people are to give up their greed by which they have been extracting and stealing the wealth from the LORD's people by using false measures. The LORD's people must use just instruments of measure as they weigh and measure using accurate balances; and accurate ephahs, dry measures, and baths, which are liquid measures. The ephah and the bath shall be of one measure so that the bath may contain the tenth part of an homer, and the ephah the tenth part of an homer: the measure thereof shall be after the homer, which is about six bushels. And the shekel (approximately 2/5 ounce) shall be twenty gerahs: twenty shekels, five and twenty shekels, fifteen shekels, or 60 shekels, shall be your maneh, your rate of exchange, instead of the 50 shekels which was commonly used.

This is the offering and standard for fair trade that you shall offer; the sixth part of an ephah of an homer of wheat, and you shall give the sixth part of an ephah of an homer of barley:

Concerning the ordinance of oil, the bath of oil, you shall offer the tenth part of a bath out of the cor, which consists of one homer or ten baths; for ten baths are equivalent to an homer. One lamb out of the flock out of two hundred from out of the fat pastures of Israel are to be given as a meat offering, and for a burnt offering, and for peace offerings to make reconciliation for them, says the Lord GOD.

16 All the people of the land shall give this oblation for the prince in Israel.
17 And it shall be the prince's part to give burnt offerings, and meat offerings, and drink offerings, in the feasts, and in the new moons, and in the sabbaths, in all solemnities of the house of Israel: he shall prepare the sin offering, and the meat offering, and the burnt offering, and the peace offerings, to make reconciliation for the house of Israel.

All the people of the land who are outside the holy land and who desire to join in the spirit that is provided as the example for them to follow shall offer this oblation for the people who provide the representation of the prince of Israel in their example of living. It is the prince of Israel's responsibility to give the burnt offerings, meat offerings, and drink offerings in the feasts and Sabbaths of the house of Israel. Each prince of Israel must prepare his offering to make reconciliation to the children of Israel says the Lord GOD.

18 Thus saith the Lord GOD; In the first month, in the first day of the month, thou shalt take a young bullock without blemish, and cleanse the sanctuary:
19 And the priest shall take of the blood of the sin offering, and put it upon the posts of the house, and upon the four corners of the settle of the altar, and upon the posts of the gate of the inner court.
20 And so thou shalt do the seventh day of the month for every one that erreth, and for him that is simple: so shall ye reconcile the house.

The Lord GOD says that in the first day of the first month, each person who desires to enter into the house of Israel, the spiritual house of the LORD, must take a young bullock without blemish, the symbol of a person who desires to come to the LORD, and cleanse the sanctuary which is the holy place within one's self, and offer one's self to the priest, the representative of the LORD on earth. The priest will take the sin offering of the person's wrong behavior and take the blood of the sin offering and put it on the door posts of the house of Israel, and upon the four corners of the settle, the upper ledge, of the altar, and upon the gates of the inner court of the holy place that the person desires to enter to serve the LORD. The person shall do the seventh day, the holy day of the LORD, to let the spirit of the LORD flow through himself for every one that errs against him knowingly or for him that is simple and does not understand: This is the way that each person shall reconcile the house of the LORD in one's own experience.

21 In the first month, in the fourteenth day of the month, ye shall have the passover, a feast of seven days; unleavened bread shall be eaten.
22 And upon that day shall the prince prepare for himself and for all the people of the land a bullock for a sin offering.
23 And seven days of the feast he shall prepare a burnt offering to the LORD, seven bullocks and seven rams without blemish daily the seven days; and a kid of the goats daily for a sin offering.
24 And he shall prepare a meat offering of an ephah for a bullock, and an ephah for a ram, and an hin of oil for an ephah.

As this process of spiritual expression continues, then in the fourteenth day of the month, after several cycles of right behavior in letting the spirit of the LORD flow through one's experience, then the passover, the spirit of the LORD moving through, passing over, the human equipment shall occur. The unleavened bread of life from the LORD to the person shall be eaten, experienced, and the person will be filled, fulfilled, made whole. On that day, the prince shall prepare for himself and all the people of the land, a burnt offering of the bullock, the symbol of the fallen identity, for a sin offering, an offering that the person will not sin against the LORD. During the seven days of the feast, he shall prepare the burnt offering to the LORD, seven bullocks and seven rams without blemish for seven days which are symbols of an unblemished nature to replace the sinful human nature of man; the kid of goats daily for a sin offering are the small sins which come up from one's own experience in one's consciousness that will be replaced daily by a clean nature. The offering of one's self in service to the LORD shall replace the importance of material measures and treasures that tarnish man and keep him in the fallen state.

The Testimony of the Major Prophets

25 In the seventh month, in the fifteenth day of the month, shall he do the like in the feast of the seven days, according to the sin offering, according to the burnt offering, and according to the meat offering, and according to the oil.

In the seventh month the symbol of the completed cycle, in the fifteenth day of the month, as spiritual behavior becomes a way of life, then the person shall do the feast of the seven days every day as he lets the sin offering from his past pass away as they are burned in the spirit of the LORD according to the ability to allow his flesh reveal the spirit because of his love, his oil, for the spirit of the LORD.

CHAPTER 46

1 Thus saith the Lord GOD; The gate of the inner court that looketh toward the east shall be shut the six working days; but on the sabbath it shall be opened, and in the day of the new moon it shall be opened.
2 And the prince shall enter by the way of the porch of that gate without, and shall stand by the post of the gate, and the priests shall prepare his burnt offering and his peace offerings, and he shall worship at the threshold of the gate: then he shall go forth; but the gate shall not be shut until the evening.
3 Likewise the people of the land shall worship at the door of this gate before the LORD in the sabbaths and in the new moons.

The Lord GOD speaking through the prophet, Ezekiel, says that the gate of the inner court facing the east, the symbol of the future, shall be shut for the six working days. The six days of labor during which time the gate is shut is the process by which man in the fallen state is working for himself and not for the spirit of the LORD. But on the Sabbath day and the day of the new moon, the new reflection of the human consciousness is the response to the radiation from the LORD, and the east gate shall be opened. The new moon is the reflection of the sun as the darkness of the sky is lightened and brightened by the new moon as it changes to its pattern of fullness. In like manner, the consciousness of the spirit of the LORD within man increases as the person reflects the radiation from the spirit of the LORD. This is due to the fact that there is understanding that what is generated in human consciousness shall produce corresponding material forms which reveal the thought patterns.

The prince, the spiritual son of the King, shall enter by way of the porch of that east gate and he shall stand by the post of the gate as he enters into the realm of the world of form from the world of the spirit. In true identity, every person is a spiritual prince, a Son of the King, who has entered the world of form. The priests shall prepare his burnt offering and his peace offerings for distribution into the world of forms and materiality. The prince shall worship at the threshold of the gate: then he shall go forth; but the gate shall not be shut until evening, the end of the day of that person, the end of life in form on earth. The gate between the realm of spirit to the realm of form shall not be shut until the evening. Just as the priests received the message from the prince of the spirit of the king, likewise the people of the land shall worship at the door of this gate before the Sabbaths and follow the instruction of the priests as the priests were instructed at the door of this gate by the prince, who is the representative of the king.

4 And the burnt offering that the prince shall offer unto the LORD in the sabbath day shall be six lambs without blemish, and a ram without blemish.
5 And the meat offering shall be an ephah for a ram, and the meat offering for the lambs as he shall be able to give, and an hin of oil to an ephah.
6 And in the day of the new moon it shall be a young bullock without blemish, and six lambs, and a ram: they shall be without blemish.
7 And he shall prepare a meat offering, an ephah for a bullock, and an ephah for a ram, and for the lambs according as his hand shall attain unto, and an hin of oil to an ephah.

The Testimony of the Major Prophets

8 And when the prince shall enter, he shall go in by the way of the porch of that gate, and he shall go forth by the way thereof.

The burnt offering that the prince shall offer to the LORD in the Sabbath day, which is the day of the LORD, shall be six lambs without blemish and a ram without blemish to symbolize the perfection that is available in spirit. The ram is the symbol for the positive expression of the spirit of the LORD which is differentiated into the aspects of the spirit of the LORD symbolized by the lambs which came from the spirit. And the meat offering shall be an ephah for a ram, and the meat offering for the lambs as he shall be able to give, and an hin of oil to an ephah. In symbolic language, this exchange means that what is offered to the LORD in material form without blemish is returned by the LORD with an increase in of spirit, an increase of spiritual substance. And in the day of the new moon, it shall be a young bullock without blemish, and six lambs, and a ram: they shall be without blemish. A person who seeks the spirit of the LORD, symbolized by the unblemished ram and the unblemished lambs, must come as an unblemished bullock which symbolizes a person with a clean mind and heart.

And he, the person who desires to receive the blessing of the LORD, shall prepare a meat offering, an offering of his own flesh in service to the LORD, and he shall receive an ephah of the LORD's spiritual substance for a bullock, and an ephah of spiritual substance for a ram; the same measure to receive the spirit of the LORD which is being sent by the LORD. The lambs, the symbols of the radiation from the LORD, shall be received according to the ability and capacity that his hand of control can contain. A hin of oil, the symbol of the love from the LORD, which is equal to —— is available for the ephah provided by man. The prince, the son and heir of the King, enters and goes forth into the world of form from the world of spirit by way of the gate of the porch which is the future from the material point of view.

9 But when the people of the land shall come before the LORD in the solemn feasts, he that entereth in by the way of the north gate to worship shall go out by the way of the south gate; and he that entereth by the way of the south gate shall go forth by the way of the north gate: he shall not return by the way of the gate whereby he came in, but shall go forth over against it.
10 And the prince in the midst of them, when they go in, shall go in; and when they go forth, shall go forth.
11 And in the feasts and in the solemnities the meat offering shall be an ephah to a bullock, and ephah to a ram, and to the lambs as he is able to give, and an hin of oil to an ephah.

When the people of the land shall come before the LORD in the solemn feasts, they must do so in the present moment. North is the symbol of the direction which receives the radiation from the sun in the present moment; south is the direction in the present moment which is the source of the radiation from the sun. The person that enters in by the way of the north gate to worship shall go out by the way of the south gate. In symbolic language, the person who observes the radiation of spirit in another enters the north gate of the present moment and he will depart a different way, the way of the south gate, as he becomes a source of the radiation which he has observed. He that enters by the way of the south gate of the present moment because he is radiating the spirit of the LORD through his capacities shall go forth by the way of the north gate as he becomes a point of orientation for others to observe: he shall not return by the way of the gate whereby he came in, but shall go forth over against it. They will depart as changed people as they experience the spirit of the prince.

And the spirit of the prince shall be in the midst of them; when they go in, the prince shall go in; and when they go forth, the prince shall go forth because the spiritual prince is with them always as they allow his spirit to move through them so that the spirit and the form become one. And in the feasts and in the solemnities, which are the experience with the spirit of the prince, the meat offering shall be an ephah of the spirit to a bullock of the person's clean offering, and ephah to a ram which symbolizes the spirit of the LORD, and to the lambs, which symbolize the offspring of the spirit of the LORD through the body of the person as he is able to give, and an hin of oil, the flow of love from the LORD to an ephah, that the person is able to receive. A hin is approximately 1½ gallons; an ephah is approximately 10 gallons.

12 Now when the prince shall prepare a voluntary burnt offering or peace offerings voluntarily unto the LORD, one shall then open him the gate that looketh toward the east, and he shall prepare his burnt offering and his peace offerings, as he did on the sabbath day: then he shall go forth; and after his going forth one shall shut the gate.

13 Thou shalt daily prepare a burnt offering unto the LORD of a lamb of the first year without blemish: thou shalt prepare it every morning.
14 And thou shalt prepare a meat offering for it every morning, the sixth part of an ephah, and the third part of an hin of oil, to temper with the fine flour; a meat offering continually by a perpetual ordinance unto the LORD.
15 Thus shall they prepare the lamb, and the meat offering, and the oil, every morning for a continual burnt offering.

Now when the prince, the son of the king, prepares a burnt offering of love through himself or peace offerings to the LORD, one who is in agreement with the prince shall then open the gate that looks toward the east, the direction from which the LORD enters into the earth. The person in agreement with the prince shall prepare his burnt offering and his own specific peace offerings, as he did on the sabbath day: then, the person shall go forth in the spirit of the LORD. After he goes forth, the gate is shut which symbolizes the spirit is with him and he has become a co-creator and representative with the LORD on earth. The person has a divine commission to represent, to re-present, the spirit of the LORD which he has experienced.

The person shall, daily, prepare a burnt offering unto the LORD of a lamb of the first year without blemish; and he shall prepare it, the spirit of the LORD moving through him into the world, every morning as symbolized by the sixth part of an ephah, and the third part of an hin of oil, to temper with the fine flour; a meat offering continually by a perpetual ordinance unto the LORD. In this manner, a person shall prepare the lamb of the LORD's spirit through the meat offering of his own flesh, and the oil of the LORD's love, shall be seen every morning for a continual burnt offering for others to observe on earth. The goal for each person is to let the oil of the spirit of the LORD burn in the flesh, the meat, of the servant of the LORD.

16 Thus saith the Lord GOD; If the prince give a gift unto any of his sons, the inheritance thereof shall be his sons'; it shall be their possession by inheritance.
17 But if he give a gift of his inheritance to one of his servants, then it shall be his to the year of liberty; after it shall return to the prince: but his inheritance shall be his sons' for them.
18 Moreover the prince shall not take of the people's inheritance by oppression, to thrust them out of their possession; but he shall give his sons inheritance out of his own possession: that my people be not scattered every man from his possession.
19 After he brought me through the entry, which was at the side of the gate, into the holy chambers of the priests, which looked toward the north: and, behold, there was a place on the two sides westward.

The word of the Lord GOD is that if the prince, the son of the king on earth, shall give a gift of his spirit to any of his sons, his spiritual offspring, then the inheritance which the prince received from the king, shall be bequeathed to his sons, the sons of the prince. It shall be their possession by inheritance. But if the prince gives the gift of the spirit of the LORD to one of his servants, then the gift of spirit shall bless the servant until the year of his liberty; afterward, after the spirit of the prince has blessed the servant and the servant has not generated the spirit of the LORD for and through himself, then the spirit of the LORD shall return to the prince. But the person who receives the inheritance of the prince, and becomes his spiritual son, shall have the spirit of the prince by inheritance.

Moreover, the prince shall not take the people's inheritance of the spirit of the LORD away from them by oppression to thrust them out of their possession. It is the responsibility of the prince to provide the LORD's spirit to his sons and the LORD's spirit is in the possession of the prince. The prince shall give his sons the inheritance of the LORD so that the LORD's people will not be scattered. After the person understood the function of a son of the prince, he brought me through the entry, which was at the side of the gate, into the holy chambers of the priests, which looked toward the north: and, behold, there was a place on the two sides westward where the person could observe the past, his own past, and the sinful behaviors which have prevented the individual from knowing the spirit of the LORD.

20 Then said he unto me, This is the place where the priests shall boil the trespass offering and the sin offering, where they shall bake the meat offering; that they bear them not out into the outer court, to sanctify the people.

The Lord GOD said to Ezekiel that this is the place where the priests shall boil the trespass offering and the sin offering and bake the meat offering. The person realized that in this position he or she is a priest ordained by the LORD. The place where the past behavior can be reviewed is the place where the trespass offering, the sinful behavior, shall be

The Testimony of the Major Prophets

seen as the path which led the person to where he presently is as a priest of the spirit of the LORD. The past experience, whatever it was, is to be boiled away and seen without guilt and sadness. This place is also the place where the meat offering of what the person will do to serve the spirit of the LORD is to be baked to offer to the LORD's people. The purpose of this step is to allow the sins to be "boiled away" and to prevent the past sins from being taken into the outer court to be passed on to others. The people in the fallen state are to be sanctified by the truth of the LORD's spirit and not the sins of the past from human nature. People in the fallen state love to talk about their sins; people in the ascended state love to reveal the LORD's spirit.

21 Then he brought me forth into the outer court, and caused me to pass by the four corners of the court; and, behold, in every corner of the court there was a court.
22 In the four corners of the court there were courts joined of forty cubits long and thirty broad: these four corners were of one measure.
23 And there was a row of building round about in them, round about them four, and it was made with boiling places under the rows round about.
24 Then said he unto me, These are the places of them that boil, where the ministers of the house shall boil the sacrifice of the people.

Then the Lord GOD brought me forth into the outer court, and caused me to pass by the four corners of the court that were the limits of his own state of consciousness; and, behold, in every corner of the court there was a court that was the area of another person's consciousness. In the four corners of the court there were courts joined of forty cubits long and thirty broad: these four corners were of one measure. The one measure was that these courts were equal in measure and that they were the courts that contain the spirit and the consciousness of the LORD.

And there was a row of building round about in them, round about them four, and these buildings contained the human, sinful, experiences of man in the fallen state. Each building was made with boiling places under the rows round about. Then said the LORD unto me, These are the places of them that boil, where the ministers of the house shall boil the sacrifice of the people, the sins that people are willing to relinquish as offerings to the LORD.

CHAPTER 47

1 Afterward he brought me again unto the door of the house; and, behold, waters issued out from under the threshold of the house eastward: for the forefront of the house stood toward the east, and the waters came down from under from the right side of the house, at the south side of the altar.
2 Then brought he me out of the way of the gate northward, and led me about the way without unto the outer gate by the way that looketh eastward; and, behold, there ran out waters on the right side.
3 And when the man that had the line in his hand went forth eastward, he measured a thousand cubits, and he brought me through the waters; the waters were to the ancles.
4 Again he measured a thousand, and brought me through the waters; the waters were to the knees. Again he measured a thousand, and brought me through; the waters were to the loins.
5 Afterward he measured a thousand; and it was a river that I could not pass over: for the waters were risen, waters to swim in, a river that could not be passed over.

Afterward, the spiritual man who has served as guide and mentor to Ezekiel brought him to the door of the house which symbolized the house of his own being; and, behold the waters of the truth of being issued out from under the threshold eastward, into the future: for the front of the house faced east, the direction of the future from where the truth of being originates and flows into the present. The waters came down from under the right side, the clean side of the house of one's being, at the south side of the altar which is the symbol of the present time.

Then the spiritual man brought Ezekiel out of the way of the gate northward, the symbol of the present time in earthly forms, and led Ezekiel to the way out to the outer gate by the way that looks eastward, the way of the future; and behold, there ran out waters of the truth of being on the right side. When the spiritual man that had the line in his hand that measured the way in which they were going went eastward into the future, he measured a thousand cubits, and he brought Ezekiel through the waters which were to his ankles. As they proceeded, the spiritual man measured another thousand cubits and brought him through waters which were up to his knees. Again the spiritual man measured a thousand cubits and brought Ezekiel through waters which were to his loins. Afterward, he measured a thousand; and it was a river that Ezekiel could not pass over because the waters were risen, waters to swim in, a river that could not be passed over with the feet touching the ground. It is obvious that the more that Ezekiel follows the spiritual man, the more Ezekiel is aware that he is more deeply immersed in the river of spirit. Ezekiel is in the river of water, which is the material symbol for the river of the spirit of truth, with the spiritual man who has been his guide.

6 And he said unto me, Son of man, hast thou seen this? Then he brought me, and caused me to return to the brink of the river.
7 Now when I had returned, behold, at the bank of the river were very many trees on the one side and on the other.
8 Then said he unto me, These waters issue out toward the east country, and go down into the desert, and go into the sea: which being brought forth into the sea, the waters shall be healed.

The Testimony of the Major Prophets

The spiritual man said to Ezekiel, Son of man, have you seen this? have you seen that the more you proceed into the waters of being, the waters which symbolize the flow of the spirit, the deeper it gets? Then the spiritual man caused Ezekiel to return to the brink of the river. Ezekiel is consciously aware that he is a spiritual being who has returned to stand on the brink of the river where he can observe the flow of the river of spirit from the LORD which is every where and in every thing.

Now when Ezekiel had returned, behold, at the bank of the river were very many trees on the one side and on the other. He was not alone and not the only person on the bank of the river. The trees symbolize people who are aware of the truth of spirit as it flows through human beings. Then the spiritual man told Ezekiel that these waters, that represent the truth of the spirit of life, the truth of Being, issue out toward the east country, and go down into the desert of the world, which is barren and desolate due to the lack of water and life. The waters in the sea symbolizes mankind in the fallen state: As the living waters of the LORD from on high, which symbolize the restored, ascended people, are brought forth into the sea, the waters of the sea that symbolize mankind in the fallen state shall be healed by the waters from on high.

9 And it shall come to pass, that every thing that liveth, which moveth, whithersoever the rivers shall come, shall live: and there shall be a very great multitude of fish, because these waters shall come thither: for they shall be healed; and every thing shall live whither the river cometh.

The spiritual man tells Ezekiel that it shall come to pass, that everything that lives, which moves, contains the spirit of the truth of life from wherever the rivers shall come, shall live and there shall be a very great multitude of fish, the symbols of people, who swim in the waters of the LORD, because the waters of truth shall come there in the fallen state. They shall be healed; and everything shall live where the river of the LORD comes through people who carry the spirit of the LORD.

10 And it shall come to pass, that the fishers shall stand upon it from Engedi even unto Eneglaim; they shall be a place to spread forth nets; their fish shall be according to their kinds, as the fish of the great sea, exceeding many.
11 But the miry places thereof and the marshes thereof shall not be healed; they shall be given to salt.
12 And by the river upon the bank thereof, on this side and on that side, shall grow all trees for meat, whose leaf shall not fade, neither shall the fruit thereof be consumed: it shall bring forth new fruit according to his months, because their waters they issued out of the sanctuary: and the fruit thereof shall be for meat, and the leaf thereof for medicine.

And it shall come to pass, that the fishers, the fishers who are the spiritual guides that carry the spirit of the LORD and search to aid fallen men, shall stand upon the bank of the river from Engedi even unto Eneglaim, which are cities located on the Dead Sea; they, the spiritually-aware people who stand on the banks, shall be a place to spread forth nets to capture the fish, the fallen people who do not know the LORD; the fish that they catch, the fallen human beings that they save, shall be according to their kinds, as the fish of the great sea, exceeding many. But the miry places thereof and the marshes where the fish hide to escape the nets and they who resist capture shall not be healed; they shall be given to salt. There will be those "fish", people, who will be in places that are difficult to catch. They shall be given to salt, return to the salt of the sea as humans return to the dust of the ground.

And the people who dwell on the bank of the river, on this side and on that side, shall grow all trees for meat, whose leaf shall not fade, neither shall the fruit thereof be consumed: it shall bring forth new fruit according to his months, because their waters, the truth of their beings, issued out of the sanctuary of the holy place: and the fruit thereof shall be for meat to the people of the fallen state, and the leaf thereof shall be used for medicine to heal the nations

13 Thus saith the Lord GOD; This shall be the border, whereby ye shall inherit the land according to the twelve tribes of Israel: Joseph shall have two portions.
14 And ye shall inherit it, one as well as another: concerning the which I lifted up mine hand to give it unto your fathers: and this land shall fall unto you for inheritance.
15 And this shall be the border of the land toward the north side, from the great sea, the way of Hethlon, as men go to Zedad;

16 Hamath, Berothah, Sibraim, which is between the border of Damascus and the border of Hamath; Hazar-hatticon, which is by the coast of Hauran.
17 And the border from the sea shall be Hazar-enan, the border of Damascus, and the north northward, and the border of Hamath. And this is the north side.
18 And the east side ye shall measure from Hauran, and from Damascus, and from Gilead, and from the land of Israel by Jordan, from the border unto the east sea. And this is the east side.
19 And the south side southward, from Tamar even to the waters of strife in Kadesh, the river to the great sea. And this is the south side southward.
20 The west side also shall be the great sea from the border, till a man come over against Hamath. This is the west side.
21 So shall ye divide this land unto you according to the tribes of Israel.

The Lord GOD has said; This shall be the border whereby you shall inherit the land according to the twelve tribes of Israel. The expansion of the divine design of the spirit of the LORD moving through man was to be accomplished through the twelve sons of Jacob who became Israel, the spiritually enlightened man. According to the blessing from Israel, Joseph was to have two portions for his two sons. The spiritual children of Israel shall inherit the land of the spirit as the Lord GOD has lifted up his hand to give it to the fathers of the children of Israel as an inheritance. The spiritual inheritance must be made manifest in the physical land that is occupied by the children wherever they are. At that time, the border of the land toward the north, east and south ranged from the great sea, the Mediterranean, to the land that approximates the borders at the time of David and Solomon. This land was to be divided and occupied according to the tribes of Israel as they expressed the spirit of the LORD in their living. The problem, of course, was that the people did not express the spirit of the LORD in their living of life.

22 And it shall come to pass, that ye shall divide it by lot for an inheritance unto you, and to the strangers that sojourn among you, which shall beget children among you: and they shall be unto you as born in the country among the children of Israel; they shall have inheritance with you among the tribes of Israel.
23 And it shall come to pass, that in what tribe the stranger sojourneth, there shall ye give him his inheritance, saith the Lord GOD.

If the people do become the spiritual representatives of the LORD by becoming the spiritual children of Israel, then it shall come to pass that they shall divide the land as an inheritance for themselves and the strangers who sojourn among them who will beget spiritual children among themselves. The offspring among the children of Israel and the strangers shall be as though they were born in the country among the children of Israel. They shall have the inheritance from the LORD with you among the tribes of Israel.

And it shall come to pass, that in whatever tribe the stranger lives, there shall you give them their inheritance says the Lord GOD. It should be obvious that the inheritance from the LORD is available to all of His children, but the nucleus to begin the expansion must put in an appearance through the twelve tribes of Israel. The twelve tribes are to reveal the same spirit that was received and expressed by their father, Israel. the spirit of GOD must be magnified on earth.

The sons of Jacob were not revealing the spirit exemplified by their father, Israel, who called attention to the fallen nature of his sons at the time of his death. (See, *The Symbolic Version of Genesis.*) The descendants of Israel are alive at the time of Ezekiel. The twelve tribes and the strangers who sojourn on earth with them can accept the spirit of the LORD and inherit the land which the LORD will give them.

CHAPTER 48

1 Now these are the names of the tribes. From the north end to the coast of the way of Hethlon, as one goeth to Hamath, Hazar-enan, the border of Damascus northward, to the coast of Hamath; for these are his sides east and west; a portion for Dan.
2 And by the border of Dan, from the east side unto the west side, a portion for Asher.
3 And by the border of Asher, from the east side even unto the west side, a portion for Naphtali.
4 And by the border of Naphtali, from the east side unto the west side, a portion for Manasseh.
5 And by the border of Manasseh, from the east side unto the west side, a portion for Ephraim.
6 And by the border of Ephraim, from the east side even unto the west side, a portion for Reuben.
7 And by the border of Reuben, from the east side unto the west side, a portion for Judah.
8 And by the border of Judah, from the east side unto the west side, shall be the offering which ye shall offer of five and twenty thousand reeds in breadth, and in length as one of the other parts, from the east side unto the west side: and the sanctuary shall be in the midst of it.

Ezekiel lists the names of the leaders of the tribes to the north who have the responsibility for the children of Israel. The land runs from east side to the west side which symbolizes the future connected to the past. The borders of the land are connected to each other illustrating that the people in the lands must live together in the brotherhood. The brotherhood is only possible because all the brothers are the sons of the same father, Israel, the focus of spirit. The brothers who have the responsibility for the land to the north are Dan, Asher, Naphtali, Manesseh, Ephraim, Reuben and Judah. A portion of land bordering Judah has special conditions attached to it. Its length from east to west shall equal the tribal portions. A parcel of land 25,000 reeds in length and width shall be an offering, and a sanctuary shall be in the midst of it.

9 The oblation that ye shall offer unto the LORD shall be of five and twenty thousand in length, and of ten thousand in breadth.
10 And for them, even for the priests, shall be this holy oblation; toward the north five and twenty thousand in length, and toward the west ten thousand in breadth, and toward the east ten thousand in breadth, and toward the south five and twenty thousand in length: and the sanctuary of the LORD shall be in the midst thereof.
11 It shall be for the priests that are sanctified of the sons of Zadok; which have kept my charge, which went not astray when the children of Israel went astray, as the Levites went astray.
12 And this oblation of the land that is offered shall be unto them a thing most holy by the border of the Levites.

The offering to the LORD shall be 25,000 reeds in length and 10,000 reeds in breadth: this area is for the priests. It shall be 25,000 reeds long on the north side, 10,000 reeds wide on the west side, 10,000 reeds wide on the east side, and 25,000 reeds long on the south side. In the center of it will be the sanctuary of the LORD. This shall be for the priests of the sons of Zadok who have kept the charge, the commandments and the responsibility from the LORD by not going astray, when the children of Israel went astray from the spirit of the LORD and the Levites went astray. This offering

The Symbolic Version of Ezekiel

of land shall be to them as a land most holy on the border of the Levites, who were the tribe that had the responsibility to serve the LORD and, as a tribe, they did not do so. A segment of the tribe, the sons of Zadok, kept the charge from the LORD and they were honored for their faithfulness. The Levites were positioned next to the priesthood to remind them of their failure and with the opportunity to serve the LORD in close proximity to the priesthood.

13 And over against the border of the priests the Levites shall have five and twenty thousand in length, and ten thousand in breadth: all the length shall be five and twenty thousand, and the breadth ten thousand.
14 And they shall not sell of it, neither exchange, nor alienate the firstfruits of the land: for it is holy unto the LORD.

Adjacent to the border of the land of the priests, the Levites had a portion of land 25,000 reeds in length and 10,000 reeds in width. The instruction for them was they should not sell this land, exchange it nor alienate the first fruits of the land because it is holy to the LORD. What occurs in the land is holy to the LORD because the power of the LORD is used to produce what is happening and transpiring even though the people are distorting the way of the LORD. The earth and its inhabitants still belong to the LORD. The Levites must live in proximity to the priesthood and not move away to forget their disobedience. The land is holy to the LORD and the Levites will see the example of the priesthood in action and learn to serve the spirit of the LORD where they are. The tribe of the Levites will be used to remind the children of Israel that there is a choice of a holy place and a choice of a profane place that can come forth on earth through man from the spirit of the LORD.

15 And the five thousand, that are left in the breadth over against the five and twenty thousand, shall be a profane place for the city, for dwelling, and for suburbs: and the city shall be in the midst thereof.
16 And these shall be the measures thereof; the north side four thousand and five hundred, and the south side four thousand and five hundred, and on the east side four thousand and five hundred, and the west side four thousand and five hundred.
17 And the suburbs of the city shall be toward the north two hundred and fifty, and toward the south two hundred and fifty, and toward the east two hundred and fifty, and toward the west two hundred and fifty.
18 And the residue in length over against the oblation of the holy portion shall be ten thousand eastward, and ten thousand westward: and it shall be over against the oblation of the holy portion; and the increase thereof shall be for food unto them that serve the city.

The portion of the land occupied by the Levites, which is 25,000 reeds in length and 5,000 reeds in width, shall be a profane place for the city, for the dwelling and for suburbs of those who profane the spirit of the LORD. The city of those who profane the LORD shall be in the midst of the tribe of Levites who should carry the responsibility for serving the LORD on earth, and who do not. This land is half the total portion of the land of the Levites. It symbolizes the human half and not the divine half. Human nature is profane; the divine nature from the LORD is not profane.

The profane portion of 5,000 reeds of the city is divided into a square of land which is 4,500 reeds on each side: equal measures on the north and south which symbolize the expressions of the people in the present time whether those expressions are original with the person or a reflection of the behavior of the fallen leaders; and the east and west which symbolize the future and the past expressions of the inhabitants. The suburbs of the city, which symbolize the overflow or the outflow of the people in the profane city, shall be 250 reeds on each side of the city in each direction to complete the 5,000 reeds of the land of the Levites (4500 plus 250 plus 250.) The suburbs of the city symbolize new land that is to be inhabited and cultivated as a new beginning is made when one leaves the ways of the old city of the fallen state.

19 And they that serve the city shall serve it out of all the tribes of Israel.
20 All the oblation shall be five and twenty thousand by five and twenty thousand: ye shall offer the holy oblation foursquare, with the possession of the city.
21 And the residue shall be for the prince, on the one side and on the other of the holy oblation, and of the possession of the city, over against the five and twenty thousand of the oblation toward the east border, and westward over against the five and twenty thousand toward the west border, over against the portions for the prince: and it shall be the holy oblation; and the sanctuary of the house shall be in the midst thereof.

The Testimony of the Major Prophets

The fallen state of the children of Israel is not limited to the tribe of the Levites. The fallen state that is illustrated by the profane city is expressed by the people is from of all the tribes of Israel. The offering of the priesthood and the Levites taken together shall be foursquare, 25,000 reeds in length and 25,000 reeds in width. The people who inhabit this land shall offer the holy expression from the LORD through themselves into the environment in order for the LORD to possess the city, in order for the city to be a holy city as holiness comes through the people so that the land will be holy unto the LORD, who is the King.

The residue of the land which remains on both sides of the area formed by the sacred portion and the city property shall be for the prince. It will extend eastward from the 25,000 reeds of the sacred portion to the eastern border, and westward from the 25,000 reeds to the western border. Both of these portions shall belong to the prince and the sacred portion with the temple sanctuary shall be in the midst of them.

22 Moreover from the possession of the Levites, and from the possession of the city, being in the midst of that which is the prince's, between the border of Judah and the border of Benjamin, shall be for the prince.
23 As for the rest of the tribes, from the east side unto the west side, Benjamin shall have a portion.
24 And by the border of Benjamin, from the east side unto the west side, Simeon shall have a portion.
25 And by the border of Simeon, from the east side unto the west side, Issachar a portion.
26 And by the border of Issachar, from the east side unto the west side, Zebulun a portion.
27 And by the border of Zebulun, from the east side unto the west side, Gad a portion.
28 And by the border of Gad, at the south side southward, the border shall be even from Tamar unto the waters of strife in Kadesh, and to the river toward the great sea.
29 This is the land which ye shall divide by lot unto the tribes of Israel for inheritance, and these are their portions, saith the Lord GOD.

Moreover, from the possession of the Levites, and from the possession of the city, which is in the midst of the land which belongs to the prince, shall be between the border of Judah and the border of Benjamin. The rest of the tribes shall have a portion from the east side to the west side: the tribes of Benjamin, Simeon, Issachar, Zebulon, and Gad shall each have a portion of land. The border of the land on the south side of Gad shall run from Tamar to the waters of Kadesh, about 50 miles south of Beer-sheba and along the river which flows northwest toward the great sea where it enters the Mediterranean about 50 miles south of Gaza. It marked the southern most boundary of Solomon's kingdom.

This is the land, that land which shall be divided by lot to the tribes of Israel for an inheritance and these are their portions, says the Lord GOD through Ezekiel.

30 And these are the goings out of the city on the north side, four thousand and five hundred measures.
31 And the gates of the city shall be after the names of the tribes of Israel: three gates northward; one gate of Reuben, one gate of Judah, one gate of Levi.
32 And at the east side four thousand and five hundred: and three gates; and one gate of Joseph, one gate of Benjamin, one gate of Dan.
33 And at the south side four thousand and five hundred measures: and three gates; one gate of Simeon, one gate of Issachar, one gate of Zebulun.
34 At the west side four thousand and five hundred, with their three gates; one gate of Gad, one gate of Asher, one gate of Naphtali.
35 It was round about eighteen thousand measures: and the name of the city from that day shall be, The LORD is there.

These are the gates, the exits, as the spirit of the LORD goes forth from the holy city on the north side which is 4,500 reeds long. The gates on the north side will be the gate of Reuben, the gate of Judah and the gate of Levi.

The exits from the holy city on the east side, which is 4500 reeds long, outward shall be the three gates of Joseph (the father of Ephraim and Manessah), Benjamin and Dan.

The Symbolic Version of Ezekiel

The exits from the holy city on the south side, which is 4500 reeds long, outward shall be the three gates of Simeon, Issachar and Zebulon.

The exits from the holy city on the west side, which is 4500 reeds long, outward shall be the three gates of Gad Asher and Naphtali.

It should be noticed that the locations of the children of Israel in the vision of Ezekiel has changed from the position and the lands which they presently occupy. All the tribes are required to change their locations to occupy new lands as they leave the familiar ways of the fallen world to let the new world of the spirit of the LORD take form through the people who compose the tribes. The people in the twelve tribes erroneously thought that the land belonged to them as separate tribes instead of the LORD.

The separation of the two tribes of Ephraim and Manasseh, the two sons of Joseph, shall be reversed and they shall unite and combine as one people into the tribe of Joseph. The unified tribe of Joseph shall then combine with the tribes of Benjamin and Dan (from the west) to form the three east gates. The tribes of Issachar and Zebulon on the north shall join Simeon in the south to form the three south gates. The tribes of Asher and Naphtali from the north shall join Gad from the east to form the three west gates. The tribes of Reuben and Judah in the south shall join with the tribe of Levi to form the three north gates.

The LORD speaking through Ezekiel understands that the twelve tribes cannot be the children of Israel and release the spirit of the LORD through His people as long as they are separated into twelve tribal identities. Israel was one person who revealed the spirit of the LORD. There cannot a northern kingdom and a southern kingdom of Israel. There cannot be twelve separate tribes and twelve separate lands to reveal an integrated Israel.

The gates round about the holy city added up to 18,000 measures (4 x 4,500). The gates or exits from the holy city are exits from the holy city to the twelve tribes through the leaders of the twelve tribes who are the descendants of physical form of Jacob, who became the spirit of Israel. The gates are not only exits from the city, but they are also entrances to the holy city through the lands of the twelve tribes and the holy, whole people who dwell or sojourn in these lands.

The holy city is available to those who approach the holiness of the city in search of the LORD. The name of the city shall be from that time on, The LORD is there. The LORD is there to be experienced. It is the LORD's spirit that is experienced in the holy city. Ezekiel has used the parable of this temple and the twelve tribes to make people aware that the spirit of the LORD is available to be experienced on earth as it was available at the time of Israel, and also at the time of Ezekiel. Ezekiel has used the spiritual pattern of the holy city within himself in covenant-agreement with the LORD as the model and the design to build the holy city in physical form. Ezekiel knew that each person has the spiritual pattern of the holy city within him or her.

The physical manifestation of the holy city can be built on earth but the spirit of the LORD must be used by the people who build it. The name of the city is, The LORD is there, for the son of man who are the people in the darkened fallen state. The name of the city for the Son of man, man restored, is, **The LORD is Here.**

Anthony John Monaco   **July 10, 1998**

The Symbolic Version of
<u>Jeremiah</u>

Anthony John Monaco
A Stars of the Scriptures Series

FOREWORD

The name, Jeremiah, means, "one who gives glory or exaltation to the LORD". The glory of the LORD was known by Jeremiah as he let the LORD's spirit be released into the earth through his individual heart, mind and physical body. If, indeed, the spirit of the LORD were flowing clearly and cleanly through the human equipment of Jeremiah, then he would be a prophet of the LORD. But, if, the information coming forth through the human equipment were generated by selfish desires and wants, then, that person would be a false prophet.

The word "prophesy" can mean to let the spirit of the LORD—which is everywhere and moving through every living thing simultaneously in the present moment of time—move through the human consciousness to produce instruction and guidance to those who can be blessed by the information thus received. The people, human beings, in the Holy Bible, who let their minds and hearts be moved by the flowing spirit of the LORD would prophesy the spirit of the LORD and they, in turn, would be known as prophets of the LORD. They were dedicated to the LORD and letting His spirit move through their hearts and minds. The present conditions of the world and the conditions that have appeared throughout recorded history are proof that although the prophets of the LORD may have prophesied, their messages have not been taken to heart. If the spirit of the LORD produced the messages that appeared through His prophets, then the people who heard the prophets in the past ignored the Word of the LORD that was revealed through the spoken and written words of the prophets.

The word "prophecy" can also mean to foretell the future by predicting future events as though the future events are cast in stone and can be predicted in advance many years before they actually occur. This view presupposes that the state of the human consciousness will never change, that humans will never repent of their rebellion away from the spirit of the LORD which evicted man, male and female, from the Garden of God on earth. The very fact that people want to predict and know the future is so that they can be prepared to live their lives "better" without the on-going, guiding direction of the spirit of the LORD. As long as man is in the fallen state, he is more interested in seeing the prophecy of things in the future than he is in prophesying the way of the spirit of the LORD through individual human flesh on a moment by moment basis.

If the methods used by the prophets to prophesy and express this spirit of the LORD through each of them, then the words of the prophets can have meaning to us in the present time because we can learn to prophesy the spirit of the LORD moving through ourselves in our daily living. The teachings of the prophets of the past—Isaiah, Jeremiah, Ezekiel, and Daniel—can have meaning for us today if we understand our personal responsibility to prophesy the spirit of the LORD to bring His kingdom to the earth.

Jeremiah considered God as the Creator of all that exists and that God is very much concerned about His people and both their responsibility and accountability to Him. Jeremiah and Ezekiel are known as the "prophets of individual responsibility". The prophets emphasized the relationship between sin, the behavior of fallen man, and the inevitable

The Testimony of the Major Prophets

consequences, as a result of the working of Divine Law. The word "sin" derives from an old English term in archery meaning, to be off-the-mark.

The Book of Jeremiah is the longest book in the Holy Bible, containing more words than any other book.
It reveals his personal experience in prophesying the spirit of the LORD and how that experience affected his experience of life and the lives of those around him during the reign of three kings of Judah. Does this Book have personal application to us today?! Let us consider *The Symbolic Version of Jeremiah*.

CHAPTER 1

1 The words of Jeremiah the son of Hilkiah, of the priests that were in Anathoth in the land of Benjamin:
2 To whom the word of the LORD came in the days of Josiah the son of Amon king of Judah, in the thirteenth year of his reign.
3 It came also in the days of Jehoiakim the son of Josiah king of Judah, unto the end of the eleventh year of Zedekiah the son of Josiah king of Judah, unto the carrying away of Jerusalem captive in the fifth month.

Jeremiah was the son of Hilkiah who descended from a priestly family that may have dated back to the time of King Solomon. The family lived in Anathoth, one of four Levitical towns located a few miles northeast of Jerusalem in the tribal land of Benjamin. The word of the LORD first came to Jeremiah in 626 BC in the days of Josiah, the son of Amon, who was king of Judah (640-609) and in the thirteenth year of his reign. The word of the LORD also came to Jeremiah in the reign of Jehoiakim (609-598), the son of Josiah, king of Judah, until the eleventh year of Zedekiah (597-586). The fall of Jerusalem occurred in 586 BC and the people were carried away as captives in the fifth month of that year.

4 Then the word of the LORD came unto me, saying,
5 Before I formed thee in the belly I knew thee; and before thou camest forth out of the womb I sanctified thee, and I ordained thee a prophet unto the nations.

Jeremiah describes his covenant-experience with the LORD which gave Jeremiah the authority from the LORD to speak on earth to others. The covenant-agreement (see *The Symbolic Version of Genesis*) relates to a conscious knowing based in individual experience that man, male and female, is a part of God. The LORD informed Jeremiah that the LORD knew the spirit that is now within Jeremiah **before** the LORD formed the body of Jeremiah in the belly from which he was born on earth which is indication that the spirit exists before the flesh is gathered around it. Jeremiah was sanctified by the LORD in the world of the spirit where he was ordained as a prophet to the nations before he came forth from the womb in a physical form. Jeremiah is shocked by the actual experience with the LORD and by the fact that he has been told by the LORD of his mission on earth. Jeremiah feels inadequate to carry out this task.

6 Then said I, Ah, Lord GOD! behold, I cannot speak: for I am a child.
7 But the LORD said unto me, Say not, I am a child: for thou shalt go to all that I shall send thee, and whatsoever I command thee thou shalt speak.
8 Be not afraid of their faces: for I am with thee to deliver thee, saith the LORD.
9 Then the LORD put forth his hand, and touched my mouth. And the LORD said unto me, Behold, I have put my words in thy mouth.
10 See, I have this day set thee over the nations and over the kingdoms, to root out, and to pull down, and to destroy, and to throw down, to build, and to plant.

The Testimony of the Major Prophets

Jeremiah tells the Lord GOD to behold his inadequacy for the task. He cannot speak to the nations because he is as a child of the spirit even though he is a physically grown man. The LORD tells Jeremiah not to say that he is a child. Jeremiah is to go to all the people to whom the LORD will send him, and say whatever the LORD commands him to speak. The LORD instructs Jeremiah not to be afraid of the faces of the people to whom he is being sent because the LORD is with Jeremiah to deliver him.

Then, the LORD put forth His hand and touched the mouth of Jeremiah, and told Jeremiah to Behold and be aware of the fact that the LORD has put His words into the mouth of Jeremiah. Also, on this day, the LORD has set Jeremiah over the nations and over the kingdoms to root out and to pull down, to destroy and to throw down the conditions of the fallen state that have been built by man in his separation from the spirit of the LORD. Jeremiah is also instructed to build, and to plant the things which reveal the spirit of the LORD. The things that Jeremiah does in the spirit of the LORD will reveal to Jeremiah the nature of the spirit of the LORD, constantly moving through his capacities, which gives him life.

11 Moreover the word of the LORD came unto me, saying, Jeremiah, what seest thou? And I said, I see a rod of an almond tree.
12 Then said the LORD unto me, Thou hast well seen: for I will hasten my word to perform it.

When the word of the LORD came to Jeremiah and asks him what he sees, Jeremiah answers that he sees the design of the LORD's kingdom symbolized by the rod of discipline required to build the almond tree, the symbol of the orderly design for mankind, which shall come from the LORD. The LORD tells Jeremiah that he has seen well and the LORD will move hastily to do His word to deliver the orderly divine design for man into the world which will produce much fruit.

13 And the word of the LORD came unto me the second time, saying, What seest thou? And I said, I see a seething pot; and the face thereof is toward the north.

When the word of the LORD came to Jeremiah the second time asking what he sees, Jeremiah understands that the divine design cannot appear on earth as long as the false design, the counterfeit, distorted state, is occupying the space needed to build the true design. Jeremiah understands that a seething pot, the symbol of the destruction of the shape and form of things, must be used to destroy the present false design. The focus or the face of the attention of the seething pot is toward the north, the symbol of the appearance in the present moment of the wrong design in physical manifestation which is occupying the space which should contain the divine design of the LORD.

14 Then the LORD said unto me, Out of the north an evil shall break forth upon all the inhabitants of the land.
15 For, lo, I will call all the families of the kingdoms of the north, saith the LORD; and they shall come, and they shall set every one his throne at the entering of the gates of Jerusalem, and against all the walls thereof round about, and against all the cities of Judah.
16 And I will utter my judgments against them touching all their wickedness, who have forsaken me, and have burned incense unto other gods, and worshipped the works of their own hands.

Then the LORD said to Jeremiah, Out of the false design existing in the present moment, an evil, a disintegration, shall come to break forth upon all the inhabitants of the land. The LORD will call all the families of the separate kingdoms of the north, and they shall come and set their individual thrones at the entrance of the gates of city of Jerusalem. The thrones of self-centered separate behaviors must be left outside the walls round about the city. People cannot enter into the holy city, the city of the LORD, while they have these false designs which have been constructed against all the cities of Judah. The LORD utters His judgments against all the people as His spirit comes and touches the wickedness in all the people who have forsaken the LORD their God; the people who have burned incense to other gods, and who have worshipped the material works of their own hands; the people are worshipping their own creations. The sin is not the burning of the incense; the sin is the allegiance to a god of stone, a god of materiality, over the living God which is moving through God's people.

17 Thou therefore gird up thy loins, and arise, and speak unto them all that I command thee: be not dismayed at their faces, lest I confound thee before them.

The Symbolic Version of Jeremiah

18 For, behold, I have made thee this day a defenced city, and an iron pillar, and brasen walls against the whole land, against the kings of Judah, against the princes thereof, against the priests thereof, and against the people of the land.
19 And they shall fight against thee; but they shall not prevail against thee; for I am with thee, saith the LORD, to deliver thee.

The LORD has commanded Jeremiah to stand tall, gird up his loins in strength, and arise to the task of speaking to all the people that the LORD commands. Jeremiah is not to be dismayed at the expressions upon their faces. If Jeremiah becomes dismayed by the expressions of disappointment and disbelief on the faces of the people, then he will appear to be confounded before the very people that he is to be leading in the name of the LORD.

Jeremiah is to behold, that the LORD has made a defended city, a city of the true design that is defended by the spirit of the LORD. The spiritual city begins to take form as an iron pillar, the first strong pillar of the new spiritual city is in place and the strong brass walls against the whole land of the fallen state which is against the kings of Judah, the princes of Judah, the priesthood, and against all the people of the land which is in the fallen state that is not the divine design of the LORD. Jeremiah, the prophet of the LORD, is the first pillar of the new Jerusalem of the LORD which is the spiritual city made manifest. The kings, the princes, the priesthood and the people of the fallen state will fight against Jeremiah as he expresses the word of the LORD but they will not prevail against Jeremiah; because the LORD is with Jeremiah to deliver Jeremiah to the people so that he can deliver the word which he has received from the LORD.

CHAPTER 2

1 Moreover the word of the LORD came to me, saying,
2 Go and cry in the ears of Jerusalem, saying, Thus saith the LORD; I remember thee, the kindness of thy youth, the love of thine espousals, when thou wentest after me in the wilderness, in a land that was not sown.
3 Israel was holiness unto the LORD, and the firstfruits of his increase: all that devour him shall offend; evil shall come upon them, saith the LORD.

Moreover, the word of the LORD came to Jeremiah, saying, Go and cry aloud the message from the LORD into the ears of the people of Jerusalem. The LORD remembers the kindness of the people of Jerusalem in their youth, the love that they espoused to the LORD, when they went to search for the LORD in the wilderness in a land that was not sown with the seed of the LORD. Israel, the ascended state of man who rose up from the repentant fallen state that was symbolized and personified in Jacob, was in the covenant with the LORD, was holiness to the LORD. The first fruits, the first expressions and behaviors through man, are to increase the spirit of the LORD on earth through people. All or anything that devours or distorts the spirit of the LORD and who do not use the spirit of the LORD to create beauty through people offends the LORD; evil, the distortion of the truth, shall come upon the people who do not serve the spirit of the LORD in their way of life.

4 Hear ye the word of the LORD, O house of Jacob, and all the families of the house of Israel:
5 Thus saith the LORD, What iniquity have your fathers found in me, that they are gone far from me, and have walked after vanity, and are become vain?
6 Neither said they, Where is the LORD that brought us up out of the land of Egypt, that led us through the wilderness, through a land of deserts and of pits, through a land of drought, and of the shadow of death, through a land that no man passed through, and where no man dwelt?
7 And I brought you into a plentiful country, to eat the fruit thereof and the goodness thereof; but when ye entered, ye defiled my land, and made mine heritage an abomination.

The word of the LORD which is to be heard by the house of Jacob, who symbolizes people in the repentant fallen state of human nature, and all the families of the house of Israel, who represent the people who heard the word of the LORD is as follows: The LORD asks, What iniquity have the fathers of Jacob and Israel found in the LORD that they are gone so far away from the ways of the LORD in their living, so that they have walked after the vanity of their own wants and desires and become vain in the process?

The people who fell from the precious state, where they knew the glory of the LORD in the past, asked where is the LORD who brought them out of the Land of Egypt, through the wilderness, the deserts and pits, drought and death, through a land where no man passed through and dwelt? It was the LORD who bought them to a plentiful country to eat the fruit and the goodness thereof. But when the people entered into the land, they defiled the land of the LORD

The Symbolic Version of Jeremiah

and they made their spiritual heritage an abomination by the distortion introduced through their impure hearts and selfish minds.

8 The priests said not, Where is the LORD? and they that handle the law knew me not: the pastors also transgressed against me, and the prophets prophesied by Baal, and walked after things that do not profit.
9 Wherefore I will yet plead with you, saith the LORD, and with your children's children will I plead.
10 For pass over the isles of Chittim, and see; and send unto Kedar, and consider diligently, and see if there be such a thing.
11 Hath a nation changed their gods, which are yet no gods? but my people have changed their glory for that which doth not profit.

The priests of the LORD, who did bear the prime responsibility since the time of Moses, did not ask, Where is the LORD? and the scribes who handle the laws did not know the LORD: the pastors transgressed against the LORD, while the prophets prophesied by the teachings of Baal and walked in ways that did not profit or reveal the LORD. Even so, even with all this rebellion by the people, the LORD will continue to plead with the children's children. The hearers of the word of the LORD are advised to pass over the isles of Chittim, the nations to the west, and see; or, send to Kedar, the nations to the east, to see if there has been such a thing among other people or other gods that are worshipped by the people. The LORD asks if other nations have changed the gods which they worship which are not gods? But the LORD's people have changed the God which gave them their glory of life for false gods which have not profited them at all.

12 Be astonished, O ye heavens, at this, and be horribly afraid, be ye very desolate, saith the LORD.
13 For my people have committed two evils; they have forsaken me the fountain of living waters, and hewed them out cisterns, broken cisterns, that can hold no water.

The people who have ignored the LORD should be astonished, in the heavens of their consciousness, that they have done this to the Lord GOD. The people who ignore God should be horribly afraid and very desolate because their actions worship false gods. The LORD's people have committed two evils; first, they have forsaken the fountain of the living waters, the symbol of the moving spirit of the truth of the LORD which is flowing to them, and, second, they have hewed out for themselves cisterns, broken cisterns, that can hold no water of the spirit of truth from the LORD. A cistern is a container used to hold physical water from the environment. It is a symbol of the container of beliefs of men in the fallen state who worship false gods. There is a difference between people who have access to the living water of the truth of spirit and those who have access to the polluted water of the broken containers filled with beliefs of fallen human nature. There is a difference between Israel, the ascended state of the **S**on of man, and Jacob, the fallen state of the **s**on of man who needs to become Israel. There is a need for Jacob to rise up!

14 Is Israel a servant? is he a homeborn slave? why is he spoiled?
15 The young lions roared upon him, and yelled, and they made his land waste: his cities are burned without inhabitant.
16 Also the children of Noph and Tahapanes have broken the crown of thy head.
17 Hast thou not procured this unto thyself, in that thou hast forsaken
the LORD thy God, when he led thee by the way?

The LORD asks if Israel, the true state of man, man made in the image and likeness of God, is a servant? Is man truly a servant of the false gods or is man a server of the spirit of the true God? Is man created by God to be a home-born slave to the rulers of the environment? Why is man in the fallen state spoiled, rotted, unless it is because he ignores the glory of the LORD which is flowing through him to give him life?

The young lions, the destructive immature rulers of the fallen world, roared upon a fearful and desolate fallen man, yelled at him, and made his land a waste: his cities have been burned without an inhabitant in them. The children of the towns of Noph and Tahapanes in the delta region of Egypt have used their earthly power to break the crown of spiritual authority from the LORD which is the heavenly crown of your head. The LORD asks if the people have not brought these conditions upon themselves because they have forsaken the LORD their God who always led them in the way of righteousness?

The Testimony of the Major Prophets

18 And now what hast thou to do in the way of Egypt, to drink the waters of Sihor? or what hast thou to do in the way of Assyria, to drink the waters of the river?
19 Thine own wickedness shall correct thee, and thy backslidings shall reprove thee: know therefore and see that it is an evil thing and bitter, that thou hast forsaken the LORD thy God, and that my fear is not in thee, saith the Lord GOD of hosts.
20 For of old time I have broken thy yoke, and burst thy bands; and thou saidst, I will not transgress; when upon every high hill and under every green tree thou wanderest, playing the harlot.
21 Yet I had planted thee a noble vine, wholly a right seed: how then art thou turned into the degenerate plant of a strange vine unto me?

Now that you are in this predicament, which you brought upon yourself by your own behavior and by your decision to ignore the LORD, what will you have to do in Egypt to drink the Egyptian waters of Sihor (the Nile) to survive your captivity? or what do you have to do to in Assyria to drink the water of their beliefs from their river?

The wickedness of the people who should have turned to the LORD for help, but did not, has produced conditions which shall correct them if they learn the error of their ways. Any backsliding from the way of the LORD shall reprove and correct the people to make them aware of their wrong function. The people should know and understand that it is an evil thing, and has bitter consequences, when they forsake the spirit of the LORD, and the fear and consequences of disobedience are not in the people to keep them on the path of the LORD.

In a time long ago, the LORD broke the yoke and burst the bonds of man where the LORD could control the thoughts and actions of man. Man said that he would not transgress from the way of the LORD, but he has wandered upon every high hill and under every green tree playing the harlot by looking for selfish pleasure for himself everywhere. Yet, man knows that the LORD has planted mankind as a noble vine, a wholly right seed. The question of the LORD to fallen man is how then has he turned into the degenerate plant of this strange vine, this weed, in the LORD's garden of Earth? Is the problem with man an external or an internal one? Is the problem from the environment, or from man's strained and distorted relationship with the spirit of God?

22 For though thou wash thee with nitre, and take thee much soap, yet thine iniquity is marked before me, saith the Lord GOD.
23 How canst thou say, I am not polluted, I have not gone after Baalim? see thy way in the valley, know what thou hast done: thou art a swift dromedary traversing her ways;
24 A wild ass used to the wilderness, that snuffeth up the wind at her pleasure; in her occasion who can turn her away? all they that seek her will not weary themselves; in her month they shall find her.
25 Withhold thy foot from being unshod, and thy throat from thirst: but thou saidst, There is no hope: no; for I have loved strangers, and after them will I go.

Even though man would physically wash himself with nitre (a salt of potassium or sodium nitrate), and use much soap, the iniquity of man is marked before the LORD because of the fallen and unclean relationship of the impure thoughts and emotions of fallen man with the LORD. How can man continue to say, I am not polluted, I have not gone after Baalim? Baalim symbolizes the many local forms of false gods worshipped by the people. Fallen man is admonished by the LORD to see the way that he has fallen into the valley and know what he has done and why he is in the condition in which he finds himself. Fallen man is like a swift dromedary (camel) traversing ways which are familiar; a wild ass who is used to living in the wilderness and sniffs the wind in her physical pleasure while she is in heat; who can resist her and turn her away? All who seek physical pleasure shall find her at the time of mating. The people have been taught to withhold their foot from being unshod and their throats from thirst—they have been taught to restrain these desires and emotions: but, fallen man has said that there is no hope for him in this condition. Fallen man has physically loved strangers and he will go after them.

26 As the thief is ashamed when he is found, so is the house of Israel ashamed; they, their kings, their princes, and their priests, and their prophets,
27 Saying to a stock, Thou art my father; and to a stone, Thou hast brought me forth: for they have turned their back unto me, and not their face: but in the time of their trouble they will say, Arise, and save us.

The Symbolic Version of Jeremiah

28 But where are thy gods that thou hast made thee? let them arise, if they can save thee in the time of thy trouble: for according to the number of thy cities are thy gods, O Judah.
29 Wherefore will ye plead with me? ye all have transgressed against me, saith the LORD.
30 In vain have I smitten your children; they received no correction: your own sword hath devoured your prophets, like a destroying lion.

As a thief is ashamed when he is caught, so is the house of Israel ashamed; they enjoyed their rebellion from the LORD until they were caught and must face the consequences of their actions. They, the house of Israel, their kings, their princes, their priests and their prophets have been saying to a stock, a wooden idol, that it is their father; and to a stone idol, that the stone has brought them forth. The fallen people have turned their back to the LORD, but not their face that continues to pray to false gods. However, in time of trouble, they will say to the LORD, Arise and save us from these conditions (which they have sown by their own behavior).

But where are the false gods of wood and stone that you have made to worship so that you could continue in your wicked ways? Let them arise and save you in our time of trouble! The people of Judah have as many gods as the number of their cities. They have ignored the one God. Why and wherefore will you plead with the true God? You have all transgressed against me, says the LORD. In vain, in your vanity, the LORD has smitten you and brought you to your just punishment; you have received no correction or learned the lesson of your transgression. Your own sword, your own power, has been used to devour your true prophets from the LORD like a destroying lion.

31 O generation, see ye the word of the LORD. Have I been a wilderness unto Israel? a land of darkness? wherefore say my people, We are lords; we will come no more unto thee?
32 Can a maid forget her ornaments, or a bride her attire? yet my people have forgotten me days without number.
33 Why trimmest thou thy way to seek love? therefore hast thou also taught the wicked ones thy ways.
34 Also in thy skirts is found the blood of the souls of the poor innocents: I have not found it by secret search, but upon all these.

The generation of wrong function through people is admonished to see the word of the LORD which is spoken to them through Jeremiah. Has the LORD been a wilderness to Israel? a land of darkness? Or has the LORD given Life, Light and blessings to the people. Why and wherefore do the LORD's people come to Him and say, We are lords on our own; we will come to You no more?

The LORD speaking through Jeremiah asks if a maid can forget the ornaments which she has been given by her owner, or a bride forget her attire, the reason that she is getting married? Have the people forgotten that the LORD has given them ornaments of hearts, minds and bodies? Has the bride forgotten the Bridegroom? Yet the LORD's people have forgotten the LORD for days without number. Why do the LORD's people trim and restrict the ways that they seek to love the LORD. As they cease to love the LORD, they have also taught the wicked ones their ways. As a person ceases to love the LORD, he automatically becomes wicked! In your skirts, in your private area of responsibility, is found the blood of innocent people who have been harmed by your actions. The LORD has not found these sinful behaviors by searching you but by observation of the people that you harmed.

35 Yet thou sayest, Because I am innocent, surely his anger shall turn from me. Behold, I will plead with thee, because thou sayest, I have not sinned.
36 Why gaddest thou about so much to change thy way? thou also shalt be ashamed of Egypt, as thou wast ashamed of Assyria.
37 Yea, thou shalt go forth from him, and thine hands upon thine head: for the LORD hath rejected thy confidences, and thou shalt not prosper in them.

Yet, you say that because you are innocent, surely the anger of the LORD will turn away from you. Behold, the LORD will plead with you because you say that you have not sinned, when the results of your sin is upon the people that you have harmed. Why have you gadded about trying to change the way, the circumstance, in which you find yourself? You should be ashamed of yourself and your past behavior toward the LORD as you have been ashamed of the behavior of Egypt and as you were ashamed of the behavior of Assyria.

The Testimony of the Major Prophets

Yes, you shall go forth from the LORD and your hands shall be on your own head for the circumstances in which you find yourself: for the LORD has rejected your confidences in the people in the fallen state, and their idols, in whom you have confidence. You shall not prosper by following and emulating them in lieu of following and emulating the way of the spirit of the LORD which is moving through you.

CHAPTER 3

1 They say, If a man put away his wife, and she go from him, and become another man's, shall he return unto her again? shall not that land be greatly polluted? but thou hast played the harlot with many lovers; yet return again to me, saith the LORD.

Jeremiah uses the familiar example of divorce in which a man puts away his wife who then becomes the wife of another to make the point that the LORD's love is different than that of man in the fallen state. Shall that man who told his wife to go return to her again after he has put her away? Shall not that land, that woman, be greatly polluted in his eyes since he already rejected her? But man in the fallen state has played the harlot with many lovers as he has left the LORD and become emotionally involved with all the material treasures of the environment. Man has polluted himself in his way of judgment when he judged the things of the environment to be of more value than the LORD. Yet, even though the LORD has been ignored by man who left the LORD to worship false idols, the LORD keeps the door open for man to return to Him whereas man would not take the wife back that he had put away in divorce. The LORD will take His "wife" back; fallen man will not!

2 Lift up thine eyes unto the high places, and see where thou hast not been lien with. In the ways hast thou sat for them, as the Arabian in the wilderness; and thou hast polluted the land with thy whoredoms and with thy wickedness.
3 Therefore the showers have been withholden, and there hath been no latter rain; and thou hadst a whore's forehead, thou refusedst to be ashamed.
4 Wilt thou not from this time cry unto me, My father, thou art the guide of my youth?
5 Will he reserve his anger for ever? will he keep it to the end? Behold, thou hast spoken and done evil things as thou couldest.

The LORD tells man in the fallen state to lift up his eyes to high places, to observe with a higher vision, so that he can see where he has not been lien, where he has not been held and bound to the material world of idols. Man has sat for the treasures and pleasures of the environment as an Arabian alone in the wilderness; and you, fallen man, have polluted the land with your whoredom and your wickedness in the sight of the LORD whom you have disregarded. The circumstances of the world, the pollution, is everywhere because of your wickedness.

Therefore, the showers of the spirit of the LORD which come to you from on high have been withheld and there has been no rain from heaven to you lately; you have had a whore's forehead, you have thought as a whore, and you refused to be ashamed of your behavior which has kept you in the fallen state.

Will you not, from this present time forward cry to the LORD, call to your Father, and admit that the LORD has been the guide of your youth before you strayed from the way of the LORD? Will the LORD your Father withhold his anger forever? will he keep his anger in check until the end of your days on earth? Behold, you have spoken and done evil things as quickly as you could think of them.

The Testimony of the Major Prophets

6 The LORD said also unto me in the days of Josiah the king, Hast thou seen that which backsliding Israel hath done? she is gone up upon every high mountain and under every green tree, and there hath played the harlot.
7 And I said after she had done all these things, Turn thou unto me. But she returned not. And her treacherous sister Judah saw it.
8 And I saw, when for all the causes whereby backsliding Israel committed adultery I had put her away, and given her a bill of divorce; yet her treacherous sister Judah feared not, but went and played the harlot also.

The LORD also said to Jeremiah in the days of Josiah the king, Have you not seen the result of what the people of Israel have done because of their backsliding from the way of the LORD? She, the fallen people of the land of Israel, has gone up on every mountain where the view seemed favorable to her and under every green tree, where pleasure and comfort seemed to be, and she has played the harlot by giving herself in exchange for emotional, mental and physical pleasures. The LORD said, after the people had done these wicked things, Turn again to the LORD. But the people of Israel refused to repent and return to the LORD. The people of Judah, the treacherous sister of Israel, saw what was done.

Jeremiah saw, when for all the reasons that the people of Israel committed adultery because of their backsliding behavior, the LORD had put her away and given her a bill of divorce as punishment for rebelling against the spirit of the LORD; yet the people of Judah, the treacherous sister of Israel, saw the punishment of Israel and did not fear the LORD. The nation of Judah went the fallen way of the nation of Israel and played the harlot also.

9 And it came to pass through the lightness of her whoredom, that she defiled the land, and committed adultery with stones and with stocks.
10 And yet for all this her treacherous sister Judah hath not turned unto me with her whole heart, but feignedly, saith the LORD.

And it came to pass that through the wrong function and behavior which seemed light and insignificant to the people in the fallen state, the people caused the land to be defiled and committed adultery, false practice of pagan love, with material idols made of stones and wood, things made of atoms and molecules which were more important to them than the spirit of the LORD. And yet, even though this fallen behavior was observed by the people of Judah, they behaved as a treacherous sister and did not turn to the LORD wholeheartedly. The people of Judah feigned, pretended, to return to the LORD.

11 And the LORD said unto me, The backsliding Israel hath justified herself more than treacherous Judah.
12 Go and proclaim these words toward the north, and say, Return, thou backsliding Israel, saith the LORD; and I will not cause mine anger to fall upon you: for I am merciful, saith the LORD, and I will not keep anger for ever.
13 Only acknowledge thine iniquity, that thou hast transgressed against the LORD thy God, and hast scattered thy ways to the strangers under every green tree, and ye have not obeyed my voice, saith the LORD.

The LORD said to Jeremiah, The backsliding people of Israel, who did slide away from the way of the LORD, has justified herself more than the treacherous people of Judah. Jeremiah is commanded by the LORD to go and proclaim these words to the north, the people of Israel, and say, Return, you backsliding people of Israel, and the LORD will not keep his anger, the working of the Law of the LORD, forever. If the people repent, the LORD will not cause his anger to fall upon them: for the LORD is merciful to those who repent and change their behavior, but the LORD will not keep his anger, the working of the Law of Sowing and Reaping forever. The people of Israel must acknowledge their iniquity, that they have transgressed the way of the LORD their God, and by so doing they have scattered their wicked ways to strangers, by their wrong example. The pollution is spreading under every green tree, every person who is alive and growing, because the people of Israel have not obeyed the voice of the LORD.

14 Turn, O backsliding children, saith the LORD; for I am married unto you: and I will take you one of a city, and two of a family, and I will bring you to Zion:
15 And I will give you pastors according to mine heart, which shall feed you with knowledge and understanding.

16 And it shall come to pass, when ye be multiplied and increased in the land, in those days, saith the LORD, they shall say no more, The ark of the covenant of the LORD: neither shall it come to mind: neither shall they remember it; neither shall they visit it; neither shall that be done any more.

The word of the LORD spoken through Jeremiah is that the backsliding people of Israel are to turn, to repent of their behavior and return to the LORD, because the LORD is married to them. In symbolic language to illustrate the relationship, the LORD is the "husband" and the people are His "wife". The LORD will take them to Zion, the spiritual place of the covenant with the LORD. The LORD will provide them with pastors who have the LORD's spirit in their hearts to feed them with knowledge and understanding from the LORD. If the people do this, then it shall come to pass, that when they are increased and multiplied in the land, they shall no more say, The ark of the covenant of the LORD: the physical structure of the ark of the covenant which carried the books of Moses shall not come into their minds as the holy place of the LORD; they shall not remember the symbol of the ark of the covenant: they shall not visit it; neither shall that form of worship be done anymore. The worship of the ark of the covenant, as something separate from them, is to replaced by something else.

17 At that time they shall call Jerusalem the throne of the LORD; and all the nations shall be gathered unto it, to the name of the LORD, to Jerusalem: neither shall they walk any more after the imagination of their evil heart.
18 In those days the house of Judah shall walk with the house of Israel, and they shall come together out of the land of the north to the land that I have given for an inheritance unto your fathers.
19 But I said, How shall I put thee among the children, and give thee a pleasant land, a goodly heritage of the hosts of nations? and I said, Thou shalt call me, My father; and shalt not turn away from me.
20 Surely as a wife treacherously departeth from her husband, so have ye dealt treacherously with me, O house of Israel, saith the LORD.

When the people repent and follow the spirit of the LORD as it moves through them, then, at that time, they shall call the city of Jerusalem the throne of the LORD. The ark of the covenant which held the five books of Moses and symbolized the place of the LORD should be replaced by the city of Jerusalem. This cannot occur unless the people repent and rise up to reveal the spirit of the LORD flowing through them. The people of Israel shall not walk anymore after the imaginations that come forth from their evil hearts.

In those days the house of Judah shall walk in spiritual agreement with the house of Israel, and they shall come together out of the land of the north, the physical land which they inhabit to the spiritual land that the LORD has given for an inheritance to their fathers. The LORD asks the rhetorical question, How shall I put you among the LORD's children and give you a pleasant land on earth which is a goodly heritage of the hosts of all the nations? The LORD supplies the answer when He says, You shall call me, My Father; and you shall not turn away from the LORD and act as though you were not the sons and daughters of the LORD, the children of God. Surely as a wife treacherously departed from her husband, so have you dealt treacherously with me, O house of Israel. The nations of Judah and Israel can come together as they accept the spirit of the LORD as Father to both nations.

21 A voice was heard upon the high places, weeping and supplications of the children of Israel: for they have perverted their way, and they have forgotten the LORD their God.
22 Return, ye backsliding children, and I will heal your backslidings. Behold, we come unto thee; for thou art the LORD our God.
23 Truly in vain is salvation hoped for from the hills, and from the multitude of mountains: truly in the LORD our God is the salvation of Israel.
24 For shame hath devoured the labour of our fathers from our youth; their flocks and their herds, their sons and their daughters.
25 We lie down in our shame, and our confusion covereth us: for we have sinned against the LORD our God, we and our fathers, from our youth even unto this day, and have not obeyed the voice of the LORD our God.

Then a voice was heard upon the high places in the consciousness of those people who heard the word of the LORD, which caused weeping and supplications of the children of Israel who realized that they had indeed perverted their true way on earth, and that they have forgotten the LORD their God who had created them. The LORD commanded the children, the backsliding children, who heard his voice to return to the place from where they had fallen, and

The Testimony of the Major Prophets

the LORD would heal their backsliding in that place. The people who responded to the word of the LORD through Jeremiah answered, Behold, LORD, we come to You for You are the LORD our God.

The people who respond to the word of the LORD by returning to their true position as the children of God and say, Truly, salvation from the hills and the multitude of mountains, the high places in the human state, are in vain; they can see that, truly, the salvation of Israel is in the LORD our God who is the Father, the spiritual reality for everyone. The people who repent of their former ways can comprehend that it was the shame of their own shameful behavior that devoured the labor of their fathers from their youth; their flocks, herds, sons and daughters were all wasted. The shameful behavior of the people in the fallen state caused them to lie down in their shame and the shame of their behavior confused and covered the sinful people. The people who respond to the call of the word of the LORD can readily see that they have sinned against the LORD their God; not only themselves alone in their own generation, but also they could see that they and their fathers, from their youth even unto this day, they have not obeyed the voice of the LORD God.

The people who desire to return to the word of the LORD God must in fact must give up the behaviors of the fallen ways and return to the expression of the spirit of the LORD which is the ascended or risen way.

CHAPTER 4

1 If thou wilt return, O Israel, saith the LORD, return unto me: and if thou wilt put away thine abominations out of my sight, then shalt thou not remove.
2 And thou shalt swear, The LORD liveth, in truth, in judgment, and in righteousness; and the nations shall bless themselves in him, and in him shall they glory.

The word of the LORD through Jeremiah to the people of Israel is an invitation for them to return to the LORD against whom they have ignored and rebelled. The invitation is issued through the prophet, Jeremiah; the people of Israel must decide whether or not they are willing to respond to the invitation to return to the LORD. The return to the LORD must be voluntary and the return must be preceded by a willingness to return to the way of the LORD. The LORD is very clear in that the people in the fallen state must put away their abominations, their abominable behavior out of the sight of the LORD. Since the spirit of the LORD is everywhere at all times, the abominable behaviors must be eliminated from the expressions of the people who shall not remove themselves from the position of cleanness and holiness that characterizes the spirit of the LORD. The people of Israel who choose to live in the spirit of the LORD shall then swear the LORD lives in truth, judgment and righteousness through each of them. The people cannot swear that the LORD was **in** them unless the spirit of the LORD is moving **through** them. Then the nations shall bless themselves in the spirit of the LORD which is moving through the people and the people shall be blessed in the spirit of the LORD which will give them the glory of the LORD as it flows through them. It can be no other way.

3 For thus saith the LORD to the men of Judah and Jerusalem, Break up your fallow ground, and sow not among thorns.
4 Circumcise yourselves to the LORD, and take away the foreskins of your heart, ye men of Judah and inhabitants of Jerusalem: lest my fury come forth like fire, and burn that none can quench it, because of the evil of your doings.
5 Declare ye in Judah, and publish in Jerusalem; and say, Blow ye the trumpet in the land: cry, gather together, and say, Assemble yourselves, and let us go into the defenced cities.

The invitation is not limited to the people who live in Israel. The word of the LORD is also offered through Jeremiah to the men who live in Judah and Jerusalem. They are to break up the fallow, uncultivated holy ground within themselves and to not sow the seeds of their behaviors among the thorns that have grown from their past behaviors. The people of Judah and Jerusalem are to circumcise themselves, cut away all the unclean behaviors from their past, to offer themselves to the spirit of the LORD. The men of Judah and Jerusalem are to take away the symbolic foreskins that have covered their hearts and kept them away from the spirit of the LORD. In separation from the spirit of the LORD, the power of the fire of the LORD will produce a burn that will be like a fury that no one can quench because of the evil of your doings, your behaviors which do not reveal the spirit of the LORD.

The people in Judah and Jerusalem are to declare and publish in the places where they live by blowing the trumpet of the spirit of the LORD through themselves so that others can rally to the call of the trumpet of the LORD which

The Testimony of the Major Prophets

is sounded in the land. Mankind was created to be the trumpet of the LORD, the means through which the LORD's spirit is heard on earth. The people who cry, who loudly express and declare, that the spirit of the LORD is moving through them, will assemble the people together in the spirit of the LORD to defend the spiritual city in the power of the LORD.

6 Set up the standard toward Zion: retire, stay not: for I will bring evil from the north, and a great destruction.
7 The lion is come up from his thicket, and the destroyer of the Gentiles is on his way; he is gone forth from his place to make thy land desolate; and thy cities shall be laid waste, without an inhabitant.
8 For this gird you with sackcloth, lament and howl: for the fierce anger of the LORD is not turned back from us.

The standard for the people to follow is toward Zion, the spiritual holy place of the LORD that is within each person. As the people retire and rest in the spirit of the LORD, they are not to stay in Jerusalem and Judah because the destructive power of the LORD is moving toward them from the north. The lion, which symbolizes the Babylonian invaders, has come out of his lair and is determined to destroy the Gentiles, the nations foreign to the spirit of the LORD, by making the land desolate and the cities shall be laid waste without an inhabitant. The people should prepare or gird themselves for defeat as the power from Babylon comes upon them. The people will wear sackcloth, lament and howl at their misfortune. The fierce anger of the LORD, which is a distortion of the LORD's spirit that appears on earth through His people, manifesting through the Babylonians will not be turned back, turned away, from the people of Jerusalem who are reaping the results of what has been sown in the past. The Law of Sowing and Reaping is at work and behaviors which have been sown shall come to pass.

9 And it shall come to pass at that day, saith the LORD, that the heart of the king shall perish, and the heart of the princes; and the priests shall be astonished, and the prophets shall wonder.
10 Then said I, Ah, Lord GOD! surely thou hast greatly deceived this people and Jerusalem, saying, Ye shall have peace; whereas the sword reacheth unto the soul.
11 At that time shall it be said to this people and to Jerusalem, A dry wind of the high places in the wilderness toward the daughter of my people, not to fan, nor to cleanse,
12 Even a full wind from those places shall come unto me: now also will I give sentence against them.
13 Behold, he shall come up as clouds, and his chariots shall be as a whirlwind: his horses are swifter than eagles. Woe unto us! for we are spoiled.

The LORD speaking through the prophet Jeremiah says that it shall come to pass that the hearts of the king and the princes shall perish; the priests shall be astonished and the prophets shall wonder at the destruction of Jerusalem by the Babylonians. Then Jeremiah said, Ah, Lord GOD, surely the people of Jerusalem have been deceived because they expected peace from the LORD and they have received the destructive sword that reaches into their soul. The people have erroneously thought that the LORD will bring peace on earth even if they rebel against the LORD.

At that time, when it was widely believed that the LORD will bring peace through the impure hearts of mankind, it shall be said to these mistaken people and to Jerusalem, A dry wind of the high places in the wilderness, which symbolizes the powerful scorching wind that carries sand and dust, shall blow toward the daughter of my people, not to fan, nor to cleanse, even a full wind from those places shall come unto me: now also will I give the sentence of retribution against the people for their behavior that has ignored the LORD. Behold, the retribution shall come up as destructive clouds in the form of the Babylonians, and his chariots shall be as a whirlwind: his horses are swifter than eagles. The people will cry, Woe unto us! for we are spoiled and ruined by the invaders.

14 O Jerusalem, wash thine heart from wickedness, that thou mayest be saved. How long shall thy vain thoughts lodge within thee?
15 For a voice declareth from Dan, and publisheth affliction from mount Ephraim.
16 Make ye mention to the nations; behold, publish against Jerusalem, that watchers come from a far country, and give out their voice against the cities of Judah.
17 As keepers of a field, are they against her round about; because she hath been rebellious against me, saith the LORD.
18 Thy way and thy doings have procured these things unto thee; this is thy wickedness, because it is bitter, because it reacheth unto thine heart.

The Symbolic Version of Jeremiah

Even though the invaders from Babylon have come upon the people of Jerusalem, they can begin to return to the LORD whom they have ignored, The prescription for salvation from the LORD always remains the same. The people in the fallen state must wash their hearts from wickedness so that they may be saved. The LORD speaking through Jeremiah asks, How long shall your vain thoughts of independence and separation from the LORD remain lodged within you? The voices of the people from far-away Dan, which is close to the northern border of Israel, and as close as Ephraim, which is a few miles north of Jerusalem, declare and proclaim the impending disaster of invasion by Babylonians.

The people of the nations of the children of Israel in the south, Jerusalem and the cities of Judah, are warned that the advance guard are coming from a far country and they are as close as keepers of a field who are ready to move into the field that they are observing. Jeremiah states that these things have come to pass because the children of Israel have been rebellious against the LORD. The wicked ways of the people have brought these things upon them. It is a direct result of the wickedness of the people who have ignored the LORD. The words may sound bitter to the hearers of the word because the truth of the message reaches into their hearts.

19 My bowels, my bowels! I am pained at my very heart; my heart maketh a noise in me; I cannot hold my peace, because thou hast heard, O my soul, the sound of the trumpet, the alarm of war.
20 Destruction upon destruction is cried; for the whole land is spoiled: suddenly are my tents spoiled, and my curtains in a moment.
21 How long shall I see the standard, and hear the sound of the trumpet?
22 For my people is foolish, they have not known me; they are sottish children, and they have none understanding: they are wise to do evil, but to do good they have no knowledge.

The people who hear the word of the LORD through Jeremiah cry in anguish that their bowels, their inner depths of their emotions, are feeling the effects in the hearts of their emotions. The people have been touched at the level of their hardened hearts which is making a noise in them that has disturbed their peace. This has occurred only because they have heard the alarm of war through the trumpet of the messengers from the north who report the advance of the Babylonians. Destruction after destruction is reported that describes the spoil of the land by the invader. Suddenly, in an instant, the shelter of the people, symbolized by their tents and curtains, is seen to be at an end. How long will it be before the people of Jerusalem and Judah see the battle standard of the invader and hear the sound of the trumpet, the noise of the activity of the invader. The LORD speaking through Jeremiah states that the people of Jerusalem and Judah are foolish; they have not known the LORD in their individual or collective experience. As senseless children without understanding of how things work on earth, they have been very wise to do evil, but to do good for the LORD, they have no knowledge of how to act. They have ignored the fact that everything that transpires begins with the LORD and the view of conditions from the LORD.

23 I beheld the earth, and, lo, it was without form, and void; and the heavens, and they had no light.
24 I beheld the mountains, and, lo, they trembled, and all the hills moved lightly.
25 I beheld, and, lo, there was no man, and all the birds of the heavens were fled.
26 I beheld, and, lo, the fruitful place was a wilderness, and all the cities thereof were broken down at the presence of the LORD, and by his fierce anger.
27 For thus hath the LORD said, The whole land shall be desolate; yet will I not make a full end.
28 For this shall the earth mourn, and the heavens above be black: because I have spoken it, I have purposed it, and will not repent, neither will I turn back from it.

The LORD beheld the earth and it was without form and void from the design of the LORD's spirit; the heavens, the place in the consciousness of man where the LORD should be, has no light from the LORD. The LORD beheld the mountains and the hills, the high places in the consciousness of mankind, and they trembled and moved lightly to reveal that their is some activity, but the LORD beheld that there was no man made in the image and likeness of God and all the birds of heaven, the symbols of the heavenly thoughts from the LORD, had fled.

The LORD speaking through Jeremiah beheld the condition of the consciousness of the fallen people and observed that what should have been a fruitful place of the divine design of God was a wilderness, and all the cities built from that state of consciousness were broken down by the presence of the LORD, and by his fierce anger which results against His rebellious children. The LORD declares that the whole land that is built by fallen man shall be desolate;

The Testimony of the Major Prophets

but the LORD will not bring it to a full end. The conditions of the earth made by fallen man shall mourn the absence of the LORD, and the heavens of the consciousness of man where the LORD should be, shall be black when the light from the LORD is excluded. The LORD has spoken his punishment for rebellious man in the fallen state which has the purpose of teaching fallen man the results of rebelling against the LORD. The LORD will not repent, neither will the LORD turn back from the working of the Law which he has declared for the operation of the material conditions on earth.

29 The whole city shall flee for the noise of the horsemen and bowmen; they shall go into thickets, and climb up upon the rocks: every city shall be forsaken, and not a man dwell therein.
30 And when thou art spoiled, what wilt thou do? Though thou clothest thyself with crimson, though thou deckest thee with ornaments of gold, though thou rentest thy face with painting, in vain shalt thou make thyself fair; thy lovers will despise thee, they will seek thy life.
31 For I have heard a voice as of a woman in travail, and the anguish as of her that bringeth forth her first child, the voice of the daughter of Zion, that bewaileth herself, that spreadeth her hands, saying, Woe is me now! for my soul is wearied because of murderers.

The whole city of Jerusalem, which should be a holy city of the LORD inhabited by a holy people, shall flee the noise of the horsemen and bowmen from Babylon who rush into the area where the LORD has been excluded. The people of Jerusalem shall go into thickets and climb upon rocks: every city shall be forsaken by the LORD and there will not be a man, made in the image and likeness of God, to dwell therein. When the people are spoiled and defeated by the working of the Law of the LORD, what will they do? Even though they dress themselves with crimson garments that symbolize power and wear ornaments of gold that symbolizes wealth, even though they paint their faces to make themselves appear fair, the people who love these false symbols will despise you and seek your life and your earthly treasures.

Jeremiah has heard the travail, the cry, of the people whom he compares to a woman in labor and the anguish of her that brings forth her first child. This is the voice of the daughter of Zion, a people who have delivered the child which they have conceived from their own rebellious behavior. The people of Jerusalem are like a woman in labor who cries, Woe is me now, because of the circumstance in which she finds herself, but it is the natural result of the working of the Law. The people have reaped what they have sown as a woman delivers her child into the world. The woman, who symbolizes people everywhere, thinks that her internal pain has been caused by the invaders, the murderers from Babylon, who are in her environment but Jeremiah tells her that the people have brought their pain upon themselves by ignoring and rebelling against the LORD. In the fallen state, **all** the people are guilty of breaking their covenant-connection with the LORD.

CHAPTER 5

1 Run ye to and fro through the streets of Jerusalem, and see now, and know, and seek in the broad places thereof, if ye can find a man, if there be any that executeth judgment, that seeketh the truth; and I
will pardon it.
2 And though they say, The LORD liveth; surely they swear falsely.
3 O LORD, are not thine eyes upon the truth? thou hast stricken them, but they have not grieved; thou hast consumed them, but they have refused to receive correction: they have made their faces harder than a rock; they have refused to return.
4 Therefore I said, Surely these are poor; they are foolish: for they know not the way of the LORD, nor the judgment of their God.

The LORD tells Jeremiah to run to and fro in the streets of Jerusalem, and see for himself, now in the present moment and know for himself the rebellion of the people against the spirit of the LORD which is flowing to each of them. Jeremiah is instructed to seek in the broad and open places of the streets of Jerusalem to see if he can find a man who will execute honest judgment, that seeks the truth as to why the conditions are the way that they are; If Jeremiah finds such an honest man, the LORD will pardon the punishment intended for that honest person. There will be people who say that the LORD lives; but they swear falsely because the people in the fallen state do not know the presence of the LORD in their own experience.

Jeremiah asks the LORD if His eyes are not on the truth? The power of the LORD has stricken the people with His power for their rebellion and they have not grieved; the LORD has consumed them with punishment and they have refused to receive correction for their ways: the people in the fallen state have made their faces harder than a rock so that they are immovable; they have refused to return to the LORD to be the servants of the LORD. Therefore, Jeremiah has said these people of Jerusalem are poor in the spirit of the LORD which is available to them; they are foolish because they ignore the strength and wisdom from the LORD: they do not know the way of the LORD or the judgment of their God to reward or punish the people who magnify or ignore the spirit of the living God.

5 I will get me unto the great men, and will speak unto them; for they have known the way of the LORD, and the judgment of their God: but these have altogether broken the yoke, and burst the bonds.
6 Wherefore a lion out of the forest shall slay them, and a wolf of the evenings shall spoil them, a leopard shall watch over their cities: every one that goeth out thence shall be torn in pieces: because their transgressions are many, and their backslidings are increased.
7 How shall I pardon thee for this? thy children have forsaken me, and sworn by them that are no gods: when I had fed them to the full, they then committed adultery, and assembled themselves by troops in the harlots' houses.
8 They were as fed horses in the morning: every one neighed after his neighbour's wife.
9 Shall I not visit for these things? saith the LORD: and shall not my soul be avenged on such a nation as this?

The Testimony of the Major Prophets

10 Go ye up upon her walls, and destroy; but make not a full end: take away her battlements; for they are not the LORD's.

Jeremiah decides that he will go to the great men and speak to them for surely they have known the way of the LORD and the judgment of their God: but these people have altogether broken the yoke with the spirit of God and broken the bonds of the covenant from God to them and gone their own way without their spiritual connection with the LORD who would love and protect them if they are enfolded in His spirit. Wherefore, as a result of their rebellion against the spirit of the LORD, the symbols of destruction such as a lion of the forest, a wolf of the evening and a leopard shall watch their actions to move swiftly against them in their cities waiting for an opportunity to destroy them: everyone that goes out will be torn in pieces. This destruction of man will occur because their transgressions against the spirit of the LORD are many and their backsliding from revealing the spirit of the LORD in their expressions are increased.

How shall the LORD pardon the people who have ignored and rebelled against Him? Their children have forsaken the presence of the LORD, and sworn by the examples of their fathers to idols that are not gods. When the LORD had fed the people to the full with life, they then committed adultery, and assembled themselves by troops in the harlots' houses seeking pleasures. The fallen people were as fed horses in the morning: every one neighed after his neighbor's wife. Shall the LORD not visit punishment upon the people for these things? and shall not the LORD be avenged on such a rebellious nation as this? The LORD commands that the destructive power shall go upon the walls of Jerusalem and destroy them. But there shall not be a full end of all the people. The power of the LORD will remove all the battlements, the walls of separation, between the LORD and his creation, which are not of the design of the LORD.

11 For the house of Israel and the house of Judah have dealt very treacherously against me, saith the LORD.
12 They have belied the LORD, and said, It is not he; neither shall evil come upon us; neither shall we see sword nor famine:
13 And the prophets shall become wind, and the word is not in them: thus shall it be done unto them.
14 Wherefore thus saith the LORD God of hosts, Because ye speak this word, behold, I will make my words in thy mouth fire, and this people wood, and it shall devour them.

The LORD speaking through Jeremiah declares that the people of the house of Israel and the people of the house of Judah have dealt treacherously, treasonably, and traitorously against the kingdom of the LORD. The rebellious and devious people have lied against the LORD by saying that it is not the LORD who brings these circumstances. The LORD will not bring evil circumstances upon us and the people of Israel and Judah shall not see the sword of war or famine. The prophets who preach otherwise have become as wind, and the word of the LORD is not in them. Therefore, the retribution of the LORD God of hosts shall come upon these fallen people, and because they speak these words, behold, that the power of the LORD is like a destructive fire in the mouths of these fallen people and they are like wood, and the fire shall destroy the wood. The behaviors of the people of Israel and Judah shall cause their own destruction.

15 Lo, I will bring a nation upon you from far, O house of Israel, saith the LORD: it is a mighty nation, it is an ancient nation, a nation whose language thou knowest not, neither understandest what they say.
16 Their quiver is as an open sepulchre, they are all mighty men.
17 And they shall eat up thine harvest, and thy bread, which thy sons and thy daughters should eat: they shall eat up thy flocks and thine herds: they shall eat up thy vines and thy fig trees: they shall impoverish thy fenced cities, wherein thou trustedst, with the sword.
18 Nevertheless in those days, saith the LORD, I will not make a full end with you.

The LORD will bring a nation from far away, a mighty and ancient nation, upon you whose language you do not know or understand what they say. Their quiver is an open sepulcher that produces death; they are all mighty men. They shall eat up your harvest, and the bread which your sons and daughters should eat; they shall eat up your flocks and your herds; your vines and your fig trees; they shall impoverish with their swords the fortified cities that you trusted to defend you. Nevertheless, in those days of destruction, the LORD will not make a full end of you as a people and destroy you completely.

19 And it shall come to pass, when ye shall say, Wherefore doeth the LORD our God all these things unto us? then shalt thou answer them, Like as ye have forsaken me, and served strange gods in your land, so shall ye serve strangers in a land that is not yours.
20 Declare this in the house of Jacob, and publish it in Judah, saying,
21 Hear now this, O foolish people, and without understanding; which have eyes, and see not; which have ears, and hear not:
22 Fear ye not me? saith the LORD: will ye not tremble at my presence, which have placed the sand for the bound of the sea by a perpetual decree, that it cannot pass it: and though the waves thereof toss themselves, yet can they not prevail; though they roar, yet can they not pass over it?

It shall come to pass, when you shall ask, Why does the LORD our God do these things to us? then Jeremiah shall answer them, As you have forsaken the LORD and served strange gods in your land, so shall you serve strangers in a land that is not yours.

Jeremiah is commanded to declare this message in the house of Jacob, the people of the fallen state symbolized by Jacob who had not ascended to the covenant with the LORD as Israel. Jeremiah is to spread the word in all of Judah, saying, Hear now this, foolish people without understanding, people with eyes to see and see not; people with ears to hear and hear not: Do you not fear the LORD? Will you not tremble at the presence of the LORD who has placed the sand by the sea as a perpetual boundary? Though the waves toss themselves repeatedly over the boundary of sand, they cannot prevail; though the waves roar at the boundary, they cannot pass over it?

23 But this people hath a revolting and a rebellious heart; they are revolted and gone.
24 Neither say they in their heart, Let us now fear the LORD our God, that giveth rain, both the former and the latter, in his season: he reserveth unto us the appointed weeks of the harvest.
25 Your iniquities have turned away these things, and your sins have withholden good things from you.
26 For among my people are found wicked men: they lay wait, as he that setteth snares; they set a trap, they catch men.
27 As a cage is full of birds, so are their houses full of deceit: therefore they are become great, and waxen rich.
28 They are waxen fat, they shine: yea, they overpass the deeds of the wicked: they judge not the cause, the cause of the fatherless, yet they prosper; and the right of the needy do they not judge.

The people of Jerusalem, Judah and Israel have a revolting and rebellious heart against the spirit of the LORD; they are rebellious and gone away from the LORD. Neither do they repent and say in their hearts, Let us now fear the LORD our God, that gives rain, both the former and the latter, the spiritual rain of the truth from heaven and the physical rain of water on earth: The LORD reserves to the people the appointed weeks of the harvest based solely on the expressed behavior of the people. This is the Law.

The iniquities of the people have turned away the things of the LORD, and the sins of the people have prevented the good things from the LORD from being made manifest through the people. The LORD knows that among His people are wicked men who lay in wait as he that sets snares to set a trap to catch men. As a cage is full of birds, which are the symbols of thoughts, so are their houses full of deceits; therefore in their evil ways they have become great in an evil world and grown rich and fat. They shine as leaders of the fallen world. They overlook the deeds of the wicked. They do not judge the cause that produces the effects of the fatherless people who are poor, yet they themselves prosper. They do not judge the right of the people in need to prosper also.

30 A wonderful and horrible thing is committed in the land;
31 The prophets prophesy falsely, and the priests bear rule by their means; and my people love to have it so: and what will ye do in the end thereof?

There is a wonderful and a horrible thing which is committed in the land where the people live; the prophets who should be teaching the people the way of the LORD prophesy falsely, and the priests rule the people by means of these false teachings. The end result is that the fallen people love to have it so: they do not want it to change. And the question is what will you as an individual do to end this false state in your environment?

CHAPTER 6

1 O ye children of Benjamin, gather yourselves to flee out of the midst of Jerusalem, and blow the trumpet in Tekoa, and set up a sign of fire in Beth-haccerem: for evil appeareth out of the north, and great destruction.
2 I have likened the daughter of Zion to a comely and delicate woman.
3 The shepherds with their flocks shall come unto her; they shall pitch their tents against her round about; they shall feed every one in his place.
4 Prepare ye war against her; arise, and let us go up at noon. Woe unto us! for the day goeth away, for the shadows of the evening are stretched out.
5 Arise, and let us go by night, and let us destroy her palaces.

The LORD speaking through Jeremiah tells the children of Benjamin, the people who inhabit the territory of Benjamin which is immediately north of Judah, to gather themselves together and flee from the midst of Jerusalem. His message is to blow the trumpet, sound the alarm as a warning, in Tekoa, which is a city 6 miles south of Bethlehem and 11 miles from Jerusalem; Tekoa also means, "a trumpet". The people are also instructed to set up a sign of fire as a visible warning day and night in Beth-haccerem, which was a fire-signal point 2 miles south of Jerusalem: the reason for the warnings of sound and sight are that evil and great destruction are appearing out of the north by means of a Babylonian invasion.

The LORD has likened the daughter of Zion, a personification for the city of Jerusalem, to a comely and delicate woman. The shepherds and their flocks come to Jerusalem—as suitors are attracted to a beautiful woman—pitch their tents, camp round about the city where the people are fed. The invaders plan to prepare war against Jerusalem as they plan to go up at noon. However, the daylight is fading and the day is coming to an end as the shadows of the evening are stretched out. The invaders plan to attack Jerusalem at night and destroy the palaces which are symbols of authority.

6 For thus hath the LORD of hosts said, Hew ye down trees, and cast a mount against Jerusalem: this is the city to be visited; she is wholly oppression in the midst of her.
7 As a fountain casteth out her waters, so she casteth out her wickedness: violence and spoil is heard in her; before me continually is grief and wounds.
8 Be thou instructed, O Jerusalem, lest my soul depart from thee; lest I make thee desolate, a land not inhabited.

The LORD of hosts is the LORD of everyone on the planet including the Babylonians whom the LORD will use for divine retribution against the sinners of Jerusalem. The LORD of hosts says to the invaders, Hew down the trees and cast a mount, an incline of siege ramps against Jerusalem which is the target of their attack, the city to be visited. Jerusalem is a city filled with people who oppress each other. As a fountain casts forth water, Jerusalem casts forth wickedness: violence and spoil is contained in Jerusalem; grief and wounds come forth from the city. Jerusalem is instructed that the power of the LORD shall make the land of Jerusalem desolate and uninhabited.

9 Thus saith the LORD of hosts, They shall throughly glean the remnant of Israel as a vine: turn back thine hand as a grapegatherer into the baskets.
10 To whom shall I speak, and give warning, that they may hear? behold, their ear is uncircumcised, and they cannot hearken: behold, the word of the LORD is unto them a reproach; they have no delight in it.
11 Therefore I am full of the fury of the LORD; I am weary with holding in: I will pour it out upon the children abroad, and upon the assembly of young men together: for even the husband with the wife shall be taken, the aged with him that is full of days.
12 And their houses shall be turned unto others, with their fields and wives together: for I will stretch out my hand upon the inhabitants of the land, saith the LORD.

The LORD of hosts speaking through Jeremiah states that the invaders shall glean through the remnant of Israel as a vine is plucked of its fruit: they shall thoroughly gather with their hands as a grape-gatherer plucks ripe grapes into his baskets.

To whom shall the LORD speak and give warning of the invasion so that the people of Jerusalem will hear? The ear of the people is described as uncircumcised which restricts their hearing and they cannot hear the warning through the sinful covering over their hearts. Behold, they interpret the word of the LORD as a reproach; they have no delight in hearing the word of the LORD.

13 For from the least of them even unto the greatest of them every one is given to covetousness; and from the prophet even unto the priest every one dealeth falsely.
14 They have healed also the hurt of the daughter of my people slightly, saying, Peace, peace; when there is no peace.
15 Were they ashamed when they had committed abomination? nay, they were not at all ashamed, neither could they blush: therefore they shall fall among them that fall: at the time that I visit them they shall be cast down, saith the LORD.

All the inhabitants of Jerusalem, the supposed holy city, from the least to the greatest of them are covetous people; and from the prophet to the priest, every one deals falsely with one another. The priests and the prophets in the city healed the people slightly by saying Peace, Peace, when there is no peace. Were the people of Jerusalem ashamed when they committed the abominations? No, they were not at all ashamed; they do not even know how to blush: therefore, they shall fall among the people who fall at the hands of the invaders. At the time that the LORD visits them, they shall be cast down by the Babylonian invasion.

16 Thus saith the LORD, Stand ye in the ways, and see, and ask for the old paths, where is the good way, and walk therein, and ye shall find rest for your souls. But they said, We will not walk therein.
17 Also I set watchmen over you, saying, Hearken to the sound of the trumpet. But they said, We will not hearken.
18 Therefore hear, ye nations, and know, O congregation, what is among them.
19 Hear, O earth: behold, I will bring evil upon this people, even the fruit of their thoughts, because they have not hearkened unto my words, nor to my law, but rejected it.
20 To what purpose cometh there to me incense from Sheba, and the sweet cane from a far country? your burnt offerings are not acceptable, nor your sacrifices sweet unto me.
21 Therefore thus saith the LORD, Behold, I will lay stumblingblocks
before this people, and the fathers and the sons together shall fall
upon them; the neighbour and his friend shall perish.

When the voice of the LORD through Jeremiah advises the people to stand in the ways of the spirit of the LORD and see the effect of doing that, to ask for the old paths, the good way to walk therein, so that they will find rest for their souls, they said that, they will not walk in the way of the spirit of the LORD moving through themselves.

The LORD has set watchmen to sound the warning of the sound of the trumpet to the inhabitants of Jerusalem, but they said that they will not listen to the words of warning. Therefore, the nations and the congregations should hear what will happen to them. The power of the LORD will bring evil upon the people, even the fruit of their thoughts,

The Testimony of the Major Prophets

because they would not listen to the word of the LORD, nor the Law, because they rejected the words of warning. To what purpose do the people offer incense from Sheba and sweet cane from a country far away? The burnt offerings are not sweet and pleasant to the LORD. Therefore, the LORD will place stumbling blocks because of these unacceptable offerings before the fathers and sons who shall fall together along with the neighbors and friends.

22 Thus saith the LORD, Behold, a people cometh from the north country, and a great nation shall be raised from the sides of the earth.
23 They shall lay hold on bow and spear; they are cruel, and have no mercy; their voice roareth like the sea; and they ride upon horses, set in array as men for war against thee, O daughter of Zion.
24 We have heard the fame thereof: our hands wax feeble: anguish hath taken hold of us, and pain, as of a woman in travail.
25 Go not forth into the field, nor walk by the way; for the sword of the enemy and fear is on every side.

The LORD speaking through Jeremiah announces the retribution for the wrong behavior of the people of Jerusalem. Behold, a people who are a great nation come from the north country who have been raised from the sides of the earth. They shall use bow and spear; they are cruel and show no mercy; their voice roars like the sea; they ride on horses as men set for war toward the daughter of Zion, Jerusalem. The fame of the invaders has been heard and the hands of the people grow feeble; anguish and pain have taken hold of them as a woman in childbirth. The people are advised not to go out into the field or walk by the way of the invaders; for the fear of the power of the enemy is at hand on every side.

26 O daughter of my people, gird thee with sackcloth, and wallow thyself in ashes: make thee mourning, as for an only son, most bitter lamentation: for the spoiler shall suddenly come upon us.
27 I have set thee for a tower and a fortress among my people, that thou mayest know and try their way.
28 They are all grievous revolters, walking with slanders: they are brass and iron; they are all corrupters.
29 The bellows are burned, the lead is consumed of the fire; the founder melteth in vain: for the wicked are not plucked away.
30 Reprobate silver shall men call them, because the LORD hath rejected them.

Jeremiah warns the people to prepare themselves emotionally for certain defeat at the hands of the Babylonians by putting on their sackcloth and covering themselves with ashes, the traditional practice of mourning: the people are advised to make a great and grievous mourning as for the loss of an only son, which would end the bloodline of that father; for the spoiler shall suddenly come upon us. The LORD has set Jerusalem as a tower and a fortress among the people so that the people may know what the invaders will do to them. The invaders are grievous revolters against the way of the LORD who walk with slanders and evil in their hearts; they are as false as brass and as strong as iron; all of them are corrupters of the way of the LORD. They are the destructive sword of the LORD.

The bellows that accelerates the destructive power, the fire of the LORD, will have a destructive effect on the people of Jerusalem as the fire burns hot to melt the lead which is consumed in the fire to refine the metal; the founder, the originator, of the process of purification melts the metal in vain for the wicked are not plucked away in the process. The people are as reprobate silver, degenerate and base, because the LORD has rejected them because they have rebelled and ignored the LORD; they will not repent and return to the LORD to express the spirit of the LORD through each of them. Jeremiah allowed the spirit of the LORD to flow through him.

CHAPTER 7

1 The word that came to Jeremiah from the LORD, saying,
2 Stand in the gate of the LORD's house, and proclaim there this word, and say, Hear the word of the LORD, all ye of Judah, that enter in at these gates to worship the LORD.
3 Thus saith the LORD of hosts, the God of Israel, Amend your ways and your doings, and I will cause you to dwell in this place.
4 Trust ye not in lying words, saying, The temple of the LORD, The temple of the LORD, The temple of the LORD, are these.
5 For if ye thoroughly amend your ways and your doings; if ye thoroughly execute judgment between a man and his neighbour;
6 If ye oppress not the stranger, the fatherless, and the widow, and shed not innocent blood in this place, neither walk after other gods to your hurt:
7 Then will I cause you to dwell in this place, in the land that I gave to your fathers, for ever and ever.
8 Behold, ye trust in lying words, that cannot profit.

The word that came to Jeremiah from the LORD, saying, Stand in the gate of the LORD's house by letting the spirit of the LORD flow through the gate, the body, mind and heart of Jeremiah, to proclaim this message: Hear the word of the LORD all people of Judah, that enter in at these gates, the gates which are the symbols of their bodies, minds and hearts, to worship the LORD by letting the LORD's spirit flow out **through** them. This is not the word of Jeremiah; it is the word of the LORD of hosts, the God of Israel, that commands the people to amend their ways and their behaviors, and the LORD will cause the people who do it to dwell in this holy place.

The people are advised by Jeremiah not to trust in lying words that repeat the phrase, The temple of the LORD over and over again, or, the temple of the LORD is thus and so. The spirit of the LORD moving through a person produces actions which are observable. If a person thoroughly amends their human ways and doings to let the spirit of the LORD produce new actions; if you thoroughly execute the LORD's judgment between a man and his neighbor; if you do not oppress the stranger, the fatherless, and the widow, and do not shed innocent blood, neither walk after other gods that lead you to hurt; then the LORD will cause you to dwell in the holy place in the land that the LORD gave to your fathers forever and ever. Behold, that you who trust in lying words, cannot profit by the truth of the spirit of the LORD.

9 Will ye steal, murder, and commit adultery, and swear falsely, and burn incense unto Baal, and walk after other gods whom ye know not;
10 And come and stand before me in this house, which is called by my name, and say, We are delivered to do all these abominations?
11 Is this house, which is called by my name, become a den of robbers in your eyes? Behold, even I have seen it, saith the LORD.

The Testimony of the Major Prophets

Can a person steal, murder, commit adultery, swear falsely, burn incense to Baal and other false gods whom you do not know and also come and stand before the LORD in the house of the LORD, the holy place available within each person which is called by the name of the LORD, I AM. In this holy place can you truly say that you were delivered here on earth to do all these abominations? Is the holy house, which is called by the name of the LORD, I AM, become a den of robbers that steal the power of the LORD to do abominations? Behold, the LORD has seen these abominations that the people have been doing because the LORD is present with you, in the holy place within you, the holy place that has been defiled by the action of man in the fallen state.

12 But go ye now unto my place which was in Shiloh, where I set my name at the first, and see what I did to it for the wickedness of my people Israel.
13 And now, because ye have done all these works, saith the LORD, and I spake unto you, rising up early and speaking, but ye heard not; and I called you, but ye answered not;
14 Therefore will I do unto this house, which is called by my name, wherein ye trust, and unto the place which I gave to you and to your fathers, as I have done to Shiloh.
15 And I will cast you out of my sight, as I have cast out all your brethren, even the whole seed of Ephraim.

The people who will not repent and change are directed to go to the place, the tabernacle which was set up in Shiloh after the conquest of Canaan, and see what the LORD has done to it because of the wickedness of His people, Israel. The holy place of the tabernacle was destroyed. Now, because you have done all these evil works, broken the commandments that were spoken to you and ignored the call of the LORD to return to Him and you did not answer, therefore the LORD will do to the house of your being, where the LORD dwells, what has been done to the tabernacle at Shiloh. The people who do not hear the call of the LORD will be cast out of the sight of the LORD as the LORD has cast out the sight of all your brethren before you, even the whole seed of Ephraim, the seed which could have been fruitful.

16 Therefore pray not thou for this people, neither lift up cry nor prayer for them, neither make intercession to me: for I will not hear thee.
17 Seest thou not what they do in the cities of Judah and in the streets of Jerusalem?
18 The children gather wood, and the fathers kindle the fire, and the women knead their dough, to make cakes to the queen of heaven, and to pour out drink offerings unto other gods, that they may provoke me to anger.
19 Do they provoke me to anger? saith the LORD: do they not provoke themselves to the confusion of their own faces?
20 Therefore thus saith the Lord GOD; Behold, mine anger and my fury shall be poured out upon this place, upon man, and upon beast, and upon the trees of the field, and upon the fruit of the ground; and it shall burn, and shall not be quenched.

The spirit of the LORD speaking through Jeremiah instructs the people who hear His word to not pray for the people who have heard the word of the LORD and refused to heed the call. People are not to intercede on behalf of those who have ignored and refused the spirit of the LORD. The LORD will not hear their prayers. Do you not see what they do in the cities of Judah and on the streets of Jerusalem? The people who have fallen away from the LORD go about their own ways: their children gather wood, and the fathers kindle the fire, and the women knead their dough, to make cakes to the queen of heaven, and to pour out drink offerings to other gods, that they may provoke the LORD to anger. Do they provoke the LORD to anger? Do they not provoke themselves to the confusion of their own faces?

Therefore the Lord GOD says; Behold, mine anger and my fury shall be poured out upon this place, upon man, and upon beast, and upon the trees of the field, and upon the fruit of the ground; and it shall burn, and shall not be quenched. It is the working of the Law that the creative love of the LORD will be replaced by the destructive power of the LORD to those who ignore and rebel against the LORD.

21 Thus saith the LORD of hosts, the God of Israel; Put your burnt offerings unto your sacrifices, and eat flesh.
22 For I spake not unto your fathers, nor commanded them in the day that I brought them out of the land of Egypt, concerning burnt offerings or sacrifices:

23 But this thing commanded I them, saying, Obey my voice, and I will be your God, and ye shall be my people: and walk ye in all the ways that I have commanded you, that it may be well unto you.
24 But they hearkened not, nor inclined their ear, but walked in the counsels and in the imagination of their evil heart, and went backward, and not forward.

The LORD of hosts, the God of Israel, speaking through Jeremiah tells the people to put aside their burnt offerings and eat the flesh themselves. The LORD did not speak to command the people to make burnt offerings and sacrifices when they were brought out of the land of Egypt. The LORD commanded the people to walk in the ways that the LORD has commanded you so that it would be well for the people. The people did not listen and to the commandments of the LORD but they walked in the counsel of their own imagination and evil, impure hearts which cause them to backslide, go backward, from the way of the LORD instead of forward to the individual expression of the LORD's spirit.

25 Since the day that your fathers came forth out of the land of Egypt unto this day I have even sent unto you all my servants the prophets, daily rising up early and sending them:
26 Yet they hearkened not unto me, nor inclined their ear, but hardened their neck: they did worse than their fathers.
27 Therefore thou shalt speak all these words unto them; but they will not hearken to thee: thou shalt also call unto them; but they will not answer thee.
28 But thou shalt say unto them, This is a nation that obeyeth not the voice of the LORD their God, nor receiveth correction: truth is perished, and is cut off from their mouth.
29 Cut off thine hair, O Jerusalem, and cast it away, and take up a lamentation on high places; for the LORD hath rejected and forsaken the generation of his wrath.
30 For the children of Judah have done evil in my sight, saith the LORD: they have set their abominations in the house which is called by my name, to pollute it.
31 And they have built the high places of Tophet, which is in the valley of the son of Hinnom, to burn their sons and their daughters in the fire; which I commanded them not, neither came it into my heart.

Since the day that your fathers came forth from the land of Egypt until this day, the LORD has always sent His servants, the prophets, with the word of the LORD and the people did not listen; in fact, they hardened their necks and would not turn to hear the word of the LORD: they did worse than their fathers before them. Therefore, you shall speak all these words to the people and they will not listen; you shall call them, and they will not answer. But you shall say to them, This is a nation that does not obey the voice of the LORD their God and does not receive correction: truth is perished and is cut off from their mouth, their expression.

Cut off your hair, people of Jerusalem, and cast it away and take up a lamentation on high places, to demonstrate your sorrow for the predicament in which you find yourselves. These acts of sorrow for yourselves will do no good for the LORD has rejected and forsaken the generation of his wrath. The children of Judah have done evil in the sight of the LORD: they have done their abominations in the house which is called by the name of the LORD, I AM, and polluted it by their behaviors. They have built high places of Tophet, which means, "betrayal", high places to worship false gods, which is in the valley, the low place, of the son of Hinnom, which means "their riches", where their earthly riches are worshipped instead of the commandments of the LORD. It is these actions which burn their sons and daughters in the fire, the destructive fire of the power of the LORD which the LORD did not command them to do, nor did it ever enter into His heart.

32 Therefore, behold, the days come, saith the LORD, that it shall no more be called Tophet, nor the valley of the son of Hinnom, but the valley of slaughter: for they shall bury in Tophet, till there be no place.
33 And the carcases of this people shall be meat for the fowls of the heaven, and for the beasts of the earth; and none shall fray them away.
34 Then will I cause to cease from the cities of Judah, and from the streets of Jerusalem, the voice of mirth, and the voice of gladness, the voice of the bridegroom, and the voice of the bride: for the land shall be desolate.

Therefore, Behold. The days come that it shall no more be called Tophet, betrayal, or the valley of the son of Hinnom, the valley where they will seek their earthly riches, but, it shall be called the valley of slaughter, the slaughter which was caused by the rebellion of the people who would not heed the word of the LORD. The carcasses of the people shall be meat for the fowls of heaven and the beasts of the field; and there shall be no people left to frighten them away.

The Testimony of the Major Prophets

Then, the LORD shall cause to cease from the cities of Judah and the streets of Jerusalem, the voice of mirth and the voice of gladness, the voice of the bridegroom and the voice of the bride: for the land and the people shall be desolate from the invasion of the Babylonians.

CHAPTER 8

1 At that time, saith the LORD, they shall bring out the bones of the kings of Judah, and the bones of his princes, and the bones of the priests, and the bones of the prophets, and the bones of the inhabitants of Jerusalem, out of their graves:
2 And they shall spread them before the sun, and the moon, and all the host of heaven, whom they have loved, and whom they have served, and after whom they have walked, and whom they have sought, and whom they have worshipped: they shall not be gathered, nor be buried; they shall be for dung upon the face of the earth.
3 And death shall be chosen rather than life by all the residue of them that remain of this evil family, which remain in all the places whither I have driven them, saith the LORD of hosts.

At the time of the invasion, and the destruction and desolation which accompanies it, says the LORD to Jeremiah, the invaders shall bring forth the bones of the leaders who were kings of Judah along with the bones of his princes, priests, prophets and the inhabitants of Jerusalem were taken out of their graves to spread their bones before the sun and the moon, and all the host of heaven. The invaders open the sacred crypts to demonstrate that they control the material heritage and that nothing from the past, present or future is beyond their control as they intimidate and humiliate their captives. The bones of the leaders shall be spread before all that they have served, or sought, or those who they walked after and worshipped: these people shall not be gathered nor buried; they shall be as dung which disintegrates and is used as fertilizer upon the face of the earth. The conditions will be so horrible that death will be preferred and chosen rather than life by all those who remain alive in the places which the LORD has driven the fallen people by means of the working of the Law.

4 Moreover thou shalt say unto them, Thus saith the LORD; Shall they fall, and not arise? shall he turn away, and not return?
5 Why then is this people of Jerusalem slidden back by a perpetual backsliding? they hold fast deceit, they refuse to return.
6 I hearkened and heard, but they spake not aright: no man repented him of his wickedness, saying, What have I done? every one turned to his course, as the horse rusheth into the battle.
7 Yea, the stork in the heaven knoweth her appointed times; and the turtle and the crane and the swallow observe the time of their coming; but my people know not the judgment of the LORD.

Moreover, Jeremiah shall say to them as the messenger of the LORD, when he said, Shall not all the leaders and the people of Jerusalem fall and not arise? Shall the LORD turn away and never return? Why do the people of Jerusalem slide back from the way of the LORD as a perpetual backslider? The fallen people hold fast to deceit, and they refuse to return to the service of the LORD. Jeremiah hearkened and listened intently but the people in the fallen state did not speak correctly and uprightly. There was no man who repented of his own wickedness, saying, What have I done? Everyone proceeded on his own course as the horse rushes into battle. Yes, the stork in the heaven knows her

The Testimony of the Major Prophets

appointed time, and the turtle dove, the crane and the swallow observe the time of their coming; but the people do not know the time that the judgment of the LORD should come upon them.

8 How do ye say, We are wise, and the law of the LORD is with us? Lo, certainly in vain made he it; the pen of the scribes is in vain.
9 The wise men are ashamed, they are dismayed and taken: lo, they have rejected the word of the LORD; and what wisdom is in them?
10 Therefore will I give their wives unto others, and their fields to them that shall inherit them: for every one from the least even unto the greatest is given to covetousness, from the prophet even unto the priest every one dealeth falsely.
11 For they have healed the hurt of the daughter of my people slightly, saying, Peace, peace; when there is no peace.
12 Were they ashamed when they had committed abomination? nay, they were not at all ashamed, neither could they blush: therefore shall they fall among them that fall: in the time of their visitation they shall be cast down, saith the LORD.

How is it that the fallen people can say, We are wise and the law of the LORD is with us? Lo, they have made that statement in vain, in vanity, because it is not true. The pen of the scribes is in vain. The wise men of the fallen state are ashamed, dismayed and taken; they have rejected the word of the LORD; and what wisdom is in the people who have rejected the spirit of the LORD? therefore the LORD will give their wives to others, and their fields to them that shall inherit them by force. In the fallen state, where everyone is controlled by greed and covets his neighbors goods from the least to the greatest person, from the priest to the prophet, everyone deals falsely with each other.

The priest and the prophet of the fallen state have healed and helped the daughter of the LORD's people only slightly, saying, Peace, Peace, when there is no peace. Were the people in the fallen state ashamed when they had committed abomination? No, they were not at all ashamed, neither could they blush: therefore shall they fall among them that fall: in the time of their visitation by the working of the Law, they shall be cast down, says the LORD.

13 I will surely consume them, saith the LORD: there shall be no grapes on the vine, nor figs on the fig tree, and the leaf shall fade; and the things that I have given them shall pass away from them.
14 Why do we sit still? assemble yourselves, and let us enter into the defenced cities, and let us be silent there: for the LORD our God hath put us to silence, and given us water of gall to drink, because we have sinned against the LORD.
15 We looked for peace, but no good came; and for a time of health, and behold trouble!
16 The snorting of his horses was heard from Dan: the whole land trembled at the sound of the neighing of his strong ones; for they are come, and have devoured the land, and all that is in it; the city, and those that dwell therein.
17 For, behold, I will send serpents, cockatrices, among you, which will not be charmed, and they shall bite you, saith the LORD.

The LORD states emphatically that he will consume the people who do not follow the way of the LORD: there shall be no grapes on the vine, nor figs on the fig tree, and the leaf shall fade; and the things that the LORD has given them as blessings shall pass away from them. The people in the fallen state ask why do they sit still? They can assemble themselves and enter the gates of the defended cities and they can be silent there: they begin to realize that the power of the LORD has put them to silence and given them water of gall to drink, the symbol of terrible conditions, because they have sinned against the LORD.

We looked for peace, but no peace came; and for a time of health, and behold, trouble! The snorting of the horses of the invader was heard from the distant land of Dan: the whole land trembled at the sound of the neighing of his strong ones; for they are come, and have devoured the land, and all that is in it; the city, and those that dwell therein. Behold, the LORD will send serpents, cockatrices, among you as symbols of people who contain venom. The serpents will not be charmed, and they shall bite you to cause sickness and pain, says the LORD.

18 When I would comfort myself against sorrow, my heart is faint in me.
19 Behold the voice of the cry of the daughter of my people because of them that dwell in a far country: Is not the LORD in Zion? is not her king in her? Why have they provoked me to anger with their graven images, and with strange vanities?

The Symbolic Version of Jeremiah

20 The harvest is past, the summer is ended, and we are not saved.
21 For the hurt of the daughter of my people am I hurt; I am black; astonishment hath taken hold on me.
22 Is there no balm in Gilead; is there no physician there? why then is not the health of the daughter of my people recovered?

When Jeremiah who knows the law of the LORD tries to comfort himself in the sorrow of the terrible circumstances of the invasion, his heart is faint within him. He is able to behold the cry of the daughter of his people, Jerusalem, because of the invaders from the far country of Babylonia. He asks if the LORD is not in Zion, the spiritual hill within each person? Is not the king in her? Why have the fallen people provoked the LORD to anger with their worship of graven images and their strange vanities?

The harvest is past, the summer is ended and we as a people are not saved from our fallen behavior. For the hurt of the daughter of my people, Jeremiah is hurt; he is black with the absence of light; astonishment has taken hold on me. Is there no balm in Gilead; is there no physician there? Why then is not the health of the daughter of my people recovered? Why do they remain in the fallen state when the ascended state is also available and at hand?

CHAPTER 9

1 Oh that my head were waters, and mine eyes a fountain of tears, that I might weep day and night for the slain of the daughter of my people!
2 Oh that I had in the wilderness a lodging place of wayfaring men; that I might leave my people, and go from them! for they be all adulterers, an assembly of treacherous men.
3 And they bend their tongues like their bow for lies: but they are not valiant for the truth upon the earth; for they proceed from evil to evil, and they know not me, saith the LORD.

The spirit of the LORD moving through the physical form—the emotional heart, the mind and the body— of Jeremiah is saddened by the plight and circumstances of the city of Jerusalem and the kingdoms of Judah and Israel which are victims to the invaders from Babylon. He wishes that his head were filled with waters and his eyes a fountain of tears so that he could weep day and night for the slain people of the daughter of his people. The "daughter" of his people are the people in the fallen state who have attached themselves to the materialistic idols of the environment as a daughter attaches herself and submits to a parent. Jeremiah wishes that he had a dwelling place in the wilderness as a lodging place for the wayfaring men who had strayed from the path of the LORD so that Jeremiah could leave his people and depart from them and the sadness which they have brought upon themselves. All the people are adulterers who have attached themselves and blended with the things of the environment made of physical forms, atoms and molecules, which they deemed more important than the spirit of the LORD. This choice of earthly matter over the spirit of the LORD made all of them an assembly of treacherous men. They bend their tongues, like bows are bent, to tell lies: they are not valiant and steadfast for the truth to come on earth through a straight tongue which does not distort the truth of the spirit of the LORD; they proceed from evil to evil as they express themselves and they do not know the LORD who is being made manifest for them through Jeremiah.

4 Take ye heed every one of his neighbour, and trust ye not in any brother: for every brother will utterly supplant, and every neighbour will walk with slanders.
5 And they will deceive every one his neighbour, and will not speak the truth: they have taught their tongue to speak lies, and weary themselves to commit iniquity.
6 Thine habitation is in the midst of deceit; through deceit they refuse to know me, saith the LORD.

Jeremiah tells the fallen people that each one of them should take heed for his neighbor, to pay attention to their expression and example, and not to trust any of their brothers: for every one of them will utterly supplant, will inevitably replace the spirit of the LORD which is flowing through each of them with a distortion of the spirit. Every one of their neighbors will walk with slanders against the way of the LORD. They will deceive their neighbors and they will not speak the truth. In the fallen state, they have taught their tongue to speak lies and they weary themselves in their efforts to commit iniquity instead of letting the spirit of the LORD to be made visible and manifest itself on earth. Their habitation, their dwelling place, is in the midst of deceit in the fallen world, and it is through this deceit that they refuse to know the presence of the LORD.

7 Therefore thus saith the LORD of hosts, Behold, I will melt them, and try them; for how shall I do for the daughter of my people?
8 Their tongue is as an arrow shot out; it speaketh deceit: one speaketh peaceably to his neighbour with his mouth, but in heart he layeth his wait.
9 Shall I not visit them for these things? saith the LORD: shall not my soul be avenged on such a nation as this?

Therefore the LORD of the hosts of all the people says, Behold, I will melt them and try them in the furnace of wrong effects which they have made; for how else shall the LORD offer correction for the daughter, the fallen state, who has rebelled against the spirit of the LORD? Their tongue, their collective expression, is as an arrow shot out of a bow; it speaks deceit: one speaks peaceably with his mouth to his neighbor but in the evil of his heart he lays in wait to harm him. Shall not the LORD visit them for these evil things that they do? Shall not the LORD be avenged on such a rebellious nation as this?

10 For the mountains will I take up a weeping and wailing, and for the habitations of the wilderness a lamentation, because they are burned up, so that none can pass through them; neither can men hear the voice of the cattle; both the fowl of the heavens and the beast are fled; they are gone.
11 And I will make Jerusalem heaps, and a den of dragons; and I will make the cities of Judah desolate, without an inhabitant.
12 Who is the wise man, that may understand this? and who is he to whom the mouth of the LORD hath spoken, that he may declare it, for what the land perisheth and is burned up like a wilderness, that none passeth through?

Jeremiah states that for the mountains, the high divine potential, that the people could be, he will take up weeping for their loss, and for their habitations as they dwell in the wilderness of their own making; he will lament for them because they are burned up in the furnace of wrong effects so that no one can pass through them. Neither can men hear the voice of the cattle, the symbol of the animals that they have become, which is not man made in the image and likeness of God. The fowl, which symbolize thoughts of the heaven in one's consciousness, and the beast of the field, which symbolize the effects of those thoughts, have fled, they have gone away; the distinction between the heavenly behavior and the earthly behavior are gone from the consciousness of man when they are seen as one continuous progression from the heaven to the earth. The earthly form is a continuation of the heavenly image.

The result of this fall of man is that the LORD will make Jerusalem heaps of destructive debris and a den of the dragons that fallen people have become. The working of the law of the LORD, the Law of Sowing and Reaping, will make the cities of Judah desolate, without an inhabitant. Who is the wise man that may understand this working of the Law? and who is he to whom the mouth of the LORD, the spokesman for the LORD that Jeremiah is, has spoken and that person has truly heard so that he may declare the truth of it in his own experience. What land perishes and is burned up like the wilderness that no man in the fallen state has passed through?

13 And the LORD saith, Because they have forsaken my law which I set before them, and have not obeyed my voice, neither walked therein;
14 But have walked after the imagination of their own heart, and after Baalim, which their fathers taught them:
15 Therefore thus saith the LORD of hosts, the God of Israel; Behold, I will feed them, even this people, with wormwood, and give them water of gall to drink.
16 I will scatter them also among the heathen, whom neither they nor their fathers have known: and I will send a sword after them, till I have consumed them.

The LORD said that because the fallen people have forsaken His law, the Law of Sowing and Reaping, which the LORD has set before them, and the people have not obeyed the voice of the LORD nor walked in the way that the LORD commanded; but the people walked after the imaginations of their own hearts, and after Baalim, the false gods, which their fathers taught them to do: Therefore, the action of the LORD of hosts, the God of Israel, will feed the people the bitter wormwood and give them gall to drink which are symbols of a distorted and fallen environment. The LORD will scatter the people among the heathen whom neither they nor their forefathers have known: and the sword of truth will be sent by the LORD after them until all the people of the fallen state have been consumed. The LORD

The Testimony of the Major Prophets

does not desire the people to be consumed with disintegration and death; they can also be consumed by repentance and the return to the LORD.

17 Thus saith the LORD of hosts, Consider ye, and call for the mourning women, that they may come; and send for cunning women, that they may come:
18 And let them make haste, and take up a wailing for us, that our eyes may run down with tears, and our eyelids gush out with waters.
19 For a voice of wailing is heard out of Zion, How are we spoiled! we are greatly confounded, because we have forsaken the land, because our dwellings have cast us out.
20 Yet hear the word of the LORD, O ye women, and let your ear receive the word of his mouth, and teach your daughters wailing, and every one her neighbour lamentation.
21 For death is come up into our windows, and is entered into our palaces, to cut off the children from without, and the young men from the streets.

The LORD of hosts of all the people says that all the people in the fallen state, should consider their predicament. The LORD through Jeremiah calls for the mourning women that they may come, and He sends for the cunning women so that they may repent and come. The mourning women and the cunning women symbolize the hearts and minds of the people in the fallen state. Let them make haste and take up a wailing and longing for the spirit of the LORD so that the eyes and eyelids of Jeremiah and the LORD will run down with tears of joy and gladness at their return.

A voice of wailing is heard out of Zion, the spiritual dwelling place of the LORD and His people, exclaiming, How are we spoiled! There is a knowing of the answer as to why the people in the fallen state are spoiled because they have left Zion, the dwelling place of the LORD and His people. The answer is that we, the people in the fallen state, are greatly confounded because we have forsaken the land, the spiritual land, for the dwellings in the world of forms which have cast us out of the world of spirit.

Yet the women of the fallen state, male and female, are called to hear the word of the LORD. The people are to hear with their ears the words from the mouth of Jeremiah who speaks the word of the LORD so that they can teach their daughters and their neighbors, repentance so they will weep and long for the spirit of the LORD from which they have separated. The return to the LORD is desirable because death has come to the windows and entered our individual palaces where it can be seen. It is only a matter of time until death destroys the children and the young men from off the streets and they will be no more.

22 Speak, Thus saith the LORD, Even the carcases of men shall fall as dung upon the open field, and as the handful after the harvestman, and none shall gather them.
23 Thus saith the LORD, Let not the wise man glory in his wisdom, neither let the mighty man glory in his might, let not the rich man glory in his riches:
24 But let him that glorieth glory in this, that he understandeth and knoweth me, that I am the LORD which exercise lovingkindness, judgment, and righteousness, in the earth: for in these things I delight, saith the LORD.

The LORD speaks through Jeremiah that even the carcasses of the men shall fall as dung, human fertilizer, upon the open field and as plentiful grain after the one who harvests it, and no one shall gather them. The LORD warns and cautions that in the fallen state, the wise man should not glory in his wisdom, the mighty man should not glory in his might nor the rich man glory in his riches. But let the person, who likes glory, glory in the fact that he understands and knows that I AM the LORD which exercises loving kindness, judgment and righteousness in the earth. The LORD delights in these positive things.

25 Behold, the days come, saith the LORD, that I will punish all them which are circumcised with the uncircumcised;
26 Egypt, and Judah, and Edom, and the children of Ammon, and Moab, and all that are in the utmost corners, that dwell in the wilderness: for all these nations are uncircumcised, and all the house of Israel are uncircumcised in the heart.

Behold and observe, says the LORD, that the days come that the LORD will punish all of the people with the conditions that mankind has made on earth whether they are physically circumcised or not; Egypt, and Judah, and Edom, and the children of Ammon, and Moab, and all that are in the utmost corners, that dwell in the wilderness: for all these nations are uncircumcised, and all the house of Israel are uncircumcised in the heart. The evil and the uncleanness of the heart have not been cut away

CHAPTER 10

1 Hear ye the word which the LORD speaketh unto you, O house of Israel:
2 Thus saith the LORD, Learn not the way of the heathen, and be not dismayed at the signs of heaven; for the heathen are dismayed at them.
3 For the customs of the people are vain: for one cutteth a tree out of the forest, the work of the hands of the workman, with the axe.
4 They deck it with silver and with gold; they fasten it with nails and with hammers, that it move not.
5 They are upright as the palm tree, but speak not: they must needs be borne, because they cannot go. Be not afraid of them; for they cannot do evil, neither also is it in them to do good.

The LORD speaks to the house of Israel, the spiritual people in human forms that compose the people who are consciously aware that they are of the house of Israel, so that they can hear and do his word: The word is that they are not to learn the way of the heathen and to be not dismayed at the sighs of heaven, the material forms which have been made by the power from heaven, the place of cause, for the heathen are dismayed, shocked and horrified at these signs. The customs of the fallen people are vain, filled with vanity, which is demonstrated in this parable. A workman uses his hands to cut a tree out of the forest with an ax. They deck it with silver and gold, fasten it with nails and hammers, so that it does not move. These decorated pieces of wood stand upright as a palm tree but they do not speak: these idols need to be carried, borne from place to place, because they cannot go by themselves. The people are instructed to not be afraid of them, the idols, because they cannot do evil; neither is it in them to do good.

6 Forasmuch as there is none like unto thee, O LORD; thou art great, and thy name is great in might.
7 Who would not fear thee, O King of nations? for to thee doth it appertain: forasmuch as among all the wise men of the nations, and in all their kingdoms, there is none like unto thee.
8 But they are altogether brutish and foolish: the stock is a doctrine of vanities.
9 Silver spread into plates is brought from Tarshish, and gold from Uphaz, the work of the workman, and of the hands of the founder: blue and purple is their clothing: they are all the work of cunning men.
10 But the LORD is the true God, he is the living God, and an everlasting king: at his wrath the earth shall tremble, and the nations shall not be able to abide his indignation.

On the other hand, there is none like the LORD who is great and whose name, I AM, is great in might. Who would not fear the King of all nations? for it is to the individual that the might of the LORD pertains directly. Among all the wise men of the nations, and in all their kingdoms, there is none like the living LORD. But the idols of the heathen are altogether brutish and foolish: The stock of wood from which the idol is made is a doctrine of vanities. Silver spread into plates is brought from Tarshish, and gold from Uphaz, the work of the workman, and of the hands of the founder: blue and purple is their clothing: they are all the work of cunning men. But the LORD is the true God, he is the living God, and an everlasting king: at his wrath the earth shall tremble, and the nations shall not be able to abide his indignation.

11 Thus shall ye say unto them, The gods that have not made the heavens and the earth, even they shall perish from the earth, and from under these heavens.
12 He hath made the earth by his power, he hath established the world by his wisdom, and hath stretched out the heavens by his discretion.
13 When he uttereth his voice, there is a multitude of waters in the heavens, and he causeth the vapours to ascend from the ends of the earth; he maketh lightnings with rain, and bringeth forth the wind out of his treasures.
14 Every man is brutish in his knowledge: every founder is confounded by the graven image: for his molten image is falsehood, and there is no breath in them.
15 They are vanity, and the work of errors: in the time of their visitation they shall perish.
16 The portion of Jacob is not like them: for he is the former of all things; and Israel is the rod of his inheritance: The LORD of hosts is his name.

Jeremiah shall say to the people who worship the decorated wooden idols, The gods that have not made the heavens and the earth of your own forms shall perish from the earth and from under the heavens which are contained in the people of the house of Israel. The LORD has made the earth by His power, and established the earth by His wisdom, and stretched out the heavens by His discretion. When he utters his voice, there is a multitude of waters in the heavens, and he causes the vapors to ascend from the ends of the earth; He makes lightning with rain, and brings forth the wind out of his treasures. The LORD is the cause of these actions.

Every man is brutish, very limited, in his knowledge: every founder, creator or craftsman, is confounded by the graven image made from material things: for the molten image made by a brutish man is a falsehood, and there is no breath in these lifeless idols. They are vanity, and the work of errors: in the time of their visitation by the power of the LORD, they shall perish. The portion of Jacob, the symbol of the repentant human material self who seeks the LORD, is not like them: for he is the former of all things; and Israel is the spiritual rod of Jacob's material inheritance: The LORD of hosts, I AM, is the name of the rod of the spiritual inheritance.

17 Gather up thy wares out of the land, O inhabitant of the fortress.
18 For thus saith the LORD, Behold, I will sling out the inhabitants of the land at this once, and will distress them, that they may find it so.
19 Woe is me for my hurt! my wound is grievous: but I said, Truly this is a grief, and I must bear it.
20 My tabernacle is spoiled, and all my cords are broken: my children are gone forth of me, and they are not: there is none to stretch forth my tent any more, and to set up my curtains.
21 For the pastors are become brutish, and have not sought the LORD: therefore they shall not prosper, and all their flocks shall be scattered.
22 Behold, the noise of the bruit is come, and a great commotion out of the north country, to make the cities of Judah desolate, and a den of dragons.

The people, the inhabitants of the fortress of the LORD, are instructed to gather up all their wares. The LORD says, Behold, I will sling out the false inhabitants of the land at this once, and will distress them, that they may find it so. They will cry at the loss of their possessions: Woe is me for my hurt! my wound is grievous: but I said, Truly this is a grief, and I must bear it. The sadness is replaced with resolve.

The LORD proclaims that His tabernacle on earth through His creation, Man, is spoiled, and all the spiritual cords of connection with the people are broken: the LORD's children are gone forth from Him, and they are not His children any longer because His connection to them has been severed by them. There is no one to stretch forth the LORD's tent any more, and to set up His curtains. The pastors are become brutish because they worship idols, and they have not sought the LORD. Therefore, they shall not prosper, and all their flocks shall be scattered. Behold, the noise of the bruit, the reputation of the invader, is come, and a great commotion out of the north country, to make the cities of Judah desolate, and a den of dragons.

23 O LORD, I know that the way of man is not in himself: it is not in man that walketh to direct his steps.
24 O LORD, correct me, but with judgment; not in thine anger, lest thou bring me to nothing.

The Testimony of the Major Prophets

25 Pour out thy fury upon the heathen that know thee not, and upon the families that call not on thy name: for they have eaten up Jacob, and devoured him, and consumed him, and have made his habitation desolate.

Jeremiah states that the way of man is not in himself. It is not in man who walks to direct his own steps. The LORD is called upon to correct Jeremiah with loving judgment and not destructive anger lest Jeremiah be brought to nothing. Jeremiah is willing to be a servant of the LORD. Let the fury be poured out upon the heathen and families that do not call upon the LORD: for they have eaten up, consumed and devoured, Jacob, the symbol of one who desired the LORD, and his habitation is desolate within them.

CHAPTER 11

1 The word that came to Jeremiah from the LORD, saying,
2 Hear ye the words of this covenant, and speak unto the men of Judah, and to the inhabitants of Jerusalem;
3 And say thou unto them, Thus saith the LORD God of Israel; Cursed be the man that obeyeth not the words of this covenant,
4 Which I commanded your fathers in the day that I brought them forth out of the land of Egypt, from the iron furnace, saying, Obey my voice, and do them, according to all which I command you: so shall ye be my people, and I will be your God:
5 That I may perform the oath which I have sworn unto your fathers, to give them a land flowing with milk and honey, as it is this day. Then answered I, and said, So be it, O LORD.

The word of the LORD has come to Jeremiah that he is to hear the words of the covenant and speak them to the men of Judah and the people of Jerusalem. Jeremiah is to say to them that the LORD God of Israel has said, Cursed be the man that does not obey the words of this covenant which the LORD commanded your fathers in the day that He brought them forth out of the land of Egypt. The people are to obey the voice of the LORD, and to do those commandments in their individual experience. In this manner, the people will be the LORD's people and He will be their God so that He will perform the oath which the LORD swore to their fathers, to give them a land flowing with milk and honey, as it is this day. Then Jeremiah answered and said, So be it with me, O LORD.

6 Then the LORD said unto me, Proclaim all these words in the cities of Judah, and in the streets of Jerusalem, saying, Hear ye the words of this covenant, and do them.
7 For I earnestly protested unto your fathers in the day that I brought them up out of the land of Egypt, even unto this day, rising early and protesting, saying, Obey my voice.
8 Yet they obeyed not, nor inclined their ear, but walked every one in the imagination of their evil heart: therefore I will bring upon them all the words of this covenant, which I commanded them to do; but they did them not.
9 And the LORD said unto me, A conspiracy is found among the men of Judah, and among the inhabitants of Jerusalem.
10 They are turned back to the iniquities of their forefathers, which refused to hear my words; and they went after other gods to serve them: the house of Israel and the house of Judah have broken my covenant which I made with their fathers.
11 Therefore thus saith the LORD, Behold, I will bring evil upon them, which they shall not be able to escape; and though they shall cry unto me, I will not hearken unto them.

Jeremiah is to proclaim all these words in the cities of Judah and the streets of Jerusalem by saying, Hear the words of the covenant and do them. The LORD has always protested the fallen behavior of the people from the day that He brought them out of Egypt to this day. The message has remained the same, Obey My voice, the voice of the LORD. Yet they obeyed not, nor inclined their ear to listen, but every one walked in the imagination of their evil heart.

The Testimony of the Major Prophets

Therefore the LORD will bring upon them all the words of this covenant, which they were commanded to do; but they did them not.

The LORD said to Jeremiah, A conspiracy is found among the men of Judah, and among the inhabitants of Jerusalem. They have conspired among themselves to turn back to the iniquities of their forefathers, which refused to hear the words of the LORD; and they went after other gods to serve them: the house of Israel and the house of Judah have broken the covenant which the LORD made with their fathers. Therefore thus says the LORD, Behold, I will bring evil upon them, which they shall not be able to escape; and though they shall cry unto Me, I will not hearken to their pleas.

12 Then shall the cities of Judah and inhabitants of Jerusalem go, and cry unto the gods unto whom they offer incense: but they shall not save them at all in the time of their trouble.
13 For according to the number of thy cities were thy gods, O Judah; and according to the number of the streets of Jerusalem have ye set up altars to that shameful thing, even altars to burn incense unto Baal.
14 Therefore pray not thou for this people, neither lift up a cry or prayer for them: for I will not hear them in the time that they cry unto me for their trouble.
15 What hath my beloved to do in mine house, seeing she hath wrought lewdness with many, and the holy flesh is passed from thee? when thou doest evil, then thou rejoicest.
16 The LORD called thy name, A green olive tree, fair, and of goodly fruit: with the noise of a great tumult he hath kindled fire upon it, and the branches of it are broken.
17 For the LORD of hosts, that planted thee, hath pronounced evil against thee, for the evil of the house of Israel and of the house of Judah, which they have done against themselves to provoke me to anger in offering incense unto Baal.

The LORD speaking through Jeremiah states that the cities of Judah and the inhabitants of Jerusalem shall cry to the false gods to whom they offered incense: but the false gods shall not save them in the time of trouble. Judah had gods according to the number of her cities, and Jerusalem had false gods according to the number of her streets as they set up altars to shameful things, and even altars to burn incense to Baal. Jeremiah is not to pray for these people nor to lift up their prayers for them: for the LORD will not hear their prayers in the time of their troubles. What has the beloved of the LORD, the people, to do in His house when she has brought forth lewdness with many and the holy flesh has passed from her? When she does evil, she rejoices in her evil!

The LORD called the name of His creation, A green olive tree, fair, and of goodly fruit. However, with the noise of a great tumult, the LORD has kindled fire upon the beautiful creation, and the branches of it are broken. For the LORD of hosts, who planted the olive tree that symbolizes mankind, has pronounced evil against mankind, for the evil of the house of Israel and of the house of Judah, which they have done against themselves to provoke the LORD to anger in offering incense to Baal, the worship of a false god.

18 And the LORD hath given me knowledge of it, and I know it: then thou shewedst me their doings.
19 But I was like a lamb or an ox that is brought to the slaughter; and I knew not that they had devised devices against me, saying, Let us destroy the tree with the fruit thereof, and let us cut him off from the land of the living, that his name may be no more remembered.
20 But, O LORD of hosts, that judgest righteously, that triest the reins and the heart, let me see thy vengeance on them: for unto thee have I revealed my cause.

The LORD has given Jeremiah knowledge of the disobedience of the people in the fallen state and he knows the extent of the sin of the people as he was shown what they had done. But Jeremiah did not know what the people would do to him; he was as a lamb or an ox that was brought to the slaughter. Jeremiah did not know that they had devised devices to destroy the tree with the fruit that he was, and destroy him from the land of the living, that his name would not be remembered any more. But the LORD of hosts, that judges righteously, that tries the reins of the hearts of people, let Jeremiah see the vengeance of the LORD on the wicked people: the LORD revealed His cause to Jeremiah.

21 Therefore thus saith the LORD of the men of Anathoth, that seek thy life, saying, Prophesy not in the name of the LORD, that thou die not by our hand:

22 Therefore thus saith the LORD of hosts, Behold, I will punish them: the young men shall die by the sword; their sons and their daughters shall die by famine:
23 And there shall be no remnant of them: for I will bring evil upon the men of Anathoth, even the year of their visitation.

Therefore, the LORD says that the men of Anathoth (the land where Jeremiah was born and whose name means, "poverty") shall seek the life of Jeremiah, saying, Prophesy not in the name of the LORD, or you will die by our hand. The people from the city of Jeremiah want to destroy him. The LORD of hosts says, Behold, I will punish them: the young men shall die by their sword, the misuse of their spiritual power; and their sons and daughters shall die by famine. There shall be no remnant of them remaining: for the LORD will bring disaster upon the men of Anathoth, even the year of their visitation, their punishment, from the LORD.

CHAPTER 12

1 Righteous art thou, O LORD, when I plead with thee: yet let me talk with thee of thy judgments: Wherefore doth the way of the wicked prosper? wherefore are all they happy that deal very treacherously?
2 Thou hast planted them, yea, they have taken root: they grow, yea, they bring forth fruit: thou art near in their mouth, and far from their reins.
3 But thou, O LORD, knowest me: thou hast seen me, and tried mine heart toward thee: pull them out like sheep for the slaughter, and prepare them for the day of slaughter.
4 How long shall the land mourn, and the herbs of every field wither, for the wickedness of them that dwell therein? the beasts are consumed, and the birds; because they said, He shall not see our last end.
5 If thou hast run with the footmen, and they have wearied thee, then how canst thou contend with horses? and if in the land of peace, wherein thou trustedst, they wearied thee, then how wilt thou do in the swelling of Jordan?
6 For even thy brethren, and the house of thy father, even they have dealt treacherously with thee; yea, they have called a multitude after thee: believe them not, though they speak fair words unto thee.

Jeremiah sees and understands, generally, the working of the Law of the LORD, the precise application of the Law of Sowing and Reaping, yet he wants to talk with the LORD with regard to certain of His judgments particularly with respect to why does the way of the wicked seem to prosper the wicked? why are the people who behave treacherously seem to be happy? Jeremiah understands that the LORD has planted these people, and their treacherous behavior is their rebellion from the way of the LORD; he understands that the wicked grow and bring forth the fruits of their labors: he understands that the LORD is near in the expression, symbolized by their mouth, because the power of the LORD is being used to produce the effects of everyone on earth; and the LORD is also very far from controlling the reins, the direction, of the sowing done by the wicked people. The LORD has given his people, who were made in the image and likeness of God, the power to create either beauty or chaos.

By contrast, the LORD knows and sees that Jeremiah does not bring forth wicked ways because Jeremiah has chosen to express the spirit of the LORD. The LORD knows that the heart of Jeremiah is with the spirit of the LORD in covenant-agreement. Jeremiah wants the LORD to pull the wicked sheep out of the flock of the body of mankind as a sheep is pulled out for the slaughter, and prepare the wicked for the day of the slaughter. Jeremiah argues, How long shall the land mourn, and the herbs of every field wither, because of the wicked behavior of the people who dwell on earth and produce the wickedness? The beasts and the birds, the symbols of material effects and thoughts that fly through the mind, are consumed because they cannot see the end to the wickedness generated by the wicked people.

If a person has run with the footmen, and became weary doing that, then how can a person contend with horses who are more powerful? and if a person becomes weary in a land of peace, where the people can trust the working of the Law under peaceful conditions, then how will the people behave in the swelling of Jordan, when adverse conditions, come upon them? Jeremiah is shocked to tell the LORD that even the brethren of the LORD, the house of your father, have dealt treacherously with their LORD; yes, they have called a multitude after the LORD using the name of the LORD in their treachery: Jeremiah implores the LORD not to believe them even though they speak fair words to the LORD.

7 I have forsaken mine house, I have left mine heritage; I have given the dearly beloved of my soul into the hand of her enemies.
8 Mine heritage is unto me as a lion in the forest; it crieth out against me: therefore have I hated it.
9 Mine heritage is unto me as a speckled bird, the birds round about are against her; come ye, assemble all the beasts of the field, come to devour.
10 Many pastors have destroyed my vineyard, they have trodden my portion under foot, they have made my pleasant portion a desolate wilderness.
11 They have made it desolate, and being desolate it mourneth unto me; the whole land is made desolate, because no man layeth it to heart.
12 The spoilers are come upon all high places through the wilderness: for the sword of the LORD shall devour from the one end of the land even to the other end of the land: no flesh shall have peace.
13 They have sown wheat, but shall reap thorns: they have put themselves to pain, but shall not profit: and they shall be ashamed of your revenues because of the fierce anger of the LORD.

Jeremiah admits that he has forsaken the house of his cultural heritage; he has given people whom he loved into the hand of the enemies without intervening, because they chose to go in that direction because that is the way in which they were raised. Jeremiah was raised with the same cultural heritage. Jeremiah's heritage was to be as a destructive lion in the forest also. This destructive inclination has cried out against Jeremiah's peaceful way to follow the way of the LORD, but Jeremiah loved the LORD more. Therefore, Jeremiah hated his heritage that continues the rebellion against the LORD and the LORD's kingdom, the divine heritage of the promised land. Jeremiah compares his divine heritage from the LORD as a speckled bird, different and easily recognized; and the birds, the thoughts of the people with the heritage of the fallen state who surround Jeremiah, are against the example of the speckled bird, the representative of the LORD. In fact, the birds, who are against what Jeremiah stands for, call the beasts of the field, the destructive people, to come and devour Jeremiah, the speckled bird.

Jeremiah relates that many pastors, people who lead the flocks, have destroyed the vineyard that the LORD is attempting to grow. Each of them has trodden his portion of the way of the LORD under foot; they have made the promised land, the kingdom, a desolate wilderness. The wicked people have made the world of Jeremiah's environment desolate, and being desolate, it saddens him; he sees that the whole land is made desolate, because no man lays, applies, the spirit of the LORD, represented by the spirit of Jeremiah, to his own heart.

The spoilers of the environment of the earth have come upon all high places through the wilderness: the sword of the LORD, the destructive power of the LORD, shall devour the false pattern from one end of the land to the other: no flesh of man in the fallen state shall have peace. There are those who have sown wheat, but shall reap thorns sown by others because mankind is connected and it is one flesh. The people who have functioned badly have put themselves to pain of their own wickedness. They shall not profit from their wicked behavior because they have reaped what they have sown: and the people who express wickedness shall be ashamed of Jeremiah's revenues, the result of sowing the right seed, because of the fierce anger of the LORD will be visited upon them according to the working of the Law.

14 Thus saith the LORD against all mine evil neighbours, that touch the inheritance which I have caused my people Israel to inherit; Behold, I will pluck them out of their land, and pluck out the house of Judah from among them.
15 And it shall come to pass, after that I have plucked them out I will return, and have compassion on them, and will bring them again, every man to his heritage, and every man to his land.
16 And it shall come to pass, if they will diligently learn the ways of my people, to swear by my name, The LORD liveth; as they taught my people to swear by Baal; then shall they be built in the midst of my people.
17 But if they will not obey, I will utterly pluck up and destroy that nation, saith the LORD.

The word of the LORD to all the evil neighbors of Jeremiah who have touched the true inheritance from the LORD for the earth through the behavior of Jeremiah: Behold, the LORD will pluck them out of their promised land, the land of Israel, and pluck out the house of Judah, through whom the kingdom should put in an appearance, from among them. And it shall come to pass, after the LORD has plucked them out, He shall return and have compassion on them and bring to them again their heritage if the people will repent. The divine design of the LORD is always present and available to be brought into manifestation on earth. Every man will bring to the land of his own experience what he has earned by the nature of the seed that he has sown. The people, individually, have a choice as to the nature of the world in which they live.

And it shall come to pass, if the people will diligently learn the ways of the LORD's people, to swear by His name, I AM, then, the LORD lives in the LORD's people. The results experienced will be the effect of the working of the Law. The process is the same as when the leaders taught the people to swear by Baal, the false god, who produced the results of human nature, the fallen state. There will be a choice on earth as to whether the kingdom of the LORD, or the kingdom of Baal, shall be built in the midst of the LORD's people. But if they will not obey the LORD, then, the LORD will utterly pluck up and destroy that nation. It is only a matter of time for divine retribution because the Law of Sowing and Reaping is at work always.

CHAPTER 13

1 Thus saith the LORD unto me, Go and get thee a linen girdle, and put it upon thy loins, and put it not in water.
2 So I got a girdle according to the word of the LORD, and put it on my loins.
3 And the word of the LORD came unto me the second time, saying,
4 Take the girdle that thou hast got, which is upon thy loins, and arise, go to Euphrates, and hide it there in a hole of the rock.
5 So I went, and hid it by Euphrates, as the LORD commanded me.
6 And it came to pass after many days, that the LORD said unto me, Arise, go to Euphrates, and take the girdle from thence, which I commanded thee to hide there.
7 Then I went to Euphrates, and digged, and took the girdle from the place where I had hid it: and, behold, the girdle was marred, it was profitable for nothing.

Then the word of the LORD came to Jeremiah saying, Go and get a linen girdle. the symbol of a fine and beautiful covering, to cover yourself and place it upon your loins, your parts which you do not want to be exposed to other people, and do not put the linen girdle in the water to wash it because it is clean and new. Jeremiah obeyed the command of the LORD; he got a linen girdle and placed it upon his loins, and wore it proudly and with dignity. The girdle is the symbol for the covering for the spirit of the LORD.

The word of the LORD came to Jeremiah a second time saying, Take the girdle which you have obtained, which is upon your loins, and arise, go to the bank of the Euphrates River, the symbol of flowing and changing nature of life experience, and hide the linen girdle there in a hole of the rock. Jeremiah went and hid the linen girdle by the Euphrates, as the LORD commanded. It came to pass after many days, that the LORD told Jeremiah to go to the Euphrates and retrieve the girdle that the LORD commanded him to hide there. Jeremiah discovered that the girdle which had been buried and hidden was marred and it was good for nothing. The beautiful linen girdle, that symbolized the covering for the spirit of the LORD and was to have been a sign of beauty, had become dirty and deteriorated while it was hidden rather than being worn by Jeremiah, the representative symbol of what every man should do for the LORD.

8 Then the word of the LORD came unto me, saying,
9 Thus saith the LORD, After this manner will I mar the pride of Judah, and the great pride of Jerusalem.
10 This evil people, which refuse to hear my words, which walk in the imagination of their heart, and walk after other gods, to serve them, and to worship them, shall even be as this girdle, which is good for nothing.
11 For as the girdle cleaveth to the loins of a man, so have I caused to cleave unto me the whole house of Israel and the whole house of Judah, saith the LORD; that they might be unto me for a people, and for a name, and for a praise, and for a glory: but they would not hear.

The LORD explained the meaning of the parable of the linen girdle to Jeremiah by saying that when the girdle that symbolizes the covering of the spirit of the LORD is not worn the flow of the river of life will mar the pride of the

The Testimony of the Major Prophets

people of Judah and the great pride of the people of Jerusalem. The people should be wearing and revealing the clean beauty of the girdle that is in the flow of the spirit of life which is the expression of the LORD in the moment, which is symbolized by the linen girdle. The people are not to remove and not use the linen girdle that symbolizes the beautiful covering of the LORD's spirit. And the people of Judah and Jerusalem are not to set it aside and hide the linen girdle, the expression of the LORD's spirit, which is not being worn or displayed by the people who claim to be the LORD's people.

As Jeremiah begins to understand the parable, the LORD states that the people of Judah and Jerusalem are an evil people who refuse to hear the words from the LORD which flow as a river of living spirit. Instead, they walk in the imagination of their hearts, and walk after other material gods to serve them and worship them. The people who do not wear the linen girdle of the LORD's spirit have become as the marred girdle and have become good for nothing in the bringing of the LORD's divine design to the earth. As a girdle cleaves to the loins of a man, the loins which cause man to stand upright in strength, so has the LORD designed the whole house of Judah and Jerusalem to cleave to Him in covenant-agreement. The LORD tells Jeremiah that the people of Judah and Jerusalem were to be His people on earth who would carry the LORD's spirit, and consequently be the LORD's people, to carry the LORD's name and praise, and reveal the glory of the LORD: but the people would not hear, they would not listen. The people of Judah and Jerusalem have ignored their calling to be the LORD's people and to wear the girdle from the LORD. They want the blessings of the LORD on earth while they ignore the spirit of the LORD that would make manifest on earth the LORD's blessings. The material blessings from the LORD cannot appear unless the LORD's spirit is worn by His people.

12 Therefore thou shalt speak unto them this word; Thus saith the LORD God of Israel, Every bottle shall be filled with wine: and they shall say unto thee, Do we not certainly know that every bottle shall be filled with wine?
13 Then shalt thou say unto them, Thus saith the LORD, Behold, I will fill all the inhabitants of this land, even the kings that sit upon David's throne, and the priests, and the prophets, and all the inhabitants of Jerusalem, with drunkenness.
14 And I will dash them one against another, even the fathers and the sons together, saith the LORD: I will not pity, nor spare, nor have mercy, but destroy them.

Therefore Jeremiah is commanded to speak the word of the LORD God of Israel to the fallen people of Judah and Jerusalem this parable. Every bottle, which symbolizes the individual people, shall be filled with wine, the symbol of the wine of life from the spiritual vine of the LORD. The people who hear this will say, Do we not know that every bottle shall be filled with the wine of life?

Then Jeremiah shall say unto them the message of the LORD, Behold, I will fill all the inhabitants of this land, even the kings that sit upon David's throne, and the priests, and the prophets, and all the inhabitants of Jerusalem, with drunkenness. The LORD will cause the His wine of life to make the disobedient and rebellious people drunk and disorderly. As a result of the misuse of the LORD's wine (life), the people will dash themselves one against another in a pattern of disagreement, even the fathers and the sons together. The power of the LORD will not pity, nor spare, nor have mercy on the people, but destroy them for their disobedience by the working of the Law.

15 Hear ye, and give ear; be not proud: for the LORD hath spoken.
16 Give glory to the LORD your God, before he cause darkness, and before your feet stumble upon the dark mountains, and, while ye look for light, he turn it into the shadow of death, and make it gross darkness.
17 But if ye will not hear it, my soul shall weep in secret places for your pride; and mine eye shall weep sore, and run down with tears, because the LORD's flock is carried away captive.
18 Say unto the king and to the queen, Humble yourselves, sit down: for your principalities shall come down, even the crown of your glory.

Jeremiah is to warn the people that they are disobeying and rebelling against the LORD. The people should hear and not be proud, filled with self-pride, for the LORD has spoken to them His words of warning. The people are to give glory to the LORD their God before He causes darkness. the absence of the LORD's light, as they turn away from their source of light. They should repent before their feet stumble and they fall even farther than they have upon the dark mountains. Their fall is inevitable when they are off the LORD's path. While the people are looking for light on their

The Symbolic Version of Jeremiah

own without the LORD, the LORD will turn their way into the shadow of death and make their environments gross darkness. As people search the environment for light, their search leads them into darkness.

But if the people of Judah and Jerusalem will not hear and heed the LORD's warning, the soul—the body, mind and heart—of the LORD shall weep in secret places for the false pride that brings punishment upon them. The LORD's eye, His vision, shall weep and run down with tears, because the LORD's flock is carried away captive from the beauty which the LORD wants for His people. Jeremiah is to say to the king, the symbol of the spirit of the person, and to the queen, the symbol of the form of the person, Humble yourselves, sit down, cease searching for the LORD. The LORD is with you! Your principalities shall fall and come down, even the crown of your glory from the LORD which is present with you, but ignored.

19 The cities of the south shall be shut up, and none shall open them: Judah shall be carried away captive all of it, it shall be wholly carried away captive.
20 Lift up your eyes, and behold them that come from the north: where is the flock that was given thee, thy beautiful flock?
21 What wilt thou say when he shall punish thee? for thou hast taught them to be captains, and as chief over thee: shall not sorrows take thee, as a woman in travail?

The cities of the south shall be closed as they were known, and none shall open them: the nation of Judah shall be carried away captive all of it, it shall be wholly carried away captive by the invaders from the north. The people have been warned to lift up their eyes, and behold the invaders that come from the north. The people of Judah and Jerusalem are asked, Where is the flock that was given to you, the beautiful flock of the children of Israel? What will you say when the invaders shall punish you? for you have taught the people of the environment to be captains, and as chief over you who were to be the crowning creation. Shall not sorrows overtake you with labor and pain as a woman in childbirth giving birth to the fruit of her womb?

22 And if thou say in thine heart, Wherefore come these things upon me? For the greatness of thine iniquity are thy skirts discovered, and thy heels made bare.
23 Can the Ethiopian change his skin, or the leopard his spots? then may ye also do good, that are accustomed to do evil.
24 Therefore will I scatter them as the stubble that passeth away by the wind of the wilderness.
25 This is thy lot, the portion of thy measures from me, saith the LORD; because thou hast forgotten me, and trusted in falsehood.
26 Therefore will I discover thy skirts upon thy face, that thy shame may appear.
27 I have seen thine adulteries, and thy neighings, the lewdness of thy whoredom, and thine abominations on the hills in the fields. Woe unto thee, O Jerusalem! wilt thou not be made clean? when shall it once be?

And if you say in your heart, Why have these things come upon me? The answer is that the greatness of your iniquity, the adultery against the LORD's spirit, has been discovered in your unclean skirts. Your heels, which you dug in to resist the pull of the LORD, have been made bare, and it is known that you have resisted the way of the LORD. The fallen people wonder if their defeat and impending punishment will surely come to pass although they inherently know that the Law works.

Can the Ethiopian change his skin, or the leopard his spots? then may you, who were designed to do good, the will of the LORD, but who are accustomed to doing evil. Therefore the working of the Law of the LORD scatters them that do evil as the stubble that passes away by the wind of the wilderness. This is your lot, the portion of your measure, your just reward from the LORD, because you have forgotten the spirit of the LORD and trusted in falsehood. Therefore the LORD will discover your skirts upon your face in the very act of adultery with the things of the world and your shame may appear. The LORD has seen your adulteries, and your neighing, your call to the things of the environment, which you placed above the spirit of the LORD, the lewdness of your whoredom, and your behaviors which were abominations on the hills in the fields. Woe to you, O Jerusalem! Will you not be made clean when you see the evil of your behavior? When shall the clean expression of the spirit of the LORD once again put in an appearance through you?

CHAPTER 14

1 The word of the LORD that came to Jeremiah concerning the dearth.
2 Judah mourneth, and the gates thereof languish; they are black unto the ground; and the cry of Jerusalem is gone up.
3 And their nobles have sent their little ones to the waters: they came to the pits, and found no water; they returned with their vessels empty; they were ashamed and confounded, and covered their heads.
4 Because the ground is chapt, for there was no rain in the earth, the plowmen were ashamed, they covered their heads.
5 Yea, the hind also calved in the field, and forsook it, because there was no grass.
6 And the wild asses did stand in the high places, they snuffed up the wind like dragons; their eyes did fail, because there was no grass.

The word of the LORD that came to Jeremiah concerning the dearth, the scarcity, of the spirit of the LORD that inevitably was present in the people of Judah and Jerusalem as they failed to allow the spirit to flow into the world through them. The people of Judah mourned and the gates within the people through which the spirit of the LORD flowed through the inhabitants languished and diminished. The gates which should have allowed the light of the LORD to come into the earth were black due to the absence of light. The cry of sadness from the people of Jerusalem was expressed and it was gone up to be heard in the land.

The nobles of the people who wanted to do the noble thing sent their little ones, their small attempts, to the waters, the symbols of the truth from the LORD which was available to them: but they came to the pits, the empty places within themselves which once held the water of truth, and there was no water to be found. They had dried up from lack of use. The little ones returned to their parents with their vessels empty; they were ashamed and confounded by their failure and covered their heads in shame and disappointment.

Because the ground is chapt, dried and broken, for there was no rain in the earth, the plowmen, who tried to do some creative work, were ashamed; they covered their heads. Yes, the hind also calved in the field, gave birth a creative idea from the calf which is the symbol for the mind, but the father of the thought did forsake the new-born calf because it had no grass to feed it. The behaviors, symbolized by wild asses, did stand in high places as they snuffed up the wind of the spirit like dragons, the distortions that were made, by the spirit of the LORD moving through a distortion pattern; but their eyes, their perception, did fail because they had no green grass, the symbol of healthy effects in the environment, to feed them.

7 O LORD, though our iniquities testify against us, do thou it for thy name's sake: for our backslidings are many; we have sinned against thee.
8 O the hope of Israel, the saviour thereof in time of trouble, why shouldest thou be as a stranger in the land, and as a wayfaring man that turneth aside to tarry for a night?

9 Why shouldest thou be as a man astonied, as a mighty man that cannot save? yet thou, O LORD, art in the midst of us, and we are called by thy name; leave us not.

The people of the fallen state of Judah and Jerusalem in their troubles raised their voices to the LORD to acknowledge that their behaviors, their iniquities and sins, are the proof that their behaviors have distorted the spirit of the LORD. The people state that they understand that the LORD had to allow these sins to appear for the sake of the LORD's name, I AM, and the working of the Law: the people admit that their backslidings, their departures from the true way of the LORD, are many and that they have sinned against the LORD.

The people plead with the LORD that they see that the hope of Israel, the spirit of the LORD coming through the people who allow it to be so, is the savior that will aid them in the time of trouble. Why should the LORD be unknown to His people, as a stranger in the land, or as a wayfaring man that turns aside from his path to tarry for a night? The people ask, Why should the LORD be as a man, astonished, as a mighty man that cannot save His people? The people acknowledge that the LORD is in the midst of them and they also acknowledge that they are called by the LORD's name; they beg the LORD not to leave them. They are afraid of the impending consequences of their behavior.

10 Thus saith the LORD unto this people, Thus have they loved to wander, they have not refrained their feet, therefore the LORD doth not accept them; he will now remember their iniquity, and visit their sins.
11 Then said the LORD unto me, Pray not for this people for their good.
12 When they fast, I will not hear their cry; and when they offer burnt offering and an oblation, I will not accept them: but I will consume them by the sword, and by the famine, and by the pestilence.

The LORD replies to his people that they have loved to wander away from His spirit and they have not refrained their feet from doing so. Therefore, the LORD does not accept them or their plea which is made order to get them out of their trouble and pain. The LORD will remember their iniquity and visit their sins upon them according to the working of the Law.

Then the LORD said to Jeremiah, Pray not for the people for their selfish good. When they fast from their iniquity, the LORD will not hear their cry; when they offer burnt offering and an oblation, sacrifice or gift to the LORD for a selfish, self-centered purpose, the LORD will not accept gifts motivated by self-centeredness. The LORD will consume them with the sword of His power applied in the destructive cycle in accordance with the Law, by famine, which is the absence of spiritual food, and by pestilence, which is the disease caused by the absence of the LORD's spirit which is Health.

13 Then said I, Ah, Lord GOD! behold, the prophets say unto them, Ye shall not see the sword, neither shall ye have famine; but I will give you assured peace in this place.
14 Then the LORD said unto me, The prophets prophesy lies in my name: I sent them not, neither have I commanded them, neither spake unto them: they prophesy unto you a false vision and divination, and a thing of nought, and the deceit of their heart.
15 Therefore thus saith the LORD concerning the prophets that prophesy in my name, and I sent them not, yet they say, Sword and famine shall not be in this land; By sword and famine shall those prophets be consumed.
16 And the people to whom they prophesy shall be cast out in the streets of Jerusalem because of the famine and the sword; and they shall have none to bury them, them, their wives, nor their sons, nor their daughters: for I will pour their wickedness upon them.

Then Jeremiah said, Oh, Lord God, behold, their prophets say unto them, You are the children of Israel, and you shall not see the sword, the power of the LORD, used against you as a chosen people, and neither shall you have famine; and the LORD will give you an assured peace in this place.

Then the LORD said to Jeremiah, The prophets prophesy lies using the name of the LORD: the LORD did not send the false prophets or command them or speak to the people. They prophesy a false vision and divination; their teachings are a thing of nothing and the result of the deceit of their own heart which is not of the LORD. Therefore the LORD says, concerning the prophets that prophesy in His name, He did not send them. Yet the false prophets continue to say

The Testimony of the Major Prophets

that the sword of the LORD and famine shall not be in this land of Judah and Jerusalem. But, by sword and famine, which they say cannot come in the land, shall those false prophets be consumed.

And the people to whom they prophesy shall be cast out in the streets of Jerusalem because of the famine and the sword; and they shall have no one to bury them: neither them, their wives, nor their sons, nor their daughters: for the LORD will pour their own wickedness upon them.

17 Therefore, thou shalt say this word unto them; Let mine eyes run down with tears night and day, and let them cease; for the virgin daughter of my people is broken with a great breach, with a very grievous blow.
18 If I go forth into the field, then behold the slain with the sword! and if I enter into the city, then behold them that are sick with famine! yea, both the prophet and the priest go about into a land that they know not.

Therefore, Jeremiah shall say this word to them: Let the eyes of the LORD, which manifest as the spirit that observes and shines through the eyes of the fallen people in the fallen state, run down with tears night and day, and let the people cease the behaviors which cause the tears. The virgin daughter of the LORD's people, the symbol of the children of Israel, is broken with a great breach that is the result of a grievous blow to the body of people that should be carrying the name of the LORD. If the power of the LORD goes forth into the field of the environment, behold the people who were slain with the sword of the LORD's power and His Law! If the LORD enters into the city, then behold them who are sick with famine that is caused by the absence of the spirit. Yes, both the false prophet and the priest go about the land and they do not know how the conditions of the environment are the way that they are.

19 Hast thou utterly rejected Judah? hath thy soul loathed Zion? why hast thou smitten us, and there is no healing for us? we looked for peace, and there is no good; and for the time of healing, and behold trouble!
20 We acknowledge, O LORD, our wickedness, and the iniquity of our fathers: for we have sinned against thee.
21 Do not abhor us, for thy name's sake, do not disgrace the throne of thy glory: remember, break not thy covenant with us.
22 Are there any among the vanities of the Gentiles that can cause rain? or can the heavens give showers? art not thou he, O LORD our God? therefore we will wait upon thee: for thou hast made all these things.

The prophets and the priests ask, Has the LORD utterly rejected Judah? Has the LORD loathed Zion? Why has the LORD smitten us, who are His people, and why is there is no healing for us? The priests and the false prophets have looked for peace and there is no good to be found; they looked for the time of healing, and behold, they observe trouble!

The people acknowledge their wickedness and the iniquities of their fathers: they realize that father and son they have sinned against the LORD. The people pray that the LORD does not abhor them because they have sinned. They do not understand the Law of the LORD which is based on the blessings of the LORD coming through His people and not to His people without their participation. The people pray that the LORD should not disgrace the throne of the glory of the LORD as though the LORD could cause the disgrace that fallen man has made on earth. The false prophets, and priests advise and caution that the LORD should not break the covenant with His people because they do not realize that the LORD is connected with His people but His people are not connected to Him.

Are there any people among the vanity, the vain ones, of the Gentiles that can cause the rain, the spiritual rain of truth from the LORD to fall from heaven? They imply that they alone are the chosen people of the LORD and that the LORD's blessings should come to them. They mock the LORD when they ask why the LORD is withholding means of their salvation from them. They ask, Can the heavens give showers of the truth from the LORD to come on earth, or is it just imagination? Are you not He, O LORD our God? Therefore we will wait on the LORD, we shall wait on the LORD's spirit to come into the earth. It is the LORD who has made all of these things, the earth and everything on it. The people think that the LORD should make the kingdom and hand it to them.

CHAPTER 15

1 Then said the LORD unto me, Though Moses and Samuel stood before me, yet my mind could not be toward this people: cast them out of my sight, and let them go forth.
2 And it shall come to pass, if they say unto thee, Whither shall we go forth? then thou shalt tell them, Thus saith the LORD; Such as are for death, to death; and such as are for the sword, to the sword; and such as are for the famine, to the famine; and such as are for the captivity, to the captivity.
3 And I will appoint over them four kinds, saith the LORD: the sword to slay, and the dogs to tear, and the fowls of the heaven, and the beasts of the earth, to devour and destroy.
4 And I will cause them to be removed into all kingdoms of the earth, because of Manasseh the son of Hezekiah king of Judah, for that which he did in Jerusalem.

Then the LORD said to Jeremiah to emphasize the exactness and the preciseness of the working of the Law of Sowing and Reaping that even if Moses and Samuel, two of the LORD's servants, stood before Him in an attempt to intercede for the people of Judah and Jerusalem, the LORD would not change His mind toward the rebellious and arrogant people. The people are to be cast out of the LORD's sight and they are to go forth to experience the effects of what they had sown over many years.

It shall come to pass, if the people say to Jeremiah, Where shall we go? then Jeremiah shall tell them that the word of the LORD is that those who are for death shall go to their death; and such as are for the sword shall go to the sword; and such as are for the famine shall go to the famine; and such as are for the captivity shall go to their captivity. The LORD's Law will appoint over the people four kinds of destructive punishment and retribution based upon the behaviors of the people: the sword to slay; and the dogs to tear; and the fowls of the heaven, and the beasts of the earth, to devour and destroy. The power of the LORD working through the Law of Sowing and Reaping will cause the people to be repelled into all the kingdoms of the earth because of Manesseh, the son of Hezekiah, king of Judah for that which he did in Jerusalem. Manessah was the most wicked king in Judah's long history. The wickedness sown in Jerusalem must be reaped.

5 For who shall have pity upon thee, O Jerusalem? or who shall bemoan thee? or who shall go aside to ask how thou doest?
6 Thou hast forsaken me, saith the LORD, thou art gone backward: therefore will I stretch out my hand against thee, and destroy thee; I am weary with repenting.
7 And I will fan them with a fan in the gates of the land; I will bereave them of children, I will destroy my people, since they return not from their ways.
8 Their widows are increased to me above the sand of the seas: I have brought upon them against the mother of the young men a spoiler at noonday: I have caused him to fall upon it suddenly, and terrors upon the city.

The Testimony of the Major Prophets

9 She that hath borne seven languisheth: she hath given up the ghost; her sun is gone down while it was yet day: she hath been ashamed and confounded: and the residue of them will I deliver to the sword before their enemies, saith the LORD.

In the light of the absoluteness of the working of the Law, who shall have pity on the fate of Jerusalem? who shall mourn your fate? who shall ask how you are doing as you receive your just punishment? The people being punished by their own behavior are reminded that they had forsaken the LORD and they had gone backward, backsliding away from the spirit of the LORD which has been with them always: therefore, the LORD will stretch out his hand of control against them and destroy them with the results of their own behavior which has shown no repentance and no return to the spirit of the LORD.

The LORD will fan them with the wind of His spirit which constantly moves through all His creation through the gates where the spirit enters the material land. The spirit, moving in the true design of the LORD, will stop the fallen people from producing children, the symbol for the offspring or expression of fallen and wicked behavior. The movement of the spirit of the LORD will destroy the distortions of the material world contained in the consciousness of the people who do not repent of their wicked ways and return to the LORD. The LORD removes his spiritual offspring, His children, away from their material forms, their wives. This process leaves the material forms as widows.

These widows are increased in number to the LORD above the sand of the seas. The LORD has brought a spoiler at noonday against the mother of the young men who symbolize a continuation of the wicked ways of the fallen people: the LORD has caused the spoiler to fall upon the material form suddenly, and this brings terror upon the city. The widow that symbolizes the material form that has borne seven, the symbol of the completed cycle of the false design, languishes as the forms weaken and fade away: she, the material form, has given up the ghost of the spirit; her sun is gone down, the material form of the false design disintegrates, while it was yet day: the widow, the form without the spirit of the LORD has been ashamed and confounded: and the residue of them will the LORD deliver to the sword of the spirit before their enemies. The material forms must disintegrate so that the raw materials can be integrated into the true design.

10 Woe is me, my mother, that thou hast borne me a man of strife and a man of contention to the whole earth! I have neither lent on usury, nor men have lent to me on usury; yet every one of them doth curse me.
11 The LORD said, Verily it shall be well with thy remnant; verily I will cause the enemy to entreat thee well in the time of evil and in the time of affliction.
12 Shall iron break the northern iron and the steel?
13 Thy substance and thy treasures will I give to the spoil without price, and that for all thy sins, even in all thy borders.
14 And I will make thee to pass with thine enemies into a land which thou knowest not: for a fire is kindled in mine anger, which shall burn upon you.

Jeremiah speaking the word of the LORD declares that it is a woe to the LORD that the mother of the material earth has borne a man of strife and a man of contention to the whole earth! The whole earth is in the fallen state! This fallen state of mankind was delivered into the material world by the "mother" who gave birth to a child of strife and contention. The LORD has neither lent His spirit to this distorted creation—the spirit of the LORD was usurped—nor borrowed any of the distortion created by mankind; yet everyone blames the LORD and curses the LORD as the author of the distorted state.

The LORD said, Verily it shall be well with the remnant of the distorted material world which has been created truly. The LORD will cause the enemy to entreat you well in the time of evil and in the time of affliction as the distortions of the human state destroy each other. Shall the iron of Jerusalem and Judah break the northern iron and steel of the invader from the north? Both groups are in the fallen state and one is physically stronger than the other, and the outcome is obvious to the LORD.

The substance and the treasures of Jerusalem and Judah will be given—by the working of the Law of the LORD—as a spoil without price. The loss of the spoils from the people of Jerusalem and Judah are the predictable result for all the sins that occurred in all your borders. The LORD will allow the people to be taken by their enemies into a land which they know not. A destructive fire is kindled in the LORD's anger, which shall burn upon the people of Jerusalem and Judah as the Law continues to intensify to destroy evil. The people, in their misery, will cry to the LORD in self-righteousness as they attempt to deny their guilt.

15 O LORD, thou knowest: remember me, and visit me, and revenge me of my persecutors; take me not away in thy longsuffering: know that for thy sake I have suffered rebuke.
16 Thy words were found, and I did eat them; and thy word was unto me the joy and rejoicing of mine heart: for I am called by thy name, O LORD God of hosts.
17 I sat not in the assembly of the mockers, nor rejoiced; I sat alone because of thy hand: for thou hast filled me with indignation.
18 Why is my pain perpetual, and my wound incurable, which refuseth to be healed? wilt thou be altogether unto me as a liar, and as waters that fail?

The people turn their attention to the LORD as they proclaim that the LORD knows them, they want the LORD to visit them and be on their side, and they seek revenge on the invaders who persecute them; the LORD is asked that they be not taken away as captives for their sins because the LORD is long suffering, patient. The people in the fallen state believe that they have suffered rebuke for the sake of the LORD. The LORD's words were found and they were eaten, assimilated, by the people of Jerusalem and Judah. The word was a joy and a rejoicing of the heart; the people declare that they are called by the name of the LORD, the LORD God of hosts.

The people continue to declare their lies when they say that they did not sit in the assembly of the mockers, nor rejoiced; they declare that they sat alone because of the hand of control from the LORD is upon them: it is the LORD who has filled them with indignation. The people ask, Why is their pain perpetual, and their wound incurable, which refuses to be healed? Will the LORD be altogether as a liar, and His word as waters that fail?

19 Therefore thus saith the LORD, If thou return, then will I bring thee again, and thou shalt stand before me: and if thou take forth the precious from the vile, thou shalt be as my mouth: let them return unto thee; but return not thou unto them.
20 And I will make thee unto this people a fenced brasen wall: and they shall fight against thee, but they shall not prevail against thee: for I am with thee to save thee and to deliver thee, saith the LORD.
21 And I will deliver thee out of the hand of the wicked, and I will redeem thee out of the hand of the terrible.

Since the people turned to the LORD, even though their prayers were wrong, they did turn to hear the LORD and the LORD answered with the truth to ears that were inclined to hear Him. The LORD declared—speaking through Jeremiah—that if you truly return to the spirit which is present with you, then the LORD will bring you again to the position where you will stand before the LORD. If you take the precious from the LORD and separate it from the vile, the distortion, then you shall be as a mouth, the expression, of the LORD. Let the people return to the LORD but do not let the people return to the fallen ways of Jerusalem and Judah.

Therefore, the LORD says that if the people truly return to the spirit of the LORD which is available to them, at hand, then the LORD will make for this people a fenced bronze wall to separate the LORD's people from the people who try to invade the space of the LORD's people. The people who try to invade and fight against you shall not prevail because the LORD is with you to save you and deliver you from the hand of the wicked. The LORD will deliver you out of the hand of the wicked, and redeem you out of the hand of the terrible, the terrible material distortion which is not of the spirit of the LORD. The distorted material realm is a terrible and a wicked place. It is not the heaven of the LORD.

CHAPTER 16

1 The word of the LORD came also unto me, saying,
2 Thou shalt not take thee a wife, neither shalt thou have sons or daughters in this place.
3 For thus saith the LORD concerning the sons and concerning the daughters that are born in this place, and concerning their mothers that bare them, and concerning their fathers that begat them in this land;
4 They shall die of grievous deaths; they shall not be lamented; neither shall they be buried; but they shall be as dung upon the face of the earth: and they shall be consumed by the sword, and by famine;
and their carcases shall be meat for the fowls of heaven, and for the beasts of the earth.

The word of the LORD came to Jeremiah, saying, You shall not take a wife, the symbol of a material attachment and connection, and neither shall you have sons and daughters, the symbols of offspring or creations at the emotional, mental or physical level from this place, from the distorted material state. If Jeremiah, who represents the pure spirit of the word of the LORD, creates anything with a wife, the distorted material form, then, whatever will be created will be a distortion. The LORD will clarify His instruction concerning the sons and daughters, the offspring of the spirit of the LORD as the father and the material forms of the mother that are to be born in this place on earth at the material level of creation where the material forms must put in an appearance. All material things are composed of the materials from the mother, mother earth, that did bare the offspring, and the spirit of the father, that begot them in this land.

The spirit from the LORD declares that creation from the father, the symbol of the LORD, through a distorted material form as a mother shall produce new creations, offspring, that shall die grievous deaths. The distortions in form must die and pass away; they shall not be lamented; they shall not be buried with honor; they shall be as dung, as human fertilizer, on the face of the earth. They shall be consumed by the sword of the truth of the LORD, and by famine; their carcasses shall be meat for the fowls of heaven—fowl are symbols of thoughts—and these thoughts are in heaven, the place where the LORD is, and the beasts of the earth. The beasts are symbols for the effects that are created on earth in material form. The power of the spirit of the LORD was used to create the form but the form itself is a distortion, a house of mourning.

5 For thus sayeth the LORD, Enter not into the house of mourning, neither go to lament nor bemoan them; for I have taken away my peace from this people, saith the LORD, even lovingkindness and mercies.
6 Both the great and the small shall die in this land: they shall not be buried, neither shall men lament for them, nor cut themselves, nor make themselves bald for them:
7 Neither shall men tear themselves for them in mourning, to comfort them for the dead; neither shall men give them the cup of consolation to drink for their father or for their mother.
8 Thou shalt not also go into the house of feasting, to sit with them to eat and to drink.
9 For thus saith the LORD of hosts, the God of Israel; Behold, I will cause to cease out of this place in your eyes, and in your days, the voice of mirth, and the voice of gladness, the voice of the bridegroom, and the voice of the bride.

The Symbolic Version of Jeremiah

The LORD says through Jeremiah that the people should not enter into the distorted and changing material form, the house of mourning; Jeremiah and his followers should not lament or bemoan the distorted material forms produced by the fallen people at all. The loving kindness and the mercies of the LORD are not primarily in the **forms** of the people; these qualities are in the **spirit**, and the spirit is in the heaven before it can appear in the earth. The qualities of the LORD are one with and they radiate from the spirit first and then they are reflected in the earth. Both the great and the small shall die in this material land of distortion: they shall not be buried and neither shall men lament for them, nor cut themselves, nor make themselves bald for them.

Neither shall men tear themselves for the material forms of things in mourning, to comfort them for the dead; neither shall men give them the cup of consolation to drink for their father or for their mother. You shall not also go into the house of feasting, to sit with them to eat and to drink. For thus says the LORD of hosts, the God of Israel; Behold, I will cause to cease out of this place in your eyes, and in your days, the voice of mirth, and the voice of gladness, the voice of the bridegroom, and the voice of the bride. The forms of the distorted material world will be desolate because it lacks the whole and holy spirit of the LORD. The whole spirit of the LORD is symbolized by the voice of the bridegroom and the whole material form that reveals the whole of the spirit of the LORD is symbolized by the voice of the bride. The LORD will cause the person to see in their eyes, in their vision, and in their days on earth, the reason why the voice of mirth and the voice of gladness cease to be in the material forms that deny the spirit of the LORD.

10 And it shall come to pass, when thou shalt shew this people all these words, and they shall say unto thee, Wherefore hath the LORD pronounced all this great evil against us? or what is our iniquity? or what is our sin that we have committed against the LORD our God?
11 Then shalt thou say unto them, Because your fathers have forsaken me, saith the LORD, and have walked after other gods, and have served them, and have worshipped them, and have forsaken me, and have not kept my law;
12 And ye have done worse than your fathers; for, behold, ye walk every one after the imagination of his evil heart, that they may not hearken unto me:
13 Therefore will I cast you out of this land into a land that ye know not, neither ye nor your fathers; and there shall ye serve other gods day and night; where I will not shew you favour.

And it shall come to pass, when Jeremiah shows the people all these words, and they shall say to him, Why has the LORD pronounced all this great evil against us? or what is our iniquity? or what is our sin that we have committed against the LORD our God? Then Jeremiah shall say to fallen people who asked the questions, Because your fathers have forsaken the LORD, and have walked after other gods, and have served them, and have worshipped them, and have forsaken the LORD, and have not kept the law. You have done worse than your fathers; for, behold, you walk every one after the imagination of your evil heart, that the hearts of mankind may not hearken to the LORD. Therefore, the LORD will cast you out of this spiritual land into a land that you know not, neither you nor your fathers; and there, in the ever-changing material world, the LORD will not show you any favor as the Law works. You shall serve other material gods day and night;

14 Therefore, behold, the days come, saith the LORD, that it shall no more be said, The LORD liveth, that brought up the children of Israel out of the land of Egypt;
15 But, The LORD liveth, that brought up the children of Israel from the land of the north, and from all the lands whither he had driven them: and I will bring them again into their land that I gave unto their fathers.
16 Behold, I will send for many fishers, saith the LORD, and they shall fish them; and after will I send for many hunters, and they shall hunt them from every mountain, and from every hill, and out of the holes of the rocks.
17 For mine eyes are upon all their ways: they are not hid from my face, neither is their iniquity hid from mine eyes.
18 And first I will recompense their iniquity and their sin double; because they have defiled my land, they have filled mine inheritance with the carcases of their detestable and abominable things.

Therefore, behold, the days come, says the LORD, that it shall no more be said, The LORD lives, that brought up the children of Israel out of the land of Egypt; But, The LORD lives, that brought up the children of Israel from the land of the north, and from all the lands from where he had driven them: and the LORD will bring the children of Israel again into the promised land that the LORD gave to their fathers.

The Testimony of the Major Prophets

Behold, the LORD says that He will send for many fishers of men, and they shall fish for the people who choose to serve the spirit of the LORD into the earth; and afterward, the LORD will send for many hunters who shall hunt for the people who will serve the LORD from every mountain, and from every hill, and out of the holes of the rocks. The fishermen are symbols of those who fish the seas of consciousness; the hunters are those who hunt for the people who are willing to serve the spirit of the LORD in the world of form. Both fishermen and hunters serve the LORD in their respective places. For the eyes of the LORD are upon all their ways: they are not hid from the LORD's face, neither is their iniquity hid from the eyes of the LORD. And first the LORD will recompense their iniquity and their sin double; because they have defiled the LORD's land, they have filled the inheritance which the LORD sends for future generations with the carcasses of their detestable and abominable things.

19 O LORD, my strength, and my fortress, and my refuge in the day of affliction, the Gentiles shall come unto thee from the ends of the earth, and shall say, Surely our fathers have inherited lies, vanity, and things wherein there is no profit.
20 Shall a man make gods unto himself, and they are no gods?
21 Therefore, behold, I will this once cause them to know, I will cause them to know mine hand and my might; and they shall know that my name is The LORD.

Jeremiah voices his agreement with the LORD, who is the strength, the fortress, and the refuge in the days of the affliction of the distorted earthly body of mankind. Jeremiah will be the voice of the LORD and call the Gentiles, the people who do not know the covenant with the LORD, to come to the LORD from the ends of the earth. Jeremiah will say that our fathers have inherited, from their fathers before them, lies, vanity and things wherein there is no profit.

Jeremiah shall ask the people in the fallen state if man should make gods to himself to worship that are not gods? Therefore, behold and observe, that he will, this once, cause the people in the fallen state to know that the LORD will cause them to know the hand of the LORD's control on earth through a person and the might of the LORD as the spirit of the LORD flows through a human form. Then, the people shall know by a living example as the spirit of the LORD flows through the physical form of Jeremiah, that the LORD and Jeremiah are one in the covenant-agreement that is available to them.

CHAPTER 17

1 The sin of Judah is written with a pen of iron, and with the point of a diamond: it is graven upon the table of their heart, and upon the horns of your altars;
2 Whilst their children remember their altars and their groves by the green trees upon the high hills.
3 O my mountain in the field, I will give thy substance and all thy treasures to the spoil, and thy high places for sin, throughout all thy borders.
4 And thou, even thyself, shalt discontinue from thine heritage that I gave thee; and I will cause thee to serve thine enemies in the land which thou knowest not: for ye have kindled a fire in mine anger, which shall burn for ever.

The sin of Judah is the direct result of the people who lived in the nation of Judah who did not reveal in their living the spirit of the LORD their God. The results of their sin is written with a pen of iron symbolizing their hard unbending ways and behaviors which are so unbending and unmoving that the spirit of the LORD cannot move them into behaviors that would be influenced by His spirit. The behaviors of people are written with the point of diamond; this symbolizes that all behaviors make an impression on the consciousness of the people. The "writing", the distorted collective behaviors or sins are engraved upon the table of the heart, the emotional realm of the people. Instead of changing their behaviors and atoning for their sins, the people offer their sins upon the horns of the altars, the altars where the people make burnt offerings to their gods. The children of the sinful people of the fallen state remember the altars upon which their parents made offerings of the flesh of animals to God. The children also remember the high aspirations of the parents which are symbolized by orderly groves of green trees with much life that grow on high hills.

The spirit of the LORD speaking through Jeremiah addresses his people on earth as His mountain in the field and declares that He will give all the substance and the treasures of the people as a spoil to the invader, and the high places for your sinful behavior, throughout all your borders. And the people shall be discontinued from the heritage that the LORD gave to them. The people will be captives and slaves to serve their enemies in a land which they do not know since they will be taken to a strange land. These things will be done to a sinful people according to the destructive power of the Law of Sowing and Reaping which is symbolized in human terms as a fire kindled in anger which shall burn for ever.

5 Thus saith the LORD; Cursed be the man that trusteth in man, and maketh flesh his arm, and whose heart departeth from the LORD.
6 For he shall be like the heath in the desert, and shall not see when good cometh; but shall inhabit the parched places in the wilderness, in a salt land and not inhabited.
7 Blessed is the man that trusteth in the LORD, and whose hope the LORD is.
8 For he shall be as a tree planted by the waters, and that spreadeth out her roots by the river, and shall not see when heat cometh, but her leaf shall be green; and shall not be careful in the year of drought, neither shall cease from yielding fruit.

The Testimony of the Major Prophets

9 The heart is deceitful above all things, and desperately wicked: who can know it?
10 I the LORD search the heart, I try the reins, even to give every man according to his ways, and according to the fruit of his doings.
11 As the partridge sitteth on eggs, and hatcheth them not; so he that getteth riches, and not by right, shall leave them in the midst of his days, and at his end shall be a fool.
12 A glorious high throne from the beginning is the place of our sanctuary.

Jeremiah delivers the message of the LORD who says, Cursed be the man that trusts in man, and makes flesh his arm of strength, and whose heart departs from the LORD. He shall be like the heath, a bush, in the desert, and shall not see when good comes his way; but shall dwell in the parched places in the wilderness, in a salt land where no one lives. But there is an alternative to the curse that awaits him.

Blessed is the man who trusts in the LORD, and whose hope and confidence is in the LORD. He shall be as a tree planted by the waters, and that spreads out her roots by the river, and shall not see when heat comes, but her leaf shall be green. The person who trusts in the spirit of the LORD shall not worry in the year of drought in the environment and shall not cease from yielding fruit of the spirit of the LORD which flows constantly as long as a person is alive. A person's heart, a person's emotions, may not feel the confidence which is inherent in the spirit of the LORD when one perceives himself to be in a desert.

The impure heart is deceitful above all things, and desperately wicked: who can know it? The LORD who is with you always searches the heart, tries the reins to determine whether the heart is being controlled from external idols so that the LORD gives to every man according to his ways, and according to the fruit of his doings. As the partridge sits on eggs, and does not hatch them; so he that gets riches, and not by right, he gets the riches unjustly, shall leave them in the midst of his days, and at his end he shall be a fool. A glorious high throne of spirit has been given by the LORD to man from the beginning and it is the place of the sanctuary between the LORD and man. The true sanctuary is in spirit and not in material things which are in a constant state of change.

13 O LORD, the hope of Israel, all that forsake thee shall be ashamed, and they that depart from me shall be written in the earth, because they have forsaken the LORD, the fountain of living waters.
14 Heal me, O LORD, and I shall be healed; save me, and I shall be saved: for thou art my praise.
15 Behold, they say unto me, Where is the word of the LORD? let it come now.
16 As for me, I have not hastened from being a pastor to follow thee: neither have I desired the woeful day; thou knowest: that which came out of my lips was right before thee.
17 Be not a terror unto me: thou art my hope in the day of evil.
18 Let them be confounded that persecute me, but let not me be confounded: let them be dismayed, but let not me be dismayed: bring upon them the day of evil, and destroy them with double destruction.

Jeremiah has turned to the LORD, the hope for himself as well as all of Israel that reveals the spirit of the LORD. The people who depart from the example of Jeremiah—who carry and represent the spirit of the LORD—shall be written in the earth, as they identify with the material world because they have forsaken the living spirit of the LORD, who is symbolized as a fountain of living waters. The living waters of the truth of the spirit of the LORD are available to heal the people who want to be healed of their emptiness and desolation.

Heal me, O LORD, and I shall be healed; save me, and I shall be saved: as the spirit of the LORD flows through the person to reveal the praise of the LORD. The impatient people in the fallen state hear this instruction and say, Behold, where is the word of the LORD? let it come to me now. As for Jeremiah, he has not hastened from being a pastor to follow the spirit of the LORD by revealing and releasing the spirit of his LORD on earth: neither has Jeremiah desired the woeful day, the day of sadness when Jeremiah ceases to reveal the spirit of the LORD. The LORD knows that what came out of the lips of Jeremiah was right before the LORD. The presence of the LORD is not a terror to Jeremiah: the spirit of the LORD is his hope in the day of evil. Let the evil people—who do not reveal the spirit of the LORD and who persecute Jeremiah—be confounded, but do not let Jeremiah be dismayed. The working of the Law shall bring upon them who ignore the spirit of the LORD the day of evil, and destroy them with double destruction.

The Symbolic Version of Jeremiah

19 Thus said the LORD unto me; Go and stand in the gate of the children of the people, whereby the kings of Judah come in, and by the which they go out, and in all the gates of Jerusalem;
20 And say unto them, Hear ye the word of the LORD, ye kings of Judah, and all Judah, and all the inhabitants of Jerusalem, that enter in by these gates:
21 Thus saith the LORD; Take heed to yourselves, and bear no burden on the sabbath day, nor bring it in by the gates of Jerusalem;
22 Neither carry forth a burden out of your houses on the sabbath day, neither do ye any work, but hallow ye the sabbath day, as I commanded your fathers.
23 But they obeyed not, neither inclined their ear, but made their neck stiff, that they might not hear, nor receive instruction.

The word of the LORD came to Jeremiah, saying; Go and stand in the gate of the children of the people. The LORD has **spiritual** people made in His image and likeness. The children of the people are immature people who are in the fallen state and partially separated from the spirit of the LORD. The gate of the children of the people is the gate through which the spirit from the LORD comes into the earth through His people. These gates, between the world of spirit and the world of form, are the means through which the spiritual people, who are the kings of Judah, come in, enter, the earth, and the means by which they exit, they go out. This is true of all the gates of Jerusalem, the holy, spiritual city of the LORD. Jeremiah has a message from the LORD for all the spiritual people who desire to enter the ascended state through the gate; the message is not for the materialistic immature children of the people who are in the fallen state.

Jeremiah is to tell the people, Hear the word of the LORD, you kings of Judah, and all Judah, and all the inhabitants of Jerusalem, that enter in by these gates: the LORD says; Take heed to yourselves and to the expressions that come forth through you. The people are to bear no burden from the fallen distorted conditions from the materialistic world on the Sabbath day. The Sabbath day is the day of the LORD; the day when the LORD's spirit comes through His people into the earth. The Sabbath of the LORD is every day. The Sabbath is every moment of every day. The burdens of the fallen state, the sinful behavior, is not to be brought into the gates of the holy spiritual city of Jerusalem by the LORD's people who are his kings. The LORD's people are commanded not to carry forth a burden, sinful behavior, out of your houses, your body, mind and heart, on the Sabbath day, neither shall you do any work to perpetuate the fallen state any more. You are to hallow the Sabbath day, the day of the LORD, as the LORD commanded your fathers.

But the people who heard the message of the LORD through the mouth of Jeremiah obeyed not, neither inclined their ear to hear his message. On the contrary, they made their neck stiff, that they might not hear, nor receive instruction from the LORD. People have the freedom of choice to not be a stiff-necked people. It is an individual choice. The people who heard Jeremiah chose not to change their ways.

24 And it shall come to pass, if ye diligently hearken unto me, saith the LORD, to bring in no burden through the gates of this city on the sabbath day, but hallow the sabbath day, to do no work therein;
25 Then shall there enter into the gates of this city kings and princes sitting upon the throne of David, riding in chariots and on horses, they, and their princes, the men of Judah, and the inhabitants of Jerusalem: and this city shall remain for ever.
26 And they shall come from the cities of Judah, and from the places about Jerusalem, and from the land of Benjamin, and from the plain, and from the mountains, and from the south, bringing burnt offerings, and sacrifices, and meat offerings, and incense, and bringing sacrifices of praise, unto the house of the LORD.
27 But if ye will not hearken unto me to hallow the sabbath day, and not to bear a burden, even entering in at the gates of Jerusalem on the sabbath day; then will I kindle a fire in the gates thereof, and it shall devour the palaces of Jerusalem, and it shall not be quenched.

And it shall come to pass, if you diligently listen to Me, says the LORD, to bring in no burden of sin from the fallen state through the gates of this city on the Sabbath day, but hallow the Sabbath day, to do no self-centered work therein, then there shall enter into the gates of this spiritual city kings and princes sitting upon the throne of David, riding in chariots and on horses. The Sabbath day is the present moment, the time, when a person allows the spirit of the LORD to flow through the emotions, the mind and the body without resistance or interference. The spiritual kingdom of heaven shall enter into the earth. Then, they, the LORD's people, and their princes, the men of Judah, and the

The Testimony of the Major Prophets

inhabitants of Jerusalem shall be spiritual people clothed in manifest form: and this spiritual city occupied by spiritual people shall remain for ever. The holy city, spiritual Jerusalem, will be an attractive place. It will be a "new" Jerusalem that reveals the spirit of the LORD.

And the people shall come from the cities of Judah, and from the places about Jerusalem, and from the land of Benjamin, and from the plain, and from the mountains, and from the south, bringing burnt offerings, and sacrifices, and meat offerings, and incense, and bringing sacrifices of praise to the house of the LORD.

But, if you will not listen to the word of the LORD to hallow the Sabbath day, and if you choose not to relinquish your burden of sin so that you may enter into the gates of the spiritual Jerusalem on the Sabbath day, then, if you do not meet these requirements to enter the city, the Law of the LORD shall kindle a destructive fire in the gates of the holy city and the fire of the LORD shall devour the palaces of Jerusalem, and it shall not be quenched in you because of your choice.

CHAPTER 18

1 The word which came to Jeremiah from the LORD, saying,
2 Arise, and go down to the potter's house, and there I will cause thee to hear my words.
3 Then I went down to the potter's house, and, behold, he wrought a work on the wheels.
4 And the vessel that he made of clay was marred in the hand of the potter: so he made it again another vessel, as seemed good to the potter to make it.

The word of the LORD came to Jeremiah, saying, Arise, and go down to the potter's house, and there I will cause you to hear the words of instruction that will help you to teach the people. Then Jeremiah went down to the potter's house, and, behold, he wrought a work on the wheels. The vessel that he made of clay was marred in the hand of the potter: so the potter made another vessel as good as the potter could make it. This illustration of the potter making a vessel of clay is used by the LORD to explain to Jeremiah that the living spirit in the potter can reshape the same material clay to make another vessel.

5 Then the word of the LORD came to me, saying,
6 O house of Israel, cannot I do with you as this potter? saith the LORD. Behold, as the clay is in the potter's hand, so are ye in mine hand, O house of Israel.
7 At what instant I shall speak concerning a nation, and concerning a kingdom, to pluck up, and to pull down, and to destroy it;
8 If that nation, against whom I have pronounced, turn from their evil, I will repent of the evil that I thought to do unto them.
9 And at what instant I shall speak concerning a nation, and concerning a kingdom, to build and to plant it;
10 If it do evil in my sight, that it obey not my voice, then I will repent of the good, wherewith I said I would benefit them.

The word of the spirit of the LORD enlightens Jeremiah, saying, O House of Israel, cannot the LORD do with you what the potter does with clay? Behold, as the clay is in the potter's hand, so is the house of Israel in the hand of the LORD. At what instant shall the LORD speak concerning a spiritual and holy nation, and concerning a kingdom to come on earth as it is in heaven, to pluck up the nation, or to pull it down, and destroy it. If the nation, against whom the LORD has pronounced elimination, turn from their evil, the LORD will repent of the evil that which he thought to do to them. At what instant shall the LORD speak concerning a nation, and concerning a kingdom, to build and to plant it in the earth where it is needed? If the nation of people does evil in the sight of the LORD, and does not obey His voice, then the LORD will not deliver the benefits that He intended to bestow on the people because the people are the means of delivery. The people who deliver the spirit of the LORD are absolutely necessary to bring the blessings from heaven into the earth.

The Testimony of the Major Prophets

11 Now therefore go to, speak to the men of Judah, and to the inhabitants of Jerusalem, saying, Thus saith the LORD; Behold, I frame evil against you, and devise a device against you: return ye now every one from his evil way, and make your ways and your doings good.
12 And they said, There is no hope: but we will walk after our own devices, and we will every one do the imagination of his evil heart.

Jeremiah is to go and speak the word of the LORD to the men of Judah and the inhabitants of Jerusalem: Behold, the LORD will deliver evil against you based upon a device called the Law of Sowing and Reaping; everyone must return from his evil way and begin to express ways and actions that are good in the sight of the LORD. But the people said, There is no hope for the kingdom of heaven on earth: the people will continue to walk after their own devices and after the imaginations of an evil heart which will produce evil thoughts and actions.

13 Therefore thus saith the LORD; Ask ye now among the heathen, who hath heard such things: the virgin of Israel hath done a very horrible thing.
14 Will a man leave the snow of Lebanon which cometh from the rock of the field? or shall the cold flowing waters that come from another place be forsaken?
15 Because my people hath forgotten me, they have burned incense to vanity, and they have caused them to stumble in their ways from the ancient paths, to walk in paths, in a way not cast up;
16 To make their land desolate, and a perpetual hissing; every one that passeth thereby shall be astonished, and wag his head.
17 I will scatter them as with an east wind before the enemy; I will shew them the back, and not the face, in the day of their calamity.
18 Then said they, Come, and let us devise devices against Jeremiah; for the law shall not perish from the priest, nor counsel from the wise, nor the word from the prophet. Come, and let us smite him with the tongue, and let us not give heed to any of his words.

The LORD speaking through Jeremiah asks the heathen who has heard of such a thing as the virgin of Israel, the only people who have been in communion and covenant with the LORD, have done a terrible thing by refusing the spirit of the LORD. Will a man leave the snow of Lebanon which comes from the rock of the field? or shall the cold flowing waters that come from another place be forsaken? A person who thirsts for the water of truth will drink from the source of the cool water: the source of the water of truth that satisfies the thirst for God is the covenant where one receives the spirit of the LORD.

The people created by the LORD, as the potter has created a vessel, have forgotten the Creator who created them. They have burned incense to false idols in their vanity, in taking the LORD's name, I AM, in vain. Their vanity of ignoring the LORD has caused them to stumble in their ways from the ancient paths which do not have an orderly design. They make their way desolate and their land is filled with a perpetual complaint; everyone who walks by the chaos shall be astonished and wag his head in disbelief that such chaotic conditions could exist.

Therefore, the LORD will scatter them as with an east wind before the enemy; He will show them the back, and not the face, in the day of their calamity. Then said they, Come, and let us devise devices, create evil schemes, against Jeremiah; for the law shall not perish from the way that the priests have taught us, nor counsel from the people that we believe are wise, nor the word from the person that we believe to be a prophet. Come, and let us smite Jeremiah with a tongue that expresses displeasure, and let us not give heed to any of his words.

19 Give heed to me, O LORD, and hearken to the voice of them that contend with me.
20 Shall evil be recompensed for good? for they have digged a pit for my soul. Remember that I stood before thee to speak good for them, and to turn away thy wrath from them.
21 Therefore deliver up their children to the famine, and pour out their blood by the force of the sword; and let their wives be bereaved of their children, and be widows; and let their men be put to death; let their young men be slain by the sword in battle.
22 I will scatter them as with an east wind before the enemy; I will shew them the back, and not the face, in the day of their calamity.

The Symbolic Version of Jeremiah

18 Then said they, Come, and let us devise devices against Jeremiah; for the law shall not perish from the priest, nor counsel from the wise, nor the word from the prophet. Come, and let us smite him with the tongue, and let us not give heed to any of his words.

Jeremiah asks the LORD to give heed and listen to the reaction of the people that contend with the word of the LORD spoken through Jeremiah. Shall the evil behavior of the rebellious people be rewarded with good? the wicked people have dug a pit for the soul of Jeremiah. Remember that Jeremiah stood before the LORD to speak good for them and to turn away the wrath of the LORD. The wicked people have not listened to the LORD or His prophet. Therefore, deliver these children to the famine, pour out their blood to the sword; let their wives be childless and be widows; let the men be put to death: and let their young men be slain in battle. Let the Law work to consume evil away from the kingdom of the LORD.

The power of the LORD moving through the Law will scatter the rebellious people as with an east wind before the enemy; the LORD will show them the back side of defeat, and not the face of victory, in the day of their calamity when the Law of Sowing and Reaping brings the expected punishment. Then the people who were not willing to repent and change their ways said, Let us devise a plot and let us devise devices, traps and snares, against Jeremiah; for the law shall not perish from the priest, nor counsel from the wise, nor the word from the prophet. Come, and let us smite him with the tongue, and let us not give heed to any of his words. The people have rejected the word of the LORD through Jeremiah and they have plotted to entrap and harm him. The Law of Sowing and Reaping will result in disaster.

CHAPTER 19

1 Thus saith the LORD, Go and get a potter's earthen bottle, and take of the ancients of the people, and of the ancients of the priests;
2 And go forth unto the valley of the son of Hinnom, which is by the entry of the east gate, and proclaim there the words that I shall tell thee,
3 And say, Hear ye the word of the LORD, O kings of Judah, and inhabitants of Jerusalem; Thus saith the LORD of hosts, the God of Israel; Behold, I will bring evil upon this place, the which whosoever heareth, his ears shall tingle.

The LORD said to Jeremiah, Go and get a potter's vessel, take the wisest of the people and the priests, and go forth into the Valley of the son of Hinnom which is located by the entry of the east gate, the symbolic direction of the future, and proclaim the words that the LORD shall tell Jeremiah. The kings of Judah and the inhabitants of Jerusalem are to hear the word of the LORD of hosts, the LORD who is the God of Israel. The LORD declares that He will bring evil upon this place and anyone who hears the word of the LORD, his ears shall tingle. The message of the LORD will serve as a wake-up call for those who hear the message as their ears tingle, ring true, from the content of the message.

4 Because they have forsaken me, and have estranged this place, and have burned incense in it unto other gods, whom neither they nor their fathers have known, nor the kings of Judah, and have filled this place with the blood of innocents;
5 They have built also the high places of Baal, to burn their sons with fire for burnt offerings unto Baal, which I commanded not, nor spake it, neither came it into my mind:
6 Therefore, behold, the days come, saith the LORD, that this place shall no more be called Tophet, nor The valley of the son of Hinnom, but The valley of slaughter.

The ears of the people will tingle because they have forsaken the LORD by refusing to worship the LORD their God. This caused the people to be estranged from the LORD as they strayed away from the LORD's spirit. The people who strayed from revealing the spirit of the LORD in covenant agreement have turned the holy place into a strange place where they burned incense to other gods whom neither they, their fathers nor the spiritual kings of Judah had ever known. As the people ignored the spirit of the LORD, they have filled the place with the blood of innocents. They have built altars to Baal, to burn their innocent sons with fire as burnt offerings to Baal, to prove their love for the false god of Baal. The LORD did not command this sacrifice of the children: the LORD neither spoke it nor did the sacrifice of sons ever come into the mind of the LORD.

Therefore, the days will come that this strange place shall no longer be called Tophet, which means, "a place of betrayal", or, the valley of the son of Hinnom, which means, "the place where they are". This strange place holds the strange people who have rebelled against the LORD's spirit and guidance. The place will be called the valley of slaughter, the place where the children of the kings and elders of Judah and Jerusalem were sacrificed to a false god, Baal

7 And I will make void the counsel of Judah and Jerusalem in this place; and I will cause them to fall by the sword before their enemies, and by the hands of them that seek their lives: and their carcases will I give to be meat for the fowls of the heaven, and for the beasts of the earth.
8 And I will make this city desolate, and an hissing; every one that passeth thereby shall be astonished and hiss because of all the plagues thereof.
9 And I will cause them to eat the flesh of their sons and the flesh of their daughters, and they shall eat every one the flesh of his friend in the siege and straitness, wherewith their enemies, and they that seek their lives, shall straiten them.

The LORD will make void the wise counsel of Judah and Jerusalem in this wicked place which simply means that they will fall by the sword of the destructive power of the LORD before their enemies by the hand of those who seek their lives. Their carcases will be given by the LORD as meat, as creative materials, for the fowls of heaven, the symbols of the divine thoughts from the LORD, and the beasts of the earth which are the symbols of the material effects of those thoughts in the earth.

And the action of the LORD through the Law of Sowing and Reaping will make this city desolate. Every one that passes by there shall be astonished and hiss with scorn and scoff at the desolation of the city with all of its plagues which were produced by the behavior of man in the fallen state. The law of the LORD will cause the people in the fallen place, who created the desolation, to eat the flesh of their sons and the flesh of their daughters, and they shall eat every one the flesh of his friend. The people will not literally eat the flesh, but, symbolically, the people will need to live in the flesh that they produced on earth according to the working of the Law. In the siege and the straitness, the difficult predicaments of the desolate state, their enemies, and they that seek their lives, shall inflict conditions in this state where the working of the Law through the people shall discipline and chastise them.

10 Then shalt thou break the bottle in the sight of the men that go with thee,
11 And shalt say unto them, Thus saith the LORD of hosts; Even so will I break this people and this city, as one breaketh a potter's vessel, that cannot be made whole again: and they shall bury them in Tophet, till there be no place to bury.
12 Thus will I do unto this place, saith the LORD, and to the inhabitants thereof, and even make this city as Tophet:
13 And the houses of Jerusalem, and the houses of the kings of Judah, shall be defiled as the place of Tophet, because of all the houses upon whose roofs they have burned incense unto all the host of heaven, and have poured out drink offerings unto other gods.

Then, Jeremiah shall break the bottle in the sight of the men, the elders and priests, that went with him to the valley to witness this parable. Jeremiah delivers the parable from the LORD; as the LORD breaks this potter's vessel which is designed to hold water, as a human is to hold the spirit of the truth of the LORD, the human cannot be made whole again. They shall bury the distorted and fallen expressions from fallen people in Tophet, in the place of betrayal, until there is no place to bury them.

Thus the working of the Law of Sowing and Reaping of the LORD upon the inhabitants of the desolate land shall make any city as desolate as the city of Tophet. The houses of Jerusalem, and the houses of the kings of Judah, shall be defiled as the place of Tophet was defiled because of all the people who offered burnt offerings upon the roofs and houses. The people in the fallen state have burned incense ion the sight of all the host of heaven, and they have poured out drink offerings to other false gods.

14 Then came Jeremiah from Tophet, whither the LORD had sent him to prophesy; and he stood in the court of the LORD's house; and said to all the people,
15 Thus saith the LORD of hosts, the God of Israel; Behold, I will bring upon this city and upon all her towns all the evil that I have pronounced against it, because they have hardened their necks, that they might not hear my words.

Then Jeremiah returned from Tophet, the land of desolation where the LORD sent him to prophesy, to express, the true spirit of the LORD to all the people. Jeremiah prophesied that the LORD of hosts, the LORD of all the people, will bring the same fate upon all of their towns because the people refuse to hear the word of the LORD as they harden their necks so that they will not hear the words of salvation.

CHAPTER 20

1 Now Pashur the son of Immer the priest, who was also chief governor in the house of the LORD, heard that Jeremiah prophesied these things.
2 Then Pashur smote Jeremiah the prophet, and put him in the stocks that were in the high gate of Benjamin, which was by the house of the LORD.
3 And it came to pass on the morrow, that Pashur brought forth Jeremiah out of the stocks. Then said Jeremiah unto him, The LORD hath not called thy name Pashur, but Magormissabib.

The religious and political leaders did not like to hear the things that Jeremiah prophesied in the spirit of the LORD that would surely come to pass in accordance with the working of the Law. Pashur—who was a son of Immer the priest, was the chief governor in the house of the LORD, the temple—was unhappy with the preaching of Jeremiah. Pashur had Jeremiah beaten and placed in the stocks, in confinement, that was located at the north gate that opened in the direction of the land of Benjamin. The next day, when Pashur released Jeremiah from prison, Jeremiah told Pashur that the LORD has not called him by the name Pashur, whose name means, "one who magnifies the hole", but Magormissabib, which means, "fear round about". Pashur, who has been magnifying the emptiness and desolation, the hole in the environment, is now attempting to suppress the truth expressed by Jeremiah by the use of fear and beatings.

4 For thus saith the LORD, Behold, I will make thee a terror to thyself, and to all thy friends: and they shall fall by the sword of their enemies, and thine eyes shall behold it: and I will give all Judah into the hand of the king of Babylon, and he shall carry them captive into Babylon, and shall slay them with the sword.
5 Moreover I will deliver all the strength of this city, and all the labours thereof, and all the precious things thereof, and all the treasures of the kings of Judah will I give into the hand of their enemies, which shall spoil them, and take them, and carry them to Babylon.
6 And thou, Pashur, and all that dwell in thine house shall go into captivity: and thou shalt come to Babylon, and there thou shalt die, and shalt be buried there, thou, and all thy friends, to whom thou hast prophesied lies.

Jeremiah tells Pashur that according to the working of the Law of Sowing and Reaping, that the LORD will make Pashur a terror to himself and all of his friends: they will fall by the sword of their enemies who will react to the fear by destroying the source of the fear; and their eyes will observe the working of the Law. Jeremiah states that the working of the Law will bring all of Judah into the hand of control of the Babylonians who will take their treasures as spoil and take the people as captives to Babylon. The people shall be slain by the sword which is the symbol of the power of destruction that results when people use the power of the LORD outside the divine design. Jeremiah prophesies that Pashur and all his people shall go into captivity. Pashur shall be taken to Babylon and he will die and be buried there with all of his friends to whom Pashur has prophesied lies.

The Testimony of the Major Prophets

7 O LORD, thou hast deceived me, and I was deceived: thou art stronger than I, and hast prevailed: I am in derision daily, every one mocketh me.
8 For since I spake, I cried out, I cried violence and spoil; because the word of the LORD was made a reproach unto me, and a derision, daily.
9 Then I said, I will not make mention of him, nor speak any more in his name. But his word was in mine heart as a burning fire shut up in my bones, and I was weary with forbearing, and I could not stay.
10 For I heard the defaming of many, fear on every side. Report, say they, and we will report it. All my familiars watched for my halting, saying, Peradventure he will be enticed, and we shall prevail against him, and we shall take our revenge on him.

Jeremiah interpreted the beating and the imprisonment which he has received at the hand of Pashur as a deception from the LORD instead of the working of the Law. The LORD and the Law are stronger than Jeremiah and the LORD and the Law prevail. Jeremiah can prophesy for the LORD using the LORD's spirit, but the people in the fallen state hold him in derision and mock him daily because of his representation of the LORD's spirit.

Ever since Jeremiah spoke and cried out to the people of the violence and spoil that would transpire at the hands of the Babylonians, which was the outworking of the Law on a larger scale, Jeremiah has received the jeers of the people who would not see what was about to transpire. Jeremiah, due to the unpleasantness of the mockery, derision, beating and imprisonment, decided that he would not make mention of the LORD anymore. But the word of the LORD was in Jeremiah's heart as a burning fire, and although Jeremiah did not like to forbear with the punishment that he received, he could not stay silent and he could not cease to represent the spirit of the LORD. The reluctance of Jeremiah to prophesy because of the pain was overcome by the divine compulsion to serve and represent the LORD.

As Jeremiah continued to express the truth that burned in his heart, he heard the defamation and the accusations from all sides of the many people who were afraid of their circumstances. They asked Jeremiah to report the truth to them and they will report it to others. All of Jeremiah's familiar "friends" watched for his halting, his failure, saying, Peradventure Jeremiah will be enticed to slip and fall, and they shall prevail against him, and shall take their revenge on him.

11 But the LORD is with me as a mighty terrible one: therefore my persecutors shall stumble, and they shall not prevail: they shall be greatly ashamed; for they shall not prosper: their everlasting confusion shall never be forgotten.
12 But, O LORD of hosts, that triest the righteous, and seest the reins and the heart, let me see thy vengeance on them: for unto thee have I opened my cause.
13 Sing unto the LORD, praise ye the LORD: for he hath delivered the soul of the poor from the hand of evildoers

But the LORD that was with Jeremiah is a mighty and awesome One: therefore Jeremiah's persecutors shall stumble, and they shall not prevail: they shall be greatly ashamed; for they shall not prosper: their everlasting confusion shall never be forgotten. But, O LORD of hosts, that tries the righteous, and sees the reins and the heart, let me see your vengeance on them: for unto the service of the LORD has Jeremiah opened his cause. Jeremiah will continue to sing the praises of the LORD.

Jeremiah's message for everyone is the sing to the LORD, praise the LORD by revealing the LORD's spirit through the people. It is the spirit of the LORD that will deliver the soul, the body, mind and heart, of the poor from the hand of evil doers. The evil doers of the fallen state do not praise the LORD and reveal His spirit in their individual living. Instead of praise to the LORD, the people in the fallen state curse their conditions.

14 Cursed be the day wherein I was born: let not the day wherein my mother bare me be blessed.
15 Cursed be the man who brought tidings to my father, saying, A man child is born unto thee; making him very glad.
16 And let that man be as the cities which the LORD overthrew, and repented not: and let him hear the cry in the morning, and the shouting at noontide;
17 Because he slew me not from the womb; or that my mother might have been my grave, and her womb to be always great with me.
18 Wherefore came I forth out of the womb to see labour and sorrow, that my days should be consumed with shame?

The people, who do not praise the LORD for the blessings which they have received, curse the day they were born and they do not allow the day in which they were born on earth through their mother be a blessing. They curse the man who brought the tidings of his birth to their fathers, saying a man child is born to you which made the father very glad. The person in the fallen state curses his parents. He believes and espouses that he is accursed. He expresses cursings, not blessings, through his heart, mind and body. He curses the world around him which makes his environment desolate.

Let that man who curses his circumstances be as the cities which the LORD overthrew and who does not repent when he hears the cry of the people who express cursings in the morning, and the shouting at noon.
It was not the LORD who slew the fallen person who is cursing from the womb; nor was it the mother who gave birth to a living child who did not die in the grave of his mother's womb. The womb of the mother was always great to the person; the womb delivered the person into the earth; the womb was not a tomb or a grave; the womb is a womb of life.

The person born into the fallen state cannot understand why he came out of the womb of his mother to see this fallen world of labor and sorrow. The person in the fallen state cannot comprehend the world into which he was born and asks why his days are consumed with shame at the distorted conditions which he perceives?

CHAPTER 21

1 The word which came unto Jeremiah from the LORD, when king Zedekiah sent unto him Pashur the son of Melchiah, and Zephaniah the son of Maaseiah the priest, saying,
2 Inquire, I pray thee, of the LORD for us; for Nebuchadrezzar king of Babylon maketh war against us; if so be that the LORD will deal with us according to all his wondrous works, that he may go up from us.

Zedekiah was the king of Judah from 597-586 BC. The king sent Pashur the son of Melchiah, and Zephaniah the son of Maaseiah the priest, to ask Jeremiah to inquire of the LORD in regard to the fate of Judah and Jerusalem because they had heard that Nebuchadnezzar, the king of Babylon, intends to make war against them; if this is true, then they would ask the LORD to deal with them according to all his wondrous works, that the power and strength of the LORD would be on their side. It is apparent that while Jeremiah was being beaten and confined with regard to his preaching the word of the LORD, the king and his messengers recognized something of the covenant which Jeremiah had with the LORD because they asked him to inquire of the LORD with respect to the impending threat from Babylon. The word of the LORD did come to Jeremiah who gave the LORD's message to the representatives of the king of Judah.

3 Then said Jeremiah unto them, Thus shall ye say to Zedekiah:
4 Thus saith the LORD God of Israel; Behold, I will turn back the weapons of war that are in your hands, wherewith ye fight against the king of Babylon, and against the Chaldeans, which besiege you without the walls, and I will assemble them into the midst of this city.
5 And I myself will fight against you with an outstretched hand and with a strong arm, even in anger, and in fury, and in great wrath.
6 And I will smite the inhabitants of this city, both man and beast: they shall die of a great pestilence.

Jeremiah informs the envoys of the king that they should tell Zedekiah that the LORD God of Israel will use the power of the LORD moving through the invaders to turn back the weapons of war that are in the hands of the people of Judah. When the people of Judah fight against the king of Babylon and the Chaldeans, they will be besieged, and the invaders will enter into the heart of the city. The LORD will fight against king Zedekiah with an outstretched hand and with a strong arm, using the Babylonians and the Chaldeans, even in anger, and in fury, and in great wrath to smite the inhabitants of the city who will die of a great pestilence, a great scourge.

7 And afterward, saith the LORD, I will deliver Zedekiah king of Judah, and his servants, and the people, and such as are left in this city from the pestilence, from the sword, and from the famine, into the
hand of Nebuchadrezzar king of Babylon, and into the hand of their enemies, and into the hand of those that seek their life: and he shall smite them with the edge of the sword; he shall not spare them, neither have pity, nor have mercy.
8 And unto this people thou shalt say, Thus saith the LORD; Behold, I set before you the way of life, and the way of death.

The Symbolic Version of Jeremiah

9 He that abideth in this city shall die by the sword, and by the famine, and by the pestilence: but he that goeth out, and falleth to the Chaldeans that besiege you, he shall live, and his life shall be unto him for a prey.
10 For I have set my face against this city for evil, and not for good, saith the LORD: it shall be given into the hand of the king of Babylon, and he shall burn it with fire.

The LORD speaking through Jeremiah says that He will deliver Zedekiah king of Judah, and his servants, and the people, and such as are left in this city from the pestilence, from the destructive sword of the LORD's power which is moving through the Law of the LORD, and from the famine. The LORD will cause king Zedekiah to be delivered into the hand of Nebuchadnezzar king of Babylon, and into the hand of their enemies, and into the hand of those that seek their lives. The power of the LORD moving through Nebuchadnezzar shall smite the people of Judah with the edge of the sword; he shall not spare them, neither have pity, nor have mercy.

The LORD directs Jeremiah to inform the people to; Behold that He has set before you the way of life and the way of death. He that abides in this city, which shall be overrun by the Chaldeans shall die by the sword, and by the famine, and by the pestilence: but he that goes out, and falls to the Chaldeans that besiege the nation of Judah and the city of Jerusalem shall live, and his life shall be unto him for a prey, a goal. For the LORD has set His face against this city for evil, and not for good: it shall be given into the hand of the king of Babylon, and he shall burn it with destructive fire which is a symbol of the destructive aspect of the Law of Sowing and Reaping.

11 And touching the house of the king of Judah, say, Hear ye the word of the LORD;
12 O house of David, thus saith the LORD; Execute judgment in the morning, and deliver him that is spoiled out of the hand of the oppressor, lest my fury go out like fire, and burn that none can quench it, because of the evil of your doings.
13 Behold, I am against thee, O inhabitant of the valley, and rock of the plain, saith the LORD; which say, Who shall come down against us? or who shall enter into our habitations?
14 But I will punish you according to the fruit of your doings, saith the LORD: and I will kindle a fire in the forest thereof, and it shall devour all things round about it.

Jeremiah is to prophesy to the king of Judah to hear the word of the LORD. The house of David is commanded to execute judgment in the morning, and deliver him that is spoiled out of the hand of the oppressor, lest my fury go out like fire, and burn with such intensity that none can quench it, because of the evil of your doings.

Behold, the LORD is against the people of Jerusalem and the nation of Judah who are called the inhabitants of the valley, and rock of the plain. These are the inhabitants of Jerusalem and Judah who have said, Who shall come down against us? or who shall enter into our habitations? But the spirit of the LORD will punish you according to the fruit of your doings, according to the Law of Sowing and Reaping. If the design is not the design of the LORD, then the Law will kindle a fire in the forest thereof, the symbol where material things are transformed, and power of the spirit of God shall truly destroy and devour all things round about in the environment.

CHAPTER 22

1 Thus saith the LORD; Go down to the house of the king of Judah, and speak there this word,
2 And say, Hear the word of the LORD, O king of Judah, that sittest upon the throne of David, thou, and thy servants, and thy people that enter in by these gates:
3 Thus saith the LORD; Execute ye judgment and righteousness, and deliver the spoiled out of the hand of the oppressor: and do no wrong, do no violence to the stranger, the fatherless, nor the widow, neither shed innocent blood in this place.
4 For if ye do this thing indeed, then shall there enter in by the gates of this house kings sitting upon the throne of David, riding in chariots and on horses, he, and his servants, and his people.
5 But if ye will not hear these words, I swear by myself, saith the LORD, that this house shall become a desolation.

The LORD directs Jeremiah to go to king of Judah, who sits upon the throne of David with the authority and responsibility for the servants and people and tell the king to execute judgment and righteousness, and deliver the people who have been spoiled by the invader out of the hand of the oppressors, the Babylonians and the Chaldeans. The king of Judah is instructed to do no wrong, do no violence to the stranger, the fatherless, nor the widow, neither shed innocent blood in this place. If the king of Judah does wrong, then foreign kings shall enter and sit upon the throne of David, riding triumphantly in chariots and on horses, he, and his servants, and his people. The king of Judah is warned that if he does not heed the word of the LORD, then the house of Judah shall become a desolation.

6 For thus saith the LORD unto the king's house of Judah; Thou art Gilead unto me, and the head of Lebanon: yet surely I will make thee a wilderness, and cities which are not inhabited.
7 And I will prepare destroyers against thee, every one with his weapons: and they shall cut down thy choice cedars, and cast them into the fire.
8 And many nations shall pass by this city, and they shall say every man to his neighbour, Wherefore hath the LORD done thus unto this great city?
9 Then they shall answer, Because they have forsaken the covenant of the LORD their God, and worshipped other gods, and served them.
10 Weep ye not for the dead, neither bemoan him: but weep sore for him that goeth away: for he shall return no more, nor see his native country.

The message of the LORD to the king's house of Judah is that they are Gilead to the LORD and the head of Lebanon. Gilead means, "the mass" of the people who contain the word of the LORD on earth, and Lebanon means, "the whiteness, or the incense" which is contained within the head, the consciousness of the LORD's people. Even so, if the people do not carry and reveal the spirit of the LORD, then the LORD will make them a wilderness, and cities which are not inhabited by the LORD's people. If the LORD's spirit is not with the people, then the working of the Law will prepare destroyers against the inhabitants who will be cut down as choice cedars and cast into the fire of destruction.

The Symbolic Version of Jeremiah

Many nations shall pass by this city, and they shall say every man to his neighbor, Why has the LORD done this unto this great city? Then they shall answer, Because the people have forsaken the covenant of the LORD their God, and worshipped other gods, and served them. The people are advised not to weep and moan for their dead, but to weep for the LORD that has gone away from the people because He shall return no more to them, nor see his native country. The LORD does not leave the people and His native country as much as the people have ignored the spirit of the LORD and shut Him out.

11 For thus saith the LORD touching Shallum the son of Josiah king of Judah, which reigned instead of Josiah his father, which went forth out of this place; He shall not return thither any more:
12 But he shall die in the place whither they have led him captive, and shall see this land no more.
13 Woe unto him that buildeth his house by unrighteousness, and his chambers by wrong; that useth his neighbour's service without wages, and giveth him not for his work;
14 That saith, I will build me a wide house and large chambers, and cutteth him out windows; and it is cieled with cedar, and painted with vermilion.
15 Shalt thou reign, because thou closest thyself in cedar? did not thy father eat and drink, and do judgment and justice, and then it was well with him?
16 He judged the cause of the poor and needy; then it was well with him: was not this to know me? saith the LORD.
17 But thine eyes and thine heart are not but for thy covetousness, and for to shed innocent blood, and for oppression, and for violence, to do it.

The LORD touched Shallum, which means, "perfect" or "peaceable", who, as a child of the LORD is available to be touched by the LORD. (Shallum is the personal name of Jehoiakim, the son of Josiah, king of Judah, who reigned in Judah after his father). Josiah, was taken captive to Egypt in 609 BC by the Pharaoh Neco. Josiah would die in Egypt never to return from Egypt to see his kingdom any more. Jeremiah describes the woe that befalls the person who builds his house, the house of all the people in the kingdom, with unrighteousness and wrong doing, who uses his neighbor's services without wages and who does not reward him for his work; a leader who says that he will build himself a wide house with large chambers and large windows; a house which is paneled with cedar and painted vermilion.

The LORD speaking through Jeremiah asks if a king shall reign because he encloses himself in cedar? Did not his father eat and drink, do judgment and justice, and then it was well with him when he did it? The father of Jehoiakim judged the cause of the poor and needy and it was well with him. Was this service not the way to know the spirit of the LORD? But the eyes and the heart of Jehoiakim were used only to covet things for himself, to shed innocent blood, to oppress the people and for violence. The purpose and motivation of Jehoiakim was for self-centered things. His selfishness will not be missed.

18 Therefore thus saith the LORD concerning Jehoiakim the son of Josiah king of Judah; They shall not lament for him, saying, Ah my brother! or, Ah sister! they shall not lament for him, saying, Ah lord! or, Ah his glory!
19 He shall be buried with the burial of an ass, drawn and cast forth beyond the gates of Jerusalem.
20 Go up to Lebanon, and cry; and lift up thy voice in Bashan, and cry from the passages: for all thy lovers are destroyed.
21 I spake unto thee in thy prosperity; but thou saidst, I will not hear. This hath been thy manner from thy youth, that thou obeyedst not my voice.
22 The wind shall eat up all thy pastors, and thy lovers shall go into captivity: surely then shalt thou be ashamed and confounded for all thy wickedness.
23 O inhabitant of Lebanon, that makest thy nest in the cedars, how gracious shalt thou be when pangs come upon thee, the pain as of a woman in travail!

Therefore, the LORD speaking through Jeremiah, informs the hearers of the word to not lament for Jehoiakim, son of Josiah, king of Judah. The people shall not lament for him as they would a brother, or a sister, or a lord or the glory of his reign. He shall be buried as an ass is buried, drawn and cast forth beyond the gates of Jerusalem.

Instead of mourning for their selfish king, the people are advised to go up to Lebanon, the symbol of the incense of the LORD which is within them, and cry; they should lift up their voice to Bashan, a mountainous region which is devoid of the things of the world and cry from the mountain passages to the LORD their God. For all the things that they loved

The Testimony of the Major Prophets

of a material nature have been destroyed. The LORD has spoken to the people in their prosperity, but the people would not hear. This has been their manner of reaction from their youth when they did not heed and obey the voice of the LORD. The wind of change shall do away with their leaders and their lovers shall go into captivity. Surely, the people will now be ashamed and confounded with the results of their wickedness. Jeremiah asks the person, the inhabitant of Lebanon who makes his house as a nest of cedar, how gracious shall the person be when the pangs of desolation come upon them which shall be as painful as a woman in labor?

24 As I live, saith the LORD, though Coniah the son of Jehoiakim king of Judah were the signet upon my right hand, yet would I pluck thee thence;
25 And I will give thee into the hand of them that seek thy life, and into the hand of them whose face thou fearest, even into the hand of Nebuchadrezzar king of Babylon, and into the hand of the Chaldeans.
26 And I will cast thee out, and thy mother that bare thee, into another country, where ye were not born; and there shall ye die.
27 But to the land whereunto they desire to return, thither shall they not return.
28 Is this man Coniah a despised broken idol? is he a vessel wherein is no pleasure? wherefore are they cast out, he and his seed, and are cast into a land which they know not?
29 O earth, earth, earth, hear the word of the LORD.
30 Thus saith the LORD, Write ye this man childless, a man that shall not prosper in his days: for no man of his seed shall prosper, sitting upon the throne of David, and ruling any more in Judah.

The LORD speaking through Jeremiah says that even though Coniah, the son of Jehoiakim king of Judah, were the signet, the seal, upon the LORD's right hand, even so the LORD would honor the Law of Sowing and Reaping and pluck the people who have ignored Him and deliver them into the hand of Nebuchadnezzar king of Babylon, and into the hand of the Chaldeans. These are the invaders who the people of Judah fear and who seek their lives. The working of the Law of the behavior of the people which will produce its results will cast the people out into a new land where they will die. The people may desire to return to the land from which they have been cast out, but they shall not return.

Is the man, Coniah, a despised broken idol? Is he a vessel wherein there is no pleasure? The name, Coniah, means, "the strength of the LORD". The strength of the LORD is present within the people. Why are all the people cast out, with Coniah and his seed, and are cast into a land which they do not know?

Jeremiah delivers the word of the LORD. O earth, earth, earth, the physical forms created by the people on earth through their own behavior. Hear the word of the LORD! The LORD says, You should write this man childless. He may have the potential of the LORD within him but unless the potential is given birth, actualized, you must consider the man childless. The man who does not express the LORD's spirit shall not prosper in his days: for no man of his seed, a seed that is not of the LORD's seed, shall prosper, even though he sits on the throne of David. He shall not rule any more in Judah.

CHAPTER 23

1 Woe be unto the pastors that destroy and scatter the sheep of my pasture! saith the LORD.
2 Therefore thus saith the LORD God of Israel against the pastors that feed my people; Ye have scattered my flock, and driven them away, and have not visited them: behold, I will visit upon you the evil of your doings, saith the LORD.
3 And I will gather the remnant of my flock out of all countries whither I have driven them, and will bring them again to their folds; and they shall be fruitful and increase.
4 And I will set up shepherds over them which shall feed them: and they shall fear no more, nor be dismayed, neither shall they be lacking, saith the LORD.

The LORD considers all the people on earth as the sheep in His pasture. The "pasture" is the symbol for the planet Earth, and the "sheep" are the symbol for the inhabitants of the planet. The pastors or the shepherds are the people who have the responsibility to lead the people to a conscious awareness, a covenant, with the LORD. The LORD speaking through Jeremiah preaches that woe shall come to the pastors who destroy and scatter the people in the LORD's pasture instead of working to bring the people together.

The LORD God of Israel declares through Jeremiah that the lack of true leadership by the pastors who feed His people have scattered the flock, driven them away from the spirit of the LORD, and they have not visited the scattered people to exemplify the spirit of the LORD to them. Behold, the LORD will visit upon the pastors the evil of their behaviors. The LORD desires that the remnant of His people, the people who will hear the word of the LORD, be gathered from the countries where they have been driven under the power of the LORD according to his Law of Sowing and Reaping. The scattered people are to be brought again to their folds, their place of rest and protection which is the spiritual covenant of the LORD where they shall be fruitful and increase. They cannot be fruitful and productive as long as they are scattered and separated from the spirit of the LORD. Why would the LORD desire his children in the fallen state, an evil state, to be fruitful? Evil would be multiplied and destroy the fallen state that exists in manifest physical form! There is no evil in the spirit of the LORD. The LORD states the He will set up Shepherds over the people to feed them with the spirit of the LORD. If it is the spirit of the LORD that flows clearly and cleanly through the people, then the people shall not experience fear, be dismayed nor shall they experience lack; they will experience the spirit of the LORD.

5 Behold, the days come, saith the LORD, that I will raise unto David a righteous Branch, and a King shall reign and prosper, and shall execute judgment and justice in the earth.
6 In his days Judah shall be saved, and Israel shall dwell safely: and this is his name whereby he shall be called, THE LORD OUR RIGHTEOUSNESS.
7 Therefore, behold, the days come, saith the LORD, that they shall no more say, The LORD liveth, which brought up the children of Israel out of the land of Egypt;
8 But, The LORD liveth, which brought up and which led the seed of the house of Israel out of the north country, and from all countries whither I had driven them; and they shall dwell in their own land.

The Testimony of the Major Prophets

The sheep are to behold and see that the days have come when the LORD will raise a person to the level of the covenant, which David experienced as a righteous Branch, a King shall reign and prosper, and shall execute judgment and justice on earth. When the King puts in an appearance in the experience of the people, then, in His days, Judah shall be saved after she repents, and Israel, the spiritual people who represent the LORD, shall dwell safely in the land. The King shall be called the LORD OUR RIGHTEOUSNESS because the righteousness of the spirit of the LORD is moving through the people, through their bodies, minds and hearts, which is the right use of the spirit of the LORD.

When this mass release of the spirit of the LORD, is allowed to flow into the earth through the people, then, behold, the days come when the people shall no more say the LORD lives who brought the children of Israel out of the land of Egypt; but rather, the LORD lives which brought up and led the seed of the house of Israel who had been scattered to the north country and from all countries where the LORD had driven them. It is the same LORD and the same power of the LORD that moved the scattered people to dwell in their own land, the land where the spirit of the LORD moves through the land of their earthly, human equipment to shape the land upon which they walk.

9 Mine heart within me is broken because of the prophets; all my bones shake; I am like a drunken man, and like a man whom wine hath overcome, because of the LORD, and because of the words of his holiness.
10 For the land is full of adulterers; for because of swearing the land mourneth; the pleasant places of the wilderness are dried up, and their course is evil, and their force is not right.
11 For both prophet and priest are profane; yea, in my house have I found their wickedness, saith the LORD.
12 Wherefore their way shall be unto them as slippery ways in the darkness: they shall be driven on, and fall therein: for I will bring evil upon them, even the year of their visitation, saith the LORD.

The heart of the LORD which is with and in all of the people is broken and scattered among the people because of the teachings of the false prophets. The bones of the body of the LORD, which is the body of mankind, will shake when the spirit of the LORD is absent or only partially present. The LORD within His body of mankind is like a drunken man overcome with wine. The body of mankind staggers because the power and the design of LORD is being received by each person in the fallen state within the body from the LORD who is holy. The holiness from the spirit of the LORD conflicts with the body, mind, and heart of the fallen state to produce distortions. The distortions of the spirit of the LORD, which are caused by the people who have forsaken the spirit of the LORD for the seeming treasure of the environment, is like a woman who has forsaken her husband and committed adultery by an illicit attachment to the environment. Everyone in the fallen state has forsaken the LORD for some material treasure, some heart's desire, from the environment. This is committing adultery. The land is full of adulterers, people who have forsaken the spirit of the LORD for the pleasure of a distorted form. The attachment to the land causes the person to mourn; the pleasant places of the wilderness are dried up and their course is evil; their force is not right. Both the false prophet and the priest are profane because of their emotional and material connections with the material world that have priority over the spirit of God; which is wicked behavior or wickedness. Therefore the ways that the people behave shall be as slippery ways in the darkness which will cause them to fall. When the people commit adultery with the treasures of the environment, then the LORD brings evil upon them according to the working of the Law.

13 And I have seen folly in the prophets of Samaria; they prophesied in Baal, and caused my people Israel to err.
14 I have seen also in the prophets of Jerusalem an horrible thing: they commit adultery, and walk in lies: they strengthen also the hands of evildoers, that none doth return from his wickedness: they are all of them unto me as Sodom, and the inhabitants thereof as Gomorrah.
15 Therefore thus saith the LORD of hosts concerning the prophets; Behold, I will feed them with wormwood, and make them drink the water of gall: for from the prophets of Jerusalem is profaneness gone forth into all the land.

The LORD speaking through Jeremiah states that He has seen the folly of the prophets in Samaria, the way that they prophesied to the false god, Baal, and caused the LORD's people, the spiritual people of Israel, to err. Even in Jerusalem, the LORD has seen a horrible thing in the prophets of Jerusalem: they commit adultery by blending emotionally with material treasures which are more important to them than the spirit of the LORD. This false connection causes the people to walk in lies, strengthen the hands of the evil doers so that none return from their wicked ways. The LORD states that these people are to Him as the inhabitants of Sodom and Gomorrah. Therefore the LORD of hosts says, concerning the fate of the false prophets, that He will feed them with wormwood and they shall drink bitter waters of gall. This will occur because only profaneness goes forth from the people of Jerusalem into all the lands.

16 Thus saith the LORD of hosts, Hearken not unto the words of the prophets that prophesy unto you: they make you vain: they speak a vision of their own heart, and not out of the mouth of the LORD.
17 They say still unto them that despise me, The LORD hath said, Ye shall have peace; and they say unto every one that walketh after the imagination of his own heart, No evil shall come upon you.
18 For who hath stood in the counsel of the LORD, and hath perceived and heard his word? who hath marked his word, and heard it?

The LORD speaking through Jeremiah advises the people to not listen to the words of the false prophets who prophesy to you with messages that make you vain. The false prophets speak with a vision out of their own impure hearts which do not come from the mouth of the LORD, from the expression of His spirit. The false prophets promise the people that they will have peace, and they say to the people who have evil hearts that no evil will come upon them. But who has stood in the counsel of the LORD as the connecting link of the covenant-agreement between man and God to perceive the word of the LORD? Who has marked the word of the LORD which comes to man in spirit and heard the word of the LORD in one's own form as the wind of the spirit comes into the earth? The spirit can be either creative or destructive.

19 Behold, a whirlwind of the LORD is gone forth in fury, even a grievous whirlwind: it shall fall grievously upon the head of the wicked.
20 The anger of the LORD shall not return, until he have executed, and till he have performed the thoughts of his heart: in the latter days ye shall consider it perfectly.
21 I have not sent these prophets, yet they ran: I have not spoken to them, yet they prophesied.
22 But if they had stood in my counsel, and had caused my people to hear my words, then they should have turned them from their evil way, and from the evil of their doings.
23 Am I a God at hand, saith the LORD, and not a God afar off?
24 Can any hide himself in secret places that I shall not see him? saith the LORD. Do not I fill heaven and earth? saith the LORD.

Behold the whirlwind of the LORD is constantly moving grievously upon the head of the wicked. The anger of the LORD shall not return, until he has executed, and till he has performed the thoughts of his heart: in the latter days, as you become spiritually mature, you shall consider the spirit moving through one's heart, perfectly. The LORD declares that He has not sent forth these false prophets, yet they ran with the false message: the LORD has not spoken to them, yet they prophesied to the people in the name of the LORD. But if the false prophets had really stood in the LORD's counsel, and had caused the LORD's people to hear the LORD's words, then they should have turned from their evil ways, and from the evil of their doings.

Is God a God who is at hand, says the LORD, or a God who is afar off? The true God is moving through all of His creation; He is not a God that is afar off. Can any person hide himself in secret places that the LORD God shall not see him when God is everywhere? Does not Almighty God and His spirit fill heaven and earth?

25 I have heard what the prophets said, that prophesy lies in my name, saying, I have dreamed, I have dreamed.
26 How long shall this be in the heart of the prophets that prophesy lies? yea, they are prophets of the deceit of their own heart;
27 Which think to cause my people to forget my name by their dreams which they tell every man to his neighbour, as their fathers have forgotten my name for Baal.
28 The prophet that hath a dream, let him tell a dream; and he that hath my word, let him speak my word faithfully. What is the chaff to the wheat? saith the LORD.
29 Is not my word like as a fire? saith the LORD; and like a hammer that breaketh the rock in pieces?
30 Therefore, behold, I am against the prophets, saith the LORD, that steal my words every one from his neighbour.
31 Behold, I am against the prophets, saith the LORD, that use their tongues, and say, He saith.
32 Behold, I am against them that prophesy false dreams, saith the LORD, and do tell them, and cause my people to err by their lies, and by their lightness; yet I sent them not, nor commanded them: therefore they shall not profit this people at all, saith the LORD.

The Testimony of the Major Prophets

The LORD, who is present everywhere, has heard what the false prophets who prophesy lies using the name of the LORD, saying, I have dreamed, I have dreamed what I have been telling you. How long shall these false dreams be in the heart of the prophets that prophesy lies? Yes, they are prophets of the deceit of their own hearts; they cause the people to forget the name of the LORD by their dreams which they tell every man to his neighbor. Their fathers have forgotten the name of the LORD for Baal, a symbol of a false god.

The LORD speaking through Jeremiah states that the prophet that has a dream, let him tell that dream; and he that has the word of the LORD, let him speak that word faithfully. What is the chaff, the symbol of the dream state, to the wheat, the symbol of the truth from the LORD? Is not the LORD's word like a fire? and like a hammer that breaks the rock in pieces? Therefore, behold, that the LORD is against the false prophets who steal the words of the LORD from his neighbor.

Behold, I am against the prophets, says the LORD, that use their tongues, and say, falsely, The LORD says that it is so.

Behold, I am against them that prophesy false dreams, says the LORD, and do tell their false dreams to cause My people to err by their lies, and by their lightness; yet I sent them not, nor commanded them: therefore this people shall not profit at all, says the LORD.

33 And when this people, or the prophet, or a priest, shall ask thee, saying, What is the burden of the LORD? thou shalt then say unto them, What burden? I will even forsake you, saith the LORD.
34 And as for the prophet, and the priest, and the people, that shall say, The burden of the LORD, I will even punish that man and his house.
35 Thus shall ye say every one to his neighbour, and every one to his brother, What hath the LORD answered? and, What hath the LORD spoken?
36 And the burden of the LORD shall ye mention no more: for every man's word shall be his burden; for ye have perverted the words of the living God, of the LORD of hosts our God.

When the people, the prophet or the priest shall ask you, saying, What is the burden of the LORD? You shall say to them, What burden? I will even forsake you, says the LORD. However, the prophet, the priest and the people shall say that the burden of the LORD will punish that particular man or that particular house.

Thus, you shall say to all your neighbors, and every one who hears to his brother, What has the LORD answered? What has the LORD spoken? And the burden of the LORD, you shall not mention any more: for every man's word, every man's expression, in thought, word and deed, shall be his burden; if there is any perversion of the LORD, then you have perverted the words of the living God, of the LORD of hosts our God.

37 Thus shalt thou say to the prophet, What hath the LORD answered thee? and, What hath the LORD spoken?
38 But since ye say, The burden of the LORD; therefore thus saith the LORD; Because ye say this word, The burden of the LORD, and I have sent unto you, saying, Ye shall not say, The burden of the LORD;
39 Therefore, behold, I, even I, will utterly forget you, and I will forsake you, and the city that I gave you and your fathers, and cast you out of my presence:
40 And I will bring an everlasting reproach upon you, and a perpetual shame, which shall not be forgotten.

Jeremiah tells the people that when they speak to a prophet, they should ask, What has the LORD answered you? And, What has the LORD spoken? Since the false prophet says, The burden of the LORD; or, Therefore, thus says the LORD; Because, you have said, the burden of the LORD and Jeremiah has told his people, You shall not say, the burden of the LORD as though it is a heavy burden, because the burden of the LORD is light; the burden is as light as spirit. Therefore, behold, I, the LORD speaking through the physical equipment of Jeremiah, shall utterly forget you, the people who do not reveal the lightness of spirit, and forsake you, and the city that I gave you and your fathers, and cast you out of my presence: And I will bring an everlasting reproach upon you, and a perpetual shame, which shall not be forgotten.

CHAPTER 24

1 The LORD shewed me, and, behold, two baskets of figs were set before the temple of the LORD, after that Nebuchadrezzar king of Babylon had carried away captive Jeconiah the son of Jehoiakim king of Judah, and the princes of Judah, with the carpenters and smiths, from Jerusalem, and had brought them to Babylon.
2 One basket had very good figs, even like the figs that are first ripe: and the other basket had very naughty figs, which could not be eaten, they were so bad.
3 Then said the LORD unto me, What seest thou, Jeremiah? And I said, Figs; the good figs, very good; and the evil, very evil, that cannot be eaten, they are so evil.
4 Again the word of the LORD came unto me, saying,
5 Thus saith the LORD, the God of Israel; Like these good figs, so will I acknowledge them that are carried away captive of Judah, whom I have sent out of this place into the land of the Chaldeans for their good.
6 For I will set mine eyes upon them for good, and I will bring them again to this land: and I will build them, and not pull them down; and I will plant them, and not pluck them up.
7 And I will give them an heart to know me, that I am the LORD: and they shall be my people, and I will be their God: for they shall return unto me with their whole heart.

The spirit of the LORD moving through Jeremiah showed him two baskets of figs which were set before the temple of the LORD after Nebuchadnezzar king of Babylon had carried away as captives Jeconiah, the son of Jehoiakim king of Judah, and the princes of Judah, with the carpenters and smiths, from Jerusalem, and had brought them to Babylon. One basket had very good figs, even like the figs that are first ripe: and the other basket had very naughty figs, which could not be eaten, they were so bad.

Then the LORD asked, What do you see, Jeremiah? And Jeremiah said, Figs; the good figs are very good; and the evil figs are so very evil that they cannot be eaten, because they are so evil.

Again the word of the LORD came to Jeremiah to explain the parable of the two baskets of figs, saying, Like these good figs, so will the LORD acknowledge the people who are carried away as captives from Judah. "The captives have been sent out of this place into the land of the Chaldeans for their good."

The LORD will set His eyes upon them for good, and He will bring them again to this land from which they were taken. The LORD will build them, and not pull them down; and the LORD will plant them, and not pluck them up. The LORD informs Jeremiah that, as with the good figs, it is possible to build the people whose hearts are open to the LORD and they shall not be pulled down; it is possible to plant the people who are symbolized by the good figs and not pluck them up. During the period of captivity, the LORD will give them a heart to know the LORD: and the captives shall be the LORD's people, and the LORD will be their God. In season, the people who were taken captives shall return unto the LORD with their whole heart. It is obvious that the people who were taken captives did not love

The Testimony of the Major Prophets

the LORD with their whole heart. The people who did love the LORD more than others were symbolized by the basket of good figs, while the people whose hearts were turned far away from the LORD were symbolized by the basket of evil figs.

8 And as the evil figs, which cannot be eaten, they are so evil; surely thus saith the LORD, So will I give Zedekiah the king of Judah, and his princes, and the residue of Jerusalem, that remain in this land, and them that dwell in the land of Egypt:
9 And I will deliver them to be removed into all the kingdoms of the earth for their hurt, to be a reproach and a proverb, a taunt and a curse, in all places whither I shall drive them.
10 And I will send the sword, the famine, and the pestilence, among them, till they be consumed from off the land that I gave unto them and to their fathers.

The evil figs symbolize the evil people who are evil because their hearts are turned far away from the spirit of the LORD. They are so evil that they cannot be eaten as fruit, they are not useful to the plan of the LORD on earth to build a kingdom. The people, who are symbolized by the basket of evil figs, represent Zedekiah the king of Judah, and his princes, and the residue of Jerusalem, that remain in this land, and them that dwell in the land of Egypt.

These people whose hearts are turned far from the LORD, the basket of bad figs, shall be removed to all the kingdoms of the earth to be a reproach and a proverb, a taunt and a curse, in all the places that the power of the LORD shall drive them. The sword of the LORD, the power of the LORD which can destroy the evil people shall accompany the people with the impure hearts, and famine and pestilence shall dwell among them until they are consumed from off the land that the LORD gave to their forefathers. The working of the Law of Sowing and Reaping is beautifully portrayed in the parable of the fig baskets.

CHAPTER 25

1 The word that came to Jeremiah concerning all the people of Judah in the fourth year of Jehoiakim the son of Josiah king of Judah, that was the first year of Nebuchadrezzar king of Babylon;
2 The which Jeremiah the prophet spake unto all the people of Judah, and to all the inhabitants of Jerusalem, saying,
3 From the thirteenth year of Josiah the son of Amon king of Judah, even unto this day, that is the three and twentieth year, the word of the LORD hath come unto me, and I have spoken unto you, rising early and speaking; but ye have not hearkened.
4 And the LORD hath sent unto you all his servants the prophets, rising early and sending them; but ye have not hearkened, nor inclined your ear to hear.
5 They said, Turn ye again now every one from his evil way, and from the evil of your doings, and dwell in the land that the LORD hath given unto you and to your fathers for ever and ever:
6 And go not after other gods to serve them, and to worship them, and provoke me not to anger with the works of your hands; and I will do you no hurt.
7 Yet ye have not hearkened unto me, saith the LORD; that ye might provoke me to anger with the works of your hands to your own hurt.

The word of the LORD came to Jeremiah the prophet concerning all the people of Judah and all the inhabitants of Jerusalem in the fourth year of the reign of Jehoiakim, the son of Josiah king of Judah; this was the first year of Nebuchadnezzar king of Babylon. Jeremiah said that for twenty three years, beginning in the thirteenth year of the reign of Josiah the son of Amon king of Judah, he has spoken the word of the LORD to the people, but they would not listen. The LORD has also sent to the people of Judah and Jerusalem all of His servants, the prophets, and the people would not listen to the content of their messages; they did not even incline their ear, pay attention, to hear what was being said.

The message of the prophets from the LORD was always the same as they said, Turn away from the evil way, the evil of your doings and behaviors, and dwell in the land of the spirit of the LORD which was given to you and your fathers forever and ever. Do not go after any other gods to serve them or worship them. Do not provoke the LORD to anger with the work of your hands and the LORD will do you no harm. But the people have not listened to the word of the LORD through His prophets and they will bring punishment upon themselves according to the working of the Law of Sowing and Reaping.

8 Therefore thus saith the LORD of hosts; Because ye have not heard my words,
9 Behold, I will send and take all the families of the north, saith the LORD, and Nebuchadrezzar the king of Babylon, my servant, and will bring them against this land, and against the inhabitants thereof,
and against all these nations round about, and will utterly destroy them, and make them an astonishment, and an hissing, and perpetual desolations.

The Testimony of the Major Prophets

10 Moreover I will take from them the voice of mirth, and the voice of gladness, the voice of the bridegroom, and the voice of the bride, the sound of the millstones, and the light of the candle.
11 And this whole land shall be a desolation, and an astonishment; and these nations shall serve the king of Babylon seventy years.

Therefore, because the people did not listen and obey, the LORD of all the hosts of all people will send all the families of the north and Nebuchadnezzar the king of Babylon, a servant of the LORD, and bring them against this land, the inhabitants thereof, and against all the nations round about. The LORD will utterly destroy the people, make them astonished by the invasion, and bring a sadness and perpetual desolation. The desolation is the result of the working of the Law against a people who ignored and rebelled against the word of the LORD.

Moreover the working of the Law of the LORD will take from the people the voice of mirth and the voice of gladness; the voice of the bridegroom, and the voice of the bride; the sound of the millstones which means that there is grain for food, and the light of the candle which provides light for the darkness. The whole land shall be a desolation, and an astonishment because of the invasion and capture of the people; and these nations shall serve the king of Babylon for seventy years.

12 And it shall come to pass, when seventy years are accomplished, that I will punish the king of Babylon, and that nation, saith the LORD, for their iniquity, and the land of the Chaldeans, and will make it perpetual desolations.
13 And I will bring upon that land all my words which I have pronounced against it, even all that is written in this book, which Jeremiah hath prophesied against all the nations.
14 For many nations and great kings shall serve themselves of them also: and I will recompense them according to their deeds, and according to the works of their own hands.

It shall come to pass, after seventy years, that the LORD will punish the king of Babylon and his nation for their iniquity along with the land of the Chaldeans. They will be made perpetual desolations. The power of the LORD working through the Law will bring upon the land everything that the LORD has pronounced against it, even everything that is written in the Book which Jeremiah has prophesied against the fallen people. Many nations and great kings shall serve themselves instead of the LORD, and they will be punished according to their deeds and according to the works of their own hands.

15 For thus saith the LORD God of Israel unto me; Take the wine cup of this fury at my hand, and cause all the nations, to whom I send thee, to drink it.
16 And they shall drink, and be moved, and be mad, because of the sword that I will send among them.
17 Then took I the cup at the LORD's hand, and made all the nations to drink, unto whom the LORD had sent me:
18 To wit, Jerusalem, and the cities of Judah, and the kings thereof, and the princes thereof, to make them a desolation, an astonishment, an hissing, and a curse; as it is this day;
19 Pharaoh king of Egypt, and his servants, and his princes, and all his people;
20 And all the mingled people, and all the kings of the land of Uz, and all the kings of the land of the Philistines, and Ashkelon, and Azzah, and Ekron, and the remnant of Ashdod,
21 Edom, and Moab, and the children of Ammon,
22 And all the kings of Tyrus, and all the kings of Zidon, and the kings of the isles which are beyond the sea,
23 Dedan, and Tema, and Buz, and all that are in the utmost corners,
24 And all the kings of Arabia, and all the kings of the mingled people that dwell in the desert,
25 And all the kings of Zimri, and all the kings of Elam, and all the kings of the Medes,
26 And all the kings of the north, far and near, one with another, and all the kingdoms of the world, which are upon the face of the earth: and the king of Sheshach shall drink after them.

The LORD God of Israel has said to Jeremiah that he should take the wine cup of this fury, the result of the working of the Law, and cause all the nations to drink, the wine of experience that came from the fruits of their own behavior. The people shall drink the results of their own actions and be moved, be mad at the results which came about because the sword, the power of the LORD, has produced the conditions according to the working of the Law. Jeremiah must take the cup from the LORD's hand and make the people drink from the cup according to the nature of the wine which they have produced by their behavior.

The Law of Sowing and Reaping works very precisely to produce the effects that have been sown through the consciousness of the people. Behaviors of the people of Jerusalem, and the cities of Judah, the kings and the princes have made the conditions of desolation, astonishment and the curse as it exists this very day. In like manner, conditions are made in other countries through the behaviors of Pharaoh, king of Egypt, and his servants, and his princes, and all his people. The same Law of Sowing and Reaping applies to all the mingled people, and all the kings of the land of Uz, all the kings of the land of the Philistines, Ashkelon, Azzah, Ekron, the remnant of Ashdod, Edom, and Moab, and the children of Ammon.

The Law of the LORD of hosts works simultaneously upon the kings of Tyrus, kings of Zidon, the kings of the isles which are beyond the sea, Dedan, Tema, Buz, and all that are in the utmost corners of the earth. All the kings of Arabia, all the kings of the mingled people that dwell in the desert, the kings of Zimri, and all the kings of Elam, the kings of the Medes, all the kings of the north, far and near, one with another, and all the kingdoms of the world, which are upon the face of the earth; and the king of Sheshach shall drink after them. Everyone is subject to the working of the Law of the LORD including all the kings of the earth and their subjects.

27 Therefore thou shalt say unto them, Thus saith the LORD of hosts, the God of Israel; Drink ye, and be drunken, and spue, and fall, and rise no more, because of the sword which I will send among you.
28 And it shall be, if they refuse to take the cup at thine hand to drink, then shalt thou say unto them, Thus saith the LORD of hosts; Ye shall certainly drink.
29 For, lo, I begin to bring evil on the city which is called by my name, and should ye be utterly unpunished? Ye shall not be unpunished: for I will call for a sword upon all the inhabitants of the earth, saith the LORD of hosts.
30 Therefore prophesy thou against them all these words, and say unto them, The LORD shall roar from on high, and utter his voice from his holy habitation; he shall mightily roar upon his habitation; he
shall give a shout, as they that tread the grapes, against all the inhabitants of the earth.
31 A noise shall come even to the ends of the earth; for the LORD hath a controversy with the nations, he will plead with all flesh; he will give them that are wicked to the sword, saith the LORD.

The LORD of hosts, the God of Israel, directs Jeremiah to tell everyone to drink the wine, the symbol of the conditions that they have made, and be made drunk by the results of their terrible behavior, vomit it out of them and let the sinful behavior rise no more because of the power of the sword that the LORD sends among all people can destroy the source of the sinful behavior. And it shall be, if the people refuse to take the cup of the knowledge of the working of the Law from the hand of Jeremiah to drink it and make it a part of their knowledge, then Jeremiah shall say to them, the LORD of hosts commands that you shall certainly drink the cup of the working of the Law. There is no choice because the Law is at work. The LORD begins to bring evil retribution upon the city which is called by His name.

The city is a symbol of an individual person or a collection of people. The name of the person or people is the name of the LORD: I AM, or I Am. The spirit of the LORD is with all people everywhere! Shall the people who carry the LORD's name go utterly unpunished? You shall not be unpunished because the LORD of hosts will call for a sword of retribution upon all the inhabitants of the earth. A noise, the results of the working of the Law, shall come to the people even to the ends of the earth; for the LORD has a controversy with the nations. The controversy is that the LORD sends the true design in spiritual form into the earth and the people distort the spiritual design to contaminate it with their own self-centered designs. The LORD through His prophet Jeremiah will plead with all flesh; he will give the people who acknowledge that they are wicked the opportunity to repent and let the destructive aspect of the sword to eliminate evil from the earth, from themselves.

32 Thus saith the LORD of hosts, Behold, evil shall go forth from nation to nation, and a great whirlwind shall be raised up from the coasts of the earth.
33 And the slain of the LORD shall be at that day from one end of the earth even unto the other end of the earth: they shall not be lamented, neither gathered, nor buried; they shall be dung upon the ground.
34 Howl, ye shepherds, and cry; and wallow yourselves in the ashes, ye principal of the flock: for the days of your slaughter and of your dispersions are accomplished; and ye shall fall like a pleasant vessel.
35 And the shepherds shall have no way to flee, nor the principal of the flock to escape.
36 A voice of the cry of the shepherds, and an howling of the principal of the flock, shall be heard: for the LORD hath spoiled their pasture.

The Testimony of the Major Prophets

37 And the peaceable habitations are cut down because of the fierce anger of the LORD.
38 He hath forsaken his covert, as the lion: for their land is desolate because of the fierceness of the oppressor, and because of his fierce anger.

The LORD of hosts says through Jeremiah, Behold, the evil shall go forth from nation to nation, and a great whirlwind of spirit shall be raised up from the coasts of the earth. The slain of the LORD shall be at that day from one end of the earth even unto the other end of the earth: they shall not be lamented, neither gathered, nor buried; they shall be dung upon the ground Death eliminates the source of evil from the consciousness of the individual. The word of the LORD through people—who are symbolized as shepherds—must reach individuals in the fallen state **before** they die.

The LORD speaking through Jeremiah cries to his fallen children who would represent the LORD on earth as shepherds, Howl, you shepherds of the flock of the LORD, and cry aloud so that the people in the fallen state can hear your cries; wallow yourselves in the ashes of the fallen state as a principal or leader of the flock. The days of your slaughter as a false person and of your dispersion or separation from the LORD is accomplished; your sinful, false self shall fall like a pleasant vessel.

The shepherds shall have no way to flee, nor the principal of the flock to escape from the spirit of the LORD. A voice of the cry of the shepherds, and a howling of the principal of the flock, shall be heard: for the spirit of the LORD moving through the consciousness of people has spoiled their pasture which was characterized by the sinful fallen state. The pasture belongs to the LORD. The peaceable habitations are cut down because of the fierce anger, the destructive cycle, of the LORD. He has forsaken his covert, secret place as the lion who leaves his lair to hunt for food. The land created by people in the fallen state is desolate because of the fierceness of the oppressor, the fallen person who is an oppressor; and the fierce anger of the oppressor, the person in the fallen state, is the absence of love which is the spirit of the LORD.

CHAPTER 26

1 In the beginning of the reign of Jehoiakim the son of Josiah king of Judah came this word from the LORD, saying,
2 Thus saith the LORD; Stand in the court of the LORD's house, and speak unto all the cities of Judah, which come to worship in the LORD's house, all the words that I command thee to speak unto them; diminish not a word:
3 If so be they will hearken, and turn every man from his evil way, that I may repent me of the evil, which I purpose to do unto them because of the evil of their doings.
4 And thou shalt say unto them, Thus saith the LORD; If ye will not hearken to me, to walk in my law, which I have set before you,
5 To hearken to the words of my servants the prophets, whom I sent unto you, both rising up early, and sending them, but ye have not hearkened;
6 Then will I make this house like Shiloh, and will make this city a curse to all the nations of the earth.
7 So the priests and the prophets and all the people heard Jeremiah speaking these words in the house of the LORD.

At the time of the beginning of the reign of Jehoiakim the son of Josiah king of Judah there came this word of the LORD to Jeremiah who was told to stand in the court of the LORD's house and speak to all the cities of Judah, the people of Judah, who come to worship in the LORD's house. Since Jeremiah is a prophet of the LORD, the court of the LORD's house in which Jeremiah stands, is the court, the place, where Jeremiah happens to be where he is in covenant-agreement with the spirit of the LORD. The words which come to Jeremiah from the LORD are to be spoken to the people and Jeremiah is not to diminish in any way the words of the LORD. In this manner, the words that come forth from the physical mouth of Jeremiah are indeed the words of the LORD. If the people really hear the words of the LORD through the mouth of Jeremiah, then they will turn away from their evil ways, so the LORD will help the people repent of the evil of their ways. The LORD desires to help the people to repent of their wicked ways and the evil of their doings.

Jeremiah is to tell the people that if they do not listen to the word of the LORD, if they do not walk in the creative cycle of the Law of Sowing and Reaping which the LORD has set before them, if they do not hear and do the words of the LORD's servants the prophets, then the LORD will make their house like Shiloh, and the city a curse to all the nations of the earth. Shiloh was a city in Ephraim and it was one of the earliest and most sacred of the Hebrew sanctuaries. A sacred city, by example and comparison, would be a curse to the people in every city in the fallen state. So all the priests, the prophets and all the people heard Jeremiah speaking these words from the LORD while he was in the house of the LORD. Jeremiah is in the house of the LORD whenever and wherever he is in covenant-agreement with the LORD.

8 Now it came to pass, when Jeremiah had made an end of speaking all that the LORD had commanded him to speak unto all the people, that the priests and the prophets and all the people took him, saying, Thou shalt surely die.
9 Why hast thou prophesied in the name of the LORD, saying, This house shall be like Shiloh, and this city shall be desolate without an inhabitant? And all the people were gathered against Jeremiah in the house of the LORD.

The Testimony of the Major Prophets

10 When the princes of Judah heard these things, then they came up from the king's house unto the house of the LORD, and sat down in the entry of the new gate of the LORD's house.
11 Then spake the priests and the prophets unto the princes and to all the people, saying, This man is worthy to die; for he hath prophesied against this city, as ye have heard with your ears.

Now it came to pass that when Jeremiah finished speaking all that the LORD commanded him to speak, all the priests, prophets and people took him and said, You shall surely die. Why have you prophesied in the name of the LORD, saying, This house shall be like Shiloh, and this city shall be desolate without an inhabitant. All the people were gathered against Jeremiah who was in the house of the LORD.

When the princes of Judah heard these things, then they came up from the king's house, king Jehoiakim, to the house of the LORD, the physical body of Jeremiah with his mind and heart, and sat down in the entry of the new gate of the LORD's house. Jeremiah is the new gate to the LORD's house.
Then the priests and the prophets spoke to the princes and to all the people, saying, This man Jeremiah is worthy to die; for he has prophesied against this city, and the people in it, as you have heard with your ears.

12 Then spake Jeremiah unto all the princes and to all the people, saying, The LORD sent me to prophesy against this house and against this city all the words that ye have heard.
13 Therefore now amend your ways and your doings, and obey the voice of the LORD your God; and the LORD will repent him of the evil that he hath pronounced against you.
14 As for me, behold, I am in your hand: do with me as seemeth good and meet unto you.
15 But know ye for certain, that if ye put me to death, ye shall surely bring innocent blood upon yourselves, and upon this city, and upon the inhabitants thereof: for of a truth the LORD hath sent me unto you to speak all these words in your ears.
16 Then said the princes and all the people unto the priests and to the prophets; This man is not worthy to die: for he hath spoken to us in the name of the LORD our God.
17 Then rose up certain of the elders of the land, and spake to all the assembly of the people, saying,
18 Micah the Morasthite prophesied in the days of Hezekiah king of Judah, and spake to all the people of Judah, saying, Thus saith the LORD of hosts; Zion shall be plowed like a field, and Jerusalem shall become heaps, and the mountain of the house as the high places of a forest.
19 Did Hezekiah king of Judah and all Judah put him at all to death? did he not fear the LORD, and besought the LORD, and the LORD repented him of the evil which he had pronounced against them? Thus might we procure great evil against our souls.

Jeremiah told the princes and the people that the LORD sent him to prophesy the words which they had heard. Therefore, amend your ways, obey the voice of the LORD, and the LORD will repent that person of the evil which has been pronounced against you. As for Jeremiah, he simply stated that he was in the hand of their control and they should do with him what seemed good and just. But know for a certain that if you put Jeremiah to death, then you shall bring innocent blood upon yourselves; for, of a truth, the LORD has sent Jeremiah to speak the particular words into their ears.

The princes and all the people said to the priests and to the prophets; This man is not worthy to die: for he has spoken to us in the name of the LORD our God. Then, certain of the elders of the land rose up and spoke to all the assembly of the people, saying, Micah the Morasthite prophesied in the days of Hezekiah king of Judah. He spoke to all the people of Judah in the name of the LORD of hosts, saying; Zion shall be plowed like a field, Jerusalem shall become heaps, and the mountain of the house as the high places of a forest. Then they asked, Did Hezekiah king of Judah and all Judah put him to death at all? Did he not fear the LORD, and besought the LORD, and the LORD repented him of the evil which he had
pronounced against them? In this manner, if we do not heed the word of the LORD through Jeremiah, then we might procure great evil against our souls.

20 And there was also a man that prophesied in the name of the LORD, Urijah the son of Shemaiah of Kirjath-je'arim, who prophesied against this city and against this land according to all the words of Jeremiah:

21 And when Jehoiakim the king, with all his mighty men, and all the princes, heard his words, the king sought to put him to death: but when Urijah heard it, he was afraid, and fled, and went into Egypt;
22 And Jehoiakim the king sent men into Egypt, namely, Elnathan the son of Achbor, and certain men with him into Egypt.
23 And they fetched forth Urijah out of Egypt, and brought him unto Jehoiakim the king; who slew him with the sword, and cast his dead body into the graves of the common people.
24 Nevertheless the hand of Ahikam the son of Shaphan was with Jeremiah, that they should not give him into the hand of the people to put him to death.

There was also a man who prophesied in the name of the LORD whose name was Urijah the son of Shemaiah of Kirjath-je'arim, who prophesied against this city and against this land according to all the words of Jeremiah. When Jehoiakim the king and his mighty men heard the words of the prophet, they sought to put him to death. Urijah, whose name means, "the light of the LORD", heard this, he was afraid and fled to Egypt.

Jehoiakim the king sent Elnathan and certain men into Egypt. They fetched forth Urijah out of Egypt, and brought him unto Jehoiakim the king who slew him with the sword, and cast his dead body into the graves of the common people. Nevertheless, even though king Jehoiakim slew Urijah, the hand of Ahikam, whose name means, "a brother that raises up", was with Jeremiah and stood in agreement with him so that he would not be given into the hands of people who would put him to death. One person, Ahikam, in agreement with Jeremiah broke the historical pattern and Jeremiah was not put to death.

CHAPTER 27

1 In the beginning of the reign of Jehoiakim the son of Josiah king of Judah came this word unto Jeremiah from the LORD, saying,
2 Thus saith the LORD to me; Make thee bonds and yokes, and put them upon thy neck,
3 And send them to the king of Edom, and to the king of Moab, and to the king of the Ammonites, and to the king of Tyrus, and to the king of Zidon, by the hand of the messengers which come to Jerusalem unto Zedekiah king of Judah;
4 And command them to say unto their masters, Thus saith the LORD of hosts, the God of Israel; Thus shall ye say unto your masters;
5 I have made the earth, the man and the beast that are upon the ground, by my great power and by my outstretched arm, and have given it unto whom it seemed meet unto me.
6 And now have I given all these lands into the hand of Nebuchadrezzar the king of Babylon, my servant; and the beasts of the field have I given him also to serve him.
7 And all nations shall serve him, and his son, and his son's son, until the very time of his land come: and then many nations and great kings shall serve themselves of him.

In the beginning of the reign of Jehoiakim (609-598) the son of Josiah king of Judah came this word to Jeremiah from the LORD, saying, Make bonds and yokes for yourselves, put them on your necks, and send them to the king of Edom, the king of Moab, the king of the Ammonites, the king of Tyrus, and the king of Zidon, by the hand of the messengers which come to Jerusalem until the reign of Zedekiah, (597-586) king of Judah. Command them to say to their masters, the LORD of hosts, the God of Israel says that you shall speak in this manner to your masters; the LORD has made the earth, the man and the beasts that are upon the ground, by His great power and by His outstretched arm, and He has given dominion over it to whomsoever it seemed fitting and appropriate according to the operation of the Law.

Now the LORD has given all these lands and the beasts of the field into the hand of Nebuchadnezzar the king of Babylon, His servant. All nations shall serve Nebuchadnezzar, his son, and his grandson until the very time of his land come: and then many nations and great kings shall subjugate him. The power of the LORD has been focused in the reign of Nebuchadnezzar who is a servant of the LORD and his offspring.

8 And it shall come to pass, that the nation and kingdom which will not serve the same Nebuchadrezzar the king of Babylon, and that will not put their neck under the yoke of the king of Babylon, that nation will I punish, saith the LORD, with the sword, and with the famine, and with the pestilence, until I have consumed them by his hand.
9 Therefore hearken not ye to your prophets, nor to your diviners, nor to your dreamers, nor to your enchanters, nor to your sorcerers, which speak unto you, saying, Ye shall not serve the king of Babylon:
10 For they prophesy a lie unto you, to remove you far from your land; and that I should drive you out, and ye should perish.

The Symbolic Version of Jeremiah

11 But the nations that bring their neck under the yoke of the king of Babylon, and serve him, those will I let remain still in their own land, saith the LORD; and they shall till it, and dwell therein.

And it shall come to pass, that the nations and kingdoms which will not serve Nebuchadnezzar the king of Babylon, and that will not put their necks under the yoke of the king of Babylon, then that nation will be punished, by the working of the power, the sword of the LORD. The punishment will manifest as famine and pestilence until the power of the LORD has consumed the enemy.

Therefore, do not hearken and listen to your prophets, diviners, dreamers, enchanters, nor to your sorcerers, who speak to you, saying, You shall not serve the king of Babylon. They prophesy a lie to you, to remove you far from your land; so that the LORD should drive you out, and you should perish. But the nations that bring their necks under the yoke of the king of Babylon, and serve him, those will I let remain still in their own lands, says the LORD; they shall till it, and dwell therein.

12 I spake also to Zedekiah king of Judah according to all these words, saying, Bring your necks under the yoke of the king of Babylon, and serve him and his people, and live.
13 Why will ye die, thou and thy people, by the sword, by the famine, and by the pestilence, as the LORD hath spoken against the nation that will not serve the king of Babylon?
14 Therefore hearken not unto the words of the prophets that speak unto you, saying, Ye shall not serve the king of Babylon: for they prophesy a lie unto you.
15 For I have not sent them, saith the LORD, yet they prophesy a lie in my name; that I might drive you out, and that ye might perish, ye, and the prophets that prophesy unto you.
16 Also I spake to the priests and to all this people, saying, Thus saith the LORD; Hearken not to the words of your prophets that prophesy unto you, saying, Behold, the vessels of the LORD's house shall now shortly be brought again from Babylon: for they prophesy a lie unto you.
17 Hearken not unto them; serve the king of Babylon, and live: wherefore should this city be laid waste?
18 But if they be prophets, and if the word of the LORD be with them, let them now make intercession to the LORD of hosts, that the vessels which are left in the house of the LORD, and in the house of the king of Judah, and at Jerusalem, go not to Babylon.

The LORD spoke also to Zedekiah king of Judah according to all these words, saying, Bring your necks under the yoke of the king of Babylon, and serve him and his people, and live. Why will you and your people die by the sword of the Law of the LORD, by the famine, and by the pestilence, as the LORD has spoken, against the nations that will not serve the king of Babylon?

The LORD has not sent them, yet they prophesy a lie in His name; that the LORD might drive you out, and that you might perish; you, and the prophets that prophesy to you. Also the LORD spoke to the priests and to all this people, saying, Hearken not to the words of your prophets that prophesy unto you, saying, Behold, the vessels of the LORD's house shall now shortly be brought again from Babylon: for they prophesy a lie unto you. Do not listen to the false prophets; serve the king of Babylon, and live: why should this city be laid waste?

But if they be prophets, and if the word of the LORD be with them, let them now make intercession to the LORD of hosts, that the vessels which are left in the house of the LORD, and in the house of the king of Judah, and at Jerusalem, do not go to Babylon.

19 For thus saith the LORD of hosts concerning the pillars, and concerning the sea, and concerning the bases, and concerning the residue of the vessels that remain in this city,
20 Which Nebuchadrezzar king of Babylon took not, when he carried away captive Jeconiah the son of Jehoiakim king of Judah from Jerusalem to Babylon, and all the nobles of Judah and Jerusalem;
21 Yea, thus saith the LORD of hosts, the God of Israel, concerning the vessels that remain in the house of the LORD, and in the house of the king of Judah and of Jerusalem;
22 They shall be carried to Babylon, and there shall they be until the day that I visit them, saith the LORD; then will I bring them up, and restore them to this place.

The Testimony of the Major Prophets

The LORD of hosts said in regard to the temple treasures, the bronze pillars, the bronze Sea, the bases and the vessels that remained in the city which Nebuchadnezzar, king of Babylon did not take away with him when he captured Jeconiah, the son of Jehoiakim king of Judah from Jerusalem to Babylon along with all the nobles of Judah and Jerusalem

The LORD of hosts, the God of Israel, said that the vessels that remain in the house of the LORD, and in the house of the king of Judah and of Jerusalem shall be carried to Babylon, and they shall remain there until the day that the LORD visits them, brings them up, and restores them to Jerusalem.

CHAPTER 28

1 And it came to pass the same year, in the beginning of the reign of Zedekiah king of Judah, in the fourth year, and in the fifth month, that Hananiah the son of Azur the prophet, which was of Gibeon, spake unto me in the house of the LORD, in the presence of the priests and of all the people, saying,
2 Thus speaketh the LORD of hosts, the God of Israel, saying, I have broken the yoke of the king of Babylon.
3 Within two full years will I bring again into this place all the vessels of the LORD's house, that Nebuchadrezzar king of Babylon took away from this place, and carried them to Babylon:
4 And I will bring again to this place Jeconiah the son of Jehoiakim king of Judah, with all the captives of Judah, that went into Babylon, saith the LORD: for I will break the yoke of the king of Babylon.

It came to pass in the same year of the beginning of the reign of Zedekiah king of Judah (597-586 BC), in the fifth month of the fourth year, that Hananiah the son of Azur the prophet, which was of Gibeon, spoke to Jeremiah. They were in the house of the LORD in the presence of the priests and all the people. Hananiah said that the LORD of hosts, the God of Israel, had spoken to him saying that the LORD has broken the yoke of the king of Babylon.

Hananiah the false prophet declares that the LORD of hosts will bring within two full years into this place all the vessels of the LORD's house, that Nebuchadnezzar king of Babylon took away from Jerusalem and carried to Babylon. In addition, Hananiah declares that that the LORD says that He will bring again Jeconiah the son of Jehoiakim king of Judah, with all the captives of Judah, that went into Babylon, because the LORD will break the yoke of the king of Babylon.

5 Then the prophet Jeremiah said unto the prophet Hananiah in the presence of the priests, and in the presence of all the people that stood in the house of the LORD,
6 Even the prophet Jeremiah said, Amen: the LORD do so: the LORD perform thy words which thou hast prophesied, to bring again the vessels of the LORD's house, and all that is carried away captive, from Babylon into this place.
7 Nevertheless hear thou now this word that I speak in thine ears, and in the ears of all the people;
8 The prophets that have been before me and before thee of old prophesied both against many countries, and against great kingdoms, of war, and of evil, and of pestilence.
9 The prophet which prophesieth of peace, when the word of the prophet shall come to pass, then shall the prophet be known, that the LORD hath truly sent him.

Then Jeremiah said to Hananiah in the presence of the priests and all the people that stood in the house of the LORD agreed as he said, Amen: the LORD will bring the event that Hananiah has prophesied to bring the vessels of the temple that had been taken away back from Babylon to Jerusalem. Nevertheless, Hananiah, the priests and the people are to hear the words that Jeremiah speaks. The prophets of old have prophesied against many countries and kingdoms, of war, of evil and of pestilence. The prophet who prophesies of peace, when the word of the prophet comes to pass and peace is the experience of the people, then the people shall know the prophet has truly been sent by the LORD.

The Testimony of the Major Prophets

10 Then Hananiah the prophet took the yoke from off the prophet Jeremiah's neck, and brake it.
11 And Hananiah spake in the presence of all the people, saying, Thus saith the LORD; Even so will I break the yoke of Nebuchadrezzar king of Babylon from the neck of all nations within the space of two full years. And the prophet Jeremiah went his way.
12 Then the word of the LORD came unto Jeremiah the prophet, after that Hananiah the prophet had broken the yoke from off the neck of the prophet Jeremiah, saying,
13 Go and tell Hananiah, saying, Thus saith the LORD; Thou hast broken the yokes of wood; but thou shalt make for them yokes of iron.
14 For thus saith the LORD of hosts, the God of Israel; I have put a yoke of iron upon the neck of all these nations, that they may serve Nebuchadrezzar king of Babylon; and they shall serve him: and I have given him the beasts of the field also.

Then Hananiah took the yoke, which was worn as a symbol of submission, from off the neck of Jeremiah, and broke it. Hananiah spoke in the presence of all the people, saying, Thus says the LORD; Even so will I break the yoke of Nebuchadnezzar king of Babylon from the neck of all nations within the space of two full years. And the prophet Jeremiah went his way. Then the word of the LORD came to Jeremiah to go and tell Hananiah that he may have broken the yokes of wood; but Hananiah is making yokes of iron for the people. The LORD says that He has put a yoke of iron upon the neck of all these nations so that they may serve Nebuchadnezzar king of Babylon. The people who have been captured by Nebuchadnezzar shall serve him. It is the LORD's will and the working of the Law that the people serve Nebuchadnezzar and that the beasts of the field shall belong to him also.

15 Then said the prophet Jeremiah unto Hananiah the prophet, Hear now, Hananiah; The LORD hath not sent thee; but thou makest this people to trust in a lie.
16 Therefore thus saith the LORD; Behold, I will cast thee from off the face of the earth: this year thou shalt die, because thou hast taught rebellion against the LORD.
17 So Hananiah the prophet died the same year in the seventh month.

Then the prophet Jeremiah said to the Hananiah, the false prophet, the LORD has not sent Hananiah and that Hananiah has made the people trust in a lie. Therefore the LORD says, Behold, Hananiah shall be cast from the face of the earth. This year Hananiah shall die because he has taught rebellion against the LORD. So Hananiah died in the seventh month of the same year.

CHAPTER 29

1 Now these are the words of the letter that Jeremiah the prophet sent from Jerusalem unto the residue of the elders which were carried away captives, and to the priests, and to the prophets, and to all the
people whom Nebuchadrezzar had carried away captive from Jerusalem to Babylon;
2 (After that Jeconiah the king, and the queen, and the eunuchs, the princes of Judah and Jerusalem, and the carpenters, and the smiths, were departed from Jerusalem;)
3 By the hand of Elasah the son of Shaphan, and Gemariah the son of Hilkiah, (whom Zedekiah king of Judah sent unto Babylon to Nebuchadrezzar king of Babylon) saying,
4 Thus saith the LORD of hosts, the God of Israel, unto all that are carried away captives, whom I have caused to be carried away from Jerusalem unto Babylon;
5 Build ye houses, and dwell in them; and plant gardens, and eat the fruit of them;
6 Take ye wives, and beget sons and daughters; and take wives for your sons, and give your daughters to husbands, that they may bear sons and daughters; that ye may be increased there, and not diminished.
7 And seek the peace of the city whither I have caused you to be carried away captives, and pray unto the LORD for it: for in the peace thereof shall ye have peace.

Now these are the words of the letter that Jeremiah the prophet sent from Jerusalem to the residue of the elders, the priests, the prophets, and to all the people whom Nebuchadnezzar had carried away captive from Jerusalem to Babylon. This occurred after Jeconiah the king, the queen, the eunuchs, the princes of Judah and Jerusalem, the carpenters, and the smiths were departed from Jerusalem. The letter was delivered by the hand of Elasah the son of Shaphan, and Gemariah the son of Hilkiah, (whom Zedekiah king of Judah sent unto Babylon to Nebuchadnezzar king of Babylon).

The message of the LORD of hosts, the God of Israel, given to Jeremiah and sent by letter to all the people who were carried away captives from Jerusalem unto Babylon under the working of the Law was that they should build houses, and dwell in them; plant gardens, and eat the fruit of them; take wives, and beget sons and daughters; take wives for your sons, and give your daughters to husbands, that they may bear sons and daughters. The people are being instructed so that they may be increased while they are in Babylon, and not diminished in size and strength. The LORD wants the people to seek peace in the city to which the LORD has caused the people to be taken captive. The people are to pray to the LORD for the peace that comes directly from the LORD for only in the peace from the LORD shall each person have peace.

8 For thus saith the LORD of hosts, the God of Israel; Let not your prophets and your diviners, that be in the midst of you, deceive you, neither hearken to your dreams which ye cause to be dreamed.
9 For they prophesy falsely unto you in my name: I have not sent them, saith the LORD.
10 For thus saith the LORD, That after seventy years be accomplished at Babylon I will visit you, and perform my good word toward you, in causing you to return to this place.

The Testimony of the Major Prophets

11 For I know the thoughts that I think toward you, saith the LORD, thoughts of peace, and not of evil, to give you an expected end.
12 Then shall ye call upon me, and ye shall go and pray unto me, and I will hearken unto you.
13 And ye shall seek me, and find me, when ye shall search for me with all your heart.
14 And I will be found of you, saith the LORD: and I will turn away your captivity, and I will gather you from all the nations, and from all the places whither I have driven you, saith the LORD; and I will bring you again into the place whence I caused you to be carried away captive.

The LORD of hosts, the God of Israel, speaking through Jeremiah instructs the people to not let the false prophets and diviners in your midst deceive you nor listen to your own dreams, that you cause to be dreamed, because that is your own desire. These false prophets prophesy falsely to you in the name of the LORD. The LORD has not sent the false prophets into the world.

The LORD says, that after seventy years be accomplished at Babylon, He will visit you and perform His good word toward you, in causing you to return to this place. The LORD knows the thoughts that He thinks toward you are thoughts of peace, and not of evil, to give you an expected peaceful end. Then shall you call upon the LORD in peace, and you shall go and pray to the LORD and He will hearken to you.
And you shall seek the LORD and find Him when you shall search for Him with all your heart. Then, the LORD shall be found of you and He will turn away your captivity and He will gather you from all the nations, and from all the places where He has driven you. He will bring you again into the place from hence the LORD caused you to be carried away captive.

15 Because ye have said, The LORD hath raised us up prophets in Babylon;
16 Know that thus saith the LORD of the king that sitteth upon the throne of David, and of all the people that dwelleth in this city, and of your brethren that are not gone forth with you into captivity;
17 Thus saith the LORD of hosts; Behold, I will send upon them the sword, the famine, and the pestilence, and will make them like vile figs, that cannot be eaten, they are so evil.
18 And I will persecute them with the sword, with the famine, and with the pestilence, and will deliver them to be removed to all the kingdoms of the earth, to be a curse, and an astonishment, and an
hissing, and a reproach, among all the nations whither I have driven them:
19 Because they have not hearkened to my words, saith the LORD, which I sent unto them by my servants the prophets, rising up early and sending them; but ye would not hear, saith the LORD.

Since the people have said that the LORD has raised up prophets in Babylon, people who can prophesy the peace of the LORD while they have been captives in Babylon, then they should know the LORD of the king that sits on the throne of David, all the people that dwell in this city and of the brethren that have not gone forth with you into captivity. The LORD of hosts, the LORD of all people everywhere, says that He will send upon the people the sword of truth which is the working of the Law along with famine and pestilence so that the people will be like vile figs that cannot be eaten because they are so evil.

The LORD will persecute them with the sword of the working of the Law, famine and pestilence which is the punishment for people who are not of the spirit of the LORD. The LORD will remove them from the kingdoms of the earth to be a curse and an astonishment, a hissing like a serpent and a reproach among all the nations where the power of the LORD has driven them according to the working of the Law. Because they have not listened to the words of the LORD, which were sent by means of the servants, the prophets, who rose up early in the morning; but the people would not listen to the word of the LORD.

20 Hear ye therefore the word of the LORD, all ye of the captivity, whom I have sent from Jerusalem to Babylon:
21 Thus saith the LORD of hosts, the God of Israel, of Ahab the son of Kolaiah, and of Zedekiah the son of Maaseiah, which prophesy a lie unto you in my name; Behold, I will deliver them into the hand of Nebuchadrezzar king of Babylon; and he shall slay them before your eyes;
22 And of them shall be taken up a curse by all the captivity of Judah which are in Babylon, saying, The LORD make thee like Zedekiah and like Ahab, whom the king of Babylon roasted in the fire;

23 Because they have committed villany in Israel, and have committed adultery with their neighbours' wives, and have spoken lying words in my name, which I have not commanded them; even I know, and am a witness, saith the LORD.

The people, the exiles, who are held in captivity should hear the word of the LORD which was sent to Babylon from Jerusalem. The LORD of hosts, the God of Israel, shall deliver Ahab the son of Kolaiah, and of Zedekiah the son of Maaseiah, who prophesied a lie to you in the name of the LORD—they were false prophets—shall be delivered to Nebuchadnezzar who would slay them before your eyes; the slain people will be like a curse by all the captives of Judah who are in Babylon that the king of Babylon could roast them in a fire as a means of execution. This punishment is because they have committed villainy in Israel, adultery with their neighbor's wives, spoken lies in the LORD's name which the LORD has not commanded them. The LORD knows and He is a witness to all behavior because the LORD is present with everyone.

24 Thus shalt thou also speak to Shemaiah the Nehelamite, saying,
25 Thus speaketh the LORD of hosts, the God of Israel, saying, Because thou hast sent letters in thy name unto all the people that are at Jerusalem, and to Zephaniah the son of Maaseiah the priest, and to all the priests, saying,
26 The LORD hath made thee priest in the stead of Jehoiada the priest, that ye should be officers in the house of the LORD, for every man that is mad, and maketh himself a prophet, that thou shouldest put him in prison, and in the stocks.
27 Now therefore why hast thou not reproved Jeremiah of Anathoth, which maketh himself a prophet to you?
28 For therefore he sent unto us in Babylon, saying, This captivity is long: build ye houses, and dwell in them; and plant gardens, and eat the fruit of them.
29 And Zephaniah the priest read this letter in the ears of Jeremiah the prophet.

Jeremiah shall also speak to Shemaiah the Nehelamite with this message of prophesy from the LORD of hosts, the God of Israel. Shemaiah has sent letters in his own name to all the people of Jerusalem and to Zephaniah, the son of Measeiah the priest, and to all the priests. He has said that the LORD has appointed him a priest in the place of Jehoiada the priest and that they should be officers in the house of the LORD. He states that every man who is mad or declares himself a prophet should be put in prison and in the stocks. He asks the priest why they have not reproved Jeremiah of Anathoth who has made himself a prophet? Jeremiah has sent a message to Babylon saying, Your captivity shall be long so you should build houses and dwell in them; plant gardens and eat the fruits of them. Zephaniah the priest read this letter in the ears of Jeremiah the prophet.

30 Then came the word of the LORD unto Jeremiah, saying,
31 Send to all them of the captivity, saying, Thus saith the LORD concerning Shemaiah the Nehelamite; Because that Shemaiah hath prophesied unto you, and I sent him not, and he caused you to trust in a lie:
32 Therefore thus saith the LORD; Behold, I will punish Shemaiah the Nehelamite, and his seed: he shall not have a man to dwell among this people; neither shall he behold the good that I will do for my people, saith the LORD; because he hath taught rebellion against the LORD.

The word of the LORD came to Jeremiah saying, Send all of them into captivity so that they can have the experience of being a captive. The LORD says to Jeremiah concerning Shemaiah that because he prophesied to you and the LORD did not send him and he caused you to trust in a lie, therefore the LORD will punish Shemaiah and his descendants. There shall not be a man of the LORD with his people; there shall not see the good that the LORD will do for His people. This is the punishment of Shemaiah because he preached rebellion against the LORD.

CHAPTER 30

1 The word that came to Jeremiah from the LORD, saying,
2 Thus speaketh the LORD God of Israel, saying, Write thee all the words that I have spoken unto thee in a book.
3 For, lo, the days come, saith the LORD, that I will bring again the captivity of my people Israel and Judah, saith the LORD: and I will cause them to return to the land that I gave to their fathers, and they shall possess it.
4 And these are the words that the LORD spake concerning Israel and concerning Judah.
5 For thus saith the LORD; We have heard a voice of trembling, of fear, and not of peace.
6 Ask ye now, and see whether a man doth travail with child? wherefore do I see every man with his hands on his loins, as a woman in travail, and all faces are turned into paleness?
7 Alas! for that day is great, so that none is like it: it is even the time of Jacob's trouble; but he shall be saved out of it.

The word of the LORD God of Israel came to Jeremiah saying, Write all the words which were spoken to you in a book. The days come when the creative power of the LORD will bring again the captivity of the people of the nations of Israel and Judah and cause them to return to the spiritual land that was given to their forefathers so that they can possess it. The word Israel is the symbol of people who are in covenant-agreement with the LORD, as Jacob, the repentant material person became Israel, the spiritual person; the word, Judah, is a symbol for those who dwell in the land but they have not experienced a state of the covenant-agreement or oneness with the spirit of the LORD.

The words of the LORD have been spoken to His people, who dwell in the lands of Israel and Judah. The LORD has heard a voice of trembling, of fear and not of peace. The people who are in covenant with the LORD (Israel) are to ask those who are not (Jacob) whether they are having a difficult time giving birth to the spiritual child which is within each one? Why does the LORD see every man with his hands on his loins as a woman in labor trying to give birth to a spiritual expression, and all their faces are turned pale at the thought of giving birth to the expression of spirit. Alas, this is a great day so that there is none like it. It is the time of Jacob's trouble when he wrestled with the angel with the result that Jacob became Israel. Jacob, the physical identity, became Israel, the spiritual identity, and changed, or was saved, from Jacob when he transformed into Israel. The human being became a spiritual being in a human form.

8 For it shall come to pass in that day, saith the LORD of hosts, that I will break his yoke from off thy neck, and will burst thy bonds, and strangers shall no more serve themselves of him:
9 But they shall serve the LORD their God, and David their king, whom I will raise up unto them.
10 Therefore fear thou not, O my servant Jacob, saith the LORD; neither be dismayed, O Israel: for, lo, I will save thee from afar, and thy seed from the land of their captivity; and Jacob shall return, and shall be in rest, and be quiet, and none shall make him afraid.
11 For I am with thee, saith the LORD, to save thee: though I make a full end of all nations whither I have scattered thee, yet will I not make a full end of thee: but I will correct thee in measure, and will not leave thee altogether unpunished.

The Symbolic Version of Jeremiah

The LORD of hosts says that on that day the yoke will be broken from off the neck of a person in bondage, and the bonds will be broken by the LORD; strangers shall no more be served of him as they enter into the covenant. The people shall serve the LORD their God, and David their king, whom the LORD will raise up to the people. Therefore, the servant Jacob, the symbol of the person who is in the fallen state, should fear not; neither be dismayed, O Israel, symbol of the ascended state. The LORD will save you from afar and your descendants from the land of their captivity, the fallen state, in which the people have been held. Jacob, the symbol of the heart, within a person who desires to find the LORD, shall be in rest and quiet as he repents and turns to the LORD and no one shall be afraid. The LORD tells Jacob, the symbol of a person in the fallen human state who desires to experience the true spiritual state, that He is with Jacob to **save** him. Even though the LORD makes a full end of all nations, where they have been scattered, yet the LORD will not make an end to those people who long to experience the covenant with the LORD. The LORD will correct Jacob in some measure, but He will not leave Jacob altogether unpunished because of the working of the Law. A person in the fallen state (Jacob) has been wounded in the fall from the true state of man symbolized by Israel.

12 For thus saith the LORD, Thy bruise is incurable, and thy wound is grievous.
13 There is none to plead thy cause, that thou mayest be bound up: thou hast no healing medicines.
14 All thy lovers have forgotten thee; they seek thee not; for I have wounded thee with the wound of an enemy, with the chastisement of a cruel one, for the multitude of thine iniquity; because thy sins were increased.
15 Why criest thou for thine affliction? thy sorrow is incurable for the multitude of thine iniquity: because thy sins were increased, I have done these things unto thee.
16 Therefore all they that devour thee shall be devoured; and all thine adversaries, every one of them, shall go into captivity; and they that spoil thee shall be a spoil, and all that prey upon thee will I give for a prey.
17 For I will restore health unto thee, and I will heal thee of thy wounds, saith the LORD; because they called thee an Outcast, saying, This is Zion, whom no man seeketh after.

The bruise of man in the fallen state is incurable and the wound of man in the fallen state is very grievous as long as he remains in the fallen state. There is no one to plead the cause of fallen man so that he can be bound up and healed of his affliction. Fallen man has no healing medicines for the wound of fallen state. All your lovers from the fallen world have forgotten you; they do not seek you; for the LORD has wounded you with the wound of an enemy, with the chastisement of a cruel one, for the multitude of your iniquity; because your sins were increased. Why do you cry for your affliction? Your sorrow is incurable for the multitude of the iniquity: The LORD has done these things to you because your sins were increased and you remained in the sinful state.

Therefore, according to the working of the Law, all the people that devour you shall be devoured; all your adversaries, every one of them, shall go into captivity; they that spoil you shall be a spoil to others, and all that prey upon you, the LORD will give to you for a prey according to the working of the Law of Sowing and Reaping. The LORD will restore health unto you, and heal you of your wounds because they called you an Outcast as you departed the fallen state; the adversaries say, This is Zion, an imaginary place that does not exist and whom no man seeks after. They do not know the place where the LORD meets man in the covenant-agreement.

18 Thus saith the LORD; Behold, I will bring again the captivity of Jacob's tents, and have mercy on his dwellingplaces; and the city shall be builded upon her own heap, and the palace shall remain after the manner thereof.
19 And out of them shall proceed thanksgiving and the voice of them that make merry: and I will multiply them, and they shall not be few; I will also glorify them, and they shall not be small.
20 Their children also shall be as aforetime, and their congregation shall be established before me, and I will punish all that oppress them.
21 And their nobles shall be of themselves, and their governor shall proceed from the midst of them; and I will cause him to draw near, and he shall approach unto me: for who is this that engaged his heart to approach unto me? saith the LORD.

The LORD proclaims that He will bring the captivity of Jacob's tents, the symbol of those in the fallen state who seek the LORD, and He will have mercy on their dwelling places; and the city, the conscious awareness of the inhabitant of the city, shall be built upon her own heap that has been torn down on the inside of the mind and heart, and the palace of the physical body shall remain after the manner which is familiar. And out of them—the body, mind and

The Testimony of the Major Prophets

heart—there shall proceed thanksgiving and the voices of them that make merry. The LORD will multiply the children and they shall not be few; the LORD will also glorify them, and they shall not be small. Their children also shall be as aforetime, as before the fall, and their congregation of repentant ascended people shall be established before the LORD who will punish all that oppress them. Their nobles shall be of themselves, and their governor shall proceed from the midst of them; the LORD will cause him to draw near, and he shall approach the LORD. Who is this that engaged his heart to approach the LORD? He is the LORD's creation restored.

22 And ye shall be my people, and I will be your God.
23 Behold, the whirlwind of the LORD goeth forth with fury, a continuing whirlwind: it shall fall with pain upon the head of the wicked.
24 The fierce anger of the LORD shall not return, until he have done it, and until he have performed the intents of his heart: in the latter days ye shall consider it.

The people who come to the LORD in covenant-agreement and oneness shall be the LORD's people and the LORD shall be their God. Behold the whirlwind, the rapid movement of the spirit of the LORD, goes forth with a fury, a continuing whirlwind of spirit, to accomplish the purposes of the LORD. The spirit of the LORD shall fall with pain upon the head of the wicked. The fierce anger of the LORD, the burning power of the spirit, shall not return until it has been done, until He has performed the intentions of His heart. In the latter days of life, all people in human forms shall continue to yearn for the return of the spirit of the LORD as they long for eternal life.

CHAPTER 31

1 At the same time, saith the LORD, will I be the God of all the families of Israel, and they shall be my people.
2 Thus saith the LORD, The people which were left of the sword found grace in the wilderness; even Israel, when I went to cause him to rest.

The LORD, speaking through Jeremiah, says that He will be the God of all the families of Israel, all of the twelve tribes and their descendants, and the families of Israel shall be His people. The people have always been the LORD's people from the LORD's point of view; the people have not accepted an invisible God as their LORD and they preferred to worship material idols that they could see and touch to give them pleasure. This practice has kept the people from the reality of the spiritual covenant which has always been at hand, available. As the people ignored the LORD, they experienced the destructive cycle of the working of the Law of Sowing and Reaping which is the destructive aspect of the sword.

The people which were left of the sword, who survived the destructive aspect of the spiritual power of the sword in the fallen state, found grace in the wilderness. The wilderness is the remnant of the true state which manifests itself partially in the environment of the fallen state. The people can find rest in the spirit of the LORD even as did Israel when the LORD went to cause him to rest in his transition from Jacob to Israel. Israel is the spiritual pattern of Man in covenant-agreement with the LORD in which the spirit of Man is one with the spirit of the LORD; Jacob is the material pattern of man who longs in his heart to find the LORD and experience the covenant.

3 The LORD hath appeared of old unto me, saying, Yea, I have loved thee with an everlasting love: therefore with lovingkindness have I drawn thee.
4 Again I will build thee, and thou shalt be built, O virgin of Israel: thou shalt again be adorned with thy tabrets, and shalt go forth in the dances of them that make merry.
5 Thou shalt yet plant vines upon the mountains of Samaria: the planters shall plant, and shall eat them as common things.
6 For there shall be a day, that the watchmen upon the mount Ephraim shall cry, Arise ye, and let us go up to Zion unto the LORD our God.

The LORD has appeared of old in times past to other prophets who were a focus of spirit on earth as Jeremiah is in this time. The LORD has declared that He has loved His people with an everlasting love that radiates from the LORD to his people. Therefore with loving kindness which is a constant radiation, the LORD draws the people who would respond to the radiant love of His spirit. Once again, the LORD will build the truth of His people on earth, and from the LORD's perspective, the divine design through people shall be built if they become as a virgin of Israel, a pure receptacle who is willing to receive the spirit of the LORD which is radiating constantly to them. The acceptance of the LORD's spirit shall result in happiness and wholeness which is symbolized by the music and the dancing that make the people merry instead of sad. The people shall plant vines upon the mountains of Samaria and eat the fruit

The Testimony of the Major Prophets

of them as common things which are available. There shall be a day that the watchmen, the people with vision, upon mount Ephraim, which means "fruitful", shall cry, Arise and let us go up to mount Zion, the mount of the high point of spiritual expression that symbolizes the high place of the covenant with the LORD. The covenant is available to all the people who desire to enter into the covenant with the LORD. The LORD has already chosen His people; the people must choose the LORD by choosing to let the spirit of the LORD flow through them.

7 For thus saith the LORD; Sing with gladness for Jacob, and shout among the chief of the nations: publish ye, praise ye, and say, O LORD, save thy people, the remnant of Israel.
8 Behold, I will bring them from the north country, and gather them from the coasts of the earth, and with them the blind and the lame, the woman with child and her that travaileth with child together: a great company shall return thither.
9 They shall come with weeping, and with supplications will I lead them: I will cause them to walk by the rivers of waters in a straight way, wherein they shall not stumble: for I am a father to Israel, and Ephraim is my firstborn.

The LORD speaking through Jeremiah says that the people must sing with gladness for Jacob who led the way to the covenant with the LORD when he became a new person in the spirit of the LORD, and become Israel. The LORD wants everyone to shout, publish and praise using His spirit among the chiefs of all nations so that the hearers of the good news of the covenant can be magnified and the remnant of Israel, the LORD's people, can multiply on earth.

Behold, the LORD will bring the people who respond to the invitation from everywhere: the north country, and the coasts of the earth; and when they come, they will bring with them the blind and the lame, the woman with child and her that is about to deliver a child together. A great company shall return there. The LORD's people shall come with the weeping of tears of joy and with supplications of spiritual radiation will the LORD lead them. The LORD will cause them to walk by the rivers of waters in a straight way, wherein they shall not stumble for the LORD is a father to Israel, and Ephraim, the fruitful child of the spirit, is the firstborn. The word of the LORD to the covenant experience is to be proclaimed.

10 Hear the word of the LORD, O ye nations, and declare it in the isles afar off, and say, He that scattered Israel will gather him, and keep him, as a shepherd doth his flock.
11 For the LORD hath redeemed Jacob, and ransomed him from the hand of him that was stronger than he.
12 Therefore they shall come and sing in the height of Zion, and shall flow together to the goodness of the LORD, for wheat, and for wine, and for oil, and for the young of the flock and of the herd: and their soul shall be as a watered garden; and they shall not sorrow any more at all.
13 Then shall the virgin rejoice in the dance, both young men and old together: for I will turn their mourning into joy, and will comfort them, and make them rejoice from their sorrow.
14 And I will satiate the soul of the priests with fatness, and my people shall be satisfied with my goodness, saith the LORD.

The word of the LORD is to be heard by the nations and declared in far-away isles. The LORD who has scattered Israel—when the people do not obey the spirit of the LORD—can also be gathered by the LORD and kept safe as a Shepherd keeps His flock. The LORD has redeemed Jacob from the fallen state and ransomed him from the fallen culture which was stronger than he. The implication is the LORD can rescue anyone from the fallen state who is willing to come to the LORD. Therefore, the people shall come and sing in the height of Zion where they shall be in spiritual agreement and flow together in the spirit of the LORD as they do all things on earth as they grow wheat, make wine, oil, tend their flocks and herds. The soul of man—the heart, mind and body—shall be full of life as a watered garden; and the people shall not sorrow any more at all.

Then the virgin person who gives oneself spiritually to the LORD shall rejoice in the dance, both young men and old together. The LORD will turn their mourning into joy, comfort them and make them rejoice from their sorrow. The LORD will satiate the soul of the priests with fatness, and His people shall be satisfied with the goodness from the LORD.

15 Thus saith the LORD; A voice was heard in Ramah, lamentation, and bitter weeping; Rachel weeping for her children refused to be comforted for her children, because they were not.

The Symbolic Version of Jeremiah

16 Thus saith the LORD; Refrain thy voice from weeping, and thine eyes from tears: for thy work shall be rewarded, saith the LORD; and they shall come again from the land of the enemy.
17 And there is hope in thine end, saith the LORD, that thy children shall come again to their own border.
18 I have surely heard Ephraim bemoaning himself thus; Thou hast chastised me, and I was chastised, as a bullock unaccustomed to the yoke: turn thou me, and I shall be turned; for thou art the LORD my God.
19 Surely after that I was turned, I repented; and after that I was instructed, I smote upon my thigh: I was ashamed, yea, even confounded, because I did bear the reproach of my youth.
20 Is Ephraim my dear son? is he a pleasant child? for since I spake against him, I do earnestly remember him still: therefore my bowels are troubled for him; I will surely have mercy upon him, saith the LORD.

The LORD speaking through Jeremiah said that a voice of lamentation and bitter weeping was heard in Ramah, a city 5 miles north of Jerusalem through which the captive people of Jerusalem passed on their way to exile in Babylon. The sadness is compared to the weeping of Rachel who refused to be comforted because she did not have children as she wanted. The LORD says to refrain your voice from weeping and your eyes from tears. The LORD will reward your works that are done in the spirit of the LORD. The people who are sent into exile shall return again from the land of the enemy and there is hope in the end, that the children shall come again to their own border.

The LORD has surely heard Ephraim feeling sorrow for himself when the LORD chastised him with some circumstance, as a bullock is unaccustomed to the yoke. There is a willingness for a child to be turned, then the yoke of the spirit is easy and the child shall be turned because the LORD is God. Surely after the child was turned, then repentance occurred; and after the child is instructed, he hit upon his thigh and walked a new way. The person was ashamed, yes, even confounded, because he carried the memory of the reproach of his youth. The LORD asks if Ephraim continues to be his dear son? Is he a pleasant child? Since the LORD speaks against him to chastise him, this is proof that the LORD earnestly remembers him still. The LORD chastises those that He loves. Therefore, the LORD's heart is concerned for his progress, and the LORD shall surely have mercy upon him during the transition and change from the fallen state to the restored state.

21 Set thee up waymarks, make thee high heaps: set thine heart toward the highway, even the way which thou wentest: turn again, O virgin of Israel, turn again to these thy cities.
22 How long wilt thou go about, O thou backsliding daughter? for the LORD hath created a new thing in the earth, A woman shall compass a man.

A person needs to set marks along the way, symbolized by high heaps of stones along the way through life, to set one's heart toward the highway, the way to express the spirit of the LORD through one's own heart, mind and body. The person in the fallen state is called to be once again what they were created to be, a virgin of Israel, a person in oneness with the spirit of the LORD. Turn once again to these cities of the spirit which come from the LORD. Your spirit does come from the LORD and not from the fallen state of man. How long shall you go about life in the wrong and fallen way, you backsliding daughter who remains in the fallen state, and who ignores your divine inheritance? The LORD has created a new thing in the earth: the woman that symbolizes the earthly form, a male or a female, shall encompass, receive, a spiritual man from the LORD.

23 Thus saith the LORD of hosts, the God of Israel; As yet they shall use this speech in the land of Judah and in the cities thereof, when I shall bring again their captivity; The LORD bless thee, O habitation of justice, and mountain of holiness.
24 And there shall dwell in Judah itself, and in all the cities thereof together, husbandmen, and they that go forth with flocks.
25 For I have satiated the weary soul, and I have replenished every sorrowful soul.
26 Upon this I awaked, and beheld; and my sleep was sweet unto me.
27 Behold, the days come, saith the LORD, that I will sow the house of Israel and the house of Judah with the seed of man, and with the seed of beast.
28 And it shall come to pass, that like as I have watched over them, to pluck up, and to break down, and to throw down, and to destroy, and to afflict; so will I watch over them, to build, and to plant, saith the LORD.

The Testimony of the Major Prophets

The LORD of all the hosts of the people on earth, who is the God of Israel, the God of mankind in spirit, says through Jeremiah, the prophet who is in the spiritual covenant-agreement, that the people in the fallen state shall use the information and wisdom in this speech in the land of Judah when the LORD shall bring about their captivity. The people have learned the experience of what it is like to be captured by the Babylonians; the people have not learned what it is like to be captured and held in captivity by the spirit of the LORD. In the latter instance, the people would be blessed by the LORD and the people would be a habitation of justice and a mountain of holiness. Then there shall dwell in Judah and the cities thereof, husbandmen, and they that go forth with the flocks of people who are willing to be led to the LORD.

For the spirit of the LORD has satiated the weary soul and replenished every sorrowful soul. This is the vision or the dream to which Jeremiah awakened and saw so that the sleep was sweet to him. In the vision of Jeremiah, he could behold the days that would come when the LORD would sow the house of Israel (spirit) and the house of Judah (form) with the seed of Man, made in the image and likeness of God, with the seed of beast, which is man in the fallen state. This would return the divine design to earth.

It shall come to pass, that as the LORD has watched over them, to pluck up, and to break down, and to throw down, and to destroy, and to afflict in a destructive cycle; so will the LORD watch over them, to build, and to plant in a creative cycle.

29 In those days they shall say no more, The fathers have eaten a sour grape, and the children's teeth are set on edge.
30 But every one shall die for his own iniquity: every man that eateth the sour grape, his teeth shall be set on edge.
31 Behold, the days come, saith the LORD, that I will make a new covenant with the house of Israel, and with the house of Judah:
32 Not according to the covenant that I made with their fathers in the day that I took them by the hand to bring them out of the land of Egypt; which my covenant they brake, although I was an husband unto them, saith the LORD:
33 But this shall be the covenant that I will make with the house of Israel; After those days, saith the LORD, I will put my law in their inward parts, and write it in their hearts; and will be their God, and they shall be my people.
34 And they shall teach no more every man his neighbour, and every man his brother, saying, Know the LORD: for they shall all know me, from the least of them unto the greatest of them, saith the LORD: for I will forgive their iniquity, and I will remember their sin no more.

In the days when the spirit of the LORD is moving through His children on earth, there will be a negative reaction that is symbolized by the sour expression on the face when the father has eaten a sour grape, and the children's teeth are set on edge as they await punishment for their sins. But the working of the Law demands that every man who eats a sour grape shall have his teeth set on edge as he is reprimanded by the LORD.

Behold, the LORD says that a new covenant will be made with the house of Israel, and with the house of Judah. The new covenant will not be according to the covenant that was made with their fathers in the day that the LORD took them by the hand to bring them out of the land of Egypt. The people broke their covenant although the LORD was a husband to them. But in this covenant which the LORD will make
with the house of Israel, the covenant shall be placed in their inward parts, and written in their hearts. The result of this new covenant will be that the LORD will be their God, individually and personally, and they shall be His people. They shall teach no more that every man his neighbor, and every man his brother, saying, Know the LORD: Everyone **shall** know the LORD from the least of them to the greatest of them for the LORD who is present with everyone will forgive their iniquity and remember their sin no more. When the LORD is known, the right relationships are already established in spirit and previous iniquity and sin from the fallen state fade away.

35 Thus saith the LORD, which giveth the sun for a light by day, and the ordinances of the moon and of the stars for a light by night, which divideth the sea when the waves thereof roar; The LORD of hosts is his name:
36 If those ordinances depart from before me, saith the LORD, then the seed of Israel also shall cease from being a nation before me for ever.

37 Thus saith the LORD; If heaven above can be measured, and the foundations of the earth searched out beneath, I will also cast off all the seed of Israel for all that they have done, saith the LORD.

The LORD who gives the sun for a light by day, and the ordinances of the moon and stars for a light by night, which divides the sea when the waves thereof roar is indeed the LORD of hosts. If those ordinances depart from before the LORD, then the seed of Israel also shall cease from being a nation before me for ever. If heaven above can be measured, and the foundations of the earth searched out beneath, then the LORD will also cast off all the seed of Israel for all that they have done, says the LORD.

38 Behold, the days come, saith the LORD, that the city shall be built to the LORD from the tower of Hananeel unto the gate of the corner.
39 And the measuring line shall yet go forth over against it upon the hill Gareb, and shall compass about to Goath.
40 And the whole valley of the dead bodies, and of the ashes, and all the fields unto the brook of Kidron, unto the corner of the horse gate toward the east, shall be holy unto the LORD; it shall not be plucked up, nor thrown down any more for ever.

Behold, the days come that the city of Jerusalem shall be built to the glory of the LORD and the glory will expand and grow from the tower of Hananeel to the Corner Gate, the eastern and western ends of the north wall, from sunrise to sunset, all day long. The measuring line shall yet go forth over against it upon the hill Gareb, and shall compass about to Goath. The whole valley where the dead bodies are thrown, and of the ashes, and all the fields to the brook of Kidron, to the corner of the horse gate toward the east, shall be holy to the LORD; it shall not be plucked up, nor thrown down any more for ever. The spirit of the LORD can move into and use everything.

CHAPTER 32

1 The word that came to Jeremiah from the LORD in the tenth year of Zedekiah king of Judah, which was the eighteenth year of Nebuchadrezzar.
2 For then the king of Babylon's army besieged Jerusalem: and Jeremiah the prophet was shut up in the court of the prison, which was in the king of Judah's house.
3 For Zedekiah king of Judah had shut him up, saying, Wherefore dost thou prophesy, and say, Thus saith the LORD, Behold, I will give this city into the hand of the king of Babylon, and he shall take it;
4 And Zedekiah king of Judah shall not escape out of the hand of the Chaldeans, but shall surely be delivered into the hand of the king of Babylon, and shall speak with him mouth to mouth, and his eyes shall behold his eyes;
5 And he shall lead Zedekiah to Babylon, and there shall he be until I visit him, saith the LORD: though ye fight with the Chaldeans, ye shall not prosper.

This is the word that came to Jeremiah from the LORD in the tenth year of Zedekiah king of Judah, which was the eighteenth year of Nebuchadnezzar. At that time, the king of Babylon's army besieged Jerusalem and Jeremiah the prophet was shut up in the court of the prison, which was in the king of Judah's house.

Jeremiah was imprisoned by Zedekiah king of Judah who asked why Jeremiah prophesied, using the name of the LORD, with the message that the city would be given into the hand of the king of Babylon, and he shall take it. Zedekiah king of Judah shall not escape out of the hand of the Chaldeans, but he shall surely be delivered into the hand of the king of Babylon, who shall speak with him mouth to mouth, and eye to eye. The LORD shall lead Zedekiah to Babylon, and he shall remain there until the LORD deals with him according to the Law. Although Zedekiah and his army may fight with the Chaldeans, they shall not succeed.

6 And Jeremiah said, The word of the LORD came unto me, saying,
7 Behold, Hanameel the son of Shallum thine uncle shall come unto thee, saying, Buy thee my field that is in Anathoth: for the right of redemption is thine to buy it.
8 So Hanameel mine uncle's son came to me in the court of the prison according to the word of the LORD, and said unto me, Buy my field, I pray thee, that is in Anathoth, which is in the country of Benjamin: for the right of inheritance is thine, and the redemption is thine; buy it for thyself. Then I knew that this was the word of the LORD.
9 And I bought the field of Hanameel my uncle's son, that was in Anathoth, and weighed him the money, even seventeen shekels of silver.

The word of the LORD came to Jeremiah saying, Behold, Hanameel, the son of Shallum your uncle, shall ask that you buy his field in Anathoth, the place of Jeremiah's birth. In accordance with the ancient law of redemption, Jeremiah, as nearest relative, has the right and duty to buy it for himself. Hanameel came to Jeremiah while he was in prison; he asked Jeremiah to buy the field and Jeremiah knew that this was the word of the LORD; so he bought the field for seventeen shekels of silver.

10 And I subscribed the evidence, and sealed it, and took witnesses, and weighed him the money in the balances.
11 So I took the evidence of the purchase, both that which was sealed according to the law and custom, and that which was open:
12 And I gave the evidence of the purchase unto Baruch the son of Neriah, the son of Maaseiah, in the sight of Hanameel mine uncle's son, and in the presence of the witnesses that subscribed the book of the purchase, before all the Jews that sat in the court of the prison.
13 And I charged Baruch before them, saying,
14 Thus saith the LORD of hosts, the God of Israel; Take these evidences, this evidence of the purchase, both which is sealed, and this evidence which is open; and put them in an earthen vessel, that they may continue many days.

Jeremiah signed the deed of purchase, sealed it and paid for the land before witnesses. The deed was given to Baruch the son of Neriah, the son of Maaseiah, in the sight of Hanameel and in the presence of the witnesses that signed the deed before all the Jews that sat in the court of the prison. In their presence, Jeremiah instructed Baruch that the LORD of hosts, the God of Israel has said that the deed for the land, the evidence of the purchase, both the sealed and the open copy, are to be put in an earthen vessel, so that they will be preserved and last a long time.

15 For thus saith the LORD of hosts, the God of Israel; Houses and fields and vineyards shall be possessed again in this land.
16 Now when I had delivered the evidence of the purchase unto Baruch the son of Neriah, I prayed unto the LORD, saying,
17 Ah Lord GOD! behold, thou hast made the heaven and the earth by thy great power and stretched out arm, and there is nothing too hard for thee:
18 Thou shewest lovingkindness unto thousands, and recompensest the iniquity of the fathers into the bosom of their children after them: the Great, the Mighty God, the LORD of hosts, is his name,
19 Great in counsel, and mighty in work: for thine eyes are open upon all the ways of the sons of men: to give every one according to his ways, and according to the fruit of his doings:
20 Which hast set signs and wonders in the land of Egypt, even unto this day, and in Israel, and among other men; and hast made thee a name, as at this day;
21 And hast brought forth thy people Israel out of the land of Egypt with signs, and with wonders, and with a strong hand, and with a stretched out arm, and with great terror;
22 And hast given them this land, which thou didst swear to their fathers to give them, a land flowing with milk and honey;
23 And they came in, and possessed it; but they obeyed not thy voice, neither walked in thy law; they have done nothing of all that thou commandedst them to do: therefore thou hast caused all this evil to come upon them:
24 Behold the mounts, they are come unto the city to take it; and the city is given into the hand of the Chaldeans, that fight against it, because of the sword, and of the famine, and of the pestilence: and what thou hast spoken is come to pass; and, behold, thou seest it.
25 And thou hast said unto me, O Lord GOD, Buy thee the field for money, and take witnesses; for the city is given into the hand of the Chaldeans.

The LORD of hosts, the God of Israel has said through Jeremiah that houses, fields and vineyards shall be possessed again in this land that has been invaded and conquered by the Babylonians. Now after Jeremiah had delivered the deed to Baruch, he prayed to the LORD, saying, Ah Lord GOD! Who has made the heaven and the earth by Your great power and stretched out arm, there is nothing too hard for You. You show your loving kindness to thousands, and punish the iniquity of the fathers into the bosom of their children after them according to the operation of the Law of Sowing and Reaping. The Great, the Mighty God, the LORD of hosts, is Your name; You are great in counsel, and mighty in work: for Your eyes are open upon all the ways of the sons of men to give every one according to their ways, and according to the fruit of their behaviors. The results of the behaviors through people have set the signs and wonders in the land of Egypt even to this day, and in Israel, and among other men. The operation of the Law has made the conditions exactly as they are this day.

You, LORD, have brought forth your people, Israel, out of the land of Egypt in which they were in bondage, with signs wonders, a strong hand, a stretched out arm, and with great terror. You have given Your people this land flowing with milk and honey which You had sworn to their fathers. Their fathers came in and possessed the land but they did not

The Testimony of the Major Prophets

obey the voice of the LORD nor did they walk in the way of the Law of Sowing and Reaping. They have done nothing that You commanded them to do. Therefore, You have caused all this evil to come upon them. Behold, the mounts, the invaders on horses, have come to the city to take it; and the city is given into the hand of the Chaldeans, that fight against Jerusalem, because of the sword, and of the famine, and of the pestilence which are the destructive cycle of the power of the LORD. What You have spoken has come to pass; and, behold, You see it. Even though all this destruction is happening, the LORD has said to Jeremiah to buy the field which is presently in the hands of Chaldeans for money, and to take witnesses to the purchase.

26 Then came the word of the LORD unto Jeremiah, saying,
27 Behold, I am the LORD, the God of all flesh: is there any thing too hard for me?
28 Therefore thus saith the LORD; Behold, I will give this city into the hand of the Chaldeans, and into the hand of Nebuchadrezzar king of Babylon, and he shall take it:
29 And the Chaldeans, that fight against this city, shall come and set fire on this city, and burn it with the houses, upon whose roofs they have offered incense unto Baal, and poured out drink offerings unto other gods, to provoke me to anger.
30 For the children of Israel and the children of Judah have only done evil before me from their youth: for the children of Israel have only provoked me to anger with the work of their hands, saith the LORD.
31 For this city hath been to me as a provocation of mine anger and of my fury from the day that they built it even unto this day; that I should remove it from before my face,
32 Because of all the evil of the children of Israel and of the children of Judah, which they have done to provoke me to anger, they, their kings, their princes, their priests, and their prophets, and the men of Judah, and the inhabitants of Jerusalem.

The LORD of all flesh replied to Jeremiah by asking if there is anything too hard for Him? The LORD says that He will give the city into the hand of the Chaldeans, and into the hand of Nebuchadnezzar king of Babylon, and he shall take it: the Chaldeans, shall come and set fire on this city, and burn it with the houses, upon whose roofs they have offered incense unto Baal, and poured out drink offerings unto other gods, to provoke the LORD to anger. The children of Israel and the children of Judah have only done evil from their youth as they provoked the LORD to anger with the work of their hands. This city has provoked the destructive cycle of the Law from the day that the people built it even to this day; the LORD shall remove the material evidence from before His face because of all the evil works done by the children of Israel and of the children of Judah, their kings, their princes, their priests, their prophets, the men of Judah, and the inhabitants of Jerusalem, which provoked the anger. The Law works!

33 And they have turned unto me the back, and not the face: though I taught them, rising up early and teaching them, yet they have not hearkened to receive instruction.
34 But they set their abominations in the house, which is called by my name, to defile it.
35 And they built the high places of Baal, which are in the valley of the son of Hinnom, to cause their sons and their daughters to pass through the fire unto Molech; which I commanded them not, neither came it into my mind, that they should do this abomination, to cause Judah to sin.

The people who should have served the LORD turned their backs and not their faces to Him even though He has risen early to teach them, they have not paid attention to receive instruction. They have set their abominations in the house which is called by the name of the LORD, I Am, to defile it. They have built altars to Baal, the false god, in the valley of Hinnom to cause their sons and daughters to be sacrificed in the fire to Molech, the god of the Ammonites, which the LORD commanded them not to do and which never came into the mind of the LORD. The people did this abomination to cause Judah to sin.

36 And now therefore thus saith the LORD, the God of Israel, concerning this city, whereof ye say, It shall be delivered into the hand of the king of Babylon by the sword, and by the famine, and by the pestilence;
37 Behold, I will gather them out of all countries, whither I have driven them in mine anger, and in my fury, and in great wrath; and I will bring them again unto this place, and I will cause them to dwell safely:
38 And they shall be my people, and I will be their God:
39 And I will give them one heart, and one way, that they may fear me for ever, for the good of them, and of their children after them:

The Symbolic Version of Jeremiah

40 And I will make an everlasting covenant with them, that I will not turn away from them, to do them good; but I will put my fear in their hearts, that they shall not depart from me.
41 Yea, I will rejoice over them to do them good, and I will plant them in this land assuredly with my whole heart and with my whole soul.

Therefore, the LORD has delivered the city into the hand of the king of Babylon by the sword, famine and pestilence to destroy the evil practices. Behold, in time and repentance, the LORD will gather the people once again and return them to this place from the countries where they were driven by the anger, fury and wrath which are the working of the Law. In time, the LORD will cause them to dwell safely: they shall be the LORD's people, and He will be their God: He will give them one heart, and one way, that they may fear the LORD for ever, for the good of them, and of their children after them. The LORD will make an everlasting covenant with them, and He will not turn away from them, to do them good; but the LORD will put His fear in their hearts, that they shall not depart from me. Yes, the LORD will rejoice over them to do them good, and He will plant them in this land assuredly with His whole heart and with His whole soul.

42 For thus saith the LORD; Like as I have brought all this great evil upon this people, so will I bring upon them all the good that I have promised them.
43 And fields shall be bought in this land, whereof ye say, It is desolate without man or beast; it is given into the hand of the Chaldeans.
44 Men shall buy fields for money, and subscribe evidences, and seal them, and take witnesses in the land of Benjamin, and in the places about Jerusalem, and in the cities of Judah, and in the cities of the mountains, and in the cities of the valley, and in the cities of the south: for I will cause their captivity to return, saith the LORD.

The LORD speaking through Jeremiah states that as He has brought great evil upon the people, so will He bring all the good that has been promised to them. Fields shall be bought in this land where you have said that it is desolate without man nor beast and given into the hands of the Chaldeans. Men shall buy fields for money and take witnesses in the land of Benjamin, the places about Jerusalem, in the cities of Judah, in the cities of the mountains, the valley and the south: for the LORD will cause their captivity to Him to return. The LORD purchased land through Jeremiah to indicate His love and final victory for the people.

CHAPTER 33

1 Moreover the word of the LORD came unto Jeremiah the second time, while he was yet shut up in the court of the prison, saying,
2 Thus saith the LORD the maker thereof, the LORD that formed it, to establish it; the LORD is his name;
3 Call unto me, and I will answer thee, and shew thee great and mighty things, which thou knowest not.
4 For thus saith the LORD, the God of Israel, concerning the houses of this city, and concerning the houses of the kings of Judah, which are thrown down by the mounts, and by the sword;
5 They come to fight with the Chaldeans, but it is to fill them with the dead bodies of men, whom I have slain in mine anger and in my fury, and for all whose wickedness I have hid my face from this city.
6 Behold, I will bring it health and cure, and I will cure them, and will reveal unto them the abundance of peace and truth.
7 And I will cause the captivity of Judah and the captivity of Israel to return, and will build them, as at the first.
8 And I will cleanse them from all their iniquity, whereby they have sinned against me; and I will pardon all their iniquities, whereby they have sinned, and whereby they have transgressed against me.
9 And it shall be to me a name of joy, a praise and an honour before all the nations of the earth, which shall hear all the good that I do unto them: and they shall fear and tremble for all the goodness and for all the prosperity that I procure unto it.

The word of the LORD came to Jeremiah the second time while he was in the court of the prison saying that the LORD who made the earth, formed it and established is indeed the LORD; He commands Jeremiah to call upon Him and He will answer and show Jeremiah great and mighty things which he does not know. The LORD, the God of Israel, says this about the houses of Jerusalem and the houses of the kings of Judah which have been destroyed by the horses and the sword of the truth of the working of the Law. The people of Israel and Judah think that they have come to fight with the Chaldeans, but the battle is to provide the invaders with the dead bodies of men that the LORD has slain in his anger and fury for their behavior which was so wicked that the LORD withheld His face from it. The LORD withholding His face is symbolic language to illustrate that the LORD will allow the Law to work and the destruction to occur.

Behold, the LORD will bring Jerusalem and Judah health and cure, will cure the people and will reveal to them the abundance of peace and truth. The LORD will cause the captivity of Judah and the captivity of Israel to return, and will build them, as at the first. The LORD will cleanse them from all their iniquity, pardon all their iniquities, whereby they have sinned, and whereby they have transgressed against the LORD. This restored body of people who express the spirit of the LORD shall be a joy, a praise and an honor before all the nations of the earth, which shall hear all the good that the LORD does to them. They shall fear and tremble at the awareness of the presence of the LORD for all the goodness and for all the prosperity that the LORD procures for the body of people that reveals the spirit of the LORD on earth.

The Symbolic Version of Jeremiah

10 Thus saith the LORD; Again there shall be heard in this place, which ye say shall be desolate without man and without beast, even in the cities of Judah, and in the streets of Jerusalem, that are desolate, without man, and without inhabitant, and without beast,
11 The voice of joy, and the voice of gladness, the voice of the bridegroom, and the voice of the bride, the voice of them that shall say, Praise the LORD of hosts: for the LORD is good; for his mercy endureth for ever: and of them that shall bring the sacrifice of praise into the house of the LORD. For I will cause to return the captivity of the land, as at the first, saith the LORD.
12 Thus saith the LORD of hosts; Again in this place, which is desolate without man and without beast, and in all the cities thereof, shall be an habitation of shepherds causing their flocks to lie down.
13 In the cities of the mountains, in the cities of the vale, and in the cities of the south, and in the land of Benjamin, and in the places about Jerusalem, and in the cities of Judah, shall the flocks pass again under the hands of him that telleth them, saith the LORD.

The LORD said again that there shall be heard, in these desolate places without man or beast, even in the cities of Judah and the streets of Jerusalem, the voice of joy, gladness, the voices of the bridegroom and the bride, and the voice of them who say, Praise the LORD of hosts: for the LORD is good; for His mercy endures forever: and of them that bring the sacrifice of praise into the house of the LORD. The sacrifice of praise to the LORD is the only requirement to cause the sowing of the right seed to produce the effect of the reaping of the promised land as it was at the first.

The LORD also states through Jeremiah that these desolate places without man or beast shall be a habitation of shepherds who represent the LORD on earth and will cause their flocks of human followers to lie down in green pastures of the promised land. The shepherds who represent the LORD and reveal His spirit shall teach their flocks to praise the LORD in all that they do which will return the divine design to the cities of the mountains, the cities of the vale, the cities of the south, in the land of Benjamin, the places about Jerusalem, and in the cities of Judah

14 Behold, the days come, saith the LORD, that I will perform that good thing which I have promised unto the house of Israel and to the house of Judah.
15 In those days, and at that time, will I cause the Branch of righteousness to grow up unto David; and he shall execute judgment and righteousness in the land.
16 In those days shall Judah be saved, and Jerusalem shall dwell safely: and this is the name wherewith she shall be called, The LORD our righteousness.
17 For thus saith the LORD; David shall never want a man to sit upon the throne of the house of Israel;
18 Neither shall the priests the Levites want a man before me to offer burnt offerings, and to kindle meat offerings, and to do sacrifice continually.

Behold, in time and in accord with the working of the Law, the days will come when the LORD will perform the good things that He has promised to the house of Israel and the house of Judah. In those days and at that time, the LORD will cause the Branch of righteousness to grow up to the spirit that was within David and he shall execute judgment and righteousness in the land. In those days Judah shall be saved, and Jerusalem shall dwell safely. This is the name that the people and her inhabitants shall be called, The LORD our righteousness. Righteousness is the right use of the equipment of heart, mind and body for the purposes of the LORD. The LORD says that neither David nor the priests of the Levites shall ever want a man to sit upon the throne of the house of Israel to offer burnt offerings, and to kindle meat offerings, and to do sacrifices continually.

19 And the word of the LORD came unto Jeremiah, saying,
20 Thus saith the LORD; If ye can break my covenant of the day, and my covenant of the night, and that there should not be day and night in their season;
21 Then may also my covenant be broken with David my servant, that he should not have a son to reign upon his throne; and with the Levites the priests, my ministers.
22 As the host of heaven cannot be numbered, neither the sand of the sea measured: so will I multiply the seed of David my servant, and the Levites that minister unto me.

The word of the LORD came to Jeremiah saying that man cannot break the permanence of the covenant with the LORD and man. If man can break the covenant with the day and with the night, so that there would no longer be a

The Testimony of the Major Prophets

day and a night in its proper season, then he could also break the covenant with the LORD. Then also the LORD's covenant with David, His servant, could be broken so that the LORD would not have a son to reign upon the spiritual throne of David; there would be no priests from the Levites to function as David's ministers. Since the covenant cannot be broken, the LORD will multiply the seed of David and the seed of the Levites that minister to the LORD in quantities comparable to the hosts of the heaven in spiritual form which cannot be numbered nor the sand of the sea be measured.

23 Moreover the word of the LORD came to Jeremiah, saying,
24 Considerest thou not what this people have spoken, saying, The two families which the LORD hath chosen, he hath even cast them off? thus they have despised my people, that they should be no more a nation before them.
25 Thus saith the LORD; If my covenant be not with day and night, and if I have not appointed the ordinances of heaven and earth;
26 Then will I cast away the seed of Jacob, and David my servant, so that I will not take any of his seed to be rulers over the seed of Abraham, Isaac, and Jacob: for I will cause their captivity to return, and have mercy on them.

Moreover, the word of the LORD came to Jeremiah saying that he should not consider what the people in the fallen state are repeating when they say that the LORD has cast off and rejected the two families of Israel and Judah. The people who spread these lies despise the LORD's people and they no longer regard them as a nation so that they will not have to serve the LORD on earth and bring His kingdom. The LORD says that if He has no covenant with the day and the night, and if He has not established the ordinances of the heaven and the earth, then the LORD will cast away the seed of Jacob and David the LORD's servant. The support of the LORD on earth for the people who will bring His kingdom and reveal the LORD's nature is as certain as day and night, and the continuous operation of the Law of Cause and Effect. The LORD will not take any of the seed of the people who ignore Him, a rebellious and untrustworthy seed, to be the rulers over the seed of Abraham. Isaac and Jacob. Since the LORD is eternal and the people who rebel against the spirit of the LORD are temporal, then the LORD will cause the seed of Abraham, Isaac, Jacob and David to return to Jerusalem and Judah and have mercy on them.

CHAPTER 34

1 The word which came unto Jeremiah from the LORD, when Nebuchadrezzar king of Babylon, and all his army, and all the kingdoms of the earth of his dominion, and all the people, fought against Jerusalem, and against all the cities thereof, saying,
2 Thus saith the LORD, the God of Israel; Go and speak to Zedekiah king of Judah, and tell him, Thus saith the LORD; Behold, I will give this city into the hand of the king of Babylon, and he shall burn it with fire:
3 And thou shalt not escape out of his hand, but shalt surely be taken, and delivered into his hand; and thine eyes shall behold the eyes of the king of Babylon, and he shall speak with thee mouth to mouth, and thou shalt go to Babylon.
4 Yet hear the word of the LORD, O Zedekiah king of Judah; Thus saith the LORD of thee, Thou shalt not die by the sword:
5 But thou shalt die in peace: and with the burnings of thy fathers, the former kings which were before thee, so shall they burn odours for thee; and they will lament thee, saying, Ah lord! for I have pronounced the word, saith the LORD.

While Nebuchadnezzar king of Babylon, and all his army, and all the people from his kingdoms fought against Jerusalem, the word of the LORD came to Jeremiah directing him to go to Zedekiah, king of Judah with this message from the LORD: Behold, the operation of the Law of the LORD will give this city into the hand of the king of Babylon, and he shall burn it with fire and you shall not escape out of his hand, but you shall surely be taken and delivered into his hand. Your eyes shall behold the eyes of the king of Babylon, and he shall speak with you mouth to mouth, and you shall go to Babylon.

The word of the LORD for Zedekiah is that he will not die by the sword but he shall die in peace. Zedekiah will have funeral fires in his honor as did his fathers before him, the former kings, who were honored with incense and lamentations by his people who would remember him as a lord and king. This is the word of the LORD to Zedekiah through Jeremiah.

6 Then Jeremiah the prophet spake all these words unto Zedekiah king of Judah in Jerusalem,
7 When the king of Babylon's army fought against Jerusalem, and against all the cities of Judah that were left, against Lachish, and against Azekah: for these defenced cities remained of the cities of Judah.
8 This is the word that came unto Jeremiah from the LORD, after that the king Zedekiah had made a covenant with all the people which were at Jerusalem, to proclaim liberty unto them;
9 That every man should let his manservant, and every man his maidservant, being an Hebrew or an Hebrewess, go free; that none should serve himself of them, to wit, of a Jew his brother.
10 Now when all the princes, and all the people, which had entered into the covenant, heard that every one should let his manservant, and every one his maidservant, go free, that none should serve themselves of them any more, then they obeyed, and let them go.

The Testimony of the Major Prophets

11 But afterward they turned, and caused the servants and the handmaids, whom they had let go free, to return, and brought them into subjection for servants and for handmaids.

Then Jeremiah the prophet spoke all these words to Zedekiah king of Judah in Jerusalem, when the king of Babylon's army fought against Jerusalem, and against all the cities of Judah that were left, against Lachish, and Azekah: for these were the only fortified cities that remained in Judah. This is the word that came to Jeremiah from the LORD, after that the king Zedekiah had made a covenant with all the people which were at Jerusalem, to proclaim liberty unto them. The covenant that Zedekiah proclaimed to his people was that every man should let his servants who were Hebrew, male or female, go free; no Jew should have another Jew for a servant.

Now when all the princes, and all the people, which had entered into the covenant, heard that every one should let his servants go free, they obeyed, and let them go. But afterward they turned, and caused the servants and the handmaids, whom they had let go free, to be brought again into subjection as servants and handmaids. The king had freed the servants but the people brought them back into subjection.

12 Therefore the word of the LORD came to Jeremiah from the LORD, saying,
13 Thus saith the LORD, the God of Israel; I made a covenant with your fathers in the day that I brought them forth out of the land of Egypt, out of the house of bondmen, saying,
14 At the end of seven years let ye go every man his brother an Hebrew, which hath been sold unto thee; and when he hath served thee six years, thou shalt let him go free from thee: but your fathers hearkened not unto me, neither inclined their ear.
15 And ye were now turned, and had done right in my sight, in proclaiming liberty every man to his neighbour; and ye had made a covenant before me in the house which is called by my name:
16 But ye turned and polluted my name, and caused every man his servant, and every man his handmaid, whom ye had set at liberty at their pleasure, to return, and brought them into subjection, to be unto you for servants and for handmaids.

The word of the LORD came to Jeremiah saying that the LORD, the God of Israel, made a covenant with your fathers when they were brought out of bondage in the land of Egypt. The agreement was that at the end of seven years, their fathers were to free every servant that had been sold to them who was a Hebrew. When the servant had served six years, their fathers were to let them go free, but they did not obey the word of the LORD.

Now, you had done right in the sight of the LORD by proclaiming liberty for the servants; you made a covenant in the house which is called by the name of the LORD, I AM. But you turned and polluted the LORD's name when you brought into subjection the brothers that you had set free.

17 Therefore thus saith the LORD; Ye have not hearkened unto me, in proclaiming liberty, every one to his brother, and every man to his neighbour: behold, I proclaim a liberty for you, saith the LORD, to the sword, to the pestilence, and to the famine; and I will make you to be removed into all the kingdoms of the earth.
18 And I will give the men that have transgressed my covenant, which have not performed the words of the covenant which they had made before me, when they cut the calf in twain, and passed between the parts thereof,
19 The princes of Judah, and the princes of Jerusalem, the eunuchs, and the priests, and all the people of the land, which passed between the parts of the calf;
20 I will even give them into the hand of their enemies, and into the hand of them that seek their life: and their dead bodies shall be for meat unto the fowls of the heaven, and to the beasts of the earth.

Therefore, the LORD said, since you have not listened to proclaim liberty to your brother, then behold, the LORD has proclaimed a liberty, your choice, for you. The choice that you have chosen is the destructive power of the sword of the LORD, to the pestilence and to famine. The LORD will make you to be removed from the kingdom of the LORD into the fallen kingdoms of the earth. The LORD will give the people, who transgressed His covenant by refusing to honor the agreement that they made with the LORD, their punishment. The LORD will treat the rebellious people like the calf that they cut in two and distributed the parts thereof. The princes of Judah, and the princes of Jerusalem, the eunuchs, and the priests, and all the people of the land which passed between the parts of the calf will be given into the hand of their enemies, and into the hand of them that seek their life: and their dead bodies shall be for food for the fowls of the heaven, and the beasts of the earth.

21 And Zedekiah king of Judah and his princes will I give into the hand of their enemies, and into the hand of them that seek their life, and into the hand of the king of Babylon's army, which are gone up from you.
22 Behold, I will command, saith the LORD, and cause them to return to this city; and they shall fight against it, and take it, and burn it with fire: and I will make the cities of Judah a desolation without an inhabitant.

Zedekiah, the king of Judah, and his princes will be given into the hand of the enemies who seek their lives and into the hand of the king of Babylon's army which has withdrawn from you. Behold, the LORD will command and cause them to return to Jerusalem. They will fight against it, take it and burn it with fire. The LORD will make the cities of Judah a desolation without an inhabitant. The LORD has punished the people who were given sufficient time to free their Hebrew brothers who were delivered from bondage in Egypt. The LORD would not want His children, held in bondage by Hebrews, their own brothers, in Judah and Israel.

CHAPTER 35

1 The word which came unto Jeremiah from the LORD in the days of Jehoiakim the son of Josiah king of Judah, saying,
2 Go unto the house of the Rechabites, and speak unto them, and bring them into the house of the LORD, into one of the chambers, and give them wine to drink.
3 Then I took Jaazaniah the son of Jeremiah, the son of Habaziniah, and his brethren, and all his sons, and the whole house of the Rechabites;
4 And I brought them into the house of the LORD, into the chamber of the sons of Hanan, the son of Igdaliah, a man of God, which was by the chamber of the princes, which was above the chamber of Maaseiah the son of Shallum, the keeper of the door:
5 And I set before the sons of the house of the Rechabites pots full of wine, and cups, and I said unto them, Drink ye wine.

The word of the LORD came to Jeremiah in the days of Jehoiakim, (609-598), the son of Josiah, who were the kings of Judah prior to Zedekiah. Jeremiah was to go the house of the Rechabites and bring them into the house of the LORD and give them wine to drink. The Rechabites were a family who obeyed their forefather's command to free the servants and they served as a reminder and a rebuke to the people of Judah who had disobeyed the LORD by not giving freedom to their servants. Jeremiah the prophet took Jaazaniah, whose name means "attentive to the LORD", the son of Jeremiah, the son of Habaziniah and his brethren, and all his sons, and the whole house of Rachabites, and brought them into the house of the LORD into the chamber of the sons of Hanan, the son of Igdaliah, a man of God. This chamber was by the chamber of the princes, which was above the chamber of Maaseiah, the son of Shallum, the keeper of the door. The name Shallum, means "perfect". Jeremiah set pots full of wine and cups to drink before the sons of the Rechabites.

6 But they said, We will drink no wine: for Jonadab the son of Rechab our father commanded us, saying, Ye shall drink no wine, neither ye, nor your sons for ever:
7 Neither shall ye build house, nor sow seed, nor plant vineyard, nor have any: but all your days ye shall dwell in tents; that ye may live many days in the land where ye be strangers.
8 Thus have we obeyed the voice of Jonadab the son of Rechab our father in all that he hath charged us, to drink no wine all our days, we, our wives, our sons, nor our daughters;
9 Nor to build houses for us to dwell in: neither have we vineyard, nor field, nor seed:
10 But we have dwelt in tents, and have obeyed, and done according to all that Jonadab our father commanded us.
11 But it came to pass, when Nebuchadrezzar king of Babylon came up into the land, that we said, Come, and let us go to Jerusalem for fear of the army of the Chaldeans, and for fear of the army of the Syrians: so we dwell at Jerusalem.

The Rechabites, who were attentive to the word of the LORD, said that they would drink no wine because Jonadab, whose name means "earnest", son of Rechab their father commanded the family never to drink wine for ever. They were not to build a house, sow seed, or plant a vineyard; they were to dwell in tents and live many days in the land where they will be strangers. They obeyed the word of their father.

But when Nebuchadnezzar king of Babylon came up into the land, they decided to go to Jerusalem for fear of the army of the Chaldeans, and the army of the Syrians.

12 Then came the word of the LORD unto Jeremiah, saying,
13 Thus saith the LORD of hosts, the God of Israel; Go and tell the men of Judah and the inhabitants of Jerusalem, Will ye not receive instruction to hearken to my words? saith the LORD.
14 The words of Jonadab the son of Rechab, that he commanded his sons not to drink wine, are performed; for unto this day they drink none, but obey their father's commandment: notwithstanding I have spoken unto you, rising early and speaking; but ye hearkened not unto me.

At that time, long before the reign of Zedekiah, the LORD directed Jeremiah to go to the people of Judah and the inhabitants of Jerusalem and ask them why they will not hear the words of the LORD? The words of Jonadab are followed by the Rechabites who obey their father's commandments. But the LORD has spoken to the people of Judah and Jerusalem and they have not listened.

15 I have sent also unto you all my servants the prophets, rising up early and sending them, saying, Return ye now every man from his evil way, and amend your doings, and go not after other gods to serve them, and ye shall dwell in the land which I have given to you and to your fathers: but ye have not inclined your ear, nor hearkened unto me.
16 Because the sons of Jonadab the son of Rechab have performed the commandment of their father, which he commanded them; but this people hath not hearkened unto me:
17 Therefore thus saith the LORD God of hosts, the God of Israel; Behold, I will bring upon Judah and upon all the inhabitants of Jerusalem all the evil that I have pronounced against them: because I have spoken unto them, but they have not heard; and I have called unto them, but they have not answered.
18 And Jeremiah said unto the house of the Rechabites, Thus saith the LORD of hosts, the God of Israel; Because ye have obeyed the commandment of Jonadab your father, and kept all his precepts, and done according unto all that he hath commanded you:
19 Therefore thus saith the LORD of hosts, the God of Israel; Jonadab the son of Rechab shall not want a man to stand before me for ever.

The LORD has sent all of his servants, the prophets, with the message for the people of Judah to repent from their evil way and amend their behaviors. If they do not worship false gods, they will dwell in the land which the LORD has given to their fathers; but they would not listen.

Because the Rechabites have listened to the command of their father and the people of Judah and Jerusalem have not listened to the LORD, therefore, The LORD will bring upon the people of Judah and Jerusalem all the evil of the sword, the pestilence and the famine that has been pronounced against them because the LORD has spoken to them and they have not answered. They shall receive the punishment of disobedience and ignoring the word of the LORD. This was said by Jeremiah before the reign of Zedekiah.

Jeremiah also delivered the word of the LORD to the house of the Rechabites at that time. Because the Rechabites had obeyed the commandment of Jonadab their father, and kept all his precepts, and done according unto all that he had commanded you, therefore the LORD of hosts, the God of Israel said that Jonadab the son of Rechab shall not lack a man to stand in obedience before the LORD forever. Years later, during the reign of Zedekiah, the Rechabites were still obedient to commands of their father.

CHAPTER 36

1 And it came to pass in the fourth year of Jehoiakim the son of Josiah king of Judah, that this word came unto Jeremiah from the LORD, saying,
2 Take thee a roll of a book, and write therein all the words that I have spoken unto thee against Israel, and against Judah, and against all the nations, from the day I spake unto thee, from the days of Josiah, even unto this day.
3 It may be that the house of Judah will hear all the evil which I purpose to do unto them; that they may return every man from his evil way; that I may forgive their iniquity and their sin.
4 Then Jeremiah called Baruch the son of Neriah: and Baruch wrote from the mouth of Jeremiah all the words of the LORD, which he had spoken unto him, upon a roll of a book.
5 And Jeremiah commanded Baruch, saying, I am shut up; I cannot go into the house of the LORD:
6 Therefore go thou, and read in the roll, which thou hast written from my mouth, the words of the LORD in the ears of the people in the LORD's house upon the fasting day: and also thou shalt read them in the ears of all Judah that come out of their cities.
7 It may be they will present their supplication before the LORD, and will return every one from his evil way: for great is the anger and the fury that the LORD hath pronounced against this people.
8 And Baruch the son of Neriah did according to all that Jeremiah the prophet commanded him, reading in the book the words of the LORD in the LORD's house.

In the fourth year of Jehoiakim the son of Josiah king of Judah, the word of the LORD came to Jeremiah instructing him to take a scroll and write all the words that the LORD has spoken to him against Israel, Judah, and all the nations, from the days of Josiah to this day. This shall be written so that the house of Judah will hear all the evil which the LORD will bring upon them according to the working of the Law. The people of Judah will be warned so that they may return from their evil way and so the LORD may forgive their iniquity and their sin for which they shall surely pay in accord with the Law of Sowing and Reaping if they do not repent.

Then Jeremiah called Baruch the son of Neriah to record all the words of the LORD which Jeremiah dictated to him. Jeremiah tells Baruch that he is confined and cannot go into the temple. Therefore, Baruch should go and read the scroll containing the words of the LORD into the ears of the people on a day of fasting and into the ears of the people who come out of their cities. It may be they will present their supplication before the LORD, and will repent from their evil ways. The people should repent because the anger and the fury that the LORD has pronounced against the people is great because the sins of the people against the way of the LORD are great. Baruch the son of Neriah did what Jeremiah the prophet commanded him by reading the words of the LORD in the temple on a day of fasting.

9 And it came to pass in the fifth year of Jehoiakim the son of Josiah king of Judah, in the ninth month, that they proclaimed a fast before the LORD to all the people in Jerusalem, and to all the people that came from the cities of Judah unto Jerusalem.

10 Then read Baruch in the book the words of Jeremiah in the house of the LORD, in the chamber of Gemariah the son of Shaphan the scribe, in the higher court, at the entry of the new gate of the LORD's house, in the ears of all the people.
11 When Michaiah the son of Gemariah, the son of Shaphan, had heard out of the book all the words of the LORD,
12 Then he went down into the king's house, into the scribe's chamber: and, lo, all the princes sat there, even Elishama the scribe, and Delaiah the son of Shemaiah, and Elnathan the son of Achbor, and Gemariah the son of Shaphan, and Zedekiah the son of Hananiah, and all the princes.
13 Then Michaiah declared unto them all the words that he had heard, when Baruch read the book in the ears of the people.
14 Therefore all the princes sent Jehudi the son of Nethaniah, the son of Shelemiah, the son of Cushi, unto Baruch, saying, Take in thine hand the roll wherein thou hast read in the ears of the people, and come. So Baruch the son of Neriah took the roll in his hand, and came unto them.
15 And they said unto him, Sit down now, and read it in our ears. So Baruch read it in their ears.

In the ninth month of the fifth year of Jehoiakim king of Judah a fast was declared before the LORD for all the people of Jerusalem and to all the people that came from the cities of Judah into Jerusalem. Then Baruch read the words of Jeremiah in the temple in the chamber of Gemariah in the higher court at the entry of the new gate so that all the people could hear the words of Jeremiah. When Michaiah the son of Gemariah heard the words of the LORD to Jeremiah spoken by Baruch, he went down to the king's house into the scribe's chamber where sat all the princes and the pre-eminent scribes, such as, Elishama the scribe, and Delaiah the son of Shemaiah, and Elnathan the son of Achbor, and Gemariah the son of Shaphan, and Zedekiah the son of Hananiah.

Michaiah declared to the scribes of the king all that he had heard when Baruch read the words of the LORD in the book that was heard by all the people. Therefore, all the princes sent Jehudi, the son of Nathaniah to Baruch asking him to bring the scroll, which he had read to the people, and come to them. The princes wanted Baruch to read the scroll into their ears so that they could hear the words directly.

16 Now it came to pass, when they had heard all the words, they were afraid both one and other, and said unto Baruch, We will surely tell the king of all these words.
17 And they asked Baruch, saying, Tell us now, How didst thou write all these words at his mouth?
18 Then Baruch answered them, He pronounced all these words unto me with his mouth, and I wrote them with ink in the book.
19 Then said the princes unto Baruch, Go, hide thee, thou and Jeremiah; and let no man know where ye be.

After the princes heard the words of Jeremiah which were read to them by Baruch, they were afraid and they told Baruch that they would tell the king of all of these words. When the princes asked how Baruch wrote all the words that came from the mouth of Jeremiah, Baruch said that Jeremiah spoke the words and Baruch wrote them with ink on a scroll. The princes were afraid of the king's reaction and they told Baruch to take Jeremiah and hide where no man would know where they are hidden.

20 And they went in to the king into the court, but they laid up the roll in the chamber of Elishama the scribe, and told all the words in the ears of the king.
21 So the king sent Jehudi to fetch the roll: and he took it out of Elishama the scribe's chamber. And Jehudi read it in the ears of the king, and in the ears of all the princes which stood beside the king.
22 Now the king sat in the winterhouse in the ninth month: and there was a fire on the hearth burning before him.
23 And it came to pass, that when Jehudi had read three or four leaves, he cut it with the penknife, and cast it into the fire that was on the hearth, until all the roll was consumed in the fire that was on the hearth.
24 Yet they were not afraid, nor rent their garments, neither the king, nor any of his servants that heard all these words.
25 Nevertheless Elnathan and Delaiah and Gemariah had made intercession to the king that he would not burn the roll: but he would not hear them.
26 But the king commanded Jerahmeel the son of Hammelech, and Seraiah the son of Azriel, and Shelemiah the son of Abdeel, to take Baruch the scribe and Jeremiah the prophet: but the LORD hid them.

The Testimony of the Major Prophets

The princes went to the king in his court but they laid the scroll in the chamber of Elishama the scribe and told the king the words of Jeremiah. The king sent Jehudi to fetch the scroll who retrieved it from Elishema the scribe's chamber. Jehudi read the scroll to the king and the princes who stood beside him. The king sat in the winter house in the ninth month and a fire was burning in the hearth. And when Jehudi had read two or three leaves from the scroll, he cut it and cast it into the fire that was on the hearth until the entire scroll was consumed by fire.

Yet neither the king nor any of his servants who heard these words of the LORD were afraid of the charge and the punishment that the LORD would bring upon them. Elnathan and Delaiah and Gemariah made intercession to the king that he would not burn the roll: but the king would not hear them. But the king commanded Jerahmeel the son of Hammelech, and Seraiah the son of Azriel, and Shelemiah the son of Abdeel, to take Baruch the scribe and Jeremiah the prophet into captivity: but the LORD hid them.

27 Then the word of the LORD came to Jeremiah, after that the king had burned the roll, and the words which Baruch wrote at the mouth of Jeremiah, saying,
28 Take thee again another roll, and write in it all the former words that were in the first roll, which Jehoiakim the king of Judah hath burned.
29 And thou shalt say to Jehoiakim king of Judah, Thus saith the LORD; Thou hast burned this roll, saying, Why hast thou written therein, saying, The king of Babylon shall certainly come and destroy this land, and shall cause to cease from thence man and beast?
30 Therefore thus saith the LORD of Jehoiakim king of Judah; He shall have none to sit upon the throne of David: and his dead body shall be cast out in the day to the heat, and in the night to the frost.
31 And I will punish him and his seed and his servants for their iniquity; and I will bring upon them, and upon the inhabitants of Jerusalem, and upon the men of Judah, all the evil that I have pronounced against them; but they hearkened not.
32 Then took Jeremiah another roll, and gave it to Baruch the scribe, the son of Neriah; who wrote therein from the mouth of Jeremiah all the words of the book which Jehoiakim king of Judah had burned in the fire: and there were added besides unto them many like words.

After the king burned the scroll, the word of the LORD came to Jeremiah that he should take another scroll and write on it all the former words which Jehoiakim king of Judah had burned. Jeremiah was to tell the king that the LORD knows that Jehoiakim has burned the scroll which contained the words of the LORD and that he has asked why Jeremiah has written that the king of Babylon shall come and destroy the land, and kill both man and beast?

The word of the LORD to Jehoiakim king of Judah was that He shall have no one to sit on the throne of David: his dead body shall be cast out in the day to the heat and in the night to the frost. The LORD will punish him and his descendants for their iniquity; the LORD will bring upon them, and upon the inhabitants of Jerusalem, and upon the men of Judah, all the evil that the LORD has pronounced against them; but the people did not obey the LORD by repentance and change. Jeremiah dictated to Baruch on another scroll the words which the king destroyed in the fire and recorded his additional disobedience.

CHAPTER 37

1 And king Zedekiah the son of Josiah reigned instead of Coniah the son of Jehoiakim, whom Nebuchadrezzar king of Babylon made king in the land of Judah.
2 But neither he, nor his servants, nor the people of the land, did hearken unto the words of the LORD, which he spake by the prophet Jeremiah.
3 And Zedekiah the king sent Jehucal the son of Shelemiah and Zephaniah the son of Maaseiah the priest to the prophet Jeremiah, saying, Pray now unto the LORD our God for us.
4 Now Jeremiah came in and went out among the people: for they had not put him into prison.
5 Then Pharaoh's army was come forth out of Egypt: and when the Chaldeans that besieged Jerusalem heard tidings of them, they departed from Jerusalem.
6 Then came the word of the LORD unto the prophet Jeremiah, saying,
7 Thus saith the LORD, the God of Israel; Thus shall ye say to the king of Judah, that sent you unto me to inquire of me; Behold, Pharaoh's army, which is come forth to help you, shall return to Egypt into their own land.
8 And the Chaldeans shall come again, and fight against this city, and take it, and burn it with fire.
9 Thus saith the LORD; Deceive not yourselves, saying, The Chaldeans shall surely depart from us: for they shall not depart.
10 For though ye had smitten the whole army of the Chaldeans that fight against you, and there remained but wounded men among them, yet should they rise up every man in his tent, and burn this city with fire.

Nebuchadnezzar king of Babylon made Zedekiah the son of Josiah king in the land of Judah instead of Coniah the son of Jehoiakim. However, neither Zedekiah, nor his servants, nor the people of the land, did hearken to the words of the LORD, which he spoke by the prophet Jeremiah. Zedekiah the king sent Jehucal the son of Shelemiah and Zephaniah the son of Maaseiah the priest to the prophet Jeremiah, saying, Pray now to the LORD our God for us. Now Jeremiah came in and went out among the people: for they had not put him into prison.

In the meantime, Pharaoh's army had come forth out of Egypt. When the Chaldeans that besieged Jerusalem heard tidings of the coming of the Egyptians, they departed from Jerusalem. Then came the word of the LORD through the prophet Jeremiah for the king of Judah that sent Jeremiah to inquire of the LORD; Behold, Pharaoh's army, which is come forth to help you, shall return to Egypt into their own land. The Chaldeans shall come again, and fight against this city, and take it, and burn it with fire.

The LORD tells them to not deceive themselves by saying that he Chaldeans shall surely depart from Jerusalem; for they shall not depart. Even though you had smitten the whole army of the Chaldeans that fight against you, and there remained but wounded men among them, yet should they rise up every man in his tent, and burn this city with fire. The destruction of Jerusalem is inevitable. Iniquity must be destroyed. The Law must work.

The Testimony of the Major Prophets

11 And it came to pass, that when the army of the Chaldeans was broken up from Jerusalem for fear of Pharaoh's army,
12 Then Jeremiah went forth out of Jerusalem to go into the land of Benjamin, to separate himself thence in the midst of the people.
13 And when he was in the gate of Benjamin, a captain of the ward was there, whose name was Irijah, the son of Shelemiah, the son of Hananiah; and he took Jeremiah the prophet, saying, Thou fallest away to the Chaldeans.
14 Then said Jeremiah, It is false; I fall not away to the Chaldeans. But he hearkened not to him: so Irijah took Jeremiah, and brought him to the princes.
15 Wherefore the princes were wroth with Jeremiah, and smote him, and put him in prison in the house of Jonathan the scribe: for they had made that the prison.
16 When Jeremiah was entered into the dungeon, and into the cabins, and Jeremiah had remained there many days;
17 Then Zedekiah the king sent, and took him out: and the king asked him secretly in his house, and said, Is there any word from the LORD? And Jeremiah said, There is: for, said he, thou shalt be delivered into the hand of the king of Babylon.

When it came to pass that the army of the Chaldeans had withdrawn from Jerusalem for fear of Pharaoh's army, Jeremiah went out from Jerusalem to go into the land of Benjamin, where he had purchased land. When he was in the gate of Benjamin, a captain of the ward was there—whose name was Irijah, the son of Shelemiah, the son of Hananiah—and took Jeremiah the prophet, saying, Jeremiah was deserting to the Chaldeans. Jeremiah denied that he was deserting to the Chaldeans but Irijah did not believe him and took Jeremiah to the princes.

Wherefore the princes were angry with Jeremiah; they beat him and put him in prison in the house of Jonathan the scribe which had been made into a prison. Jeremiah was placed into the dungeon, and remained there many days. Then Zedekiah the king sent, and took Jeremiah out of the dungeon and asked him secretly if there is any word from the LORD? And Jeremiah told the king that he shall be delivered into the hand of the king of Babylon.

18 Moreover Jeremiah said unto king Zedekiah, What have I offended against thee, or against thy servants, or against this people, that ye have put me in prison?
19 Where are now your prophets which prophesied unto you, saying, The king of Babylon shall not come against you, nor against this land?
20 Therefore hear now, I pray thee, O my lord the king: let my supplication, I pray thee, be accepted before thee; that thou cause me not to return to the house of Jonathan the scribe, lest I die there.
21 Then Zedekiah the king commanded that they should commit Jeremiah into the court of the prison, and that they should give him daily a piece of bread out of the bakers' street, until all the bread in the city were spent. Thus Jeremiah remained in the court of the prison.

Jeremiah asked king Zedekiah what offense had been done against the king, his servants or the people that he has been put in prison? Jeremiah asked the king where are the prophets who advised the king saying the king of Babylon shall not come against the king or the land? Jeremiah asks the king to not return him to the house of Jonathan as a prisoner, lest he should die there. Zedekiah commanded that Jeremiah be placed into the courtyard of the prison and that he be given a piece of bread daily until all the bread of the city is gone. Jeremiah remained in the courtyard of the prison.

CHAPTER 38

1 Then Shephatiah the son of Mattan, and Gedaliah the son of Pashur, and Jucal the son of Shelemiah, and Pashur the son of Malchiah, heard the words that Jeremiah had spoken unto all the people, saying,
2 Thus saith the LORD, He that remaineth in this city shall die by the sword, by the famine, and by the pestilence: but he that goeth forth to the Chaldeans shall live; for he shall have his life for a prey, and shall live.
3 Thus saith the LORD, This city shall surely be given into the hand of the king of Babylon's army, which shall take it.
4 Therefore the princes said unto the king, We beseech thee, let this man be put to death: for thus he weakeneth the hands of the men of war that remain in this city, and the hands of all the people, in speaking such words unto them: for this man seeketh not the welfare of this people, but the hurt.
5 Then Zedekiah the king said, Behold, he is in your hand: for the king is not he that can do any thing against you.

The word of the LORD has been heard through Jeremiah by four people who took heed to the advice; they were, Shephatiah, Gedaliah, Jucal, and Pashur. The warning of the LORD was that the people who remained in the city of Jerusalem would die by the sword, the famine and the pestilence; but the people that go forth to the Chaldeans shall live. If life is their prey, their target or objective, they shall live. The city shall surely be given into the hand of control of the king of Babylon's army which shall take it.

Therefore the princes told the king to let Jeremiah be put to death because he weakened the hands of the men of war who remained in the city, and he weakened the hands of all the people, in speaking such words to them: for this man seeks not the welfare of this people, but the hurt. Then Zedekiah the king said, Behold, Jeremiah is in your hand: your king is not the person to do any thing against you for what you do.

6 Then took they Jeremiah, and cast him into the dungeon of Malchiah the son of Hammelech, that was in the court of the prison: and they let down Jeremiah with cords. And in the dungeon there was no water, but mire: so Jeremiah sunk in the mire.
7 Now when Ebed-melech the Ethiopian, one of the eunuchs which was in the king's house, heard that they had put Jeremiah in the dungeon; the king then sitting in the gate of Benjamin;
8 Ebed-melech went forth out of the king's house, and spake to the king, saying,
9 My lord the king, these men have done evil in all that they have done to Jeremiah the prophet, whom they have cast into the dungeon; and he is like to die for hunger in the place where he is: for there is no more bread in the city.

The princes took Jeremiah and cast him into the dungeon of Malchiah that was in the courtyard of the prison: they let Jeremiah down with cords. There was no water in the dungeon, so he sank into the mire.
When Ebed-melech the Ethiopian, one of the eunuchs in the king's house, heard that they had put Jeremiah in the dungeon or a cistern, Ebed-melech went out of the king's house, and told the king, who was sitting in the gate of

The Testimony of the Major Prophets

Benjamin, what these men have done evil to Jeremiah the prophet. Jeremiah is likely to die of hunger in the place where he is: for there is no more bread in the city.

10 Then the king commanded Ebed-melech the Ethiopian, saying, Take from hence thirty men with thee, and take up Jeremiah the prophet out of the dungeon, before he die.
11 So Ebed-melech took the men with him, and went into the house of the king under the treasury, and took thence old cast clouts and old rotten rags, and let them down by cords into the dungeon to Jeremiah.
12 And Ebed-melech the Ethiopian said unto Jeremiah, Put now these old cast clouts and rotten rags under thine armholes under the cords. And Jeremiah did so.
13 So they drew up Jeremiah with cords, and took him up out of the dungeon: and Jeremiah remained in the court of the prison.
14 Then Zedekiah the king sent, and took Jeremiah the prophet unto him into the third entry that is in the house of the LORD: and the king said unto Jeremiah, I will ask thee a thing; hide nothing from me.
15 Then Jeremiah said unto Zedekiah, If I declare it unto thee, wilt thou not surely put me to death? and if I give thee counsel, wilt thou not hearken unto me?
16 So Zedekiah the king sware secretly unto Jeremiah, saying, As the LORD liveth, that made us this soul, I will not put thee to death, neither will I give thee into the hand of these men that seek thy life.

The king commanded Ebed-melech the Ethiopian to take thirty men and remove Jeremiah from the dungeon or cistern before he dies. Ebed-melech and the men went into the house of the king under the treasury and took old clothes and rags and let them down into the cistern or dungeon. The rags were put under the armholes and they drew Jeremiah out of the cistern where he remained in the courtyard of the prison.

Then Zedekiah the king sent, and took Jeremiah the prophet to him into the third entrance of the house of the LORD where he spoke to Jeremiah in confidence asking the prophet to be honest with him. Jeremiah asked the king that if Jeremiah did give a truthful answer, will not the king put Jeremiah to death? and if Jeremiah gives true counsel to the king, will the king really listen? So Zedekiah the king swore secretly to Jeremiah, saying, As the LORD lives who made him, he will not put Jeremiah to death, or give him into the hand of the men that seek his life.

17 Then said Jeremiah unto Zedekiah, Thus saith the LORD, the God of hosts, the God of Israel; If thou wilt assuredly go forth unto the king of Babylon's princes, then thy soul shall live, and this city shall not be burned with fire; and thou shalt live, and thine house:
18 But if thou wilt not go forth to the king of Babylon's princes, then shall this city be given into the hand of the Chaldeans, and they shall burn it with fire, and thou shalt not escape out of their hand.
19 And Zedekiah the king said unto Jeremiah, I am afraid of the Jews that are fallen to the Chaldeans, lest they deliver me into their hand, and they mock me.
20 But Jeremiah said, They shall not deliver thee. Obey, I beseech thee, the voice of the LORD, which I speak unto thee: so it shall be well unto thee, and thy soul shall live.
21 But if thou refuse to go forth, this is the word that the LORD hath shewed me:
22 And, behold, all the women that are left in the king of Judah's house shall be brought forth to the king of Babylon's princes, and those women shall say, Thy friends have set thee on, and have prevailed against thee: thy feet are sunk in the mire, and they are turned away back.
23 So they shall bring out all thy wives and thy children to the Chaldeans: and thou shalt not escape out of their hand, but shalt be taken by the hand of the king of Babylon: and thou shalt cause this city to be burned with fire.

Jeremiah gave Zedekiah the word from the LORD, the God of hosts, the God of Israel. If Zedekiah surrenders to the princes of the king of Babylon, he and his family will live, and the city shall not be burned with fire. But if he does not surrender to the princes of the king of Babylon, then the city shall be given to the Chaldeans who will burn it with fire, and Zedekiah shall not escape from their hands.

And Zedekiah told Jeremiah that he was afraid of the Jews taken captive by the Chaldeans who might deliver him into their hand, and they would mock and mistreat the fallen king. But Jeremiah said, They shall not deliver you. Jeremiah beseeches Zedekiah to obey the voice of the LORD which Jeremiah is speaking to him: it shall be well with you and your soul shall live. But if you refuse to surrender, this is the word that the LORD has showed Jeremiah: all the women that are left in the king of Judah's house shall be brought forth to the king of Babylon's princes, and those women shall say, Your friends have set themselves, have misled and prevailed against you: your feet are sunk in the mire, and your friends have turned their backs on you. So the princes shall bring out all your wives and your children to the Chaldeans: you shall not escape out of their hand, but shall be taken by the hand of the king of Babylon: and you shall cause this city to be burned with fire.

24 Then said Zedekiah unto Jeremiah, Let no man know of these words, and thou shalt not die.
25 But if the princes hear that I have talked with thee, and they come unto thee, and say unto thee, Declare unto us now what thou hast said unto the king, hide it not from us, and we will not put thee to death; also what the king said unto thee:
26 Then thou shalt say unto them, I presented my supplication before the king, that he would not cause me to return to Jonathan's house, to die there.
27 Then came all the princes unto Jeremiah, and asked him: and he told them according to all these words that the king had commanded. So they left off speaking with him; for the matter was not perceived.
28 So Jeremiah abode in the court of the prison until the day that Jerusalem was taken: and he was there when Jerusalem was taken.

Zedekiah tells Jeremiah to let no man know of this conversation and he shall not die. If the princes hear that the king has come to Jeremiah, they will want to know the nature of their conversations. If Jeremiah does not tell them, they will threaten to put him to death. Jeremiah is to tell the princes that he is praying that the king will not cause him to return to Jonathan's house to die there. Jeremiah told the princes everything that the king had ordered him to say. Jeremiah remained in prison until Jerusalem was taken.

CHAPTER 39

1 In the ninth year of Zedekiah king of Judah, in the tenth month, came Nebuchadrezzar king of Babylon and all his army against Jerusalem, and they besieged it.
2 And in the eleventh year of Zedekiah, in the fourth month, the ninth day of the month, the city was broken up.
3 And all the princes of the king of Babylon came in, and sat in the middle gate, even Nergal-sharezer, Samgar-nebo, Sarse-chim, Rab-saris, Nergal-sharezer, Rab-mag, with all the residue of the princes of the king of Babylon.
4 And it came to pass, that when Zedekiah the king of Judah saw them, and all the men of war, then they fled, and went forth out of the city by night, by the way of the king's garden, by the gate betwixt the two walls: and he went out the way of the plain.
5 But the Chaldeans' army pursued after them, and overtook Zedekiah in the plains of Jericho: and when they had taken him, they brought him up to Nebuchadrezzar king of Babylon to Riblah in the land of Hamath, where he gave judgment upon him.
6 Then the king of Babylon slew the sons of Zedekiah in Riblah before his eyes: also the king of Babylon slew all the nobles of Judah.
7 Moreover he put out Zedekiah's eyes, and bound him with chains, to carry him to Babylon.
8 And the Chaldeans burned the king's house, and the houses of the people, with fire, and brake down the walls of Jerusalem.

In the tenth month of the ninth year of Zedekiah king of Judah, Nebuchadnezzar king of Babylon came with all his army against Jerusalem, and besieged the city. In the ninth day of the fourth month of the eleventh year the city was broken up. All the princes of the king of Babylon came in, and sat in the middle gate, even Nergal-sharezer, Samgar-nebo, Sarse-chim, Rab-saris, Nergal-sharezer, Rab-mag, with all the residue of the princes of the king of Babylon.

And it came to pass, that when Zedekiah the king of Judah saw them, and all the men of war, they fled, and departed the city by night, by way of the king's garden, by the gate between the two walls by way of the plains. But the Chaldeans' army pursued after them, and overtook Zedekiah in the plains of Jericho. When they had taken him, they brought him up to Nebuchadnezzar king of Babylon to Riblah in the land of Hamath, where he gave judgment upon him. The king of Babylon slew the sons of Zedekiah in Riblah before his eyes and he slew all the nobles of Judah. Moreover he put out Zedekiah's eyes, and bound him with chains, to carry him to Babylon. The Chaldeans burned the king's house, and the houses of the people, with fire, and broke down the walls of Jerusalem.

9 Then Nebuzaradan the captain of the guard carried away captive into Babylon the remnant of the people that remained in the city, and those that fell away, that fell to him, with the rest of the people that remained.
10 But Nebuzaradan the captain of the guard left of the poor of the people, which had nothing, in the land of Judah, and gave them vineyards and fields at the same time.
11 Now Nebuchadrezzar king of Babylon gave charge concerning Jeremiah to Nebuzaradan the captain of the guard, saying,

The Symbolic Version of Jeremiah

12 Take him, and look well to him, and do him no harm; but do unto him even as he shall say unto thee.
13 So Nebuzaradan the captain of the guard sent, and Nebushasban, Rabsaris, and Nergalsharezer, Rabmag, and all the king of Babylon's princes;
14 Even they sent, and took Jeremiah out of the court of the prison, and committed him unto Gedaliah the son of Ahikam the son of Shaphan, that he should carry him home: so he dwelt among the people.

Nebuzaradan the captain of the guard carried away into Babylon the remnant of the people that remained in the city, and those that had gone over to him with the rest of the people that remained. The people who did not run away were allowed to live. Nebuzaradan the captain of the guard left of the poor people, which had nothing, in the land of Judah, and gave them vineyards and fields at the same time.

Now Nebuchadnezzar king of Babylon gave charge concerning Jeremiah to Nebuzaradan the captain of the guard, saying, Take him, and look well to him, and do him no harm; but do to him as he shall say to you. So Nebuzaradan the captain of the guard sent, and Nebushasban, Rabsaris, and Nergalsharezer, Rabmag, and all the king of Babylon's princes sent, and took Jeremiah out of the court of the prison, and committed him to Gedaliah the son of Ahikam the son of Shaphan, to carry him home to dwell among his own people.

15 Now the word of the LORD came unto Jeremiah, while he was shut up in the court of the prison, saying,
16 Go and speak to Ebed-melech the Ethiopian, saying, Thus saith the LORD of hosts, the God of Israel; Behold, I will bring my words upon this city for evil, and not for good; and they shall be accomplished in that day before thee.
17 But I will deliver thee in that day, saith the LORD: and thou shalt not be given into the hand of the men of whom thou art afraid.
18 For I will surely deliver thee, and thou shalt not fall by the sword, but thy life shall be for a prey unto thee: because thou hast put thy trust in me, saith the LORD.

Now the word of the LORD came to Jeremiah, while he was shut up in the courtyard of the prison, saying, Go and speak to Ebed-melech the Ethiopian, with the message that the LORD of hosts, the God of Israel will bring His words upon this city for disaster and not for prosperity; and they shall be accomplished and fulfilled in the day that is before you. But the LORD will deliver you in that day: you shall not be given into the hands of the men of whom you are afraid. For the LORD will surely deliver you and you shall not fall by the sword, but your life shall be an objective for you to enjoy because you have put your trust in the LORD.

CHAPTER 40

1 The word that came to Jeremiah from the LORD, after that Nebuzaradan the captain of the guard had let him go from Ramah, when he had taken him being bound in chains among all that were carried away captive of Jerusalem and Judah, which were carried away captive unto Babylon.
2 And the captain of the guard took Jeremiah, and said unto him, The LORD thy God hath pronounced this evil upon this place.
3 Now the LORD hath brought it, and done according as he hath said: because ye have sinned against the LORD, and have not obeyed his voice, therefore this thing is come upon you.
4 And now, behold, I loose thee this day from the chains which were upon thine hand. If it seem good unto thee to come with me into Babylon, come; and I will look well unto thee: but if it seem ill unto thee to come with me into Babylon, forbear: behold, all the land is before thee: whither it seemeth good and convenient for thee to go, thither go.
5 Now while he was not yet gone back, he said, Go back also to Gedaliah the son of Ahikam the son of Shaphan, whom the king of Babylon hath made governor over the cities of Judah, and dwell with him among the people: or go wheresoever it seemeth convenient unto thee to go. So the captain of the guard gave him victuals and a reward, and let him go.

The word came to Jeremiah from the LORD after Nebuzaradan the captain of the guard had let him go from Ramah, when he had taken him being bound in chains among all that were carried away as captives of Jerusalem and Judah into Babylon. And the captain of the guard took Jeremiah, and said to him, The LORD God has pronounced this evil upon this place. Now the LORD has brought it, and done according as He has said because the people have sinned against the LORD, and have not obeyed his voice; therefore this thing is come upon you.

And now, behold, I will release you today from the chains which were upon your wrists. If it seems good to you to come with me into Babylon, come; and I will look well after you: but if it seems ill to you to come with me into Babylon, forbear. Behold, all the land is before you: wherever it seems good and convenient for you to go, go there. Now before Jeremiah had turned to go, Nebuzaradan said, Go back also to Gedaliah the son of Ahikam the son of Shaphan, whom the king of Babylon has made governor over the cities of Judah, and dwell with him among the people: or go wherever it seems convenient for you to go. So the captain of the guard gave him victuals and a reward, and let him go.

6 Then went Jeremiah unto Gedaliah the son of Ahikam to Mizpah; and dwelt with him among the people that were left in the land.
7 Now when all the captains of the forces which were in the fields, even they and their men, heard that the king of Babylon had made Gedaliah the son of Ahikam governor in the land, and had committed
unto him men, and women, and children, and of the poor of the land, of them that were not carried away captive to Babylon;

The Symbolic Version of Jeremiah

8 Then they came to Gedaliah to Mizpah, even Ishmael the son of Nethaniah, and Johanan and Jonathan the sons of Kareah, and Seraiah the son of Tanhumeth, and the sons of Ephai the Netophathite, and Jezaniah the son of a Maachathite, they and their men.
9 And Gedaliah the son of Ahikam the son of Shaphan sware unto them and to their men, saying, Fear not to serve the Chaldeans: dwell in the land, and serve the king of Babylon, and it shall be well with you.
10 As for me, behold, I will dwell at Mizpah to serve the Chaldeans, which will come unto us: but ye, gather ye wine, and summer fruits, and oil, and put them in your vessels, and dwell in your cities that ye have taken.

Jeremiah went to Gedaliah and dwelt with him who had been made governor of the people who were left in the land. Now when all the captains of the forces which were in the fields heard that the king of Babylon had made Gedaliah governor in the land, and had committed to him men, and women, and children, and of the poor of the land, who were not carried away captive to Babylon; they came to Gedaliah at Mizpah. Among the captains were Ishmael the son of Nethaniah, Johanan, Jonathan the sons of Kareah, Seraiah the son of Tanhumeth, the sons of Ephai the Netophathite, and Jezaniah the son of a Maachathite. Gedaliah swore to them and to their men, saying, Fear not to serve the Chaldeans: dwell in the land, and serve the king of Babylon, and it shall be well with you. As for me, behold, I will dwell at Mizpah to serve the Chaldeans, which will come to us: but you may gather wine, summer fruits, and oil, and put them in your vessels, and dwell in your cities that you have taken.

11 Likewise when all the Jews that were in Moab, and among the Ammonites, and in Edom, and that were in all the countries, heard that the king of Babylon had left a remnant of Judah, and that he had set over them Gedaliah the son of Ahikam the son of Shaphan;
12 Even all the Jews returned out of all places whither they were driven, and came to the land of Judah, to Gedaliah, unto Mizpah, and gathered wine and summer fruits very much.
13 Moreover Johanan the son of Kareah, and all the captains of the forces that were in the fields, came to Gedaliah to Mizpah,
14 And said unto him, Dost thou certainly know that Baalis the king of the Ammonites hath sent Ishmael the son of Nethaniah to slay thee? But Gedaliah the son of Ahikam believed them not.
15 Then Johanan the son of Kareah spake to Gedaliah in Mizpah secretly, saying, Let me go, I pray thee, and I will slay Ishmael the son of Nethaniah, and no man shall know it: wherefore should he slay thee, that all the Jews which are gathered unto thee should be scattered, and the remnant in Judah perish?
16 But Gedaliah the son of Ahikam said unto Johanan the son of Kareah, Thou shalt not do this thing: for thou speakest falsely of Ishmael.

When all the Jews that were in Moab, Ammon, Edom, and all the countries, heard that the king of Babylon had left a remnant of Judah, and that he had set Gedaliah over them, then all the Jews returned out of all places where they were driven, and came to the land of Judah to gather wine and summer fruits.
Moreover Johanan the son of Kareah, and all the captains of the forces that were in the fields, came to Gedaliah to Mizpah, and said to him, Do you certainly know that Baalis the king of the Ammonites has sent Ishmael the son of Nethaniah to slay you? But Gedaliah the son of Ahikam did not believe them.

Then Johanan the son of Kareah spoke to Gedaliah in Mizpah secretly, saying, Let me go, I pray you, and I will slay Ishmael the son of Nethaniah, and no man shall know it: why should he slay you that all the Jews which are gathered to you should be scattered, and the remnant in Judah perish? But Gedaliah the son of Ahikam said to Johanan the son of Kareah, You shall not do this thing for you speak falsely of Ishmael.

CHAPTER 41

1 Now it came to pass in the seventh month, that Ishmael the son of Nethaniah the son of Elishama, of the seed royal, and the princes of the king, even ten men with him, came unto Gedaliah the son of Ahikam to Mizpah; and there they did eat bread together in Mizpah.
2 Then arose Ishmael the son of Nethaniah, and the ten men that were with him, and smote Gedaliah the son of Ahikam the son of Shaphan with the sword, and slew him, whom the king of Babylon had made governor over the land.
3 Ishmael also slew all the Jews that were with him, even with Gedaliah, at Mizpah, and the Chaldeans that were found there, and the men of war.
4 And it came to pass the second day after he had slain Gedaliah, and no man knew it,
5 That there came certain from Shechem, from Shiloh, and from Samaria, even fourscore men, having their beards shaven, and their clothes rent, and having cut themselves, with offerings and incense in their hand, to bring them to the house of the LORD.

Now it came to pass in the seventh month, that Ishmael who was of royal blood, and the princes of the king, even ten men with him, came to visit Gedaliah at Mizpah where they ate bread together. Then Ishmael, and the ten men that were with him, struck Gedaliah with the sword, and slew him, whom the king of Babylon had made governor over the land. Ishmael also slew all the Jews that were with Gedaliah, at Mizpah, the Chaldeans that were present there, and the men of war. On the second day after he had slain Gedaliah, and no man knew it, eighty men with their beards shaven, and their clothes rent, and having cut themselves, with offerings and incense in their hand came from Shechem, from Shiloh, and from Samaria to bring them to the house of the LORD.

6 And Ishmael the son of Nethaniah went forth from Mizpah to meet them, weeping all along as he went: and it came to pass, as he met them, he said unto them, Come to Gedaliah the son of Ahikam.
7 And it was so, when they came into the midst of the city, that Ishmael the son of Nethaniah slew them, and cast them into the midst of the pit, he, and the men that were with him.
8 But ten men were found among them that said unto Ishmael, Slay us not: for we have treasures in the field, of wheat, and of barley, and of oil, and of honey. So he forbare, and slew them not among their brethren.
9 Now the pit wherein Ishmael had cast all the dead bodies of the men, whom he had slain because of Gedaliah, was it which Asa the king had made for fear of Baasha king of Israel: and Ishmael the son of Nethaniah filled it with them that were slain.

Ishmael the son of Nethaniah went forth from Mizpah to meet the eighty men, weeping as he went. When he met them, he said, Come to Gedaliah the son of Ahikam. When they came into the midst of the city, Ishmael and his men slew them, and cast them into the midst of the pit. But ten men were found among them that said unto Ishmael, Slay us not: for we have treasures in the field, of wheat, barley, oil, and honey. So Ishmael did not kill them. Now the pit where Ishmael had cast all the dead bodies of the men whom he had slain because of Gedaliah, was the one which

The Symbolic Version of Jeremiah

king Asa of Judah had made for fear of attack by Baasha king of Israel approximately 300 years before: Ishmael the son of Nethaniah filled it with the dead.

10 Then Ishmael carried away captive all the residue of the people that were in Mizpah, even the king's daughters, and all the people that remained in Mizpah, whom Nebuzaradan the captain of the guard had committed to Gedaliah the son of Ahikam: and Ishmael the son of Nethaniah carried them away captive, and departed to go over to the Ammonites.
11 But when Johanan the son of Kareah, and all the captains of the forces that were with him, heard of all the evil that Ishmael the son of Nethaniah had done,
12 Then they took all the men, and went to fight with Ishmael the son of Nethaniah, and found him by the great waters that are in Gibeon.
13 Now it came to pass, that when all the people which were with Ishmael saw Johanan the son of Kareah, and all the captains of the forces that were with him, then they were glad.
14 So all the people that Ishmael had carried away captive from Mizpah cast about and returned, and went unto Johanan the son of Kareah.
15 But Ishmael the son of Nethaniah escaped from Johanan with eight men, and went to the Ammonites.
16 Then took Johanan the son of Kareah, and all the captains of the forces that were with him, all the remnant of the people whom he had recovered from Ishmael the son of Nethaniah, from Mizpah, after that he had slain Gedaliah the son of Ahikam, even mighty men of war, and the women, and the children, and the eunuchs, whom he had brought again from Gibeon:
17 And they departed, and dwelt in the habitation of Chimham, which is by Bethlehem, to go to enter into Egypt,
18 Because of the Chaldeans: for they were afraid of them, because Ishmael the son of Nethaniah had slain Gedaliah the son of Ahikam, whom the king of Babylon made governor in the land.

Ishmael carried away as captives all the people that were in Mizpah, even the king's daughters, whom Nebuzaradan the captain of the guard had committed to Gedaliah. Ishmael departed to go over to the Ammonites. But when Johanan the son of Kareah, and all the captains of the forces that were with him, heard of all the evil that Ishmael had done, they took all their men, and went to fight with Ishmael, and found him by the great waters that are in Gibeon. When all the people who were taken captive with Ishmael were glad to see Johanan and all the captains of the forces that were with him and they went over to him. But Ishmael escaped from Johanan with eight men, and went to the Ammonites.

Then Johanan and his forces led away all the people of Mizpah whom he had recovered from Ishmael after the assassination of Gedaliah—mighty men of war, women, children, and eunuchs, whom he had brought from Gibeon—and they departed, and dwelt in the habitation of Chimham, which is by Bethlehem. Johanan prepared to enter into Egypt, because of the Chaldeans: they were afraid of them, because Ishmael had slain Gedaliah, whom the king of Babylon made governor of the land.

CHAPTER 42

1 Then all the captains of the forces, and Johanan the son of Kareah, and Jezaniah the son of Hoshaiah, and all the people from the least even unto the greatest, came near,
2 And said unto Jeremiah the prophet, Let, we beseech thee, our supplication be accepted before thee, and pray for us unto the LORD thy God, even for all this remnant; (for we are left but a few of many, as thine eyes do behold us:)
3 That the LORD thy God may shew us the way wherein we may walk, and the thing that we may do.
4 Then Jeremiah the prophet said unto them, I have heard you; behold, I will pray unto the LORD your God according to your words; and it shall come to pass, that whatsoever thing the LORD shall answer you, I will declare it unto you; I will keep nothing back from you.

Then, all the captains of the forces, Johanan, Jezaniah, and all the people from the least even unto the greatest came near and said to Jeremiah the prophet, Let, we beseech you, our supplication be accepted before you and pray for us to the LORD for all this remnant. The remnant of people are few in number, for we are left but a few of many, as your eyes can see. The people want the LORD to show them the way wherein they may walk, and the thing that they may do. Then Jeremiah the prophet said that he has heard them and will pray to the LORD God according to their words; and whatsoever the LORD answers, Jeremiah will declare it and keep nothing back from you.

5 Then they said to Jeremiah, The LORD be a true and faithful witness between us, if we do not even according to all things for the which the LORD thy God shall send thee to us.
6 Whether it be good, or whether it be evil, we will obey the voice of the LORD our God, to whom we send thee; that it may be well with us, when we obey the voice of the LORD our God.
7 And it came to pass after ten days, that the word of the LORD came unto Jeremiah.
8 Then called he Johanan the son of Kareah, and all the captains of the forces which were with him, and all the people from the least even to the greatest,
9 And said unto them, Thus saith the LORD, the God of Israel, unto whom ye sent me to present your supplication before him;
10 If ye will still abide in this land, then will I build you, and not pull you down, and I will plant you, and not pluck you up: for I repent me of the evil that I have done unto you.
11 Be not afraid of the king of Babylon, of whom ye are afraid; be not afraid of him, saith the LORD: for I am with you to save you, and to deliver you from his hand.
12 And I will shew mercies unto you, that he may have mercy upon you, and cause you to return to your own land.

Then the people said to Jeremiah, The LORD be a true and faithful witness between us, if we do not perform according to all things which the LORD your God shall send to us through you. Whether it be good, or whether it be evil, we will obey the voice of the LORD our God, to whom we send you as our representative. The people sense that all will go well with them when they obey the voice of the LORD their God. And it came to pass after ten days, that the word of the LORD came to Jeremiah.

Jeremiah called Johanan, the captains of the forces which were with him, and all the people from the least to the greatest, to deliver to them the word from the LORD to whom they sent Jeremiah to present their prayer to the LORD. The LORD says that if they will still abide in this land, then the LORD will build you, and not pull you down, and the LORD will plant you, and not pluck you up: for the LORD will show compassion on you to remove the evil that has befallen you according to the working of the Law of Sowing and Reaping through the consciousness of man.

Be not afraid of the king of Babylon says the LORD Who is with you to save you, and to deliver you from the hand of the king of Babylon. The LORD will show mercies to you, so that the mercy of the LORD shall be upon you, and cause you to return to your own land.

13 But if ye say, We will not dwell in this land, neither obey the voice of the LORD your God,
14 Saying, No; but we will go into the land of Egypt, where we shall see no war, nor hear the sound of the trumpet, nor have hunger of bread; and there will we dwell:
15 And now therefore hear the word of the LORD, ye remnant of Judah; Thus saith the LORD of hosts, the God of Israel; If ye wholly set your faces to enter into Egypt, and go to sojourn there;
16 Then it shall come to pass, that the sword, which ye feared, shall overtake you there in the land of Egypt, and the famine, whereof ye were afraid, shall follow close after you there in Egypt; and there ye shall die.
17 So shall it be with all the men that set their faces to go into Egypt to sojourn there; they shall die by the sword, by the famine, and by the pestilence: and none of them shall remain or escape from the evil that I will bring upon them.

But if you say, We will not dwell in this land, neither obey the voice of the LORD your God, saying, No; but we will go into the land of Egypt, where we shall see no war, nor hear the sound of the trumpet, nor have hunger of bread; and there will we dwell: therefore hear the word of the LORD, you remnant of Judah; Thus says the LORD of hosts, the God of Israel; If you wholly set your faces to enter into Egypt, and go to sojourn there; then it shall come to pass, that the sword, which you feared, shall overtake you there in the land of Egypt, and the famine, of which you were afraid, shall follow close after you there in Egypt; and there you shall die. So shall it be with all the men that set their faces to go into Egypt to sojourn there; they shall die by the sword, by the famine, and by the pestilence: and none of them shall remain or escape from the evil that the LORD will bring upon them in Egypt.

18 For thus saith the LORD of hosts, the God of Israel; As mine anger and my fury hath been poured forth upon the inhabitants of Jerusalem; so shall my fury be poured forth upon you, when ye shall enter into Egypt: and ye shall be an execration, and an astonishment, and a curse, and a reproach; and ye shall see this place no more.
19 The LORD hath said concerning you, O ye remnant of Judah; Go ye not into Egypt: know certainly that I have admonished you this day.
20 For ye dissembled in your hearts, when ye sent me unto the LORD your God, saying, Pray for us unto the LORD our God; and according unto all that the LORD our God shall say, so declare unto us, and we will do it.
21 And now I have this day declared it to you; but ye have not obeyed the voice of the LORD your God, nor any thing for the which he hath sent me unto you.
22 Now therefore know certainly that ye shall die by the sword, by the famine, and by the pestilence, in the place whither ye desire to go and to sojourn.

For thus says the LORD of hosts, the God of Israel; As His anger and fury have been poured forth upon the inhabitants of Jerusalem; so shall His fury be poured forth upon you, when you shall enter into Egypt: and you shall be an abomination, and an astonishment, and a curse, and a reproach; and you shall see this place no more. The LORD has said concerning you, O you remnant of Judah; Go not into Egypt: know certainly that the LORD has admonished you this day. For you dissembled in your hearts, when you sent me to the LORD your God, saying, Pray for us to the LORD our God; and according to all that the LORD our God shall say, so declare to us, and we will do it.

And now I have this day declared it to you; but you have not obeyed the voice of the LORD your God, nor anything for which the LORD has sent me to you. Now therefore know certainly that you shall die by the sword, by the famine, and by the pestilence, in the place where you desire to go, to settle and to dwell.

CHAPTER 43

1 And it came to pass, that when Jeremiah had made an end of speaking unto all the people all the words of the LORD their God, for which the LORD their God had sent him to them, even all these words,
2 Then spake Azariah the son of Hoshaiah, and Johanan the son of Kareah, and all the proud men, saying unto Jeremiah, Thou speakest falsely: the LORD our God hath not sent thee to say, Go not into Egypt to sojourn there:
3 But Baruch the son of Neriah setteth thee on against us, for to deliver us into the hand of the Chaldeans, that they might put us to death, and carry us away captives into Babylon.
4 So Johanan the son of Kareah, and all the captains of the forces, and all the people, obeyed not the voice of the LORD, to dwell in the land of Judah.
5 But Johanan the son of Kareah, and all the captains of the forces, took all the remnant of Judah, that were returned from all nations, whither they had been driven, to dwell in the land of Judah;
6 Even men, and women, and children, and the king's daughters, and every person that Nebuzaradan the captain of the guard had left with Gedaliah the son of Ahikam the son of Shaphan, and Jeremiah the prophet, and Baruch the son of Neriah.
7 So they came into the land of Egypt: for they obeyed not the voice of the LORD: thus came they even to Tahpanhes.

And it came to pass, when Jeremiah finished telling the people all the words of the LORD their God—everything that the LORD had sent Jeremiah to tell them—then spoke Azariah, and Johanan, and all the proud men accusing Jeremiah of speaking falsely. The LORD has not sent you to say, Go not into Egypt to settle there. Baruch the son of Neriah has set you against us to deliver us into the hand of the Chaldeans, that they might put us to death, and carry us away as captives into Babylon.

So Johanan and all the captains of the forces, and all the people, did not obey the voice of the LORD, to dwell in the land of Judah. The leaders took all the remnant of Judah, that were returned from all nations, from where they had been driven, to dwell in the land of Judah; men, and women, and children, and the king's daughters, and every person that Nebuzaradan the captain of the guard had left with Gedaliah and Jeremiah the prophet, and Baruch the son of Neriah, and they came to the land of Egypt. They did not obey the voice of the LORD. They came even to Tahpanhes, a city in the eastern delta region of Egypt.

8 Then came the word of the LORD unto Jeremiah in Tahpanhes, saying,
9 Take great stones in thine hand, and hide them in the clay in the brickkiln, which is at the entry of Pharaoh's house in Tahpanhes, in the sight of the men of Judah;
10 And say unto them, Thus saith the LORD of hosts, the God of Israel; Behold, I will send and take Nebuchadrezzar the king of Babylon, my servant, and will set his throne upon these stones that I have hid; and he shall spread his royal pavilion over them.
11 And when he cometh, he shall smite the land of Egypt, and deliver such as are for death to death; and such as are for captivity to captivity; and such as are for the sword to the sword.

12 And I will kindle a fire in the houses of the gods of Egypt; and he shall burn them, and carry them away captives: and he shall array himself with the land of Egypt, as a shepherd putteth on his garment; and he shall go forth from thence in peace.
13 He shall break also the images of Beth-she'mesh, that is in the land of Egypt; and the houses of the gods of the Egyptians shall he burn with fire.

Then came the word of the LORD to Jeremiah in Tahpanhes, saying, Take great stones in your hand, and hide them in the clay in the brick kiln, which is at the entry of Pharaoh's house in Tahpanhes, in the sight of the men of Judah. And say to them, Thus says the LORD of hosts, the God of Israel; Behold, I will send and take Nebuchadnezzar the king of Babylon, my servant, and will set his throne upon these stones that I have hid; and he shall spread his royal canopy over them.

When Nebuchadnezzar comes, he shall strike and defeat the land of Egypt, and deliver such as are for death to death; and such as are for captivity to captivity; and such as are for the sword to the sword.
And the power of the LORD working through Nebuchadnezzar will kindle a fire in the houses of the gods of Egypt; and he shall burn them, and carry them away captives. He shall array himself with the land of Egypt, as a shepherd puts on his garment; and he shall go forth from there in peace. He shall break also the images of Beth-she'mesh, that is in the land of Egypt; and the houses of the gods of the Egyptians shall he burn with fire.

CHAPTER 44

1 The word that came to Jeremiah concerning all the Jews which dwell in the land of Egypt, which dwell at Migdol, and at Tahpanhes, and at Noph, and in the country of Pathros, saying,
2 Thus saith the LORD of hosts, the God of Israel; Ye have seen all the evil that I have brought upon Jerusalem, and upon all the cities of Judah; and, behold, this day they are a desolation, and no man dwelleth therein,
3 Because of their wickedness which they have committed to provoke me to anger, in that they went to burn incense, and to serve other gods, whom they knew not, neither they, ye, nor your fathers.
4 Howbeit I sent unto you all my servants the prophets, rising early and sending them, saying, Oh, do not this abominable thing that I hate.
5 But they hearkened not, nor inclined their ear to turn from their wickedness, to burn no incense unto other gods.
6 Wherefore my fury and mine anger was poured forth, and was kindled in the cities of Judah and in the streets of Jerusalem; and they are wasted and desolate, as at this day.

The word that came to Jeremiah from the LORD concerning all the Jews that dwell in the land of Egypt— at Migdol, at Tahpanhes, at Noph, and in the country of Pathros—saying, thus says the LORD of hosts, the God of Israel: You have seen all the evil that the LORD has brought upon Jerusalem, and upon all the cities of Judah; and, behold, this day they are a desolation, and no man dwells therein because of their wickedness which they have committed to provoke the LORD to anger by the destructive aspect of the working of the Law. The people disobeyed the LORD in that they went to burn incense, and to serve other gods, whom they knew not, neither they, you, nor your fathers.

How is it that the LORD sent to you all my servants the prophets, rising early and sending them, saying, Oh, do not this abominable thing that I hate. But they hearkened not, nor inclined their ear to turn from their wickedness, to burn no incense to other gods. Wherefore the fury and the anger of the LORD was poured forth to destroy the practices which are not of the LORD's design; the destructive process was kindled in the cities of Judah and in the streets of Jerusalem; and they are wasted and desolate, as at this day.

7 Therefore now thus saith the LORD, the God of hosts, the God of Israel; Wherefore commit ye this great evil against your souls, to cut off from you man and woman, child and suckling, out of Judah, to leave you none to remain;
8 In that ye provoke me unto wrath with the works of your hands, burning incense unto other gods in the land of Egypt, whither ye be gone to dwell, that ye might cut yourselves off, and that ye might be a curse and a reproach among all the nations of the earth?
9 Have ye forgotten the wickedness of your fathers, and the wickedness of the kings of Judah, and the wickedness of their wives, and your own wickedness, and the wickedness of your wives, which they have committed in the land of Judah, and in the streets of Jerusalem?
10 They are not humbled even unto this day, neither have they feared, nor walked in my law, nor in my statutes, that I set before you and before your fathers.

The Symbolic Version of Jeremiah

Therefore, the LORD, the God of hosts, the God of Israel says; Why do you commit this great evil against your souls, to cut off from you man and woman, child and suckling, out of Judah, to leave you none to remain? In that you provoke the LORD to wrath with the works of your hands, burning incense to other gods in the land of Egypt, where you have gone to dwell, that you might cut yourselves off from the spirit of the LORD, and that you might be a curse and a reproach among all the nations of the earth?

Have you forgotten the wickedness of your fathers, the wickedness of the kings of Judah, the wickedness of their wives, your own wickedness, and the wickedness of your wives, which they have committed in the land of Judah, and in the streets of Jerusalem? They are not humbled even unto this day, neither have they feared, nor walked in the law of the LORD, nor in the statutes that the LORD has set before you and before your fathers.

11 Therefore thus saith the LORD of hosts, the God of Israel; Behold, I will set my face against you for evil, and to cut off all Judah.
12 And I will take the remnant of Judah, that have set their faces to go into the land of Egypt to sojourn there, and they shall all be consumed, and fall in the land of Egypt; they shall even be consumed by the sword and by the famine: they shall die, from the least even unto the greatest, by the sword and by the famine: and they shall be an execration, and an astonishment, and a curse, and a reproach.
13 For I will punish them that dwell in the land of Egypt, as I have punished Jerusalem, by the sword, by the famine, and by the pestilence:
14 So that none of the remnant of Judah, which are gone into the land of Egypt to sojourn there, shall escape or remain, that they should return into the land of Judah, to the which they have a desire to return to dwell there: for none shall return but such as shall escape.

Therefore the LORD of hosts, the God of Israel says; Behold, I will set my face against you for evil, and to cut off all Judah. I will take the remnant of Judah that have set their faces to go into the land of Egypt to settle there, and they shall all be consumed, and fall in the land of Egypt; they shall even be consumed by the sword and by the famine: they shall die, from the least even unto the greatest, by the sword and by the famine: and they shall be an abomination, an astonishment, a curse, and a reproach. For the LORD will punish them that dwell in the land of Egypt, as the working of the Law of the LORD has punished Jerusalem, by the sword, by the famine, and by the pestilence. The final result is that none of the remnant of Judah, the people who have gone into the land of Egypt to settle there, shall escape or remain, to return into the land of Judah, to which they have a desire to return to dwell there. No one shall return but such as shall escape.

15 Then all the men which knew that their wives had burned incense unto other gods, and all the women that stood by, a great multitude, even all the people that dwelt in the land of Egypt, in Pathros, answered Jeremiah, saying,
16 As for the word that thou hast spoken unto us in the name of the LORD, we will not hearken unto thee.
17 But we will certainly do whatsoever thing goeth forth out of our own mouth, to burn incense unto the queen of heaven, and to pour out drink offerings unto her, as we have done, we, and our fathers, our kings, and our princes, in the cities of Judah, and in the streets of Jerusalem: for then had we plenty of victuals, and were well, and saw no evil.
18 But since we left off to burn incense to the queen of heaven, and to pour out drink offerings unto her, we have wanted all things, and have been consumed by the sword and by the famine.
19 And when we burned incense to the queen of heaven, and poured out drink offerings unto her, did we make her cakes to worship her, and pour out drink offerings unto her, without our men?

Then all the men who knew that their wives had burned incense to other gods, and all the women that stood by, a great multitude, even all the people that dwelt in the land of Egypt, in Pathros, answered Jeremiah, saying, As for the word that you have spoken to us in the name of the LORD, we will not hearken to you. But we will certainly do whatsoever thing goes forth out of our own mouth, to burn incense to the queen of heaven (the queen of heaven is the earth), and to pour out drink offerings to her, as we have done—we, our fathers, our kings, and our princes, in the cities of Judah, and in the streets of Jerusalem. Then, we had we plenty of victuals, and were well, and saw no evil.

But since we ceased to burn incense to the queen of heaven, the earth, and to pour out drink offerings to her, we have wanted all things, and have been consumed by the sword and by the famine. And when we burned incense to the queen

The Testimony of the Major Prophets

of heaven, and poured out drink offerings to her, did we make cakes to worship her, and pour out drink offerings to her, without our men?

20 Then Jeremiah said unto all the people, to the men, and to the women, and to all the people which had given him that answer, saying,
21 The incense that ye burned in the cities of Judah, and in the streets of Jerusalem, ye, and your fathers, your kings, and your princes, and the people of the land, did not the LORD remember them, and came it not into his mind?
22 So that the LORD could no longer bear, because of the evil of your doings, and because of the abominations which ye have committed; therefore is your land a desolation, and an astonishment, and a curse, without an inhabitant, as at this day.
23 Because ye have burned incense, and because ye have sinned against the LORD, and have not obeyed the voice of the LORD, nor walked in his law, nor in his statutes, nor in his testimonies; therefore this evil is happened unto you, as at this day.

Then Jeremiah said to all the people who had given him that answer, saying, the incense that you burned in the cities of Judah, and in the streets of Jerusalem, you, your fathers, your kings, your princes, and the people of the land, did not the LORD remember them, and came it not into His mind? The LORD could no longer bear, because of the evil of your doings, and because of the abominations which you have committed; therefore your land is a desolation, and an astonishment, and a curse, without an inhabitant, as at this day. Because you have burned incense, and because you have sinned against the LORD, and have not obeyed the voice of the LORD, nor walked in His law, nor in His statutes, nor in His testimonies; therefore this evil is happened to you, as it is at this day.

24 Moreover Jeremiah said unto all the people, and to all the women, Hear the word of the LORD, all Judah that are in the land of Egypt:
25 Thus saith the LORD of hosts, the God of Israel, saying; Ye and your wives have both spoken with your mouths, and fulfilled with your hand, saying, We will surely perform our vows that we have vowed, to burn incense to the queen of heaven, and to pour out drink offerings unto her: ye will surely accomplish your vows, and surely perform your vows.
26 Therefore hear ye the word of the LORD, all Judah that dwell in the land of Egypt; Behold, I have sworn by my great name, saith the LORD, that my name shall no more be named in the mouth of any man of Judah in all the land of Egypt, saying, The Lord GOD liveth.

Moreover Jeremiah said to all the people, and to all the women, Hear the word of the LORD, all Judah that are in the land of Egypt: Thus says the LORD of hosts, the God of Israel, saying; You and your wives have both spoken with your mouths, and fulfilled with your hand, saying, We will surely perform our vows that we have vowed, to burn incense to the queen of heaven, and to pour out drink offerings to her: you will surely accomplish your vows, and surely perform your vows.

Therefore hear you the word of the LORD, all Judah that dwells in the land of Egypt; Behold, I have sworn by My great name, says the LORD, that My name shall no more be named in the mouth of any man of Judah in all the land of Egypt, saying, The Lord GOD lives.

27 Behold, I will watch over them for evil, and not for good: and all the men of Judah that are in the land of Egypt shall be consumed by the sword and by the famine, until there be an end of them.
28 Yet a small number that escape the sword shall return out of the land of Egypt into the land of Judah, and all the remnant of Judah, that are gone into the land of Egypt to sojourn there, shall know whose words shall stand, mine, or theirs.
29 And this shall be a sign unto you, saith the LORD, that I will punish you in this place, that ye may know that my words shall surely stand against you for evil:
30 Thus saith the LORD; Behold, I will give Pharaoh-hophra king of Egypt into the hand of his enemies, and into the hand of them that seek his life; as I gave Zedekiah king of Judah into the hand of Nebuchadrezzar king of Babylon, his enemy, and that sought his life.

Behold, The LORD will watch over the people in Egypt for evil, and not for good: and all the men of Judah that are in the land of Egypt shall be consumed by the sword and by the famine, the visible evidence of the operation of the Law, until there be an end of them. Yet, only a small number of people that escape the sword shall return out of the land of Egypt into the land of Judah. All the remnant of Judah, that have gone into the land of Egypt to settle there, shall know whose words shall stand, Mine, or theirs.

And this shall be a sign unto you, says the LORD, that I will punish you in this place, that you may know that My words shall surely stand against you for evil: the LORD says; Behold, I will give Pharaoh-hophra king of Egypt into the hand of his enemies, and into the hand of them that seek his life; as I gave Zedekiah king of Judah into the hand of Nebuchadnezzar king of Babylon, his enemy that was seeking his life. (Pharaoh-hophra was killed by his Egyptian rivals during a power struggle.)

CHAPTER 45

1 The word that Jeremiah the prophet spake unto Baruch the son of Neriah, when he had written these words in a book at the mouth of Jeremiah, in the fourth year of Jehoiakim the son of Josiah king of Judah, saying,
2 Thus saith the LORD, the God of Israel, unto thee, O Baruch;
3 Thou didst say, Woe is me now! for the LORD hath added grief to my sorrow; I fainted in my sighing, and I find no rest.
4 Thus shalt thou say unto him, The LORD saith thus; Behold, that which I have built will I break down, and that which I have planted I will pluck up, even this whole land.
5 And seekest thou great things for thyself? seek them not: for, behold, I will bring evil upon all flesh, saith the LORD: but thy life will I give unto thee for a prey in all places whither thou goest.

The word that Jeremiah the prophet spoke to Baruch the son of Neriah, when he had written these words in a book dictated from the mouth of Jeremiah, in the fourth year of Jehoiakim the son of Josiah king of Judah, saying, Thus says the LORD, the God of Israel, to you, O Baruch; You did say, Woe is me now! for the LORD has added grief to my sorrow; I fainted in my sighing, and I find no rest. Baruch is blaming the LORD as the source of woe, grief and sorrow. Baruch is blaming the LORD for the weakness of his sighing and the fact that he has found no rest.

Jeremiah, the prophet of the LORD says to Baruch to write for everyone to hear and know what the LORD says: Behold, that which the LORD has built, the LORD will break down, and that which the LORD has planted, the LORD will pluck up, even this whole land. The LORD is the power that does it all according to the working of the Law through the hearts and minds of mankind. The design is in the spirit of the LORD through each person.

And seek you great things for yourself? Seek them not! A person who seeks great things for himself is not letting the spirit of the LORD find expression through the person's heart, mind and body. Behold, the LORD will bring evil upon all flesh, says the LORD: but your life, the life that comes from the LORD, everlasting life, will the LORD give to you for an objective in all places where you go. The LORD has promised the constant flow of His life as the objective for a person while he is in flesh on earth. The prey, the objective, the target, is life.

CHAPTER 46

1 The word of the LORD which came to Jeremiah the prophet against the Gentiles;
2 Against Egypt, against the army of Pharaoh-necho king of Egypt, which was by the river Euphrates in Carchemish, which Nebuchadrezzar king of Babylon smote in the fourth year of Jehoiakim the son of Josiah king of Judah.
3 Order ye the buckler and shield, and draw near to battle.
4 Harness the horses; and get up, ye horsemen, and stand forth with your helmets; furbish the spears, and put on the brigandines.
5 Wherefore have I seen them dismayed and turned away back? and their mighty ones are beaten down, and are fled apace, and look not back: for fear was round about, saith the LORD.
6 Let not the swift flee away, nor the mighty man escape; they shallstumble, and fall toward the north by the river Euphrates.
7 Who is this that cometh up as a flood, whose waters are moved as the rivers?
8 Egypt riseth up like a flood, and his waters are moved like the rivers; and he saith, I will go up, and will cover the earth; I will destroy the city and the inhabitants thereof.
9 Come up, ye horses; and rage, ye chariots; and let the mighty men come forth; the Ethiopians and the Libyans, that handle the shield; and the Lydians, that handle and bend the bow.
10 For this is the day of the Lord GOD of hosts, a day of vengeance, that he may avenge him of his adversaries: and the sword shall devour, and it shall be satiate and made drunk with their blood: for the Lord GOD of hosts hath a sacrifice in the north country by the river Euphrates.

The word of the LORD came to Jeremiah the prophet against the Gentiles, which are the nations that are not the nation of the LORD. The word of the LORD through Jeremiah begins against Egypt, against the army of Pharaoh-necho king of Egypt. This Egyptian army was by the river Euphrates in Carchemish, which Nebuchadnezzar king of Babylon, in the first year of his reign, attacked in the fourth year of Jehoiakim the son of Josiah king of Judah. Egypt's defeat by the Babylonians was one of the most decisive battles of the ancient world ending Egypt's power in the area. The spirit of the LORD is destroying the distortions to the LORD's design that exists in the Egyptian Pharaohs. There is a call to victory over Egypt by the Babylonians.

Make ready your buckler and shield, and draw near to battle. Harness the horses; and get up, you horsemen, and stand forth with your helmets; furbish the spears, and put on protective armor.
Why has Jeremiah seen the Egyptians dismayed and turned back? their mighty ones are beaten down, and they flee in haste as they do not look back as they retreat: for fear was everywhere, says the LORD.

Let not the swift flee away, nor the mighty man escape; they shall stumble and fall toward the north by the river Euphrates. Who is this that comes up as a flood, whose waters are moved as the rivers? Egypt rises up like a flood, and his waters are moved like the rivers; and he says, I will go up, and will cover the earth; I will destroy the city and the inhabitants thereof. Come up, you horses; and rage, you chariots; and let the mighty men of Egypt come forth; the

The Testimony of the Major Prophets

Ethiopians and the Libyans that handle the shield; and the Lydians, that handle and bend the bow. For this is the day of the Lord GOD of hosts, a day of vengeance, that He may avenge Him of his adversaries: and the sword shall devour, and it shall be satisfied and made drunk with their blood: for the Lord GOD of hosts has a sacrifice in the north country by the river Euphrates as the Law of the LORD is in operation to destroy a design that is not of the LORD.

11 Go up into Gilead, and take balm, O virgin, the daughter of Egypt: in vain shalt thou use many medicines; for thou shalt not be cured.
12 The nations have heard of thy shame, and thy cry hath filled the land: for the mighty man hath stumbled against the mighty, and they are fallen both together.
13 The word that the LORD spake to Jeremiah the prophet, how Nebuchadrezzar king of Babylon should come and smite the land of Egypt.
14 Declare ye in Egypt, and publish in Migdol, and publish in Noph and in Tahpanhes: say ye, Stand fast, and prepare thee; for the sword shall devour round about thee.
15 Why are thy valiant men swept away? they stood not, because the LORD did drive them.
16 He made many to fall, yea, one fell upon another: and they said, Arise, and let us go again to our own people, and to the land of our nativity, from the oppressing sword.
17 They did cry there, Pharaoh king of Egypt is but a noise; he hath passed the time appointed.

Go up into Gilead, and take balm, O virgin, the daughter of Egypt: in vain shall you use many medicines; for you shall not be cured of this defeat. The nations have heard of your shame, and your cry has filled the land: for the mighty man has stumbled against the mighty, and they are fallen both together.

The word that the LORD spoke to Jeremiah the prophet, relates to how Nebuchadnezzar king of Babylon should come and defeat the land of Egypt. Declare you in Egypt, and publish in Migdol, and publish in Noph and in Tahpanhes: say you, Stand fast, and prepare yourself; for the sword shall devour round about you. Why are your valiant men swept away? they stood not, because the LORD did drive them. He made many to fall, yes, one fell upon another: and they said, Arise, and let us go again to our own people, and to the land of our nativity, from the oppressing sword. They did cry aloud there that Pharaoh king of Egypt is but a noise; he has passed the time appointed and his reign is at an end.

18 As I live, saith the King, whose name is the LORD of hosts, Surely as Tabor is among the mountains, and as Carmel by the sea, so shall he come.
19 O thou daughter dwelling in Egypt, furnish thyself to go into captivity: for Noph shall be waste and desolate without an inhabitant.
20 Egypt is like a very fair heifer, but destruction cometh; it cometh out of the north.
21 Also her hired men are in the midst of her like fatted bullocks; for they also are turned back, and are fled away together: they did not stand, because the day of their calamity was come upon them, and the time of their visitation.
22 The voice thereof shall go like a serpent; for they shall march with an army, and come against her with axes, as hewers of wood.
23 They shall cut down her forest, saith the LORD, though it cannot be searched; because they are more than the grasshoppers, and are innumerable.
24 The daughter of Egypt shall be confounded; she shall be delivered into the hand of the people of the north.
25 The LORD of hosts, the God of Israel, saith; Behold, I will punish the multitude of No, and Pharaoh, and Egypt, with their gods, and their kings; even Pharaoh, and all them that trust in him:
26 And I will deliver them into the hand of those that seek their lives, and into the hand of Nebuchadrezzar king of Babylon, and into the hand of his servants: and afterward it shall be inhabited, as in the days of old, saith the LORD.

As I live, says the King, whose name is the LORD of hosts, As surely as Tabor is among the mountains, and as Carmel by the sea, so shall the LORD come. O you daughter dwelling in Egypt, furnish yourself to go into captivity: for Noph shall be waste and desolate without an inhabitant. Egypt is like a very fair heifer, but destruction comes to a heifer; it comes out of the north. Also her hired men, the mercenaries, in the midst of her ranks, are like fatted bullocks; for they also are turned back, and are fled away together: they did not stand, because the day of their calamity was come upon them, and the time of their visitation from superior power to be punished.

The Symbolic Version of Jeremiah

The voice thereof shall go like a serpent; for they shall march with an army, and come against her with axes, as hewers of wood. They shall cut down her forest, says the LORD, though it cannot be searched; because they are more than the grasshoppers, and are innumerable. The daughter of Egypt shall be confounded; she shall be delivered into the hand of the people of the north.

The LORD of hosts, the God of Israel, speaking through Jeremiah says; Behold, I will punish the multitude of No, and Pharaoh, and Egypt, with their gods, and their kings; even Pharaoh, and all them that trust in him: The Law of the LORD will deliver them into the hand of those that seek their lives, and into the hand of Nebuchadnezzar king of Babylon, and into the hand of his servants: and afterward, Egypt shall be inhabited, as in the days of old, says the LORD.

27 But fear not thou, O my servant Jacob, and be not dismayed, O Israel: for, behold, I will save thee from afar off, and thy seed from the land of their captivity; and Jacob shall return, and be in rest and at ease, and none shall make him afraid.
28 Fear thou not, O Jacob my servant, saith the LORD: for I am with thee; for I will make a full end of all the nations whither I have driven thee: but I will not make a full end of thee, but correct thee in measure; yet will I not leave thee wholly unpunished.

Fear not, Jacob, the symbol of the material nature of man, who desires to ascend to the covenant of the LORD, and be not dismayed, O Israel, the spiritual nature of man which comes from the spirit of the LORD: for, behold, the LORD will save you from afar off, and your seed, your descendants, from the land of their captivity; and Jacob shall return, and be in rest and at ease, and none shall make him afraid. Fear not, O Jacob, the LORD's servant of the flesh, for the LORD is with you; for He will make a full end of all the distorted nations where the LORD has driven you by the operation of the Law: but the LORD will not make a full end of you, but correct you in measure according to the Law; yet the LORD will not leave you wholly unpunished during the corrective, creative process.

CHAPTER 47

1 The word of the LORD that came to Jeremiah the prophet against the Philistines, before that Pharaoh smote Gaza.
2 Thus saith the LORD; Behold, waters rise up out of the north, and shall be an overflowing flood, and shall overflow the land, and all that is therein; the city, and them that dwell therein: then the men shall cry, and all the inhabitants of the land shall howl.
3 At the noise of the stamping of the hoofs of his strong horses, at the rushing of his chariots, and at the rumbling of his wheels, the fathers shall not look back to their children for feebleness of hands;
4 Because of the day that cometh to spoil all the Philistines, and to cut off from Tyrus and Zidon every helper that remaineth: for the LORD will spoil the Philistines, the remnant of the country of Caphtor.
5 Baldness is come upon Gaza; Ashkelon is cut off with the remnant of their valley: how long wilt thou cut thyself?
6 O thou sword of the LORD, how long will it be ere thou be quiet? put up thyself into thy scabbard, rest, and be still.
7 How can it be quiet, seeing the LORD hath given it a charge against Ashkelon, and against the sea shore? there hath he appointed it.

The word of the LORD came to Jeremiah the prophet against the Philistines, before Pharaoh attacked them at Gaza, saying, Behold, waters as a symbol of the collective consciousness of an attacking army rise up out of the north, and shall be an overflowing flood as the army invades the land, and shall overflow the land, and all that is therein; the "waters" of the attackers shall flood the city and them that dwell therein: then the Philistine men who have been defeated in battle shall cry, and all the inhabitants of the land shall howl at the overwhelming defeat.

At the noise of the stamping of the hoofs of the strong Egyptian horses, at the rushing of their chariots, and at the rumbling of their wheels, the fathers shall not look back to their children for feebleness of the efforts of their hands; Because of the day that comes to spoil all the Philistines, and to cut them off from Tyrus and Zidon every helper from the north that remains. The LORD will spoil the Philistines, the remnant of the country of the coasts of Caphtor. (The Philistines were believed to have originated from one of the islands in the Mediterranean.)

Baldness that symbolizes a sign of mourning is come upon Gaza; Ashkelon is cut off with the remnant of their valley: how long will you cut yourself? O you sword of the LORD, the destructive cycle that eliminates the false creation by fallen man, how long will it be before you will be quiet? Put yourself into your scabbard, rest, and be still. How can it be quiet, seeing the LORD has given it a charge against Ashkelon, a city north of Gaza, and against the sea shore to destroy the people who serve the false gods of the earth? There has the LORD appointed His sword, His destructive power of the working of the Law, to destroy the false design that appears in the fabric of mankind. Jeremiah is aware that when the divine design of the LORD does not appear on earth, then the power of the sword of the LORD is at work in its destructive cycle and power to eliminate the distortion in the area. The action of the destructive cycle of the sword of the LORD has been described by Jeremiah against the Egyptians and the Philistines; he will inform of us the action against Moab.

CHAPTER 48

1 Against Moab thus saith the LORD of hosts, the God of Israel; Woe unto Nebo! for it is spoiled: Kiriathaim is confounded and taken: Misgab is confounded and dismayed.
2 There shall be no more praise of Moab: in Heshbon they have devised evil against it; come, and let us cut it off from being a nation. Also thou shalt be cut down, O Madmen; the sword shall pursue thee.
3 A voice of crying shall be from Horonaim, spoiling and great destruction.
4 Moab is destroyed; her little ones have caused a cry to be heard.
5 For in the going up of Luhith continual weeping shall go up; for in the going down of Horonaim the enemies have heard a cry of destruction.
6 Flee, save your lives, and be like the heath in the wilderness.
7 For because thou hast trusted in thy works and in thy treasures, thou shalt also be taken: and Chemosh shall go forth into captivity with his priests and his princes together.
8 And the spoiler shall come upon every city, and no city shall escape: the valley also shall perish, and the plain shall be destroyed, as the LORD hath spoken.

The LORD of hosts, the God of Israel, speaking through his prophet Jeremiah speaks of woe that will come upon Moab. Moab is a small nation, located on the eastern side of the Dead Sea, but it is proud and defiant like Assyria and Babylon. Specifically, three cities are mentioned because of the woe which will come upon these places due to the fallen behavior of the inhabitants and the operation of the Law of Sowing and Reaping. Nebo is described as spoiled due to the fallen behavior of the people; Kiriathaim is confounded and taken with the wrong example of others; Misgab is confounded and overwhelmed by the behavior of their neighbors.

There shall be no more praise of Moab which is perceived as an aggressor and an expansionist nation. In Heshbon, a city to the north which has a history of being a Levitical town with a religious heritage, they have devised evil against Moab to cut it off from being a nation. Also they shall be cut down because they are called madmen; the sword of the destructive cycle of the LORD shall pursue them and destroy them.
A voice of crying against Moab is spreading to other cities, such as Horonaim, who is spoiling for a great destruction due to its sins. Moab is destroyed; her little ones have caused a cry to be heard. For in the going up of Luhith, continual weeping shall go up; for in the going down of Horonaim, the enemies have heard a cry of destruction.

Flee, save your lives, and be like the heath, the bush, in the wilderness which survives its environment.
Because you have trusted in your deeds and in your material treasures, you shall also be taken. Chemosh, the national god of Moab, shall go forth into captivity with his priests and his princes together. The spoiler in the form of the sword of retribution shall come upon every city, and no city shall escape: the valley also shall perish, and the plain shall be destroyed, as the LORD has spoken that evil shall be destroyed.

The Testimony of the Major Prophets

9 Give wings unto Moab, that it may flee and get away: for the cities thereof shall be desolate, without any to dwell therein.
10 Cursed be he that doeth the work of the LORD deceitfully, and cursed be he that keepeth back his sword from blood.
11 Moab hath been at ease from his youth, and he hath settled on his lees, and hath not been emptied from vessel to vessel, neither hath he gone into captivity: therefore his taste remained in him, and his scent is not changed.
12 Therefore, behold, the days come, saith the LORD, that I will send unto him wanderers, that shall cause him to wander, and shall empty his vessels, and break their bottles.
13 And Moab shall be ashamed of Chemosh, as the house of Israel was ashamed of Bethel their confidence.
14 How say ye, We are mighty and strong men for the war?

Give wings of repentance and change to Moab, that it may flee and get away from its intended destruction due to the operation of the Law of the LORD: otherwise, the cities thereof shall be desolate, without any people to dwell in them. Cursed be he that does the work of the LORD deceitfully, and cursed be he that keeps back his sword, his body, mind and heart, from the blood of the spirit of the LORD. If people do not reveal the spirit of the LORD in their living, they shall be cursed instead of blessed. The people of Moab have been at ease, lazy, from their youth in the revelation of the spirit of the LORD. The people of Moab, who live in vineyards, have settled on their lees, their residues or dregs, and they have not been emptied from vessel to vessel to separate the dregs from the wine. They have become a contaminated people. They have not been taken into captivity where they could have learned new ways from their captors; therefore their taste remained within them, and their scent has not changed. In symbolic language, they have remained fallen sinners who have not purified themselves over the generations.

Therefore, behold, the days come, when the LORD will send them to wander, which shall cause the people to empty their vessels of consciousness and lose the dregs which symbolize their sins, and break their bottles of the old wine and replace it with new wine. Then, Moab shall be ashamed of Chemosh, their false god, as the house of Israel was ashamed of Bethel when they put their confidence in the northern kingdom of Israel instead of the LORD. How can either group say, We are mighty and strong men for the war?

15 Moab is spoiled, and gone up out of her cities, and his chosen young men are gone down to the slaughter, saith the King, whose name is the LORD of hosts.
16 The calamity of Moab is near to come, and his affliction hasteth fast.
17 All ye that are about him, bemoan him; and all ye that know his name, say, How is the strong staff broken, and the beautiful rod!
18 Thou daughter that dost inhabit Dibon, come down from thy glory, and sit in thirst; for the spoiler of Moab shall come upon thee, and he shall destroy thy strong holds.
19 O inhabitant of Aroer, stand by the way, and espy; ask him that fleeth, and her that escapeth, and say, What is done?

Moab is spoiled due to the sinful behavior of her people, and their evil behavior has gone up out of her cities, and their chosen young men whom the LORD has sent to them are gone down to the slaughter, says the King, whose name is the LORD of hosts. The fall of Moab is at hand and destruction will come quickly. All you that live among the people of Moab, who are in a state of decay, mourn his fallen condition; and all you that know the loss of his glory, exclaim, How is the strong staff that symbolizes material form be broken, and also the spiritual discipline and strength of the beautiful rod! The decay of Moab will spread to other cities. Other cities are personified as the daughter that inhabits the city of Dibon. It too will come down from its glory and sit in thirst for a better way. The spoiler, the fallen state of the absence of the spirit of the LORD, which is destroying Moab shall also come upon you and destroy your strongholds. The inhabitant of Aroer, stand by the way, and espy, perceive the flight of the people of Moab and ask him that flees and her that escapes, What is done? What has happened to cause you to flee and escape?

20 Moab is confounded; for it is broken down: howl and cry; tell ye it in Arnon, that Moab is spoiled,
21 And judgment is come upon the plain country; upon Holon, and upon Jahazah, and upon Mephaath,
22 And upon Dibon, and upon Nebo, and upon Beth-diblatha'im,
23 And upon Kiriathaim, and upon Bethgamul, and upon Bethmeon,
24 And upon Kerioth, and upon Bozrah, and upon all the cities of the land of Moab, far or near.

25 The horn of Moab is cut off, and his arm is broken, saith the LORD.
26 Make ye him drunken: for he magnified himself against the LORD: Moab also shall wallow in his vomit, and he also shall be in derision.
27 For was not Israel a derision unto thee? was he found among thieves? for since thou spakest of him, thou skippedst for joy.
28 O ye that dwell in Moab, leave the cities, and dwell in the rock, and be like the dove that maketh her nest in the sides of the hole's mouth.
29 We have heard the pride of Moab, (he is exceeding proud) his loftiness, and his arrogancy, and his pride, and the haughtiness of his heart.

Moab is confounded and broken down: howl and cry; tell it and spread the word along the Arnon river that Moab is spoiled and destroyed. Judgment is come upon the country of the plain; upon Holon, Jahazah, Mephaath, Dibon, Nebo, Beth-diblatha'im, Kiriathaim, Bethgamul, Bethmeon, Kerioth, Bozrah, and upon all the cities of the land of Moab, far or near. The horn, the collective means of expression through the people of Moab is cut off, and the strength of his mighty arm is broken, says the LORD.

Moab has behaved as a drunken people for he magnified himself against the LORD: the drunkenness of Moab was caused by the intoxication that results from disobeying the LORD, not drinking the wine of life, and Moab shall wallow in his vomit, and he shall be held in derision, scorn, ridicule and mockery. Was not Israel held in derision in the sight of the LORD? Was he found among thieves? for since you speak of him, you skip for joy. O you people that dwell in Moab, leave the cities, and dwell in the rock, away from the bad example of the people of Moab; be like the dove that makes her nest all alone in the sides of the opening to a cave. We have heard the pride of Moab, (he is exceeding proud) his loftiness, and his arrogance, and his pride, and the haughtiness of his heart. These fallen characteristics are the evidence of the pride that led to the fall of Moab.

30 I know his wrath, saith the LORD; but it shall not be so; his lies shall not so effect it.
31 Therefore will I howl for Moab, and I will cry out for all Moab; mine heart shall mourn for the men of Kirheres.
32 O vine of Sibmah, I will weep for thee with the weeping of Jazer: thy plants are gone over the sea, they reach even to the sea of Jazer: the spoiler is fallen upon thy summer fruits and upon thy vintage.
33 And joy and gladness is taken from the plentiful field, and from the land of Moab; and I have caused wine to fail from the winepresses: none shall tread with shouting; their shouting shall be no shouting.
34 From the cry of Heshbon even unto Elealeh, and even unto Jahaz, have they uttered their voice, from Zoar even unto Horonaim, as an heifer of three years old: for the waters also of Nimrim shall be desolate.
35 Moreover I will cause to cease in Moab, saith the LORD, him that offereth in the high places, and him that burneth incense to his gods.

The LORD knows the wrath of the people of Moab that led to its destruction; but it shall not remain and survive that way. The lies of the Moabites shall not change the outcome of their demise which was ordained by the operation of the Law. Therefore the LORD will cry out for all Moab to repent and change; His heart shall mourn for the men of Kirheres in southern Moab. The LORD, whose vine and branches are the people in the true design on earth, is aware of the vine and the branches composed of the people in the false and distorted design that will be destroyed. The LORD will weep for the people who compose the vine of Sibmah and Jazer which are north and west of the Dead Sea. The plants of the counterfeit design have spread as for as Jazer. The spoiler of the distorted design is fallen upon the summer fruits and upon the vintage, the harvest, so that joy and gladness is taken from the plentiful field, and from the land of Moab.

The action of the Law of the LORD causes the wine of life to fail from the winepresses that symbolize that which comes forth from the expression of people: none of the people shall tread with shouting because they are a part of the counterfeit design of the fallen state; their shouting shall be no shouting. From the cry of the people in the cities of Heshbon to Elealeh, from Zoar to Horonaim, and to Jahaz, they uttered their voices, as an heifer of three years old which is to be sacrificed. The waters also of Nimrim shall be desolate and dried up. Moreover the LORD will cause to cease in Moab, the person that offers sacrifices in the high places and burns incense to his false gods.

The Testimony of the Major Prophets

36 Therefore mine heart shall sound for Moab like pipes, and mine heart shall sound like pipes for the men of Kirheres: because the riches that he hath gotten are perished.
37 For every head shall be bald, and every beard clipped: upon all the hands shall be cuttings, and upon the loins sackcloth.
38 There shall be lamentation generally upon all the housetops of Moab, and in the streets thereof: for I have broken Moab like a vessel wherein is no pleasure, saith the LORD.
39 They shall howl, saying, How is it broken down! how hath Moab turned the back with shame! so shall Moab be a derision and a dismaying to all them about him.

Therefore the heart of the LORD within His fallen people shall sound like pipes, flutes, for Moab and the men of Kirheres because the riches that he has gotten from the LORD are perished and gone. Every head shall be bald, every beard cut off, all hands slashed and all loins covered with sackcloth as symbols of mourning. There shall be lamentation generally upon all the housetops and streets of Moab for the LORD has broken Moab like a vessel wherein there is no pleasure. They shall howl, saying, How is it broken down! how has Moab turned her back with shame! Moab shall be a derision and a dismaying to everyone round about him.

40 For thus saith the LORD; Behold, he shall fly as an eagle, and shall spread his wings over Moab.
41 Kerioth is taken, and the strong holds are surprised, and the mighty men's hearts in Moab at that day shall be as the heart of a woman in her pangs.
42 And Moab shall be destroyed from being a people, because he hath magnified himself against the LORD.
43 Fear, and the pit, and the snare, shall be upon thee, O inhabitant of Moab, saith the LORD.
44 He that fleeth from the fear shall fall into the pit; and he that getteth up out of the pit shall be taken in the snare: for I will bring upon it, even upon Moab, the year of their visitation, saith the LORD.
45 They that fled stood under the shadow of Heshbon because of the force: but a fire shall come forth out of Heshbon, and a flame from the midst of Sihon, and shall devour the corner of Moab, and the crown of the head of the tumultuous ones.
46 Woe be unto thee, O Moab! the people of Chemosh perisheth: for thy sons are taken captives, and thy daughters captives.
47 Yet will I bring again the captivity of Moab in the latter days, saith the LORD. Thus far is the judgment of Moab.

Behold, the LORD says, that His spirit shall fly as an eagle, and shall spread his wings in victory over Moab. Kerioth is taken, the strong holds are surprised, and the mighty men's hearts in Moab at that day shall be as the heart of a woman in her pangs as she labors to give birth to her child. Moab shall be destroyed from being a people, because he has magnified himself against the LORD, which is rebellion and disobedience.

The LORD says that fear, the pit, and the snare shall be upon the inhabitants of Moab. The person that flees from fear shall fall into the pit; and he that gets up out of the pit shall be taken in the snare: there is no escape from the Law which the LORD brings upon the people of Moab in the year of their punishment.

They that fled from Moab stood under the shadow of Heshbon, a city between Reuben and Gad, because of the force: but a fire shall come forth out of Heshbon, and a flame from the midst of Sihon, and shall devour the corner of Moab, and the crown of the head of the tumultuous ones. There is no escape from the operation of the Law of the LORD. Woe be unto you, people of Moab! the people who worship the false god of Moab, Chemosh, shall perish: for your sons and your daughters are taken captives for their distorted expressions, or sins, against the LORD. Yet the LORD will bring again the captivity of Moab in latter days into the design of the LORD but only if the people repent and change their fallen ways. Thus far is the judgment of Moab.

CHAPTER 49

1 Concerning the Ammonites, thus saith the LORD; Hath Israel no sons? hath he no heir? why then doth their king inherit Gad, and his people dwell in his cities?
2 Therefore, behold, the days come, saith the LORD, that I will cause an alarm of war to be heard in Rabbah of the Ammonites; and it shall be a desolate heap, and her daughters shall be burned with fire: then shall Israel be heir unto them that were his heirs, saith the LORD.
3 Howl, O Heshbon, for Ai is spoiled: cry, ye daughters of Rabbah, gird you with sackcloth; lament, and run to and fro by the hedges; for their king shall go into captivity, and his priests and his princes together.
4 Wherefore gloriest thou in the valleys, thy flowing valley, O backsliding daughter? that trusted in her treasures, saying, Who shall come unto me?
5 Behold, I will bring a fear upon thee, saith the Lord GOD of hosts, from all those that be about thee; and ye shall be driven out every man right forth; and none shall gather up him that wandereth.
6 And afterward I will bring again the captivity of the children of Ammon, saith the LORD.

This is what the LORD speaking through Jeremiah asks concerning the Ammonites, the people who lived in Ammon, the land east of the Jordan and north of Moab: Has Israel no sons? The sons of Israel were to occupy various portions of the promised land; the land of the twelve tribes. Is there no son of Israel to occupy this land or go to the defense of his brother? Has Israel no heir among all the people in the twelve tribes to occupy the land? Why then does their king, the king of the Ammonites, inherit Gad by invading it, and why do his people dwell in the cities of Gad, who was one of the sons of Israel? The Ammonites have expanded their influence and power into the west, into the land of Gad.

Therefore, behold, the days are coming when the LORD will cause an alarm of war to be heard in Rabbah, a metropolis, of the Ammonites; and the city shall be a desolate heap of ruins, and her daughters, the symbol of her surrounding villages, shall be set on fire: then Israel shall be the heir to them that were his heirs when Israel drives out the Ammonites away from Rabbah. Howl, O Heshbon, the city between the nations of Reuben and Gad, because the city of Ai is spoiled: cry, you villages of Rabbah in Ammon; gird yourselves with sackcloth to demonstrate your sorrow; lament and run to and fro by the hedges which serve as battle lines as the destructive results of war are inflicted on both sides. Jeremiah prophesies that the king of Ammon shall go into captivity along with his priests and his princes.

Why glorify yourselves in the valleys, your flowing valley, O backsliding daughter? who trusted in her treasures, saying, Who shall come to me? Behold, the Lord GOD of hosts will bring a fear upon you, from all those around you; and you every man shall be driven out forthright; and no one shall gather up the fugitives who wander. And afterward, the LORD will bring again the captivity of the children of Ammon into the house of the LORD as earthly kingdoms fall and return into the divine design.

7 Concerning Edom, thus saith the LORD of hosts; Is wisdom no more in Teman? is counsel perished from the prudent? is their wisdom vanished?

The Testimony of the Major Prophets

8 Flee ye, turn back, dwell deep, O inhabitants of Dedan; for I will bring the calamity of Esau upon him, the time that I will visit him.
9 If grapegatherers come to thee, would they not leave some gleaning grapes? if thieves by night, they will destroy till they have enough.
10 But I have made Esau bare, I have uncovered his secret places, and he shall not be able to hide himself: his seed is spoiled, and his brethren, and his neighbours, and he is not.
11 Leave thy fatherless children, I will preserve them alive; and let thy widows trust in me.

Thus says the LORD of hosts concerning Edom, the land to the south of Moab and the dead Sea, when He asks if there is no more wisdom in Teman? Teman was a city known for its wisdom. Has wise counsel perished from the prudent people who live in Teman? Has their wisdom vanished? The inhabitants of the city of Dedan are instructed to flee the city, turn back and dwell in caves for the LORD will bring the calamity of Esau upon him, when the power of the Law of the LORD visits Edom, which is the land of Esau.

If grape gatherers come to you, would they not leave some gleaning grapes for those who follow them? If thieves come by night, they will destroy until they have enough. But the power of the LORD will strip Esau (the brother of Jacob, who became Israel) bare. The LORD will uncover his secret places, so that he shall not be able to hide himself. His seed (his descendants) are spoiled, along with his brethren, and his neighbors, and he will be no more. Leave your fatherless children, and let your widows trust in the LORD who will let them live.

12 For thus saith the LORD; Behold, they whose judgment was not to drink of the cup have assuredly drunken; and art thou he that shall altogether go unpunished? thou shalt not go unpunished, but thou shalt surely drink of it.
13 For I have sworn by myself, saith the LORD, that Bozrah shall become a desolation, a reproach, a waste, and a curse; and all the cities thereof shall be perpetual wastes.
14 I have heard a rumour from the LORD, and an ambassador is sent unto the heathen, saying, Gather ye together, and come against her, and rise up to the battle.
15 For, lo, I will make thee small among the heathen, and despised among men.
16 Thy terribleness hath deceived thee, and the pride of thine heart, O thou that dwellest in the clefts of the rock, that holdest the height of the hill: though thou shouldest make thy nest as high as the eagle, I will bring thee down from thence, saith the LORD.

The LORD says, Behold, if the people, whose judgment was not to drink of the cup of the effects that are brought to them, must drink it, then why should you who are guilty go unpunished? You shall not go unpunished, but you shall surely drink the wine of effects from grapes which have been expressed. For the LORD has sworn that by the operation of the Law, Bozrah, a major city, shall become a desolation, a reproach, a waste, and a curse; and all the cities of the Ammonites shall be perpetual wastes.

Jeremiah has heard a message from the LORD, that an ambassador has been sent to the heathen, saying, Gather you together, and come against her, and rise up to the battle. But the power of the LORD will make you small among the heathen, and despised among men. Your terrible behavior and the pride of your heart has deceived you, the people that dwell in the clefts of the rock and who hold the height of the hill. The LORD says that though you should make your nest as high as the eagle, the power of the LORD will bring you down from there.

17 Also Edom shall be a desolation: every one that goeth by it shall be astonished, and shall hiss at all the plagues thereof.
18 As in the overthrow of Sodom and Gomorrah and the neighbour cities thereof, saith the LORD, no man shall abide there, neither shall a son of man dwell in it.
19 Behold, he shall come up like a lion from the swelling of Jordan against the habitation of the strong: but I will suddenly make him run away from her: and who is a chosen man, that I may appoint over her? for who is like me? and who will appoint me the time? and who is that shepherd that will stand before me?
20 Therefore hear the counsel of the LORD, that he hath taken against Edom; and his purposes, that he hath purposed against the inhabitants of Teman: Surely the least of the flock shall draw them out: surely he shall make their habitations desolate with them.
21 The earth is moved at the noise of their fall, at the cry the noise thereof was heard in the Red sea.

22 Behold, he shall come up and fly as the eagle, and spread his wings over Bozrah: and at that day shall the heart of the mighty men of Edom be as the heart of a woman in her pangs.

Edom shall be a desolation: every one that goes by it shall be astonished, and shall hiss their astonishment at all the plagues that take place there. As in the overthrow of Sodom and Gomorrah, and the neighbor cities, says the LORD, no man shall abide there, neither shall a son of man dwell in it. Behold, the Edomites shall come up to battle like a destructive lion, they shall rise up as the swelling of Jordan against the habitation of the strong: but the power of the LORD will suddenly chase them away from the army with the LORD's power. After the victory over the Edomites, who is a chosen man, that the LORD may appoint over her that has been vanquished? Who is like the LORD? Who will take the time to represent the LORD? Who is that shepherd that will stand before the LORD? The LORD is looking for a leader to represent Him on earth.

Therefore hear the counsel that the LORD has taken against Edom and His purposes against the inhabitants of Teman: Surely the least of the flock shall draw them out: surely he shall make their habitations desolate with them. The earth is moved at the noise of their fall and the cry of the noise of their defeat was heard previously at the Red sea when the LORD had a victory over the Egyptians under the leadership of Moses. Behold, a leader shall come up and fly as the eagle, and spread his wings over Bozrah: and at that day shall the hearts of the mighty men of Edom be as the heart of a woman in the pangs of labor. As earthly kingdoms fall, the LORD will take captive the people who were trapped in the pattern of the Ammonites.

23 Concerning Damascus. Hamath is confounded, and Arpad: for they have heard evil tidings: they are fainthearted; there is sorrow on the sea; it cannot be quiet.
24 Damascus is waxed feeble, and turneth herself to flee, and fear hath seized on her: anguish and sorrows have taken her, as a woman in travail.
25 How is the city of praise not left, the city of my joy!
26 Therefore her young men shall fall in her streets, and all the men of war shall be cut off in that day, saith the LORD of hosts.
27 And I will kindle a fire in the wall of Damascus, and it shall consume the palaces of Ben-ha'dad.

The LORD speaking through Jeremiah expressed these words concerning Damascus. Hamath and Arpad, cities in Aram (Syria) are confounded, for they have heard evil tidings: they are fainthearted; there is sorrow in the troubled hearts of the sea of their consciousness; it cannot be quieted. Damascus is grown more feeble; she has turned herself to flee, and fear has seized on her: anguish and sorrows have taken her, as a woman in the pains of labor that cannot think of anything else.

How is the city of praise not left, the city of my joy! The people have become more feeble, weak and disheartened and they have lost their strength. Therefore, according to the operation of the Law of Sowing and Reaping, her young men shall fall in her streets, and all the men of war shall be cut off in that day, says the LORD of hosts. And the LORD will kindle a fire in the wall of Damascus, and it shall consume the palaces of Ben-ha'dad. As this earthly kingdom falls, the LORD has taken captive the people who were in the false pattern. They have an opportunity to return to the LORD.

28 Concerning Kedar, and concerning the kingdoms of Hazor, which Nebuchadrezzar king of Babylon shall smite, thus saith the LORD; Arise ye, go up to Kedar, and spoil the men of the east.
29 Their tents and their flocks shall they take away: they shall take to themselves their curtains, and all their vessels, and their camels; and they shall cry unto them, Fear is on every side.
30 Flee, get you far off, dwell deep, O ye inhabitants of Hazor, saith the LORD; for Nebuchadrezzar king of Babylon hath taken counsel against you, and hath conceived a purpose against you.
31 Arise, get you up unto the wealthy nation, that dwelleth without care, saith the LORD, which have neither gates nor bars, which dwell alone.
32 And their camels shall be a booty, and the multitude of their cattle a spoil: and I will scatter into all winds them that are in the utmost corners; and I will bring their calamity from all sides thereof, saith the LORD.
33 And Hazor shall be a dwelling for dragons, and a desolation for ever: there shall no man abide there, nor any son of man dwell in it.

The Testimony of the Major Prophets

The word of the LORD through Jeremiah concerning Kedar, and concerning the kingdoms of Hazor, which Nebuchadnezzar king of Babylon shall attack, says, Arise, go up to Kedar, and destroy the men of the east. Take away their tents and their flocks: their curtains, all their vessels, and their camels. They shall cry to them, Fear is on every side. Flee, get you far away, hide deep in caves you inhabitants of Hazor, says the LORD. Nebuchadnezzar, king of Babylon has taken counsel against you, and has conceived a plan against you.

Arise, get you up to the wealthy nation, that dwells without care, says the LORD, which has neither gates nor bars, which dwell alone. Their camels shall be a booty, and the multitude of their cattle a spoil of war: the power of the LORD will scatter into all winds, in all directions, the people that are in the utmost corners; and the power of the Law will bring their calamity from all sides. And Hazor shall be a dwelling for predators, and a desolation for ever: there shall no man abide there, nor any son of man dwell in it. As this earthly kingdom falls, the LORD of hosts extends an opportunity for the people who were in that pattern to return to the LORD.

34 The word of the LORD that came to Jeremiah the prophet against Elam in the beginning of the reign of Zedekiah king of Judah, saying,
35 Thus saith the LORD of hosts; Behold, I will break the bow of Elam, the chief of their might.
36 And upon Elam will I bring the four winds from the four quarters of heaven, and will scatter them toward all those winds; and there shall be no nation whither the outcasts of Elam shall not come.
37 For I will cause Elam to be dismayed before their enemies, and before them that seek their life: and I will bring evil upon them, even my fierce anger, saith the LORD; and I will send the sword after them, till I have consumed them:
38 And I will set my throne in Elam, and will destroy from thence the king and the princes, saith the LORD.
39 But it shall come to pass in the latter days, that I will bring again the captivity of Elam, saith the LORD.

The word of the LORD of hosts came to Jeremiah the prophet against the province of Elam in the beginning of the reign of Zedekiah king of Judah, saying, Behold, I will break the bow, the symbol of the cause of their might, that gives strength to Elam. The power of the LORD moving through the people will bring the four winds, the four directions of the moving spirit from the four quarters of heaven, the place of cause in the consciousness of people through which the spirit moves, and the action of spirit on earth will scatter the people of Elam toward all those winds; and there shall be no nation where the exiles, the outcasts of Elam, shall not come as they disperse in disarray.

The power of the LORD will cause Elam to be dismayed before their enemies, and before them that seek their lives: and the power of the LORD in its destructive cycle will bring evil upon them, even the fierce anger of the LORD, Who send the destructive power of the sword after them, till the LORD has consumed them. The LORD will set His throne, his presence of power, in Elam, will destroy the king and the princes, who ruled Elam. But it shall come to pass, in the latter days, eventually, that the LORD will bring again the captivity of the people of Elam into the courtyards of the LORD. As earthly kingdoms fall, the pieces may be used to build the kingdom of the LORD on earth through those who will be His servants.

CHAPTER 50

1 The word that the LORD spake against Babylon and against the land of the Chaldeans by Jeremiah the prophet.
2 Declare ye among the nations, and publish, and set up a standard; publish, and conceal not: say, Babylon is taken, Bel is confounded, Merodach is broken in pieces; her idols are confounded, her images are broken in pieces.
3 For out of the north there cometh up a nation against her, which shall make her land desolate, and none shall dwell therein: they shall remove, they shall depart, both man and beast.
4 In those days, and in that time, saith the LORD, the children of Israel shall come, they and the children of Judah together, going and weeping: they shall go, and seek the LORD their God.

The word that the LORD spoke against Babylon and against the land of the Chaldeans by Jeremiah the prophet. Declare among the nations, people who hear the words, publish and set up a standard, a banner; and do not conceal the information that Babylon will be taken, Bel, a false god, will be confounded with terror, Merodach will be broken in pieces; her idols are confounded and her images broken in pieces. A nation will come out of the north against the Babylonians, which shall make the land of Babylon desolate; no one shall dwell therein as both man and beast depart. In those days, and in that time, says the LORD, the children of Israel shall come, they and the children of Judah together, going and weeping: they shall go, and seek the LORD their God and weep because they have not found the LORD.

5 They shall ask the way to Zion with their faces thitherward, saying, Come, and let us join ourselves to the LORD in a perpetual covenant that shall not be forgotten.
6 My people hath been lost sheep: their shepherds have caused them to go astray, they have turned them away on the mountains: they have gone from mountain to hill, they have forgotten their restingplace.
7 All that found them have devoured them: and their adversaries said, We offend not, because they have sinned against the LORD, the habitation of justice, even the LORD, the hope of their fathers.
8 Remove out of the midst of Babylon, and go forth out of the land of the Chaldeans, and be as the he goats before the flocks.
9 For, lo, I will raise and cause to come up against Babylon an assembly of great nations from the north country: and they shall set themselves in array against her; from thence she shall be taken: their arrows shall be as of a mighty expert man; none shall return in vain.
10 And Chaldea shall be a spoil: all that spoil her shall be satisfied, saith the LORD.

They shall ask the way to Zion with their faces thitherward, facing in that direction, as they have turned to the LORD, saying, Come, and let us join ourselves to the LORD in a perpetual covenant that shall not be forgotten. This is an admission that they have turned away from the LORD. Jeremiah declares that his people have been lost sheep: their shepherds have caused them to go astray, they have turned them away on the mountains of material goals: they have gone from mountain to hill which symbolizes that they are changing from high materialistic goals to lower goals; they have forgotten their resting place is in the spirit of the LORD their God. All the people who found them in this

The Testimony of the Major Prophets

weakened condition without the full force of the spirit of the LORD moving through them have devoured them: and their adversaries said, We do not offend the LORD, because they have sinned against the LORD, who is the habitation of justice, and the hope of their fathers.

The LORD's people must be removed out of the midst of Babylon and the land of the Chaldeans, and be as the he-goats that lead the flocks to safe pasture. For, lo, the LORD will raise and cause to come up against Babylon an assembly of great nations from the north country: and they shall set themselves in array against her; from there, she shall be taken captive: their arrows shall be as of a mighty expert man which hit the mark and none shall return in vain. And Chaldea shall be a spoil of war: all that plunder her shall be satisfied, says the LORD.

11 Because ye were glad, because ye rejoiced, O ye destroyers of mine heritage, because ye are grown fat as the heifer at grass, and bellow as bulls;
12 Your mother shall be sore confounded; she that bare you shall be ashamed: behold, the hindermost of the nations shall be a wilderness, a dry land, and a desert.
13 Because of the wrath of the LORD it shall not be inhabited, but it shall be wholly desolate: every one that goeth by Babylon shall be astonished, and hiss at all her plagues.
14 Put yourselves in array against Babylon round about: all ye that bend the bow, shoot at her, spare no arrows: for she hath sinned against the LORD.
15 Shout against her round about: she hath given her hand: her foundations are fallen, her walls are thrown down: for it is the vengeance of the LORD: take vengeance upon her; as she hath done, do unto her.
16 Cut off the sower from Babylon, and him that handleth the sickle in the time of harvest: for fear of the oppressing sword they shall turn every one to his people, and they shall flee every one to his own land.

The LORD through Jeremiah speaks to the destroyers of His heritage, the heritage which is the kingdom of the LORD on earth. The disobedient people have failed in their responsibility to serve the LORD and be His people that carry His spirit. They disobeyed the LORD because they were glad and rejoiced in their own self-centeredness; they have grown fat as the heifer at grass, and they bellow their selfish wants as bulls. Your mother that bore you shall be sorely confounded and ashamed; behold, the least guilty of the nations shall be a wilderness, a dry land, and a desert. Due to the operation of the Law of Sowing and Reaping which produced the wrath of the LORD, instead of the blessing that the environment could have been, the land shall not be inhabited, but it shall be wholly desolate: every one that goes by Babylon shall be astonished, and hiss at the astonishment and deterioration of all her plagues.

The people are advised to put themselves in array, to line up, against the wrong example that produced the fallen state of Babylon everywhere. All you that bend the bow from your own source of cause that contributes to the conditions of the fallen world, shoot at her, and spare no arrows: for the material example of Babylon has sinned against the LORD. Shout against her everywhere; she has given her hand of control to others; her foundations are fallen, her walls are thrown down: for it is the vengeance of the LORD that has produced her fall: take vengeance upon her; as she has done, do to her. This is the working of the Law. Cut off the sower from Babylon, and him that handles the sickle, the reaping, in the time of harvest: for fear of the oppressing sword in which the LORD rewards or punishes the people according to the seed that they sow, then, people shall return to His people, and every one shall flee to his own land where everyone is a lamb to the LORD.

17 Israel is a scattered sheep; the lions have driven him away: first the king of Assyria hath devoured him; and last this Nebuchadrezzar king of Babylon hath broken his bones.
18 Therefore thus saith the LORD of hosts, the God of Israel; Behold, I will punish the king of Babylon and his land, as I have punished the king of Assyria.
19 And I will bring Israel again to his habitation, and he shall feed on Carmel and Bashan, and his soul shall be satisfied upon mount Ephraim and Gilead.
20 In those days, and in that time, saith the LORD, the iniquity of Israel shall be sought for, and there shall be none; and the sins of Judah, and they shall not be found: for I will pardon them whom I reserve.

The people of Israel, the true state of spiritual mankind on earth, are like scattered sheep; the more powerful lions have driven the sheep away: first the king of Assyria has devoured them; and last this Nebuchadnezzar king of Babylon has broken their bones. Therefore thus says the LORD of hosts, the God of Israel; Behold, I will punish the king of

The Symbolic Version of Jeremiah

Babylon and his land, as I have punished the king of Assyria. And I will bring Israel, the spiritual people of the LORD, again to his habitation, and he shall feed on Carmel and Bashan, and his soul shall be satisfied upon mount Ephraim and Gilead. In those days, and in that time, says the LORD, the iniquity of Israel, the spiritual person, shall be sought for, and there shall be no one who disobeys the LORD; and the sins of Judah shall be searched for in the distorted material conditions, and they shall not be found: for the LORD will pardon the remnant of people whom the LORD spares and reserves. The divine design of the LORD, the garden of Eden, shall return to the earth in manifest form.

21 Go up against the land of Merathaim, even against it, and against the inhabitants of Pekod: waste and utterly destroy after them, saith the LORD, and do according to all that I have commanded thee.
22 A sound of battle is in the land, and of great destruction.
23 How is the hammer of the whole earth cut asunder and broken! how is Babylon become a desolation among the nations!
24 I have laid a snare for thee, and thou art also taken, O Babylon, and thou wast not aware: thou art found, and also caught, because thou hast striven against the LORD.
25 The LORD hath opened his armoury, and hath brought forth the weapons of his indignation: for this is the work of the Lord GOD of hosts in the land of the Chaldeans.
26 Come against her from the utmost border, open her storehouses: cast her up as heaps, and destroy her utterly: let nothing of her be left.
27 Slay all her bullocks; let them go down to the slaughter: woe unto them! for their day is come, the time of their visitation.

Go up against the land of Merathaim, which means, "double rebellion against the LORD", and against the inhabitants of Pekod, which means, "punishment": waste and utterly destroy after them, says the LORD, and do according to all that I have commanded you. A sound of battle is in the land, and of great destruction. How is the hammer of the whole earth cut asunder and broken! how is Babylon become a desolation among the nations! The LORD has laid a snare for you and you are also taken, O Babylon, and you were not aware that the LORD was at work: you are found, and also caught, because you have disobeyed and opposed the LORD. The LORD has opened his armory, and has brought forth the weapons of his indignation according to the operation of the Law for this is the work of the Lord GOD of hosts in the land of the Chaldeans. Come against her from the utmost border, open her storehouses: cast her up as heaps, and utterly destroy her: let nothing of her be left. Slay all her bullocks; let them go down to the slaughter: woe unto them! for their day is come, the time of their visitation by the punishment of the LORD according to the evil that they have produced. The LORD is calling for the return of the kingdom of Zion.

28 The voice of them that flee and escape out of the land of Babylon, to declare in Zion the vengeance of the LORD our God, the vengeance of his temple.
29 Call together the archers against Babylon: all ye that bend the bow, camp against it round about; let none thereof escape: recompense her according to her work; according to all that she hath done, do unto her: for she hath been proud against the LORD, against the Holy One of Israel.
30 Therefore shall her young men fall in the streets, and all her men of war shall be cut off in that day, saith the LORD.

The voice of them that flee and escape out of the land of Babylon, the distorted materialistic state, to declare in Zion, the true restored state of the LORD on earth, demonstrates the vengeance of the LORD our God, the vengeance of his temple. As people representing Zion sow, so they shall reap. Call together the archers against Babylon: all you that bend the bow to send the arrows of your expressions into the world, camp against the environmental world round about which is a terrible distortion of the true design; let none thereof escape: recompense her according to her work; according to all that she has done, do to her: for she has been filled with pride and defied the LORD and been against the Holy One of Israel. Therefore shall Babylon's young men fall in the streets, and all her men of war shall be cut off in that day, the day when the way of the LORD comes through His creation of man.

31 Behold, I am against thee, O thou most proud, saith the Lord GOD of hosts: for thy day is come, the time that I will visit thee.
32 And the most proud shall stumble and fall, and none shall raise him up: and I will kindle a fire in his cities, and it shall devour all round about him.

The Testimony of the Major Prophets

33 Thus saith the LORD of hosts; The children of Israel and the children of Judah were oppressed together: and all that took them captives held them fast; they refused to let them go.
34 Their Redeemer is strong; the LORD of hosts is his name: he shall throughly plead their cause, that he may give rest to the land, and disquiet the inhabitants of Babylon.

Behold, the LORD, I AM, against you, O you most proud, Babylon, the symbol of all who are against the LORD, says the Lord GOD of hosts: for your day is come, the time that the LORD will visit you. And the most proud of the fallen state shall stumble and fall, and no one shall raise him up: and the LORD will kindle a fire in his cities, and it shall devour everything that is not of the LORD round about him. Thus says the LORD of hosts; The children of Israel, who are spiritual children, and the children of Judah, who are fallen and distorted material children who desire to return to the LORD were oppressed together: and all that took them captives held them fast; they refused to let them go.

Their Redeemer, the Redeemer of both the children of Israel and the children of Judah, is strong; the LORD of hosts is his name: the LORD shall thoroughly plead their cause, so that he may give rest to the land, and disquiet the inhabitants of Babylon who are the sinners of the fallen state.

35 A sword is upon the Chaldeans, saith the LORD, and upon the inhabitants of Babylon, and upon her princes, and upon her wise men.
36 A sword is upon the liars; and they shall dote: a sword is upon her mighty men; and they shall be dismayed.
37 A sword is upon their horses, and upon their chariots, and upon all the mingled people that are in the midst of her; and they shall become as women: a sword is upon her treasures; and they shall be robbed.
38 A drought is upon her waters; and they shall be dried up: for it is the land of graven images, and they are mad upon their idols.
39 Therefore the wild beasts of the desert with the wild beasts of the islands shall dwell there, and the owls shall dwell therein: and it shall be no more inhabited for ever; neither shall it be dwelt in from generation to generation.
40 As God overthrew Sodom and Gomorrah and the neighbour cities thereof, saith the LORD; so shall no man abide there, neither shall any son of man dwell therein.
41 Behold, a people shall come from the north, and a great nation, and many kings shall be raised up from the coasts of the earth.
42 They shall hold the bow and the lance: they are cruel, and will not shew mercy: their voice shall roar like the sea, and they shall ride upon horses, every one put in array, like a man to the battle, against thee, O daughter of Babylon.
43 The king of Babylon hath heard the report of them, and his hands waxed feeble: anguish took hold of him, and pangs as of a woman in travail.

The LORD says that there is a sword, the sword of the power of the spirit of the LORD, which is upon the Chaldeans, upon the inhabitants of Babylon, upon her princes, and upon her wise men. A sword is upon the liars of Babylon; and they shall dote: a sword is upon her mighty men; and they shall be dismayed. A sword is upon their horses, chariots, and upon all the people that are mingled in the midst of Babylon; and they shall become as women: a sword is upon her treasures; and they shall be robbed. A drought is upon her waters; and they shall be dried up: for Babylon is the symbol of the land of graven images, and they are mad with their attachments to their idols. Therefore the wild beasts of the desert with the wild beasts of the islands shall dwell there, and the owls shall dwell within the fallen state of Babylon that fallen man has made: and this fallen state shall be inhabited no more for ever; neither shall it be dwelt in from generation to generation by those who love the LORD.

As God overthrew Sodom and Gomorrah, and the neighbor cities thereof, says the LORD; so shall no man abide there in the fallen state, neither shall any son of man dwell therein. Behold, a people shall come from the north, and a great nation, and many kings shall be raised up from the coasts of the earth to destroy the people of Babylon. They shall hold the bow and the lance: they are cruel, and they will not show mercy: their voice shall roar like the sea, and they shall ride upon horses, every one put in an orderly array, like a man to the battle against you, O daughter of Babylon, who symbolizes the sinful and distorted state of mankind. The king of Babylon has heard the report of them that will invade and destroy him and his land; and his hands grow more feeble: anguish took hold of him, and pangs of pain as of a woman in labor.

The Symbolic Version of Jeremiah

44 Behold, he shall come up like a lion from the swelling of Jordan unto the habitation of the strong: but I will make them suddenly run away from her: and who is a chosen man, that I may appoint over her? for who is like me? and who will appoint me the time? and who is that shepherd that will stand before me?
45 Therefore hear ye the counsel of the LORD, that he hath taken against Babylon; and his purposes, that he hath purposed against the land of the Chaldeans: Surely the least of the flock shall draw them out: surely he shall make their habitation desolate with them.
46 At the noise of the taking of Babylon the earth is moved, and the cry is heard among the nations.

Behold, Babylon shall come up like a lion from the swelling of Jordan to the habitation of the strong: but the LORD will make them suddenly run away from her: and who is a chosen man, who represents the spirit of the LORD, that the LORD may appoint over Babylon? for who is like the LORD? and who will give the LORD the time to let the spirit of the LORD come to focus in a body? and who is that shepherd that will stand before the LORD?

Therefore each person should hear the counsel of the LORD, that He has taken against Babylon; and the LORD's plan against the land of the Chaldeans: Surely the least of the flock of the sheep of the LORD shall draw out the Babylonians: surely the power of the LORD shall make their habitation desolate with them. At the noise of the capture of Babylon, the earth is moved by the victory of the spirit, and the cry of victory is heard among the nations.

CHAPTER 51

1 Thus saith the LORD; Behold, I will raise up against Babylon, and against them that dwell in the midst of them that rise up against me, a destroying wind;
2 And will send unto Babylon fanners, that shall fan her, and shall empty her land: for in the day of trouble they shall be against her round about.
3 Against him that bendeth let the archer bend his bow, and against him that lifteth himself up in his brigandine: and spare ye not her young men; destroy ye utterly all her host.
4 Thus the slain shall fall in the land of the Chaldeans, and they that are thrust through in her streets.
5 For Israel hath not been forsaken, nor Judah of his God, of the LORD of hosts; though their land was filled with sin against the Holy One of Israel.

The LORD speaking through Jeremiah says; Behold, the power of the LORD will raise up a destroying wind, a destructive movement of the spirit, against Babylon, and against them that dwell in the midst of them that rise up against the LORD; and will send fanners, people who carry a like spirit to fan her and increase the force that empties the land of Babylon: for in the day of trouble they shall be against her on every side. Let the archer bend his bow against him that bends a bow against him and the person who lifts himself up in his armor: and do not spare her young men; destroy utterly all her hosts. Thus the slain shall fall in the land of the Chaldeans, and they that are thrust through in her streets. For Israel, the spiritual man, nor Judah, the material man in the fallen state, has not been forsaken, of his God, of the LORD of hosts; though their land was filled with sin against the Holy One of Israel.

6 Flee out of the midst of Babylon, and deliver every man his soul: be not cut off in her iniquity; for this is the time of the LORD's vengeance; he will render unto her a recompence.
7 Babylon hath been a golden cup in the LORD's hand, that made all the earth drunken: the nations have drunken of her wine; therefore the nations are mad.
8 Babylon is suddenly fallen and destroyed: howl for her; take balm for her pain, if so be she may be healed.
9 We would have healed Babylon, but she is not healed: forsake her, and let us go every one into his own country: for her judgment reacheth unto heaven, and is lifted up even to the skies.

Flee from out of the midst of Babylon, and let every man deliver his soul—his heart, mind and body—to the LORD: be not cut off from the spirit of the LORD in the iniquity of Babylon; for this is the time of the LORD's vengeance Who will render a recompense to her. Babylon has been a golden cup in the LORD's hand, that made all the earth drunk: the nations have drunken of her wine; therefore the nations have gone mad with the wine of Babylon. Babylon is suddenly fallen and destroyed: howl for her; take balm for her pain, if so be, she may be healed. We would have healed Babylon, but she is not healed: forsake her because she does not want to be healed; let every one go into his own country: for her judgment reaches to heaven, and is lifted up even to the skies where the LORD shall wreak vengeance on Babylon according to the Law.

The Symbolic Version of Jeremiah

10 The LORD hath brought forth our righteousness: come, and let us declare in Zion the work of the LORD our God.
11 Make bright the arrows; gather the shields: the LORD hath raised up the spirit of the kings of the Medes: for his device is against Babylon, to destroy it; because it is the vengeance of the LORD, the vengeance of his temple.
12 Set up the standard upon the walls of Babylon, make the watch strong, set up the watchmen, prepare the ambushes: for the LORD hath both devised and done that which he spake against the inhabitants of Babylon.
13 O thou that dwellest upon many waters, abundant in treasures, thine end is come, and the measure of thy covetousness.

The LORD has brought forth our righteousness: come, and let us declare in Zion, the place of spirit within each of us, the work of the LORD our God. Make bright the arrows; gather the shields: the LORD has raised up the spirit of the kings of the Medes: for his device is against Babylon, to destroy it; because it is the vengeance of the LORD, the vengeance of his temple. Set up the standard upon the walls of Babylon, make the watch strong, set up the watchmen, prepare the ambushes: for the LORD has both devised and done that which He spoke against the inhabitants of Babylon. O you that dwell upon many waters, abundant in treasures, your end is come, and the measure of your covetousness.

14 The LORD of hosts hath sworn by himself, saying, Surely I will fill thee with men, as with caterpillers; and they shall lift up a shout against thee.
15 He hath made the earth by his power, he hath established the world by his wisdom, and hath stretched out the heaven by his understanding.
16 When he uttereth his voice, there is a multitude of waters in the heavens; and he causeth the vapours to ascend from the ends of the earth: he maketh lightnings with rain, and bringeth forth the wind out of his treasures.
17 Every man is brutish by his knowledge; every founder is confounded by the graven image: for his molten image is falsehood, and there is no breath in them.
18 They are vanity, the work of errors: in the time of their visitation they shall perish.
19 The portion of Jacob is not like them; for he is the former of all things: and Israel is the rod of his inheritance: the LORD of hosts is his name.

The LORD of hosts has sworn that He shall fill the earth with men, as He fills the earth with caterpillars that turn into butterflies; and they shall lift up a shout against the fallen state of man. The LORD has made the earth by His power, established the world by His wisdom, and has stretched out the heaven by His understanding. When he utters His voice, there is a multitude of waters in the heavens that respond to His voice; and He causes the vapors from the waters to ascend from the ends of the earth: He makes lightning with rain, and brings forth the wind of the spirit out of his treasures.

Every man is brutish compared to the extent of His knowledge; every founder, every man on earth, is confounded by the graven image which he sees in his consciousness: for his molten image, the material image that he sees in his consciousness, is a falsehood, and there is no breath, no living spirit of the LORD, in the false images. The false images of fallen man are vanity, the work of errors: in the time of their punishment they shall perish. The portion of Jacob that is from the LORD is not like counterfeit man in the fallen state; for ascended man is the former of all things that led to man in the ascended state that became Israel as the caterpillar became a butterfly: and Israel, the spirit from the LORD in man, is the rod of his inheritance: the LORD of hosts is his name.

20 Thou art my battle axe and weapons of war: for with thee will I break in pieces the nations, and with thee will I destroy kingdoms;
21 And with thee will I break in pieces the horse and his rider; and with thee will I break in pieces the chariot and his rider;
22 With thee also will I break in pieces man and woman; and with thee will I break in pieces old and young; and with thee will I break in pieces the young man and the maid;
23 I will also break in pieces with thee the shepherd and his flock; and with thee will I break in pieces the husbandman and his yoke of oxen; and with thee will I break in pieces captains and rulers.

The Testimony of the Major Prophets

24 And I will render unto Babylon and to all the inhabitants of Chaldea all their evil that they have done in Zion in your sight, saith the LORD.

Man in his true state, the ascended state not the fallen state, is the battle ax and the weapons of war for the LORD: for with man in His hand, the LORD will break in pieces the nations, and destroy kingdoms; And with ascended man the LORD will break in pieces the horse and his rider, the chariot and his rider; man and woman; the old and young; the young man and the maid; the shepherd and his flock; the husbandman and his yoke of oxen; captains and rulers. The LORD with His spirit moving through a body of man in His hand will render to Babylon and to all the inhabitants of Chaldea according to the Law of Sowing and Reaping all the evil that they have done in Zion, the true spiritual design on earth, so that you can see it in your own sight, says the LORD.

25 Behold, I am against thee, O destroying mountain, saith the LORD, which destroyest all the earth: and I will stretch out mine hand upon thee, and roll thee down from the rocks, and will make thee a burnt mountain.
26 And they shall not take of thee a stone for a corner, nor a stone for foundations; but thou shalt be desolate for ever, saith the LORD.

Behold, the LORD is against the fallen state of man, who is compared to a destroying mountain, a destructive volcano, which destroys all the earth: and the LORD will stretch out His hand upon fallen man and roll you down from the rocks, and will make you a burnt mountain. And the people who are wise and who are builders shall not take of you a stone for a corner, nor a stone for foundations; but you shall be desolate for ever, says the LORD as the wise men leave you alone.

27 Set ye up a standard in the land, blow the trumpet among the nations, prepare the nations against her, call together against her the kingdoms of Ararat, Minni, and Ashchenaz; appoint a captain against her; cause the horses to come up as the rough caterpillers.
28 Prepare against her the nations with the kings of the Medes, the captains thereof, and all the rulers thereof, and all the land of his dominion.
29 And the land shall tremble and sorrow: for every purpose of the LORD shall be performed against Babylon, to make the land of Babylon a desolation without an inhabitant.
30 The mighty men of Babylon have forborn to fight, they have remained in their holds: their might hath failed; they became as women: they have burned her dwellingplaces; her bars are broken.
31 One post shall run to meet another, and one messenger to meet another, to shew the king of Babylon that his city is taken at one end,
32 And that the passages are stopped, and the reeds they have burned with fire, and the men of war are affrighted.

The true state of man shall set up a standard in the land, blow the trumpet among the nations, prepare the nations against the distortion that is Babylon. Call together against Babylon the kingdoms of Ararat in Turkey, Minni in Armenia, and Ashchenaz in the upper Euphrates; appoint a captain against her; cause the horses to come up under divine control as the rough caterpillars. Prepare against Babylon the nations with the kings of the Medes, the captains, all the rulers thereof, and all the land of his dominion.

And the land shall tremble and sorrow: for every purpose of the LORD shall be performed against Babylon, to make the land of Babylon a desolation without an inhabitant, without a member of the fallen state. The mighty men of Babylon have stopped fighting, they have remained in their holds: their might has failed; they became as women: they have burned her dwelling places; her bars are broken. One post shall run to meet another, and one messenger to meet another, to show the king of Babylon that his city is taken at one end, the passages are stopped, the reeds have burned with fire, and the men of war are afraid.

33 For thus saith the LORD of hosts, the God of Israel; The daughter of Babylon is like a threshingfloor, it is time to thresh her: yet a little while, and the time of her harvest shall come.
34 Nebuchadrezzar the king of Babylon hath devoured me, he hath crushed me, he hath made me an empty vessel, he hath swallowed me up like a dragon, he hath filled his belly with my delicates, he hath cast me out.
35 The violence done to me and to my flesh be upon Babylon, shall the inhabitant of Zion say; and my blood upon the inhabitants of Chaldea, shall Jerusalem say.

The Symbolic Version of Jeremiah

The LORD of hosts, the God of Israel says the daughter of Babylon, who symbolizes the offspring of the fallen state, is like a threshing floor, it is time to thresh her: yet a little while, and the time of her harvest shall come. Nebuchadnezzar the king of Babylon has devoured the spirit of the LORD in His people; Nebuchadnezzar has crushed the spirit of the LORD, he has made the spirit of the LORD an empty vessel, he has swallowed the spirit of the LORD up like a dragon, he has filled his belly with the delicacies of the spirit of the LORD, and he has cast the spirit of the LORD out of Babylon. The violence done to the spirit of the LORD and to the flesh of the spirit of the LORD be upon Babylon, the inhabitant of Zion, the spirit within Zion, shall say; Jerusalem shall say that the blood of the people of Judah is upon the inhabitants of Chaldea.

36 Therefore thus saith the LORD; Behold, I will plead thy cause, and take vengeance for thee; and I will dry up her sea, and make her springs dry.
37 And Babylon shall become heaps, a dwellingplace for dragons, an astonishment, and an hissing, without an inhabitant.
38 They shall roar together like lions: they shall yell as lions' whelps.
39 In their heat I will make their feasts, and I will make them drunken, that they may rejoice, and sleep a perpetual sleep, and not wake, saith the LORD.
40 I will bring them down like lambs to the slaughter, like rams with he goats.
41 How is Sheshach taken! and how is the praise of the whole earth surprised! how is Babylon become an astonishment among the nations!
42 The sea is come up upon Babylon: she is covered with the multitude of the waves thereof.
43 Her cities are a desolation, a dry land, and a wilderness, a land wherein no man dwelleth, neither doth any son of man pass thereby.
44 And I will punish Bel in Babylon, and I will bring forth out of his mouth that which he hath wallowed up: and the nations shall not flow together any more unto him: yea, the wall of Babylon shall fall.
45 My people, go ye out of the midst of her, and deliver ye every man his soul from the fierce anger of the LORD.

Therefore, Behold, the LORD will plead your cause, and take vengeance for you against Babylon, the symbol of the fallen state; dry up her sea, and make her springs dry so that the fallen state cannot continue to grow and multiply. And Babylon shall become heaps of ruins, a dwelling place for dragons, a place of astonishment, and a place to hiss and boo against, without an inhabitant. The people in the fallen state of Babylon shall roar together like lions: they shall yell as lions' whelps. In the heat of their anger and destructiveness, the LORD will cause them to have feasts, and make themselves drunk and disorderly, so that they may rejoice in their drunkenness, sleep a perpetual sleep, and not wake, says the LORD. The LORD will bring them down like lambs, rams and goats to the slaughter.

How is Sheshach taken! Sheshach is a cryptogram formed by substituting the first consonant of the Hebrew alphabet for the last, the second consonant for the next to last, etc. Consonants are used and not vowels. In symbolism, consonants refer to form, while vowels refer to spirit. There is no **spirit** of the LORD in the cryptogram. The consonants are in reverse sequence to create a chaotic mishmash of the letters. The fallen state is a distorted chaotic state that uses the material building blocks without the spirit of the LORD. The spirit of the LORD must be present and used to create divine order. The creation of the fallen state, symbolized by Babylon, is like the cryptogram: it is incomplete and not whole. Babylon has received the praise of the whole earth. It is surprising that a distorted state could receive such praise!

How has Babylon become an astonishment among the nations! The sea of distortion in the consciousness of fallen people has risen up and come to focus in Babylon: she is covered with the multitude of the waves of consciousness to produce the results of the magnification of the fallen state. Her cities are a desolation, a dry land, and a wilderness, a land wherein no spiritual man dwells, neither does any son of a spiritual man pass by. And the LORD will punish Bel, the name of an idol, in Babylon, and bring forth out of the mouth of his expression that which he has wallowed up as the idol of the false god obtained by groveling in the material world: and the nations shall not flow together any more to him: yes, the wall of Babylon shall fall. The LORD's people should go out of the midst of her, and every man should deliver his soul, his body, mind and heart, from the fierce anger of the LORD which will come to bear upon Babylon as the joy of the LORD.

The Testimony of the Major Prophets

46 And lest your heart faint, and ye fear for the rumour that shall be heard in the land; a rumour shall both come one year, and after that in another year shall come a rumour, and violence in the land, ruler against ruler.
47 Therefore, behold, the days come, that I will do judgment upon the graven images of Babylon: and her whole land shall be confounded, and all her slain shall fall in the midst of her.
48 Then the heaven and the earth, and all that is therein, shall sing for Babylon: for the spoilers shall come unto her from the north, saith the LORD.
49 As Babylon hath caused the slain of Israel to fall, so at Babylon shall fall the slain of all the earth.
50 Ye that have escaped the sword, go away, stand not still: remember the LORD afar off, and let Jerusalem come into your mind.
51 We are confounded, because we have heard reproach: shame hath covered our faces: for strangers are come into the sanctuaries of the LORD's house.

And lest your heart faint, and you fear for the rumors that shall be heard in the land, one year and the next, about violence in the land of ruler against ruler. Therefore, behold, the days come, that the LORD will do judgment upon the graven images of Babylon: and her whole land shall be confused, and all her slain shall fall in the midst of her. Then the heaven and the earth, and all that is therein, shall sing for the disintegration of Babylon because of the spoilers that come to her from the north. As Babylon has caused the slain of Israel to fall, so at Babylon shall fall the slain of all the earth. Jeremiah is calling attention to the fact that what Babylon has done to Jerusalem, the same fate will befall Babylon on a greater scale on the earth.

You that have escaped the sword of the power of the LORD in operation at Babylon, the symbol of the fallen state, go away from the distorted state and do not stand still: the word of the LORD is to, Come out of her My people. Remember the LORD afar off and let Him come closer, and let the new Jerusalem and the spirit of the LORD come into your mind. We are confounded, because we have heard the reproach of the LORD toward a disobedient and fallen people: shame has covered our faces because we are aware that strangers, sinful people, have come into the sanctuaries of the LORD's house.

52 Wherefore, behold, the days come, saith the LORD, that I will do judgment upon her graven images: and through all her land the wounded shall groan.
53 Though Babylon should mount up to heaven, and though she should fortify the height of her strength, yet from me shall spoilers come unto her, saith the LORD.
54 A sound of a cry cometh from Babylon, and great destruction from the land of the Chaldeans:
55 Because the LORD hath spoiled Babylon, and destroyed out of her the great voice; when her waves do roar like great waters, a noise of their voice is uttered:
56 Because the spoiler is come upon her, even upon Babylon, and her mighty men are taken, every one of their bows is broken: for the LORD God of recompences shall surely requite.
57 And I will make drunk her princes, and her wise men, her captains, and her rulers, and her mighty men: and they shall sleep a perpetual sleep, and not wake, saith the King, whose name is the LORD of hosts.

Wherefore, behold, the days come, when the LORD will do judgment upon the graven images of Babylon, which are the environmental conditions of the fallen state: and through all her land, the wounded shall groan. Even though Babylon should try to climb up to heaven, and though she should fortify the height of her strength, yet spoilers shall come to her, says the LORD. A sound of a cry comes from Babylon, and great destruction from the land of the Chaldeans:
because the LORD has spoiled Babylon, and destroyed out of her the great voice; when the waves of her people do roar like great waters, a noise of their voice is uttered: because the spoiler, the destructive power of the LORD, is come upon Babylon. Her mighty men are taken and every one of their bows is broken: for the LORD God of recompenses shall surely repay evil according to the working of the Law.
The destructive power of the LORD will make drunk her princes, and her wise men, her captains, and her rulers, and her mighty men: and they shall sleep a perpetual sleep, and not wake, says the King, whose name is the LORD of hosts.

58 Thus saith the LORD of hosts; The broad walls of Babylon shall be utterly broken, and her high gates shall be burned with fire; and the people shall labour in vain, and the folk in the fire, and they shall be weary.

The Symbolic Version of Jeremiah

59 The word which Jeremiah the prophet commanded Seraiah the son of Neriah, the son of Maaseiah, when he went with Zedekiah the king of Judah into Babylon in the fourth year of his reign. And this Seraiah was a quiet prince.
60 So Jeremiah wrote in a book all the evil that should come upon Babylon, even all these words that are written against Babylon.

The LORD of hosts says that the broad walls of Babylon shall be utterly broken, and her high gates shall be burned with fire; the people shall labor in vain, and the folk in the fire of adversity, the destructive aspect of the fire of love, shall be weary. The word which Jeremiah the prophet commanded Seraiah the son of Neriah, the son of Maaseiah, when he went with Zedekiah the king of Judah into Babylon in the fourth year of his reign. And this Seraiah was a quiet prince. So Jeremiah wrote in a book all the evil that should come upon Babylon, even all these words that are written against Babylon.

61 And Jeremiah said to Seraiah, When thou comest to Babylon, and shalt see, and shalt read all these words;
62 Then shalt thou say, O LORD, thou hast spoken against this place, to cut it off, that none shall remain in it, neither man nor beast, but that it shall be desolate for ever.
63 And it shall be, when thou hast made an end of reading this book, that thou shalt bind a stone to it, and cast it into the midst of Euphrates:
64 And thou shalt say, Thus shall Babylon sink, and shall not rise from the evil that I will bring upon her: and they shall be weary. Thus far are the words of Jeremiah.

And Jeremiah said to Seraiah, When you come to Babylon, and you shall see with your own eyes, and you shall read all these words; Then shall you say, O LORD, you have spoken against this place, to cut it off, that none shall remain in it, neither man nor beast, but that it shall be desolate for ever.

And it shall be, when you have made an end of reading this book, that you shall bind a stone to it, and cast it into the midst of Euphrates where it shall sink like a stone in the river of life wrapped in the word of the LORD. And you shall say, Thus shall Babylon sink, and shall not rise from the evil that I will bring upon her: and the people who resist the coming of the kingdom of the LORD shall be weary and sad at the fate of Babylon. Thus far are the words of Jeremiah: the words of Jeremiah end here.

CHAPTER 52

1 Zedekiah was one and twenty years old when he began to reign, and he reigned eleven years in Jerusalem. And his mother's name was Hamutal the daughter of Jeremiah of Libnah.
2 And he did that which was evil in the eyes of the LORD, according to all that Jehoiakim had done.
3 For through the anger of the LORD it came to pass in Jerusalem and Judah, till he had cast them out from his presence, that Zedekiah rebelled against the king of Babylon.
4 And it came to pass in the ninth year of his reign, in the tenth month, in the tenth day of the month, that Nebuchadrezzar king of Babylon came, he and all his army, against Jerusalem, and pitched against it, and built forts against it round about.
5 So the city was besieged unto the eleventh year of king Zedekiah.
6 And in the fourth month, in the ninth day of the month, the famine was sore in the city, so that there was no bread for the people of the land.
7 Then the city was broken up, and all the men of war fled, and went forth out of the city by night by the way of the gate between the two walls, which was by the king's garden; (now the Chaldeans were by the city round about:) and they went by the way of the plain.
8 But the army of the Chaldeans pursued after the king, and overtook Zedekiah in the plains of Jericho; and all his army was scattered from him.
9 Then they took the king, and carried him up unto the king of Babylon to Riblah in the land of Hamath; where he gave judgment upon him.
10 And the king of Babylon slew the sons of Zedekiah before his eyes: he slew also all the princes of Judah in Riblah.
11 Then he put out the eyes of Zedekiah; and the king of Babylon bound him in chains, and carried him to Babylon, and put him in prison till the day of his death.

Zedekiah was twenty one years old when he began to reign, and he reigned eleven years in Jerusalem. His mother's name was Hamutal the daughter of Jeremiah of Libnah. He did that which was evil in the eyes of the LORD, according to all that Jehoiakim had done. For through the anger of the LORD according to the Law, it came to pass in Jerusalem and Judah, when Zedekiah rebelled against the king of Babylon and cast them out from his presence.

And it came to pass in the ninth year of his reign, in the tenth month, in the tenth day of the month, that Nebuchadnezzar king of Babylon came with all his army against Jerusalem, and built forts against it round about. So the city was besieged unto the eleventh year of king Zedekiah. In the fourth month, in the ninth day of the month, the famine was sore in the city, so that there was no bread for the people of the land.

Then the city was broken up, and all the men of war fled, and went forth out of the city by night by the way of the gate between the two walls, which was by the king's garden; (now the Chaldeans were by the city round about:) and they went by the way of the plain. But the army of the Chaldeans pursued after the king, and overtook Zedekiah in the

The Symbolic Version of Jeremiah

plains of Jericho; and all his army was scattered from him. Then they took the king, and carried him up to the king of Babylon to Riblah in the land of Hamath; where he gave judgment upon him. The king of Babylon slew the sons of Zedekiah before his eyes: he slew also all the princes of Judah in Riblah. Then he put out the eyes of Zedekiah and bound him in chains, carried him to Babylon, and put him in prison until the day of his death.

12 Now in the fifth month, in the tenth day of the month, which was the nineteenth year of Nebuchadrezzar king of Babylon, came Nebuzaradan, captain of the guard, which served the king of Babylon, into Jerusalem,
13 And burned the house of the LORD, and the king's house; and all the houses of Jerusalem, and all the houses of the great men, burned he with fire:
14 And all the army of the Chaldeans, that were with the captain of the guard, brake down all the walls of Jerusalem round about.
15 Then Nebuzaradan the captain of the guard carried away captive certain of the poor of the people, and the residue of the people that remained in the city, and those that fell away, that fell to the king of Babylon, and the rest of the multitude.
16 But Nebuzaradan the captain of the guard left certain of the poor of the land for vinedressers and for husbandmen.
17 Also the pillars of brass that were in the house of the LORD, and the bases, and the brasen sea that was in the house of the LORD, the Chaldeans brake, and carried all the brass of them to Babylon.
18 The caldrons also, and the shovels, and the snuffers, and the bowls, and the spoons, and all the vessels of brass wherewith they ministered, took they away.
19 And the basons, and the firepans, and the bowls, and the caldrons, and the candlesticks, and the spoons, and the cups; that which was of gold in gold, and that which was of silver in silver, took the captain of the guard away.

Now in the fifth month, in the tenth day of the month, which was the nineteenth year of Nebuchadnezzar king of Babylon, came Nebuzaradan, captain of the guard, which served the king of Babylon, in Jerusalem, and burned the house of the LORD, the king's house; all the houses of Jerusalem, and all the houses of the great men, with fire: And all the army of the Chaldeans, that were with the captain of the guard, broke down all the walls of Jerusalem round about. Then Nebuzaradan the captain of the guard carried away captive certain of the poor of the people, the residue of the people that remained in the city, those that came over to the king of Babylon, and the rest of the multitude. But Nebuzaradan the captain of the guard left certain of the poor of the land for vinedressers and for husbandmen.

Also the pillars of brass that were in the house of the LORD, the moveable bases, and the bronze sea were broken by the Chaldeans who carried all the brass of them to Babylon. The captain of the guard took away the caldrons, the shovels, the snuffers, the bowls, the spoons, and all the vessels of brass that they ministered in the temple. The basins, firepans, bowls, caldrons, candlesticks, spoons, and cups that were made of gold and silver were taken away by the captain of the guard.

20 The two pillars, one sea, and twelve brasen bulls that were under the bases, which king Solomon had made in the house of the LORD: the brass of all these vessels was without weight.
21 And concerning the pillars, the height of one pillar was eighteen cubits; and a fillet of twelve cubits did compass it; and the thickness thereof was four fingers: it was hollow.
22 And a chapiter of brass was upon it; and the height of one chapiter was five cubits, with network and pomegranates upon the chapiters round about, all of brass. The second pillar also and the pomegranates were like unto these.
23 And there were ninety and six pomegranates on a side; and all the pomegranates upon the network were an hundred round about.
24 And the captain of the guard took Seraiah the chief priest, and Zephaniah the second priest, and the three keepers of the door:
25 He took also out of the city an eunuch, which had the charge of the men of war; and seven men of them that were near the king's person, which were found in the city; and the principal scribe of the host, who mustered the people of the land; and threescore men of the people of the land, that were found in the midst of the city.
26 So Nebuzaradan the captain of the guard took them, and brought them to the king of Babylon to Riblah.
27 And the king of Babylon smote them, and put them to death in Riblah in the land of Hamath. Thus Judah was carried away captive out of his own land.

The Testimony of the Major Prophets

The two pillars, one sea, and twelve bronze bulls that were under the bases, which king Solomon had made in the house of the LORD: the brass of all these vessels was immeasurable, without weight. And concerning the pillars, the height of one pillar was eighteen cubits; and a fillet of twelve cubits did compass it; and the thickness thereof was four fingers: it was hollow. And a chapiter, the top molding of a pillar, of brass was upon it; and the height of one chapiter was five cubits, with network and pomegranates upon the chapiters round about, all of brass. The second pillar also and the pomegranates were like unto these. And there were ninety pomegranates on a side; and all the pomegranates upon the network were a hundred round about.

And the captain of the guard took Seraiah the chief priest, and Zephaniah the second priest, and the three keepers of the door: He took also out of the city a eunuch, which had the charge of the men of war; and seven men of them that were near the king's person, which were found in the city; and the principal scribe of the host, who mustered the people of the land; and threescore men of the people of the land, that were found in the midst of the city. So Nebuzaradan the captain of the guard took them, and brought them to the king of Babylon to Riblah. Riblah was a place between Palestine and Babylonia where the kings of Babylonia remained while directing the operations of their armies. And the king of Babylon struck them, and put them to death in Riblah in the land of Hamath. Thus was Judah taken away captive out of his own land.

28 This is the people whom Nebuchadrezzar carried away captive: in the seventh year three thousand Jews and three and twenty:
29 In the eighteenth year of Nebuchadrezzar he carried away captive from Jerusalem eight hundred thirty and two persons:
30 In the three and twentieth year of Nebuchadrezzar Nebuzaradan the captain of the guard carried away captive of the Jews seven hundred forty and five persons: all the persons were four thousand and six hundred.
31 And it came to pass in the seven and thirtieth year of the captivity of Jehoiachin king of Judah, in the twelfth month, in the five and twentieth day of the month, that Evilmerodach king of Babylon in the first year of his reign lifted up the head of Jehoiachin king of Judah, and brought him forth out of prison,
32 And spake kindly unto him, and set his throne above the throne of the kings that were with him in Babylon,
33 And changed his prison garments: and he did continually eat bread before him all the days of his life.
34 And for his diet, there was a continual diet given him of the king of Babylon, every day a portion until the day of his death, all the days of his life.

This is the number of people whom Nebuchadnezzar carried away captive: in the seventh year 3,023 Jews. In the eighteenth year of Nebuchadnezzar he carried away captive from Jerusalem 832 persons. In the twenty-third year of Nebuchadnezzar, Nebuzaradan the captain of the guard carried away 745 Jews: all the persons were 4,600.

And it came to pass in the thirty-seventh year of the captivity of Jehoiachin king of Judah, in the twelfth month, in the twenty-fifth day of the month, that Evilmerodach king of Babylon in the first year of his reign lifted up the head of Jehoiachin king of Judah, and brought him forth out of prison. He spoke kindly to him, changed his prison garments and set his throne above the thrones of the kings that were with him in Babylon. Jehoiachin did continually eat bread before him all the days of his life. And for his diet, there was a continual diet given him by the king of Babylon every day a portion all the days of his life until the day of his death.

Anthony John Monaco   **August 31, 1998**

The Symbolic Version of
Lamentations

Anthony John Monaco

A Stars of the Scriptures Series

FOREWORD

Lamentations is the title of this book of the Holy Bible that was given to it in the Greek Septuagint and the Latin Vulgate. The Hebrew title of the book is *'ekah* (How..!) which is the first word of the first, second and fourth chapters. This is an appropriate beginning word that asks the main question: How could the city of Jerusalem have suffered such a tragic end in 586 BC when it was pillaged, burned and destroyed by the Babylonians under king Nebuchadnezzar? How could such a lamentable thing have happened to Jerusalem? Hebrew tradition refers to this book, because of its subject matter, as *qinot*, "Lamentations". Lamentations shares the sense of loss and the darkness that followed the destruction of the city, its temple, its rituals, the removal of its religious symbols and the captivity and exile of the inhabitants of Jerusalem.

Orthodox Jews customarily read the Book of Lamentations aloud in its entirety on the ninth day of month of Ab, the traditional date of the destruction of Solomon's temple in 586 BC, as well as the date of the destruction of Herod's temple in 70 AD. Many people today read the Book of Lamentations each week at the Western Wall in the Old City of Jerusalem which is known as the "Wailing Wall". In Roman Catholic liturgy, the Book of Lamentations is read during the last three days of Holy Week between the crucifixion and the Resurrection of Jesus the Christ.

The Symbolic Version of Lamentations follows the Symbolic Version of Jeremiah. Although the author of Lamentations is anonymous, ancient Jewish and Christian tradition ascribes it to Jeremiah. Jeremiah as a prophet of the LORD wrote and preached the word of the LORD to the LORD's people. The people did not listen to his message to let the spirit of the LORD build the kingdom and unite the divided kingdoms of Israel and Judah. The Book of Jeremiah ends with the destruction of Jerusalem, the pillage of the temple, the disposition of the temple treasures and the exact number of the 4,600 captives taken into exile. Jeremiah, although beaten and imprisoned, warned three kings of Judah of the impending disaster to Jerusalem and Judah. Jeremiah had reason to lament over the destruction of the city which he warned against and for which he was rebuked. The author of Lamentations understands very clearly that the Babylonians were the unknowing human agents of divine retribution in the destruction of Jerusalem based upon the operation of the Law of Sowing and Reaping.

However passionate, emotional and sad that the lamentations appear to be, they were constructed with great care. Each of the five laments contains 22 verses (except for the third chapter which contains 66 verses—3 times 22). There are 22 letters in the Hebrew alphabet. The first four lamentations are alphabetic acrostics: this means that each of the verses begins with the successive letter of the Hebrew alphabet. In the third chapter, the LORD—who has caused Jerusalem and the temple to be destroyed—is described as a God of hope, love, faithfulness and salvation. The people were punished because they broke the covenant with the LORD and disobeyed and ignored the LORD and his prophets. This was the message of the LORD through Jeremiah to the people which was ignored at that time.

The book begins with lament and rightly ends in repentance. Let us consider the Book of Lamentations which the author assumes to be written by Jeremiah to determine whether the message has application today. Let us consider

The Testimony of the Major Prophets

whether or not the LORD still offers His divine Kingdom of Heaven from the world of spirit to become manifest in physical form on earth. Let us consider whether man in his fallen state continues to refuse to let the spirit of the LORD create the divine design on earth through the people. Let us consider *The Symbolic Version of Lamentations*.

CHAPTER 1

1 How doth the city sit solitary, that was full of people! how is she become as a widow! she that was great among the nations, and princess among the provinces, how is she become tributary!
2 She weepeth sore in the night, and her tears are on her cheeks: among all her lovers she hath none to comfort her: all her friends have dealt treacherously with her, they are become her enemies.
3 Judah is gone into captivity because of affliction, and because of great servitude: she dwelleth among the heathen, she findeth no rest: all her persecutors overtook her between the straits.

Jeremiah contemplates the fact that the city of Jerusalem has been robbed, defiled and destroyed by the Babylonians and Chaldeans under king Nebuchadnezzar. This is no surprise to Jeremiah who has been giving the message from the LORD as a warning to the people, their leaders, princes and three different kings of this fate for many years. Jeremiah is lamenting the fact that the people did not give heed to the word of the LORD that could have prevented this destruction of Jerusalem. Jerusalem was to have been the Holy City, the city of the LORD on earth in which the LORD's people would live and exert the LORD's spirit and influence into the world.

She, Jerusalem, was to be a city of light that would shine as a beacon in the fallen world as an example of the beauty, compassion and love from the LORD made manifest through people who would reveal the spirit of the LORD through themselves. The city did not live up to its potential because the inhabitants of the city did not live up to their potential as people made in the image and likeness of God. The people denied this divine starting point! Generally, people reject the idea of being made in the image and likeness of God even though they know and quote from memory the way that God created Man.

Jeremiah asks his readers in any generation, How does the city of Jerusalem, personified as a woman, sit solitary and alone in a destroyed city that was once full of people! How is she (Jerusalem) become as a widow who has lost her husband! She, Jerusalem, that was great among the nations, a princess, a daughter of her spiritual Father among the provinces, how has she become tributary, a small branch of the flow the spirit instead as the main recipient of the flow of spirit from the LORD to the earth! These are not questions; these are exclamations of the stupidity of man in the fallen state.

The woman that symbolizes the people of Jerusalem weeps bitterly in the night that symbolizes the darkness and sadness of the world in which she lives. Her tears are on her cheeks so that she knows the depth of the sorrow in her heart. The tears of sadness and despair are hers. She has had many lovers from all the people who lived in Jerusalem but now she has no one to comfort her in her misery to make the sadness and loneliness depart. She has no Comforter. All of her friends have dealt treacherously with her; they have become her enemies as the survivors have accepted the yoke of Babylon.

The Testimony of the Major Prophets

The captives blame their leaders for their present fate. All of Judah is gone into captivity because of the affliction by the Babylonians and Chaldeans and because of the great servitude that the captives must render to their captors. The people of Jerusalem, personified by a woman, dwell among the heathen, the outsiders who do not know the LORD, and she finds no rest as a slave and captive: all the persecutors, the oppressors from Babylonia, overtook her people who tried to flee to escape the dire straits of captivity, and the people of Jerusalem find no rest in the hands of her captors.

*4 The ways of Zion do mourn, because none come to the solemn feasts: all
her gates are desolate: her priests sigh, her virgins are afflicted, and she is in bitterness.
5 Her adversaries are the chief, her enemies prosper; for the LORD hath afflicted her for the multitude of her transgressions: her children are gone into captivity before the enemy.
6 And from the daughter of Zion all her beauty is departed: her princes are become like harts that find no pasture, and they are gone without strength before the pursuer.*

The ways of Zion are the ways of holiness and spiritual living are known by the people of the LORD who participate in the solemn feasts of the spiritual covenant with the LORD. No one comes to the solemn feasts. All the gates to the covenant with the LORD—which are always open to be entered—are desolate because people do not choose to enter the gate. They do not know that the gate is open. Her priests sigh because they are captives, and the virgins, the symbol of the people who should receive the spirit of the LORD, their Lover, into their bodies which they bring into the temple, are afflicted because they are not receiving the fullness of the spirit from the LORD which inevitably results in a bitter experience.

The adversaries of Jerusalem have become her chief and her enemies prosper. She has exchanged the true but invisible God of love for a visible false chief, or god, in the visible, material form of Babylonians. The LORD has afflicted Jerusalem for the multitude of her transgressions and she has transgressed against the LORD whom she proclaimed to be her God. This is the reason that her offspring, the symbols of her behaviors that have come forth through her, have gone into captivity before the enemy. The daughter of Zion, the potential of the beauty which was possible through Jerusalem has departed from the city which is in ruins: her princes, who should be courting her, have become like deer that find no pasture. They are gone without strength, in a state of weakness, to challenge or resist their pursuer, or hide from him.

*7 Jerusalem remembered in the days of her affliction and of her miseries all her pleasant things that she had in the days of old, when her people fell into the hand of the enemy, and none did help her: the adversaries saw her, and did mock at her sabbaths.
8 Jerusalem hath grievously sinned; therefore she is removed: all that honoured her despise her, because they have seen her nakedness: yea, she sigheth, and turneth backward.
9 Her filthiness is in her skirts; she remembereth not her last end; therefore she came down wonderfully: she had no comforter. O LORD, behold my affliction: for the enemy hath magnified himself.*

Jerusalem, in the days after she had become afflicted and experienced her miseries, remembered all the pleasant things that she had in days of old, now that her people have fallen into the hand of the enemy and no one was available to help her. The invaders saw her and mocked at her Sabbaths to an invisible God that was to protect her. The fact of the matter is that the people of Jerusalem had sinned grievously and has become a weak people; that is the reason that she was removed from her position of power: all who honored her greatness in the past, now despise her as they see her nakedness and weakness before the LORD. Yes Jerusalem has sighed, that she could not help herself and she has turned backward, away from the LORD. Her filthiness is in her skirts, the symbol of the garment that covers her hidden uncleanness; she has forgotten her last end, the purpose of her presence on earth that would bring a divine future under the guidance of the impulse of the spirit from the LORD. Therefore she came down, she fell, astonishingly fast because she had no comforter to provide her with stability and steadfastness. Jerusalem in her weakness could only pray with words asking the LORD to behold the affliction of people and conditions of Jerusalem as though the LORD, Who is omniscient and omnipresent, was not aware of the observable facts. Jerusalem could cry in sorrow that, by comparison, the enemy from Babylon had magnified himself with a great force.

The Symbolic Version of Lamentations

10 The adversary hath spread out his hand upon all her pleasant things: for she hath seen that the heathen entered into her sanctuary, whom thou didst command that they should not enter into thy congregation.
11 All her people sigh, they seek bread; they have given their pleasant things for meat to relieve the soul: see, O LORD, and consider; for I am become vile.

The invader from Babylon has spread out his hand of greed upon all the pleasant things of Jerusalem. She has seen the heathen enter into her sanctuary of the temple that the LORD did command that the heathen should not enter into the sanctuary of the LORD's congregation. All the people of Jerusalem sigh that seek bread to sustain themselves; they have given their pleasant things as meat to the invaders to relieve the pressure of the invaders upon them so that they can survive. Jerusalem asks the LORD to look upon them and consider how fallen the people have become. Jerusalem knows that she has indeed become vile.

12 Is it nothing to you, all ye that pass by? behold, and see if there be any sorrow like unto my sorrow, which is done unto me, wherewith the LORD hath afflicted me in the day of his fierce anger.
13 From above hath he sent fire into my bones, and it prevaileth against them: he hath spread a net for my feet, he hath turned me back: he hath made me desolate and faint all the day.
14 The yoke of my transgressions is bound by his hand: they are wreathed, and come up upon my neck: he hath made my strength to fall, the Lord hath delivered me into their hands, from whom I am not able to rise up.

The woman who personifies the defeated Jerusalem asks, Is it nothing to you people who pass by? Behold and see if there is any sorrow anywhere that is like the sorrow that is being experienced by Jerusalem that has been done by the working of the Law by the LORD who has afflicted Jerusalem in the day of his fierce anger. The fierce anger of the LORD is the operation of the destructive cycle of the Law of Sowing and Reaping.

The LORD has sent fire of His burning love from above into the bones of Jerusalem, and the fire, the symbol of the power of the LORD, has prevailed against the people of Jerusalem. The LORD has set a net for the feet of the woman who personifies the city that was going in the wrong direction and the LORD has captured Jerusalem and turned her back. The LORD has done this by making Jerusalem weak and desolate all the day. Jerusalem has transgressed and the yoke of control of her transgression is held by the hand of the LORD. The transgressions are woven together as a wreath that come up to her neck to choke her. The LORD has made her strength to fall, and the LORD has delivered Jerusalem into the hands of the Babylonians, and she is not able to rise up from their control.

15 The Lord hath trodden under foot all my mighty men in the midst of me: he hath called an assembly against me to crush my young men: the Lord hath trodden the virgin, the daughter of Judah, as in a winepress.
16 For these things I weep; mine eye, mine eye runneth down with water, because the comforter that should relieve my soul is far from me: my children are desolate, because the enemy prevailed.
17 Zion spreadeth forth her hands, and there is none to comfort her: the LORD hath commanded concerning Jacob, that his adversaries should be round about him: Jerusalem is as a menstruous woman among them.

The LORD has trodden under foot, using the Babylonians and the Chaldeans, all the mighty men of Jerusalem that were in her midst of the city. The LORD has called an assembly of aggressive invaders against Jerusalem to crush her young men; the power of the LORD has trodden the virgin, the daughter of Judah, the daughter who has fallen from the height of Zion to the depths of Judah, as grapes are trodden in a winepress.

Jerusalem weeps for these things; her eye, her vision, which is filled and overflows with tears of sadness because the comforter that should relieve her soul is far from her. There is an awareness that a comforter is available to relieve discomfort and sadness, but this comforter is far from the people of Jerusalem. The children, the offspring, are desolate because the enemy prevailed against the city. Zion spreads forth her hands and there is no one to comfort her. The LORD has commanded concerning Jacob, who was the symbol of the fallen state that did arise to the restored state called Israel, that the adversaries of Jacob should be round about him, outside his heart, mind and body, where the adversaries would not trouble Jacob. Jacob could represent the spirit of the LORD to his adversaries and not be troubled by them. If Jacob represents the LORD, his heart will not be troubled because his heart is open to the LORD and not to the environment. Jerusalem, by contrast, is a menstruous woman whose blood, the symbol of life, is flowing into the ground.

The Testimony of the Major Prophets

18 The LORD is righteous; for I have rebelled against his commandment: hear, I pray you, all people, and behold my sorrow: my virgins and my young men are gone into captivity.
19 I called for my lovers, but they deceived me: my priests and mine elders gave up the ghost in the city, while they sought their meat to relieve their souls.
20 Behold, O LORD; for I am in distress: my bowels are troubled; mine heart is turned within me; for I have grievously rebelled: abroad the sword bereaveth, at home there is as death.
21 They have heard that I sigh: there is none to comfort me: all mine enemies have heard of my trouble; they are glad that thou hast done it: thou wilt bring the day that thou hast called, and they shall be like unto me.
22 Let all their wickedness come before thee; and do unto them, as thou hast done unto me for all my transgressions: for my sighs are many, and my heart is faint.

The woman who symbolizes Jerusalem begins to see that she is in distress and calls upon the LORD: she tells the LORD that her inner physical body is in torment; the heart of her emotions is turned within her; she is also aware of the reason for her misery and discomfort is because she has grievously rebelled against the LORD. Outside the city the sword of the enemy can end bereavement and sorrow, but at home in Jerusalem, there is a condition that is as death. A person in this state wishes that they were dead because of the emotional pain.

There are those who have heard that Jerusalem sighs and grieves but there is no one to comfort me, the fallen and beaten survivors of Jerusalem. All of my enemies who have heard of my troubles say that they are glad that the LORD has done this thing to Jerusalem. They understand the operation of the Law that says the LORD will bring around the day that the LORD has called, and their experience of the Law of Sowing and Reaping shall be like what has happened to Jerusalem. Jerusalem proclaims in her misery that the LORD should let their wickedness come before the LORD and let the LORD do to them as the LORD has done to Jerusalem for all her transgressions. The woman who symbolizes Jerusalem states that her sighs and groans are many and her heart is faint.

CHAPTER 2

1 How hath the Lord covered the daughter of Zion with a cloud in his anger, and cast down from heaven unto the earth the beauty of Israel, and remembered not his footstool in the day of his anger!

Jeremiah makes a rhetorical exclamation when he asks, How has the LORD covered the daughter of Zion, who symbolizes the potential beauty of city of Jerusalem, with a cloud of His anger, the destructive power of the LORD in action against Jerusalem and its inhabitants! The LORD constantly casts down from heaven into the earth the beauty of Israel. Israel is the spiritual design from the LORD which is perfect, and that perfection can be seen on earth in the harmony of the natural systems in operation on earth. Could it be that the LORD has not remembered his footstool, the city of Jerusalem, the holy city, in which the LORD would have a place for His foot on earth in the process of bringing the kingdom of heaven into the earth! Could it be that the LORD would not remember anything!

2 The Lord hath swallowed up all the habitations of Jacob, and hath not pitied: he hath thrown down in his wrath the strong holds of the daughter of Judah; he hath brought them down to the ground: he hath polluted the kingdom and the princes thereof.
3 He hath cut off in his fierce anger all the horn of Israel: he hath drawn back his right hand from before the enemy, and he burned against Jacob like a flaming fire, which devoureth round about.
4 He hath bent his bow like an enemy: he stood with his right hand as an adversary, and slew all that were pleasant to the eye in the tabernacle of the daughter of Zion: he poured out his fury like fire.

Jacob is the physical symbol of man in the fallen state who is in position to repent and ascend into Israel, the symbol of the spiritual state of man. The physical form of Jacob is the container for Israel who was in the covenant-agreement with the LORD. The covenant-agreement is the condition of oneness which occurs in the place where the consciousness of man rises up to know that his spirit is a part of the spirit of the LORD. The **spirit** of man is the true identity, not the **form** of man. The spirit is eternal; the form is temporal. Jacob became Israel when Jacob ascended in consciousness to oneness with the LORD. The LORD swallows up the habitations of Jacob with the spiritual presence of Israel; the eternal spirit has dominance over the physical form. The physical personality of Jacob becomes the identity of Israel. The LORD has no pity when this occurs. In the fallen state of man, the caterpillar must turn into the butterfly. The LORD has expressed his wrath toward the strongholds of the daughter of Judah, the fallen physical connections of Judah to the material world. As Jacob is the material form of man who is in position to turn into Israel in the return to the true state of material man in the covenant with the LORD, then Judah is the material form which has developed strong cords of connection with the world of the environment while ignoring the spirit of the LORD. The LORD's anger is to destroy the strong emotional ties that bind material man to the environmental world that the LORD wants to bring down to the ground and eliminate. It is Judah, the symbol of man in the fallen state, who has polluted the kingdom of the LORD and the princes, the sons of the King, who should be living in the kingdom. The LORD wants to destroy this usurper of the LORD's kingdom and power so that the true design of Israel, the true identity, shall appear.

The Testimony of the Major Prophets

The LORD, in the fierce anger of the destructive cycle of His creative power, has cut off all the beautiful music that should be coming through the horn, the instrument of expression, of Israel, of man made in the image of the spirit of the LORD. The LORD has withdrawn his powerful right hand of divine control, and He uses the power of spirit, symbolized by a flaming fire, to burn against Jacob, the material covering of man made of atoms and molecules, which devours the false material form that does not reveal the spirit of the LORD round about. The LORD has bent His bow, the bow of the material form of mankind, through which His divine spirit is to deliver the material kingdom of the LORD into the earth, and bent it as an enemy, an enemy who was fighting the spirit of the LORD instead of coming into covenant-agreement with the spirit of the LORD. The rebellion and the disobedience of man has caused the LORD to use His powerful, strong and clean right hand as an adversary against His rebellious creation. The LORD slew, destroyed, all the material things that were pleasant to the eye of the daughter of Zion, the inhabitants of Jerusalem, who worshipped their temple and the temple vessels, instead of the LORD their God. The LORD poured out his fury like fire to destroy the sinful nation that Jerusalem and Judah had become.

5 The Lord was as an enemy: he hath swallowed up Israel, he hath swallowed up all her palaces: he hath destroyed his strong holds, and hath increased in the daughter of Judah mourning and lamentation.
6 And he hath violently taken away his tabernacle, as if it were of a garden: he hath destroyed his places of the assembly: the LORD hath caused the solemn feasts and sabbaths to be forgotten in Zion, and hath despised in the indignation of his anger the king and the priest.

The Lord, the fallen Lord, who should have been the representative of the LORD in heaven on earth, was as an enemy: he has swallowed up Israel, the ascended state of true man in covenant-agreement with the LORD and he has swallowed up all her spiritual palaces that represent the divine design of God: he has destroyed the strong holds, the spiritual connections with the LORD and by so doing, he has increased the mourning and the lamentation known by the daughter of Judah, the material people in the fallen state by the usurpation and misuse of the power of the LORD. He has violently taken away his tabernacle as though it were a garden: he has destroyed his places of the assembly. The corrective power of the LORD has caused the solemn feasts and Sabbaths to be forgotten in Zion, the symbol of the high spiritual place in consciousness and has despised the king and the priest in the indignation of his anger because they did not represent the LORD.

7 The Lord hath cast off his altar, he hath abhorred his sanctuary, he hath given up into the hand of the enemy the walls of her palaces; they have made a noise in the house of the LORD, as in the day of a
solemn feast.

The Lord, the fallen Lord, has cast off his altar, the holy place within himself where he should worship the LORD God; he has abhorred his sanctuary which is the holy place where he should be in covenant-agreement with his LORD; he has given up into the hands of the enemies, the fallen people of the environment, the walls of the palaces that belong to the LORD. The enemies have made a noise in the house of the LORD, which should have been as a day of a solemn feast. Raucous living by the enemy is taking place in the house of the LORD. The LORD of heaven cannot allow this blasphemy on earth to continue without punishment.

8 The LORD hath purposed to destroy the wall of the daughter of Zion: he hath stretched out a line, he hath not withdrawn his hand from destroying: therefore he made the rampart and the wall to lament; they languished together.
9 Her gates are sunk into the ground; he hath destroyed and broken her bars: her king and her princes are among the Gentiles: the law is no more; her prophets also find no vision from the LORD.

The LORD has deliberated planned to destroy the material wall of the daughter of Zion that symbolizes the material city of Jerusalem with its temple. The LORD is not disconnected from the earth. He has stretched out a line of connection in spirit and His spirit has not withdrawn His hand of control from destroying the false designs that are not of the LORD. Therefore, the LORD made the rampart and the wall, that symbolizes the material world which is controlled by the spirit of the LORD. On one side of the wall, the LORD's side, the wall provides protection; the distorted side of the wall provides a place for lamentation. The distorted or false side of the wailing wall allows for a view; that brings sadness and mourning. The true rampart allows the view of the material world that is characterized by joy and thanksgiving. The rampart and the wall languish and deteriorate together when man in the fallen state rebels against the LORD.

When the walls around the city are broken, her gates are sunk into the ground; he has destroyed and broken the bars on the gates which were to protect the king and the princes who are now captive among the Gentiles in the form of Babylonians and Chaldeans. The word "Gentiles" rightly applies to any person who is outside the covenant-agreement of the LORD. The law of the kings and princes of Judah is no more; the prophets of Judah also find no vision from the LORD. The connection with the LORD, the covenant-agreement that was to be made manifest in the Holy City of Jerusalem has been broken.

10 The elders of the daughter of Zion sit upon the ground, and keep silence: they have cast up dust upon their heads; they have girded themselves with sackcloth: the virgins of Jerusalem hang down their heads to the ground.
11 Mine eyes do fail with tears, my bowels are troubled, my liver is poured upon the earth, for the destruction of the daughter of my people; because the children and the sucklings swoon in the streets of the city.
12 They say to their mothers, Where is corn and wine? when they swooned as the wounded in the streets of the city, when their soul was poured out into their mothers' bosom.

The elders of the daughter of Zion symbolize the spiritual elders who are available to enter into the city of Jerusalem. They sit upon the ground and keep their silence because they have no experiences of success to pass on to the material forms in which the spirit dwells. In their material fallen state of identity, they have sprinkled dust upon their heads and wrapped themselves with sackcloth to demonstrate their sorrow and mourning; the virgins of Jerusalem, who have not given themselves to the spirit of the LORD, hang down their heads to the ground in shame.

The eyes of Jeremiah fail to see clearly as they are filled with tears; he experiences inner torment and vomits his gall upon the earth because of the destruction of Jerusalem and the sight of infants and children lying faint in the streets of the city. They ask their mothers, Where is the corn to eat and the wine to drink? when they faint for lack of food and pour out their souls in their mother's bosoms for emotional support and solace.

13 What thing shall I take to witness for thee? what thing shall I liken to thee, O daughter of Jerusalem? what shall I equal to thee, that I may comfort thee, O virgin daughter of Zion? for thy breach is great like the sea: who can heal thee?

Jeremiah is at a loss to know what to do for the suffering of the people; he feels helpless at the extent of the devastation and destruction. What can he see to help the situation? What thing in his experience can he compare to the condition of the daughter of Jerusalem so that he might comfort the virgin daughter of spiritual Zion which is so far from her divine potential in this fallen condition? The breach between the divine design of the spiritual offspring of Zion and the destroyed material appearance of the daughter of Jerusalem is as great as the sea: Jeremiah asks, Who can heal this condition?!

14 Thy prophets have seen vain and foolish things for thee: and they have not discovered thine iniquity, to turn away thy captivity; but have seen for thee false burdens and causes of banishment.
15 All that pass by clap their hands at thee; they hiss and wag their head at the daughter of Jerusalem, saying, Is this the city that men call The perfection of beauty, The joy of the whole earth?
16 All thine enemies have opened their mouth against thee: they hiss and gnash the teeth: they say, We have swallowed her up: certainly this is the day that we looked for; we have found, we have seen it.

The false prophets of Jerusalem have seen vain and foolish things for the city: they have seen vain things because they were vain people; they saw foolish things because they ignored the covenant of the LORD and the operation of the Law of Sowing and Reaping through human behavior. The false prophets did not observe or discover the iniquity of the people of Jerusalem in her relationship with the LORD, which, if corrected, would have turned away her ultimate captivity. Instead of accepting the responsibility of the inhabitants of the Holy City toward the LORD of the Holy City, the false prophets saw false burdens for the people which led to the causes of banishment from the holy city. They were not holy people.

The Testimony of the Major Prophets

All that pass by clap their hands in agreement that the hypocrisy of the people of Jerusalem has been discovered and punished; they hiss and boo, they shake their heads at the daughter of Jerusalem, saying in derision, Is this the city that men call, The perfection of beauty, The joy of the whole earth?

All your enemies have opened their mouths against you: they hiss and gnash the teeth: they say, We have totally swallowed up the fate of your city with great satisfaction: certainly this is the day that we looked for; we have found, we have seen it. Jerusalem has received her just desserts, her divine retribution.

17 The LORD hath done that which he had devised; he hath fulfilled his word that he had commanded in the days of old: he hath thrown down, and hath not pitied: and he hath caused thine enemy to rejoice over thee, he hath set up the horn of thine adversaries.
18 Their heart cried unto the Lord, O wall of the daughter of Zion, let tears run down like a river day and night: give thyself no rest; let not the apple of thine eye cease.
19 Arise, cry out in the night: in the beginning of the watches pour out thine heart like water before the face of the Lord: lift up thy hands toward him for the life of thy young children, that faint for hunger in the top of every street.

The LORD, working through the operation of His Law, has done that which He had devised and planned; He has fulfilled his word that He had commanded through His commandments in the days of old: He has thrown down and destroyed that which does not belong in His world, and has not pitied the destruction of the false material design: and He has caused your enemy to rejoice over you; He has set up the horn, the sound of the people who are your adversaries, to be heard in the land.

Their hearts cried to the Lord of the fallen state, the fallen angel, who has rebelled and disobeyed the LORD to bring about this material destruction, the material circumstances symbolized by the wailing wall of the daughter of Zion. The cry of the hearts of the people in the fallen state is to let their tears run down like a river day and night: give yourselves no rest; let not the true vision of Jerusalem which you saw as the apple of your eye cease and become an object of your sadness. Arise, cry out in the night: in the beginning of the watches each day, pour out your heart like water before the face of the Lord (in the fallen state) who has led you into this predicament: lift up your hands toward him for the life of your young children, that faint for hunger in the top of every street.

20 Behold, O LORD, and consider to whom thou hast done this. Shall the women eat their fruit, and children of a span long? shall the priest and the prophet be slain in the sanctuary of the Lord?
21 The young and the old lie on the ground in the streets: my virgins and my young men are fallen by the sword; thou hast slain them in the day of thine anger; thou hast killed, and not pitied.
22 Thou hast called as in a solemn day my terrors round about, so that in the day of the LORD's anger none escaped nor remained: those that I have swaddled and brought up hath mine enemy consumed.

The people in the fallen state, who have been punished for their iniquity by the operation of the Law with the destruction of Jerusalem, ask the LORD of the heaven to behold and consider to whom He has done this punishment, as though the LORD has made a mistake by doing these terrible things to them. They ask the LORD if the women should eat their fruit, the children, that they have cared for? They ask if the priest and the prophet shall be slain in the physical sanctuary of building of the Lord?

The Lord of the fallen state, who is the spokesman and leader for the people who have been punished for their disobedience by the operation of the Law, tells the LORD that the young and old lie on the ground in the streets: his virgins and his young men are fallen by the sword of the power of the LORD; the LORD has slain them in the day of His anger; the LORD has killed, and not pitied. The LORD has summoned, as the LORD calls the people to temple on a solemn day, the terrors that are seen everywhere. In the day of the LORD's anger, no one escaped or survived.

The Lord of the fallen state, the spokesman for the fallen human nature of his community, has admitted only that the people that he has swaddled and brought up, cared for and reared within his culture have been consumed by his enemies, the Babylonians and the Chaldeans as instruments of the LORD. Who is this Lord, this spokesman for every man in the fallen state?

CHAPTER 3

1 I am the man that hath seen affliction by the rod of his wrath.
2 He hath led me, and brought me into darkness, but not into light.
3 Surely against me is he turned; he turneth his hand against me all the day.

The Lord of the fallen state is the symbol of a human being, singularly or collectively, who has seen affliction to himself in the material world in which he dwells which has been delivered to him by the rod of His wrath, the wrath of the LORD of heaven. It is the Lord of the fallen state on earth who has brought man into darkness, but not into the light. Surely, He is turned against me and He has turned the hand of His control against man all day long because of his disobedience to the LORD of heaven.

4 My flesh and my skin hath he made old; he hath broken my bones.
5 He hath builded against me, and compassed me with gall and travail.
6 He hath set me in dark places, as they that be dead of old.
7 He hath hedged me about, that I cannot get out: he hath made my chain heavy.
8 Also when I cry and shout, he shutteth out my prayer.
9 He hath inclosed my ways with hewn stone, he hath made my paths crooked.
10 He was unto me as a bear lying in wait, and as a lion in secret places.
11 He hath turned aside my ways, and pulled me in pieces: he hath made me desolate.
12 He hath bent his bow, and set me as a mark for the arrow.
13 He hath caused the arrows of his quiver to enter into my reins.

The LORD has made the flesh and the skin of man old, and broken his bones. The LORD has built and compassed fallen man with gall and travail, bitterness and pain. The LORD has set man in places of darkness as were they who were dead of old times past. He has built a hedge about man that man cannot get out and He has given man on earth a heavy chain to bear.

When man cries and shouts, the Lord of the fallen state shuts out his prayer. He has enclosed my ways with blocks of stone and made my paths crooked. The Lord of the fallen state was like a powerful bear lying in wait or a destructive lion lying in wait in a secret place ready to pounce upon me and do bodily harm. He has diverted my way from the true path and pulled me in pieces: he has made me desolate. The Lord of the fallen state has bent his bow and made me a mark for his arrow. He has caused the harmful arrows in his quiver enter into the reins of each person's control.

14 I was a derision to all my people; and their song all the day.
15 He hath filled me with bitterness, he hath made me drunken with wormwood.
16 He hath also broken my teeth with gravel stones, he hath covered me with ashes.
17 And thou hast removed my soul far off from peace: I forgat prosperity.

The Testimony of the Major Prophets

I was a derision to all my people who looked at me with disdain and mocked me with their song all day long. The Lord of the fallen state has filled me with bitterness and drunk with wormwood wine which poisons my soul. He has broken my teeth with gravel stones and covered me with the ashes of sadness. He has removed my soul so far away from peace that I forgot what prosperity felt like. I need to remember what prosperity felt like when I knew what it was. There is a need to remember the prosperity that comes from the LORD.

18 And I said, My strength and my hope is perished from the LORD:
19 Remembering mine affliction and my misery, the wormwood and the gall.
20 My soul hath them still in remembrance, and is humbled in me.
21 This I recall to my mind, therefore have I hope.
22 It is of the LORD's mercies that we are not consumed, because his compassions fail not.
23 They are new every morning: great is thy faithfulness.
24 The LORD is my portion, saith my soul; therefore will I hope in him.
25 The LORD is good unto them that wait for him, to the soul that seeketh him.
26 It is good that a man should both hope and quietly wait for the salvation of the LORD.

Then I said, My strength and my hope is perished from the LORD: my connection with the LORD of heaven has been forgotten and severed in my consciousness. As I remembered my affliction and my misery, the wormwood and the gall of my misery, then, the soul of my body, mind and heart, had these miserable memories of my experience of life and they humbled me.

Then I recalled this to mind which gave me hope. It is of the LORD's mercies that we are not consumed, because His compassion to us is that we do not fail. The blessings from the LORD are new every morning: great is the faithfulness of the LORD in sending His blessings to us constantly. The LORD is my portion of love, life, truth and eternity, says my human soul composed of a heart that receives love, a mind that receives the truth and a body that receives life; therefore, I will hope in the LORD who has eternal values.

The LORD is good to them that wait for Him, that serve Him and His spirit into the world. The LORD is good to them that seek the spirit of the LORD by seeking His spirit to express His spirit which is in every person to be expressed. It is good that a man should both hope and quietly wait for the salvation of the LORD to come through him from the inside and not to him from the environment of the outside. The yoke with the spirit of the LORD is within man.

27 It is good for a man that he bear the yoke in his youth.
28 He sitteth alone and keepeth silence, because he hath borne it upon him.
29 He putteth his mouth in the dust; if so be there may be hope.
30 He giveth his cheek to him that smiteth him: he is filled full with reproach.
31 For the Lord will not cast off for ever:
32 But though he cause grief, yet will he have compassion according to the multitude of his mercies.
33 For he doth not afflict willingly nor grieve the children of men.
34 To crush under his feet all the prisoners of the earth,
35 To turn aside the right of a man before the face of the most High,
36 To subvert a man in his cause, the Lord approveth not.

It is good for a man that he bear the yoke of the spirit of the LORD in his youth so that he can learn the discipline of the spirit at an early age and it will be natural to him. Once he has learned the discipline of the spirit, he can sit alone by himself and keep silence because he has borne the spirit upon him and he speaks to others of the spirit.

He puts his mouth, his expression of the spirit, into the material pattern of the dust of the ground to see if there is any response to the spirit; if so, then there may be hope. The person with the discipline of the spirit gives his cheek, the spiritual attention that comes through his face, to the material person who strikes the spiritual expression that comes through him: If the spirit strikes the material person, he will be filled full with reproach. For the Lord of the fallen state will not express the distortion from his spirit forever.

The Symbolic Version of Lamentations

But though the spiritual man may cause grief to the material man, yet will he have compassion according to the multitude of his mercies which come forth through him. The spiritual man does not afflict willingly nor intend to grieve the children of men; or, to crush under his feet all the prisoners of the earth, to turn aside the right of a man to appear before the face of the most High, or to subvert a man in his cause to find and express the LORD. The Lord of the fallen state would not approve of the mission of the spiritual man.

37 Who is he that saith, and it cometh to pass, when the Lord commandeth it not?
38 Out of the mouth of the most High proceedeth not evil and good?
39 Wherefore doth a living man complain, a man for the punishment of his sins?

Who is He that says, and it comes to pass, when the Lord of the fallen state commands it not to happen? It happens anyway. Therefore the power is greater and higher than the Lord of the earth. Does not both good and evil proceed out of the mouth of the most High? Why does a living man complain, particularly a man who is being punished for his sins?

40 Let us search and try our ways, and turn again to the LORD.
41 Let us lift up our heart with our hands unto God in the heavens.
42 We have transgressed and have rebelled: thou hast not pardoned.
43 Thou hast covered with anger, and persecuted us: thou hast slain, thou hast not pitied.
44 Thou hast covered thyself with a cloud, that our prayer should not pass through.
45 Thou hast made us as the offscouring and refuse in the midst of the people.

The author of Lamentations says, Let us search and try our ways, our behaviors, to examine the nature of our expression to determine if there is a need to turn again to the LORD. If there is a need for repentance and change, then let us lift up our hearts with our hands to God in the heavens. We have transgressed and have rebelled: God has not pardoned our transgression if we do not repent and change. God has covered us with anger, and persecuted us with the effect of the Law of Sowing and Reaping: God has slain and not pitied at the application of the Law. God has covered Himself with a cloud that our prayers will not pass through because his Law is very just and very fair. When we do not obey the Law of God, He has made us as the scum and refuse to be seen in the midst of the people so that the people can see the nature of our expression is from the fruit that is within us. Our enemies can see what is within us by the fruit of our expression. As we express ourselves, people know what is in our minds and hearts by our fruits, by our expressions.

46 All our enemies have opened their mouths against us.
47 Fear and a snare is come upon us, desolation and destruction.
48 Mine eye runneth down with rivers of water for the destruction of the daughter of my people.
49 Mine eye trickleth down, and ceaseth not, without any intermission,
50 Till the LORD look down, and behold from heaven.
51 Mine eye affecteth mine heart because of all the daughters of my city.
52 Mine enemies chased me sore, like a bird, without cause.
53 They have cut off my life in the dungeon, and cast a stone upon me.
54 Waters flowed over mine head; then I said, I am cut off.

All our enemies have opened their mouths to speak against our behaviors which reveal the conditions of our hearts to produce the sinfulness of Jerusalem. The LORD has used the enemy to punish us. Fear and a snare have come upon us to produce desolation and destruction. The eye of Jeremiah runs down with rivers of tears for the destruction of the daughter of My people, the people of Jerusalem and the other captives. His eye trickles down, and ceases not, without any intermission, as long as the LORD looks down, and beholds from heaven to see the justness of the divine punishment for disobeying the LORD God.

Those who were Jeremiah's enemies without cause chased him like a bird. They tried to cut off his life in a dungeon, and cast stones upon him. Waters flowed over his head; then he said, I am cut off.

55 I called upon thy name, O LORD, out of the low dungeon.
56 Thou hast heard my voice: hide not thine ear at my breathing, at my cry.

The Testimony of the Major Prophets

57 Thou drewest near in the day that I called upon thee: thou saidst, Fear not.

Jeremiah called upon the LORD of heaven out of his dungeon. The LORD heard Jeremiah's voice. He did not hide His ear at the difficulty in Jeremiah's breathing and his cry for help. The LORD drew near to Jeremiah in the day that Jeremiah called upon Him. The LORD said, Fear not.

58 O Lord, thou hast pleaded the causes of my soul; thou hast redeemed my life.

The Lord of the fallen state who had pleaded the cause of his soul, his physical body, mind and heart, to the LORD of heaven. The LORD of heaven has redeemed the life of the Lord of the fallen state, Jeremiah. Jeremiah, in his turning and calling to the LORD, has experienced the covenant-agreement with the LORD as a result of true repentance.

59 O LORD, thou hast seen my wrong: judge thou my cause.
60 Thou hast seen all their vengeance and all their imaginations against me.
61 Thou hast heard their reproach, O LORD, and all their imaginations against me;
62 The lips of those that rose up against me, and their device against me all the day.
63 Behold their sitting down, and their rising up; I am their musick.
64 Render unto them a recompence, O LORD, according to the work of their hands.
65 Give them sorrow of heart, thy curse unto them.
66 Persecute and destroy them in anger from under the heavens of the LORD.

Jeremiah understands that the LORD has been with him always and seen all of his behaviors. The LORD has always been in position to see and judge the cause of Jeremiah's actions. The feelings and thoughts in the consciousness of Jeremiah were the cause of all of his actions. The LORD knows that He provides the power of the spirit to each spiritual person who then can use that power to serve the LORD as a co-creator with and for the LORD, or he can use the power in self-centeredness. The LORD has seen all their vengeance and all their imaginations that actions have brought against him. The LORD has heard the reproach and all the imaginations of the working of the Law against Jeremiah; the lips of those that rose up against him, and their device against him all the day. The LORD has heard it all and Jeremiah is aware of it. Everything that is done by everyone is subject to the operation of the Law of Sowing and Reaping.

Behold their sitting down, and their rising up; all the activities generated by people in the world of their environment in the material world. Jeremiah understands, I am their music: the spirit that I Am which comes from the LORD, I AM, is the heavenly music that sounds on earth to produce conditions according to the Law. Render to them a recompence, O LORD, according to the work of their hands: As people sow, let them reap! Give them sorrow of heart when they sow the wrong seed, which is the LORD's curse to them so that they will know that they are planting the wrong seed which is not of the LORD, which is not of love. If people continue to sow the seeds that are not of the LORD, then the destructive power will persecute and destroy them in anger from under the heavens of the LORD. Jeremiah, in covenant-agreement with the LORD, understands the operation of the Law.

CHAPTER 4

1 How is the gold become dim! how is the most fine gold changed! The stones of the sanctuary are poured out in the top of every street.
2 The precious sons of Zion, comparable to fine gold, how are they esteemed as earthen pitchers, the work of the hands of the potter!
3 Even the sea monsters draw out the breast, they give suck to their young ones: the daughter of my people is become cruel, like the ostriches in the wilderness.
4 The tongue of the sucking child cleaveth to the roof of his mouth for thirst: the young children ask bread, and no man breaketh it unto them.

The LORD in heaven sends His power into the earth. Gold is an earthly symbol of love from heaven. The LORD sends His spirit of love, His gold, into the earth to be what it is, gold. Gold is a beautiful symbol for love from the LORD because gold does not tarnish or change. How does the gold of the spirit of love leave heaven, enter the earth, and become dim?! The LORD has sown the gold of love from heaven into mankind on earth where He should reap the gold of love on earth. How is the gold of the LORD become dim! How is the most fine gold changed?! The LORD sends His divine BEING into the earth to build the kingdom. The stones of the sanctuary, the earthly materials, are poured out in the top of every street for man to build the temple of God on earth. The LORD sends divine Beings to build a divine world. Man in the fallen state has come to believe that he is "only human" thereby exchanging his divine heritage for a mess of pottage, an "only human" identity. Man is made in the image and likeness of God! The collective being of Mankind, Man, on earth is composed of the precious sons of Zion, the high place of spiritual consciousness in the spiritual men who are in covenant-agreement with God.

The precious sons of Zion are comparable to fine gold. How are they esteemed as earthen pitchers, earthen pitchers that symbolize that they are "only human", only earth, but made by the work of the hands of the potter! Man is not an earthen pitcher. The sons of Zion are comparable to fine gold, the spirit of love, that is in the earthen pitcher. The fine gold in man draws its power from the gold of the LORD. Even the sea monsters, great whales, draw milk out the breast of their mothers as they suckle their young ones. The young ones grow to be what they were designed to be. The daughter, the offspring, of the LORD's people has become cruel like the ostriches in the wilderness. Man in the fallen state is like a wild bird lost in the wilderness. The tongue of the sucking child cleaves to the roof of his mouth because of its thirst which is an illustration that the young child is ready to drink the milk of divine kindness to nourish its body but there is no one to provide the milk. As they grow, the young children ask for the bread from heaven, and no man breaks the heavenly bread of the spirit to give it to them. The people are hungry for spiritual food. It is the nature of fine gold to be gold. It is the nature of a child of the LORD to seek the LORD.

5 They that did feed delicately are desolate in the streets: they that were brought up in scarlet embrace dunghills.
6 For the punishment of the iniquity of the daughter of my people is greater than the punishment of the sin of Sodom, that was overthrown as in a moment, and no hands stayed on her.

The Testimony of the Major Prophets

7 Her Nazarites were purer than snow, they were whiter than milk, they were more ruddy in body than rubies, their polishing was of sapphire:
8 Their visage is blacker than a coal; they are not known in the streets: their skin cleaveth to their bones; it is withered, it is become like a stick.

The people who were "only human" are the people in the fallen state who did feed lightly, sparingly, from the spiritual food from the divine source, and, consequently, they are desolate in the streets. The people who were raised with earthly treasures, symbolized by scarlet or royal purple, are the desolate people who embrace dunghills. The punishment for the weakness of the iniquity of the daughter of my people is greater than the punishment of the sin of Sodom, that was overthrown in a moment, and no hands stayed on her.

The Nazarites were those special people who chose a life of total devotion to the LORD. As emissaries of the Father, they were as princes of the earthly kingdom. Her princes, the Nazarites were purer than snow, whiter than milk, more ruddy in body than rubies, and their polishing was of sapphire. In the fallen state of Jerusalem, their visage, their countenance, was blacker than a coal; they are not known in the streets: their skin cleaves to their bones; it is withered, it is become like a stick.

9 They that be slain with the sword are better than they that be slain with hunger: for these pine away, stricken through for want of the fruits of the field.
10 The hands of the pitiful women have sodden their own children: they were their meat in the destruction of the daughter of my people.
11 The LORD hath accomplished his fury; he hath poured out his fierce anger, and hath kindled a fire in Zion, and it hath devoured the foundations thereof.

The desolation of Jerusalem left people in such dire straits that the ones who were killed quickly by the sword were better off than those slain slowly by hunger who would pine away, stricken for the lack of food from the fruits of the field. The hands of the pitiful women have cooked their own children for food during the destruction and the aftermath of the people. The LORD has accomplished His fury; he has poured out his fierce anger which is the destructive aspect to the Law in action. The LORD has kindled a fire in Zion, the symbol of the high place in spiritual consciousness, that has devoured the material foundations of the evil thereof.

12 The kings of the earth, and all the inhabitants of the world, would not have believed that the adversary and the enemy should have entered into the gates of Jerusalem.
13 For the sins of her prophets, and the iniquities of her priests, that have shed the blood of the just in the midst of her,
14 They have wandered as blind men in the streets, they have polluted themselves with blood, so that men could not touch their garments.
15 They cried unto them, Depart ye; it is unclean; depart, depart, touch not: when they fled away and wandered, they said among the heathen, They shall no more sojourn there.

The kings of the earth, and all the inhabitants of the world, would not have believed that the adversary and the enemy should have entered into the gates of Jerusalem. It was because of the sins of her prophets, and the iniquities of her priests who have shed the blood of the just in the midst of the people for whom they were to set a good example as a representative of the LORD. These leaders have wandered as blind men in the streets, who could not see their true purpose of representing the spirit of the spirit of the LORD to the people, they have polluted themselves with the blood of the sinful fallen state, so that men could not touch their spiritual garments. The prophets and priests are so polluted and defiled that no one wants to follow their example. The people who see them say, Depart you who are unclean; depart, do not touch us: when they fled away and wandered, they said among the heathen, They shall sojourn there in the "holy" city no more.

16 The anger of the LORD hath divided them; he will no more regard them: they respected not the persons of the priests, they favoured not the elders.
17 As for us, our eyes as yet failed for our vain help: in our watching we have watched for a nation that could not save us.

18 They hunt our steps, that we cannot go in our streets: our end is near, our days are fulfilled; for our end is come.
19 Our persecutors are swifter than the eagles of the heaven: they pursued us upon the mountains, they laid wait for us in the wilderness.
20 The breath of our nostrils, the anointed of the LORD, was taken in their pits, of whom we said, Under his shadow we shall live among the heathen.

The anger of the destructive power of the LORD has divided the people of Jerusalem and Judah; He will regard them no more: the people in the destroyed conditions did not respect the leaders, the priests and the elders. As for us, our eyes for our vain help, the vanity of our leadership provided a false example. In our search, we watched for a nation that could not save us.

The invaders pursue our steps so that we cannot go into the streets: our end is near, our days are fulfilled; for our end is come. Our persecutors who chase us are swifter than the eagles of the heaven: they pursued us upon the mountains and laid wait for us in the wilderness. Jeremiah, the anointed of the LORD who was the breath of life to our nostrils, was taken and placed in their pits as a prisoner. We believed that under his shadow, under his example, we would live and survive among the heathen.

21 Rejoice and be glad, O daughter of Edom, that dwellest in the land of Uz; the cup also shall pass through unto thee: thou shalt be drunken, and shalt make thyself naked.
22 The punishment of thine iniquity is accomplished, O daughter of Zion; he will no more carry thee away into captivity: he will visit thine iniquity, O daughter of Edom; he will discover thy sins.

The message of Jeremiah was to rejoice and be glad, daughter of Edom that dwells in the land of Uz, a large territory east of Jordan that symbolizes the heathen of the fallen state. The cup of retribution of the Law of the LORD shall pass to you and you must drink it, be made drunk by it, be made naked, and be exposed for your sins so that you are aware of your sins. The punishment of your iniquity is then accomplished. You will not be exiled away from the LORD any longer; He will visit you exactly where you are; He will discover your sins where you are. He will not punish you at some future time for your sins; He will punish you with the conditions created by your sins.

CHAPTER 5

1 Remember, O LORD, what is come upon us: consider, and behold our reproach.
2 Our inheritance is turned to strangers, our houses to aliens.
3 We are orphans and fatherless, our mothers are as widows.
4 We have drunken our water for money; our wood is sold unto us.
5 Our necks are under persecution: we labour, and have no rest.

The people of Jerusalem and Judah who have been exiled and punished have not really learned or comprehended the operation of the Law. They ask the LORD for mercy to remove them from their circumstances of the moment which were the result of the operation of the Law. They pray to the LORD to change their circumstances by having the LORD become aware of what devastation that they have been through. Remember, O LORD, what is come upon us: consider, and behold our reproach and how terrible that it has been. The LORD is asked to feel sorry for the people that He has punished.

The inheritance of the promised land has been turned to strangers; our houses to aliens. We, as a punished people, are orphans and fatherless, our mothers are as widows. We have had to pay money to get our water; our wood is sold unto us. Our necks are under constant persecution: we labor, and have no rest.

6 We have given the hand to the Egyptians, and to the Assyrians, to be satisfied with bread.
7 Our fathers have sinned, and are not; and we have borne their iniquities.
8 Servants have ruled over us: there is none that doth deliver us out of their hand.
9 We gat our bread with the peril of our lives because of the sword of the wilderness.
10 Our skin was black like an oven because of the terrible famine.

We have given the hand of our control over to the Egyptians, and to the Assyrians, to get enough bread to survive. Our fathers have sinned, and are not here to bear the burden of their decisions; and we have borne their iniquities. Servants have ruled over us: there is no one like Moses to deliver us out of their control. We get our bread with the peril of our lives because of the destructive cycle of the power of the sword of the LORD in the wilderness. Our skin was black like an oven because of the terrible famine of the absence of the living bread of the spirit of the LORD which would nourish us.

11 They ravished the women in Zion, and the maids in the cities of Judah.
12 Princes are hanged up by their hand: the faces of elders were not honoured.
13 They took the young men to grind, and the children fell under the wood.
14 The elders have ceased from the gate, the young men from their musick.

The Symbolic Version of Lamentations

The conquerors ravished the women in Zion, and the maids in the cities of Judah. Princes are hanged up by their hands: the faces of elders were not honored or shown the respect due to old age. They took the young men to grind at the millstones, and the children fell under heavy loads of wood. The elders are gone from congregating at the gate, and the young men have stopped making their music. The people are unhappy and sad.

15 The joy of our heart is ceased; our dance is turned into mourning.
16 The crown is fallen from our head: woe unto us, that we have sinned!
17 For this our heart is faint; for these things our eyes are dim.
18 Because of the mountain of Zion, which is desolate, the foxes walk upon it.

The joy of our heart is ceased; our dance is turned into mourning. The crown is fallen from our head: woe unto us, that we have sinned! For this our heart is faint; for these things our eyes are dim. Because of the mountain of Zion, the high holy place within us, which is desolate, the foxes walk upon the uninhabited land.

19 Thou, O LORD, remainest for ever; thy throne from generation to generation.
20 Wherefore dost thou forget us for ever, and forsake us so long time?
21 Turn thou us unto thee, O LORD, and we shall be turned; renew our days as of old.
22 But thou hast utterly rejected us; thou art very wroth against us.

O LORD, You remain for ever; Your throne exists from generation to generation. Wherefore and why do you forget us for ever, and forsake us so long time? Turn us to You, O LORD, and we shall be turned; renew our days as of old. But You, LORD, have utterly rejected us; You are very wroth against us. If any changes are to occur, the changes are up to the LORD. The people pray for the LORD to turn them back to Him and then, after they are turned, everything will be as it was in the sinful days of old which the people thought were the good old days.

Jeremiah is sad and laments the condition that the people want the LORD to turn them rather than the people use their freedom of choice to turn themselves to the LORD, which is the only true repentance. Jeremiah knows that the LORD is present and His spirit is flowing through all the people on earth because he knows that the spirit of the LORD is flowing through him. As long as the people in any generation wait for the LORD to turn them, they will wait forever. Jeremiah knows that when the people repent, and magnify the spirit of the LORD through each of them individually, as though they were the only person on earth, then, they will come to know the spirit that they express, the spirit of the of the LORD.

The LORD has chosen them but they have not chosen to serve the LORD, to wait on the LORD, to let the LORD's spirit flow through them so that they will know eternal life. The covenant with the LORD is available to everyone. The fact that the people have not turned to serve the LORD their God is lamentable.

Anthony John Monaco   September 3, 1998

The Symbolic Version of
Daniel

Anthony John Monaco

A Stars of the Scriptures Series

FOREWORD

The name Daniel means, "the judgment of God", or, "God is my judge". Daniel is a prophet who descended from the royal family of David. He was captured and taken to Babylon when he was very young. Daniel is known for his ability to interpret dreams and the symbolic versions of these dreams will be considered in the following text.

There is a widely held view that the Book of Daniel is fictional. This viewpoint is based on the assumption that long-range predictive prophecy is impossible. Some scholars believe that the Book of Daniel was not written until the Second Century BC after the fulfillment of the prophecies had taken place. The word, **prophecy**, relates to the ability **to foretell the future**. We are more interested in the word, **prophesy**, which is to speak in the spirit of the LORD in the present moment.

The author believes that Daniel had the ability to prophesy the spirit of the LORD during the time in which he lived. The ability to prophesy the spirit of the LORD is the result of a person who is in the covenant-agreement with the LORD. The covenant is the agreement on the part of a human being to let the spirit of the LORD flow through the heart, mind and body of a person so that the invisible spirit of the LORD is made visible on earth. In this covenant-agreement with the spirit of the LORD, the person is able to see with the vision of the LORD Who sees things in the material world exactly as they are. The material world is the clothing of the invisible spirit. The person in the covenant with the LORD also lets a portion of the divine design enter the earth because of his or her submission to the spirit. This relationship with the spirit of the LORD flowing clearly and cleanly through the heart, mind and physical body of a person gives that person the authority to prophesy and to speak the truth. The person with the authority to prophesy is regarded as a prophet.

Daniel was not alone or unique in being referred to as a prophet of the LORD. The prophets of Judah following king David and king Solomon who ruled over the United Kingdom were Isaiah, Jeremiah, Ezekiel and Daniel. Isaiah and Jeremiah were prophets at the time of the rulership of the kings of Judah until the fall of Jerusalem in 586 BC. Ezekiel and Daniel lived during the time of the Jews in exile until the fall of Babylon by king Cyrus, the founder of the Persian empire, in 539 BC. Daniel lived from 605-530 BC.

These four prophets spoke with the authority of the LORD. There is an experience which gave these prophets the authority to speak the word of the LORD and that experience is the covenant-agreement between the LORD and a person. The prophets spoke in a way to encourage others to listen to the word of the LORD and serve the spirit of the LORD in their own living of life on earth. The prophets encouraged others to participate in the expression of the spirit of the LORD which was not exclusive to them. In actual fact, the spirit of the LORD is moving through everyone who is alive.

Let us consider that the words in the Book of Daniel are not only a prophecy to predict the future hundreds of years later. Instead, let us also consider the Book of Daniel as the articulated words of Daniel the prophet who would

The Testimony of the Major Prophets

prophesy the spirit of the LORD in the living of his life while he was a captive in Babylon. Let us not change the words of the King James version of the Book of Daniel but let us consider a new interpretation of the words that depart from a literal translation to an allegorical, symbolic or spiritual interpretation of the very same words.

Let us consider The Symbolic Version of Daniel to determine if the words of Daniel written long ago have meaning for us in the here and now as we read the words today.

CHAPTER 1

1 In the third year of the reign of Jehoiakim king of Judah came Nebuchadnezzar king of Babylon unto Jerusalem, and besieged it.

Jehoiakim, king of Judah, ruled from 609-598 BC. In the third year of the reign of Jehoiakim king of Judah, which according to the Babylonian system of counting calendar years was 605 BC, king Nebuchadnezzar of Babylon came to Jerusalem, and besieged it. (According to the Judahite system, which counted the year of accession to the throne as the first year, this would be the fourth year of the reign of king Jehoiakim. This difference of one year is a piece of evidence that gives credence to the fact that the Book of Daniel was written by Daniel who was educated by the Babylonians after he had been taken captive as a young boy.)

The city of Jerusalem, which was besieged by Nebuchadnezzar in 605 BC, did not fall until 586 BC. The first deportation of Jews who were taken captive included young Daniel in the year 605 BC; the second deportation of Jews included Ezekiel in 597 BC; and the third deportation of Jews occurred when the Babylonians destroyed Jerusalem and the temple in 586 BC. The defeat of the people of Judah and the destruction of Jerusalem came about because the people did not keep their portion of the agreement of the covenant with the LORD. This led the disobedient people into the destructive cycle of the spiritual Law of Sowing and Reaping. If the people do not reveal the spirit of the LORD on earth, then the distorted effects of the working of the Law through people will put in an appearance in the world of form on earth. The distortions of the divine spiritual design of the LORD are referred to as being caused by the diminished and distorted design of the Lord (small letters) produced by people in the fallen state.

2 And the Lord gave Jehoiakim king of Judah into his hand, with part of the vessels of the house of God: which he carried into the land of Shinar to the house of his god; and he brought the vessels into the treasure house of his god.

The operation of the destructive cycle of the Law placed king Jehoiakim into the hand of control of Nebuchadnezzar, king of Babylon. Some of the vessels of the house of God, the temple, in Jerusalem were carried by representatives of the king of Babylon into the land of Shinar—the ancient name of the tract of land through which the Tigris and Euphrates Rivers flowed, also known as Chaldea or Babylonia—to the house of his god, a false god. A false god is a material object made by a person to represent someone's idea of a deity; the true God created the person who is worshipping the false god. The material vessels of the temple in Jerusalem were delivered into the treasure house of the god of Babylon.

3 And the king spake unto Ashpenaz the master of his eunuchs, that he should bring certain of the children of Israel, and of the king's seed, and of the princes;
4 Children in whom was no blemish, but well favoured, and skilful in all wisdom, and cunning in knowledge, and understanding science, and such as had ability in them to stand in the king's palace, and whom they might teach the learning and the tongue of the Chaldeans.

The Testimony of the Major Prophets

5 And the king appointed them a daily provision of the king's meat, and of the wine which he drank: so nourishing them three years, that at the end thereof they might stand before the king.

King Nebuchadnezzar spoke to Ashpenaz the master of his eunuchs, that he should bring certain of the children of Israel, who were descendant's of the king of Judah and of the princes. These children should be without physical defects, be well favored, skillful in all wisdom, cunning in knowledge, understanding science, and have the ability in them to stand in the king's palace where they might be taught the learning and the tongue of the Chaldeans. The king assigned these selected children a daily provision of the king's meat, and of the wine from the king's table. In addition to the physical food from the king's table, the meat and wine also symbolized the traditions, teachings and beliefs of the culture which would be assimilated along with the meals. The children were to be nourished and taught for three years, and at the end of that time, they would stand before the king, who would decide if they could be of service to Nebuchadnezzar. The act of taking the young children of the defeated king and princes was a common practice to abort the legacy of the defeated king. The victors took the seed, the children, of the defeated royalty and transplanted them to the customs and culture of the new master in order to prevent revolt.

6 Now among these were of the children of Judah, Daniel, Hananiah, Mishael, and Azariah:
7 Unto whom the prince of the eunuchs gave names: for he gave unto Daniel the name of Belteshazzar; and to Hananiah, of Shadrach; and to Mishael, of Meshach; and to Azariah, of Abednego.
8 But Daniel purposed in his heart that he would not defile himself with the portion of the king's meat, nor with the wine which he drank: therefore he requested of the prince of the eunuchs that he might not defile himself.

Now among these children of Judah were Daniel, Hananiah, Mishael, and Azariah: Daniel means, "the judgment of God"; Hananiah means, "the LORD shows grace"; Mishael means, "Who is what God is?" and Azariah means, "the LORD helps". In symbolic and allegorical terms, Daniel can be seen as the focus of a **spirit** of God; Hananiah can be seen as the focus of the spirit moving through the **heart**; Mishael can be seen as the focus of spirit moving through the **mind**; and Azariah can be seen as the focus of spirit moving through the **physical body**.

The prince of the eunuchs gave Daniel and his three friends Babylonian names: Daniel became Belteshazzar, which means, "Bel or Marduk (names of false gods) protect his life"; Hananiah became Shadrach, which means, "command of Aku", the moon-god; Mishael became Meshach which means, "Who is what Aku is?"; Azariah became Abednego which means, "a servant of Nego", a Babylonian god. The prince of the eunuchs changed the meanings of the names of Daniel and his 3 friends from an invisible God to the names of visible material gods of the Babylonians. This transition indicates a fall from spiritual identity to a material identity. The idols of the Babylonians are given glory.

Although these select children of Judah were promised and guaranteed to be fed from the king's table, Daniel resolved in his heart that he would not defile himself with the portion of the king's meat, nor with the wine which he drank. The captives considered the food from the king's table as unclean and contaminated because the first portion of the food was offered to idols and a portion of the wine was poured out on a pagan altar. Daniel, who did not want to partake of the "unclean" food and wine therefore requested from the prince of the eunuchs that he, Daniel, might not defile himself in the sight of the LORD by eating unclean food and drink, (and also assimilating the beliefs of the Babylonians).

9 Now God had brought Daniel into favour and tender love with the prince of the eunuchs.
10 And the prince of the eunuchs said unto Daniel, I fear my lord the king, who hath appointed your meat and your drink: for why should he see your faces worse liking than the children which are of your sort? then shall ye make me endanger my head to the king.

Now God had brought Daniel into favor and tender love with the prince of the eunuchs. When Daniel asked the prince of the eunuchs that he be excused from eating the unclean food from the table of the king, the prince of the eunuchs said to Daniel, that he feared king Nebuchadnezzar, who assigned Daniel meat and drink from the king's table: and when the king sees your faces looking worse than the children which are your age, then the prince of eunuchs might lose his head for catering to Daniel.

11 Then said Daniel to Melzar, whom the prince of the eunuchs had set over Daniel, Hananiah, Mishael, and Azariah,
12 Prove thy servants, I beseech thee, ten days; and let them give us pulse to eat, and water to drink.
13 Then let our countenances be looked upon before thee, and the countenance of the children that eat of the portion of the king's meat: and as thou seest, deal with thy servants.
14 So he consented to them in this matter, and proved them ten days.

Then Daniel said to Melzar, the steward whom the prince of the eunuchs had set over Daniel and his three friends, Hananiah, Mishael, and Azariah, to test his servants for ten days by giving them pulse, which is leguminous vegetables such as peas and beans, to eat, and water to drink. Legumes are rich in protein. Then let our countenances be looked upon compared to the faces of the children that eat of the portion of the king's meat. Then, deal with your servants according to what you see. So the guard consented to them in this matter, and tested them for ten days.

15 And at the end of ten days their countenances appeared fairer and fatter in flesh than all the children which did eat the portion of the king's meat.
16 Thus Melzar took away the portion of their meat, and the wine that they should drink; and gave them pulse.

At the end of ten days, the countenances of Daniel and his three friends appeared fairer and fatter in flesh, more muscular, than all the children which did eat the diet of the king's table. If Daniel is seen as a focus of spirit, and his three friends are seen as symbols of the heart, the mind and the physical body, then the story of Daniel has application to everyone. As a result of the test, Melzar took away the portion of the meat that the children would eat from the king's table, and the wine that they should drink; and he gave them the same food that Daniel and his three friends were eating. The culture and the ways of Daniel, a servant of the LORD, has been accepted and utilized by his captor.

17 As for these four children, God gave them knowledge and skill in all learning and wisdom: and Daniel had understanding in all visions and dreams.
18 Now at the end of the days that the king had said he should bring them in, then the prince of the eunuchs brought them in before Nebuchadnezzar.
19 And the king communed with them; and among them all was found none like Daniel, Hananiah, Mishael, and Azariah: therefore stood they before the king.
20 And in all matters of wisdom and understanding, that the king inquired of them, he found them ten times better than all the magicians and astrologers that were in all his realm.
21 And Daniel continued even unto the first year of king Cyrus.

As for these four children, God gave them knowledge and skill in all learning and wisdom from the Babylonian and Chaldean culture: and Daniel had an innate understanding in all visions and dreams which would prove valuable to him. Although Daniel was not of the Babylonian culture, he learned to function within that world but not be controlled by it.

Now at the end of the three years that the king had provided them for orientation and education, the prince of the eunuchs brought them in before Nebuchadnezzar. The king communed with them; and, among them all, none was found like Daniel, Hananiah, Mishael, and Azariah. Therefore, they stood before the king. In all matters of wisdom and understanding that the king inquired of them, he found them ten times better than all the established magicians and astrologers that were in all his realm. Daniel and his three friends had found favor in the eyes of the king of Babylon.

And Daniel continued to be looked upon with favor by king Nebuchadnezzar even to the first year of king Cyrus, the Persian, who defeated Babylon in 539 BC, the time in which king Cyrus freed the hostages from Babylon and allowed the captives to return to Judah. Daniel was alive until 537 BC, which meant that Daniel saw the exiles return to Judah.

CHAPTER 2

1 And in the second year of the reign of Nebuchadnezzar Nebuchadnezzar dreamed dreams, wherewith his spirit was troubled, and his sleep brake from him.
2 Then the king commanded to call the magicians, and the astrologers, and the sorcerers, and the Chaldeans, for to shew the king his dreams. So they came and stood before the king.
3 And the king said unto them, I have dreamed a dream, and my spirit was troubled to know the dream.
4 Then spake the Chaldeans to the king in Syriack, O king, live for ever: tell thy servants the dream, and we will shew the interpretation.

In 604 BC, the second year of the reign of Nebuchadnezzar, Nebuchadnezzar dreamed dreams, whereby his heart and mind were troubled, and he was unable to sleep. In symbolic comparison with Daniel who has three "friends", it can be seen that king Nebuchadnezzar has a heart, a mind and a physical body that are troubled and "unfriendly" to him. It is apparent that he lacks the spiritual awareness that Daniel possesses as a servant of the LORD. The king, who is in a state of discomfort, commanded all the magicians, the astrologers, the sorcerers, and the Chaldeans, to show the king his dreams. So, the wise men of the land came and stood before their king.

The king told them that he had dreamed a dream, and his spirit was troubled to know the dream. Then the Chaldeans spoke to the king in Syriack, in the language of Syria, Aramaic. Aramaic, the language of the Syrians, was the language which almost everyone understood. Since astrologers were of every racial background, Aramaic was used as the official court language. The Chaldeans greeted their king with the customary phrase, O king, live for ever: tell your servants the dream, and we will show you the interpretation of it.

5 The king answered and said to the Chaldeans, The thing is gone from me: if ye will not make known unto me the dream, with the interpretation thereof, ye shall be cut in pieces, and your houses shall be made a dunghill.
6 But if ye shew the dream, and the interpretation thereof, ye shall receive of me gifts and rewards and great honour: therefore shew me the dream, and the interpretation thereof.

The king told his advisers that the troubling dream was gone from his memory. If the astrologers did not tell the king what his dream was and its interpretation, they would be cut in pieces and their houses would be turned into a dunghill. But, if they show the king the dream with its interpretation, they will receive gifts, rewards and great honor. The king demanded that the astrologers not only reveal the nature of his dream but he also demanded that they reveal the interpretation of it.

7 They answered again and said, Let the king tell his servants the dream, and we will shew the interpretation of it.
8 The king answered and said, I know of certainty that ye would gain the time, because ye see the thing is gone from me.

The Symbolic Version of Daniel

9 But if ye will not make known unto me the dream, there is but one decree for you: for ye have prepared lying and corrupt words to speak before me, till the time be changed: therefore tell me the dream, and I shall know that ye can shew me the interpretation thereof.

The astrologers and wise men asked the king again to tell them his dream and then, after they had heard the dream, they would show him the interpretation of it. The king replied that they were trying to gain time because they see that the dream is gone from his memory. The king will not tell the advisors of his dream so that he can test their powers; he has not really forgotten his dream. If the wise men will not make the dream known to the king, then there is but one decree for them. The king believes that his advisors have prepared lying and corrupt words to speak to him until the situation will change. The king insists that his wise men tell him the dream—as proof of their abilities—so that the king shall know that they can show him the interpretation of it.

10 The Chaldeans answered before the king, and said, There is not a man upon the earth that can shew the king's matter: therefore there is no king, lord, nor ruler, that asked such things at any magician, or astrologer, or Chaldean.
11 And it is a rare thing that the king requireth, and there is none other that can shew it before the king, except the gods, whose dwelling is not with flesh.
12 For this cause the king was angry and very furious, and commanded to destroy all the wise men of Babylon.
13 And the decree went forth that the wise men should be slain; and they sought Daniel and his fellows to be slain.

The Chaldeans answered the king, and said, There is not a man upon the earth that can meet the king's request. There also has never been a king, lord, or ruler that asked such things of any magician, astrologer, or Chaldean. It is a rare thing that the king requires, and there is no one, except the gods, whose dwelling is not with flesh, that can show the king what he asks. For this cause the king was angry and very furious, and commanded his guard to destroy all the wise men of Babylon. He issued a decree that all the wise men should be slain. The king's guard also sought Daniel and his fellows, who were considered to be wise men, so that they could be slain as their king commanded.

14 Then Daniel answered with counsel and wisdom to Arioch the captain of the king's guard, which was gone forth to slay the wise men of Babylon:
15 He answered and said to Arioch the king's captain, Why is the decree so hasty from the king? Then Arioch made the thing known to Daniel.
16 Then Daniel went in, and desired of the king that he would give him time, and that he would shew the king the interpretation.

Daniel spoke with words of counsel and wisdom to Arioch, the captain of the king's guard who had been ordered to slay the wise men of Babylon. Daniel asked Arioch the reason for the hasty decree from the king since he had not been present when the order was given. After Arioch explained the situation to Daniel, Daniel went to see the king and asked the king for time and he would reveal the details of the dream to the king, as well as the interpretation of the dream.

17 Then Daniel went to his house, and made the thing known to Hananiah, Mishael, and Azariah, his companions:
18 That they would desire mercies of the God of heaven concerning this secret; that Daniel and his fellows should not perish with the rest of the wise men of Babylon.

Daniel returned to his house, and made the situation—which he considered an opportunity—known to Hananiah, Mishael, and Azariah, his three companions. In symbolic language, Daniel and his three friends, the spirit and his heart, mind and body, went to the house of the LORD which is a place of spirit. They would desire and ask for the mercies of God of heaven, they would pray to God, concerning this secret so that Daniel and his fellows should continue to serve the LORD and that they should not perish with the rest of the wise men of Babylon.

19 Then was the secret revealed unto Daniel in a night vision. Then Daniel blessed the God of heaven.
20 Daniel answered and said, Blessed be the name of God for ever and ever: for wisdom and might are his:
21 And he changeth the times and the seasons: he removeth kings, and setteth up kings: he giveth wisdom unto the wise, and knowledge to them that know understanding:
22 He revealeth the deep and secret things: he knoweth what is in the darkness, and the light dwelleth with him.

The Testimony of the Major Prophets

23 I thank thee, and praise thee, O thou God of my fathers, who hast given me wisdom and might, and hast made known unto me now what we desired of thee: for thou hast now made known unto us the king's matter.

When the secret of the king's dream was revealed to Daniel in a night vision, a dream from the One God who had also given the dream to Nebuchadnezzar, Daniel blessed and gave praise and thanks to the God of heaven with the following words: Blessed be the name of God for ever and ever: for the wisdom and might are His: He changes the times and the seasons: He removes kings, and sets up kings: He gives wisdom to the wise, and knowledge to them that know understanding: He reveals the deep and secret things: He knows what is in the darkness, and the light dwells with Him. I thank You, and praise You, O God of my fathers, Who has given me wisdom and might, and has made known to me now what we desired of You: for You have now made known to us the king's dream.

Daniel has given the glory to God.

24 Therefore Daniel went in unto Arioch, whom the king had ordained to destroy the wise men of Babylon: he went and said thus unto him; Destroy not the wise men of Babylon: bring me in before the king, and I will shew unto the king the interpretation.
25 Then Arioch brought in Daniel before the king in haste, and said thus unto him, I have found a man of the captives of Judah, that will make known unto the king the interpretation.
26 The king answered and said to Daniel, whose name was Belteshazzar, Art thou able to make known unto me the dream which I have seen, and the interpretation thereof?

Therefore, Daniel went to Arioch, whom the king had ordained to destroy the wise men of Babylon, and said to him; Do not destroy the wise men of Babylon: bring me in before the king, and I will show the king the interpretation of his dream. Arioch hastily brought Daniel before the king and told him that one of the captives of Judah can interpret the king's dream. The king answered and said to Daniel, whose Babylonian name was Belteshazzar, Are you able to make known to me the dream which I have seen, and the interpretation thereof?

27 Daniel answered in the presence of the king, and said, The secret which the king hath demanded cannot the wise men, the astrologers, the magicians, the soothsayers, shew unto the king;
28 But there is a God in heaven that revealeth secrets, and maketh known to the king Nebuchadnezzar what shall be in the latter days. Thy dream, and the visions of thy head upon thy bed, are these;
29 As for thee, O king, thy thoughts came into thy mind upon thy bed, what should come to pass hereafter: and he that revealeth secrets maketh known to thee what shall come to pass.
30 But as for me, this secret is not revealed to me for any wisdom that I have more than any living, but for their sakes that shall make known the interpretation to the king, and that thou mightest know the thoughts of thy heart.

Daniel told the king that the secret which the king has demanded cannot be shown to him by the wise men, the astrologers, the magicians, and the soothsayers. But there is a God in heaven that reveals secrets, and makes known to king Nebuchadnezzar things that shall be in the days to come. The king's dream and the visions that were seen in the king's head while he was alone upon his bed, are these: The thoughts that came into your mind while you were on your bed are things that shall come to pass hereafter: and God in heaven that reveals secrets makes known to you what shall come to pass. This secret of your dream was not revealed to Daniel because Daniel has more wisdom than any other living person but for the sake of the people who will benefit when the interpretation to the king's dream is made known to the king and the king will know the thoughts of his own heart. (The spirit moving through the king is from the same Source as the spirit that is moving through Daniel.) Daniel tells the king of the nature of his dream which was known only by the king and God.

31 Thou, O king, sawest, and behold a great image. This great image, whose brightness was excellent, stood before thee; and the form thereof was terrible.
32 This image's head was of fine gold, his breast and his arms of silver, his belly and his thighs of brass,
33 His legs of iron, his feet part of iron and part of clay.
34 Thou sawest till that a stone was cut out without hands, which smote the image upon his feet that were of iron and clay, and brake them to pieces.

35 Then was the iron, the clay, the brass, the silver, and the gold, broken to pieces together, and became like the chaff of the summer threshingfloors; and the wind carried them away, that no place was found for them: and the stone that smote the image became a great mountain, and filled the whole earth.
36 This is the dream; and we will tell the interpretation thereof before the king.

Daniel tells the king that in his dream he saw a great image. This great image, whose brightness was excellent, stood before him; and the form of the image was terrible, awesome. This image's head was of fine gold, his breast and his arms of silver, his belly and his thighs of brass, his legs of iron, his feet part of iron and part of clay. The king saw the image until a stone, that was cut out without hands, struck the image upon his feet that were a mixture of iron and clay, and broke them to pieces. Then, the iron, the clay, the brass, the silver, and the gold were all broken to pieces and became like the chaff of the summer threshing floors. The wind carried them away, that no place was found for them: and the stone that struck the image became a great mountain, and filled the whole earth. This is the dream; and Daniel will tell the interpretation of it before the king.

37 Thou, O king, art a king of kings: for the God of heaven hath given thee a kingdom, power, and strength, and glory.
38 And wheresoever the children of men dwell, the beasts of the field and the fowls of the heaven hath he given into thine hand, and hath made thee ruler over them all. Thou art this head of gold.
39 And after thee shall arise another kingdom inferior to thee, and another third kingdom of brass, which shall bear rule over all the earth.
40 And the fourth kingdom shall be strong as iron: forasmuch as iron breaketh in pieces and subdueth all things: and as iron that breaketh all these, shall it break in pieces and bruise.

You, O king, are a king of kings. The God of heaven has given you a kingdom, power, and strength, and glory. The God of heaven has given into your hand and made you ruler over wherever the children of men, the beasts of the field and the fowls of the heaven dwell, and He has made you ruler over them all. You are this head of gold, and gold, the most precious metal, is the symbol of the power of love that comes to earth from God.

After you shall arise another kingdom that is inferior to you (which is symbolized by silver, a precious metal that tarnishes and becomes black), and then, another third kingdom of brass, which shall bear rule over all the earth. Brass has the appearance of gold but brass is not gold; it is a counterfeit. The kingdom of brass, a fallen kingdom shall rule over the whole earth. A fourth kingdom shall be strong as iron: for as iron has the property to break in pieces and subdue all things, the kingdom, symbolized by iron shall break in pieces and bruise others. The kingdoms on earth are decreasing in material value and increasing in their destructiveness that will subsequently break the image into pieces and the image which represents mankind in the fallen state shall be destroyed.

41 And whereas thou sawest the feet and toes, part of potters' clay, and part of iron, the kingdom shall be divided; but there shall be in it of the strength of the iron, forasmuch as thou sawest the iron mixed with miry clay.
42 And as the toes of the feet were part of iron, and part of clay, so the kingdom shall be partly strong, and partly broken.
43 And whereas thou sawest iron mixed with miry clay, they shall mingle themselves with the seed of men: but they shall not cleave one to another, even as iron is not mixed with clay.

And whereas you saw the feet and toes, part of potters' clay, and part of iron, the kingdom shall be divided; but there shall be in it of the strength of the iron, for as you saw the iron mixed with miry clay. As the toes of the feet were part of iron, and part of clay, so the kingdom shall be partly strong, and partly broken. This kingdom shall have potential strength of iron but the weakness of clay, which is dirt or dust. Where you saw iron mixed with miry clay, this symbolizes the people who shall mingle themselves with the seed of men: but they shall not cleave one to another, even as iron does not mix with clay. The dream has portrayed a vision of the deterioration of mankind in the fallen state without the spirit of God and as a progressive disintegration of man made in a disintegrating image that is not of God. (In symbolism, the feet illustrate understanding, or the lack of it.)

The Testimony of the Major Prophets

44 And in the days of these kings shall the God of heaven set up a kingdom, which shall never be destroyed: and the kingdom shall not be left to other people, but it shall break in pieces and consume all these kingdoms, and it shall stand for ever.
45 Forasmuch as thou sawest that the stone was cut out of the mountain without hands, and that it brake in pieces the iron, the brass, the clay, the silver, and the gold; the great God hath made known to the king what shall come to pass hereafter: and the dream is certain, and the interpretation thereof sure.

And in the days of these kings, the God of heaven shall set up a spiritual kingdom whose true design is in the spirit, which shall never be destroyed: and the kingdom, this kingdom of heaven from God, shall not be left to other people, but it shall break in pieces and consume all these material kingdoms, and the kingdom of spirit shall stand for ever.

For as you saw, the stone of God's true design in spirit was cut out of the mountain without human hands. The spiritual stone cannot be cut with hands because it is a spiritual stone with spiritual power from God. It is this spiritual stone cut without human hands that broke the iron, the brass, the clay, the silver, and the gold into pieces. The great God has made known to the king what shall come to pass hereafter: the dream is certain, and the interpretation thereof is sure. God's design is the only true design that will last and only those who submit to the God in heaven can bring God's kingdom on earth.

46 Then the king Nebuchadnezzar fell upon his face, and worshipped Daniel, and commanded that they should offer an oblation and sweet odours unto him.
47 The king answered unto Daniel, and said, Of a truth it is, that your God is a God of gods, and a Lord of kings, and a revealer of secrets, seeing thou couldest reveal this secret.
48 Then the king made Daniel a great man, and gave him many great gifts, and made him ruler over the whole province of Babylon, and chief of the governors over all the wise men of Babylon.
49 Then Daniel requested of the king, and he set Shadrach, Meshach, and Abednego, over the affairs of the province of Babylon: but Daniel sat in the gate of the king.

Then king Nebuchadnezzar fell upon his face, and worshipped Daniel, and commanded that his subjects should offer an oblation and sweet odors to him. The king answered Daniel, the bearer of the message from the God of heaven, and said, Of a truth it is, that your God is a God of gods, a Lord of kings, and a revealer of secrets, seeing that Daniel could reveal this secret known only to Nebuchadnezzar.

Then, the king made Daniel a great man, gave him many great gifts, and made him ruler over the whole province of Babylon, and chief of the governors over all the wise men of Babylon. But Daniel knew his place in the design of God On earth: Daniel requested of the king, and received the king's permission to set Shadrach, Meshach, and Abednego over the affairs of the province of Babylon to represent and magnify the spirit of God: but Daniel sat in the gate of the king, to be in close agreement with the king as the messenger of God who would prophesy the spirit of God. Daniel's presence would remind king Nebuchadnezzar that he is the earthly lord of lords of the fallen state who represents the head of gold in the image of the body of mankind.

CHAPTER 3

1 Nebuchadnezzar the king made an image of gold, whose height was threescore cubits, and the breadth thereof six cubits: he set it up in the plain of Dura, in the province of Babylon.

King Nebuchadnezzar was told by Daniel, the prophet of the LORD who interpreted his dream, that he would be the ruler of a kingdom that was symbolized by the head of gold in the image of an idol. The idol represented all of mankind in the fallen state. Gold was the symbol of love. The kingdom that is symbolized by gold should be a kingdom of love from the LORD. The kingdom was to be the LORD's spiritual kingdom of love made manifest on earth. Nebuchadnezzar immediately accepted the information from Daniel which came from the God of heaven, but he interpreted it **literally**. Nebuchadnezzar decided that the substance of gold should be worshipped instead of the LORD and the LORD's kingdom.

He directed his craftsmen to build an image of gold that was 60 cubits in height (approximately 90 feet) and 6 cubits in width (approximately 9 feet). King Nebuchadnezzar set up this golden image in the plain of Dura a few miles south of Babylon. Gold is the symbol of a metal that endures forever and does not tarnish with age. Every earthly king would love to have his earthly kingdom endure forever. This perpetual kingdom was the desire of Nebuchadnezzar and he erected this golden idol for his people to see and worship at the entrance to Babylon. The Babylonians were idol-worshippers and Nebuchadnezzar gave them a new idol of gold, the most valuable of the earthly treasures. Nebuchadnezzar was not aware of the fact that gold is a symbol for the treasured power of the love that comes from the invisible God of heaven. He wanted all of his subjects to worship the golden image.

2 Then Nebuchadnezzar the king sent to gather together the princes, the governors, and the captains, the judges, the treasurers, the counsellors, the sheriffs, and all the rulers of the provinces, to come to the dedication of the image which Nebuchadnezzar the king had set up.
3 Then the princes, the governors, and captains, the judges, the treasurers, the counsellors, the sheriffs, and all the rulers of the provinces, were gathered together unto the dedication of the image that Nebuchadnezzar the king had set up; and they stood before the image that Nebuchadnezzar had set up.
4 Then an herald cried aloud, To you it is commanded, O people, nations, and languages,
5 That at what time ye hear the sound of the cornet, flute, harp, sackbut, psaltery, dulcimer, and all kinds of musick, ye fall down and worship the golden image that Nebuchadnezzar the king hath set up:
6 And whoso falleth not down and worshippeth shall the same hour be cast into the midst of a burning fiery furnace.
7 Therefore at that time, when all the people heard the sound of the cornet, flute, harp, sackbut, psaltery, and all kinds of musick, all the people, the nations, and the languages, fell down and worshipped the golden image that Nebuchadnezzar the king had set up.

Nebuchadnezzar the king commanded the princes, the governors, the captains, the judges, the treasurers, the counselors, the sheriffs, and all the rulers of the provinces to come to the dedication of the golden image which he had set up to

The Testimony of the Major Prophets

honor himself as the lord of lords of his earthly kingdom, which was based on the strength of his accumulated earthly power. The power structure of the kingdom of Babylon with its hierarchy of officials—the princes, the governors, the captains, the judges, the treasurers, the counselors, the sheriffs, and all the rulers of the provinces—were gathered together at the dedication ceremony of the image that Nebuchadnezzar the king had commanded to be erected; and everyone stood before the image that Nebuchadnezzar had ordered built to be worshipped as an idol.

Then a herald cried aloud to all the people, nations and languages the command from the king to make an earthly kingdom work: Whenever you hear the sound of the musical instruments such as the cornet, flute, harp, sackbut, psaltery, dulcimer, and all kinds of music, which is the ceremonial music of the king, you shall fall down and worship the golden image that Nebuchadnezzar the king has set up. The golden image is the earthly idol that the king built for the people to worship to maintain his kingdom and authority. Whoever does not fall down and worship shall, in the same hour, be cast into the midst of a burning fiery furnace. The fiery furnace could be real or it could be the fiery wrath of the authorities who represented the king. The people who did not worship the image were to be burned for their disobedience, punished, or put to death immediately. Symbolically, the fiery furnace has greater application in the world today if it is seen as the fiery wrath of the people in power.

Therefore, at that time, when all the people heard the sound of the cornet, flute, harp, sackbut, psaltery, and all kinds of music, all the people, the nations, and the languages fell down and worshipped the golden image that Nebuchadnezzar the king had set up. The instruments that make the music and the noise can be seen as symbols of the leaders who sound the praises and policies of the king, the people who carry out the commands of the earthly king by means of the power of the kingdom. People are the instruments that play the tune of the earthly king. The system, the strength of the kingdom and its continuity, depended on the obedience to the commands of the king which were enforced by punishment and death to the disobedient. The worship of the idol by the people identified the people who supported the king. The people who did not bow down to the idols, when the music played, were easily identified and eliminated. The enforcement of the harsh punishment hastened compliance to the required and acceptable behavior. It would take unusual people who would not bow down to worship the idol.

8 Wherefore at that time certain Chaldeans came near, and accused the Jews.
9 They spake and said to the king Nebuchadnezzar, O king, live for ever.
10 Thou, O king, hast made a decree, that every man that shall hear the sound of the cornet, flute, harp, sackbut, psaltery, and dulcimer, and all kinds of musick, shall fall down and worship the golden image:
11 And whoso falleth not down and worshippeth, that he should be cast into the midst of a burning fiery furnace.
12 There are certain Jews whom thou hast set over the affairs of the province of Babylon, Shadrach, Meshach, and Abednego; these men, O king, have not regarded thee: they serve not thy gods, nor worship the golden image which thou hast set up.

Wherefore at that time certain Chaldeans came near, and accused the Jews who did not fall down to worship the golden image when the music played. The Jews did not worship material idols and images; they worshipped the invisible God Who is the Source of life moving through them to give them life. The Chaldeans who accused the Jews spoke and said to king Nebuchadnezzar, O king, live for ever. They acknowledged the earthly position of the king. The routine greeting for the king to live forever is a form of mind-conditioning to keep the king in power forever; the people who address the king in this manner would think of no other king as long as the king was alive. No earthly king lives forever as does the heavenly King! The earthly king attempts duplicate the eternal nature of the heavenly kingdom of the King and perpetuate his earthly kingdom by the process of succession of his offspring to his earthly throne at the time of his death.

The people who have an interest in perpetuating the status quo would report any deviations in the behavior of others that may harm their earthly kingdom in which they have a self interest. The Chaldeans call to the attention of the king that he has made a decree, that every man that hears the sound of the cornet, flute, harp, sackbut, psaltery, and dulcimer, and all kinds of music, shall fall down and worship the golden image. Whoever does not fall down and worship should be cast into the midst of a burning fiery furnace as punishment for their non-conformity. There are certain Jews—Shadrach, Meshach, and Abednego—whom the king has set over the affairs of the province of Babylon and these men have not regarded the king's commands: they do not serve the gods of the king nor do they worship the golden image which the king has erected. There are three people in the "golden" kingdom who are disobeying the

The Symbolic Version of Daniel

king of the earthly material world. Today, the king of Babylon could be seen as the head of a country, a corporation, the earthly establishment who wields power. The three friends of Daniel, the focus of spirit, can be seen as the heart, the mind and the body of anyone in this predicament. The person in authority is in a rage and he is furious as the fire burns within him.

13 Then Nebuchadnezzar in his rage and fury commanded to bring Shadrach, Meshach, and Abednego. Then they brought these men before the king.
14 Nebuchadnezzar spake and said unto them, Is it true, O Shadrach, Meshach, and Abednego, do not ye serve my gods, nor worship the golden image which I have set up?
15 Now if ye be ready that at what time ye hear the sound of the cornet, flute, harp, sackbut, psaltery, and dulcimer, and all kinds of musick, ye fall down and worship the image which I have made; well: but if ye worship not, ye shall be cast the same hour into the midst of a burning fiery furnace; and who is that God that shall deliver you out of my hands?

Then Nebuchadnezzar in his rage and fury commanded that Shadrach, Meshach, and Abednego be brought before him and he asked the three men if it were true that they do not serve his gods, nor worship the golden image which he has set up? The king gives the three men the two choices which are available to them: If you hear the hear the sound of the cornet, flute, harp, sackbut, psaltery, and dulcimer, and all kinds of music, the music of the earthly kingdom, if you fall down and worship the image which the king has made; well and good. But if you do not worship, you shall be cast—in the very same hour—into the midst of a burning fiery furnace, symbolizing the punishment that will destroy you.

Shadrach, Meshach and Abednego—who have been given Babylonian names and who are in positions of power in a land to which they have been exiled and held as captives—are given the choice to obey the earthly rules of the material kingdom, react to the music like everyone else, or die. Shadrach, Meshach and Abednego are in the power structure of the Babylonians and they have been given a choice by the king himself who asks them, Who is that God that shall deliver you out of the hands of the king? If Nebuchadnezzar were really the representative of the LORD of Lords, he would have delivered Shadrach, Meshach and Abednego from destruction by direct order since he was king and had earthly power. But Nebuchadnezzar serves his own kingdom, not the kingdom of the LORD.

16 Shadrach, Meshach, and Abednego, answered and said to the king, O Nebuchadnezzar, we are not careful to answer thee in this matter.
17 If it be so, our God whom we serve is able to deliver us from the burning fiery furnace, and he will deliver us out of thine hand, O king.
18 But if not, be it known unto thee, O king, that we will not serve thy gods, nor worship the golden image which thou hast set up.
19 Then was Nebuchadnezzar full of fury, and the form of his visage was changed against Shadrach, Meshach, and Abednego: therefore he spake, and commanded that they should heat the furnace one seven times more than it was wont to be heated.
20 And he commanded the most mighty men that were in his army to bind Shadrach, Meshach, and Abednego, and to cast them into the burning fiery furnace.

Shadrach, Meshach, and Abednego, answered and said to king Nebuchadnezzar that they would not even be careful to answer the king in this matter, the choice of living to worship an idol, or dying by being thrown into a fiery furnace. Shadrach, Meshach, and Abednego clearly state their position and their choice with regard to idol worship or death. If it be so, the God whom they serve is able to deliver them from the burning fiery furnace on themselves, their hearts, minds and bodies. Their God will deliver them out of the hand of the king. But, even if God does not deliver them from death, they want the king to know that they will not serve his gods, nor worship the golden image of the material idol which he has erected.

Then Nebuchadnezzar was full of fury, and the form of his facial expression changed to reveal his inner fury against Shadrach, Meshach, and Abednego: therefore he spoke, and commanded that they should heat one of the furnaces seven times hotter than usual. In his fury, the king was not content to burn and destroy the three people who would not do what he wanted them to do, but he wanted the furnace to be heated seven times hotter than usual. This intense condition reveals his intense inner rage at not being worshipped by his subjects. He demonstrated his earthly power even further when he commanded the maximum force of his most mighty men that were in his army to bind Shadrach,

The Testimony of the Major Prophets

Meshach, and Abednego with strong cords so that they would be unable to escape and to make them feel more helpless as they were cast into the burning fiery furnace. The king was jealous and enraged by the loyalty to an invisible God of the three friends who would not be intimidated by pain and death.

21 Then these men were bound in their coats, their hosen, and their hats, and their other garments, and were cast into the midst of the burning fiery furnace.
22 Therefore because the king's commandment was urgent, and the furnace exceeding hot, the flame of the fire slew those men that took up Shadrach, Meshach, and Abednego.
23 And these three men, Shadrach, Meshach, and Abednego, fell down bound into the midst of the burning fiery furnace.

Then these men, who were wearing their coats, their trousers, their hats, and their other garments, were cast into the midst of the burning fiery furnace. Since the king's commandment was urgent, and the furnace extraordinarily hot, the flame of the fire slew those men that took up Shadrach, Meshach, and Abednego. The men who were leading Shadrach, Meshach and Abednego suffered and were destroyed by the intensity of the fire within their own experience. These three men, Shadrach, Meshach, and Abednego, fell down bound into the midst of the burning fiery furnace. They were in the fiery furnace which was created by the king and his followers. How would they react?!

24 Then Nebuchadnezzar the king was astonied, and rose up in haste, and spake, and said unto his counsellors, Did not we cast three men bound into the midst of the fire? They answered and said unto the king, True, O king.
25 He answered and said, Lo, I see four men loose, walking in the midst of the fire, and they have no hurt; and the form of the fourth is like the Son of God.

Nebuchadnezzar the king was astonished, rose up in haste and said to his counselors, Did we not cast three men who were bound with earthly bonds into the midst of the fire? They answered and said, True, O king. The king answered and said, Lo, I see four men loose, walking in the midst of the fire, and they are unharmed; and the form of the fourth is like the Son of God. Nebuchadnezzar is able to discern that there is a fourth person in the fire and that He is like the Son of God. Nebuchadnezzar could only see the Son of God when Shadrach, Meshach and Abednego were in the fiery furnace of the situation. The behavior or the three friends in the intense heat of the fiery furnace is the only means through which king Nebuchadnezzar could see the fourth person, the invisible person, who is like the Son of God, who was in the furnace with them. Symbolically, the spirit of the one like the Son of God comes forth in the time of trouble of the individual body, mind and heart; or death, that separates the spirit from the human forms. The end of the physical human equipment is not the end of the one like the Son of God.

26 Then Nebuchadnezzar came near to the mouth of the burning fiery furnace, and spake, and said, Shadrach, Meshach, and Abednego, ye servants of the most high God, come forth, and come hither. Then Shadrach, Meshach, and Abednego, came forth of the midst of the fire.
27 And the princes, governors, and captains, and the king's counsellors, being gathered together, saw these men, upon whose bodies the fire had no power, nor was an hair of their head singed, neither were their coats changed, nor the smell of fire had passed on them.

Then Nebuchadnezzar came near to the mouth of the burning fiery furnace, and spoke, and said, Shadrach, Meshach, and Abednego, you servants of the most high God, come forth, and come here. Then Shadrach, Meshach, and Abednego, came forth from the midst of the fire. The princes, governors, captains, and the king's counselors, being gathered together, saw these men, upon whose bodies the fire had no power, nor was a hair of their head singed, neither were their coats changed, nor the smell of fire had passed on them.

28 Then Nebuchadnezzar spake, and said, Blessed be the God of Shadrach, Meshach, and Abednego, who hath sent his angel, and delivered his servants that trusted in him, and have changed the king's word, and yielded their bodies, that they might not serve nor worship any god, except their own God.
29 Therefore I make a decree, That every people, nation, and language, which speak any thing amiss against the God of Shadrach, Meshach, and Abednego, shall be cut in pieces, and their houses shall be made a dunghill: because there is no other God that can deliver after this sort.
30 Then the king promoted Shadrach, Meshach, and Abednego, in the province of Babylon.

The Symbolic Version of Daniel

Then Nebuchadnezzar spoke, and said, Blessed be the God of Shadrach, Meshach, and Abednego, who has sent his angel, and delivered his servants that trusted in Him. Their brave actions have changed the king's word, with their willingness to yield their bodies, rather than serve or worship any god, except their own God.

Therefore Nebuchadnezzar made a decree, That every people, nation, and language, which speak any thing amiss against the God of Shadrach, Meshach, and Abednego, shall be cut in pieces, and their houses shall be made a dunghill: because there is no other God that can deliver in this manner. Then the king, who had been successfully defied by three servants of God, rewarded their loyalty and courage to the God of heaven, as he promoted Shadrach, Meshach, and Abednego in the province of Babylon.

Symbolically, the experience of Shadrach, Meshach and Abednego produced an experience of victory in the circumstance in which they found themselves. They were willing to die, to lose their life, in order to find their life. Life is with the one like unto the Son of God, who is the spirit of Life. Life can be known by the friends of Life, the body, the mind and heart, which are the forms of life. But Life is with the spirit of the One who dwells, the child of God, the One Who is like unto the Son of God.

CHAPTER 4

1 Nebuchadnezzar the king, unto all people, nations, and languages, that dwell in all the earth; Peace be multiplied unto you.
2 I thought it good to shew the signs and wonders that the high God hath wrought toward me.
3 How great are his signs! and how mighty are his wonders! his kingdom is an everlasting kingdom, and his dominion is from generation to generation.
4 I Nebuchadnezzar was at rest in mine house, and flourishing in my palace:
5 I saw a dream which made me afraid, and the thoughts upon my bed and the visions of my head troubled me.
6 Therefore made I a decree to bring in all the wise men of Babylon before me, that they might make known unto me the interpretation of the dream.
7 Then came in the magicians, the astrologers, the Chaldeans, and the soothsayers: and I told the dream before them; but they did not make known unto me the interpretation thereof.

Nebuchadnezzar the king has changed his mind and heart toward the LORD because of the spiritual influence of Daniel, the interpretations of the dreams and the unusual things which he has been privileged to see. As Nebuchadnezzar changes his feelings to accept and come into agreement with Daniel, the servant of the invisible LORD, the king, unknowingly, also moves into closer agreement with the spirit of the LORD made manifest through Daniel. The king proclaims to all people, nations, and languages, that dwell in all the earth; Peace be multiplied to you. Nebuchadnezzar thought it good to show the signs and wonders that the high God has wrought toward him as he exclaimed, How great are His signs! and how mighty are His wonders! His kingdom is an everlasting kingdom, and His dominion is from generation to generation while Nebuchadnezzar, the symbol of earthly identity, is mortal.

Nebuchadnezzar recalls when he was at rest in his house, and flourishing in his palace when he
saw a dream which made him afraid. The thoughts which he had while he lay upon his bed and the visions of his head troubled the king. Therefore, he made a decree to bring in all the wise men of Babylon before him, that they might make known to him the interpretation of the dream. When the magicians, the astrologers, the Chaldeans, and the soothsayers came in, the king told all of them that he had a dream and this time he related the details; but none of them could interpret the king's dream.

8 But at the last Daniel came in before me, whose name was Belteshazzar, according to the name of my god, and in whom is the spirit of the holy gods: and before him I told the dream, saying,
9 O Belteshazzar, master of the magicians, because I know that the spirit of the holy gods is in thee, and no secret troubleth thee, tell me the visions of my dream that I have seen, and the interpretation thereof.
10 Thus were the visions of mine head in my bed; I saw, and behold a tree in the midst of the earth, and the height thereof was great.
11 The tree grew, and was strong, and the height thereof reached unto heaven, and the sight thereof to the end of all the earth:

12 The leaves thereof were fair, and the fruit thereof much, and in it was meat for all: the beasts of the field had shadow under it, and the fowls of the heaven dwelt in the boughs thereof, and all flesh was fed of it.

Finally, Daniel, whose name had been changed to Belteshazzar (which means "the lord protect his life") according to the name of the god of Nebuchadnezzar, came before the king. Nebuchadnezzar was convinced that in Daniel was the spirit of the holy gods. The king told Daniel (Belteshazzar) to come to him, and tell him the interpretation of the visions of his dream. Nebuchadnezzar related the visions that he saw in his head while he was in his bed; he saw a tree in the midst of the earth, and the height of it was great. The tree grew, and was strong, and the height of it reached the sky, and the sight of it could be seen from the ends of the earth. The leaves of the tree were fair, and there was much fruit on it. The tree had food for everyone, the beasts of the field had shade under it for them, and the fowls of the heaven dwelt in the boughs of the tree. All flesh was fed from the tree in Nebuchadnezzar's dream.

13 I saw in the visions of my head upon my bed, and, behold, a watcher and an holy one came down from heaven;
14 He cried aloud, and said thus, Hew down the tree, and cut off his branches, shake off his leaves, and scatter his fruit: let the beasts get away from under it, and the fowls from his branches:
15 Nevertheless leave the stump of his roots in the earth, even with a band of iron and brass, in the tender grass of the field; and let it be wet with the dew of heaven, and let his portion be with the beasts in the grass of the earth:
16 Let his heart be changed from man's, and let a beast's heart be given unto him; and let seven times pass over him.
17 This matter is by the decree of the watchers, and the demand by the word of the holy ones: to the intent that the living may know that the most High ruleth in the kingdom of men, and giveth it to whomsoever he will, and setteth up over it the basest of men.

In the vision which the king had in his mind while lying on his bed, he beheld a holy messenger come down from heaven, who cried aloud and said, Hew down the tree, cut off its branches, shake off its leaves, and scatter its fruit. Let the beasts get away from under it and the fowls from its branches. Nevertheless, leave the stump of the roots of the tree in the earth, bound with iron and brass in the tender grass of the field. Let it be wet with the dew of heaven, and let his portion be with the beasts in the grass of the earth Let his heart be changed from man's, and let a beast's heart be given unto him; and let seven times pass over him.

This matter is by the decree of the messengers from heaven, and the demand by the word of the holy ones: to the intent that the living may know that the most High rules in the kingdom of men, and gives it to whomsoever He will, and sets up over it the lowliest of men.

18 This dream I king Nebuchadnezzar have seen. Now thou, O Belteshazzar, declare the interpretation thereof, forasmuch as all the wise men of my kingdom are not able to make known unto me the interpretation: but thou art able; for the spirit of the holy gods is in thee.
19 Then Daniel, whose name was Belteshazzar, was astonied for one hour, and his thoughts troubled him. The king spake, and said, Belteshazzar, let not the dream, or the interpretation thereof, trouble thee. Belteshazzar answered and said, My lord, the dream be to them that hate thee, and the interpretation thereof to thine enemies.

This dream of king Nebuchadnezzar has been seen and Belteshazzar (Daniel) is to declare the interpretation of it since all the wise men of the kingdom are not able to make the interpretation: but Daniel is able; for the spirit of the holy gods is in him. Then Daniel, whose name was Belteshazzar, was astonished for one hour, and his thoughts troubled him. The king spoke, and said, Belteshazzar, let not the dream, or the interpretation thereof, trouble you. Belteshazzar answered and said, My lord, the dream is about them that hate you, and the interpretation thereof, will reveal your enemies to you.

20 The tree that thou sawest, which grew, and was strong, whose height reached unto the heaven, and the sight thereof to all the earth;
21 Whose leaves were fair, and the fruit thereof much, and in it was meat for all; under which the beasts of the field dwelt, and upon whose branches the fowls of the heaven had their habitation:
22 It is thou, O king, that art grown and become strong: for thy greatness is grown, and reacheth unto heaven, and thy dominion to the end of the earth.

The Testimony of the Major Prophets

Daniel explains that the tree—which the king saw in his dream that grew, was strong, whose height reached to the heaven, and the sight of it is visible in all the earth; the tree whose leaves were fair, and the fruit was abundant, and in the tree was food for all; under which the beasts of the field dwelt, and upon whose branches the fowls of the heaven had their habitation—is the symbol of king Nebuchadnezzar who has grown and become strong: for the greatness is grown, and reaches to heaven, and his dominion extends to the end of the earth.

23 And whereas the king saw a watcher and an holy one coming down from heaven, and saying, Hew the tree down, and destroy it; yet leave the stump of the roots thereof in the earth, even with a band of iron and brass, in the tender grass of the field; and let it be wet with the dew of heaven, and let his portion be with the beasts of the field, till seven times pass over him;
24 This is the interpretation, O king, and this is the decree of the most High, which is come upon my lord the king:
25 That they shall drive thee from men, and thy dwelling shall be with the beasts of the field, and they shall make thee to eat grass as oxen, and they shall wet thee with the dew of heaven, and seven times shall pass over thee, till thou know that the most High ruleth in the kingdom of men, and giveth it to whomsoever he will.

And whereas the king saw a watcher, who observes and judges, and a holy one, who claims to represent god, coming down from heaven, and saying, Hew the tree down, and destroy it; yet leave the stump of the roots thereof in the earth, even with a band of iron and brass, in the tender grass of the field; and let it be wet with the dew of heaven, and let his portion be with the beasts of the field, till seven times pass over him; This is the interpretation, O king, and this is the decree of the most High, which is come upon my lord the king: your enemies shall drive you from men, and your dwelling shall be with the beasts of the field, and they shall make you to eat grass as oxen, and they shall wet you with the dew of heaven, and seven times shall pass over you, till you know that the most High rules in the kingdom of men, and gives it to whomsoever He will. Nebuchadnezzar can be moved physically from his position in the spiritual design, but his roots will remain in the spiritual divine design. However, there is a way to return to his spiritual roots from which he has been removed. This is the way of repentance and change to reveal that the spirit of the LORD from the heavens do rule the earth.

26 And whereas they commanded to leave the stump of the tree roots; thy kingdom shall be sure unto thee, after that thou shalt have known that the heavens do rule.
27 Wherefore, O king, let my counsel be acceptable unto thee, and break off thy sins by righteousness, and thine iniquities by shewing mercy to the poor; if it may be a lengthening of thy tranquillity.

And whereas they commanded to leave the stump of the tree roots; your kingdom shall be sure to you, after you know that the spirit in the heavens do rule the earth. Wherefore, O king, let the counsel of Daniel be acceptable to you. Break off your sins by righteousness, and your iniquities by showing mercy to the poor and it may be that your peace, tranquility and prosperity be lengthened.

28 All this came upon the king Nebuchadnezzar.
29 At the end of twelve months he walked in the palace of the kingdom of Babylon.
30 The king spake, and said, Is not this great Babylon, that I have built for the house of the kingdom by the might of my power, and for the honour of my majesty?

All this came upon king Nebuchadnezzar as his palace was returned to him. At the end of twelve months, he walked in the palace of the kingdom of Babylon and asked, Is not this the great city of Babylon which he has built for the house of his kingdom by the might of his power, and for the honor of his majesty? The king forgot that he is ruler of the kingdom only by the fact that he will do the will of the LORD. The king asserts that this is indeed his personal kingdom. The king, in his self-righteousness, contends with the spirit of the LORD and in so doing, he will be repulsed and removed by the spirit of the LORD from his spiritual roots. The removal of the king will be accomplished by the spirit of the LORD moving through other people who are perceived as enemies of the king.

31 While the word was in the king's mouth, there fell a voice from heaven, saying, O king Nebuchadnezzar, to thee it is spoken; The kingdom is departed from thee.

32 And they shall drive thee from men, and thy dwelling shall be with the beasts of the field: they shall make thee to eat grass as oxen, and seven times shall pass over thee, until thou know that the most High ruleth in the kingdom of men, and giveth it to whomsoever he will.
33 The same hour was the thing fulfilled upon Nebuchadnezzar: and he was driven from men, and did eat grass as oxen, and his body was wet with the dew of heaven, till his hairs were grown like eagles' feathers, and his nails like birds' claws.

While the word was in the king's mouth proclaiming that he alone had built the kingdom of Babylon, there fell a voice from heaven, saying, O king Nebuchadnezzar, to you it is spoken; The kingdom is departed from you. You will be driven from men by your enemies, and your dwelling place shall be with the beasts of the field: they shall make you eat grass as oxen, and seven times shall pass over you until you know that the most High rules in the kingdom of men, and gives it to whomsoever He will. The same hour was the thing fulfilled upon Nebuchadnezzar: and he was driven from men, did eat grass as oxen, his body was wet with the dew of heaven, his hairs were grown like eagles' feathers, and his nails like birds' claws.

34 And at the end of the days I Nebuchadnezzar lifted up mine eyes unto heaven, and mine understanding returned unto me, and I blessed the most High, and I praised and honoured him that liveth for ever, whose dominion is an everlasting dominion, and his kingdom is from generation to generation:
35 And all the inhabitants of the earth are reputed as nothing: and he doeth according to his will in the army of heaven, and among the inhabitants of the earth: and none can stay his hand, or say unto him, What doest thou?
36 At the same time my reason returned unto me; and for the glory of my kingdom, mine honour and brightness returned unto me; and my counsellors and my lords sought unto me; and I was established in my kingdom, and excellent majesty was added unto me.
37 Now I Nebuchadnezzar praise and extol and honour the King of heaven, all whose works are truth, and his ways judgment: and those that walk in pride he is able to abase.

And at the end of the days, Nebuchadnezzar lifted up his eyes to heaven, and his understanding returned him. He blessed the most High, praised and honored Him that lives for ever, whose dominion is an everlasting dominion, and His kingdom is from generation to generation. And all the inhabitants of the earth are reputed as nothing: and He does according to His will in the army of heaven, and among the inhabitants of the earth: and none can stay His hand, or say unto Him, What are You doing?

At the very same time that Nebuchadnezzar acknowledged that his kingdom belonged to the LORD, then his reason returned to him; the glory of his kingdom, his honor and his brightness returned to him. The king's counselors and his lords sought him. Nebuchadnezzar was established in his kingdom, and excellent majesty was added to him.

Now Nebuchadnezzar praises, extols and honors the King of heaven, Whose works are truth, and His ways are the ways of righteous judgment. The message for people everywhere is that King of Heaven is able to bring low those people like himself that walk in pride because the material design of life is in spirit, in the heaven, and not in the earth.

CHAPTER 5

1 Belshazzar the king made a great feast to a thousand of his lords, and drank wine before the thousand.
2 Belshazzar, whiles he tasted the wine, commanded to bring the golden and silver vessels which his father Nebuchadnezzar had taken out of the temple which was in Jerusalem; that the king, and his princes, his wives, and his concubines, might drink therein.
3 Then they brought the golden vessels that were taken out of the temple of the house of God which was at Jerusalem; and the king, and his princes, his wives, and his concubines, drank in them.
4 They drank wine, and praised the gods of gold, and of silver, of brass, of iron, of wood, and of stone.

Belshazzar, whose name means, "let the idol, Bel, protect the king", is now the king of Babylon and the successor to Nebuchadnezzar. Belteshazzar (Daniel) is the representative of the LORD and His spiritual kingdom of heaven; Belshazzar the king is a representative of himself and the kingdom of Babylon. The reader should note the slight difference in the names of Belshazzar, the king, and Belteshazzar, who is Daniel, the servant of the LORD.

Belshazzar made a great feast to a thousand of his lords, and drank wine, made a toast, before the thousand, the multitude of the people who were engaged in an orgy of revelry and blasphemy. While he tasted the wine, he commanded that the golden and silver vessels which his father, Nebuchadnezzar, had taken out of the temple in Jerusalem be brought to him so that the king, his princes, his wives, and his concubines, might drink from them. His servants brought the golden vessels that were taken out of the temple of the house of God at Jerusalem and the king, his princes, his wives, and his concubines, drank in them. The perditious king and his company symbolized the unholy people who were drinking from the vessels of the holy temple at Jerusalem. They drank wine, and praised the gods of gold, and of silver, of brass, of iron, of wood, and of stone—all the materials which were considered valuable to the material world which they believed to be theirs instead of the LORD's. The vessels of the temple used to praise the LORD were being used to praise the material things of the world. The vessels of the temple of the LORD are symbols for the people who come to the temple to be filled with an increased awareness of the spirit of the LORD which is moving through each of them as long as they are alive. The vessels are material things whose only spiritual value is that they represent the LORD's people, the people who reveal the LORD's spirit..

5 In the same hour came forth fingers of a man's hand, and wrote over against the candlestick upon the plaister of the wall of the king's palace: and the king saw the part of the hand that wrote.
6 Then the king's countenance was changed, and his thoughts troubled him, so that the joints of his loins were loosed, and his knees smote one against another.
7 The king cried aloud to bring in the astrologers, the Chaldeans, and the soothsayers. And the king spake, and said to the wise men of Babylon, Whosoever shall read this writing, and shew me the interpretation thereof, shall be clothed with scarlet, and have a chain of gold about his neck, and shall be the third ruler in the kingdom.
8 Then came in all the king's wise men: but they could not read the writing, nor make known to the king the interpretation thereof.

The Symbolic Version of Daniel

9 Then was king Belshazzar greatly troubled, and his countenance was changed in him, and his lords were astonied.

In the same hour that the king and his lords were drinking from the vessels from the temple in Jerusalem giving praise to the material goods of the world, there came forth fingers of a man's hand, and wrote over against the candlestick upon the plaster of the wall of the king's palace: and the king saw the part of the hand that wrote. Then, the king's countenance was changed as his face turned pale, his thoughts troubled him, so that the joints of his loins were loosed as his legs gave way, and his knees knocked together in fear.

The king cried aloud to bring in the astrologers, the Chaldeans, and the soothsayers. And the king spoke, and said to the wise men of Babylon, Whosoever shall read this writing, and show me the interpretation thereof, shall be clothed with scarlet, and have a chain of gold about his neck, and shall be the third ruler in the kingdom. All the king's wise men could not read the writing, nor make known to the king the interpretation thereof. Then king Belshazzar was greatly troubled, and his countenance was changed in him from regal bearing to fear, and his lords were astonished at the sudden change due to the troubled heart of the king.

10 Now the queen, by reason of the words of the king and his lords, came into the banquet house: and the queen spake and said, O king, live for ever: let not thy thoughts trouble thee, nor let thy countenance be changed:
11 There is a man in thy kingdom, in whom is the spirit of the holy gods; and in the days of thy father light and understanding and wisdom, like the wisdom of the gods, was found in him; whom the king Nebuchadnezzar thy father, the king, I say, thy father, made master of the magicians, astrologers, Chaldeans, and soothsayers;
12 Forasmuch as an excellent spirit, and knowledge, and understanding, interpreting of dreams, and shewing of hard sentences, and dissolving of doubts, were found in the same Daniel, whom the king named Belteshazzar: now let Daniel be called, and he will shew the interpretation.

Now the queen, who heard the words of the king and his lords, came into the banquet house and said, O king, live for ever: let not your thoughts trouble you, or let your face be changed by a troubled heart.
There is a man in your kingdom, in whom is the spirit of the holy gods; and in the days of your father, light and understanding and wisdom, like the wisdom of the gods, was found in him. Your father, king Nebuchadnezzar made him master of the magicians, astrologers, Chaldeans, and soothsayers. Let Daniel, whom the king named Belteshazzar, be called and he will show you the interpretation for he has an excellent spirit, and knowledge, and understanding, interpreting dreams, showing the meaning of hard sentences, and dissolving the doubts engendered by them.

13 Then was Daniel brought in before the king. And the king spake and said unto Daniel, Art thou that Daniel, which art of the children of the captivity of Judah, whom the king my father brought out of Jewry?
14 I have even heard of thee, that the spirit of the gods is in thee, and that light and understanding and excellent wisdom is found in thee.
15 And now the wise men, the astrologers, have been brought in before me, that they should read this writing, and make known unto me the interpretation thereof: but they could not shew the interpretation of the thing:
16 And I have heard of thee, that thou canst make interpretations, and dissolve doubts: now if thou canst read the writing, and make known to me the interpretation thereof, thou shalt be clothed with scarlet, and have a chain of gold about thy neck, and shalt be the third ruler in the kingdom.

When Daniel was brought in before the king, he was asked if he were that person, Daniel, who was taken captive from Judah by his father who brought him out of Jewry? The king said that he has heard of Daniel and that the spirit of the gods is in him which gives him the light and understanding and the excellent wisdom that is found in him. The king tells Daniel that the wise men, the astrologers, had been brought before him to read the writing, and make known to the king the interpretation of it, but they could not do it. The king has heard that Daniel can make interpretations, and dissolve his doubts. If Daniel can read the writing, and make known the interpretation thereof, he shall be rewarded with clothes of scarlet, have a chain of gold about his neck, and be the third ruler in the kingdom.

17 Then Daniel answered and said before the king, Let thy gifts be to thyself, and give thy rewards to another; yet I will read the writing unto the king, and make known to him the interpretation.
18 O thou king, the most high God gave Nebuchadnezzar thy father a kingdom, and majesty, and glory, and honour:

The Testimony of the Major Prophets

19 And for the majesty that he gave him, all people, nations, and languages, trembled and feared before him: whom he would he slew; and whom he would he kept alive; and whom he would he set up; and whom he would he put down.
20 But when his heart was lifted up, and his mind hardened in pride, he was deposed from his kingly throne, and they took his glory from him:
21 And he was driven from the sons of men; and his heart was made like the beasts, and his dwelling was with the wild asses: they fed him with grass like oxen, and his body was wet with the dew of heaven; till he knew that the most high God ruled in the kingdom of men, and that he appointeth over it whomsoever he will.

Daniel answered the king, Let your gifts remain in your possession and give the rewards to another. Daniel neither requires nor wants material gifts and he will read the writing to the king, and he will make the interpretation known to him.

King Belshazzar is told by Daniel that the Most High God gave Nebuchadnezzar, his father a kingdom, and majesty, and glory, and honor. And for the majesty that God gave to Nebuchadnezzar, all people, nations, and languages, trembled and feared, were in awe, before him: whom He would, he would slay; and whom He would, he would keep alive; and whom He would, he would set up; and whom He would, he would put down. Nebuchadnezzar was an instrument of the Most High God.

But when king Nebuchadnezzar's heart was lifted up in vanity, and his mind hardened in pride, he was deposed from his kingly throne, and they took his glory from him. He was driven from the sons of men; and his heart (emotional realm) was made like the beasts, and his dwelling was with the wild asses: they fed him with grass like oxen, and his body was wet with rain. This fallen and degraded situation continued until he knew that the Most High God ruled in the kingdom of men, and that He appointed over it whomsoever He will. There is a spiritual God over the greatest of the earthly kings

22 And thou his son, O Belshazzar, hast not humbled thine heart, though thou knewest all this;
23 But hast lifted up thyself against the Lord of heaven; and they have brought the vessels of his house before thee, and thou, and thy lords, thy wives, and thy concubines, have drunk wine in them; and thou hast praised the gods of silver, and gold, of brass, iron, wood, and stone, which see not, nor hear, nor know: and the God in whose hand thy breath is, and whose are all thy ways, hast thou not glorified:

And you his son, O Belshazzar, have not humbled your heart, though you knew all this. Instead, you have lifted up yourself against the Lord of heaven; and they have brought the vessels of His house before you, and you as a fallen lord of your kingdom, your lords, your wives, and your concubines, have drunk wine in them; and you have praised the gods of silver, and gold, of brass, iron, wood, and stone, which see not, nor hear, nor know. You have glorified inanimate materials and you have not glorified the God in Whose hand your breath is, and Who is the Source of all your ways. God has sent king Belshazzar a message!

24 Then was the part of the hand sent from him; and this writing was written.
25 And this is the writing that was written, MENE, MENE, TEKEL, UPHARSIN.
26 This is the interpretation of the thing: MENE; God hath numbered thy kingdom, and finished it.
27 TEKEL; Thou art weighed in the balances, and art found wanting.
28 PERES; Thy kingdom is divided, and given to the Medes and Persians.

Then was the part of the hand of God sent from Him; and this writing was a message from God written to Belshazzar. And this is the writing that was written, MENE, MENE, TEKEL, UPHARSIN.

This is the interpretation of the thing:

>MENE—God has numbered your kingdom, and finished it. The message is repeated for emphasis of its importance.

>MENE—God has numbered your kingdom of self-centeredness and it will come to an end and be finished.

The Symbolic Version of Daniel

TEKEL—You are weighed in the balances, and you are found wanting.

PERES—Your kingdom is divided, and given to the Medes and Persians.

Daniel has interpreted the message to emphasize the fact that the kingdom of Belshazzar of the Chaldeans has been given to the control of the Medes and the Persians.

29 Then commanded Belshazzar, and they clothed Daniel with scarlet, and put a chain of gold about his neck, and made a proclamation concerning him, that he should be the third ruler in the kingdom.
30 In that night was Belshazzar the king of the Chaldeans slain.
31 And Darius the Median took the kingdom, being about threescore and two years old.

Then, Belshazzar commanded that Daniel be clothed with scarlet, ordered a chain of gold put about his neck, and proclaimed that he should be the third ruler in the kingdom.

In that very night, Belshazzar the king of the Chaldeans was slain.

And Darius the Median was placed in charge of the kingdom of the Babylonians and the Chaldeans, when he was about sixty-two years old. The Most High God has numbered the days of Belshazzar's kingdom, weighed Belshazzar's behaviors in the balance of the Law of Sowing and Reaping and found him wanting, and gave his kingdom to the Medes and the Persians.

The message of this chapter is obvious. The kingdoms of this world which are not in agreement with the divine plan of God will be overthrown and replaced by another ruler who will be given the opportunity to bring the kingdom of the LORD on earth in manifest form. Belshazzar, the son of Nebuchadnezzar, did not succeed in his desire to rule the kingdom in self-centered human ways.

CHAPTER 6

1 It pleased Darius to set over the kingdom an hundred and twenty princes, which should be over the whole kingdom;
2 And over these three presidents; of whom Daniel was first: that the princes might give accounts unto them, and the king should have no damage.
3 Then this Daniel was preferred above the presidents and princes, because an excellent spirit was in him; and the king thought to set him over the whole realm.
4 Then the presidents and princes sought to find occasion against Daniel concerning the kingdom; but they could find none occasion nor fault; forasmuch as he was faithful, neither was there any error or fault found in him.

It pleased Darius, the Mede, to set a hundred and twenty princes to be over the whole kingdom. Three presidents, of whom Daniel was first, were established over the 120 princes so that the princes would report to the 3 presidents and suffer no damage to Darius from the princes who were once loyal to Belshazzar of Babylon. In this manner, Darius could continue to use the machinery of the kingdom, the hierarchy of Belshazzar who were known by the majority of the people, but the princes must report to three new presidents who were loyal to Darius.

Daniel was preferred above the presidents and princes, because an excellent spirit was in him because Daniel served and represented the spirit of God. Darius sensed something very special about Daniel that caused him to set Daniel over the whole realm. The other presidents and princes, in their jealousy, envy and resentment, sought to find some occasion of fault against Daniel concerning the kingdom for which he was very responsible and trustworthy. The presidents and the princes could find no occasion nor fault in Daniel; for as much as Daniel was faithful, to the spirit of his God, there was not any error or not any fault found in him as he did the right thing in each moment.

5 Then said these men, We shall not find any occasion against this Daniel, except we find it against him concerning the law of his God.
6 Then these presidents and princes assembled together to the king, and said thus unto him, King Darius, live for ever.
7 All the presidents of the kingdom, the governors, and the princes, the counsellors, and the captains, have consulted together to establish a royal statute, and to make a firm decree, that whosoever shall ask a petition of any God or man for thirty days, save of thee, O king, he shall be cast into the den of lions.
8 Now, O king, establish the decree, and sign the writing, that it be not changed, according to the law of the Medes and Persians, which altereth not.
9 Wherefore king Darius signed the writing and the decree.

Then these men who were trying to put down Daniel said, We shall not find any occasion against this Daniel, except we find it against him concerning the law of his God. The presidents and princes assembled themselves together, went to the king, and greeted him with the familiar salutation for the ruling monarch: King Darius, live for ever. (This is the

The Symbolic Version of Daniel

same untruthful greeting that they used for Nebuchadnezzar and Belshazzar, Live for ever. They were aware that no earthly king lives forever.)

All the presidents of the kingdom, the governors, the princes, the counselors, and the captains, have consulted together to establish a royal statute, and to make a firm decree, that whosoever shall ask a petition of any God or man for thirty days, except to king Darius, that person shall be cast into the den of lions. After they appealed to the vanity of the king with a petition designed to honor him, they asked king Darius to establish the decree and sign the writing, that it be not changed, according to the law of the Medes and Persians. The law of the Medes and Persians stated that once a law was reduced to writing, then everyone should abide by it and no one shall alter it. King Darius signed the writing and issued the decree not knowing that it was a clever trap for Daniel.

10 Now when Daniel knew that the writing was signed, he went into his house; and his windows being open in his chamber toward Jerusalem, he kneeled upon his knees three times a day, and prayed, and gave thanks before his God, as he did aforetime.
11 Then these men assembled, and found Daniel praying and making supplication before his God.
12 Then they came near, and spake before the king concerning the king's decree; Hast thou not signed a decree, that every man that shall ask a petition of any God or man within thirty days, save of thee, O king, shall be cast into the den of lions? The king answered and said, The thing is true, according to the law of the Medes and Persians, which altereth not.

Now when Daniel knew that the writing was signed, he went into the privacy of his house to pray; and his windows being open in his chamber toward Jerusalem, he kneeled upon his knees three times a day, and prayed, and gave thanks before his God, as he had always done. Daniel would not cease to pray to the LORD his God nor would he place any earthly king above his heavenly King.

As they had planned, these jealous, envious and resentful officials assembled together, and they observed Daniel praying and making supplication before his God. They came and spoke to the king concerning the decree that the king had signed stating that every man who asks a petition of any God or man within thirty days, except for king Darius, shall be cast into the den of lions. The king acknowledged that it was true, that he had signed the decree and that it cannot be altered according to the law of the Medes and Persians, which meant that once the command was written, it shall be done.

13 Then answered they and said before the king, That Daniel, which is of the children of the captivity of Judah, regardeth not thee, O king, nor the decree that thou hast signed, but maketh his petition three times a day.
14 Then the king, when he heard these words, was sore displeased with himself, and set his heart on Daniel to deliver him: and he laboured till the going down of the sun to deliver him.
15 Then these men assembled unto the king, and said unto the king, Know, O king, that the law of the Medes and Persians is, That no decree nor statute which the king establisheth may be changed.

Then they told the king, that Daniel, who was one of the children taken captive out of the land of Judah, has no regard for the king, nor the decree that the king has signed. Daniel makes his petition three times a day to his God. (They did not use Daniel's Babylonian name, Belteshazzar!) When the king heard these words, he was sorely displeased with himself that he had been trapped and set his heart on Daniel to try to find some way to deliver him: and king labored until the going down of the sun for some way to deliver Daniel from the decree designed to eliminate Daniel from the service of the king. Then the men who had concocted this plot reminded the king that according to the law of the Medes and Persians no decree nor statute which the king established in writing may be changed. The decree must be obeyed by everyone, including the king.

16 Then the king commanded, and they brought Daniel, and cast him into the den of lions. Now the king spake and said unto Daniel, Thy God whom thou servest continually, he will deliver thee.
17 And a stone was brought, and laid upon the mouth of the den; and the king sealed it with his own signet, and with the signet of his lords; that the purpose might not be changed concerning Daniel.

The Testimony of the Major Prophets

Then the king commanded that Daniel be brought and cast into the den of lions. Now the king spoke and said to Daniel, Your God whom you serve continually will deliver you. A stone was brought and laid upon the mouth of the den; and the king sealed it with his own signet, his own seal, and with the signet, the stamp of approval, of his lords that the purpose might not be changed concerning Daniel. If the seals were broken, that would indicate that Daniel had been removed from the lion's den.

18 Then the king went to his palace, and passed the night fasting: neither were instruments of musick brought before him: and his sleep went from him.
19 Then the king arose very early in the morning, and went in haste unto the den of lions.
20 And when he came to the den, he cried with a lamentable voice unto Daniel: and the king spake and said to Daniel, O Daniel, servant of the living God, is thy God, whom thou servest continually, able to deliver thee from the lions?

Then the king went to his palace, and passed the night fasting: neither were instruments of music brought to play to him and he was unable to sleep. Neither food and drink, music or sleep was used to divert the concern of Darius for Daniel. Darius kept a vigil for the safety of Daniel all night long without ceasing. The king arose very early in the morning, and went in haste to the den of lions. When he came to the den, he cried with a lamentable voice to Daniel: and the king spoke and said, O Daniel, servant of the living God, is your God, whom you serve continually, able to deliver you from the lions?

21 Then said Daniel unto the king, O king, live for ever.
22 My God hath sent his angel, and hath shut the lions' mouths, that they have not hurt me: forasmuch as before him innocency was found in me; and also before thee, O king, have I done no hurt.
23 Then was the king exceeding glad for him, and commanded that they should take Daniel up out of the den. So Daniel was taken up out of the den, and no manner of hurt was found upon him, because he believed in his God.
24 And the king commanded, and they brought those men which had accused Daniel, and they cast them into the den of lions, them, their children, and their wives; and the lions had the mastery of them, and brake all their bones in pieces or ever they came at the bottom of the den.

Then Daniel said to the king, O king, live for ever. My God has sent His angel, and has shut the lions' mouths, that they have not hurt me. Daniel tells the king that he was innocent before his God and also before king Darius, he has done no harm. Then, the king was exceedingly glad for him, and commanded that they should take Daniel up out of the den It was discovered that no manner of hurt was found upon him, because he believed in his God commended his spirit and his safety to his God. Then the king commanded that the men, who had accused Daniel, be cast into the den of lions, with their children, and their wives, which was the custom at that time. The lions had the mastery of them, and broke all their bones in pieces before they came to the bottom of the den.

25 Then king Darius wrote unto all people, nations, and languages, that dwell in all the earth; Peace be multiplied unto you.
26 I make a decree, That in every dominion of my kingdom men tremble and fear before the God of Daniel: for he is the living God, and stedfast for ever, and his kingdom that which shall not be destroyed, and his dominion shall be even unto the end.
27 He delivereth and rescueth, and he worketh signs and wonders in heaven and in earth, who hath delivered Daniel from the power of the lions.
28 So this Daniel prospered in the reign of Darius, and in the reign of Cyrus the Persian.

Then king Darius wrote to all people, nations, and languages, that dwell in all the earth: Peace be multiplied to you. King Darius made a decree that, in every dominion of his kingdom, men shall tremble and fear before the God of Daniel: for He is the living God, the living representative of God on earth and steadfast for ever, and His kingdom is that which shall not be destroyed; His dominion shall be even unto the end. It is God who delivers and rescues, and He works signs and wonders in heaven and in earth. It is God who has delivered Daniel from the power of the lions. King Darius has written this decree and it was subject to the law of the Medes and the Persians. So this Daniel, the Daniel who trusted in the spirit of God, prospered in the reign of Darius, and in the reign of Cyrus the Persian.

The Symbolic Version of Daniel

While it is highly unlikely that people who are alive today will be physically cast into an actual den of lions, it should be remembered that, in symbolism, the lion represents a destructive force that can harm or destroy an individual. The destructive aspects of man in the fallen state have been described as a "den of lions" or a "fiery furnace" to destroy a person—who does the right thing in the sight of the LORD—by the use of others as surrogates. There are many individuals who desire to cast their "enemies", the people who hold different views, to the lions or into the fire of destruction to remove them from the opposition.

CHAPTER 7

1 In the first year of Belshazzar king of Babylon Daniel had a dream and visions of his head upon his bed: then he wrote the dream, and told the sum of the matters.
2 Daniel spake and said, I saw in my vision by night, and, behold, the four winds of the heaven strove upon the great sea.
3 And four great beasts came up from the sea, diverse one from another.

The Book of Daniel has described that Belshazzar, the son of Nebuchadnezzar, has been slain because he has not ruled in the spirit of the LORD and that Darius, his successor, has expressed his love and concern for Daniel. In the first year of Belshazzar king of Babylon, Daniel had a dream and visions passed through his mind while he was lying on his bed: Daniel wrote the dream to record the sum of the matters, the total content of the dream, as he remembered it. Daniel said that he saw in his vision by night, that he had seen the four winds of the heaven having their effect on the great sea. In symbolism, the great sea is the symbol for the total consciousness of mankind. Each individual person represents a thimbleful of the total consciousness of the body of mankind. And four great beasts came up from the sea, each one was diverse or different from another. There were four great beasts that came up from the sea of the mass consciousness of man.

The four winds from heaven symbolize the forces of spirit that originate in heaven, from the Divine Source. The four winds from heaven will produce four effects on earth because heaven and earth are connected; heaven and earth are one. The four effects on earth are described as four beasts. Since the consciousness of mankind is in the fallen state, the sea is polluted with the sinful nature of man, the four winds of the spirits from heaven, which contain the true design of God, produce four beasts, four distortions, which are contained within the fallen sea of the consciousness of mankind. The distortions are from the earth and not from the heaven of the spirit. The distortions in the sea of consciousness can be observed in the distortions in the four beasts of the earth.

4 The first was like a lion, and had eagle's wings: I beheld till the wings thereof were plucked, and it was lifted up from the earth, and made stand upon the feet as a man, and a man's heart was given to it.
5 And behold another beast, a second, like to a bear, and it raised up itself on one side, and it had three ribs in the mouth of it between the teeth of it: and they said thus unto it, Arise, devour much flesh.
6 After this I beheld, and lo another, like a leopard, which had upon the back of it four wings of a fowl; the beast had also four heads; and dominion was given to it.

The beasts which arise from out of the sea of consciousness of mankind are beastly regimes which have their destructive effects upon the condition of mankind. The first destructive effect is depicted as a lion which had eagle's wings. Daniel beheld the lion, the symbol of destructiveness, which came out of the sea of the consciousness of mankind, and it had eagle's wings. Wings are the symbol of high vision and the eagle's wings depict a very high vision. Daniel beheld the eagle's wings until they were plucked, until the lion lost his wings, lost his vision. A transition occurred as the

The Symbolic Version of Daniel

wingless, visionless lion was lifted up from the earth and made to stand upon the feet as a man, and a man's heart was given to it. A destructive lion rises up from the sea of the consciousness of mankind and takes the form of a man, a man's body, and a man's feet, the symbol of his understanding, and a man's heart, his emotional realm, is given to it. The wings of the eagle were used to symbolize the fact that the destructive lion has more vision, more ability to visualize and to create compared to a traditional lion. The beast of man in the fallen state is portrayed as a destructive lion with more vision to increase its destructiveness. The beast of man is not "man made in the image and likeness of God" which would naturally be produced by the winds of the spirit that originate in the heaven, in the place where God is. Man has become a beast like a destructive lion. There are other beasts to rise up out of the sea of the consciousness of mankind.

And behold another beast arose out of the sea of the mass consciousness, a second beast, that was like a bear. The bear in the vision, symbolizes the great physical power and strength inherent in a bear, raised itself up on one side, and it had three ribs in its mouth and between its teeth: this symbolizes that the great power of the bear is used to destroy its prey. The prey can be seen when the bear raises itself up on one side, at which time the three ribs in its mouth can be observed to illustrate that the bear has already killed its prey and is feasting on it. The people in the dream, who are observing the activity of the powerful bear, said, Arise, devour much flesh with your power; eat up the enemy.

After this, Daniel saw another beast arise out of the sea of consciousness of the body of mankind and it was like a leopard. A leopard is a very swift animal, characterized by its speed, who feeds quietly at night in darkness, but this symbolic leopard had upon its back four wings of a fowl. Wings are used as symbols to depict the ability to fly, to rise above the level of the ground, to enable the beast with four wings to see with greater vision and more quickly than a beast with only two wings. The leopard had four wings so it can be seen that as the animals have additional wings, its speed and vision also increases with wings that can take the vision higher than the first beast. The beast had also four heads which symbolize its ability to see in four directions: north; south; east; and west. Increased dominion and authority was given to this third beast who looks in each direction to swiftly catch and devour its prey. Destructiveness, power and speed are the attributes of the first three beasts that arise out of the consciousness of the fallen state of man.

7 After this I saw in the night visions, and behold a fourth beast, dreadful and terrible, and strong exceedingly; and it had great iron teeth: it devoured and brake in pieces, and stamped the residue with the feet of it: and it was diverse from all the beasts that were before it; and it had ten horns.

After this, Daniel saw in his night visions a fourth beast, dreadful, terrible, and exceedingly strong. The fourth great beast had great iron teeth. It devoured, broke in pieces, and stamped the residue, those that remained, with its feet. It was different from all the three beasts that were before it; and it had ten horns. Horns are the symbols of the ability to magnify sound and be heard. The ten horns are symbols that the sounds of the fourth beast are able to be magnified greatly when all the horns sound. The fourth beast is the symbol of the beast of all mankind in the fallen state.

8 I considered the horns, and, behold, there came up among them another little horn, before whom there were three of the first horns plucked up by the roots: and, behold, in this horn were eyes like the eyes of man, and a mouth speaking great things.
9 I beheld till the thrones were cast down, and the Ancient of days did sit, whose garment was white as snow, and the hair of his head like the pure wool: his throne was like the fiery flame, and his wheels as burning fire.
10 A fiery stream issued and came forth from before him: thousand thousands ministered unto him, and ten thousand times ten thousand stood before him: the judgment was set, and the books were opened.

As Daniel considered the ten horns of the fourth beast, which is more ghastly, more destructive, more powerful and quicker than the first three beasts, behold, there came up among the ten horns that magnify its sound of evil, another little horn, before whom there were three of the first horns plucked up by the roots. Behold, in this little horn were eyes like the eyes of man, and a mouth speaking great things. The little horn symbolizes the potential of the Son of man which is inherent in each child born on earth. The little horn symbolizes that word of God must be sounded on earth through each individual person. The sound of the little horn with its divine message will magnify on earth until it casts down the beasts.

The Testimony of the Major Prophets

Daniel beheld this condition until the thrones of the evil beasts were cast down, and the Ancient of days, a figure of ancient deity, did sit upon the thrones, whose garment was white as snow, and the hair of his head like the pure wool. White is the symbol of cleanliness and purity, and the head of the white hair which was like the radiance of wool which grew from many years experience. The throne of the Ancient of days was like the fiery flame that symbolizes the cleansing power of righteousness. His wheels, the symbols of His instrument of action on earth, the bodies of men and women, were as wheels of burning fire. The Ancient of days must work through His wheels, and His wheels are the machinery of people.

A fiery stream, the power of fire, issued and came forth from before Him, the Ancient of days, the symbol of Deity: the symbol of Almighty God. A thousand thousands, millions, ministered to Him, and ten thousand times ten thousand, a hundred million, stood before Him: the judgment of God was set in the earth through the four beasts which arose from out of the sea of the consciousness of man in the fallen state, and the books were opened for people to understand that the regimes of mankind in the fallen state are all represented by beasts. The fiery power of God has been misused and abused to produce destructive beasts instead of creative man made in the image and likeness of God. The destructive aspect of the fire will destroy the beasts; the creative aspect of the fire will recreate man on earth.

11 I beheld then because of the voice of the great words which the horn spake: I beheld even till the beast was slain, and his body destroyed, and given to the burning flame.
12 As concerning the rest of the beasts, they had their dominion taken away: yet their lives were prolonged for a season and time.

Daniel, whose name means "the judgment of God", then saw and understood because of the voice of the great words which the horn, the horn of the Ancient of days, spoke. Daniel beheld the vision until he had seen the beast was slain, his body destroyed, and given to the burning flame. As concerning the rest of the three beasts, they had their dominion taken away. Yet, their lives were prolonged for a season and time. It would take time for the dominion of the beasts to be destroyed from the consciousness of mankind.

13 I saw in the night visions, and, behold, one like the Son of man came with the clouds of heaven, and came to the Ancient of days, and they brought him near before him.
14 And there was given him dominion, and glory, and a kingdom, that all people, nations, and languages, should serve him: his dominion is an everlasting dominion, which shall not pass away, and his kingdom that which shall not be destroyed.

Daniel saw in the night visions of his mind that, behold, one like the Son of man came with the clouds of heaven, and came to the Ancient of days, and they brought him near before him. The Son of man is the restored state of man, man made in the image and likeness of God, that must put in an appearance with the clouds of heaven, the heavenly atmosphere and radiance that comes forth from the Son of man. The one like the Son of man is brought to the Ancient of days; the people in the fallen state, each individual person, must bring one like the Son of man before the Deity symbolized by the Ancient of days.

And there was given to the restored Son of man, dominion, and glory, and a kingdom, that all people, nations, and languages, should serve him: his dominion is an everlasting dominion, which shall not pass away, and his kingdom that which shall not be destroyed. The Son of man, man made in the image and likeness of God, is the true inhabitant of planet Earth.

15 I Daniel was grieved in my spirit in the midst of my body, and the visions of my head troubled me.
16 I came near unto one of them that stood by, and asked him the truth of all this. So he told me, and made me know the interpretation of the things.

Daniel was grieved in his spirit in the midst of his body, and the visions of his mind troubled him. Daniel came near to one of the people in the vision that stood by, and asked him the truth of all this. So the person in the vision told Daniel, and made him know the interpretation of the things that were seen in his vision.

17 These great beasts, which are four, are four kings, which shall arise out of the earth.

18 But the saints of the most High shall take the kingdom, and possess the kingdom for ever, even for ever and ever.

These great beasts, which are four in number, are four kings, which shall arise out of the earth. The first three beasts, of the total of four beasts, symbolize the destructive aspects from the physical, the mental and the emotional expressions of the fallen individuals which are magnified collectively to compose the beasts. Each destructive act by an individual on the physical, mental or emotional level adds to the strength of the three beasts. Each beastly act is performed by the choice of a human being who usurps the creative power of God for a destructive purpose. This is a temporary action that may seem successful to the fallen human nature point of view. These are actions taken by the fallen angels.

But the saints of the most High shall take the kingdom, and possess the kingdom forever, even forever and ever. The four kings of the fallen state are the kings of the destructive cycle of fallen man who rule the kingdom while it is in the fallen state. But their destructive cycle will not endure forever. They will be replaced by the people who will represent and serve the spirit of the most High. The people who represent and serve the spirit of the most High on Earth are the saints of the most High.

19 Then I would know the truth of the fourth beast, which was diverse from all the others, exceeding dreadful, whose teeth were of iron, and his nails of brass; which devoured, brake in pieces, and stamped the residue with his feet;
20 And of the ten horns that were in his head, and of the other which came up, and before whom three fell; even of that horn that had eyes, and a mouth that spake very great things, whose look was more stout than his fellows.

Then Daniel, and those who hear his words, would know the truth of the fourth beast, which was diverse and different from all the others: The fourth beast of mankind in the fallen state is exceedingly dreadful, whose teeth were of iron, and his nails of brass; which devoured, broke in pieces, and stamped the residue with his feet to leave the imprint of his fallen behavior on the next generation of people.

The ten horns that were in the head of the fourth beast, and of the others which came up, and before whom three fell; even of that little horn that had the eyes of a man, a mouth that spoke very great things and whose look, whose vision, was more stout, fuller and more encompassing, than his fellows.

21 I beheld, and the same horn made war with the saints, and prevailed against them;
22 Until the Ancient of days came, and judgment was given to the saints of the most High; and the time came that the saints possessed the kingdom.

Daniel beheld, and the same little horn, the same single focus of man in the fallen human state, the person who says that he is "only human", made war with the saints, and prevailed against them; Until the Ancient of days, the spirit of the most High, the Divine Spirit, came, and the true judgment of man was given to the saints of the most High, the people who carry the spirit of the most High in their living. The flow of the spirit of the most High, the Ancient of days, the Father, carries with it the true judgment of man made in the image and likeness of God which produces the saints of the most High. And in time, the time came that the saints possessed the kingdom. The time for the saints cannot occur until the people repent.

23 Thus he said, The fourth beast shall be the fourth kingdom upon earth, which shall be diverse from all kingdoms, and shall devour the whole earth, and shall tread it down, and break it in pieces.
24 And the ten horns out of this kingdom are ten kings that shall arise: and another shall rise after them; and he shall be diverse from the first, and he shall subdue three kings.

Thus, the Ancient of days said, The fourth beast shall be the fourth kingdom upon earth, the magnified fallen state, which shall be different and more destructive than all kingdoms, and shall devour the whole earth, and shall tread it down, and break it in pieces. The fourth beast will destroy mankind in the fallen state.

The fourth beast will self-destruct. And the ten horns out of this kingdom are ten kings that shall arise: and another shall rise after them; and he shall be more different from the first, and he shall subdue three kings. The ten horns, the leadership from within the fourth beast, will lead to self-destruction, will destroy itself. The fourth beast is the rebellion of the fallen state which arises through the consciousness of fallen man.

The Testimony of the Major Prophets

25 And he shall speak great words against the most High, and shall wear out the saints of the most High, and think to change times and laws: and they shall be given into his hand until a time and times and the dividing of time.
26 But the judgment shall sit, and they shall take away his dominion, to consume and to destroy it unto the end.

And he shall speak great words against the most High, and shall wear out the saints of the most High, and think to change times and laws: and they shall be given into his hand until a time and times and the dividing of time. But the judgment shall sit, and they shall take away his dominion, to consume and to destroy it to the end.

27 And the kingdom and dominion, and the greatness of the kingdom under the whole heaven, shall be given to the people of the saints of the most High, whose kingdom is an everlasting kingdom, and all dominions shall serve and obey him.
28 Hitherto is the end of the matter. As for me Daniel, my cogitations much troubled me, and my countenance changed in me: but I kept the matter in my heart.

And the kingdom and dominion, and the greatness of the kingdom under the whole heaven, shall be given to the people of the saints of the most High, whose kingdom is an everlasting kingdom, and all dominions shall serve and obey him. Dominion shall be restored from the beasts of the fallen state to the true state of man made in the image and likeness of God. This was the end of the matter, the end of the vision. As for Daniel, his thoughts and meditations on the vision troubled him greatly, and his countenance changed within him: but he kept the matter in his heart.

CHAPTER 8

1 In the third year of the reign of king Belshazzar a vision appeared unto me, even unto me Daniel, after that which appeared unto me at the first.
2 And I saw in a vision; and it came to pass, when I saw, that I was at Shushan in the palace, which is in the province of Elam; and I saw in a vision, and I was by the river of Ulai.
3 Then I lifted up mine eyes, and saw, and, behold, there stood before the river a ram which had two horns: and the two horns were high; but one was higher than the other, and the higher came up last.
4 I saw the ram pushing westward, and northward, and southward; so that no beasts might stand before him, neither was there any that could deliver out of his hand; but he did according to his will, and became great.

In the third year of the reign of king Belshazzar a vision appeared to Daniel two years after the vision which appeared to him in the first year of the king's reign. Daniel saw in a vision; and the vision actually came to pass, when he was in the palace at a city east of Babylon, Shushan (Suza), which is in the province of Elam; and in the vision, he was by the river of Ulai.

Then Daniel lifted up his eyes, and saw, standing before the river a ram which had two horns. A ram symbolizes a country whose army is of a positive expression of power charging forward. The ram had two horns with which to inflict its damage to anyone who got in the way. The two horns which developed after a matter of time, were high; but one was higher than the other, and the higher came up last after it had experience of success by its charges into new territory. Daniel saw the ram pushing westward, and northward, and southward; so that no beasts might stand before him, neither was there any that could deliver out of his hand, out of his control; but the country symbolized by the ram did according to his will, as he chose to do to fill his desires, and thus became great.

In symbolic language, the ram is the symbol for the Medo-Persian Empire which was in power from 539-330 BC. The two horns of different size represented the lands of the Medes and the Persians: the longer of the two horns represented the predominant position of Persia. The ram that symbolized Medo-Persia was charging, expanding northward, westward and southward and no country was strong enough to stop the advance.

5 And as I was considering, behold, an he goat came from the west on the face of the whole earth, and touched not the ground: and the goat had a notable horn between his eyes.
6 And he came to the ram that had two horns, which I had seen standing before the river, and ran unto him in the fury of his power.
7 And I saw him come close unto the ram, and he was moved with choler against him, and smote the ram, and brake his two horns: and there was no power in the ram to stand before him, but he cast him down to the ground, and stamped upon him: and there was none that could deliver the ram out of his hand.

The Testimony of the Major Prophets

And as Daniel was considering the ram, behold, a male goat came from the west on the face of the whole earth, and touched not the ground: and the goat had a notable horn between his eyes. The male goat came to the ram that had two horns, which Daniel had seen standing before the river, and ran toward him in the fury of his power. Daniel saw the goat come closer to the ram and charge him with a great rage and strike the ram breaking his two horns. There was not sufficient power in the ram to stand before charge of the goat. The goat cast the ram to the ground, and stamped upon him: and there was none that could deliver the ram out of his hand.

In symbolic language, the he-goat represented the Greek empire which included the Ptolomies and the Seleucids. The Greek empire was in power from 330-63 BC. The Greek invasion would come from the west on the face of the whole earth in numbers so great that the entire western horizon was covered with the evidence of their power. The symbolism of the fact that they did not touch the ground indicates that the warriors came in ships on the sea and chariots on the land.

8 Therefore the he goat waxed very great: and when he was strong, the great horn was broken; and for it came up four notable ones toward the four winds of heaven.
9 And out of one of them came forth a little horn, which waxed exceeding great, toward the south, and toward the east, and toward the pleasant land.
10 And it waxed great, even to the host of heaven; and it cast down some of the host and of the stars to the ground, and stamped upon them.

The Greek empire, symbolized by the he-goat, grew great. Greece was led by one great horn, it spoke with one voice of a united country rather than the two horns of the ram. The one great horn which was broken at the height of the power of the Greek empire symbolized Alexander the Great, "the first great king". After the death of Alexander in 323 BC, the four notable horns, the four countries, that grew out of the head of the goat toward the four winds of heavens, in four different directions were as follows:

(1.) Macedon and Greece under the leadership of Antipater and Cassander;
(2.) Thrace and Asia Minor under the leadership of Lysimachus;
(3.) Syria under Seleucus; and,
(4.) Palestine and Egypt under the leadership of Ptolomy.

Out of one of the four came forth a little horn in the person of Antiochus IV Epiphanes that would grow exceedingly great toward the south, the east and toward the pleasant land which Daniel considered the Holy Land of Jerusalem. And the little horn that symbolized Antiochus waxed great, as it grew to the host of heaven, the people who lived under the heaven on the earth, to include everyone; and it cast down some of the host and of the stars to the ground, and stamped upon them as it expanded and grew in size.

11 Yea, he magnified himself even to the prince of the host, and by him the daily sacrifice was taken away, and the place of his sanctuary was cast down.
12 And an host was given him against the daily sacrifice by reason of transgression, and it cast down the truth to the ground; and it practised, and prospered.

Yes, the little horn of Antiochus magnified himself even to the position of the prince of the host, the pretender who usurped the position of the son of the King on earth. He elevated himself higher than anyone else in his own view of himself. In the last few years of his reign from 168-164 BC, he made a determined effort to destroy the Jewish faith. He set himself up as an equal to God and ordered the daily sacrifices to God to end; and the place of His sanctuary, the temple, was cast down. And a host of believers in God gave their lives in rebellion against Antiochus for taking away the daily sacrifice. As Antiochus ground the truth into the ground, he prospered in everything that he did as he gained control of material wealth.

13 Then I heard one saint speaking, and another saint said unto that certain saint which spake, How long shall be the vision concerning the daily sacrifice, and the transgression of desolation, to give both the sanctuary and the host to be trodden under foot?
14 And he said unto me, Unto two thousand and three hundred days; then shall the sanctuary be cleansed.

The Symbolic Version of Daniel

Then Daniel heard one saint, a representative of God on earth, speaking, and another saint said to that certain saint which spoke with authority, How long shall be the vision concerning the end of the daily sacrifice, and the rebellion that causes desolation, the surrender of the sanctuary and the people be trodden under foot? The answer was a total of 2,300 morning and evening sacrifices which would be 1,150 days since there were two sacrifices a day; and then the sanctuary shall be cleansed.

The army of Judas Maccabeus recaptured Jerusalem and rededicated the temple to the LORD on Kislev 25, 165 BC which was three years after Antiochus set up his pagan altar three years earlier on Kislev 25, 168 BC, which was a period of 1,095 days. Since the pagan altar was set up approximately 2 months after the LORD's altar was destroyed, this difference of 55 days would add up to 1,150 days or 2,300 offerings.

15 And it came to pass, when I, even I Daniel, had seen the vision, and sought for the meaning, then, behold, there stood before me as the appearance of a man.
16 And I heard a man's voice between the banks of Ulai, which called, and said, Gabriel, make this man to understand the vision.
17 So he came near where I stood: and when he came, I was afraid, and fell upon my face: but he said unto me, Understand, O son of man: for at the time of the end shall be the vision.

And it came to pass, when Daniel, had seen the vision, and sought for the meaning, then, behold, there stood before him as the appearance of a man. Daniel heard a man's voice between the banks of Ulai, from the middle of the river, which called, and said, Gabriel, make this man to understand the vision. So Gabriel came near where Daniel stood: and when he came, Daniel was afraid, and fell upon his face: but Gabriel said to Daniel, Understand, O son of man: for at the time of the end shall be the vision, the vision is about the end of the exile in the future.

18 Now as he was speaking with me, I was in a deep sleep on my face toward the ground: but he touched me, and set me upright.
19 And he said, Behold, I will make thee know what shall be in the last end of the indignation: for at the time appointed the end shall be.
20 The ram which thou sawest having two horns are the kings of Media and Persia.
21 And the rough goat is the king of Grecia: and the great horn that is between his eyes is the first king.
22 Now that being broken, whereas four stood up for it, four kingdoms shall stand up out of the nation, but not in his power.
23 And in the latter time of their kingdom, when the transgressors are come to the full, a king of fierce countenance, and understanding dark sentences, shall stand up.
24 And his power shall be mighty, but not by his own power: and he shall destroy wonderfully, and shall prosper, and practise, and shall destroy the mighty and the holy people.
25 And through his policy also he shall cause craft to prosper in his hand; and he shall magnify himself in his heart, and by peace shall destroy many: he shall also stand up against the Prince of princes; but he shall be broken without hand.

Now as Gabriel was speaking, Daniel was in a deep sleep with his face toward the ground: but Gabriel touched Daniel, set him upright and said, Behold, I will make you know what shall be in the last end of the indignation: for at the time appointed, the end shall be.

The ram which you saw having two horns are the kings of Media and Persia and the rough goat is the king of Greece: and the great horn that is between his eyes is the symbol of the first king who is the authority, the point of focus, for the kingdom of Greece.

Now, when that Greek kingdom was broken and divided into segments, four stood up for it, four kingdoms shall rise up out of the one great nation, but not in his great collective power before the division occurred. The total collective power will be divided among four kingdoms. In the latter time of their kingdoms, when the transgressors are come to the full, a king of fierce countenance, and understanding dark sentences, shall stand up. His power shall be mighty, but it is not by his own power: he will usurp power from the LORD. He shall destroy successfully, and shall prosper as he practices destruction, and he shall destroy the mighty and the holy people. He is a destroyer. But through his policy,

The Testimony of the Major Prophets

he shall also cause crafts to prosper in his hand; and he shall magnify himself in his heart, and by peace shall destroy many. He shall also stand up against the Prince of princes, the Son of the King, the true spiritual power who should rule on earth; eventually the rebellious usurper of divine power shall be broken, but not by the hand of human power. If the destruction is not by human power, it must be by divine power.

26 And the vision of the evening and the morning which was told is true: wherefore shut thou up the vision; for it shall be for many days.
27 And I Daniel fainted, and was sick certain days; afterward I rose up, and did the king's business; and I was astonished at the vision, but none understood it.

And the vision of the evening and the morning, the dream that occurred between the evening and the morning, which was told is true: therefore, you should seal up the vision in writing and keep it for others to read for the message in it shall be for many days into the future.

Daniel fainted at the distress that the effect of the vision had upon his own body, mind and heart, and he was sick for several days; afterward he rose up, returned to work and did the king's business. Daniel was astonished at the vision, but no one understood it because it applied to what would unfold hundreds of years into the future.

CHAPTER 9

1 In the first year of Darius the son of Ahasuerus, of the seed of the Medes, which was made king over the realm of the Chaldeans;
2 In the first year of his reign I Daniel understood by books the number of the years, whereof the word of the LORD came to Jeremiah the prophet, that he would accomplish seventy years in the desolations of Jerusalem.
3 And I set my face unto the Lord God, to seek by prayer and supplications, with fasting, and sackcloth, and ashes:
4 And I prayed unto the LORD my God, and made my confession, and said, O Lord, the great and dreadful God, keeping the covenant and mercy to them that love him, and to them that keep his commandments;
5 We have sinned, and have committed iniquity, and have done wickedly, and have rebelled, even by departing from thy precepts and from thy judgments:
6 Neither have we hearkened unto thy servants the prophets, which spake in thy name to our kings, our princes, and our fathers, and to all the people of the land.

In the first year, 539-538 BC, of Darius the son of Ahasuerus, a descendent of the Medes, who was made king over the kingdom of the Chaldeans; in the first year of his reign, Daniel understood from the Scriptures, according to the word of the LORD to the prophet Jeremiah, that the desolation of Jerusalem would last 70 years. So Daniel set his face, turned his attention, to the LORD God, to seek by prayer and supplications using the customs and rituals of the time. The rituals were fasting, and the wearing of sackcloth and ashes to demonstrate the sadness and the repentance of a person who acknowledges that he is in the fallen state, which is a personal sinful state. Daniel opened his heart and prayed to the LORD God.

Daniel prayed to the LORD, the great and awesome God, Who keeps the covenant and offers mercy to the people that love Him, and keep His commandments. Daniel must admit that he and others have sinned, and committed iniquity, done wickedly, rebelled, and departed from His precepts judgments. Daniel also admits that he, and the fallen people that he represents, has not listened to the prophets who came and spoke in the name of the LORD to our kings, our princes, and our fathers, and to all the people of the land.

7 O Lord, righteousness belongeth unto thee, but unto us confusion of faces, as at this day; to the men of Judah, and to the inhabitants of Jerusalem, and unto all Israel, that are near, and that are far off, through all the countries whither thou hast driven them, because of their trespass that they have trespassed against thee.
8 O Lord, to us belongeth confusion of face, to our kings, to our princes, and to our fathers, because we have sinned against thee.
9 To the Lord our God belong mercies and forgivenesses, though we have rebelled against him;
10 Neither have we obeyed the voice of the LORD our God, to walk in his laws, which he set before us by his servants the prophets.

The Testimony of the Major Prophets

Daniel acknowledges that righteousness belongs to the LORD, but to the people in the fallen state there is confusion on their faces this day. Daniel sees and understands that the men of Judah, the inhabitants of Jerusalem, and all Israel, who are near and far off in all the countries to which the LORD has driven them by the working of the Law of Sowing and Reaping because of their trespasses against the spirit of the LORD.

Daniel acknowledges that he sees that the confusion is on the faces of the people, to our kings, to our princes, and to our fathers, because we have sinned against the LORD. The covenant of the LORD has been broken by the people, not the LORD. As long as a person is alive, the connection between the LORD and His creation is intact but not known by the person who has ignored the LORD. The LORD continues to be merciful and offers forgiveness to the people even though the people have fallen away from the LORD because they rebelled against Him. People have not obeyed the voice of the LORD God, to walk in His laws, which He set before them and which were made known to them by His servants the prophets. The people have heard the word of the LORD but they have ignored and rebelled against the word of the LORD which they were commanded to live by. Instead of the people obeying the commandments of the LORD while they are on earth, the fallen people have developed beliefs that no one is able to keep the commandments. This belief keeps the people in the fallen state and out of an awareness of the covenant that the LORD is indeed with them always.

11 Yea, all Israel have transgressed thy law, even by departing, that they might not obey thy voice; therefore the curse is poured upon us, and the oath that is written in the law of Moses the servant of God, because we have sinned against him.
12 And he hath confirmed his words, which he spake against us, and against our judges that judged us, by bringing upon us a great evil: for under the whole heaven hath not been done as hath been done upon Jerusalem.
13 As it is written in the law of Moses, all this evil is come upon us: yet made we not our prayer before the LORD our God, that we might turn from our iniquities, and understand thy truth.
14 Therefore hath the LORD watched upon the evil, and brought it upon us: for the LORD our God is righteous in all his works which he doeth: for we obeyed not his voice.
15 And now, O Lord our God, that hast brought thy people forth out of the land of Egypt with a mighty hand, and hast gotten thee renown, as at this day; we have sinned, we have done wickedly.
16 O Lord, according to all thy righteousness, I beseech thee, let thine anger and thy fury be turned away from thy city Jerusalem, thy holy mountain: because for our sins, and for the iniquities of our fathers, Jerusalem and thy people are become a reproach to all that are about us.

Yes, Daniel sees and acknowledges that all the people of Israel have transgressed God's law, even by departing from the spirit of the LORD, so that they might not obey the voice of the LORD's commands. Daniel comprehends that this is why the curse of terrible conditions is poured upon the rebellious and stiff-necked people, and the oath that is written in the law of Moses, the servant of God, that all this evil has come upon the people who disobey the commandments. The curse of the LORD is the direct result of the people who have disobeyed the LORD. The LORD has confirmed His words, which He spoke against us, and against our judges that judged us, by bringing a great evil upon the people. Daniel sees that under the whole heaven, a punishment has not been done with such caring detail as has been done to Jerusalem. Other people were not instructed by the servants of the LORD as were the children of Israel.

As it is written in the law of Moses, all this evil has come upon the people who disobeyed the LORD's commandments and yet they have not made a prayer of repentance and sorrow before the LORD our God; repentance requires that the people turn from their iniquities, and understand the truth of the LORD. Daniel observes that the people who express iniquity actually experience the way of iniquity which is a warning to repent and return to the LORD. The iniquity expressed in thought, word or deed carries its own immediate punishment.

Therefore, the LORD who remains in covenant-agreement with His people observes the evil that was brought upon the people who disobeyed and rebelled against His spirit: the LORD God is righteous in all His works which He does: it is the people who have not obeyed His voice. Now, Daniel sees that the LORD that brought His people out of the land of Egypt with a mighty hand, and has obtained renown for the deeds that He can do when the people obey His word, but the LORD cannot work through a people whose hearts, minds and bodies have sinned and done wickedly.

The Symbolic Version of Daniel

Daniel's prayer to the spirit of the Lord that is moving through him, according to all the righteousness of the LORD, is to let the anger and the fury, the destructive cycle of the LORD's spirit, be turned away from His city, Jerusalem, His holy mountain: the anger and the fury are present because of the sins and the iniquities of the people alive today and their fathers before them. Jerusalem and its people have become a reproach to all who are round about us. Daniel acknowledges and begins to see with the divine vision of the LORD that the problem is with the people who disobeyed the spirit of the LORD and who produced the chaos that resulted from their own actions. The people reaped exactly what they sowed as they mis-used and abused the creative power of the LORD.

17 Now therefore, O our God, hear the prayer of thy servant, and his supplications, and cause thy face to shine upon thy sanctuary that is desolate, for the Lord's sake.
18 O my God, incline thine ear, and hear; open thine eyes, and behold our desolations, and the city which is called by thy name: for we do not present our supplications before thee for our righteousnesses, but for thy great mercies.
19 O Lord, hear; O Lord, forgive; O Lord, hearken and do; defer not, for thine own sake, O my God: for thy city and thy people are called by thy name.
20 And whiles I was speaking, and praying, and confessing my sin and the sin of my people Israel, and presenting my supplication before the LORD my God for the holy mountain of my God;
21 Yea, whiles I was speaking in prayer, even the man Gabriel, whom I had seen in the vision at the beginning, being caused to fly swiftly, touched me about the time of the evening oblation.

Daniel prays to God to hear the prayer of his servant, and cause God's face to shine upon His sanctuary that is desolate: God's desolate sanctuary is His desolate people. The presence of the LORD on earth can appear through people who let it be so. Daniel prays to God to incline His ear, to listen, and to open His eyes to see the desolation of the people and the conditions of the city that should bear the name of God. Daniel asks God to hear his supplications and prayer not because the people have been righteous but because the LORD is merciful. Daniel is praying for the LORD to change His mind: Daniel does not understand the simple application of the Law. Daniel needs to pray to the **Lord within himself** to listen, to forgive and to repent.

O Lord, hear; O Lord, forgive; O Lord, listen and do; do not procrastinate: for Your city and Your people are called by the name of the Lord. And while Daniel confessing his own sin and the sin of his people, Israel, before the LORD God, then the man Gabriel, the angel Gabriel, whom Daniel had seen in the vision at the beginning, touched him about the time of the evening sacrifice.

22 And he informed me, and talked with me, and said, O Daniel, I am now come forth to give thee skill and understanding.
23 At the beginning of thy supplications the commandment came forth, and I am come to shew thee; for thou art greatly beloved: therefore understand the matter, and consider the vision.
24 Seventy weeks are determined upon thy people and upon thy holy city, to finish the transgression, and to make an end of sins, and to make reconciliation for iniquity, and to bring in everlasting righteousness, and to seal up the vision and prophecy, and to anoint the most Holy.

Gabriel said, Daniel, I am now come forth to give you skill and understanding. At the very beginning of your prayers to God, the commandment came forth, and I am come to show you; for you are greatly beloved by God: therefore understand the matter, and consider the vision.

In the vision, the angel Gabriel declares that seventy weeks are determined for your people and your holy city, to finish the transgression and put an end to sins, to make reconciliation for iniquity, to bring in everlasting righteousness, to seal up the vision and prophecy, and to anoint the most Holy within themselves. Gabriel has instructed Daniel that he and the people must repent of their sins and obey the LORD to bring about the vision and the prophecy and to anoint the most Holy by letting the spirit of the most Holy flow through the human equipment.

25 Know therefore and understand, that from the going forth of the commandment to restore and to build Jerusalem unto the Messiah the Prince shall be seven weeks, and threescore and two weeks: the street shall be built again, and the wall, even in troublous times.

The Testimony of the Major Prophets

26 And after threescore and two weeks shall Messiah be cut off, but not for himself: and the people of the prince that shall come shall destroy the city and the sanctuary; and the end thereof shall be with a flood, and unto the end of the war desolations are determined.

27 And he shall confirm the covenant with many for one week: and in the midst of the week he shall cause the sacrifice and the oblation to cease, and for the overspreading of abominations he shall make it desolate, even until the consummation, and that determined shall be poured upon the desolate.

Gabriel tells Daniel that in order for him to know and understand that from the going forth, the expression, of the commandment of the LORD to let His spirit go forth through Daniel and through his people to restore and to build Jerusalem, the Holy City of the people so that the habitation of the Messiah the Prince to dwell there shall be seven weeks, and followed by 62 weeks. The angel Gabriel has told Daniel that the Messiah, the Prince of the King, the spirit of the Son of God, is to dwell in the people. The people must not let the spirit of the LORD move through them for only seven weeks and then, cease their activity; but the people must continue to let the spirit of the LORD flow through them for another sixty two weeks. At the end of this time, the new pattern of behavior should be established. Then the street of the Holy City, the street upon which the people shall walk in the spirit of the LORD, shall be built again, and the wall, the wall to protect the street that has been built for the LORD's people to walk upon, will be built also, even in troubled times round about. The street and the wall are to be built by and with the spirit of the LORD moving through the people.

And after 62 weeks, Messiah, the anointed One from the LORD, shall be cut off, but not for Himself: the spirit of the Messiah shall be with His people, and the people of the prince that shall come to express the spirit of the Messiah, shall destroy the fallen city and the fallen sanctuary which were built by people who disobeyed and rebelled against the LORD. The end thereof shall be with a flood of the spirit of the Messiah from the spirit of truth from God that is released through the people. This will be a war between the constant and consistent flow of the spirit of God and the forms of desolation that remain. At the end of the war, the absence of desolations are determined. The responsibility of Daniel and the responsibility of the children of Israel is to release the spirit of the LORD into the earth.

The LORD shall confirm His covenant with many for one week: and in the midst of the week, the LORD shall cause the sacrifice and the oblation to Him to cease because the people in covenant-agreement with the LORD need not worship and make sacrifices to the LORD because the LORD's spirit is moving through them. As the LORD moves through the people in covenant-agreement with Him, there are no abominations being generated, and the LORD will make the area around them desolate of abominations. The consummation of the fallen state in people is replaced by the ascended state of the covenant, and when that spirit of the LORD is desired and determined by a person, the spirit of the LORD shall be poured upon the people who are desolate.

CHAPTER 10

1 In the third year of Cyrus king of Persia a thing was revealed unto Daniel, whose name was called Belteshazzar; and the thing was true, but the time appointed was long: and he understood the thing, and had understanding of the vision.
2 In those days I Daniel was mourning three full weeks.
3 I ate no pleasant bread, neither came flesh nor wine in my mouth, neither did I anoint myself at all, till three whole weeks were fulfilled.
4 And in the four and twentieth day of the first month, as I was by the side of the great river, which is Hiddekel;
5 Then I lifted up mine eyes, and looked, and behold a certain man clothed in linen, whose loins were girded with fine gold of Uphaz:
6 His body also was like the beryl, and his face as the appearance of lightning, and his eyes as lamps of fire, and his arms and his feet like in colour to polished brass, and the voice of his words like the voice of a multitude.

In the third year of Cyrus king of Persia, the third year after his conquest of Babylonia in 539 BC, a revelation was revealed to Daniel, whose Babylonian name was Belteshazzar; the vision was true, but the time appointed for it to take place was lengthy; it would take many years for the revelation to unfold: Daniel understood the vision.

In those days, Daniel was mourning three full weeks. During this time, he ate no pleasant bread, flesh or wine as he fasted, neither did he anoint himself at all until the three whole weeks were passed. In the 24th day of the first month, as Daniel was by the side of the great river, which is Hiddekel, the name of a river leaving the Garden of Eden, he lifted his eyes and saw a certain man clothed in linen, whose loins were girded with fine gold of Uphaz. His body also was like the beryl, and his face as the appearance of lightning, his eyes as lamps of fire, his arms and his feet like in color to polished brass, and the voice of his words like the voice of a multitude.

7 And I Daniel alone saw the vision: for the men that were with me saw not the vision; but a great quaking fell upon them, so that they fled to hide themselves.
8 Therefore I was left alone, and saw this great vision, and there remained no strength in me: for my comeliness was turned in me into corruption, and I retained no strength.
9 Yet heard I the voice of his words: and when I heard the voice of his words, then was I in a deep sleep on my face, and my face toward the ground.
10 And, behold, an hand touched me, which set me upon my knees and upon the palms of my hands.
11 And he said unto me, O Daniel, a man greatly beloved, understand the words that I speak unto thee, and stand upright: for unto thee am I now sent. And when he had spoken this word unto me, I stood trembling.
12 Then said he unto me, Fear not, Daniel: for from the first day that thou didst set thine heart to understand, and to chasten thyself before thy God, thy words were heard, and I am come for thy words.

The Testimony of the Major Prophets

Daniel alone saw the vision: for the men that were with him did not see it; but a great quaking fell upon them so that they fled to hide themselves. Daniel saw a great vision which left him with little strength.
The goodness that Daniel thought was in him turned into corruption, and he felt very weak. Yet Daniel, who was in a deep sleep with his face to the ground, heard the voice of his words.

In the vision, a hand touched Daniel, which set him upon all fours, upon his knees and the palms of his hands. The man told Daniel that he was greatly beloved and that he should stand upright and hear the words spoken to him. Daniel trembled when he heard the words spoken to him in the vision. Then the man in the vision said, Fear not, Daniel, for from the first day that you set your heart to understand, and to chasten yourself before God, your words were heard, and I am come because of your words.

13 But the prince of the kingdom of Persia withstood me one and twenty days: but, lo, Michael, one of the chief princes, came to help me; and I remained there with the kings of Persia.
14 Now I am come to make thee understand what shall befall thy people in the latter days: for yet the vision is for many days.
15 And when he had spoken such words unto me, I set my face toward the ground, and I became dumb.
16 And, behold, one like the similitude of the sons of men touched my lips: then I opened my mouth, and spake, and said unto him that stood before me, O my lord, by the vision my sorrows are turned upon me, and I have retained no strength.
17 For how can the servant of this my lord talk with this my lord? for as for me, straightway there remained no strength in me, neither is there breath left in me.

The prince of the kingdom of Persia withstood the spiritual being, the messenger, for 21 days: but, lo, Michael, one of the chief princes in the heaven of the world of spirit, came to help me; and the spiritual messengers from heaven remained there with the kings of Persia. The spiritual messengers had been "visiting" the kings of Persia and now one has come to make Daniel understand what will happen to his people in the days to come. The vision is a long range view and the spiritual messenger wants Daniel to understand.

When the messenger had spoken these words to Daniel, he became dumbstruck and put his face toward the ground. Then, one like the similitude of the sons of men touched Daniel's lips and he could speak: Daniel told the messenger that the vision had given him sorrow and made him so weak that he would fall to the ground. How can the **material** servant of his lord talk with the lord of his **spirit**? How can the human capacities of its lord within talk with the Lord, the Being of its spirit? How can oneness be realized? Daniel admits that he is weak and breathless from his encounter with a spiritual messenger. Daniel has "wrestled" with an angel.

18 Then there came again and touched me one like the appearance of a man, and he strengthened me,
19 And said, O man greatly beloved, fear not: peace be unto thee, be strong, yea, be strong. And when he had spoken unto me, I was strengthened, and said, Let my lord speak; for thou hast strengthened me.
20 Then said he, Knowest thou wherefore I come unto thee? and now will I return to fight with the prince of Persia: and when I am gone forth, lo, the prince of Grecia shall come.
21 But I will shew thee that which is noted in the scripture of truth: and there is none that holdeth with me in these things, but Michael your prince.

Then there came again and touched him, one who had the appearance of a man, and he strengthened him.
The messenger said, O man greatly beloved, fear not: peace be to you, be strong, yes, be strong. And when the man had spoken to Daniel, he was strengthened, and said, Let my lord speak; for you have strengthened me.

Then he said, Do you know why I come to you? Now the spiritual messenger will return to fight with the prince of Persia to keep him occupied and distracted. When Daniel is told that the spiritual messenger has gone forth to distract the prince of Persia, lo, the prince of Greece shall come.

But the spiritual messenger will show Daniel that which is noted in the scripture of truth from God: and there is no one that supports in these things, but Michael your prince, the archangel, in the heaven of the spirit who protects the people of God who are in form on earth. Daniel understands that spiritual Beings can influence and affect the people who are on earth.

CHAPTER 11

1 Also I in the first year of Darius the Mede, even I, stood to confirm and to strengthen him.
2 And now will I shew thee the truth. Behold, there shall stand up yet three kings in Persia; and the fourth shall be far richer than they all: and by his strength through his riches he shall stir up all against the realm of Grecia.
3 And a mighty king shall stand up, that shall rule with great dominion, and do according to his will.
4 And when he shall stand up, his kingdom shall be broken, and shall be divided toward the four winds of heaven; and not to his posterity, nor according to his dominion which he ruled: for his kingdom shall be plucked up, even for others beside those.

In the first year of Darius the Mede, Daniel stands to confirm the position of the king and to strengthen him. Daniel will show king Darius the truth. Behold, there shall be three kings in Persia. While Daniel does not give the names and years that the 3 kings reign, history does: Cambyses (530-522 BC); Guamata (522BC); and Darius (522-486 BC); and a fourth king, Xerxes I (486-455 BC) shall be far richer than them all. His strength and his riches shall stir up everyone against the kingdom of Greece. Xerxes tried to conquer Greece in 480 BC.

A mighty king shall stand up, Alexander the Great (336-323 BC) that shall rule with great dominion, and do according to his will, whatever he chooses to do. And when Alexander shall stand up, be seen in his earthly glory and finish his career, his kingdom shall be broken, and it shall be divided toward the four winds of heaven as it is divided into four parts; his kingdom shall not be divided to his posterity, nor according to his dominion which he ruled. His kingdom shall be plucked up, uprooted and given to others.

5 And the king of the south shall be strong, and one of his princes; and he shall be strong above him, and have dominion; his dominion shall be a great dominion.
6 And in the end of years they shall join themselves together; for the king's daughter of the south shall come to the king of the north to make an agreement: but she shall not retain the power of the arm; neither shall he stand, nor his arm: but she shall be given up, and they that brought her, and he that begat her, and he that strengthened her in these times.
7 But out of a branch of her roots shall one stand up in his estate, which shall come with an army, and shall enter into the fortress of the king of the north, and shall deal against them, and shall prevail:
8 And shall also carry captives into Egypt their gods, with their princes, and with their precious vessels of silver and of gold; and he shall continue more years than the king of the north.

And the king of the south, who history identifies as Ptolemy I Soter (323-285 BC), shall become strong, and one of his princes Seleucus I Nicator (311-280 BC) will become even stronger than he, and have dominion; his dominion shall be a great dominion. After many years, they shall join themselves together; for the king's daughter of the south, Berenice, daughter of Ptolemy II Philadelphus (285-245 BC) shall come to the king of the north, Antiochus II Theos (261-246 BC) of Syria to make an agreement. The agreement is to unite the two kingdoms through a marriage between children.

The Symbolic Version of Daniel

A treaty cemented the marriage of Berenice to Antiochus. She shall not retain her power of the arm that symbolizes the extension of power; neither shall he stand, nor his arm of extension of power through marriage. Laodice, the former wife of Antiochus, conspired to have Berenice and Antiochus put to death. Daniel predicts that Berenice shall be given up, along with they that brought her, and he that fathered her, and he that strengthened her in these times. Berenice's father, Ptolemy, died at about the same time.

But out of a branch of her roots, Berenice's brother Ptolemy III Euergetes (246-221 BC), shall stand up in his estate, which shall come with an army, and shall enter into the fortress of the king of the north, which was built by king Antiochus of Syria, and shall deal against them, and shall prevail. Ptolemy III carried captives into Egypt along with the images of their gods, their princes, and with their precious vessels of silver and of gold. He shall continue more years, live longer, than the king of the north.

9 So the king of the south shall come into his kingdom, and shall return into his own land.
10 But his sons shall be stirred up, and shall assemble a multitude of great forces: and one shall certainly come, and overflow, and pass through: then shall he return, and be stirred up, even to his fortress.
11 And the king of the south shall be moved with choler, and shall come forth and fight with him, even with the king of the north: and he shall set forth a great multitude; but the multitude shall be given into his hand.
12 And when he hath taken away the multitude, his heart shall be lifted up; and he shall cast down many ten thousands: but he shall not be strengthened by it.

So the king of the south, Ptolemy III Euergetes, shall come into his kingdom, and shall return into his own land. But his sons shall be stirred up, and shall assemble a multitude of great forces: and one shall certainly come, and overflow, and pass through: then shall he return, and be stirred up, even to his fortress. And the king of the south, Ptolomy IV Philopater (221-203 BC) of Egypt shall be moved with rage, and shall come forth and fight with the king of the north, Antiochus III: and he shall set forth a great multitude; but the multitude shall be given into his hand. And when he has taken away the multitude, his heart shall be lifted up; and he shall cast down many ten thousands: but he shall not be strengthened by it. The battle took place at Raphia, a city between Jerusalem and Babylon, Ptolemy's fortress in southern Palestine. The historian Polybius records that Antiochus lost nearly 10,000 infantrymen at Raphia.

13 For the king of the north shall return, and shall set forth a multitude greater than the former, and shall certainly come after certain years with a great army and with much riches.
14 And in those times there shall many stand up against the king of the south: also the robbers of thy people shall exalt themselves to establish the vision; but they shall fall.
15 So the king of the north shall come, and cast up a mount, and take the most fenced cities: and the arms of the south shall not withstand, neither his chosen people, neither shall there be any strength to withstand.

For the king of the north shall return, and shall set forth a multitude, an army of people, greater than the former, and shall certainly come after certain years with a great army and with much riches. And in those times there shall many stand up against the king of the south, Ptolemy V Epiphanes of Egypt (203-181 BC): also the robbers of Daniel's people, Jews who joined the forces of Antiochus, shall exalt themselves to establish the vision; but they shall fall. The Ptolemaic general Scopas crushed the rebellion in 200 BC.

So the king of the north, Antiochus, shall come, and cast up a mount, a tower used to attack walls of cities, and capture the most fortified cities: such as the Mediterranean city of Sidon. The arms of the south shall not withstand the invasion, neither his chosen people, neither shall there be any strength to withstand the invasion from the north. The invader, Antiochus, was in control of Palestine by 197 BC.

16 But he that cometh against him shall do according to his own will, and none shall stand before him: and he shall stand in the glorious land, which by his hand shall be consumed.
17 He shall also set his face to enter with the strength of his whole kingdom, and upright ones with him; thus shall he do: and he shall give him the daughter of women, corrupting her: but she shall not stand on his side, neither be for him.
18 After this shall he turn his face unto the isles, and shall take many: but a prince for his own behalf shall cause the reproach offered by him to cease; without his own reproach he shall cause it to turn upon him.

The Testimony of the Major Prophets

19 Then he shall turn his face toward the fort of his own land: but he shall stumble and fall, and not be found.

But he that comes against Antiochus shall do so if he chooses but none shall succeed and stand in victory before him: and he shall stand in the glorious land of Israel, which, by his hand, many inhabitants were killed. Antiochus shall also set his face to enter with the strength of his whole kingdom into Egypt; thus shall he do: and he shall give him the daughter of women, corrupting her: but she shall not stand on his side, neither be for him. Antiochus gave his daughter, Cleopatra I, in marriage to Ptolemy V in 194 BC. to overthrow the kingdom but his plans will not succeed.

After this, Antiochus shall turn his face toward the isles, the coastlands of Asia Minor, and he shall take many captives: but a prince functioning on his own behalf, the Roman consul Lucius Cornelius Scipio Asiaticus, defeated Antiochus in Asia Minor in 190 BC. Then Antiochus shall turn his face toward the fort of his own land: he shall retreat, but he shall stumble and fall, and not be found. Antiochus died in 187 BC while attempting to plunder a temple in Elymais.

20 Then shall stand up in his estate a raiser of taxes in the glory of the kingdom: but within few days he shall be destroyed, neither in anger, nor in battle.
21 And in his estate shall stand up a vile person, to whom they shall not give the honour of the kingdom: but he shall come in peaceably, and obtain the kingdom by flatteries.
22 And with the arms of a flood shall they be overflown from before him, and shall be broken; yea, also the prince of the covenant.

Then, the son of Antiochus the Great, Seleucus IV Philopater (187-175 BC), a raiser of taxes, shall stand up in his estate in the glory of the kingdom: but within few days he shall be destroyed, neither in anger, nor in battle. Seleucus was the victim of a conspiracy engineered by his finance minister, Heliodorus.

He was replaced by a vile person, his younger brother Antiochus IV Epiphanes (175-164 BC) to whom they shall not give the honor royalty of the kingdom: but he shall come in peaceably, and obtain the kingdom by flatteries and intrigue, rather than the force of war that kills many people. And with a flood of an overwhelming army, they shall overflow before him, and they shall be broken; yes, the defeated army and the prince of the covenant, Ptolemy VI Philometor (181-146 BC).

23 And after the league made with him he shall work deceitfully: for he shall come up, and shall become strong with a small people.
24 He shall enter peaceably even upon the fattest places of the province; and he shall do that which his fathers have not done, nor his fathers' fathers; he shall scatter among them the prey, and spoil, and riches: yea, and he shall forecast his devices against the strong holds, even for a time.
25 And he shall stir up his power and his courage against the king of the south with a great army; and the king of the south shall be stirred up to battle with a very great and mighty army; but he shall not stand: for they shall forecast devices against him.
26 Yea, they that feed of the portion of his meat shall destroy him, and his army shall overflow: and many shall fall down slain.
27 And both these kings' hearts shall be to do mischief, and they shall speak lies at one table; but it shall not prosper: for yet the end shall be at the time appointed.

After the league, an agreement, made between Antiochus IV Epiphanes and Ptolemy VI Photometer, Antiochus shall work deceitfully: for he shall come up, and shall become strong and rise to power with a small number of people. He shall enter peaceably even upon the wealthiest places of the province; and he shall do that which his fathers nor his fore-fathers have not done; he shall distribute the plunder, loot, and the riches among his followers: yes, and he shall forecast and plot the overthrow of strongholds and fortresses for a time.

Antiochus IV Epiphanes shall stir up his power and his courage by assembling his army against the king of the south, Ptolemy VI; and the king of the south shall be stirred up to battle with a very great and mighty army; but he shall not stand against the plans against him. The people who eat from the king's table shall destroy him, and his army shall go forth to battle: and many shall be slain. Both these kings' hearts, which are bent on evil, shall speak lies to each other at one table; but it will be to no avail because the end will come at the appointed time.

28 Then shall he return into his land with great riches; and his heart shall be against the holy covenant; and he shall do exploits, and return to his own land.
29 At the time appointed he shall return, and come toward the south; but it shall not be as the former, or as the latter.
30 For the ships of Chittim shall come against him: therefore he shall be grieved, and return, and have indignation against the holy covenant: so shall he do; he shall even return, and have intelligence with them that forsake the holy covenant.
31 And arms shall stand on his part, and they shall pollute the sanctuary of strength, and shall take away the daily sacrifice, and they shall place the abomination that maketh desolate.

The king of the north, Antiochus IV Epiphanes, shall return to his land with great riches; and his heart shall be against the holy covenant. He will and he shall do exploits, and return to his own land. Antiochus plundered the temple in Jerusalem, set up a garrison there and massacred many Jews in the city. At the appointed time, he shall invade the south again; but this time the outcome shall not be as it was before. The ships of Chittim on the western coast shall come against him: therefore he shall be grieved, and reward the people who forsake, and have indignation against, the holy covenant. He shall even return, and have intelligence with them that forsake the holy covenant. His arms and power will rise up to desecrate the temple fortress, destroy the sanctuary, and abolish the daily sacrifice. They will set up the abomination that makes desolation in the holy place. The altar to the pagan god, Zeus Olympus, was set up by Antiochus Epiphanes in 168 BC.

32 And such as do wickedly against the covenant shall he corrupt by flatteries: but the people that do know their God shall be strong, and do exploits.
33 And they that understand among the people shall instruct many: yet they shall fall by the sword, and by flame, by captivity, and by spoil, many days.
34 Now when they shall fall, they shall be holpen with a little help: but many shall cleave to them with flatteries.
35 And some of them of understanding shall fall, to try them, and to purge, and to make them white, even to the time of the end: because it is yet for a time appointed.

Antiochus IV Epiphanes will corrupt with flattery those people who do wickedly against the covenant: but the people that do know their God shall be strong, and do no exploits to deny their God. They, that have wisdom and understanding among the people, shall instruct many: yet they shall fall by the sword, by flame, by captivity, and by spoil for many days.

Now when they fall, they shall receive little help: but many who are not sincere shall cleave to them with flatteries. And some of the wise shall fall, to try them, and to purge them and make them spotless until the time of the end which will come at the appointed time.

36 And the king shall do according to his will; and he shall exalt himself, and magnify himself above every god, and shall speak marvellous things against the God of gods, and shall prosper till the indignation be accomplished: for that that is determined shall be done.
37 Neither shall he regard the God of his fathers, nor the desire of women, nor regard any god: for he shall magnify himself above all.
38 But in his estate shall he honour the God of forces: and a god whom his fathers knew not shall he honour with gold, and silver, and with precious stones, and pleasant things.
39 Thus shall he do in the most strong holds with a strange god, whom he shall acknowledge and increase with glory: and he shall cause them to rule over many, and shall divide the land for gain.

Antiochus the king shall do as he pleases according to his will. He shall exalt and magnify himself above every god, and shall speak marvelously wicked things against the God of gods. He shall prosper for a time until the indignation be accomplished: the determination for his punishment shall be done. He shall neither regard the God of his fathers, nor the desire of women, nor regard any god: for he shall magnify himself above all.

In his fallen state Antiochus shall honor the God of forces: and he shall honor a god, whom his fathers knew not, with gold, silver, with precious stones, and pleasant things. Thus shall he do in the most strong holds with a strange god,

40 And at the time of the end shall the king of the south push at him: and the king of the north shall come against him like a whirlwind, with chariots, and with horsemen, and with many ships; and he shall enter into the countries, and shall overflow and pass over.
41 He shall enter also into the glorious land, and many countries shall be overthrown: but these shall escape out of his hand, even Edom, and Moab, and the chief of the children of Ammon.
42 He shall stretch forth his hand also upon the countries: and the land of Egypt shall not escape.
43 But he shall have power over the treasures of gold and of silver, and over all the precious things of Egypt: and the Libyans and the Ethiopians shall be at his steps.

At the time of the end of the king of the north, Antiochus IV, and his kingdom, the king of the south from Egypt shall push at him: and the king of the north shall come against him like a whirlwind, with chariots, and with horsemen, and with many ships; and he shall enter into the countries, and shall overflow and pass over. He shall enter also into the glorious land, and many countries shall be overthrown: but these lands shall escape out of his hand of control, even Edom, and Moab, and the chief of the children of Ammon.

Antiochus IV and his armies shall stretch forth his hand also upon the countries: and the land of Egypt shall not escape. But he shall have power over the treasures of gold and of silver, and over all the precious things of Egypt: and the Libyans and the Ethiopians shall be at his steps to acknowledge defeat.

44 But tidings out of the east and out of the north shall trouble him: therefore he shall go forth with great fury to destroy, and utterly to make away many.
45 And he shall plant the tabernacles of his palace between the seas in the glorious holy mountain; yet he shall come to his end, and none shall help him.

But tidings out of the east and out of the north shall trouble him: therefore, Antiochus IV Epiphanes shall go forth with great fury to destroy, and utterly annihilate many. He shall plant the tabernacles of his palace between the seas in the glorious holy mountain of Jerusalem; yet he shall come to his end, and no one shall help him.

CHAPTER 12

1 And at that time shall Michael stand up, the great prince which standeth for the children of thy people: and there shall be a time of trouble, such as never was since there was a nation even to that same time: and at that time thy people shall be delivered, every one that shall be found written in the book.
2 And many of them that sleep in the dust of the earth shall awake, some to everlasting life, and some to shame and everlasting contempt.
3 And they that be wise shall shine as the brightness of the firmament; and they that turn many to righteousness as the stars for ever and ever.
4 But thou, O Daniel, shut up the words, and seal the book, even to the time of the end: many shall run to and fro, and knowledge shall be increased.

At that time Michael the Archangel shall stand up, the great prince who stands and protects the children of your people: and there shall be a time of trouble, such as never before since the time that there was a nation: and at that time your people shall be delivered, every one that shall be found written in the book of life, the book of the body of mankind which is on earth.

Many of them, who are, from an earthly viewpoint, spirits that sleep in the dust of the earth of their own bodies, minds and hearts, shall awake to their divine heritage: the "sleeping" spirits shall awaken; some to everlasting life; and some to shame and everlasting contempt. They who are wise shall shine as the brightness of the firmament of heaven as they let the spirit of the covenant flow through them; and they that turn many to righteousness as the stars for ever and ever to discover their eternal nature. The Being portion of the "human being" will become aware that they are divine and eternal beings while they are in earthly bodies. The spirit that a human person believed would survive and go to heaven when they died is awake and alive while they are on earth in human form. The human person does not have or possess a spirit; the spirit has or occupies a human form. The truth is that person is a spirit in human form.

But you, Daniel, close up the words, and seal the words in the book, even to the time of the end, the end of the fallen state on earth, when many shall run to and fro in the earth looking for knowledge on how to rise up and ascend out of the fallen state to the true state. Knowledge shall be increased because of what you have written, sealed and verified in your own experience.

5 Then I Daniel looked, and, behold, there stood other two, the one on this side of the bank of the river, and the other on that side of the bank of the river.
6 And one said to the man clothed in linen, which was upon the waters of the river, How long shall it be to the end of these wonders?
7 And I heard the man clothed in linen, which was upon the waters of the river, when he held up his right hand and his left hand unto heaven, and sware by him that liveth for ever that it shall be for a time, times, and an half; and when he shall have accomplished to scatter the power of the holy people, all these things shall be finished.

The Testimony of the Major Prophets

8 And I heard, but I understood not: then said I, O my Lord, what shall be the end of these things?

Then Daniel looked, and, behold, there stood two others: one on this side of the bank of the river, and one on the other side of the river. One said to the man clothed in linen, which was upon the waters of the river of truth, How long shall it be to the end of these wonders? And Daniel heard the man clothed in linen, who was upon the waters of the river; the Man that Daniel heard clothed in white linen who was upon the river of life, was the voice of the LORD. When the LORD held up his right hand, the clean hand, and his left hand, the normally unclean hand, to heaven, and swore by Him that lives for ever, God Almighty, that it shall be for a time, times, and an half; the times are a time of transition from a physical orientation (time), through a mental and emotional orientation (times) to a beginning understanding that the true nature of man is the spirit of God (half a time) when the LORD will meet you half way and lead you to the covenant-agreement with Him. When the LORD shall have accomplished the work to scatter the power of the holy people, the people who reveal in their living the spirit of the LORD, then, all these things shall be finished.

Daniel heard, but he did not understand. Then he said, O my Lord, what shall be the end, the outcome of all these things?

9 And he said, Go thy way, Daniel: for the words are closed up and sealed till the time of the end.
10 Many shall be purified, and made white, and tried; but the wicked shall do wickedly: and none of the wicked shall understand; but the wise shall understand.
11 And from the time that the daily sacrifice shall be taken away, and the abomination that maketh desolate set up, there shall be a thousand two hundred and ninety days.

And the Lord said, Go your way, Daniel: for the words are closed up and sealed until the time of the end. The end refers to the end of the fallen state of mankind on earth. The end of the fallen state on earth is the point in time when all the children of God are awake and aware that they are on earth to represent, re-present, the spirit of their King.

Many shall be purified individually, and made white, and tried; but the wicked shall do wickedly; they shall choose to continue to be wicked people: and none of the wicked shall understand the things of the spirit; but the wise shall understand as they let the spirit of the LORD flow through them. The wise ones who express the spirit shall know the spirit because everyone knows what they express in the moment of expression.

And from the time that the daily sacrifice to the LORD, who is perceived as separate from man, shall be taken away because man is in oneness with God in the covenant-agreement; and the abomination that makes desolate shall be set up so that the person can see the abomination of desolation stand in the holy place, there shall be 1,290 days.

In the symbolism of numbers, the number 1,000 is the symbol of the covenant. The number, 1, is the symbol of Almighty God in heaven; the three 0's are the symbols of the open body, open mind and open heart that symbolize that the spirit of God is finding expression through three human capacities on earth. The 290 days are the days which an individual may need to experience "nothingness", or, oneness with the LORD. The number 290, 2+9+0 adds up to the number 11, or 2. The number, **2**, is the symbol of God in action on earth through man, **Jehovah**. It is any symbolic number that adds up to 2. God Almighty in **heaven** (1) is God in action on **earth** through a man (2). The Garden of Eden is restored. Heaven and earth are one! There is no separation between God in heaven and a spirit of God on earth.

12 Blessed is he that waiteth, and cometh to the thousand three hundred and five and thirty days.
13 But go thou thy way till the end be: for thou shalt rest, and stand in thy lot at the end of the days.

Blessed is he that waits and serves the spirit of the LORD into the earth, and comes to the 1,335 days; a number which contains the symbolism of the covenant with the LORD. The number 1,000 is the number of the covenant-agreement. The number 335, 3+3+5 adds up to 11 which adds up to **2**. Jehovah. But you, each person, go your way until the end comes for you. The end of your days is the end of the fallen state for you; it is also the beginning of the ascended or risen state for you. You shall rest, and rise in your lot at the end of the days to receive your divine inheritance, which is the experience of the covenant. You are made in the image and likeness of God. In the covenant-agreement, Almighty God is number **1**; you, a point of focus, a child, a spirit of God, are number **2**; your temporary earthly human capacities, made of the dust of the ground—of heart, mind and physical body—are number **3**. In true identity, you are not the dust of the ground; you are a spirit, the child of your Father in heaven. **Be who you really are!**

Anthony John Monaco **September 23, 1998**

ABOUT THE AUTHOR

As a health care professional, Anthony John Monaco was interested in the cause of disease in the individual. His scientific approach led him to investigate spiritual approaches to health. His analysis of the major scriptures of the world has led to symbolic interpretations of the works of the original authors who were responsible for the religious thought of mankind that are relevant today. These books containing the works of Isaiah, Ezekiel, Jeremiah, and Daniel are presented with detailed explanations of the symbolism used to lead people in the fallen state out of bondage into a covenant-agreement with the LORD.

Printed in the United States
20416LVS00001B/3-10